CONTENTS

W9-DIG-558

Contents

ON THE ROAD WITH FODOR'S

WE'RE ALWAYS THRILLED to get letters from readers, especially one like this:

It took us an hour to decide what book to buy and we now know we picked the best one. Your book was wonderful, easy to follow, very accurate, and good on pointing out eating places, informal as well as formal. When we saw other people using your book, we would look at each other and smile.

Our editors and writers are deeply committed to making every Fodor's guide "the best one"—not only accurate but always charming, brimming with sound recommendations and solid ideas, right on the mark in describing restaurants and hotels, and full of fascinating facts that make you view what you've traveled to see in a rich new light.

About Our Writers

Our success in achieving our goals—and in helping to make your trip the best of all possible vacations—is a credit to the hard work of our extraordinary writers.

Helen Ayers is a freelance journalist and student of the metaphysical. She was the first female editor of the Fremantle Gazette and currently serves as a Fremantle city councillor. She travels extensively both at home and abroad.

After writing travel articles while being based in London, Singapore, and Jakarta, **Jane Carstens** returned to her native Queensland, where she covered that vast state top to bottom for Fodor's. A self-confessed foodie, she used to review restaurants in Southeast Asia, which accounts for her ever-so-tempting additions of Thai, Malaysian, and Indonesian restaurants to the Queensland chapter this year.

Terry Durack is the leading light of Australian food journalism. As restaurant critic for the Sydney morning *Herald,* author of several cookbooks, and columnist for *Australian Gourmet Traveller, Elle,* and *Mode* magazines, he writes about food in much the same way as he eats it— with passion, intrigue, and great joy.

British by birth, American by education, and Australian since 1979—after a stint as a Kiwi as well—**Michael Gebicki** is a freelance travel writer and photographer based in Sydney. Dashing articles about his global wanderings appear regularly in travel publications in North America, Europe, and Asia.

Chips Mackinolty is our man in the Outback. A writer and graphic artist, he lives in Darwin with his Australian red heeler cattle dog, Madge. A lover of extreme weather conditions, he has lived in the Northern Territory for 15 years, much of that time traveling and working in remote Aboriginal communities in the Territory and the Kimberley, from the heart of the desert to the northern wetlands.

English-born **Anne Matthews** started "reading" the family atlas at the age of four. Since then she's been using it to check off the places she's been. As an adventure travel guide she lived in Nepal and India and, judging from the marks on that atlas, made it to Bolivia, China, Israel, Jordan, Kenya, Papua New Guinea, Peru, Tibet, and Zimbabwe, at least. As a freelance travel writer and photographer, she has contributed to 25 books, several of them on Sydney and Australia.

Gary Walsh is a Melbourne-based travel writer whose work appears regularly in major Australian newspapers and magazines. Wanderlust has seen him contribute to guidebooks on Australia and Greece. He also has an offbeat column on sports for the *Sunday Age* newspaper and follows with sometimes dangerous intensity the fortunes of the Essendon Australian Football League team.

New This Year

Because of outstanding contributions from all of our writers this year, Fodor's *Australia '98* is hands down the best guide to the country that we have ever published. Terry Durack has once again delivered excruciatingly delicious reviews of Sydney and Melbourne restaurants. He also poured out a refreshing new article, "The Shocking Truth about Australian Wine," that prompted this editor to raid the Aussie stock of his local vintner.

Anne Matthews has let us in for the first time on the secrets of the Southern Highlands near Sydney—that spectacular countryside where *Babe* was filmed—and filled out our unique coverage of pristine Lord Howe Island. Likewise Gary Walsh wrote two essential sections on Southern Australia from the ground up: the historic Clare Valley wine region to the north of Adelaide (which prompted yet another buyout at the local wine shop) and the picturesque Fleurieu Peninsula to the south. For the past three years Chips Mackinolty has advised us about Aboriginal issues in Australia; this year he rolled his experience with Aborignal peoples into an informative new portrait, "The First Australians." Jane Carstens joined us this year and heroically whipped the massive Queensland chapter into tip-top shape, which includes major new coverage of the mid-coast Townsville and Magnetic Island. And Michael Gebicki rejoined the fold to take on Sydney with his typical wit and charm. Hats off for the great work!

Also this year, Fodor's joins Rand McNally, the world's largest commercial mapmaker, to bring you a detailed color map of Australia. Just detach it along the perforation and drop it in your tote bag.

We're also proud to announce that the American Society of Travel Agents has endorsed Fodor's as its guidebook of choice. ASTA is the world's largest and most influential travel trade association, operating in more than 170 countries, with 27,000 members pledged to adhere to a strict code of ethics reflecting the Society's motto, "Integrity in Travel." ASTA shares Fodor's devotion to providing smart, honest travel information and advice to travelers, and we've long recommended that our readers consult ASTA member agents for the experience and professionalism they bring to the table.

On the Web, check out Fodor's site (www.fodors.com/) for information on major destinations around the world and travel-savvy interactive features. The Web site also lists the 85-plus stations nationwide that carry the Fodor's Travel Show, a live call-in program that airs every weekend. Tune in to hear guests discuss their wonderful adventures—or call in to get answers for your most pressing travel questions.

How to Use This Book
Organization

Up front is the **Gold Guide,** an easy-to-use section divided alphabetically by topic. Under each listing you'll find tips and information that will help you accomplish what you need to in Australia. You'll also find addresses and telephone numbers of organizations and companies that offer destination-related services and detailed information and publications.

The first chapter in the guide, Destination: Australia, helps get you in the mood for your trip. What's Where gets you oriented, New and Noteworthy cues you in on trends and happenings, Pleasures and Pastimes describes the activities and sights that really make Australia unique, Fodor's Choice presents our top picks, and Festivals and Seasonal Events alerts you to special events you'll want to seek out.

Chapters in *Australia '98* are arranged beginning with Sydney, cover the southeastern states, then work their way west from Queensland. Each city chapter begins with an Exploring section subdivided by neighborhoods; each subsection recommends a walking or driving tour and lists sights in alphabetical order. Each regional chapter is divided by geographical area; within each area, towns are covered in logical geographical order, and attractive stretches of road and minor points of interest between them are indicated by the designation *En Route*. Throughout, Off the Beaten Path sights appear after the places from which they are most easily accessible. And within town sections, all restaurants and lodgings are grouped together.

To help you decide what to visit in the time you have, all chapters begin with recommended itineraries; you can mix and match those from several chapters to create a complete vacation. The A-to-Z section that ends all chapters covers getting there and getting around. It also provides helpful contacts and resources.

At the end of the book you'll find Portraits, wonderful essays about Ozzie (or Aussie) wine, culture, life on the plains, and Aborigines, followed by suggestions for pre-trip reading, both fiction and nonfiction, and movies on tape with Australia as a backdrop.

Icons and Symbols

★   Our special recommendations
✕   Restaurant
▦   Lodging establishment
✕▦   Lodging establishment whose restaurant warrants a special trip
⚠   Campgrounds
🦆   Good for kids (rubber duckie)
☞   Sends you to another section of the guide for more information
✉   Address
☎   Telephone number
🕙   Opening and closing times
💰   Admission prices (those we give apply to adults; substantially reduced fees are almost always available for children, students, and senior citizens)

Numbers in white and black circles that appear on the maps, in the margins, and within the tours correspond to one another.

Dining and Lodging

The restaurants and lodgings we list are the cream of the crop in each price range. Except in the Sydney chapter, price charts appear in the Pleasures and Pastimes section that follows each chapter introduction.

Hotel Facilities

We always list the facilities that are available—but we don't specify whether they cost extra: When pricing accommodations, always ask what's included. In addition, assume that all rooms have private baths unless otherwise noted.

Restaurant Reservations and Dress Codes

Reservations are always a good idea; we note only when they're essential or when they are not accepted. Book as far ahead as you can, and reconfirm when you get to town. Unless otherwise noted, the restaurants listed are open daily for lunch and dinner. We mention dress only when men are required to wear a jacket or a jacket and tie. Look for an overview of local habits in the Gold Guide.

Credit Cards

The following abbreviations are used: **AE**, American Express; **DC**, Diners Club; **MC**, MasterCard; and **V**, Visa.

Please Write to Us

You can use this book in the confidence that all prices and opening times are based on information supplied to us at press time; Fodor's cannot accept responsibility for any errors. Time inevitably brings changes, so always confirm information when it matters—especially if you're making a detour to visit a specific place. In addition, when making reservations be sure to mention if you have a disability or are traveling with children, if you prefer a private bath or a certain type of bed, or if you have specific dietary needs or other concerns.

Were the restaurants we recommended as described? Did our hotel picks exceed your expectations? Did you find a museum we recommended a waste of time? If you have complaints, we'll look into them and revise our entries when the facts warrant it. If you've discovered a special place that we haven't included, we'll pass the information along to our correspondents and have them check it out. So send us your feedback, positive *and* negative: email us at editors@fodors.com (specifying the name of the book on the subject line) or write the Australia editor at Fodor's, 201 East 50th Street, New York, New York 10022. Have a wonderful trip!

Karen Cure

Karen Cure
Editorial Director

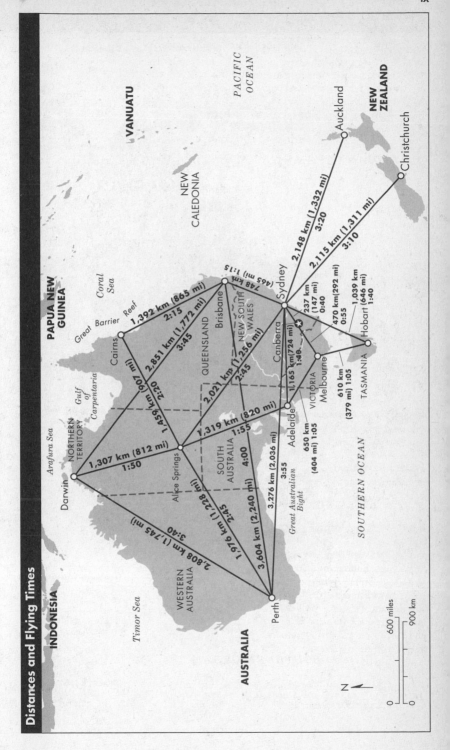

Distances and Flying Times

x

INDONESIA Timor

Timor Sea

KAK.

Darwin

Katherine

INDIAN OCEAN

Kununurra

KIMBERLEY REGION

Halls
Creek

NORTHERN

Broome Derby

Great Northern Hwy.

Port
Hedland

GREAT SANDY DESERT

TANAMI DESERT
WILDLIFE
SANCTUARY

Dampier

RUDALL RIVER
NATIONAL PARK

Exmouth

Tropic of Capricorn

KARIJINI
NATIONAL
PARK Newman

Tom Price

Uluru
(Ayers Rock)

WESTERN
AUSTRALIA

BROWNE RANGE
NATURE RESERVE

87

Carnarvon

Great Northern Hwy.

GREAT VICTORIA DESERT

Monkey
Mia

Meekatharra

North West Coastal Hwy.

GREAT VICTORIA
DESERT
NATURE RESERVE

Coober P

95

NULLARBOR PLAIN

Geraldton

NAMBUNG
NATIONAL
PARK

95

Kalgoorlie

New Norcia

Coolgardie

94

Merredin

1

Perth

Fremantle

Narrogin

Eyre Hwy.

1

Bunbury
Busselton

95

Esperance

Great Australian Bight

Margaret
River

1

Albany

N

SOUTHERN OCEAN

Bass Strait

King Island

Burnie
Launceston

Strahan

St. Marys

TASMANIA

0 ——————— 400 miles

0 ——————— 600 km

Hobart Port
Arthur

Arafura Sea

KADU NATIONAL PARK

ARNHEM LAND

PAPUA NEW GUINEA

Gulf of Carpentaria

Weipa

CAPE YORK PENINSULA

Coral Sea

Laura

Cooktown

Port Douglas

Mareeba

Burketown

Cairns

Normanton

Innisfail

GREAT

Georgetown

Ingham

TERRITORY

QUEENSLAND

Townsville

Ayr

BARRIER

Tennant Creek

Mt. Isa

Cloncurry

REEF

Stuart Hwy

Alice Springs

66

Hughenden

Mackay

Bedourie

Longreach

66

Emerald

Rockhampton

Blackwater

Bruce Hwy

Birdsville

Windorah

71

Gladstone

Charleville

54

Oodnadatta

Rama

Kingaroy

Nambour

Lake Eyre

71

Cunnamulla

Dalby

Brisbane

Toowoomba

Pedy

SOUTH

Goondiwindi

Warwick

Lismore

AUSTRALIA

Marree

Bourke

Moree

Pacific Hwy

Lake Torrens

FLINDERS RANGES NATIONAL PARK

Walgett

NEW

Armidale

Grafton

Ceduna

Port Augusta

32

Broken Hill

71

Nyngan

SOUTH WALES

Coffs Harbour

Port Pirie

Mitchell Hwy

Dubbo

Kempsey

1

EYRE PENINSULA

Renmark

Orange

Port Macquarie

Port Lincoln

Mildura

Hay

Bathurst

Cowra

Newcastle

Adelaide

Stuart Hwy

Young

GREAT

Sydney

Kangaroo Island

Bordertown

VICTORIA

Shepparton

Albury

Wollongong

Canberra

Bendigo

Cooma

Mt. Gambier

Ballarat

Seymour

Melbourne

Bega

Portland

Coolac

Geelong

Orbost

Warrnambool

Wonthaggi

Sale

Bairnsdale

King Island

Bass Strait

Flinders Island

TASMANIA

SMART TRAVEL TIPS A TO Z

Basic Information on Traveling in Australia, Savvy Tips to Make Your Trip a Breeze, and Companies and Organizations to Contact

A
AIR TRAVEL

The major gateways to Australia include Sydney, Melbourne, Perth, Brisbane, and Cairns. Flights leave from Los Angeles, San Francisco, Honolulu, New York, Toronto, and Vancouver, as well as London, Frankfurt, and Rome. Depending on your airline and route, you can elect to stop over in Honolulu, Fiji, Tahiti, or Auckland from the U.S.; Singapore or Bangkok from Europe. Nonstop service is available to Sydney from Los Angeles or San Francisco.

Flying times from New York to Sydney (via Los Angeles) are about 21 hours; from Chicago to Sydney (via Los Angeles) about 19 hours; from Los Angeles or San Francisco to Sydney (nonstop) about 15 hours; from Los Angeles to Melbourne (via Auckland) around 16 hours; and from London to Sydney or Melbourne about 20½ hours via Singapore or Bangkok.

MAJOR AIRLINE OR LOW-COST CARRIER?

Most people choose a flight based on price. Yet there are other issues to consider. Major airlines offer the greatest number of departures; smaller airlines—including regional, low-cost, and no-frill airlines—usually have a more limited number of flights daily. Major airlines have frequent-flyer partners, which allow you to credit mileage earned on one airline to your account with another. Low-cost airlines offer a definite price advantage and fewer restrictions, such as advance-purchase requirements. Safety-wise, low-cost carriers as a group have a good history, but **check the safety record before booking** any low-cost carrier; call the Federal Aviation Administration's Consumer Hotline (☞ Airline Complaints, *below*).

➤ FROM THE U.S.: Nonstop service is available to Sydney from Los Angeles or San Francisco. **Air New Zealand** (☎ 800/262–1234 in the U.S., 800/663–5494 in Canada; 13–2476 in Australia). **Canadian Air International** (☎ 800/665–1177 in Canada, 800/426–7000 in the U.S.; 02/9299–7843 in Australia). **Delta** (☎ 800/221–1212) to Sydney. **Qantas** (☎ 800/227–4500; 13–1313 in Australia) to Sydney, Melbourne, Brisbane, Cairns, Perth. **United** (☎ 800/538–2929; 13–1777 in Australia) to Sydney, Melbourne.

➤ FROM THE U.K.: From the United Kingdom to Australia **British Airways** (☎ 0345/222–111) and **Qantas** (☎ 0345/747–767 or 0800/747–767) are the major carriers. Qantas has the greatest number of flights and serves nine Australian cities, offering daily flights to Sydney and Perth. Other carriers flying from Britain to Australia are **Air New Zealand** (☎ 0181/741–2299), **Cathay Pacific** (☎ 0171/747–8888; 13–1747 in Australia), **Japan Airlines** (☎ 0171/408–1000), and **Singapore Airlines** (☎ 0181/747–0007; 13–1011 in Australia).

➤ WITHIN AUSTRALIA: **Ansett** (☎ 800/366–1300 in the U.S. and Canada; ☎ 0171/434–4071 in the U.K.; 13–1300 in Australia) and its regional subsidiaries such as **Kendall** (☎ 1800/33–8894 in Australia), **Hazelton, Flight West,** and **Airlines of Tasmania** (☎ 03/6248–5030 or 03/6391–8755 or 1800/03–0550 in Australia); and **Qantas** (☎ 13–1313 in Australia), and its subsidiaries of **Eastern Australia, Southern Australia, Sunstate,** and **Airlink,** are the major domestic airlines. In South Australia: **Air Kangaroo Island** (☎ 13–1301), **Augusta Airways** (☎ 08/8234–3000).

GET THE LOWEST FARE

The least-expensive airfares to Australia are priced for round-trip travel. Major airlines usually require that you **book far in advance and stay at least seven days** and no more than 30 to get the lowest fares. Ask about "ultrasaver" fares, which are the cheapest; they must be booked 90 days in advance and are nonrefundable. A little more expensive are "supersaver" fares, which require only a 30-day advance purchase. Remember that penalties for refunds or scheduling changes are stiffer for international tickets, usually about $150. International flights are also sensitive to the season: **plan to fly in the off season** for the cheapest fares. If your destination or home city has more than one gateway, **compare prices to and from different airports.** Also price flights scheduled for off-peak hours, which may be significantly less expensive.

To save money on flights from the United Kingdom and back, **look into an APEX or Super-PEX ticket.** APEX tickets must be booked in advance and have certain restrictions. Super-PEX tickets can be purchased at the airport on the day of departure—subject to availability.

DISCOUNT PASSES

Qantas has a **Discover Australia Fare,** which gives a 30% discount off the normal full economy fare on its domestic routes. These fares can either be purchased before arrival, or once you have arrived in Australia.

Qantas's **Boomerang Pass** is a discount air-travel pass valid for a minimum of two and a maximum of 10 sectors of economy-class air travel. Two price levels apply to Australian cities and those in other Qantas destinations, such as New Zealand and Fiji. Flights to the less expensive "zone-one" cities cost $160 per sector. Flights to "zone-two" locations, such as Perth, Ayers Rock, some of the resort islands, and flights to New Zealand and Fiji, cost $200 per sector. The two "zone" options can be combined to suit your flight plans. The pass must be purchased outside Australia.

Ansett's **Visit Australia/New Zealand Pass** must also be purchased overseas, and a minimum of two and maximum of 10 sectors also applies. The basic "one-zone" pass costs $160 and allows travel throughout *either* east-

ern *or* western Australia, as well as sectors *within* New Zealand with the exception of Auckland–Queenstown and Rotorua–Queenstown flights. "Two-zone" cross zones: for example flights from eastern to western zones in Australia and flights from Australia to New Zealand. Ansett's **See Australia Fare** cuts up to 30% off normal economy-class fares without restrictions; tickets must be purchased before you leave home or within 30 days of your arrival. The company's flights between Sydney and Auckland, New Zealand, are not included in See Australia discounts, only the sector-based passes mentioned above.

DON'T STOP UNLESS YOU MUST

When you book, **look for nonstop flights** and **remember that "direct" flights stop at least once.** International flights on a country's flag carrier are almost always nonstop; U.S. airlines often fly direct. Try to **avoid connecting flights,** which require a change of plane. Two airlines may jointly operate a connecting flight, so ask if your airline operates every segment—you may find that your preferred carrier flies you only part of the way.

USE AN AGENT

Travel agents, especially those who specialize in finding the lowest fares (☞ Discounts & Deals, *below*), can be especially helpful when booking a plane ticket. When you're quoted a price, **ask your agent if the price is likely to get any lower.** Good agents know the seasonal fluctuations of airfares and can usually anticipate a sale or fare war. However, waiting can be risky: The fare could go *up* as seats become scarce, and you may wait so long that your preferred flight sells out. A wait-and-see strategy works best if your plans are flexible, but if you must arrive and depart on certain dates, don't delay.

CHECK WITH CONSOLIDATORS

Consolidators buy tickets for scheduled flights at reduced rates from the airlines then sell them at prices that beat the best fare available directly from the airlines, usually without advance restrictions. Sometimes you can even get your money back if you need to return the ticket. Carefully

THE GOLD GUIDE / SMART TRAVEL TIPS

read the fine print detailing penalties for changes and cancellations, and **confirm your consolidator reservation with the airline.**

➤ CONSOLIDATORS: United States Air Consolidators Association (✉ 925 L St., Suite 220, Sacramento, CA 95814, ☎ 916/441–4166, FAX 916/441–3520).

AVOID GETTING BUMPED

Airlines routinely overbook planes, knowing that not everyone with a ticket will show up, but sometimes everyone does. When that happens, airlines ask for volunteers to give up their seats. In return these volunteers usually get a certificate for a free flight and are rebooked on the next flight out. If there are not enough volunteers the airline must choose who will be denied boarding. The first to get bumped are passengers who checked in late and those flying on discounted tickets, **so get to the gate and check in as early as possible,** especially during peak periods.

ENJOY THE FLIGHT

If you don't like airline food, **ask for special meals when booking.** These can be vegetarian, low-cholesterol, or kosher, for example.

To avoid jet lag try to maintain a normal routine while traveling. When flying to Australia that means **getting a full night's sleep.** For the rest of the flight, **eat light meals, drink water (not alcohol), and move about the cabin** to stretch your legs.

Some carriers have prohibited smoking throughout their systems; others allow smoking only on certain routes or even certain departures from that route, so **contact your carrier regarding its smoking policy.**

COMPLAIN IF NECESSARY

If your baggage goes astray or your flight goes awry, complain right away. Most carriers require that you file a claim immediately.

➤ AIRLINE COMPLAINTS: U.S. Department of Transportation **Aviation Consumer Protection Division** (✉ C-75, Washington, DC 20590, ☎ 202/366–2220). **Federal Aviation Administration (FAA) Consumer Hotline** (☎ 800/322–7873).

AIRPORTS

The major airports are **Sydney Kingsford-Smith Airport, Melbourne Tullamarine Airport, Brisbane Airport,** and **Cairns International Airport.**

➤ AIRPORT INFORMATION: **Sydney Kingsford-Smith Airport** (☎ 61-29/667–9111). **Melbourne Tullamarine Airport** (☎ 61-39/297–1600). **Brisbane Airport** (☎ 61-73/860–8600). **Cairns International Airport** (☎ 61-70/52–38–77).

B

BUS TRAVEL

Most Australian towns are well served by bus. Route networks of large express companies cover the nation's major highways and link up with regional operators that serve smaller communities. Buses are usually air-conditioned, with toilets and, on some routes, hostesses. Drivers run videos from time to time on overhead monitors. One advantage of bus touring is that drivers also act as guides, sharing their considerable knowledge of the countryside, blending illuminating descriptions of the areas you traverse with anecdotes about local characters.

In addition to the national bus passes on sale overseas (☞ Discount Passes, *above*), regional passes can be bought in Australia. An example is the Tasmanian Redline Coaches *Tassie Wilderness Pass*, which is valid for 7-, 14-, or 30-day periods. Costs range from $99 to $199.

Following are some travel times and approximate one-way costs at press time: Sydney–Melbourne (15 hours, $56); Sydney–Adelaide (23 hours, $99); Sydney–Brisbane (17 hours, $72); Brisbane–Cairns (25 hours, $143); Melbourne–Adelaide (10 hours, $56); Adelaide–Perth, (35 hours, $207); Adelaide–Alice Springs (20 hours, $148); Alice Springs–Ayers Rock (6 hours, $81).

➤ BUS LINES: The major national bus lines are **Greyhound Pioneer Australia** (☎ 13–2030 in Australia) and **McCafferty's** (☎ 13–1499), which run between most major cities.

DISCOUNT PASSES

Greyhound Pioneer Australia operates the national bus network and offers passes that result in considerable savings, especially when purchased overseas. Most can be bought on arrival in Australia, but at a 10%–15% higher price.

The **Aussie Pass** offers a variety of unlimited travel itineraries over the entire Greyhound Pioneer network, for periods ranging from 7 to 90 non-consecutive days, within time limits of 30–180 days. Prices vary from $475 to $2,335 for adults, with 10% discounts (except on the 90-day pass) applying to children, YHA card holders, and VIP and ISIC Backpacker card holders. Holders of International Student Cards are eligible for a 20% reduction. McCafferty's offers comparable **Travel Australia** passes, along with a number of regional passes. These passes, some varieties of which include discounts for accommodations and sightseeing, are available in the United States and Canada through **ATS Tours** (☎ 800/423–2880, FAX 310/643–0032, on-demand doc. 510) and in Canada through **Goway Travel** (☎ 800/387–8850).

BUSINESS HOURS

As a rule, business hours in Australia are weekdays 9–5; this applies to post offices as well. Banks are open Monday–Thursday 9:30–4, Friday 9:30–5. In some states a few banks are open on Saturday mornings. Shops are normally open weekdays 8:30–5:30, with one late closing at 9 PM. On Saturday shops are open from 8:30 to between noon and 4. Some stores, particularly those in the tourist areas of major cities, may be open a few hours on Sunday. In the Northern Territory, hours are most commonly 8:00–4:40 for government departments.

C

CAMERAS, CAMCORDERS, & COMPUTERS

Always **keep your film, tape, or computer disks out of the sun.** Carry an extra supply of batteries, and **be prepared to turn on your camera, camcorder, or laptop** to prove to security personnel that the device is real. Always **ask for hand inspection of film,** which becomes clouded after successive exposure to airport x-ray machines, and **keep videotapes and computer disks away from metal detectors.**

➤ PHOTO HELP: Kodak Information Center (☎ 800/242–2424). *Kodak Guide to Shooting Great Travel Pictures,* available in bookstores or from Fodor's Travel Publications (☎ 800/533–6478; $16.50 plus $4 shipping).

CUSTOMS

Before departing, **register your foreign-made camera or laptop with U.S. Customs** (☞ Customs & Duties, *below*). If your equipment is U.S.-made, call the consulate of the country you'll be visiting to find out whether the device should be registered with local customs upon arrival.

CAR RENTAL

Rates in Sydney begin at $41 a day and $246 a week for an economy car with air conditioning, a manual transmission, and 100 free kilometers. Rates in Auckland begin at $48 a day and $270 a week. This does not include tax on car rentals, which is 1.5% in Sydney and 12.5% in Auckland. Travelers renting a car in Sydney must purchase mandatory collision insurance, which is included in the price.

➤ MAJOR AGENCIES: **Budget** (☎ 800/527–0700, 0800/181181 in the U.K.). **Dollar** (☎ 800/800–4000; 0990/565656 in the U.K., where it is known as Eurodollar). **Hertz** (☎ 800/654–3001, 800/263–0600 in Canada, 0345/555888 in the U.K.). **National InterRent** (☎ 800/227–3876; 0345/222525 in the U.K., where it is known as Europcar InterRent).

➤ LOCAL AGENCIES: For renting within Australia, **Brits** (1800/331–454) is the only national rental group specializing in long-distance campervan and 4-wheel-drive vehicles that they allow across all state borders.

CUT COSTS

To get the best deal, **book through a travel agent who is willing to shop around.**

Also **ask your travel agent about a company's customer-service record.** How has it responded to late plane

THE GOLD GUIDE / SMART TRAVEL TIPS

arrivals and vehicle mishaps? Are there often lines at the rental counter, and, if you're traveling during a holiday period, does a confirmed reservation guarantee you a car?

Be sure to **look into wholesalers,** companies that do not own fleets but rent in bulk from those that do and often offer better rates than traditional car-rental operations. Prices are best during off-peak periods. Rentals booked through wholesalers must be paid for before you leave the United States.

➤ RENTAL WHOLESALERS: The **Kemwel Group** (☎ 914/835–5555 or 800/678–0678, FAX 914/835–5126).

NEED INSURANCE?

When driving a rented car you are generally responsible for any damage to or loss of the vehicle. You also are liable for any property damage or personal injury that you may cause while driving. Before you rent, **see what coverage you already have** under the terms of your personal auto-insurance policy and credit cards.

BEWARE SURCHARGES

Before you pick up a car in one city and leave it in another, **ask about drop-off charges or one-way service fees,** which can be substantial. Note, too, that some rental agencies charge extra if you return the car before the time specified on your contract. To avoid a hefty refueling fee, **fill the tank just before you turn in the car,** but be aware that gas stations near the rental outlet may overcharge.

MEET THE REQUIREMENTS

In Australia your own driver's license is accepted at some rental companies. An International Driver's Permit is required at others; it's available from the American or Canadian automobile association, or in the United Kingdom from the Automobile Association or Royal Automobile Club.

CHILDREN & TRAVEL

CHILDREN IN AUSTRALIA

Be sure to plan ahead and **involve your youngsters** as you outline your trip. When packing, include things to keep them busy en route. On sightseeing days try to schedule activities of special interest to your children. If you

are renting a car don't forget to **arrange for a car seat** when you reserve.

BABY SUPPLIES

Department and drugstores (called **chemists** locally) in Australia carry a wide range of baby products such as disposable diapers (ask for napkins or **nappies**), formula, and baby food.

DINING

In Australia, eating out with children is no problem in **family restaurants,** which cater to children with high chairs and booster seats. This type of restaurant is usually found in suburbs rather than city centers. For more casual eating, coffee shops, delis, bistros, and fast-food eateries, both international chains and Aussie versions such as Hungry Jack's, welcome children.

HOTELS

Most hotels in Australia allow children under a certain age to stay in their parents' room at no extra charge, but others charge them as extra adults; be sure to **ask about the cutoff age for children's discounts.**

In hotels in Australia, roll-away beds are usually free, and children under 12 sharing a hotel room with adults either stay free or receive a discount rate. Few hotels have separate facilities for children. Exceptions include some of the Great Barrier Reef resorts.

Home hosting provides an ideal opportunity for visitors to stay with a local family, either in town or on a working farm. For information on home and farm stays, home exchange, and apartment rentals, *see* Lodging, *below.*

➤ BEST CHOICES: The **Hyatt hotels** (☎ 13–1234) located in Sydney, Sanctuary Cove, Coolum Beach, Perth, Melbourne, Canberra, and Adelaide allow children under 18 to stay free when sharing a room with parents. The Hyatt Regency Sanctuary Cove and Hyatt Regency Coolum Beach both have a Camp Hyatt program for children.

FLYING

As a general rule, infants under two not occupying a seat fly at greatly reduced fares and occasionally for free. If your children are two or older **ask about children's airfares.**

In general the adult baggage allowance applies to children paying half or more of the adult fare. When booking, **ask about carry-on allowances for those traveling with infants.** In general, for babies charged 10% of the adult fare you are allowed one carry-on bag and a collapsible stroller, which may have to be checked; you may be limited to less if the flight is full.

According to the FAA it's a good idea to use safety seats aloft for children weighing less than 40 pounds. Airlines, however, can set their own policies: U.S. carriers allow FAA-approved models but usually require that you buy a ticket, even if your child would otherwise ride free, since the seats must be strapped into regular seats. Airline rules vary regarding their use, so it's important to **check your airline's policy about using safety seats during takeoff and landing.** Safety seats cannot obstruct any of the other passengers in the row, so get an appropriate seat assignment as early as possible.

When making your reservation, **request children's meals or a free-standing bassinet** if you need them; the latter are available only to those seated at the bulkhead, where there's enough legroom. Remember, however, that bulkhead seats may not have their own overhead bins, and there's no storage space in front of you—a major inconvenience.

GROUP TRAVEL

If you're planning to take your kids on a tour, look for companies that specialize in family travel.

➤ FAMILY-FRIENDLY TOUR OPERATORS: **Grandtravel** (✉ 6900 Wisconsin Ave., Suite 706, Chevy Chase, MD 20815, ☎ 301/986–0790 or 800/247–7651) for people traveling with grandchildren ages 7–17. **Rascals in Paradise** (✉ 650 5th St., Suite 505, San Francisco, CA 94107, ☎ 415/978–9800 or 800/872–7225, FAX 415/442–0289).

CONSUMER PROTECTION

Whenever possible, **pay with a major credit card** so you can cancel payment if there's a problem, provided that you can provide documentation. This is a good practice whether you're buying travel arrangements before your trip or shopping at your destination.

If you're doing business with a particular company for the first time, **contact your local Better Business Bureau and the attorney general's offices** in your state and the company's home state, as well. Have any complaints been filed?

Finally, if you're buying a package or tour, always **consider travel insurance** that includes default coverage (☞ Insurance, *above*).

➤ LOCAL BBBs: **Council of Better Business Bureaus** (✉ 4200 Wilson Blvd., Suite 800, Arlington, VA 22203, ☎ 703/276–0100, FAX 703/525–8277).

CUSTOMS & DUTIES

When shopping, **keep receipts** for all of your purchases. Upon reentering the country, **be ready to show customs officials what you've bought.** If you feel a duty is incorrect, appeal the assessment. If you object to the way your clearance was handled, get the inspector's badge number. In either case, first ask to see a supervisor, then write to the port director at the address listed on your receipt. Send a copy of the receipt and other appropriate documentation. If you still don't get satisfaction you can take your case to customs headquarters in Washington.

ENTERING AUSTRALIA

Australia has strict laws prohibiting or restricting the import of weapons and firearms. Animals and certain foodstuffs are subject to quarantine. Anti-drug laws are strictly enforced, and penalties are severe. Nonresidents over 18 years of age may bring in 250 cigarettes, or 250 grams of cigars or tobacco, and 1.125 liters of liquor, provided this is carried with them. Other taxable goods to the value of $400 for adults and $200 for children may be included in personal baggage duty free.

ENTERING THE U.S.

You may bring home $400 worth of foreign goods duty-free if you've been out of the country for at least 48 hours and haven't already used the $400 allowance or any part of it in the past 30 days.

Travelers 21 and older may bring back 1 liter of alcohol duty-free. In addition, regardless of your age, you are allowed 200 cigarettes and 100 non-Cuban cigars. (At press time, a federal rule restricting tobacco access to persons 18 years and older did not apply to importation.) Antiques, which the U.S. Customs Service defines as objects more than 100 years old, enter duty-free, as do original works of art done entirely by hand, including paintings, drawings, and sculptures.

You may also send packages home duty-free: up to $200 worth of goods for personal use, with a limit of one parcel per addressee per day (and no alcohol or tobacco products or perfume worth more than $5); label the package PERSONAL USE, and attach a list of its contents and their retail value. Do not label the package UNSOLICITED GIFT, or your duty-free exemption will drop to $100. Mailed items do not affect your duty-free allowance on your return.

➤ INFORMATION: **U.S. Customs Service** (Inquiries, ✉ Box 7407, Washington, DC 20044, ☎ 202/927–6724; complaints, ✉ Commissioner's Office, 1301 Constitution Ave. NW, Washington, DC 20229; registration of equipment, ✉ Resource Management, 1301 Constitution Ave. NW, Washington DC, 20229, ☎ 202/927–0540).

ENTERING CANADA

If you've been out of Canada for at least seven days you may bring in C$500 worth of goods duty-free. If you've been away for fewer than seven days but more than 48 hours, the duty-free allowance drops to C$200; if your trip lasts 24–48 hours, the allowance is C$50. You may not pool allowances with family members. Goods claimed under the C$500 exemption may follow you by mail; those claimed under the lesser exemptions must accompany you.

Alcohol and tobacco products may be included in the seven-day and 48-hour exemptions but not in the 24-hour exemption. If you meet the age requirements of the province or territory through which you reenter Canada you may bring in, duty-free, 1.14 liters (40 imperial ounces) of

wine or liquor *or* 24 12-ounce cans or bottles of beer or ale. If you are 16 or older you may bring in, duty-free, 200 cigarettes and 50 cigars; these items must accompany you.

You may send an unlimited number of gifts worth up to C$60 each duty-free to Canada. Label the package UNSOLICITED GIFT—VALUE UNDER $60. Alcohol and tobacco are excluded.

➤ INFORMATION: **Revenue Canada** (✉ 2265 St. Laurent Blvd. S, Ottawa, Ontario K1G 4K3, ☎ 613/993–0534, 800/461–9999 in Canada).

ENTERING THE U.K.

From countries outside the EU, including Australia, you may import, duty-free, 200 cigarettes or 50 cigars; 1 liter of spirits or 2 liters of fortified or sparkling wine or liqueurs; 2 liters of still table wine; 60 milliliters of perfume; 250 milliliters of toilet water; plus £136 worth of other goods, including gifts and souvenirs.

➤ INFORMATION: **HM Customs and Excise** (✉ Dorset House, Stamford St., London SE1 9NG, ☎ 0171/202–4227).

D

DINING

Some Australian restaurants offer a fixed-price dinner, but the majority are à la carte. It's wise to **make a reservation** and **inquire if the restaurant has a liquor license** or is "BYOB" or "BYO" (Bring Your Own Bottle). Some are both BYOB and licensed to sell beer, wine, and liquor.

Down Under, entrée means appetizer and main courses are American entrées—more logical than what we call them in the States, in fact. You'll also encounter the term "silver service," which indicates upscale dining. "Bistro" generally refers to a relatively inexpensive place. French fries are called chips; if you want ketchup, ask for tomato sauce.

Breakfast is usually served between 7 and 10, lunch 11:30–2:30, and dinner service begins around 6:30. Outside of these times it may be hard to find anything but snacks, particularly in the countryside. And despite the vast array of restaurants in the cities—the Melbourne metropolitan area alone has some 1,500—it's sometimes difficult in business districts to locate a restaurant where you can sit at a table for lunch, since Australian workers tend to eat fast food or order their food to go. Look in shopping areas instead, where arcade tearooms and cafés serve lunch and afternoon tea. Don't be surprised if someone joins you at your table in the more humble cafés. You also might try a counter lunch in a pub bar; the food is similar to that in England, and pies and pasties, sausage and mash (potatoes), and a ploughman's lunch of bread, cheese, and pickles are the common fare. You can eat similar food in the many wine bars that have sprung up, accompanied by a glass of one of Australia's excellent wines.

DISABILITIES & ACCESSIBILITY

ACCESS IN AUSTRALIA

➤ LOCAL RESOURCES: The **Australian Council for Rehabilitation of the Disabled** (ACROD, 33 Thesiger Ct., Deakin, ACT 2605, ☎ 02/6282–4333) is one source of information on facilities. Since provisions vary from state to state, for additional information contact the ACROD offices in the states you plan to visit: Australian Capital Territory, ☎ 02/6282–4333; New South Wales, ☎ 02/9809–4488; Northern Territory, ☎ 08/8947–0681; Queensland, ☎ 07/3367–1605; South Australia, ☎ 08/8244–5529; Tasmania, ☎ 03/6223–6086; Victoria, ☎ 03/9690–2266; Western Australia, ☎ 08/9221–9066.

TIPS AND HINTS

When discussing accessibility with an operator or reservationist, **ask hard questions.** Are there any stairs, inside *or* out? Are there grab bars next to the toilet *and* in the shower/tub? How wide is the doorway to the room? To the bathroom? For the most extensive facilities meeting the latest legal specifications, **opt for newer accommodations,** which are more likely to have been designed with access in mind. Older buildings or ships may offer more limited facilities. Be sure to **discuss your needs before booking.**

➤ COMPLAINTS: **Disability Rights Section** (✉ U.S. Department of Justice, Box 66738, Washington, DC 20035–6738, ☎ 202/514–0301 or 800/514–0301, FAX 202/307–1198, TTY 202/514–0383 or 800/514–0383) for general complaints. Aviation **Consumer Protection Division** (☞ Air Travel, *above*) for airline-related problems. **Civil Rights Office** (✉ U.S. Department of Transportation, Departmental Office of Civil Rights, S-30, 400 7th St. SW, Room 10215, Washington, DC, 20590, ☎ 202/366–4648) for problems with surface transportation.

AIR TRAVEL

In addition to making arrangements for wheelchair-using passengers, both Qantas and Ansett Airlines accommodate trained dogs accompanying sight- and hearing-impaired passengers. On Air New Zealand, wheelchairs for in-flight mobility are standard equipment; seat-belt extensions, quadriplegic harnesses, and padded leg rests are also available. Ask for the company's brochure "Air Travel for People with Disabilities."

CAR RENTAL

Only **Budget** (☎ 800/527–0700 in the U.S. and Canada) offers cars fitted with hand controls, but supplies are limited. **Hertz** (☎ 800/654–3131 in the U.S., and 800/263–0600 Canada) will fit hand-held controls onto standard cars in some cities.

LODGING

The major hotel chains (such as Regent, Sheraton, InterContinental, Ramada, Hilton, Holiday Inn, and Hyatt) provide three or four rooms with disabled facilities in most of their properties.

The **National Roads and Motorists Association (NRMA)** (✉ 151 Clarence St., Sydney, NSW 2000, ☎ 13–2132) publishes the $10 *Accommodation Directory,* indicating which properties have independent wheelchair access and which provide wheelchair access with assistance. Another source of information is the "Disabled Travellers Guide to Australia, Accessible Motels and Hotels" from the **Council of Disabled Motorists** (✉ 2A Station St., Coburg, VIC 3058, ☎ 03/9386–0413).

TAXIS

In Australia, wheelchair-accessible taxis are available in most state capitals: **Adelaide** (☎ 08/8234–6444), **Brisbane** (☎ 07/3391–1000), **Darwin** (☎ 08/8981–8777), **Melbourne** (☎ 03/9345–3455 or 13–2227), **Perth** (☎ 08/9322–0111 or 08/9333–3377), **Sydney** (☎ 02/9339–0200).

TRAIN TRAVEL

Passengers on mainline passenger trains in Australia can request collapsible wheelchairs to negotiate narrow interior corridors. However, compact toilet areas and platform access problems make long-distance train travel difficult. Countrylink's (New South Wales) XPLORER and XPT trains have specially designed wheelchair access toilets, and ramps for boarding and disembarking are provided.

Both **Countrylink,** the New South Wales state rail company, and **V/Line** (Victoria) issue brochures detailing assistance available on metropolitan, country and interstate trains. To request these, call 13–1500 (Sydney metropolitan) or 13–2232 (NSW country and interstate) in Sydney, or 03/9619–2189 for V/Line in Melbourne.

TRAVEL AGENCIES & TOUR OPERATORS

The Americans with Disabilities Act requires that travel firms serve the needs of all travelers. That said, you should note that some agencies and operators specialize in making travel arrangements for individuals and groups with disabilities.

➤ TRAVELERS WITH MOBILITY PROBLEMS: **Access Adventures** (✉ 206 Chestnut Ridge Rd., Rochester, NY 14624, ☎ 716/889–9096), run by a former physical-rehabilitation counselor. **Accessible Journeys** (✉ 35 W. Sellers Ave., Ridley Park, PA 19078, ☎ 610/521–0339 or 800/846–4537, FAX 610/521–6959), for escorted tours exclusively for travelers with mobility impairments. **Hinsdale Travel Service** (✉ 201 E. Ogden Ave., Suite 100, Hinsdale, IL 60521, ☎ 630/325–1335), a travel agency that benefits from the advice of wheelchair traveler Janice Perkins. **Wheelchair Journeys** (✉ 16979 Redmond Way, Redmond, WA 98052, ☎ 206/885–2210 or 800/313–4751), for general travel arrangements.

➤ TRAVELERS WITH DEVELOPMENTAL DISABILITIES: Sprout (✉ 893 Amsterdam Ave., New York, NY 10025, ☎ 212/222–9575 or 888/222–9575, FAX 212/222–9768).

DISCOUNTS & DEALS

Shop intelligently: **compare all your options before making a choice.** A plane ticket bought with a promotional coupon may not be cheaper than the least expensive fare from a discount ticket agency. For high-price travel purchases, such as packages or tours, keep in mind that what you get is just as important as what you save. Just because something is cheap doesn't mean it's a bargain.

LOOK IN YOUR WALLET

When you use your credit card to make travel purchases you may get free travel-accident insurance, collision-damage insurance, and medical or legal assistance, depending on the card and the bank that issued it. American Express, MasterCard, and Visa provide one or more of these services, so **get a copy of your credit card's travel-benefits policy.** If you are a member of the American Automobile Association (AAA) or an oil-company-sponsored road-assistance plan, always **ask hotel or car-rental reservationists about auto-club discounts.** Some clubs offer additional discounts on tours, cruises, or admission to attractions. And don't forget that auto-club membership entitles you to free maps and trip-planning services.

DIAL FOR DOLLARS

To save money, **look into "1-800" discount reservations services,** which use their buying power to get a better price on hotels, airline tickets, even car rentals. When booking a room, always **call the hotel's local toll-free number** (if one is available) rather than the central reservations number—you'll often get a better price. Always ask about special packages or corporate rates.

When shopping for the best deal on hotels and car rentals **look for guaranteed exchange rates,** which protect you against a falling dollar. With your rate locked in you won't pay more even if the price goes up in the local currency.

➤ AIRLINE TICKETS: ☎ 800/FLY–4–
LESS.

➤ HOTEL ROOMS: **Steigenberger
Reservation Service** (☎ 800/223–
5652). **Travel Interlink** (☎ 800/888–
5898). **VacationLand** (☎ 800/
245–0050).

SAVE ON COMBOS

Packages and guided tours can both
save you money, but don't confuse
the two. When you buy a package
your travel remains independent, just
as though you had planned and
booked the trip yourself. Fly/drive
packages, which combine airfare and
car rental, are often a good deal.

JOIN A CLUB?

Many companies sell discounts in the
form of travel clubs and coupon
books, but these cost money. You
must use participating advertisers to
get a deal, and only after you recoup
the initial membership cost or book
price do you begin to save. If you
plan to use the club or coupons
frequently you may save considerably.
Before signing up, find out what
discounts you get for free.

➤ DISCOUNT CLUBS: **Entertainment
Travel Editions** (✉ Box 1068, Trum-
bull, CT 06611, ☎ 800/445–4137;
$28–$53, depending on destination).
Great American Traveler (✉ Box
27965, Salt Lake City, UT 84127,
☎ 800/548–2812; $49.95 per year).
**Moment's Notice Discount Travel
Club** (✉ 7301 New Utrecht Ave.,
Brooklyn, NY 11204, ☎ 718/234–
6295; $25 per year, single or family).
Privilege Card International (✉ 201
E. Commerce St., Suite 198,
Youngstown, OH 44503, ☎ 330/
746–5211 or 800/236–9732; $74.95
per year). **Sears's Mature Outlook**
(✉ Box 9390, Des Moines, IA 50306,
☎ 800/336–6330; $14.95 per year).
Travelers Advantage (✉ CUC Travel
Service, 3033 S. Parker Rd., Suite
1000, Aurora, CO 80014, ☎ 800/
548–1116 or 800/648–4037, $49
per year, single or family). **Worldwide
Discount Travel Club** (✉ 1674
Meridian Ave., Miami Beach, FL
33139, ☎ 305/534–2082; $50 per
year family, $40 single).

DRIVING

Driving is easy in Australia, once you
adjust to traveling on the left. The
catch-phrase is: **Drive left, look right.**
"Look right" is the pedestrian's
caveat—and a serious one. For Americans, stepping into the street means
looking left for oncoming traffic. Do
that Down Under and you could be in
trouble. Repeat: Drive left, look right.

Except for some expressways in and
around the major cities, the majority
of highways are two-lane roads with
frequent passing lanes. Roads are
usually paved and well maintained,
though traffic lanes are narrower than
in the United States. Always **take
precautions when you drive through
the Outback,** however. **Road Trains**
(i.e. truck trains) can get up to fifty
yards long, and passing them at that
length becomes a matter of great
caution, especially on roads in the
bush. There are **no speed limits** on the
open road in the Northern Territory.

Many **Outback** roads are unpaved,
traffic is very light, and temperatures
can be extreme. **Carry plenty of water
and always tell someone your
itinerary and schedule.** Flash floods
from sudden rain showers can occur
on low-lying roads. Don't try to
outdrive them—**get to higher ground
immediately when it rains.**

Service stations are generally plentiful,
although full service is common only
in rural areas. The cost of gasoline
("petrol") varies around the country
from about 70¢ per liter in Sydney to
about 90¢ per liter in the Outback.
Speed limits are 60 kilometers per
hour (kph) in populated areas, and
100–110 kph on open roads—the
equivalent of 37 and 62–68 mph,
respectively. Surveillance of speeders
and "drink-driving" (the legal limit is
a tough .05% blood alcohol level) is
thorough and penalties are high. Seat
belts are mandatory nationwide for
drivers and all passengers.

Road regulations differ from state to
state and even city to city. At designated intersections in Melbourne's
Golden Mile (the central business
district), you must get into the left
lane to make a right-hand turn—
watch for the sign RIGHT HAND TURN
FROM LEFT LANE ONLY. Traffic circles
are widely used at intersections
throughout Australia; cars that have
already entered the circle have the
right-of-way. It's wise to **pick up a
copy of the Highway Code** of any

THE GOLD GUIDE / SMART TRAVEL TIPS

state or territory in which you plan to drive from the local automobile club. The Australian Automobile Association has a branch in each state, known as the National Roads and Motorists' Association (NRMA) in New South Wales and Canberra, the Automobile Association in the Northern Territory (AANT), and the Royal Automobile Club (RAC) in all other states. It is affiliated with AAA worldwide and offers reciprocal services to American, Canadian, and British members, including emergency road service and discounts on car rental, accommodations, and other services. Reservations must be made through an NRMA or RAC office.

When planning a driving itinerary, it's vital to bear in mind the **huge distances** involved. Queensland's Brisbane is 1,031 kilometers (640 miles) by road from Sydney, 1,718 kilometers (1,067 miles) from Melbourne, and almost the same distance from Cairns in its own state. The journey from Sydney to Alice Springs, the gateway to Ayers Rock, is 2½ hours by jet and a grueling 52 hours by bus. Between major cities, flying is usually advised.

Jet lag is a good reason to avoid a long drive after your arrival in Australia. There is a **high accident rate** for jet-lagged people who undertake long rural drives.

➤ AUTO CLUBS: In the U.S., **American Automobile Association** (☎ 800/564–6222). In the U.K., **Automobile Association** (AA, ☎ 0990/500–600), **Royal Automobile Club** (RAC, membership ☎ 0990/722–722; insurance 0345/121–345).

E
ELECTRICITY

To use your U.S.-purchased electric-powered equipment, **bring a converter and adapter.** The electrical current in Australia is 240 volts, 50 cycles alternating current (AC); wall outlets take slanted three-prong plugs (but not the U.K. three-prong) and plugs with two flat prongs set in a V.

If your appliances are dual-voltage, you'll need only an adapter. Don't use 110-volt outlets, marked FOR SHAVERS ONLY, for high-wattage appliances such as blow-dryers. Most laptops

operate equally well on 110 and 220 volts and so require only an adapter.

G
GAY & LESBIAN TRAVEL

Politically and socially, Australia is one of the gay-friendliest countries in the world, ranking right up there with the Netherlands, Denmark, and Canada. Queer tourism associations are well established and have plenty to offer lesbian and gay tourists.

Australia is famous for its many festivals and parties, several of which are gay-oriented. In March, more than 500,000 onlookers are drawn to the **Sydney Gay and Lesbian Mardi Gras.** Sydney is the country's leading lesbian and gay destination, with Melbourne not far behind. **Midsumma** is Melbourne's queer festival, with parties and events running from January through early February. Most other Australian cities and resort areas, especially on the east and southeast coasts, are fairly tolerant. In the west, Perth has a relatively small community, but there still is plenty going on. The one part of the country still rather closed-minded about queer life is Tasmania; however, the island still has a number of gay guest houses and B&Bs. Darwin and the Outback are also areas where same-sex traveling companions might want to exercise discretion.

➤ U.S. TOUR OPERATORS: **Atlantis Events** (⊠ 9060 Santa Monica Blvd., Suite 310, West Hollywood, CA 90069, ☎ 310/281–5450 or 800/628–5268), for mixed gay and lesbian travel. **Men on Vacation** (4715 30th St., Suite 6, San Diego, CA 92116, ☎ 619/641–7085), for group tours to Australia and New Zealand. **Toto Tours** (⊠ 1326 W. Albion Ave., Suite 3W, Chicago, IL 60626, ☎ 773/274–8686 or 800/565–1241, FAX 773/274–8695), for groups.

➤ AUSTRALIAN GAY- AND LESBIAN-FRIENDLY TRAVEL AGENCY: **Australian Gay and Lesbian Tourism Association** (Box 208, Darlinghurst, New South Wales, 2010, ☎ 02/9362–0900) for names and information on local tour operators, agencies, accommodations, and other businesses of interest to the lesbian and gay community.

➤ U.S. Gay- and Lesbian-Friendly Travel Agencies: **Advance Damron** (✉ 1 Greenway Plaza, Suite 800, Houston, TX 77046, ☎ 713/682–2002 or 800/695–0880, FAX 713/888–1010). **Club Travel** (✉ 8739 Santa Monica Blvd., West Hollywood, CA 90069, ☎ 310/358–2200 or 800/429–8747, FAX 310/358–2222). **Islanders/Kennedy Travel** (✉ 183 W. 10th St., New York, NY 10014, ☎ 212/242–3222 or 800/988–1181, FAX 212/929–8530). **Now Voyager** (✉ 4406 18th St., San Francisco, CA 94114, ☎ 415/626–1169 or 800/255–6951, FAX 415/626–8626). **Yellowbrick Road** (✉ 1500 W. Balmoral Ave., Chicago, IL 60640, ☎ 773/561–1800 or 800/642–2488, FAX 773/561–4497). **Skylink Women's Travel** (✉ 3577 Moorland Ave., Santa Rosa, CA 95407, ☎ 707/585–8355 or 800/225–5759, FAX 707/584–5637), serving lesbian travelers.

➤ Publications: **Gay Maps Australia** (Box 1401, Bondi, Junction, NSW 2022, ☎ 02/9369–2738), for maps detailing gay attractions and businesses in Sydney, Brisbane, and Melbourne. The **G'day Guide** (Rainbow Travel Australia, 4 Baker St., St. Kilda, VIC 3182, ☎ 03/9525–4040, FAX 03/9534–3224) lists more than 150 gay and gay-friendly accommodations throughout Australia.

You'll find plenty of information on nightlife, travel, and queer life in *Campaign* (☎ 02/9332–3620, FAX 02/9361–5962) and *Outrage* (☎ 02/9360–4088), two monthly glossies on gay Australia. Some newspapers and magazines are also available at lesbigay bookstores in North America and the United Kingdom. Additionally, most major cities—including Sydney, Brisbane, Melbourne, Perth, and Adelaide—publish queer newspapers and/or have gay lesbian business directories.

H
HEALTH

Hygiene standards in Australia are high and well monitored, so **don't worry about drinking the water or eating fresh produce** in Australia. The major health hazard is sunburn or sunstroke: Australians suffer one of the world's highest incidences of skin cancer from overdoses of sun. Even

people who are not normally bothered by strong sun should cover up with a long-sleeve shirt, a hat, and long pants or a beach wrap. Keep in mind that at higher altitudes you will burn more easily. **Apply sunscreen liberally** before you go out—even for a half hour—and wear a visored cap or sunglasses.

You are also advised to protect yourself from mosquito bites during the summer months (particularly in the north of the continent) by applying a reliable insect repellent.

Dehydration is a serious danger that can be easily avoided, so be sure to carry water and drink often. Above all, **limit the amount of time you spend in the sun** for the first few days until you are acclimatized, and always avoid sunbathing in the middle of the day.

You may take a four weeks' supply of prescribed medication into Australia (more with a doctor's certificate).

MEDICAL PLANS

No one plans to get sick while traveling, but it happens, so **consider signing up with a medical-assistance company.** Members get doctor referrals, emergency evacuation or repatriation, 24-hour telephone hot lines for medical consultation, cash for emergencies, and other personal and legal assistance. Coverage varies by plan, so **review the benefits carefully.**

➤ Medical-Assistance Companies: **International SOS Assistance** (✉ Box 11568, Philadelphia, PA 19116, ☎ 215/244–1500 or 800/523–8930; ✉ Box 466, pl. Bonaventure, Montréal, Québec H5A 1C1, ☎ 514/874–7674 or 800/363–0263; ✉ 7 Old Lodge Pl., St. Margarets, Twickenham TW1 1RQ, England, ☎ 0181/744–0033). **MEDEX Assistance Corporation** (✉ Box 5375, Timonium, MD 21094, ☎ 410/453–6300 or 800/537–2029). **Traveler's Emergency Network** (✉ 3100 Tower Blvd., Suite 1000B, Durham, NC 27707, ☎ 919/490–6055 or 800/275–4836, FAX 919/493–8262). **TravMed** (✉ Box 5375, Timonium, MD 21094, ☎ 410/453–6380 or 800/732–5309). **Worldwide Assistance Services** (✉ 1133 15th St. NW, Suite 400, Washington, DC 20005, ☎ 202/331–1609 or 800/821–2828, FAX 202/828–5896).

DIVERS' ALERT

If you intend to take advantage of Australia's absolutely phenomenal opportunities for underwater exploration, **do not fly within 24 hours of scuba diving.**

I

INSURANCE

Travel insurance is the best way to **protect yourself against financial loss.** The most useful policies are trip-cancellation-and-interruption, default, medical, and comprehensive insurance.

Without insurance you will lose all or most of your money if you cancel your trip, regardless of the reason. It's essential that you **buy trip-cancellation-and-interruption insurance,** particularly if your airline ticket, cruise, or package tour is nonrefundable and cannot be changed. When considering how much coverage you need, look for a policy that will cover the cost of your trip plus the nondiscounted price of a one-way airline ticket, should you need to return home early. Also **consider default or bankruptcy insurance,** which protects you against a supplier's failure to deliver.

Medicare generally does not cover health-care costs outside the United States, nor do many privately issued policies. If your own policy does not cover you outside the United States, **consider buying supplemental medical coverage.** Remember that travel health insurance is different from a medical-assistance plan (☞ Health, *above*).

Citizens of the United Kingdom can buy an annual travel-insurance policy valid for most vacations during the year in which it's purchased. If you are pregnant or have a preexisting medical condition, make sure you're covered.

If you have purchased an expensive vacation, particularly one that involves travel abroad, comprehensive insurance is a must. **Look for comprehensive policies that include trip-delay insurance,** which will protect you in the event that weather problems cause you to miss your flight, tour, or cruise. A few insurers sell waivers for preexisting medical conditions. Companies that offer both features include

Access America, Carefree Travel, Travel Insured International, and Travel Guard (☞ *below*).

Always **buy travel insurance directly from the insurance company**; if you buy it from a travel agency or tour operator that goes out of business you probably will not be covered for the agency or operator's default, a major risk. Before you make any purchase, **review your existing health and home-owner's policies** to find out whether they cover expenses incurred while traveling.

➤ TRAVEL INSURERS: In the U.S., **Access America** (✉ 6600 W. Broad St., Richmond, VA 23230, ☎ 804/285–3300 or 800/284–8300), **Carefree Travel Insurance** (✉ Box 9366, 100 Garden City Plaza, Garden City, NY 11530, ☎ 516/294–0220 or 800/323–3149), **Near Travel Services** (✉ Box 1339, Calumet City, IL 60409, ☎ 708/868–6700 or 800/654–6700), **Travel Guard International** (✉ 1145 Clark St., Stevens Point, WI 54481, ☎ 715/345–0505 or 800/826–1300), **Travel Insured International** (✉ Box 280568, East Hartford, CT 06128–0568, ☎ 860/528–7663 or 800/243–3174), **Travelex Insurance Services** (✉ 11717 Burt St., Suite 202, Omaha, NE 68154-1500, ☎ 402/445–8637 or 800/228–9792, FAX 800/867–9531), **Wallach & Company** (✉ 107 W. Federal St., Box 480, Middleburg, VA 20118, ☎ 540/687–3166 or 800/237–6615). In Canada, **Mutual of Omaha** (✉ Travel Division, 500 University Ave., Toronto, Ontario M5G 1V8, ☎ 416/598–4083, 800/268–8825 in Canada). In the U.K., **Association of British Insurers** (✉ 51 Gresham St., London EC2V 7HQ, ☎ 0171/600–3333).

L

LANGUAGE

To an outsider's ear, Australian English can be mystifying. Not only is the accent thick and slightly slurred, but Australians have developed a vibrant vernacular quite distinct from that of any other English-speaking country. You can soon learn the idiom and how to speak "strine"—as Aussies (who also call themselves "Ozzies") pronounce "Australian"—with a copy of Danielle Martin's

Australians Say G'Day, which comes with a cassette tape recording to help you interpret the book's dialogues. Other useful guides to the intricacies of Australian terminology are *Australian Slang* by Lenie Johansen, and *The Best of Aussie Slang* by John Blackman. All of these books are available in Aussie bookstores.

LODGING

Except for designated bed-and-breakfasts and farm stays, the majority of prices listed by hotels are for room only, although resorts in remote areas may offer American Plan (three meals included) or Modified American Plan (two meals). Surcharges sometimes apply on weekends, long weekends, and during holiday seasons.

APARTMENT AND VILLA RENTALS

If you want a home base that's roomy enough for a family and comes with cooking facilities, **consider a furnished rental.** These can save you money, however some rentals are luxury properties, economical only when your party is large. Home-exchange directories list rentals (often second homes owned by prospective house swappers), and some services search for a house or apartment for you (even a castle if that's your fancy) and handle the paperwork. Some send an illustrated catalog; others send photographs only of specific properties, sometimes at a charge. Up-front registration fees may apply.

➤ RENTAL AGENTS: **Europa-Let/Tropical Inn-Let** (✉ 92 N. Main St., Ashland, OR 97520, ☎ 541/482–5806 or 800/462–4486, ☏ 541/482–0660). **Property Rentals International** (✉ 1008 Mansfield Crossing Rd., Richmond, VA 23236, ☎ 804/378–6054 or 800/220–3332, ☏ 804/379–2073). **Rent-a-Home International** (✉ 7200 34th Ave. NW, Seattle, WA 98117, ☎ 206/789–9377 or 800/488–7368, ☏ 206/789–9379).

CAMPING

Think twice before camping outside of designated campgrounds, particularly in the Outback, where such unexpected, and potentially fatal, dangers as flash floods can catch you by surprise. A four-wheel-drive vehicle is a necessity for any safari into the bush. Once there it is equally important to know what to look out for. Be sure to speak with the nearest park rangers before setting out.

The **National Roads and Motorists Association** (NRMA) (✉ 151 Clarence St., Sydney, NSW 2000, ☎ 13–2132) puts out the booklet "Outback Motoring" (free to members, $4 for nonmembers). Another NRMA publication, "Caravan and Camping Directory," lists campgrounds and costs $10 for nonmembers.

HOME & FARM STAYS

Home and farm stays, which are very popular with visitors to Australia, offer not only comfortable accommodations but a chance to get to know the lands and their people. Most operate on a bed-and-breakfast basis, though some also offer an evening meal. Farm accommodations vary from modest shearers' cabins to elegant homesteads. Guests can join in farm activities or explore the countryside. Some hosts offer day trips, as well as horseback riding, hiking, and fishing. For two people, the cost varies from $100–$250 per night, including all meals and some or all farm activities. Home stays, the urban equivalent of farm stays, are less expensive.

➤ RESERVATIONS: For information and reservations in the United States contact: **Australian Home Accommodation, represented by ATS/Sprint** (☎ 800/423–2880); **Australian Farm Host and Farm Holidays,** represented by ATS/Sprint, SO/PAC (☎ 800/551–2012), and **Pacific Destination Center** (☎ 800/227–5317); **Victoria Host Farms** and **Bed & Breakfast Australia,** represented by SO/PAC. Pacific Destination Center also represents **Grand Country Estates** and **Houseguest,** offering B&B accommodations in private homes.

A number of Queensland sheep and cattle stations offering farm and country vacations have banded together as the **Queensland Host Farm Association.** For information and reservations, contact the **Royal Automobile Club of Queensland** (RACQ) Travel Service (Box 537, Fortitude Valley, QLD 4006, ☎ 07/3361–2390, ☏ 07/3257–1504).

HOTELS AND MOTELS

Hotel and motel rooms generally have private bathrooms with a combined shower/tub—called "en suites"—although some bed-and-breakfast hotels and hostels require guests to share bathrooms. Tea and coffeemakers are a fixture in almost every type of accommodation, refrigerators are found in virtually all motels, and stocked minibars are the norm in deluxe hotels. You can expect a swimming pool, health club, tennis courts, and spas in many resort hotels, some of which also have their own golf courses. Motel chains, such as Flag International, are usually reliable and much less expensive than hotels. You often can check into a motel without booking ahead, but reservations are required for weekends and holidays.

➤ HOTEL CHAINS: Most major international hotel chains are represented in Australia. Reservations for Australia can be made with the following chains: **Best Western International** (☎ 800/528–1234); **Conrad International Hotels and Hilton International** (☎ 800/445–8667); **Holiday Inns** (☎ 800/HOLIDAY); **Hyatt Hotels** (☎ 800/233–1234); **Inter-Continental Hotels** (☎ 800/327–0200); **Marriott Hotels** (☎ 800/228–9290); **Quality Inns International** (☎ 800/228–5151); **Radisson Hotels** (☎ 800/333–3333); **Ramada International and Renaissance Hotels and Resorts** (☎ 800/228–9898); **Regent International** (☎ 800/545–4000); **Ritz-Carlton Hotels** (☎ 800/241–3333 in the U.S., 800/341–8565 in Canada); **Sheraton Corporation** (☎ 800/325–3535); **Federal Hotels & Resorts and P & O Resorts** (☎ 800/225–9849); **Flag International Hotels & Resorts** (☎ 800/624–3524); **Pan Pacific Hotels Corporation** (☎ 800/937–1515); **Southern Pacific Hotel Corporation** (☎ 800/835–7742). Reservations for many Great Barrier Reef and beach resorts can be made in the United States through such groups as **Utell International** (☎ 800/44–UTELL).

M

MAIL

RATES

Mail service in Australia is normally efficient. Postage rates are 45¢ for domestic letters, $1.05 per 20-gram (28.35 grams = 1 ounce) airmail letter, and 95¢ for airmail postcards to North America; the same service costs $1.20 and $1 to the United Kingdom. Overseas fax service costs around $10 for the first page plus $4 for each additional page. You can send printed material by Economy Air, which travels via surface mail within Australia but by airmail across the Pacific, at a cost of $19 for up to a kilogram (a little more than 2 pounds).

RECEIVING MAIL

You can receive mail care of General Delivery (known as Post Restante in Australia) at the General Post Office or any branch post office; the service is free and mail is held one month. It is advisable to know the **correct Australian postcode,** obtainable by telephoning the nearest Australian Consulate General (☞ *below*).

To find out the zip code (postcode in Australia) of the area you are visiting, call the nearest Australian Consulate General: **Houston** (☎ 713/629–9131); **Los Angeles** (☎ 213/469–4300); **New York** (☎ 212/245–4000); **San Francisco** (☎ 415/362–6160); **Washington** (☎ 202/797–3222); **Ottawa** (☎ 613/236–0841); **Toronto** (☎ 416/323–1155); **Vancouver** (☎ 604/684–1177). The zip code will allow you to receive mail care of Poste Restante (General Delivery) at the area's General Post Office. You will need identification to pick up mail.

Alternatively, American Express offers free mail collection at its main city offices. For a list of addresses, call 800/528–4800 (in the NY metropolitan area, 212/477–5700).

MONEY

All prices listed in this guide are quoted in Australian dollars.

Australia's currency operates on a decimal system, with the dollar (A$) as the basic unit and 100 cents (¢) equaling $1. Bills come in $100, $50, $20, $10, and $5 denominations; which are differentiated by color and size. Coins are minted in $2, $1, 50¢, 20¢, 10¢, and 5¢ denominations. At press time, the exchange rate was about A$1.30 to the U.S. dollar,

$1.03 to the Canadian dollar, $2.05 to the pound sterling, and 80¢ to the New Zealand dollar.

ATMS

Before leaving home, **make sure that your credit cards have been programmed for ATM use in Australia.** Note that Discover is accepted mostly in the United States. Local bank cards often do not work overseas or may access only your checking account; **ask your bank about a MasterCard/ Cirrus or Visa debit card,** which works like a bank card but can be used at any ATM displaying a MasterCard/ Cirrus or Visa logo. These cards, too, may tap only your checking account; check with your bank about their policy.

➤ ATM LOCATIONS: **Cirrus** (☎ 800/ 424–7787). A list of **Plus** locations is available at your local bank.

COSTS

It is difficult to accurately represent prices for 1998 because at press time most companies had not set their rates, and prices for goods and services can be volatile. Still, those cited below may be used as an approximate guide, since variation should rarely exceed 10%.

Despite the growing perception in North America that Australia is an expensive destination, it has become more price competitive. Although prices appear high at Sydney's five-star hotels, virtually all offer discounts of up to 30% on published "rack" rates. There are also plenty of cheaper dining and lodging alternatives. Medium-priced hotels and hotel-apartments abound in city centers and inner suburbs. For example, double-occupancy rates at the luxury Regent of Sydney start at $215 (weekend rate) or $280 (during the week) a night, whereas the tariff at Victoria Court, a bed-and-breakfast hotel classified as a landmark by the National Trust, is in the region of $120–$150, including breakfast. Melbourne and Sydney tend to be more expensive than other cities.

Fares on international flights are usually lower between June and September, and many hotels offer lower tariffs in their off-peak season: April–September in the south, November–March in the Top End.

Another way to save money is to buy passes, available for everything from hotels and interstate transportation to local bus and train services (☞ Bus Travel, *above*).

The following are sample costs in Australia at press time:

Cup of coffee $2–$3; glass of beer in a bar $2–$2.50; take-out ham sandwich or meat pie $2.50–$4; hamburger in a café $4–$9; room-service sandwich in a hotel $12–$15; a 2-kilometer (1¼-mile) taxi ride $5.30.

CURRENCY EXCHANGE

For the most favorable rates, **change money at banks.** Although fees charged for ATM transactions may be higher abroad than at home, Cirrus and Plus exchange rates are excellent, because they are based on wholesale rates offered only by major banks. You won't do as well at exchange booths in airports or rail and bus stations, in hotels, in restaurants, or in stores, although you may find their hours more convenient. To avoid lines at airport exchange booths, **get a small amount of local currency before you leave home.**

➤ EXCHANGE SERVICES: **International Currency Express** (☎ 888/842–0880 on the East Coast or 888/278–6628 on the West Coast for telephone orders). **Thomas Cook Currency Services** (☎ 800/287–7362 for telephone orders and retail locations).

TRAVELER'S CHECKS

Whether or not to buy traveler's checks depends on where you are headed. **Take cash if your trip includes rural areas** and small towns, traveler's checks to cities. If your checks are lost or stolen, they can usually be replaced within 24 hours. To ensure a speedy refund, buy your checks yourself (don't ask someone else to make the purchase). When making a claim for stolen or lost checks, the person who bought the checks should make the call.

O
OUTDOOR ACTIVITIES & SPORTS

GOLF

Generally speaking, clubs can be rented, but you'll need your own shoes. In Australia, greens fees at public courses are generally under $20 for 18 holes.

HIKING

Despite the term "national," parks are operated by the individual states in which they are located. For information, contact the National Parks and Wildlife Service in the capital of the state in which you are interested. In Western Australia, contact the Department of Conservation and Land Management. Organized hiking tours can be arranged through the bushwalking clubs listed in the telephone directory of each capital city. In this guide, national parks most often appear in a separate section at the end of each chapter.

To protect your skin against the sun, **wear a hat and sunglasses and put on sun block** to protect your skin against the sun. At higher altitudes, where the air is thinner, you will burn more easily. Sun reflected off of snow, sand, or water can be especially strong. Apply sunscreen liberally before you go out—even if only for a half hour—and wear a visored cap or sunglasses.

Out in the hot Aussie sun, **be careful about heatstroke.** Symptoms include headache, dizziness, and fatigue, which can turn into convulsions, unconsciousness, and can lead to death. If someone in your party develops any of these conditions, have one person seek emergency help while others move the victim into the shade, wrap him or her in wet clothing (is a stream or lake nearby?) to cool him or her down.

Likewise, **avoid dehydration.** This underestimated danger can be very serious, especially considering that one of the major symptoms is the inability to swallow. It may be the easiest hazard to prevent, however: Simply **drink every 10–15 minutes,** up to a gallon of water per day in intense summer heat.

Temperatures can vary widely from day to night. Be sure to **bring enough warm clothing** for hiking and camping, along with **wet weather gear.** Weather in a number of hiking hotspots in Australia can change quickly at almost any time of year. If you are not dressed warmly enough, hypothermia can be a problem. Expo-

sure to the degree that body temperature dips below 95°F (35°C) produces the following symptoms: chills, tiredness, then uncontrollable shivering and irrational behavior, with the victim not always recognizing that he or she is cold. If someone in your party is suffering from any of this, wrap him or her in blankets and/or a warm sleeping bag immediately and try to keep him or her awake. The fastest way to raise body temperature is through skin-to-skin contact in a sleeping bag. Drinking warm liquids also helps.

Remember to **never drink from streams or lakes,** no matter how clear they may be. Giardia organisms can turn your stomach inside out. The easiest way to purify water is to dissolve a water purification tablet in it. Camping equipment stores also carry purification pumps. Boiling water for 15 minutes is always a reliable method, if time- and fuel-consuming.

For information on camping, *see* Lodging, *above.*

P

PACKING FOR AUSTRALIA

If you need to pack for both the tropical north and the cooler south, try to put the woolen clothes in one suitcase and lighter clothes in another, so you don't have to delve into both at each stop. Valuables, such as jewelry, should always be packed in your carry-on luggage. Likewise, pack prescription medicines, as well as any allergy medication you may need, in hand luggage.

The wisest approach to dressing Down Under is to **wear layered outfits.** Frequently, particularly at the change of seasons, weather can turn suddenly. You'll appreciate being able to remove or put on a jacket. A light raincoat and umbrella are worthwhile accessories, but remember that plastic raincoats and nonbreathing polyester are uncomfortable in the tropics. **Don't wear lotions or perfume in the tropics** either, since they attract mosquitoes and other bugs. It is also recommended that you carry insect repellent. Bring a hat with a brim to provide protection from the strong sunlight (☞ Health *above*).

Dress is fairly casual in most cities, though top resorts and restaurants may require a jacket and tie. In Melbourne and Sydney, the younger set tends to be trendy; women might want to take along a cocktail dress for evening dining. In autumn, a light sweater or jacket will suffice for evenings in coastal cities, but winter demands a heavier coat—a raincoat with a zip-out wool lining is ideal. **Comfortable walking shoes are a must.** You should have a pair of running shoes or the equivalent if you're planning to trek, and rubber-sole sandals or canvas shoes are needed for walking on reef coral.

Bring an extra pair of eyeglasses or contact lenses in your carry-on luggage, and if you have a health problem, **pack enough medication** to last the entire trip or have your doctor write you a prescription using the drug's generic name, because brand names vary from country to country. It's important that you **don't put prescription drugs or valuables in luggage to be checked**: it might go astray. To avoid problems with customs officials, carry medications in the original packaging. Also, don't forget the addresses of offices that handle refunds of lost traveler's checks.

LUGGAGE

In general, you are entitled to check two bags on flights within the United States and on international flights leaving the United States. A third piece may be brought on board, but it must fit easily under the seat in front of you or in the overhead compartment.

Keep in mind that **within Australia weight limits are stricter** than they are for entering the country. If you are flying between two foreign destinations, note that baggage allowances may be determined not by piece but by weight—generally 88 pounds (40 kilograms) in first class, 66 pounds (30 kilograms) in business class, and 44 pounds (20 kilograms) in economy. If your flight between two cities abroad *connects* with your transatlantic or transpacific flight, the piece method still applies.

Airline liability for baggage is limited to $1,250 per person on flights within the United States. On international flights it amounts to $9.07 per pound or $20 per kilogram for checked baggage (roughly $640 per 70-pound bag) and $400 per passenger for unchecked baggage. Insurance for losses exceeding these amounts can be bought from the airline at check-in for about $10 per $1,000 of coverage; note that this coverage excludes a rather extensive list of items, which is shown on your airline ticket.

Before departure, **itemize your bags' contents** and their worth, and label the bags with your name, address, and phone number. (If you use your home address, cover it so that potential thieves can't see it readily.) Inside each bag, **pack a copy of your itinerary.** At check-in, **make sure that each bag is correctly tagged** with the destination airport's three-letter code. If your bags arrive damaged or fail to arrive at all, file a written report with the airline before leaving the airport.

PASSPORTS & VISAS

Once your travel plans are confirmed, **check the expiration date of your passport.** It's also a good idea to **make photocopies of the data page**; leave one copy with someone at home and keep another with you, separated from your passport. If you lose your passport, promptly call the nearest embassy or consulate and the local police; having a copy of the data page can speed replacement.

U.S. CITIZENS

All U.S. citizens, even infants, need a valid passport to enter Australia for stays of up to 90 days. A visa is also required.

Qantas passengers may obtain an Australian visa from that airline; otherwise, application forms are available from one of the offices listed below. Children traveling on a parent's passport do not need a separate application form, but should be included under Item 16 on the parent's form. The completed form and passport must be sent or brought in person to an issuing office, together with a recent passport-type photograph signed on the back (machine photographs are *not* acceptable).

Visitors planning to stay more than three months must pay a fee. Check

SMART TRAVEL TIPS / THE GOLD GUIDE

with the Consulate-General to ascertain the cost, since it varies with the exchange rate. At press time, a visa costs $21. If you travel on an under-three-month visa and decide to extend it while in Australia, the fee rises; currently it's $200. If applying by mail, enclose a 12½" X 9½", stamped, self-addressed envelope and allow 21 days for processing.

➤ INFORMATION: **Office of Passport Services** (☎ 202/647–0518).

➤ VISAS: For Australian visa application forms contact the nearest Australian Consulate-General: **Honolulu** (✉ 1000 Bishop St., Penthouse, Honolulu, HI 96813-9998, ☎ 808/524–5050, FAX 808/523–1906); **Houston** (✉ 1990 Post Oak Blvd., Suite 800, Houston, TX 77056-9998, ☎ 713/629–9131, FAX 713/622–6924); **Los Angeles** (✉ 611 N. Larchmont Blvd., Los Angeles, CA 90004, ☎ 213/469–4300, FAX 213/469–9176); **New York** (✉ International Bldg., 636 5th Ave., New York, NY 10111-0050, ☎ 212/245–4000, FAX 212/265–4917); **San Francisco** (✉ 1 Bush St., San Francisco, CA 94104, ☎ 415/362–6160, FAX 415/986–5440); **Washington** (✉ Australian Embassy, 1601 Massachusetts Ave. NW, Washington, DC 20036-4673, ☎ 202/797–3222, FAX 202/797–3168).

CANADIANS

You need a valid passport to enter Australia for stays of up to 90 days.

Australian visa requirements for Canadians are the same as for Americans. Visitors planning to stay more than three months must pay a $30 processing fee. (If you travel on an under-three-month visa and decide to extend it while there, the fee rises to about $150.) Contact the nearest Australian Consulate General for visa application forms.

➤ INFORMATION: **Passport Office** (☎ 819/994–3500 or 800/567–6868).

➤ VISAS: For Australian visa application forms contact the nearest Australian Consulate-General: **Ottawa** (✉ Australian High Commission, 50 O'Connor St., Suite 710, Ottawa, Ontario K1P 6L2, ☎ 613/236–0841); **Toronto** (✉ 175 Bloor St. E, Suite 314, Toronto, Ontario M4W 3R8, ☎ 416/323–1155); **Vancouver** (✉ World Trade Center Office Complex, 999 Canada Pl., Suite 602, Vancouver, British Columbia V6C 3E1, ☎ 604/684–1177).

U.K. CITIZENS

Citizens of the United Kingdom need only a valid passport to enter Australia for stays of up to 90 days.

Australian visa application forms for longer stays are available from most travel agents and in the Australian Tourist Commission's brochure, "Australia, A Traveller's Guide." You may also apply in person at the Australian High Commission or at the Australian consulates in Manchester and Edinburgh. Visitors planning to stay more than three months must pay a £15 processing fee. (If you travel on an under-three-month visa and decide to extend it while there, the fee rises to about £45.) Apply at least two weeks in advance if making your application by mail.

➤ INFORMATION: **London Passport Office** (☎ 0990/21010) for fees and documentation requirements and to request an emergency passport.

➤ VISAS: Australian visa application forms are available at the **Australian High Commission** (✉ Australia House, Strand, London WC2B 4LA, ☎ 0171/379–4334).

S

SENIOR-CITIZEN TRAVEL

Few, if any, of the discounts that Australian senior citizens enjoy are available to visitors, because an Australian "pensioner's card" is usually required as proof of age.

To qualify for age-related discounts, **mention your senior-citizen status up front** when booking hotel reservations (not when checking out) and before you're seated in restaurants (not when paying the bill). Note that discounts may be limited to certain menus, days, or hours. When renting a car, **ask about promotional car-rental discounts,** which can be cheaper than senior-citizen rates.

➤ EDUCATIONAL TRAVEL PROGRAMS: **Elderhostel** (✉ 75 Federal St., 3rd floor, Boston, MA 02110, ☎ 617/426–7788). **Interhostel** (✉ University of New Hampshire, 6 Garrison Ave., Durham, NH 03824, ☎ 603/862–

1147 or 800/733–9753, FAX 603/
862–1113).

SHOPPING

Bargains are hard to come by in
Australia. Quality is good and prices
are high, particularly in such clothing
as hand-knitted wool sweaters, wool
suits, and designer dresses and
sportswear. Bargain hunters are best
advised to **join one of the shopping
tours in Melbourne and Sydney,** which
visit one or two factory outlets.
Check with your hotel concierge or
the state tourist office for information
about these tours.

There is no sales tax added to purchases in Australia, but an excise tax
is levied on some luxury goods. Many
department stores and specialty
shops, such as those selling opals, will
deduct this tax—allowing you substantial savings—upon presentation
of your passport and airline ticket.
You can also **avoid paying excise tax**
by shopping in one of the many duty-
free stores scattered through the main
cities. Prices on many items compare
favorably with those in duty-free
ports, such as Singapore and Hong
Kong. In some Australian cities you
don't even have to go to the store if
you buy from certain duty-free
shops—you can order goods by
phone, and your purchases will be
delivered to the airport for your
departure.

SPORTS

➤ BICYCLING: A network of rural
trails for cyclists is being developed,
and several books, such as *A Guide
to Cycle Touring in the Southern
Highlands and Adjacent Coastal Area
of N.S.W.,* by Richard D. Kenderdine,
can help guide you. For more information on touring, contact **Bicycle
New South Wales** (⊠ GPO Box 272,
Sydney, NSW 2001, ☎ 02/9283–
5200, FAX 02/9283–5246), who can
advise you on cycling in NSW and
also provide contact details for other
states if required.

➤ BOATING AND SAILING: If you're
looking for a day on the water, contact the **Australian Yachting Federation** (⊠ Locked Bag 806, Milsons
Point, NSW 2061, ☎ 02/9922–4333,
FAX 02/9923–2883).

➤ DIVING: For information about
scuba diving and all underwater

sports, contact the **Australian Underwater Federation** (⊠ Box 1006, Civic
Sq., Canberra, ACT 2608, ☎ 02/
6247–5554, FAX 02/6257–3018).
Check other city telephone directories
in Australia for branches.

➤ GOLF: Among U.S. operators
offering golf packages are **Classic
Australian Golf Tours** (☎ 800/426–
3610), **ITC Golf Tours** (☎ 800/257–
4981), and **Swain Australian Tours**
(☎ 800/227–9246).

STUDENTS

Students and backpackers are entitled
to reductions on the Greyhound
Pioneer Australia unlimited travel
Aussie Pass (☞ Bus Travel, *above*).
These 10%–20% discounts are ob-
tained by presenting an International
Student Card, YHA cards, and VIP or
ISIC Backpacker cards. Some accom-
modation discounts are also available
in conjunction with the pass.

Victoria Street in Sydney's Kings
Cross, near the rear entrance to the
Kings Cross subway station, is a
gathering spot for international backpackers. There you can sometimes find
drivers looking for a rider to share car
expenses while exploring the country,
or someone heading home who is
selling a car. However, several backpackers were murdered in New South
Wales in the early 1990s, and backpackers are strongly advised against
hitchhiking anywhere in the country. If
you are sharing a car and expenses, it
would be prudent to let someone
know the vehicle's registration number, the people you will be traveling
with, and your estimated time of
arrival before you depart. Also, as well
as you can, be sure that your aims and
personalities are compatible.

To save money, **look into deals available through student-oriented travel
agencies.** To qualify you'll need a
bona fide student ID card. Members
of international student groups are
also eligible.

DISCOUNT PASSES

For a free guide to backpacker hostels, contact **V.I.P. Backpackers Resorts of Australia** (⊠ Box 600,
Cannon Hill, QLD 4170, ☎ 07/
3268–5733, FAX 07/3268–4066);
enclose US$3 for postage and han-
dling. This organization also sells a
V.I.P. Backpacker card, available for

$20, plus $5 for postage, which entitles you to discounts at all Australian backpacker hostels and on **Greyhound Pioneer Australia,** and several other bus lines.

The **NSW Discovery Pass YHA,** available for $199 to any member of the YHA or its overseas affiliates, allows unlimited economy travel on all Countrylink rail and coach services throughout New South Wales for one month. The pass is available from Countrylink Travel Centres (☎ 13–2232 for details).

For information on the Backpackers Discounts, a bus pass for young budget travelers, contact SO/PAC (☎ 800/551–2012) for information and reservations.

➤ STUDENT IDs AND SERVICES: **Council on International Educational Exchange** (✉ CIEE, 205 E. 42nd St., 14th floor, New York, NY 10017, ☎ 212/822–2600 or 888/268–6245, FAX 212/822–2699), for mail orders only, in the United States. **Travel Cuts** (✉ 187 College St., Toronto, Ontario M5T 1P7, ☎ 416/979–2406 or 800/667–2887) in Canada.

➤ HOSTELING: **Hostelling International—American Youth Hostels** (✉ 733 15th St. NW, Suite 840, Washington, DC 20005, ☎ 202/783–6161, FAX 202/783–6171). **Hostelling International—Canada** (✉ 400-205 Catherine St., Ottawa, Ontario K2P 1C3, ☎ 613/237–7884, FAX 613/237–7868). **Youth Hostel Association of England and Wales** (✉ Trevelyan House, 8 St. Stephen's Hill, St. Albans, Hertfordshire AL1 2DY, ☎ 01727/855215 or 01727/845047, FAX 01727/844126). Membership in the U.S., $25; in Canada, C$26.75; in the U.K., £9.30.

➤ STUDENT TOURS: **Contiki Holidays** (✉ 300 Plaza Alicante, Suite 900, Garden Grove, CA 92840, ☎ 714/740–0808 or 800/266–8454, FAX 714/740–0818).

T

TAXES

AIRPORT

Everyone leaving Australia pays a departure tax (now known as a Passenger Movement Charge) of $27–this amount is prepaid with your airline ticket.

HOTEL

No service charge or tax is levied for accommodations in Australia, except in the Northern Territory, where there is a 2.5% room tax.

TELEPHONES

The country code for Australia is 61. From the U.S., dial 011, then 61, then the local area code. From the U.K., dial 00, then 61. When dialing an Australian number from abroad, drop the initial 0 from the local area code.

CALLS WITHIN AUSTRALIA

Pay phones accept either coins (40¢ for a local call on a public phone) or locally purchased Phone Cards (for use with silver phones). Long-distance calls can be dialed directly using the city code or area code: Sydney and Canberra are 02, for example, Melbourne and Hobart are 03, Brisbane and Cairns are 07, and Adelaide, Darwin, and Perth come under the 08 code.

Long distance rates are divided into three time periods: day (Mon.–Fri. 8–6); night (Mon.–Fri. 6–8); and economy (Mon.–Fri. 8 PM–8 AM and all weekend–from Fri. 8 PM–Mon. 8 AM). A $2.80 service fee is charged for operator-connected calls when direct dialing is possible. Area codes are listed in the white pages of local telephone directories.

A note on phone numbers: Since 1994, virtually all telephone numbers in Australia have gradually been converted from six or seven digits to eight-digit numbers. Exceptions are toll-free numbers (see below) and numbers with the prefix 13. The latter are country-wide and thus carry no area code at all. The conversion process is expected to be completed by the end of 1997, but for at least six months after a number has changed, callers to the old number will be redirected automatically or advised by recorded message that a number has changed. If you have difficulty reaching a number, ring directory assistance on 013 for a local number, or 0175 for others.

➤ NATIONAL NUMBERS: Australian numbers with a 13 prefix can be dialed country-wide for the cost of a local call: 40¢. For example, dialing a 13-number for a company in Melbourne when you are in Sydney will be billed as a local call.

➤ TOLL-FREE NUMBERS: Toll-free numbers in Australia have an 1800 prefix. Unless otherwise noted, toll-free numbers in this book are accessible only within Australia.

CALLING HOME

Calls from Australia to the United States, Canada, and the U.K. cost about $1.00 per minute (plus a 12¢ connection fee) in off-peak hours. These are Mon.–Fri. 6 PM–9 AM, and all day on weekends. Operator-assisted calls can be made from any phone with IDD (International Direct Dialing) access—check local telephone directories for international operator numbers. A $3 fee is charged on person-to-person calls, and an $8 fee on collect calls, known in Australia as "reverse charges."

For international directory assistance call 0103. The number for information on international call costs is 0102.

Before you go, **find out the local access codes** for your destinations. AT&T, MCI, and Sprint long-distance services make calling home relatively convenient, but you may find the local access number blocked in many hotel rooms. First ask the hotel operator to connect you. If the hotel operator balks, ask for an international operator, or dial the international operator yourself. One way to improve your odds of getting connected to your long-distance carrier is to travel with more than one company's calling card (a hotel may block Sprint, for example, but not MCI). If all else fails, call your phone company collect in the United States or call from a pay phone in the hotel lobby.

➤ TO OBTAIN ACCESS CODES: **AT&T USADirect** (☎ 800/874–4000). **MCI Call USA** (☎ 800/444–4444). **Sprint Express** (☎ 800/793–1153).

Trying to figure out just what time it is Down Under can get dizzying, especially because of cross-hemisphere daylight savings times and multi-time-zone countries. Without

daylight savings times, Sydney is 15 hours ahead of New York; 16 hours ahead of Chicago and Dallas; 18 hours ahead (or count back six hours and add a day) from Los Angeles; and ten hours ahead of London.

From Canada and the States, in order to avoid waking up some Aussie in the middle of the night, **call Australia after 7 PM.** If you're calling Western Australia, call after 9. From the U.K. or Europe, it isn't quite as complicated: call early in the morning or very late at night. **When faxing,** it's usually not a problem to ring discreet fax numbers at any time of day.

TIPPING

Hotels and restaurants do not add service charges, but it is a widely accepted practice to tip a waiter 10%–12% for good service, although many Australians consider it sufficient to leave only $3 or $4. It is not necessary to tip a hotel doorman for carrying suitcases into the lobby, but porters could be given $1 a bag. Room service and housemaids are not tipped except for special service. Taxi drivers do not expect a tip, but you may want to leave any small change. Guides, tour bus drivers, and chauffeurs don't expect tips either, though they are grateful if someone in the group takes up a collection for them. No tipping is necessary in beauty salons or for theater ushers.

TOUR OPERATORS

Buying a prepackaged tour or independent vacation can make your trip to Australia less expensive and more hassle-free. Because everything is prearranged you'll spend less time planning.

Operators that handle several hundred thousand travelers per year can use their purchasing power to give you a good price. Their high volume may also indicate financial stability. But some small companies provide more personalized service; because they tend to specialize, they may also be more knowledgeable about a given area.

For additional information on **adventure tour operators**—who run everything from camel treks to sea-kayaking to Antarctic fly-overs—*see* Chapter 13.

A GOOD DEAL?

The more your package or tour includes, the better you can predict the ultimate cost of your vacation. Make sure you know exactly what is covered, and **beware of hidden costs.** Are taxes, tips, and service charges included? Transfers and baggage handling? Entertainment and excursions? These can add up.

If the package or tour you are considering is priced lower than in your wildest dreams, **be skeptical.** Also, **make sure your travel agent knows the accommodations** and other services. Ask about the hotel's location, room size, beds, and whether it has a pool, room service, or programs for children, if you care about these. Has your agent been there in person or sent others you can contact?

BUYER BEWARE

Each year consumers are stranded or lose their money when tour operators—even very large ones with excellent reputations—go out of business. So **check out the operator.** Find out how long the company has been in business, and ask several agents about its reputation. **Don't book unless the firm has a consumer-protection program.**

Members of the National Tour Association and United States Tour Operators Association are required to set aside funds to cover your payments and travel arrangements in case the company defaults. Nonmembers may carry insurance instead. Look for the details, and for the name of an underwriter with a solid reputation, in the operator's brochure. Note: When it comes to tour operators, **don't trust escrow accounts.** Although there are laws governing charter-flight operators, no governmental body prevents tour operators from raiding the till. For more information, *see* Consumer Protection, *above.*

➤ TOUR-OPERATOR RECOMMENDATIONS: **National Tour Association** (✉ NTA, 546 E. Main St., Lexington, KY 40508, ☎ 606/226–4444 or 800/755–8687). **United States Tour Operators Association** (✉ USTOA, 342 Madison Ave., Suite 1522, New York, NY 10173, ☎ 212/599–6599, FAX 212/599–6744).

USING AN AGENT

Travel agents are excellent resources. When shopping for an agent, however, you should **collect brochures from several sources**; some agents' suggestions may be skewed by promotional relationships with tour and package firms that reward them for volume sales. If you have a special interest, **find an agent with expertise in that area** (☞ Travel Agents, *below*). Don't rely solely on your agent, who may be unaware of small-niche operators. Note that some special-interest travel companies only sell directly to the public and that some large operators only accept bookings made through travel agents.

SINGLE TRAVELERS

Prices for packages and tours are usually quoted per person, based on two sharing a room. If traveling solo, you may be required to pay the full double-occupancy rate. Some operators eliminate this surcharge if you agree to be matched with a roommate of the same sex, even if one is not found by departure time.

GROUP TOURS

Among companies that sell tours to Australia, the following are nationally known, have a proven reputation, and offer plenty of options. The classifications used below represent different price categories, and you'll probably encounter these terms when talking to a travel agent or tour operator. The key difference is usually in accommodations, which run from budget to better, and better-yet to best.

➤ SUPER-DELUXE: **Abercrombie & Kent** (✉ 1520 Kensington Rd., Oak Brook, IL 60521-2141, ☎ 630/954–2944 or 800/323–7308, FAX 630/954–3324). **Travcoa** (✉ Box 2630, 2350 S.E. Bristol St., Newport Beach, CA 92660, ☎ 714/476–2800 or 800/992–2003, FAX 714/476–2538).

➤ DELUXE: **Globus** (✉ 5301 S. Federal Circle, Littleton, CO 80123-2980, ☎ 303/797–2800 or 800/221–0090, FAX 303/347–2080). **Maupintour** (✉ 1515 St. Andrews Dr., Lawrence, KS 66047, ☎ 913/843–1211 or 800/255–4266, FAX 913/843–8351). **Tauck Tours** (✉ Box 5027, 276 Post Rd. W, Westport, CT 06881-5027, ☎ 203/226–

6911 or 800/468–2825, FAX 203/
221–6828).

➤ FIRST-CLASS: **AAT King's Australian
Tours** (⊠ 9430 Topanga Canyon
Blvd., #207, Chatsworth, CA 91311,
☎ 800/353–4525, FAX 818/700–
2647). **Brendan Tours** (⊠ 15137
Califa St., Van Nuys, CA 91411,
☎ 818/785–9696 or 800/421–8446,
FAX 818/902–9876). **Collette Tours**
(⊠ 162 Middle St., Pawtucket, RI
02860, ☎ 401/728–3805 or 800/
832–4656, FAX 401/728–1380). **Down
Under Answers** (⊠ 12115 100th Ave.
NE, Kirkland, WA 98034, ☎ 206/
814–0777 or 800/788–6685, FAX 206/
820–5571). **Gadabout Tours** (⊠ 700
E. Tahquitz Canyon Way, Palm
Springs, CA 92262–6767, ☎ 619/
325–5556 or 800/952–5068). **Newmans South Pacific Vacations** (⊠ 6033
W. Century Blvd., Ste. 1270, Los
Angeles, CA 90045, ☎ 310/348–8282
or 800/421–3326, FAX 310/215–9705).
South Pacific Your Way (⊠ 2819 1st
Ave., #280, Seattle, WA 98121-1113,
☎ 206/441–8682 or 800/426–3615,
FAX 206/441–8862). **Swain Australia
Tours** (⊠ 6 W. Lancaster Ave., Ard-
more, PA 19003, ☎ 610/896–9595 or
800/227–9246, FAX 610/896–9592).

➤ BUDGET: **Cosmos** (☞ **Globus**,
above).

PACKAGES

Like group tours, independent vacation packages are available from
major tour operators and airlines. The
companies listed below offer vacation
packages in a broad price range.

➤ AIR/HOTEL: **Qantas Vacations**
(⊠ 300 N. Continental Blvd., #610,
El Segundo, CA 90245, ☎ 800/641–
8772, FAX 310/524–9771). **United
Vacations** (☎ 800/328–6877).

➤ FLY/DRIVE: **Qantas Vacations**
(☞ Air/Hotel, *above*). **United Vacations** (☞ Air/Hotel, *above*).

Also contact **Budget WorldClass
Drive** (☎ 800/527–0700, 0800/
181181 in the U.K.) for self-drive
itineraries.

➤ HOTEL/SIGHTSEEING: **AAT King's
Australian Tours** (☞ Group Tours,
above). **Down Under Answers** (☞
Group Tours, *above*). **Newmans South
Pacific Vacations** (☞ Group Tours,
above). **South Pacific Your Way** (☞

Group Tours, *above*). **Swain Australia
Tours** (☞ Group Tours, *above*).

➤ FROM THE U.K.: For holiday
packages contact **British Airways
Holidays** (⊠ Astral Towers, Betts
Way, London Rd., Crawley, West
Sussex RH10 2XA, ☎ 01293/723–
191), **Kuoni Travel** (⊠ Kuoni
House, Dorking, Surrey RH5 4AZ,
☎ 01306/741–111), or **Qantas
Holidays** (⊠ Sovereign House, 361
King St., Hammersmith, London W6
9NJ, ☎ 0990/673–464).

THEME TRIPS

➤ BICYCLING: **Backroads** (⊠ 801
Cedar St., Berkeley, CA 94710-1800,
☎ 510/527–1555 or 800/462–2848,
FAX 510/527–1444.

➤ CUSTOMIZED PACKAGES:
**Australia/New Zealand Down Under
Travel** (☞ Australia Specialists,
above). **Down Under Connections**
(⊠ 6160 Peachtree Dunwoody Rd.,
Ste. 205-B, Atlanta, GA 30328,
☎ 770/481–0717 or 800/937–7878,
FAX 770/481–0608). **Pacific Experience** (⊠ 185 Spring St., Newport, RI
02840, ☎ 800/279–3639, FAX 203/
618-0121).

➤ FISHING: **Fishing International**
(⊠ Box 2132, Santa Rosa, CA
95405, ☎ 800/950–4242). **Rod &
Reel Adventures** (⊠ 3507 Tully Rd.,
Suite B6, Modesto, CA 95356-1052,
☎ 209/524–7775 or 800/356–6982,
FAX 209/524–1220).

➤ GOLF: **Australia/New Zealand
Down Under Travel** (☞ Customized
Packages, *above*). **ITC Golf Tours**
(⊠ 4134 Atlantic Ave., #205, Long
Beach, CA 90807, ☎ 310/595–6905
or 800/257–4981).

➤ HORSEBACK RIDING: **Equitour FITS
Equestrian** (⊠ Box 807, Dubois, WY
82513, ☎ 307/455–3363 or 800/
545–0019, FAX 307/455–2354).

➤ LEARNING: **Earthwatch** (⊠ Box
9104, 680 Mount Auburn St., Water-
town, MA 02272, ☎ 617/926–8200
or 800/776–0188, FAX 617/926–
8532) for research expeditions. **Natural Habitat Adventures** (⊠ 2945
Center Green Ct., Boulder, CO
80301, ☎ 303/449–3711 or 800/
543–8917, FAX 303/449–3712).
Nature Expeditions International
(⊠ 6400 El Dorado Circle, Suite 210,

THE GOLD GUIDE / SMART TRAVEL TIPS

Tucson, AZ 85715, ☎ 520/721–6712 or 800/869–0639, FAX 520/721–6719). **Questers** (✉ 381 Park Ave. S, New York, NY 10016, ☎ 212/251–0444 or 800/468–8668, FAX 212/251–0890). **Smithsonian Study Tours and Seminars** (✉ 1100 Jefferson Dr. SW, Room 3045, MRC 702, Washington, DC 20560, ☎ 202/357–4700, FAX 202/633–9250).

➤ MUSIC: **Dailey-Thorp Travel** (✉ 330 W. 58th St., #610, New York, NY 10019-1817, ☎ 212/307–1555 or 800/998–4677, FAX 212/974–1420).

➤ SCUBA DIVING: **Down Under Answers** (☞ Group Tours, *above*). **Rothschild Dive Safaris** (✉ 900 West End Ave., #1B, New York, NY 10025-3525, ☎ 800/359–0747, FAX 212/749–6172). **See & Sea Travel** (✉ 50 Francisco St., #205, San Francisco, CA 94133, ☎ 415/434–3400 or 800/348–9778, FAX 415/434–3409). **Tropical Adventures** (✉ 111 2nd Ave. N, Seattle, WA 98109, ☎ 206/441–3483 or 800/247–3483, FAX 206/441–5431).

➤ SINGLES AND YOUNG ADULTS: **Contiki Holidays** (✉ 300 Plaza Alicante, #900, Garden Grove, CA 92840, ☎ 714/740–0808 or 800/266–8454, FAX 714/740–0818).

➤ SPAS: **Spa-Finders** (✉ 91 5th Ave., #301, New York, NY 10003-3039, ☎ 212/924–6800 or 800/255–7727).

➤ SPORTS: **Championship Tennis Tours** (✉ 7350 E. Stetson Dr., #106, Scottsdale, AZ 85251, ☎ 602/990–8760 or 800/468–3664, FAX 602/990–8744).

➤ YACHT CHARTERS: **Alden Yacht Charters** (✉ 1909 Alden Landing, Portsmouth, RI 02871, ☎ 401/683–1782 or 800/662–2628, FAX 401/683–3668). **Huntley Yacht Vacations** (✉ 210 Preston Rd., Wernersville, PA 19565, ☎ 610/678–2628 or 800/322–9224, FAX 610/670–1767). **Lynn Jachney Charters** (✉ Box 302, Marblehead, MA 01945, 617/639–0787 or 800/223–2050, FAX 617/639–0216). **The Moorings** (✉ 19345 U.S. Hwy. 19 N, 4th floor, Clearwater, FL 34624-3193, ☎ 813/530–5424 or 800/535–7289, FAX 813/530–9474). **Ocean Voyages** (✉ 1709 Bridgeway, Sausalito, CA 94965, ☎ 415/332–4681 or 800/299–4444, FAX 415/332–7460).

TRAIN TRAVEL

Australia has a network of interstate, country, and urban trains offering first- and economy-class service. The major interstate trains are the *Indian-Pacific* from Sydney to Perth via Adelaide (26 hours Sydney–Adelaide, 38 hours Adelaide–Perth); the *Ghan* from Adelaide to Alice Springs (20½ hours; ☞ Chapter 10); the *Overland* (night service) and *Daylink* from Melbourne to Adelaide (12 hours); and the *XPT* (Express Passenger Train) from Sydney to Brisbane (14½ hours). Service between Melbourne and Sydney is on the daytime or overnight *XPT* (10½ hours). The current decrease in air fares is occasioning cutbacks in service, as well as slashed rail fares, so there may be variations from what has been listed. Check in advance, and book early whenever possible, especially for the *Indian-Pacific* and the *Ghan* during peak times (August–October and Christmas holidays).

➤ RAIL AUSTRALIA: For more information on Australia's network of rural and urban trains, or to make reservations or purchase discount passes, contact **Rail Australia:** in the United States (☎ 800/423–2880; ATS Tours, ☎ 818/841–1030; Austravel Inc., ☎ 800/633–3404), in Canada (Goway Travel, ☎ 800/387–8850), and in the United Kingdom (☎ 071/828–4111).

DISCOUNT PASSES

With the exception of the **NSW Discovery Pass,** the following rail passes are available only to overseas visitors. However, they can be purchased in Australia on presentation of your passport. Passes must be presented to the ticket office prior to the commencement of any journey. Rail passes do not include sleeping berths or meals.

The **Austrailpass** allows unlimited first-class travel on any passenger train in the country. The **Budget Austrailpass** allows unlimited economy-class travel. Passes are available for 14, 21, 30, 60, or 90 days at prices ranging from $780 to $1,950 for first-class travel, and $460 to $1,180 for economy-class travel.

The **Austrail Flexipass** allows unlimited travel on the national rail network. However, since its value is not ebbing away on days when you are not traveling, many will find this more cost-effective than the Austrailpass. Four passes are available—those detailed below, plus others for 22 days and 29 days. The 8-day pass allows eight days of travel in a 6-month period and costs $380 for economy class, $650 for first class. The 15-day pass allows 15 days of travel in the same period and costs $550 for economy, $915 for first class. The 8-day pass does not allow travel west of Crystal Brook in South Australia, which means that this pass is not valid for service to Perth or to Alice Springs.

The **NSW Discovery Pass** allows unlimited economy class travel on all Countrylink rail and coach services throughout New South Wales for one month; the pass costs $249.

Advance purchase fares, which afford a 10%–40% discount between some major cities, are better bought before departure for Australia, as they tend to be booked up far in advance. It is advisable to make all rail reservations well in advance, particularly during peak tourist seasons. Contact your travel agent or the appropriate Rail Australia office.

TRAVEL AGENCIES

A good travel agent puts your needs first. **Look for an agency that specializes in your destination, has been in business at least five years, and emphasizes customer service.** If you're looking for an agency-organized package or tour, your best bet is to choose an agency that's a member of the National Tour Association or the United States Tour Operator's Association (☞ Payments *and* Tour Operators, *above*).

➤ LOCAL AGENT REFERRALS: **American Society of Travel Agents** (✉ ASTA, 1101 King St., Suite 200, Alexandria, VA 22314, ☎ 703/739–2782, FAX 703/684–8319). **Alliance of Canadian Travel Associations** (✉ Suite 201, 1729 Bank St., Ottawa, Ontario K1V 7Z5, ☎ 613/521–0474, FAX 613/521–0805). **Association of British Travel Agents** (✉ 55–57 Newman St., London W1P 4AH, ☎ 0171/637–2444, FAX 0171/637–0713).

TRAVEL GEAR

Travel catalogs specialize in useful items, such as compact alarm clocks and travel irons, that can **save space when packing.** They also offer dual-voltage appliances, currency converters, and foreign-language phrase books.

➤ MAIL-ORDER CATALOGS: **Magellan's** (☎ 800/962–4943, FAX 805/568–5406). **Orvis Travel** (☎ 800/541–3541, FAX 540/343–7053). **TravelSmith** (☎ 800/950–1600, FAX 800/950–1656).

U
U.S. GOVERNMENT

The U.S. government can be an excellent source of inexpensive travel information. When planning your trip, **find out what government materials are available.**

➤ ADVISORIES: **U.S. Department of State American Citizens Services Office** (✉ Room 4811, Washington, DC 20520); enclose a self-addressed, stamped envelope. Interactive hot line (☎ 202/647–5225, FAX 202/647–3000). Computer bulletin board (☎ 202/647–9225).

➤ PAMPHLETS: **Consumer Information Center** (✉ Consumer Information Catalogue, Pueblo, CO 81009, ☎ 719/948–3334) for a free catalog that includes travel titles.

V
VISITOR INFORMATION

For general information contact the national and regional tourism bureaus below. For a free information-packed booklet "Destination Australia," call 800/333–0262. If you've got specific questions about planning your trip, the Australian Tourism Commission runs the **Aussie Help Line** (☎ 847/296–4900), which operates from 8 AM to 7 PM, Central Standard Time. Before you go, contact **Friends Overseas Australia** (✉ 68–01 Dartmouth St., Forest Hills, NY 11375, ☎ 718/261–0534) to be put in touch with Australians who share your interests. Membership is $25.

➤ COUNTRYWIDE INFORMATION: U.S.: Australian Tourist Commission (✉ 2049 Century Park E., Los Angeles, CA 90067, ☎ 310/229–4870, FAX 310/

552–1215). U.K.: ✉ Gemini House, 10–18 Putney Hill, Putney, London SW15 6AA, ☎ 0181/780–2227, FAX 0181/780–1496. New Zealand: (✉ Level 13, 44–48 Emily Pl., Box 1666, Auckland 1, ☎ 09/379–9594).

➤ REGIONAL INFORMATION: **Queensland Tourist & Travel Corporation** (✉ 1800 Century Park E, Suite 330, Los Angeles, CA 90067, ☎ 310/788–0997). **Australian Travel Headquarters** (✉ 1600 Dove St., Ste. 215, Newport Beach, CA 92660, ☎ 714/852–2270 or 800/546–2155, FAX 714/852–2277) for information on South Australia. **Australia's Northern Territory** (✉ 3601 Aviation Blvd., Ste. 2100, Manhattan Beach, CA 90266, ☎ 310/643–2636, FAX 310/643–2637).

➤ IN THE U.K.: **Australian Tourist Commission** (✉ Gemini House, 10–18 Putney Hill, Putney, London SW15 6AA, ☎ 0990/022–000 [information] or 0990/561–434 [brochure line], FAX 0181/940–5221).

W

WHEN TO GO

Australia is in the Southern Hemisphere, which means that **seasons are reversed**—it's winter Down Under during the American and European summer.

The ideal time to visit the north, particularly the Northern Territory's Kakadu National Park, is early in the dry season (around May). Bird life remains profuse on the drying flood plains, and waterfalls are still spectacular and accessible. The Dry (April–October) is also a good time to visit northern Queensland's beaches and rain forests. You can swim off the coast without fear of dangerous stinging box jellyfish, which infest ocean waters between November and March. In rain forests, heat and humidity are lower than later in the

year, and crocodile viewing is at its prime, as the creatures tend to bask on riverbanks rather than submerge in the colder water.

During school holidays, Australians take to the roads in droves. Accommodations and attractions are crowded and surcharges are often added to car rentals and hotel tariffs. The worst period is mid-December to the end of January, which is the equivalent of the U.S. and British summer break. The dates of other school vacations vary from state to state, but generally fall around Easter, mid-June to July, and late September to mid-October.

CLIMATE

Australia's climate is temperate in southern states, such as Victoria and Tasmania, particularly in coastal areas, and tropical in Australia's far north. The Australian summer north of the Tropic of Capricorn is a steam bath—remember that by comparison no parts of North America or Europe are anywhere near as close to the equator. From the end of October to December (the Australian spring), or from February through April (late summer–autumn), southern regions are generally sunny and warm, with only occasional rain in Sydney, Melbourne, and Adelaide. Perth and the south of Western Australia are at their finest in springtime, when wildflowers blanket the land. Some people would say that spring and fall are the best times to travel to Oz, unless you're dying to get away from a northern winter.

➤ FORECASTS: **Weather Channel Connection** (☎ 900/932–8437), 95¢ per minute from a Touch-Tone phone.

The following are average daily maximum and minimum temperatures for some major Australian cities.

Climate in Australia

SYDNEY

Jan.	79F	26C	May	67F	19C	Sept.	67F	17C
	65	18		52	11		52	11
Feb.	79F	26C	June	61F	16C	Oct.	72F	22C
	65	18		49	9		56	13
Mar.	76F	24C	July	61F	16C	Nov.	74F	23C
	63	17		49	9		61	16
Apr.	72F	22C	Aug.	63F	17C	Dec.	77F	25C
	58	14		49	9		63	17

MELBOURNE

Jan.	79F	26C	May	63F	17C	Sept.	63F	17C
	58	14		47	8		47	8
Feb.	79F	26C	June	58F	14C	Oct.	67F	19C
	58	14		45	7		49	9
Mar.	76F	24C	July	56F	13C	Nov.	72F	22C
	56	13		43	6		52	11
Apr.	68F	20C	Aug.	59F	15C	Dec.	76F	24C
	52	11		43	6		54	12

HOBART

Jan.	72F	22C	May	58F	14C	Sept.	59F	15C
	54	12		45	7		43	6
Feb.	72F	22C	June	54F	12C	Oct.	63F	17C
	54	12		41	5		47	8
Mar.	68F	20C	July	52F	11C	Nov.	67F	19C
	52	11		40	4		49	9
Apr.	63F	17C	Aug.	56F	13C	Dec.	70F	21C
	49	9		41	5		52	11

CAIRNS

Jan.	90F	32C	May	81F	27C	Sept.	83F	28C
	74	23		67	19		65	18
Feb.	90F	32C	June	79F	26C	Oct.	86F	30C
	74	23		65	18		68	20
Mar.	88F	31C	July	79F	26C	Nov.	88F	31C
	74	23		61	16		70	21
Apr.	85F	29C	Aug.	81F	27C	Dec.	90F	32C
	70	21		63	17		74	23

ALICE SPRINGS

Jan.	97F	36C	May	74F	23C	Sept.	81F	27C
	70	21		47	8		49	9
Feb.	95F	35C	June	67F	19C	Oct.	88F	31C
	70	21		41	5		58	14
Mar.	90F	32C	July	67F	19C	Nov.	94F	34C
	63	17		40	4		65	18
Apr.	81F	27C	Aug.	74F	23C	Dec.	97F	36C
	54	12		43	6		68	20

THE GOLD GUIDE / SMART TRAVEL TIPS

DARWIN

Jan.	90F	32C	May	92F	33C	Sept.	92F	33C
	77	25		74	23		74	23
Feb.	90F	32C	June	88F	31C	Oct.	94F	34C
	77	25		70	21		77	25
Mar.	92F	33C	July	88F	31C	Nov.	94F	34C
	77	25		67	19		79	26
Apr.	92F	33C	Aug.	90F	32C	Dec.	92F	33C
	76	24		70	21		79	26

PERTH

Jan.	85F	29C	May	69F	20C	Sept.	70F	21C
	63	17		53	12		50	10
Feb.	85F	29C	June	64F	18C	Oct.	76F	24C
	63	17		50	10		53	12
Mar.	81F	27C	July	63F	17C	Nov.	81F	27C
	61	16		48	9		57	14
Apr.	76F	24C	Aug.	67F	32C	Dec.	83F	28C
	57	14		48	9		61	16

1 Destination: Australia

THE ROAD FROM BOTANY BAY

WE WERE COOKING steak and sausages over an open fire, Rupert Murdoch and I, looking up at the rolling green hills on which the media magnate raises sheep and cattle near Canberra. "I love Australia for the birds," my fellow expatriate enjoined, as swans and then pelicans flew overhead. "Coming out here I feel my Australianness again."

For all their cherished "bushman" legend, however, 80% of the 18 million Australians cluster in the suburbs of the "Boomerang Coast"—a thin arc stretching 1,600 km (1,000 mi) around the southeastern seaboard from Adelaide to Brisbane. Few Australians have visited much of their huge, empty land, yet their souls dwell in the dusty, Technicolor Outback.

To realize the sparseness of the sixth-largest country in the world, imagine a land the size of the United States with virtually no human population for the first 3,200 km (2,000 mi) inland from the West Coast—as if nothing but sand and spinifex lay between Los Angeles and Chicago. In Australia, sheep outnumber people.

Despite the immensity of the land, local cultural variations, and a sectionalism that often has the six states snarling at one another, Australia is a nation of one texture. The same Australian accent flattens the vowels from Cape York to Hobart and puts the same cozy suffixes on words ("Brissy" for Brisbane, "Fre-o" for Fremantle) from the Kimberley in the far northwest to Melbourne nearly 2,900 km (1,800 mi) away in the southeast.

The harsh yet beautiful land beguiles me as much as anything about Australia after two decades of living in the United States. But you don't need to head into the Outback to sense the land's enormous power. Whereas in Europe and America, cities intrude upon the countryside, in Australia the country tends to invade the cities. When the British founded Sydney more than 200 years ago, they called the area Botany Bay because of the profusion of flowers and trees. Even today, with a population of nearly

3.8 million, Sydney seems to be, above all, a slice of nature. On hills around a sparkling blue harbor, red-tile roofs are softened by plants and flowering shrubs.

In the large, stately city of Melbourne you find a high, vast sky whose light overwhelms, and a silence that allows you to hear the rustle of a gum (eucalyptus) tree as you exit from the airport terminal. With its gray-green acacias and purple-flowering jacarandas, much of Brisbane looks like a horticultural exhibit, and one can become lost in dreams strolling through King's Park in Perth, where a riot of boronia, orchid, and kangaroo paw spreads beneath magnificent gums.

For tens of thousands of years the Aborigines and nature shared this continent together. The Aborigines arrived during the Ice Age, before sea levels rose and isolated Australia from the rest of Asia. The British took Australia in casual stages, without ever dealing fully with the fact that it had already been occupied. Some 300,000 Aborigines existed when Captain Cook arrived in 1770. As Europeans caught fish and the new settlements drove away kangaroos and other animals, natives lost their sources of food. And although they welcomed some of the European accoutrements, they could not cope with alcohol, and many thousands died from smallpox, venereal disease, and other infections. Aborigines were simply pushed aside, and Aboriginal life declined.

The days when Australia was a penal colony are not so distant. All four of my grandparents were alive in Victoria when the last convict ships reached Western Australia in 1868. Australia's unique origin as a place of crime and punishment haunted Australians for a century and a half. It was only after World War II that most people could bring themselves to talk about their criminal ancestry. Today, it is fashionable to boast of it.

I see a legacy of the convict era in some Australian attitudes. This is a society that looks to the government for solutions to its problems. In part, geographic necessity dictates the posture—private enterprise won't build an unprofitable railroad in the sparse north, for example—but it also stems from the nation's origins as a government camp.

Paradoxically, Australians also have an antiauthoritarian streak that seems to echo the contempt of the convict for his keepers and "betters." This attitude, too, has been perpetuated by geographic realities. The farmer in the tough Outback was not inclined—and still isn't—to respect the city bureaucrat who does not know how to mend a fence or cook a meal in the desert. Thus, in one and the same Australian you find both the government-dependent mindset and the anti-authoritarian rhetoric. It is no coincidence, then, that the historical figure who stands out most clearly as an Australian hero is Ned Kelly, a bushranger (highwayman) who killed policemen.

Out of this past, distance from European norms, and nature's influence have fostered a casual and easygoing lifestyle. A businessman can sound as folksy as a worker, and an academic can look like a worker as he boozes and barracks at a football game. Some of the rich parade their wealth, but what does it mean to parade their status in a land that began as a prison colony? It is still an insult to a cab driver for any man traveling alone to ride in the back seat.

The nation's spirit dwells somewhere within a triangle, the points of which are diffidence, innocence, and skepticism. Aussies can neither be easily fooled nor easily enthused. They like to believe others will be reasonable, but at arm's length many a proposed scheme will seem flawed or not worth the bother. In spite of that skepticism, there is a seductive softness to Aussie life. People still say "sorry" if they bump into you on the street, and the word for thank you, "ta," is uttered even after you yourself have said thank you in a shop or restaurant. And whether the topic is the weather, the stupidity of politicians, or the way the world is going to pot, Australians tend to want your agreement.

This desire for affirmation may be due, in part, to the fact that Australians lived in the shadow of Great Britain for so long, during which time they developed something of an inferiority complex. Not so long ago, "a pie and tea" or "fish-and-chips" were a staple that, in an unspoken way, were defiantly asserted to be adequate

"tucker" for any "real Australian." Today it is different, thanks largely to immigration. Although bare-armed and sandaled, diners in Melbourne and Sydney do peer lengthily at wine lists, fuss over the right sauce for duckling, and dispute the most appropriate seasoning for lamb.

The emergence of an Australian culinary tradition is part of a growing nationalism in which Australia can be seen to be moving away from Great Britain and forging an identity of its own. Internationally successful films, Aboriginal art, a respected wine industry, and a vibrant theater have given Australians new cultural confidence in themselves.

IT TAKES TIME to establish an identity rooted in one's own geographic and climatic experience, however, and Australia can seem quite British at times and somewhat American at others. Political, legal, and educational institutions derive from Britain. Each state capital is named after a colonial politician (Perth, Brisbane, Sydney, Hobart, Melbourne) or a British royal figure (Adelaide). Dry, sunscorched towns bear names from England's green, temperate land. Each day in the leading newspapers a "Vice Regal" column lists the activities and visitors at the state and national government houses, where the representative of the English queen is the formal head of the governmental structure. Only since 1984 has it been required that a civil servant in Australia be an Australian—previously it was sufficient to be British.

American culture influences entertainment, technology, defense arrangements, and business. Television channels are well stocked with American programs, and American popular music and clothing styles attract youth in Sydney and Melbourne, as they do in much of the world. Books from the United States have made a major advance in Australian intellectual circles since the 1960s. American ideas of management and problem-solving are sweeping away cobwebs as the presence of multilateral corporations grows and public service sheds its British legacy of amateurism.

"Aussie-born, eh?" the immigration officer at Sydney airport remarked as he flipped through my American passport on a recent visit. "Yeah," I grunted in my best Australian accent. "Good—there's not many of us left," said the middle-aged officer with a smile.

The changes wrought by immigration impress a returning native son. Nearly half of Australia's inhabitants were either born outside Australia or have at least one parent who was. So far, less than 10% of the population is Asian, even though Asians comprise more than half the immigrants who have arrived in recent years. Under 2% are Aborigines.

The approach of a Eurasian Australia has been made possible by some basic changes in Australian policy and behavior. A flood of Europeans following World War II accustomed Australians to new arrivals who brought different foods, languages, and values. The long-standing British quality of Australia became diluted as Greeks, Italians, and Yugoslavs settled in the big cities. Tourist travel by Australians to Southeast Asia and Japan liberalized Australian racial attitudes, and so has the presence of thousands of Asian students who have graduated from Australian universities in recent decades. In the 1970s, as the arrival of Vietnamese refugees began an era of Asian immigration, both Labor and conservative (Liberal-National) governments put forward the doctrine of multiculturalism to express ethnic pluralism. Having tried to ward off Asia for so many years, Australia has finally begun to accept its geographic location in the world and is realigning itself accordingly. Today, Indonesia (as a defense worry) and Japan (as an economic partner) outweigh in priority any European country in Australia's foreign policy.

Australian urban life has become more cosmopolitan, with Chinese restaurants, Italian cafés, and Vietnamese and Lebanese grocery stores in virtually every suburb. Greeks and Yugoslavs teach school classes that are half Vietnamese and Chinese— yesterday's students teaching today's— with gum trees outside the window and cricket played during the sports hour.

AUSTRALIA HAS REMAINED pleasant and peaceable by a practical (if sometimes hit-or-miss) approach to issues, a lack of compelling ideologies, an agreeable climate,

and a beautiful landscape. Some Australians wonder if this approach will adequately address tomorrow's challenges. Government ministers have suggested that Australia should forget about being the "lucky country" and strive to be a "clever country"—competing in Asia through high-tech development, ingenuity, and flexibility.

For now, Australia is a young nation with few glorious moments in its past and with an identity that is still crystallizing. Its last half-century has brought it to an exciting stage of development. Greater ethnic diversity, creative excellence, and the pleasures of a comfortable, safe, and healthy life have instilled in its people new pride and sophistication.

— Ross Terrill

Australian-born Ross Terrill is the author of *The Australians* and many books on China, including *Mao, Madame Mao,* and *China in Our Time.* Now an American citizen, he is a research associate at Harvard University's Fairbanks Center for East Asian Research.

NEW AND NOTEWORTHY

Australia's inflation rate has remained low, and most travelers will find that an Australian holiday is good value for the money, especially outside major cities.

In the Northern Territory there is growing recognition of local and tourist interest in **Aboriginal culture** and its relationship to the land. You'll see this in the changeover of some Anglo place names to Aboriginal names—for example, Uluṟu, the original name for Ayers Rock, is gaining place in common parlance. So we now use the word Uluṟu, along with the Aboriginal name for its close neighbor, Kata Tjuṯa (formerly the Olgas to Westerners). And the Northern Territory Tourist Commission publishes a booklet detailing Aboriginal tours in the Top End and the Red Centre.

In the aftermath of the tragic killings at the Port Arthur Historic Site, where 35 people died, twenty-nine-year-old Tasmanian Martin Bryant has pleaded guilty to the murders, and has been imprisoned for the term of his natural life. The Broad Arrow café has been demolished, and a memorial garden will eventually be constructed on the site.

WHAT'S WHERE

Geography

Visitors to Australia are inevitably surprised by its vastness. The phrase "tyranny of distance" entered Australian parlance almost at the very beginning of white settlement. Although the country occupies almost the same land mass as the continental United States, its population is strikingly smaller: just over 18 million Australians compared with 251 million Americans.

Australia is an ancient land. Originally part of the Gondwanaland supercontinent that included present-day South America, Africa, Antarctica, and New Zealand, the island continent began to migrate to its current position around 100 million years ago. Since then it has been weathered flat—the country's highest peak, Mt. Kosciusko (pronounced ko-zee-os-ko), is only 7,317 ft. The eastern seaboard is backed by the Great Dividing Range, which parallels the coastline from Cape York in northern Queensland all the way south into western Victoria. Watered by swift rivers, this littoral region is clothed with rolling pasturelands and lush rain forests. Off of Queensland the banks of coral reef known collectively as the Great Barrier Reef run from Cape York 2,000 km (1,250 mi) southward. Inland, beyond the Great Dividing Range, semiarid plains cover much of Queensland, New South Wales, Victoria, and South Australia. This is grazing land, drawing its moisture from the 3,719-km (2,310-mi) waterways of the Murray River—Australia's Mississippi—and its tributaries, the Darling and the Murrumbidgee. Much of the rest of the country is desert, including a large portion of Western Australia and the lower Northern Territory, known as the Red Centre. Tasmania floats south of the mainland, looking on maps like it's plunging toward the Antarctic.

If you're coming from the northern hemisphere, remember that the compass is turned upside down: The farther north you go *toward* the equator, the hotter it gets. And where Australia is bisected by the tropic of Capricorn—meaning that overall it is rather close to the equator—the U.S. and Europe lie much closer to the pole, well above the Tropic of Cancer.

Sydney

The vibrant, cosmopolitan gateway to Australia covers the waterfront with audacious Aussie attitude, sprawl, and pop culture. Down under, of course, that includes beaches. It also means some of the most astonishing food on the current world scene, a Eurasian cornucopia overflowing with seafood and exotic flavor. You're bound to spend at least a couple of days here—take hold of them with both hands.

New South Wales

Although its capital city may be the ultimate urban experience south of Hong Kong, New South Wales plays virtually all of the continent's rural and coastal variations: historical towns, mountain ranges, seductive sands, subtropical rain forest, and a vineyard-strewn river valley. For sport, it provides in turn hiking, scuba diving, fishing, skiing, trail riding, cave exploring, and white-water rafting.

Canberra and the A.C.T.

Located between Sydney and Melbourne in the Australian Capital Territory, in the midst of mountain ranges and rivers, Canberra is the nation's spacious and immaculately landscaped capital city. Possessed of interesting architecture and museums, it is the closest of cities to some of Australia's greatest national parks.

Melbourne and Victoria

Melbourne (say *mel*-burn), is the urbane, cultivated sister of brassy Sydney. To the extent that culture is synonymous with sophistication—except when it comes to watching Australian Rules football or the Melbourne Cup—some call it the cultural capital of the continent. Outside of the city, watch the sundown race of fairy penguins on Phillip Island, marvel at the sculpted South Ocean coastline, sample some of the country's tasty wine in and around charming Victorian towns, or bushwalk in a splendid variety of national parks.

Tasmania

From the Freycinet Peninsula to the Nut to the wilds of Southwest National Park,

Tasmania is a place of unsurpassable natural beauty. The island is a hiker's dream. For time-travelers, convict lore from the state's early days as a penal colony is a stinging contrast to the well-preserved old towns where the rest of us would have lived. But the greatest call comes from the great outdoors—Tasmania is rich with coastal and inland parks both known and loved and wilderness still unexplored.

Queensland and the Great Barrier Reef

A fusion of Florida, Las Vegas, and the Caribbean Islands, Queensland and the Great Barrier Reef are meccas for crowd lovers and escapists alike, whether you wish to be awash in the Coral Sea, to stroll from cabana to casino with your favorite cocktail, to pose in front of the monumental kitsch of the Sunshine Coast, or to cruise rivers and rain forests with crocs and other legendary creatures of the tropics.

Adelaide and South Australia

Come to park-enveloped Adelaide for its biennial Festival of the Arts or simply for a calmer urban experience. Elsewhere in the state, step back in time on the quiet, entirely relaxing Kangaroo Island; explore some of Australia's celebrated wineries and the transplanted German heritage of the Barossa Valley; unwind on a Murray River cruise, as your own pilot if you choose; catch a glimpse of the great variety of Australian wildlife; live underground with opal miners; or tramp around one of the best Outback national parks.

The Red Centre

The light in the Red Centre—named for the deep color of its desert soils—has a purity and vitality that photographs only begin to approach. Like the ancient desert landscapes, the quality of light is humanized in the heritage of the Aboriginal people who have occupied this vast territory for tens of thousands of years. Uluru, also known as Ayers Rock, symbolizes these traditions, as do so many Aboriginal sites alive in the Centre's mountain ranges, gorges, dry riverbeds, and spinifex plains. At the center of all this lies Alice Springs, Australia's only desert city.

Darwin, the Top End, and the Kimberley

From sunset over Darwin Harbour to sunrise over the rocky domes and towers of Purnululu National Park, the Top End and the Kimberley's stunning and diverse landforms are virtual time lines of life on the planet, tracing the ancient and living heritage of Aboriginal rock art alongside of contemporary pursuits. Darwin and Broome—both far closer to the cities of Asia than to any Australian counterparts—host the most racially diverse populations of the nation: Aborigines, Anglos, and Asians sharing a relaxed tropical lifestyle.

Perth and Western Australia

Despite the tyranny of distance, those who make it to the "undiscovered country" are stunned by the sheer diversity of places to go and things to do. Relax on beautiful beaches; hang out in Fremantle or on Rottnest Island; explore gold country east of Perth or the historic towns, wineries, and seaside national parks of the Southwest; wonder at coastal limestone formations in Nambung National Park; or swim with dolphins, manta rays, and whale sharks at Monkey Mia or Ningaloo Reef Marine Park to the north.

PLEASURES AND PASTIMES

As much or more than any other countries, Australians love sports—professional, amateur, and any variety of weekend sports. You'll see a number of them listed below. If it's hard or soft adventure that you're looking for, turn to Adventure Vacations, Chapter 13, for specific package-oriented trips beyond what appears in the regional chapters of this guide. If you want to strike out on your own, the chapter can also point out desirable regions for activities to take on without guides.

Other pleasures and pastimes described below include dining, lodging, shopping, and wine and beer. Be sure to look in the Gold Guide for more specific information on some of the categories listed in this section.

Australian Rules Football

Despite its name—"Australian Rules football"—novice observers frequently ask the question: "What rules?" This fast, vigorous game, played between teams of

18, is one of four kinds of football down under. Aussies also play rugby league, rugby union, and soccer, but Aussie Rules, widely known as "footie," is the one to which Victoria, South Australia, the Top End, and Western Australia subscribe. It is the country's most popular spectator sport.

Because it is gaining an international television audience, the intricacies of Aussie Rules football are no longer the complete mystery they once were to the uninitiated: The ball can be kicked or punched in any direction, but never thrown. You'll see players make spectacular leaps vying to catch a kicked ball before it touches the ground, for which they earn a free kick. The game is said to be at its finest in Melbourne, although the recent defeat of a Melbourne team in a grand final was widely interpreted as a sign of moral lassitude in the state of Victoria.

New South Wales and Queensland devote themselves to two versions of rugby. Rugby league, the professional game, is a faster, more exciting version of rugby union, the darling of purists.

Beaches
Australia is renowned for its beaches. Along its coastline are miles and miles of pristine sand where you can sunbathe in solitary splendor. It is advisable, however, to swim only at designated areas where lifeguards are on duty. Surf is often rough, and many beaches have a treacherous undertow. Volunteer lifesavers monitor almost all metropolitan and town beaches.

Sydney has 34 ocean beaches, with such well-known names as Bondi, Manly, Coogee, Bronte, and Maroubra. Daily reports are given on the state of the ocean in metropolitan newspapers and on the radio. The Gold Coast of Queensland's 32-km (20-mi) stretch of clean beach is washed by warm, moderate surf. This area does not have the box jellyfish that plague the coast farther north (but not the Great Barrier Reef islands) from November to April. Perth's ocean beaches are excellent, too. From South Fremantle on up, there are 19 beaches along the Indian Ocean with wide swathes of sand and good surf. On most Australian beaches, women sunbathe topless; some beaches, like Sydney's Lady Jane and Perth's Swan-

bourne, are for those who prefer their sunning and swimming au naturel.

Beer
Some might say that beer is a way of life in Oz. True or not, pub life is a legitimate subculture worth looking into to get an earful of some local talk, and a mug-full of some local grog. Traditional beer is strong and similar to Danish and German beer, although lighter, low-alcohol beer is now readily available. Draft from the tap is the brew of choice, served ice-cold with little head.

Bicycling
Australia's flat terrain is perfect for long-distance cycling. It's equally enjoyable to rent a bike and take a spin through the city parks, most of which have bicycle trails, and a network of rural trails is being developed.

Boating and Sailing
Australians are passionate sailors. Close to a million families own some sort of craft, and sailing charters on either bare-boat or crewed yachts abound, particularly in the Whitsunday Islands inside the Great Barrier Reef.

Bushwalking
With so much bird life, flora, and fauna to admire, hiking—Ozzies call it bushwalking—is a pleasurable and popular pastime. Every weekend thousands of people head to the tranquillity of national parks in nearby ranges either individually or with one of the many bushwalking clubs. Get yourself out into one of the country's parks—the Australian bush is a national treasure.

Fodor's Choice, *below*, highlights some of the country's finest parks.

Cricket
Although Australians are often fiercely divided by their allegiance to winter sports, the nation is united in its obsession with the summer sport of cricket. Played between teams of 11 players, this often slow—and incomprehensible to outsiders—game can take place over the course of a day. Test matches, full-scale international games, last for five days.

So leisurely is the pace of this game that to the uninitiated it looks more like an esoteric religious ritual than a sport. Despite the gentlemanly white garb and the tea breaks, however, cricket is a game of power and torrid passions.

Test matches against the Windies (West Indies), Pakistan, India, Sri Lanka, New Zealand, South Africa, and England are played in all capital cities except Darwin and Canberra on a rotating basis. The ultimate cricketing prize, The Ashes, is fought solely between Australia and England. Because of its history, The Ashes means more to either side than any other test series.

This rather odd name for a sporting event, and its trophy, is derived from a series of events that occurred early in the history of Aussie-English competition. In 1882, the colonial upstarts scored their first win on British soil, which shocked the English to the core. One sportswriter at the time declared that English cricket died that day, and that the body would be cremated and its ashes taken to Australia.

The following season, the English team toured Australia. Some local wit had the fine idea to burn the bails—part of the wooden stumps that batsmen defend much as baseball batters defend the strike zone—then presented "The Ashes" to the English team's captain. Years later, in the 1920s, these ashes were given to the English cricketing establshment and enshrined in an urn at Lords, the holiest of English cricket holies.

The cricket season runs from October to March.

Dining

Dining out in Australia was not always a pleasurable experience. For much of its history, Australian cuisine labored under the worst traditions of bland English fare. Happily, post-World War II migration changed that. First European migrants brought Continental, Slavic, and Mediterranean cooking, then Middle Eastern and Asian immigrants introduced a whole new spicy repertoire. Today every conceivable type of cuisine is available in the capitals, and often in regional towns, too.

Contemporary Australian cuisine usually emphasizes fresh ingredients, such as seasonal vegetables and fish. Each state boasts its own specialties, particularly seafood. In the Northern Territory, for instance, grilled barramundi fish is prized as a delicacy. Yabbies, or "Moreton Bay bugs,"

a crayfishlike crustacean, are also highly regarded. Recently, "bushtucker," the food native to Australia, has been rediscovered, and there is scarcely a fashionable "modern Australian" school restaurant that does not have some bush food on its menu. Although ingredients such as wattle seed, lemon aspen, emu (a smaller relative of the ostrich), marron (a large freshwater crustacean), rocket (arugula), and stingray might not all be familiar, they provide an astonishing range of ingredients, and chefs with skill and imagination have leapt at the chance to create truly "Australian" dishes. The result is a sort of hybrid of Mediterranean and Asian techniques and spices using these uniquely Australian ingredients—quite delicious.

Reminders of Australia's pioneer days are evoked in two bush staples: damper (an unleavened bread cooked over a fire) and billy tea (brewed in an open pot). Traditionally, Australians have been big meat eaters, although the days of the plate-size steak smothered in tenacious sauce are long gone. Chicken (sometimes called "chook") is becoming more popular as health consciousness grows. However, cholesterol concerns have not taken over Australian thinking: It is difficult to find substitute eggs in a restaurant, though they are available in stores, and requests for nonfat milk (known as slim milk or skim milk) meet with varying success.

Diving

With 36,735 km (22,827 mi) of coast bordering two oceans and four seas, Australians spend a good deal of their time in and on the water. Opportunities are abundant for scuba diving, snorkeling, surfing, water-skiing, and windsurfing. The best known area for scuba diving and snorkeling, of course, is the Great Barrier Reef. Prime diving season is September–December, though diving is still good until late April. Western Australia's Ningaloo Marine Park, 2,400 km (1,500 mi) of Indian Ocean coral reefs off the central coast near Exmouth, is quickly gaining a reputation among international divers. Unlike the Great Barrier Reef, these reefs lie only a few hundred yards offshore. For an unusual diving experience, visit Western Australia's Rowley Shoals, 14 hours by boat from Broome, where you can "fly" with the tides through canyons formed by mountains close to the surface.

If time is short, look no further than metropolitan areas. Good diving is to be found right in Sydney Harbour at North Head, and off-shore at south-of-the-harbor beaches, Port Hacking and Broken Bay. Shipwrecks are the lure in Melbourne's Port Phillip Bay, particularly near the bay's entrance. Close to Adelaide is Port Noarlunga Reef, a marine reserve popular with local divers. Rottnest Island, off Perth's port of Fremantle, is a major diving attraction for both marine life and wrecks.

Fishing

Records for marlin are frequently broken off the east coast, and the region around Cairns and Lizard Island has won world acclaim for giant black marlin. Fighting fish, including black and blue marlin, mackerel, tuna, barracuda, and sailfish, are found all the way down the east coast. Game fishing for marlin, tuna, and sharks is particularly good at Bermagui in southern New South Wales, and is less expensive than at Cairns. September through November is the best time for catching marlin off Cairns; off Bermagui, the end of November to June.

Barramundi, jack, tarpon, and mackerel attract anglers to the fresh and sea waters of the Northern Territory's Top End, around Darwin and Bathurst Island. Barramundi run from June to November. Rainbow and brown trout thrive in the lake-fed streams of Tasmania, the rivers of the Australian Alps in both Victoria and New South Wales, and in the Onkaparinga River on the outskirts of Adelaide. Fishing seasons vary according to the area but are generally December–May.

Golf

Australia has more than 1,400 golf courses. Some private clubs extend reciprocal rights to overseas club members on proof of membership; check whether your club maintains reciprocal membership rights with Australian clubs. You can always arrange a round on a municipal course, although you may have to contend with a kangaroo or two watching your form from the rough.

Sea-Kayaking and White-Water Rafting

Favored areas for white-water canoeing or rafting are Tasmania's wild Franklin River and the Nymboida and Gwydir

rivers in northern New South Wales. The Snowy River in Victoria's High Country, and Kosciusko National Park streams in nearby southern New South Wales, are also popular choices. Local adventure travel operators offer guided trips on all of these rivers. Try sea-kayaking off Tasmania's rugged coast or in the calmer waters around the Great Barrier Reef.

Shopping

The best buys in Australia are woolen goods, fashionable leather clothing, sheepskin rugs and car seat covers, arts and crafts, Aboriginal art, and gemstones—particularly opals, diamonds, and pearls. Fine gems can be found in reputable jewelers throughout Australia, but consider going to the source. For opals, look for South Australia's Coober Pedy "milky" stones, and New South Wales's Lightning Ridge mines' coveted black opals. Western Australia is the place for rare "pink" diamonds—from the Kimberley's Argyle Diamond Mine—gold, and pearls produced in the waters off Broome in the north. Sapphires and other gemstones are mined in Queensland's ranges. Darwin, Alice Springs, and Kununurra in the Kimberley region are good places to look for Aboriginal art and artifacts.

Skiing

You can ski in Australia from late June through September. Ski resorts admittedly don't compare too favorably with those in the United States and Europe, mostly due to less significant snowfall and vertical rise, but they retain an appealing natural bushland character. Cross-country skiing may in fact be more rewarding than downhill because of the vast size of the snowfields and the unusual flora and fauna. The major downhill areas are in the Snowy Mountains region of New South Wales—Thredbo, Perisher Blue, comprising the resorts of Perisher Valley, Smiggin Holes, Guthega and Mt. Blue Cow, and Mt. Selwyn—and in Victoria's High Country—Mt. Buller, Falls Creek, and Mt. Hotham, and Tasmania has snowfields, too. The principal cross-country areas are in Koscuisko and in Victoria's Alps.

'Strine

Getting an earful of 'strine is one of the distinct pleasures of a trip to Oz. "'Strine" is an Aussie contraction of "Australian"—say it with an accent and you'll start to hear the sound. "Oz" is another nickname: say "Aussie" with hard esses and you end up with "Ozzie." Shorten that and you end up in the land of Oz, what they call the Lucky Country.

Down Under, you'll hear Melbourne pronounced *mil*-bin, Darwin pronounced *daeh*-wun and odd phrases like "back 'o Bourke" (middle of nowhere), words like "thingo" (thingamajig)—or "esky" (eskimo cooler) and "shellacking" (getting trounced) if you're watching a game of "footie" (rugby or Australian Rules football).

Surfing

Most Australians spend at least part of their youth on surfboards, and the country is well represented in the ranks of world champions. The best surfing beaches are found in New South Wales, Victoria, and Western Australia. Bell's Beach in Victoria and Margaret River in Western Australia are legendary in the surfing world, and several beaches about an hour from the center of Sydney have surfable waves. For those who prefer warmth, Byron Bay in northern New South Wales has been a hangout since the days of the Malibu board. Surf shops are a common sight in most coastal towns in southern states, and boards and wet suits are generally available for hire.

Tennis

Tennis courts, both municipal and private, are everywhere, and most resorts have courts as well. Call the nearest tennis club to arrange a game. Rackets can usually be rented, but you'll have to bring your own shoes.

Wine

Australian wine has become such a phenomenon—from the shiraz and semillon that you find in your wine shop near home to the tokay and muscat that you'll have to bring back from your trip Down Under. Quite literally, it is made to be tasted with food, and contemporary Australian food is itself so phenomenal that we decided to have our Sydney and Melbourne food writer properly take on the subject. So after glancing at the note on wine tasting that follows, turn straight to Chapter 14, Portraits of Australia, for Terry Durack's lip-smacking piece on Aussie wine—and the foods you might be shocked to pair with it.

WINE TASTING> If you plan to visit wineries and have never done it before, you may find the following to be helpful. Generally, when sampling more than one variety of wine, begin with a light, aromatic white, like Riesling, and move on to heavier whites. Repeat the same process with red wine. Sweet and fortified wine should be left until last. You are not expected to sample a winery's entire range—to do so would overwhelm your taste buds. Inform the tasting-room staff of your preferences and let them suggest wine for you to sample.

FODOR'S CHOICE

The Real Oz

★**Bondi Beach** on a warm summer evening, Sydney

★**Ferry ride** across Sydney Harbour to Manly, Sydney

★**Mount Wilson** in autumn, Blue Mountains, New South Wales

★**Riding the Zig Zag Railway,** Blue Mountains, N.S.W.

★**Cross-country skiing** through snow gums, Kosciusko National Park, N.S.W.

★**Gliding** over farmland at Lake Keepit, N.S.W.

★**Coffee at an open-air café** in Lygon Street, Carlton, on the bohemian fringe of inner-city Melbourne

★**Watching whales** at Warrnambool, Victoria

★**Saturday morning** at Salamanca Market, Hobart, Tasmania

★**A late-afternoon walk** through Allendale Gardens (near Smithton), Tasmania

★**The Skyrail Cableway over the rain forest** and mountains behind Cairns, Queensland

★**The first view of Heron Island** by helicopter, Queensland

★**Afternoon tea** in the Adelaide Hills, South Australia

★**The drive into Seppeltsfield,** Barossa Valley, S.A.

★**Taking the Coober Pedy–Oodnadatta Mail Run** with the local postman through the smallest town, the largest cattle station, and a helluva lot of dust, Outback, S.A.

★**A walk through King's Canyon,** the Red Centre

★**Sunrise and sunset** over Uluṟu, Ayers Rock, the Red Centre

★**Studying Aboriginal rock art** at Nourlangie Rock, Kakadu National Park, the Top End

★**A sunset cruise** on Yellow Water, Kakadu National Park, the Top End

★**Spring wildflowers** in King's Park, Perth, Western Australia

★**Sipping cappuccino** in Fremantle's sidewalk cafés, W.A.

★**Wine tasting** at the vineyards of Margaret River, W.A.

National Parks and Natural Wonders

★**The Three Sisters** formation in Blue Mountains National Park, New South Wales

★**The waterfalls** and rain forest of Dorrigo National Park, N.S.W.

★**The peaks, subtropical forest, beaches, and coral reef** of Lord Howe Island, N.S.W.

★**The alpine landscape** and flora of Kosciusko National Park, N.S.W.

★**Horseback riding** through the "Man from Snowy River" mountain country, Victoria.

★**Twelve Apostles rock formation** just off the coast of Port Cambell National Park, Victoria

★**The mountainous** Grampians (Gariwerd) National Park, Victoria

★**Rafting** on the Franklin River, West Coast, Tasmania

★**The rain forest** of Bellenden Ker National Park, Queensland

★**The waters, islands, and coral** of the Great Barrier Reef

★**The crashing seas,** the rocks, and wildlife of Flinders Chase National Park on Kangaroo Island, South Australia

★**Uluṟu** (Ayers Rock) and **Kata Tjuṯa** (the Olgas) in the Red Centre

★**The cuts and gorges** of the MacDonnell Ranges, the Red Centre

★**Jim Jim and Twin falls** in Kakadu National Park, the Top End

★**Tiger-striped,** beehive-shaped sandstone hills in Purnululu National Park, The Kimberley

★**The coastal scenery** and caves of Cape Leeuwin–Naturaliste National Park, Western Australia

★**The otherworldly limestone formations** of the Pinnacles in Nambung National Park, W.A.

Experiencing Wildlife

★**Birding** in Royal National Park, Sydney, New South Wales

★**Taronga Zoo,** Sydney

★**The twilight spectacle** of the return of the fairy penguins, Phillip Island, Victoria

★**The seabirds,** kangaroos, wombats, and koalas of Wilson's Promontory National Park, Victoria

★**Watching Tasmanian devils** feed at Cradle Mountain Lodge in Cradle Mountain–Lake St. Clair National Park, Tasmania

★**Cuddling a koala** at Lone Pine Koala Sanctuary, Brisbane, Queensland

★**Hand-feeding giant potato cod** at Cod Hole off Lizard Island, Great Barrier Reef

★**The variety of Australian fauna** at Cleland Conservation Park, South Australia

★**Walking among sea lions** at Seal Bay, Kangaroo Island, S.A.

★**Crocodile-spotting** on the Yellow Water cruise, Kakadu, the Top End

★**Visiting raptors** at Eagles Heritage, Margaret River, Western Australia

★**Swimming with whale sharks** or tagging nesting turtles at Exmouth, W.A.

Dining

★**Rockpool**'s devastating dishes virtually define the modern Australian culinary vocabulary's fusion of Mediterranean and Asian techniques. Sydney *$$$$*

★**Tetsuya.** Nothing quite compares with chef Tetsuya Wakuda's holistic and principled blend of Western technique and Japanese ingredients. Sydney $$$

★**Sea Treasure.** When you need your fix of out-of-this-world Cantonese food—possibly the best on the continent—look no further. Sydney $$

★**Flower Drum,** as some have said, would even rate among the best Cantonese restaurants if it were in Hong Kong. Melbourne $$$

★**Café Di Stasio.** Crisply roasted duck, chargrilled baby squid, *orecchiette* pasta with turnip tops—the choice is yours. Melbourne $$

★**Il Bacaro,** in the style of a Venetian wine bar, is the perfect place to choose from any number of wines by the glass and pair them with some very stylish Italian cooking. Melbourne $$

★**Ali Akbar**'s food will take you a lot farther away than Tasmania—it's a delightful change of scenery and a culinary trip to Lebanon. Hobart, Tasmania $$

★**Pier 9.** River views, an assortment of fresh oysters, and a late-harvest Australian riesling are a great way to start a fine evening in Brisbane, Queensland. $$–$$$

★**Spirit House.** For a taste of Thailand on the Sunshine Coast, this Yandina favorite is almost as memorable for its garden setting as it is for its food. Queensland $$$

★**Nediz tu**'s Franco-Sino-Vietnamese fare, like chili squid with whitebait fish or lobster mille-feuille with champagne butter, is one of Adelaide's top taste treats. South Australia $$$

★**Hanuman** is Darwin's Asian sensation, where clean, aromatic Thai-Malaysian flavors are as dazzling as the peacock-blue and gold decor. Darwin $$–$$$

★**Mead's Fish Gallery.** Views of mansions, immaculate white yachts, and a squadron of pelicans gliding over the Swan River—and dishes like Thai parcel of king prawns and snapper served with fresh mango—make Mead's nearly irresistible. Perth $$$

Beach Resorts

★**Aanuka Beach Resort.** Banana trees outside, teak furniture and Indonesian antiques inside, and a Pacific-coast white-sand beach a stroll away—this may be New South Wales's finest beach resort. Coffs Harbour, New South Wales. $$$

★**Hyatt Regency Resort.** Set between Mount Coolum and a mile of beach and surf—and equipped to the nines—this Hyatt is a must for tennis, golf, and fitness enthusiasts. Sunshine Coast, Queensland $$$

★**Heron Island Resort** is actually on the Great Barrier Reef, which means great diving and snorkeling just a flipper's length away. It also happens to be a nesting sight for loggerhead turtles and seabirds. Great Barrier Reef $$$–$$$$

★**Hayman Island Resort** spells luxury with its superbly designed building and grounds and stylish dining venues. The island itself comes with secluded beaches, rain forests, and fringing coral. G.B.R. $$$$

★**Lady Elliot Island.** To see the reef more affordably, look to this coral cay for its coral beaches, great nearby diving, and reef walking. G.B.R. $$

City Lodging

★**Park Hyatt.** Luxurious and cosmopolitan, this Hyatt has the best location in Sydney in the historic Rocks district. Sydney $$$$

★**The Russell.** For Old World character—and a view of the harbor from the roof garden—The Russell is Sydney's classy, century-old bargain. Sydney $$

★**Windsor Hotel.** While in the state of Victoria, take in the Victorian-era air of this grandame of Melbourne, where high tea is still an institution. Melbourne $$$$

★**Robinson's by the Sea,** a terrace house overlooking St. Philip Bay, is the B&B of choice in Melbourne's cosmopolitan St. Kilda neighborhood. $$

★**Lenna of Hobart.** Colonial-era decor virtually oozes the romance of travel, and the Lenna is Hobart's answer for romantics. Tasmania $$$

★**The Heritage.** Splendid public spaces, river views from all rooms, and remarkably attentive service make this *the* top-end choice in Brisbane. $$$$

★**Royal Albert Boutique Hotel.** Staying in a small hotel has its benefits, such as personal service. This one also has a heritage-listed building and in-room kitchenettes to recommend it. Brisbane $$$

★**Thornbury House.** Breakfast in a courtyard garden, waffle-weave bathrobes, and a glass of port in the evening make staying in this historic B&B one of Brisbane's pleasures. $$

★**Directors Studios and Suites.** You can't beat rooms that are as well fitted as those in most luxury hotels, but that come at almost half the price, as they do here. Adelaide $$

★**Miss Maud Swedish Hotel** is Perth's Old World charmer, where pine furniture, Scandinavian blue, and a smorgasbord have won the Miss Maud its rightful share of fans. Perth $$

Country Lodging

★**Jemby Rinjah Lodge.** For an all-out getaway within relatively close range of Sydney in appropriately Aussie rusticity, set yourself up in the wilds of the Blue Mountains in one of these fully equipped timber cabins. N.S.W. $$

★**Villa Dalmeny.** Come here prepared to be swept off your feet by European hospitality, sensational cooking, and a host of tasteful touches. Southern Highlands, N.S.W. $$$

★**Taylors.** Natural charm—in this district that means riots of junglelike vegetation—along with elegant antique furnishings and fantastic breakfasts, are all woven into the luxurious atmosphere at Taylors. North Coast. N.S.W. $$$

★**Avoca House.** Vine-covered verandas, comfortable rooms, and a hearty home-cooked breakfast make this century-old brook-side house a country classic. Hunter Valley, N.S.W. $$

★**Quamby Homestead.** Native birdcalls, English-style gardens all-round, and breakfast and dinner included in the rates make this both a great escape and a great value. West Coast, Victoria $$

★**Silky Oaks Lodge.** The combination of open-air living and delicious food in a wilderness setting—at Silky Oaks you're smack in the middle of a tropical rain forest—is unforgettable. Mossman Gorge, Queensland $$$$

★**Mercure Grand Hotel Mount Lofty House.** Vineyards, farms, and forests below, clean air all around, and sumptuous food keep all senses satisfied at this deluxe mountainside lodge. Adelaide Hills, S.A. $$$$

★**Apple Tree Cottage and Gum Tree Cottage,** set in irresistible rolling farm country, are a pair of antique-filled brick and stone cottages that come with log-burning fireplaces and fully equipped kitchens. Adelaide Hills, S.A. $$$

★**The Lodge.** In one of Australia's finest wine regions, this bluestone aristocrat, surrounded by gardens and orchards, is a classic Barossa Valley image of the finest country pleasures. Barossa Valley, S.A. $$$$

★**Collingrove.** The Barossa is all about history, and though you stay in very comfortable former servants' quarters at historic Collingrove, you can no less indulge in the fantasy of the privileged country life. Barossa Valley, S.A. $$

★**Seven Spirit Bay.** To call this remote is an understatement. But the isolation translates into superb bushwalking and wildlife watching, which happens to come with cuisine fresh enough to complement all the fresh air. Cobourg Peninsula, the Top End $$$$

★**El Questro Cattle Station.** Atop a cliff overlooking a river, El Questro is a working ranch. You can join a roundup or just watch, go for incredible hikes in nearby gorges, and dunk in a river, all in this remarkable part of Australia's stained-red Outback. Kununurra, The Kimberley $–$$$$

★**Cape Lodge.** Right in the heart of Western Australia's wine country, birdsong, inspired decor, and paddling in an adjacent lake are the ingredients for this country idyll. Margaret River, W.A. $$$

FESTIVALS, SEASONAL EVENTS AND NATIONAL HOLIDAYS

Annual and biennial events range from international cultural festivals and sporting matches to uniquely Australian celebrations with a distinctly tongue-in-cheek flavor. With the opening of performing arts centers in most capital cities, arts festivals have become major features on the Australian calendar. The dates of some of these festivals may change, so call ahead to check. And remember that the northern winter is Australia's summer.

SUMMER

DEC. 25 AND 26➤ **Christmas Day,** when almost everything is closed nationwide, and **Boxing Day,** are observed as holidays in all states except South Australia. (The name for the latter holiday stems from the era when English squires "boxed" the remains of their Christmas dinners for their tenants.)

JAN. 1➤ **New Year's Day** is observed as a holiday nationwide.

JAN.➤ Beginning with harborside fireworks on New Year's Eve, the **Sydney Festival** (✉ Sydney Festival Ltd., St. Martin's Tower, 31 Market St., Level 11, Sydney, NSW 2000, ☎ 02/9265–0444, FAX 02/9264–9495) is a month-long, multicultural celebration of art,

music, and theater. The whole city is in party mode. See outdoor movies, circuses, arts workshops, ferryboat races, and fringe theater events. Jazz and rock bands, symphony orchestras, and the Australian Opera stage free outdoor performances in the Domain.

JAN. 26➤ **Australia Day** is a country-wide holiday that celebrates the founding of the nation.

FEB.–MAR.➤ **Sydney Gay and Lesbian Mardi Gras** (✉ Box 557, Newtown, NSW 2042, ☎ 02/9557–4332, FAX 02/9516–4446) fêtes lesbian and gay life with a month of theater, performances, art and photography exhibitions, culminating in a spectacular parade in early March.

FEB.–MAR.➤ Regarded by many as Australia's most prestigious feast of arts and culture, the **Adelaide Festival** (✉ GPO Box 1269, Adelaide, SA 5001, ☎ 08/8226–8111, FAX 08/8226–8100) is held every second year, with the next occurring in 1998. The month-long celebration features international music, drama, dance, opera and visual arts, as well as the offbeat and highly entertaining Festival Fringe.

AUTUMN

MAR.➤ The **Canberra Festival** (✉ Box 173,

Civic Sq., Canberra, ACT 2608, ☎ 02/6207–6477, FAX 02/6207–6472) is the national capital's major annual event, lasting for 10 days, with a colorful hot-air balloon fiesta, music, concerts, and a street parade.

2ND AND 3RD WEEK OF MAR.➤ **The Melbourne Moomba Festival** (✉ 117 Sturt St., Southbank, Melbourne VIC 3006, ☎ 03/9699–4022, FAX 03/9699–9879) is Melbourne's lighthearted end of summer celebration, with fun high on the agenda. The street parade concluding the festival is the biggest and best in the country.

MAR. OR APR.➤ **Easter** holiday is observed Good Friday through Easter Monday.

MAR. OR APR.➤ The **Barossa Vintage Festival** (✉ Barossa Wine and Tourism Association, Box 420, Tanunda, SA 5352, ☎ 008/812–662, FAX 08/8563–0616), the best known wine-region harvest celebration, bears the stamp of the valley's Germanic heritage and is based on the joys of wine, food, music, and culture. The festival is held around Easter every second (odd-numbered) year, with the next in 1999.

APR. 25➤ **Anzac Day** is a solemn holiday honoring fallen members of Australia's armed forces.

WINTER

WINTER

2ND MON. IN JUNE➤ **The Queen's Birthday** holiday is observed in every state but Western Australia, which celebrates it in September or October.

AUG.➤ The **Beer Can Regatta** in Darwin is an event that shows a fine sensitivity to recycling—the sailing craft are constructed from used beer cans! It takes place just before the **Festival of Darwin** celebrating the dry season, and at about the same time as the fabulous horse racing carnival, the **Darwin Cup.**

SPRING

SEPT.➤ **Warana Festival,** usually held over a 10-day period, celebrates Brisbane in spring blossom with arts, entertainment, and a series of gala happenings, including a festive parade.

LATE SEPT. OR EARLY OCT.➤ **Henley-On-Todd Regatta** in Alice Springs is a boat race with a difference—it's held on a dry riverbed. Crews "wear" the boats, and leg power replaces rowing.

MID-OCT. OR EARLY NOV.➤ **Melbourne International Festival of the Arts** (✉ Box 7550, Melbourne, VIC 3004, ☎ 03/9866–8866, FAX 03/9820–3611), formerly the Spoleto Festival, features Australia's top performing artists, along with outstanding international productions, at the Victorian Arts Centre and venues around Melbourne. Weekend ticket packages are available.

MID-OCT.➤ **Fun in the Sun Festival** in Cairns highlights the city's tropical setting. A grand parade with floats climaxes a week of entertainment, exhibitions, a yacht race, and a fun run.

1ST TUES. IN NOV.➤ The **Melbourne Cup** is one of Australia's most famous sporting events—a horse race that brings the nation to a virtual standstill!

2 Sydney

The vibrant, cosmopolitan gateway
to Australia wraps its spectacular
waterfront with audacious Aussie
attitude, sprawl, and pop culture.
Down Under, that includes beaches.
It also means some of the most
astonishing food on the current
world scene, a Eurasian cornucopia
overflowing with seafood and exotic
flavor. You're bound to spend at least
a couple of days here—take hold of
them with both hands.

TAKE A TAXI FROM SYDNEY AIRPORT and chances are that the driver will not say "G'day" with the broad accent you might expect. Probe a little further and you

By Michael
Gebicki and
Anne
Matthews

will probably discover that he was not born in Australia. Like the United States, Australia is a society of immigrants, and Sydney has been a major destination for many of these new arrivals. Over the past half century the city's original Anglo-Irish immigrants have been enriched by successive waves of Italians, Greeks, Yugoslavs, Turks, Lebanese, and, more recently, Southeast Asians. This intermingling has created a cultural vibrancy and energy that were missing only a generation ago.

Sydney is a city in a hurry. The traffic is fast and impatient, and for most drivers, the instinctive reaction to a yellow light is to accelerate. This city of over 3.7 million people works hard and plays harder—moderation is something practiced by people from Melbourne. Sydney has the tallest buildings, the most expensive real estate, the finest beaches, and the seediest nightlife of any Australian city. Most Australians regard its loud, brash ways with a mixture of fear and fascination, although Sydneysiders prefer to think of their city as virile rather than vulgar.

British writer Lawrence Durrell once lamented that Americans seem to live out of sync with their natural surroundings. The same could be said of Sydney, which seems determined to ignore its position on the cusp of a barren, unforgiving continent. In many ways Sydney has turned its cosmopolitan back on the heartland and established itself as a separate entity altogether. For the average Sydneysider, life unfolds in one of the red-roofed suburbs that sprawl around the city, and these suburban streets are the true terrain of Australia—bush talk is reserved for pubs and foreigners.

Sydney may have forsaken the hinterland, but it embraces its harbor with passion. And why not? The harbor is a shining gem, studded with small bays and inlets and crowned by the billowing sails of the Opera House. Even two-plus centuries back, when he first set eyes on this harbor on January 26, 1788, First Fleet Captain Arthur Phillip swooned, in his way: "We had the satisfaction of finding the finest harbor in the world, in which a thousand ships of the line may ride in the most perfect security." It was not an easy beginning, however. Passengers on board the 11 ships of the First Fleet were not the "huddled masses yearning to breathe free" that migrated to the United States, but wretched inmates flushed from overcrowded jails in England and sent halfway around the globe. It says much of those early days that when the women prisoners came ashore two weeks after the men, an orgy ensued.

Sydney has long since outgrown the stigma of its convict origins, but the passage of time has not tamed its spirit. Other Australian cities can claim the title of the nation's cultural capital with more justification, but Sydney's panache and appetite for life are unchallenged. A walk among the scantily clad bathers at Bondi Beach or through the raucous nightlife district of Kings Cross provides evidence enough.

Visiting Sydney is an essential part of an Australian experience, but the city is no more synonymous with Australia than New York is with the United States. Sydney has joined the ranks of the great cosmopolitan cities whose characters are essentially international. For visitors from European or North American cities, Sydney's architecture, customs, and cuisine will be no more than a variation on a familiar theme.

Pleasures and Pastimes

Although Sydney is well endowed with galleries, museums, and some splendid examples of Georgian and Victorian architecture, the city exercises a far greater hold on the body than on the mind. Sydney's warm, sunny climate, spectacular setting, and addiction to the great outdoors make this a place to wine, dine, splash in the surf, or shop till you drop.

Beaches and Waterways

The boom of the surf could well be Sydney's summer theme song: Forty beaches, including world-famous Bondi, lie within the Sydney metropolitan area. With their fine, golden sand, average water temperature of 68°F, and a choice of sheltered harbor waters or crashing breakers, it's little wonder these beaches have Sydneysiders addicted to the pleasures of sun, sea, sand, and surfing. If you wish to try your hand at the latter, surfboards can be rented at most ocean beaches.

The city is also a paradise for other water-based activities. Sydney Harbour, its coves and associated waterways, and its beaches are ideal for boating, sailing, windsurfing, and diving. You can hire craft of all types, or join a skippered sailing excursion to explore these delightful waters.

Dining

It is highly advisable to come to Sydney hungry.

Oyster and banana blossom salad; spiced duck cake with beetroot; tea-smoked sea scallops with seaweed noodles; crispy-skinned spatchcock with black rice pancake; prawn ravioli with ginger, soy, and coriander—this is the stuff of mod-Oz (modern Australian) cooking, and Sydney is where it flourishes, fuelled by local produce and steered by Mediterranean and Asian techniques. In recent years, the dining scene has become as sunny and cosmopolitan as the city itself, and there are diverse and highly charged culinary adventures to suit every appetite. A meal at Tetsuya's, Paramount, Bayswater Brasserie, Darley Street Thai, or any of Neil Perry's several eateries will be a crash course in this dazzling culinary language.

Food lovers on holiday in Sydney are especially in luck, for many of Sydney's top sightseeing spots are of equal food interest. Although the Opera House has Bennelong, and Darling Harbour has Star Grill, the historic Rocks area has Rockpool, bel mondo, Sailors Thai, and more. Then there are the food 'burbs of Bondi, Balmain, Surry Hills, and Darlinghurst, where the smells of good espresso, a sizzling grill, or an aromatic stir fry seem to hover in the air.

Seafood is a definite highlight. You'll find a variety of fish and shellfish that nearly boggles the mind: rudderfish, warehou, barramundi, blue-eye cod, kingfish, princess fish, John Dory, ocean perch, and parrot fish; then Yamba prawns, Balmain bugs, sweet Sydney rock oysters, mud crab, spanner crab, yabbies (small lobsters), and marrons (freshwater lobsters). A visit to the Pyrmont fish markets, just a few minutes' drive out of the city, can tell you more about Sydney than any museum.

Of course, Sydney food tastes so much better when taken outdoors—at a sidewalk table, in a sun drenched courtyard, or best of all, in full view of that glorious harbor—keeping in mind the general rule: the better the view, the bigger the bill.

National Parks and Wildlife

Anyone who wishes to sample the sights and sounds of wild Australia or experience the country's Aboriginal heritage can choose from a dozen or so national parks (and numerous nature reserves) in the Greater Sydney region. Close to the heart of the city you can enjoy the surprisingly unspoiled Sydney Harbour National Park, and Ku-ring-gai Chase and Garigal to the north and Royal National Park to the south encompass large tracts of natural coastline, foreshore, and bushland.

Although Sydney's wildlife is generally restricted to birds and small creatures like lizards and possums, several wildlife parks around the city display the full range of unique native fauna. These are ideal places to learn more about koalas, kangaroos, the strange, egg-laying mammals (the echidna and platypus), birds, and reptiles (☞ Around Sydney, *below*).

Sports

Whether it's watching or playing, Sydneysiders are devoted to their sport, and the city's generally benign climate makes outdoor sporting activity a year-round possibility. There are some 80 golf courses within easy reach of the city. Many of these are open to the public, and greens fees are modest compared with most countries. Tennis is also popular, with dozens of centers hiring out courts for both day and night use.

By far the most popular summer sport is cricket, when Australia plays international test matches against England, the West Indies, Sri Lanka, Pakistan, and India at the legendary Sydney Cricket Ground. The biggest winter game is Rugby League, but Rugby Union, soccer, and Australian Rules football also have substantial followings. Many of these winter matches take place at the Sydney Football Stadium.

Shopping

Sydney is a great place to shop for knitwear and woolen goods, sheep skin items, Aboriginal art and artifacts, innovative beach, leisure and resort wear (raised to a virtual art form in this city of beaches), opals, gemstones, and crafts. There are also plenty of outlets for local clothing designers, ranging from high fashion to bush- and country-wear manufacturers. Look for such names as Carla Zampatti, Trent Nathan, George Gross, Simona, R. M. Williams, Dorian Scott, and Adele Weiss. Duty-free shopping is excellent in Sydney—prices are very competitive in the dozens of duty-free shops.

EXPLORING SYDNEY

Sydney is a giant, stretching almost 97 km (60 mi) from top to bottom and about 55 km (35 mi) across. It is divided into north and south by the harbor, with most of the headline attractions located on the south shore. The area bounded by Chinatown in the south, Harbour Bridge in the north, Darling Harbour to the west, and the beaches and coastline to the east has plenty to occupy any visitor for several days. North of Harbour Bridge lie the important commercial center of North Sydney and the pleasant, leafy, north-shore suburbs. Ocean beaches, Taronga Zoo, and Ku-ring-gai Chase National Park are the only reasons most visitors find to venture north of the harbor.

We have divided Sydney into seven exploring areas and an Around Sydney section. Tours cover sights historical and modern, from the city's earliest convict days to the colonial era to the construction of the Sydney Opera House, the very symbol of cosmopolitan, contemporary Australia. Walks begin at Circular Quay, a central point in Sydney as well as the docking area for harbor ferries, and the Pitt Street Mall, the heart of the main shopping district. Sydney Harbour is a ferry tour, and the Kings Cross and Paddington itinerary requires some bus travel, but the rest can be done easily on foot. Around Sydney covers various places of interest that are farther afield.

There are areas of spectacular scenic beauty outside Sydney, but the city's sheer size and somewhat inadequate road system do not facilitate the quick escape. It is possible to make day trips to such areas as the Blue Mountains or the vineyards of the Hunter Valley (both of which are covered in Chapter 3), and several coach companies can get you there (☞ Guided Tours *in* Sydney A to Z, *below*), but the long and tedious shuffle through suburban Sydney is a bit daunting for a day trip. If you want more than a fleeting glimpse of these places—and the Blue Mountains in particular deserve more—you would do far better to plan an overnight stop.

Numbers in the text correspond to numbers in the margin and on the Sydney Harbour, Central Sydney, and Greater Sydney maps.

Great Itineraries

You really need three days in Sydney to see the essential city center, while seven days would allow more time to explore the beaches and inner suburbs. A stay of 10 days would allow trips outside the city and give you time to explore a few of Sydney's lesser known delights.

IF YOU HAVE 3 DAYS

Start with an afternoon **Sydney Harbour Explorer cruise** for one of the best impressions of the city (☞ Guided Tours *in* Sydney A to Z, *below*). Follow the cruise with a walking tour of the historic **Rocks,** the nation's birthplace, and take a walk up onto the **Sydney Harbour Bridge** for great views. The following day, take a **Sydney Explorer** tour. If you're feeling energetic, there will still be enough time to see the famous **Sydney Opera House** and relax at sunset in the nearby **Royal Botanic Gardens** and **Domain** parkland. On day three, explore the **city center** highlights, with another spectacular panorama from the top of **Sydney Tower.** Include a walk around the **Macquarie Street** area, a living reminder of Sydney's colonial history, and the contrasting experience of futuristic **Darling Harbour,** with its museums, aquarium, and lively shopping center.

IF YOU HAVE 6 DAYS

Follow the three-day itinerary above, then take the **Kings Cross, Darlinghurst, and Paddington** bus and walking trip on day four. You could also continue to **Bondi,** Australia's most famous beach. The next day, catch the ferry to **Manly** to visit that beach, the historic Quarantine Station, and the Oceanworld aquarium. From here, take an afternoon bus tour to the **northern beaches,** or return to the city to shop or spend more time in one of the many museums. Day six options could include a visit to a **wildlife** or **national park, Taronga Zoo,** or take a trip west of the city to tour the Sydney 2000 **Olympic Games site.**

IF YOU HAVE 10 DAYS

In this amount of time it is possible to see most of the above, then travel farther afield by rental car or with an organized tour. Take day trips to the **Blue Mountains** (☞ Chapter 3), **Ku-ring-gai Chase National Park,** the **Hawkesbury River,** or the historic city of **Parramatta** to Sydney's west. You may also like to explore some lesser known corners of the city. Travel on the **Bondi & Bay Explorer** bus around the eastern suburbs to Vaucluse House, the charming harborside village of Watsons Bay, and its beaches. You could take a boat tour to the historic harbor island of **Fort Denison,** play a round of golf or some tennis, or just spend a day shopping or do more relaxing on the beach.

When to Tour Sydney

The best times to visit Sydney are late spring and early fall. October and November are pleasantly warm, although the ocean is a bit too cold in October for swimming. December is hot but dry, unlike the muggy months of January and February, when heavy, almost tropical downpours are frequent. In March and April, weather is stable and comfortable, outdoor city life is still in full swing, and the ocean is at its warmest.

If you're interested in two of the city's major festivals, you'll just have to live with the heat. January is the time of the Sydney Festival, with outdoor music, theater, circuses, and general mayhem. All of this takes an interesting turn in February and March during the Sydney Gay and Lesbian Mardi Gras, which includes a glittering and raunchy parade.

Sydney Harbour

Governor Arthur Phillip, the first European to sail into these waters, called Sydney Harbour "in extent and security, very superior to any other that I have ever seen—containing a considerable number of coves, formed by narrow necks of land, mostly rocks, covered with timber." The wooded splendor he described may now be altered, but few would dispute that the harbor is one of nature's extraordinary creations.

Officially titled Port Jackson, the harbor is in its depths a river valley carved by the Parramatta and Lane Cove rivers and the many creeks that flow in from the north. The rising sea level at the end of the last Ice Age submerged the floor of the valley, leaving only the walls. In the earliest days of the colony, the military laid claim to much of the harbor's 240 km (150 mi) of waterfront. It is for this reason that so much of the foreshore has survived in its natural splendor. Several pockets of land are now protected within Sydney Harbour National Park. Such areas as North, South, and Middle heads, and the harbor islands that you'll pass on the harbor cruise, are in general remarkably unspoiled.

This tour is based on the route followed by the State Transit Authority ferries on their thrice-daily Harbour Cruises (☞ Contacts and Resources *in* Sydney A to Z, *below*). The Coffee Cruise run by Captain Cook Cruises follows a similar course. The tour takes in the eastern half of the harbor, from the city to the Heads and Middle Harbour. This is the glamorous side of the waterway, but the western shore has its areas of historic and natural distinction, including Homebush Bay, the main site for the Olympic Summer Games in 2000 (☞ Around Sydney, *below*).

A Good Cruise

As the vessel leaves the ferry wharves at Circular Quay, it crosses **Sydney Cove** ①, the area where the soldiers and convicts of the First Fleet established their initial makeshift village in January 1788. After rounding Bennelong Point (named after an early Aboriginal inhabitant) and the Sydney Opera House, the boat turns east and crosses **Farm Cove** ②, passing the Royal Botanic Gardens. The tall, Gothic Revival chimneys just visible above the trees belong to Government House, the former official residence of the state governor and now frequently open to the public.

Garden Island ③, the country's largest naval dockyard, is easily identifiable across Woolloomooloo (say "*wool-uh-muh-loo*") Bay by its squadrons of sleek, gray warships. Visiting ships of the U.S. Navy's Pacific fleet can often be seen tied up here. Darling Point is the next headland, dominated by several tall apartment blocks and marking the beginning of Sydney's desirable eastern suburbs. Across Double Bay, **Point Piper** ④ is famous as the ritziest address in the country. The large expanse of water to the east of Point Piper is **Rose Bay** ⑤, bordered by another highly desirable, but somewhat more affordable, harborside suburb.

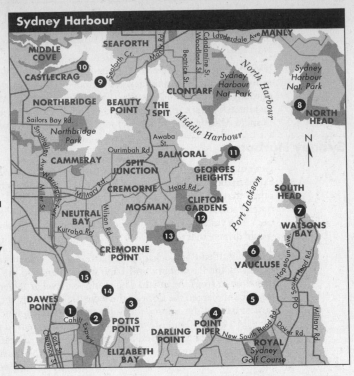

Sydney Harbour

Vaucluse ⑥ is yet another suburb that conveys social stature, beyond Rose Bay. The area is named after **Vaucluse House,** the sandstone mansion built by 19th-century explorer, publisher, and politician William Wentworth. The house is hidden from view, but you can see the Grecian columns of Strickland House, which was used as a convalescent home until a few years ago. The beach to the east surrounds Shark Bay, which is part of **Nielsen Park** and has one of the most popular of the harbor bathing beaches (☞ Beaches, *below*). **Watsons Bay** ⑦, a former fishing village, is the easternmost south shore suburb. Beyond here, South Head presides over the meeting of harbor and ocean. It is one of the two giant sandstone headlands that protect Port Jackson.

North Head is the boat's next landmark, followed by the beachside suburb of **Manly** (☞ Beaches, *below*), and the **Quarantine Station** ⑧. The station was used to protect Sydney from disease, and it is a remnant of a fascinating chapter in the nation's history. The vessel then enters **Middle Harbour** ⑨—formed by creeks that spring from the forested peaks of Ku-ring-gai Chase National Park (☞ Around Sydney, *below*)—where you'll pass the beach at Clontarf and sail through the opening in the Spit Bridge. On the way back to the bridge after exploring Middle Harbour, you'll cruise by the suburb of **Castlecrag** ⑩, founded by Walter Burley Griffin, the American architect responsible for the layout of Canberra.

On returning to the main body of the harbor, look for the popular beach at Balmoral and **Middle Head** ⑪, part of Sydney Harbour National Park and the site of mid-19th-century cannons and fortifications. During that period, Sydney Harbour became a regular port of call for American whaling ships, the crews of which were responsible for the name of nearby **Chowder Bay** ⑫. Sailing deeper into the harbor, the vessel passes **Taronga Zoo** ⑬, where you might catch a glimpse of some of the animals through the foliage.

The vessel now heads back toward Harbour Bridge. On the way, the tiny island of **Fort Denison** ⑭, Sydney's most prominent fortification, occupies a prime position near the Opera House, was fortified progressively during the 19th century. On the point at **Kirribilli** ⑮, almost opposite the Opera House, you will catch glimpses of two colonial-style houses—the official Sydney residences of the governor-general and prime minister, who are otherwise based in Canberra. Still on the north side, but west of Harbour Bridge, lies Luna Park, Sydney's defunct amusement park.

From the north side of the harbor, the vessel crosses back to Circular Quay, where the tour ends.

TIMING

This scenic cruise takes 2½ hours and operates year-round. Refreshments are available on the boat's lower deck and, for the best view, you should begin the voyage on the right side of the vessel.

The cruise passes several places—such as Vaucluse House, the Quarantine Station, Taronga Zoo, and Fort Denison—that you may wish to visit later. These can all be reached either via ferry from Circular Quay, or on one of the Explorer buses. The State Transit Authority ferry tour described above runs morning and afternoon. Sunset and city-lights tours ply the waters on different but equally scenic routes.

Sights to See

⑩ **Castlecrag.** This Middle Harbour suburb was founded by Walter Burley Griffin after he designed Canberra. In 1924, after working on the national capital and in Melbourne, the American architect moved to Sydney and built a number of houses that are notable for their sympathy to the surrounding bushland—a radical departure from the domestic architecture of the time. About eight of his houses survive, although none are visible from the harbor.

⑫ **Chowder Bay.** The oysters and other shellfish collected from these rocky shores decades ago have their part in the naming of this bay. Nineteenth-century American whalers made their chowder here. They once anchored off what is now army land to the southwest of Middle Head. The bay's location is identifiable by a cluster of wooden buildings at water's edge and twin oil-storage tanks.

② **Farm Cove.** Now the location of the **Royal Botanic Gardens** (☞ *below*), the shore of this bay was where the first, unsuccessful attempts were made to establish gardens to feed the convict settlers. The long sea wall was constructed from the 1840s onward to enclose the previously swampy foreshore.

⑭ **Fort Denison.** For a brief time in the early days of the colony, convicts who committed petty offenses were kept on this harbor island. The island was progressively fortified from 1841, when it was decided to strengthen the existing defenses at Dawes Point Battery, under Harbour Bridge. Work was abandoned when cash ran out and not completed until 1857, when fears of Russian expansion in the Pacific spurred further fortification. Today, the firing of the fort's cannon signals not an imminent invasion, but merely the hour—one o'clock. The National Parks and Wildlife Service runs two-hour-long tours to Fort Denison. Tours depart from Cadman's Cottage, 110 George Street, The Rocks. ⊠ *Sydney Harbour,* ☎ *02/9247–5033.* ☜ *$9.* ☉ *Tour daily at 10, noon, and 2.*

③ **Garden Island.** During the 1941–45 War of the Pacific, Garden Island, Sydney's large naval base and dockyard, was a frontline port for Allied ships. On the night of May 31, 1942, this battle fleet was the target of three Japanese midget submarines that were launched from a mother submarine at sea. One of the three penetrated the antisubmarine net that had been laid across the harbor and sank the HMAS *Kuttabul,* a ferry being used as a naval depot ship, with a loss of 21 lives. In the chaos that followed one midget submarine escaped, but the other two were sunk.

Garden Island isn't open to the public, but the naval base may eventually be relocated outside of Sydney, and there are plans to transform this prime harborside location into a recreational area.

⑮ **Kirribilli.** Residents of this attractive suburb opposite the city and Opera House have million-dollar views, an excellent little theater, and two of Sydney's most important mansions. The larger of the two is **Admiralty House**—the Sydney residence of the governor-general, the Queen's representative in Australia. The other is **Kirribilli House,** which is the official Sydney home of the prime minister. These impressive residences are rarely and unpredictably open for inspection.

⑨ **Middle Harbour.** Except for the buzz of Jet Skis and the sight of yachts moored in the sandy coves, the upper reaches of Middle Harbour are exactly as they were when the first Europeans set eyes on Port Jackson, just over 200 years ago. This area of bush and parkland also has tranquil, desirable residential suburbs that are only a short drive from the city. Many of the houses here on the northern side of the harbor are set back from the waterline behind bushland; by the time these were built, planning authorities no longer allowed direct water frontage.

⑪ **Middle Head.** Despite its benign appearance now, Sydney Harbour once bristled with armaments. In the middle of the last century, faced with expansionist European powers hungry for new colonies, artillery positions were erected on the headlands to guard harbor approaches. At Middle Head you can still see the rectangular gun emplacements set into the cliff face.

④ **Point Piper.** Many of this exclusive harborside suburb's magnificent dwellings are home to Sydney's rich and famous. At the height of the real-estate boom during the late 1980s, several waterfront mansions here changed hands for close to $20 million.

⑧ **Quarantine Station.** From the 1830s onward, ships and passengers that arrived with contagious diseases were isolated on this outpost in the shadow of North Head until pronounced free of illness. Among the last to be quartered here were the victims of Cyclone Tracy, which devastated Darwin in 1974. Ten years later, after its brief use as a staging post for a group of Vietnamese orphans, the Quarantine Station was closed, its grim purpose finally brought to an end by modern medicine. You can take a 90-minute guided tour of the station with a ranger from the National Parks and Wildlife Service, caretakers of the site. Another interesting option is a three-hour nocturnal Ghost Tour—the station reputedly has its fair share of ghosts—which includes supper. Two-hour children's tours ($7) are also available for those under 11. Tour reservations are essential. Catch a ferry to Manly from Circular Quay, then Bus 135 from Manly Wharf. ✉ *North Head, Manly,* ☎ *02/9977–6229.* ▦ *$8, basic tour $17, Ghost Tour $17.* ◷ *Basic tour daily at 1:10; Ghost Tour Wed., Fri., and weekends 7:30; children's tour Tues. and Thurs. at 7.*

⑤ **Rose Bay.** This large bay was once a base for the Qantas flying boats that provided the only passenger air service between Australia and America and Europe. The last flying boat departed Rose Bay in the 1960s, but the "airstrip" is still used by floatplanes on scenic flights connecting Sydney with the Hawkesbury River and the Central Coast.

❶ Sydney Cove. Enclosed by Bennelong Point and the Sydney Opera House to the east and Circular Quay West and the Rocks on the other side, the cove was named after Lord Sydney, the British Home Secretary at the time the colony was founded. The settlement itself was to be known as New Albion, but the name never caught on. Instead the city took its name from this tiny bay.

★ �™ ⓭ **Taronga Zoo.** In a natural bush setting on the northern shore of the harbor, Sydney's zoo has an especially extensive collection of Australian fauna, including everybody's favorite marsupial—the koala. Over the past few years, the zoo has made great progress in creating spacious enclosures that closely simulate natural habitats. It is set on a hillside, and a complete tour can be tiring, so you may want to pick up the free map at the entrance gate that outlines a less strenuous route. Children's strollers are provided free of charge, but they are rather basic.

The easiest way to get to the zoo from the city is by ferry. From Taronga Wharf, a bus or the cable car will take you up the hill to the main entrance. The ZooPass, a combined ferry-zoo ticket, is available at Circular Quay. ✉ *Bradleys Head Rd., Mosman,* ☎ *02/9969–2777.* 🎫 *$21.* ⊙ *Daily 9–5.*

❻ Vaucluse. One of the most attractive harbor suburbs, the palatial homes of Vaucluse offer a glimpse of Sydney's high society. The small beaches at Nielsen Park and Parsley Bay offer safe swimming and are packed with families in summer.

A large part of this area once belonged to the estate of **Vaucluse House,** one of Sydney's most illustrious remaining historic mansions. Most of the Gothic Revival building was constructed in the 1830s for William Charles Wentworth, the "Father of the Australian Constitution," and his family. The 15-room house is furnished in period style, and its delightful gardens are managed by the Historic Houses Trust and open to the public. There are also famous old-style **tearooms** on the grounds. You can get to the house on the Bondi & Bay Explorer Bus. ✉ *Wentworth Rd., Vaucluse,* ☎ *02/9388–7922.* 🎫 *$5.* ⊙ *Tues.–Sun. 10–4:30.*

❼ Watsons Bay. Established as a military base and fishing settlement in the colony's early years, Watsons Bay is a charming suburb that has held onto its rare, village atmosphere. Camp Cove, the main beach here, is of some historical importance: It was intended that the convicts who were to be Australia's first settlers would establish a community at Botany Bay, which had been explored by Captain Cook in 1770. However, as Captain Phillip found when he arrived 18 years later, the lack of fresh water at that site made settlement impossible. After a few days, he set off to explore Port Jackson, which had been named but not visited by Cook. Phillip rounded the heads and landed on a beach that he named Camp Cove. To his delight, Cook found a far more workable and pleasing site for settlement farther east along the harbor, at the present-day site of Circular Quay.

The Rocks and Sydney Harbour Bridge

The Rocks is the birthplace not just of Sydney but of modern Australia. It was here that the 11 ships of the First Fleet dropped anchor in 1788, and this stubby peninsula enclosing the western side of Sydney Cove became known simply as The Rocks.

The first crude wooden huts erected by the convicts were followed by simple houses made from mud bricks cemented together by a mixture of sheep's wool and mud. The rain soon washed this rough mortar away, and no buildings in the Rocks survive from the earliest period of convict settlement. Most of the architecture dates from the Victorian era, by which time Sydney had become a thriving port. Warehouses lining the waterfront were backed by a row of tradesmen's shops, banks, and taverns, and above them ascending Observatory Hill rose a tangled mass of alleyways lined with the cottages of seamen and wharf laborers. By the late 1800s all who could afford to had moved out of the area, and it was widely regarded as a rough, tough, squalid part of town. As late as 1900 bubonic plague swept through The Rocks, prompting the government to offer a bounty for dead rats in an effort to exterminate their disease-carrying fleas.

The character of the Rocks area changed considerably when the Sydney Harbour Bridge was built during the 1920s and '30s, when many old houses, and even entire streets, were demolished to make room for the bridge's southern approach route. The bridge took almost nine years to build and replaced the ferries that once carried passengers and freight across the harbor.

It is only in the last decade or so that The Rocks has become appreciated for its historic significance and extensive restoration has transformed the area. Here you can see the evolution of a society almost from its inception to the present, and yet The Rocks is anything but a stuffy tutorial. History stands side by side with shops, outdoor cafés, and some excellent museums.

A Good Walk

Begin at **Circular Quay,** the lively waterfront area where Sydney's ferry, bus, and train systems converge. Follow the quay toward Harbour Bridge and, as you round the curve, turn left and walk about 20 paces into First Fleet Park. The map on the platform in front of you describes the colony of 1808. The **Tank Stream** entered Sydney Cove at this very spot. This tiny watercourse brought the colony its fresh water—the necessity that decided the location of the first European settlement on Australian soil.

Return to the waterfront and take the paved walkway toward Harbour Bridge. The massive Art Deco–style building to your left is the **Museum of Contemporary Art** ⑯, which is devoted to painting, sculpture, film, video, and kinetic art made during the past 20 years.

Continue on this walkway around **Circular Quay West,** and when you reach the fig trees in the circular bed, look left. The bronze statue beneath the trees is the figure of **William Bligh** ⑰ of HMAV *Bounty* fame. To the right is a two-story, cream-color stone house. This is **Cadman's Cottage** ⑱. Built in 1816, it is the oldest surviving house in the city of Sydney. The large modern building ahead of you on the waterfront is the **Overseas Passenger Terminal** ⑲, the main mooring for passenger liners in Sydney.

Have a look inside Cadman's Cottage and then climb the stairs leading to George Street. Note the original gas streetlamp at the top of these steps. Turn right and immediately on the right is **The Rocks Heritage and Information Centre** ⑳, which has a small museum and can provide you with useful leaflets and details on the area.

After leaving the Information Centre, turn right past the redbrick facade of the Australian Steam Navigation Company. Continue down the hill and steps to **Campbell's Cove** ㉑ and its warehouses. This carefully restored precinct contains numerous restaurants and cafés and is a great spot for harbor watching and a drink or meal.

Walk back up the steps beside the warehouses and cross to upper **George Street,** lined with restored 19th-century buildings. Across the road is **Atherden Street,** Sydney's shortest street. Note the small garden of staghorn ferns that has been painstakingly cultivated on tiny rock ledges at the end of this street. Just behind the Westpac Bank on the corner of George and Playfair streets is the **Westpac Banking Museum** ㉒, which has a collection of currency from the earliest days of settlement. After leaving the museum, return to George Street and on the left is the **Merchants House** ㉓, a restored example of the dwellings that served as both home and storeroom for the city's merchant classes in the mid-1800s.

Continue up George Street toward Harbour Bridge until you are directly beneath the bridge's massive girders. Note the small, green, iron cubicle standing on the landward side of George Street. This is a gentlemen's toilet, modeled on the Parisian pissoir. At the turn of the century these were fairly common on the streets of Sydney, but they have since lost place to the more discreet brick constructions (a modern toilet stands at the back of this sole survivor).

Walk under the bridge to **Dawes Point Park** ㉔ for excellent views of the harbor, including the Opera House and the small island of **Fort Denison** ㉕. This park also provides an unusual perspective on the **Sydney Harbour Bridge** ㉖—an unmistakable symbol of the city. It is among the world's widest long-span bridges.

Turn your back on the harbor and walk up **Lower Fort Street** ㉗, which runs to the right of the Harbour View Hotel. Ring the bell at number 53, the curious **Colonial House Museum,** and you will probably be ushered inside by Mrs. Shirley Ball, director of the museum as well as the occupant of the house above.

Continue up Lower Fort to the corner of Windmill Street, where you'll find the wedge-shape **Hero of Waterloo,** one of the oldest pubs in the city.

Lower Fort Street ends at **Argyle Place,** built by Governor Macquarie and named after his home county in Scotland. The houses and other buildings here in the mini-suburb of Millers Point are worth an inspection—particularly **Holy Trinity Church** ㉘ on the left-hand side, and the **Lord Nelson Hotel** beyond the "village" green.

Argyle Place is dominated by **Observatory Hill** ㉙, the site of the colony's first windmill and, later, a signal station. If you have the energy to climb the steps that lead to the hill, you will reach a park shaded by giant Moreton Bay fig trees and the reward of one of the finest views in Sydney. On top of the hill the **Sydney Observatory** ㉚, now a museum of astronomy, is worth a visit. You can also follow the path behind the Observatory to the National Trust Centre and the **S.H. Ervin Gallery** ㉛, which mounts changing exhibitions with Australian themes.

Leave Argyle Place and walk down **Argyle Street** into the dark tunnel of the **Argyle Cut** ㉜. On the lower side of the cut and to the left, the **Argyle Stairs** lead up through an archway. Don't take these steps unless you have the energy for several steep flights. This part of the walk takes you up to Harbour Bridge and into the **South East Pylon** for a dizzying view of the Opera House and the city, which is the best city view from the bridge. To get to the Sydney Harbour Bridge walkway from the top of the stairs, cross the road and walk left for 20 yards,

28

The Rocks and Sydney Harbour Bridge

Argyle Cut, **32**
Argyle Stores, **33**
William Bligh
Statue, **17**
Cadman's Cottage, **18**
Campbell's Cove, **21**
Dawes Point Park, **24**
S.H. Ervin Gallery, **31**
Fort Denison, **25**
Holy Trinity Church, **28**
Lower Fort Street, **27**
Merchants House, **23**
Museum of
Contemporary Art, **16**
Nurses Walk, **35**
Observatory Hill, **29**
Overseas Passenger
Terminal, **19**
The Rocks Heritage and
Information Centre, **20**
Suez Canal, **34**
Sydney Harbour
Bridge, **26**
Sydney Observatory, **30**
Westpac Banking
Museum, **22**

Macquarie Street and the Domain South

Art Gallery of New
South Wales, **52**
Customs House, **36**
The Domain south, **51**
Garden Palace Gates, **42**
History House, **41**
Hyde Park Barracks, **48**
Lands Department, **38**
Macquarie Place, **37**
Museum of Sydney, **39**
Royal Australasian
College of Physicians, **43**
St. James Church, **49**
St. Mary's Cathedral, **50**
State Library of New
South Wales, **44**
State Parliament
House, **45**
Sydney
Conservatorium of
Music, **40**
Sydney Hospital, **46**
Sydney Mint
Museum, **47**

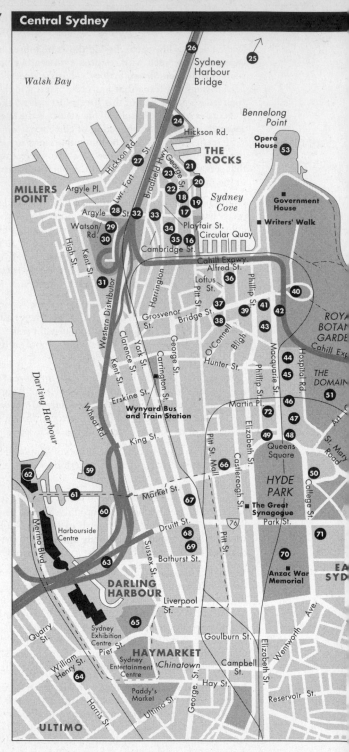

Central Sydney

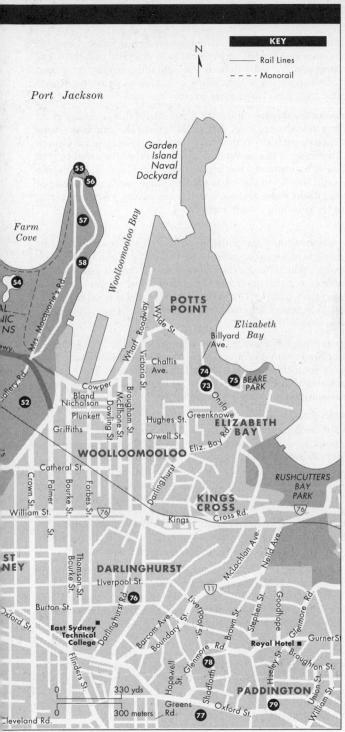

The Opera House, the RBG, and the Domain North
Andrew (Boy) Charlton Pool, **58**
The Domain north, **57**
Mrs. Macquarie's Chair, **56**
Mrs. Macquarie's Point, **55**
Royal Botanic Gardens, **54**
Sydney Opera House, **53**

Darling Harbour
Australian National Maritime Museum, **62**
Chinese Garden, **65**
Darling Harbour Olympic Showcase, **60**
IMAX Theatre, **63**
Powerhouse Museum, **64**
Pyrmont Bridge, **61**
Sydney Aquarium, **59**

Sydney City Center
Australian Museum, **71**
Hyde Park, **70**
Martin Place, **72**
Queen Victoria Building, **67**
St. Andrew's Cathedral, **69**
Sydney Tower, **66**
Sydney Town Hall, **68**

Elizabeth Bay and Kings Cross, Darlinghurst, and Paddington
Arthur McElhone Reserve, **74**
Beare Park, **75**
Elizabeth Bay House, **73**
Juniper Hall, **79**
Shadforth Street, **78**
Sydney Jewish Museum, **76**
Victoria Barracks, **77**

then follow the signs to the walkway and pylon. You should allow at least 1½ hours for this detour.

The walk resumes at the foot of the steps on Argyle Street. Continue down the street and turn left under the archway inscribed with the words **Argyle Stores** ㉝. The old warehouses around this courtyard have been converted to upmarket fashion shops and galleries. Leave the Argyle Stores and cross onto Harrington Street.

The **Gumnut Tea Garden** on the left-hand side of this street is a good place for a refreshment stop. Ten yards beyond the café is the **Suez Canal** ㉞, a narrow laneway that runs down the incline toward George Street. Turn right at **Nurses Walk** ㉟, another of the area's historic and atmospheric back streets, then left into Surgeons Court and left again into George Street. On the left is the handsome sandstone facade of the former **Rocks Police Station,** now a crafts gallery. From this point, Circular Quay is only a short walk away.

TIMING

The attractions of the Rocks are many, so to walk this route, even without lingering in museums or galleries, or walking up to the Sydney Harbour Bridge, you should allow around half a day. If you spend a reasonable amount of time in the Museum of Contemporary Art, Sydney Observatory, and the S.H. Ervin Gallery, a full day is required. The other Rocks museums are small, and an inspection of each should not take more than half an hour.

The area is often very crowded on weekends, when the Rocks Market in George Street with its crafts, souvenir items, and hand-made Australiana presents a serious distraction from sightseeing. The Rocks is also packed with interesting shops, so be forewarned that your time can disappear rapidly if you're tugged by the lure of goods.

Sights to See

㉜ **Argyle Cut.** Argyle Street links Argyle Place with George Street, and the thoroughfare is dominated by the Argyle Cut and its massive walls. In the days before the cut was made, the sandstone ridge here was a major barrier to traffic crossing between Circular Quay and Millers Point. In 1843, convict work gangs hacked at the sandstone with hand tools for 2½ years before the project was abandoned due to lack of progress. Work restarted in 1857, when drills, explosives, and paid labor completed the job. The **Argyle Stairs** lead off this street up to the Sydney Harbour Bridge walkway, and a spectacular view from the South East Pylon (*see* Sydney Harbour Bridge, *below*, for details).

Argyle Place. Unusual for Sydney, this charming enclave in the suburb of Millers Point has all the traditional requirements of an English green: a pub at one end, church at the other, and grass in between. Argyle Place is lined with 19th-century houses and cottages on its northern side and flanked by Observatory Hill to the south.

NEED A
BREAK?
While in the west end of Argyle Place, consider the liquid temptations of the **Lord Nelson,** Sydney's oldest hotel, which has been licensed (to serve alcohol) since 1842. The sandstone pub has its own brewery on the premises, and one of its specialties is Quayle Ale, named after the U.S. vice president who "sank a schooner" here during his 1989 visit to Australia. ✉ *19 Kent St., Millers Point,* ☎ *02/9251-4044.*

㉝ **Argyle Stores.** These solid old warehouses date from the late 1820s. The building emerged from a total re-fit at the end of 1996 and now houses several chic gift and souvenir shops, clothes boutiques, and cafés. ✉ *Argyle St. opposite Harrington St.*

⑰ **William Bligh Statue.** Yes, this is the infamous captain—cursed both at sea and on land. After his incident on the *Bounty,* Bligh became governor of New South Wales in 1806. Two years later he faced his second mutiny. Bligh had made himself unpopular with the soldiers of the New South Wales Corps, popularly known as the Rum Corps, who were the real power in the colony. When he threatened to end their lucrative liquor trade monopoly, he was imprisoned in an incident known as the Rum Rebellion. He spent the next two years as a captive until his successor, Lachlan Macquarie, arrived. Ironically, the statue's gaze frequently rests on HMAV *Bounty,* a replica of Bligh's ship, as it sails around the harbor on daily sightseeing cruises.

⑱ **Cadman's Cottage.** Although of modest proportions, the city's oldest building has an interesting history. John Cadman was a convict who was sentenced for life to New South Wales for stealing a horse. He later became superintendent of government boats, a position that entitled him to live in the upper story of this house. The water once lapped almost at Cadman's doorstep, and the original seawall still stands at the front of the house. The small extension on the side of the cottage was built to lock up the oars of Cadman's boats, since oars would have been desirable to any convict attempting to escape by sea. The upper floor of Cadman's Cottage now contains a useful National Parks and Wildlife Service bookshop and information center. ⊠ *110 George St.,* ☎ *02/9247– 8861.* ⊙ *Mon. 10–3, Tues.–Fri. 9–4:30, weekends 11–4.*

㉑ **Campbell's Cove.** Robert Campbell was a Scottish merchant who is sometimes referred to as "the father of Australian commerce." Campbell broke the stranglehold that the British East India Company exercised over seal and whale products, which were New South Wales's only exports in those early days. Built from 1838 onward, the cove's atmospheric, sandstone **Campbells Storehouse** now serves as a home for waterside restaurants. The pulleys that were used to hoist cargoes still hang on the upper level of the warehouses.

The cove is also the mooring place for Sydney's fully operational tall ships—**HMAV** *Bounty,* an authentic replica of the original 18th-century vessel, and the rebuilt 1902 *Solway Lass*—which offer theme cruises around the harbor (☞ Guided Tours *in* Sydney A to Z, *below*).

㉔ **Dawes Point Park.** Named after William Dawes, a First Fleet marine and astronomer who established the colony's first basic observatory nearby in 1788, this was also once the site of a fortification known as Dawes Battery. The cannon on the hillside pointing toward the Opera House came from the ships of the First Fleet. The park provides wonderful views of the harbor, Fort Denison, and Harbour Bridge.

㉛ **S.H. Ervin Gallery.** Housed in the impressive National Trust Centre just behind Observatory Hill, this gallery concentrates on Australian art and architecture from a historical perspective. The changing exhibitions are of a consistently high standard and have shown the work of such renowned artists as Lloyd Rees, Sidney Nolan, Hans Heysen, and Russell Drysdale. The gallery has a bookshop, and there is a very good National Trust gift shop next door. ⊠ *National Trust Centre, Observatory Hill, Watson Rd., Millers Point,* ☎ *02/9258–0174.* ⊡ *$6–$10.* ⊙ *Tues.–Fri. 11–5, weekends 2–5.*

Harrington Street area. The small precinct around this street forms one of the Rocks's most interesting areas. Many old cottages, houses, and even warehouses here have been converted to hotel accommodations, and there are some fascinating lanes and alleyways to explore. ☞ **Suez Canal** and ☞ **Nurses Walk** are among them.

28 **Holy Trinity Church.** Every morning redcoats would march to this 1840 Argyle Place church from Dawes Point Battery, and it became commonly known as Garrison Church. As the regimental plaques and colors around the walls testify, it still retains a close association with the military. The tattered ensign on the left wall was carried into battle by Australian troops during the Boer War, in which Australians were enlisted to help the empire fight Dutch South Africans. ✉ *Argyle Pl., Millers Point.* ☉ *Daily, generally 9–5, but times vary.*

27 **Lower Fort Street.** At one time the handsome Georgian houses along this street, originally a rough track leading from the Dawes Point Battery to Observatory Hill, were among the best addresses in Sydney. Elaborate wrought-iron lacework still graces many of the facades—restoration is underway, but many of the houses are rather rundown.

The street's rambling **Colonial House Museum** is the singular domain of Shirley Ball, one of the many remarkable characters of the district—a longtime resident and a vocal campaigner in the fight to preserve the area. The museum is her personal indulgence, a vast and mostly unlabeled collection that includes a penny-farthing bicycle, documents from the convict era, cigarette cards from World War I, old bottles, carpet beaters, ships in bottles, and even a bowl of plastic fruit. Some of the most interesting exhibits are photographs of the Rocks taken before Harbour Bridge was built, forever altering the area. Essentially a haphazard social history of early Australian life, this museum adds flesh and blood to any tour of the area. Both Shirley and her husband are elderly and hard-of-hearing, and sometimes you will have to ring several times; however, their enthusiasm more than compensates for this minor inconvenience. ✉ *53 Lower Fort St.,* ☎ *02/9247–6008.* 🎫 *$1.* ☉ *Daily 10–5.*

Hero of Waterloo, which dates from 1844, is Sydney's second oldest hotel. Gold fever struck the colony during the middle of the 19th century, and it was not uncommon for an entire ship's crew to desert and head for the goldfields as soon as the ship reached Sydney. Captains often resorted to skulduggery to recruit a new crew, and legend has it that many a lad who drank with a generous sea captain in the Hero would awake the next morning on a heaving deck, already out of sight of land. The building dates from 1844 and is the city's second oldest hotel. ✉ *81 Lower Fort St.,* ☎ *02/9252–4553.* ☉ *Daily 10 AM–11 PM.*

23 **Merchants House.** This fully restored 1848 dwelling incorporates the Australian Childhood Collection, a display of rare books, illustrations, and toys. Although the house and its period furnishings are essentially simple, the relatively generous dimensions of the rooms and the decorative touches—French doors that open to the upper-story balcony, for example—identify its owners as members of a privileged elite. The house also features changing exhibitions. ✉ *43 George St.,* ☎ *02/ 9241–5099.* 🎫 *$2.* ☉ *Wed.–Sun. 10–4.*

16 **Museum of Contemporary Art.** Andy Warhol, Roy Lichtenstein, Cindy Sherman, and local artists Juan Devila, Maria Kozic, and Imants Tillers are just some of the well-known names whose works hang in this ponderous Art Deco building on Circular Quay West. Needless to say, the MCA houses Australia's most important collection of modern art. Unfortunately, it's hard to say that the exhibitions always challenge or inspire. In spite of that, the museum's café, with outdoor seating beside the harbor, is a pleasant, inexpensive option for breakfast and lunch. ✉ *Circular Quay W,* ☎ *02/9252–4033.* 🎫 *$8.* ☉ *Daily 11–6.*

35 **Nurses Walk.** Cutting across the area of the colony's first hospital, Nurses Walk bears its name out of the colony's earliest illnesses. Seven hundred and thirty-six convicts survived the voyage from Portsmouth, England, aboard First Fleet's eleven ships. Many of them arrived suffering from dysentery, smallpox, scurvy, and typhoid. A few days after he landed at Sydney Cove, Governor Phillip established a tent hospital to care for the worst cases.

Only 40 convicts of the 776 who left England had died onboard Phillip's ships, a mortality rate (5%) that was considered a triumph at the time. In comparison, by the time the Second Fleet dropped anchor in Sydney Cove in 1790, a quarter of its convicts had died and a great many more were critically ill. One of the ships in the Second Fleet carried a prefabricated hospital, which was erected and filled almost immediately.

Beyond Nurses Walk, the old **Rocks Police Station** on George Street dates from 1882 and now contains a variety of good crafts shops. Note the police truncheon thrust into the lion's mouth above the doorway, an architectural motif that appears on at least one other of Sydney's Victorian police stations.

NEED A
BREAK?

The **Gumnut Tea Garden** is more than just an ideal refreshment stop. In this second-oldest (1830) building in the Rocks—originally the residence of blacksmith William Reynolds—a painless history lesson comes with a delicious lunch. The restaurant tucked away in his sandstone cottage serves tasty salads, pies, and cakes. The best tables are at the back in the shady garden. The Gumnut has a devoted clientele, and reservations are necessary at lunchtime. If you're staying in the area, breakfast in the courtyard is a great start to the day. Prices are moderate. ⊠ *28 Harrington St.,* ☎ *02/9247-9591.*

❷❾ **Observatory Hill.** The city's highest point at 145 ft, this was known originally as Windmill Hill because the first windmill in the colony once stood here—but not for long. Soon after it was built, the canvas sails were stolen, the machinery was damaged in a storm, and the foundations cracked. Before it was 10 years old, the mill was useless. Several other windmills were erected in the area, however, and this part of the Rocks is still known as Millers Point. In 1848 the signal station at the top of the hill was built. This later became an astronomical observatory, and Windmill Hill changed its name to Observatory Hill. Until 1982 the metal ball on the tower of the observatory was cranked up the mast and dropped at precisely 1 PM so that ship captains could set their chronometers.

❶❾ **Overseas Passenger Terminal.** Busy Circular Quay West is dominated by the structure and dock of this maritime station. The terminal was rebuilt in 1987 to accommodate the enormous ships that often call into Sydney as part of their cruise itineraries. There are a couple of excellent waterfront restaurants at the terminal's northern end, and it's worth taking the escalator to the upper deck for a good view of the harbor and Opera House.

❷⓿ **The Rocks Heritage and Information Centre.** Once a sailor's home that provided inexpensive accommodations for mariners, this building now offers insight into the history of the Rocks, with displays of artifacts and a short video. Center staff can answer questions about the area and make travel bookings, and the informative Rocks Walking Tours depart from here. The building also contains a couple of good places to eat—the very popular **Sailors Thai** (☞ Dining, *below*) restaurant and its less-expensive canteen. ⊠ *106 George St.,* ☎ *02/9255–1788.* ☉ *Mar.–Oct., daily 9–5; Nov.–Feb., daily 9–6.*

③ **Suez Canal.** This narrow alley got its name before drains were installed, when rainwater would pour down its funnel-like passageway and gush across George Street. It was a haunt of the notorious Rocks gangs of the late 19th century, when robbery and crime were rife in the area.

㉖ **Sydney Harbour Bridge.** Known affectionately by Sydneysiders as "the old coat hanger," Harbour Bridge was a monumental engineering feat when it was completed in 1932. The roadway is supported by the arch above, not by the massive stone pylons, which were added for aesthetic rather than structural reasons. The 1,650-ft-long bridge is 160 ft wide and contains two railways tracks, eight road lanes, a cycleway, and a footpath. Actor Paul Hogan worked for several years as a rigger on the bridge, long before he tamed the world's wildlife and lowlife as the star of the film *Crocodile Dundee.*

The best way to experience the bridge and its spectacular views is to follow the walkway from its access point near the **Argyle Stairs** (☞ *above*) to the **South East Pylon.** This structure houses a display on the bridge's construction, and you can climb the 200 steps to the lookout and its unbeatable harbor panorama. ⊠ *S. East Pylon, Sydney Harbour Bridge,* ☎ *02/9247–3408.* ⌸ *$2.* ⊙ *Daily 10–5.*

㉚ **Sydney Observatory.** No longer used for serious sky-gazing, because few stars can be seen through the glow of Sydney's lights, this struc-ture on top of Observatory Hill has become an entertaining museum. The Observatory features a number of hands-on displays, including constellation charts, talking computers, and games designed to illus-trate principles of astronomy. During evening shows, you'll have a close-up view of such wonders as the rings of Saturn, the moons of Jupiter, distant galaxies, and the enormous, multicolor clouds of gas known as nebulae. Reservations are required for the show. ⊠ *Observatory Hill, Watson Rd., Millers Point,* ☎ *02/9217–0485.* ⌸ *Evening show $6.* ⊙ *Observatory weekdays 2–5, weekends 10–5; show Nov.–Mar., Thurs.–Tues. at 8:30; Apr.–Oct., Thurs.–Tues. at 6:15 and 8:15.*

Upper George Street. With its well-restored, 19th-century dwellings and old storehouses that now contain shops, this part of George Street is a charming section of the Rocks. The covered Rocks Market is held here on weekends. ☞ **Merchants House** is at number 43.

㉒ **Westpac Banking Museum.** Duck behind George Street to get the story of Australian banking. The Westpac museum uses its collection of early Australian coins to chart the economic fortunes of the infant colony. ⊠ *6–8 Playfair St.,* ☎ *02/9251–1419.* ⊙ *Tues.–Fri. 10:30–4, Sat.–Mon. 1–4.*

Macquarie Street and the Domain South

This walk will introduce you to two of the most remarkable figures in Australian history—Governor Lachlan Macquarie and his govern-ment architect, Francis Greenway. Descended from Scottish clan chief-tains, Macquarie was an accomplished soldier and a man of vision—the first governor to foresee a role for New South Wales as a free society rather than an open prison. Macquarie laid the foundations for that society by establishing a plan for the city, constructing significant pub-lic buildings, and advocating that reformed convicts be readmitted to society. Francis Greenway was himself such a former prisoner.

Macquarie's policies may seem perfectly reasonable today, but in the early 19th century they marked him as a radical. Because his vision of a free society threatened to blur distinctions between soldiers, free set-tlers, and convicts, Macquarie was forced to resign in 1821. He was buried on his Scottish estate three years later, his gravestone inscribed with the words "the Father of Australia."

Macquarie's grand plans for the construction of Sydney might have come to nothing were it not for Francis Greenway. The governor had been continually frustrated by his masters in the Colonial Office in London, who saw no need for an architect in a penal colony. Then, in 1814, fate delivered Greenway into his hands. He had trained as an architect in England, where he was convicted of forgery and sentenced to 14 years in New South Wales. Macquarie seized this opportunity, gave Greenway a ticket of leave that allowed him to work outside the convict system, and set him to work transforming Sydney.

For all his brilliance as an architect, Greenway was a difficult and temperamental man. When his patron Macquarie returned to England in 1822, Greenway quickly fell from favor and retired to his farm north of Sydney. Some years later he was charged with misappropriating this property, but he was able to produce a deed giving him title to the land. It is now believed that the signature on the title deed is a forgery. Greenway was depicted on one side of the old $10 notes until they went out of circulation early in the 1990s.

Only in Australia would a convicted forger be depicted on the currency.

A Good Walk

This historically based walk roughly follows the perimeter of the Royal Botanic Gardens and the Domain. A shady park bench is never far away.

Begin at Circular Quay. Turn your back on the harbor and cross Alfred Street, which runs parallel to the waterfront. The only building of historic distinction along Alfred is the **Customs House** ㊱. When it was built in the late 1880s, the sandstone structure was surrounded by warehouses storing the fleeces that were the principal source of the colony's prosperity.

Walk up Loftus Street, which runs to the right of the Customs House. In Customs House Lane at the rear you can still see a pulley that was used to lower the wool bales to the dockyard from the top floor of Hinchcliff's Wool Stores.

Follow Loftus Street to the small triangular park on your right, **Macquarie Place** ㊲, with its interesting historical monuments. The southern side of the park is bordered by busy **Bridge Street,** named for the bridge that once crossed the Tank Stream at the bottom of this V-shape street. Across Bridge Street, the **Lands Department** ㊳ is one of the finest examples of Victorian public architecture in Sydney. Walk up Bridge Street past the facade of the Department of Education. The **Museum of Sydney** ㊴ is on the next block. Built on the site of the first Government House, the museum chronicles the history of the city between 1788 and 1850.

Continuing up Bridge Street, the next sandstone building on the left is the old Treasury Building, now part of the Hotel Inter-Continental. James Barnet's **Colonial Secretary's Office**—he also designed the Lands Department—is opposite. Note the buildings' similarities, right down to the figures in the corner niches.

Pause for a moment at the corner of Macquarie Street. The figure on horseback about to gallop down Bridge Street is Edward VII, successor to Queen Victoria. The castellated building behind him is the **Sydney Conservatorium of Music** ㊵, originally built in 1819 as stables for Government House, which is screened by trees near the Opera House.

Turn right into **Macquarie Street** (north). On the right at Number 133 is elegant 1850s **History House** ㊶, headquarters of the Royal Australian Historical Society. On the opposite side are the **Garden Palace Gates** ㊷, an elegant wrought-iron entrance to the Royal Botanic Gardens. A little farther along Macquarie Street (Number 145) is the **Royal Australasian College of Physicians** ㊸. The patrician facade of this building gives some idea of the way Macquarie Street looked in the 1840s, when it was lined with the homes of the colonial elite.

The ponderous brown building ahead and to the left is the **State Library of New South Wales** ㊹. Cross the road toward this building, passing the **Light Horse Monument** and the **Shakespeare Memorial.** Australian cavalrymen fought with distinction in several Middle Eastern campaigns during World War I, and the former statue is dedicated to their horses—which were not allowed to return due to Australian quarantine regulations.

Continue along Macquarie Street toward the gates of **State Parliament House** ㊺, a building with an intriguing history. It's the northern wing of the Rum Hospital, built with profits from the rum trade. In a stroke of political genius, Governor Macquarie persuaded two merchants to build a hospital for convicts in return for an extremely lucrative three-year monopoly on the importation of rum.

The next building on the left is the Victorian-style **Sydney Hospital** ㊻, constructed to replace the central section of the Rum Hospital, which had begun to fall apart almost as soon as it was completed. Beyond the hospital is the **Sydney Mint Museum** ㊼, originally the Rum Hospital's southern wing. It is devoted to the history of gold in Australia.

Next door is the **Hyde Park Barracks** ㊽. Before Macquarie arrived, convicts were left to roam freely at night, and there was little regard for the sanctity of life or property on the streets of Sydney after dark. As the new governor, Macquarie was determined to establish law and order, and he commissioned Greenway to design this building to house prisoners.

Cross **Queens Square** to the other side of the road, where the figure of Queen Victoria presides over Macquarie Street. This area is the heart of Sydney's legal district and the location of the 1970s high-rise **Law Court** building, opposite Hyde Park Barracks. To Victoria's left is another Greenway building, **St. James Church** ㊾, originally designed as a court of law.

Return to the other side of Macquarie and walk along College Street to **St. Mary's Cathedral** ㊿ (the main entrance is on Cathedral Street). This is Sydney's Roman Catholic cathedral, the Gothic Revival design of which is based on Lincoln Cathedral in England. As you walk along the side of the cathedral, note the pointed arches above the doors and the flying buttresses—the arches that connect the side of the cathedral to supporting piers—both signatures of Gothic style.

At the rear of the cathedral, cross St. Mary's Road to Art Gallery Road. You are now in the **Domain south**'s ○51 parklands, which extend north to the harbor, bordering the Royal Botanic Gardens and ending at Mrs. Macquarie's Point. Continue past the statue of **Robert Burns**, the Scottish writer. The large trees on the left with enormous roots and drooping limbs are the widely planted Moreton Bay figs, which bear inedible fruit. Directly ahead is the **Art Gallery of New South Wales** ○52, housed in a grand Victorian building with modern extensions. It contains the state's largest collection of artwork.

This is where the tour ends. From the Art Gallery, you can return to Macquarie Street by crossing the Domain or wandering for a half mile through the Royal Botanic Gardens. If you have an Explorer bus pass, you can catch the bus back to the city center from the front of the gallery.

TIMING

To simply walk the outlined itinerary should take no more than a morning or afternoon—other than the rise from Circular Quay to Macquarie Street, the walking is flat and easy. Extended stops, however, at the main attractions of the Museum of Sydney, Sydney Mint Museum, Hyde Park Barracks, and the Art Gallery of New South Wales could easily turn this walk into a daylong event.

Sights to See

52 **Art Gallery of New South Wales.** This gallery permanently exhibits Aboriginal, Asian, and European art, as well as the work of some of the best-known Australian artists. A distinctly Australian style evolves, from early painters who saw the country through European eyes to such painters as Russell Drysdale, whose strident colors and earthy realism give a very different impression of the Australian landscape.

Twentieth-century art is displayed on the entrance level, where large windows frame their own spectacular view of the harbor. Below ground level, in the gallery's major extensions, the Yiribana Gallery displays one of the nation's most comprehensive collections of Aboriginal and Torres Strait Islander art. If you want a change from the usual postcards of kookaburras, kangaroos, and koalas, the bookshop on the ground floor has an offbeat collection. ⊠ *Art Gallery Rd., the Domain,* ☎ *02/ 9225–1744.* ☒ *Free, special-exhibition fee varies.* ⊘ *Daily 10–5.*

Bridge Street. Formerly the site of the 1789 Government House and the colony's first bridge, a number of grandiose Victorian architectural specimens line its sidewalks. One of Bridge Street's most impressive buildings is the ☞ **Lands Department.**

36 **Customs House.** Close to the site where the British flag was raised on the First Fleet's arrival in 1788, this impressive 1840s–1890s building was in use until 1990, originally as the city's customs house and later as offices. Since its closure many schemes have been proposed for its use, but the building is now earmarked for a $24 million refurbishment. The Customs House will ultimately serve as a multiuse cultural and tourism facility, including a museum, which is expected to open in late 1997. ⊠ *Customs House Sq., Alfred St., Circular Quay.*

51 **The Domain south.** Laid out by Governor Macquarie in 1810 as his own personal "domain" and originally including what is now the Royal Botanic Gardens, this large area of parkland is a tranquil haven at the city's eastern edge. Used mainly by office workers for lunchtime recreation, the park is also the venue for free outdoor concerts during the Festival of Sydney, held in January.

42 **Garden Palace Gates.** The gates are all that remains of the Garden Palace, a massive glass pavilion that was erected for the Sydney International Exhibition of 1879 and destroyed by fire three years later. The gates show the dome of the palace, and the stone pillars on either side are engraved with Australian wildflowers. ⊠ *Macquarie St. between Bridge and Bent Sts.*

41 **History House.** You're welcome to visit the home of the Royal Australian Historical Society and its collection of books and other material. The society offers its considerable resources to anyone who wishes to delve into Australiana. ⊠ *133 Macquarie St.,* ☎ *02/9247–8001.* ☒ *Library $5.* ⊘ *Weekdays 9:30–4:30.*

48 **Hyde Park Barracks.** This 1819 building is considered Greenway's architectural masterpiece. Essentially a simple structure, its restrained, classical lines are hallmarks of the Georgian era. The clock on the tower is the oldest functioning public timepiece in New South Wales. Today the Hyde Park Barracks houses a collection of artifacts from the convict era and later years, when it was used as an asylum for Irish orphans and "unprotected women." A surprising number of relics from this period were preserved by rats, which carried away scraps of clothing for their nests beneath the floorboards—a bizarre detail that is graphically illustrated in the foyer. A room on the top floor is strung with hammocks, exactly as it was when the building housed convicts. Try one for size—or you can even spend the night here as part of a unique Sydney "convict experience" that the Historic Houses Trust occasionally organizes. ⊠ *Queen's Sq., Macquarie St.,* ☎ *02/9223–8922, 02/9692–8366 lodging inquiries.* 🎫 *$5.* ☉ *Daily 10–5.*

NEED A
BREAK?

On a sunny day, the courtyard tables of the **Hyde Park Barracks Café** provide one of the finest places in the city to enjoy an outdoor lunch. The café serves a selection of light, imaginative meals, salads, and open sandwiches, with a wine list including Australian wine. Prices are moderate. ⊠ *Queen's Sq., Macquarie St.,* ☎ *02/9223–1155.*

38 **Lands Department.** The figures residing in the niches at the corners of this 1890 sandstone building are early Australian explorers and politicians. James Barnet's building stands among other fine Victorians on Bridge Street, near the intersection of Macquarie Place.

37 **Macquarie Place.** This park, once a special Aboriginal site, contains a number of important monuments, including the obelisk once used as the point from which all distances from Sydney were measured. On a stone plinth at the bottom of the park is the anchor of HMS *Sirius*, flagship of the First Fleet, which struck a reef and sank off Norfolk Island in 1790. The bronze statue of the gentleman with his hands on his hips represents Thomas Mort, who more than a century ago became the first person to ship refrigerated cargo. The implications of this shipment were enormous. Mutton suddenly became a valuable export commodity, and for most of the next century the Australian economy rode on sheep's backs.

Macquarie Street (north). Sydney's most elegant boulevard was masterminded by Governor Macquarie who, from 1810 until he was ousted, planned the transformation of the cart track leading to Sydney Cove into a stylish street of dwellings and government buildings. Fortunately, many of the 19th-century architectural delights here escaped demolition—such as ☞ **History House** and the ☞ **Royal Australasian College of Physicians.**

39 **Museum of Sydney.** Built on the site of the first modest Government House, this museum documenting Sydney's beginnings opened in 1995. One of the most interesting features is outside—the striking "Edge of the Trees" sculpture, with its 29 columns that "speak" and contain remnants of Aboriginal and early European occupation. Inside the museum, Aboriginal culture, convict society, and the gradual transformation of the settlement at Sydney Cove are woven into the single most evocative portrayal of life in the early days of Australia. Many of the exhibits are very innovative, using ultramodern technology and ingenious display methods. The museum has a popular café, and a shop that stocks unusual gifts and other items. ⊠ *Bridge and Phillip Sts.,* ☎ *02/9251–5988.* 🎫 *$6.* ☉ *Daily 10–5.*

43 **Royal Australasian College of Physicians.** Once the home of a wealthy Sydney family, the building now houses a different elite—the city's most eminent physicians, many of whom perform their surgeries here. ⊠ *Macquarie St. between Bridge and Bent Sts.*

49 **St. James Church.** Begun in 1822, Colonial Georgian–style St. James is Sydney's oldest church, and another fine Francis Greenway design. The original law court building was half completed when Commissioner Bigge, who had been sent from England to investigate Macquarie's administration, ordered that the structure be converted into a church. Now lost among the skyscrapers, the church's tall spire once served as a landmark for ships entering the harbor.

Enter St. James through the door in the Doric portico. The interior walls of the church are covered with plaques commemorating early Australian explorers and administrators. Inscriptions on the plaques testify to the hardships of those early days, when death either at sea or at the hands of Aborigines seems to have been a common fate. ⊠ *Queen's Sq., Macquarie St.,* ☎ *02/9232–3022.* ☉ *Daily 9–5.*

50 **St. Mary's Cathedral.** The first St. Mary's was built here in 1821, but the chapel was destroyed by fire, and work on the present cathedral began in 1868. The building has not been completed, however—due to a shortage of funds, spires that were planned for the south front towers have never been built. St Mary's has some particularly fine stained-glass windows and a terrazzo mosaic floor in the crypt, where exhibitions are often held. The large rose window came from England, and the Stations of the Cross were painted by the French artist Crovet.

At the front of the cathedral are **statues of Cardinal Moran and Archbishop Kelly,** two Irishmen who were prominent in the Roman Catholic Church in Australia. Due to the high proportion of Irish men and women in the convict population, the Roman Catholic Church was often the voice of the oppressed in 19th-century Sydney, where anti-Catholic feeling ran high among the Protestant rulers. Australia's first cardinal, Patrick Moran, was a powerful exponent of Catholic education and a diplomat who did much to heal the rift between the two faiths. By contrast, Michael Kelly, his successor as head of the church in Sydney, was excessively pious and politically inept; Kelly and Moran remained at odds until Moran's death in 1911. ⊠ *College and Cathedral Sts.,* ☎ *02/9220–0400.* ▭ *Tour free.* ☉ *Weekdays 6:30–6:30, Sat. 8–7:30, Sun. 6:30 AM–7:30 PM; tour Sun. at noon.*

44 **State Library of New South Wales.** This large complex is based around the Mitchell and Dixson libraries, which house the world's largest collection of Australiana. A modern extension on Macquarie Street is generally of more interest, however. The extension has an excellent book and gift shop, a café, free films, the general reference library, and changing exhibitions with Australian historical and cultural themes in the upstairs gallery.

The foyer inside the heavy glass doors of the imposing 1910 Mitchell Wing contains one of the earliest maps of Australia. It is a copy in marble mosaic of a map made by Abel Tasman, the Dutch navigator. Tasman was not the first European to set eyes on the Australian coastline, but his voyages established that Australia was not the fabled Great South Land for which the Dutch had been searching, believing it to possess great riches. On his first voyage to Australia in 1642–43, Tasman sailed along the southern coast of Australia and discovered Tasmania, which he named Van Diemen's Land in honor of his patron, the governor of the Dutch East Indies. On his next voyage in 1644, Tasman explored much of the north coast of Australia. On the mosaic map the two ships of the first voyage are shown off the south coast in the Great Australian Bight; the ships of the second voyage are shown off the northwest coast. Marble for the map came from Wombeyan, about 160 km (100 mi) southwest of Sydney.

Beyond the map and through the glass doors is the vast reading room of the Mitchell Library, but you need a reader's ticket (establishing that you are pursuing legitimate research) to enter. You can, however, take a free escorted tour of either or both of the library's buildings. ⊠ *Macquarie St.,* ☎ *02/9230–1414.* ⊙ *Weekdays 9–9, weekends 11–5; General Reference Library tour Tues.–Thurs. at 2:30; Mitchell Library tour Tues. and Thurs. at 11.*

45 **State Parliament House.** This 1816 Rum Hospital building, with its simple facade and shady verandas, is a classic example of Australian colonial architecture. From 1829, two rooms of the old hospital were used for meetings of the executive and legislative councils, which had been set up to advise the governor. The functions of these advisory bodies grew until New South Wales became self-governing in the 1840s, at which time Parliament occupied the entire building. The Legislative Council Chamber—the upper house of the parliament, identifiable by its red color scheme—is a cast-iron, prefabricated structure that was originally intended to be a church on the goldfields of Victoria.

State Parliament generally sits between mid-February and late May, and again between mid-September and late November. The New South Wales Parliament has a reputation as one of the rowdiest and toughest legislatures in the world, and visitors are welcome to the public gallery to watch the vocal Westminster system of democracy in action. On weekdays, generally between 9:30 and 4, you can tour the building's public areas, which contain a number of portraits and paintings. You must make reservations. ⊠ *Macquarie St.,* ☎ *02/9230–2111.* ⊙ *Sitting days 9–whenever House rises, nonsitting days 9:30–4; tour and visiting times vary according to House schedule.*

40 **Sydney Conservatorium of Music.** Once the governor's stables, this fortresslike, Gothic Revival, Francis Greenway building presents a marked departure from his normally simple and elegant designs. The cost of constructing the stables caused a storm among Governor Macquarie's superiors in London and eventually helped bring about the downfall of both Macquarie and his architect.

Although held on an irregular basis, this establishment's talented students give free lunchtime (usually Wednesday and Friday) and evening concerts—check with the Conservatorium for current details. ⊠ *Conservatorium Rd. off Macquarie St.,* ☎ *02/9230–1222.*

46 **Sydney Hospital.** Completed in 1894 as the replacement for the main Rum Hospital building, this institution offered an infinitely better medical option—by all accounts, admission to the Rum Hospital was only slightly preferable to death itself. Convict nurses stole patients' food, and abler patients stole from the weaker. The kitchen sometimes doubled as a mortuary, and the kitchen table was occasionally used to perform operations.

In front of the hospital is a bronze figure of a boar. This is **Il Porcellino,** a copy of a statue that stands in Florence, Italy. According to the inscription, if you make a donation in the coin box and rub the boar's nose, "you will be endowed with good luck." Sydney citizens seem to be a superstitious bunch, as the boar's nose is very shiny indeed.

47 **Sydney Mint Museum.** The south wing of Greenway's 1816 Rum Hospital became a branch of the Royal Mint after the 1850s Australian gold rushes—a series of events that lured many thousands of gold diggers from around the world. Appropriately, this refined, verandaed structure is now a museum focusing on the discovery of gold and its ensuing impact on the nation. Containing a large range of gold-crafted jewelry, ornaments, and trophies, many with an Australian theme, the museum also has a coining factory where you can strike your own souvenir coin. The shop sells quality gold, silver, and precious gem products, including bullion. ⊠ *Macquarie St.,* ☎ *02/9217-0311.* ☲ *$5.* ☉ *Daily 10–5.*

The Opera House, the RBG, and the Domain North

Bordering Sydney Cove, Farm Cove, and Woolloomooloo (that's "*wool*-uh-muh-loo") Bay, this section of Sydney includes the iconic, symbolic Sydney Opera House, as well as extensive gardens and parkland that create a delightful harborside haven.

The colony's first farming attempt was made here in 1788, and the Botanic Gardens were initiated in 1816. The most dramatic change to the enclave came in 1959, however, when work began on the site for the Sydney Opera House at Bennelong Point. This promontory was originally a small island, then the site of 1819 Fort Macquarie, and later a tram depot that did little to enhance the cityscape.

A Good Walk

From Circular Quay, walk around Sydney Cove along Circular Quay East. This walkway is also known as **Writers' Walk;** brass plaques embedded into the sidewalk commemorate prominent Australian writers, playwrights, and poets.

Unmistakably ahead, on the Bennelong Point promontory, is the **Sydney Opera House** ⑤③. Its distinctive white concrete sails and prominent position jutting into the harbor make this the most widely recognized landmark of urban Australia. Country-wide, the Opera House has been a source of enormous controversy and debate. Australians have alternately called it "a bunch of mussels stuck in the mud," "the building of the century," and "the greatest political public-relations stunt since the Pyramids." Whatever its merits, the Opera House leaves no visitor unmoved.

The **Royal Botanic Gardens** ⑤④ are behind the Opera House, combining with the rolling parkland of the Domain to form the eastern border of the city. You can either walk around the Farm Cove pathway, or head inland to spend some time exploring the gardens, including a stop at **Government House,** before returning to the waterfront.

The pathway around the cove leads to a peninsula, **Mrs. Macquarie's Point** ⑤⑤ in the northern part of the Domain. It is named for Elizabeth Macquarie, the governor's wife, who planned the road through the parkland. As you round the peninsula and turn toward the naval dockyard at Garden Island, notice the small bench carved into the rock with an inscription identifying it as **Mrs. Macquarie's Chair** ⑤⑥.

Continue through **the Domain north** ⑤⑦ on Mrs. Macquarie's Road to the **Andrew (Boy) Charlton Pool** ⑤⑧, built over Woolloomooloo Bay. It's a great spot for a summer swim. From the pool there are good views of the Garden Island naval base and the suburb of Potts Point, across the bay.

This road eventually takes you to the southern part of the Domain (☞ Macquarie Street *and* the Domain South, *above*). The once-continuous Domain is divided into two sections by the Cahill Expressway, which leads up to the Sydney Harbour Bridge and down into the **Sydney Har-**

bour Tunnel. The tunnel was completed in the early 1990s and has helped to alleviate traffic congestion on the bridge.

At the end of the walk, you can return to Circular Quay by crossing the Domain to Macquarie Street, or by reentering the Botanic Gardens through the Woolloomooloo Gate near the roadway over the Cahill Expressway. If you have time, the latter option will allow you to see much more of this delightfully verdant city center haven.

TIMING

A walk around the Sydney Opera House, Royal Botanic Gardens, and the northern section of the Domain can easily be accomplished in a morning or afternoon. Allow more time if you wish to explore the gardens more thoroughly—these are delightful at any time of year, but spring blooms make the area particularly attractive.

Sights to See

58 **Andrew (Boy) Charlton Pool.** Named after one of Australia's famous swimmers, this Olympic-size, saltwater pool is extremely popular with locals in summer. It's the perfect place to cool off if you are walking this route on a hot day. ⊠ *The Domain north*, ☎ *02/9358–6686.* ▨ *$2.* ☉ *Oct.–Apr., weekdays 6 AM–7 PM, weekends 6:30–6.*

57 **The Domain north.** The northern part of the Domain adjoins the Royal Botanic Gardens and extends from Mrs. Macquarie's Point to the Cahill Expressway. Surrounded by Farm Cove and Woolloomooloo Bay, this is a pleasant harbor-fringed area of parkland that encompasses all sights mentioned in this section, excluding the Opera House on Bennelong Point.

Government House. Completed in 1843, this two-story, sandstone, Gothic Revival building served as the residence of the Governor of New South Wales—who represents the British crown in local matters—until the Labour Party Government handed it back to the public in 1996. The building was designed by the prominent English architect Edward Blore, who completed the plan without ever setting foot in Australia. The house has impressive reception, drawing, and dining rooms on the ground floor. Their prim, almost sterile quality belies their public function. The house's stencilled ceilings, which were repainted in the 1980s, are its most impressive feature. Paintings hanging on the walls bear the signatures of some of Australia's best-known artists, incuding Roberts, Streeton, and Drysdale. You are free to wander about Government House's gardens, which lie within the Royal Botanic Gardens, on your own, but you must join a guided tour to see the house's interior. ⊠ *Royal Botanic Gardens*, ☎ *02/9931–5200.* ▨ *Free.* ☉ *House Fri.–Sun. 10–3; gardens daily 10–4.*

56 **Mrs. Macquarie's Chair.** During the early 1800s, Elizabeth Macquarie often sat on the point in the Domain at the east side of Farm Cove, at the rock where a seat has been hewn in her name. The point is, of course, also named for her.

55 **Mrs. Macquarie's Point.** With excellent views of the harbor and north shore, the point and its waterside lawns are a popular place for picnics, especially on warm summer evenings when the sunset makes a spectacular backdrop to the Opera House and Harbour Bridge. Being the governor's partner, her fondness for this part of the Domain was cause enough to name it after her.

54 **Royal Botanic Gardens.** Groves of palm trees, duck ponds, a cactus garden, restaurant, greenhouses, and acres of lawns come together in Sydney's finest gardens, where the convicts of the First Fleet established a farm. Their early attempts at agriculture were disastrous, and for the first couple of years the prisoners and their guards survived on the verge of starvation. The colony was eventually saved by the arrival of a supply ship in 1790.

The gardens were founded in 1816 and greatly expanded by the 1830s. The wonderful collection of plants and trees are both native Australians and exotics from around the world, and garden highlights include the Sydney Tropical Centre, housed in the Pyramid and Arc glass houses, with a superb collection of tropical plants and the lush Sydney Fernery. The Visitor Centre and Gardens Shop is worth a visit, as is the excellent Botanic Gardens restaurant. Tours leave from the Visitor Centre, near the Art Gallery of New South Wales. ✉ *The Domain,* ☏ *02/9231–8125.* ✉ *Sydney Tropical Centre $5, tour free.* ☉ *Sydney Tropical Centre daily sunrise–sunset (generally from 6:30 AM); Sydney Tropical Centre and Sydney Fernery daily 10–4; tour daily at 10:30.*

53   **Sydney Opera House.** Considering everything that happened during its construction, it's no minor miracle that the Opera House exists at all. In 1954, the state premier appointed a committee to advise the government on the building of an opera house. The site chosen was Bennelong Point—until that time, the site of a tram depot. The premier's committee launched a competition to find a suitable plan, and a total of 233 submissions came in from architects from all over the world. One of them was a young Dane named Joern Utzon.

His plan was brilliant, but it had all the markings of a monumental disaster. The structure was so narrow that stages would have miniscule wings, and the soaring "sails" that formed the walls and roof could not be built by existing technology. (The cathedral in Florence, Italy, started its life with a similar predicament—no dome.)

Nonetheless, Utzon's dazzling, dramatic concept caught the judges' imagination, and construction of the giant podium began in 1958. From the very beginning, the contractors faced a cost blowout—a problem that was to plague the Opera House throughout its construction. The building that was projected to cost $7 million and take four years to erect would eventually require $102 million and 15 years. Taxpayers paid virtually nothing, however, since construction was funded by a state-run lottery.

Initially it was thought that the concrete exterior of the building would have to be cast in place, which would have meant building an enormous birdcage of scaffolding at even greater expense. Then, as he was peeling an orange one day, Utzon had a flash of inspiration. Why not construct the shells from segments of a single sphere? The concrete ribs forming the skeleton of the building could be prefabricated in just a few molds, hoisted into position, and joined together. These ribs are clearly visible inside the Opera House, especially in the foyers and staircases of the Concert Hall.

In 1966, Utzon resigned as Opera House architect and left Australia, embittered by his dealings with unions and the government (he has never returned to see his masterpiece). A team of young Australian architects carried on, completing the exterior one year later. Until that time, however, nobody had given much thought to the *interior.* The shells created awkward interior spaces, and conventional performance areas were simply not feasible. It is a tribute to the architectural team's ingenuity that the exterior of the building is matched by the aesthetically pleasing and acoustically sound theaters inside.

In September 1973 the Australian Opera performed *War and Peace* in the Opera Theatre; a month later, Queen Elizabeth II officially opened the building in a ceremony capped by an astonishing fireworks display. Nowadays, the controversies that raged around the building seem moot. Poised majestically on its peninsula, with Circular Quay and Harbour Bridge on one side and the Royal Botanic Gardens on the other, it has become a loved and potent national symbol.

The building is actually far more versatile than its name implies. In reality, it is an entertainment complex allowing a wide range of performances and activities—dance, drama, films, opera, and jazz in the forecourt, as well as four restaurants and cafés, and several bars that cater to the hordes of patrons. Guided one-hour tours of the Opera House depart at frequent intervals from the tour office, on the lower forecourt level, 9:15–4 on most days. All tours can be restricted or suspended due to performances or rehearsals; call in advance. ☎ *02/9250–7111.* 🎫 *$13.50, tour $9.*

Darling Harbour

Until the mid-1980s, this horseshoe-shape bay on the western edge of the city center was a wasteland of disused docks and railway yards. Then, in an explosive burst of activity, the whole area was redeveloped and opened in time for Australia's bicentennial in 1988. Now there's plenty to take in at the Darling Harbour complex: the National Maritime Museum, the large Harbourside shopping and dining center, the Sydney Aquarium, and a gleaming Exhibition Centre whose masts and spars recall the square riggers that once berthed here. At the harbor's center is a large park shaded by palm trees, and the complex is laced together by a series of waterways and fountains.

The Powerhouse Museum is within easy walking distance, and immediately to the south are Chinatown, the vast indoor Paddy's Market (open only on weekends), and the Sydney Entertainment Centre. A 1995 addition to the area is the Sydney Harbour Casino, located at nearby Pyrmont but probably best visited as a separate excursion.

Darling Harbour's emphasis is on lighthearted fun, including free music, and other entertainment, especially on weekends. This is a particularly good place to bring children—the area's aquarium and museums should keep most young travelers entertained for hours.

A Good Walk

Start at the Market Street end of Pitt Street Mall, Sydney's main pedestrian shopping precinct. Take the monorail—across Market Street and above ground level on the right-hand side of Pitt Street—from here to the next stop (Darling Park), passing the large Queen Victoria Building on your left. Get off at this stop and go down the steps and escalator to **Sydney Aquarium** (59)—the city's first-class fishbowl full of exotic fins, flippers, and reptilians—on your right.

Walk from the Aquarium under Pyrmont Bridge to the **Darling Harbour Olympic Showcase** (60) on the SS *South Steyne,* an old steam ferry that's moored in the bay. The ferry is now the showcase for Sydney's Summer Olympic Games in 2000.

From here, take the escalator back up to historic **Pyrmont Bridge** (61) and walk across to the **Australian National Maritime Museum** (62), the large white-roof building on your right. Documenting Australia's vital links with the ocean, the museum features everything from Aboriginal canoes to ships and surfboards.

After visiting the Maritime Museum you can either explore the Harbourside center (a good place for a drink or a meal) and then walk through Darling Harbour, or take the monorail from Harbourside to the Haymarket stop. The curved building beside the elevated freeway with the checkerboard painted on its side is the **IMAX Theatre** ⑥₃, the world's largest movie screen, featuring a series of stunning special-effect presentations.

From Haymarket, turn left for a short walk along a covered walkway to the entertaining **Powerhouse Museum** ⑥₄, which is inside an old power station with extensive modern additions. This complex is by far the city's largest museum, with a vast collection from the Museum of Applied Arts and Sciences.

From the Powerhouse, walk back to the Haymarket monorail station, turn left onto another walkway, continue down to Darling Harbour and then underneath the expressway to the **Chinese Garden** ⑥₅. With its distinctive pagodas and white walls, this exotic garden is hard to miss.

You can return to the city center on the monorail from the Haymarket station, or take a short walk (between the Pumphouse Tavern and Entertainment Centre, and then up the lane on the other side of Harbour Street) to stroll around the colorful streets, shops, markets, and restaurants of Chinatown.

TIMING

Although the distance covered on this walk is relatively small, it is full of engrossing and time-consuming places to stop. You'll need at least a half day to see the best of the area. Darling Harbour is very popular with locals and the area is often very crowded on weekends—better to come during the week, if you can.

If you aren't so interested in the museums, a good time to visit is in the evening, when the tall city buildings reflect the sunset and cast magical images on the water—and you might pop over to Chinatown for dinner. Later, pubs, cafés, and nightclubs turn on lights and music for a party that lasts well past midnight.

Sights to See

🦢 ⑥₂ **Australian National Maritime Museum.** This soaring, futuristic white building is divided into six galleries that tell the story of Australia and the sea. In addition to figureheads, model ships, and the brassy apparati of nautical enterprise, there are antique racing yachts, and the jet-powered *Spirit of Australia,* current holder of the water speed record. Many displays are interactive. Among the many spectacular exhibits is the fully rigged *Australia II,* the famous 12-meter yacht with winged keel that finally broke the Newport Yacht Club's hold on the America's Cup in 1983. An outdoor section features numerous vessels moored at the museum's wharves—including HMAS *Vampire,* a World War II destroyer, a Russian submarine, and a northern Australian pearling lugger. ⊠ *Darling Harbour (west),* ☎ *02/9552–7777.* 🎟 *$15.* ⊙ *Daily 9:30–6.*

⑥₅ **Chinese Garden.** The nation's long and enduring links with China— prospectors came to the Australian goldfields as far back as the 1850s— are symbolized by this tranquil walled enclave. Designed by Chinese landscape architects, the garden includes bridges, lakes, waterfalls, and Cantonese-style pavilions. This is the perfect spot for a break from sightseeing and Darling Harbour's crowds. ⊠ *Darling Harbour (south),* ☎ *02/9281–6863.* 🎟 *$2.* ⊙ *Daily 9:30–sunset.*

⑥⓪ **Darling Harbour Olympic Showcase.** Sydney is progressively gearing up for the 2000 Olympic and Paralympic Games, and this series of displays, on board the beautifully restored 1938 SS *South Steyne*, documents the city's progress toward the event. Designed to increase public awareness of the games, and to raise money for the Australian Olympic team (a proportion of admission fees go to this cause), the showcase presents plans of the Olympics site, an informative multiscreen video presentation, and stories of Australia's Olympic gold medalists. ⊠ *SS South Steyne, Darling Harbour (east),* ☎ *02/9267–0099.* ⊒ *$2.* ⊙ *Daily 9–7.*

⑥③ **IMAX Theatre.** Both in size and dramatic impact, this eight-story-tall movie screen is overwhelming. Inside, three one-hour presentations take you on an astonishing wide-angle voyage of discovery—into space, under the sea, or through the human body. Movies are changed every couple of months. The complex also includes the **Star Grill** (☞ Dining, *below*), a brasserie that overlooks Darling Harbour. ⊠ *Darling Harbour (south),* ☎ *02/9281–3300.* ⊒ *$13.95.* ⊙ *Daily 10–10.*

☙ ⑥④ **Powerhouse Museum.** An architectural amalgam of old and new, this extraordinary museum of applied arts and sciences is housed in the 1890s electricity station that once powered Sydney's trams. Exhibits include costumes and jewelry, a whole floor of working steam engines, a pub, space modules, airplanes suspended from the ceiling, state-of-the-art computer gadgetry, and a 1930s Art Deco–style movie-theater auditorium. Hands-on displays encourage participation, and older children will be intrigued by the opportunities that these present.

A highlight of the museum is the top-level Powerhouse Garden Restaurant—painted in spectacularly vibrant colors and patterns by famous local artist Ken Done and his team. ⊠ *500 Harris St., Ultimo,* ☎ *02/ 9217–0444 or 02/9217–0111.* ⊒ *$8.* ⊙ *Daily 10–5.*

⑥① **Pyrmont Bridge.** Dating from 1902, this is the world's oldest electrically operated swing-span bridge. The structure once carried motor traffic, but it is now a walkway that links Darling Harbour's east and west sides. The Monorail runs above the bridge, but the center span still swings open to allow tall-masted ships into Cockle Bay, the landward portion of Darling Harbour.

☙ ⑤⑨ **Sydney Aquarium.** The city's largest aquarium is a fascinating underwater world, with everything from saltwater crocodiles to giant sea turtles to delicate, multicolor reef fish and corals. The displays about the Great Barrier Reef and Australia's largest river system, the Murray-Darling, are excellent. Children will particularly enjoy the Touch Pool and the Marine Mammal Sanctuary with its playful seals. The highlights of the aquarium are two transparent tunnels submerged in an oceanarium—a footpath takes you safely through the water while sharks, eels, and stingrays glide overhead. The aquarium is often very crowded on weekends. ⊠ *Aquarium Pier, Wheat Rd., Darling Harbour (east),* ☎ *02/9262–2300.* ⊒ *$14.90.* ⊙ *Daily 9:30–9.*

Sydney City Center

Most travelers visit Sydney's city center primarily for shopping, but there are several buildings and other places of interest among the myriad office blocks, department stores, and shopping centers.

This walk takes in the best view in Sydney, several historic buildings, the shopping and architectural delights of the Queen Victoria Building, the city's premier park, and the wonderful Australian Museum.

A Good Walk

Begin at the Market Street end of Pitt Street Mall. Turn left into Market Street and walk a few meters to the Centrepoint entrance and the high-speed elevators that will take you to the top of **Sydney Tower** ⑥. The spectacular view from the city's tallest structure will give you an excellent idea of the lay of the land.

Return to Market Street and walk in the other direction to George Street. Turn left and continue to the Sydney Hilton Hotel, on the left-hand side. For a little refreshment now or later in the day, take the steps down below street level to the Marble Bar, an opulent basement watering hole with extraordinary decor and architecture.

Back up on George Street cross the road to enter the **Queen Victoria Building** ⑥, a massive Victorian structure that occupies an entire city block. The shops are many and varied, and the meticulous restoration work is impressive.

After browsing in the QVB, exit at the Druitt Street end and cross this road to the rather elaborate **Sydney Town Hall** ⑥, the domain of Sydney City Council and a popular performance space. Next door is **St. Andrew's Cathedral** ⑥, Sydney's foremost Anglican church.

Cut across George Street and walk along Park Street to the southern section of **Hyde Park** ⑦. This is the city center's largest green space and the location of the **Anzac War Memorial,** which commemorates Australians who fought and died in the service of their country.

Continue through the park to College Street, cross the road and walk a few more feet to the **Australian Museum** ⑦. An excellent natural history museum, it has some of the country's best exhibits on anthropology, culture, and Australian and Pacific-region fauna.

From the museum, cross College Street and then Park Street and walk through the northern half of Hyde Park. This area contains a tree-covered walkway and the impressive **Archibald Memorial Fountain.** Continue to the northern end of Hyde Park and cross the road to Macquarie Street. As you walk north on Macquarie, you'll pass the **Hyde Park Barracks, Sydney Mint Museum,** and **Sydney Hospital** (☞ Macquarie Street and the Domain South, *above*). In front of the hospital, cross the road to the large semi-pedestrian precinct of **Martin Place** ⑦ and walk the length of the plaza to George Street: Note the impressive Victorian and more recent banks and public buildings, and the Cenotaph war memorial near the far end.

From here you can return to the Pitt Street Mall via Pitt Street, or walk north on George Street to Circular Quay.

TIMING

The walk itself should take no longer than a couple of hours. Plan more time for an extended tour of the Australian Museum, or for shopping in the Queen Victoria Building. Weekday lunchtimes (generally 1–2) in the city center are manic, with working people trying to make the most of their brief break. It's best to avoid the shops and eating places at this time.

Sights to See

⑦ **Australian Museum.** Bear in mind, after your initial greeting by the skeleton of a sperm whale suspended from the ceiling, that this natural history museum is best known for its cultural exhibitions. The Aboriginal section of the museum is particularly informative and rewarding, especially in its treatment of the impact of white European society on the first Australians (for an introduction to Aboriginal history, *see* "The

World of the First Australians" *in* Chapter 14). Native fauna and the tribal cultures of Papua New Guinea are also well represented, and the museum has a comprehensive gems and minerals display, an excellent book and gift shop, and a lively café. ✉ *6 College St., near William St.*, ☎ *02/9320–6000.* 🎫 *$5.* ⊙ *Daily 9:30–5.*

⑩ Hyde Park. Declared public land by Governor Phillip in 1792 and used for the colony's earliest cricket matches and horse races, this area was made into a park in 1810. Gardens are formal, with fountains, statuary, and tree-lined walks. The park provides some welcome city-center tranquillity and is popular with office workers at lunchtime.

In Hyde Park's southern section (near Liverpool Street), the 1934 Art Deco–style **Anzac War Memorial** pays tribute to those who have died at war, and commemorates the proud ANZAC (Australian and New Zealand Army Corps) tradition that dates back to World War I. The memorial has some poignant sculptures, and there is an interesting war-related photographic exhibition on the lower level. ✉ *Hyde Park S,* ☎ *02/9267–7668.* ⊙ *Mon.–Sat. 10–4, Sun. 1–4.*

NEED A
BREAK?

> **MARBLE BAR –** Stop in for a drink alongside a masterpiece of Victorian extravagance. The 1890 Marble Bar was formerly another hotel's bar much favored by gentlemen of the racing fraternity. Threatened with demolition in the 1970s, the whole bar was moved—marble arches, colored glass ceiling, elaborately carved woodwork, paintings of voluptuous nudes, and all—to its present site beneath the Sydney Hilton. By night, it becomes the backdrop for jazz and other music. ✉ *Sydney Hilton Hotel, basement, 259 Pitt St.*, ☎ *02/9266–0610. Closed Sun.*

⑫ Martin Place. Sydney's largest pedestrian precinct, flanked by banks, offices, and the MLC Shopping Centre, forms the hub of the central business district. There are some grand buildings here—including the beautifully refurbished Commonwealth Bank on the Pitt Street corner (have a look inside), and the 1870s Venetian Renaissance–style General Post Office building, with its 230-ft clocktower. Toward the George Street end of the plaza the simple 1929 Cenotaph war memorial commemorates Australians who died in World War I. Every weekday from about 12:30, the amphitheater near Castlereagh Street is the site for well-attended, free lunchtime concerts with sounds from all corners of the music world—from police bands to string quartets to rock-and-rollers. ✉ *Between Macquarie and George Sts.*

⑥⑦ Queen Victoria Building. Originally the city's produce market, this vast 1898 sandstone structure had become a maze of shabby offices by the time it disappeared under scaffolding in 1981. When the wraps came off five years later, the building was adorned with sweeping staircases, enormous stained-glass windows, and the 1-ton Royal Clock, which is suspended from the glass roof. Other restoration highlights in this 650-ft-long building include the period-style tiling on the ground floor, the central glass dome, and Victorian-era toilets on the Albert Walk level. The QVB is also excellent for shopping—the complex includes over 200 boutiques, with those on the upper floors generally more upmarket and exclusive—and the basement level has a variety of inexpensive eating options. ✉ *George, York, Market, and Druitt Sts.*, ☎ *02/9264–9209.* ⊙ *Daily 24 hrs.*

⑥⑨ St. Andrew's Cathedral. Sydney's Gothic Revival–style Anglican cathedral (the country's oldest) was founded in 1819 and consecrated in 1868. The church was built with local sandstone and designed by Edmund Blacket, Sydney's most famous church architect—highlights include the ornamental windows illustrating the life of Christ, and the great east window with its images relating to the life of St. Andrew. ⊠ *Sydney Sq., George St., next to Town Hall,* ☎ *02/9265–1661.* ☉ *Mon., Tues., Thurs., and Fri. 7:30–5:30; Wed. 7:30 AM–8 PM; Sat. 9–4; Sun. 7:30 AM–8 PM; tour weekdays 11 and 1:45, Sun. noon.*

66 **Sydney Tower.** Short of taking a scenic flight, a visit to the top of this 1,000-ft golden-minaret-topped spike is the best way to view Sydney's spectacular layout. This is the tallest building in the city, and if you come here on a smog-free day, the views from its observation deck are astounding. The panorama encompasses the entire Sydney metropolitan area of more than 1,560 square km (600 square mi), and you can often see as far as the Blue Mountains, over 80 km (50 mi) away. The tower includes two revolving restaurants, and dining here at night overlooking the city lights is a magical experience. ⊠ *Centrepoint, 100 Market St., between Pitt and Castlereagh Sts.,* ☎ *02/9229–7444.* ▦ *$9.* ☉ *Sun.–Fri. 9:30–9:30, Sat. 9:30 AM–11:30 PM.*

68 **Sydney Town Hall.** This elaborate, multilayered Victorian sandstone building is often rather unkindly likened to a wedding cake. The city's Town Hall, however, has some grand interior spaces, especially the Vestibule and large Centennial Hall, and performs many functions. The building houses council offices, but is also used as a performance venue, including lunchtime organ concerts that star the massive Grand Organ, one of the world's most powerful. Tours of the building run from time to time—call ahead for details. ⊠ *George and Druitt Sts.,* ☎ *02/9265–9007, 02/9231–4629 tour.* ☉ *Weekdays 9–5.*

Elizabeth Bay and Kings Cross, Darlinghurst, and Paddington

This bus and walking tour takes you into some of the city's inner east suburbs and looks at the people's Sydney—from the mansions of the colonial aristocracy and the humble laborers' cottages of the same period, to the modernized terrace houses of Paddington, one of Sydney's most charming suburbs. You'll also pass through Kings Cross and Darlinghurst, the best-known nightlife district in the country, and visit the acclaimed Sydney Jewish Museum.

A Good Walk

Begin at the bus stop on Alfred Street just behind Circular Quay and catch Bus 311, which leaves from the stop at the Harbour Bridge end of the street. This bus carries the sign RAILWAY VIA KINGS CROSS or RAILWAY VIA ELIZABETH BAY. Ask the driver to drop you off at Elizabeth Bay House and take a seat on the left side of the bus.

You'll wind your way through the city streets to Macquarie Street, past the State Library, the New South Wales Parliament, Hyde Park Barracks, and St. Mary's Cathedral. The bus then follows the curve of Woolloomooloo Bay, where it passes **Harry's Café de Wheels,** a unique Sydney institution, and beneath the bows of naval vessels at the Garden Island Dockyard, the main base for the Australian navy. Visiting ships from other Pacific Ocean navies can often be seen along this wharf.

Just before the Garden Island gates, the bus turns right and climbs through the shady streets of Potts Point and **Elizabeth Bay** to **Elizabeth Bay House** ⑦₃, an aristocratic Regency-style mansion. Built some 150 years ago by Alexander Macleay, the colonial secretary, this is one of Australia's finest historic homes.

After a spin through Elizabeth Bay House, cross to the **Arthur McElhone Reserve** ⑦₄ for a pleasant resting spot with the bonus of harbor views. Take the stone steps leading down from the park to Billyard Avenue. Near the lower end of this street is a walled garden with cypress trees and banana palms reaching above the parapets. Through the black iron gates of the driveway, you can catch a glimpse of Boomerang—a sprawling, Spanish-style villa built by the manufacturer of the harmonica of the same name. Just beyond the house, turn left to **Beare Park** ⑦⑤ overlooking the yachts in Elizabeth Bay.

Return to Billyard Avenue. Wait at the bus stop opposite the first gate of Boomerang for Bus 311, but make sure that you catch one marked RAILWAY, *not* CIRCULAR QUAY. This bus threads its way through the streets of Kings Cross, Sydney's nightlife district, and Darlinghurst. During the day the Cross is only half awake, although the doormen of the various strip clubs are never too sleepy to lure passersby inside to watch nonstop video shows. Ask the driver to deposit you at the stop near the corner of Darlinghurst Road and Burton Street. From here, the moving and thought-provoking **Sydney Jewish Museum** ⑦⑥ is just across the road.

After leaving the museum, walk along the remainder of Darlinghurst Road to Oxford Street. Turn left, and about 300 yards up Oxford Street, on your right, is a long sandstone wall—the perimeter of **Victoria Barracks** ⑦⑦ and its **Army Museum.** These barracks were built in the middle of the last century to house the British regiments stationed in the colony. The troops were withdrawn in 1870 and replaced by Australian soldiers.

Almost opposite the main entrance to the barracks is the start of **Shadforth Street** ⑦⑧, along which you'll see some of the oldest houses in Paddington. At the first intersection Shadforth Street changes its name to Liverpool Street and terrace houses begin.

Continue downhill on Liverpool Street and turn right at the intersection with Glenmore Road, where the terrace houses are even more elaborate. Follow this road past the intersection with Brown Street to the colorful collection of shops known as Five Ways. The **Royal Hotel** on the far corner has a fine pub—a good place to stop for something cool.

Walk up Broughton Street to the right of the Royal Hotel. Turn right at Union Street, left into Underwood, and right at William Street. You are now among the boutique shops of Paddington and may want to spend some time browsing here before completing the walk. On the right, **Sweet William** (✉ 4 William St., Paddington, ☎ 02/9331–5468) is a shop for chocolate lovers. If you're in the mood, don't miss Oxford Street's offbeat clothing and curio shops.

Walk toward the city along Oxford Street to the restored colonial mansion of **Juniper Hall** ⑦⑨, which marks the end of this tour—unless you'd like to make a refreshment break down the street at **New Edition Tea Rooms** your last stop.

There are buses back to the city from the other side of Oxford Street. But if the sun is shining, consider heading out to Bondi Beach, a mere 20-minute ride on Bus 380.

TIMING

Allow the better part of a day to make your way through these neighborhoods, especially if you have a good look around Elizabeth Bay House and the Sydney Jewish Museum. If you wish to tour Victoria Barracks, take this trip on a Thursday and get there by 10 AM, which pretty much means going there first and seeing the preceding places in the afternoon.

There is an additional diversion on Saturday, when the famous Paddington Bazaar (☞ Shopping, *below*) is held in the area. The walk around

Paddington is not particularly long, but some of the streets are rather steep.

Sights to See

74 Arthur McElhone Reserve. Another of the city's welcome havens, the reserve has tree ferns, a gushing stream, a stone bridge over a carp pond, and excellent views up the harbor. ✉ *Onslow Ave., Elizabeth Bay.*

75 Beare Park. Almost as a rule, local favorites are worth checking out— so it is with this waterfront park. With its pleasant harbor views, it's a favorite recreation spot with Elizabeth Bay locals. The adjoining wharf is often busy with sailors coming and going to their yachts, moored out in the bay. ✉ *Off Ithaca Rd., Elizabeth Bay.*

Elizabeth Bay. Much of this densely populated but still charming harborside suburb was originally part of the extensive Elizabeth Bay House grounds. Wrought-iron balconies and French doors on some of the older apartment blocks give the area a Mediterranean feel, and during the 1920s and 1930s this was a fashionably bohemian quarter of the city.

73 Elizabeth Bay House. Regarded in its heyday as "the finest house in the colony," this 1835–9 mansion has retained little of its original furniture, but the rooms have been restored in the style of its early life. The house's most striking feature is an oval-shape salon, naturally lit through glass panels in a dome roof, with a staircase that winds its way to the upper floor. The colonial secretary Macleay lived here for only six years before suffering crippling losses in the colonial depression of the 1840s. In return for settling his father's debts, his son William took possession of the house and most of its contents and promptly evicted his father. ✉ *7 Onslow Ave., Elizabeth Bay,* ☎ *02/9356–3022.* ✉ *$5.* ☉ *Tues.–Sun. 10–4:30.*

OFF THE
BEATEN PATH

HARRY'S CAFÉ DE WHEELS – The attraction of this dockyard nighttime food stall is not so much the pies and coffee Harry dispenses as the clientele. Harry's is a famous Sydney institution, and famous opera singers, actors, and international rock-and-roll stars have been spotted here rubbing shoulders with shift workers and taxi drivers. Sampling one of the stall's famous meat pies with peas is a must. ✉ *1 Cowper Wharf Rd., Woolloomooloo.*

79 Juniper Hall. Built by a gin distiller in 1824, Robert Cooper, this Paddington notable was named for the juniper berries used to make the potent beverage. Cooper did everything on a grand scale—and that included raising and housing his family. He built Juniper Hall for his third wife, Sarah, whom he married when he was 46 and who bore 14 of his 24 children. The house later became an orphanage. It was renovated at considerable public expense and opened as a museum during the 1980s. Due to lack of funds the house is now closed to the public and contains offices. ✉ *248 Oxford St., Paddington.*

NEED A
BREAK?

The Oxford Street **New Edition Tea Rooms** is a bright daytime restaurant serving croissants, salads, and crusty French loaves filled with ham or smoked salmon, as well as cakes, herbal teas, and cappuccino. The best tables are near the windows at the front, and the restaurant has a good selection of international magazines and newspapers. Prices are moderate and the tearooms are open daily. ✉ *328 Oxford St., entry through New Edition Bookshop, Paddington,* ☎ *02/9361–0744.*

Paddington. Most of this suburb's elegant two-story houses were built during the 1880s, when the colony experienced a long period of economic growth following the gold rushes of the 1860s. The balconies are trimmed with decorative wrought iron, sometimes known as Paddington lace, that initially came from England and later was produced in Australian foundries. If you look closely at the patterns, you may be able to distinguish between the rose-and-thistle design that came from England and the flannel flower, fern, and lyre-bird feather designs made in Australia.

During the depression of the 1890s, Paddington's boom came to an abrupt end. The advent of the automobile and motorized public transport just a few years later meant that people could live in more distant suburbs, surrounded by gardens and trees. Such inner-city neighborhoods as Paddington became unfashionable. The area declined further during the depression of the 1930s, when many terrace houses were converted into low-rent accommodations and most of the wrought-iron balconies were boarded up to create extra rooms.

In the late 1960s inner-city living suddenly gained appeal, and many young couples began to buy these dilapidated, quaint houses at bargain prices. Renovated and repainted, the now-stylish Paddington terrace houses give the area its characteristic, villagelike charm. Today you can expect to pay at least $400,000 for a small terrace house.

Royal Hotel. The pub inside the hotel is back in line with its original Victorian state, with leather couches and stained-glass windows. On the floor above the pub there is a balconied restaurant that is particularly popular on sunny afternoons. ⊠ *237 Glenmore Rd.,* ☎ *02/331–2604. AE, MC, V.*

❼❽ Shadforth Street. Built at about the same time as Elizabeth Bay House, the tiny stone houses in this street were assembled to house the workers who built and serviced the ☞ **Victoria Barracks.** Their design was copied from the simple laborers' cottages of England.

❼❻ Sydney Jewish Museum. This, one of Sydney's best-curated museums, simultaneously presents Jewish history in Australia and memorializes the 6 million Jews who were killed in the Holocaust. Exhibits are brilliantly arranged on eight levels, which lead upward in chronological order and address everything from the handful of Jews who arrived on the First Fleet in 1788, to the founding of the State of Israel, to wartime survivors who now live in Australia. ⊠ *Darlinghurst Rd. and Burton St., Darlinghurst,* ☎ *02/9360–7999.* ☞ *$6.* ☉ *Mon.–Thurs. 10–4, Fri. 10–2, Sun. 11–5.*

❼❼ Victoria Barracks. Built by soldiers and convicts from 1841 on to replace the colony's original Observatory Hill barracks—and still occupied by the army—this vast building is an excellent example of Regency-style architecture. The 740-ft-long sandstone facade is particularly impressive. Most of the area within the walls is taken up by a parade ground, and an army band performs here from 10 AM every Thursday, when anyone is welcome on a free tour of the complex. Dress uniforms have been abolished in the Australian army, so the soldiers wear their parade-ground dress, which includes the famous slouch hat: The brim is cocked on the left side, allowing soldiers to present arms without knocking off their hats.

The **Army Museum** is on the far side of the parade ground, in the former military prison. Exhibits cover Australia's military history from the early days of the Rum Corps to the Malayan conflict of the 1950s. Its volunteer staff is knowledgeable and enthusiastic, and students of military history will not be disappointed. ⊠ *Oxford St., Paddington,* ☎ *02/9339–3000.* ☉ *Museum Thurs. 10–noon, Sun. 10–3:30; tour Thurs. 10 AM; barracks mid-Feb.–early Dec.*

Around Sydney

The Sydney area has numerous activities of interest that are well away from the city center and inner suburbs. These include historic townships, the Sydney 2000 Olympics site, national parks in which to enjoy the Australian bush, and wildlife and theme parks that will appeal particularly to children.

Other points of interest are the beach cultures-plus of **Bondi** and **Manly,** the historic city of **Parramatta,** founded in 1788 and 26 km (16 mi) to the west, and the magnificent **Hawkesbury River** that winds its way around the city's western and northern borders. Also **Balmain** has an interesting Saturday craft market (☞ Shopping, *below*).

Visiting many of these places by public transport would take a considerable amount of time and effort, so it may be smarter to rent a car or go with one of the tour operators that offer excursions and day trips (☞ Guided Tours *in* Sydney A to Z, *below*).

TIMING

To really experience each of the sights below (and allow for traveling time) you'll need the best part of a day. Some tour companies combine visits within a particular area—for example, a trip west to the Olympic Games site, Australian Wildlife Park, and the Blue Mountains—making it possible to see much more in one day.

Sights to See

☺ ⑧⑤ **Australian Wildlife Park.** Part of the ☞ **Australia's Wonderland** complex, this park delivers close encounters with the widest array of animals of Sydney area parks, including koalas, kangaroos, and other cuddly Australian fauna, as well as the chance to view crocodiles and rainforest birds. Also in the park is the **Outback Woolshed,** where sheep are rounded up and shorn in a 30-minute demonstration of a time-honored Australian tradition. ⊠ *Wallgrove Rd., Eastern Creek,* ☎ *02/9830–9100.* ⌨ *$9.95; free if you also visit Australia's Wonderland.* ☉ *Daily 9–5.*

☺ ⑧⑤ **Australia's Wonderland.** The largest amusement park in the Southern Hemisphere is landscaped and choreographed for total fun. Action ranges from a Ferris wheel to a roller coaster to the ☞ **Australian Wildlife Park.** The complex is in the metropolitan region's west, and admission prices cover all rides and entry fees, including the wildlife park and woolshed. ⊠ *Wallgrove Rd., Eastern Creek,* ☎ *02/9830–9100.* ⌨ *$31.95.* ☉ *Sat. 10–10, Sun. 10–5.*

⑧⓪ **Bondi.** In spite of its glorious beach and sparkling views, the suburb of Bondi has only recently acquired social status. Bondi—an Aboriginal word meaning "place of breaking waters"—was developed during the 1920s and 30s. But the spare, redbrick architecture, lack of trees, and generally flat terrain did their share to reduce the town's appeal. Over the years, Bondi acquired a seedy image fostered by low rents and a free-and-easy lifestyle that the suburb afforded. Author Peter Corris—Australia's Raymond Chandler—used Bondi as a tawdry, neon-lit backdrop for his 1980s thriller, *The Empty Beach.*

During the 1990s, Bondi's proximity to the city and affordable real estate have attracted young and upwardly mobile residents. Most of the old apartment blocks have been smartly renovated, and Campbell Parade has been populated with a row of glittering cafés and gourmet delicatessens. **Onzain** and **Sean's Panorama** both appear in our Dining section, *below*.

Greater Sydney

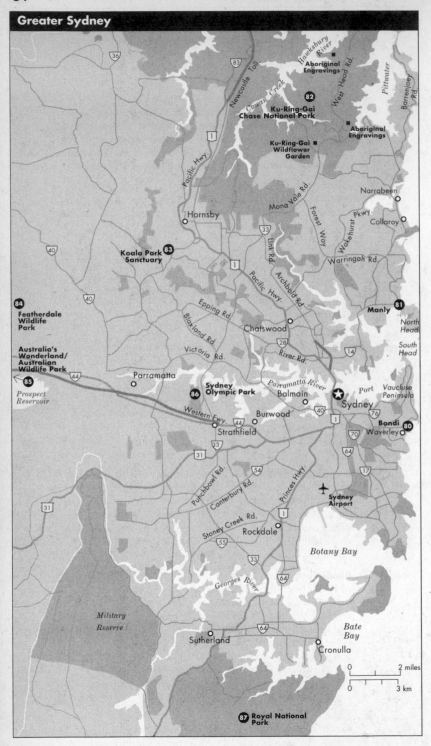

Aboriginal Engravings

82 Ku-Ring-Gai Chase National Park

Ku-Ring-Gai Wildflower Garden

Aboriginal Engravings

Hawkesbury River

Cowan Creek

Newcastle Toll

Pittwater

Barrenjoey Rd.

West Head Rd.

Narrabeen

Collaroy

Hornsby

Mona Vale Rd.

Forest Way

Wakehurst Pkwy.

Warringah Rd.

Pacific Hwy.

Link Rd.

Archbold Rd.

83 Koala Park Sanctuary

84 Featherdale Wildlife Park

Australia's Wonderland/ Australian Wildlife Park

85 Prospect Reservoir

Epping Rd.

Blaxland Rd.

Victoria Rd.

Chatswood

River Rd.

Manly **81**

North Head

South Head

Parramatta

Parramatta River

86 Sydney Olympic Park

Balmain

Port

Vaucluse Peninsula

SYDNEY

76

Bondi **80**

Waverley

Western Fwy.

Burwood

Strathfield

Punchbowl Rd.

Canterbury Rd.

Princes Hwy.

Stoney Creek Rd.

Rockdale

Sydney Airport

Botany Bay

Georges River

Military Reserve

Sutherland

Bate Bay

Cronulla

87 Royal National Park

0   2 miles

0   3 km

Apart from a pleasant day at the beach (☞ Beaches, *below*), Bondi's main appeal is sociology. This is where Sydney sheds its clothes and most of its inhibitions. Many of the city's sporting subcultures congregate here—among them cyclists, anglers, surfers, bodybuilders, and skateboarders—as do a healthy crowd of exhibitionists and eccentrics. The promenade along the back of the beach is the best place to take all of this in.

To get to Bondi, take Bus 380 or 382 from Circular Quay via Elizabeth and Oxford streets; or catch a train from the city to Bondi Junction, then board Bus 380 or 382. A higher-cost option is the **Bondi & Bay Explorer** bus (☞ Guided Tours *in* Sydney A to Z, *below*).

🖐 ㉘ **Featherdale Wildlife Park.** Located northwest of the city, this park is home to a roll call of Australia's extraordinary fauna in their native bush setting—creatures that even most Australians won't ever see in the wild. ✉ *217 Kildare Rd., Doonside,* ☎ *02/9622–1644.* 🖃 *$9.50.* ⊙ *Daily 9–5.*

🖐 ㉓ **Koala Park Sanctuary.** At this private park on Sydney's northern outskirts, you can cuddle, feed, and photograph a koala. The sanctuary also houses dingoes, kangaroos, emus, and wallaroos, and there are sheep shearing and boomerang throwing demonstrations. Feeding times are 10:20, 11:45, 2, and 3. ✉ *84 Castle Hill Rd., West Pennant Hills,* ☎ *02/9484–3141.* 🖃 *$9.50.* ⊙ *Daily 9–5.*

㉒ **Ku-Ring-Gai Chase National Park.** Originally inhabited by the Guringai Aboriginal tribe, for which the park is named, this is the site of many ancient Aboriginal rock engravings and paintings. The creation of the park in the 1890s also ensured the survival of large stands of eucalypts, as well as small pockets of rain forest in moist gullies. The wildlife here includes swamp wallabies, possums, and goannas (Australian monitor lizards), as well as a wide range of bird species. The many trails that traverse the park are a delight and are mostly designed for easy-to-moderate hikes. Among them, the 3-km (2-mi) Garigal Aboriginal Heritage Walk at West Head takes in ancient rock-art sites, and the short Topham and America tracks lead down to Cowan Water from West Head Road. There are many trails in the Bobbin Head area, and from Mt. Ku-ring-gai train station you can walk the 3-km (2-mi) Ku-ring-gai track to Appletree Bay. Another track, the 30-minute Discovery Trail, is negotiable in a wheelchair and offers an excellent introduction to the region's flora and fauna. Leaflets on all of the walks are available at the park's entry stations and from the Kalkari Visitor Centre and the Wildlife Shop at Bobbin Head.

The park is only 24 km (15 mi) north of Sydney. Railway stations at Mt. Ku-ring-Gai, Berowa, and Cowan, close to the park's western border, provide access to walking trails (on Sunday, for example, you can walk from Mt. Ku-ring-gai station to Appletree Bay then Bobbin Head, where a bus can take you to the Turramurra rail station). By car, take the Pacific Highway to Pymble, then turn into Bobbin Head Road, or continue on the highway to Mt. Colah and turn off into the park on Ku-ring-gai Chase Road. Another approach: follow the Pacific Highway to Pymble, then drive along the Mona Vale Road to Terry Hills and take the West Head turnoff.

Camping in the park is permitted only at the Basin in Pittwater. Sites must be booked in advance (☎ 02/9451–8124). Rates are $15 per night for two people during peak periods and $10 in the off-season. Each additional person is $2; children under 5 are free. Supplies can be purchased in Palm Beach.

For more information, contact **Ku-ring-gai Chase National Park Visitors Centre.** ✉ *Box 834, Hornsby 2077,* ☎ *02/9457–9322 weekdays, 02/9457–9310 weekends.*

㉛ Manly. Until the Sydney Harbour Bridge was built in the 1930s, Manly's air of distant enchantment and ease made it a popular holiday resort. Many Sydneysiders can still recall childhood holidays spent at Manly, embroidered with sandcastles, dribbling ice creams, and visits to the Manly Aquarium and the amusement park on Manly Pier.

Sprawling across the isthmus that forms the northern haw of Sydney Harbour, the suburb of Manly has an ocean beach as well as a harbor beach (☞ Beaches, *below*). The area was named by Governor Phillip, the colony's first governor, when he noted the "manly behavior" of the local Aborigines. Two years later, he might have reconsidered his choice of words when those same Aborigines speared him in the shoulder at Manly Cove.

Manly is more family oriented than Bondi—better mannered, better shaded, and well equipped with cafés—although it does lack its southern sister's sheer entertainment value. If you're thinking about spending the day in Manly, there are also the Quarantine Station (☞ Sydney Harbour, *above*) and Oceanworld aquarium to visit, and a trip out to North Head is worthwhile for its panoramic views. To get to Manly, take a ferry or JetCat from Circular Quay; from its landing point the beach is a 10-minute walk. The Northern Beaches Explorer bus (☞ Guided Tours *in* Sydney A to Z, *below*) also travels to Manly.

★ **㊳ Royal National Park.** Established in 1879 on the coast south of Sydney, the Royal has the distinction of being the first national park in Australia and the second in the world, after Yellowstone. Originally set aside as a combination botanical and zoological garden for city dwellers, the park remains popular among Sydneysiders on long weekends and holidays. Surprisingly few foreign visitors visit Royal, however; those who do are guaranteed great bird-watching—more than 200 species have been recorded—and great swimming holes. Many areas were severely burned in the bushfires of January 1994, but fire is an integral part of the Australian ecosystem. Some native plant species rely on fire to crack open their seedpods, and apart from the rain forest areas, the park has regenerated rapidly.

Several walking tracks traverse the park, most of which require little or no hiking experience. The Lady Carrington Walk, a 10-km (6-mi) trek, is a self-guided tour that crosses 15 creeks and passes several historic sites. Other tracks take you along the coast past beautiful wildflower displays and through patches of rain forest. You can canoe the Hacking River upstream from the Audley Causeway; rent canoes and boats at the Audley boat shed on the Hacking River.

Royal National Park is 35 km (22 mi) south of Sydney via the Prince's Highway to Farnell Avenue (south of Loftus) or McKell Avenue at Waterfall. The Illawarra–Cronulla train line stops at Loftus, Engadine, Heathcote, Waterfall, and Otford stations, where most of the park's walking tracks begin. The park charges a $7.50 entrance fee per vehicle per day.

Although most visitors stay for only a day, campsites are available. Camping facilities at Bonnie Vale Camping Area generally require reservations and deposits at the Park Visitor Centre in Audley, especially during school vacations and long weekends. Camping fees are $10 per night for two people and $2 for each additional person over five years of age. Hot showers, toilets, and laundry facilities are available at the eastern end of Bonnie Vale, 1,650 ft from the campsite. Bush camping is currently forbidden, in order to speed recovery of vegetation affected by the bushfires. Groceries can be purchased in Bundeena, about a mile from the camping area.

Further information is available from the **Royal National Park Visitor Centre** (✉ Box 44, Sutherland 2232, ☎ 02/9542–0648) or from the **National Parks and Wildlife Service** district office (☎ 02/9542–0666).

86 **Sydney Olympic Park.** As Sydney prepares for the 2000 Olympic and Paralympic Games, the main site at Homebush Bay, to the west of the city, is gradually taking shape. As yet, however, there isn't much for all but the dedicted Olympics enthusiasts to appreciate. You can join a 45-minute guided bus tour of the existing and proposed facilities, including the Sydney International Aquatic Centre, the International Athletic Centre, and the State Sports Centre with its New South Wales Hall of Champions museum. Although this is a nonstop trip, it is possible to inspect some of the high-tech buildings more closely after the tour, and separate tours of the superb aquatic center (☎ 02/9752–3666) are also available.

The Homebush Bay Shuttle bus departs from the north side of Strathfield Station, reached by train from Town Hall or Central stations. Tours depart from Strathfield Station. ✉ *Homebush Bay,* ☎ *02/9735–4800.* 🚌 *$5.* ☉ *Tour weekdays at 9:30, 10:30, and 12:30.*

BEACHES

Numbers in the margin correspond to beaches on the Sydney Beaches map.

Sydney is a veritable smorgasbord for beach lovers—there are over 30 ocean beaches, all with golden sand and rolling surf, and there are several around the harbor with calm water and safe swimming. If your hotel is on the city side of the harbor, the logical choice for a seaside sojourn is to go to the southern ocean beaches between Bondi and Maroubra. On the north side of the harbor, Manly is easily accessible by ferry, but beaches farther north involve a long trip by car or public transport.

Lifeguards are on duty at most of Sydney's ocean beaches, and the patrolled areas are indicated by flags. "Swim between the flags" is an adage that is drummed into every Australian child, with very good reason: The undertow and sidewash can be very dangerous. Topless sunbathing is common at all Sydney beaches, but full nudity is permitted only at a couple of locations, including Lady Jane Beach, close to Watsons Bay on the south side of the harbor.

Some visitors to Sydney are concerned about sharks. Although there is no shortage of sharks both inside and outside the harbor, many Sydney beaches are protected by nets, and the last shark attack in Sydney waters occurred more than 30 years ago. A more common hazard is jellyfish, known locally as bluebottles, which inflict a painful sting. Fortunately, this danger is confined to the later part of the summer, and only rarely do the wind and currents send the jellies onto the beaches in any numbers.

A more real beach-related problem is the risk of skin cancer, caused by excessive exposure to sunlight. As a result of their addiction to a powerful sun, Australians suffer from this form of cancer more than any other people on earth, and the depletion of the ozone layer has increased the risk. Precautions are simple and should be followed by every visitor: Wear a hat, as well as sunglasses, sit in the shade between 11 AM and 3 PM, and protect your skin with high-protection sun block at all times.

Details of how to reach the beaches by bus, train, or ferry are provided below, but some of the city's harbor and southern beaches are also on the **Bondi & Bay Explorer** bus route (☞ Guided Tours *in* Sydney A to Z, *below*). These are Nielsen Park, Camp Cove, Lady Jane, Bondi, Bronte, Clovelly, and Coogee.

Departing from Manly Wharf, the **Northern Beaches Explorer** bus (also known as the Boomerang Beach Bus) will take you to any of the beaches that stretch from Manly to Palm Beach, the latter being an hour's ride. You can stay on the bus for the three-hour round-trip to familiarize yourself with this delightful part of the city. The ferry ride to Manly takes about 30 minutes, and Manly beach is a 10-minute walk from there.

Inside the Harbor

★ ⑩ **Balmoral.** This long, peaceful beach is backed by parkland in one of Sydney's most exclusive northern suburbs. The Esplanade, which runs along the back of the beach, has several snack bars and cafés. You could easily combine a trip to Balmoral with a visit to Taronga Zoo. To reach Balmoral, take the ferry from Circular Quay to Taronga Zoo, then board Bus 238. ⊠ *Raglan St., Balmoral.*

⑫ **Camp Cove.** Just inside South Head, this crescent-shaped beach is where Sydney's fashionable people come to see and be seen. The gentle slope of the beach and the relatively calm water make it a safe playground for young children. A shop at the northern end of the beach sells a variety of salad rolls and fresh fruit juices, as well as the usual snacks. The grassy knoll at the southern end of the beach has a plaque to commemorate the spot where Captain Arthur Phillip, the commander of the First Fleet, first set foot inside Sydney Harbour. Parking is limited, and if you arrive by car after 10 AM on weekends, you'll have a long walk to the beach. Take Bus 324 or 325 from Circular Quay. ⊠ *Cliff St., Watsons Bay.*

⑪ **Lady Jane.** Lady Jane—officially called Lady Bay—is the most accessible of the nude beaches around Sydney. When you tire of body-watching, it is a short walk to South Head and some great city and harbor views. ⊠ *Access via Camp Cove (☞ above), then walk along path above shop and make short, difficult descent by ladder down cliff face.*

⑬ **Nielsen Park.** This beach at the end of the Vaucluse Peninsula is small by Sydney standards, but behind the sand is a large, shady park that is ideal for picnics. The headlands at either end of the beach are especially popular for their magnificent views across the harbor. Despite the crowds, it is always possible to find a quiet spot on the grass. The beach is protected by a semicircular net, so don't be deterred by the correct name of this beach—Shark Bay. The shop and café behind the beach sell drinks, snacks, and meals. Parking is often difficult on weekends. When you've had enough of the beach, a 10-minute walk will take you to historic Vaucluse House (☞ Sydney Harbour, *above*) and a very different harborside experience. Take Bus 325 from Circular Quay. ⊠ *Greycliffe Ave. off Vaucluse Rd., Vaucluse.*

South of the Harbor

★ ⑭ **Bondi.** Wide, wonderful Bondi (pronounced *bon*-dye) is the most famous and the most crowded of all Sydney beaches. It has something for just about everyone, and the droves who flock here on a sunny day

Balmoral, **10**
Bondi, **14**
Botany Bay, **20**
Bronte, **16**
Bungan, **3**
Camp Cove, **12**
Clovelly, **17**
Collaroy–Narrabeen, **5**
Coogee, **18**
Cronulla, **21**
Dee Why–Long Reef, **6**
Freshwater, **7**
Lady Jane, **11**
Manly, **8**
Maroubra, **19**
Newport, **2**
Nielsen Park, **13**
Palm Beach, **1**
Shelly, **9**
Tamarama, **15**
Warriewood, **4**

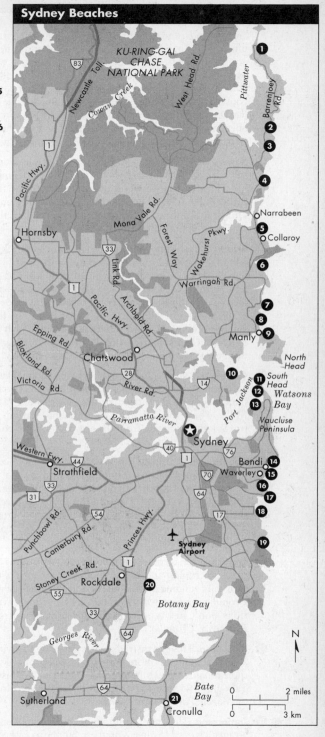

Sydney Beaches

give it a bustling, carnival atmosphere unmatched by any other Sydney beach. Facilities include toilets and showers, and many cafés, ice cream stands, and restaurants are on Campbell Parade, which runs behind the beach. Family groups tend to prefer the more sheltered northern end of the beach, though surfing is a very popular pursuit at the south end, where you'll also find a path that winds along the sea-sculpted cliffs to Tamarama and Bronte beaches. If you come out for the day, consider trying **Onzain** or **Sean's Panorama** for one of your daily meals (☞ Dining, *below*). Take Bus 380 or 382 from Circular Quay via Elizabeth and Oxford streets, or take the train from the city to Bondi Junction, then board Bus 380 or 382. ☒ *Campbell Parade, Bondi.*

⓴ **Botany Bay.** The bay's historic name, alas, doesn't rescue Lady Robinson's Beach, which stretches for several miles along the bay, from the bleak, featureless view and nearby heavy traffic that make it one of Sydney's least attractive beaches. Take Bus 302 or 303 from Circular Quay, or take the train from the city to Rockdale, then board Bus 478. ☒ *Grand Parade, Brighton-le-Sands.*

★ ⓰ **Bronte.** If you want an ocean beach close to the city that has good facilities, a choice of sand or parkland, and a terrific setting, this one is hard to beat. Bronte is surrounded by a wooded park of palm trees and Norfolk Island pines. The park includes a playground and sheltered picnic tables, and a couple of excellent cafés are in the immediate area. The breakers can be fierce here, but the sea pool at the southern end of the beach offers safe swimming at any time. Take Bus 378 from Central Station, or take the train from the city to Bondi Junction, then board Bus 378. ☒ *Bronte Rd., Bronte.*

★ ⓱ **Clovelly.** At the end of a long, keyhole-shaped inlet, swimming is safe here even on the roughest day. There are toilet facilities but no snack bars or shops in the immediate area. Take Bus 339 from Argyle Street, Millers Point (the Rocks), or Wynyard bus station; Bus 341 from Central Station; or a train from the city to Bondi Junction, then board Bus 329. ☒ *Clovelly Rd., Clovelly.*

⓲ **Coogee.** A reef protects this lively beach (pronounced *kuh*-jee, not *coo*-jee), creating calmer swimming conditions than those found at its neighbors. A grassy headland overlooking the beach has an excellent children's playground. Cafés in the shopping precinct at the back of the beach sell ice cream, pizza, and ingredients for delicious picnics. Take Bus 373 from Circular Quay or Bus 372 from Central Station. ☒ *Coogee Bay Rd., Coogee.*

㉑ **Cronulla.** Even on the hottest day you can escape the crowds at Cronulla, the southernmost and largest beach in the metropolitan area. Good surf is usually running at this beach, and the sand is backed by parkland. Cronulla is a long way from the city by train, however, and its attractions don't justify a long trip for anyone not staying nearby. ☒ *Kingsway, Cronulla.*

⓳ **Maroubra.** This expansive beach is very popular with surfers, although anyone looking for more than waves will probably be unimpressed by the rather scrappy surroundings and the lackluster shopping area. Take Bus 395 from Central Station or Bus 396 from Circular Quay. ☒ *Marine Parade, Maroubra.*

★ ⓯ **Tamarama.** This small, fashionable beach (it's also known as "Glam-a-rama") is one of Sydney's prettiest, but the rocky headlands that squeeze close to the sand on either side make it less than ideal for swimming. A café at the back of the beach sells open sandwiches, fresh fruit juices, and fruit whips. Surfing is not allowed. Take the train from the city to

Bondi Junction, then board Bus 391, or walk for 10 minutes along the cliffs from the south end of Bondi Beach. ⊠ *Tamarama Marine Dr., Tamarama*.

North of the Harbor

❸ **Bungan.** If you *really* want to get away from it all, this is the beach for you. Very few Sydneysiders have discovered Bungan, and those who have would like to keep it to themselves. As well as being relatively empty, this wide, attractive beach is one of the cleanest, due to the prevailing ocean currents. Access to the beach involves a difficult hike down a wooden staircase, and there are no facilities. Take Bus 184 or 190 from the Wynyard bus station. ⊠ *Beach Rd., off Barrenjoey Rd., Mona Vale*.

❺ **Collaroy–Narrabeen.** This is actually one beach that passes through two suburbs. Its main attractions are its size—it's almost 3 km (2 mi) long—and the fact that it's always possible to escape the crowds here. The shops are concentrated at the southern end of the beach. Take Bus 155 or 157 from Manly or Bus 182, 184, 189, or 190 from the Wynyard bus station. ⊠ *Pittwater Rd*.

❻ **Dee Why–Long Reef.** Separated from Dee Why by a narrow channel, Long Reef Beach is remoter and much quieter than its southern neighbor. However, Dee Why has better surfing conditions, a big sea pool, and several take-out shops. Take Bus 136 from Manly. ⊠ *The Strand, Dee Why*.

❼ **Freshwater.** This small beach is protected by sprawling headlands on either side, making it popular among families. The surf club on the beach has good facilities as well as a small shop that sells light refreshments. Take Bus 139 from Manly. ⊠ *The Esplanade, Harbord*.

★ ❽ **Manly.** The Bondi Beach of the north shore, Manly caters to everyone except those who want to get away from it all. The beach itself is well equipped with changing and toilet facilities, and the nearby shopping area, the Corso, is lined with cafés, souvenir shops, and ice cream parlors. Manly also has several nonbeach attractions (☞ Around Sydney, *above*). Coming from the city, the ferry ride makes a day at Manly feel more like a holiday than just an excursion to the beach. Take a ferry or JetCat from Circular Quay; from there the beach is a 10-minute walk. ⊠ *N. Steyne and S. Steyne*.

❷ **Newport.** With its backdrop of hills and Norfolk Island pines, this broad sweep of sand is one of the finest of the northern beaches. Within easy walking distance is a shopping center offering one of the best selections of cafés and take-out shops of any Sydney beach. Newport is known for its bodysurfing, and the atmosphere is fairly relaxed. Take Bus 189 or 190 from the Wynyard bus station. ⊠ *Barrenjoey Rd., Newport*.

❶ **Palm Beach.** The wide, golden sands of Palm Beach mark the northern end of Sydney's beaches—a fitting sort of best-for-last finale. The ocean beach runs along one side of a peninsula separating the large inlet of Pittwater from the Pacific Ocean. Bathers can easily cross from the ocean side to Pittwater's calm waters and sailboats, and you can take a circular ferry trip around this waterway from the wharf on the Pittwater side. The view from the lighthouse at the northern end of the beach is well worth the walk; on a windy day, the southern end of the beach affords some protection. Nearby shops and cafés sell light snacks and meals. The suburb of Palm Beach is a favorite with successful filmmakers and with Sydney's wealthy elite, many of whom own weekend houses in the area. Take Bus 190 from Wynyard bus station. ⊠ *Ocean Rd., Palm Beach*.

9 **Shelly.** This delightful little beach is protected by a headland rising behind it to form a green, shady park, and it is well endowed with food options. The snack shop and restaurant on the beach sell everything from light refreshments to elaborate meals, and there are a couple of waterfront cafés at nearby Fairy Bower Bay. On weekends the beach is crowded and parking in the area is nearly impossible—it's best to walk along the seafront from Manly. Take a ferry or JetCat from Circular Quay to Manly; from there the beach is a half mile walk. ⊠ *Marine Parade, Manly.*

4 **Warriewood.** Enticing and petite in its cove at the bottom of looming cliffs, Warriewood has excellent conditions for surfers and windsurfers. For swimmers and sunbathers, however, the beach does not justify the difficult journey down the steep cliffs. Anyone traveling by public transport faces a long walk from the nearest bus stop. Basic toilet facilities are available on the beach, but there are no shops nearby. Take Bus 184, 189, or 190 from Wynyard bus station or Bus 155 from Manly. ⊠ *Narrabeen Park Parade, Warriewood.*

DINING

By Terry
Durack

Although most Sydney restaurants are now licensed to serve alcohol, the few that aren't generally allow you to bring your own bottle (BYOB). Reservations are generally required with a few noticeable exceptions where no bookings at all are taken. Lunch is normally served between noon and 2:30, and dinner is served, usually in a single sitting, between 7 and 10:30. A 10% tip is customary, and there may be a corkage fee in BYOB restaurants, but there is no sales tax or service charge. Some establishments may add a small surcharge on weekends and holidays.

CATEGORY	COST*
$$$$	over $60
$$$	$40–$60
$$	$20–$40
$	under $20

per person, excluding drinks and tip

The Rocks and Circular Quay

Australian

$$$$ ✕ **Bennelong.** Sydney's essential sightseeing stop, the Opera House,
★ is now an essential dining stop thanks to the refined cooking talents of Gay Bilson and Janni Kyritsis. The food here is as well constructed and as dramatically spectacular as Joern Utzon's world-famous architecture, running from a classic French repertoire to more innovative efforts that neatly showcase the best of local produce. Roasted pigeon, *tripes Lyonnaise,* and a salad of veal trotters, tongue, and sweetbreads all bring the house down. ⊠ *Sydney Opera House, Bennelong Point,* ☎ *02/9250–7578 or 02/9250–7548. Reservations essential. AE, DC, MC, V. Closed Sun. No lunch.*

$$$$ ✕ **Kables.** The Regent's executive chef, Serge Dansereau, is Sydney's unofficial patron saint of local food suppliers and growers. His encouragement has enabled many of Australia's more innovative growers and breeders not only to survive, but to flourish. Naturally this fine produce regularly finds its way onto Kable's elegantly draped tables along with some rare vintages of Australia's finest wines. Do try the Western Australian marron (freshwater lobster) with parsnip brandade, Illabo lamb (a young New South Wales lamb) with hothouse artichokes, or grilled Kobe-style Wagyu beef. ⊠ *Regent of Sydney, 199*

George St., the Rocks, ☎ 02/9238–0000. Reservations essential.
Jacket and tie. AE, DC, MC, V. No lunch Mon.–Wed.

\$\$\$\$ ✕ **Rockpool.** Glide up an undulating gangplank into this shipshape,
★ brave new world of chrome and glass. Originally known for its local
seafood, Rockpool has blossomed into something far more difficult to
categorize, rolling with consummate ease from Mediterranean to Thai
to Chinese. Such dishes as Yamba prawns with goat cheese ravioli, Chinese pressed duck with fresh mango, tea-smoked ocean trout, mud crab
and sweet pork salad, and grilled John Dory fillet in Indian pastry
bounce around the palate like a pinball. Chef Neil Perry is a perfectionist,
and his meticulously honed flavors make Rockpool a serious contender
for Australia's best restaurant. ☒ 107 George St., the Rocks, ☎ 02/9252–
1888. Reservations essential. AE, DC, MC, V. Closed Sun. No lunch Sat.

\$\$ ✕ **The Wharf.** As the name implies, this popular restaurant is at the tip
of an old timber-cargo wharf, and it affords spectacular views of the
Harbour Bridge and nearby Luna Park. Because it shares its lodgings
with the adjacent Sydney Theatre Company, it is the ideal spot for a
pre-theater dinner or a post-theater supper. The menu combines modern Mediterranean techniques with good old baby-boomer favorites.
Dishes include smoked cod's roe taramasalata served with char-grilled
olive bread; grilled kingfish with creamed spinach; and polenta cake with
egg, tomato, and roasted garlic. ☒ Pier 4, Hickson Rd., Walsh Bay, ☎
02/9250–1761. Reservations essential. AE, DC, MC, V.

French

\$\$\$\$ ✕ **Bilson's.** The only way you'll get a better view of Sydney Harbour
is to fly over it, but then you wouldn't be able to enjoy Guillaume
Brahimi's classy and meticulous French cooking. Brahimi has worked
for the master, Joel Robuchon in Paris, and it shows in every mouth-
ful. He doesn't dare take his delicate, basil-infused tuna and beef tenderloin with Paris mash and Merlot sauce off the menu, yet such newer
dishes as roasted veal sweetbreads with risotto and lamb jus, and
seared blue-eye cod on celeriac puree are winning their share of fans.
☒ Overseas Passenger Terminal, Circular Quay W, ☎ 02/9251–5600.
Reservations essential. AE, DC, MC, V. No lunch Sat.

Italian

\$\$\$\$ ✕ **bel mondo.** After 13 years at Restaurant Manfredi in Ultimo, the
★ Manfredi family has moved into a restored 1913 warehouse space on
top of the Argyle Department store in the Rocks, and the town hasn't
stopped raving. With its glamorous big-night-out feel and dramatic,
raised, open kitchen, the place is pure theater. But the food keeps
crowds coming back, from a quick antipasto and a spaghetti at the an-
tibar to the sublimely tender roasted Illabo lamb, light-as-air gnocchi
with crabmeat, and gasp-inducing licorice sushi. ☒ Level 3, Argyle Department Store, 18–24 Argyle St., the Rocks, ☎ 02/9241–3700.
Reservations essential. AE, DC, MC, V. No dinner Sun.

Japanese

\$\$\$\$ ✕ **Unkai.** Roughly translated, unkai means "ocean of clouds," but with
luck, there won't be any clouds to obscure one of the best views in town.
Thirty-six floors above Sydney Harbour, Unkai provides that classic
mix of ceremony and freshness that is uniquely Japanese, and its menu
caters to everyone. Sushi is highly recommended, grilled dishes are uni-
formly good, and the multicourse kaiseki (formal, Kyoto-style) banquets are a feast for the eyes and the palate. ☒ ANA Hotel, 176
Cumberland St., Level 36, the Rocks, ☎ 02/9250–6123. Reservations
essential. Jacket and tie. AE, DC, MC, V. No lunch Sat.

64

Central Sydney Dining and Lodging

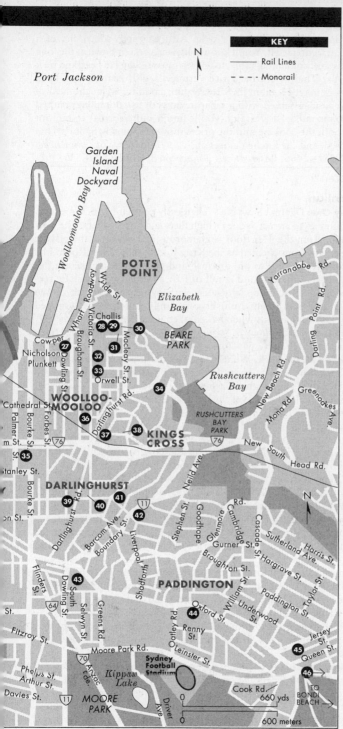

Port Jackson

KEY

—— Rail Lines

- - - Monorail

Garden
Island
Naval
Dockyard

POTTS
POINT

Elizabeth
Bay

Challis

BEARE
PARK

Yarranabbe Rd.

Cowper

Nicholson

Plunkett

Rushcutters
Bay

New Beach Rd.

Darling Point Rd.

Mona Rd.

Greenoaks Ave.

WOOLLOO-
MOOMOO

Cathedral St

RUSHCUTTERS
BAY
PARK

Palmer St.

Bourke St.

Forbes St.

Darlinghurst Rd.

KINGS
CROSS

New South Head Rd.

Stanley St.

DARLINGHURST

Bourke St.

Darlinghurst Rd.

Barcom Ave.

Boundary St.

Liverpool St.

Stephen St.

Neild Ave.

Glenmore Rd.

Goodhope St.

Cambridge St.

Cascade St.

Hargrave St.

Sutherland Ave.

Harris St.

Gurner St.

Broughton St.

William St.

Paddington St.

Taylor St.

Flinders
St.

South Dowling St.

Selwyn St.

Greens Rd.

PADDINGTON

Underwood St.

Oxford St.

Jersey St.

Queen St.

Fitzroy St.

Moore Park Rd.

Oxley Rd.

Renny St.

Leinster St.

Sydney
Football
Stadium

TO
BONDI
BEACH

Phelps St.

Arthur St.

Anzac Pde.

Kippax
Lake

Driver Ave.

Cook Rd.

Davies St.

MOORE
PARK

0   660 yds

0   600 meters

Lodging

ANA Hotel, **12**

Brooklyn Bed and
Breakfast, **21**

Challis Lodge, **28**

Harbour Rocks
Hotel, **9**

Hotel Inter-Continental
Sydney, **15**

The Hughenden, **45**

Jackson Hotel, **32**

Observatory Hotel, **11**

Park Hyatt Sydney, **2**

Ravesi's on Bondi
Beach, **46**

Regent of
Sydney, **13**

Ritz-Carlton,
Sydney, **14**

The Russell, **10**

Sebel of Sydney, **34**

Stafford Quest
Sydney, **8**

Sullivans Hotel, **43**

Sydney Travellers Rest
Hotel, **22**

Trickett's, **20**

Victoria Court
Sydney, **33**

Woolloomooloo Waters
Apartment Hotel, **27**

Thai

$ ✕ **Sailor's Thai Canteen.** This slick communal noodle bar in the old Sailor's Home in the historic Rocks district is turning into something of a tourist attraction itself. You'll know why when you sit down at the long stainless steel communal table, take a sip of your Sing Ha beer, and tuck into a Pat Thai of stir-fried rice vermicelli with peanuts and bean sprouts, or maybe Kanom Jin Saow Nahm, a traditional lunchtime dish of Thai noodles served with a separate bowl of fish dumplings bathed in coconut milk. Downstairs, you'll find a more formal restaurant where both the cooking and the prices move up a notch. Sailor's Thai is licensed, and the kitchen closes at 8. ⊠ *106 George St., the Rocks,* ☎ *02/9251–2466. Reservations not accepted. AE, DC, MC, V.*

City Center Area

Australian

$$$$ ✕ **Forty-One.** Dietmar Sawyere's relentlessly popular big-ticket restaurant continues to attract Sydney's high fliers and heavy hitters. The view of Sydney from the 41st floor is glamorous and glorious, the private dining rooms (now themed as the Krug Room, the Cartier Room, the Christofle Room and so on) are lush and plush, and the Asian-influenced, lightly classical food is full of flair and finesse. Especially recommended is artichoke vichyssoise with oysters and caviar, crown roast of hare with oriental mushrooms, and truffled squab wrapped in wet clay that hardens when baked, then is cracked off. ⊠ *Level 41, Chifley Tower, 2 Chifley Sq., Sydney,* ☎ *02/9221–2500. Reservations essential. AE, DC, MC, V. Closed Sun. No lunch Sat.*

$$$ ✕ **Pavilion on the Park.** What it says is what it is: a gloriously refurbished pavilion smack dab in the middle of parkland in Sydney's famous Domain. The Botanic Gardens are next door, the Art Gallery of New South Wales is just over the road, and the harbor is a stroll away. Although it also operates as a kiosk and a café, it is the restaurant that attracts the most attention, featuring Anthony Mussara's Mediterranean-inspired cooking. Once you've tucked into a lunch of his spiced duck cake with beetroot, seared tuna and potato cake with caperberries, or oxtail crepinettes with lentils, you'll probably be glad that there are so many pleasant walks to choose from. ⊠ *1 Art Gallery Rd., the Domain (south),* ☎ *02/9232–1322. Reservations essential. AE, DC, MC, V. Closed Sun. No dinner.*

$$$ ✕ **Star Grill.** Darling Harbour is more known for tourist attractions—the Maritime Museum, the Aquarium, and the Casino—than it is for fine dining. However, Neil Perry of Rockpool fame is determined to change all that with his new, light-bright future world of a restaurant tucked into the ground floor of the big screen Panasonic Imax Theatre. The food runs from an easygoing bar menu that includes freshly shucked oysters or penne pasta with braised oxtail sauce to Perry's Sicilian garfish salad; boiled rock lobster with aioli; and golden, spice-rubbed chicken grilled on the rotisserie. ⊠ *Panasonic Imax Theatre, Southern Promenade, Darling Harbour,* ☎ *02/9211–9888. Reservations essential. AE, DC, MC, V.*

$$ ✕ **Restaurant CBD.** It's a pub, it's a pool hall, it's a function center, and it's a restaurant, depending on what floor you happen to be on. Normal Friday nights it may take you a while to fight your way through the after-work revellers at the ground floor bar—but get those elbows up and keep moving toward the stairs to get to the tastefully restored first floor dining room. Luke Mangan's Britpack-take on French cooking is well worth the effort, especially his terrine of caramelized witlof (Belgian endive) and truffles, pheasant breast with sweet potato puree, and homemade crab ravioli. ⊠ *75 York St.,* ☎ *02/9299–8911. Reservations essential. AE, DC, MC, V. Closed weekends.*

Chinese

$$ ✗ **Golden Century.** This is sheer Cantonese seafood heaven with its wall-to-wall fish tanks filled with crab, lobster, abalone, baskets of tiny clams, and schools of barramundi, parrot fish, perch, and silver bream. At least you won't have to ask if the food is fresh—most of it is swimming around you as you eat. The atmosphere is no-frills and the noise level can be deafening, but the eating is very good indeed, especially if you order king crab three ways: half steamed with shallots, half wok-fried with pepper, and its roe served with noodles. ⊠ *393–399 Sussex St.,* ☎ *02/9212–3901. AE, DC, MC, V.*

East Sydney and Darlinghurst

Café

$ ✗ **bill's.** In this relaxed unpretentious place, where the Split Rock mineral water doubles as decor, a mixed-up group that represents every race, creed, and hairstyle shares a big central table. The crowd changes from suits at midweek breakfast to Vuitton-bag ladies at lunch, with a reassuring assortment of young post-grunge types in between. At breakfast, ricotta hotcakes with honeycomb butter are a way of life, and at lunch the food runs from spring onion pancakes with gravlax to the most famous steak sandwich in town. ⊠ *433 Liverpool St., Darlinghurst,* ☎ *02/9360–9631. Reservations not accepted. No credit cards. BYOB. Closed Sun. No dinner.*

European

$$ ✗ **Mohr's.** Hans Mohr made his name in Sydney first as a master salmon smoker and then as a fish-and-chip maestro at Mohr Fish at Surry Hills. Now he's turned his hand to meatier matters at this comfortable, no-frills inner city diner. This is the place to tuck into melt-in-the-mouth pâté, fall-apart, old-fashioned beef brisket, a full-blown cassoulet with the works, and a totally irresistible roast suckling pig with crackling you can hear up and down Crown Street. ⊠ *527 Crown St., Surry Hills,* ☎ *02/9319–5682. Reservations essential. AE, MC, V. Closed Sun. No lunch Tues. or Sat.*

Greek

$$$ ✗ **Cosmos.** In Australia, Greek food so often used to mean no-thrills cafés that churn out platters of commercial dips and regulation souvlaki that sit for hours under heat lamps. That was before Peter Conistis came along. At his cozy East Sydney restaurant, this talented chef has combined his Greek background with his Sydney bistro-cooking experience to produce some highly original, highly delicious food. Conistis's "moussaka" is a sublime combination of sea scallops, eggplant, and taramasalata, his "baklava" is filled with sand crab and spiced custard, and his rabbit and black olive pie "Cephalonian" style must be seen—and tasted—to be believed. ⊠ *185A Bourke St., East Sydney,* ☎ *02/9331–5306. Reservations essential. AE, DC. No lunch.*

Italian

$$$ ✗ **Mario's.** It's not the best Italian food in town, and the wine list leaves a little to be desired. Nevertheless, if you want to capture the very essence of Sydney high life this is the place to be. At lunch, pop stars rub shoulders with tycoons, television personalities, and half of ad-land as they all tuck into bowls of pasta Mario (curly pasta with tomato cream and meat), simple plates of crumbed veal, and tall glasses of Peroni beer and Italian mineral water. At night it all gets a bit *Melrose Place,* but it's still worth the effort. ⊠ *38 Yurong St., Darlinghurst,* ☎ *02/9331–4945. Reservations essential. AE, DC, MC, V. Closed Sun. No lunch Sat.*

Middle Eastern

$–$$ ✕ **Fez.** The chalkboard menu meanders around the Middle East in much
the same way that co-owner Hugh Foster himself did during his mis-
spent youth. Turkish, Moroccan, and Israeli influences are all evident
in Turkish bread with dips, lamb and vegetable couscous, and barbecued tuna in *chermoula* (a spicy Moroccan sauce with garlic, olive oil,
cumin, paprika, cayenne, and coriander). While Fez works well at
night, this is a restaurant designed for sultry summer lunchtimes, with
windows that slide open to the street corner, giant padded cushions,
and aqua-stucco paint. ⊠ *247 Victoria St., Darlinghurst,* ☎ *02/9360–
9581. Reservations not accepted. No credit cards.*

Seafood

$–$$ ✕ **Fishface.** Don't expect sea views here. In fact, the largest nearby vol-
ume of water is swirling in washing machines at the laundromat next
door. Nevertheless, Fishface specializes in some of the freshest, best-value
seafood in town. It's a cozy, street-smart sort of place full of fashionably thin types who don't mind waiting for one of the six tables. Paul
Wrightson's small menu depends on what didn't get away that morning and often includes such rarities as rudderfish ceviche, barbecued warehou fish on bok choy cabbage, and barbecued monkfish with polenta.
⊠ *132 Darlinghurst Rd., Darlinghurst,* ☎ *02/9332–4803. Reservations
not accepted. No credit cards. No lunch Mon.–Wed. or Sat.*

Thai

$–$$ ✕ **Prasit's Northside on Crown.** The golden-haired Prasit Prateeprasen
has new Thai restaurants the way the rest of us have Thai dinners, but
his latest effort in the middle of hot and happening Surry Hills has a
reassuring feeling of permanence. The place is buzzy and loud, with
equally loud gold and purple decor to match. The food is a step up
from the usual suburban Thai as it ranges from Prasit's renowned roast
duck curry to the more unusual smoked crispy-Princess-fish salad,
and steamed baby Atlantic salmon in lemon, chili, and garlic. ⊠ *415
Crown St., Surry Hills,* ☎ *02/9319–4803. Reservations essential. AE,
MC, V. BYOB. No lunch Mon.–Wed. or Sat. Closed Sun.*

Kings Cross

Australian

$$ ✕ **Bayswater Brasserie.** By opening the Brasserie way back in 1982,
★ New Zealand–born Tony Papas was one of the pioneers of the Syd-
ney bistro style and its mod-Med, Cal–Ital–Pac-Rim, East-meets-West
plus-the-kitchen-sink influences. He hasn't skipped a beat since and is
still pulling in the faithful with offerings as diverse as herring salad with
beetroot, Thai-style chicken curry, and corned beef with garlic mash.
If Sting or Elton is in town, this is probably where you'll find him. ⊠
32 Bayswater Rd., Kings Cross, ☎ *02/9357–2177. Reservations not
accepted. AE, MC, V.*

Thai

$$$ ✕ **Darley Street Thai.** Seeing well beyond the hit-and-run fixes of
★ sugar-pot green curries, chef David Thompson has pared down his tech-
nique to an authentic purity of style that is rare even in Thailand. In
such dishes as full-on Chiang Mai buffalo sausage with curry paste,
oyster and banana blossom salad, and a lush curry of pheasant with
kaffir lime leaves, this food takes no prisoners. The decor is as dramatic as the food, with hot-pink walls, bright green cushions, and gold
leaf–adorned walls. ⊠ *28–30 Bayswater Rd., Kings Cross,* ☎ *02/9358–
6530. Reservations essential. AE, DC, MC, V. No lunch Mon.*

Paddington

Italian

$$$ ✕ **Buon Ricordo.** Dinner at Buon Ricordo is a night at the theater, in
★   the back streets of Florence, and at home curled up on the couch all
       rolled into one. Owner and chef Armando Percuoco invests classic
       Neapolitan and Tuscan techniques with personal, inventive touches to
       produce sighs with results like warmed figs with gorgonzola and prosci-
       utto; a much loved truffled egg pasta; and orecchiette with broccoli,
       pancetta, and chili. Everything comes with Italian style that you can
       see, feel, smell, and taste. ⊠ *108 Boundary St., Paddington,* ☎ *02/9360–
       6729. Reservations essential. AE, MC, V. Closed Sun. No dinner
       Mon.– Thurs.*

$$ ✕ **la mensa.** In Italian, la mensa refers to a student cafeteria, but in
      spite of the slide-along trays and the serve-yourself cutlery stands, this
      is like no cafeteria you've ever seen. The place has Milanese chic, with
      its pressed-metal surfaces and designer park bench seating, and the crowd
      looks shipped in from a fashion preview. Food runs from filled baguettes
      and homey soups to Asian-inspired stir fries and piled-high roast lamb
      and potatoes. And if you think you'll still feel like eating later on, you
      can shop for bread, fruit and vegetables, oils, and preserves to take away.
      ⊠ *257 Oxford St., Paddington,* ☎ *02/9332–2963. Reservations not
      accepted. AE, DC, MC, V.*

Potts Point

Asian

$$$ ✕ **Wockpool.** The pony-tailed serial restaurateur wunderkind Neil
       Perry of Rockpool fame does it again with four floors of serious buzz
       and a kitchen that chops and woks its way through the sweet, sour,
       salty tastes of Southeast Asia. If there were a culinary hall of fame, then
       his Szechuan duck confit with mandarin pancakes and spanner crab
       omelet would surely take its place in the modern Asian wing. The Perry
       magic is also available if you're on a budget—at the ground floor noo-
       dle bar such one-pot wonders as Vietnamese pho noodle soup and stir-
       fried hokkien noodles are worth queuing up for. ⊠ *155 Victoria St.,
       Potts Point,* ☎ *02/9368–1771. Reservations essential. No lunch.*

Australian

$$$ ✕ **Morans.** Just a short walk from the bustling nerve center of King's
★   Cross is equally bustling Morans. Stark white walls and contrastingly
       black-clad clientele create a perpetual party time feeling that makes the
       place a regular pit stop for locals and tourists alike. If you know any-
       one in Sydney, this is where you just might find them, huddled over
       chef Matthew Moran's roast duckling with parsnip puree, baked
       salmon with spiced lentils, and Moroccan reef fish hot pot. ⊠ *61–63
       Macleay St., Potts Point,* ☎ *02/9356–2223. Reservations essential. AE,
       DC, MC, V.*

$$$ ✕ **Paramount.** With its wraparound fiberglass decor, Paramount is all
★   curves and swerves and softness and light, emitting a glow that oozes
       out the front window like the aura of a giant glowworm. Chef Chris
       Manfield and partner Margie Harris run a snappy place full of bright,
       good-looking food and bright, good-looking people. Manfield's salt
       and pepper lamb's brains with pepper noodles, crispy-skinned "twice
       cooked" corn-fed chicken, and iced pyramid of mango sorbet and co-
       conut ice cream are all inspirational. ⊠ *73 Macleay St., Potts Point,*
       ☎ *02/9358–1652. Reservations essential. AE, DC, MC, V.*

French

$$$
★
✕ Cicada. Chef Peter Doyle's French-driven take on mod-Oz cooking and sommelier Philippe Morin's encyclopaedic wine list make a heady combination. At night the fashionable and the famished scramble for a table in the main dining room, while at lunch the sun-drenched balcony is a magnet for the darkest sunglasses in town. Doyle's distinction shines through in his prawn ravioli with ginger, soy, and coriander; his boned lamb rack with spiced eggplant; and his apricot and peach schnapps soufflé. ⊠ *29 Challis Ave., Potts Point,* ☎ *02/9358–1255. Reservations essential. AE, DC, MC, V. Closed Sun. No lunch Sat.– Tues.*

Sydney Area Dining

Australian

$$$$
★
✕ Tetsuya's. Regarded by many as Sydney's finest and most passionate chef, Tetsuya Wakuda is one of the living treasures of the Sydney restaurant scene. Yet his restaurant is totally unassuming with its plain, sensible good looks, crisp white tablecloths, gum-leaf green decor, and soft-spoken painting and sculpture. It is as if nothing is allowed to interfere with the food. Wakuda's unique blend of Western technique and Japanese ingredients continually breaks old rules and sets new standards. Such dishes as his wondrous slow-cooked ocean trout, ostrich carpaccio, and blue cheese *bavarois* leave even other chefs gasping. ⊠ *729 Darling St., Rozelle,* ☎ *02/9555–1017. Reservations essential. MC, V. Closed Sun. and Mon. No lunch Tues.*

$$$
✕ Area. Double Bay is the closest Sydney gets to Beverly Hills, so it might not be so surprising that this home away from home for the tanned and Donna Karan–clad locals positively glows with Californian chic. A slide projector beams a Kandinsky onto a blank wall, while well-known faces talk business over designer *pizze* in the back courtyard, and the young and the dangerous cavort around vodka martinis in the front bar. Order whatever's turning 'round on the wood-fired rotisserie and count your lucky stars if it happens to be legs of local Illabo lamb. ⊠ *29 Bay St., Double Bay,* ☎ *02/9363–3656. Reservations essential. AE, DC, MC, V.*

$$$
✕ Bathers' Pavilion. Mick Jagger loved it. George Miller practically lives here. Even Barbara Bush said nice things about her lunch here. This former beachside bathing shed is now one of Sydney's prettiest restaurants. You could be in the South of France, except the view wouldn't be quite as good—nor, necessarily, the food. Genevieve Harris's contemporary Australian cuisine blows kisses from the Mediterranean and sends postcards from the Orient, in the form of crispy-skinned spatchcock (young chicken) with black rice pancake, rare tuna steak with eggplant and tofu, and tea-smoked sea scallops with seaweed noodles. ⊠ *4 The Esplanade, Balmoral,* ☎ *02/9968–1133. AE, DC, MC, V.*

$$$
✕ Catalina Rose Bay. To experience the essential Sydney in a single meal head straight for Catalina. Every night here resembles a glittering charity premiere, as personalities and famous faces toy with their roasted five-spice-marinated quail, hot smoked salmon risotto, and jasmine tea–poached chicken breast. By day, all eyes are on the harbor as boats, sea planes, and the odd pelican drift by. Bright, light, and white, this is a gorgeously modern restaurant bustling with gorgeously modern food. ⊠ *Lyne Park off New South Head Rd., Rose Bay,* ☎ *02/9371– 0555. Reservations essential. Jacket and tie. AE, MC, V.*

$$
✕ Onzain. No, you haven't come to the wrong place. To get to this bright and boppy Bondi bistro, you first have to pass through the portals of the venerable Digger's Club for returned servicemen, with its retro reception desk and whirring poker machines. Once you've ma-

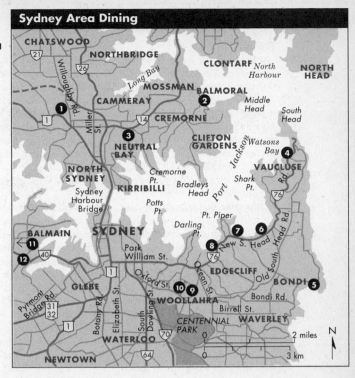

Sydney Area Dining

neuvered your way up the stairs to the second floor, you'll be rewarded by an awesome view of Australia's most famous beach and some of the eater-friendliest food in Sydney. Chef Laif Etournard's mainly French-inspired cooking has presence and precision that far outstrips the very reasonable prices. ⊠ *Bondi Diggers Club, 232 Campbell Parade, Bondi,* ☎ *02/9365–0763. Reservations essential. AE, DC, MC, V. No lunch Mon.–Thurs.*

Cafés

$$$ ✕ **Sean's Panaroma.** It may look like a cross between a half-finished bomb shelter and a neglected beach house, but this beachside café is home to one of Sydney's brightest young chefs. Working in a specially designed "eco kitchen," where water and energy waste are kept to a minimum, Sean Moran cooks with a lean and clean assurrance that is astonishing. Such dishes as beef brisket with mustard and mushroom sauce, barramundi pan fried with black butter and capers, and roast quail salad with lentils have a big-time feel. The weekend breakfasts are legendary. ⊠ *270 Campbell Parade, North Bondi,* ☎ *02/9365–4924. Reservations essential. No credit cards. BYOB. No dinner Sun. or lunch weekdays.*

Chinese

$$ ✕ **Sea Treasure.** It may be a Chinese restaurant in the suburbs, but a suburban Chinese restaurant it most definitely is not. This is home to some of the most authentic Cantonese cooking you'll find this side of Tsim Sha Tsui. The daily dim sum lunch is one of Sydney's finest (save room for *wor tip* potsticker dumplings), while at night, king crab with pepper butter sauce, chili lobster, and steamed parrot fish are all showstoppers. If in doubt, put yourself in the capable hands of Ying Tam, the affable restaurant manager. Do whatever he says and you won't go wrong. A dim sum lunch is served daily. ✉ *46 Willoughby Rd., Crows Nest,* ☎ *02/99906–6388. AE, MC, V.*

French

$$$$ ✕ **Claude's.** For some 20 years this charming little dining room, with
★ Limoges dinner service neatly hanging from the walls, has been a bastion of exquisite French cooking. Today that tradition is admirably carried on by the talented Tim Pak Poy, who has polished his craft until it positively gleams. With such dishes as farm cockerel baked in salt, grilled ribs of salt-meadow hogget (mature sheep fed with sweet prairie grass), and pot-roasted pigeon with parsnip and cabbage, he is one of the few new-wave young chefs who refuses to sacrifice painstaking technique for trendiness. ✉ *10 Oxford St., Woollahra,* ☎ *02/9331–2325. Reservations essential. Jacket and tie. AE, MC, V. Closed Sun. and Mon. No lunch.*

$$ ✕ **Bistro Deux.** Damien Pignolet, who turned French bistro into an art form at his mega popular Bistro Moncur in Woollahra, has brought his failsafe formula to Balmain with equally pleasing results. Although the feeling of Bistro Deux is similar to its eastern suburbs sibling with its smart black-and-white mural; long-aproned waiters; and pâté, steak, and pommes frites-riddled menu, chefs George Sinclair and Simon Fenwick both have a deft touch and a light hand that rises far above the basics. So feel free to be adventurous. ✉ *599 Darling St., Rozelle,* ☎ *02/9555–7788. Reservations not accepted. AE, DC, MC, V. Closed Mon.*

$$ ✕ **Bistro Moncur.** After building Claude's into a gastronomic jewel, Damien Pignolet went around the corner and down-market to open a loud and proud bistro that spills over with happy-go-lucky patrons who don't mind waiting half an hour for a table. Here it is relaxing in itself to watch others enjoying the food. How refreshing—to order salmon and get salmon, to order sausages and get sausages, and have no disappointments. Even the coffee at the end of the meal is the ultimate coffee. And the bill, though not cheap, is appropriate to the bistro nature of the place. ✉ *Woollahra Hotel, 116 Queen St., Woollahra,* ☎ *02/9363–2782. Reservations not accepted. AE, DC, MC, V. Closed Mon.*

Japanese

$ ✕ **Shimbashi Soba.** Yoshi Shibazaki is one of only 50 chefs recognized by the Japanese government as a master of *soba* (buckwheat noodles) and *udon* (thick wheat noodles). So it's hardly surprising that this small, family-run restaurant concentrates on noodles. Indeed, you could make an entire meal of soba here, starting with small, crisp, fried soba chips, then moving to one of 17 different main noodle courses, and finishing with a refreshing dessert, such as a buckwheat mousseline slice, all washed down with distilled spirits and hot liquid derived from boiled soba—uncanny, delicious, and satisfying. ✉ *Shop 1, 24 Young St., Neutral Bay,* ☎ *02/9908–3820. AE, DC, MC, V. Closed Sun.*

Seafood

$$$ ✕ **Pier.** Chefs Greg Doyle and Steve Hodges know their fish so well, it's a wonder they're both not covered in fine little scales. The food here reaches beyond the predictable char-grills and fish-and-chips without having to resort to unnecessary gimmickry. The freshness of the produce itself sings in such dishes as blue-eyed cod on spiced potato galette, carpaccio of Queensland scallops, and grilled reef fish fillet with spinach and laksa butter. The food is so good that you might forget to look at the surrounding harbor views. ✉ *594 New South Head Rd., Rose Bay,* ☎ *02/9327–4187. Reservations essential. AE, DC, MC, V.*

$$ ✕ **Doyle's on the Beach.** After the Harbour Bridge and the Opera House, an alfresco lunch of fish-and-chips at Doyle's ranks as one of Sydney's most popular tourist draws. And why not? Views across the harbor are spectacular, people-watching is first-rate, and—on a sunny day—a chilled glass of Riesling and a dozen oysters is hard to beat. Phone for details of the restaurant's own water taxi for the ulitmate experience. ⊠ *11 Marine Parade, Watsons Bay,* ☎ *02/9337–2007. Reservations essential. DC, MC, V.*

LODGING

Sydney has plenty of big, glamorous, international-style hotels that charge $250-plus per night, but quality bed-and-breakfast accommodation at under $150 per night is scarce. However, even expensive five-star hotels slash rates on weekends, when their high-paying corporate customers return home. Weekend discounts of up to 30% are typical. The most desirable hotel location is undoubtedly the Rocks area, which combines harbor views, proximity to major historic and cultural attactions, and a tranquil atmosphere. The area around Kings Cross has several hotels and guest houses that offer easy access to the city's raunchy nightlife district.

If you arrive in Sydney without a hotel reservation, the best place to start looking is the **Tourism New South Wales information counter** at the international airport, or the **New South Wales Travel Centre** (☞ Visitor Information *in* Sydney A to Z, *below*). Both act as clearinghouses for hotel rooms, and they can usually give you significant savings on published room rates.

CATEGORY	COST*
$$$$	over $265
$$$	$180–$265
$$	$100–$180
$	under $100

All prices are for a standard double room.

The Rocks and Circular Quay

$$$$ ▥ **ANA Hotel.** The largest hotel in Sydney, this towering, modern building occupies a premier position in the Rocks immediately beside Harbour Bridge. Rooms are opulent, decorated with a subdued Asian theme. Although north-facing rooms have exceptional views across the harbor, views on the other sides—Darling Harbour, the city, or the eastern suburbs—are only marginally less impressive. On the 36th floor, the Horizons Bar has the cosmopolitan touches of a plush cocktail bar and a glass wall that provides front-row seats on Sydney's finest harbor view, which is pure magic in the evening, when the setting sun bleeds across the harbor, and the city lights come on. On the same floor, **Unkai** (☞ Dining, *above*) is one of the city's best Japanese restaurants. ⊠ *176 Cumberland St., 2000,* ☎ *02/9250–6000,* ℻ *02/9250–6250. 573 rooms with bath. 3 restaurants, 2 bars, no-smoking rooms, indoor pool, saunas, exercise room, business services. AE, DC, MC, V.*

$$$$ ▥ **Hotel Inter-Continental Sydney.** The heart of this hotel is the Treasury Building, which dates from 1851. By incorporating the honey-color sandstone structure into the hotel's public areas, the architects have instilled a feeling of warmth and tradition in this sleek, sophisticated international hotel. Opened in 1985, it is near the harbor and within easy walking distance of Circular Quay, the Opera House, and the central business district. Australian motifs have been used extensively in the stylish rooms. The best views are from the rooms facing north, which overlook Harbour Bridge, or from the rooms on the eastern side of the hotel, which look without obstruction on the Royal Botanic Gardens and the harbor. Three executive floors offer valet and limousine service to and from the airport, and complimentary breakfast and evening cocktails are served in the private lounges. ☒ *117 Macquarie St., 2000,* ☎ *02/ 9230–0200,* FAX *02/9240–1240. 498 rooms with bath. 4 restaurants, lounge-bar dining area, bar, 2 no-smoking floors, indoor pool, saunas, exercise room, business services. AE, DC, MC, V.*

$$$$ 🏨 **Observatory Hotel.** A 1993 addition to Sydney's five-star ranks, this
★   small, elegant hotel is a popular choice for many VIPs and corporate travelers who prefer a less conspicuous city address. Operated by the same company that runs the *Orient Express* train and the Hotel Cipriani in Venice, the 96-room property is in a part of the Rocks that has not lost its character due to development. Throughout the hotel, Regency furnishings and the extensive use of cedar, accented by Venetian and Asian mementos, create a warm, opulent character that evokes the mood of a gracious Georgian country house. Guest rooms are extremely spacious and decorated in a restrained color scheme with quality fabrics and walnut furnishings; the best are the junior suites, in particular rooms 313 and 310. The health club is the finest of any city hotel, with a 20-m pool where you glide beneath a starry canopy depicting the southern night skies. The four-story hotel's single weakness is its views, which consist on one side of a Rocks streetscape, and on the other a panorama of Darling Harbour and Walsh Bay with a container terminal in the foreground. ☒ *89–113 Kent St., 2000,* ☎ *02/9256– 2222,* FAX *02/9256–2233. 2 restaurants, bar, indoor pool, sauna, steam room, exercise room. AE, DC, MC, V.*

$$$$ 🏨 **Park Hyatt Sydney.** Moored in the shadow of Harbour Bridge on
★   the western side of Circular Quay, this is the city's most expensive hotel, with the finest location of any in Sydney. Its character is luxurious, cosmopolitan, and distinguished by the extra dash of sophistication (such as butler service) that is the hallmark of Park Hyatts. The color scheme is dominated by sandstone and earth tones, and the decor combines reproductions of classical statuary with contemporary bronzes and Australian artwork. Most rooms in the four-story hotel overlook Campbell's Cove, some the Opera House; most have balconies. The white and honey–color marble bathrooms are among the biggest and best in town, and all rooms have a walk-in wardrobe and CD and videocassette players. ☒ *7 Hickson Rd., 2000,* ☎ *02/9241–1234,* FAX *02/ 9256–1555. 158 rooms with bath. 2 restaurants, bar, pool, sauna, spa, exercise room, business services. AE, DC, MC, V.*

$$$$ 🏨 **Regent of Sydney.** Completed in 1983 and extensively renovated since,
★   this glossy, glamorous harborfront hotel skirting Circular Quay and the Rocks is a favorite with corporate clients and well-heeled vacationers. Each floor has an attendant who unpacks guests' luggage, handles laundry, and arranges all tour, entertainment, and restaurant bookings. Rooms are luxuriously equipped, and many are decorated with light wood and a cocoa-and-gray color scheme. About half the rooms have unobstructed views of the Opera House and Harbour Bridge, but cityside lower floor rooms have unexceptional views. If you are comfortable with $500-per-night rooms, junior suites are the best in town. **Kables,** one of the hotel's restaurants, is a Sydney notable (☞ Dining, *above*). ☒ *199 George St., 2000,* ☎ *02/9238–0000,* FAX *02/9251–2851. 594 rooms with bath. 3 restaurants, 2 bars, pool, beauty salon, sauna, exercise room, business services. AE, DC, MC, V.*

$$$$ 🏨 **Ritz-Carlton, Sydney.** Opened in 1990, this is the aristocrat of the
★   city's deluxe elite hotels. It is in a prime position close to the Opera House, Circular Quay, the Royal Botanic Gardens, and the central business district. Decor throughout is a mixture of marble, antiques, warm-

toned fabrics, and soft lighting—an intimate and opulent blend that evokes the European hotel tradition. Service is polished, professional, and friendly. Rooms are large and luxurious, and most have French doors leading to a small balcony. For a view of the Botanic Gardens and the Opera House, request a room on the east side of the hotel. ⊠ *93 Macquarie St., 2000,* ☎ *02/9252–4600,* FAX *02/9252–4286. 106 rooms with bath. Restaurant, dining room, bar, pool, sauna, exercise room. AE, DC, MC, V.*

$$$ ▦ **Harbour Rocks Hotel.** This converted, historic, Rocks wool store and its accompanying cottages offers reasonable value for location, but limited character. Top-floor rooms on the eastern side of the four-story building afford glimpses of Circular Quay and the Opera House. Room 119, a "superior" on a lower floor, is spacious and particularly suitable for a family, but it has only street views. The rooms—many of which are decorated in a muted pink-and-blue color scheme—are neat and well kept. In order to preserve the character of the building, the hotel is air-conditioned only in the public areas, and there are no guest elevators. ⊠ *34–52 Harrington St., 2000,* ☎ *02/9251–8944,* FAX *02/9251–8900. 54 rooms with shower. Restaurant, bar, laundry service. AE, DC, MC, V.*

$$$ ▦ **Stafford Quest Sydney.** Opened in 1989, this sleek hotel in a peaceful corner of the Rocks offers reasonable value and well-equipped rooms. The lower floor consists of two-story terrace units, with a kitchen and lounge on the lower floor and a bedroom and bathroom above. At the rear is a block of spacious studios and apartments with full kitchen facilities. The rooms and the apartments have a clean-cut Scandinavian feel that is both elegant and uncluttered. Rooms on the fourth through sixth floors have views across Circular Quay to the Opera House. ⊠ *75 Harrington St., 2000,* ☎ *02/9251–6711,* FAX *02/9251– 3458. 54 apartments, 7 houses. Pool, sauna, exercise room, laundry facilities. AE, DC, MC, V.*

$$ ▦ **The Russell.** For charm, character, and central location, it would be ★ hard to beat this small, century-old hotel on the edge of the Rocks. No two of its rooms are quite the same, and rates vary considerably depending on room size and facilities. The spacious double rooms at the front have views of Circular Quay, while there are somewhat quieter, standard-size double rooms overlooking Nurses Walk or opening onto an internal courtyard. Five rooms classified as small doubles are the least expensive, but they are tiny and bathroom facilities are shared. The decor is a blend of Australian colonial-style furnishings and Victorian color schemes. In keeping with the Victorian character of the hotel, rooms are not air-conditioned and some have televisions only upon request. The pleasant roof garden has views of the harbor and Circular Quay area. ⊠ *143A George St., 2000,* ☎ *02/9241–3543,* FAX *02/9252–1652. 29 rooms, 3 with bath, 16 with shower. Restaurant. AE, DC, MC, V.*

City Center Area

$$ ▦ **Sydney Travellers Rest Hotel.** This friendly, medium-size hotel—extensively renovated and upgraded in 1995—is extremely good value, although street noise makes it unlikely that you'd get much rest during daylight hours. Guest rooms are comfortable and spacious and include a private en suite, color TV, bar-fridge, and other facilities. Accommodations range from "premier" to "deluxe," and well-priced family rooms sleep up to six. The hotel is conveniently located at the southern edge of the city center, with the shops and restaurants of Chinatown at the doorstep and Darling Harbour within easy walking distance. ⊠ *37 Ultimo Rd., Haymarket 2000,* ☎ *02/9281–5555,* FAX *02/*

9281–2666. *85 rooms with bath. Restaurant, laundry facilities. AE, DC, MC, V.*

Paddington and Woollahra

$$ ⊡ **The Hughenden.** This Victorian mansion has recently been converted to accommodate travelers at its genteel address. Rooms are small but prettily decorated, and each has an en suite bathroom. Rooms 21, 23, 24, and 25 are the largest, although they overlook the moderately busy street below. Set in the prestige suburb of Woollahra, close to many of Sydney's finest antique shops and art dealers, the hotel is relatively near Oxford Street, Centennial Park, and Paddington. The city and the eastern beaches are about 15 minutes by public transport. A full, cooked breakfast is included in the tariff. ⊠ *14 Queen St., Woollahra 2025,* ☎ *02/9363–4863,* ℻ *02/9362–0398. 33 rooms with shower. Restaurant, bar. AE, DC, MC, V.*

$ ⊡ **Sullivans Hotel.** This small, friendly, family-owned and operated hotel is an exceptional value. Just a 15-minute walk from the city in fashionable Paddington, the hotel is close to the shops, cafés, restaurants, movie theaters, and nightlife of Oxford Street. The best rooms are those overlooking the central courtyard, pool, and the terrace houses at the rear. Those that overlook the city are more likely to be affected by traffic noise. Rooms are decorated in a contemporary style, and families can book adjoining rooms for a modest additional charge. Those at the front are subject to considerable traffic noise. ⊠ *21 Oxford St., Paddington 2021,* ☎ *02/9361–0211,* ℻ *02/9360–3735. 62 rooms with shower. Restaurant, pool, bicycles. AE, DC, MC, V.*

Potts Point, Elizabeth Bay, and Woolloomooloo

$$$$ ⊡ **Sebel of Sydney.** Situated close to the center of Sydney's nightlife in Kings Cross, this hotel's clubby atmosphere is its greatest strength, which makes it a favorite with visiting rock stars and senior executives alike. Bedrooms on the west side of the hotel afford glimpses of the city, and those on the east overlook the yacht basin in Rushcutters Bay. Below the seventh floor, however, views are restricted. Rooms are spacious and well equipped, and the solid wood furnishings and heavy fabrics used throughout set a comfortable and conservative yet modern tone. The column-studded rooftop pool area is a charmer. ⊠ *23 Elizabeth Bay Rd., Elizabeth Bay 2011,* ☎ *02/9358–3244 or 008/22–2266,* ℻ *02/9357–1926. 166 rooms with bath. Restaurant, bar, pool, sauna, health club, business services. AE, DC, MC, V.*

$$ ⊡ **Jackson Hotel.** The rooms in this century-old terrace house are neat, trim, and reasonably priced, if small. A Continental breakfast is served in a pleasant conservatory. The hotel is situated on a tree-lined street within a five-minute walk of Kings Cross. ⊠ *94 Victoria St., Potts Point 2011,* ☎ *02/9358–5144,* ℻ *02/9357–4935. 17 rooms, 8 with bath. AE, DC, MC, V.*

$$ ⊡ **Victoria Court Sydney.** Set on a leafy street near Kings Cross, this small, smart hotel is appealing for more than just its reasonable rates. Hand-painted tiles and etched-glass doors recall its Victorian ancestry, yet the rooms come with the modern blessings of en-suite bathrooms and comfortable beds. ⊠ *122 Victoria St., Potts Point 2011,* ☎ *02/9357–3200,* ℻ *02/9357–7606. 22 rooms with shower. AE, DC, MC, V.*

$$ ⊡ **Woolloomooloo Waters Apartment Hotel.** Guest suites in this modern, apartment-style hotel are spacious and attractively priced, although the hotel itself is not in a prime location—it's a 15-minute walk from the city, and the immediate surroundings have little to offer in the way of restaurants, nightlife, or charm. Apartments come in four

styles, from "superior" to two-bedroom suites, and each has a well-equipped kitchen. Rooms are decorated in muted pastels with a gray-fleck carpet, and all but the standard suites have a washer and dryer in the bathroom. ⊠ *88 Dowling St., Woolloomooloo 2011,* ☎ *02/9358–3100,* FAX *02/9356–4839. 94 rooms with bath. Restaurant, bar, indoor pool, sauna, spa. AE, DC, MC, V.*

Sydney Area Lodging

$$ ⊞ **Ravesi's on Bondi Beach.** This small, boutique hotel looks out on Australia's most famous beach and offers a dash of style at a moderate tariff. All rooms are spacious, well kept, and uncluttered, decorated in a stylish sand-and-blue color scheme enhanced by Art Deco touches, in keeping with the building's origins. Oceanfront rooms have the best views, in particular Room 6. For family-size space, the split-level suites, which have their own terrace, are recommended. Least expensive are the basic doubles without air-conditioning. The second-floor restaurant is popular and noisy; request a room on the top floor for peace and privacy. Frequent bus service takes 25 minutes to get to the city. ⊠ *Campbell Parade and Hall St., Bondi Beach 2026* ☎ *02/9365–4422,* FAX *02/9365–1481. 16 rooms, 13 with bath, 3 with shower. Restaurant, bar. AE, DC, MC, V.*

$$ ⊞ **Trickett's.** This converted Victorian mansion—whose character is evident in such features as 13-ft ceilings, a ballroom, and hallway elegantly enhanced with Oriental rugs and porcelain—is set in a quiet neighborhood close to the city center. Guest rooms are vast, although simply furnished, and each has a bathroom, with robes supplied. The city is a 10-minute bus ride away, the immediate vicinity offers a wide choice of dining, and two waterfront parks are within easy walking distance. A Continental breakfast is included in the tariff. ⊠ *270 Glebe Point Rd., Glebe 2037* ☎ *02/9552–1141,* FAX *02/9692–9462. 7 rooms with shower. No credit cards.*

$ ⊞ **Brooklyn Bed and Breakfast.** Tucked away in an inner-west suburb, this late-Victorian guest house offers accommodations with character and exceptional value. Bedrooms are on the upper level, and except for the single room at the rear, all are large and comfortable and equipped to sleep three. The front room with balcony is especially recommended. Breakfasts here include muesli and other cereals, stewed fruits, croissants and toast, orange juice, and tea and coffee. The house is close to Petersham station, a 15-minute train ride from the city. The cafés and restaurants of Norton Street, Sydney's "little Italy," are within a 10-minute walk. Owner Angela Finnigan is convivial and helpful. ⊠ *25 Railway St., Petersham 2049,* ☎ *02/9564–2312. 5 rooms share 2 baths, 2 showers. MC, V.*

NIGHTLIFE AND THE ARTS

The Arts

The most comprehensive listing of upcoming events is in the "Metro" section of the *Sydney Morning Herald* published on Friday; on other days, browse through the entertainment section of the same paper. Tickets for almost all stage presentations can be purchased through **Ticketek** agencies. In the city this agency is in the Grace Bros. department store on the corner of Market and George streets. For credit-card bookings (AE, DC, MC, V) call the **Ticketek Phone Box Office** (☎ 02/9266–4800). Alternatively, you can buy tickets for Opera House performances and the major musical and theatrical shows through **Firstcall** (☎ 02/9320–9000), who also take credit-card bookings (AE, MC, V). The **Halftix Booth** (☎ 0055/26655) sells tickets for each night's performances at half price on a cash-only basis. The booth is in Martin Place near Macquarie Street and opens at noon. For recorded information on **current stage and screen attractions,** you can phone ☎ 02/ 11681.

Ballet, Opera, Classical Music

Sydney Opera House. Despite its name, this famous building is actually a showcase for all the performing arts: It has five theaters, only one of which is devoted to opera. The Opera House is the home of the Australian Ballet and the Sydney Dance Company, as well as the Australian Opera Company. The complex also includes two stages for theater and the 2,700-seat Concert Hall, where the Sydney Symphony Orchestra and the Australian Chamber Orchestra perform regularly. ⊠ *Bennelong Point,* ☎ *02/9250–7777.* ☉ *Box office Mon.–Sat. 9–8:30.*

Dance

Aboriginal Islander Dance Theatre. This troupe presents both traditional and modern interpretations of Aboriginal dances, and performances are notably witty and inventive. The company performs in its headquarters near the Rocks. ⊠ *Bond Store 3, Windmill St., Millers Point,* ☎ *02/9252–0199.*

Sydney Dance Company. Innovative contemporary dance is the specialty of this internationally acclaimed group, who generally perform at the Opera House when they are not touring outside Sydney. ⊠ *Pier 4, Hickson Rd., Walsh Bay,* ☎ *02/9221–4811.*

Theater

Belvoir Street Theatre. The two stages here are often home to innovative and challenging political and social drama. The theater is a 10-minute walk from Central Station. ⊠ *25 Belvoir St., Surry Hills,* ☎ *02/9699–3444.*

Capitol Theatre. The 100-year-old Capitol building, which fell into disrepair during the 1980s, has been gloriously renovated and transformed into the city's most elaborate performance space. The 2,000-seat theater presents musicals and other major theatrical events. ⊠ *13 Campbell St., Haymarket,* ☎ *02/9320–9122.*

Her Majesty's Theatre. This is a showcase for musical hits imported from Broadway and the West End. ⊠ *107 Quay St., Haymarket,* ☎ *02/9212–3411.*

Stables Theatre. Dedicated to experimental works, this small theater occasionally shines with brilliant displays of young, local talent. ⊠ *10 Nimrod St., Kings Cross,* ☎ *02/9361–3817.*

Theatre Royal. This big mid-city house is a regular venue for imported productions. ⊠ *MLC Centre, King St.,* ☎ *02/9320–9111.*

The Wharf Theatre. Located on a redeveloped wharf in the shadow of Harbour Bridge, this is the home of the Sydney Theatre Company, one of the most original and highly regarded companies in Australia. For large-scale productions, the company usually performs in the Opera House. ⊠ *Pier 4, Hickson Rd., Walsh Bay,* ☎ *02/9250–1777.*

Nightlife

"Satan made Sydney," wrote Mark Twain, quoting a citizen of the city, and no more iniquitous thread is there in the city's fabric than that entwining **King's Cross,** Sydney's most notorious nightlife district. Temptations are varied and openly displayed, and although the area is reasonably safe, it is no place for the fainthearted. Strictly speaking, Kings Cross refers to the intersection of Victoria Street and Darlinghurst Road, although the name "the Cross" applies to a much wider area. Essentially, it is a quarter mile stretch of bars, burlesque shows, cafés, video shows, and massage parlors. The area does not come to life much before 10 PM, and the action runs hot for most of the night (especially weekends).

Sydneysiders in search of late-night action are more likely to head for Oxford Street, between Hyde Park and Taylor Square, where the choice ranges from pubs to the hottest discos in town. Oxford Street is also the nighttime focus for Sydney's large gay population.

The entertainment section published daily in the *Sydney Morning Herald* is the most informative guide to current attractions in the city's pubs and clubs. For inside information on the club scene—who's been seen where and what they were wearing—pick up a free copy of *3-D World*, available at just about any Oxford Street café.

Comedy Clubs

Comedy Store. This smartly renovated pub about 5 km (3 mi) from the city is Sydney's leading comedy venue, offering shows and an optional dinner. ⊠ *Crystal St. and Parramatta Rd., Petersham,* ☏ *02/ 9564–3900.* ⊒ *$6–$25, dinner $15.* ☉ *Tues.–Sun.*

Harold Park Hotel. Formerly best known for its "Writers in the Park" literary evenings, this ordinary-looking inner-west hotel, about a mile from the city, now also presents innovative comedy, improvised theater, and other offbeat events. ⊠ *115 Wigram Rd., Glebe,* ☏ *02/ 9552–1791 or 02/9692–0564.* ⊒ *Usually $12.* ☉ *Mon.–Sat. from 8:30 PM.*

Gambling

Sydney Harbour Casino. Gambling is an Australian passion, and although a multitude of clubs have long provided poker machines, Sydney's casino opened only in 1995. In two smartly renovated shipping wharves near Darling Harbour, the casino offers such options as roulette, craps, blackjack, baccarat, and the classic Australian game of two-up. This is a temporary location only, however—the permanent casino is scheduled to open at Darling Harbour in 1998. ⊠ *Wharves 12 and 13, off Jones Bay Rd., Pyrmont Bay,* ☏ *02/9777–9000.* ☉ *Daily 24 hrs.*

Gay Bars

Albury Hotel. The first and still one of the most popular of Sydney's gay pubs, it's especially popular with under-35s. ⊠ *6 Oxford St., Paddington,* ☏ *02/9361–6555.* ☉ *Daily 2 PM–2 AM.*

Club 77. This is the major lesbian club in the city area. ⊠ *77 William St., East Sydney,* ☏ *02/9361–4981.* ⊒ *$5.* ☉ *Fri. and Sat. 8 PM–3 AM.*

Midnight Shift. This mainly gay nightclub is renowned for its dance floor and laser light show. ⊠ *85 Oxford St., Darlinghurst,* ☏ *02/9360–4319.* ⊒ *$10.* ☉ *Tues.–Sun. 8 PM–3 AM.*

Jazz Clubs

The Basement. Close to the waterfront at Circular Quay, this subterranean club is a regular venue for top Australian and overseas jazz, blues, and funk musicians. Dinner is also available. ⊠ *29 Reiby Pl., Circular Quay,* ☏ *02/9251–2797.* ⊒ *$8–$30.* ☉ *Daily usually 7:30 PM–1 AM.*

Harbourside Brasserie. With the lights of Harbour Bridge twinkling in the background, this nightclub is a popular place to dine while listening to music. The entertainment varies from rock to dance acts, but the club is best known as a contemporary jazz venue. A wide range of food, from light snacks to steaks with all the trimmings, is available until midnight. ⊠ *Pier 1, Hickson Rd., Walsh Bay,* ☏ *02/9252–3000.* ⊒ *$5–$20.* ☉ *Tues.–Sun. usually 7 PM–3 AM.*

Strawberry Hills Hotel. This city-center fringe pub is a reliable venue for local jazz talent, and music is on offer every night of the week. The hotel also has bistro dining. ⊠ *453 Elizabeth St., at Devonshire St., Surry Hills,* ☎ *02/9698–2997.* ☞ *Weekdays $5–$7.* ☉ *Daily 11 AM–midnight.*

Nightclubs

Bobby McGees. Set in a spectacular waterfront location at Darling Harbour, this fantasy nightclub includes a restaurant, cocktail lounge, and disco. Competitions and talent shows feature prominently in the action, and the waiters and waitresses are likely to break into a song or a dance routine at any moment. The clientele is mostly between 25 and 35, but the club appeals to anyone in the mood for a party. ⊠ *South Pavilion, Level 2, Harbourside, Darling Harbour,* ☎ *02/9281–3944.* ☞ *Thurs.–Sat. $10, free for diners.* ☉ *Mon.–Sat. noon–2 AM, Sun. 11–9.*

The Cauldron. This disco and its accompanying quality restaurant near Kings Cross is the place where Sydney's well-heeled sophisticates gather. Despite the name, the club is spacious and airy, except on weekends, when it's packed to the rafters. ⊠ *207 Darlinghurst Rd., Darlinghurst,* ☎ *02/9331–1523.* ☞ *Fri. and Sat. after 9 $10–$15.* ☉ *Tues.–Sat. usually 6 PM–3 AM.*

The Craig Brewery. This large and popular pub has three bars and an open-air restaurant during the day, all of which becomes a nightclub after dark—a lively disco from Thursday through Saturday and a band on Sunday afternoon. ⊠ *225 Harbourside, Darling Harbour,* ☎ *02/9281–3922.* ☞ *Thurs.–Sat. $5–$10.* ☉ *Mon.–Wed. 10 AM–midnight, Thurs.–Sat. 10 AM–3 AM, Sun. 10 AM–midnight.*

Juliana's. This dimly lit, sophisticated nightclub is for those who like to dress up and dance. The entertainment usually begins with a floor show, which is followed by a disco. Prices are high and patrons are mostly over 25. ⊠ *Sydney Hilton Hotel, 259 Pitt St.,* ☎ *02/9266–0610.* ☞ *$5–$15.* ☉ *Wed.–Sat. 9 PM–3 AM.*

Kinselas. A nightclub inside a former funeral parlor might sound bizarre, but this one, on a busy corner just off Oxford Street, attracts a large and avant-garde crowd. Stairs from the café-bar on the ground floor lead to a disco-dance club on the floor above, and the place also has pool tables, a cocktail bar, theater shows, and live music. ⊠ *Bourke and Campbell Sts., Taylor Sq.,* ☎ *02/9331–3100.* ☞ *Shows and live music $5–$20, dance club $10.* ☉ *Mon.–Wed. 6 PM–2 AM, Thurs.–Sat. 6 PM–3 AM, Sun. 6 PM–midnight.*

Riva. The best nightclub in any Sydney hotel, this impressive venue has a variety of very different entertainment experiences, from fashion parades to a disco, and live funk or rhythm and blues. The clientele reads like a *Who's Who* of social Sydney. ⊠ *Sheraton on the Park, 138 Castlereagh St.,* ☎ *02/9286–6666.* ☞ *$12.* ☉ *Wed.–Sat. 10 PM–5 AM.*

Sky. One of Sydney's favorite nightspots for the young and fashion-conscious, this dance club spins house music under high-tech lighting. ⊠ *Level 3, Skygarden, 77 Castlereagh St,* ☎ *015/402–138.* ☞ *$10.* ☉ *Fri. and Sat. 9 PM–4 AM.*

Soho Bar. This trendy Kings Cross bar and dance club offers a variety of entertainment. The main downstairs area features live bands and music from DJs, and the upper-level lounge bar is a quieter chill-out spot with pool tables and city views. ⊠ *171 Victoria St., Potts Point,* ☎ *02/9358–6511.* ☞ *Sat. $8.* ☉ *Daily 6 PM–3 AM.*

Pubs with Music

Mercantile Hotel. In the shadow of Harbour Bridge, this hotel is Irish and very proud of it. You can hear fiddles, drums, and pipes rising above the clamor in the bar, and lilting accents lifted in song, seven nights a week. ⊠ *25 George St., the Rocks,* ☎ *02/9247–3570.* ☾ *Mon.–Wed. 10 AM–midnight, Thurs.–Sat. 10 AM–1 AM, Sun. 10 AM–midnight.*

Rose, Shamrock and Thistle. Popularly known as the Three Weeds, this friendly, boisterous pub 5 km (3 mi) from the city center is one of the best places to hear music—generally from Thursday to Saturday—in a traditional Aussie hotel. ⊠ *193 Evans St., Rozelle,* ☎ *02/9555–7755.* ▣ *Music nights $5–$10.* ☾ *Mon.–Wed. 4–midnight, Thurs.–Sat. noon–midnight, Sun. noon–10.*

Theater-Restaurants

The Tilbury Hotel. This unpretentious hotel, a short walk from the city center, is famous for its innovative cabaret, comedy, and theater shows. Despite its small performance area, the Tilbury attracts some of Sydney's most extraordinary talent and has become deservedly famous. It offers dinner-theater–style evenings, but you can also opt for the show without dinner. ⊠ *Forbes and Nicholson Sts., Woolloomooloo,* ☎ *02/ 9358–1295.* ▣ *Show $25, á la carte dinner extra.* ☾ *Dinner Mon.– Sat. at 7; show Mon.–Sat. at 9; Sun. at noon, 2, 6, and 8.*

OUTDOOR ACTIVITIES AND SPORTS

Cricket

For Australians, the pinnacle of excitement is the Ashes, when the team takes the field against their age-old rivals and forebears—the English. It happens every other summer (December–January), and the two nations take turns hosting the event. The season runs from October to March. The Ashes is next scheduled for Australia in '97–'98.

You can take a guided tour (Monday–Saturday) of the famous Sydney Cricket Ground and its interesting museum with **Sportspace Tours** (☎ *02/9380–0383).* ⊠ *Sydney Cricket Ground, Moore Park, Paddington,* ☎ *02/9360–6601.* ☾ *Oct.–Mar.*

Football

Rugby league, known locally as footie, is Sydney's winter addiction. This is a fast, gutsy, physical game—one of the two Aussie rugby variants—that bears some similarities to North American football, although the action is more constant and the ball cannot be passed forward. The season falls between April and September.

Major rugby league games are played at the Sydney Football Stadium, which you can tour daily except Sunday with **Sportspace Tours** (☎ *02/ 9380–0383).* ⊠ *Sydney Football Stadium, Moore Park, Paddington,* ☎ *02/9360–6601.* ☾ *Apr.–Sept.*

Golf

More than 80 golf courses lie within a 40-km (25-mi) radius of the Sydney Harbour Bridge, 35 of them public courses where visitors are welcome. Golf clubs and electric carts are usually available for hire, but caddies are not.

Bondi Golf Club is a nine-hole public course offering challenging play on the cliffs overlooking famous Bondi Beach. ⊠ *5 Military Rd., North Bondi,* ☎ *02/930–1981.* ▣ *Greens fee $11.*

Moore Park Golf Club is a gently undulating course barely a mile from the city center. Visitors must make advance arrangements with the pro shop. ⊠ *Cleveland St. and Anzac Parade, Moore Park,* ☎ *02/9663– 4966.* ▣ *Greens fee weekdays $20, weekends $24.*

A 90-minute drive northwest of Sydney, **Riverside Oaks Golf Club** is a spectacular course in a classic bush setting on the banks of the Hawkes-

bury River. ✉ *O'Brien's Rd., Cattai,* ☎ *02/4560–3299.* ✍ *Greens fee weekdays $60, weekends $75.*

Running

One of the finest paths in the city is the route from the **Opera House to Mrs. Macquarie's Chair,** along the edge of the harbor through the Royal Botanic Gardens. At lunchtime on weekdays, this track is crowded with corporate joggers.

In the eastern suburbs, an official running track runs south along the cliffs from **Bondi Beach to Tamarama**; it is marked by distance indicators and includes a number of exercise stations.

The **Manly** beachfront is good for running. If you've got legs for it, you can run down to Shelly Beach, or pop over the hill to Freshwater Beach and follow it all the way to check out Curl Curl's huge waves.

Sailing and Boating

At **Eastsail,** near Kings Cross, you can hire, for about $95 per half day, a small boat to sail or motor yourself around the harbor. It's also possible to charter a skippered yacht for a full day's excursion for around $1,500. ✉ *D'Albora Marine, New Beach Rd., Rushcutters Bay,* ☎ *02/ 9327–1166.*

The **Northside Sailing School** at Middle Harbour hires out small sailboats like Lasers and Mirrors. Rates start at $20 per hour, and you can also book an instructor to show you the ropes. ✉ *The Spit, Mosman,* ☎ *02/9969–3972.*

Scuba Diving

Pro Dive offers courses and shore- or boat-diving around the harbor and city beaches. Some of the best dive spots are close to the eastern suburbs' beaches of Clovelly and Coogee, where Pro Dive is based. A full day out with an instructor or dive master costs around $100, including lunch and rental equipment. ✉ *27 Alfreda St., Coogee,* ☎ *02/ 9665–6333.*

Surfing

Several international surfing competitions are held on Sydney's beaches, including the Coca-Cola Classic in April, the O'Neill Pro at Bondi Beach in March, and the Mambo Pro in December, also at Bondi Beach. For dates of international and local events, see the entertainment pages of the *Sydney Morning Herald.*

Just what beaches are best for surfing is a matter of personal opinion, but ocean beaches are generally great. You almost can't go wrong south of Bondi, and to the north, stay between Manly and Newport for good waves. In summer, surfing reports are a regular feature of radio news broadcasts—that's Sydney. ☞ Beaches, *above.*

Tennis

Cooper Park Tennis Courts is a complex of eight synthetic grass courts in a park surrounded by bush about 5 km (3 mi) east of the city center. ✉ *Off Suttie Rd., Cooper Park, Double Bay,* ☎ *02/9389–9259.* ✍ *Weekdays 7 AM–dusk $16 per hr, dusk–10 $19; weekends 8 AM–dusk $17 per hr, dusk–10 $20 per hr.*

Parklands Sports Centre has nine courts set in a shady park approximately 2½ km (1½ mi) from the city center. ✉ *Lang Rd. and Anzac Parade, Moore Park,* ☎ *02/9662–7033.* ✍ *Weekdays 8 AM–5 PM $15 per hr, 6–9 PM $17 per hr; weekends 8 AM–6 PM $17 per hr.*

Windsurfing

The bays and inlets of Sydney Harbour afford great windsurfing opportunities, and **Rose Bay Aquatic Hire** rents out windsurfers and gives individual lessons for $35 per hour. Catamarans are also available for hire. ⊠ *1 Vickery Ave., Rose Bay,* ☎ *02/9371–7036.* ⊒ *$15 per hr, high-performance board $20.* ☉ *Oct.–Mar., daily during daylight, weather permitting.*

SHOPPING

Sydney is Australia's shopping capital. Some of the finest souvenirs are in Aboriginal art galleries, opal shops, crafts galleries, or even weekend flea markets. If you're concerned about buying genuine Australian products, look carefully at the labels: Stuffed koalas and kangaroos made in Taiwan have become a standing joke in Australia. In the city, shops are generally open on weekdays between 9 and 5:30. Thursday night, most shops stay open until 9, although some close at 7. On Saturday shopping hours are 9 to 4. Department stores in the city and shops in such tourist areas as the Rocks and Darling Harbour are open Sunday. The most widely accepted credit cards are American Express, MasterCard, and Visa.

Department Stores

David Jones. "Dee Jays," as it's known locally, is the largest department store in the city, with a reputation for excellent service and high-quality goods. Clothing by many of Australia's finest designers is on display here, and the store also markets its own fashion label at reasonable prices. The basement level of the men's store is a food hall with a range of treats from all over the world. ⊠ *Women's store, Elizabeth and Market Sts.; men's store, Castlereagh and Market Sts.,* ☎ *02/9266–5544.* ☉ *Mon.–Wed. and Fri. 9–6, Thurs. 9–9, Sat. 9–5, Sun. 11–5.*
Grace Bros. Located near the Queen Victoria Building, the store has moderately priced merchandise and includes an optician's shop and a Ticketek theater and events booking agency. *George and Market Sts.,* ☎ *02/ 9238–9111.* ☉ *Mon.–Wed. and Fri. 9–6, Thurs. 9–9, Sun. 11–5.*

Duty-Free Shops

Overseas visitors can take advantage of great bargains on electrical goods, cameras, perfume, and liquor at the many duty-free shops scattered throughout the city. In fact, most of the prices in Sydney's duty-free shops are comparable with those in the duty-free bargain centers of Singapore and Hong Kong. Although you can purchase goods at any time with the display of a ticket to leave Australia and a passport, you have to collect them from the shop only 48 hours before you leave. You must carry the goods, which are sealed in plastic carrier bags, on the plane as hand luggage, and you cannot open the goods until you clear immigration formalities at the airport. In a survey of Sydney's duty-free shops published in the *Sydney Morning Herald,* Downtown Duty-Free shops (☞ *below*) offered the best prices, but only by a small margin on most goods. Downtown also operates the duty-free shop at Sydney's international airport, where prices are identical to those at the store's city shops—however, the range of perfumes, liquor, and electrical and electronic items at the airport store is less extensive than in town.

Angus and Coote. Sydney's specialist jeweler offers a wide selection of duty-free watches and gemstones. ⊠ *496 George St., beneath Sydney Hilton Hotel,* ☎ *02/9267–1363.* ☉ *Mon.–Sat. 10–6, Sun. 12:30–6.*
Downtown Duty Free. With two city outlets, Downtown is popular among airline flight crews, who are generally a reliable indicator of the best prices. ⊠ *Strand Arcade, basement level, off Pitt St. Mall,* ☎

02/9233–3166; ⊠ 105 Pitt St., ☎ 02/9221–4444. ⊙ Mon.–Wed. 9–5:30, Thurs. 9–8:30, Sat. 9–5, Sun. 11–4.

Flea Markets

Balmain Market. This Saturday market has a rustic appeal that is a relaxing change from city-center shopping. The 140-odd stalls display some unusual and high-quality bric-a-brac, craftwork, and jewelry. Inside the church hall you can buy a truly international range of snacks, from Indian samosas to Indonesian satays to Australian meat pies. It is set in a leafy churchyard less than 5 km (3 mi) from the city. ⊠ *St. Andrew's Church, Darling St., Balmain.* ⊙ *Sat. 8:30–4.*

Paddington Bazaar. Popularly known as Paddington Market, the stalls crammed with essential oils and tribal jewelry give this busy churchyard bazaar a New Age feel, although it's also a great place to shop for children's clothing and socks at bargain prices. The market is also a major outlet for a number of avant-garde but unknown dress designers, whose clothing is still affordable. Even if you are not interested in shopping, the market is a lively, entertaining environment that acts as a magnet for buskers and some of the flamboyant characters of the area. While you're in the neighborhood, check out **Oxford Street's** offbeat clothing and curio shops. ⊠ *St. John's Church, Oxford St., Paddington.* ⊙ *Sat. 10–4.*

The Rocks Market. Weekends, this sprawling covered bazaar transforms the upper end of George Street into a cultural collage of music, food, arts, crafts, and entertainment. ⊠ *Upper George St. near Argyle St., the Rocks.* ⊙ *Weekends 10–5.*

Shopping Centers and Arcades

Harbourside. The shopping area of the Darling Harbour complex contains more than 200 clothing, jewelry, and souvenir shops. However, its attraction as a shopping area is due not so much to the shops themselves as to its striking architecture and spectacular waterside location. The shopping center is open daily and has many cafés, restaurants, and bars that overlook the harbor. ⊠ *Darling Harbour.*

Pitt Street Mall. The pedestrian plaza in the heart of Sydney's shopping area includes the Mid-City Centre, Centrepoint Arcade, Imperial Arcade, Skygarden, and the charming and historic Strand Arcade—five multilevel shopping plazas crammed with more than 450 shops, most of which sell clothing. ⊠ *Between King and Market Sts.*

Queen Victoria Building. A sprawling example of Victorian architecture near Town Hall in the middle of the city, the QVB contains more than 200 boutiques, cafés, and antiques shops. Even if you have no intention of shopping, the meticulously restored 1890s building itself is worth a look. The QVB is open 24 hours a day, although the shops trade at the usual hours. ⊠ *George, York, Market, and Druitt Sts.,* ☎ *02/9264–9209.*

Specialty Stores

ABORIGINAL ART

Aboriginal art includes functional items, such as boomerangs and spears, as well as paintings and ceremonial implements that testify to a rich culture of legends and dreams. Although much of this artwork remains strongly traditional in character, the tools and colors used in Western art have fired the imaginations of many Aboriginal artists. Elsewhere in the country, the two outstanding sources of Aboriginal art are Arnhem Land and the Central Desert Region, which are close to Darwin and Alice Springs, respectively. Although there is no shortage of Aboriginal artwork in either place, much of the best finds its way into the galleries of Sydney and Melbourne.

Aboriginal Art Centres. This chain of variously named shops sells Aboriginal work, from large sculpture and bark paintings to such small collectibles as carved emu eggs. ⊠ *Aboriginal and Tribal Art Centre, 117*

George St., Level 1, the Rocks, ☎ 02/9247–9625; *Dreamtime Gallery*, ⊠ *the Rocks Centre, Playfair St., the Rocks,* ☎ 02/9247–1380; *Aboriginal Art Shop,* ⊠ *Opera House, Upper Concourse,* ☎ 02/9247–4344. ⊙ *Aboriginal and Tribal Art Centre daily 10–5, Dreamtime Gallery daily 9:30–5:30, Aboriginal Art Shop daily 10–6.*

Coo-ee Aboriginal Art. A wide selection of "wearable" Aboriginal artwork includes jewelry and T-shirts painted with abstract designs, at moderate prices. ⊠ *98 Oxford St., Paddington,* ☎ 02/9332–1544. ⊙ *Mon.–Sat. 10–6, Sun. 11–5.*

BOOKS

Ariel Booksellers. This large, bright browser's delight at the lower end of Paddington is the place to go for anything new or avant-garde. It also has the best collection of art books in Sydney. ⊠ *42 Oxford St., Paddington,* ☎ 02/9332–4581. ⊙ *Daily 10 AM–midnight.*

The Travel Bookshop. Stop in here for Sydney's most extensive range of maps, guides, armchair travel books, and histories. ⊠ *6 Bridge St.,* ☎ 02/9241–3554. ⊙ *Weekdays 9–6, Sat. 10–5, Sun. noon–5.*

BUSH APPAREL AND CAMPING AND OUTDOOR GEAR

Paddy Pallin. For serious bush adventurers—or serious fashion pretenders—heading for the Amazon, Annapurna, or wild Australia, Paddy's should be your first stop. You'll find maps, books, and mounds of gear tailored especially for the Australian outdoors. ⊠ *507 Kent St.,* ☎ 02/9264–2685. ⊙ *Mon.–Wed. 9–5:30, Thurs. 9–9, Fri. 9–6, Sat. 9–5, Sun. 10–4.*

R. M. Williams. This is the place to buy your trendy Australian country wear, including an Akubra hat, Drizabone riding coat, plaited kangaroo-skin belt, and moleskin trousers. ⊠ *389 George St.,* ☎ 02/9262–2228. ⊙ *Mon.–Wed. and Fri. 9–5:30, Thurs. 9–9, Sat. 9–4, Sun. 11–4.*

CDS AND TAPES

Folkways. If you're looking for a range of Australian bush, folk, and Aboriginal records, Folkways has an especially impressive selection. ⊠ *282 Oxford St., Paddington,* ☎ 02/9361–3980. ⊙ *Mon. 9–6, Tues.–Wed. and Fri. 9–7, Thurs. 9–9, Sat. 9:30–6:30, Sun. 11–6.*

CRAFTS

Australian Craftworks. Many of the wares here—superb woodwork, ceramics, knitwear, and glassware, as well as small souvenirs made by leading Australian crafts workers—are displayed in the cells of this former police station. ⊠ *127 George St., the Rocks,* ☎ 02/9247–7156. ⊙ *Mon.–Sat. 9–7, Sun. 10–7.*

The Craft Centre Shop. The beautiful creations in glass, wood, ceramic, and metal sold here have been crafted for the connoisseur. ⊠ *88 George St., the Rocks,* ☎ 02/9247–7984. ⊙ *Weekdays 10–5:30, weekends 10–5.*

KNITWEAR

Dorian Scott. A wide range of all-Australian knitwear for men, women, and children includes bright, bold high-fashion garments as well as sweaters and scarves in natural colors. ⊠ *105 George St., the Rocks,* ☎ 02/9247–4090. ⊙ *Mon.–Sat. 9:30–6, Sun. 10–6.*

OPALS

Australia has a virtual monopoly on the world's supply of this fiery gemstone. The least expensive stones are doublets, which consist of a thin shaving of opal mounted on a plastic base. Sometimes the opal is covered by a quartz crown, in which case it becomes a triplet. The most expensive stones are solid opals, which cost anything from a few hundred dollars to a few thousand. Opals are sold at souvenir shops all over the city, but anyone who intends to buy a valuable stone should visit an opal specialist.

Flame Opals. Selling nothing but solid opals, set in either sterling silver or 18-karat gold, the shop has a wide selection of black, white, and Queensland boulder opals, which have a distinctive depth and luster. The sales staff is very helpful. ⊠ *119 George St., the Rocks,* ☏ *02/ 9247–3446.* ☉ *Weekdays 9–7, Sat. 10–5, Sun. 11:30–5.*

Van Brugge House. This duty-free store has the world's largest retail supply of opals. You can watch as artisans cut and polish the stones, or look at a video of the miners at work. ⊠ *37 Pitt St.,* ☏ *02/9251– 2833.* ☉ *Mon.–Sat. 10–7, Sun. 11–7.*

T-SHIRTS AND BEACHWEAR

Done Art and Design. Prominent artist Ken Done catches the sunny side of Sydney with vivid, vibrant colors and bold brush strokes. His shops sell a variety of practical products carrying his distinctive designs, including bed linens, sunglasses, beach towels, beach and resort wear, and T-shirts. ⊠ *123 George St., the Rocks,* ☏ *02/9251–6099.* ☉ *Weekdays 9–7, Sat. 9–6, Sun. 10–6; 141 Harbourside Festival Marketplace,* ☏ *02/9281–3818.* ☉ *Weekdays 9–6, Sat. 10–6, Sun. 10–6.*

SYDNEY A TO Z

Arriving and Departing

By Bus

Bus service is available to all major cities from Sydney. Purchase tickets for long-distance buses from travel agents, by telephone with a credit card, or at bus terminals. **Greyhound Pioneer Australia** (☏ 13–2030) and **McCafferty's** (☏ 02/9212–3433) operate from the Central Station (Eddy Avenue) terminus just south of the City Center. Lockers are available in the terminal.

By Car

Driving in and out of Sydney has become slightly easier thanks to an improved freeway system. With the assistance of a good road map or street directory, you shouldn't have too many problems.

Remember that distances between major Australian cities are large, and two days would be required to comfortably cover the route to or from Melbourne or Brisbane. These may be called "highways," but most major Australian roads are modest by North American or European standards.

The main roads to and from other state capitals are: the **Pacific Highway** (Hwy. 1) north to Brisbane (610 mi), the **Hume Highway** (Hwy. 31) southwest to Canberra (208 mi) and Melbourne (543 mi), and the **Princes Highway** (Hwy. 1) to the NSW south coast and Melbourne (645 mi). Adelaide is 1,425 km (885 mi) away via the Hume and Sturt (Hwy. 20) highways, and Perth is a long and not particularly recommended 4,135-km (2,566-mi) drive via Adelaide.

By Plane

AIRLINES

International airlines serving Sydney from North America, Europe, and major Southeast Asian cities include **Air New Zealand, Ansett Australia, British Airways, Canadian Airlines International** (connecting with Qantas via Honolulu), **Cathay Pacific Airways, Japan Airlines, Qantas Airways, Singapore Airlines,** and **United Airlines.**

Domestic flights into Sydney include those of **Ansett Australia, Qantas Airways,** and **Hazelton Airlines.**

Qantas flights with numbers from QF1 to QF399 depart from the international terminal; QF400 and higher depart from the domestic terminal.

☞ Air Travel *in* the Gold Guide for airline telephone numbers.

AIRPORTS

Kingsford–Smith is Sydney's main airport, 8 km (5 mi) south of the city. Trolleys are available in the baggage area of the international terminal. You can convert your money to Australian currency at the **Thomas Cook** bureaux, in both the arrivals and departures areas, open from about 5 AM to 10 PM or later, depending on flight arrival or departure times.

Tourism New South Wales has two information counters in the international terminal's arrivals hall. One provides free maps and brochures and handles general inquiries, while the other deals with accommodations bookings. Both counters are open daily from approximately 6 AM to 11 PM.

Kingsford–Smith's **domestic and international terminals** are 3 km (2 mi) apart. To get from one terminal to the other, you can take a taxi for about $7, use the Airport Shuttle Bus, or catch the **Airport Express** bus. The latter departs approximately every 10–15 minutes, between about 5 AM and 11 PM and costs $2.50.

BETWEEN SYDNEY AIRPORT AND CENTER CITY

The green-and-yellow **Airport Express** bus provides a fast, comfortable link between the airport terminals and the city and Kings Cross, and for those traveling with fewer than four people, the cost compares favorably with the cost of a taxi. Bus 300 takes two routes—one to Central Station only, and the other to Circular Quay via George Street and the Rocks. The Bus 350 stops at Central Station, Elizabeth Street, Liverpool Street, Oxford Street, and Darlinghurst Road, ending its route with a circuit through Kings Cross, Potts Point, and Elizabeth Bay. All three services depart regularly (from every 10 minutes on weekdays to every 30 minutes on weekends) from the airport, generally from around 5 AM to 11 PM. Refer to timetables outside the airport terminals for full details, or call the State Transit Infoline (☎ 13–1500). ▱ *One-way $5, round-trip $8.*

Taxis are available from the ranks outside the terminal buildings. The fare to city hotels is about $30, about $25 to Kings Cross.

A chauffeured **limousine** to the city hotels costs about $75. Waiting time is charged at the rate of $60 per hour. Operators include **Premier Limousines** (☎ 02/9313–4277) and **Astra Hire Cars** (☎ 02/9693–5300).

By Ship

Cruise ships call frequently at Sydney as part of their South Pacific itineraries. Passenger ships generally berth at the **Sydney Cove Passenger Terminal** at Circular Quay. The terminal is in the shadow of Harbour Bridge, close to many of the city's major attractions as well as to the bus, ferry, and train networks. Otherwise, passenger ships berth at the **Darling Harbour Passenger Terminal,** which is a short walk from the city center. For information on ship arrivals and departures, call the **Maritime Services Board** (☎ 02/9364–2800; after hours, 02/9364–2000).

By Train

The main terminal for long-distance and intercity trains is **Central Station** (✉ Eddy Ave.), about a mile south of the city center. Two daily services (morning and evening) between Sydney and Melbourne are available on the XPT train; the trip takes about 10 hours. Three "Explorer" trains make the four-hour trip to Canberra daily. The

Indian-Pacific leaves Sydney on Monday and Thursday afternoons for Adelaide (26 hours) and Perth (64 hours). The overnight *Brisbane XPT* makes the 15-hour Sydney–Brisbane journey every day. Call **Countrylink** (☎ 13–2232) between 6:30 AM and 10 PM daily for information about fares and timetables.

Tickets for long-distance train travel can be purchased from **Countrylink Travel Centres** at Central Station, Circular Quay (✉ 1 Alfred St.), Wynyard Station (✉ 11–31 York St.), and Town Hall Station (✉ lower level of Queen Victoria Bldg., George and Park Sts.).

Getting Around

Despite its vast size, Sydney's primary attractions are packed into a fairly small area, and such areas as the Rocks, Darling Harbour, and the Opera House are best explored on foot. Getting to and from these places is simple on Sydney's buses, ferries, and trains—except during rush hours. Mostly you will find public transport an efficient, economical way to see the city.

A **Travelpass** applies to public transport and allows you unlimited travel within a designated area for a week or more. The most useful is probably the week-long Blue Travelpass ($17.10), which covers the city and eastern suburbs and inner-harbor ferries (ferries to Manly will cost extra). Travelpasses are available from railway and bus stations and from most news agents on bus routes.

If you're planning on spending three days or less in Sydney and taking the Airport Express bus, the guided Sydney Explorer and Bondi & Bay Explorer buses, and any of the three sightseeing cruises operated by the State Transit Authority, **Sydneypass** ($60 for three days) will save you money. The pass also allows unlimited travel on any public bus or harbor ferry. Five- and seven-day passes are also available. Purchase passes from the **Tourism New South Wales counter** on the ground floor of the international airport terminal, and from the **New South Wales Travel Centre** (✉ 11–31 York St., ☎ 02/13–2077).

For route, timetable, and ticket price information on Sydney's buses, ferries, and trains, call the **State Transit Infoline** (☎ 13–1500) daily 6 AM–10 PM. If you plan to make extensive use of the city's public transport systems, consider buying the **"Sydney Bus, Rail & Ferry Guide,"** available for $2.50 from most news agents and the New South Wales Travel Centre (☞ *above*).

By Bus

On Sydney's well-developed bus system, journeys and as a result fares are measured by sections. The minimum one-section bus fare ($1.20) applies to trips throughout the inner-city area. You would pay the minimum fare, for example, for a ride from Circular Quay to Kings Cross, or from Park Street to Oxford Street in Paddington. Tickets may be purchased from the driver. Discounted fares are available in several forms, including **Travelten** passes (valid for 10 journeys), which start at $8 and are available from bus stations and most news agents.

By Car

Driving a car around Sydney is not particularly recommended. Although the signage and highway system has improved greatly in recent years, many other roads are poorly marked, and harbor inlets and hilly terrain allow for few straight streets. Parking space is limited; furthermore, Sydney drivers are best known for speed and intolerance. If you do decide to take the plunge and drive, a detailed street directory (available from bookshops and news agents) would be a great asset.

By Ferry

No finer introduction to the city is to be found than aboard one of the commuter ferries that ply Sydney Harbour. The hub of the ferry system is **Circular Quay,** and ferries run to almost 30 spots the length and breadth of the harbor between about 6 AM and 11:30 PM. One of the most popular sightseeing trips is aboard the Manly ferry, a 30-minute journey from Circular Quay that provides glimpses of harborside mansions and the sandstone cliffs and bushland along the north shore. On the return journey from Manly, consider taking the JetCat, which skims the waves in an exhilarating 15-minute trip back to the city.

The one-way Manly ferry fare is $3.60, and the JetCat costs $4.80; fares for shorter inner harbor journeys are $2.80 and $1.40 respectively. You can also buy economical ferry-and-entrance-fee passes, available from the Circular Quay ticket office, to such attractions as Taronga Zoo and Sydney Aquarium.

By Limousine

Chauffeur-driven limousines are available for trips around Sydney, and at your request, the driver will give a commentary on the major sights. Limousines can be rented for approximately $80 per hour. Operators include **Premier Limousines** (☎ 02/9313–4277) and **Astra Hire Cars** (☎ 02/9693–5300).

By Monorail

The monorail (☎ 02/9552–2288) is one of the fastest and most relaxing forms of public transport, but its use is limited to travel between the city center, Darling Harbour, and the Chinatown area. The flat-rate fare is $2.50, but $6 all-day passes are better value if you intend to use the monorail to explore. The monorail operates every two–six minutes, generally from 7AM to late evening, but times vary seasonally.

By Taxi

Taxis are a relatively economical way to cover short to medium distances in Sydney. A 3-km (2-mi) trip from Circular Quay to the eastern suburbs costs around $12. Drivers are entitled to charge more than the metered fare if the passenger's baggage exceeds 55 pounds, if the taxi has been booked by telephone, or if the passenger crosses Harbour Bridge, where a toll is levied. Taxis are licensed to carry four passengers. Many drivers accept payment by American Express or Diners Club cards. Taxis can be hailed on the street, hired from a taxi rank, or booked by phone. Taxi ranks can be found outside most bus and railway stations as well as the larger hotels. On the south side of the harbor, the most efficient telephone booking service is provided by **Taxis Combined Services** (☎ 02/9332–8888). North of the bridge, try **Premier Cabs** (☎ 13–1017).

By Train

For journeys in excess of 7 km (4 mi), Sydney's trains are considerably faster than buses. However, the rail network has been designed primarily for rapid transit between outlying suburbs and the city. Apart from the City Circle line, which includes the Circular Quay and Town Hall stations, the spur line to Kings Cross and Bondi Junction, and over Harbour Bridge to Milsons Point, the system does not serve areas of particular interest to visitors. Travelers using trains should remember the following axioms: All trains pass through Central Station; Town Hall is the "shoppers" station; the bus, ferry, and train systems converge at Circular Quay. Trains generally operate from 4:30AM to midnight.

As an example of fare prices, a one-way ticket from Town Hall Station to Bondi Junction costs $1.80. A variety of discounted fares is also available, including **Off-Peak** tickets that apply on weekends and after 9AM on weekdays.

By Water Taxi

A fun, fast, but somewhat expensive way to get around is by water taxi. These operate to and from practically anywhere on Sydney Harbour that has wharf or steps access. Contact **Harbour Taxi Boats** (☎ 02/9555–1155) or **Taxis Afloat** (☎ 02/9955–3222) for details and bookings.

Contacts and Resources

Car Rentals

All major rental companies, as well as a number of smaller operators, are represented in Sydney. Generally, the larger companies charge higher prices but offer unrestricted mileage and a greater number of pickup and drop-off facilities. Expect to pay about $80 per day for a medium-size automatic and about $70 for a compact standard model from a major operator, although some companies vary their rates considerably on a day-to-day basis. Small local operators often restrict travel to within a 50-km (30-mi) radius of the city center. Nevertheless, some real bargains are to be found, and a one-year-old model can cost as little as $40 per day. For rentals of one month or more with unrestricted travel, the rate on a new, medium-size sedan is anything from $50–$70 per day.

Major car-rental operators are **Avis** (☎ 02/9353–9000), **Budget** (☎ 13–2727), **Hertz** (☎ 13–3039), and **Thrifty** (☎ 008/652–008). Smaller companies include **Dollar** (☎ 02/9223–1444) and **Bayswater** (☎ 02/9360–3622).

Consulates

U.S. Consulate General. ⊠ *19–29 Martin Pl., Level 59,* ☎ 02/9373–9200.

British Consulate General. ⊠ *Gateway Building, 1 Macquarie Pl., Level 16,* ☎ 02/9247–7521.

Canadian Consulate General. ⊠ *111 Harrington St., Level 5,* ☎ 02/9364–3000.

New Zealand Consulate General. ⊠ *1 Alfred St., Level 14, Circular Quay,* ☎ 02/9247–1999.

Doctors and Dentists

Doctors and dentists are widely available throughout the city, and there are many medical centers where apppointments are not necessary. You can contact any of the services and establishments listed below or, alternatively, ask for recommendations at your hotel.

Dental Emergency Information Service (☎ 02/9369–7050) can provide you with the name and number of a nearby duty dentist, but this service is available only after 7 PM daily.

Hotel Doctor Service (☎ 02/9962–6000) operates 24 hours and will send a doctor out on request to any Sydney hotel.

Royal North Shore Hospital has an accident and emergency department and is 7 km (4 mi) northwest of city center. ⊠ *Pacific Hwy., St. Leonards,* ☎ 02/9926–7111.

St. Vincent's Public Hospital, 2½ km (1½ mi) east of city center, provides emergency treatment. ⊠ *Victoria and Burton Sts., Darlinghurst,* ☎ *02/9339–1111.*

Emergencies

Dial 000 for **fire, police,** or **ambulance** services. You can also make nonemergency police inquiries through the **Sydney Police Centre** (☎ 02/9281–0000.)

Guided Tours

The following is a sample of the dozens of guided tours that operate in Sydney and the surrounding area. Options include everything from a shopping tour to abseiling (rappelling) in the Blue Mountains (which are covered in Chapter 3, *below*). The Sydney Visitors Information Centre (and the other booking and information centers detailed under Visitor Information below) can provide you with many more suggestions and recommendations.

BOAT TOURS AND CRUISES

A replica of Captain Bligh's HMAV *Bounty* is alive and afloat on Sydney Harbour, and **Bounty Cruises** has various harbor excursions. A lunch cruise departs weekdays and travels east along the harbor. Subject to wind and weather, most of the voyage is made under sail, and, in the best nautical tradition, all on board are encouraged to take a turn with the ropes and the wheel. A commentary is provided, and the cruise focuses as much on square-rigger sailing and the *Bounty*'s history as on the sights of Sydney Harbour. For photographers, the nightly dinner cruise offers spectacular possibilities. Cruises depart from Campbell's Cove, in front of the Park Hyatt Hotel. ☎ 02/9247–1789. ⌨ *Lunch cruise $45, weekend lunch $65, dinner cruise $70.* ☉ *Lunch cruise weekdays at 12:30, dinner cruise daily at 7.*

Captain Cook Cruises is the largest cruise operator on the harbor. Its best introductory trip is the 2½-hour **Coffee Cruise,** which follows the southern shore of the harbor to Watsons Bay, crosses to the north shore to explore Middle Harbour, and returns to Circular Quay. The **Sydney Harbour Explorer** cruise allows passengers to disembark from the cruise boat at the Opera House, Watsons Bay, Taronga Zoo, or Darling Harbour, explore, and catch any following Captain Cook explorer cruise. Four explorer cruises depart daily from Circular Quay at two-hour intervals, beginning at 9:30 AM. Dinner, sunset, and showtime cruises are also available. They all depart from Wharf 6, Circular Quay. ☎ 02/9206–1111. ⌨ *Coffee cruise $32, Explorer cruise $20.* ☉ *Coffee cruise daily at 10 and 2.*

The **State Transit Authority** runs the following three cruises aboard harbor ferries, often at lower costs than those of privately operated cruises. Light refreshments are available on board. All cruises depart from Wharf 4 at the Circular Quay terminal.

The **Morning Harbour–River Cruise** focuses on the early days of the colony during a 2½-hour trip around five of the harbor islands that lie east and west of the city. ☎ 13–1500. ⌨ *$16.* ☉ *Daily at 10 AM.*

The **Afternoon Harbour Cruise** is a leisurely 2½-hour tour that takes in the scenic eastern suburbs and Middle Harbour, home to many of Sydney's wealthiest residents. (For the cruise itinerary, *see* Sydney Harbour in Exploring, *above*.) ☎ 13–1500. ⌨ *$16.* ☉ *Weekdays at 1, weekends at 1:30.*

The 1½-hour **Evening Harbour Lights Cruise** takes you into Darling Harbour for a nighttime view of the city from the west, then passes the Garden Island naval base to view the Opera House and Kings Cross. ☎ 13–1500. ⌨ *$14.* ☉ *Departs Mon.–Sat. at 8.*

EXCURSIONS AND DAY TRIPS

Several coach companies run a wide variety of day trips in and around the Sydney region. There are city tours and excursions to such places as the Blue Mountains, the Hunter Valley wine region, Canberra, wildlife parks, and the 2000 Olympics site at Homebush Bay. The following major operators all have a 24-hour inquiry and reservation service. **AAT King's** (☎ 02/9252–2788), **Australian Pacific Tours** (☎ 13–1304), **Murrays Australia** (☎ 02/9252–3590).

NATIONAL PARKS AND THE BUSH

Morrell Adventure Travel (☎ 02/9388–1200) has mountain biking tours, ranging in duration from half a day to three days, of Sydney's eastern suburbs, the Southern Highlands, and south coast. National park, hiking, abseiling (rappelling), and whitewater rafting trips are also available. Prices start from around $45 for a half-day bike ride.

Sydney Day Tours (☎ 02/9251–6101), although essentially a coach touring company, have some off-the-beaten-path outings. You can spend an afternoon viewing Garigal National Park just north of the city and bushwalking at Palm Beach. An option farther afield is a day of four-wheel driving and hiking in the Blue Mountains area. A half-day trip costs around $70 per person.

Wild Escapes (☎ 02/9482–2881) specializes in ecotour and national park excursions, including trips to the Blue Mountains and Hawkesbury River. You can also visit the northern beaches and Ku-ring-gai Chase National Park to view Aboriginal carvings. Charters are available, but standard prices range from $69 (half-day) to $180 (full-day).

ORIENTATION TOURS

Tickets for either of the following State Transit Authority bus tours cost $20. They are valid for one day and can be purchased on board the buses, or from the New South Wales Travel Centre. ⊠ *11-31 York St.,* ☎ *02/13–2077.*

The only guided bus tour of the inner city is the **Sydney Explorer** bus, with its 35-km (22-mi) circuit of all the major attractions in the city, including the Rocks, Kings Cross, Darling Harbour, Chinatown, and across Harbour Bridge to Milsons Point. Ticket holders can board or leave the bus at any of the 28 stops along the route and catch any following Explorer bus. The bright red buses follow one another every 20 minutes, and the service operates 9–7 daily. If you wish to stay on board, the entire circuit takes around two hours.

The **Bondi & Bay Explorer** bus runs a guided bus tour of the eastern suburbs. The blue bus begins its 35-km (22-mi) journey at Circular Quay and travels through Kings Cross, Double Bay, Vaucluse, and Watsons Bay to the Gap, then returns to the city via Bondi, Bronte, and other beaches; Centennial Park; and Oxford Street. You can leave the bus at any of its 20 stops and catch a following bus, or remain on board for a round-trip of about two hours. Buses follow one another at 30-minute intervals between 9 and 6 daily.

SPECIAL-INTEREST TOURS

Australian Special Interest Tours (☎ 02/9973–1673) provide personalized service on their small-group day tours around the Sydney area. You can take an Aboriginal art and culture tour; play golf; go surfing with an instructor, sailboarding, or birdwatching; or take a sightseeing trip to the Northern Beaches. Prices vary considerably according to the tour, but they start around $40.

Eastcoast Motorcycle Tours (☎ 02/9545–4321) is just one of several companies that offer exciting chauffeur-driven (you ride as a passenger) Harley-Davidson tours to such places as the city's beaches, the Blue Mountains, Royal National Park, Hawkesbury River, and the Hunter Valley wineries. A two-hour tour costs $115 per person, and a full day excursion is around $325.

South Pacific Seaplanes (☎ 02/9544–0077) fly over the region from Rose Bay in the eastern suburbs. Options include Sydney Harbour, the Northern Beaches, the Blue Mountains, and charters for fishing, romantic getaways, or beach picnics. Prices start at $70 per person for a 15-minute flight.

WALKING TOURS

The Rocks Walking Tours offer introductions to the Rocks (the site of Sydney's original settlement) with an emphasis on the buildings and personalities of the convict period. The tour, which lasts for 1½ hours, travels at a gentle pace and involves little climbing. ✉ *106 George St., the Rocks,* ☎ *02/9247–6678.* 🎫 *$10.* ⏲ *Weekdays at 10:30, 12:30, and 2:30; weekends at 11:30 and 2.*

Sydney Guided Tours with Maureen Fry are an excellent introduction to Sydney. More of a stroll than a walk, standard tours cost $12 and cover the colonial buildings along Macquarie Street, a ramble through the historic waterside suburbs of Glebe and Balmain, or Circular Quay and the Rocks area. Theme tours include art galleries, shops, Sydney's fish markets, and a fascinating tour of the Opera Centre, where operas are rehearsed before they move to the Sydney Opera House (☎ 02/9660–7157).

Late-Night Pharmacies

Your best bet for a late-night pharmacy is in the major city hotels, or in the Kings Cross and Oxford Street (Darlinghurst) areas. You can also call the Pharmacy Guild's 24-hour number for advice and assistance (☎ 02/9235–0333).

Travel Agencies

Scarcely a shopping plaza or main street in Sydney lacks a travel agency. Both **American Express Travel Service** (✉ 92 Pitt St., ☎ 02/9239–0666) and **Thomas Cook** (✉ 175 Pitt St., ☎ 02/9231–2877) are in the heart of the city, as well as in a number of suburbs.

Visitor Information

In addition to the services detailed below, there are tourist information booths throughout the city, including Circular Quay, Martin Place, the Pitt Street Mall, and Darling Harbour.

The **Backpacker's Travel Centre** specializes in tours, accommodations, and information for the budget traveler. ✉ *Shop 33, Imperial Arcade, off Pitt St. near Market St.,* ☎ *02/9232–5166.*

The **Sydney Visitors Information Centre,** in the same building as The Rocks Heritage and Information Centre, is the major source of information, brochures, and maps for Sydney and New South Wales. Center staff will assist with inquiries and make all hotel, travel, and tour bookings. ✉ *106 George St.,* ☎ *02/9255–1788,* FAX *02/9241–5010.*

Countrylink, the state rail authority, is another source of brochures and general Sydney and New South Wales travel information. ✉ *11–31 York St.,* ☎ *02/13–2077.*

The **Sydney Information Line** has useful recorded service and entertainment information. ☎ *02/9911–7700.*

The **Tourist Information Service** is a free phone-in facility that provides information on accommodations, tours, and shopping. It also provides other tips on what to see and do in Sydney. ☎ *02/9669–5111.*

3 New South Wales

Although its capital city may be the ultimate urban experience south of Hong Kong, New South Wales plays virtually all of the continent's rural and coastal variations: historic towns, mountain ranges, seductive sands, subtropical rain forest, and a vineyard-strewn river valley. For sport, it provides excellent hiking, scuba diving, fishing, skiing, golf, trail riding, cave exploring, and white-water rafting.

FOR MANY TRAVELERS, SYDNEY *is* New South Wales,
and they look to the other, less-populated states for
the kind of wilderness experiences for which Australia
is famous. Although there is no substitute for Queensland's Great Barrier Reef or the Northern Territory's Kakadu National Park, anyone
with limited time for traveling around Australia would be wise to concentrate on New South Wales. The state contains the World Heritage
areas of Lord Howe Island and the rain forests that back the northern
coast, and gives a taste of most of the natural wonders that Australia
has to offer—from desert Outback to subtropical rain forest to snow-covered mountains—all within easy reach of the country's largest,
most glamorous city.

By Michael
Gebicki

Updated by
Anne
Matthews

New South Wales was named by Captain James Cook during his voyage of discovery in 1770: The area's low, rounded hills reminded him
of southern Wales. It was the first state to be settled by the British, whose
plan to establish a penal colony at Botany Bay in 1788 was scrapped
in favor of a site a short distance to the north—Sydney Cove. Successive waves of convicts helped swell the state's population, but the discovery in 1850 of gold at Bathurst on the western edge of the Great
Dividing Range sparked a population explosion. The state's economic
might was bolstered by gold and was further strengthened by the discovery of huge coal seams in the Hunter Valley. Timber and wool industries also thrived.

With almost 6.2 million people, New South Wales is Australia's most
populous state. Although this is crowded by Australian standards, it's
worth remembering that New South Wales is larger than every U.S.
state except Alaska. The state can be divided into four main regions:
In the east, a coastal plain reaching north to Queensland varies in width
from less than a mile to almost a hundred miles. This plain is bordered
to the west by a chain of low mountains known as the Great Dividing
Range that tops off at about 7,000 ft in the Snowy Mountains in the
state's far south. On the western slopes of this range is a belt of pasture and farmland. Beyond that are the western plains and Outback,
an arid, sparsely populated region that takes up two-thirds of the
state.

Eighty km (50 mi) west of Sydney in the Great Dividing Range are the
Blue Mountains, a domain of tall eucalyptus trees, deep river valleys,
and craggy sandstone outcrops that provide the perfect environment
for hiking and adventure activities. The mountains are also famous for
their charming guest houses and lush, cool-climate gardens. Looking
about 100 km (63 mi) south from Sydney, the Southern Highlands form
a cool upland region that is geographically similar to the Blue Mountains. The difference here is a rather more genteel atmosphere, and the
added attraction of the nearby temperate South Coast beaches. The
wine-growing Hunter Valley region is a little farther afield. Taste its
wine, dine very well, explore historic towns, and relax in the tranquil
countryside.

The North Coast stretches almost 600 km (375 mi) up to the Queensland border, its seaside delights contrasting with the rest of the state's
rural splendor. With its sandy beaches, surf, and warm climate, the area
is a perfect holiday playground. Finally, way out in the Pacific Ocean,
Lord Howe Island is a small wonder, ringed with fringing coral, stacked
with towering, forested peaks and hills that are great for climbing—
all around flapping and swimming with bird and undersea life.

New South Wales

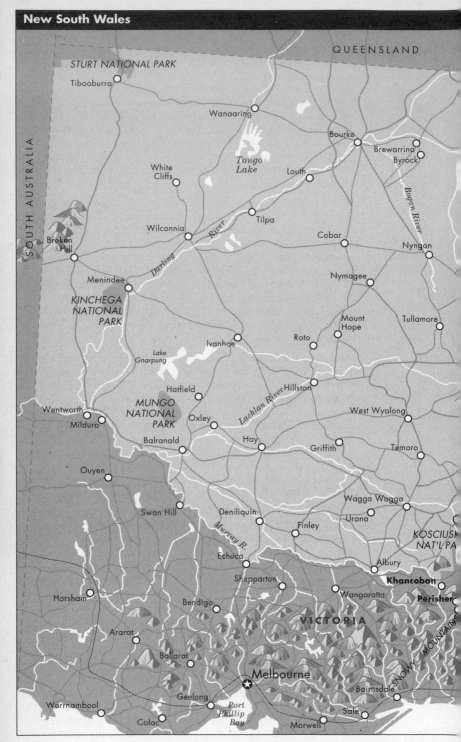

QUEENSLAND

STURT NATIONAL PARK
Tibooburra

Wanaaring

Bourke

Brewarrina
Byrock

SOUTH AUSTRALIA

White
Cliffs

Tongo
Lake

Louth

Bogan River

Wilcannia

River

Tilpa

Cobar

Nyngan

Broken
Hill

Darling

Nymagee

Menindee

KINCHEGA
NATIONAL
PARK

Mount
Hope

Tullamore

Ivanhoe

Roto

Lake
Gnarpung

Hatfield

Hillston

Lachlan River

West Wyalong

Wentworth
Mildura

MUNGO
NATIONAL
PARK

Oxley

Balranald

Hay

Griffith

Temora

Ouyen

Wagga Wagga

Swan Hill

Deniliquin

Urana

KOSCIUS
NAT'L PA

Murray R.

Finley

Echuca

Shepparton

Albury

Khancoban

Horsham

Bendigo

Wangaratta

Perisher

VICTORIA

Ararat

Ballarat

SNOWY MOUNTAINS

Melbourne

Bairnsdale

Warrnambool

Geelong

Port
Phillip
Bay

Sale

Colac

Morwell

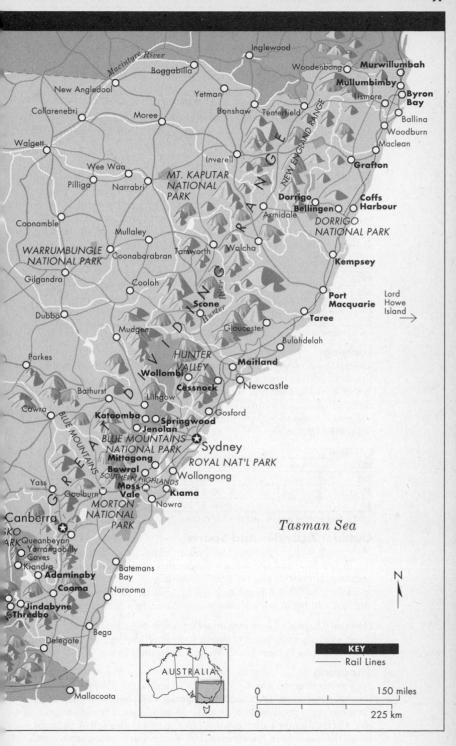

Inglewood

Macintyre River

Boggabilla

Woodenbong

Murwillumbah

New Angledool

Yetman

Mullumbimby

Lismore

Byron Bay

Collarenebri

Moree

Bonshaw

Tenterfield

Ballina

Woodburn

Walgett

Inverell

Maclean

Wee Waa

Grafton

Pilliga

Narrabri

MT. KAPUTAR NATIONAL PARK

NEW ENGLAND RANGE

Dorrigo

Coffs Harbour

Coonamble

Mullaley

Armidale

Bellingen

DORRIGO NATIONAL PARK

WARRUMBUNGLE NATIONAL PARK

Coonabarabran

Tamworth

Walcha

Gilgandra

Coolah

Kempsey

Dubbo

Mudgee

Gloucester

Port Macquarie

Lord Howe Island →

Taree

Bulahdelah

Parkes

HUNTER VALLEY

Maitland

Bathurst

Wollombi

Cessnock

Newcastle

Cowra

Lithgow

Gosford

Katoomba

Springwood

Jenolan

BLUE MOUNTAINS NATIONAL PARK

☆ **Sydney**

Yass

Mittagong

ROYAL NAT'L PARK

Bowral

SOUTHERN HIGHLANDS

Wollongong

Goulburn

Moss Vale

Kiama

MORTON NATIONAL PARK

Nowra

Canberra

Tasman Sea

KO

☆

ARK

Queanbeyan

Yarrangobilly Caves

Batemans Bay

Kiandra

Narooma

Adaminaby

Coома

Jindabyne

Thredbo

Bega

Delegate

BLUE MOUNTAINS

GREAT DIVIDING RANGE

Hunter River

Peter River

AUSTRALIA

Mallacoota

Pleasures and Pastimes

Dining

Dining standards vary dramatically throughout New South Wales—from superb city-standard restaurants to average country-town fare. As popular weekend retreats for well-heeled Sydneysiders, the Blue Mountains and Southern Highlands have a number of fine restaurants and cozy tearooms that are perfect for light lunches or afternoon teas. In the Hunter Valley, there are several excellent restaurants to match the fine wines. The Snowy Mountains region is not gastronomically distinguished, though it is famous for its trout.

In spite of the North Coast's excellent seafood and exotic fruits, fine dining is rare away from such major resort centers as Coffs Harbour and Port Macquarie. The small far north town of Byron Bay stands out, however, for its wide selection of excellent and reasonably priced vegetarian, whole-food, and Asian restaurants. And although located far out in the ocean, tiny Lord Howe Island has several surprisingly stylish restaurants that serve good modern Australian–style cuisine.

CATEGORY	COST*
$$$$	over $50
$$$	$35–$50
$$	$20–$35
$	under $20

*per person, excluding drinks

Lodging

The state's accommodation scene includes everything from run-of-the-mill motels to large, glossy seaside resorts, and historic guest houses in the Blue Mountains and Southern Highlands. Bear in mind that room rates are often much lower weekdays than weekends, particularly in the areas closest to Sydney (the Blue Mountains, Hunter Valley, and Southern Highlands).

CATEGORY	COST*
$$$$	over $250
$$$	$150–$250
$$	$100–$150
$	under $100

*All prices are for a standard double room.

Outdoor Activities and Sports

New South Wales just about has it all, from hiking and serious climbing in the Blue and the Snowy mountains to good walking in the Southern Highlands and on Lord Howe Island, and from diving and snorkeling to fishing, horseback riding, golfing, white-water rafting, and just soaking in the sun on some of Australia's finest beaches.

Note: ☞ Chapter 13 for more information on bicycling, bushwalking, camel trekking, cross-country skiing, four-wheel-driving, horseback riding, and rafting in New South Wales's great outdoors.

Shopping

Locally made crafts are the state-wide standout for shopping. Byron Bay has good work, and the Blue Mountains and Southern Highlands have especially good outlets for crafts and antiques. The obvious purchase in the Hunter Valley is wine, but the area is also full of antiques shops (particularly in Pokolbin and Wollombi), arts-and-crafts shops, and galleries that display the works of local artists and potters.

Exploring New South Wales

As New South Wales covers such a large area, and it is unlikely that you'll have the time to explore far beyond the eastern fringe, we have selected six of the state's most interesting, accessible, and scenic regions.

Great Itineraries

It is wise to decide in advance whether you'd like to cover a lot of ground quickly or choose one or two places to linger awhile. If you have four days or less, stick close to Sydney in the Blue Mountains or the Southern Highlands, or just hop on a plane to Lord Howe Island as the ultimate counterpoint to time in Sydney. In a very busy week you could visit the Blue and Snowy mountains and either the Hunter Valley or Southern Highlands, while two weeks would allow a Blue Mountains–North Coast–Lord Howe circuit or brief stops in most of the six regions.

IF YOU HAVE 4 DAYS

Start with a visit to the **Blue Mountains**—you could cover our round-trip itinerary from Sydney in a fairly hectic day or, preferably, spend a night in **Katoomba** or **Leura** and make it a two-day excursion. Return to Sydney, then head north to the **Hunter Valley.** A two-day/one-night driving visit here would be enough to see the main sights and spend time touring the wineries before traveling back to Sydney on day four. Alternatives would be a quick visit to the Blue Mountains, then a tour of the **Southern Highlands,** or you could fly to **Cooma** from Sydney for an escape to Australia's highest alpine region, the **Snowy Mountains.** Then again, you might want to chuck all of that and fly out to **Lord Howe Island** for beaches, reefs, soaring mountains, and a perfect holiday pace.

IF YOU HAVE 7 DAYS

In this period of time, you could visit the **Blue Mountains** and **Hunter Valley** as described above, then continue to the **North Coast.** In three days of driving you wouldn't get much farther than **Coffs Harbour** (with overnights there and in **Port Macquarie**), and this would be rushing it, but it's possible to fly back to Sydney from Coffs. Of course, if the North Coast appeals, head straight there from the Blue Mountains and give yourself a chance to take in more of it. Another option: Spend three days in the **Southern Highlands,** then drop over to the **Snowy Mountains** for some alpine air, trout fishing, and bushwalking.

IF YOU HAVE 14 DAYS

Divide and conquer: Choose three areas and give yourself four days in each, taking into account travel time between them to round out the fortnight. The following combinations would allow for optimal encounters with the varied best of the state: wine, water, and wide-open spaces with the **Hunter Valley–North Coast–Snowy Mountains;** rocks, rain forests, and reefs with the **Blue Mountains–North Coast–Lord Howe Island;** or a watery triad of the **Southern Highlands–North Coast–Lord Howe.**

When to Tour New South Wales

For many visitors the Australian summer (December to February), which complements the northern winter, has great pull. During these months the north and south coast and Lord Howe Island are in full holiday mode, while such upland areas as the Blue Mountains and Southern Highlands offer a relief from city and coastal heat. This is also the ideal season for bushwalking in the cool Snowy Mountains, but be aware that some of the hotels here close from October to May—the off season for skiing. The best times to visit the Hunter Valley are during the

February-March grape harvest season, and for the September Hunter Food and Wine Festival.

Remember that although the North Coast holiday region is at its peak (and its most crowded) in summer, autumn (March to May) and spring (September to November) are also good times to visit—especially the far north, which is usually quite hot and humid in summer.

On Lord Howe Island, February is the driest (and hottest), and August is the windiest month. Keep in mind that many of the island's hotels and restaurants close for at least part of the June-to-August period. Summer is the best bet, especially for swimming, snorkeling, and diving, but from Christmas through the first half of January the island is booked solid months in advance.

There are some wonderful options if you are in New South Wales in winter (officially June, July, and August). The Snowy Mountains ski season runs from early June to early October. And the "Yulefest" season from June to August is a popular time to visit the Blue Mountains, with blazing log fires and Christmas-style celebration packages.

THE BLUE MOUNTAINS

Sydneysiders have been doubly blessed by nature. Not only do they have a magnificent coastline right at their front door, but a 90-minute drive west puts them in the midst of one of the most spectacular wilderness areas in Australia—Blue Mountains National Park, which is currently being considered for a World Heritage listing. Standing at 3,500-plus ft high, these "mountains" didn't exactly rise; they gradually emerged over the course of eons as forces of wind and water carved them out of a high sandstone plateau, creating superb examples of this continent's rugged beauty. Richly forested hills, crisp mountain air, gardens that blaze with autumn color, vast sandstone chasms where waterfalls shatter on the rocks, and little towns of timber and stone are just part of a broad repertoire of wonders. The mountains' distinctive blue coloring is caused by the evaporation of oil from the dense eucalyptus forests. This disperses light in the blue colors of the spectrum, a phenomenon known as Rayleigh Scattering.

For a quarter of a century after European settlement, these mountains marked the limits of westward expansion. Early attempts to cross them ended at sheer cliff faces or impassable chasms. For convicts, many of whom believed China lay on the far side, the mountains offered a tantalizing possibility of escape. But not until 1813 did explorers finally forge a crossing by hugging the mountain ridges—the route that the Great Western Highway to Bathurst follows today.

When a railway line from Sydney was completed at the end of the 19th century, the mountains suddenly became fashionable, and guest houses and hotels flourished. Wealthy Sydney businesspeople built grand weekend homes here, cultivating cool-climate gardens that are among the area's man-made glories. Mountain walking being as popular an activity then as it is now, people of the time created a splendid network of trails crisscrossing the hills and valleys. Combined with the natural beauty of the area, the history and charm of local villages enhance the appeal of traveling through the Blue Mountains.

It is possible to see much of the area on a day trip from Sydney, but an overnight stop will allow you to begin to get your feet on the ground. Our coverage of the area follows the route of the Great Western Highway from its ascent of the mountains to their western edge before leading you back to Sydney by a more northerly route, the Bells Line of Road.

Numbers in the margin correspond to points of interest on the Blue Mountains map.

Springwood and the Lower Blue Mountains

72 km (45 mi) northwest of Sydney.

Such lower Blue Mountains towns as Glenbrook, Blaxland, and Springwood aren't particularly alluring, but it is worth stopping at the useful **Blue Mountains Information Centre** beside the highway at Glenbrook, 61 km (38 mi) from Sydney. The office is open Monday–Saturday 8:30–5 and Sunday 8:30–4:30. Just outside of the town of Springwood, a sign points to the right, indicating the way to an interesting museum.

❶ Dedicated to the Australian artist and writer, the National Trust–listed **Norman Lindsay Gallery and Museum** is one of the cultural highlights of the Blue Mountains. Lindsay is best known for his paintings, etchings, and drawings, but he also built model boats, sculpted, and wrote poetry and children's books, among which *The Magic Pudding* has become an Australian classic. Some of his most famous paintings were inspired by Greek and Roman mythology and depict voluptuous nudes. Lindsay lived in this house during the latter part of his life (he died in 1969), and it contains a representative selection of his superb work (featured, interestingly enough, in the film *Sirens*). The landscaped gardens, containing several of Lindsay's sculptures, are delightful, and you can also take a short but scenic bushwalk beyond the garden. The gallery is off the highway, between Springwood and Faulconbridge. ⊠ *14 Norman Lindsay Crescent, Faulconbridge,* ☎ *02/ 4751–1067.* ▨ *$6.* ◷ *Wed.–Mon. 10–4.*

Wentworth Falls

26 km (16 mi) west of Springwood.

This attractive township has numerous crafts and antiques shops, a lake, and a popular golf course. Wentworth Falls straddles both sides of the highway, but most points of interest and views of the Jamison Valley and Blue Mountains National Park are to the south side of the road.

❷ Built largely from New Zealand kauri pine, the elegant 1888 Victorian house of **Yester Grange** has been painstakingly restored and filled with period antiques and dozens of 19th-century paintings. There are excellent tearooms here, and the balcony at the front of the house overlooks lush green lawns, which contrast with the rugged backdrop of the Jamison Valley. Wentworth Falls, the best known of the many mountain waterfalls, is only about 440 yards from the house, but the trail is not marked. The house is reached by turning left off the highway just before town. ⊠ *Yester Rd., Wentworth Falls,* ☎ *02/4757–1110.* ▨ *$5.* ◷ *Weekdays 10–4, weekends 10–5.*

★ ❸ From a lookout in the **Falls Reserve,** south of the town of Wentworth Falls, there are magnificent views both out across the Jamison Valley to the Kings Tableland and of the 935-ft-high **Wentworth Falls** themselves. On the far side of the falls, steps cut in the sheer cliff lead to one of the finest walking trails in the mountains, the National Pass. This trail doubles back beneath the falls and follows a narrow cliff ledge to the delightful Valley of the Waters. From this point another trail leads up past a succession of cascades to the Conservation Hut (☞ *below*). The round-trip hike demands plenty of stamina, sturdy shoes, and at

The Blue Mountains

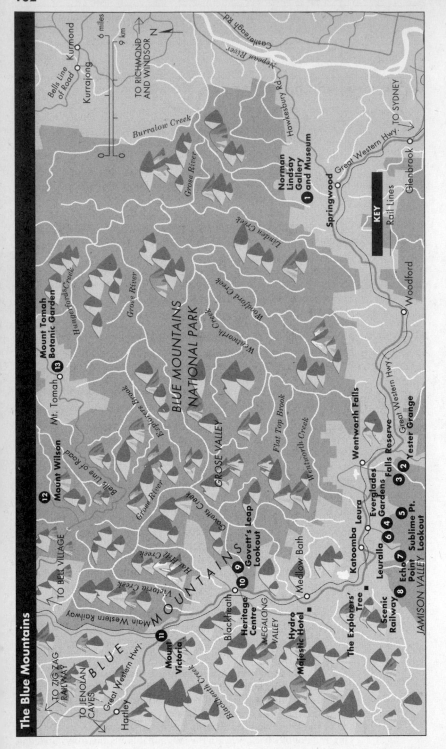

least three hours of your time. ⊠ *Falls Rd., 2 km (1¼ mi) along highway from Yester Grange.*

Dining

$ ✕ **Conservation Hut.** Situated within the Blue Mountains National Park on top of the cliffs overlooking the Jamison Valley, this spacious, nonsmoking, mud-brick bistro serves simple savory fare and stunning cakes to the strains of classical music. An open balcony is a real delight on warm days, and a fire blazes in the cooler months. A hiking trail from the bistro leads down into the Valley of the Waters, one of the splendors of the mountains—but take the walk before, rather than after, a meal. ⊠ *Fletcher St., Wentworth Falls,* ☎ *02/4757–3827. MC, V. BYOB. No dinner Sun.–Thurs.*

Leura

5 km (3 mi) west of Wentworth Falls.

Leura is one of the prettiest of all of the mountain towns—with charming old buildings dotting an entire main street that has been registered by the National Trust. There are plenty of shops in town, as well as some excellent cafés and restaurants.

❹ Leura's delightful **Everglades Gardens** is one of the best public gardens in the Blue Mountains region. This cool-climate arboretum and nature reserve was begun in the 1930s. Plantings include native bushland and exotic flora, a rhododendron garden, an alpine plant area, and formal European-style terraces. Everglades also has an interesting art gallery, and from the gardens the views of the Jamison Valley and the rugged escarpment and cliff are quite magnificent. ⊠ *37 Everglades Ave., Leura,* ☎ *02/4784–1938.* ⊠ *$5.* ☉ *Sept.–Feb., daily 10–5; Mar.–Aug., daily 10–4.*

★ ❺ You'll get another great view of the Jamison Valley and the generally spectacular Blue Mountains scenery from the **Sublime Point Lookout,** just outside of Leura. This less well-known, and therefore far less crowded, vantage point provides a completely different perspective of the famous **Three Sisters** rock formation at nearby Katoomba. ⊠ *Sublime Point Rd., Leura.*

❻ The mansion of **Leuralla** dates from 1911 and once belonged to the family of Dr. H. V. ("Doc") Evatt (1894–1965), the first president of the General Assembly of the United Nations, and later the leader of the Australian Labor Party. The historic house contains a collection of 19th-century Australian art as well as a small museum dedicated to Dr. Evatt. ⊠ *Olympian Parade and Balmoral Rd., Leura,* ☎ *02/4784–1169.* ⊠ *$6.* ☉ *Daily 10–5.*

Dining and Lodging

$$$ ✕ **Silks Brasserie.** Regarded as one of the very best restaurants in the Blue Mountains, this excellent eatery offers Sydney-standard food, wine, and service. Wholesome dishes include such delights as potato and herb gnocchi with burnt butter and sage, kangaroo fillet in a peppered red wine sauce, and Atlantic salmon on mashed potato with a chive cream sauce—as well as a range of tempting desserts and a cheese plate. The simple but elegant interior is enhanced in colder months by a log fire. ⊠ *128 The Mall, Leura,* ☎ *02/4784–2534. AE, MC, V.*

$$ ✕ **Cafe Bon Ton.** Situated at the lower end of Leura Mall, this bright, ★ elegant café is a good choice either for breakfast, coffee and cake, or a three-course dinner. The food, like the decor, is essentially Italian, with well and simply prepared meals—various pasta and pizza dishes, a selection of crisp, well-stuffed baguettes, and a good choice of meat, fish, and vegetarian fare. In winter a log fire burns in the grate, and

on warm summer days the shady garden at the front is ideal for lunch. The café serves some of the best coffee in the mountains. ⊠ *192 The Mall, Leura,* ☎ *02/4782–4377. AE, MC, V. BYOB. No dinner Tues.*

$$$ ☂ **Fairmont Resort.** Rising dramatically from the edge of the cliffs, Fairmont is the largest hotel in the mountains, and although it provides a wide range of facilities, its scale might be overwhelming for some. Rooms are luxuriously equipped and decorated with honey-color wood furnishings. The valley rooms have better views. Guests have access to the adjoining Leura Golf Course, the finest in the mountains. ⊠ *1 Sublime Point Rd., Leura, 2780,* ☎ *02/4782–5222,* FAX *02/4784–1685. 210 rooms with bath. 2 restaurants, bar, indoor and outdoor pools, sauna, spa, tennis courts, exercise room, squash. AE, DC, MC, V.*

$$ ☂ **Little Company Retreat.** Built at the turn of the century, this sprawling, single-story guest house has a solid, imposing character befitting its former status as a convent. The house is surrounded by a tall hedge and flower-filled gardens and separated from tennis courts on the property by an avenue of conifers. Bedrooms are modest in size, but each has its own en suite bathroom, and the living rooms are invitingly equipped with comfortable chairs, magazines, and board games. A full-size croquet lawn is at the back of the house, and the town is within walking distance. The guest house operates seven local four-bedroom houses that are ideal for families or small groups. Bookings are heavy on weekends. Rates include breakfast and dinner. ⊠ *2 Eastview Ave., Leura 2781,* ☎ *02/4782–4023,* FAX *02/4782–5361. 13 rooms with bath. Pool, tennis courts, putting green. AE, DC, MC, V.*

En Route   From Leura, there is a dazzling, 19-km (12-mi) route named the **Cliff Drive** that leads to Echo Point at Katoomba and beyond. The road skirts the rim of the Jamison Valley, often only yards from the cliff edge, and provides truly spectacular Blue Mountains views. Begin at the southern end of Leura Mall, the town's main street.

Katoomba

2 km (1¼ mi) west of Leura.

Easily the largest town in the Blue Mountains, Katoomba developed in the early 1840s as a coal-mining settlement, turning its attention to tourism later in the 19th century. The town center has its share of shops, cafés, and places to stay, but the breathtaking local scenery is the real reason to come.

❼   The best views around Katoomba are from **Echo Point,** which overlooks the densely forested Jamison Valley and the soaring sandstone pillars known as the **Three Sisters.** The name comes from an Aboriginal legend, which relates how three sisters were turned to stone by their witch-doctor father to save them from the clutches of a mythical monster. This formation also illustrates the geological character of the Blue Mountains. The whole area was once a seabed that lifted over a long period and subsequently eroded, leaving behind such formations of sedimentary rock as the Three Sisters. From Echo Point you can clearly see the horizontal sandstone bedding in the rock. The formation is floodlit at night. ⊠ *Follow Katoomba St. south out of Katoomba to Echo Point Rd. and point.*

Echo Point is also the location for a **Blue Mountains Visitor Information Centre,** which can provide useful information on bushwalks from Katoomba. Several walks, varying in duration from ½ hour (an easy stroll to the Three Sisters) to a far more challenging four hours, start from the Echo Point area. ⊠ *Echo Point Rd., Katoomba,* ☎ *02/4739–6266.* ⊙ *Daily 9–5.*

❽ Far below Echo Point, the **Scenic Railway** was built into the cliff face during the 1880s to haul coal and shale from the mines in the valley. When the supply of shale was exhausted, the railway was abandoned until the 1930s, when the Katoomba Colliery began using the carts to give tourists the ride of their life on the steep incline. Today the carriages are far more comfortable, but the ride down to the foot of the cliffs is no less exciting. Just a few steps from the railway is the **Scenic Skyway,** a cable car that carries passengers for a short ride across the gorge, with a 1,000-ft drop below. If you're going to pick one, the railway is more spectacular. ⊠ *Cliff Dr. and Violet St., Katoomba,* ☎ *02/4782–2699.* 🎫 *Return fare for railway and skyway $4.50.* ⊙ *Daily 9–5.*

A very different Katoomba attraction is **The Edge Maxvision Cinema.** This giant cinema screen is about the height of a six-story building, and runs a variety of films. The most worthwhile is *The Edge,* an exciting 40-minute movie on the region's valleys, gorges, cliffs, waterfalls, and other dramatic scenery. The large complex includes a café and gift shop, and at night the cinema screens regular feature films. ⊠ *225–237 Great Western Hwy., Katoomba,* ☎ *02/4782–8928.* 🎫 *$11.50.* ⊙ *Daily;* The Edge *begins daily at 10.*

Dining and Lodging

$ ✕ **Paragon Cafe.** In the center of Katoomba, this 1916 restaurant offers a glimpse into the past. With its wood paneling, chandeliers, gleaming cappuccino machine, and bas-relief figures above the booths, the Paragon recalls the Blue Mountains in their heyday. The menu has all-day fare, including homemade soups, grills, pasta dishes, famous Paragon meat pies, seafood, and wonderful cakes and waffles. Afternoon tea—hot scones with whipped cream, jam, and coffee or tea—is delicious. But be warned that the place closes at 5 sharp. ⊠ *65 Katoomba St., Katoomba,* ☎ *02/4782–2928. AE, MC, V. Closed Mon. No dinner.*

$$$$ ✕🏨 **Lilianfels Blue Mountains.** Incorporating a historic country house in its design, this elegant hotel combines the manners and patrician airs of a traditional country hotel with five-star accommodations. Located in a separate wing from the original house, guest rooms are spacious and plushly decorated in warm fabrics and colors. To fully savor the magnificent panoramas, reserve one of the slightly more expensive rooms with a valley view. The dining room, Darleys, serves exceptional modern Australian food to both guests and nonguests. Game dishes often appear on the winter menu; reservations are essential. The hotel is a member of the Small Luxury Hotels of the World group. ⊠ *Lilianfels Ave., Echo Point, Katoomba, 2780,* ☎ *02/4780–1200,* FAX *02/4780–1300. 81 rooms with bath, 5 suites. 2 restaurants, bar, indoor pool, sauna, steam room, spa, tennis courts, gymnasium, mountain bikes. AE, DC, MC, V.*

$$$ 🏨 **Echoes.** Perched precipitously above the Jamison Valley, this striking guest house offers traditional Blue Mountains warmth and comfort and an excellent restaurant. Wentworth, the room on the corner of the top floor, has particularly good views on two sides. The hotel is close to the Three Sisters and the network of trails that lead down into the Jamison Valley. Smoking is not permitted. Rates include breakfast. ⊠ *3 Lilianfels Ave., Katoomba, 2780,* ☎ *02/4782–1966,* FAX *02/4782–3707. 12 rooms with bath. Bar, sauna. AE, MC, V.*

$$ ⊞ **Mountain Heritage Country House Retreat.** Set on a ridge close to the center of Katoomba and overlooking the Jamison Valley, this elegant country house offers some of the best views in the mountains. The atmosphere is both warm and welcoming, and the house is steeped in history. Furnished throughout in a warm, country-house style that makes extensive use of Australian motifs, the hotel offers accommodation with a variety of room styles, which are all of a high standard but reasonably priced. The two very private Valley View suites come with their own verandas, kitchens, lounge rooms with fireplaces, and whirlpool baths. Comfortable lounges and blazing log fires provide the perfect environment in which to enjoy some of the Jamison Views Restaurant's fine food. ⊠ *Apex and Lovel Sts., Katoomba, 2780,* ☎ *02/4782– 2155,* 𝔽𝔸𝕏 *02/4782–5323. 36 rooms with bath, 4 suites. Bar, pool, games room, volleyball, gym, mountain bikes. AE, DC, MC, V.*

En Route   West of Katoomba, the Cliff Drive ends and returns you to the Great Western Highway via Narrow Neck Road. From there, the highway winds along the ridge top, passing a couple of points of interest between Katoomba and the next main town of Blackheath.

About a half mile beyond where Narrow Neck Road joins the highway, the **Explorers' Tree** on the left marks an important historic site. George Blaxland, William Charles Wentworth, and William Lawson, the men who finally pioneered the route across these mountains in 1813, carved their initials into the trunk of this tree, which in time has grown over the traces of their passing.

At the small village of Medlow Bath, 4 km (2½ mi) beyond the Explorers' Tree, it is impossible to miss the enormous **Hydro Majestic Hotel** on the left-hand side of the highway. Originally a European-style spa, this sprawling Art Deco building was a fashionable hotel in the 1930s, especially popular with honeymoon couples. Since that time the "Hydro" has fallen on hard times, but, in spite of some not entirely successful restoration work, it has great character, and the view from the lounge room across the Megalong Valley is outstanding. The ballroom to the left of the main entrance is worth a look, too. During World War II the U.S. Army used the hotel as a hospital for soldiers wounded in the Pacific. You can call in here for breakfast, lunch, or afternoon tea, and seekers of atmosphere will be drawn to the hotel's bar, which takes on a slightly Hitchcockian mood after dark—arrive at dusk for a drink on the terrace while the sun is still lighting the valley below. ⊠ *Great Western Hwy., Medlow Bath,* ☎ *02/4788–1002.*

Blackheath

12 km (7½ mi) north of Katoomba.

The site of Blackheath, at the summit of the mountains (3,495 ft), was visited and named by Governor Macquarie in 1815 after a rough road had been constructed through here to the town of Bathurst, beyond the mountains. As with most of the Blue Mountains towns, the main attractions are the magnificent views—this time over terrain to the east of the highway that includes the Grose Valley and a different section of the Blue Mountains National Park than you've been seeing. Blackheath also has delightful gardens, antiques shops, and the interesting National Parks and Wildlife Heritage Centre.

❾ Blackheath's most famous view is from the **Govett's Leap Lookout,** with its striking panorama of the Grose Valley and Bridal Veil Falls to the right. Govett was a surveyor who mapped this region extensively in the 1830s. He estimated the perpendicular drop near the falls to be 528 ft. ⊠ *End of Govett's Leap Rd., Blackheath.*

⑩ Located close to Govett's Leap Lookout, the **Heritage Centre,** operated by the National Parks and Wildlife Service, offers useful information on historic sites, camping, guided walks, and hiking in Blue Mountains National Park. The center also features videos, interactive educational displays, exhibitions, and a nature-oriented gift and souvenir shop. ⊠ *Govett's Leap Rd., Blackheath,* ☎ *02/4787–8877.* ☉ *Daily 9–4:30.*

In a deep mountain valley off the Great Western Highway 15 km (9 mi) from Blackheath, the **Megalong Valley Heritage Farm** is a working sheep and cattle property and demonstration farm, with displays of farm animals and pioneer farm skills. Events begin at 10:30 AM and include a cattle show, a Clydesdale horse show, tractor rides, and sheep-shearing—most of which should appeal to children. There is also a baby animal nursery here, and both adults and children can go horseback riding around the farm's 2,000 acres. If you'd like to go farther afield, you can join an overnight muster ride. ⊠ *Megalong Valley Rd., Blackheath,* ☎ *02/4787–9165.* 🔲 *Weekdays during school terms $3, weekends $9.50.* ☉ *Daily 10:30–4.*

Dining and Lodging

$$$$ ✕🏠 **Cleopatra.** Tucked away in the leafy mountain village of Black-
★ heath, this charming farmhouse is decorated with baskets of wildflowers, botanical prints, and antiques. The finest accommodations are in the Apartment, which has its own private sitting room and a bedroom upstairs. Below the house, an informal garden is planted with Japanese maples, arbutus trees, rhododendrons, and a wisteria-covered pergola. Cleopatra Restaurant serves country French food, with chef Dany Chouet conjuring up the rich country cooking of her native Dordogne. The fixed-price menu is limited to a choice of three to five dishes for each course. A typical summer menu might include a starter of sweetbreads with puff pastry and wild mushrooms, and a main course of roasted loin of lamb. Keep in mind that you must bring your own wine to the restaurant (Barmans shop in Leura can send bottles to Cleopatra for you; ☎ 02/4784–1981). The enormous popularity of both the restaurant and the guest house makes it advisable to book well in advance. Meals are included in room rates. ⊠ *118 Cleopatra St., Blackheath, 2785,* ☎ *02/4787–8456,* 🕾 *02/4787–6092. 5 rooms, 3 with bath. Restaurant, tennis court. MC, V.*

$$ 🏠 **Jemby Rinjah Lodge.** Set in bushland on the edge of the Blue Moun-
★ tains National Park, this environmentally sensitive lodge is the perfect retreat for escapists in search of a wilderness experience. Each of the self-contained timber cabins consists of a large lounge–dining room, kitchen, and two bedrooms that sleep up to six. Furnishings are of natural wood, and a large picture window in each cabin opens onto a small deck. Couples should reserve one of the one-bedroom "tree houses," cottages on stilts that put guests on the same level as the kookaburras that abound in the trees. Several less-expensive lodges without kitchens have recently been added. The main building's comfortable lounge area has an open circular fireplace, and Isopogons Restaurant serves wholesome healthy meals. The award-winning lodge is close to walking trails leading into the Grose Valley, and activities include free guided walks on the Grand Canyon trail, feeding wild parrots, and spotlighting possums at night. ⊠ *336 Evans Lookout Rd., Blackheath, 2785,* ☎ *02/4787–7622,* 🕾 *02/4787–6230. 9 cabins with bath, 15 lodge rooms share 6 baths. MC, V.*

Horseback Riding

At the foot of the Blue Mountains, 10 km (6 mi) from Blackheath, **Werriberri Trail Rides** conduct reasonably priced half- to three-hour horseback rides through the beautiful Megalong Valley. Everyone is catered to—with quiet horses for beginners, ponies on leads for young children, and excellent mounts for experienced riders. All rides are guided, and hard hats are supplied. ⊠ *Megalong Rd., Megalong Valley,* ☎ *02/ 4787–9171.*

Mount Victoria

⑪ *7 km (4 mi) northwest of Blackheath.*

Little has changed over the past few decades in the settlement of Mount Victoria, which is classified as an Urban Conservation Area. A walk around the village reveals charming houses, a few antiques shops, the atmospheric Victoria and Albert Hotel, and a small local history museum. Mount Victoria is at the far side of the mountains at the western limit of this region, and there are a couple of off-the-beaten-path attractions that are best reached from this village.

OFF THE   The wondrous world of the **Jenolan Caves** is a labyrinth of underground
BEATEN PATH   rivers and vast limestone chasms filled with stalactites, stalagmites, columns, and shawls carved out on multiple levels. The caves were created by underground rivers, and because of that they are mostly interconnected. There may be as many as 300 of them in the Jenolan area.

The first European to set eyes on the caves was James McKeown, an escaped convict who preyed on the stagecoaches traveling across the mountains and who used them as a hideout in the 1830s. A search party eventually followed his horse's tracks, and the capture of McKeown made his secret caves suddenly famous. Tours were organized soon thereafter, but the most spectacular caves weren't found for another twenty-odd years.

Three caves near the surface can be explored without a guide, but to see the very best formations, you need to take a guided tour. Nine of these caves are open to the public: they are graded according to difficulty, and even the easiest entails a total of 300 stairs interspersed throughout the cave. The Lucas Cave tour in particular is a good challenge. Tours depart every 15 minutes on weekends, approximately every 30 minutes on weekdays, and last from one to two hours. Cave lovers may want to inquire about the caves in Abercrombie and Wombeyan (☞ Southern Highlands and the South Coast, *below*) to the west and south of Jenolan.

To reach the caves, follow the Great Western Highway north out of Mount Victoria as it winds through rural hill country, then turn after Hartley southwest toward Hampton. Jenolan Caves is 59 km (37 mi) from Mount Victoria. ⊠ *Jenolan,* ☎ *02/6359-3311.* 🎟 *Lucas, Chifley, and Imperial caves $12; Orient, Temple of Baal, and River caves $14; Cerberus, Julibee, and Ribbon caves $16.* ☼ *Daily; tour begins weekdays 10, weekends 9:30, with last tour leaving at 5.*

★ The **Zig Zag Railway** will delight train buffs. Dramatic views and the huff-and-puff of a vintage steam engine make this cliff-hugging, 16-km (10-mi) round-trip ride a thriller. Built in 1869, this was the main line across the Blue Mountains until 1910. The track is laid on the cliffs in a giant "Z," and the train climbs the steep incline by chugging backward and then forward along alternating sections of the track—hence its name. The steam engine operates on weekends and public holidays, and during weekdays in school holiday times. A vintage self-propelled diesel-powered rail car is used at other times. The railway is 19 km (12 mi) northwest of Mount Victoria. Take the Darling Causeway north out of town, then turn northwest on Bells Line of Road in Bell. ⊠ *Clarence, Bells Line of Rd.,* ☎ *02/6353–1795.* ☜ *$11.* ☉ *Daily; trains depart weekdays at 11, 1, and 3 and weekends at 10:30, 12:15, 2, and 3:30.*

Dining

$ ✕ **Bay Tree Tea Shop.** This cozy café is delightful at any time, but particularly welcoming on chilly afternoons when a fire is burning in the grate and scones are served piping hot from the kitchen. The menu includes hearty soups, salads, ploughman's lunch, a fantastic "meat pie hotpot," lasagna, and quiches. Almost everything is made on the premises—bread, cakes, and even jam that comes with cream tea. ⊠ *26 Station St., Mount Victoria,* ☎ *02/4787–1275. No credit cards. Closed Tues. and Wed. No dinner.*

En Route   The **Bells Line of Road** (reached by taking the Darling Causeway north out of Mount Victoria and turning right at the village of Bell) provides an interesting alternative route back to Sydney. Named after explorer Archibald Bell, who discovered a path over the mountains from Richmond, and built by convicts in 1841, this scenic road runs from Lithgow to Richmond and winds its way along the mountain ridges. Along the way you will pass gardens, apple orchards, and small villages with roadside fruit stalls.

Mount Wilson

⑫   *30 km (17 mi) northeast of Mount Victoria.*

This enchanting village lies off the Bells Line of Road at the end of Five Mile Road, which snakes along a sandstone ridge. Built more than a century ago by wealthy families seeking a retreat from the summer heat of Sydney, the settlement was planted with avenues of elms, beeches, and plane trees that give it a distinctly European air. The town is at its prettiest during spring and autumn, and many of the gardens are open for inspection. The cool, shady woodland of the **Cathedral of Ferns** is perhaps the most attractive of the lovely gardens in Mount Wilson.

Mount Tomah

25 km (15½ mi) southeast of Mount Wilson.

Located on the Bells Line of Road, the area around the village of Mount Tomah has strong appeal for garden lovers.

⑬   The cool climate branch of Sydney's Royal Botanic Gardens, the **Mount Tomah Botanic Garden** provides a spectacular setting for many native and imported plant species. At 3,280 ft above sea level, the moist, cool environment is perfect for rhododendrons, conifers, maples, and a wide variety of European deciduous trees. The delightful gardens also have a restaurant, shop, visitor center, and picnic areas, and guided walks are available by arrangement. ⊠ *Bells Line of Rd.,* ☎ *02/4567–2154.* ☜ *$5 per car.* ☉ *Mar.–Sept., daily 10–4, Oct.–Feb., daily 10–5.*

En Route   The Bells Line of Road continues toward Sydney past the villages of Bilpin and Kurrajong (there is a terrific panorama of the Sydney metropolitan region from a lookout near Kurrajong), then the towns of Richmond and Windsor. These latter settlements were founded in 1810 and contain several historic churches and other buildings from the mid-1800s—if you have time, it's worth having a look around both towns. From Richmond, Sydney is about a 60-minute drive away.

Blue Mountains A to Z

Arriving and Departing

BY CAR

Leave Sydney via Parramatta Road and the M4 Motorway, which leads to Lapstone at the base of the Blue Mountains. From there, continue on the Great Western Highway and follow the signs to Katoomba. The 100-km (62-mi) journey to Katoomba takes between 90 minutes and two hours.

BY TRAIN

The Blue Mountains are served by Sydney's Cityrail commuter trains, with frequent services to and from the city between 5 AM and 11 PM. The round-trip fare on weekdays between Sydney's Central Station and Katoomba, the main station in the Blue Mountains—and the only town where you can rent a car—is $18.80. If you travel on weekends, or begin travel after 9 AM on weekdays, the fare falls to $11. For more information on schedules and fares, call ☎ 13–1500.

Getting Around

BY BUS

Public buses operate between the various towns of the Blue Mountains, although the areas of greatest scenic beauty are some distance from the towns. So if you want to see the best that the Blue Mountains have to offer, take a guided tour or hire a vehicle and drive from Sydney.

BY CAR

Renting a car is the best plan, and you can rent either in Sydney or in Katoomba. Distances between Blue Mountains towns are short, roads are generally in good condition, and there are many scenic routes and lookouts that are realistically accessible only by car.

BY TRAIN

Train services from Sydney stop at most of the many small stations that dot the railway line from the base of the mountains to Mount Victoria on the western side. Again, however, you will be very limited in the scope of what you can see if traveling by train only.

Contacts and Resources

CAR RENTALS

If you plan to rent a car in Katoomba, be sure to reserve a car from the following companies in advance: **Thrifty** (☎ 02/4784–2888) and **Cales** (☎ 02/4782–2917). If you intend to drive to the Blue Mountains from Sydney, *see* Sydney A to Z *in* Chapter 2.

EMERGENCIES

Ambulance, fire brigade, and **police.** ☎ *000.*

GUIDED TOURS

As one of Sydney's most popular escapes, the Blue Mountains are extremely well served by tour operators of all varieties. You can day-trip from Sydney with one of many coach touring companies, or make your own way to the mountains and then link up with a guided tour. If you are interested in adventure activities, the region is great for such sports as mountain biking, rappelling, rock climbing, hiking, and horseback riding. *See* Chapter 13 for other outdoor outfitters in the area.

Adventure Sports. Blue Mountains Adventure Company (✉ Box 242, Katoomba 2780, ☎ 02/4782–1271, FAX 02/4782–1277) offers rappelling, canyoning, mountain biking, and caving for all levels of ability. The Katoomba-based company began as the Blue Mountains Climbing School, and rock climbing remains a specialty. Most outings (☞ $89 for a one-day trip) are of a one-day duration, and costs include equipment, lunch, and transportation from Katoomba. **Great Australian Walks** (☎ 02/9555–7580, FAX 02/9810–6429), based in Sydney, offers a three-day guided walk along the historic Six Foot Track from Katoomba to Jenolan Caves (☞ from $330, including wine and all meals). Walkers—typically about a dozen—sleep in a lodge one night and tents the other, and carry only a light day pack. Guides are artists, writers, musicians, or naturalists, and the walks appeal to cultivated tastes. **Outland Expeditions** (☎ 02/9804–7411, FAX 02/9804–7202; ☞ from $75 for a one-day trip) operates canyoning and other guided adventure trips in the Blue Mountains, as well as courses in rappelling, rock climbing, and canyoning. One-, two-, and five-day trips are available, as is transportation from Sydney.

Four Wheel Drive Tours. The local Blue Mountains company **Cox's River Escapes** (✉ P.O. Box 81, Leura, 2780, ☎ 02/4784–1621 or 015/400–121, FAX 02/4784–2450; ☞ from $85 for a half-day tour) has off the beaten track half- or full-day four-wheel-drive tours—taking a maximum of six people in an air-conditioned vehicle. Operator Ted Taylor knows the region and its flora and fauna intimately, and provides a highly personalized service, complete with home-cooked morning or afternoon teas and lunches. Such activities as horseback riding, rappelling, or trout fishing can be incorporated, and guided bushwalking trips can also be arranged. Bookings are essential. **Wild Escapes** (✉ Box 116, Asquith, 2077, ☎ 02/9482–2881, FAX 02/9477–3114; ☞ from $199 for a one-day tour, including meals and wine) has various small-group day trips from Sydney to the Blue Mountains. The most popular trip is the four-wheel-drive High Country Ecotour, which departs the beaten track near Katoomba and snakes back to Sydney through private trails in the Jamison Valley, with bushwalks and a champagne picnic en route.

Orientation Tours. Australian Pacific Tours (✉ Circular Quay W, Sydney, ☎ 13–1304) has daily bus tours from Sydney to the Blue Mountains (from $62) and to Jenolan Caves (from $79). The company also offers daily departures for a two-day Jenolan Caves/Blue Mountains tour, which includes accommodations at Jenolan Caves Guest House (from $197). Buses depart from the Overseas Shipping Terminal, on the Harbour Bridge side of Circular Quay. Free hotel pickup is available upon request. **Fantastic Aussie Tours** (✉ 283 Main St., Katoomba, ☎ 02/4782–1866) has a number of options that it can arrange. On **weekends** and public holidays from 9:30 AM to 4:30 PM, the **Blue Mountains Explorer Bus** ($16) meets trains from Sydney at the Katoomba Railway Station. The double-decker makes 18 stops on its 50-minute circuit, including many of the major attractions around Katoomba and Leura. You are free to leave the tour at any point and join a following bus. On **weekdays**, a three-hour Blue Mountains Highlights bus tour ($29) departs from Katoomba Station at 10:30, 11:30, and 2, connecting with Sydney's Central Station's 8:20, 9, and 11 trains, respectively (train schedules might change, so call ahead; ☞ Arriving and Departing, *above*). At the end of the tour, the bus returns to Katoomba Station to reconnect with a Sydney-bound train. Fantastic Aussie Tours has other half- and full-day bus and four-wheel-drive tours around the Blue Mountains region.

VISITOR INFORMATION
Blue Mountains Information Centres are at Echo Point in Katoomba, and at the foot of the mountains on the Great Western Highway at Glenbrook. ☎ *02/4739–6266.* ☼ *Daily 9–5.*

Sydney Visitors Information Centre has information on Blue Mountains accommodation, tours, and sights. ✉ *106 George St. (The Rocks), 2000,* ☎ *02/9255–1788,* ℻ *02/9241–5010.*

THE SOUTHERN HIGHLANDS AND SOUTH COAST

By Anne
Matthews

This fertile upland region just over 100 km (62 mi) southwest of Sydney was first settled during the 1820s by farmers in search of grazing lands. Later during the 19th century, wealthy Sydney folk built grand country houses here, primarily to escape the city's summer heat and humidity. Farming still prevails today, but the area's rolling hills, small fields, gentle green hues, and refined townships have long attracted visitors. Although the region is often likened to England, Australia's ruggedness manages to dramatize even this picturesque rural scene—in the form of the steep sandstone gorges and impenetrable forest of Morton National Park. An added bonus to visiting the inland Southern Highlands is that the South Coast—with its excellent surfing and swimming beaches—is just a short drive away.

At its altitude of around 2,100 ft above sea level, the Southern Highlands, unlike most of Australia, experiences four distinct seasons. It is pleasantly cool here in summer, snow occasionally falls in winter, and the area comes alive with the rich colors of falling leaves in autumn (March to May). The Highlands are famous for their country hotels, guest houses and restaurants, antiques and crafts, and English-style gardens—as well as hiking, golf, horseback riding, and other outdoor activities.

The towns and sights of the Southern Highlands make an ideal two- to four-day round-trip either from Sydney or as a stopover on the way to Canberra or the Snowy Mountains. Distances between towns and villages are so small that you might consider basing yourself in Bowral, one of the most attractive towns that has most of the accommodation, and taking day trips from there. If you are heading back to Sydney after seeing the Highlands, take the South Coast route past beaches and the attractive seaside township of Kiama.

Mittagong

103 km (64 mi) southwest of Sydney.

Although it's known as the gateway to the Southern Highlands, the commercial center of Mittagong doesn't have a great deal to stop for. You can shop for crafts and antiques here, and you might want to look into the Tourism Southern Highlands Information Centre on Main Street for maps and local brochures.

OFF THE
BEATEN PATH

From Mittagong, you can take a detour through rugged mountain scenery to the spectacular and delicate limestone formations of **Wombeyan Caves.** Five caves are open to the public—you can look around the Fig Tree Cave on your own, but you must be accompanied by a guide to visit the others. Guided tours take place at regular intervals throughout the day. There are also bushwalking trails and wildlife in the area. The caves are just 66 km (41 mi) from Mittagong, but the journey along the narrow, winding, and partly unsealed road takes about 1½ hours each way. ✉ *Wombeyan Caves Rd., via Mittagong,* ☎ *02/ 4843-5976.* ☞ *Self-guided cave tour $10, guided 1-cave tour $12, guided 2-cave tour $18.* ⊙ *Daily 8:30–5:30.*

Berrima

14½ km (9 mi) southwest of Mittagong.

Founded in 1829, charming Berrima is Australia's best preserved Georgian settlement—due largely to the fact that the 1860s Sydney-to-Melbourne railway line bypassed the township. The entire English-style town is virtually a museum in itself, full of early colonial sandstone and brick buildings (many of them built by convicts), such as the National Trust–listed Harpers Mansion and Holy Trinity Church. The 1839 Berrima Gaol is still in use, and the 1834 Surveyor General Inn is Australia's oldest continuously licensed hotel. To learn more about the town's history, pick up a copy of the self-guided walking tour at the Courthouse, or join one of the extremely knowledgeable local guides (☞ Guided Tours *in* Southern Highlands A to Z, *below*).

In addition to its historic buildings, restaurants, and tea shops, Berrima is a shopper's paradise—look for antiques, crafts, and traditional Australian knitwear. And although Berrima is rather small, it would be easy to spend a day exploring it in detail.

The 1838 **Berrima Courthouse,** with its grand, classical facade, is the town's architectural highlight. The impressive sandstone complex contains the original courtroom and holding cells, and in its current function as a museum it presents a reenactment of an infamous murder trial and has audiovisual and conventional displays of such items as iron shackles and a cat-o-nine tails that was once used on recalcitrant convicts. The courthouse also serves as the main information center. ⊠ *Wilshire St., Berrima,* ☎ *02/4877–1505.* ⊑ *Museum $2.50.* ⊙ *Daily 10–4.*

Dining

$$ ✕ **White Horse Inn.** This meticulously restored inn is not just a fine example of colonial Australian architecture. The atmospheric 1832 hotel (which is reputed to have a resident ghost) is an ideal spot for lunch and morning or afternoon tea, with both indoor and courtyard seating. The lunch menu features soups, salads, open sandwiches, excellent focaccias, and a good range of desserts. If you are visiting Berrima in the evening, rather more expensive contemporary Australian fare is served in the inn's traditionally decorated formal dining rooms. ⊠ *Market Pl., Berrima,* ☎ *02/4877–1204. AE, DC, MC, V.*

Shopping

The Bell Gallery. The craftwork at Berrima's classiest gallery includes unusual glassware, pottery, fabrics, and other handmade items. ⊠ *10 Jellore St., Berrima,* ☎ *02/4877–1267.* ⊙ *Fri.–Tues. 10–4 (Wed. and Thurs. by appointment only).*

Peppergreen in Berrima. Among the town's numerous antiques shops, this one is outstanding both for its size and its extraordinary range of old wares. In addition to the more predictable jewelry, silver, glassware, and china items, Peppergreen stocks buttons, books, an array of old lace and linen, and various other intriguing collectables. ⊠ *Market Pl., Berrima,* ☎ *02/4877–1488.* ⊙ *Weekdays 10–5, weekends 9–5.30.*

Bowral

9½ km (6 mi) east of Berrima.

The commercial center for the Southern Highlands, genteel Bowral has provided a desirable country address for the wealthy since the 1880s. This is now the region's largest town, with a burgeoning population of around 7,500: a figure that includes many city retirees. In addition to its fine old houses and antiques and crafts shops, Bowral is famous for its tree-lined streets as well as its parks and private gardens, which are the focus of the colorful spring **Tulip Time Festival,** held every September and October. For panoramic views of Bowral, Mittagong, and the surrounding countryside, don't miss the scenic drive up 2,830-ft-high **Mount Gibraltar,** atop which there are four short walking trails with fine views.

Bowral's main attraction (at least for cricket fans) is the **Bradman Museum.** The town was the childhood home of Australia's legendary cricketer Sir Donald Bradman, who played for and captained Australia between 1928 and 1948, and the museum commemorates "The Don's" remarkable achievements. Featuring film footage, photographs, and a great deal of sporting memorabilia, this excellent museum also pays tribute to the game of cricket—one of Australia's enduring obsessions. The center includes a shop and tearooms, and the museum is located next to the town's idyllic cricket oval. ⊠ *Glebe Park, St. Jude St., Bowral,* ☎ *02/4862–1247.* ⊠ *$5.* ⊘ *Daily 10–4.*

Dining and Lodging

$$$ ✕ **Grand Bar and Brasserie.** Located next to Bowral's Grand Hotel, this lively city-style brasserie is open all day, and its modern Australian menu changes seasonally. Appetizers might include a "grand" Caesar salad with smoked chicken, pancetta, and a soft-poached egg, or tempura king prawns with guacamole and a mango, capsicum, and pinenut salad. Recent main dishes have been lightly steamed Atlantic salmon with lemon-and-dill dressing, and smoked beef fillet with a mixed mushroom sauté, asparagus, creamy mash, and a red wine sauce. A tempting range of desserts and a wine list that includes a good selection of Australian reds and whites also deserve attention. ⊠ *The Grand Arcade, 295 Bong Bong St., Bowral,* ☎ *02/4861–4783. AE, DC, MC, V.*

$ ✕ **Janeks Cafe.** This small, casual café is one of the few eateries in Bowral that has outdoor seating. Come for breakfasts, milk shakes, smoothies, cakes, waffles, and an all-day menu that lists toasted sandwiches, soups, focaccias, pastas, and salads. At dinner, look for such mod-Oz dishes as steamed mussels with lemongrass, chilli, and coriander; or roast lamb rump with lentil ragout, greens, and potatoes, or a delicious warm salad with wild duck, mesclun, artichokes, and balsamic dressing. ⊠ *Corbett Plaza, Wingecarribee St., Bowral,* ☎ *02/4861–4414. Reservations essential. MC, V. BYOB. Closed Sun. No dinner Mon.–Wed.*

$$$$ ✕▣ **Milton Park.** Set in 20 acres of English-style gardens on a forested 700-acre estate 13 km (8 mi) east of Bowral, this once was the country home of a wealthy Sydney family. The extended and refurbished mansion is now regarded by many as the ultimate (it's certainly the most expensive) Southern Highland address, and it is a popular venue for weddings and conferences. Warm yellow tones prevail in the decor, and there are superb furnishings and original artwork. Common areas include a lounge and drawing room. Most guest rooms lead onto an internal courtyard; all have king-size beds. The six suites have four-poster or sleigh beds and spa baths, and some rooms include a fireplace. Breakfast and lunch are served in the airy garden court, and dinner, contemporary Australian fare with European and Asian influences, is set out in the elegant Hordern Room (nonresidents are welcome to dine here). Rates include guided walks, a large country breakfast, and à la carte dinner. ⊠ *Horderns Rd., Bowral, 2576,* ☎ *02/4861–1522,* ℻ *02/4861–4716. 34 rooms with bath, 6 suites. 2 restaurants, bar, pool,* *massage, yoga, 3 tennis courts, bocce, croquet, horseback riding, mountain bikes. AE, DC, MC, V.*

$$ ✕⛟ **Links House Small Hotel.** This friendly, stylish hotel, in a quiet location directly opposite the Bowral golf course, has been catering to visitors since 1928. It is rather small, as the name suggests, but rooms are tastefully appointed, and the suites are ideal for families. If you book well in advance, you may be fortunate enough to secure number 20—a delightful cottage-style room in the hotel's gardens. The two comfortable lounge areas are beautifully decorated, and fires blaze in them in winter. A full, cooked breakfast is included in the rates, and you can also have dinner in-house in the popular Basil's Restaurant, which serves excellent contemporary Australian cuisine. ⊠ *17 Links Rd., Bowral, 2576,* ☎ *02/4861–1408,* 🆁🅰🆇 *02/4862–1706. 13 rooms with shower, 4 suites. Pool, tennis court, bocce, croquet. AE, DC, MC, V.*

Moss Vale

10 km (6 mi) southeast of Berrima.

Founded as a market center for the surrounding farming districts, which now concentrate on horses, sheep, and dairy and stud cattle, Moss Vale is a pleasant township with abundant antiques and crafts shops. It is a good place to shop and stroll, and the attractive Leighton Gardens, in the center of town, are also worth a visit.

Situated on the banks of the Wingecarribee River, just to the north of Moss Vale, the lagoon and swamplands of the **Cecil Hoskins Nature Reserve** have been a wildlife sanctuary since the 1930s. This important wetland area is home to over 80 species of local and migratory waterfowl, including pelicans and black swans. You may even be fortunate enough to see a reclusive platypus here. The reserve has hides for birdwatching, a picnic area, and several easy walking tracks that provide excellent views of the river and wetlands. ⊠ *Moss Vale–Bowral Rd., Bowral,* ☎ *02/4887–7270.* ☉ *Daily dawn–dusk.*

Golf

With its well-groomed greens and on-course accommodation, the par 71 **Moss Vale Golf Club** (⊠ Arthur St., ☎ 02/4868–1503 or 02/4868–1811) is regarded as one of the best and most challenging in this golf-crazy area. Visitors are welcome every day except Saturday, but it is best to phone first. Greens fees are $20.

Sutton Forest and Bundanoon

6–13 km (4–8 mi) south of Moss Vale.

If you've come to the Southern Highlands to take in some rural splendor, don't miss the drive from Moss Vale through the tranquil southern villages, a region of dairy farms and premier horse studs. Although relatively unimportant today, **Sutton Forest** was the focus of the area's early settlement. In later years, this small township became the country seat of the Governors of New South Wales, who periodically based themselves at the grand country house, Hillview. The village, 6 km (4 mi) from Moss Vale, also contains a few shops and the pleasant Sutton Forest Inn. Labeled after its far larger English namesake, the nearby hamlet of **Exeter** is where you'll find the 1895 St. Aidans Church, complete with a vaulted timber ceiling and beautiful stained-glass windows.

Six kilometers (4 miles) south of Sutton Forest, **Bundanoon** (Aboriginal for "place of deep gullies") was once an extremely busy weekend getaway for Sydneysiders. This popularity was due to its location—on the main railway line to Melbourne, at a bracing elevation of 2,230

ft, perched above the northern edge of spectacular Morton National
Park. The now quiet village is still delightful, and provides the best access to the park's western section. There are a few antiques and crafts
shops, and Bundanoon is also the focus of the annual Brigadoon Festival, held in April, a lively event that features pipe bands, highland
games, and all things Scottish.

Dining and Lodging

$$ ✕ **Gambells on the Park.** Set among 5 acres of gardens, this friendly
and relaxed country home's delightful restaurant offers a lunch and
dinner blackboard menu that changes weekly. The cuisine is modern
Australian, and you might find roast tomato soup with pesto, or
smoked salmon and corn frittata. Main courses range from savory stuffed
chicken breast to Atlantic salmon to gnocchi with roasted tomato
sauce and crispy prosciutto. The locally made wood-fired bread and
tasty desserts are an additional temptation. The restaurant has indoor
and garden seating. ⊠ *Gullies Rd., Bundanoon,* ☎ *02/4883–6892.
AE, DC, MC, V. BYOB. Closed Mon.–Wed.*

$$$ ✕🄷 **Peppers Mount Broughton.** Adjoining the Mount Broughton golf
course and set in 185 acres of gardens and pastureland, this elegant
country resort is based around a grand 1920s family home. The old
homestead's baronial Great Hall has a high vaulted ceiling, leadlight
windows, and a blazing fire in winter, and there are five traditionally
decorated guest rooms. Other accommodations, with either colonial-
or country-style decor, are located in the bright, modern Garden Wing.
Three suites are also available, and the two-bedroom Elms Cottages
are ideal for families or small groups. Both guests and nonresidents can
dine in the hotel's stylish Seasons Restaurant, which serves fresh local
produce in its innovative Australian country cuisine-style preparations. Rates include a hearty country breakfast. The hotel is located
just outside Moss Vale, on the road to Sutton Forest. ⊠ *Kater Rd., Sutton Forest, 2577,* ☎ *02/4868–2355,* 𝔽𝔸𝕏 *02/4868–3257..40 rooms with
bath or shower, 3 suites. Restaurant, cocktail lounge, golf, 2 floodlit
tennis courts, outdoor saltwater pool, mountain bikes, volleyball, croquet. AE, DC, MC, V.*

Outdoor Activities and Sports

GOLF

The rather exclusive Scottish-style **Mount Broughton Golf & Country
Club** (⊠ Kater Rd., Sutton Forest, ☎ 02/4869–1597) has a picturesque,
par 72, 18-hole championship course, rated among the top 100 in Australia, and facilities of a very high standard. Visitors are welcome, but
call in advance. Greens fees are $45 on weekdays, $55 on weekends.

HORSEBACK RIDING

If you're interested sitting astride a horse and stepping back into rural
time, the superbly equipped **Highlands Equestrian Centre** (⊠ Sutton
Farm, Illawarra Hwy., Sutton Forest, ☎ 02/4868–2584) offers classes
for everyone from beginners to advanced riders who are capable of dres-
sage and show jumping. Pony rides are available for $10, and escorted
trail rides start at $26. Reservations are essential. The farm also offers
accommodation in its historic 1830s homestead.

Morton National Park and Fitzroy Falls

19 km (12 mi) southwest of Moss Vale.

With an area of over 400,000 acres, rugged **Morton National Park** is
one of the state's largest national parks. This superb region encompasses
sheer sandstone cliffs and escarpments, scenic lookouts, waterfalls, and

densely forested valleys and is very popular with bushwalkers and bird-watchers. The Bundanoon area of the park has a variety of walks, many of which can be completed in less than an hour. These include short hikes to the historic Erith Coal Mine, the lookout at Mount Carnarvon, Fairy Bower Falls, and Ferntree Gully. You can also walk to Glow Worm Glen, a small sandstone grotto that is home to fungus gnat larvae that glow at night with a bright blue luminescence. The track to the glen is accessible after dark. Information on all walks is available from the National Parks and Wildlife Service Fitzroy Falls Visitor Centre.

The highlight of vast Morton National Park's eastern section is Fitzroy Falls, which tumble 270 ft off the craggy sandstone escarpment. A board-walk leads to lookouts that provide spectacular views of the falls and the heavily forested Yarrunga Valley. Several marked bushwalks of varying lengths along the escarpment's eastern and western edges allow further exploration of the area. The park's birdlife is prolific—look for kookaburras, a wide variety of parrots, and even the elusive lyrebird. The **Fitzroy Falls Visitor Centre,** operated by the National Parks and Wildlife Service, is open daily from 8:30 to 5 and includes a shop, information displays, and a pleasant café. ⊠ *Nowra Rd., Fitzroy Falls,* ☎ *02/4887–7270.*

OFF THE BEATEN PATH
From Fitzroy Falls you can take a short scenic drive to the northeast via the sleepy hamlets of Myra Vale and Wildes Meadow. Originally an 1860s timber village, **Burrawang** has retained much of its original charm, with weatherboard houses and buildings like the 1870s **Burrawang General Store** having changed little in recent decades. On weekends pay a visit to the **Old School House**—for an excellent collection of antiques and a dining room that serves delicious lunches, cakes, teas, and coffees. Burrawang is 11 km (7 mi) from Fitzroy Falls.

The main claim to fame of the attractive farming area around **Robertson,** 8 km (5 mi) east of Burrawang, is that this is where the internationally successful movie *Babe* was filmed—all those green, English-looking fields were in fact located in Australia's Southern Highlands. You can also explore the temperate rain forest of **Robertson Nature Reserve** on a short walk, and call in at the rustic local pub for a drink.

Kangaroo Valley

18 km (11 mi) southeast of Fitzroy Falls.

After dropping down the steep, winding road that traverses Barren-garry Mountain—from which there are wonderful views of the plains and coast below—you reach Kangaroo Valley, a lush dairy farming region that was first settled during the early 1800s. Many old buildings remain here, and the entirely charming, verdant region is National Trust classified. The Kangaroo Valley township has some good cafés and craft shops, and you can hire a canoe, golf, swim in the river, or go hiking. The entrance to the village is marked by the rather grand, medieval-style Hampden Bridge, which was erected over the Kangaroo River in 1897.

Next to Hampden Bridge, the **Pioneer Settlement Reserve** has a unique perspective on the valley's history. The site includes Pioneer Farm, a re-creation of a late–19th-century homestead, complete with artifacts from the period and a variety of forest and woodland bushwalks. ⊠

Moss Vale Rd., Kangaroo Valley, ☎ *02/4465–1306.* 🖃 *$3.* ☼ *Daily 9:30–4:30.*

En Route   After leaving the township, take the scenic Kangaroo Valley Road east to the delightful Princes Highway town of **Berry.** Styling itself as the "Town of Trees," this roadside settlement has carefully preserved its 19th-century heritage and architecture. The 1886 bank now serves as an interesting museum, and the main street is lined with shops and attractive old buildings.

From Berry you can either travel to Kiama along the Princes Highway, or take a more scenic coastal route via the sands and wild surf of spectacular **Seven Mile Beach,** and the quiet seaside villages of **Gerroa** and **Gerringong.** It is 26 km (16 mi) to Kiama along this alternative route.

Kiama

47 km (29 mi) northeast of Kangaroo Valley.

First "discovered" by the intrepid explorer George Bass, who sailed here from Sydney in his small whaleboat in 1797, this small coastal township (pop. 18,000) began life as a fishing port. Kiama has long been a popular holiday center, however, due to its mild climate, fine beaches, pleasant walks, and easy rail access from Sydney. And now it has the distinction of having been proclaimed "Australia's Tidiest Town."

Unlike most coastal Australian towns, Kiama has managed to retain a sense of charm with its 19th-century buildings—such as the National Trust–listed weatherboard cottages on Collins Street, the Presbyterian church, and Manning Street's surprisingly grand post office. The Kiama Visitors Centre has a Heritage Walks brochure that describes points of interest around the town center.

The town's beaches—including Kendalls, Easts, the aptly named Surf Beach, and nearby Bombo—are excellent for swimming and surfing. Other popular activities around Kiama are fishing and scuba diving. Several boat operators based in the attractive harbor offer game, sports, and deep-sea fishing trips, and others cater to divers.

Two of Kiama's most visited sights are located at **Blowhole Point**—these are the blowhole itself, through which, given the right conditions, the sea noisily spurts, and the impressive 1887 Kiama Lighthouse.

OFF THE   One of the Kiama area's highlights is a short excursion to the delightful
BEATEN PATH   old settlement of **Jamberoo,** 9 km (5½ mi) inland. Settlers first came to
               this tranquil farming valley in the 1820s and the village contains some
               interesting shops and several old stone buildings, including the 1875
               National Trust–classified Schoolhouse. The old-style Jamberoo Pub is a
               good spot for an ice cold beer on a hot day.

Dining and Lodging

$$ ✕ **Chachis.** Located in one of Collins Street's historic 1880s cottages, this friendly and reasonably priced Italian-style ristorante serves lunch, dinner, and snacks. There is a wide range of soups, starters, and salads, and penne, spaghetti, fettuccine, and ravioli are available with a choice of eight sauces. Meat, seafood, and vegetarian main courses are also available, and the dessert menu is extensive and tempting. Dining is either indoors, or at a table on the veranda. ⊠ *The Terraces, Collins St., Kiama,* ☎ *02/4233–1144. AE, MC, V. BYOB.*

$$$ ✕🔲 **Villa Dalmeny l'Hotel Privé**. A stay at this charming 1895 National Trust listed mansion is nothing less than magical—a spell woven by the combination of chic decor, fresh, innovative food, remarkable attention to detail, and the warm hospitality of French-Swiss host and chef Jacqueline Noss-Ferrero, who ran a popular Manhattan restaurant for 12 years. The four luxurious and very individual guest rooms—named Aix-en-Provence, Santa Fe, Siena, and La Coquille—vary in decor and ambience, and each has its own modern marble bathroom. Five-course dinner-party "events" take place in the dramatic Valentine's dining room, and Jacqueline's exciting (again five-course) breakfasts are served on the deck outdoors (weather permitting). This intimate French-style private hotel pampers you in inimitable style, and a two-night stay is highly recommended. Rates include breakfast, and dinner is included in the higher weekend prices. Smoking is not permitted inside the house, and children are not catered for. Nonresidents are welcome for dinner by arrangement. ✉ *72 Shoalhaven St., Kiama, 2533,* ☎ *02/ 4233–1911,* FAX *02/4233–1912. 4 rooms with shower. No credit cards.*

En Route   Between Kiama and Sydney, the Princes Highway loops inland, skirting Lake Illawarra and the port and major industrial center of **Wollongong,** the state's third largest city. Other than beaches, a museum, and an art gallery, there is not a great deal of interest in Wollongong itself, but you should leave the highway at the Bulli turnoff, and follow the scenic coastal route. This winding road passes small townships and beaches, then climbs the escarpment to **Stanwell Park,** a famous hang-gliding launch point with fantastic views down the coast. From Stanwell Park, it will take about an hour to reach central Sydney.

Southern Highlands A to Z

Arriving and Departing

BY BUS

Greyhound Pioneer Australia (☎ 13–2030), and **McCaffertys** (☎ 13–1499) offer daily service between Sydney and Mittagong. The journey takes 2½ hours, and the round-trip fare is $52. The same companies also run daily buses from Canberra (2 hours), at $44 round-trip.

BY CAR

From central Sydney, head west along Parramatta Road and follow the signs to the Hume Highway (Hwy. 5). Join the Hume at Ashfield and drive southwest on the F5 Freeway until you reach the Mittagong exit. Mittagong is 103 km (64 mi) southwest of Sydney, and the drive should take 1½–2 hours.

BY TRAIN

Sydney's **Cityrail** (☎ 13–1500) commuter line trains has frequent daily service to Mittagong, Bowral, Moss Vale, and Bundanoon. Trains from Sydney also stop daily at Kiama. Round-trip fares are the same to both the Southern Highlands (Bowral) and Kiama—$21.20, or $12.60 for an off-peak ticket.

Getting Around

BY BUS

Local buses run between the main Highlands towns, but these will not take you to the out of the way attractions. Renting a car is the best way to see most of the area.

BY CAR

Distances between towns and attractions are small, and roads are generally in very good condition and scenic—all the more reason to drive them yourself.

Contacts and Resources

CAR RENTALS

For details of renting a car in Sydney, *see* Sydney A to Z *in* Chapter 2. In the Southern Highlands, you can hire a car from **Avis** (✉ Ampol Service Station, Station and Wingecarribee Sts., Bowral, ☎ 02/4861–2575), **Hertz** (✉ Chadwick's BP Sales & Service, Kirkham Rd., Bowral, ☎ 02/4862–1755), and **Thrifty** (✉ Mobil Service Station, Hume Hwy., Mittagong, ☎ 02/4871–1777). Call ahead to reserve a car.

EMERGENCIES

Ambulance, fire brigade, and **police.** ☎ *000.*

GUIDED TOURS

With the local Southern Highlands operator **Highland Trips & Treks** (✉ Burrawang, ☎ 02/4886–4202 or 015/24–4714) you can explore the region in air-conditioned 4WD luxury. The company offers several full-day excursions for small groups and arranges hiking trips into Morton National Park. Fees start at $90 per person for a full-day trip. Lunch and morning and afternoon teas are included in rates. The best way to see the old buildings and other attractions of Berrima is on an informative stroll with **Historic Berrima Village Guided Walking Tours** (☎ 02/4877–1505; ✆ $5). Tours depart from the Berrima Courthouse on Wilshire Street daily at 11:30, 1, and 2:30. **Wild Escapes** (☎ 02/9482–2881; ✆ from $199) has a full-day tour from Sydney that includes Kiama, Kangaroo Valley, and the Southern Highlands. Wild Escapes specializes in small-group travel, with an emphasis on the natural environment. Prices include lunch and drinks.

VISITOR INFORMATION

Kiama Visitors Centre has information on the Kiama, Jamberoo, and Minnamurra areas. ✉ *Blowhole Point, Kiama, 2533,* ☎ *02/4232–3322 or 1800/80–3897.*
Sydney Visitors Information Centre has information on Southern Highlands and South Coast accommodation, tours, and sights. ✉ *106 George St. (The Rocks), 2000,* ☎ *02/9255–1788,* FAX *02/9241–5010.*
Tourism Southern Highlands Information Centre. ✉ *62–70 Main St., Mittagong, 2575,* ☎ *02/4871–2888 or 1800/65–6176.*

THE HUNTER VALLEY

The meandering waterway that gives this valley its name is one of the most extensive river systems in the state. The Hunter Valley covers an area of almost 25,103 square km (9,650 square mi), stretching from the town of Gosford north of Sydney to Taree, 177 km (110 mi) farther north along the coast, and almost 300 km (186 mi) inland. From its source on the rugged slopes of the Mount Royal Range, the Hunter River flows through rich grazing country and past the horse stud farms around Scone in the upper part of the valley, home of some of Australia's wealthiest farming families. In the Lower Hunter region, the river crosses the vast coal deposits of the Greta seam. Coal mining, both open-cut and underground, is an important industry for the Hunter Valley, and the mines in this area provide the fuel for the steel mills of Newcastle, the state's second-largest city, which lies at the mouth of the Hunter River.

To almost everyone in Sydney, however, the Hunter Valley conjures up visions not of coal mines or cows but of wine. The Hunter is the largest grape-growing area in the state, with over 50 wineries and a reputation for producing high- (and, alas, low-) quality vintages. Much of it has found a market overseas, and visiting wine lovers might recognize the Hunter Valley labels of Rosemount or Lindemans.

In recent years the area has become a favorite weekend destination for Sydneysiders. In addition to wine tasting, the Hunter Valley's historic towns, bushland walks, and several excellent restaurants draw crowds. During the week you'll find quiet roads, empty picnic grounds, spare tables in restaurants—and less expensive accommodations.

The arrangement of towns and sights below follows a logical order for anyone arriving from Sydney. Starting at the Hunter Valley gateway town of Cessnock, move on to Pokolbin and the main Lower Hunter wineries, followed by an optional detour to historic Wollombi, and then on to the Upper Hunter Valley settlements of Muswellbrook and Scone. The easiest return route to Sydney from the Upper Hunter is via the historic town of Maitland, and then by joining the Sydney–Newcastle Freeway.

Cessnock

185 km (115 mi) north of Sydney.

The large town of Cessnock is better known as the entrance to the Lower Hunter Valley than for any particular attraction in the town itself. Between 1890 and 1960 this was an important coal-mining area, but when coal production began to decline during the 1950s, the mines gradually gave way to vines.

Any tour of the area's vineyards should begin at the **Cessnock Visitor Information Centre** at Turner Park, Aberdare Road. The center can provide maps of the vineyards, brochures, and copies of *Wine Hunter* magazine, which has vineyard news and tasting notes.

At **Rusa Park Zoo,** 3 km (2 mi) north of Cessnock, animals from all over the world mingle with such Australian fauna as koalas, wallabies, kangaroos, wombats, snakes, and lizards in a 24-acre bushland park. There are over 90 species of animals and birds here, including monkeys, deer, and antelope. Barbecue and picnic facilities are provided. ⊠ *Lomas La., Nulkaba,* ☎ *02/4990–7714.* ☜ *$6.* ⊙ *Daily 9:30–4:30.*

Golf
Cessnock Golf Club (⊠ Lindsay St., ☎ 02/4990–1876) is one of the Hunter Valley's more notable courses. The club welcomes visitors on most days, but it's best to check beforehand. Greens fees are $12–$15.

Wollombi

31 km (19 mi) southwest of Cessnock.

Nothing seems to have changed in the atmospheric town of **Wollombi** since the days when the Cobb & Co. stagecoaches rumbled through town. Founded in 1820, Wollombi was the overnight stop for the coaches on the second day of the journey from Sydney along the convict-built Great Northern Road—at that time the only route north. The town is full of delightful old sandstone buildings, a museum, and antiques shops, and the local hotel, the Wollombi Tavern, serves its own exotic brew, which goes by the name of Dr. Jurd's Jungle Juice. The pub also scores high marks for its friendliness and local color.

Lodging
$$ ⊞ **Avoca House.** Overlooking the Wollombi Brook just outside of ★ town, this charming century-old house, with its vine-covered verandas and central courtyard, is a country classic. Rooms are tastefully furnished, and the owners, Russell and Kay Davies, pay great attention to detail to ensure that their guests have a comfortable and memorable stay. There are three rooms to choose from—the largest is the

self-contained suite, with its queen-size bedroooom and sitting room—
and the layout of the house guarantees privacy. Rates include a hearty
country-style breakfast. Dinner is available by arrangement. ⊠ *Wollombi Rd., Wollombi, 2325,* ☎ *02/4998–3233,* FAX *02/4998–3319. 2
rooms without bath, 1 suite. MC, V.*

Pokolbin

10 km (6 mi) northwest of Cessnock.

The Lower Hunter wine growing region is centered around the village
of Pokolbin, where there are dozens of wineries. Here are suggestions
about a few to visit.

On the lower slopes of Mt. Bright, one of the loveliest parts of the Lower
Hunter region, is **Drayton's Family Wines.** Wine making is a Drayton
family tradition dating back to the middle of the 19th century, when
Joseph Drayton first cleared these slopes and planted vines. Today, the
Chardonnay, Semillon, and Shiraz made by this winery are some of
the most consistent award winners around, and a full range of wines
is available for tasting. ⊠ *Oakey Creek Rd., Pokolbin,* ☎ *02/4998–
7513.* ⊙ *Weekdays 9–5, weekends 10–5.*

The **Lindemans Hunter River Winery** has been the home of Lindemans,
one of the largest and most prestigious wine makers in the country,
since the early 1900s. In addition to its Hunter Valley vineyards, the
company also owns property in South Australia and Victoria, and a
wide range of outstanding wine from these vineyards can be sampled
in the tasting room—try Red Burgundy and Semillon Chardonnay. The
winery also has two picnic areas—one near antique wine-making
equipment beside the parking lot, and the other next to the willow trees
around the dam. ⊠ *McDonalds Rd., Pokolbin,* ☎ *02/4998–7684.* ⊙
Weekdays 9–5, weekends 10–5.

As its name suggests, **Verona Vineyard and the Small Winemakers Centre** is the showcase for the small Hunter Valley boutique wineries, some
of which are off the beaten track. The wine available for tasting comes
mainly from Reynolds Estate, Broke Estate, Simon Whitlam, and
Verona itself—all prestigious small wineries. The center also has a café,
and a well-stocked delicatessen, which serves cheeses, fruit, preserves,
and cold foods, as well as gourmet picnics. ⊠ *McDonalds Rd., Pokolbin,* ☎ *02/4998–7668.* ⊙ *Daily 10–5.*

The low stone and timber buildings of the **McGuigan Hunter Village**
is the heart of the Pokolbin wine-growing district. This large complex
includes a resort and convention center, a crafts gallery, restaurants, a
cheese factory, and two tasting rooms—those of the McGuigan Brothers Winery itself, and the underground rooms of the Hunter Cellars.
At the lower end of the complex you'll find a large, shady picnic area
with barbecues and an adventure playground. ⊠ *Broke and McDonalds Rds., Pokolbin,* ☎ *02/4998–7466.* ⊙ *Daily 10–5.*

Dining and Lodging

$$$$ ✕ **Robert's at Pepper Tree.** Built around a century-old heritage-listed
★   pioneer's cottage and surrounded by grapevines in one of the prettiest
parts of the Lower Hunter, this restaurant is the brainchild of Robbie
Molines, who had established a solid reputation as chef at the Pokolbin Cellar. The country fare menu has been heavily influenced by regional French and Italian cooking. In the Australian country-style
cottage, with chunky beams, bare timber floors, antiques, and a big
stone fireplace, first courses might include char-grilled quails and a
seafood salad of octopus, tuna, prawns, and mussels. Among the main

courses are fillet of hare on leaves of homemade pasta with a black-berry sauce, and baked lamb with pumpkin and cabbage, but the menu changes regularly to use the freshest local produce. ⊠ *Halls Rd., Pokolbin,* ☎ *02/4998-7330. AE, DC, MC, V.*

$ ✕ **Café Max.** Located above the tasting room of the Small Winemak-ers Centre, this café specializes in light, wholesome meals that are salt free. The menu features an eclectic range of dishes from Europe, the Mediterranean, and Asia, including a selection of salads, soups, an-tipasto, Thai dishes, pastas, pies, and a variety of desserts. Vegetari-ans are well catered to, and you can purchase wine for your meal from the downstairs center. ⊠ *Small Winemakers Centre, McDonalds Rd., Pokolbin,* ☎ *02/4998-7899. MC, V. BYOB. No dinner.*

$$$ ✕🖭 **Casuarina Country Inn.** Unspoiled beauty and luxury best de-scribe this guest house, set amid a sea of grapevines in the shadow of the Brokenback Range. The palatial split-level guest suites are furnished according to particular themes: the infamous French Bordello suite with a mirrored, canopied four-poster bed; the Victorian suite, with stun-ning antique walnut furnishings and an elaborate iron balustrade; and the equally delightful Colonial, Oriental, British Empire, Mariner's, Fed-eration, and Edwardian suites. For families and groups, the spaciously designed self-contained cottages are ideal. The wonderful **Casuarina Restaurant,** a stroll from the inn, offers innovative "Mediter-Asian" cuisine and makes for an elegant night out. Flambéed dishes, which are theatrically prepared at your table, are a specialty—the chilli lob-ster and prawn flambé is a must—as is the king-size raspberry souf-flé. The inn is a member of Small Luxury Hotels of the World. There is a minimum two-night booking on weekends. ⊠ *Hermitage Rd., Pokol-bin, 2320,* ☎ *02/4998-7888,* 🅵🅰🆇 *02/4998-7692. 8 suites, 3 cottages. Restaurant, pool, sauna, tennis court. AE, MC, V.*

$$$ ✕🖭 **Peppers Guest House Hunter Valley.** In a grove of wild pepper-corn trees you'll find a cluster of houses built as reproductions of clas-sic Australian homesteads—long, low buildings with corrugated-iron roofs surrounded by flagstone verandas. The country atmosphere con-tinues in the luxurious guest rooms, decorated with scrubbed-pine furnishings and floral-print fabrics. The award-winning hotel has a de-voted following who cherish its relaxed country manners and the Chez Pok restaurant's fine cuisine and wine. Under the auspices of execu-tive chef Jamie Hartcher, Chez Pok offers country-style fare with French, Asian, and Italian influences, and a menu that changes regu-larly to take advantage of seasonal produce. The guest house is often booked well in advance for weekends. ⊠ *Ekerts Rd., Pokolbin, 2320,* ☎ *02/4998-7596,* 🅵🅰🆇 *02/4998-7739. 47 rooms with shower, 1 4-bed-room homestead. Restaurant, bar, indoor pool, sauna, spa, tennis court. AE, DC, MC, V.*

$$$$ 🖭 **Convent Pepper Tree.** Housing the most luxurious accommoda-tions in the Hunter Valley, this imposing two-story timber building, once a convent, was transported 605 km (375 mi) from its original home in western New South Wales. Rooms are cozy, spacious, and elegantly furnished, and each has doors that open onto a wide veranda. The house is surrounded by the vineyards of the Pepper Tree Winery. The nearby **Robert's at Pepper Tree** restaurant (☞ *above*) enhances the experience with fabulous French and Italian-inspired dishes. Rates include a full country breakfast. ⊠ *Halls Rd., Pokolbin, 2320,* ☎ *02/4998-7764,* 🅵🅰🆇 *02/4998-7323. 17 rooms with bath. Restaurant, tennis, spa, out-door pool, bikes. AE, DC, MC, V.*

$ 🖭 **Glen Ayr Cottages.** Tucked away in the Pokolbin bushland, these trim, colonial-style timber cottages have fully equipped kitchens, fam-

ily-size space, en suite bathrooms, and marvelous views from their verandas. The cottages are built on a ridge with vineyards on one side
and eucalyptus forest on the other. The furnishings are simple but comfortable, and neither televisions, radios, nor telephones are allowed to
compete with the birds. Three of the cottages will sleep four comfortably, and both the Morrison and the two-story Ferguson sleep eight.
⊠ *Box 188, Cessnock, 2325,* ☎ *02/4998–7784,* 𝖥𝖠𝖷 *02/4998–7476.*
1 cottage with bath, 5 with shower. MC.

$ ⊞ **Vineyard Hill Country Motel.** This motel sits on a rise in a secluded
★   part of the Hunter Valley with views across the vineyards to the Pokolbin State Forest. Its smart, modern one- and two-bedroom lodgings
are an exceptional value. Each pastel-color suite has its own high-ceiling lounge area and a kitchen equipped with a coffee infuser and a choice
of microwave or convection oven. French doors open onto a private
deck. The reception area has a wide selection of prepared dishes ready
for the oven in your room, as well as meats, salads, pâtés, and cheeses,
and full, cooked breakfasts are available. The best views are from Rooms
4 through 8. There is a minimum stay of two nights on weekends. ⊠
Lovedale Rd., Pokolbin, 2320, ☎ *02/4990–4166,* 𝖥𝖠𝖷 *02/4991–4431.*
8 rooms with shower. Pool. AE, MC, V.

En Route   From Pokolbin, you can drive around the scenic vineyard countryside
between here and Rothbury, and then take Branxton Road to the village of Branxton on the New England Highway. From Branxton, it is
71 km (44 mi) via the town of Singleton to Muswellbrook and the Upper
Hunter Valley.

Muswellbrook

111 km (69 mi) northwest of Pokolbin.

First settled in the 1820s as cattle farming land, the Upper Hunter Valley town of Muswellbrook is an agricultural and coal mining center
with few attractions other than the Regional Art Gallery and some historic buildings. There are numerous wineries around the nearby village of Denman, however, including Arrowfield Wines and the excellent
Rosemount Estate, and the area's tranquil scenery takes in rolling hills
and rich farmlands.

Scone

26 km (16 mi) north of Muswellbrook.

Noted for its high-quality horse and cattle studs and penchant for playing polo—the town is known as the horse capital of Australia—the
charming Upper Hunter farming town of Scone contains some historic
mid–19th-century buildings and a local museum, and there are particularly fine accommodations in the area.

Dining and Lodging

$$$$ ✕⊞ **Belltrees Country House.** Located on a working sheep and cattle
★   property a few miles from Scone and about an hour's drive from the
Lower Hunter wineries, this outstanding rural retreat offers its guests
a taste of the finer side of Australian country life. You are welcome to
watch the station hands at work with the livestock, or you can enjoy
such activities as horseback riding, polo, archery, clay pigeon shooting,
or a four-wheel-drive trip into the surrounding mountains. The historic
1830s property has its own schoolhouse, store, and church, and the house
is surrounded by extensive gardens and vibrant bird life. The large, comfortable guest rooms are in a modern building about a 10-minute walk
from the homestead. Bring your own wine to dinner at the house. Rates
include breakfast, dinner, and a tour of the property. Another Belltrees

accommodation option is the secluded, romantic Mountain Retreat—atop a 5,000-ft mountain and with a superb panorama of the region. ⊠ *Gundy Rd., Scone, 2337,* ☎ *02/6545–1668,* FAX *02/6546–1122. 8 rooms with bath. Pool, tennis. MC, V.*

Maitland

121 km (75 mi) southeast of Scone.

A good way to return to Sydney from the Upper Hunter is to travel back along the New England Highway to Muswellbrook and Singleton, then on to the historic town of Maitland. This settlement has a number of colonial buildings, and its history is best absorbed by strolling along High Street, which has been classified by the National Trust as a conservation area. Leading off this thoroughfare, Church Street has some handsome two-story Georgian homes, a couple of which are of particular interest and open to the public.

In one of Church Street's Georgian houses, the **Maitland City Art Gallery** contains both a permanent collection and changing exhibitions. ⊠ *Brough House, Church St.,* ☎ *02/4933–1657.* ◷ *Weekdays 1–4, Sat. 1:30–5, Sun. 10:30–5.*

The National Trust's **Grossman House** adjoins Maitland's art gallery. The 1870 house reopened in mid-1995 after extensive restoration, and is furnished as a Victorian merchant's town house—it contains an interesting collection of colonial antiques. ⊠ *Church St.,* ☎ *02/4933–6452.* 🎫 *$2.* ◷ *Weekends 1:30–4:30; also by appointment.*

OFF THE
BEATEN PATH — The riverside village of **Morpeth** is a scenic 5-km (3-mi) country drive from Maitland. Due to the settlement's comparative isolation, its quaint shop fronts, wharves, and even the hitching posts have survived from the time when this was an important trading station for the Hunter River Steam Navigation Company. Today the town is a backwater of the best possible kind—a place for browsing through crafts shops or just sitting under a tree by the riverbank.

Dining and Lodging

$$$$ ✗⋔ **Old George and Dragon.** In an old coaching inn in East Maitland, ★ this is one of the finest country restaurants in the state. Its atmosphere evokes the privileged air of an English country house—antique oak furnishings, Victorian watercolors in gilt frames, a blazing fire on winter evenings, vases brimming with fresh flowers. You might come across such appetizers as warm oysters and raspberries in puff pastry and a croustade of king prawns and leeks, then move on to Tasmanian salmon with wild mushroom pâté in a champagne sauce, beef fillet with Stilton cheese sauce, and duck with oranges and Grand Marnier. Desserts are rich and exotic, and the wine list has a selection of about 250 varieties. Accommodations are available in another part of the inn; guest rooms, all with private bath, are decorated in a style similar to the restaurant. Room 3 is particularly recommended. ⊠ *48 Melbourne St., East Maitland, 2323,* ☎ *02/4933–7272,* FAX *02/4934–1481. Reservations essential. AE, DC, MC, V. Closed Sun. and Mon. Lunch by arrangement Tues.–Sat.*

Golf

Maitland Golf Club (⊠ Sinclair St., East Maitland, ☎ 02/4933–7512 or 02/4933–4141) is another of the Hunter Valley's notable courses. The club welcomes visitors on most days, but it's best to check beforehand. Greens fees are $12–$15.

Hunter Valley A to Z

Arriving and Departing

BY BUS

Keans Express Travel (☎ 008/04–3339 or 02/4990–5000) buses make the 2½-hour journey from Sydney's Central Coach Terminal on Eddy Avenue (near Central Station) to Cessnock daily. The round-trip fare is $40.

BY CAR

Leave Sydney by the Harbour Bridge or Harbour Tunnel and follow the signs for Newcastle. Just before Hornsby this road joins the Sydney–Newcastle Freeway. Take the exit from the freeway that is sign-posted "Hunter Valley Vineyards via Cessnock." From Cessnock, the route to the vineyards is clearly marked. Allow 2½ hours for the 185-km (115-mi) journey from Sydney.

Getting Around

BY CAR

If you plan to spend several days exploring the area, you will need a car. Other than taking a guided tour on arrival, this is by far the best way to visit the wineries and travel to more off-the-beaten-path attractions, such as the villages of Wollombi and Morpeth.

Contacts and Resources

CAR RENTALS

For details of renting a car in Sydney, *see* Sydney A to Z *in* Chapter 2. In the Hunter Valley you can rent from **Hertz** (✉ Aberdare Rd., Lot 1A, Cessnock, ☎ 02/4991–2500). Prebook prior to arrival.

EMERGENCIES

Ambulance, fire brigade, and **police.** ☎ *000.*

GUIDED TOURS

Several Sydney-based bus companies tour the Hunter Valley. Alternative ways to explore the region are by horse-drawn carriage, bicycle, motorbike, or even in a hot-air balloon. Full details are available from the Cessnock Visitor Information Centre (☞ *below*).

Ballooning. Drifting across the valley while the vines are still wet with dew is an unforgettable way to see the Hunter Valley. **Balloon Aloft** offers flights from the Rothbury area of about an hour's duration, and serves a champagne breakfast upon your return. ☎ *02/4938–1955.* 🎟 *Weekdays $185, weekends $200.*

Bus Tours. The major touring company **AAT King's** operates a one-day bus tour of the Hunter Valley and Wollombi from Sydney on Tuesday, Thursday, and Sunday. Buses depart from the Overseas Passenger Terminal on the Harbour Bridge side of Circular Quay. Free hotel pickup is available on request. ☎ *02/9252–2788.* 🎟 *$88, including lunch and wine tasting.*

Horse-Carriage Tours. Somerset Carriages offers half-day or full-day horse-drawn carriage tours of the wineries, with the full-day tour including a gourmet picnic. ✉ *Pokolbin,* ☎ *02/4998–7591.* 🎟 *½-day tour from $150 per couple, full-day tour $250 per couple.*

VISITOR INFORMATION

Cessnock Visitor Information Centre. ✉ *Turner Park, Aberdare Rd., Cessnock, 2325,* ☎ *02/4990–4477.*
Scone (Upper Hunter) Tourist Information Centre. ✉ *Kelly and Susan Sts., Scone, 2337,* ☎ *02/6545–1526.*

Sydney Visitors Information Centre has information on Hunter Valley accommodation, tours, and sights. ✉ *106 George St. (The Rocks), 2000,* ☎ *02/9255–1788,* FAX *02/9241–5010.*

THE NORTH COAST

The North Coast is one of the most glorious and seductive stretches of terrain in Australia. An almost continuous line of beaches follows the coast, and the Great Dividing Range rises to the west. These natural borders frame a succession of rolling green pasturelands, mossy rain forest, towns dotted by red-roof houses, and waterfalls that tumble in glistening arcs from the escarpment.

A journey along the coast leads through a series of rich agricultural districts, beginning with grazing country in the south and moving into plantations of bananas, sugarcane, mangoes, avocados, and macadamia nuts. There are interesting parks for getting your feet on some native soil and for seeing unusual bird life, such as Dorrigo National Park outside of Bellingen, and Muttonbird Island in Coffs Harbour. The North Coast is also a major vacation playground, studded with resort towns that offer a modest dose of sophistication.

The tie that binds the North Coast is the Pacific Highway. Crowded, slow, and deadly dull, this highway rarely affords glimpses of the Pacific Ocean. If you take the time to explore some of the side roads, however, the rewards will more than compensate for the length of the journey. The following description of towns and other sights generally follows the route of the highway as it leads north to the Queensland border. There are several off-highway diversions—to particularly attractive or historic stretches of coastline, and some interesting inland towns and natural attractions.

In addition to general water-based activities like surfing, swimming, and boating, which are popular right through this region, a couple of North Coast spots are particularly good for scuba diving. Coffs Harbour and Byron Bay both have excellent diving, as well as several dive operators who provide trips and instruction. White-water rafting is a popular and exciting adventure sport in the Coffs Harbour region.

It is feasible to drive the entire length of the North Coast in a single day, but allow at least three—or, better still, a week—to sample properly some of the attractions.

Numbers in the margin correspond to points of interest on the North Coast map.

Taree

⑭ *335 km (208 mi) north of Sydney.*

The first major town along the North Coast, Taree is the commercial center of the Manning River district. But apart from a few fine beaches in the area, or perhaps to make an overnight stop, there is little reason to linger here on the way north.

Lodging

$$ ⊞ **Clarendon Forest Retreat.** If you're looking for affordable luxury in a forest setting, this is a fine choice. The six self-contained, self-catering cottages are spread throughout the valley to guarantee privacy. Each is spotlessly kept and equipped with a kitchen, laundry, two bedrooms, and a loft room. Recent additions are The Chapel, The Summer House, and The Sanctuary—sandstone cottages with sunken spa pools and antique furnishings. Activities on the 1,000-acre beef-cattle property in-

The North Coast

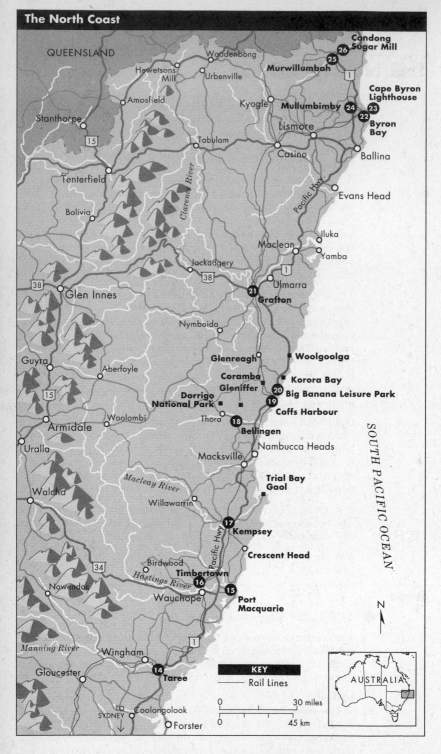

QUEENSLAND

Woodenbong

Hewetsons Mill

Urbenville

Murwillumbah

Condong Sugar Mill

26

25

1

Amosfield

Kyogle

Mullumbimby

24

Cape Byron Lighthouse

23

Stanthorpe

Lismore

22

Byron Bay

15

Tabulam

Casino

Ballina

Tenterfield

Clarence River

Evans Head

Bolivia

Iluka

Maclean

Yamba

1

Jackadgery

38

Glen Innes

38

Ulmarra

21

Grafton

Nymboida

Guyra

Woolgoolga

Glenreagh

Aberfoyle

Coramba

Korora Bay

15

Gleniffer

20

Big Banana Leisure Park

Dorrigo National Park

19

Coffs Harbour

Armidale

Woolombi

Thora

18

Uralla

Bellingen

Nambucca Heads

Walcha

Macksville

Macleay River

Trial Bay Gaol

Willawarrin

Kempsey

17

Birdwood

Crescent Head

34

Timbertown

Hastings River

16

Nowendoc

15

Wauchope

Port Macquarie

Manning River

1

Wingham

14

Taree

Gloucester

TO SYDNEY

Coolongolook

Forster

SOUTH PACIFIC OCEAN

N

KEY
— Rail Lines

0 ___ 30 miles

0 ___ 45 km

AUSTRALIA

clude tennis, fishing, swimming, bushwalking, and wildlife watching. There are also 30 horses, and riders of all standards are welcome. The nearest surf beach is a 15-minute drive. Book at least three months in advance. A two-night minimum stay is required. ⊠ *Coates Rd., Failford via Taree, 2430,* ☎ *02/6554–3162,* ℻ *02/6554–3242. 6 cottages. MC, V.*

Port Macquarie

⓯ *82 km (51 mi) north of Taree.*

Set at the mouth of the Hastings River, Port Macquarie was founded as a convict settlement in 1821. The town was chosen for its isolation to serve as an open jail for prisoners convicted of second offenses in New South Wales. By about 1830 the pace of settlement was so brisk that the town was no longer isolated, and its usefulness as a jail had ended. Today's Port Macquarie has few reminders of its convict past and is flourishing as a vacation and retirement area.

🐨 Operated by the Koala Preservation Society of NSW, the town's **Koala Hospital** is both a worthy cause and a popular attraction. The Port Macquarie region supports a fairly large number of these extremely appealing but endangered marsupials, and the hospital cares for 150 to 200 sick and injured koalas each year. You can walk around the grounds to view the recuperating animals. Try to time your visit during feeding hours—generally at 7:30 and 3. ⊠ *Macquarie Nature Reserve, Lord St., Port Macquarie,* ☎ *02/6584–1522.* ☉ *Daily 7–5.*

The award-winning **Sea Acres Rainforest Centre** comprises 178 acres of coastal rain forest on the southern side of Port Macquarie. There are over 170 plant species here, including 300-year-old cabbage tree palms, as well as native mammals, reptiles, and prolific birdlife. An elevated boardwalk allows you to stroll through the lush environment without disturbing the vegetation. The center has informative guided tours, as well as a gift shop and pleasant rain forest café. ⊠ *Pacific Dr., Port Macquarie,* ☎ *02/6582–3355.* 🎟 *$8.50.* ☉ *Daily 9–4:30.*

Housed in a historic two-story shop near the Hastings River is the eclectic **Hastings District Historical Museum,** displaying period costumes, memorabilia from both world wars, farm implements, antique clocks and watches, and relics from the town's convict days. This wide-ranging collection represents the town's social history in a manner at once entertaining and enlightening. ⊠ *22 Clarence St., Port Macquarie,* ☎ *02/ 6583–1108.* 🎟 *$4.* ☉ *Mon.–Sat. 9:30–4:30, Sun. 1–4:30.*

St. Thomas Church is in the same area as the museum. It is the country's third-oldest church, built by convicts using local cedar and stone blocks cemented together with powdered seashells. ⊠ *Hay and William Sts., Port Macquarie.* ☉ *Weekdays 9–noon and 2–4.*

🐨 **⓰** **Timbertown** is a busy theme park that re-creates life and work in a typical pioneer town of the late 1800s. Puffing bullock teams haul giant logs to a steam-powered sawmill, shingles and rails are split with axes, and the blacksmith's forge rings with the sound of a hammer on horseshoes. You can wander through fully furnished houses and a church and school, and travel around the 100-acre site on horse-drawn drays or a steam train. The park is 21 km (13 mi) inland from Port Macquarie. ⊠ *Oxley Hwy., Wauchope,* ☎ *02/6585–2322.* 🎟 *$16.* ☉ *Daily 9:30–3:30.*

En Route A scenic alternative to taking the Pacific Highway north from Port Macquarie is the 31-km (19-mi) rough gravel road that runs beside a single, vast, and mostly deserted beach to **Crescent Head**—a beach renowned in the surfing world. Take the vehicular ferry across the Hastings River from Port Macquarie to reach the road, and you can rejoin the highway near Kempsey.

Kempsey

⑰ *48 km (30 mi) north of Port Macquarie.*

The next major Pacific Highway town is Kempsey, inland on the Macleay River. It is the center for a large farming and timber region, and there isn't a great deal of interest in the town itself other than several historic buildings, the Macleay River Historical Society Museum, and various pottery and crafts shops. But the nearby coastline (☞ *above and below*) is worth a look.

OFF THE
BEATEN PATH
Just south of Kempsey, a road leads northeast to the village of South West Rocks and **Trial Bay Gaol,** 37 km (23 mi) from town. Built in the 1870s and 1880s by convicts, this jail occupies a dramatic position on the cliffs above the sea. The purpose of the jail was to teach prisoners useful skills, but the project proved too expensive and was abandoned in 1902. During World War I, the prison became an internment camp for about 500 Germans. ⊠ *Arakoon State Recreation Area,* ☎ *02/ 6566–6168.* ☞ *$3.* ☉ *Daily 9–5.*

Bellingen

⑱ *100 km (62 mi) north of Kempsey.*

Set in a river valley a few miles off the Pacific Highway, Bellingen is one of the prettiest towns along the coast, and the detour will probably come as a welcome relief if you've been droning along the Pacific Highway. Many of Bellingen's buildings have been classified by the National Trust, and the picturesque town has a museum and plenty of cafés, galleries, and crafts outlets.

OFF THE
BEATEN PATH
If you have an hour to spare, cross the Bellinger River at Bellingen and take an 18-km (11-mi) excursion to **Gleniffer.** This spectacular, rambling journey leads through farmlands and wooded valleys and across Never Never Creek to—yes, that's right—the Promised Land. Several swimming holes and picnic areas are along this road.

Dining and Lodging

$ ✕ **Carriageway Café.** Part of a magnificently restored emporium, this modish café has a wide selection of light, healthful meals. The menu includes breakfasts, rolls, soups, salads, pasta dishes, cakes, and fresh fruit juices, as well as one of the best cups of coffee on the North Coast. ⊠ *77 Hyde St., Bellingen,* ☎ *02/6655–1672. AE, MC, V.* ☉ *Mon.– Sat. 8:30–5:30, Sun. 9–3:30.*

$ ⌂ **Koompartoo.** Set on a hillside overlooking Bellingen, these self-contained open plan–style cottages are superb examples of local craftsmanship, particularly in the extensive use of timbers from surrounding forests. Each has a complete kitchen and family room, and they are very reasonably priced. You can also book a small guest room closer to the main house. Breakfast is available by arrangement. ⊠ *Rawson and Dudley Sts., Bellingen, 2454,* ☎ FAX *02/6655–2326. 4 cottages with shower. Spa. MC, V.*

En Route   An alternative, much longer, and far more spectacular route back to the Pacific Highway from Bellingen to Coffs Harbour leads you inland along the river, then climbs more than 1,000 ft up the heavily wooded escarpment to the **Dorrigo Plateau.**

★ At the top of the plateau is **Dorrigo National Park** (☎ 02/6657–2309), a small but outstanding subtropical rain forest that is included on the World Heritage List. Signposts along the main road indicate walking trails. The Satinbird Stroll is a short rain forest walk, and the 6-km (4-mi) Cedar Falls Walk leads to the most spectacular of the park's many waterfalls. The excellent **Dorrigo Rainforest Centre** offers information, educational displays, and a shop, and from here you can walk out high over the forest canopy along the Skywalk boardwalk. The national park is approximately 31 km (19 mi) from Bellingen.

Beyond Dorrigo township, a gravel road completes the loop to the town of **Coramba,** and the nearby village of Moleton. This is the location for **George's Gold Mine.** Perched on a ridge high above the Orara Valley, this 250-acre cattle property still uses the slab huts and mustering yards built in the region's pioneering days. Owner George Robb is one of the legendary old-timers of the area, and his tour of his gold mine is a vivid account of the personalities and events from the days when "gold fever" gripped these hills. In addition to the mine and its historic equipment, the property has its own rain forest, mountain springs, stand of rare red cedars, and a barbecue-picnic area. The last tour of the property departs at about 3 PM. From Coramba it is only 16 km (10 mi) to Coffs Harbour ⊠ *Bushmans Range Rd., Moleton,* ☎ 02/ 6654–5355. ☜ *$8.50.* ☼ *Wed.–Sun. 10–5.*

Coffs Harbour

⑲ *35 km (22 mi) northeast of Bellingen via the Pacific Highway, 103 km (64 mi) from Bellingen following the inland scenic route along the Dorrigo Plateau.*

The major industry of Coffs Harbour is obvious well before you arrive. This is the state's "banana republic," and the surrounding hillsides are covered with long, neat rows of banana palms. Set at the foot of steep green hills, the town also has great beaches and a mild climate—an idyllic combination that has made it one of the most popular vacation spots along the coast. Coffs is a convenient halfway point in the 1,000-km (620-mi) journey between Sydney and Brisbane.

The town has a lively and attractive harbor in the shelter of **Muttonbird Island,** and a stroll out to the island is delightful in the evening. To get there follow the signs to the Coffs Harbour Jetty and park near the fish cooperative. A wide path leads out along the breakwater and up the side of the island. The trail is steep, but the views from the top are worth the effort. The island is named after the muttonbirds (also known as shearwaters) that nest here between September and April, spending their days at sea and returning to their burrows in the evening. In late April, the birds begin their annual migration to New Zealand, the Philippines, and past Japan to the Aleutian Islands between eastern Siberia and Alaska.

Near the port in Coffs Harbour, the giant **Pet Porpoise Pool** aquarium includes sharks, colorful reef fish, turtles, seals, and dolphins. A 90-minute sea circus show can be viewed at 10:30 or 2:15. Children may help feed the dolphins and seals. ⊠ *Orlando St., Coffs Harbour,* ☎ 02/6652–2164. ☜ *$10.50.* ☼ *Daily 9–4:30.*

On the northern side of town, impossible to miss, is the Big Banana—the symbol of Coffs Harbour. This monumental piece of kitsch is part ⑳ of the **Big Banana Leisure Park** complex, which offers a fascinating look at the past, present, and future of horticulture. After a preliminary video, a shuttle takes you on a 2½-km (1½-mi) elevated train ride across plantations containing an incredible variety of tropical fruits. Modern horticultural techniques, such as hydroponics, are illustrated during the entertaining tour, and the ride concludes with a look at futuristic horticulture on a space station. At the end of the tour, you can wander down the hill to the farmer's market to purchase some of the 1,000 varieties of tropical fruit grown at the complex. ⊠ *Pacific Hwy., Coffs Harbour,* ☎ *02/6652–4355.* ⊡ *Shuttle $9.50.* ☉ *Daily 9–3.*

<table>
<tr><td>OFF THE
BEATEN PATH</td><td>Located in the tiny village of Glenreagh about 35 km (22 mi) northwest of Coffs Harbour, the Golden Dog is a fine example of an atmospheric bush pub. The place is full of character and old local memorabilia, and it's famous for its eccentricities—you might even see a horse or motorbike in the bar! The pub includes a bistro that is open daily for lunch, as well as dinner on Friday and Saturday, but a particularly good time to visit is on Sunday lunchtimes, when jazz, bush, or folk bands often perform in the beer garden. ⊠ Coramba Rd., Glenreagh, ☎ 02/6649–2162.</td></tr>
</table>

Dining and Lodging

$$ ✕ **Avanti.** Located on High Street near the harbor, in an area known as the Strip—a row of a dozen restaurants—this is a very popular place for Italian food. The decor is traditional outside-of-Italy Italian, and the menu includes a range of freshly cooked, homemade pastas—the crab ravioli is particularly recommended—as well as fish, meat, and chicken dishes. ⊠ *368 High St., Coffs Harbour,* ☎ *02/6652–4818. AE, MC, V. BYOB. Closed Sun.*

$$ ✕ **Seafood Mamas.** The specialty of this popular hilltop restaurant is southern Italian seafood dishes with mouthwatering sauces. Other popular menu choices are a barbecued seafood platter and Mediterranean beef dish. Tables on the eastern side of the restaurant overlook the ocean. The restaurant is 6 km (4 mi) north of Coffs Harbour. ⊠ *Pacific Hwy., Korora,* ☎ *02/6653–6733. AE, DC, MC, V. No lunch Sat.–Tues.*

$$$ ⊡ **Aanuka Beach Resort.** Clustered in cabanas amid banana trees, ★ palms, frangipani, and hibiscus, each of the individual ground-floor cedar suites at this glamorous resort has its own lounge, kitchen facilities, laundry, and private two-person spa bath set in a glass-ceiling bathroom. All suites feature beautifully crafted teak furniture and antiques collected from the islands of Indonesia and the South Pacific. The landscaping at this world-class environmentally friendly resort is exotic and imaginative—the pool, for example, is immersed in a miniature rain forest with a waterfall and cave jacuzzi. The resort fronts a secluded white sandy beach and the blue waters of the Pacific Ocean. Rates include a tropical buffet breakfast. ⊠ *Box 266, Firman Dr., Coffs Harbour, 2540,* ☎ *02/6652–7555,* ℻ *02/6652–7053. 48 suites. 2 restaurants, 2 bars, pool, sauna, whirlpool, tennis, exercise room. AE, DC, MC, V.*

$$$ ⊡ **Pelican Beach Travelodge Resort.** This terraced, Mediterranean-style complex is one of the most striking resorts on the North Coast. Rooms are decorated in pastel blues and salmons, with cane chairs and glass tables. Each guest room also has a private balcony facing either the sea or the mountains to the west. Facilities are stylish and well designed, including a huge saltwater swimming pool resembling a tropical lagoon. Children have their own playroom, a video arcade, fishponds, and an outdoor junior gym. ⊠ *Pacific Hwy., Coffs Harbour,*

2450, ☎ *02/6653–7000,* FAX *02/6653–7066. 114 rooms with bath. Restaurant, 2 bars, sauna, whirlpool, tennis. AE, DC, MC, V.*

Outdoor Activities and Sports

SCUBA DIVING

The warm seas around Coffs Harbour mark the southernmost limit of coral formations, making this particular part of the coast, with its moray eels, manta rays, turtles, and gray nurse sharks, a scuba diver's favorite. **Island Snorkel & Dive** (☎ 02/6654–2860) and **Dive Quest** (☎ 02/6654–1930) have both equipment and diving tours, as well as snorkeling trips and complete tuition for novice scuba divers.

WHITE-WATER RAFTING

The highly regarded local adventure company **Wildwater Adventures** offers one-, two-, and four-day rafting trips down the Nymboida River. This is a genuine white-water river, suitable for novices but wild enough to satisfy even the most adventurous. Between shooting the rapids, the rafts travel through quiet rain forest and steep-sided gorges. Trips begin from Bonville, 14 km (9 mi) south of Coffs Harbour on the Pacific Highway, but pickups from Coffs can be arranged. ⊠ *26 Butler's Rd., Bonville,* ☎ *02/6653–4469.* 🖅 *1-day trip from $120, including meals.*

Shopping

Hidden by gum trees 16 km (10 mi) north of Coffs Harbour, the four-level **Lake Russell Gallery** houses a first-rate collection of contemporary Australian art and craftwork. Prices are comparatively low, and the complex includes pleasant tearooms. ⊠ *Smiths Rd. and Pacific Hwy., Coffs Harbour,* ☎ *02/6656–1092.* ◐ *Daily 10–5.*

En Route A few miles north of the Big Banana, the Pacific Highway loops through banana plantations toward the sea. A short detour off this road will take you to **Korora Bay,** a small crescent of sand cradled between rocky headlands. About 10 km (6 mi) north of Korora Bay, a wide, shallow lagoon formed by **Moonee Creek** offers safe, sheltered bathing for children. Note that the beaches between Korora Bay and Moonee are often unsafe for swimming because of wild pounding surf and the absence of lifeguards outside of school holiday periods.

A little farther north is **Woolgoolga**—"Woopi" to locals—known for its large Sikh population, whose ancestors came to Australia from India at the end of the 19th century. The Guru Nanak Sikh Temple is the town's main attraction—request entrance at the Temple View Restaurant opposite. Woolgoolga is 58 km (36 mi) from Grafton.

Grafton

㉑ *84 km (52 mi) north of Coffs Harbour.*

The largish city of Grafton is at the center of the Clarence Valley, a rich agricultural district with a number of sugarcane farms. The highway bypasses Grafton, but it's worth detouring to see some of the notable Victorian buildings on Fitzroy, Victoria, and Prince streets. The city is famous for its jacaranda trees, which erupt in a mass of purple flowers in the spring. During the last week of October, when the trees are at their finest, Grafton holds its **Jacaranda Festival.** Festivities include arts-and-crafts shows, novelty races, children's rides, and a parade.

En Route Between Grafton and the far north coast, the Pacific Highway enters sugarcane country, where tiny sugarcane trains and thick, drifting smoke from burning cane fields are ever present. The highway passes

the fishing and resort town of **Ballina**—beaches are its prime feature—
and the best option is to continue north to Byron Bay.

Byron Bay

㉒ *176 km (109 mi) north of Grafton (exit right from the highway at Bangalow or Ewingsdale).*

Byron Bay is the easternmost point of the continent and one of the symbols of Australia's nickname, the "Lucky Country." Fabulous beaches, awesome whales, storms that leave rainbows in glistening arches across the mountains behind the town, and a sunny, relaxed style cast a spell over practically everyone who visits. For many years Byron Bay was a mecca for surfers lured by abundant sunshine, perfect waves on Wategos Beach, and tolerant locals who allowed them to sleep on the sand. These days Byron Bay has been discovered by a more upscale clientele, but fortunately the beachfront has—as yet—been spared from high-rise resorts. The town is at its liveliest on the first Sunday of each month, when Butler Street becomes a country market.

㉓ Byron Bay is dominated by the **Cape Byron Lighthouse,** the most powerful beacon on the Australian coastline. The headland above the parking lot near the lighthouse is a launching point for hang-gliders, who soar for hours on the warm thermals. This is also a favorite place for whale-watching between June and September, when migrating humpback whales often come close inshore. The headland is the highlight of the **Cape Byron Walking Track,** which circuits a 150-acre reserve and passes through grasslands and rain forest. There are several vantage points along the track, from which you may spot dolphins, sharks, or manta rays in the waters below. ⊠ *Lighthouse Rd., Byron Bay,* ☎ *02/6685–8565.* ⊙ *Lighthouse grounds daily 8–5:30.*

Located in the Byron headland's Lighthouse Cottage, the **Byron Bay Whale Centre** is an interactive information center and museum featuring hands-on activities, CD-Roms, spectacular audiovisuals, and stunning photography. Displays focus on such topics as Byron Bay's whaling history, whale migrations and behavior, and environmental awareness. ⊠ *Lighthouse Rd., Byron Bay,* ☎ *02/6685–8799.* ⊡ *$4.* ⊙ *Daily 9–5 (last entry at 4).*

Several superb **beaches** lie in the vicinity of Byron Bay. Situated in front of the town, **Main Beach** offers safe swimming, and **Clarks Beach,** closer to the cape, has better surf. The most famous surfing beach, however, is **Wategos,** the only north-facing beach in the state. To the south of the lighthouse, **Tallow Beach** extends for 6 km (4 mi) to a rocky stretch of coastline around Broken Head, which features a number of small sandy coves. Beyond Broken Head is **Seven Mile Beach.**

Dining and Lodging

$$$ ✕ **Fig Tree Restaurant.** In its 100-year-old farmhouse with distant
★ views of Byron Bay and the ocean, the Fig Tree offers creative "Oz" cuisine in magnificently forested surroundings. Local produce fresh from the owners' farm stands out on a menu that will take you from an appetizer of ravioli with fresh mussels and prawns in butter sauce to main dishes like Moroccan-style honeyed chicken breast served with char-roasted pumpkin and chermoula. Ask for a table on the veranda. The restaurant is 5 km (3 mi) inland from Byron Bay. ⊠ *4 Sunrise La., Ewingsdale,* ☎ *02/6684–7273. AE, DC, MC, V. BYOB. Closed Sun.–Tues. No lunch Wed.*

$$ ✕ **Café D.O.C.** This smart, breezy town-center café makes good use of a wide range of locally made salamis and hams in its robust and imaginative Italian-influenced fare. Pasta dishes, which can be as simple as a spinach linguine teamed with fresh tomato, herbs, and Parmesan, are a specialty. In winter, Lisa Middleton creates dinners based on the cooking of the Italian provinces where she lived for several years. ⊠ *Shop 7, Middleton St., Byron Bay,* ☎ *02/6685–5252. MC, V. No dinner Fri.–Tues.*

$ ✕ **Beach Café.** A Byron Bay legend, this outdoor café is a perfect place
★ to sit in the morning sun and watch the waves. The café opens at 7:30 daily, and breakfasts are wholesome and imaginative—the fresh juices and tropical fruits alone are worth the 10-minute stroll along the beach from town. ⊠ *Clarks Beach, Byron Bay,* ☎ *02/6685–7598. MC, V. No dinner.*

$$$ ▥ **On the Bay Beach House.** Overlooking Byron Bay's Main Beach, this large, modern guest house offers an exceptional standard of comfort, style, and facilities. Local fabrics and furniture have been used extensively in the house, and all guest rooms have ocean views and access to sun decks. The Penthouse offers extra space and luxury at a slightly higher price. Children under 15 are not accommodated. Rates include breakfast. ⊠ *44 Lawson St., Byron Bay, 2481,* ☎ *02/6685–5125,* ℻ *02/6685–5198. 5 rooms with bath. Pool. MC, V.*

$$$ ▥ **Taylors.** Buried in a jungle of strangler figs and camphor laurel in
★ the hills behind Byron Bay, this luxurious guest house brings sophistication to the natural charm of the North Coast. Guest rooms are large and sumptuously furnished with antiques. Breakfasts are excellent, relying on the fresh fruits and eggs from the 15-acre property. The property is open all year. Children are not accommodated. Rates include breakfast. ⊠ *McGettigans La., Ewingsdale, 2481,* ☎ *02/6684–7436,* ℻ *02/6684–7526. 5 rooms with bath, 1 house. Pool. DC, MC, V.*

$ ▥ **Wheel Resort.** In a secluded bushland setting adjacent to the beach, this delightful resort has facilities especially tailored to wheelchair users, but everyone is welcome here. Wide pathways afford easy access to the 6½-acre surroundings, accommodations have been modified for safety and convenience, and the pool has a gently sloping ramp. Self-contained timber cabins, available with either one or two bedrooms, have cork-tile floors, cool cream and natural wood colors, and exposed rafters. The resort is 2½ km (1½ mi) south of Byron Bay. ⊠ *39–51 Broken Head Rd., Byron Bay, 2481,* ☎ *02/6685–6139,* ℻ *02/6685–8754. 6 cabins with shower. Restaurant, pool, spa. MC, V.*

Nightlife

With nine main venues, the small town of Byron Bay offers an unusually wide choice of music and entertainment every night of the week. **The Carpark** (⊠ The Plaza, Jonson St., ☎ 02/6685–6170) is a nightclub-restaurant featuring Thai and Mediterranean-style food and live bands. **Cocomangas Restaurant and Nightclub,** a Philippine-style club, serves up fine food and live dance music until late. ⊠ *32 Jonson St.,* ☎ *02/ 6685–8493.*

Scuba Diving

The **Byron Bay Dive Centre** offers snorkeling and scuba-diving trips for all levels of experience, gear rentals, instruction, and courses. The best local diving is at Julian Rocks, some 3 km (2 mi) offshore, where the confluence of warm and cold currents supports a profusion of marine life. ⊠ *Bay Lane, Byron Bay,* ☎ *02/6685–7149.*

Shopping

Byron Bay is a shopper's delight, with a wide range of crafts and handmade items for sale. Leather goods, offbeat designer clothing, essential oils, natural cosmetics, and housewares are just some of what's available.

Colin Heaney Hot Glass Studio. Exquisite hand-blown glassware in the form of goblets, wineglasses, paperweights, and sculpture are sold here, but another attraction is watching the glassblowers at work (weekdays 9–4). ⊠ *6 Acacia St., Industrial Estate, Byron Bay,* ☎ *02/6685–7044.* ⊙ *Weekdays 9–5, weekends 10–4.*

Mullumbimby

㉔ *23 km (14 mi) northwest of Byron Bay.*

Affectionately known as "Mullum," Mullumbimby is a peaceful inland town with some historic buildings, interesting arts and crafts shops, and a reputation for attracting alternative-lifestyle types. The town is at the center of a fertile banana and subtropical fruit-growing region, well worth a short detour off the Pacific Highway.

Dining and Lodging

$$$$ ✕▥ **Sakura Farm.** Genzan Kosaka, the owner, is a Zen Buddhist priest, and a stay at his farm is a unique experience of Japanese culture. Guests share a three-bedroom house—simple, neat, and Western in style—just inland from Mullumbimby. The chance to sample authentic Japanese cooking is a big attraction, but chef Seiko Kosaka also prepares French meals from time to time. Other options include shiatsu massage, instruction in Buddhist meditation, and taking Japanese-style open-air baths. To benefit fully from the experience, plan to stay at least two nights. Rates include all meals. ⊠ *Left Bank Rd., Lot 5, Mullumbimby, 2482,* ☎ 𝔽𝔸𝕏 *02/6684–1724. 1 cottage. MC, V.*

Murwillumbah

㉕ *53 km (33 mi) northwest of Byron Bay.*

Dominated by the towering, cone-shape peak of 3,800-ft Mount Warning, pleasant, rambling Murwillumbah is situated amid sugarcane plantations on the banks of the Tweed River. Apart from the seaside resort of Tweed Heads, Murwillumbah is the last town of any size before the Queensland border.

㉖ At the **Condong Sugar Mill,** on the banks of the Tweed River some 5 km (3 mi) north of town, you can take an informative tour during the crushing season, July through November. The one-hour visit begins with a video, followed by a hands-on tour of the mill during which you are invited to sample sugar and some of the other products manufactured at the complex. ⊠ *Pacific Hwy., Murwillumbah,* ☎ *02/6670–1700.* ▤ *$4.50.* ⊙ *Tour July–Nov., daily 9–3, weather permitting.*

North Coast A to Z

Arriving and Departing

BY BUS
Greyhound Pioneer Australia (☎ 13–2030), **McCafferty's** (☎ 13–1499), and **Pioneer Motor Service** (☎ 02/9281–2233) operate frequently between Sydney and Brisbane, with stops at all major North Coast towns. Sydney to Coffs Harbour is a 9-hour ride, Byron Bay 12.

BY CAR
From Sydney, head north via the Harbour Bridge or Harbour Tunnel and follow the signs to Hornsby and Newcastle. Join the Sydney–Newcastle Freeway, then continue up the Pacific Highway (Hwy. 1), the main route along the 604-km (375-mi) Taree-to-Queensland coast. Taree is 335 km (208 mi) north of Sydney.

From Sydney, **Ansett Australia** and **Impulse Airlines** (☎ 13–1300) operate frequent services to Port Macquarie, Kempsey, Coffs Harbour, Ballina (close to Byron Bay), and Coolangatta (just over the Queensland border, but convenient for the far north of N.S.W.). **Qantas Airways** and its subsidiary **Eastern Australia Airlines** (☎ 13–1313) fly into Taree, Port Macquarie, Kempsey, Coffs Harbour, Grafton, and Coolangatta.

BY TRAIN

Trains stop at the towns of Taree, Kempsey, Coffs Harbour, Grafton, Byron Bay, and Murwillumbah, but much of the Sydney–Brisbane railway line runs inland, and the service is not particularly useful for seeing the North Coast. Call **Countrylink** (☎ 13–2232), the NSW rail operator, for details of fares and services.

Getting Around

BY BUS

The long-distance buses mentioned above are more than adequate for travel between the coast's main centers, and all of the larger towns provide local bus services. Bus travel, however, is not recommended for getting off the beaten track, or exploring beyond the major towns.

BY CAR

A car is essential for exploring the North Coast's off-highway attractions and to travel at your own pace.

Contacts and Resources

CAR RENTALS

Car-rental agencies are represented in several North Coast towns: **Avis** (✉ Lismore near Byron Bay, ☎ 02/6621–9022; ✉ Coffs Harbour, ☎ 02/6651–3600), **Budget** (✉ Coffs Harbour, ☎ 02/6651–4994), **Hertz** (✉ Byron Bay, ☎ 02/6685–6522; ✉ Coffs Harbour, ☎ 02/6651–1899; ✉ Port Macquarie, ☎ 02/6583–6599). You can also rent a car in Sydney if you plan to make the drive up the coast (☞ Sydney A to Z *in* Chapter 2).

EMERGENCIES

Ambulance, fire brigade, and **police.** ☎ *000*.

GUIDED TOURS

Macquarie Mountain Tours (☎ 02/6585–9242) offers a full-day, four-wheel-drive trip into World Heritage–listed Werrikimbe National Park and the rain forest surrounding **Port Macquarie.** The tour costs $75. A barbecue lunch is included. **Mountain Trails 4WD Tours** (☎ 02/6658–3333) offers half- and full-day tours of the rain forests, waterfalls, and historic attractions of the Great Dividing Range to the west of **Coffs Harbour** in luxurious vehicles—a seven-seat Toyota Safari or a 14-seat, Australian-designed four-wheel-drive. The region is rich in natural and historic attractions, and the award-winning tours have a long-standing reputation for excellence. The half-day tour costs $48, and the full-day tour is $72, including lunch.

VISITOR INFORMATION

Byron Bay Visitor Information Centre. ✉ *Jonson St.,* ☎ *02/6685–8050.*
Coffs Harbour Visitor Information Centre. ✉ *Rose Ave. and Marcia St.,* ☎ *02/6652–1522 or 1800/02–5650.*
Murwillumbah Visitors Centre. ✉ *Pacific Hwy. and Alma St.,* ☎ *1800/67–4414 or 02/6672–1340.*
Port Macquarie Tourist Information Centre. ✉ *Hay and Clarence Sts.,* ☎ *1800/02–5935 or 02/6583–1077.*

Sydney Visitors Information Centre has information on North Coast accommodation, tours, and sights. ✉ *106 George St. (The Rocks), 2000,* ☎ *02/9255–1788,* FAX *02/9241–5010.*

LORD HOWE ISLAND

By David
McGonigal

Updated by
Anne
Matthews

A tiny crescent of land 782 km (485 mi) northeast of Sydney, Lord Howe Island is the most remote and arguably the most beautiful part of New South Wales. With the sheer peaks of Mount Gower (2,870 ft) and Mount Lidgbird (2,548 ft) richly clad in palms, ferns, and grasses, its golden sandy beaches, and the clear turquoise waters of the lagoon, this is a remarkably lovely place. Apart from the barren spire of Ball's Pyramid, a stark volcanic outcrop 16 km (10 mi) across the water to the southeast, the Lord Howe Island Group stands alone in the South Pacific. In 1982 the area was placed on UNESCO's World Heritage list as a "natural area of universal value and outstanding beauty." That's a fair assessment of why it is a favorite among certain Australians trying to get away from it all—and why they've been keeping it to themselves for so long.

The island's history is no less fascinating. It may be that the first ship to sight it did so in 1788, when it passed Lord Howe on its way to the Norfolk Island penal settlement farther out in the Pacific. And evidence, or lack of it, suggests that Lord Howe was uninhabited by humans until three Europeans and their Maori wives and children settled it in the 1830s. English and American whaling boats then began calling in for supplies, and by the 1870s the small population included a curious mixture of people from America (including whalers and a former slave), England, Ireland, Australia, South Africa, and the Gilbert Islands. Many of the descendants of these early settlers still live on Lord Howe. In the 1870s, when the importance of whale oil declined, islanders set up an export industry of the seeds of the endemic Kentia (*Howea forsteriana*), the world's most popular indoor palm. It's still a substantial business, but rather than seeds, seedlings are now sold.

Lord Howe is a remarkably safe and relaxed place, where cyclists and walkers far outnumber the few cars, and where locals and visitors alike leave doors unlocked and bags unattended. There are plenty of walks, both flat and rather precipitous, and fine beaches. Among the many bird species is the rare, endangered, flightless Lord Howe woodhen (*Tricholimnas sylvestris*). In the sea below the island's fringing reef is the world's southernmost coral reef, with more than 50 species of hard corals and over 500 fish species. For its size, the island has enough to keep you alternately occupied and unoccupied for at least five days.

Less than 300 people live here, which is part of the reason that much of the island shows so little impact from its 150-plus years of sustained human habitation. Visitor numbers are limited to 400 at any given time, and at present there are only 393 tourist beds. The allocation of those remaining seven is the subject of local controversy.

Exploring

The first view of Lord Howe Island rising sheer out of the South Pacific is spectacular. The sense of wonder only grows as you set out around the island, which, at a total area of 3,220 acres (about 1 by 7 mi), is pretty manageable. You don't have to allow much time to see the town. Most of the community is scattered along the rolling hills at the northern end of the island. There's a school, a hospital, a few shops, and three churches. Everything else is either a home or lodge.

As one of the very few impediments to winds sweeping across the South Pacific, the mountains of Lord Howe Island create their own weather. Visually, this can be spectacular as you stand in sunshine on the coast watching cap clouds gather around the high peaks. The average annual rainfall of about 62 inches mostly comes down in winter. Note that, except during the period of Australia's summer daylight saving time (when Lord Howe and Sydney are on the same time), island time is a curious half hour ahead of Sydney. It's also important to be aware that many of the lodges, restaurants, and tour operators close in winter—generally from June to August—and accommodation prices are reduced considerably during that period.

Sights to See

In town, a good first stop is the **museum.** The sign on the door is typical of the island's sense of time—"The museum is staffed entirely by volunteers . . . if there is no one in attendance by 2:15 pm it should be assumed that the museum will not be open on that day." Inside there's an interesting display of historical memorabilia and a less impressive collection of marine life and stuffed land animals. ✉ *Lagoon Rd.,* ✆ *$4.* ⊙ *Daily 2–4.*

A very enjoyable way of filling a sunny day is to take a picnic down to **Neds Beach,** on the eastern side of the island, where you'll find green lawns sloping down to a sandy beach and clear blue waters. This is a fantastic place for swimming and snorkeling—fish swim close to the shore, and the coral is just a few yards out.

There is a variety of **walks** all around the island, short, moderate, and considerable. The short to moderate category includes a flat, easy walk around forested Stevens Reserve, right in the heart of town, trips to surf-pounded **Blinky Beach,** to great views from the **Clear Place** and at **Middle Beach,** and to a good snorkeling spot under the heights of Mt. Gower by **Little Island.** The moderate climbs up **Mt. Eliza** and **Malabar** at the island's northern end are more strenuous than the other walks, although much less so than Mt. Gower, and they afford tremendous views of the island, including its hulking, mountainous southern end and the waters and islets all around.

The ultimate challenge on Lord Howe is the climb up the southernmost peak of **Mount Gower,** which rises straight out of the ocean to an astonishing 2,870 ft above sea level. The all-day hike starts at 7:30 AM, and you'll need to bring lunch, drinks, jackets, and walking shoes. After a scramble along the shore, the ascent into the forest begins. There's time for a break at the Erskine River crossing by some pretty cascades, then it's a solid slog to the summit. The views, the lush vegetation, and the chance to see the rare woodhen all make the hike well worthwhile. The national park requires that you use a guide. *Call Jack Shick,* ✆ *02/6563–2218.* ✆ *$25.* ⊙ *Thurs.; other days by appointment; meet at Little Island Gate at 7:30 AM sharp.*

Dining and Lodging

$$ ✕ **Aunty Sue's.** This delightful restaurant, located just behind the village, provides both indoor and outdoor dining. The decor is light and modern, with polished floorboards and painted timber walls, and the covered deck overlooks lush gardens. Marcia Branson, previously head chef at an acclaimed Sydney restaurant, creates delicious modern Australian dishes with fresh produce, much of which is from the island. Dine on stir-fried king prawns with chilli jam, or a Brie, tomato, and walnut pesto pizza, or Thai red chicken curry, vegetable pie with mashed potato, or roast duckling with Chinese vegetables. The lunch specialty is a variety of tasty pizzas. Desserts might include Greek walnut cake, or warm apple tart with ice cream. The restaurant is open daily all year for lunch and dinner. ⊠ *Anderson Rd.,* ☎ *02/6563–2093. MC, V.*

$$ ✕ **Beachcomber Lodge.** If you prefer traditional home-cooked fare, the Beachcomber provides a good-value buffet of hot and cold dishes in its licensed dining room on Thursday evening, as well as a popular "island fish fry" dinner on Sunday. The locally caught fish is cooked in beer batter and accompanied by chips and salads. Main courses are followed by a variety of desserts, a cheese platter, and coffee. ⊠ *Anderson Rd.,* ☎ *02/6563–2032. AE, DC, MC, V.*

$ ✕ **Trader Nick's Lagoon Café.** Lord Howe Island needed this bright new café in the middle of the main settlement. The meals are good and well priced, kid-size portions are available, and you dine outdoors. Tea and excellent coffee and cakes are a good draw, and the café serves beer, wine, and cocktails as well. The menu lists such snacks as salads, nachos, pizzas, potato wedges, and antipasto plates, and more substantial meals might include fish-and-chips, enormous burgers, and chicken tortillas. The café is generally open daily from 9–5, but extends its hours one evening each week. ⊠ *Lagoon Rd.,* ☎ *02/6563–2019. AE, MC, V.*

$$$$ ✕🖫 **Capella Lodge.** This is the pick of the accommodations on Lord Howe. Where to some it may seem a bit out of the way on the island's south end (of course the island is out of the way to begin with), you'll be taking advantage of Lord Howe's best lookout. The lodge's veranda looks over beaches, the ocean, and green fields to the dramatic skyline filled with the high peaks of Mount Lidgbird and Mount Gower. The nine high-ceiling guest suites are tastefully decorated with unique textiles with marine motifs, and shuttered doors that let light in while maintaining privacy. The equally attractive and stylish **White Gallinule Restaurant**— the best on the island—serves all guest meals. Presentation is excellent, and the culinary skills of chef Richard Tapper are evident in every dish. The menu changes daily. Non-guests can come for dinner, too—call ahead for reservations (☎ 02/6563–2008), and allow time for the lodge's mini-bus to pick you up. The owners also operate the luxurious Capella Apartments, at the other end of the island, if you are looking for a more central accommodation option. Rates include breakfast. ⊠ *Lagoon Rd., Lord Howe Island, 2898;* ☎ *02/9290–1922 Sydney booking office,* 🆕 *02/9290–1615. 9 rooms with bath and shower. Restaurant, bar, snorkeling, canoeing, mountain bikes. AE, MC, V.*

$$$ ✕🖫 **Trader Nick's.** This intimate hotel is tucked away at the north end of the island beside a Kentia and banyan tree forest. Set in tropical gardens, the spacious self-contained suites are beautifully furnished and decorated and feature well-equipped kitchens, separate lounge areas, ceiling fans, private decks, and luxurious bathrobes—there are no televisions to disturb the tranquillity. The hotel is close to a delightful beach and a short distance from the village. Mountain bikes are available for hire, and a complimentary transport service is also available. Guests and nonresidents can dine at the excellent brasserie-style Williams Restaurant (☎ 02/6563–2002), which serves fine wine and light modern cuisine—perhaps local kingfish, a grilled beef fillet, or pan-roasted chicken breast on coconut rice—nightly. Hydroponic lettuces and herbs are grown on the property, and all cakes, breads, and pastas are made at the restaurant. Attractive barbecue areas are also provided for you to cook your own food. ⊠ *Old Settlement Beach, Lord Howe Island, 2898;* ☎ *02/9299–2211 Sydney booking office,* 🆕 *02/9299–4644. 7 suites. Restaurant, bar, snorkeling, fishing. AE, MC, V.*

$$ ✕🖫 **Pinetrees.** Run by descendants of the island's first settlers, this is the largest resort on the island and one of the few accommodations that is open all year. The location is very convenient—opposite the main lagoon beach and near shops and the museum. The 1884 homestead forms part of the resort, but most accommodation is in undistinguished, single-story motel-style units, which have verandas leading into well-established gardens. Five Garden Cottages provide a higher standard of accommodation, with a living–dining–kitchen area, a master bedroom, and a private courtyard. At Pinetrees restaurant (☎ 02/6563–2177), you have a selection from a limited but well-balanced menu at each meal. At lunch you may have such dishes as deep-fried kingfish or leg-ham salad. In the evening, you might begin with a lightly curried cauliflower and parsnip soup, move on to crumbed chicken breast fillet or pork medallions with apple and sun-dried bell peppers, and finish with a chocolate mascarpone torte. Non-guests can also dine at Pinetrees. A number of tour operators call here at breakfast, and the staff can arrange any other activities you wish. Rates include all meals. ✉ *Booking office: 72 Erskine St., Sydney, 2000,* ☎ *02/9262–6585,* FAX *02/9262–6638. 33 rooms with shower. Restaurant, bar, tennis court, billiards. AE, DC, MC, V (credit cards accepted at booking office only, not on island).*

$$$ 🏨 **Somerset.** Established in 1946 by the descendants of Somerset, Massachusetts–born whaler Nathan Chase Thompson, one of Lord Howe's early settlers, this is the island's largest self-catering lodge. Set in well-groomed subtropical gardens with plantings of Kentia palms and hibiscus, the blocks of one-bedroom units are divided into three separate sections, creating a sense of privacy and seclusion. Although not overly luxurious, the spacious units have separate living rooms and private verandas and are well appointed. A television, ceiling fans, fridge, microwave, toaster, kettle, and cookware come in all units, as do beach towels, backpacks, and water bottles for hiking. Bikes, helmets, and snorkeling gear are available for rental. The grounds contain several pleasant barbecue areas for guests to cook their own meals, and laundry facilities are also provided. The lodge is in an ideal location—on level ground close to two beaches, shops, and the island's main facilities. ✉ *Neds Beach Rd., Lord Howe Island, 2898,* ☎ *02/6563–2061,* FAX *02/6563–2110. 25 units with shower. Barbecues. AE.*

Outdoor Activities and Sports

Fishing

Fishing is a major preoccupation on Lord Howe. There are several well-equipped boats that regularly go for kingfish, yellowfin tuna, marlin, and wahoo. These include the ***Belle Chase*** (☎ 02/6563–2032), **MV Barracuda** (☎ 02/6563–2155 or 02/6563–2185), and **TSMV** *Lulawai* (☎ 02/6563–2010). A half-day trip, including tackle and bait, costs around $50, and it's best to arrange an excursion after arriving on the island.

Golf

Visitors are welcome at the spectacularly located 9-hole **Lord Howe Island Golf Club,** and you can rent clubs and buggies rather than exceed your airline baggage allowance by bringing them from the mainland. ☎ *02/6563–2051 or 02/6563 2195.* ⛳ *Greens fee $10 for 9 or 18 holes.*

Scuba Diving

The reefs of Lord Howe Island provide a unique opportunity for diving in coral far from the equator and, unlike many of the Queensland islands, superb diving and snorkeling is literally just offshore, rather than a long boat trip away. Even though the water is warm enough for coral, most divers use a 5mm wetsuit. It's all boat diving with good equipment, operated by **Pro Dive** under the expert eye of Jeff Deacon. Although there isn't the Barrier Reef's profusion of coral, you'll see fine displays of plate coral, black coral trees, and an impressive array of fish—from lion fish and bull rays to leopard fish, box fish, and the ubiquitous parrot fish. Dives can be arranged on the day; in mid-summer there are up to four dive trips a day. Although certified divers are catered for throughout the winter, dive courses are not operated in June and July. If you are going to Lord Howe specifically for diving, contact **Pro Dive Travel** (☎ 02/9232–5733 or 1800/80–6820, FAX 02/9232–5788) in Sydney, which has packages that include accommodations, airfares, and diving.

Snorkeling

If you're not interested in diving, snorkeling is also excellent off Lord Howe Island. The best spots are on the reef that fringes the lagoon, at Neds Beach and North Bay, and around the Sylph Hole off Old Settlement Beach—a spot that turtles frequent. Snorkeling gear can be rented from your lodge, or from **Wilson's Hire Service** on Lagoon Road. A good way to get to the reef, and view the coral en route, is on a glass-bottom boat trip—both the *Blue Petrel* and *Coral Princess* offer two-hour cruises that include snorkeling gear in the $15 charge. **Pro Dive** (☞ *above*) also runs educational snorkeling tours for $15.

Lord Howe Island A to Z

Arriving and Departing

BY PLANE

Unless you have your own boat, the only practical way of getting to Lord Howe Island is by **Qantas** (☎ 13–1313) from Brisbane or Sydney. In both cases, the flying time is about two hours. Your hosts on Lord Howe Island will pick you up from the airport. There is a $20 Island Service Levy (paid on departure) for each adult, and you should note that the baggage allowance is only 31 lbs per person. Special discounts on airfares to the island are often available for overseas visitors if you purchase tickets outside of Australia.

Getting Around

BY BICYCLE

Despite the island's hills and high peaks, much of the terrain is fairly flat, and bicycles are the ideal form of transport. These can be hired through your lodge, or from **Wilson's Hire Service** on Lagoon Road, for approximately $4 per day. By law, helmets must be worn, and they are supplied with the bikes.

BY CAR

There are just six rental cars on the island. Your lodge can arrange one for you (if any are available) for about $50 per day. However, with 24 km (15 mi) of roads on the island, even cutting the 15 mph maximum permissible driving speed in half, you'll soon run out of places to go.

Contacts and Resources

EMERGENCIES

Ambulance, fire brigade, and **police.** ☎ *000*.
Doctor. ☎ 02/6563–2056.
Hospital. ☎ 02/6563–2000.

GUIDED TOURS

Ron's Ramble (☎ 02/6563–2010; ☞ $12.50) is a scenic and highly informative three-hour stroll around a small section of the island, with knowledgeable guide Ron Matthews explaining much about Lord Howe's geology, history, and plant and animal life. Groups are limited to 16 people, and the relaxed pace makes the walk suitable for all ages. The rambles take place on Monday, Wednesday, and Friday afternoons, and reservations can be made through Thompson's Store or the Lagoon Cafe. **Islander Cruises** (☎ 02/6563–2021; ✇ North Bay ferry $5 each way, snorkeling or sunset cruise $20) has several tours around the island, including ferries and cruises to North Bay for snorkeling and, weather permitting, a two-hour sunset cocktail cruise on the lagoon. Private charters are also available. **Whitfield's Island Tours** (☎ 02/6563–2115; ✇ $18) runs a half-day air-conditioned bus tour that provides a good overview of the island's history and present-day life. The tours include morning or afternoon tea at the Whitfield home, and will give you a good idea of where to return on your own. Arrange this tour through Thompson's Store.

MONEY MATTERS

Although most major credit cards are widely accepted, there are no ATMs on the island and visitors should carry adequate cash or traveler's checks in addition to their credit cards.

VISITOR INFORMATION

Contact the **Lord Howe Island Board** (✉ Lord Howe Island, NSW 2898, ☎ 02/6563–2066, FAX 026563–2127) for advance information on the island. Although the island Howe has a **Visitors Centre** (☎ 02/6563–2114), which can provide general information, most of the tours and activities should be arranged through either **Thompson's Store** on Neds Beach Road, the **Lagoon Cafe** on Lagoon Road, or **Joy's Shop** on Middle Beach Road. A notice board outside the center indicates which trips should be booked where.

Sydney Visitors Information Centre. ✉ *106 George St. (The Rocks), 2000,* ☎ *02/9255–1788,* FAX *02/9241–5010.*

THE SNOWY MOUNTAINS

Down by Kosciusko, where the pine-clad ridges raise
Their torn and rugged battlements on high,
Where the air is clear as crystal, and the white stars fairly blaze,
At midnight in the cold and frosty sky . . .

Aside from his 1890 poem, "The Man from Snowy River," what remains of Banjo Paterson's stuff of life and lore is scattered throughout the Snowys in the form of a hundred-odd old settlers' huts. Then there are the mountains and valleys themselves.

Reaching north from the border with Victoria, this section of the Great Dividing Range is an alpine wonderland. The entire region is part of Kosciusko (pronounced "ko-zee-os-ko") National Park, the largest alpine area in Australia, which occupies a 6,764-square-km (2,600-sq-mi) chunk of New South Wales. The national park also contains Australia's highest point in Mount Kosciusko, which reaches a modest—on a worldwide scale—7,314 ft. Mountain peaks and streams, high meadows, forests, caves, glacial lakes, and wildflowers provide for a wealth of outdoor activities.

This wilderness region is perfect for walking and all kinds of adventure activities outside of the winter skiing season. The area's self-guided walking trails are excellent, and in addition to the popular Mount Kosciusko summit walk (☞ **Thredbo Village**), there are many others that are wholly enjoyable. Two in particular are recommended: the **Blue Lake Trail** from Charlotte Pass, which is part of a 21-km (13-mi) loop connecting a number of peaks and a couple of other glacial lakes, and the **Goldseeker's Track,** off the Snowy Mountains Highway on the way to Cabramurra. In addition, local operators, and others based in Sydney, offer hiking, climbing, mountain biking, white-water rafting, and horseback riding tours and excursions.

A number of lakes—Jindabyne, Eucumbene, Tooma, and Tumut Pond reservoirs—and the Murray River provide excellent trout fishing opportunities. Khancoban's lake is a favorite for anglers, and Adaminaby is another fishing center. Tackle can be rented in a few towns, and a local operator offers excursions and instruction. The trout fishing season extends from the beginning of October to early June.

Although the downhill skiing isn't what Americans and Europeans are used to—Australian slopes are gentle and snow is less abundant—cross-country skiing has become popular in the Snowy Mountains for good reason. The numerous bushwalking tracks mean that nordic skiing opportunities are almost limitless, and the landscape and broad panoramas are breathtaking—non-Aussies will find the appearance of gum trees in snow almost surreal. Trails from Cabramurra in the Jagungal Wilderness, or from Kiandra, Charlotte Pass, or Thredbo to Kosciusko are very good. Ask locals about their favorites. The ski season officially runs from the June holiday weekend (second weekend of the month) to the October holiday weekend (first weekend).

Après-ski action in the Snowys is focused on the hotels in Thredbo, the large Perisher Blue resort, and the subalpine town of Jindabyne. Most hotel bars have live music in the evenings during the ski season, ranging from solo-piano to jazz to rock bands. Thredbo tends toward the cosmopolitan end of the scale, and Jindabyne makes up with energy what it lacks in sophistication. Note, however, that many of the hotels close from October to May (room rates are considerably cheaper during these months in hotels that stay open), and nightlife is much quieter out of the ski season.

This itinerary loops through the middle of the national park, beginning and ending at the region's main town of Cooma. Allow at least a few days for the round-trip, part of which follows slower but very scenic gravel roads. Or use Cooma, Jindabyne, or Thredbo as bases for exploring the area. If you plan to see the Yarrangobilly Caves, you may want to drive there straight from Cooma on the Snowy Mountains Highway. Bear in mind that the national park is about 305 km (190 mi) closer to Canberra than to Sydney, and be sure to call ahead to confirm snow conditions if you intend to ski.

Note: ☞ Chapter 13 for more information on local outdoor outfitters.

Cooma

419 km (260 mi) southwest of Sydney, 114 km (71 mi) south of Canberra.

The gateway to the Snowy Mountains and the ideal place to gather some information on the region (from the Visitors Centre), Cooma is a relatively attractive town with some interesting, albeit recent, history. Cooma is the headquarters for the **Snowy Mountains Hydroelectric Authority.** Between 1949 and 1974, over 100,000 people from more than 30 different countries were employed in the construction of the Snowy Mountains Scheme. The 16 major dams, 7 power stations, lakes, tunnels, and pipelines that make up the extensive scheme can generate almost 4 million kilowatts of electricity, which is distributed to Victoria, South Australia, New South Wales, and the Australian Capital Territory. The hydroelectric authority's **Snowy Information Centre** offers films and displays that explain the technical workings of this huge, complicated project—one of the world's modern engineering wonders.

There are also three power stations in the Snowy Mountains region (including those at Khancoban and Cabramurra; ☞ *below*) that are open for visits and tours—bookings can be made at the center in Cooma. ✉ *Monaro Hwy., Cooma North,* ☎ *02/6453–2004 or 1800/ 62–3776.* ☉ *Weekdays 8–5, weekends 8–1.*

Fishing
Based in Cooma, the **Alpine Angler** (☎ 02/6452–5538) has trout fly-fishing excursions for both novices and advanced anglers throughout the Snowy Mountains region. Lessons, equipment, transportation, and even accommodation are available.

Jindabyne

63 km (39 mi) south of Cooma.

This resort town was built in the 1960s on the shores of Lake Jindabyne, a man-made lake that flooded the original town when the Snowy River was dammed. There is a variety of outdoor activities in summer centering on the lake, and plenty of hiking, boating, and fishing equipment is available to rent or buy if you need it. For information on park trails and activities, stop in at the **Snowy Region Visitor Centre** (☎ 02/6450–5600), located in the centre of Jindabyne on the main Kosciusko Road. Here you can find information on hikes, flora and fauna, and all that Kosciusko National Park has to offer. The park entry fee is $12 per vehicle for a 24-hour period, or $4 for bus passengers. In winter, Jindabyne becomes a major base for budget skiers, with plenty of inexpensive local chalets and apartments.

Dining and Lodging

$$ ✕ **Balcony Bistro.** Huge steaks and seafood are the house specials at this very popular restaurant—on busy winter weekends you have to wait in line to grill your selections. The bistro is small, dark, and intimate, and on a balcony above the dining area is a bar with some tables on the outside deck overlooking Lake Jindabyne. ✉ *Old Town Centre, Level 3, Jindabyne,* ☎ *02/6456–2144. Reservations not accepted. AE, DC, MC, V. No lunch Mon. or Tues.*

$$ ✕ **Crackenback Cottage.** On the road to Thredbo on the outskirts of Jindabyne, this stone-and-timber bistro glows with rustic warmth. Expect robust servings of traditional favorites—soup, salad, roasts, pie, and mountain trout—as well as wood-fired pizzas. The restaurant also serves scones and afternoon tea, and is famous for its *gluhwein* (mulled wine) and Australia's largest selection of schnapps. ✉ *Alpine Way, Thredbo Valley,* ☎ *02/6456–2601. AE, DC, MC, V.*

$ ✕ **Brumby Bar and Bistro.** Only the lighting is subdued in this lively bistro, which is as popular for its live entertainment as it is for its food. The menu includes grilled steaks, chicken, beef Stroganoff, panfried trout and other seafood, lasagna, and schnitzels. Help yourself to the salad and vegetable bar. ✉ *Alpine Gables Motel, Kalkite St. and Kosciusko Rd., Jindabyne,* ☎ *02/6456–2526. Reservations not accepted. MC.*

$$$ 🏨 **Station Resort.** Set on 50 tranquil rural acres and accommodating over 1,400 guests, this is by far the largest resort in the Snowy Mountains. Popular with the under 35s and families, the hotel offers relatively inexpensive lodging, spacious, comfortable rooms, and dining choices of a bistro, chargrill, or a pizza station. Guest rooms sleep from two to seven people. A daily shuttle service connects the hotel with the Skitube Terminal. Rates can include meals and ski lift tickets. The resort is 6 km (4 mi) from Jindabyne. ✉ *Dalgety Rd., Jindabyne, 2627,*

☎ 02/6456–2895, ⅎ 02/6456–2544. *250 rooms with shower. 3 restaurants, bars, nightclub. AE, DC, MC, V.*

$$ ⬚ **Alpine Gables Motel.** These split-level suites in the village of Jind-abyne each have cooking facilities, a lounge, and a separate bedroom upstairs. The modern decor makes extensive use of wood and glass, and warm, earth tones predominate. Suites can accommodate up to six people. ⬚ *Kalkite St. and Kosciusko Rd., Jindabyne, 2627,* ☎ *02/ 6456–2555,* ⅎ *02/6456–2815. 42 rooms with bath. Restaurant, bar, sauna, spa, games room. AE, DC, MC, V.*

$ ⬚ **Eagles Range.** The two cedar lodges on this 300-acre sheep prop-
★   erty offer perhaps the best combination of comfort and value in the mountains. For families or small groups, self-catering accommoda-tions are available in a three-bedroom lodge. Other guests are housed on a dinner, bed, and breakfast basis in a four-bedroom, two-story chalet. Both lodges are charmingly rustic, with pine walls, exposed wood rafters, country-style furniture, and great views of the sur-rounding ranges. The larger lodge has an open fireplace set in a stone wall, and the smaller one has a wood-burning stove. The property is on a ridge about 12 km (7½ mi) from Jindabyne. ⬚ *Box 298, Dal-gety Rd., Jindabyne, 2627,* ☎ ⅎ *02/6456–2728. 2 rooms with bath, 2 with shared bath, 1 3-bedroom lodge with shared bath. Horseback riding, mountain bikes, spa. MC.*

Nightlife

In winter, the nightclub and bars inside **The Station Resort** usually rock until at least 1 AM, and the **Jindabyne Hotel** has a long-standing rep-utation for its party atmosphere.

Outdoor Outfitters

Paddy Pallin is a clothing and equipment specialist for outdoor ad-venturers. In addition to retail sales, the shop also rents out everything needed for a week in the wilderness, from Gore-Tex jackets to moun-tain bikes and all kinds of ski gear. The shop also has guided expedi-tions of all kinds (☞ Guided Tours *in* Snowy Mountains A to Z, *below*). ⬚ *Kosciusko Rd., Thredbo turnoff,* ☎ *02/6456–2922.*

BP Ski Hire (⬚ BP Service Station, Kosciusko Rd., Jindabyne, ☎ 02/ 6456–1959) rents snowboards and downhill or cross-country skis and equipment. The same equipment is available in Thredbo Village as well as from **Thredbo Sports** (☞ *below*).

En Route   From Jindabyne, divergent roads lead to two major destinations for walking, skiing, and generally exploring magnificent Kosciusko Na-tional Park. One is Kosciusko Road, which takes you to the northern route and Perisher Blue, and the other is the Alpine Way to the Ski-tube Terminal and Thredbo Village.

Kosciusko Road heads north to Sawpit Creek, from which point you need snow chains between June 1 and October 10. Rent chains from gas stations in Cooma and Jindabyne. This road continues to the vast ☞ **Perisher Blue** ski region (including the resorts of Smiggin Holes, Per-isher Valley, Mount Blue Cow, and Guthega), as well as the less-com-mercial skiing area around **Charlotte Pass,** which is at the very end of the road but accessible by over-snow transport during winter.

In the other direction from Jindabyne, the **Alpine Way** runs southwest to **Thredbo Village** and past the **Skitube Terminal** at Bullocks Flat, ap-proximately 21 km (13 mi) from Jindabyne. The 8-km (5-mi) Skitube (☎ 02/6456–2010) has an underground-overground shuttle train that transports skiers to the terminals at Perisher (10 minutes) and Mount Blue Cow (19 minutes). The service operates 24 hours daily in winter, and is open year-round.

Perisher Blue

30 km (18½ mi) west of Jindabyne.

The four adjoining skiing areas of Smiggin Holes, Perisher Valley, Mount Blue Cow, and Guthega have merged to become the megaresort of "Perisher Blue." This is the largest snowfield in Australia, with 50 lifts and T-bars that serve all standards of slopes. Because it is a snowfield area, Perisher Blue virtually closes down between October and May, but some lodges and cafés stay open, especially around the Christmas holidays.

Dining and Lodging

$$$$ ✕⊞ **Perisher Valley Hotel.** With a location on the slopes of Perisher Blue, this is a true "ski-in and ski-out" hotel. Each of the 31 luxurious suites accommodate between two and six people, and gourmet meals are served in Snowgums Restaurant, which has stunning views of the mountain scenery. This hotel, renowned for its outstanding service and facilities, is open only during ski season. Rates include breakfast, dinner, and over-snow transport to the hotel. ⊠ *Mt. Kosciusko Rd., Perisher Valley, 2627,* ☎ *02/6459–4455,* ⊠ *02/6457–5177. 31 suites. Restaurants, bars, sauna, spa, shops. AE, DC, MC, V. Closed Oct.–May.*

$$$ ⊞ **Perisher Manor.** In its place at the base of the main chairlift in Perisher, this is another ski-in, ski-out hotel. Perisher Manor has spacious and affordable accommodations—from budget rooms to stylish, deluxe suites with good views. All rooms are centrally heated and very comfortable, and the hotel has 24-hour reception, a lobby lounge with an open fireplace, drying rooms, and ski lockers. It is open only in season. ⊠ *Perisher Valley Rd., Perisher Valley, 2630,* ☎ *02/6457–5291,* ⊠ *02/6457–5064. 47 rooms with bath. Restaurant, café, 2 bars. AE, MC, V. Closed Oct.–May.*

Nightlife

Perisher Manor stages rock bands on several nights throughout the ski season. If you want to join the après-ski set, drop in at the cocktail bar of the **Perisher Valley Hotel.**

Skiing

Lift tickets for use at any of the **Perisher Blue** (☎ 02/6456–2010) ski areas are currently $60 per day, $255 for five days. From the Bullocks Flat Skitube Terminal, combined Skitube and lift tickets are $70 per day. From here, skiers can schuss down the mountain to a choice of four high-speed quad chairlifts and a double chair. **Blue Cow** has a good choice of beginner- and intermediate-level runs, but no accommodations are available at the area.

Thredbo Village

32 km (20 mi) southwest of Jindabyne.

Nestled in a valley at the foot of Mount Crackenback, this resort has a European feeling that is unique on the Australian snowfields. Along with having some of the best skiing in the country, this is an excellent center for summer bushwalking, rappelling, fly fishing, canoeing, and white-water rafting. The resort has tennis courts, mountain bike trails, a 9-hole PGA-rated golf course, and a 2,300-ft-long alpine slide. This pollution-free high-country environment is also the home of the Australian Institute of Sport's Thredbo Alpine Training Centre, designed primarily for the use of elite athletes, but it is open to the public. Facilities include a swimming pool; squash, basketball, badminton, volleyball, and netball courts; and a well-equipped gymnasium.

The **Crackenback Chairlift** provides easy access to Mount Kosciusko, Australia's tallest peak, with great views of the Aussie alps. From the upper chairlift terminal at 6,447 ft, the journey to the 7,314-ft summit is a relatively easy 12-km (7½-mi) return hike in beautiful alpine country. You can also take a mile walk to an overlook. Hikers should be prepared for unpredictable and sometimes severe weather.

Dining and Lodging

$$$ ✕🏠 **Bernti's Mountain Inn.** Located in the heart of Thredbo within walking distance of the chairlifts, Bernti's is a unique, boutique-style mountain inn with friendly service and superb food. The rooms have delightful views, and most have king-size beds. The lounge has a welcoming fire, and a bar and pool table. Outside, there are whirlpools and plunge pools overlooking the mountains, as well as a sauna to relax tired muscles. The popular terrace café serves snacks and drinks, and at night the restaurant takes on a romantic atmosphere—and serves an eclectic array of innovative dishes alongside a comprehensive wine list. The inn is open year-round, and rates are considerably cheaper out of ski season. ✉ *Mowamba Pl., Thredbo, 2627,* ☎ *02/6457–6332,* FAX *02/6457–6348. 27 rooms with bath. Sauna, spa. AE, DC, MC, V.*

$$$ 🏠 **Novotel Lake Crackenback Resort.** En route to Thredbo and poised on the banks of a lake that mirrors the surrounding peaks of the Crackenback Range, these luxury apartments offer family-size accommodations. The apartments in this all-season resort come in several configurations, from one bedroom plus loft (which can sleep up to four) to three bedrooms. Each has a modern kitchen, a laundry with drying racks, under-floor heating as well as a fireplace, and such thoughtful extras as undercover parking and lockable ski racks outside the rooms. ✉ *Alpine Way, via Jindabyne, 2627,* ☎ *02/6456–2960,* FAX *02/6456– 1008. 44 rooms with bath. Restaurant, bar, indoor pool, sauna, tennis courts, 9-hole golf course, exercise room. AE, DC, MC, V.*

$$ 🏠 **Thredbo Alpine Hotel.** Within easy reach of the ski lifts at Thredbo, the rooms at this hotel are spacious and comfortable, decorated in warm autumn colors, and furnished with contemporary wood and glass. The hotel has a good choice of restaurants and après-ski facilities. Rates include Continental breakfast. ✉ *Box 80, Thredbo Village, 2625,* ☎ *02/6459–4200,* FAX *02/6459–4201. 64 rooms with bath. 3 restaurants, bars, pool, sauna, spa. AE, DC, MC, V.*

Nightlife

At the center of the village, the **Thredbo Alpine Hotel** has a popular nightclub and a choice of three bars.

Skiing

Among downhill resorts of the area, Thredbo has the most challenging runs—with the only Australian giant-slalom course approved for World Cup events—and the most extensive snowmaking in the country. ☎ *02/6459–4100.* 🎫 *Lift ticket $58 per day, $250 for 5 days.*

Thredbo Sports rents downhill and cross-country skis and snowboards. ✉ *Ski-lift terminal, Thredbo Village,* ☎ *02/6459–4100.*

En Route   Between Thredbo and Khancoban, the Alpine Way turns south and then west as it skirts the flanks of **Mount Kosciusko.** This 40-km (25-mi) gravel section of the highway, often impassable in winter but reasonable at other times, leads through heavily forested terrain, with pleasant views to the south. Nineteen kilometers (12 miles) past Dead Horse Gap is the turnoff to **Tom Groggin,** the highest point of the Murray

River accessible by road. Australia's longest river travels west for another 2,515 km (1,560 mi) before it meets the sea south of Adelaide.

Khancoban

81 km (50 mi) northwest of Thredbo.

Once a dormitory town for workers on the Snowy Mountains Hydroelectric Scheme—it's close to a dam and two of the project's power stations—Khancoban is now a favorite with anglers who try their luck in the lake created by the damming of the Swampy Plain River.

In a picturesque valley outside Khancoban, the Snowy Mountains Scheme's **Murray 1 Power Station,** with its 10 turbine generators, is open for interesting free guided tours each day. Reservations are essential. ⊠ *Alpine Way, via Khancoban,* ☎ *02/6453–2004 or 1800/ 62–3776.* ☼ *Daily, guided tour daily hourly 10–2.*

En Route The road north from Khancoban leads past the Tooma and Tumut Pond reservoirs and Round Mountain to **Cabramurra,** the highest town in Australia.

Just north of Cabramurra there is another major component of the Snowy Mountains Hydroelectric Scheme—the **Tumut 2 Power Station.** You can tour the station and go inside the mountain to explore some of the scheme's workings. Bookings are essential. ⊠ *Elliot Way, via Cabramurra,* ☎ *02/6453–2004 or 1800/62–3776, 02/6452–6301 winter bookings.* ☼ *Guided tour Sept.–Apr., daily hourly 11–2; May–Aug. by appointment.*

This is the long, but very scenic, way back around to Adaminaby and Cooma. Before you get there you'll pass through **Kiandra,** a small, now-tranquil village that was the site of a frantic early 1860s gold rush. Kiandra is 81 km (50 mi) from Khancoban.

OFF THE BEATEN PATH **Yarrangobilly Caves** is a famous network of limestone grottoes full of stalactites, stalagmites, and other rock formations. A few of the caves are open to the public; one of them, South Glory Cave, has a self-guided tour. Four other caves must be toured with a guide. You can also bathe in 80°F thermal pools, an enjoyable complement to the 53°F chill of the caves. The caves are within Kosciusko National Park and the area contains pristine wilderness, including the spectacular Yarrangobilly Gorge. The caves are about 21 km (13 mi) north of Kiandra. ⊠ *Visitor Centre,* ☎ *02/6454–9597.* 🎟 *Self-guided tour $6, guided tour $10.* ☼ *Daily 9–5, subject to winter road conditions.*

Adaminaby

40 km (25 mi) southeast of Kiandra, 50 km (31 mi) northwest of Cooma.

Halfway between Kiandra and Cooma, this is the town closest to **Lake Eucumbene,** the main storage dam for the Snowy Mountains Scheme. The lake holds eight times as much water as Sydney Harbour. Adaminaby was moved to its present site in the 1950s, when the lake was created, and the area is now best known for its horseback riding holidays (☞ Reynella, *below*) and recreational fishing—the town's most famous structure is an 18-yd-long fiberglass trout.

Lodging

$$ 🏨 **Reynella.** Set in undulating country near the highest point in Australia, this sheep and cattle property offers guests a chance to saddle ★ up, don a Drizabone riding coat, and head off into *The Man from Snowy River* country. Reynella has been in operation for over 25 years, and

it is renowned for its three- and five-day horseback riding safaris into Kosciusko National Park—all levels of riding ability are welcome. The homestead provides a relaxing atmosphere, and basic but comfortable lodge-style accommodations with shared facilities. The entire experience is a unique taste of backcountry Australia. In winter, the property provides a perfect base for both downhill and cross-country skiing. It is 9 km (5½ mi) south of Adaminaby and off the Snowy Mountains Highway. Rates include all meals. ⊠ *Bolaro Rd., Adaminaby, 2630,* ☎ *02/6454–2386,* FAX *02/6454–2530. 20 rooms with shared baths. Horseback riding, tennis courts, fishing. MC, V.*

Snowy Mountains A to Z

Arriving and Departing

BY BUS

Greyhound Pioneer Australia (☎ 13–2030) runs between Sydney and the Snowy Mountains via Canberra daily. The bus stops at Cooma, Berridale, Jindabyne, and Thredbo, with additional stops at the Skitube Terminal and Perisher Blue during the ski season. It is a seven-hour ride to Thredbo from Sydney, three hours from Canberra.

BY CAR

Take Parramatta Road from Sydney to the juncture with the Hume Highway at Ashfield, about 8 km (5 mi) from the city center. Follow the highway to just south of Goulburn and then turn onto the Federal Highway to Canberra. The Monaro Highway runs south from Canberra to Cooma. The 419-km (260-mi) journey takes at least five hours.

BY PLANE

Impulse Airlines (reservations through Ansett Australia, ☎ 13–1300) operates daily flights between Sydney and Cooma. From Cooma's airport, it is a half-hour drive to Jindabyne.

Getting Around

BY BUS

In winter, shuttle buses connect the regional towns with the ski fields. At other times of the year, the only practical way to explore the area is by rental car or on a guided tour.

BY CAR

To visit anything beyond the main ski resort areas, a car is a necessity. Be aware, however, that driving these often steep and winding mountain roads in winter can be hazardous, and you must carry snow chains from June to October.

BY SKITUBE

The Skitube shuttle train (running from the Alpine Way, between Jindabyne and Thredbo, to the Perisher Blue area) operates year-round, and is a useful means of reaching either of these resorts. For full details of services and fares, contact the Skitube information office (☎ 02/6456–2010).

Contacts and Resources

CAR RENTALS

Rent cars in Cooma from **Thrifty Car Rental** (⊠ Sharpe St., ☎ 02/6452–5300), which also has an office at the airport.

EMERGENCIES

Ambulance, fire brigade, and **police.** ☎ *000.*

GUIDED TOURS

Adventure Sports. In addition to joining up with one of the tour operators listed here, you could also, if you are an experienced walker, undertake one of the area's many fine walks without a guide. Talk to staff at the Snowy Region Visitor Centre in Jindabyne (☞ *below*) for suggestions and trail maps.

Sydney-based **Morrell Adventure Travel** (⊠ 8 Newcastle St., Rose Bay, 2029, ☎ 02/9388–1200) has various guided hiking and mountain-biking trips in the Snowy Mountains between November and April. Trips range from three to nine days, and transportation from Sydney is available. Jindabyne's **Paddy Pallin** (⊠ Kosciusko Rd., Thredbo turnoff, Jindabyne, 2627, ☎ 02/6456–2922 or 1800/62–3459) offers a wide range of activities for outdoor adventurers, including bushwalking, mountain biking, white-water rafting and canoeing, and horseback riding. An outstanding choice of cross-country ski programs is also available, from introductory weekends to snow-camping trips.

Bus Tours. Murrays Australia (☎ 13–2251 or 02/6295–3611) operate both skiing/accommodation packages and a transportation service (during the ski season only) to the Snowy Mountains from Canberra: These depart from the Jolimont Tourist Centre, Alinga Street and Northbourne Avenue.

VISITOR INFORMATION
Cooma Visitors Centre. ⊠ *119 Sharpe St., Cooma,* ☎ *02/6450–1740 or 02/6450–1742.*
Snowy Region Visitor Centre. ⊠ *Kosciusko Rd., Jindabyne* ☎ *02/ 6450–5600.*
Sydney Visitors Information Centre. ⊠ *106 George St. (The Rocks), 2000,* ☎ *02/9255–1788,* FAX *02/9241–5010.*

4 Canberra and the A.C.T.

Located between Sydney and Melbourne in the Australian Capital Territory, in the midst of mountain ranges and rivers, Canberra is the nation's spacious, immaculately landscaped capital city. Possessed of interesting architecture and museums, it is the city closest to some of Australia's greatest national parks.

By Michael
Gebicki

Updated by
Anne
Matthews

AUSTRALIANS have strong opinions on many subjects, but as you travel around the country, you will hear few more strongly expressed than those on the subject of the nation's capital. Its detractors use pejorative epithets to describe it: "Monumentsville," "a city without a soul," "the bush capital," "the city with the gray flannel mind," and "a great waste of prime sheep country." Those in favor refer to Canberra as "the garden city of the Commonwealth" or "the front window of the nation," and those who live there will give you the unanswerable proclamation that "to know Canberra is to love it."

The need for a national capital arose only in 1901, when the previously quite separate Australian states were joined into a federation. An area of about 2,330 square km (900 square mi) of undulating, sheep-grazing country in southeastern New South Wales was set aside and designated the Australian Capital Territory (A.C.T.). The inland site was chosen partly for reasons of national security and partly to end the bickering between Sydney and Melbourne, both of which claimed to be the country's legitimate capital. The name Canberry—an Aboriginal word meaning "meeting place" that had been previously applied to this area—was changed to Canberra for the new city. Like everything else about it, the name was controversial, and debate has raged ever since over which syllable should be stressed. These days, "*Can*-bra" is more common than "Can-*ber*-ra."

From the very beginning this was to be a totally planned city. An international design competition was won by Walter Burley Griffin, a Chicago architect and associate of Frank Lloyd Wright. Griffin arrived in Canberra in 1913 to supervise construction, but progress was slowed by two world wars and the Great Depression. By 1947 Canberra was little more than a country town with only 15,000 inhabitants.

Development increased during the 1950s, and the current population of more than 300,000 makes it by far the largest inland city in Australia. Griffin's original plan has largely been fulfilled in the wide, tree-lined avenues and spacious parklands of present-day Canberra. The major public buildings are arranged on low knolls on either side of man-made Lake Burley Griffin, the focus of the city. Satellite communities—using the same radial design of crescents and cul-de-sacs employed in Canberra, but with a shopping center at their nucleus—have been created to house the city's growing population.

The overall impression in Canberra is one of spaciousness, calm, verdure, and an almost unnatural order. There are no advertising billboards, no strident colors, and very few buildings more than a dozen stories high. Canberra verges on being a one-company town: almost 50% of the workforce is employed in government, giving the city a peculiar homogeneity. It is paradoxically unlike anywhere else in Australia, however—the product of a brave attempt to create an urban utopia—and its success or failure has fueled many a pub debate.

Pleasures and Pastimes

Canberra's two very distinct and seemingly disparate faces—urban and bush—make it a most unusual city. There is first a showcase of national talent, in the city's galleries, libraries, sports academy, and technical institutions representing the high temples of mainstream Australian culture. Canberra's other most obvious facet is its superb natural setting, clean air, and proximity to unspoiled parks and bushland.

Dining

Canberra has never exactly been famous for the quality of its restaurants, but the city's dining scene has improved immeasurably in recent years. Canberra now claims to have more restaurants per person than any other city in Australia, and there are plenty of opportunities to taste interesting modern Australian fare and other international delights.

CATEGORY	COST*
$$$$	over $40
$$$	$25–$40
$$	$15–$25
$	under $15

per person, excluding drinks and service

Galleries, Museums, and Public Buildings

With over 30 national institutions, Canberra has an impressive array of museums, art galleries, and public buildings to visit. Completed in 1988, the vast, modern Parliament House is the most famous of these, but the National Gallery of Australia, the National Science and Technology Centre (Questacon), the Australian Institute of Sport, and the Australian War Memorial provide no less fascinating glimpses into the nation's past, present, and future.

Lodging

Most hotels in the city have sprung up since the 1960s, and few offer more than modern, utilitarian facilities. Exceptions are the country homesteads tucked away in the surrounding mountain ranges. These expansive country dwellings give you a chance to experience life on working sheep and cattle farms, often in magnificently rugged surroundings, without sacrificing creature comforts. In some cases these places are too remote from Canberra to serve as a practical base for exploring the national capital. But that may be just what you want.

CATEGORY	COST*
$$$$	over $250
$$$	$150–$250
$$	$80–$150
$	under $80

All prices are for a standard double room.

Parks, Reserves, and the Great Outdoors

Canberra's surrounding mountain ranges and river valleys, and the crisp spring and autumn weather, give the city a wide range of healthy outdoor pursuits for everyone to enjoy. Within the A.C.T. itself, there is a national park, a nature reserve, and vast areas of bush and parkland that are great for walks. And Lake Burley Griffin and its surrounds provide the perfect location for easy strolls, cycling, and water-based sports and activities. Kosciusko National Park and the New South Wales snowfields are also within easy reach of the capital—far closer than they are to Sydney.

EXPLORING CANBERRA AND THE A.C.T.

Canberra's most important public buildings are located within the "Parliamentary Triangle," formed by the lake on the north side and two long avenues, Commonwealth and Kings, which radiate out from Capital Hill, the city's political and geographical epicenter. The triangle itself can be explored comfortably on foot, but you'll need transportation for the rest of your stay in the city.

Although locals maintain otherwise, with its radial roads, erratic signage, and often large distances between suburbs, Canberra can be notoriously difficult to negotiate by car. The best solution is to buy a good street map, and try to relax about missing turnoffs and ending up on the wrong radial road. If you don't rent a car, Canberra's ACTION buses and the Murrays Canberra Explorer (☞ Central Canberra *and* Canberra and the A.C.T. A to Z, *below*) can get you around town comfortably and without stress.

Numbers in the text correspond to numbers in the margin and on the Canberra map.

Great Itineraries

Most of Canberra's galleries, museums, and public buildings can be seen in a couple of days, while the capital's parks and gardens, and Namadgi National Park to the south, brimming with remarkable flora and fauna, can easily lure you to spend another day or so wandering through these quiet oases. There are also several lesser-known museums and public buildings, and outlying A.C.T. attractions, such as Lanyon Homestead, that warrant a visit.

IF YOU HAVE 2 DAYS

In two fairly hectic days you will be able to see most of the main city attractions. You could start day one with the spectacular view from the **Telstra Tower** ⑯, then visit the **National Capital Exhibition** ③ for a good look into Canberra's planning and history. Next stop should be the **Parliamentary Triangle,** where you can easily spend the remainder of the day visiting the National Gallery of Australia, Questacon, Old Parliament House, and Parliament House. Fill in the city center gaps on the second day—the **Australian National Botanic Gardens** ⑮, **Australian War Memorial** ⑭, the **National Film and Sound Archive** ①, and perhaps take a cruise on **Lake Burley Griffin.**

IF YOU HAVE 4 DAYS

In a stay of this duration you will be able to see all of the above, but four days allows more time to linger in the many absorbing galleries and museums. Some suggestions for days three and four are to visit the **Australian Institute of Sport, St. John the Baptist Church and the Schoolhouse Museum** ⑬, and the **Royal Australian Mint,** and then take a drive around the pleasant suburb of **Yarralumla** ⑩ en route to the **National Aquarium** ⑱ and the **National Museum of Australia**'s visitor center ⑰. You should also be able to fit in a visit to **Lanyon Homestead** and **Tidbinbilla Nature Reserve,** to the city's south. Or take a day and head to **Namadgi National Park** for a walk or hike.

IF YOU HAVE 6 DAYS

Within six days your itinerary could easily cover the above suggestions, with time to spare for a gentle bicycle ride around **Lake Burley Griffin,** a day hike in **Namadgi National Park,** and perhaps a visit to the fascinating **Deep Space Communications Complex** at Tidbinbilla. You could also take a trip a few miles north of the city to **Cockington Green** and the shopping complexes at **Gold Creek Village.** Or spend a couple of days in **Kosciusko National Park**—114 km (71 mi) away in southern New South Wales. Summer activities include hiking, fishing, horse riding, or knocking around caves, while in winter (June through October) both cross-country and downhill skiing are options.

When to Tour Canberra and the A.C.T.

One particularly good time to visit the national capital is in the fall, when the city comes alive with the red and gold colors of autumn leaves, as well as the theater, dance, musical productions, open-air film festival, and jazz and rock concerts of the March Canberra Festival. This festival now incorporates the colorful international Hot Air Balloon

156

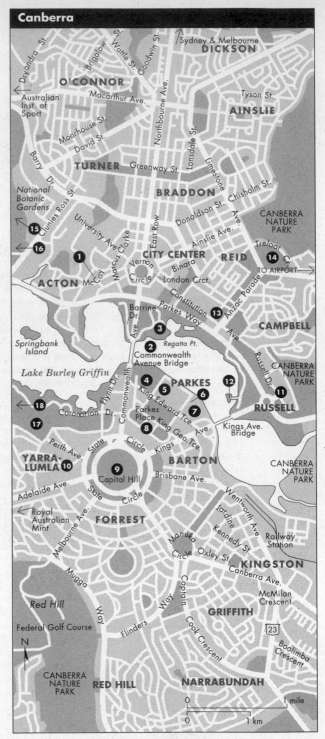

Fiesta. The spring flower celebration, Floriade, takes place in September and October.

Central Canberra

The first part of the following driving or bus tour takes in virtually all of central Canberra's major sights—including the Parliamentary Triangle buildings, the lakeside sights, and the Australian War Memorial. It is certainly possible to follow the suggested route by car, but an easier and far more relaxing (and informative) option is to take the Murrays Canberra Explorer bus tour, which departs hourly every day and provides a driver commentary. The Explorer bus does not cover the sights in the second part of the tour (the Australian National Botanic Gardens, Telstra Tower, National Museum of Australia, and the National Aquarium). To reach them you will need to use the government-operated ACTION bus number 904.

For full details of the Explorer and ACTION 904 buses, *see* Canberra and the A.C.T. A to Z, *below.*

A Good Tour

From the city center, the bus first heads to the **National Film and Sound Archive** ①, located within the grounds of the Australian National University. You could give this a miss if you're short of time, but the center repays interest in Australia's radio, film, and television history.

The bus then stops at Regatta Point, where there are excellent views of **Lake Burley Griffin** and the **Captain Cook Memorial Jet** ②, a spectacular fountain that rockets a plume of water far above the lake. This is also the location for the **National Capital Exhibition** ③, which explains how the city was planned and built, and reveals the civic secrets of Canberra present and future with videos, models, and audiovisual displays.

There is plenty to see at the next stop, over Commonwealth Avenue Bridge to the lake's southern shore and the Parliamentary Triangle: the **National Library of Australia** ④, the interactive **Questacon–The National Science and Technology Centre** ⑤, the **High Court of Australia** ⑥, and the **National Gallery of Australia** ⑦, the nation's premier art gallery. It would be easy to spend an entire morning or afternoon exploring Questacon and the National Gallery. Admittedly, the Library and High Court are of less interest.

Nearby, **Old Parliament House** ⑧ was once the hub of national politics, but this gracious old building now houses a variety of displays from the National Museum of Australia, the National Portrait Gallery, and the Australian Archive Gallery. Farther up Capital Hill, sprawling **Parliament House** ⑨ presents a striking contrast to its humble predecessor. This ultramodern glass, steel, and concrete construction deserves an extended visit.

Back on the bus, you'll circle around the attractive suburban **Yarralumla Diplomatic Missions** ⑩ before crossing Kings Avenue Bridge to return to the lake's northern shore. Beyond the end of the bridge, you'll be able to see the distinctive **Australian-American Memorial** ⑪, and to the left stands the elegant **National Carillon** ⑫.

The bus then heads up **Anzac Parade,** where you stop in at **St. John the Baptist Church and the Schoolhouse Museum** ⑬, the oldest buildings in the Canberra region. The final stop on this first part of the tour takes in the monument and extensive museum of the **Australian War Memorial** ⑭, one of the nation's most popular attractions.

From the War Memorial, the Canberra Explorer returns to the city center, where you can then connect with an ACTION 904 bus for the second section of the tour. After passing the Australian National University, the bus stops at the **Australian National Botanic Gardens** ⑮, which contains superb displays of native flora. Nearby Black Mountain is capped by the 600-ft-high **Telstra Tower** ⑯, from the top of which are spectacular views of the city, lake, and surrounding countryside.

Bus 904 then continues around the lake's western shore to visit the **National Museum of Australia** ⑰ at its Yarramundi Visitor Centre site, and the **National Aquarium and Australian Wildlife Sanctuary** ⑱, where you can end your day gawking at indigenous birds, animals, and marine life.

TIMING

You could certainly take on this entire tour in one day, but it would not do justice to Parliament House or any of the major museums or galleries. To accommodate these, split the first part of the tour into two parts—take a break after the National Gallery of Australia, and resume your sightseeing on the following day at Old Parliament House. You can then easily cover the outer (904 bus route) leg of the tour in a morning or afternoon.

The major galleries and museums (particularly the Australian War Memorial, National Gallery, and Questacon) become very crowded on weekends, so explore these, if you can, on a weekday.

Sights to See

⑪ **Australian-American Memorial.** For Americans, this slender memorial with an eagle at its summit will have particular significance. It was unveiled in 1954 to commemorate the role of American forces in the defense of Australia during World War II. The monument is located near the northern side of Kings Avenue Bridge. ⊠ *Russell Dr., Russell.*

⑮ **Australian National Botanic Gardens.** Australian plants and trees have evolved in complete isolation from the rest of the world, and these delightful gardens on the lower slopes of Black Mountain display the world's best collection of the continent's unique flora. The rain forest, rockery, Tasmanian alpine garden, and the eucalyptus lawn—with more than 600 eucalypt species—are the 125-acre site's highlights. Two self-guided "arrow trails" start from the rain forest gully, and free guided tours depart from the visitor center at 11 on Wednesday, Friday, and Sunday, and at 2 on Saturday and Sunday. ⊠ *Clunies Ross St., Black Mountain, Acton,* ☎ *02/6250–9540.* ☼ *Gardens daily 9–5 (until 8 in Jan.), Visitor Centre daily 9:30–4:30.*

⑭ **Australian War Memorial.** In a prominent position at the top of Anzac Parade, this vast monument honors the troops who have served the nation in wartime, and it is a superb museum of military weaponry and memorabilia. Built roughly in the shape of a Byzantine church, the memorial is the most popular tourist attraction in the national capital, and one of the most visited sights in the whole of Australia. Exhibits cover the period from the Sudan campaign of the late 19th century to the Vietnam War. Displays include a Lancaster bomber, a Spitfire, tanks, landing barges, the giant German Amiens Gun, and sections of two of the Japanese midget submarines that infiltrated Sydney Harbour during World War II. The memorial is the focus of the Anzac Day ceremony in Canberra, held on April 25. Free guided tours are available at regular intervals each day. ⊠ *Limestone Ave., Campbell,* ☎ *02/6243–4211.* ☼ *Daily 10–5.*

The impressive facade of the War Memorial is best appreciated by approaching it from along the broad avenue of **Anzac Parade.** Anzac is an acronym for the Australian and New Zealand Army Corps, formed during World War I. The avenue is flanked by several memorials commemorating the army, navy, and air force, as well as some of the campaigns in which Australian troops have fought, including the most recent—the Vietnam War.

② **Captain Cook Memorial Jet.** Out in Lake Burley Griffin, off Commonwealth Park's Regatta Point, this jet, which commemorates James Cook's discovery of the east coast of Australia in 1770, sends a great plume of water into the sky. On windless days the waterspout reaches a height of 450 ft—making this one of the world's highest fountains.

Lake Burley Griffin. At the very heart of the city, this large lake is one of Canberra's most welcome features. Its flat, level surrounds are great for walking and cycling, and you can hire catamarans, canoes, or a variety of boats to float around on the water from Acton Park on the northern shore.

⑥ **High Court of Australia.** As its name implies, this gleaming concrete and glass structure is the ultimate court of law in the nation's judicial system. The court of seven justices convenes only to determine constitutional matters or major principles of law. Inside the main entrance of the building, the public hall contains a number of murals depicting various constitutional and geographic themes. Each of the three courtrooms over which the justices preside has a public gallery, and you can observe the proceedings when the court is in session. ⊠ *King Edward Terr., Parkes,* ☎ *02/6270−6850.* ☉ *Daily 9:45−4:30.*

⑱ **National Aquarium and Australian Wildlife Sanctuary.** Although rather small and not really worthy of a "National" title (except that it is in the A.C.T.), this complex nonetheless brings the sensations of the Great Barrier Reef and Australia's river lands to the shores of Lake Burley Griffin. A submerged walk-through tunnel gives fish-eye views of the underwater world, and there are 26 display tanks alive with corals, marine animals, and exotic fish. The adjoining 15-acre wildlife sanctuary is a bushland park that provides a habitat for many of the more remarkable species of Australia's fauna: emus, koalas, penguins, dingoes, kangaroos, and Tasmanian devils. ⊠ *Lady Denman Dr., Scrivener Dam, Yarralumla,* ☎ *02/6287−1211.* ☐ *$10.* ☉ *Daily 9−5:30.*

③ **National Capital Exhibition.** Photographs, models, plans, audiovisual displays, and a laser model inside this lakeside pavilion illustrate the past, present, and future development of the national capital. From the pavilion's terrace there are sweeping views of the Parliamentary Triangle across the lake: The National Library on the right and the National Gallery on the left form the base of the Parliamentary Triangle, which rises toward its apex at Parliament House on Capital Hill. The terrace is a great spot from which to photograph these buildings, and to look out over Lake Burley Griffin and the **Captain Cook Memorial Jet.** The restaurant and kiosk on the terrace serve both full meals and light snacks, and if the sun is shining, sit down at a table, relax, and enjoy the scenery. ⊠ *Regatta Point, Commonwealth Park,* ☎ *02/ 6257−1068.* ☉ *Daily 9−5 (9−6 during summer).*

⑫ **National Carillon.** The tall, elegant bell tower on the Lake Burley Griffin's Aspen Island was a gift from the British government to mark Canberra's 50th anniversary in 1963. The carillon consists of 53 bells, and 45-minute recitals are played by carillonists daily—at 12:45 on weekdays (Wednesday only in winter), 2:45 on weekends and public holidays, and at 5:45 on Thursday during summer. The music ranges from popular songs to hymns and special carillon compositions. ⊠ *Aspen Island, off Wendouree Dr., Acton,* ☎ *02/6257−1068.*

① **National Film and Sound Archive.** Australia's movie industry was booming during the early years of this century—as an important spur of the nascent industry—but ultimately it could not compete with the sophistication and volume of imported films. Concern that film stock and sound recordings of national importance would be lost prompted the construction of this edifice to preserve Australia's movie and musical heritage. The archive contains an impressive display of Australian moviemaking skills, including a short film that was shot on Melbourne Cup Day in 1896—the oldest in the collection. In the Sound and Moving Image Exhibition you can watch and listen to a representative selection of the archive's diverse collection—including radio programs, historic newsreels, TV advertisements, CD recordings, and highlights from feature movies that date from the late 1800s to the present day. ⊠ *McCoy Circuit, Acton,* ☎ *02/6209–3111.* ⬚ *$3.* ☉ *Daily 9–5.*

❼ National Gallery of Australia. The nation's premier art gallery contains a sprinkling of works by the masters, including Rodin, Picasso, Pollock, and Warhol, but its real strength lies in its Australian artwork. The gallery houses the most comprehensive exhibition of Australian art in the country, with superlative collections of Aboriginal art as well as paintings by such famous native sons as Arthur Streeton, Sir Sidney Nolan, Tom Roberts, and Arthur Boyd. There is an excellent bookshop with an extensive selection of Australian art postcards, as well as a licensed restaurant. Free guided tours commence from the foyer at 11 and 2 each day. An additional charge usually applies to special-interest exhibitions that often feature artwork from around the world. ⊠ *Parkes Pl., Parkes,* ☎ *02/6240–6411.* ⬚ *$3.* ☉ *Daily 10–5, with extended hours for special exhibitions.*

NEED A   The National Gallery has two good spots to catch your wits amid the
BREAK?   Parliamentary Triangle's assault of history, culture, and science. Snacks,
                meals, and coffee are available at both the **National Gallery Brasserie**
                and the **Mirrabook Outdoor Restaurant,** which is located in the pleasant
                Sculpture Garden. The Brasserie is open daily from 10 to 4:30, while
                the outdoor eatery serves food and drinks from noon to 4. ⊠ *Parkes Pl.,*
                ☎ *02/6240–6411.*

❹ National Library of Australia. Based loosely on the design of the Parthenon in Athens, this treasury of knowledge contains more than 4 million books and 500,000 aerial photographs, maps, drawings, films, and recordings of oral history. Changing exhibitions from the library's various collections are displayed in the foyer and in the mezzanine gallery. Guided one-hour tours of the library leave the foyer at 2 on Tuesday, Wednesday, and Thursday. ⊠ *Parkes Pl., Parkes,* ☎ *02/6262–1111.* ☉ *Mon.–Thurs. 9–9, Fri. and Sat. 9–5, Sun. 1:30–5.*

❿ National Museum of Australia (Yarramundi Visitor Centre). While this relatively new national institution awaits its permanent site, the museum's exhibits are currently based in two locations—☞ **Old Parliament House** and the Yarramundi Visitor Centre, on the shores of Lake Burley Griffin. The visitor center has exhibitions, tours, nature trails, and other activities that relate to its three main themes—Aboriginal and Torres Strait Islander Cultures, Australian Society and History, and People and the Environment. ⊠ *Lady Denman Dr., Yarralumla,* ☎ *02/6256–1126.* ☉ *Daily 10–4.*

❽ Old Parliament House. Built in 1927, this long white building was meant to serve only as a temporary seat of government, but it was more than 60 years before its much larger successor was finally completed on the hill behind it. Now that the politicians have moved out, the beautifully renovated building is open for public inspection. Guided tours, which depart from Kings Hall at 30-minute intervals, take you through the legislative chambers, party rooms, and suites that once belonged to the prime minister and the president of the Senate. Old Parliament House also contains the **National Portrait Gallery,** displays from the ☞ **National Museum of Australia,** and the **Australian Archive Gallery,** all of which have frequently changing exhibitions. In the old House of Representatives, you can watch an interesting 45-minute sound and light show entitled, appropriately, *Order! Order!* While you're in the area, take a stroll through the delightful **Senate Rose Gardens.** ✉ *King George Terr., Parkes,* ☏ *02/6270–8222.* ✉ *$2, including sound and light show.* ⊙ *Daily 9–4, sound and light show 10:30 and 2:30.*

❾ Parliament House. Much of this vast and very modern structure is covered by a domed glass roof that follows the contours of Capital Hill. From a distance, the most striking feature of the billion-dollar building is its 250-ft flagpole—the tallest stainless-steel structure in the world. Although it might look only as big as a postage stamp, the Australian flag that flies night and day from the top is actually the size of a double-decker bus.

The design for the new Parliament House was chosen in an international contest that attracted more than 300 entries. The contest was won by the New York firm of Mitchell, Guirgola & Thorp, whose design merged structural elegance with the natural environment. Work commenced in 1980, and the building was completed for the Australian Bicentennial in 1988.

You approach the Parliament building across a vast courtyard featuring a central mosaic entitled *Meeting Place,* designed by Aboriginal artist Nelson Tjakamarra. Native timber has been used almost exclusively throughout the building, and the work of some of Australia's finest contemporary artists hangs on the walls.

Parliament generally sits on weekdays (except Friday) between mid-February and late June and mid-August to mid-December. Both chambers have public galleries, but debate in the House of Representatives—where the prime minister sits—is livelier and more newsworthy than in the Senate. The best time to be present in the House of Representatives is during Question Time, starting at 2 PM, when the government and the opposition are most likely to be at each other's throats. To secure a ticket for Question Time, contact the sergeant-at-arms' office (☏ 02/6277–4889). Book a week in advance, if possible. Guided tours are available every half hour from 9 AM, and you are free to wander around much of the building at your own leisure. ✉ *Capital Hill,* ☏ *02/6277–5399.* ⊙ *Daily 9–5 (later when Parliament is sitting).*

〄 ❺ Questacon–The National Science and Technology Centre. This exciting, interactive center is the city's most entertaining museum. Built around a central "drum," Questacon entertains and educates with about 200 hands-on exhibits. High-tech computer gadgetry is used along with anything from pendulums and feathers to illustrate principles of mathematics, physics, and human perception. Staff are on hand to explain the scientific principles behind the exhibits, and intriguing science shows are performed regularly. This stimulating, participative environment is highly addictive and great fun—you might have trouble getting out in less than a couple of hours. ✉ *King Edward Terr., Parkes,* ☏ *02/6270–2800.* ✉ *$8.* ⊙ *Daily 10–5.*

⓭ St. John the Baptist Church and the Schoolhouse Museum. These are the oldest surviving buildings in the Canberra district—when they were constructed in the 1840s, the land was part of a 4,000-acre property that belonged to Robert Campbell, a well-known Sydney merchant. The homestead, Duntroon, remained in the Campbell family until it was purchased by the government as a site for the military academy. The schoolhouse is now a small museum with relics from the early history of the area. ⊠ *Constitution Ave., Reid,* ☏ *02/6249–6839.* ▣ *$1.50.* ◷ *Museum Wed. 10–noon, weekends 2–4; church daily 9–5.*

⑯ **Telstra Tower.** The city's tallest landmark—this 600-ft structure on the top of Black Mountain—is one of the best places to begin any tour of the national capital. Three viewing platforms give breathtaking views of the entire city as well as the mountain ranges to the south, and the tower houses an exhibition on the history of telecommunications in Australia, and a revolving restaurant with a spectacular nighttime panorama. The structure provides a communications link between Canberra and the rest of the country and serves as a broadcasting station for radio and television networks. Its massive scale and futuristic style caused a public outcry when it was built more than a decade ago, but the focus of architectural debate has since shifted to the buildings within the Parliamentary Triangle. ⊠ *Black Mountain Dr., Acton,* ☏ *02/6248–1911 or 1800/80–6718.* ▣ *$3.* ◷ *Daily 9 AM–10 PM.*

⑩ **Yarralumla Diplomatic Missions.** The expensive and leafy suburb of Yarralumla, located west and north of nearby Parliament House, contains many of the the city's 70 or so diplomatic missions. Some of these were established when Canberra was little more than a small country town, and it was only with great reluctance that many ambassadors and their staffs were persuaded to transfer from the temporary capital in Melbourne.

On Coronation Drive you will find the unmistakable **Chinese Embassy,** while the **British High Commission** is on Commonwealth Avenue, and State Circle contains the handsome white neoclassical building of the **South African Embassy.** Nearby Moonah Place is home to the Williamsburg-style **U.S. Embassy,** the **Indian High Commission,** and the **Embassy of the Philippines.** Some of these embassies and high commissions open their doors for public inspection on special occasions—for more details, contact the Canberra Visitor Information Centre (⊠ 330 Northbourne Ave., Dickson, ☏ 02/6205–0044).

Around Canberra and the A.C.T.

In addition to the city center public buildings, galleries, and museums, Canberra's suburbs, the A.C.T., and its surrounds offer a good variety of attractions. These include the interesting Australian Institute of Sport, a nature reserve complete with native animals, two national parks, a historic homestead, and Canberra's important contribution to the space race. You will need a car to reach these attractions, as they are not on any of the sightseeing bus routes.

TIMING

Unless you plan to use the section below as a see-all checklist, choose a few places to visit over the course of a day or two. The Australian Institute of Sport, Cockington Green, and the Royal Australian Mint are withing 15 minutes of the city, and the Canberra Deep Space Communications Complex and Lanyon Homestead are twice that far out. Farther south and west, Namadgi National Park and Tidbinbilla Nature Reserve are between 45 and 60 minutes away. A trip to Kosciusko National Park warrants a day or more in itself.

Sights to See

Australian Institute of Sport. Established in 1980 to improve the performance of Australia's elite athletes, this 150-acre site north of the city includes athletic fields, a swimming center, an indoor sports stadium, and a sports medicine center. Hour-and-a-half-long tours guided

by AIS athletes depart daily at 11:30 and 2:30, with additional tours
at 10 and 1 on weekends and public holidays. Half of the tour takes
in visits to the various facilities, where you may be able to watch some
of the institute's squads in training. The remaining time is spent in the
new Ansett Visitors Centre—here, displays and a video wall focus on
AIS athletes and the achievements of Australian sporting stars, and there
is a variety of fun hands-on exhibits. You are also welcome to use some
of the institute's facilities—including the swimming pool and tennis
courts—for a reasonable fee. ⊠ *Leverrier Crescent, Bruce,* ☎ *02/
6252–1111, tours 02/6252–1444.* ▣ *Guided tour $7.* ⊙ *Weekdays
9–5, weekends 11–4.*

Canberra Deep Space Communications Complex. Managed and operated by the Commonwealth Scientific and Industrial Research Or-
ganisation, this is one of the long-distance arms of the U.S. National
Aeronautics and Space Administration (NASA). The function of the
four giant antennae at the site is to relay commands and data between
NASA and space vehicles or orbiting satellites—the first pictures of men
walking on the moon were transmitted to this tracking station. The
station is not open to the public, but the visitors information center
houses models, audiovisual displays, and memorabilia from space missions. ⊠ *Off Paddy's River Rd., Tidbinbilla, 40 km (25 mi) southwest
of Canberra,* ☎ *02/6201–7838.* ⊙ *Daily 9–5 (9–8 in summer).*

🖐 **Cockington Green.** Thatch-roof houses, castles, canals, and a football
pitch have been reproduced in small scale to create a miniature slice
of England on this 5-acre site. The display also has the Heritage Rose
Walk, with its splendid display of roses, and The Parsons Nose Restaurant, which serves such suitably British dishes as steak-and-kidney pie
and roast beef with Yorkshire pudding. The park is located about 11
km (7 mi) north of the city center, off the Barton Highway. ⊠ *11 Gold
Creek Rd., Gold Creek Village, Gungahlin,* ☎ *02/6230–2273.* ▣
$7.95. ⊙ *Daily 9:30–4:30.*

Kosciusko National Park. Kosciusko (pronounced "koh-zee-*os*-ko") is
a wonderful alpine park—Australia's largest, in fact. It is actually located in New South Wales, although a segment of its boundary does
touch the A.C.T. The gateway city, Cooma, is only 114 km (71 mi)
from Canberra. (☞ The Snowy Mountains *in* Chapter 3.)

Lanyon Homestead. On the plain beside the Murrumbidgee River, this
classic homestead from pioneering days has been magnificently restored.
When it was built in 1859, the house was the centerpiece of a self-contained community, and many of the outbuildings and workshops have
been preserved. The adjacent **Nolan Gallery** (☎ 02/6237–5192) displays
a selection of the well-known Ned Kelly paintings by the famous Australian painter Sir Sidney Nolan. The property is 30 km (19 mi) south
of Canberra off the Monaro Highway. ⊠ *Tharwa Dr., Tharwa,* ☎ *02/
6237–5136.* ▣ *Homestead $5, gallery $2.* ⊙ *Tues.–Sun. 10–4.*

Namadgi National Park. Covering almost half the total area of the Australian Capital Territory—in the southwest—this national park encompasses trout streams, mountain ranges, some of the most accessible
subalpine forests in the country, and a well-maintained network of walking trails. Parts of the park were once used for grazing. These pastures,
now emptied of sheep and cattle, are grazed by herds of eastern gray
kangaroos that often number in the hundreds. You're most likely to
see them in the early morning and late afternoon. The park has 150
km (93 mi) of marked walking tracks, and at Yankee Hat, off the
Boboyan Road, you can visit an Aboriginal rock art site.

If you are an experienced navigator of wild country, the remote parts of the park have superb terrain. At higher altitudes, the park is covered in snow from about June through September. The **Namadgi Visitors Centre** (open daily 9–4) is located on the Naas/Boboyan Road, 3 km (1¾ mi) south of the village of Tharwa. For information, contact the Park Manager. ⊠ *Namadgi National Park, via Tharwa, 2620,* ☎ *02/6207–2900.*

Royal Australian Mint. If you really want to know how to make money, this is the place to visit. The Observation Gallery inside the mint has a series of windows where visitors can watch Australian coins being minted, from the time the blanks are brought up from the basement storage level to the furnaces where the blanks are softened, and finally to the presses where the coins are stamped. The foyer has a display of rare coins, and silver and gold commemorative coins are on sale. ⊠ *Denison St., Deakin,* ☎ *02/6202–6999.* ⊙ *Weekdays 9–4, weekends 10–3; no coin production on weekends or noon–12:40 weekdays.*

Tidbinbilla Nature Reserve. Set in eucalyptus forests in the mountain ranges 40 km (25 mi) southwest of Canberra, this 12,000-acre reserve has large walk-through enclosures where you can observe kangaroos, wallabies, and koalas in their native environment. The walking trails cross rocky mountaintops, open grassland, or gullies thick with tree ferns. The reserve also has some unusual rock formations, including Hanging Rock—a granite outcrop once used as a shelter by the Aboriginal inhabitants of the area. Bird watchers should plan to visit the reserve during the 2:30 PM feeding time, when many colorful species can be seen and photographed at close quarters. Ranger-guided walks—including evening wildlife spotlighting tours, and strolls in search of koalas and platypus—are available on weekends and during school holidays, and the Visitor Centre features a slide show and nocturnal animals exhibit. ⊠ *Paddy's River Rd., Tidbinbilla,* ☎ *02/6237–5120.* ⊠ *$8 per car.* ⊙ *Daily 9–6 (9 PM in summer); Visitor Centre weekdays 10–4, weekends 9–5:30.*

DINING

By Betty Forrest

Updated by Anne Matthews

Canberra City and Northern Suburbs

AUSTRALIAN

$$$$ ✕ **The Republic.** Canberra's most famous brasserie follows a formula that has been tried and tested in Australia's dining capitals, and the result has won the hearts and minds of the locals. The mod-Oz menu specializes in seafood, with simplicity and clean flavors guiding preparations. The decor—from aluminum water jugs to glass panels on the walls—brings a dash of Sydney style to capital-city dining. ⊠ *20 Allara St., Canberra City,* ☎ *02/6247–1717. AE, DC, MC, V. Closed Sun. No lunch Mon. or Sat.*

$$$ ✕ **Charcoal Restaurant.** Practically unchanged since it opened for business in the 1960s, this restaurant still serves the capital's best beef. Politicians and businesspeople flock here for lunch—it sometimes seems more like a gentlemen's club than a restaurant. Wooden panels and wine racks line the walls, and at night soft lights and maroon upholstery provide a romantic glow. The superb King Island steaks vary from a half-pound sirloin to a monster two-pounder. A limited range of fish and poultry dishes is also available. The wine list has more than 100 varieties of Australian reds, including some local wines. ⊠ *61 London Circuit, Canberra City,* ☎ *02/6248–8015. AE, DC, MC, V. Closed Sun. No lunch Sat.*

$$$ ✕ **Vivaldi.** This restaurant within the national university's Arts Centre is known for its generous servings, and you should exercise cau-
★

Dining
Barocca Cafe, **2**
Café Lella, **18**
Cavalier Carousel
Restaurant, **14**
Charcoal Restaurant, **5**
Green Square Deli, **19**
Gus' Coffee Lounge, **5**
The Oak Room, **12**
The Republic, **11**
Tang Dynasty, **17**
Tosolini's, **8**
Vivaldi, **4**

Lodging
Argyle Executive
Apartments, **9**
Avalanche
Homestead, **21**
Brindabella Station, **13**
Capital Parkroyal, **10**
Country Comfort
Inn, **1**
Down Town Speros
Motel, **3**
Hyatt Hotel
Canberra, **12**
Manuka Park Serviced
Apartments, **20**
Olims Canberra
Hotel, **7**
Rydges Capital Hill, **15**
Telopea Inn on the
Park, **16**

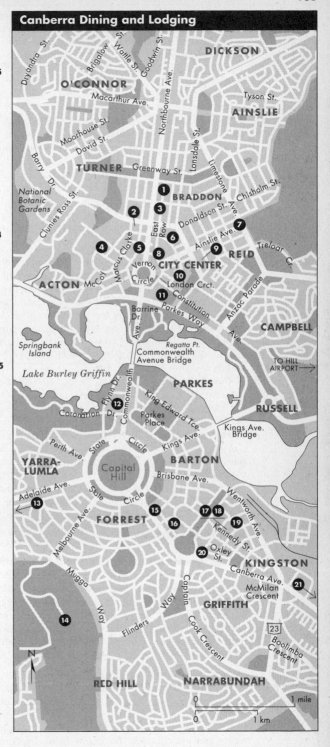

Canberra Dining and Lodging

tion before ordering a three-course meal. Typical items on Vivaldi's modern Australian menu might include a salad of artichokes, asparagus, and grilled scallops; spatchcock marinated in lemon, garlic, and oregano; and veal fillet stuffed with smoked salmon and leeks; and for dessert, almond and lemon-curd tart with amaretto-praline ice cream. The courtyard is especially recommended on sunny days. ⊠ *University Ave., Acton,* ☎ *02/6257–2718. AE, DC, MC, V. Closed Sun. and first 2 wks in Jan. No lunch Sat.*

$$ ✕ **Barocca Cafe.** This smart, attractive place is a good choice if you
★ want a dash of style at a reasonable price in the heart of the city. A cross-section of the Mediterranean menu would find Caesar salad, various pasta dishes, pizzas, and several char-grilled dishes—seafood especially. Dark wood furnishings, a neutral color scheme, and Art Deco motifs show a sophistication rarely seen outside the most expensive dining rooms in Canberra. The lunch crowd mainly consists of upwardly mobile public servants. ⊠ *60 Marcus Clarke St., Canberra City,* ☎ *02/ 6248–0253. AE, DC, MC, V. Closed Sun. No lunch Sat.*

INTERNATIONAL

$$ ✕ **Tosolini's.** A current favorite with Canberra's café society, this bustling, Italian-accented brasserie has a choice of indoor or sidewalk table eating and a menu that works hard from breakfast through dinner, with fresh fruit juices, fruit shakes, focaccia, and a small selection of main meals that usually includes pasta. The coffee is particularly good, and the cakes have an enthusiastic sweet-tooth following. Try to plan lunch around the noon to 2 crush. ⊠ *East Row and London Circuit, Canberra City,* ☎ *02/6247–4317. AE, DC, MC, V. BYOB (bottled wine only). No dinner Sun.*

$ ✕ **Gus' Coffee Lounge.** During the early 1970s the owner of this café incurred the wrath of city planning authorities when he placed tables outside on the sidewalk, and having coffee and a slice of cheesecake at Gus' became a gesture of wild defiance in staid, stolid Canberra. Now there are at least a half dozen outdoor cafés nearby, but Gus' has hardly changed, from its strains of Stephane Grappelli's fiddle rising over the noise of traffic to the eclectic range of magazines inside the café—and the cappuccino. The all-day (7:30 AM until late) menu is somewhere between New York and Vienna, with pastas, seafood dishes, bagels, croissants, waffles, and frankfurters with sauerkraut. ⊠ *Bunda St. and Garema Pl., Canberra City,* ☎ *02/6248–8118. No credit cards. BYOB.*

Southern Suburbs

CHINESE

$$$ ✕ **Tang Dynasty.** In Canberra it's hard to beat the upscale northern Chinese and Szechuan specialties at Tang Dynasty, decorated with period reproductions and a not-so-period grand piano. The popular first course of mermaid's tresses—shredded Chinese broccoli deep-fried with sugar— is a must. Also consider Peking shredded beef, marinated and deep-fried with a touch of garlic, chili, coriander, and vinegar; or boned chicken, panfried and served with Peking sauce. ⊠ *27 Kennedy St., Kingston,* ☎ *02/6295–0122. AE, DC, MC, V. Closed Sun. No lunch Sat.*

FRENCH

$$$$ ✕ **The Oak Room.** Located in the Hyatt Hotel Canberra, this is the city's
★ most elegant sophisticate—a must for a special occasion. In the two dining rooms, an atmosphere of refinement is complemented by Art Deco surroundings and soft lighting. The menu rates high for originality and presentation. Selections from the dinner menu might be smoked kangaroo and crispy eggplant salad, served with sweet and sour cherries; char-grilled sea perch accompanied by a broccoli flan and tomato marmalade in a saffron sauce; or veal cutlet with woodland

mushrooms, accompanied by a Spanish onion compote and truffle blini resting on rosemary sauce. ✉ *Hyatt Hotel Canberra, Commonwealth Ave., Yarralumla,* ☎ *02/6270–8977. Reservations essential. Jacket required. AE, DC, MC, V. Closed Sun. and Mon. No lunch Sat.*

INTERNATIONAL

$$$ ✕ **Cavalier Carousel Restaurant.** The change of name and ownership of the long-running Jean Pierre Le Carousel has been marked by a new menu that uses native Australian ingredients along with typical French dishes of frogs' legs and snails. The menu might include appetizers of scampi with king prawns in champagne and saffron sauce or warm salad of quail. Main courses on the summer menu range from rack of spring lamb with garlic and spinach to baby barramundi steamed in banana leaves, or kangaroo with quandong (a tart, plumlike native fruit) and chili sauce. The view from the restaurant, set astride Red Hill, takes in the entire city and the surrounding ranges. ✉ *Red Hill Lookout, Red Hill,* ☎ *02/6273–1808. AE, DC, MC, V. Closed Sun. No lunch Sat.*

$ ✕ **Green Square Deli.** Ideal for lunch or an evening meal, this café in a leafy square serves salads, pizzas, sandwiches, bagels, and rolls with such imaginative fillings as smoked kangaroo meat with wild plum sauce, avocado, and Brie; or smoked venison, goat cheese, and red-currant jelly. Pies are made on the premises, and fruit salads and whips are a summer treat. ✉ *Jardine Sq., Kingston,* ☎ *02/6295–7845. No credit cards. BYOB.*

ITALIAN

$ ✕ **Café Lella.** This cheerful little indoor-outdoor café is popular with locals, but unless you're in the area, neither the food nor the surroundings would justify a special excursion. The menu offers Italian-style salads, pasta dishes, cakes, and homemade gelato. Smoking is not permitted. ✉ *Jardine St., Green Sq., Kingston,* ☎ *02/6239–6383. No credit cards. BYOB. No dinner Sat.–Tues.*

LODGING

Canberra City and Northern Suburbs

$$$ 🏨 **Capital Parkroyal.** In a prime location between the city center and the National Convention Centre, this modern, atrium-style hotel has good facilities and a moderate level of luxury. Decorated in cream and honey tones, guest rooms are large, comfortable, and well equipped. Public areas have a cool, contemporary style, with plenty of chrome and glass, giant potted plants, and fresh flowers. ✉ *1 Binara St., Canberra City, 2601,* ☎ *02/6247–8999,* FAX *02/6257–4903. 293 rooms with bath. 2 restaurants, 2 bars, heated pool, sauna, exercise room. AE, DC, MC, V.*

$$ 🏨 **Argyle Executive Apartments.** Located within a five-minute walk
★ of the city center, these smart, stylish, fully self-contained, two- and three-bedroom apartments offer good value for a family or small group. Each unit has a spacious living and dining area, a separate kitchen with a microwave oven and dishwasher, and a laundry area. Set amid gardens, each has either a balcony or a private courtyard. The standby rate—available for on-the-spot bookings—is significantly less than the standard rate. Apartments are serviced daily. ✉ *144 Argyle Sq., Currong and Boolee Sts., Reid, 2601,* ☎ *02/6275–0800,* FAX *02/6275–0888. 24 apartments with bath. AE, DC, MC, V.*

$$ 🏨 **Country Comfort Inn.** The rooms and facilities here rival those in some of Canberra's more expensive hotels. The dark timber furnishings, piano, and open fire create a cozy, clublike atmosphere in the reception area, and the olive-and-cinnamon color scheme and gum-leaf motif in the rooms give them a very Australian feel. The hotel is close to the city center, but it unfortunately overlooks one of the city's major arteries, so light sleep-

ers should request a poolside room at the back of the hotel. ✉ *102 Northbourne Ave., Braddon, 2601,* ☎ *02/6249–1411,* FAX *02/6249–6878. 77 rooms with bath. Restaurant, bar, pool. AE, DC, MC, V.*

$$ 🏨 **Down Town Speros Motel.** This recently refurbished boutique-style motel offers modern facilities and excellent value for money—both the price and the proximity to the city center make this a good choice for budget travelers. There are three types of rooms, some of which have kitchens, and the place is kept spotless. ✉ *82 Northbourne Ave., Braddon, 2601,* ☎ *02/6249–1388,* FAX *02/6247–2523. 65 rooms with bath. Restaurant, gymnasium, laundry. AE, DC, MC, V.*

$$ 🏨 **Olims Canberra Hotel.** With its original National Heritage–listed building, and a modern addition built around a landscaped courtyard, this former pub has double rooms, split-level suites with kitchens, and two- and three-bedroom suites. Furnishings and decor are contemporary in style, with laminated, pinelike wood finishes, fabrics and carpets tinged with red ocher, and beige walls. Rates are reduced between Friday and Sunday nights. The hotel is about 1 km (½ mi) east of the city center, close to the Australian War Memorial. ✉ *Ainslie and Limestone Aves., Braddon, 2601,* ☎ *02/6248–5511,* FAX *02/6247–0864. 125 rooms with bath. 2 restaurants, bar. AE, DC, MC, V.*

Canberra South

$$$ 🏨 **Hyatt Hotel Canberra.** This elegant hotel is the finest in the national
★   capital. Resurrected from its former life as the National Heritage–listed Canberra Hotel, the Hyatt dates from Art Deco days and reflects that style. Rooms are large, with luxurious furnishings, and the hotel has 18 spacious suites. Warm peach and earth colors predominate, and the enormous black-and-white marble bathrooms will appeal to anyone who enjoys a good soak in the tub. The hotel has extensive gardens and is within easy walking distance of the Parliamentary Triangle. Afternoon tea, held daily between 2:30 and 5 in the gracious Tea Lounge, with all of the charm and style that the ritual demands, is one of Canberra's most popular traditions. ✉ *Commonwealth Ave., Yarralumla, 2600,* ☎ *13–1234,* FAX *02/6281–5998. 249 rooms with bath. 3 restaurants, 2 bars, indoor pool, sauna, spa, tennis court, gymnasium, business services. AE, DC, MC, V.*

$$$ 🏨 **Rydges Capital Hill.** This, one of Canberra's most luxurious hotels, attracts a largely business clientele. The atrium ceiling is composed of immense fabric sails. Rooms are large and well maintained, and although they include a number of thoughtful extras (such as irons and ironing boards), their character is bland, like that of the rest of the hotel. The 38 Spa Suites and two Premier Suites are particularly sumptuous. The hotel is close to Parliament House, and in the evening its bar always has a stimulating flow of political gossip from parliamentary staff and members of the press, who drop in regularly. ✉ *Canberra Ave., Forrest, 2603,* ☎ *02/6295–3144,* FAX *02/6295–3325. 186 rooms with bath. Restaurant, bar, indoor pool, sauna, spa, health club, business services. AE, DC, MC, V.*

$$ 🏨 **Manuka Park Serviced Apartments.** Considering that each of the comfortable one- or two-bedroom apartments and interconnecting suites in this low-rise building has cooking facilities, a living room, laundry area, and separate bedroom, the cost is just slightly more than that for a standard motel room. The fully carpeted, open-plan rooms have a clean, contemporary feel. Located in a leafy suburb within easy walking distance of the restaurants, boutiques, and antiques shops of the Manuka shopping district, and surrounded by landscaped gardens, the apartments are serviced daily, and each has a private balcony or courtyard. ✉ *Manuka Circle and Oxley St., Manuka, 2603,* ☎ *02/6285–1175,* FAX *02/6295–7750. 39 apartments with bath. Pool. AE, DC, MC, V.*

$$ ⊞ **Telopea Inn on the Park.** This motel lies in a tranquil area bordered by parklands in a leafy southern suburb, close to Parliament House; its rooms are small but a good value. Larger family rooms with kitchenettes are also available. ⊠ *16 New South Wales Crescent, Forrest, 2603,* ☎ *02/6295–3722,* ℻ *02/6239–6373. 45 rooms with bath. Restaurant, bar, indoor pool, sauna, spa. AE, MC, V.*

Outside Canberra

$$$$ ⊞ **Avalanche Homestead.** Set on a hillside above the thickly forested valleys of the Tinderry Mountains, this large, modern homestead offers its guests a luxurious taste of the "real" Australia. Rooms are spacious and comfortable, individually furnished with French antiques and plenty of wood; one room has a water bed. Dinners are splendid banquets, served in the house's vast Baronial Hall. Daily activities for guests include horseback riding, cattle mustering, sheep shearing, trout fishing, and bushwalking. The property is bordered by an 80,000-acre nature reserve, and you're likely to see kangaroos, wombats, foxes, and/or dingoes around. The homestead is 45 km (28 mi) south of Canberra, and transfers from the city are available. Rates include all meals. ⊠ *Box 544, Burra Creek, Queanbeyan, 2620,* ☎ *02/6236–3245,* ℻ *02/6236–3302. 6 rooms with shower, 1 with bath. Pool. AE, DC, MC, V.*

$$$$ ⊞ **Brindabella Station.** Sitting in a valley between the Kosciusko, Namadgi, and Brindabella national parks, this meticulously renovated turn-of-the-century Australian homestead combines the traditional lifestyle of a farm holiday with the added attraction of historic pioneer surroundings. Guest numbers are normally limited to a maximum of two couples at a time. Activities on the property include trout fishing in the Goodradidgbee River, bushwalking, swimming, mountain biking, canoeing, and watching the abundant wildlife, which includes birds, kangaroos, wombats, and platypus. You are also welcome to join in the daily activities of the sheep and cattle property. The station is 60 km (38 mi) west of Canberra, and transfers from the city·can be arranged. Rates include all meals, beverages, and activities. Smoking is not permitted in the homestead. ⊠ *Brindabella Valley, Brindabella, 2611,* ☎ *02/6236–2121,* ℻ *02/6236–2128. 4 rooms with bath. MC, V.*

NIGHTLIFE AND THE ARTS

Canberra after dark has a reputation for being dull. Actually, the city isn't quite as boring as the rest of Australia thinks, nor again as lively as the citizens of Canberra would like to believe. There is no nightclub district—clubs are scattered throughout the city and suburban shopping centers. Except on weekends, few places offer live music. The Thursday edition of the *Canberra Times* has a "What's On" section.

The Arts

Canberra Theatre Centre. The city's premier arts and theater venue is used by the local opera company, theatrical troupe, and symphony orchestra. Performances by such major national companies as the Australian Ballet are frequently held here. For a listing of current events, check the entertainment pages of the *Canberra Times.* ⊠ *Civic Sq., London Circuit,* ☎ *02/6257–1077.*

Nightlife

Bobby McGee's. The party atmosphere at this flamboyant, American-style restaurant and entertainment lounge complex appeals to a varied group. In the restaurant, Cinderella might seat you, a matador offer you cocktails, and a Roman centurion wait on your table. The music in the entertainment lounge ranges from "Heartbreak Hotel" to this week's Top 40. Service is slick and professional, the staff are gregarious and spontaneous—it would require effort not to have a good time. ⊠ *Rydge's Canberra Hotel, London Circuit,* ☎ *02/6257–7999.* ⊡ *$5 Fri. after 8.* ⊙ *Weekdays 5 PM–3 AM, Sat. 6 PM–4 AM.*

Casino Canberra. An attempt has been made at this "boutique-style" casino to create a European-style facility by leaving out slot machines in favor of the more sociable games of roulette, blackjack, poker, minibaccarat, pai gow, and keno. There are 40 gaming tables here, and the complex includes two restaurants, two bars, and a nightclub. ⊠ *21 Binara St.,* ☎ *02/6257–7074.* ⊙ *Daily noon–6 AM.*

Pandora's at Night & Wally's Bar. The disco on the upper level of this two-story bar-and-entertainment center is one of the liveliest in the city, especially on Saturday night, when it attracts a large crowd of under-25s. ⊠ *Mort and Alinga Sts.,* ☎ *02/6248–7405.* ⊡ *Thurs. $3.* ⊙ *Thurs.–Sat. 9 PM–5 AM.*

The Private Bin. One of Canberra's longest-running night spots, this large, loud club incorporates a bar, a beer garden, pool tables, and a disco on three levels. The clientele is mostly under 25, but the Waffles Piano Bar attracts an older, more sophisticated group of patrons. The comedy nights, held every Wednesday from about 8 PM, are recommended. ⊠ *50 Northbourne Ave.,* ☎ *02/6247–3030.* ⊙ *Varying hours for different bars, but generally Mon.–Sat. noon–about 2 AM, Sun. 7 PM–1 AM.*

OUTDOOR ACTIVITIES AND SPORTS

Bicycling

Canberra has almost 160 km (100 mi) of cycle paths, and the city's relatively flat terrain and dry, mild climate make it a perfect place to explore on two wheels. One of the most popular cycle paths is the 40-km (25-mi) circuit around Lake Burley Griffin.

Mr. Spokes Bike Hire has a wide range of bikes as well as tandems, baby seats, backpacks, and rollerblades. Bikes cost $8 for the first hour including helmet rental and are charged at a declining rate thereafter. ⊠ *Barrine Dr., Acton Park,* ☎ *02/6257–1188.* ⊙ *Closed Mon. and Tues.*

Boating

You can rent aquabikes, surf-skis, paddleboats, canoes, and catamarans daily (except during the winter months of June, July, and August) for use on Lake Burley Griffin from **Dobel Boat Hire.** Rates start at $9 for half an hour. ⊠ *Barrine Dr., Acton Park,* ☎ *02/6249–6861.*

Golf

On the lower slopes of Red Hill, the **Federal Golf Course** is regarded as the most challenging of the city's courses. Nonmembers are welcome on most weekdays—still, contact the club professional in advance. ⊠ *Red Hill Lookout Rd., Red Hill,* ☎ *02/6281–1888.* ⊡ *Greens fee $40 for 18 holes.*

An undulating 27-hole course on the edge of the lake, **Royal Canberra** is the city's premier golf club—due not only to the course itself but also to its membership list, which includes leading politicians from both sides of the government. The club welcomes nonmembers who can show evidence of membership in another golf club. Open days are generally Monday, Thursday, and Friday, but call first. ⊠ *Westbourne Woods, Yarralumla,* ☎ *02/6282–2655.* ⊡ *Greens fee $200 for 18 holes.*

Hiking

Namadgi National Park, Tidbinbilla Nature Reserve, and **Kosciusko National Park** have excellent bushwalking tracks (☞ Around Canberra and the A.C.T., *above*).

Running

A favorite running track is the circuit formed by the lake and its two bridges—Kings Avenue Bridge and Commonwealth Avenue Bridge.

Tennis

The **National Sports Club** offers play on synthetic grass courts. ⊠ *Mouat St., Lyneham,* ☎ *02/6247–0929.* ☛ *$8 per hr during daylight, $14 per hr under lights.* ☉ *Daily 8:30 AM–10 PM.*

At the **Australian Institute of Sport,** you can play on either indoor or outdoor courts. ⊠ *Leverrier Crescent, Bruce,* ☎ *02/6252–1111.* ☛ *$8 per hr outdoors, $12–$20 indoors.* ☉ *Weekdays 8 AM–10 PM, weekends 9–8.*

SHOPPING

Canberra is not famed for its shopping, but there are a number of high-quality arts and crafts outlets where you are likely to come across some unusual gifts and souvenirs. The city's markets are excellent, and the galleries and museums are also good for interesting and often innovative Australian-designed and -made items. In addition to the following suggestions, there are several malls and shopping centers in Canberra City.

Cuppacumbalong Craft Centre, a pioneering homestead near the Murrumbidgee River, has now become a crafts gallery for potters, weavers, painters, and woodworkers, many of whom have their studios in the outbuildings. The quality of the work is universally high and there is an opportunity to meet and talk with the artisans. The center is located about 34 km (21 mi) south of Canberra, off the Monaro Highway. The restaurant in the homestead serves healthy country food. ⊠ *Naas Rd., Tharwa,* ☎ *02/6237–5116.* ☉ *Wed.–Sun. 11–5.*

Federation Square. Located next to Cockington Green (☞ Around Canberra and the A.C.T., *above*) on the city's northern outskirts, this award-winning complex of over 20 specialty shops offers excellent shopping for clothes, crafts, pottery, and gifts. The large center also has a restaurant and coffee shop, as well as a children's playground and a walk-in aviary. ⊠ *O'Hanlon Pl., Gold Creek Village, Gungahlin,* ☎ *0411/10–3075.* ☉ *Daily 10–5.*

Gorman House Markets. These central city markets, which are located in and around a heritage building that also serves as an arts center, sells excellent arts and crafts, old books, secondhand clothes, and has live music, puppet shows, and great food. ⊠ *Ainslie Ave,* ☎ *02/6249–7377.* ☉ *Sat. 10–4, Sun. noon–4.*

Old Bus Depot Markets. This old bus depot, south of the lake in the suburb of Kingston, is now home to a lively Sunday market. Handmade goods, antiques, and other collectibles are the staples here, while exotic inexpensive food and buskers add to the shopping experience. ⊠ *49 Wentworth Ave., Kingston,* ☎ *02/6292–8391.* ☉ *May–Oct., Sun. 10–3; Nov.–Apr., Sun. 9–4.*

CANBERRA AND THE A.C.T. A TO Z

Arriving and Departing

By Bus

The main terminal for intercity coaches is the **Jolimont Tourist Centre** (⊠ 65–67 Northbourne Ave.). Canberra is served by two major coach lines, both of which have at least three daily services to and from Sydney: **Greyhound Pioneer Australia** (☎ 13–2030), and **Murrays** (☎ 13–2251).

By Car

From Sydney, take the Hume Highway to just south of Goulburn and then turn south onto the Federal Highway to Canberra. Allow 3½ to 4 hours for the 300-km (190-mi) journey. From Melbourne, follow the Hume Highway to Yass and turn right beyond the town onto the Barton Highway. The 655-km (410-mi) trip takes around 8 hours.

By Plane

Canberra Airport is located 7 km (4½ mi) east of the city center. ☞ Air Travel *in* the Gold Guide for information on airlines.

BETWEEN THE AIRPORT AND CITY

ACT Minibuses (☎ 02/6280–0000) operates a shuttle service between the airport and any Canberra address. Pick-up points are located outside both Ansett and Qantas terminals, and the minibus meets most incoming flights. The cost is $5 for one passenger, $8 for two.

Taxis are available from the rank at the front of the terminal. The fare between the airport and the city is about $12.

By Train

The Canberra Railway Station (☎ 02/6239–0111) is located on Wentworth Avenue, Kingston, about 5 km (3 mi) southeast of the city center. EXPLORER trains make the 4-hour trip between Canberra and Sydney three times daily—call **Countrylink** (☎ 13–2232) for details. A daily coach–rail service operates on the 10-hour run between Canberra and Melbourne. Passengers must travel between Canberra and Yass Junction by bus, a distance of 60 km (38 mi).

Getting Around

By Bus

Canberra's only public transportation system is the **ACTION** bus network. Buses operate weekdays between 6:30 AM and 11:30 PM, Saturday between 7 AM and 11:30 PM, and Sunday between 8 AM and 7 PM. Buses charge a flat fare of $2. If you plan to travel extensively on buses, purchase a Day Sightseeing ticket ($6.70), which allows unlimited travel on the entire bus network.

This ticket also allows travel on the "900 series" ACTION sightseeing buses. These buses depart daily from bus bay 11 on Mort Street in the city center and visit most of the major attractions in the city and its surroundings. Bus 901 departs every half hour from 9:35 to 4:05 on weekdays, and hourly from 10:06 to 4:06 on weekends, and visits the War Memorial, Regatta Point, the Parliamentary Triangle, and the Yarralumla Diplomatic Missions. Bus 904 takes in the Botanic Gardens, Telstra Tower, National Museum of Australia, and the National Aquarium, with hourly departures from 10:20 to 3:20 on weekdays, and from 10:20 to 4:20 on weekends. Tickets, maps, and timetables are available from the tourist bureau and from the **Bus Information Centre** (✉ East Row and Alinga St., Civic, ☎ 02/6207–7611).

By Car

Canberra is not an easy city to drive in, and you may well find yourself confused by the radial road system and its turnoffs. Still, because sights are scattered about and not easily connected on foot or by public transport, a car is a good way to see the city and sights in the Australian Capital Territory as well. So purchase a good map and persist.

By Taxi

Taxis can be summoned by phone or hired from ranks, but you cannot flag them down in the street. **Aerial Taxis** (☎ 02/6285–9222).

Contacts and Resources

Car Rentals

National car-rental operators with agencies in Canberra include **Avis** (⊠ 17 Lonsdale St., Braddon, ☎ 02/6249–6088 or 008/22–5533), **Budget** (⊠ Shell Service Station, Girrahween St., Braddon, ☎ 02/6257–2200), **Hertz** (⊠ 32 Mort St., Braddon, ☎ 02/6257–4877 or 1800/13–3039), and **Thrifty** (⊠ 29 Lonsdale St., Braddon, ☎ 02/6247–7422). A local operator that offers discount car rentals is **Rumbles Rent A Car** (⊠ 17/157 Gladstone St., Fyshwick, ☎ 02/6280–7444).

Doctors

Woden Valley Public Hospital has a casualty department that is open 24 hours. ⊠ *Yamba Dr., Garran,* ☎ *02/6244–2222.*

Embassies and High Commissions

British High Commission. ⊠ *Commonwealth Ave., Yarralumla,* ☎ *02/ 6270–6666.* ☉ *Weekdays 8:45–5.*
Canadian High Commission. ⊠ *Commonwealth Ave., Yarralumla,* ☎ *02/6273–3844.* ☉ *Weekdays 8:30–12:30 and 1:30–4:30.*
New Zealand High Commission. ⊠ *Commonwealth Ave., Yarralumla,* ☎ *02/6270–4211.* ☉ *Weekdays 8:45–5.*
U.S. Embassy. ⊠ *Moonah Pl., Yarralumla,* ☎ *02/6270–5000.* ☉ *Weekdays 8:30–12:30.*

Emergencies

Ambulance, fire brigade, and **police.** ☎ *000.*

Guided Tours

BOAT TOURS
Canberra Cruises offers 1½-hour guided cruises that travel the length of Lake Burley Griffin, departing daily at 10:30 and 12:30. A dinner cruise operates Wednesday through Saturday at 7:30, although services may be canceled due to insufficient demand. All cruises depart from the Acton Ferry Terminal on the north side of the lake, beside the Commonwealth Avenue Bridge. Reservations are essential. ☎ *02/6295–3544.* ☜ *Prices vary, but day cruises cost about $12.*

ORIENTATION TOURS
Murrays Canberra Explorer offers an economical introduction to Canberra. In its 25-km (16-mi) circuit of the city, the red Explorer bus stops at most of the major sights, including Parliament House, the National Gallery, the embassies, and the Australian War Memorial. A driver provides commentary, and you are free to leave the bus at any of the 19 stops and board any following Explorer bus. You can also take a one-hour nonstop trip—a good orientation. Tours leave from the Jolimont Tourist Centre at 65–67 Northbourne Avenue every hour from 10:15 to 4:15. The cost is $18 for a full day ticket, $7 for the one-hour trip. Murrays also offers a range of day or half-day sightseeing tours of Canberra and the surrounding area. ☎ *13–2251.*

Travel Agencies

American Express Travel. ⊠ *Centrepoint, Gallery Level, City Walk and Petrie Plaza,* ☎ *02/6247–2333.*
Thomas Cook. ⊠ *Canberra Centre, Bunda St.,* ☎ *02/6257–2222.*

Visitor Information

Visitor Information Centre. If you are entering Canberra by road from Sydney or the north, this is the most accessible information source. ⊠ *330 Northbourne Ave., Dickson,* ☎ *02/6205–0044.* ☉ *Weekdays 9–5, weekends 8:30–5.*
Canberra Centre. The ground floor kiosk in the Canberra Centre is another useful source of information. ⊠ *Bunda and Akuna Sts.* ☉ *During shopping hours.*

5 Melbourne and Victoria

Melbourne (say mel-burn) is the urbane, cultivated sister of brassy Sydney. To the extent that culture is synonymous with sophistication— except when it comes to watching Australian-rules football or the Melbourne Cup—some call this city the cultural capital of the continent. Outside the city, watch the sundown race of fairy penguins on Phillip Island, marvel at the sculpted South Ocean coastline, sample some of the country's tasty wine in and around charming Victorian towns, or bushwalk in a splendid variety of national parks.

By Walter
Glaser and
Michael
Gebicki

Updated by
Gary Walsh

SEPARATED from New South Wales by the mighty Murray River and fronted by a rugged and beautiful coastline, Victoria's terrain is as varied as any in the country. If you're expecting an Australian norm of big sky and vast desert horizons, you may be surprised by lush farms, vineyards, forests, and mountain peaks. And though it's younger than its rival, New South Wales, Victoria possesses a sense of history and continuity often missing in other Australian states, where humanity's grasp on the land appears temporary and precarious—even the smallest rural communities in Victoria erect some kind of museum.

If, like its dowager namesake, Victoria is a little stuffy and old-fashioned, then the state capital of Melbourne is positively Old World. For all the talk of Australia's egalitarian achievements, Melbourne society displays an almost European obsession with class. The city is the site of the nation's most prestigious schools and universities, and nowhere is it more important to have attended the right one. In a country whose convict ancestors are the frequent butt of jokes, Melburnians pride themselves on the fact that unlike Sydney, their city was founded by free men and women who came to Victoria of their own accord.

Nonetheless, whatever appearances they maintain, Melburnians do love their sports. The city is sports mad—especially when it comes to the glorious, freewheeling Melbourne Cup. On the first Tuesday of each November, everyone heads out to Flemington Racetrack for the horse race that brings the entire nation to a grinding halt. Gaily dressed in all manner of outrageous costume, like tutus and tiaras, blue-collar workers and society dames converge here to sip champagne, picnic, and cheer on their favorite ponies before making the rounds of Cup parties.

Perhaps the mania displayed at almost all Melbourne sporting events is a reawakening of the raucous excitement that blossomed in the city during the days of the gold rush. When gold was discovered in 1851, fortune seekers overran Victoria. Before long, the towns of Bendigo, Castlemaine, and Ballarat were whirlwinds of activity, as miners poured in from around the country and the world to try their luck in the goldfields. These were wild times, and the diggers who rolled into nearby Melbourne to blow off steam were a colorful bunch. The lucky ones had plenty of money to spend, and spend they did. Many of the gracious buildings that line the streets today are products of that gold rush boom, which saw the population quadruple within 10 years, as those who came to seek their fortunes in Victoria settled around what was rapidly becoming a bona fide capital city.

In Australian terms, Victoria is a compact state, astonishing in its contrasts and all the more exciting for them. Beyond the urban sprawl of Melbourne, which now extends its tentacles as far as the Mornington Peninsula, the great oceanscapes of the West Coast are among the most seductive elements of Victoria's beauty. The romantic history of the gold rushes pervades central Victoria, while paddle wheelers still ply the waters of the mighty Murray River. The long stretch of the Murray region is also known for its wineries. And from the Grampians in the west to the sprawling alpine parks in the east, the great Victorian outdoors is reason enough itself to plan a trip.

Pleasures and Pastimes

The Arts
Melbourne regards itself as the artistic and cultural capital of Australia. It is home to the Australian Ballet and a range of opera, theater, and

Victoria

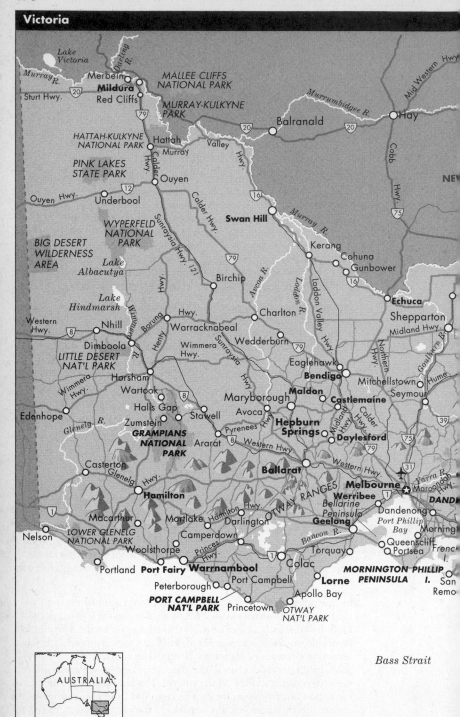

Lake Victoria

Murray R.

Sturt Hwy.

Darling R.

Merbein

Mildura

Red Cliffs

20

79

MALLEE CLIFFS
NATIONAL PARK

MURRAY-KULKYNE
PARK

Murrumbidgee R.

Mid Western Hwy

Hay

Balranald

20

20

Cobb Hwy.

NEW

HATTAH-KULKYNE
NATIONAL PARK

Hattah

Murray

Valley

Hwy.

PINK LAKES
STATE PARK

Calder Hwy.

Ouyen

16

Ouyen Hwy.

12

Underbool

BIG DESERT
WILDERNESS
AREA

WYPERFELD
NATIONAL
PARK

Lake
Albacutya

Sunraysia Hwy. 121

Hwy.

Calder Hwy.

Swan Hill

79

Birchip

Avoca R.

Murray R.

Kerang

Cohuna

Gunbower

16

Loddon R.

Loddon Valley Hwy.

Echuca

Shepparton

Lake
Hindmarsh

Western
Hwy.

8

Nhill

Dimboola

*LITTLE DESERT
NAT'L PARK*

Wimmera R.

Henry Hwy.

Borung Hwy.

Warracknabeal

Wimmera
Hwy.

Charlton

Wedderburn

79

Eaglehawk

Bendigo

Midland Hwy.

Mitchellstown

Goulburn R.

Seymour

75

Wimmera Hwy.

Horsham

Wartook

Halls Gap

Zumstein

*GRAMPIANS
NATIONAL
PARK*

8

Stawell

Sunraysia Hwy.

Maryborough

Avoca

Pyrenees Hwy.

**Hepburn
Springs**

Maldon

Castlemaine

Midland Hwy.

Calder Hwy.

Daylesford

79

39

Edenhope

Glenelg R.

Ararat

8

Western Hwy.

Casterton

Glenelg Hwy.

Hamilton

Hwy.

Western Hwy.

Ballarat

OTWAY RANGES

Melbourne

Yarra R.

Maroondah

31

DAND

Macarthur

Mortlake

Hamilton Hwy.

Darlington

Werribee

Bellarine
Peninsula

Dandenong

Port Phillip
Bay

Morning

75

1

Nelson

*LOWER GLENELG
NATIONAL PARK*

Woolsthorpe

Camperdown

Princes Hwy.

Geelong

Barwon R.

Torquay

Queenscliff

Portsea

Frenc
I.

Portland

Port Fairy

Warrnambool

Port Campbell

Colac

1

Lorne

**MORNINGTON PHILLIP
PENINSULA**

PHILLIP I.

San
Remo

Peterborough

*PORT CAMPBELL
NAT'L PARK*

Princetown

Apollo Bay

*OTWAY
NAT'L PARK*

Bass Strait

AUSTRALIA

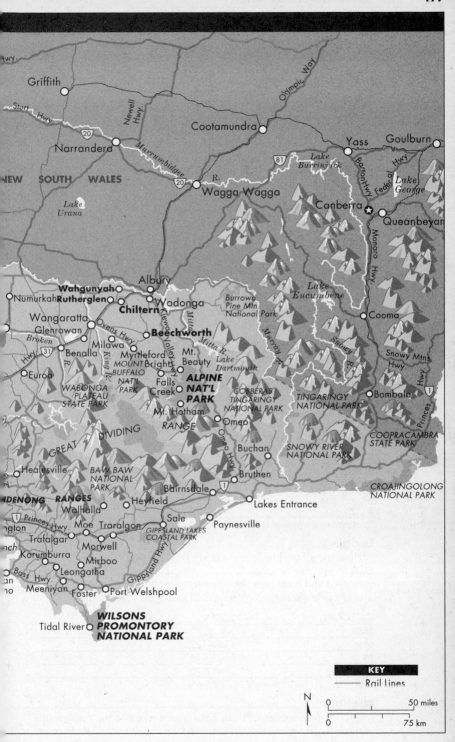

Griffith

Sturt Hwy

Newell Hwy.

Olympic Way

Cootamundra

Yass

Goulburn

Narrandera

Murrumbidgee

20

NEW SOUTH WALES

R.

Wagga Wagga

81

Lake
Burrinjuck

Barton Hwy.

Federal Hwy

Lake
George

Canberra

Queanbeyan

Lake
Urana

Lake
Eucumbene

Monaro Hwy.

Albury

Wahgunyah

Numurkah

Rutherglen

Wodonga

Chiltern

Burrowa
Pine Mtn.
National Park

Cooma

Wangaratta

Glenrowan

Ovens Hwy.

Beechworth

Mitta R.

Mitta R.

Murray R.

Snowy R.

Broken

Hwy.

31

Milawa

King R.

Myrtleford

MOUNT

Bright

Mt.
Beauty

Lake
Dartmouth

Snowy Mtns.
Hwy.

Benalla

Euroa

BUFFALO
NAT'L
PARK

Falls
Creek

ALPINE
NAT'L
PARK

GOBBERAS
TINGARINGY
NATIONAL PARK

TINGARINGY
NATIONAL PARK

Bombala

WABONGA
PLATEAU
STATE PARK

Mt. Hotham

RANGE

Omeo

SNOWY RIVER
NATIONAL PARK

COOPRACAMBRA
STATE PARK

Princes Hwy.

GREAT

DIVIDING

Omeo Hwy.

Buchan

Healesville

BAW BAW
NATIONAL
PARK

Bruthen

CROAJINGOLONG
NATIONAL PARK

DENONG

RANGES

Heyfield

Bairnsdale

1

Lakes Entrance

Walhalla

Princes Hwy.

Sale

Paynesville

gton

Moe

Traralgon

GIPPSLAND LAKES
COASTAL PARK

1

Trafalgar

Morwell

Korumburra

Mirboo

Gippsland Hwy.

Leongatha

Bass Hwy.

Meeniyan

Foster

Port Welshpool

Tidal River

WILSONS
PROMONTORY
NATIONAL PARK

N

dance companies—from the traditional to the avant garde. Many regional Victorian cities have their own smaller companies, and their own enthusiastic supporters. Art galleries, both formal and eclectic, abound throughout the state.

Dining

Few cities take their eating as seriously as Melbourne does, long hailed as the fine dining capital of Australia. Although big-night-out French- and Italian-based restaurants were once the order of the day, in recent years the dining scene has diversified into a vast smorgasbord of cuisines and dining experiences. Chinese restaurants on Little Bourke Street are the equal of anything in Hong Kong. The neighborhood of Richmond's Victoria Street convincingly reincarnates Vietnam. The central business district now boasts so many hole-in-the-wall Italian cafés that you could almost be in Rome. And a stroll down Fitzroy Street in St. Kilda is a racy, cosmopolitan walk on the wild side, where you'll find everything from sushi and Singapore *laksa* (spicy Malaysian noodle soup) to spaghetti and *som tum* (Thai green papaya salad).

Outside Melbourne one can still eat well, especially in Victoria's wine regions, where an exciting form of regional cooking is evolving at restaurants such as Arthur's on the Mornington Peninsula. Some of the best Greek food in the state can be found along the famous Great Ocean Road at Kosta's in Lorne, and city-smart food stops are popping up all around the state, as at spa-town Daylesford's Lake House.

Reservations are generally advised in the city, and although most restaurants are licensed to sell alcohol, the few that aren't will usually allow you to bring your own. Wine lists range from encyclopedic to small and selective, featuring Australian wines, which show unequaled freshness and fruit. Lunch is served between noon and 2:30, and dinner—usually a single seating—is between 7 and 10:30. A 10% tip is customary, and there may be a corkage fee in BYOB restaurants. Expect neither sales tax nor service charge.

CATEGORY	COST*
$$$$	over $60
$$$	$45–$60
$$	$30–$45
$	under $30

per person, excluding drinks and tip

Lodging

Melbourne's best hotels are world class, ranging from marble and glass properties to gracious Victorian-era edifices. Throughout the state, bed and breakfasts, host farms, and old-fashioned guest houses are welcome alternatives to hotel and motel accommodation.

CATEGORY	COST*
$$$$	over $220
$$$	$150–$220
$$	$100–$150
$	under $100

All prices are for a standard double room.

Nightlife

Many Victorians content themselves with a night at the movies, but nightclubs, live music venues, pubs, and bars are always full of action, especially in Melbourne and larger regional towns. Melbourne's nightlife mecca is King Street, where dozens of clubs and bars jostle for customers.

Outdoor Activities and Sports

Bushwalking, canoeing, fishing, hiking, rafting, riding—the choice is yours. Victoria has a variety of outstanding national parks—coastal, mountain, rain forest, and riparian environments that are havens for remarkable animal and plant life. It's a great state for getting out into the bush. Port Campbell, Grampians, Alpine, and Wilson's Promontory national parks can easily be combined with one or two of the tours or side trips in this chapter. For information on bushwalking, cross-country skiing, horseback riding, and rafting in Victoria's great outdoors beyond what's mentioned in this chapter, *see* Chapter 13.

As for spectator sports, Victorians do love a good match, like Ozzies in general. The Melbourne Cup horse race in November brings the entire city to a standstill. The same is true of Australian-rules football, one of a few varieties of "footie." This, the nation's number-one spectator sport, has its stronghold in Melbourne. The season begins in March and reaches its climax at the Grand Final, held in September, when crowds of 100,000 are commonplace. (For a description of Australian-rules football, *see* Chapter 1.)

Exploring Melbourne and Victoria

Victoria has something for almost every traveler. Urban pleasures abound in Melbourne. Along the West Coast, you'll find rugged, cliff-lined seascapes, dense forests, and charming resort towns. Traveling inland, there are historic goldfields towns, river towns along the Murray, and the delicious wine of Victoria's vineyards, particularly at smaller boutique wineries. Throughout the state, the contrasting landscape is nowhere better represented than in its national parks: the weathered offshore rock formations of Port Campbell National Park; the waterfalls, flora, and fauna of the Grampians; the high-country solitude of Alpine National Park; and the densely forested mountains and white sand beaches of Wilson's Promontory.

Great Itineraries

Because of the state's relatively small size, Victoria's principal attractions are appealingly easy to get to. Another region, another taste of this richly endowed state, is never too far away.

In five days, you can explore the glorious West Coast, particularly the stunning rock formations of Port Campbell National Park, and head into the Gold Country; traveling for a week, you can add the wineries and historic towns of the northeast. Over 10 days, you can take in more remote and little-touristed places such as the Wilson's Promontory and Alpine national parks.

IF YOU HAVE 3 DAYS

Spend your nights in ⛨ **Melbourne,** and divide your days between the city's attractions and nearby day-trip destinations. Take a full day to see the best of Melbourne. Next day, head for the hills, and a ride on **Puffing Billy** through the fern gullies and forests of the ⛨ **Dandenongs.** Continue to **Phillip Island** for the endearing Penguin Parade at Summerland Beach at dusk before returning to Melbourne. On the third day meander along the coastal roads of the **Mornington Peninsula** through such stately towns as Sorrento and Portsea and stop at a beach, or pick a Melbourne neighborhood or two to explore.

IF YOU HAVE 5 DAYS

Allow a full day or two for the sights of Melbourne, then make your way west to the **Great Ocean Road,** one of the world's finest scenic drives, stopping at **Geelong**'s fascinating **National Wool Museum** en route. In summer the beaches of the **West Coast** will be irresistible—

Fairhaven, near Lorne, is the pick of an impressive bunch. Overnight in ⊡ **Lorne,** which has a memorable setting beneath the Otway Ranges. Next day, drive west to **Port Campbell National Park** and the **Twelve Apostles** rock formation, take a walk to the beach, and continue to ⊡ **Warrnambool** for the night. Allow the morning to see the excellent Flagstaff Hill Maritime Village, before driving northeast to ⊡ **Ballarat,** the center of the goldfields region. Explore the town's 19th-century streetscapes in the evening before viewing the sound-and-light show at Sovereign Hill Historical Park. The following morning, revisit Sovereign Hill and its entertaining re-creation of the 1851 gold diggings, then return to Melbourne.

IF YOU HAVE 10 DAYS

Spend your first two days and nights in Melbourne, with an evening excursion to Phillip Island, then take the West Coast drive, overnighting in ⊡ **Lorne** before exploring in detail the delights of **Port Campbell National Park** and ⊡ **Warrnambool.** Drive 29 km (18 mi) west of Warrnambool to ⊡ **Port Fairy,** which many believe is Victoria's most beautiful town. Start early the next day for a drive via **Grampians National Park,** where you can pet the tame kangaroos at Zumstein, to ⊡ **Ballarat.** Head through **Daylesford** and the spa town of **Hepburn Springs** to ⊡ **Bendigo,** where the Golden Dragon Museum, which looks at the history of Chinese people on the goldfields, is a must. The next destination is ⊡ **Echuca,** the town that best evokes the vibrancy of life on the Murray River. Then drive via the wineries of the northeast to lovely ⊡ **Beechworth** for two nights. Spend a full day in and around the **Alpine National Park**—take a walk among the wildflowers in summer, ski in winter—before making your way back to the capital.

When to Tour Melbourne and Victoria

Melbourne—indeed, most of the state—is at its most beautiful in fall, from March through May. Days are crisp, sunny, and clear, and the foliage in parks and gardens is quite glorious. The Melbourne winter can be gloomy, but by September the weather is looking up, the football finals are on, and spirits are beginning to soar. Book early if you want to spend time in Melbourne in late October or early November when the Spring Racing Carnival and the Melbourne International Festival are in full cry; likewise in early March when the city hosts a Formula 1 motor racing grand prix.

The West Coast is a summer retreat for Melburnians, so it can be very busy, and accommodations can be hard to come by in the Christmas to New Year period. By the same token some would argue that the wild seas and leaden skies of winter provide the most suitable ambience for this dramatic scenery. Northeast winters are dry and sunny, thanks to the cloud-blocking bulk of the Great Dividing Range, and perfect for touring. Summer is extremely hot there and in gold country, where spring and fall are often perfect.

MELBOURNE

When she came to Melbourne in 1956 to make the film *On the Beach,* Ava Gardner is supposed to have said that the city *would* be a great place to make a movie about the end of the world. It turns out that an enterprising journalist had invented the comment, but these days Melburnians recall the alleged remark with humor rather than rancor, which shows how far this city of 3 million has come. And considering that the Washington, DC–based Population Crisis Committee declared Melbourne "the world's most livable city" along with Seattle and Montréal, Melburnians seem to have opinion on their side.

The symbol of Melbourne's civility, as in turn-of-the-century Budapest or in Boston, is the streetcar. Solid, dependable, going about their business with a minimum of fuss, trams are an essential part of Melbourne. For a definitive Melbourne experience, climb aboard a tram and proceed silently and smoothly up the "Paris end" of Collins Street.

As escapes from the rigors of urban life, the parks and gardens in and around Melbourne are among the most impressive features of the capital of the Garden State. More than one-quarter of the inner city has been set aside as recreational space. The profusion of trees, plants, and flowers creates a feeling of rural tranquility within the thriving city.

Exploring Melbourne

Melbourne is built on a coastal plain at the top of the giant horseshoe of Port Phillip Bay. The **city center** is an orderly grid of streets on the north bank of the Yarra River. Here stand the State Parliament, banks, multinational corporations, and splendid Victorian buildings that sprang up in the wake of the gold rush. This is Melbourne's heart, which you can explore at a leisurely pace in a couple of days. In **South Melbourne,** one of the "suburbs"—which we also refer to as neighborhoods—outside of the city center, the Southgate development has refocused Melbourne's vision on the Yarra River. Once a blighted stretch of factories and run-down warehouses, the southern bank of the river is now a vibrant, exciting part of the city, and the river itself is finally taking its rightful place in Melbourne's psyche. Take another day or two and stroll along the Esplanade in the suburb of **St. Kilda,** amble past the elegant houses of **East Melbourne,** enjoy the shops and cafés in **Fitzroy** or **Carlton,** rub shoulders with locals at the Victoria Market, nip into the Windsor for afternoon tea, or hire a canoe at Studley Park to paddle along one of the prettiest stretches of the Yarra—and you will discover Melbourne's soul as well as its heart.

Numbers in the text correspond to numbers in the margin and on the Melbourne City Center and Melbourne Suburbs maps.

City Center

Melbourne's center is an orderly grid of wide streets, framed by the Yarra River to the south and a string of parks to the east. On the river's southern bank, the Southgate development, the arts precinct around the National Gallery, and the King's Domain–Royal Botanic Gardens areas also merit attention (☞ South Melbourne and Richmond, *below*).

A GOOD WALK

One of the finest vistas of the city is from Southbank Promenade, looking across the Yarra River and its busy water traffic to the city's sparkling towers. Start here with a stroll around the shops, bars, cafés, and buskers of **Southgate** ① and a visit to the **National Gallery of Victoria** ② (☞ South Melbourne, *below*) before crossing the ornate Princes Bridge to the city proper. Take a look to the east from the bridge; the Melbourne Cricket Ground and National Tennis Centre dominate the scene. On the green banks of the Yarra, boathouses edge toward the water, and rowers glide across the river's surface.

At the corner of Swanston and Flinders streets there are three major landmarks—**Flinders Street Station** ③, with its famous clocks, **Young and Jackson's Hotel** and its infamous *Chloe,* and **St. Paul's Cathedral** ④. This corner also marks the beginning of **Swanston Street Walk,** a pedestrian roadway intended to bring people off the pavements and onto the street—ironically, that is. Once there, you have to dodge trams, tour buses, even service and emergency vehicles—better keep to the sidewalk. The gray, unsatisfying **City Square** ⑤ does little to lift

Melbourne City Center

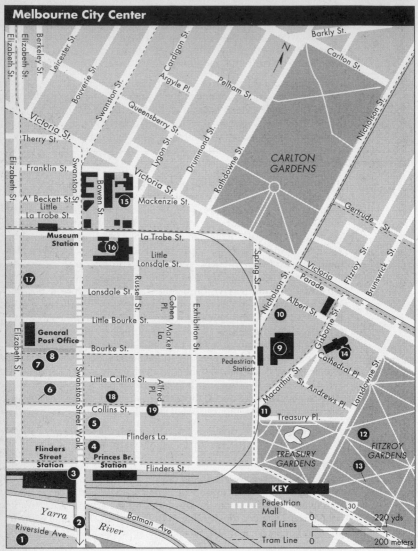

Athenaeum Theater
and Library, **18**
Block Arcade, **6**
Bourke Street Mall, **8**
Church of St.
Francis, **17**
City Square, **5**
Cook's Cottage, **13**
Fitzroy Gardens, **12**
Flinders Street
Station, **3**

Museum of Victoria
and State Library, **16**
National Gallery of
Victoria, **2**
Old Melbourne
Gaol, **15**
Old Treasury
Building, **11**
Paris End, **19**
Parliament
Gardens, **10**

Royal Arcade, **7**
St. Patrick's
Cathedral, **14**
St. Paul's
Cathedral, **4**
Southgate, **1**
State Houses of
Parliament, **9**

1>1

the spirits, but the witty statuary along this stretch of road is worth examining in some detail, and the City Square itself soon will be replaced with something more pleasing. If you walk 50 yards up the Collins Street hill on the City Square side, you'll find the **Regent Theater,** a fabulous 1930s picture palace now transformed into a live theater. It is the latest of a series of rebirths in Melbourne's classic theater life. Go west on Collins Street, along its northern side, to the **Block Arcade** ⑥, the finest example of the many arcades that Melbourne planners built to add a little invention to the strictness of the grid pattern. Turn right between the Hunt Leather and Weiss clothing shops, cross Little Collins Street, and bear slightly to the right to enter the airy, graceful **Royal Arcade** ⑦. Standing guard over the shops are Gog and Magog, the mythical giants that toll the hour on either side of Gaunt's Clock.

Bourke Street Mall ⑧ is a cluttered, always busy pedestrian zone (trams run through here, too), with an array of buskers and sidewalk artists to keep passersby entertained. Climb the Bourke Street hill to the east, with your next ports of call, the **State Houses of Parliament** ⑨ and adjacent **Parliament Gardens** ⑩, at its very end. Across the street from the gardens is the **Princess Theatre**; to the southeast, the venerable **Windsor Hotel,** an ideal spot for high tea. Walk south to the **Old Treasury Building** ⑪ and its Melbourne Exhibition, before crossing the Treasury Gardens to the **Fitzroy Gardens** ⑫ and **Cook's Cottage** ⑬. Head along Landsdowne Street to see the towering **St. Patrick's Cathedral** ⑭.

Walk west along Albert Street, which feeds into Lonsdale Street, then turn right at Russell Street. Two blocks north is the **Old Melbourne Gaol** ⑮, where you can consort briefly with assorted blackguards. Backtrack down Russell Street, turning right into La Trobe Street. At the next corner is the **Museum of Victoria and State Library** ⑯. After examining its myriad contents, perhaps the time has come to indulge in a little shopping under the inverted glass cone of Lonsdale Street's **Melbourne Central** complex. If you're there on the hour, make your way to the center of the cone and look for the massive clock, which turns into a tableaux of twittering birds and native animals to the tune of "Waltzing Matilda."

TIMING
The walk itself, without pausing at the gallery, museum, or Parliament building, or stopping for refreshments, takes around 90 minutes. But even the least keen of art and artifact viewers can spend an hour each in the National Gallery and the Museum of Victoria. Pleasant weather might tempt you to sit for a while in the lovely Fitzroy Gardens, or you might choose to descend to the grassy riverbanks east of Princes Bridge for a stress-free interlude. If shopping takes your fancy—and Block Arcade, Royal Arcade, and Melbourne Central have some of the city's finest outlets—you could while away a day in the city center.

SIGHTS TO SEE
⑱ **Athenaeum Theater and Library.** The present building, which includes an art gallery as well as a theater and library, was built in 1886. These days, the Athenaeum is used mainly for live theatrical performances, yet it is also remembered as the venue for the first talking picture show ever screened in Australia. If you don't make it to a show, take a peek inside between 8:30 and 5 on weekdays, 8:30–noon Saturday. ✉ *180 Collins St.,* ☎ *03/9650–3100.*

⑥ **Block Arcade.** Melbourne's most elegant 19th-century shopping arcade was restored in 1988 when a hundred years of grime was scraped back to reveal a magnificent mosaic floor. The arcade was built during the 1880s, when the city was flushed with the prosperity of the gold rushes, a period recalled as "Marvelous Melbourne." ✉ *282 Collins St. and 100 Elizabeth St.,* ☎ *03/9654–5244.*

NEED A
BREAK? The **Hopetoun Tea Room** (✉ Block Arcade, ☎ 03/9650-2777) has been serving Melbourne delicate sandwiches, refined cakes, and perfectly prepared cups of tea for a century. It's a slice of Melbourne circa 1890 time-warped into the present without too many modern intrusions.

⑧ Bourke Street Mall. Once the busiest east–west thoroughfare in the city, Bourke is now a pedestrian zone (but watch out for those trams!). Two of the city's biggest department stores are here, Myer (Number 314) and David Jones (Number 310). An essential part of growing up in Melbourne is being taken to Myer's at Christmas to see the window displays. ✉ *Bourke St. between Elizabeth St. and Swanston Walk.*

Carlton Gardens. The 40 acres of tree-lined paths, artificial lakes, and flower beds in this English-style 19th-century park form a backdrop for the **Exhibition Buildings** that were erected in 1880 and are still used for trade shows. The gardens are on the northeast edge of the city center, bounded by Victoria Parade and Nicholson, Carlton, and Rathdowne streets.

⑰ Church of St. Francis. This Roman Catholic church was constructed in 1845, when the city was barely a decade old. The simple, frugal design starkly contrasts with the Gothic exuberance of St. Paul's, built 40 years later. The difference illustrates just what the gold rush did for Melbourne. ✉ *Elizabeth and Lonsdale Sts.*

⑤ City Square. This messy, dismal open space is where Melbourne comes to eat lunch, listen to bands, and assemble for protest marches. Architecturally it is a disaster, and a major redevelopment, including a hotel, is planned for the site. The square features the statue of Robert Burke and William Wills, whose expedition was the first to cross Australia from south to north, from 1860 to 1861. In bronze as in life, their fate is to wander, as this statue has already been relocated several times. Proposals for a new square, to be called Federation Square, opposite Flinders Street Station are under consideration, and the awful 1960s tower blocks that once disfigured this site have been removed to allow the square to proceed. ✉ *Swanston Walk between Collins St. and Flinders La.*

⑬ Cook's Cottage. This modest stone cottage, the property of the Pacific navigator Captain James Cook, was transported stone by stone from Great Ayton in Yorkshire and reerected in the lush Fitzroy Gardens in 1934. It is believed that Cook lived in the cottage between voyages. The interior is simple and sparsely furnished—a suitable domestic realm for a man who spent much of his life in cramped quarters aboard small ships. ✉ *Fitzroy Gardens, near Landsdowne St. and Wellington Parade.* ☷ *$2.50.* ☉ *Apr.–Oct., daily 9–5; Nov.–Mar., daily 9–5:30.*

Crown Casino. Melbourne's first casino opened in 1994 at a temporary site in the World Trade Centre, and in mid-1997 it moved to its permanent site on the south bank of the Yarra. The casino is Australia's largest, and the associated development—restaurants, bars, entertainment outlets—spreads over four city blocks and includes Australia's largest hotel, with 1,000 rooms. The whole casino development has been plagued by controversy, with church and social welfare groups railing against the promotion of a "casino culture" and its supposedly adverse effects on family life. ✉ *Riverside Ave.,* ☎ *03/9685–4200.*

⑫ Fitzroy Gardens. This 65-acre expanse of European trees, manicured lawns, garden beds, statuary, and sweeping walks is Melbourne's most popular central park. Among its highlights is the **Avenue of Elms,** a majestic stand of 130-year-old trees that is one of the few in the world that have not been devastated by Dutch elm disease. ✉ *Lansdowne St. and Wellington Parade.*

❸ **Flinders Street Station.** The clocks on the front of this grand Edwardian hub of Melbourne's suburban rail network are a favorite meeting place for Melburnians. When it was proposed to replace them with television screens there was an uproar. Today, you will find both clocks and screens. ✉ *Flinders St. and St. Kilda Rd.*

⓮ **Museum of Victoria and State Library.** Set on a rise behind lawns and heroic statuary, this handsome 1853 building was constructed during the gold-rush boom. The **State Library** houses more than 1.5 million volumes, one of Australia's finest collections of manuscripts, and a vast number of maps, prints, and paintings. If you just want to take a quick look around, be sure to inspect the 115-ft dome of the Reading Room, the largest reinforced concrete dome in the world when it was built in 1913. The library's records of the Burke and Wills Expedition (whose statues are in City Square) are a highlight of its holdings.

The **Museum of Victoria** houses the state's natural history, science, and technology collections, but the state government closed the museum in mid-1997 during the construction of its new incarnation in Carlton Gardens. Until the new museum is finished in 2000, some of the existing exhibits will go on tour, others will be transferred to ☞ **Scienceworks Museum** in Spotswood, but the majority will not be on display until the reopening. ✉ *328 Swanston St.,* ☎ *03/9669–9888.* ⊙ *Library Mon. 1–9, Tues. 10–6, Wed. 10–9, Thurs.–Sun. 10–6.*

⓯ **Old Melbourne Gaol.** The city's first jail is now a museum run by the Victorian branch of the National Trust. The jail has three tiers of cells with catwalks around the upper levels. Its most famous inmate was Ned Kelly, who was hanged here in 1880. His death mask and one of the four suits of armor used by his gang are displayed in a ground-floor cell. ✉ *Russell St.,* ☎ *03/9663–7228.* ⚏ *$6.50, tour free.* ⊙ *Daily 9:30–4:30; tour daily at 11, 1, and 3.*

⓫ **Old Treasury Building.** The neoclassical brick and bluestone facade of the Old Treasury dominates the eastern end of Collins Street. It was built in 1857 to hold the gold that was pouring into Melbourne from mines in Ballarat and Bendigo. Subterranean vaults were protected by iron bars and foot-thick walls. The architect J.J. Clark designed the building when he was only 19. The **Melbourne Exhibition** occupies the entire ground floor of the tastefully restored treasury. It takes you from Aboriginal times to the present, with relics from Melbourne's past borrowed from public and private collections. ✉ *Treasury Pl. and Spring St.,* ☎ *03/9651–2233.* ⚏ *$5, gold-vault tour free.* ⊙ *Daily 9–5, tour daily at 1 and 3.*

⓳ **Paris End.** Beyond the cream and red Romanesque facade of St. Michael's Uniting Church, the eastern end of Collins Street takes on a name coined by Melburnians to identify the elegance of its fashionable shops as well as its general hauteur. Alas, modern development has seen the area lose some of its architectural appeal. Sadder still, George's, the most traditional of Melbourne's department stores, closed its doors late in 1995. **Le Louvre** is a favorite store with Melbourne's high society and a study in minimalist window dressing—no need for haute couture to trumpet its wares. ✉ *74 Collins St.,* ☎ *03/ 9650–1300.* ⊙ *Weekdays 9–5:30, Sat. 9–12:30.*

❿ **Parliament Gardens.** Stop here for a breath of cool green air in the center of the city. The gardens have a modern fountain and an excellent view of the handsome yellow facade of the ☞ **Princess Theater** across Spring Street. The gardens are also home to the lovely ☞ **St. Peter's Church.** ⊠ *Parliament, Spring, and Nicholson Sts.*

Pellegrini's Espresso Bar and Restaurant (⊠ 66 Bourke St., ☎ 03/9662–1885) serves industrial-strength coffee and bargain-priced cakes, sandwiches, and pasta dishes. At lunchtime, the narrow bar draws a mixed crowd of students, shoppers, and business executives. The restaurant at the back is usually less crowded.

Princess Theatre. A princess indeed—the ornate, 1886 wedding cake–style edifice was refurbished for a production of *Phantom of the Opera,* which was a blockbuster success. The theater, across from Parliament Gardens, is one of Melbourne's Broadway-style venues, along with the newly refurbished Regent Theatre in Collins Street. ⊠ *163 Spring St.,* ☎ *03/9662–2911.*

RIALTO TOWERS OBSERVATION DECK – If you want a bird's-eye view of Melbourne, there's no better place than from the 55th floor of the city's tallest building. The 360-degree panorama is superb, with views on a clear day extending to the Dandenong Ranges and far out into Port Phillip Bay. ⊠ *476 Flinders La.,* ☎ *03/9629-8222.* 🎟 *$6.* ☉ *Weekdays 11–11, weekends 10–11.*

❼ **Royal Arcade.** Built in 1869, this is the city's oldest shopping arcade and, despite alterations, it retains an airy, graceful elegance notably lacking in more modern shopping centers. Walk about 30 paces into the arcade, turn around, and look up to see the statues of Gog and Magog, the mythical monsters that toll the hour on either side of **Gaunt's Clock.** At the far end is a wrought-iron portico from the same period, one of the few remaining examples of the verandas that used to grace the city center. ⊠ *355 Bourke St.,* ☎ *03/0629–8888.*

⓮ **St. Patrick's Cathedral.** Begun in 1858, construction of Melbourne's Roman Catholic cathedral took 82 years to finish. Another Gothic Revival building, St. Pat's lacks the exuberant decoration of St. Paul's, Melbourne's Anglican cathedral. Ireland supplied Australia with many of its early immigrants, especially during the Irish potato famine in the middle of the 19th century, and the church is closely associated with Irish Catholicism in Australia. A statue of the Irish patriot Daniel O'Connell stands in the courtyard. ⊠ *Cathedral Pl.,* ☎ *03/9667–0377.* ☉ *Weekdays 6:30–6, weekends 7:15 AM–7:30 PM.*

❹ **St. Paul's Cathedral.** This headquarters of Melbourne's Anglican faith (completed in 1892) is regarded as one of the most important works of William Butterfield, a leader of the Gothic Revival style in England. The interior is highly decorative, right down to the patterned floor tiles. The English organ is particularly noteworthy. Outside the cathedral is the **Statue of Matthew Flinders,** who was the first seaman to circumnavigate the Australian coastline, between 1801 and 1803. ⊠ *Flinders and Swanston Sts.,* ☎ *03/9650–3791.* ☉ *Daily 7–7.*

St. Peter's Church. Two years after St. Peter's was built in 1846, Melbourne was proclaimed a city from its steps. You'll find the church, one of Melbourne's oldest buildings, at the top end of Parliament Gardens. ⊠ *Albert and Nicholson Sts.*

❾ **State Houses of Parliament.** Begun in 1856, this building was used as the National Parliament from the time of federation in 1900 until 1927, when the first Parliament House was completed in Canberra. Today, this commanding building houses the Victorian Parliament. When the state body is in session, you can watch the political process at work from the public gallery. At other times the Upper and Lower House chambers are open to the public. The Upper House, in particular the Legislative Council chamber, is a study in Victorian opulence. To view these chambers, simply ask at the reception desk inside the front door. Parliament usually sits on Tuesday afternoon and all day Wednesday and Thursday between March and July and again between August and November. The view down Bourke Street from the front steps is particularly spectacular at night. Plans to extend the building, adding the ornate dome that was in the original design but never built, were announced in 1996, but later scrapped amid political bickering. It was unclear at time of writing whether the work would indeed go ahead. ⊠ *Spring St.,* ☎ *03/9651–8911.* ◫ *Free.* ◯ *Weekdays 9–4; guided tour at 10, 11, 2, 3, and 3:45 when parliament is not in session.*

OFF THE BEATEN PATH

VICTORIA MARKET – Just north of the city center there are bargains galore, but you don't have to be a shopper to enjoy this sprawling, spirited bazaar. Built on the site of the city's first graveyard, the century-old market is the prime produce outlet, and it seems that most of inner-city Melbourne comes here to buy its strawberries, fresh flowers, and imported cheeses. On Sunday, jeans, T-shirts, bric-a-brac, and secondhand goods are the order of the day. ⊠ *Queen and Victoria Sts.,* ☎ *03/9658– 9600.* ◯ *Tues. and Thurs. 6–2, Fri. 6–6, Sat. 6–3, Sun. 9–4.*

Windsor Hotel. Not just a grand hotel, the Windsor is home to one of Melbourne's proudest institutions—the ritual of afternoon tea, served daily between 3 and 5. Recent changes have significantly altered the hotel's interiors. The Grand Dining Room, a Belle Époque extravaganza with a gilded ceiling set with seven glass cupolas through which streams tinted sunlight, is now open only to private functions (try to steal a look at the wonder anyway); the former lounge is now the restaurant, renamed 101 Spring Street; and a Hard Rock Café has emerged where once a bar existed. But afternoon tea lives on. Far more than a genteel graze, afternoon tea at the Windsor has long been an integral part of the Melbourne experience—a lesson in the city's manners and mores in what is probably the grandest hotel in the country. ⊠ *103 Spring St., Melbourne, 3000,* ☎ *03/9653–0653.* ◫ *Tea weekdays $25, Sat. $28, Sun. afternoon buffet tea $35 per person including light entertainment.*

Young and Jackson's Hotel. Pubs are not generally known for their artwork, but if you climb the steps to the bar you will find *Chloe,* a painting that has scandalized and titillated Melburnians for many decades. The larger-than-life nude, painted by George Lefebvre in Paris in 1875, has hung on the walls of Young and Jackson's Hotel for most of this century. In a more prudish era, *Chloe* was a great drawing card for the pub, although nowadays magazine covers on the newsstand outside are far more provocative. ⊠ *Swanston and Flinders Sts.,* ☎ *03/9650– 3884.*

South Melbourne and Richmond

These two riverside neighborhoods are home to the Southgate complex, King's Domain Gardens, which includes the Royal Botanic Gardens and a number of other interesting sights, the Victoria Arts Centre complex, some great restaurants, and, for lovers of sport, the Melbourne Cricket Ground.

Melbourne Suburbs

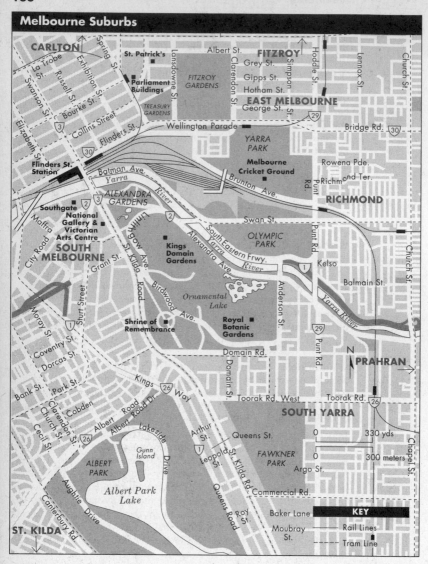

SIGHTS TO SEE

King's Domain Gardens. This expansive stretch of parkland includes Queen Victoria Gardens, Alexandra Gardens, the ☞ **Shrine of Remembrance,** Pioneer Women's Garden, the Sidney Myer Music Bowl, and the ☞ **Royal Botanic Gardens.** The floral clock in Queen Victoria Gardens talks and tells time, providing a brief recorded history of the gardens in and around Melbourne. It is situated opposite the Victorian Arts Centre on St. Kilda Road in one of the Domain's many informal gardens. ⊠ *Between St. Kilda and Domain Rds., Anderson St., and Yarra River.*

OFF THE
BEATEN PATH

MELBOURNE CRICKET GROUND – A visit here to tour its outstanding museums is essential for an understanding of Melbourne's sporting obsession. Tours cover the Australian Gallery of Sport and Olympic Museum; the famous Long Room, usually accessible only through membership of the Melbourne Cricket Club, for which there is a *20-year* waiting list; the MCC Cricket Museum and Library; the Great Southern Grandstand; and pictorial walkways. The memorabilia, especially the cricket-related bits, is some of the best in the world. And although Sydney looks forward to the 2000 Olympics, Melbourne proudly remembers the 1956 Games, for which the MCG was the main stadium. The ground is a pleasant 10-minute walk from the city center or a tram ride to Jolimont Station. ⊠ *Jolimont Terr., Jolimont,* ☎ *03/9654-8922.* ▦ *$8.* ☉ *Tours daily on the hour 10–4.*

❷ National Gallery of Victoria. This massive, moat-encompassed, blue-stone and concrete edifice opened in 1968. Among its highlights are a stained-glass ceiling in the Great Hall (best seen by lying on the floor), a collection of ancient Greek vases, Picasso's *Weeping Woman*, a series of Albrecht Dürer engravings, a number of Old Master paintings, William Blake watercolors, and works from the Australian school. ⊠ *180 St. Kilda Rd.,* ☎ *03/9208-0222.* ▦ *Free.* ☉ *Daily 10–5, several galleries closed Mon.*

OFF THE BEATEN PATH
POLLY WOODSIDE MARITIME MUSEUM – This site includes both the *Polly Woodside,* a commercial square-rigged sailing ship, and a museum devoted to maritime history. Displays cover the voyages of Captain James Cook, the First Fleet, sailors' crafts, and Victorian shipwrecks. ⊠ *Normanby Rd. and Phayer St., South Melbourne,* ☎ *03/9699-9760.* ▦ *$7.* ☉ *Daily 10–4.*

Royal Botanic Gardens. The present design and layout was the brain-child of W. R. Guilfoyle, curator and director of the gardens from 1873 to 1910. Within its 100 acres are 12,000 species of native and imported plants and trees, sweeping lawns, and ornamental lakes populated with ducks and swans that love to be fed. The oldest section of the gardens is Tennyson Lawn, where there are four English elm trees more than 120 years old. A fern gully built around an old billabong (pond) contains American swamp cypress, the tallest tree in the gardens. You can discover the gardens on your own or by joining the free guided walks that leave at 10 AM and 11 AM daily from the Plant Craft Cottage. The main entrance to the gardens is on Birdwood Avenue, near Dallas Brooks Drive. At night in summer there are al fresco performances of classic plays, usually Shakespeare, using the gardens as a set. The effect is quite magical. ⊠ *King's Domain S, Birdwood Ave.,* ☎ *03/9650-9424.* ▦ *Free.* ☉ *Nov.–Mar., daily 7:30 AM–8:30 PM; Apr., daily 7:30–6; May–Oct., daily 7:30–5:30. Friends of the Garden Shop,* ☎ *03/9820-1125.* ☉ *Daily 10–4:30. Tropical Plants Glasshouse,* ☎ *03/9650-9424.* ☉ *Daily 10–4. Plant Craft Cottage,* ☎ *03/9650-3235.* ☉ *Weekdays 10–3.*

OFF THE BEATEN PATH
SHRINE OF REMEMBRANCE – Melbourne's War Memorial, in the King's Domain Gardens, was dedicated in 1934 to commemorate the fallen in World War I, and since has grown to recognize service in World War II, Korea, Malaya, Borneo, Vietnam, and the Gulf War. The temple-style structure is designed so that at 11 AM on Remembrance Day (the 11th day of the 11th month, when in 1918 armistice for World War I was declared) a beam of sunlight passes over the Stone of Remembrance in the Inner Shrine. In the forecourt there is an Eternal Flame. ⊠ *St. Kilda Rd., Melbourne,* ☎ *03/9654-8415.* ▦ *Donations accepted.* ☉ *Daily 10–5.*

❶ Southgate. On the river's edge next to the Victorian Arts Centre, this development has successfully refocused Melbourne's attention on the Yarra and revitalized a sadly neglected part of the city. It is a prime spot for a promenade and for lingering in general. There are designer shops, classy restaurants, bars, and casual eating places and entertainment for whiling away the hours. It's especially appealing weekends, vibrant with throngs of people doing whatever they're doing.

Victorian Arts Centre. This Southbank arts precinct encompasses the Melbourne Concert Hall, Arts Complex, Performing Arts Museum, and National Gallery (☞ *above*). Although it lacks the architectural grandeur of Sydney's Opera House, the Arts Centre is Melbourne's most important cultural landmark and the venue for performances by the Australian Ballet, Australian Opera, and the Melbourne Symphony Orchestra. The **Performing Arts Museum** houses lively, imaginative exhibits that are often particularly appealing to children. One-hour tours of the complex leave at noon and 2:30 on weekdays, 10:30 and noon on Saturday, from the Smorgon Family Plaza, level five of the theater building, which is beneath the spire. A 90-minute backstage tour of the Concert Hall begins at 12:15 and 2:15 Sunday. ⊠ *100 St. Kilda Rd.,* ☎ *03/9281–8000.* ▣ *Performing Arts Museum $5, tour $9, backstage tour (no children) $12.* ⊙ *Weekdays 11–5, weekends noon–5.*

St. Kilda

The cosmopolitan bayside suburb of **St. Kilda,** 6 km (4 mi) south of the city center, is to Melbourne what Bondi is to Sydney. Whatever St. Kilda lacks in surf, it more than makes up for with its culinary offerings. It is at its best on Sunday afternoon, when half of Melbourne comes here to promenade, eat ice cream, and watch the world go by. The St. Kilda experience begins at the pier—a fine place to stroll and watch sailboats.

Sunday, the **Esplanade,** which parallels the beach, is the scene of a lively and entertaining market crowded with arts-and-crafts stalls, which form a backdrop for performances by buskers and street-theater troupes. To the south, the Esplanade curves around the **Luna Park** amusement area. **Acland Street** is St. Kilda's restaurant row—an alphabet soup of restaurants and cuisines, including Chinese, Lebanese, Italian, French, and Jewish. St. Kilda is the center for Melbourne's Jewish population, and the best-known nook to nosh in is **Scheherezade** (⊠ 99 Acland St., ☎ 03/9534–2722), opened in 1958 by Polish émigrés Masha and Avram Zeliznikow. Those with an eye for fashion prefer **Café di Stasio** (⊠ 31 Fitzroy St., ☎ 03/9525–3999), a small Italian café with personality and a gutsy menu (☞ Dining, *below*). Both Acland and **Barkley** streets have interesting and alternative shops.

By night, St. Kilda becomes Melbourne's red-light district, although it pales by comparison with Sydney's Kings Cross. To reach the suburb from the city, take Tram 10, 12, 15, or 16.

OFF THE
BEATEN PATH

LUNA PARK – The main attraction of this faded amusement park, modeled after New York's Coney Island, is the Big Dipper roller coaster. The park also has a Ferris wheel, bumper cars, and a ghost train. ⊠ *Lower Esplanade, St. Kilda,* ☎ *03/9534-0654.* ▣ *Park admission free, major rides $3.* ⊙ *Mon.–Sat. 1–5 and 7–11, Sun. 1–5.*

Fitzroy

Two km (1¼ mi) north of the city center, **Fitzroy** is Melbourne's bohemian quarter. What was once a drab, deprived part of the city is now prized by upwardly mobile white-collar workers looking for affordable housing within easy reach of city jobs. There are no inspiring monuments or grand municipal buildings to be seen here, but if you're looking for an Afghan camel bag, a secondhand bookstore, or a café where you can sit over a plate of tapas and watch Melbourne go by, Fitzroy is the place.

The main drag is **Brunswick Street. Roar Studios** (Number 115) and the **Woman's Gallery** (Number 375) specialize in the work of up-and-coming Australian artists. **On Shore** (Number 267) sells only Australian-made arts and crafts, which make excellent souvenirs. **Port Jackson Press** (Number 397) publishes and sells prints by Australian artists. The **Brunswick Street Bookstore** (Number 305) has a good range of modern Australian literature.

Along with Lygon Street in nearby **Carlton** (☞ *below*), Brunswick is also one of Melbourne's favorite eat streets. The **Black Cat Café** (✉ 252 Brunswick St., ☎ 03/9419–6230) is a delightful throwback to the fifties coffee lounge. Across the street, **Guernica** (✉ 257 Brunswick St., ☎ 03/9416–0969) is a smart, highly regarded modern Australian restaurant. **Café Provincial** (✉ 299 Brunswick St., ☎ 03/9417–2228) is a born-again pub serving pizzas cooked in a wood-fired oven and gargantuan pastas. A little farther up, **Rhumbarella's** (✉ 342 Brunswick St., ☎ 03/9417–5652), is a hot scene, forever dispensing coffee, cocktails, and rhumba juices to the hip and hungry. And **Babka Bakery Café** (✉ 358 Brunswick St., ☎ 03/9416–0091) serves everything from great breads and cheesecake to Russian breakfast blintzes. While you're in the area, don't miss the entrance gates of the **Fitzroy Nursery,** designed by Michael Leunig, Melbourne's favorite cartoonist.

Carlton

Some of inner Melbourne's finest residential streets are found in this suburb, especially in its northern reaches. It is also one of the liveliest parts of the city, with the restaurant strip of Lygon Street as its focus. Lygon Street is the city's Little Italy, with countless Italian restaurants and cafés, most of them, sadly, undistinguished. But the area has great color, particularly at night when the sidewalks are thronged with diners and strollers and a procession of high-revving muscle cars rumbling along the strip.

To see the best of **Carlton's Victorian-era architecture,** venture north of Princes Street, paying particular attention to Drummond Street, with its rows of gracious terrace houses, and Canning Street, which has a mix of workers' cottages and grander properties. The streetscapes, accented by mature trees, have gone largely unaltered since the end of the last century. The whole area repays gentle rambling.

Lygon Street also beckons, a perfect example of Melbourne's multiculturalism—where once you'd have found only Italian restaurants, you now discover Thai, Afghan, Malay, Caribbean, and Greek eateries. Walking north from Queensberry Street you'll find the monolithic **Toto's Pizza House** (✉ 101 Lygon St., ☎ 03/9347–5974), which claims to be Australia's first pizzeria. Whether or not the boast is true, Toto's serves cheap pizza, some 40 years on. For some Carribean island cooking, try the curries of **Jamaica House** (✉ 106 Lygon St., 03/663–5715), a local haunt of many years standing. At **Casa del Gelato** (Number 161) you can enjoy some of the city's best ice cream. For Southeast Asian fare, **Lemongrass Restaurant** (✉ 189 Lygon St., ☎ 03/9347–5204) serves a strain of Thai food that is more sophisticated and understated than the boisterous curries of other Thai restaurants, and **Nyonya Malasian Restaurant** is good for reasonably priced, well-prepared dishes.

Across Grattan Street is a local institution, the **University Café and Universita Bar Restaurant** (✉ 257 Lygon St., ☎ 03/9347–2132). Countless plots and revolutions have been planned at its tables. The **Lygon Food Store** (Number 263) is the place for Italian cheeses and cured meats—just eyeing the windows' piles of *parmigiano* and pendant *prosciutto* guarantees weight gain (but go ahead and pick up a picnic anyway). At **Lo Bello** (Number 275) you can gorge on luscious Italian cakes. Opposite, **Readings** (Number 338) is one of Melbourne's best-loved bookstores, and its window filled with handwritten want ads is fascinating.

The next cross street is **Faraday Street.** Venture down the hill to **Brunetti Cakes** (Number 200) for more calorie-laden delights. On Faraday's other side of Lygon Street is **Thresherman's Bakery** (Number 221), which sells excellent breads and pies. Here, too, you will find the **Carlton Moviehouse** (Number 235). Fondly known as The Bughouse, it is an old-fashioned picture theater showing a range of arthouse films.

Back on Lygon Street, King and Godfree (Number 293) is arguably Melbourne's best wine merchant. It is particularly strong on Australian and Italian wine—venture into the cellar for rare vintages. There is also a good deli selection. **Tiamo** (⌂ 303 Lygon St., ☎ 03/9347–5759) has been a trysting place for generations of Melbourne lovers, who come for the cozy atmosphere, wholesome food, and good coffee. The legendary **Jimmy Watson's Wine Bar** (⌂ 333 Lygon St., ☎ 03/9347–3985) is the spot for a convivial glass or two downstairs, or a more formal meal upstairs. At **Donnini's** (Number 398) you can buy superb homemade pasta if you're self-catering, or visit the family restaurant in neighboring Drummond Street (Number 312).

East Melbourne
Another historic enclave of Victorian houses that dates from the boom following the gold rushes of the 1850s, **East Melbourne** is less than 1 km (½ mi) from the city center. For a concise tour of the neighborhood, whose harmonious streetscapes are a great excuse for a stroll, start at the southeast corner of Fitzroy Gardens and head north on Clarendon to George Street. Turn right and take in the procession of superb terrace houses and mature European trees as you walk down the gentle slope of the street. Two blocks ahead, turn left on Simpson then again on wide, gracious Hotham Street. On either side of the grassy median that divides the roadway, the mix of terrace houses and freestanding mansions includes some of the suburb's finest architecture. Back at Clarendon, turn north. Bishopscourt, the bluestone residence of the Anglican Archbishop of Melbourne, occupies the next block. Wind right again down Gipps Street and make your way to pretty Darling Square. For different scenery on the way back, take Simpson Street south and turn right on Wellington Parade.

Around Melbourne
Como House. A splendid white Victorian mansion overlooking the Yarra, Como is Melbourne's finest example of an early colonial house. The main part of the mansion was built around 1855, and the kitchen wing predates that by 15-odd years. The gardens slope down toward the Yarra River, demonstrating the landscaping finesse of Baron von Mueller, who was also responsible for planning the city's Royal Botanic Gardens. ⌂ *16 Como Ave., South Yarra,* ☎ *03/9827–2500.* ⌂ *$7.* ☉ *Daily 10–5.*

Melbourne Zoological Gardens. Recognized as one of the finest zoos in the world, the Melbourne Zoo has recently undergone some major changes. The grounds have been transformed into gardens, and most of the animal enclosures have been renovated into "open-environment settings." Animals of particular interest are those unique to Australia, such as the koala, kangaroo, wombat, emu, and echidna. There are also a lion park, a reptile house, a butterfly pavilion, and, in a simulated African rain forest, the only group of gorillas in the country. The zoo is 4 km (2½ mi) north of Melbourne city center. ⊠ *Elliot Ave., Parkville,* ☎ *03/9285–9300.* ☜ *$12.60.* ☯ *Daily 9–5.*

Rippon Lea. Begun in the late 1860s, Rippon Lea is a sprawling polychrome brick mansion built in the Romanesque style. By the time of its completion in 1903 the original 15-room house had swollen into a 33-room mansion. The gardens were inspired by romantic Victorian concepts of landscape gardening that were fashionable in England at the time. Notable features include a grotto, a tower that overlooks the lake, a fernery, and humpback bridges. ⊠ *192 Hotham St., Elsternwick,* ☎ *03/9523–6095.* ☜ *$8.* ☯ *Daily 10–5.*

☾ **Scienceworks Museum.** A former sewage-pumping station in suburban Spotswood has been transformed into a much more glamorous place. This hands-on museum entertains while it educates—kids will have a ball. There are permanent and changing exhibits and regular programs of science-related activities. The latest exhibit is Sportsworks, where you can test your speed against an Olympic sprinter and perform other sporting feats. ⊠ *2 Booker St., Spotswood,* ☎ *03/9392–4800.* ☜ *$8.* ☯ *Daily 10–4:30.*

Dining

City Center

AUSTRALIAN

$$ ✕ **Stella.** Long and slim, with a permanent terra-cotta suntan, this city hot spot has a nice low-key glamour that attracts a lively, good-looking crowd. Beyond its looks, Stella has a seductively good wine list, while the food—including pretty-in-pink prawns with white beans, comfort-zone pumpkin tortelli, fiery Thai-style duck curry, and ingenious cherry-and-chocolate pizza—is a crash course in mod-Oz cooking. ⊠ *159 Spring St., Melbourne,* ☎ *03/9639–1555. Reservations essential. AE, DC, MC, V. No lunch weekends.*

BISTRO

$$ ✕ **Bistro 1.** You can't help but be seduced by the nostalgic bistro feel of this place, with its dark, polished floors, softly glowing table lamps, moody wooden venetians, glass-top booths, paper-over-cloth tables, and classy marble bar. The menu is full of classic comebacks, including good old grilled lamb chops, no-frills fish and chips, steak Diane, old fashioned pepper steak, a suitably dark, rich, and gooey chocolate mousse, and a back-to-the-nursery raspberry crumble (crumbles being the backbone of every Australian childhood). ⊠ *126 Little Collins St., Melbourne,* ☎ *03/9654–3343. AE, DC, MC, V.*

CHINESE

$$$ ✕ **Flower Drum.** Nobody takes the principles of Cantonese cooking
★ quite as seriously as the Flower Drum's owner, Gilbert Lau, Melbourne's undisputed Last Emperor of Chinatown. The restrained elegance of the decor and intelligence of the wine list put many French restaurants to shame, and the service is flawless. Simply ask your waiter what's special that day, and you could well wind up with a veritable feast: maybe a crisp-skinned Peking duck served with a second course of minced duck wrapped in lettuce, delicate pea shoot dumplings, a perfectly steamed Murray cod, and huge Pacific oysters daubed with black bean sauce. ⊠ *17 Market La., Melbourne,* ☎ *03/9662–3655. Reservations essential. AE, DC, MC, V. No lunch Sun.*

$ ✕ **Shark Fin House.** In the middle of Melbourne's colorful Chinatown, this bustling, three-story restaurant has a style that's pure Hong Kong—expect gleaming elevators, a bank of TV monitors, and tanks full of live fish, crabs, and lobsters. At lunchtime the place clangs with

Melbourne City Center Dining and Lodging

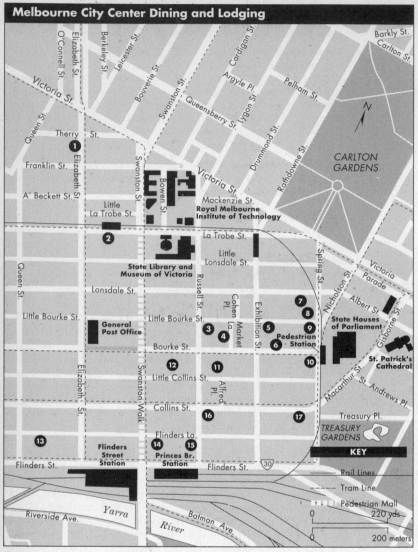

Dining

Bistro 1, **11**

Flower Drum, **4**

Il Bacaro, **12**

Madam Fang, **6**

Marchetti's Latin, **7**

Paul Bocuse
Restaurant, **2**

Ristorante
Roberto, **15**

Shark Fin House, **3**

Stella, **9**

Lodging

The Adelphi, **14**

Grand Hyatt, **16**

Hotel Sofitel
Melbourne, **17**

Oakford Gordon
Place, **8**

Rydges
Melbourne, **5**

Sebel of
Melbourne, **13**

Windsor Hotel, **10**

Hotel Y, **1**

dim sum trolleys. At night all eyes turn hungrily toward those tanks, when they're not gazing in disbelief at platters overflowing with suckling pig, roast meats, or clams and steamed abalone. ✉ *131 Little Bourke St., Melbourne,* ☎ *03/9663–1555. AE, DC, MC, V.*

FRENCH

$$$$ ✕ **Paul Bocuse Restaurant.** This temple of French cuisine may be in
★ the middle of the Japanese-owned Daimaru department store, but don't let the escalator ride put you off. Inside, you'll find all the fuss and finery of a three-star Parisian restaurant. As part of the global empire of one of France's stellar chefs, the restaurant serves many of Monsieur Bocuse's famous dishes, yet it is chef Philippe Mouchel's own subtle and assured creations that truly impress. Try his perfect braised squab, shimmering oyster terrine, sublime marinated salmon garnished with grilled salmon skin, and his famous platter of "piggy bits." ✉ *Daimaru department store, 211 La Trobe St., Level 4, Melbourne,* ☎ *03/9660–6600. Reservations essential. AE, DC, MC, V. Closed Sun. and Mon. No lunch Sat.*

ITALIAN

$$$ ✕ **Marchetti's Latin.** The Latin has been a clubby and comfortable Melbourne institution since it first opened its doors in 1919, but since Bill Marchetti took the restaurant over in 1984, it has achieved near cult status. Singer Robert Palmer called the Latin the best Italian restaurant he had ever eaten in, and Frank Sinatra, Elton John, and Bruce Springsteen have all given it thumbs-up. Even mere mortals love the tortellini filled with Queensland mud crab, sensational pumpkin-filled ravioli, and scaloppini Latino. ✉ *55 Lonsdale St., Melbourne,* ☎ *03/9662–1985. Reservations essential. AE, DC, MC, V. Closed Sun. No lunch Sat.*

$$ ✕ **Il Bacaro.** Based on the *bacari*, wine bars, of Venice, Il Bacaro promises an honest, good-value glass of wine and something worthwhile to eat. The place drips with style and glows with warm wooden tones, soft marble, and filtered sunlight. Sip espresso, nibble *panini* sandwiches, or choose from around 50 wines by the glass to enjoy with classy Italian cooking—*tagliolini* pasta with scampi, char-grilled veal rib eye, and a sensational *crema fritta* dessert. ✉ *168–170 Little Collins St., Melbourne,* ☎ *03/9654–6778. AE, DC, MC, V. Closed Sun. No dinner Mon.*

$$ ✕ **Ristorante Roberto.** Under the eagle eye of young-restaurateur-in-a-hurry, Roberto Scheriani, this buzzy, bubbly basement is full of life and light and that sparkling sense of well-being that comes from being in the right place at the right time. With its over-the-top booths and ankle-level view of the world passing by, the feel is very New York. The food, however, is unequivocally Italian, from paper thin carpaccio to house-made pasta. ✉ *31 Russell St., Melbourne,* ☎ *03/9650–3399. Reservations essential. AE, DC, MC, V. No lunch weekends.*

MODERN ASIAN

$$ ✕ **Madam Fang.** This mid-city East-meets-West culinary adventureland is one big conversation starter. The exotic decor comprises paintings and structural pieces from co-owner John Dunham's personal collection of 19th-century Indian art and artifacts. Then there are such cutely named dishes as Triple Tease, a seafood soup spiked with chilli and ginger; Green With Envy Salad; and the Miyake Platter, a fashionable, fusion-style antipasto. If you really want to get your table talking, order Silk Route Poultry—a jet-black chicken double boiled in soy stock. ✉ *27–29 Crossley St., Melbourne,* ☎ *03/9663–3199. Reservations essential. AE, DC, MC, V. Closed Sun. No lunch Sat.*

Melbourne Suburbs
AUSTRALIAN

$$$ ✕ **Jimmy Watson's.** As a wine bar and bistro, Jimmy Watson's has long been a home-away-from-home to legions of Melbourne bohemians and academics. In recent years, however, the upstairs private rooms have been converted into a serene white dining area that features the classy, classic, French-inspired cooking of Steve Szabo. All of his dishes, including caramelized pig's trotter with sweetbreads and fall-about confit of duck with fried saganaki cheese, are matched to tasting glasses of historic Australian wines from the Watsons' own cellars. ✉ *333 Lygon St., Carlton,* ☎ *03/9347–3985. AE, DC, MC, V. Closed Sun. and Mon. No lunch.*

$$ ✕ **Guernica.** With its chic tiny, frosted table lamps; retro wooden blinds; snappy, finely honed floor staff; and the kind of wine list you want to go to bed with, this is the very picture of a mod-Oz restaurant. Chef Teague Ezard has a brave, bold, and inventive style that slashes and burns its way through Asian and Mediterranean techniques. His salad of fried feta with rocket (arugula) and pomegranate molasses is a clever, contemporary take on the old deep-fried camembert. Duck leg risotto with tiny Puy lentils is a down home treat, and coconut-fried garfish with Vietnamese noodles keeps the taste buds guessing. ✉ *257 Brunswick St., Fitzroy,* ☎ *03/9416–0969. AE, DC, MC, V.*

$$ ✕ **Madame Joe Joe.** It's a dubious name in a street that used to be one of Melbourne's notorious red-light districts. But these days you'll find a good meal *and* a good time in this boppy, buzzy place, where energy levels on the dining floor are matched by the inventiveness of the kitchen. Mediterranean flavors are shaken, rattled, and rolled into such look-at-me creations as hazelnut-battered zucchini flowers, spaghettini with fried olives, barbecued Caesar salad, and pumpkin and rosewater risotto with roasted pears. ✉ *9 Fitzroy St., St. Kilda,* ☎ *03/ 9534–0000. Reservations essential. AE, DC, MC, V.D/r*

$$ ✕ **O'Connell's.** Combine classic French training with a Lebanese background and you've got some of the most intriguing food in Melbourne, served in the no-frills dining room of this reborn suburban pub. Fortunately the wine list is comprehensive enough to take on whatever chef Greg Malouf serves up, including lamb pot roast with Moroccan aromatics, salmon carpaccio, and sardine and roasted eggplant terrine. First-timers are steered toward the marvelous mezza platter of *taramasalata* (a Greek fish-roe dip), feta fritters, and lamb kebab. ✉ *Montague and Coventry Sts., South Melbourne,* ☎ *03/9699–9600. Reservations essential. AE, DC, MC, V. Closed Sun. No lunch Sat.*

BISTRO

$$ ✕ **France-Soir.** Suddenly, you're not just south of the Yarra River any-more—-you're on the Left Bank of the Seine, lost in a world of paper tablecloths, long black aprons, Kronenbourg beer, and a cool glass of muscadet. Patrons sit elbow to elbow, smelling each other's food and listening to each other's talk. Onion soup here is the genuine article, oysters are shucked strictly to order, *pommes frites* (french fries) are *fantastique,* and *andouillette* raises the humble sausage to dizzy heights. Do leave room for the work-of-art *tarte Tatin.* ✉ *11 Toorak Rd., South Yarra,* ☎ *03/9866–8569. AE, MC, V.*

CAFÉS

$ ✕ **Continental Café.** This is what café life in Melbourne is all about. In the morning, nightclubbers draped artistically over their Peroni beers rub shoulders with a few yuppies, who dig into muesli and croissants. By day, local rock stars and radio DJs—safe behind their Ray-Ban Phantoms—show up to lunch on salad, focaccia sandwiches, and mineral water. Then at night, the cooler-than-cool drift in for pasta and

Melbourne Suburbs Dining and Lodging

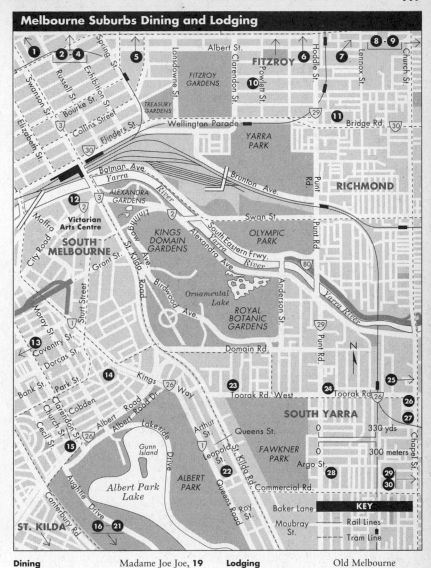

Dining

Akita, **1**
Café Di Stasio, **18**
Caffe e Cucina, **27**
Chinta Blues, **17**
Continenal Café, **29**
Est Est Est, **15**
France-Soir, **24**
Guernica, **6**
Jacques Reymond, **30**
Lo Japon, **25**
Jimmy Watson's, **5**

Madame Joe Joe, **19**
Melbourne Wine Room, **16**
Milan, **8**
O'Connell's, **13**
The Pavilion, **20**
Pho Dzung, **7**
Toofey's, **2**
Vlado's, **11**
Walter's Wine Bar, **12**

Lodging

City Park Motel, **14**
Hotel Como, **26**
Lygon Lodge Carlton, **3**
Magnolia Court Boutique Hotel, **10**
Oakford Apartments, **28**
Oakford Fairways, **22**

Old Melbourne Hotel, **5**
Pathfinder Motel, **9**
Robinson's by the Sea, **21**
The Tilba, **23**

red wine before disappearing upstairs to catch the live music. If you're not too distracted by the free-floating attitude, remember to order coffee, which many say is the best in town. ☒ *132A Greville St., Prahran,* ☎ *03/9510–2788. Reservations not accepted. AE, MC, V.*

★ ✕ **Est Est Est.** Tables are double-clothed, wine glasses are large and serious, and the food is as balanced as a tightrope walker. Chefs Donovan Cooke and Philipa Sibley-Cooke have cooked their way through the three stars of France and the rising stars of Britain, and their skills show in an appetizer of kipfer potatoes layered with lobster, freshly oven-dried tomato, and black truffle. Also memorable are scallops and roasted calamari sauced with squid ink, and a glossy chocolate pyramid filled with Valrhona chocolate. ☒ *440 Clarendon St., South Melbourne,* ☎ *03/9682–5688. Reservations essential. AE, DC, MC, V. Closed Sun. No lunch.*

FRENCH

$$$$ ✕ **Jacques Reymond.** French discipline and an Asian palette delightfully intertwine in this glamorous Victorian mansion with open fireplaces, soft candlelight, and a secret garden. The wine list is the stuff an oenophile dreams of, and service is intelligent, intuitive, and informed. The Burgundian chef uses the finest Australian produce to create such classics as guinea fowl marinated in yogurt, kangaroo with beetroot, and barramundi fillet with ginger and lime cream. ☒ *78 Williams Rd., Windsor,* ☎ *03/9525–2178. Reservations essential. AE, DC, MC, V. Closed Sun. and Mon. No lunch Sat.*

INDIAN

$ ✕ **Milan.** In too many of Melbourne's Indian restaurants dishes have an uncanny knack of tasting the same no matter what you order. Chefs Satya Prakash and Laddan Khan, however, both have a distinctive, delicate touch that separates their cooking from the pack. Milan is an Indian word for "meeting place," and in recent years more and more Indian-food-loving locals have been meeting over Satya's plump spinach-and-onion *pakoras* (fritters), tandoori lamb shanks, and tandoori barramundi. ☒ *44 Cotham Rd., Kew,* ☎ *03/9853–5379. AE, DC, MC, V. BYOB. Closed Mon.*

ITALIAN

$$ ✕ **Café Di Stasio** treads that very fine line between decadence and man-
★ nered elegance. A sleek marble bar and modishly ravaged walls contribute to the sense that you've stepped into a scene from *La Dolce Vita.* Happily, Café Di Stasio is as much a monument to chef Valerio Nucci's heavenly cooking as to Italian style. Crisply roasted duck is now a local legend, char-grilled baby squid is a sheer delight, and Nucci's pasta is always al dente. If *orecchiette* pasta with turnip tops is on the menu, do yourself a favor and order it. ☒ *31 Fitzroy St., St. Kilda,* ☎ *03/9525–3999. Reservations essential. AE, DC, MC, V.*

$$ ✕ **Caffe e Cucina.** Critics have so raved about this fashionable hole-
★ in-the-wall that soon it will be hard to get into Chapel Street, let alone the café. So if you're lucky enough to score a table, make the most of it: Order melt-in-the-mouth gnocchi, peppery arugula salad, a wonderful *panna cotta* (a pale, quivering breath of creamy custard, lighter than crème brûlée), and a glass of Victorian pinot noir. Coffee here is also great, and *tiramisù* is even better looking than the crowd. ☒ *581 Chapel St., South Yarra,* ☎ *03/9827–4139. Reservations essential upstairs, not accepted downstairs. AE, DC, MC, V.*

$$ ✕ **Melbourne Wine Room.** Wine is the driving force behind this quirky, reborn pub–dining room with 30 wines available by the glass, changing monthly. But this isn't just a restaurant with a great wine list. It's a wine room with a great food list. Chef Karen Martini's Italianate fare

is at once confident and powerfully single minded. Her pot-roasted pigeon cooked with sage, pancetta, and juniper berries is rich and warm and deep flavored, and her fresh seafood broth is a fish market in a bowl. ⊠ *25 Fitzroy St., St. Kilda,* ☎ *03/9525–5599. Reservations essential. AE, MC, V. No lunch.*

JAPANESE

$$ ✕ **Akita.** Melbourne has plenty of Japanese restaurants with beauti-
★ ful decor, dazzling tatami rooms, and a glitzy clientele. This isn't one of them. Here the fancy footwork is confined to the menu. The handwritten specials list could serve as a seasonal calendar. In summer it's awash with clams in butter and sake or vinegared crabs, while winter brings braised root vegetables and savory egg custards. There's no better Japanese restaurant in town. ⊠ *Courtney and Blackwood Sts., North Melbourne,* ☎ *03/9326–5766. AE, DC, MC, V. Closed Sun.*

JAPANESE/FRENCH

$$$ ✕ **Le Japon.** Kazu Nomura has worked in several of Melbourne's most influential fine restaurants, including the ever-so-French Paul Bocuse. Although his food is based on sound, classic Japanese technique, it now wears a distinctive French accent that harks back to the precision of nouvelle cuisine. Hence the kaiseki-inspired hors d'oueves, the sashimi, the cold noodles, and the char-grilled beef with soybean paste all take on a nearly universal sense of sophistication. ⊠ *40 Ross St., Toorak,* ☎ *03/9826–4666. Reservations essential. AE, DC, MC, V. Closed Sun. No lunch.*

MALAYSIAN

$ ✕ **Chinta Blues.** This is a curious, beckoning sort of place that man-
★ ages to combine both the charms of a Malaysian-style coffeehouse with the vibe and cool of a modern street-smart café, with barely a seam showing. Tables are simple plywood, seating is by way of communal benches, and much of the walls are covered in dark wooden shelves stocked with Asian groceries. Curry laksa—a bathtub of noodles, chicken, and prawns in a murky, spicy broth—is heaven in a bowl, and spinach blachan and spicy wok-fried noodles will soothe most hotheads. ⊠ *5 Acland St., St. Kilda,* ☎ *03/9534–9233. AE, MC, V.*

SEAFOOD

$$$ ✕ **The Pavilion.** This one-time bathing pavilion is now filled with a constant hubbub at lunch and dinnertime. Whether you're inside in the dining room, or outside on the terrace, the bay views are to die for, and the endless parade of bladers, boarders, bikers, and beach walkers is better than any floor show. Not surprisingly, chef Robert Castellani's menu teems with seafood, including char-grilled swordfish fillet, deep-fried "woven" prawns, and live Tasmanian lobster steamed or char-grilled. ⊠ *40 Jacka Blvd., St. Kilda,* ☎ *03/9534–8221. Reservations essential. AE, DC, MC, V.*

$$$ ✕ **Toofey's.** Michael Bacash's Middle Eastern background and Italian training combine in this refreshing Mediterranean approach to Australian seafood. Toofey's has the good looks of a trendy bistro and the good sense to serve only what's best at fish markets that day. It's here that you'll find Melbourne's definitive spaghetti marinara, as well as wonderful Provençale-style mussels, perfectly grilled yellowfin tuna, and an overflowing seafood risotto. ⊠ *162 Elgin St., Carlton,* ☎ *03/ 9347–9838. AE, DC, MC, V. Closed Mon. No lunch weekends.*

STEAK HOUSE

$$$ ✕ **Vlado's.** Vlado Gregurek snaps on a fresh pair of pristine white gloves every time he picks up a new cut of beef and inspects it as tenderly as if it were a newborn baby. If you love a good steak, you'll love Vlado's.

His restaurant is amazingly single-minded: Pictures of grazing cattle hang on the walls above businesspeople grazing on set menus of liver, sausage, and perfectly grilled meat. Salads may be so-so, mustards and horseradish uninspired, and strawberry pancake desserts undistinguished—just remember that you have come for the steak of your life. ⊠ *61 Bridge Rd., Richmond,* ☎ *03/9428–5833. Reservations essential. AE, DC, MC, V. Closed Sun. No lunch Sat.*

VIETNAMESE

$ ✕ **Pho Dzung.** Victoria Street, the heart of the local Vietnamese community, has become one of Melbourne's most exciting and exhilarating areas, alive with color, chatter, good food, and aromas aplenty. The Pho Dzung is little more than a soup kitchen—but oh what soup. *Pho* is to soup what cassoulet is to stew, overflowing with bits of chicken or beef and gorgeously slippery rice noodles and accompanied by a miniature garden of fresh mint, basil, and bean shoots to plunge in the broth. No wine is allowed, but you do get a free thermos of tea. ⊠ *196 Victoria St., Richmond,* ☎ *03/9427–0292. No credit cards.*

WINE BAR

$$ ✕ **Walter's Wine Bar.** Right smack in the middle of Melbourne's lively Southgate complex, this place is one nonstop party. Nibble on a classy platter of local cheeses, sip a lively Mornington pinot or a well-raised Yarra Valley chardonnay, and dine on such good, no-frills dishes as duck confit, seafood sausages, or an up-market burger. Whether you sit outside on the balcony overlooking the river, or inside with the milling throng, it is an essential Melbourne experience. ⊠ *Southgate Complex, Level 3, South Melbourne,* ☎ *03/9690–9211. Reservations essential. AE, DC, MC, V.*

Lodging

City Center

$$$$ ☷ **Grand Hyatt.** Melbourne's number one hotel for glitz, glamour, and
★   top-notch service is at the Paris End of Collins Street. Soft tones infuse the decor throughout, and the luxurious lobby is hung with quantities of roseate marble and oak paneling. A separate atrium includes two floors of elegant shops and a vast international food court that supplements the hotel's dining rooms. Top floors have attractive views, and all rooms are graced with marble bathrooms, king-size beds, and small sitting areas. Four Regency Club floors have their own check-in facility and lounge and provide complimentary Continental breakfasts and refreshments throughout the day. ⊠ *123 Collins St., Melbourne,* ☎ *03/9657–1234,* ℻ *03/9650–3491. 559 rooms with bath. 2 restaurants, 2 bars, food court, pool, tennis court, health club, nightclub, business center. AE, DC, MC, V.*

$$$$ ☷ **Hotel Sofitel Melbourne.** The glossy hotel half of this twin-towered
★   Collins Place complex was designed by architect I. M. Pei, and it combines glamour and excellent facilities with a prime location. Guest rooms, which begin on the 35th floor of the 50-story building, are built around a mirrored central atrium, and views are exceptional. A $10 million refurbishment program completed in 1995 means both the hotel's rooms and its views are the best in town. ⊠ *25 Collins St., Melbourne,* ☎ *03/9653–0000 or 008/33–1123,* ℻ *03/9650–4261. 363 rooms with bath. Restaurants, room service, health club, business center. AE, DC, MC, V.*

$$$$ ☷ **Sebel of Melbourne.** Sebel is a name most often associated with Sydney, but this intimate boutique hotel is a welcome fixture on the Melbourne scene. With only 59 one- and two-bedroom suites, it is the smallest of the city's luxury hotels. Rooms are tastefully decorated in apricot, burgundy, lemon, and pale green and are beautifully furnished. All have kitchenettes with a microwave oven and refrigerator. All guests can use the small private courtyard, inspired by the Renaissance gardens of Italy. Service standards are very high. ✉ *321 Flinders La., Melbourne,* ☎ *03/9629–4088,* FAX *03/9629–4066. 59 rooms with bath. Restaurant, bar, health club. AE, DC, MC, V.*

$$$$ 🛏 **Windsor Hotel.** The aristocrat of Melbourne hotels, the century-old
★ Windsor combines the character and patrician dimensions of the Victorian era with the modern blessings of first-rate food and comfortable beds. Guest rooms are plushly decorated with Laura Ashley–style wall coverings and rosewood furnishings; the marble bathrooms are, however, modest in size compared with those in modern hotel rooms in the same price bracket. Standard rooms are rather small, but the two-room executive suites provide good value, and the Victorian suites are vast and opulent. The hotel occupies a commanding position opposite the Victorian Parliament House and is close to theaters, parks, and some of Melbourne's finest shops. ✉ *103 Spring St., Melbourne,* ☎ *03/9653–0653,* FAX *03/9650–3233. 156 rooms with bath, 34 suites. 2 restaurants, 2 bars, business center. AE, DC, MC, V.*

$$$ 🛏 **The Adelphi.** This design-driven boutique hotel breaks new ground with its uncompromising contemporary style. Functionalist maple-and-matte–finish metal surfaces and clean, cool aesthetics might be a little brittle for some tastes, but it's all a welcome change from the run-of-the-mill. And at a one-minute walk from City Square, it's about as central as you can get. The Adelphi's pièce de résistance is a 25-m lap pool on the top floor, which has a glass bottom that juts out from the edge of the building, so that bathers literally swim into space. The view from the bar on the same floor, framed by the Gothic Revival spires of St. Paul's, is heavenly. The best rooms are those at the front, whose numbers end in "01." ✉ *187 Flinders La., Melbourne,* ☎ *03/9650–7555,* FAX *03/9650–2710. 34 rooms, 8 with bath, 26 with shower. Restaurant, 2 bars, pool. AE, DC, MC, V.*

$$$ 🛏 **Oakford Gordon Place.** Located in a historic (1883) building, this
★ is one of the most interesting and comfortable apartment hotels in the city. It's just a stone's throw from the Parliament Building and is surrounded by excellent restaurants and theaters. It is also a good value, considering its city-center setting. Apartments are modern and comfortable, and they contain washing machines, dryers, and dishwashers. Breakfast is served on a covered terrace. The studio and one- and two-bedroom apartments face a vine-covered courtyard with a 60-ft saltwater pool and a century-old palm tree. ✉ *24 Little Bourke St., Melbourne,* ☎ *03/9663–2888,* FAX *03/9639–1537. 59 apartments with bath. Restaurant, pool, sauna, spa. AE, DC, MC, V.*

$$$ 🛏 **Rydges Melbourne.** With an excellent location between the theater district and Chinatown, the Rydges Melbourne (formerly the Bryson) is a popular choice for vacationers as well as cost-conscious corporate travelers. This high-rise hotel was built in the 1970s, and its cozy lobby is decorated with traditional wood paneling, parquet floors, and a neutral color scheme. Guest rooms, also in neutral tones, are large and stylishly furnished and equipped with hair dryers, irons and ironing boards, and coffee makers. ✉ *186 Exhibition St., Melbourne,* ☎ *03/9662–0511,* FAX *03/9663–8988. 363 rooms with bath, 67 suites. Restaurant, 2 bars, pool, sauna, nightclub. AE, DC, MC, V.*

$ 🛏 **Hotel Y.** Built in 1975 for budget travelers, this motel provides clean, comfortable, no-frills accommodations. A recent upgrade ensures excellent value for money. It is within walking distance of the city center and is very near the Victoria Market. Rooms are simply furnished, each with its own bathroom. There is a central television lounge in the building, along with a gym and pool. ✉ *489 Elizabeth St., Melbourne,*

☎ *03/9329–5188,* FAX *03/9328–2931. 56 rooms with shower. Cafeteria, sauna, health club. No credit cards.*

Melbourne Suburbs

$$$$ ⊞ **Hotel Como.** Located close to the restaurants and shops of South Yarra,
★   one of Melbourne's most prestigious suburbs, this luxury hotel attracts
a large corporate clientele. The lobby is dominated by a tapestry depicting Como's history, and gray marble and chrome are prominent
throughout the smart Art Deco interior. The hotel is built in a horseshoe shape around a park, and some suites on the third and sixth floors
have access to private Japanese gardens. Rooms are appointed with king-size beds, bathrobes, alarm clocks, and Jacuzzis. Some suites have fully
equipped kitchenettes. The Como enjoys a reputation for outstanding
service. Guests receive complimentary evening drinks and valet parking. ⊠ *630 Chapel St., South Yarra,* ☎ *03/9824–0400,* FAX *03/9824–
1263. 107 suites. Indoor pool, saunas, health club. AE, DC, MC, V.*

$$$ ⊞ **Old Melbourne Hotel.** A few minutes north of the central business
district by car or tram, this hotel mimics New Orleans architecture,
with wrought-iron balconies and a cobblestone central courtyard.
There is a small reception area instead of a traditional lobby, and the
comfortable, spacious Victorian-style guest rooms are decorated with
warm colors and brass beds. ⊠ *5–17 Flemington Rd., Carlton,* ☎ *03/
9329–9344 or 008/37–3005,* FAX *03/9328–4870. 225 rooms with
bath. Restaurant, pool. AE, DC, MC, V.*

$$–$$$ ⊞ **The Tilba.** Built as a grand residence at the turn of the century, The
Tilba first became a hotel in 1920, and staying here feels like a sojourn
in a luxurious private house. During World War II it was occupied by
Ladies for the Armed Services and later fell on hard times until it was
renovated in the mid-1980s. Now you'll find a small hotel with genuine charm—something of a darling with glossy travel magazines—
filled with antiques and eclectic pieces of furniture. In one room, for
example, there is a bedstead that once did service as a gate on a
Queensland cattle ranch. The hotel overlooks Fawkner Park and is a
short stroll from the shops and restaurants of Toorak Road. ⊠ *30 Toorak
Rd. W, South Yarra,* ☎ *03/9867–8844,* FAX *03/9867–6567. 17 rooms
with bath or shower. AE, DC, MC, V.*

$$ ⊞ **City Park Motel.** Close to the parks on the south side of the city, this
ultramodern four-story motel is ideal for travelers on limited budgets.
Rooms have coffee makers and small refrigerators, and those in the
front of the redbrick building have balconies. The executive–honeymoon suite has a spa bath and sauna. There are relatively few amenities, but the city is about 1½ km (1 mi) away, and frequent tram service
is available on St. Kilda Road, a two-minute walk from the hotel. ⊠
308 Kings Way, South Melbourne, ☎ *03/9699–9811,* FAX *03/9699–
9224. 40 rooms with bath, 6 suites. Restaurant, bar, sauna, spa. AE,
DC, MC, V.*

$$ ⊞ **Oakford Apartments.** If you prefer private apartments to hotel
rooms, consider staying at these all-suite town houses at various locations in the elegant suburb of South Yarra. The studios and two- or
three-bedroom apartments are bright and comfortable, and all have
washing machines, dryers, dishwashers, and Jacuzzis. ⊠ *23 Argo St.;
631 Punt Rd.; 19 Kensington Rd.; 26 Davis Ave., South Yarra;* ☎ *03/
9820–8544 for reservations;* FAX *03/9820–8517. 20 apartments per property. Pool, tennis court. AE, DC, MC, V.*

$$ ⊞ **Oakford Fairways.** Opposite the Albert Park Lake and golf course
and just 2 km (1 mi) south of the central business district, this is another favorite with those who prefer lodging in apartments. The 1930s-style property consists of luxurious one- and two-bedroom apartments
surrounded by private lawns and manicured flower beds. Avoid the

east wing, because it faces heavily trafficked Queens Road. The St. Kilda Road tram provides easy access to the city. ⊠ *32 Queens Rd., Albert Park,* ☎ *03/9820–8544,* FAX *03/9820–8517. 48 apartments. Pool, tennis court, business center. AE, DC, MC, V.*

$$ ⊞ **Robinson's by the Sea.** This lovely terrace house overlooks Port Phillip
★ Bay, a five-minute stroll from the nightlife of Fitzroy Street, St. Kilda. The sitting room is warm and inviting and furnished with excellent antiques and objets d'art. The prize front bedroom has a large balcony, a net-shrouded king-size bed, and its own sitting area. Other rooms are smaller but quieter. This, one of Melbourne's best bed-and-breakfasts, is run by Wendy Robinson, a virtual one-woman B&B industry (she also writes guides to inns and B&Bs around the country and conducts hospitality training courses). Mrs. Robinson's famed cooked breakfasts are included in the tariff. ⊠ *335 Beaconsfield Parade, St. Kilda West,* ☎ *03/9534–2683,* FAX *03/9534–2683. 5 rooms share 3 baths. AE, DC, MC, V.*

$ ⊞ **Lygon Lodge Carlton.** In the heart of Melbourne's Little Italy and just a short tram ride from the city center, this motel is close to some of the city's best ethnic restaurants—the perfect place for the budget-conscious traveler who appreciates a colorful, lively neighborhood. Some deluxe rooms have kitchenettes, at only $11 more than standard rooms. ⊠ *220 Lygon St., Carlton,* ☎ *03/9663–6633,* FAX *03/9663–7297. 66 rooms with bath. Restaurant. AE, DC, MC, V.*

$ ⊞ **Magnolia Court Boutique Hotel.** Set in the prestigious historic suburb of East Melbourne, this small, friendly hotel profits from the area's serenity and accessibility. Rooms and furnishings are simple and spotless. Standard rooms are modest in size, but the honeymoon suite and the cottage offer more space and comfort at a moderately higher cost. A family room with a kitchen and room for six is also available. The hotel is separated from the city center by Fitzroy Gardens and is about a 12-minute walk from Spring Street. ⊠ *101 Powlett St., East Melbourne,* ☎ *03/9419–4222,* FAX *03/9416–0841. 25 rooms with bath. Café, spa. AE, DC, MC, V.*

$ ⊞ **Pathfinder Motel.** Built in the early 1960s in quiet, residential Kew, this relaxed, comfortable motel is on a direct tram line to the city, 7 km (4 mi) away. The conservative reception area and lobby, furnished with antiques, face a courtyard with a small waterfall and fish pond. Guest rooms are done in cream-color brick, with polished wood furniture and floral fabrics. ⊠ *Burke and Cotham Rds., Kew,* ☎ *03/9817–4551,* FAX *03/9817–5680. 23 rooms with bath, 1 apartment. Restaurant, room service, pool. AE, DC, MC, V.*

Nightlife and the Arts

The Arts

Melbourne Events, available from all tourism outlets, is a comprehensive monthly guide to what's happening in town. For a complete listing of performing arts events, galleries, and film, consult the EG supplement in the Friday edition of the *Melbourne Age.*

DANCE

In the 2,000-seat State Theatre at the Arts Centre, the **Australian Ballet** stages five programs annually and frequently presents visiting celebrity dancers from around the world. For information, telephone BASS (☎ 03/11–566; credit-card reservations, 03/11–500).

MUSIC

Big-name, big-drawing contemporary artists usually perform at **Melbourne Park** (⊠ Batman Ave., ☎ 03/9286–1244). The **Melbourne Sports and Entertainment Centre** (⊠ Swan St., Melbourne, ☎ 03/9429–

6288) hosts major Australian and international artists. The **Melbourne Concert Hall** (⊠ Arts Centre, 100 St. Kilda Rd., ☎ 03/9617–8211) stages major concerts in a classy atmosphere.

Open-air summertime (Dec.–Mar.) concerts can be seen at the **Sidney Myer Music Bowl** (⊠ Kings Domain near Swan St. bridge, Melbourne). Call **BASS** (☎ 03/911–566 or 03/911–500) for ticket information.

Fantastic Entertainment in Public Places (☎ 03/9663–8395) runs a varied entertainment program indoors May through September and outdoors from October through April.

The **Melbourne Symphony Orchestra** performs virtually year-round in the 2,600-seat Melbourne Concert Hall in the Arts Centre (⊠ 100 St. Kilda Rd., ☎ 03/9684–8198).

OPERA

The **Australian Opera** has regular seasons, often with performances by world-renowned stars. The length and time of seasons vary (best to call when you arrive), but all performances take place in Melbourne Concert Hall (⊠ 100 St. Kilda Rd., ☎ 03/9684–8198). Direct further inquiries to BASS (☎ 03/11–566 or 03/11–500).

THEATER

The **Half-Tix** ticket booth in the Bourke Street Mall sells tickets to a wide range of theater attractions at half price on the day of the performance. ☎ 03/9650–9420. ⊘ *Mon. 10–2, Tues.–Thurs. 11–6, Fri. 11–6:30, Sat. 10–2.*

The **Melbourne Theatre Company** (MTC, ☎ 03/9654–4000), Melbourne's first and most successful theater company, has two seasons yearly, during which classical, international, and Australian works are performed at the Russell Street Theatre (⊠ 19 Russell St.) and the Playhouse, in the Theatres Building of the Arts Centre.

The city's second-largest company, the **Playbox at the CUB Malthouse Company** (⊠ 113 Sturt St., South Melbourne, ☎ 03/9685–5111) stages about 10 primary new or contemporary productions a year. The theater, the CUB Malthouse, is a flexible space designed for a range of drama, dance, and circus companies.

The equivalent of Off Broadway in the United States, the **Universal Theatre** (⊠ UT, 13 Victoria St., Fitzroy, ☎ 03/9419–3777) is home to daring, avant-garde productions. The UT is an atmospheric, moody, oddly shaped theater that seats 300 on three sides of its stage. There is a smaller theater on the floor above.

The **Princess Theatre** (⊠ 163 Spring St., ☎ 03/9662–2911) is the home of Broadway-style blockbusters. The newly reopened **Regent Theatre** (⊠ 191 Collins St., ☎ 03/9299–9500) also presents mainstream popular productions. **Her Majesty's Theatre** (⊠ 219 Exhibition St., ☎ 03/9663–3211) sees a range of musicals. Intimate revues and plays are staged at the **Comedy Theatre** (⊠ 240 Exhibition St., ☎ 03/9662–2222).

La Mama (⊠ 205 Faraday St., Carlton, ☎ 03/9347–6142) puts on innovative, intimate, and contemporary productions in a bohemian setting. **Theatreworks** (⊠ 14 Acland St., St Kilda, ☎ 03/9534–4879) concentrates on contemporary Australian plays.

Nightlife

BARS

The 35th-floor cocktail bar at the **Hotel Sofitel** (⊠ 25 Collins St., ☎ 03/9653–0000) has spectacular views. The **Hyatt on Collins** (⊠ 123 Collins St., ☎ 03/9657–1234) is a sophisticated place. Old World charm resides at the **Windsor Hotel** (⊠ 103 Spring St., ☎ 03/9653–0653). The **Hilton on the Park** (⊠ 192 Wellington Parade, ☎ 03/9419–3311) is perfect for drinks before or after the football or cricket game at the Melbourne Cricket Ground. **Sheraton Towers** (⊠ 1 Brown St., South Melbourne, ☎ 03/9696–3100) is a good place for a drink at Southgate. **Rockman's Regency** (⊠ Exhibition and Lonsdale Sts., ☎ 03/9662–3900) has an excellent location close to Chinatown.

Live music is often played at the following spots, and bars not located in major hotels tend to be more casual. **Florentino Cellar Bar** (⊠ 80 Bourke St., ☎ 03/9662–1811) is sophisticated. **The George Hotel** (⊠ Fitzroy and Grey Sts., St. Kilda, ☎ 03/9525–5599) is a superbly renovated 19th-century building. **Cha Cha's** (⊠ 20 Chapel St., Windsor, ☎ 03/9525–1077) catches the pre-dinner crowd in busy Chapel Street. **Dog's Bar** (⊠ 54 Acland St., St Kilda, ☎ 03/9525–3599) attracts a hip, young clientele (whatever that means).

COMEDY CLUBS

Set in a historic bluestone building, the **Comedy Café** (⊠ 177 Brunswick St., Fitzroy, ☎ 03/9419–2869) is a casual, long-standing proving ground for many of Australia's most popular comedians.

The **Comedy Club** (⊠ 380 Lygon St., Carlton. ☎ 03/9348–1622) is a popular place to see top-class Australian and international acts.

The Last Laugh (⊠ 64 Smith St., Collingwood, ☎ 03/9419–8600) is a theater-restaurant where comedy artists who have graduated to television frequently return to sharpen their act in front of a critical and very vocal audience.

DANCING

Most of the central city's dance clubs are along the **King Street** strip. Popularity is a fickle thing—follow the crowds if you want the latest and hippest. But note that King Street has a growing reputation for late-night violence. Authorities and club owners are attempting to improve the situation, but common-sense caution is called for.

Chasers. One of the city's most enduring night spots, this is a good bet for anyone from 20 to 35. Music varies from night to night. Call ahead for the latest lineup. ⊠ *386 Chapel St., Prahran,* ☎ *03/9827–6615.* ▤ *$6–$10.* ☉ *Wed.–Sun. 10 PM–7 AM.*

Metro. This multilevel, high-tech nightclub has eight bars, a glass-enclosed café, and three dance floors, where the action ranges from fast to furious. Metro is one of the hottest clubs in town with Melbourne's twentysomethings. ⊠ *20–30 Bourke St.,* ☎ *03/9663–4288.* ▤ *$10.* ☉ *Thurs.–Sat. 9 PM–5 AM.*

MUSIC

Continental Cafe. This classy spot in funky Greville Street, Prahran, offers live music of the highest quality, top-name Australian acts, and international performers. ⊠ *132A Greville St., Prahran,* ☎ *03/9510–2788.* ▤ *$11.50–$21.50, dinner and show $41–$61.* ☉ *Dates vary according to artists' availability.*

Bell's Hotel (⊠ Moray and Coventry Sts., South Melbourne, ☎ 03/9690–4511) is one of Melbourne's more famed jazz haunts. **Ruby Reds** (⊠ 11 Drury La., ☎ 03/9662–1544) is the city center's jazz mainstay. The **Limerick Arms Hotel** (⊠ 364 Clarendon St., South Melbourne, ☎ 03/9690–0995) is probably the best-known jazz venue in the whole country. **Downstairs at Eric's** (⊠ Darling St. and Toorak Rd., Toorak, ☎ 03/9820–3804) is a sophisticated restaurant with live jazz Friday and Saturday. For full-on rock and roll, punk, and grunge, the **Esplanade**

Hotel (⊠ Upper Esplanade, St Kilda. ☎ 03/9534–0211) is one of Melbourne's longest-established hot spots. Dress down.

Outdoor Activities and Sports

Australian-Rules Football

This is Melbourne's choice for winter football (*see* Chapter 1 for definitions). The two most important venues for national-league games are the **Melbourne Cricket Ground** (⊠ Brunton Ave., Yarra Park, ☎ 03/9654–5511) and **Waverley Park** (⊠ Wellington Rd., Mulgrave, ☎ 03/9654–1244). Tickets are available through BASS (☎ 11–566; credit-card reservations, 11–522) or at the playing field.

Bicycling

It is estimated that Melbourne and its environs contain more than 100 km (63 mi) of bike paths, including scenic routes along the Yarra River and around Port Phillip Bay. Bikes can be rented at one of the mobile rental shops in trailers alongside the bike paths.

Boating

At the **Studley Park Boathouse,** canoes, kayaks, and rowboats are available for hire on a peaceful, delightful stretch of the Lower Yarra River, about 7 km (4 mi) east of the city center. ⊠ *Studley Park, Kew,* ☎ *03/9853–8707.* ▣ *From $16 per hr for 2 people in kayak or rowboat to $22 per hr for 4 people in rowboat.* ☾ *Daily 9:30–sunset.*

Cricket

From October through March, all big international and interstate cricket matches in Victoria are played at the **Melbourne Cricket Ground.** The stadium has lights for night games and can accommodate 100,000 people. Tickets are available at the gate or through BASS (☎ 11–566; credit-card reservations, 11–522) or at the playing field. ⊠ *Brunton Ave., Yarra Park,* ☎ *03/9654–5511.*

Golf

Melbourne has the largest number of championship golf courses in Australia, and some of the private courses, such as Metropolitan, Royal Melbourne, and Kingston-Heath, are world class. A sampling of area courses includes **Albert Park Golf Course** (⊠ Queens Rd., Melbourne, ☎ 03/9510–5588), **Brighton Golf Links** (⊠ Dendy St., Brighton, ☎ 03/9592–1388), **Ivanhoe Public Golf Course** (⊠ Vasey St., East Ivanhoe, ☎ 03/9499–7001), **Sandringham Golf Links** (⊠ Cheltenham Rd., Cheltenham, ☎ 03/9598–3590), and **Yarra Bend Golf Course** (⊠ Yarra Bend Park Rd., Fairfield, ☎ 03/9481–3729).

Horse Racing

Melbourne is the only city in the world to declare a public holiday for a horse race—the **Melbourne Cup**—held on the first Tuesday in November every year since 1861. In addition to a horse race, the Cup is also a fashion parade, and most of Melbourne society turns out in full regalia to watch, while the rest of the country comes to a standstill, with schools, shops, offices, and factories tuning in to the action.

The city has four top-class race tracks. **Flemington Race Course** (⊠ Epsom Rd., Flemington, ☎ 03/9376–4100), 3 km (2 mi) outside the city, is Australia's premier race course and home of the Melbourne Cup. **Moonee Valley Race Course** (⊠ McPherson St., Moonee Ponds, ☎ 03/9370–2633) is 6 km (4 mi) from town and holds the Cox Plate race in October. **Caulfield Race Course** (⊠ Station St., Caulfield, ☎ 03/9572–1111), 10 km (6 mi) from the city, runs the Blue Diamond in March and the Caulfield Cup in October. Finally, **Sandown Race Course** (⊠

Racecourse Dr., Springvale, ☎ 03/9572–1111), 25 km (16 mi) from the city, runs the Sandown Cup in November.

Motor Racing

Somewhat controversially, Melbourne snatched the right to host the **Australian Formula 1 Grand Prix** from the city of Adelaide. Melbourne's first GP was held in early March 1996, and was a major success despite the threat of protests and disruption by local residents and others outraged by the destruction of parkland to build the racing circuit at Albert Park, 3 km (2 mi) from the city center. The race was awarded the title of best GP of the year by the international GP organizing committee.

Running

Some of the more popular local courses are the 4-km (2½-mi) **Tan,** beginning at Anderson Street and Alexandra Avenue and looping around the perimeter of the Royal Botanic Gardens; the 5-km (3-mi) **Albert Park Lake Run** in Albert Park; and the **Bay Run,** an 18-km (11-mi) round-trip run along Port Phillip Bay, starting at Kerford Road and Beaconsfield Parade in Albert Park and continuing on to Bay Street in Brighton.

Soccer

The sport is played almost year-round in **Olympic Park** (⊠ Ovals 1 and 2, Swan St., Melbourne, ☎ 03/9429–6288).

Tennis

The **Australian Open** (☎ 03/9655–1234), held in January at Flinders Park, is one of the world's four Grand Slam events.

If you wish to get in some tennis during your stay, plan to do so on weekdays, since most courts are booked solid at night and on weekends. Public courts for hire in and around the city include **Flinders Park National Tennis Centre** (⊠ Batman Ave., Melbourne, ☎ 03/9286–1244), with 15 outdoor and 5 indoor Rebound Ace courts; **Camberwell Tennis Centre** (⊠ Bulleen and Thompson Rds., Bulleen, ☎ 03/9850–4500), with 16 outdoor Supergrass courts; **East Melbourne Tennis Centre** (⊠ Powlett Reserve, Albert St., East Melbourne, ☎ 03/9417–6511), with 4 outdoor courts; and **Collingwood Indoor Tennis Centre** (⊠ 100 Wellington St., Collingwood, ☎ 03/9419–8911), with 5 indoor synthetic grass courts.

Shopping

From the haute couture of upper Collins Street's Paris End to the shops of suburban Toorak Village, Melbourne has firmly established itself as the nation's fashion capital. Australian designer labels are available on High Street in Armadale, on Toorak Road and Chapel Street in South Yarra, and on Carlton's Lygon Street. High-quality vintage clothing abounds on Greville Street in Prahran. Most shops are open Monday through Thursday, 9–5:30, Friday until 9, and Saturday until 5. Major city stores are open Sunday until 5.

Department Stores

Daimaru (⊠ 211 LaTrobe St., Melbourne, ☎ 03/9660–6666), a multilevel department store that is part of the 200-store Melbourne Central shopping complex, brings a new level of sophistication and the world's smartest fashions to the heart of the city.

David Jones (⊠ 310 Bourke St., Melbourne, ☎ 03/9669–8200) is one of the city's finer department stores, in the Bourke Street Mall.

Myer Melbourne (⊠ 314 Bourke St., Melbourne, ☎ 03/9661–1111) is a vast department store with a long-standing reputation for quality merchandise.

Markets
Meat Market Craft Centre. The imposing Victorian building of the city's former meat market houses a vast collection of work by leading jewelers, woodworkers, printers, and ceramic artists. ⊠ *42 Courtney St., North Melbourne,* ☎ *03/9329–9966.* ⊙ *Tues.–Sun. 10–5.*
Prahran Market. This stylish suburb's market sells nothing but food—a fantastic, mouthwatering array imported from all over the world. ⊠ *177 Commercial Rd., Prahran,* ☎ *03/9522–3302.* ⊙ *Tues. and Thurs. 7:30–5, Fri. 6–6, Sat. 7–1.*

Shopping Centers, Arcades, and Malls
Australia on Collins (⊠ 260 Collins St., ☎ 03/9650–4355) is the latest downtown shopping-center entrant, with one of its floors devoted to gifts and housewares. **Aero Design, R.G. Madden,** and **Made in Japan** sell particularly striking goods.
Block Arcade (⊠ 282 Collins St. and 100 Elizabeth St., ☎ 03/9654–5244), the elegant 19th-century shopping arcade, contains the venerable **Hopetoun Tea Tooms, Melee Jewellers'** estate jewelry, **Orrefors Kosta Boda,** the **Porcelain Doll Co.,** and the **National Trust Gift Shop.**

High Street between the suburbs of Prahran and Armadale, to the east of Chapel Street, is where you are most likely to find the best collection of antiques shops in Australia.
The Jam Factory (⊠ 500 Chapel St., South Yarra, ☎ 03/9826–0537) is made up of a group of historic bluestone buildings that house fashion, food, and gift shops, as well as a branch of Georges department store.
Melbourne Central (⊠ 300 Lonsdale St., ☎ 03/9665–0000), a dizzying complex whose biggest tenant is **Daimaru** department store, is huge enough to enclose a 100-year-old shot tower (used to make bullets) in its atrium.
Royal Arcade (⊠ 355 Bourke St., ☎ 03/0629–8888), built in 1846, is Melbourne's oldest shopping arcade. It is still a lovely place to find traditional jewelers as well as eclectic shops, and it is home to splendid **Gaunt's Clock,** which tolls away the hours.
Southgate (⊠ 4 Southbank Promenade, South Melbourne, ☎ 03/9686–1000), directly opposite Flinders Street Station on the other bank of the Yarra, shelters an excellent combination of shops and eateries. The spectacular riverside location is a short walk both from the city center across Princes Bridge and from the Victorian Arts Centre, making it an excellent choice for lunch; there's lots of outdoor seating next to the Southbank promenade.
Sportsgirl Centre (⊠ 254 Collins St., ☎ 03/0650–4373) sells some of Melbourne's most popular young women's clothing labels, particularly leisurewear. You'll find food as well as fashion in the four-level shopping mall.
Toorak Road in South Yarra between Chapel and Hotham streets is where you'll find some of the ritziest boutiques in Melbourne, as well as art galleries and several fine restaurants.

Specialty Stores
BOOKS
Brunswick Street Bookstore. This Fitzroy favorite sells solid modern Australian literature, some of which you won't find outside the country. ⊠ *305 Brunswick St., Fitzroy.* ☎ *03/9416–1030.*

Hill of Content. Knowledgeable staff and an excellent selection of titles make this a Melbourne favorite. ⊠ *86 Bourke St.,* ☎ *03/9662–9472.*

CLOTHING
Sam Bear. This Melbourne institution sells everything from Ozzie outerwear to Swiss Army knives. ⊠ *225 Russell St.,* ☎ *03/9663–2191.*

JEWELRY

Altmann and Cherny is a leading jeweler that specializes in opals and offers tax-free prices to overseas tourists. ⊠ *120 Exhibition St.*, ☎ *03/9650–9685.*

Makers Mark Gallery showcases the work of some of the country's finest jewelers. ⊠ *85 Collins St.,* ☎ *03/9654–8488.*

MUSIC

Discurio has an excellent range of music, with a good selection of traditional and contemporary Australian artists represented. ⊠ *285 Little Collins St.,* ☎ *03/9654–6540.* ☉ *Mon.–Thurs. 9–6, Fri. 9–9, Sat. 10–5, Sun. noon–5.*

SOUVENIRS

You can shop for Australian-made goods at the **Australiana General Store** outlets (⊠ 1227 High St., Armadale, ☎ 03/9822–2324; and 20/45 Collins St., Melbourne, ☎ 03/9650–2075) and **Aboriginal Handcrafts** (⊠ 125–133 Swanston St., 9th Floor, Melbourne, ☎ 03/9650–4717). You might also try the **National Trust Gift Shop** (⊠ 38 Jackson St., Toorak, ☎ 03/9827–9385).

Tours

Professional shoppers might want to take advantage of **Shopping Spree Tours** (☎ 03/9596–6600), which offers lunch and escorted shopping tours to some of Melbourne's best manufacturers and importers. Tours depart weekdays at 9:15, weekends at 8. The cost is $48 per person.

Melbourne A to Z

Arriving and Departing

BY BUS

Greyhound/Pioneer (☎ 13–1238) links the city with all Australian capital cities and with major towns and cities throughout Victoria. The terminal for both is on the corner of Swanston and Franklin streets.

BY CAR

The major route into Melbourne is Hume Highway, which runs northeast to Canberra, 646 km (400 mi) distant, and Sydney, which is 868 km (540 mi) away. Princes Highway follows the coast to Sydney in one direction and to Adelaide, 728 km (455 mi) northwest of Melbourne, in the other. The Western Highway runs northwest 111 km (70 mi) to Ballarat, and the Calder Highway travels north to Bendigo, a journey of 149 km (93 mi).

BY PLANE

Melbourne Airport is 22 km (14 mi) northwest of the central business district and can be reached easily from the city on the Tullamarine Freeway. The international terminal is in the center of the airport complex; domestic terminals are found on either side. International airlines flying into Melbourne include **Air New Zealand, Ansett Australia, British Airways, Qantas,** and **United.** Domestic carriers currently serving Melbourne are **Ansett Australia/Kendell** and **Qantas.** ☞ Air Travel *in* the Gold Guide for airline telephone numbers.

Between the Airport and Center City. Skybus (☎ 03/9335–3066) is a private bus service that operates between the airport terminals and the city, but for three or more people traveling together, a taxi to the city is a better value. En route from the airport, the bus makes a loop through the city before terminating at Spencer Street Station. ⊠ *$9.* ☉ *Departures daily 6:40 AM–11:40 PM approximately every 30 min, then hourly.*

Taxis are widely available. The cost of a taxi into town is approximately $30. **Limousines** to the city cost about $55. Three of the larger limousine companies are **Astra** (☎ 03/9819–7979), **Embassy** (☎ 03/9326–6033), and **Hughes** (☎ 03/9427–0533).

Spencer Street Railway Station is at Spencer and Little Collins streets. Public transportation is available here, but cumbersome luggage would be better served by a taxi at the queue outside the station.

Getting Around

BY CAR

Melbourne's regimented layout makes it easy to negotiate by car, but two unusual road rules apply because of the tram traffic on the city's major roads. Trams should be passed on the *left*, and when a tram stops, the cars behind it also must stop, unless there is a railed safety zone for tram passengers.

At various intersections within the city, drivers wishing to turn *right* must stay in the *left* lane as they enter the intersection, then wait for the traffic signals to change before proceeding with the turn. The rule is intended to prevent traffic from impeding tram service. For complete directions, look for the black-and-white traffic signs suspended overhead as you enter each intersection where this rule applies. All other right-hand turns are made from the center. It is far easier to understand this rule by seeing it in action rather than reading about it.

The **Royal Automobile Club of Victoria** (☎ 03/9790–3333) is the major source of information on all aspects of road travel in Victoria.

BY PUBLIC TRANSPORTATION

The city's public transport system includes buses, trains, and trams (streetcars). It is the extensive tram network that you may find most useful. Melbourne has one of the world's largest tram networks, with 365 km (227 mi) of track in the inner city and suburbs, and by and large the system is a delight—fast, convenient, and oh so cheap.

The city's public transport system is operated by Metropolitan Transit (☎ 13–1638), which divides Melbourne into three zones. Zone 1 is the urban core, where you will spend most of your time. The **basic ticket** is the one-zone ticket, which can be purchased from the tram conductor for $2.20 and is valid for travel within that zone on any tram, bus, or train for a period of two hours after purchase. For most travelers, the **most useful ticket** is the Zone 1 day ticket, which costs $4.30 and is available on board any tram. For anyone intending to make extensive use of Melbourne's public transport system, a **free route map** is available from the Victoria Tourist Information Centre (✉ Little Collins St. and Swanston Street Walk). **Trams run until midnight** and can be hailed wherever you see a green and gold tram-stop sign. A free City Circle tram operates daily 10–6 on the fringe of the Central Business District, with stops in Flinders, Spencer, La Trobe, Victoria, and Spring streets. Look for the burgundy-and-cream color scheme.

BY TAXI

Taxis are metered, and empty taxis can be hailed on the street and at taxi stands or they can be ordered by phone. Melbourne's taxis are gradually adopting a yellow color scheme, and drivers are required to wear uniforms. Major taxi companies include **Silver Top** (☎ 03/9345–3455), **Northern Suburban** (☎ 03/9480–2222), **Embassy** (☎ 03/9320–0320), and **Black Cabs** (☎ 13–2227).

Contacts and Resources

B&B RESERVATION AGENCIES

Call or write for a brochure from **Bed & Breakfast Australia** (✉ Box 408, Gordon, NSW 2072, ☎ 02/9498–5344). Tourism Victoria produces a brochure, "Victorian Bed & Breakfast Getaways," available from the Victoria Tourist Information Centre (⊠ Swanston St. Walk and Little Collins St.). Another leaflet, "Melbourne's B & B's," lists 20 of the best properties in the city and suburbs. It is also available from the Tourist Information Centre.

CAR RENTALS

Avis (☎ 1800/22–5533), **Budget** (☎ 13–2727), and **Hertz** (☎ 03/9698–2555) all have offices at Melbourne Airport as well as downtown. If you hire from a major car-rental company, expect to pay between $80 and $95 per day for an automatic sedan and about $70 per day for a compact standard model. If you don't need the latest model and can return the car to the pick-up point, the smaller local rental agencies offer vehicles for as little as $35 per day including insurance. Some of these smaller agencies are **Cheapa** (☎ 03/9878–9882), **Delta** (☎ 13–1390), and **Dollar** (☎ 03/662–1188).

EMERGENCIES

Alfred Hospital. ⊠ *Commercial Rd., Prahran,* ☎ *03/9276–2000.*
Ambulance, fire brigade, and **police.** ☎ *000.*
Royal Dental Hospital. ⊠ *Elizabeth St. and Flemington Rd.,* ☎ *03/9341–0222.*
Royal Women's Hospital. ⊠ *132 Grattan St., Carlton,* ☎ *03/9344–2000.*
St. Vincent's Hospital. ⊠ *Victoria Parade, Fitzroy,* ☎ *03/9288–2211.*

GUIDED TOURS

Bay Cruises. The *Wattle* is a restored steam tug that cruises on Port Phillip Bay. The highlight of the one-hour voyage is a visit to a seal colony. The boat runs from Melbourne between mid-October and the end of June, except for summer holidays, when cruises depart from Rye on the Mornington Peninsula. ⊠ *Station Pier, Port Melbourne,* ☎ *03/9328–2739.* ☜ *$10.* ☉ *Boats depart summer, daily; fall–spring, Sun.*

Cycling Tours. Melbourne's excellent bicycle path network and flat terrain makes cycling pleasurable. **Freewheel Bicycle Tours** operates four guided half-day tours—A Taste of Melbourne, St. Kilda and the Bay, Main Yarra River Trail, and Williamstown—with all equipment supplied. Two tours are offered each day. ☎ *03/8886–0800,* FAX *03/9885–4355.* ☜ *$39 single rider, $29 each for 2 or more riders.*

Orientation Tours. Gray Line has several guided tours of Melbourne and its surroundings by coach and boat. The Melbourne Experience is a basic three-hour tour that visits the city center's main attractions and some of the surrounding parks. The tour departs daily at 9 AM from the company's headquarters. ⊠ *184 Swanston St. Walk,* ☎ *03/9663–4455.* ☜ *$38.*

Australian Pacific Tours (☎ 13–1304), **AAT Kings** (☎ 03/9663–3377), **Great Sights** (☎ 03/9639–2211), and **Melbourne Sightseeing** (☎ 03/9663–3388) all offer similar general trips and prices.

City Explorer has a do-it-yourself tour of the city on a bus that circles past major attractions, including the zoo and the parks to the east. The tour ticket is valid for one complete circuit, and it allows you to leave the double-decker bus at any of the route's eight stops and board any following City Explorer bus. The tour begins at Flinders Street Station. Buses leave hourly (except 1 PM) between 10 and 4. ☎ *03/9563–9788.* ☜ *$15.*

The City Wanderer double-decker bus travels a similar route around the city center but substitutes a detour to historic Williamstown and the Scienceworks Museum for the zoo and nearby Carlton. Buses leave at

9:30, 10:30, noon, 2, and 3:30 from Flinders Street Station. ☎ *03/9563–9788.* ☒ *$15.*

Sports Tours. Koala Golf Tours (☎ 018/329–934) specializes in golf tours around the city. The tour cost, which includes clubs and shoes if necessary, ranges from $100 to $225 per person, depending on the greens fees at the course.

Yarra River Cruises. The modern, glass-enclosed boats of the **Melbourne River Cruises** fleet take one- and two-hour cruises daily, either west through the commercial heart of the city or east through the parks and gardens, or a combination of the two. The boat departs from Berth 1, Princes Walk, on the opposite side of Princes Bridge from Flinders Street Station. ☒ *Melbourne River Tours, Vault 1, Princes Walk,* ☎ *03/9629–7233 or 03/9650–2055.* ☒ *1-hr cruise $13, 2-hr cruise $25.* ☉ *Cruises daily 10–4 every ½ hr.*

Yarra Yarra Water Taxis (☎ 0411/255–179) offers a 1950s speedboat as an alternative to the larger cruise boats. The size of the boat makes it possible to follow the Yarra as far as Dight's Falls, passing some of Melbourne's wealthiest suburbs on the way. It rents for $75 per hour and can carry up to four passengers. Picnic baskets are available.

Walking Tours. Melbourne Heritage Walks and Tours (☎ 03/9827–1085, FAX 03/9827–4263) runs a 90-minute stroll that takes its cues from the city's architecture to portray the social and political history of Melbourne. Tour guide Maxine Wood is lively and entertaining, and her contacts allow her entry to such places as the backstage chambers of Parliament House and the corridors of Government House. The tours, on Wednesday morning and Sunday afternoon, cost $20 per person. Private tours for groups also can be arranged.

LATE-NIGHT PHARMACY

Leonard Long Pharmacy (☒ Williams Rd. and High St., Prahran, ☎ 03/9510–3977) is open 9 AM–midnight.

VISITOR INFORMATION

Victoria Tourist Information Centre. ☒ *Town Hall, Swanston St. Walk and Little Collins St.,* ☎ *03/9658–9968 or 03/9658–9940.* ☉ *Weekdays 8:30–5:30, Sat. 8:30–5, Sun. 9–5; City Square and Bourke Street Mall booths Mon.–Thurs. 9–5, Sat. 10–4, Sun. 11–4; Rialto Tower Plaza Forecourt booth daily 11–6.*

City Experience Center. This new, interactive orientation facility in Melbourne Town Hall provides information in six languages with large-screen videos, touch screens, permanent displays, and daily newspapers, and there is access to the Melbourne Web site as well. The free **Melbourne Greeters** service pairs you with a local volunteer who shares your interests. You can spend two to four hours with the volunteer touring relevant parts of the city and talking about subjects such as Aboriginal culture, Australian film, parks and gardens, shopping, gay culture, history, theater, and sports. To book a Melbourne Greeter (☎ 03/9658–9524, FAX 03/9654–1054) you must give at least three days' notice, preferably more. ☒ *Swanston St. Walk and Little Collins St.,* ☎ *03/9658–9658.* ☉ *Weekdays 9–7, weekends 9–5.*

The Information Line (☎ 03/0055–34360) has a recorded listing of current events in Melbourne.

The accommodation office adjoining the Victoria Tourist Information Centre (☞ *above*) will assist you if you don't have accommodations. ☎ *03/9650–1522.* ☉ *Weekdays 8:30–5:30, Sat. 8:30–1.*

Royal Automobile Club of Victoria (☎ 03/9790–3333) can assist with booking accommodations, car rental, and holiday packages.

Department of Conservation and Natural Resources provides information on Victoria's national parks. ⊠ *240 Victoria Parade, East Melbourne,* ☎ *03/9412–4011.*

SIDE TRIPS FROM MELBOURNE

Taking day trips around Melbourne is one of the pleasures of visiting the city. To the east, in the **Dandenong Ranges,** a narrow, winding road will take you on a scenic journey through rain forests and flower-filled towns full of timber houses. South of Melbourne, the Bellarine Peninsula to the west and the **Mornington Peninsula** to the east form a horseshoe around Port Phillip Bay. Of the two, the Mornington Peninsula is more picturesque. Adrift off the bottom of the peninsula, **Phillip Island** has some gloriously rugged coastline and koalas, seals, and thousands of fairy penguins. Every evening, the seabirds push themselves out of the sea and flop back *en masse* to their burrows—this procession is Victoria's number one tourist attraction.

The Dandenongs

Melbourne comes to the Dandenong Ranges for a breath of fresh air, especially in summer, when the cool, moist hills provide a welcome relief from the heat of the city. The Dandenongs are about an hour's drive southeast of Melbourne.

Belgrave

43 km (27 mi) southeast of Melbourne.

Sherbrooke Forest is a remnant of the woodlands that once covered the ranges. Belgrave is an unexceptional town at its heart, but a place with one of Melbourne's favorite attractions. At the turn of the century, the government carved four narrow-gauge railway tracks through the forests of the Dandenongs to assist pioneers.

Ⓒ **Puffing Billy** is the sole survivor from the narrow-gauge era, a gleaming little steam engine that hauls passenger wagons from Belgrave to Emerald Lake. It is a perfectly appropriate way to take in the picture-book scenery of forests and trestle bridges. The 13-km (8-mi) trip takes almost one hour each way. ⊠ *Old Monbulk Rd., Belgrave,* ☎ *03/9754–6800.* ⊡ *$16.50.* ☉ *Trains depart weekdays 10:30, noon, and 2:30, more frequently on weekends.*

Sherbrooke

47 km (29 mi) southeast of Melbourne, 8 km (5 mi) north of Belgrave.

Deep in the lush expanse of the Dandenong Ranges National Park, the **George Tindale Memorial Garden** occupies 6 lovely acres of azaleas, camellias, and hydrangeas that spill down the hillside. ⊠ *Sherbrooke Rd., Sherbrooke,* ☎ *03/9755–2051.* ⊡ *$4.* ☉ *Mon.–Sat. 10–5.*

The mountain roads near the little settlement of Sherbrooke loop through towering forests of mountain ash and giant tree ferns. If you stop and listen for a minute, you will probably hear the tinkling calls of bellbirds and perhaps the cry of a whipbird, a piercing, drawn-out note that ends, as you might guess, with a sharp whip-crack sound. Another bird common to this area is the flightless lyrebird, an accomplished mimic that has even been known to imitate the sound of a distant chain saw.

Kallista

48 km (30 mi) southeast of Melbourne, 5 km (3 mi) northeast of Belgrave.

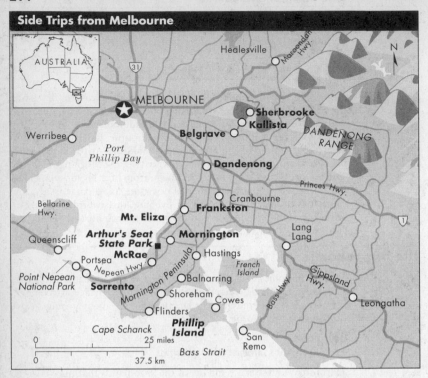

214

The **Alfred Nicholas Memorial Garden** is named for its founder, who made a fortune selling aspirin. The sprawling Art Deco mansion of the Nicholas family, which can be seen through the trees at the top of the hill, was a luxurious hotel until 1992, when it was forced to close for lack of business. The garden is particularly notable for its fuchsias and rhododendrons. Don't miss the waterfall and ornamental lake, at its best when surrounding trees are wearing their autumn colors. ⊠ *Sherbrooke Rd., Kallista,* ☎ *03/9755–2726.* 🎫 *$3.* ⊗ *Daily noon–5.*

Dining

$$$$ ✕ **Cotswold House.** One of the gastronomic gems of country Victoria, this rustic charmer sets out epicurean food in a dazzling hillside setting. The dining room overlooks trees and gardens that are illuminated at night, and dishes include sweet corn soufflé with blue-swimmer-crab sauce, and Moroccan-spiced almond and pigeon pie. On weekdays, the lunch menu is simpler and less expensive. ⊠ *Black Hill Rd., Menzies Creek,* ☎ *03/9754–7884. AE, DC, MC, V. Closed Mon. and Tues. No dinner Wed., Thurs., or Sun.*

$$$ ✕ **Olinda Chalet.** Located in a gracious old country house surrounded by gardens, fountains, and pools, this terrace restaurant offers splendid views and fine international cuisine. The blackboard menu, which changes daily, might offer pork fillet with mustard and capsicum (sweet pepper) sauce, or peppered loin of lamb baked with tomato and basil. Banana soufflé is a popular dessert. ⊠ *543 Mt. Dandenong Tourist Rd., Olinda,* ☎ *03/9751–1844. AE, DC, MC, V. Closed Mon. and Tues. No dinner Sun.*

$$ ✕ **Kenloch.** In its seat in an old mansion with sweeping gardens studded with tall trees, fern gullies, and rhododendrons, this stately and somewhat old-fashioned restaurant serves such appropriately traditional meals as beef fillet with peppercorn sauce. In the afternoon, the emphasis is on Devonshire teas, sandwiches, and small savory meals. ⊠ *Mt. Dandenong Tourist Rd., Olinda,* ☎ *03/9751–1008. AE, DC, MC, V. Closed Mon. and Tues.*

Mornington Peninsula

Mornington Peninsula rings the southeastern half of Port Phillip Bay. If you choose to set aside a sunny day for a drive down the peninsula, you'll be treated to a glimpse of life in one of Melbourne's favorite weekend and holiday retreats. Mornington has long been a favorite with moneyed Melburnians, and the tip of the peninsular boot is shod with Gatsbyesque weekenders and a scattering of stylish restaurants. If you are visiting the peninsula in summer, be sure to pack your swimsuit and take advantage of the area's wonderful beaches.

There are two things to look for as you drive down the peninsula. For one, you'll notice the timber beach huts appearing near Dromana and suddenly increasing in number around Rye. These are bathing boxes—privately leased beach huts that are one of the peculiarities of Victorian life. At some beaches they form an almost continuous line along the shore, identical in every way—in size, in shape, in proximity to each other, in the little balconies that jut out above the sea—except color. A peek inside says volumes about their owners. Some are like aquatic sports stores, complete with fishing tackle, Windsurfers, water skis, ropes, masks and flippers, and even dinghies lashed to the ceiling.

And to satisfy your botanical curiosity, that low, scrubby tree that grows prolifically along the shoreline from McRae south is the tea-tree, which appeared only in the 19th century as the original vegetation of banksias and she-oaks was burned as fuel in limestone kilns that supplied Melbourne with much of its building mortar. A species of melaleuca, tea-trees were actually used to supply a substitute tea in the early days of the colony.

Frankston
42 km (26 mi) south of Melbourne.

A bustling outer Melbourne suburb at the base of picturesque Olivers Hill, Frankston proper has a pleasant beach, but just 3 km (2 mi) south you will find two well-kept-secret beaches of locals, who come here to swim and to picnic. To reach **Pelican Point** and **Davey's Bay Yacht Club,** turn right on Old Mornington Road; follow it to the end of Marathon Drive, then turn right again onto Davey's Bay Road.

Mount Eliza
6 km (4 mi) south of Frankston, 48 km (30 mi) south of Melbourne.

Mount Eliza is a commuter suburb of Melbourne, relatively well-to-do and tree-filled, just inland from Port Phillip Bay. The **Omell Manyung Gallery,** one of the Melbourne area's most popular galleries, exhibits the work of up-and-coming Australian artists. ⊠ *1408 Nepean Hwy., Mount Eliza,* ☎ *03/9787–2953.* ⊠ *Free.* ☉ *Thurs.–Mon. 10:30–5.*

Canadian Bay Reserve, Mount Eliza's beach, is another well-kept secret. Here you'll find a boat club, and the beach has excellent picnic facilities. ⊠ *Canadian Bay Rd. off Mount Eliza Way.*

Mornington
8 km (5 mi) south of Mount Eliza, 56 km (35 mi) south of Melbourne.

The **Mornington Peninsula Arts Centre** is one of Victoria's 16 regional galleries. Names to look for among its outstanding collection of works by Australian artists include Fred Williams, Sam Fullbrook, William Dobell, Sir Russell Drysdale, and John Passmore. ⊠ *4 Vancouver St.,*

Mornington, ☎ *03/5975–4395.* 🖅 *$3.* ⊙ *Weekdays 10–4:30, weekends noon–4:30.*

Arthurs Seat

20 km (12 mi) south of Mornington; follow the Esplanade from Mornington through Mount Martha. 76 km (47 mi) south of Melbourne.

Arthurs Seat State Park has walking tracks, a public garden, and a scenic drive or ride on a chair lift to a 1,000-ft summit, which provides a sweeping view of the surrounding countryside. ⊠ *Arthur's Seat Rd., Mornington Peninsula Hwy.,* ☎ *03/5987–2565.* 🖅 *Chairlift $6.* ⊙ *Oct.–Apr., daily 11–5; May–Sept., weekends 11–5.*

McRae

2 km (1¼ mi) west of Arthurs Seat, 76 km (47 mi) south of Melbourne.

Built in 1844, the **McRae Homestead** was one of the first houses erected in this area, which is why the National Trust has it listed as a historic monument. The original furniture is on display, and guides give half-hour tours of the property. Even when the house is closed, the caretaker will often open the gate and show you around. ⊠ *8 Charles St., McRae,* ☎ *03/5981–2866.* 🖅 *$3.* ⊙ *Apr.–Nov., weekends and holidays noon–4:30; Dec.–Mar., daily noon–4:30.*

Sorrento

17 km (10 mi) from McRae, 93 km (58 mi) southwest of Melbourne.

Appropriately enough, Sorrento, with its evocative Italian name, is one of the prettiest of the bayside beach towns, with lawns backed by shade trees, a trim white gazebo, and a fish-and-chips shop out over the water that leads to a tumbledown jetty—a picturesque roost for pelicans. Sorrento developed as a fashionable resort more than a century ago when George Coppin formed a company named the Sorrento Ocean Amphitheatre Company, which built tramways through the town and linked it with Melbourne by paddle steamer. More recently, Sorrento has become the arts-and-crafts end of the peninsula, and the stretch of highway between Sorrento and Blairgowrie has no fewer than eight galleries.

Aside from extremely popular seal exhibits, you'll find more than 200 fish species swimming about at **Sorrento Marine Aquarium.** ⊠ *St. Aubin's Way, Sorrento,* ☎ *03/5984–4478.* 🖅 *$5.* ⊙ *Daily 10–5, seal feeding at noon and 3.*

En Route   At the end of the Nepean Highway, in Portsea, turn left into Back Beach Road and make a right to get to **London Bridge,** a fantastic natural bridge carved by the ocean. After you've spent your time on the beach by the arch, the sole of the Mornington Peninsula boot runs in a straight line for 28 km (17 mi), forming a long, narrow coastal park that ends at Cape Schanck, where you can visit the **Cape Schanck Lighthouse and Museum.** The sea can be violent along this coastline—in 1967, Australian prime minister Harold Holt drowned at Cheviot Beach just west of London Bridge—and swimming is advisable only where the beach is patrolled by lifeguards.

Dining

$$ ✗ **Arthurs.** Considered the Mornington Peninsula's best dining expe-
★   rience, Arthurs has three eateries, all with fine views of Port Phillip Bay: the formal Peak, the informal and much cheaper Vineyard Bistro, and a kiosk selling ice cream and snacks. In the restaurant, the baked pork fillet is sublime, as is grilled duck breast with preserved cherries. Simpler bistro lunches might feature eggplant slices rolled around a ricotta

filling. ⊠ *Arthurs Seat Scenic Rd., Arthurs Seat,* ☎ *03/5981–4444. AE, DC, MC, V. Closed Mon. and Tues.*

$$ ✕ **Licciardo's.** This noisy, bustling trattoria relies on the quality of its food, not its decor or its casual service, to keep the crowds coming. Located in a storefront, Licciardo's lists its daily specials on large blackboards on the walls. Dishes served here include tuna risotto with spicy tomato sauce, barbecued mussels with herb bread, and rabbit fillets on a bed of noodles with basil. Seafood salads are highly recommended, and pasta and antipasto dishes are generally excellent. The exquisite chocolate soufflé is often available even when it does not appear on the menu. ⊠ *84 Mount Eliza Way, Mount Eliza,* ☎ *03/9787– 7710. MC, V. No lunch Mon., Tues., or Sat.*

$$ ✕ **Poff's.** Set on a hillside with views across a vineyard to the valley below, this modern restaurant has rapidly acquired a solid reputation. The menu is small and dishes are described with an austerity that downplays their caliber. Main courses might include ocean trout, lamb kebab, roast duckling, or steak Diane—all simple and all delightful. Russian dishes, such as meat dumplings in broth flavored with soy sauce, garlic, and chili and topped with sour cream, are a specialty. Crème caramel is fantastic. ⊠ *Red Hill Rd., Red Hill, 7 km (4 mi) from McRae,* ☎ *03/5389–2566. AE, MC, V. Closed Mon.–Wed. No dinner Thurs.*

Phillip Island

★ *125 km (78 mi) south of Melbourne.*

Phillip Island looks like a chunk of Mornington Peninsula floating south toward Bass Straight. It is one home of the greatly popular fairy penguins, whose nightly waddle from the sea to their burrows in nearby dunes draws throngs of onlookers, particularly on summer weekends and holidays. Be prepared for wet and windy conditions at any time of the year.

The penguin spectacle is interesting, but the island's changing coastline may ultimately be more appealing. At the end of the Summerland Peninsula, out past the Penguin Parade, two rock formations are particularly captivating. At low tide, you can walk across a basalt causeway to the **Nobbies** and take in the splendid views along the wild northern coast of Phillip Island. Wildlife here is abundant—from September to April, thousands of shearwaters, also called muttonbirds, are in residence. After their breeding season, they return north to the Bering Straight in the Arctic.

Farther out to sea, **Seal Rocks** are home to the largest colony of Australian fur seals. In midsummer there may be 5,000 seals basking on rocky platforms and capering in the sea. You can view them through telescopes from the kiosk on the cliff above the Nobbies, or on boats that leave in season from Phillip Island's principle town of Cowes.

Unlike the large and stately emperor penguins of the Antarctic, **fairy penguins** rarely grow much bigger than a large duck. Seeing them on Phillip Island, however, is hardly a back-to-nature experience. The penguins emerge from the surf onto a floodlit beach, while a commentator in a tower describes over a public address system their progress. Spectators, who watch from concrete bleachers, may number several thousand on a busy night. For many people, the most memorable part of the experience is the sight of the fluffy young penguins, who stand outside their burrows waiting for their parents to return with food. Camera flashbulbs may not be used to film the penguins, which effectively prevents still photography. For anyone interested in seeing the animals in a less touristy setting, fairy penguins are common to most of the southern Victorian coastline, and the locals in most coastal towns will point out places where they can be seen. ✉ *Summerland Beach,* ☎ *03/5956–8300 or 03/5956–8691.* 🎟 *$7.50.*

Dining and Lodging

$$$ ✕🖭 **Rothsaye on Lovers Walk.** Whether it be for the fine beach on the doorstep or the outstanding accommodations, this seaside cottage has great appeal. The bedrooms are beautifully appointed, with thoughtful touches such as breakfast baskets, beach chairs and umbrellas, fishing lines, even sunscreen to use on your island excursions. Fresh flowers, antiques, king-size beds, and an array of magazines festoon the rooms. And there is always the floodlit delight of Lovers Walk, which you can follow into the center of Cowes from the front door. Children are not accommodated. ✉ *2 Roy Ct., Cowes,* ☎ 𝖥𝖠𝖷 *03/5952–2057. 4 rooms with bath. MC, V.*

Side Trips from Melbourne A to Z

Car Rentals

Renting a car in Melbourne and driving south is the most practical way of seeing the Mornington Peninsula in particular. Some agencies include **Avis** (☎ 1800/22–5533), **Budget** (☎ 13–2727), **Hertz** (☎ 03/9698–2555), **Cheapa** (☎ 03/9878–9882), **Delta** (☎ 13–3582), and **Dollar** (☎ 03/662–1188).

Emergencies

Ambulance, fire brigade, and **police.** ☎ *000.*

Guided Tours

Day trips from Melbourne are offered by local tour operators, including **Australian Pacific Tours** (☎ 13–1304), **Gray Line** (☎ 03/9663–4455), and **AAT Kings** (☎ 03/9663–3377)—all three of which depart from 184 Swanston Street Walk. Dandenongs tours cost about $42, Penguin Parade tours $62-$75.

Visitor Information

Victoria Tourist Information Centre. ✉ *Town Hall, Swanston St. Walk and Little Collins St.,* ☎ *03/9658–9968 or 03/9658–9940.* ⊙ *Weekdays 8:30–5:30, Sat. 8:30–5, Sun. 9–5.*
Phillip Island Information Centre. ✉ *Phillip Island Tourist Rd., Newhaven,* ☎ *03/5956–7447.*

WEST COAST REGION

Victoria's Great Ocean Road is arguably the country's most dramatic and spectacular coastal drive, heading west from Melbourne along rugged, windswept beaches. The road, built during the Great Depression atop majestic cliffs, occasionally dips down to sea level. Here in championship surfing country, some of the world's finest waves pound mile after mile of uninhabited golden sandy beaches. As you explore the coastline, don't miss Bell's Beach, site of the Easter Surfing Classic, one of the premier events of the surfing world. But be careful! Only the most competent swimmers should swim here, and then only at a lifeguard-patrolled beach with other swimmers. The fierce undertow along this coastline can be deadly.

The West Coast provides access to two of Victoria's major parks. Port Campbell National Park lies along the ocean and includes in its 30-km (19-mi) span some of Australia's most haunting coastline. And northeast of Hamilton, you can head into the mountains of Grampians National Park that begin to rise out of the plains about 80 km (50 mi) inland from the Southern Ocean.

Although this region is actually on the southeast coast of the Australian mainland, it lies to the west of Melbourne and to Melburnians it is therefore "the West Coast." From the city, you should allow two or more days for a West Coast sojourn.

Werribee

32 km (20 mi) southwest of Melbourne.

Once a country town, now a generally undistinguished outer suburb of Melbourne, Werribee is notable for the glorious Werribee Park Mansion and its attendant safari-style zoo.

The 60-room Italianate **Werribee Park Mansion,** dating from 1877, is furnished with period furniture and set on more than 10 hectares (25 acres) of formal gardens. This was one of the grandest homes in the colony, built by wealthy pastoralists Thomas and Andrew Chirnside. ⊠ *Werribee Park Mansion, K Rd., Werribee,* ☎ *03/9741–2444.* ⌷ *$8.* ⊘ *Weekdays 10–3:45, weekends 10–4:45.*

ⓒ **Werribee Zoological Park,** which is part of the original Werribee Park property, is an open-range zoo of the highest caliber. Safari buses travel through a landscape that replicates that of southern Africa, passing among giraffe, rhinoceros, zebra, hippopotamus, and other species. Australian animals also live in the park. A new walk-through section, housing cheetahs, apes, meerkats, and other African animals, again in natural conditions, was opened in December 1996. The zoo is closely aligned with the Melbourne Zoo. ⊠ *Werribee Zoological Park, K Rd., Werribee,* ☎ *03/9742–7933.* ⌷ *$14.* ⊘ *Weekdays 10:30–4, weekends 10:30–6:40.*

Geelong

72 km (45 mi) southwest of Melbourne, 40 km (25 mi) west of Werribee,

Victoria's second largest city, Geelong relies on heavy industry, notably automobile construction, for its prosperity. Its proximity to the great surf beaches of the West Coast is its greatest appeal. There is little reason to linger.

The **National Wool Museum** tells the story of this major Australian industry. There are three galleries highlighting the harvesting of wool, its manufacture into textiles, and the methods by which it is sold. Exhibits include a reconstructed shearers' hut and 1920s mill workers' cottage. Audiovisual displays tell the story in an entertaining and informative manner. ⊠ *Mooroobool and Brougham Sts.,* ☎ *03/5226–4660.* ⌷ *$7.* ⊘ *Daily 10–5.*

En Route   From Geelong, heed signs to the Torquay Road. Follow it for 23 km (13 mi) to **Torquay,** Australia's premier surfing and windsurfing resort. Bell's Beach is famous for its Easter surfing contests and its October international windsurfing competitions.

The **Great Ocean Road,** a positively magnificent coastal drive, begins at Eastern View, 10 km (6 mi) east of Lorne. The towns and hamlets along the road are set in such spectacular visual surroundings that, thankfully, no tourist attractions have been, or are likely to be, built. None could compete with what nature has wonderfully concocted.

Lorne

140 km (87 mi) southwest of Melbourne, 68 km (42 mi) southwest of Geelong, and 50 km (30 mi) southwest of Torquay.

A little town at the edge of the Otway Range, Lorne is the site of both a wild celebration every New Year's Eve and the popular Pier-to-Pub Swim held shortly thereafter. Some people make their reservations a year in advance for these New Year's events. It's also a favorite surfing, sailing, and sunbathing spot, with a pretty park beside the beach, and the site of the Great Otway Classic, a footrace held annually on the second weekend in June.

Just before the road enters Lorne, it crosses the Erskine River. From a campsite near the bridge, an 8-km (5-mi) trail winds up the **Erskine River valley.** This lush, green haven of eucalyptus, tree ferns, waterfalls, and rustic bridges is delightful; just remember to bring mosquito repellent and keep an eye out for leeches if you're bare-legged. The track passes the Sanctuary, a rock amphitheater where early pioneers gathered for religious services. If you're not in the mood for a walk, Erskine Road, which exits Lorne to the north, passes close to Erskine Falls.

Dining and Lodging

$$ ✕ **Kosta's.** Lively, bright, informal, and noisy, especially in peak sea-
★ son, this gaily decorated taverna has a wine bar and specializes in Greek food and international dishes, such as Moroccan lamb stew, a wonderful homemade *tsatsiki* (a yogurt, cucumber, and garlic dip), and char-grilled lamb. Fresh local specialties, including char-grilled fish and lobster, are also on offer. ✉ *48 Mountjoy Parade,* ☎ *03/5289–1883. MC, V. Closed Easter–Dec. 24.*

$ 🏠 **Erskine House.** Set in a 12-acre garden, Erskine House was built in 1868 and fully restored in 1930. This charming, spotless guest house, in its 30s style, is perfect if you want a relaxed, Art Deco hotel without phones, televisions, or radios. Rates include breakfast. ✉ *Mountjoy Parade,* ☎ *03/5289–1205. 72 rooms with bath, 25 suites. 8 tennis courts, putting green. AE, DC, MC, V.*

En Route After passing the charming, historic fishing town of **Apollo Bay,** 45 km (28 mi) past Lorne, the road turns inland through **Otway National Park** (✉ Otway-Beach Forest Information Centre, ☎ 03/5235–9303). Part of the Otway Ranges, the rain forest here has about 200 days of rainfall per year. In this lush, primitive natural environment, ferns and shrubs virtually define the color green. The mountain ash here are among the tallest in the world. Some roads are not paved, and the going can be bumpy and slow.

Great Ocean Road then swings out to the coast near Glenaire before heading inland again to run alongside **Melba Gully State Park.** (To reach the park, which lies between Lavers Hill and Wangerrip, turn left at Crowes.) After Melba Gulley, the road doubles back to the coastal town of Wattle Hill, where a dead-end side road will lead you to the shore at **Moonlight Head,** Otway National Park. The coastal formation was named by Matthew Flinders, the first circumnavigator of Australia, who saw the headland during a fierce storm when the moon broke through the clouds for a moment (several other ships, not his, have foundered here). The cliffs are some of the highest in the country.

The main Great Ocean Road heads inland again slightly, coming back to the coast at **Princetown.** This is the beginning of Port Campbell National Park, the most dazzling section of the drive. For the next 32 km (20 mi), the road snakes along the cliff tops for a heart-stopping, roller-coaster ride.

Port Campbell National Park

225 km (156 mi) west of Melbourne, 66 km (41 mi) east of Warr-nambool.

Stretching some 30 km (19 mi) along the southern Victoria coastline,
★ **Port Campbell National Park** is the site of some of the most famous
geological formations in Australia. Along this coast the ferocious
Southern Ocean has gnawed at limestone cliffs for ages, creating a sort
of badlands-by-the-sea, where columns of resilient rock stand 165 to
330 ft offshore. There are several scenic lookouts along the way, and
each one seems more spectacular than the last. The most famous for-
★ mation is the **Twelve Apostles,** as much a symbol for Victoria as the
Sydney Opera House is for New South Wales. Despite the name, only
eight pillars are visible—the rest have been claimed by the waves.
Equally dramatic are the formations at **Bay of Martyrs** and **Bay of Islands Coastal Reserve.** Both are less crowded with tour buses than the
Twelve Apostles, and at Bay of Islands you can watch new rock stacks
taking shape.

The level of the sea was much higher 25 million years ago, and as the
water receded, towering sediments of sand, mud, limestone, and
seashells were left standing to face the waves. The ocean is continuously carving these massive towers into strange shapes, even as they
slowly crumble into the sea.

The best time to visit the park is between January and April, when you
can also witness events on nearby **Muttonbird Island.** Toward nightfall, hundreds of hawks and kites circle the island in search of hungry
baby muttonbirds emerging impatiently from their protective burrows. Sometimes hovering on the predatory edge of success, the hawks
and kites beat a hasty retreat at the sight of thousands of adult shearwaters approaching with food for their chicks as the last light fades
from the sky.

Generally speaking, you don't come to Port Campbell to bush walk,
but if you want to explore the area on foot, pick up the self-guided
Discovery Walk at the Visitors Centre. The walk begins near Port
Campbell Beach and takes about 1½ hours to complete. It is safe to
swim only at this beach—the pounding surf and undertow are treacherous at other nearby beaches. Swimmers should opt instead for the
few isolated pools found in sheltered coves along the coastline.

Lodging
Both the visitor center and the campground are in Port Campbell. Campsites at the Port Campbell Recreation Reserve with hot water and
showers cost $12.50 per day for a site without electricity, $15.50 for
a site with power. Advance reservations are suggested (☎ 03/5598-
6369).

Arriving and Departing
The town of Port Campbell itself is 250 km (155 mi) southwest of Mel-
bourne via Geelong. The area is accessible by car along the Great
Ocean Road between Princetown and Peterborough.

Visitor Information
Port Campbell National Park. ⊠ *Tregea St., Port Campbell, VIC 3269,*
☎ *03/5598-6382.*
Department of Conservation and Natural Resources. ⊠ *240 Victoria
Parade, East Melbourne,* ☎ *03/9412-4011.*

Warrnambool

*262 km (163 mi) west of Melbourne, 122 km (76 mi) west of Lorne,
and 66 km (41 mi) west of Port Campbell.*

The nearest major population center to Port Campbell National Park,
Warrnambool is in the midst of wool and dairy-farm country. It's a
friendly city of robust, hardy people who live off the land and sea. The
area is great for fishing in surf and stream.

★ The sheltered bay at **Logan's Beach,** 3 km (2 mi) from the center of
Warrnambool, is a nice place for a stroll. Winter offers the added fascination of watching **southern right whales** close to the shore, where
they give birth to their calves. They take up residence here for a considerable stretch of time and are easily observed from the shore, where
there is a cliffside viewing platform. They are known as right whales
because they were once hunted extensively along this coast and, therefore, were "right" for killing. The **Warrnambool Tourist Information
Centre** (☎ 03/5564–7837) can advise you of their presence and direct you to the best observation points.

☼ A highlight in Warrnambool is **Flagstaff Hill Maritime Village,** a re-cre-
ated 19th-century village built around a fort constructed in 1887, during one of the Russian scares that intermittently terrified the colony.
In the village, visit an 1853 lighthouse that's still in use, wander
through the old fort, or board the *Reginald M,* a trading ship from the
South Australian Gulf. ⊠ *Merri and Banyan Sts.,* ☎ *03/5564–7841.*
☞ *$9.50.* ☉ *Daily 9–5.*

The **Wunta Fiesta,** held in February, includes whale-boat races, a ball,
a seafood and wine carnival, and children's activities.

☼ **Lake Pertobe Adventure Playground** is a children's paradise set on 86
acres. Facilities include lakes with children's powerboats, paddleboats,
kayaks, canoes, pleasure boats, and junior sailing craft, as well as a
playground, barbecue facilities, horse trails, and walking tracks. ⊠ *Pertobe Rd., Warrnambool,* ☎ *03/5564–7800.* ☞ *Free.* ☉ *Daily.*

☼ Collect your **Kid's Country Treasure Hunt Guide** kit at the Warrnambool Tourist Information Centre (⊠ 600 Raglan Parade, ☎ 03/5564–
7837). Children who answer the questions on the "treasure map"
(designed to introduce them to Warrnambool and its surroundings) get
a free badge, book, or decal from the Information Centre.

Hopkins Falls, 13 km (8 mi) northeast of Warrnambool, makes for a
pleasant side trip. After parking your car, you can inspect the waterfalls on foot or hire a horse. Ponies are available at **St. Mary's Pony
Farm** (⊠ Wangoom, ☎ 03/5567–1184).

Tower Hill State Game Reserve is a half-hour drive northwest of Warrnambool on an extinct volcano abounding with flora and fauna. Its
Natural History Centre provides extensive background information on
the site. The reserve is an attempt to return part of the land to a native state by introducing local flora and fauna. Spend some time at the
displays and walking around the reserve on its trails. ⊠ *Box 60, Ko-
roit,* ☎ *03/5565–9202.* ☞ *Free.* ☉ *Reserve daily 8–5, Natural History Centre daily 9:30–12:30 and 1:30–4:30.*

Dining and Lodging

$$ ✕ **Mahogany Ship.** Decorated in a loosely nautical theme, this restau-
rant above the Flagstaff Hill Maritime Village has splendid views of
the harbor at Lady Bay and the ocean beyond. Local crayfish (claw-
less lobster) are a specialty; steak and poultry dishes are also available.

Children are served from a separate menu, which includes that traditional Australian favorite, fish-and-chips. The tavern next door serves a basic selection of less expensive meals. ⊠ *Flagstaff Hill Maritime Village, Merri St.,* ☎ *03/5561–1833. AE, DC, MC, V. Closed Mon. No lunch Sat.*

$$ ✕⊞ **Quamby Homestead.** This magnificent century-old homestead is
★ furnished with Australian antiques and is an ideal base from which to explore the Warrnambool area. Guests are accommodated in modern rooms with en suite facilities in former staff quarters, which are set apart from the homestead and surrounded by an English-style garden, where native birdcalls compete with the shrieks of peacocks. The dining room, in the homestead, serves fine country meals, which are available to nonresident guests on weekends. Rates include breakfast and dinner. Children under 12 are not accommodated. ⊠ *Caramut Rd., Woolsthorpe, 26 km (16 mi) north of Warrnambool,* ☎ *03/5569–2395. 7 rooms with bath. MC, V.*

$$ ✕⊞ **Yellangip Country House.** Tucked away in secluded grazing country in western Victoria—well away from Warrnambool itself—this vast turn-of-the-century homestead has outstanding atmosphere, a dash of luxury, and fine country cooking. Guest rooms are plushly decorated with antiques and chintz fabrics, and big bunches of wildflowers. The master bedroom, overlooking the front garden, is recommended. Dinner is available by arrangement; the cooking draws its inspiration from northern Italy. Breakfast is included in the room rate. The house is off the Hamilton Highway, under an hour's drive northeast of Warrnambool, and two hours' drive west of Melbourne. ⊠ *Pura Pura Rd., Darlington, 72 km (45 mi) from Warrnambool,* ☎ *03/5597–9203,* FAX *055/97–9276. 5 rooms with bath. Tennis court. MC, V.*

$ ⊞ **Central Court Motel.** On Princes Highway opposite the Tourist Information Centre, this neat, contemporary two-story motel is just a 10-minute walk from the main shopping center. ⊠ *581 Raglan Parade, Princes Hwy.,* ☎ *03/5562–8555. 36 rooms with bath, 2 suites. Restaurant, pool, baby-sitting. AE, DC, MC, V.*

$ ⊞ **Mid City Motor Inn.** This modern, two-story motel, on Princes Highway, is set in a neatly manicured garden a short distance from the town center. Dinner dances are held here on Saturday night. ⊠ *525 Raglan Parade,* ☎ *03/5562–3866. 60 rooms with bath, 2 suites. Restaurant, bar, room service, pool, baby-sitting. AE, DC, MC, V.*

Outdoor Activities and Sports

BICYCLING

The **Melbourne to Warrnambool Road Race** is a cycling classic held annually on the second Saturday in October. The race starts at 7:15 AM at Port Melbourne and finishes at Raglan Parade in Warrnambool at approximately 2:30 PM.

CAR RACING

The **Grand Annual Sprintcar Classic** (☎ 03/5562–8229) is held at Premier Speedway in Allansford east of Warrnambool during the Australia Day long weekend in late January.

FISHING

Warrnambool and the surrounding district offer great fishing, in rivers and in the surf. A 28-day fishing license costs $10 and is required for fishing the rivers and streams of Victoria. Contact **Warrnambool Shooters and Anglers Shop** (⊠ Liebig St., Warrnambool, ☎ 03/5562–3502) for further information.

GOLF

The **Warrnambool Golf Course** (☎ 03/5562–2108) is a first-class 18-hole course off Younger Street. Club tournaments are held at Easter and in September. Greens fees are $17; buggy and club rental is $10.

Shopping

For crafts and homegrown produce, visit the **Warrnambool Town and Country Crafts Community Market** (✉ Swan Reserve, Raglan Parade), which is held on the second Saturday morning of each month. The Warrnambool **Saturday Market** is held on the first Saturday of each month in the Safeway parking lot.

Port Fairy

291 km (182 mi) west of Melbourne, 29 km (18 mi) west of Warrnambool.

Port Fairy wins the vote of many a Victorian as the state's prettiest village. The second-oldest town in Victoria, it was originally known as Belfast, and there are indeed echoes of Ireland in the landscape and architecture. Founded during the whaling heyday in the 19th century, Port Fairy was once one of the largest ports in Victoria. It was originally a whaling station, with sturdy old bluestone buildings set near the banks of the River Moyne, and the town still thrives as the base for a fishing fleet. More than 50 of the cottages and bluestone buildings in Port Fairy have been classified as landmarks by the National Trust, and few towns repay a leisurely stroll so richly.

The **Historical Society Museum** contains relics from whaling days and from the many ships that have foundered along this coast. ✉ *Old Courthouse, Gipps St., no phone.* 🖃 *$2.* ☉ *Wed. and weekends 2–5.*

Mott's Cottage is a restored limestone-and-timber cottage built by Sam Mott, a member of the whaling crew that discovered the town in the cutter *Fairy.* Light meals are available inside. ✉ *5 Sackville St.,* ☎ *03/9654–4711.* ☉ *Weekdays 10–noon, weekends 2–4.*

Dining and Lodging

$ ✕ **Lunch.** Lunch is open for, well, lunch, as well as brunch and morning and afternoon tea. You might snack on scrambled eggs with smoked salmon, or focaccia with a variety of fillings, or sample more substantial fare such as falafel and *babaganouj* (an eggplant appetizer) with tsatsiki sauce. Ploughman's lunch is on the menu, along with chili con carne and such specialties as a charcuterie plate. With notice, picnic baskets can be prepared. ✉ *20 Bank St.,* ☎ *03/5568–2642. MC, V. BYOB. Closed Mon. and Tues. No dinner.*

$$ ✕🖫 **Dublin House Inn.** This solid stone building was built in 1855 and is furnished in period style. Chef Wendy Ryan concentrates on the freshest local produce, creating dishes that incorporate everything from seafood to free-range chicken, duckling, and local beef. Lobster, crab chowder, and (in winter) game pie are especially recommended. Next door, Ryan's daughter runs a food shop for those who prefer to pick up ingredients for a picnic. The 32-seat dining room is open weekends only, but extra nights are added in summer. Dublin House Inn also has rooms for an overnight stay—functional rather than luxurious, but no less pleasant for their period style. ✉ *57 Bank St.,* ☎ *03/5568–1822. MC, V. BYOB. No lunch; no dinner Sun.–Thurs.*

$ 🖫 **Goble's Mill House.** An imaginative refurbishment of an 1865 flour mill on the banks of the Moyne River transformed the various levels of the mill into five bedrooms and a spacious sitting area, all furnished with antiques. The upper-story loft bedroom is especially appealing, with a balcony overlooking the ever-active river. You can also enjoy a spot of fishing off the Mill House's private jetty. Breakfast is included in the room rate. ⊠ *75 Gipps St.,* ☎ *03/5568–1118. 5 rooms with bath. AE, MC, V.*

Hamilton

290 km (181 mi) west of Melbourne, 82 km (50 mi) north of Port Fairy, 97 km (61 mi) southeast of Halls Gap at Grampians National Park.

One of western Victoria's principal inland cities, Hamilton is set in rich grazing country. It has a lovely botanical garden and a lake made from damming the Grange Burn. There is a beach on the lake, and the water is full of trout. The town is the original seat of the Ansett family (of Down Under airline fame), and there is evidence of their fortune in and around town. Also, note that you can see the Grampians Mountains to the north from Hamilton, and you might consider heeding their call and going the 100-odd km (60-odd mi) into their forested, craggy surround, **Grampians National Park** (☞ *below*).

The **Hamilton Art Gallery**'s highly respected collection of watercolors, engravings, pottery, antique silver, and porcelain from the Mediterranean is well worth a visit. ⊠ *Brown St.,* ☎ *03/5573–0460.* ▣ *Donations accepted.* ⊙ *Tues.–Fri. 10–5, Sat. 10–noon and 2–5, Sun. 2–5.*

Dining

$$ ✕ **Stirring Pot.** Located in a converted hillside mansion, this restaurant–art gallery is decorated in turn-of-the-century style. The international cuisine concentrates on huge, juicy steaks, beef with hot pepper sauce, rack of lamb, and local seafood. A two-course meal is available at a very reasonable price. As an alternative to the four cozy dining rooms inside the house, guests can dine in the garden on warm evenings. ⊠ *212 Coleraine Rd.,* ☎ *03/5572–2535. AE, DC, MC, V. BYOB. Closed Sun. and Mon. No lunch.*

West Coast Region A to Z

Arriving and Departing

BY CAR

Take the Princes Highway west from Melbourne to Geelong. From here, take the Torquay Road south to Torquay, where you will connect with the Great Ocean Road. For an alternative inland route to Warrnambool, much quicker but vastly less interesting, take the Princes Highway.

BY TRAIN

The West Coast railway operates daily services between Melbourne and Warrnambool (☎ 03/5226–6500).

Getting Around

BY CAR

Driving is the most convenient way to see the region, and the only way to really enjoy the Great Ocean Road. Distances are considerable, and the going may be slow on the most scenic routes, especially during the summer holiday period.

BY TRAIN

Geelong is fed by small, fast, and frequent Sprinter trains from Melbourne, and the West Coast Railway, a newly formed private company, serves points farther west. Although the train provides a restful means of getting to main centers, it runs inland and doesn't provide the extraordinary views you can see by car.

Contacts and Resources

EMERGENCIES

Ambulance, fire brigade, and **police.** ☎ *000.*

GUIDED TOURS

AAT Kings (☎ 03/9663–3377) has a choice of one- or two-night tours of the Great Ocean Road from Melbourne. The one-day tour costs $83. A choice of accommodations is available on the two-day tour, and the price varies from $194 to $225.

The Wayward Bus (☎ 1800/88–2823) is a minibus that takes three days to make a meandering journey from Melbourne to Adelaide via the Great Ocean Road, Mount Gambier, and the Coorong, with overnight stops at Port Fairy and Beachport. Aimed primarily at backpackers, the tour is enjoyable, informative, inexpensive, and highly recommended. Passengers can leave the bus at either overnight stop and catch the following bus. The tours depart Melbourne on Tuesday and Saturday, more frequently in summer. The cost is $135 per person, including picnic lunches, but excluding accommodations.

VISITOR INFORMATION

Geelong Tourist Information Centre. ⊠ *Moorabool St., Geelong,* ☎ *1800/ 62–0888.* ☉ *Daily 9–5.*
Port Fairy Tourist Information Centre. ⊠ *Bank St., Port Fairy,* ☎ *03/ 5568–2682.* ☉ *Weekdays 10–4, weekends 10–12:30 and 1:30–4.*
Warrnambool Tourist Information Centre. ⊠ *600 Raglan Parade,* ☎ *03/5564–7837.* ☉ *Weekdays 9–5, weekends 10–4.*

GRAMPIANS NATIONAL PARK

★ The **Grampians** combine stunning mountain scenery, abundant native wildlife, and a variety of invigorating outdoor activities. Close to the western border of Victoria, this 412,000-acre region of sharp sandstone peaks was forced up from an ancient seabed, sculpted by eons of wind and rain, then carpeted with a fantastic array of wildflowers. More than 900 wildflower species, 200 species of birds, and 35 species of native mammals populate the park.

"Gariwerd" is the Aboriginal name for this area. The abundant food supply made these ranges a natural refuge for Aboriginal groups. More than a hundred caves have been found daubed with their painting, which are relatively simpler than the complex iconography of the Arnhem Land or Western Desert Aboriginal people.

The park has more than 160 km (100 mi) of walking trails, from short, easy tracks to challenging overnight expeditions through rugged terrain. For anything more than a short stroll, water and warm, waterproof clothing is a must. Some of the best short walks are the 2½-hour climb to the summit of Mt. William, the 2½-hour hike to the Pinnacle from the Wonderland Turntable (which leads past fantastic rock formations to a magnificent view), and the two-hour walk to MacKenzie Falls from Zumstein. In recent years, Grampians National Park has become popular with rock climbers, who focus their activities on Mt. Arapiles.

There are, as well, spectacular drives through the park. The circuit of the Wonderland Range from Halls Gap, the 15-km (8-mi) drive from Halls Gap to Zumstein via the Mount Victory Road, and the drive between Halls Gap and Dunkeld, at the southern entrance to the park, are highly recommended.

The gateway to the Grampians is Halls Gap, a small, busy town where koalas can sometimes be found snoozing in the trees and kangaroos graze on the outskirts in the evening. The best time to visit the park is between October and December, when wildflowers are in bloom, the weather is mild, and summer crowds have yet to arrive.

Don't miss the **Brambuk Cultural Centre** (⊠ Dunkeld Rd, Halls Gap. ☎ 03/5356–4452), which provides a living history of Aboriginal culture in this part of Victoria.

Dining and Lodging

The main base for the national park is Halls Gap, which offers a choice of motels, guest houses, host farms, and caravan parks. Sixteen camping grounds exist within the national park. The fee is $7.50 per site for up to six people, and the rule is first come, first served. Pick up a permit at the Visitor Centre (☞ *below*).

$–$$ ✕ **Kookaburra.** At what is currently the best local bet for food, try the venison, duckling, veal, or pork and finish with a traditional pudding. ⊠ *Grampians Rd., Halls Gap,* ☎ *03/5356–4222. AE, MC, V.*

$$ ⊞ **Glenisla Homestead.** For an atmospheric alternative to motel accommodation, this 1842 B&B on the western side of the national park is highly recommended. ⊠ *Off Hamilton-Horsham Rd., Cavendish,* ☎ *03/5380–1532.*

Arriving and Departing

BY CAR

Halls Gap is reached via Ballarat and Ararat on the Western Highway (Hwy. 8). The town is 260 km (160 mi) northwest of Melbourne, 97 km (61 mi) northeast of Hamilton, 146 km (91 mi) west of Ballarat.

Guided Tours

Gray Line (☎ 03/9663–4455) operates a one-day tour of the Grampians ($79) that departs Melbourne at 8:50 AM Monday and Saturday.

Visitor Information

Grampians National Park Visitor Centre. ⊠ Dunkeld Rd., Halls Gap, VIC 3381, ☎ 03/5356–4381.

Department of Conservation and Natural Resources. ⊠ 240 Victoria Parade, East Melbourne, ☎ 03/9412–4011.

GOLD COUNTRY

Victoria was changed forever in the mid-1850s by the discovery of gold in the center of the state. Fantastic news of gold deposits caused immigrants from every corner of the world to pour into Victoria to seek their fortunes as "diggers"—a name that has become synonymous with Australians ever since. Few miners became wealthy from their search, however—the real money was made by those supplying goods and services to the thousands who had succumbed to gold fever.

Gold towns that sprang up like mushrooms to accommodate these fortune seekers prospered until the gold rush receded, when they became ghost towns or turned to agriculture to survive. Today, Victoria's gold is again being mined in limited quantities, but these historic old towns remain interesting relics of Australia's past.

If you are planning to go to Grampians National Park (☞ *above*), its principal service town of Halls Gap is some 150 km (93 mi) west of Ballarat. And from Bendigo at the end of this section, Echuca on the Murray River (☞ *below*) is an easy 90-km (55-mi) drive north.

Ballarat

106 km (66 mi) northwest of Melbourne, 146 km (91 mi) east of Grampians National Park.

In the local Aboriginal language, the name Ballarat means "resting place," since a plentiful supply of food was to be found around Lake Wendouree, to the north of the present township. The town flourished when gold was discovered here in 1851. This was not Australia's first major gold strike. That honor belongs to Bathurst, in western New South Wales, but Victoria in 1851 *was* El Dorado; 90% of the gold mined in Australia during the boom years of the 19th century came from Victoria. The biggest finds were at Ballarat and then Bendigo, and the Ballarat diggings proved to be among the richest alluvial goldfields in the world. In 1854, Ballarat was the scene of the battle of the Eureka Stockade, a skirmish that took place between miners and authorities, primarily over the extortionate gold license fees that miners were forced to pay. More than 20 men died in the battle, the only time that Australians have taken up arms in open rebellion against their government.

Montrose Cottage and Eureka Museum of Social History. Built in 1856 by a Scottish miner, Montrose Cottage was the first bluestone house in Ballarat. Inside you can see furniture and handwork of the period. Adjoining the cottage is a museum building with an impressive display of artifacts from Ballarat's gold-mining days and an excellent display on the women of Eureka. The tours conducted by Laurel Johnson, the owner of the museum, are lively and informative. ⊠ *111 Eureka St.,* ☎ *03/5332–2554.* ⊡ *$4.50.* ☉ *Daily 9:30–5.*

NEED A BREAK?
Priscilla's Cottage makes the most of its history with a cozy, cloistered atmosphere and lace cloths draped over its tables. The menu offers a choice of inexpensive light meals, such as ploughman's lunch, Devonshire tea, soups, and salads. ⊠ *109 Eureka St.,* ☎ *03/5331–5705. Closed Mon. May–Oct.*

The prosperity of the gold rush left Ballarat well endowed with handsome buildings, and the short stretch of **Lydiard Street** around Sturt has a number of notable examples.

One of the historic edifices of Lydiard Street is the **Ballarat Fine Arts Gallery,** which contains paintings by several famous Australian painters, including Russell Drysdale, Sidney Nolan, and Fred Williams. Its most impressive exhibit is the tattered remains of the original Southern Cross flag that was flown defiantly by the rebels at the Eureka Stockade. Many Australians advocate the adoption of the Southern Cross in preference to the present Australian flag, which features the Union Jack, regarded as an anachronistic symbol of the country's link with Great Britain. ⊠ *40 Lydiard St.,* ☎ *03/5331–5622.* ⊡ *Free.* ☉ *Tues.–Fri. 10:30–4:30, weekends 12:30–4:30.*

On the shores of Lake Wendouree, Ballarat's **Botanic Gardens** are identifiable by the brilliant blooms of the flower gardens and classical statuary. At the rear of the gardens, the Begonia House is the focus of events during the town's Begonia Festival, held annually in February or March. Many of the garden's trees are on the National Trust's Register of Significant Trees, including swamp cypress, California redwood, and a druid's oak. Busts on the Avenue of the Prime Ministers and 19th-century Italian marble sculpture provide interesting statuary. ⊠ *Wendouree Parade, no phone.* ⊡ *Free.*

☙ **Sovereign Hill Historical Park** is built on the site of the Sovereign Hill Quartz Mining Company's mines. This is an authentic re-creation of life, work, and play on the gold diggings at Ballarat following the discovery of gold here in 1851. On the lowest part of the site are the tent camp and diggings, which were built in the first months of the gold rush, when gold was panned from creeks or dug from the earth with picks and shovels. On Main Street, running uphill from the diggings, are the shops, workshops, and public buildings that existed on the site between 1854 and 1861. Notice the New York Hotel and the T. Murphy California Tentmaker shop, a reminder that many of the miners came from the United States. At the top of the hill lies the third stage of Sovereign Hill—the mine and the pithead equipment. When the surface gold gave out, miners were forced to dig along the ancient watercourses that lay deep underground, and this was where the real treasure lay. It was in such a mine on the Ballarat goldfields that the Welcome Nugget was discovered in 1858 by a group of Cornish miners. At today's prices, it would be worth just over a million dollars.

Near the entrance to the complex is the **Voyage to Discovery,** an indoor museum designed to provide an overview of society and the world at large at the time of the gold rush. The museum is excellent, with imaginative dioramas and computer terminals that encourage you to become an active participant in the process of discovery of gold.

Across Bradshaw Street from the historical park is the **Gold Museum,** which displays an extensive collection of nuggets from the Ballarat diggings as well as some examples of finished gold in the form of jewelry.

Between October and May, Sovereign Hill is the backdrop for **Blood on the Southern Cross,** a 90-minute sound-and-light spectacular that focuses on the Eureka uprising. The story is told with passion and dramatic technical effects, although the sheer wealth of historical detail clouds the story line. The climax of the show is the battle of the Eureka Stockade. Be prepared for chilly nights, even in midsummer. Numbers are limited and advance bookings are recommended. ⊠ *Sovereign Hill Park, Bradshaw St.,* ☎ *03/5331–1944.* ☞ *$17.50, including Gold Museum; Blood on the Southern Cross $20.50; Sovereign Hill and Blood on the Southern Cross $36.* ☉ *Park daily 9:30–5; Gold Museum Sun.–Fri. 10–5:30, Sat. 12:30–5:30; Blood on the Southern Cross 2 shows Mon.–Sat. in summer, 1 Mon.–Sat. fall–spring. Closed July 31–Aug. 18.*

🐨 **Ballarat Wildlife and Reptile Park.** This bushland park is home to native Australian wildlife from a wide range of habitats. Animals include saltwater crocodiles, snakes, lizards, wombats, echidnas, and kangaroos. A koala tour takes place daily at 11. The park also has a café, and barbecue and picnic areas. ⊠ *Fussel and York Sts., East Ballarat,* ☎ *03/5333–5933.* ☞ *$9.* ☉ *Daily 9–5:30.*

Dining and Lodging

$$$ ✕ **Alibis.** Inside a historic bluestone building, this elegant restaurant
★   takes its culinary cues from a worldwide list of fashionable cuisines. Selections from the menu include prawns coated with garlic and coriander; ravioli filled with minced chicken, basil, and leeks; and Middle Eastern–style rack of lamb served in yogurt. ⊠ *10 Camp St., Ballarat,* ☎ *03/5331–6680. MC, V. Closed Sun. and Mon. No lunch.*

$$ ✕ **Dyer's Steak Stable.** Set in a former hotel stable, this restaurant relies on a simple formula of robust food, fine wine, and a welcoming atmosphere. Game dishes and a range of steaks with various sauces are the house specialties. ⊠ *Little Bridge St., Ballarat,* ☎ *03/5331–2850. AE, DC, MC, V. Closed Sun. No lunch Sat.*

$$ ✕ **Porter's.** Informal dining with a touch of class and reasonable prices are the billings of this onetime corner pub with an Art Deco overlay.

The changing menu draws from a variety of culinary styles to provide something for every appetite, at any time of the day. From Thursday through Saturday evenings the restaurant has live entertainment, usually a vocalist with piano accompaniment. Service is friendly and professional, and the wine list is a showcase of the best of central Victoria. ⊠ *Mair and Peel Sts., Ballarat,* ☎ *03/5331–4320. AE, DC, MC, V. Closed Sun. No lunch Sat. or Mon.*

$$–$$$ ✕⚏ Ansonia. Built in the 1870s as professional offices, the Ansonia
★   is now an excellent boutique hotel and restaurant, having been rescued from oblivion by the current owners, who refurbished a derelict shell. The restaurant is open from 7 AM to late, featuring a sumptuous breakfast, all-day snacks, lunch, and dinner. The fare is eclectic—Malay beef curry sits alongside Caesar salad and steaks. There are four different styles of accommodation, from two-room apartments to studios, all of which are beautifully furnished and appointed. ⊠ *32 Lydiard St. South, Ballarat,* ☎ *03/5332–4678,* ⅢⅩ *03/5332–4698. 20 rooms with bath. Restaurant. AE, DC, MC, V.*

$–$$ ⚏ Ravenswood. Tucked away behind a garden brimming with peach trees, pussy willows, fuchsias, and climbing roses, this three-bedroom timber cottage is ideal for anyone looking for family-size accommodation with kitchen facilities. The house has been decorated with contemporary furniture, carpeting, and chintz fabrics to a high standard of comfort. The cottage is a little less than 1½ km (1 mi) from the center of Ballarat. Supplies for breakfast are provided. ⊠ *Private Box 1360, Ballarat Mail Centre, 404 Havelock St., 3354,* ☎ *03/5332–8296,* ⅢⅩ *03/5331–3358. 1 cottage with bath. No credit cards.*

Golf

Ballarat Golf Club (⊠ Sturt St., West Ballarat, ☎ 03/5334–1023). Greens fees are $13; call the pro shop (☎ 053/34–1573) for bookings. Clubs are available for rent.

Shopping

The **Gold Museum** (☎ 03/5331–1944) and **Sovereign Hill** (☎ 03/5331–1944) in Ballarat have extensive souvenir shops.

Daylesford and Hepburn Springs

109 km (68 mi) northwest of Melbourne, 45 km (28 mi) northeast of Ballarat.

Nestled in the slopes of the Great Dividing Range, Daylesford and its nearby twin, Hepburn Springs, constitute the spa capital of Australia. The water table here is naturally aerated with carbon dioxide and rich in soluble mineral salts. This concentration of natural springs was first noted during the gold rush, and a spa was established at Hepburn Springs in 1875, at the time when spa resorts were fashionable in Europe. After a long decline, this spa has been revived in a 90s, health-conscious style.

The main attraction is the **Hepburn Springs Spa Centre.** This bright, modern complex offers a variety of mineral baths and treatments, including communal spa pools, private aerospa baths, massages, facials, saunas, and float tanks. ⊠ *Main Rd., Mineral Springs Reserve,* ☎ *03/ 5348–2034.* ⚏ *Relaxation pool $9 weekends, $8 weekdays; single aerospa bath $19 weekends, $17 weekdays; double aerospa bath $28 weekends, $26 weekdays; float tank $45 weekends, $25 per hr weekdays; 45-min massage $42 weekdays, $45 weekends; ½-day pass $22 weekends, $17 weekdays.* ☉ *Daily 10–8.*

Above the Hepburn Springs Spa Centre, a path winds through the **Mineral Springs Reserve** past a series of mineral springs, each with a slightly different chemical composition—and a significantly different taste. Any empty bottles you have can be filled free of charge with the mineral water of your choice.

Perched on a hillside overlooking Daylesford, the **Convent Gallery** is a former nunnery that has been restored to its lovely Victorian state. It displays contemporary Australian pottery, glassware, jewelry, sculpture, and prints, all for sale. At the front of the gallery is **Bad Habits**, a sunny café that serves light lunches and snacks. ⊠ *Daly St.,* ☎ *03/ 5348–3211.* 🖅 *$3.* ⊙ *Daily 10–6.*

Dining and Lodging

$$–$$$ ✕🏨 **Lake House Restaurant.** Consistently rated one of the outstand-
★ ing restaurants of central Victoria, this rambling lakeside pavilion brings a touch of glamour to spa country. Summer main courses on the seasonal menu might include panfried tuna steak in a pepper crust with grilled peppers, and a selection of imaginative Asian-accented and vegetarian dishes—all presented with style and imagination. Tables on the deck are especially recommended for lunch on a warm day. The wine list features some of the finest vintages of the surrounding vineyards. Guest rooms in the lodge have a breezy, contemporary feel. Those at the front open to a terrace and better views, but slightly less privacy, than those at the back, which are screened from neighboring rooms by rose-entwined trellises. Children are not accommodated on weekends. Breakfast is included in the room rate. ⊠ *King St., Daylesford,* ☎ *03/5348–3329,* ℻ *03/5448–3995. 11 rooms with bath. Restaurant, bar, pool. AE, MC, V.*

$$ ✕🏨 **Dudley House.** On Hepburn Springs's main street, it's hard to miss this timber Federation classic—similar to the Queen Anne style in England and the United States—in cream and maroon behind a neat hedge and picket gate. The house was painstakingly restored and, with antique furnishings and cozy atmosphere, offers comfort and romance. The white room at the front and the blue room at the rear are the ones to ask for. The town's spa baths are within walking distance. Neither smoking nor children under 16 are allowed; dinner is available by arrangement. Rates include breakfast. ⊠ *101 Main St., Hepburn Springs,* ☎ *03/5348–3033. 4 rooms, 1 with bath, 3 with shower. No credit cards.*

$$ 🏨 **Holcombe Homestead.** This is country living at its aristocratic best: a century-old farmhouse that is one of the architectural glories of rural Victoria, complete with kangaroos, kookaburras, and a trout stream. The house has been furnished in keeping with its Victorian character, and to preserve its architectural integrity, guests share one bathroom. Those who arrive midweek often have the entire house to themselves. Guests can arrange to cook their own meals, and the owners, who live in a neighboring house, will prepare box lunches and dinner on request. Breakfast is included in the room rate. ⊠ *RMB 3638, Glenyon, Holcombe Rd., 3461, 15 km (9 mi) from Daylesford,* ☎ *03/5348–7514. 3 rooms share bath. Tennis court, fishing, mountain bikes. No credit cards.*

Castlemaine

119 km (74 mi) northwest of Melbourne, 38 km (23 mi) north of Daylesford.

Castlemaine is another gold-mining town, yet the gold here was mostly found on the surface. Lacking the deeper reef gold where the real riches lay, the town never reached the prosperity of Ballarat or Bendigo, as is evidenced by its comparatively modest public buildings.

Castlemaine Market, built in 1862 to resemble an ancient Roman basilica, is an exception among the town's generally unadorned public buildings. The statue on top of the building is Ceres, Roman goddess of the harvest.

Buda House is a tribute to the diversity of talents drawn to the gold rush in the middle of the past century. Built in 1861, it was purchased two years later by Ernest Liviny, a Hungarian jeweler who established a business on the Castlemaine goldfields. It was the last of his six daughters, Hilda, who left the house and its entire contents to the state when she died in 1981.

Buda House is simple, essentially, yet it shows an Eastern European love of culture. Twentieth-century woodcuts in the hall are especially fine, and the work of several important artists is displayed. Look for prints by Margaret Preston, whose native flowers of the 1920s show a strong, stylized design sense. The house contains a number of Ernest Leviny's own designs, as well as photographs, painting, sculpture, and embroidery created by his industrious and talented daughters. The gardens are delightful, with a fresh discovery at every turn. ⊠ *42 Hunter St.,* ☎ *03/5472–1032.* ⌸ *$5.* ☉ *Daily 9:30–5.*

Maldon

137 km (85 mi) northwest of Melbourne, 16 km (10 mi) northwest of Castlemaine.

Relative isolation has preserved Maldon, a former mining town, almost intact, and today the entire main street is a magnificent example of vernacular goldfields architecture. (Look for bullnose roofing over verandas, a feature now back in architectural vogue.) Maldon's charm has become a marketable commodity—now the town is busy with tourists and thick with tea shops and antiques sellers. Its atmosphere is best absorbed in a short stroll along the main street.

Three km (2 mi) south of Maldon is **Carman's Tunnel,** a gold mine that has remained unaltered since it closed in 1884. The mine, which can be seen only on a candlelight tour, offers fascinating insight into the ingenious techniques used by early gold miners. The 1,870-ft tunnel is dry, clean, and spacious, and the tour is suitable for all ages. ⊠ *Parkin's Reef Rd.,* ☎ *03/5475–2453.* ⌸ *$2.50.* ☉ *Tour weekends 1:30–4.*

☙ **Castlemaine & Maldon Railway.** This 45-minute loop aboard a historic steam train winds through forests of eucalyptus and wattle that are spectacular in spring. ⊠ *Maldon,* ☎ *03/5475–2966.* ⌸ *$9.* ☉ *Departs Maldon Station Mar.–Jan., Sun. at 12:30, 2, and 3.30 (daily Dec. 26–Jan. 12).*

Bendigo

150 km (93 mi) northwest of Melbourne, 36 km (22 mi) northeast of Maldon, 92 km (58 mi) south of Ecucha on the Murray River.

Gold was discovered in Bendigo district in 1851, and the boom lasted well into the 1880s. The city's magnificent public buildings bear witness to the richness of its mines. Today Bendigo is a bustling, enterprising small city—not as relaxing as other goldfields towns, but its architecture is noteworthy. Most of Bendigo's distinguished buildings are arranged on either side of **Pall Mall** in the city center. These include the **Shamrock Hotel, General Post Office,** and **Law Courts,** all majestic examples of late-Victorian architecture.

Despite its unprepossessing exterior, the **Bendigo Art Gallery** houses a notable collection of contemporary Australian painting, including the work of Jeffrey Smart, Lloyd Rees, and Clifton Pugh. Pugh once owned a remote outback pub infamous for its walls daubed with his own pornographic cartoons. The gallery also houses some significant 19th-century French Realist and Impressionist works, bequeathed by a local surgeon. ⊠ *42 View St.,* ☎ *03/5443–4991.* ⊞ *Free.* ⊙ *Weekdays 10– 5, weekends 2–5.*

The 1,665-ft mine shaft of the **Central Deborah Gold-Mine** yielded almost a ton of gold before it closed in 1954. For an experience of life underground, take a guided tour of the mine. An elevator descends 200 ft below ground level. ⊠ *Violet St.,* ☎ *03/5443–8322.* ⊞ *$12.50. Combined entry with Vintage Talking Tram $18.* ⊙ *Daily 9:30–5.*

Joss House (Temple of Worship) was built in gold rush days by Chinese miners on the outskirts of the city. No longer used for sacred purposes, the temple was built of handmade bricks and painted a brilliant red. Joss House is a reminder of the Chinese presence in the Victorian goldfields. At the height of the boom in the 1850s and '60s, about a quarter of the miners were Chinese. These men were usually dispatched from villages on the Chinese mainland, and they were expected to work hard and return as quickly as possible to their villages with their fortunes intact. Very few Chinese women ever accompanied the men, and apart from their graveyards and temples, there is little evidence of any Chinese presence in the goldfields. The Chinese were scrupulously law-abiding, ingenious, and hard-working—qualities that did not always endear them to other miners—and anti-Chinese riots were common. In some areas, an Office of the Chinese Protector was established to safeguard their interests. ⊠ *Finn St., Emu Point,* ☎ *03/5442–1685.* ⊞ *$3.* ⊙ *Daily 10–5.*

The superb **Golden Dragon Museum** evokes the Chinese community's role in Bendigo life, past and present. Its centerpieces are the century-old Loong imperial ceremonial dragon and the Sun Loong dragon, which, at more than 106 yards in length, is said to be the world's longest. When carried in procession, it requires 52 carriers and 52 relievers—the head alone weighs 64 pounds. Also on display are other ceremonial objects, costumes, and historic artifacts. ⊠ *5–9 Bridge St.,* ☎ *03/5441–5011.* ⊞ *$6.* ⊙ *Daily 9:30–5.*

A good introduction to Bendigo is a tour aboard the **Vintage Talking Tram,** which includes a taped commentary on the town's history. The tram departs on its 8-km (5-mi) circuit every hour on the half hour between 9:30 and 3:30 from the ☞ **Central Deborah Gold-Mine.** You can get off and on at any stop. ⊠ *Violet St.,* ⊞ *$7, combined tram ride and Central Deborah Gold-Mine $18.*

Dining and Lodging

$$ ✕ **Bazzani.** This new restaurant fuses a mainly Italian menu with Asian influences. Try carrot soup with coconut milk and chili, or beef fillet with spiced butter. Desserts are excellent, such as the chocolate marquise with black Sambuca jelly and plum sauce. There is a good selection of local and Pyrenées wines, all very well priced. There are some lighter alternatives on the lunch menu, and a café for coffee and snacks. ⊠ *Howard Place, Bendigo.* ☎ *03/5441–3777. AE, DC, MC, V. No lunch Sat.*

$$ ✕ **Metropolitan.** In a classic Australian country pub with wide verandas and distinctive stained-glass windows, this restaurant offers a choice of all-day dining in the brasserie, against a background of unobtrusive rock music, or in the more refined atmosphere of the Grill-

room. Both have an identical menu that features pasta dishes, sand-wiches, salads, steaks, and seafood. Children have their own special menu. ⊠ *244 Hargreaves St., Bendigo,* ☎ *03/5443–4916. Reservations not accepted. AE, DC, MC, V.*

$$ 🏠 **Nanga Gnulle.** On a hillside on the outskirts of Bendigo, Rob and Peg Green have created a haven in mud brick and timber, surrounded by a superb garden that does justice to their name. Pronounced "nanga nully," the name means "small stream" in the local Aboriginal language. The atmosphere is extremely relaxing and friendly, and the decor is warm, with lots of wood furniture and details and natural fabrics. The larger of the two rooms is on the lower part of the contemporary split-level house. Smoking and children under 16 are not allowed inside. Breakfast is included in the room rate. ⊠ *40 Harley St.,* ☎ *03/5443–7891,* FAX *03/5443–3397. 2 rooms with bath. MC, V.*

$$ 🏠 **Shamrock Hotel.** This landmark Victorian hotel at the city center offers a choice of accommodation, from simple, traditional pub rooms without en suite facilities to large suites. If you're looking for luxury, ask for the Amy Castles Suite, which comes at a very reasonable price. Rooms are spacious and well maintained, but furnishings are dowdy and strictly functional. The hotel's central location and character are the real drawing cards. ⊠ *Pall Mall and Williamson Sts.,* ☎ *03/54/3–0333. 24 rooms, most with bath. 2 restaurants, 3 bars. AE, DC, MC, V.*

Shopping
Bendigo Mohair Farm (⊠ Maryborough Rd., Lockwood, ☎ 03/5435–3341) is a working Angora-goat stud farm. The showroom displays hand-knit sweaters, mohair rugs, scarves, hats, ties, and toys for purchase. The farm also has barbecue and picnic facilities.

Sports
GOLF
Bendigo Golf Club (⊠ Golf Links Rd., Epsom, ☎ 03/5448–4206). Greens fees are $10; rent clubs for $10 per round.

TENNIS
Bendigo Indoor Grass Tennis. The five artificial grass courts here are open daily. ⊠ *Edwards Rd., Bendigo,* ☎ *03/5442–2411.* 🎾 *$12 per hr 9–4, $18 per hr 5–midnight.* ☉ *Daily approximately 9* AM*–midnight.*

En Route From Bendigo, Ecucha and the Murray River region are just under 100 km (62 mi) away. ☞ **Northeast Wineries and Murray River,** *below.*

Gold Country A to Z

Arriving and Departing
BY CAR
To reach Bendigo, take the Calder Highway northwest from Melbourne; for Ballarat, take the Western Highway. The mineral springs region and Maldon lie neatly between the two main cities.

BY TRAIN
Good rail service to Ballarat or Bendigo is available. For timetables and rates, contact **V-Line** (☎ 03/9619–3333) or the **Royal Automobile Club of Victoria** (☎ 03/9790–3333).

Getting Around
BY CAR
For leisurely exploration of the goldfields region, a car is essential. Although public transport serves the main centers adequately, access to

smaller towns is less assured, and even in the bigger towns, attractions tend to be widely dispersed.

BY TRAIN

If you want to visit only Ballarat or Bendigo, rail services from Melbourne are frequent and efficient, but there are no connections between the two Gold Country centers or to any of the smaller towns.

Contacts and Resources

EMERGENCIES

Ambulance, fire brigade, and **police.** ☎ *000.*

GUIDED TOURS

Operators who cover this area include **Gray Line** (☎ 03/9663–4455), **Australian Pacific Tours** (☎ 13–1304), and **AAT Kings** (☎ 03/9663–3377); all three depart from 184 Swanston Street Walk in Melbourne.

VISITOR INFORMATION

Ballarat Tourist Information Centre. ⊠ *39 Sturt St., Ballarat,* ☎ *03/5332–2694.* ⊙ *Weekdays 9–5, weekends 10–4.*
Bendigo Tourist Information Centre. ⊠ *26 High St. [Calder Hwy.], Kangaroo Flat,* ☎ *1800/81–3153.* ⊙ *Daily 9–5.*
Daylesford Tourist Information Centre. ⊠ *49 Vincent St., Daylesford,* ☎ *03/5348–1339.* ⊙ *Daily 10–4.*

MURRAY RIVER REGION

From its birthplace on the slopes of the Great Dividing Range in southern New South Wales, the Mighty Murray winds 2,574 km (1,609 mi) in a southwesterly course before it empties into Lake Alexandrina, south of Adelaide. On the driest inhabited continent on earth, such a river, the country's largest, assumes great importance. Irrigation schemes that tap the river water have transformed its thirsty surroundings into a garden of grapevines and citrus fruits.

Once prone to flooding and droughts, the river has been laddered with dams that control the floodwaters and form reservoirs for irrigation. The lakes created in the process have become sanctuaries for native birds. In the pre-railroad age of canals, the Murray was an artery for inland cargoes of wool and wheat, and old wharves in such ports as Echuca bear witness to the bustling and colorful riverboat era.

Victoria, Tasmania, New South Wales, and Western Australia were planted with vines during the 1830s, fixing roots for an industry that has earned its international repute. One of the earliest sponsors of Victorian viticulture was Charles LaTrobe, the first Victorian governor. LaTrobe had lived at Neuchâtel in Switzerland and married the daughter of the Swiss Counsellor of State. As a result of his contacts, several Swiss wine makers emigrated to Australia and developed some of the earliest Victorian vineyards in the Yarra Valley, east of Melbourne.

Digging for gold was a thirst-producing business, and the gold rushes stimulated the birth of an industry. By 1890 well over half the total Australian production of wine came from Victoria. But just as it devastated the vineyards of France, the strain of tiny plant lice, phylloxera, arrived from Europe and wreaked havoc in Victoria. In the absence of wine, Australians turned to beer, and not until the 1960s did wine regain national prominence as a drink for the masses. Although most wine specialists predict that Victoria will never recover its preeminence in the Australian viticulture, high-quality grapes are grown in several parts of the state, each with its own distinction. The area is best known for muscat, tokay, and port. The Rutherglen area in the northeast produces the finest fortified wine in the country, and anyone who enjoys the after-dinner "stickies" is in for a treat when touring this area.

All wineries in this region have tasting rooms where you are welcome to sample before you buy. However, each of them produces several wines, and mouthfuls of the whole range will leave your taste buds confused and jaded. Before you begin, indicate your general preference to the sales staff and allow them to guide you.

Southeast of Rutherglen, the town of Beechworth is a fine example of a goldfields town. In addition to enjoying historical credentials, Beechworth has a choice of charming guest houses. The town is also a logical point from which to detour to Alpine National Park (☞ *below*), where days' worth of bush-walking trails wind through Victoria's highest peaks.

The Murray River region covered in this section stretches some 460 km (290 mi) between Rutherglen in the northeast to Mildura in the northwest. So short of devoting a week or more to the area, it's best to pick one or two sections to explore. A tour of the Rutherglen wineries and the Beechworth locale makes a convenient break on the drive between Sydney and Melbourne on the Hume Freeway (Rte. 31). You could take this all in in a single day, though more time would be rewarded. If you'd rather start in Echuca, Melbourne—as well as the gold country town of Bendigo—are good jumping-off points. West of Echuca, long stretches of open country separate interesting locales— the way to go if you're headed on to Adelaide. (Although the Murray River Valley Highway parallels the course of the river, it is only by making a detour that you will actually glimpse the brown river, lined with river red gums.)

Beechworth

271 km (169 mi) northeast of Melbourne, 96 km (60 mi) from Alpine National Park.

One of the prettiest towns in Victoria, Beechworth flourished during the gold rush. When gold ran out, Beechworth was left with all the apparatus of prosperity—fine Victorian banks, imposing public buildings, breweries, parks, prisons, and hotels wrapped in wrought iron—but with scarcely two nuggets to rub together. However, poverty preserved the town from such modern amenities as aluminum window frames, and many historic treasures that might have been destroyed in the name of progress have been restored and brought back to life.

A stroll along **Ford Street** is the best way to absorb the character of the town. You pass several notable buildings—among them **Tanswell's Commercial Hotel** and the **government buildings,** note the jail—antiques shops, and the sequoia trees in **Town Hall Gardens.** Much of Beechworth's architecture is made of the honey-color granite found outside of town.

This is also Kelly country. Australia's favorite outlaw, **Ned Kelly,** once rode these hills, and Beechworth's most conspicuous public building is the handsome sandstone jail where Kelly was held before he was taken to Melbourne to be tried and hanged.

The **Burke Museum** takes its name from Robert Burke, who with William Wills became one of the first white explorers to cross Australia from south to north, in 1861. Burke was superintendent of police in Beechworth between 1856 and 1859. Paradoxically but not surprisingly, the small area and few mementos dedicated to Burke are overshadowed by the **Ned Kelly** exhibits, which include letters, photographs, and memorabilia that give genuine insight into the man and his misdeeds. Following the shooting of the police at Stringybark Creek, Kelly and his gang were seen in the hills 5 km (3 mi) from Beechworth. The man who set out to report their whereabouts had to pass six pubs along the way, and he arrived at Beechworth so drunk that the police refused to believe his story and locked him up. A day later, the man sobered up, and the police realized their mistake and mounted a raid—but too late. The museum also displays a reconstructed streetscape of Beechworth in the 1880s. ⊠ *Loch St.,* ☎ *03/5728–1420.* ⊠ *$4; combined ticket to museum, Carriage Museum, and Powder Magazine $6.50.* ⊙ *Daily 10:30–3:30.*

The **Carriage Museum** is in a corrugated-iron building that was once a stable. Displays range from simple farm carts and buggies to Cobb & Co. stagecoaches, some of which were modeled on U.S. designs. ⊠ *Railway Ave.* ⊠ *$1.50; combined ticket to museum, Carriage Museum, and Powder Magazine $6.50.* ⊙ *Daily 10:30–12:30 and 1:30–4:30.*

OFF THE BEATEN PATH
If you don't want to go all the way to Alpine National Park, visit much-loved **Mt. Buffalo National Park,** a beautiful corner of the Victorian alps about 50 km (31 mi) south of Beechworth. Anderson Peak and the Horn both top 5,000 ft, and the park is full of interesting granite formations, waterfalls, animal and plant life, and more miles of walking tracks than you're likely to cover. The gorge walk is particularly scenic. Lake Catani has swimming and a camping area. Primary access to the park is from Myrtleford and Porepunkah. Both towns have hotels and motels.

Dining and Lodging

$$ ✕ **Bank Restaurant.** This restaurant has a refined, dignified ambience befitting its former status as a bank, although paper napkins strike a discordant note among the starched tablecloths and Rococo Revival balloon-back chairs. The food is proficiently prepared and presented with style, but the menu rarely strays into adventurous territory. Main courses include Scotch fillet with french fries and salad, and noisette of lamb with lemon rind, herbs, garlic, and honey sauce. A selection of inexpensive pasta dishes is available Monday through Wednesday nights. Thursday through Saturday is reserved for more formal, à la carte dining, and a family-style carvery is available Sunday. ⊠ *86 Ford St., Beechworth,* ☎ *03/5728–2223. AE, DC, MC, V. No lunch Mon.–Sat.*

$$ ✕🏠 **Kinross.** Just a two-minute walk from the center of Beechworth, ★ this former manse has been completely renovated to offer atmospheric accommodations with a good complement of creature comforts. Rooms are decorated with chintz fabrics and furnished with heavy, dark-wood antiques. Sink into one of the big armchairs or plush sofas and enjoy the fireplace. Each room has one, as well as electric blankets and eiderdown pillows on the beds. Room 2, at the front of the house, is the largest. Four-course dinners presented by the owners—Anne Fanning preparing and her husband, Steve, serving—will be a highlight of your stay here. Children are accommodated by prior arrangement. Rates include breakfast. ⊠ *34 Loch St.,* ☎ *03/5728–2351. 5 rooms with bath. AE, MC, V.*

$ 🏠 **Country Rose.** In a quiet back street about 1 km (½ mi) from the center of Beechworth, this converted garage adjoining a family home is large and extremely good value for anyone looking for comfort, privacy, and tranquility. The decor is frilly, with plenty of pink and an antique iron bedstead, and there's a fully equipped kitchen. The house is surrounded by a commercial rose garden, through which guests are welcome to wander. Rates include breakfast. ⊠ *Malakoff St.,* ☎ *03/ 5728–1107. 1 room with bath. No credit cards.*

$ 🏠 **Rose Cottage.** Tucked away behind a pretty cottage garden close to the center of town, this small, timber guest house oozes country charm. Guest rooms are comfortable, with French doors that open onto the garden. It's easy to see why "a trip down memory lane" is a popular sentiment in the guest book. The house is filled with antiques, Tiffany-style stained-glass lamps, knickknacks, and draped with lace—which might be a bit overpowering for some. Children are accommodated by prior arrangement. At these prices, rooms are often booked in advance. Rates include breakfast. ⊠ *42 Camp St.,* ☎ *03/5728–1069. 4 rooms with bath. DC, MC, V.*

Ballooning
Balloon Flights Victoria (☎ 03/5798–5417, FAX 03/5798–5457) pilots hot-air balloon flights over farmland in the shadow of the Strathbogie Ranges in northeastern Victoria. A one-hour dawn flight costs $175 per person, including a champagne breakfast upon touchdown. The flights, generally available between March and November, depart from a farm at Longwood near Euroa, on the Hume Highway, a 90-minute drive from Melbourne.

Shopping
Buckland Gallery sells a range of Australian crafts and souvenirs that are far superior to the average, including soft toys, hats, woolen and leather wear, edible Australiana, turned-wood candlesticks, lamp bases, and dolls, pottery, and children's wear. ⊠ *Ford and Church Sts., Beechworth,* ☎ *03/5728–1432.* ⊙ *Daily 9–5:30.*

Chiltern

274 km (171 mi) northeast of Melbourne, 31 km (19 mi) north of Beechworth.

Originally known as Black Dog Creek—pretty evocative—Chiltern is another gold-rush town that fell into a coma when gold ran out. The main street of this tiny village is an almost perfectly preserved example of a 19th-century rural Australian streetscape, a fact not unnoticed by contemporary filmmakers. Notable buildings include the **Athenaeum Library and Museum,** the **Pharmacy,** the **Federal Standard Office,** and the **Star Hotel,** which has in its courtyard the largest grapevine in the country, with a girth of almost 6 ft at its base.

Lake View House is the childhood home of Henry Handel Richardson (pen name of noted 19th-century novelist Ethel Florence), whose best-known works are *The Getting of Wisdom* and *The Fortunes of Richard Mahony.* In her novel *Ultima Thule,* one of Richardson's characters reflects on Chiltern, which Richardson fictionalized as Barambogie: "Of all the dead-and-alive holes she had ever been in, this was the deadest." Among the memorabilia from her life on display in the house is the Ouija board she used for seances. ⊠ *Victoria St.,* ☎ *03/5726–1317.* 🎟 *$2.* ⊙ *Weekends 10:30–noon and 1–4:30.*

En Route From Chiltern, you might find the 40-km (25-mi) drive southeast, through hilly countryside to the picturesque gold mining town of **Yackandandah,** worth a two-hour detour. The town has interesting old buildings, a variety of new shops, a couple of pubs, and places to have Devonshire teas.

Rutherglen

274 km (171 mi) northeast of Melbourne, 18 km (11 mi) northwest of Chiltern.

Rutherglen itself has little to delay the traveler—it is an agricultural area, part of whose produce happens to be very fine grapes. And in fact the surrounding red loam soil signifies the beginning of the Rutherglen wine growing district, the source of Australia's finest fortified wines. If the term conjures up visions of sticky, cloying ports, you're in for a surprise. "Like Narcissus drowning in his own reflection, one can lose oneself in the aroma of a great old muscat"—that is the verdict of James Halliday in his authoritative *Australian Wine Compendium*.

Chambers Rosewood Winery was established in the 1850s and is one of the heavyweight producers of fortified wines. Bill Chambers's muscats are legendary, with blending stocks that go back more than a century; don't miss the chance to sample them. ⊠ *Off Corowa Rd., Rutherglen*, ☎ *03/6032–9641.* ☉ *Mon.–Sat. 9–5, Sun. 10–5.*

Despite the slick image proffered by **Campbell's Rutherglen Winery**, this is a family business that dates back more than 120 years. Ask for Campbell Family Vintage Reserve, available only at the cellar door, and you can wander freely through the winery, glass in hand, on a self-guided tour. Campbell's Merchant Prince Brown Muscat, Second Edition, is highly regarded by connoisseurs. ⊠ *Murray Valley Hwy.,* ☎ *03/6032–9458.* ☉ *Mon.–Sat. 9–5, Sun. 10–5.*

Another long-established winery, **Buller's Calliope Vineyard** was recently modernized, and many of its vintage stocks of muscat and fine sherry were released through the cellar door. Also on the winery's grounds is **Buller Bird Park**. ⊠ *Three Chains Rd. and Murray Valley Hwy.,* ☎ *03/6032–9660.* ☉ *Mon.–Sat. 9–5, Sun. 10–5.*

Pfeiffer Wines. Along with soil, climate, and heritage that favor exceptional fortified wine, the winery claims fine varietal wine; Pfeiffer chardonnay is an outstanding example. At this small, rustic winery, you can wine as well as dine on picnic baskets stuffed with crusty bread, pâté, cheese, fresh fruit, wine, and smoked salmon sold by the winery, but be sure to order a basket in advance. Wine maker Chris Pfeiffer sets up tables on the old wooden bridge that spans Sunday Creek, just down from the winery. Phone ahead to book a table on the bridge. ⊠ *Distillery Rd., Wahgunyah, 9 km (5 mi) from Rutherglen,* ☎ *03/6033–2805.* ☉ *Mon.–Sat. 9–5, Sun. 11–4.*

All Saints Vineyards & Cellars. This castellated winery has been in business since 1864, and although it was taken over by another wine maker from northeast Victoria, Brown Brothers, in 1991, the All Saints traditions and label remain. Pay particular attention to the Lyrebird Liqueur Muscat, a complex wine full of rich berry flavors, followed by a clean, dry finish. ⊠ *All Saints Rd., Wahgunyah, 9 km (5 mi) from Rutherglen,* ☎ *03/6033–1922.* ☉ *Daily 10–4:30.*

Dining and Lodging

$$ ✕ **Terrace Restaurant.** Part of the All Saints estate, the restaurant offers a wine suggestion to accompany each dish. Grilled chicken with herbed gnocchi or quail wrapped in vine leaves are good choices. Desserts are excellent, especially when combined with a formidable northeast fortified wine. ⊠ *All Saints Rd., Wahgunyah,* ☎ *03/6033–1922. AE, DC, MC, V. No dinner Sun.–Fri.*

$ ✕ **Mrs. Mouse's Teahouse.** Decorated from top to toe with toy mice, this quaint country tea house north of Rutherglen sells traditional scones and tea by day and wholesome country meals at night. The food

relies on local produce, including the delicious berries and stone fruits
of the Warby Ranges. Main courses include chicken breast with quince
cream sauce, and Thai-style fish with chili. Next door in the former
pantry there is a food shop. ✉ *12 Foord St., Wahgunyah, 9 km (5 mi)
north of Rutherglen,* ☎ *03/6033–1102. Reservations not accepted. MC,
V. No dinner Sun.–Wed.*

$ 🖫 **Wine Village Motor Inn.** In the heart of Rutherglen, this motel has
a pool for relaxing during hot northeastern summer days. ✉ *217 Main
St.,* ☎ *03/6032–9900. 16 rooms with bath. Pool. AE, DC, MC, V.*

Festivals

The main event in the region is the **Rutherglen Wine Festival,** held over
the three days of Labor Day weekend in March. The festival is a celebration of food, wine, and music, in particular jazz, folk, and country. Events are held at all surrounding wineries, as well as in town. For
more information contact the **Rutherglen Tourist Information Centre**
(☎ 03/6032–9784).

En Route   Traveling west and north of Rutherglen, distances multiply considerably. Echuca is 194 km (12 mi) to the west, and Mildura, at the north-
westernmost extent of this area, is 554 km (346 mi) distant. Plan
accordingly.

Echuca

*206 km (128 mi) north of Melbourne, 194 km (120 mi) west of Ruther-
glen, 92 km (58 mi)·north of Bendigo.*

Echuca's name derives from a local Aboriginal word meaning "meeting of the waters," a reference to the town's setting at the confluence
of the Murray, Campaspe, and Goulburn rivers. In colonial times these
rivers conveyed products from the interior. When the railway from Melbourne reached Echuca in 1864, the town became a junction at which
the cargoes of wool and wheat that came down on barges from far up
the Darling River in western New South Wales were transferred to railroad cars. During the second half of the 19th century, Echuca was Australia's largest inland port. River trade languished when the railway
network extended into the interior, but reminders of Echuca's colorful heyday remain in the restored riverboats, barges, historic hotels,
and the Red Gum Works, the town's sawmill, now a working museum.
Echuca's importance was recognized in the 1960s, when the National
Trust declared the port a historic area. Nowadays it is a busy town of
almost 10,000, the closest of the river towns to Melbourne.

If you're starting out on foot, it may help to know that **High Street,**
the main street of shops and cafés, will take you to the river. **Hare Street**
is the locus of things practical.

A tour of the historic river precincts begins in the **Star Hotel,** where
you can purchase a "passport" that gives admission to the hotel, the
Bridge Hotel, and the Historic Wharf area. The Star Hotel displays a
collection of machinery and equipment associated with the riverboat
trade. ✉ *Murray Esplanade,* ☎ *03/5482–4248.* 🖪 *Historic Wharf,
Bridge Hotel cruise on PS* Pevensey *or PS* Alexander Arbuthnot *and
guided or self-guided tour $16; without cruise $7.* ☉ *Daily 9–5.*

In the **Historic Wharf,** the heavy-duty side of the river trade business
is on view, including a warehouse, old railroad tracks, and riverboats.
Unlike those of the Mississippi or the Danube, the small, squat, utilitarian workhorses of the Murray are no beauties. Among the vessels
docked at the wharf, all original, is the **PS** *Adelaide,* Australia's old-

est operating paddle steamer. The Adelaide cannot be boarded, but it occasionally gets stoked up, with the attendant puff-puffs, chug-chugs, and toot-toots. For steam buffs, the mill engine, once used to power a local sawmill, is a sighing, hissing treat.

The **Bridge Hotel** (☞ Dining and Lodging, *below*) was built by Henry Hopwood, ex-convict father of Echuca, who had the foresight to establish a punt and later build a bridge at this commercially strategic point on the river. The hotel is rather sparsely furnished, however, and it takes great imagination to re-create what must have been a roistering, rollicking pub frequented by river men, railway workers, and drovers. ⊠ *1 Hopwood Pl.,* ☎ *03/5482–2247.*

Red Gum Works. Timber from the giant, river red gums that flourish along the Murray was once a major industry in Echuca. Stop and watch the wood turners, whose work is for sale in the gallery next door. ⊠ *Murray Esplanade,* ☎ *03/5480–6407.* ☞ *Free.* ⊙ *Daily 9–5.*

Sharp's Movie House and Penny Arcade is a nostalgic journey back to the days of the penny arcades. Have your fortune told, test your strength, dexterity, and lovability, and watch a peep show that was once banned in Australia. There are 34 machines here, the largest collection of operating penny arcade machines in the country. The movie house shows edited highlights of Australian movies that date back to 1896. A visit is highly recommended. ⊠ *Bond Store, Murray Esplanade,* ☎ *03/5482–2361.* ☞ *$8.50,* ⊙ *Daily 9–5.*

The **Echuca Coachhouse and Carriage Collection** houses 35 horse-drawn carriages collected from around the world. On weekends and during school holidays, carriages are available for rides at the front of the museum. ⊠ *57 Murray Esplanade,* ☎ *03/5482–5244.* ☞ *$3.* ⊙ *Daily 9–4.*

Life-size wax effigies of U.S. presidents may be the last thing you would expect to find in Echuca, but the **World in Wax Museum** has a Washington, Lincoln, and Kennedy—along with Fidel Castro, T.E. Lawrence (of Arabia), Queen Elizabeth II, and Australian celebrities and native sons. ⊠ *630 High St.,* ☎ *03/5482–3630.* ☞ *$6.* ⊙ *Daily 9–5:30.*

Riverboat trips along the Murray are especially relaxing if you've been following a hectic touring schedule. Several riverboats make short, one-hour excursions along the river, including the **PS** *Pevensey* and the **PS** *Canberra.* River traffic is limited to a few speedboats, small fishing skiffs, and an occasional kayak. The banks are thickly forested with river red gums, the spectacular eucalyptus with smooth white trunks, which require as much as half a ton of water per day. ⊠ *PS Pevensey tickets, Star Hotel, Murray Esplanade,* ☎ *03/5482–4248.* ☞ *$12.* ⊙ *Departs daily at 10:15, 11:30, 2, and 3:15.* ⊠ *PS Canberra tickets, Bond Store, Murray Esplanade,* ☎ *03/5482–2711.* ☞ *$9.* ⊙ *Departs daily at 10, 11:30, 12:45, 2, and 3:15.*

Dining and Lodging

$$ ✕ **Bridge Hotel Restaurant.** Set on the ground floor of a historic hotel, this popular riverside restaurant offers generous country meals that make the most of regional produce. Dishes that feature local yabbies (crayfish) and beef are particularly recommended. The restaurant occupies three rooms that were redecorated in 1992 in Victorian style and furnished with period antiques. Adjoining the restaurant is a bistro that serves simpler, less expensive fare. Choices on the menu include fish tempura with garlic mayonnaise, and chicken and Italian sausage cassoulet. When the sun shines, request a table in the garden. ⊠ *1 Hop-*

wood Pl., Echuca. ☎ *03/5482–2247. AE, DC, MC, V. No lunch weekdays.*

$$ ⌦ **Murray House.** As soon as you step inside Murray House you know
★ that you're entering a much-loved home. Since superb host-owners Len
Keeper and Doug Hall moved in, they have transformed their 1920s
building with unique pieces that they have gathered over the years from
around the world. Rooms are tastefully and individually decorated. The
sitting room and the lovely cottage garden are ideal places to while away
the hours. And there is a self-contained two-bedroom cottage in the
grounds and plans to renovate former stables for accommodation. Rates
include breakfast. ⊠ *55 Francis St., Echuca,* ☎ *03/5482–4944.* ☎ *03/
5480–6432. 4 rooms with bath, 1 cottage. MC, V.*

$$ ⌦ **River Gallery Inn.** Opened in mid-1992 in a renovated 19th-century
building, this hotel consists of large suites, offering a high standard of
comfort at a reasonable price. Each room is decorated and furnished
according to a different theme, such as the pretty French provincial room,
the opulent Victorian suite, or the mock-rustic early Australia suite. Rooms
are above an arts-and-crafts gallery. Although four rooms overlook the
street, none are affected by street noise. Two rooms have whirlpool baths;
the larger rooms can sleep four. Rates include breakfast. ⊠ *578 High
St.,* ☎ *03/5480–6902. 6 rooms with bath. AE, MC, V.*

Outdoor Activities and Sports

BOATING

Echuca Boat and Canoe Hire (⊠ Victoria Park Boat Ramp, ☎ 03/5480–
6208) offers one-person kayaks, canoes, and motorboats for river
cruises. Combination camping/canoeing trips are also available. A
canoe costs $15 for one hour, $50 for a full day; a kayak is $12 per
hour, $25 for a full day. Hours are 8–6 daily.

FISHING

No license is required to fish the Murray River on the Victorian side.
Rods and bait are available from **Echuca Boat and Canoe Hire** (☞ *above*).

GOLF

Rich River Golf Club (⊠ West of Moama, across Murray River from
Echuca on New South Wales side, ☎ 03/5482–2444), a superb 36-
hole championship course, charges $15 greens fees and $12 for clubs
and cart rental.

WATERSKIING

The **Southern 80 Water-Ski Race,** held during the first weekend in February, is best viewed from the Echuca Boat Ramp. The race consists of
high-power boats that pull two skiers apiece for 80 km (50 mi) through
the twists and turns of the Murray River.

Swan Hill

*97 km (60 mi) northwest of Echuca, 251 km (155 mi) southeast of
Mildura.*

Named in 1836 by the explorer Major Thomas Mitchell for the swans
that kept him awake at night, Swan Hill is a prosperous town surrounded
by rich citrus groves and vineyards.

The 12-acre **Swan Hill Pioneer Settlement** evokes life in a 19th-cen-
tury Victorian river port with its displays of replicas of pioneer homes,
stores, machinery, and the landlocked paddle wheeler *The Gem,* once
the largest cargo-passenger boat on the Murray. Today it houses a restaurant, art gallery, and souvenir shop. At night, the settlement becomes
the backdrop for a sound-and-light show, which uses state-of-the-art

lighting effects to bring the history of Swan Hill to life. ✉ *Horseshoe Bend, Swan Hill,* ☎ *03/5032–1093.* 🎫 *$12; sound-and-light show $8; combined entry, sound-and-light show, and PS* Pyap *cruise $23.* ⊙ *Daily 8:30–5, show begins about 1 hr after sunset.*

Dining and Lodging

$$ ✕ **Gem Restaurant.** Stroll on board the vintage paddle steamer PS *Gem,* moored high and dry in Pioneer Settlement, for an evening meal. The menu includes some unusual Australian bush tucker—including witchetty grubs and kangaroo tail soup—but its real strengths are the excellent local yabbies, Murray cod, beef, and lamb dishes. The dining room's candlelit elegance of brass and redwood brings an air of gauzy romance to the evening. ✉ *Pioneer Settlement,* ☎ *03/5032–2463. AE, DC, MC, V. No lunch.*

$ 🏨 **Lady Augusta Motor Inn.** Completed in 1991, this two-story motel is a short stroll from the town center. It surrounds a tree-lined courtyard and allows a choice of moderately large double rooms, two-bedroom suites, and spa suites. All are well maintained. ✉ *375 Campbell St.,* ☎ *03/5032–9677,* 🗏 *03/5032–9573. 24 rooms with bath. Restaurant, bar, pool. AE, DC, MC, V.*

En Route From Swan Hill, the Murray Valley Highway traverses farm country that has seen many years of irrigation—the only green in this rust-color semidesert is that of the citrus crops and vineyards. Unfortunately in some cases the land has been spoiled by excess salinity, one of the side effects of irrigation. Experiments are underway to plant salt-tolerant native trees in affected areas. After passing the south end of Hattah-Kulkyne National Park, which is full of kangaroos and interesting bird life, turn right onto the Calder Highway (Hwy. 79) and proceed north through Red Cliffs, which has a Sunday market, into Mildura.

Mildura

251 km (155 mi) northwest of Swan Hill, 557 km (348 mi) northwest of Melbourne.

Claiming more hours of sunshine per year than Queensland's Gold Coast, Mildura is known for dried fruit, wine, citrus, and avocados, as well as its hydroponic vegetable-growing industry. The town was developed in 1885 by two Canadians, George and William Chaffey, who were persuaded to emigrate by the Victorian premier, Alfred Deakin. The Chaffey brothers were world pioneers in irrigation. The irrigated vineyards of the Riverland region are enormously productive, and provide Australians with much of their inexpensive cask wines—although rarely does a premium table wine bear a Riverland label.

At the **Pioneer Cottage,** you can get a good idea of what life was like in the days when Mildura was one antipodean frontier of European settlement. ✉ *3 Hunter St.,* ☎ *03/5023–3742.* 🎫 *$2.50.* ⊙ *Daily 9–5.*

It's worth a peek into the **Workingman's Club** (☎ 03/5023–0531) on Deakin Avenue just to see the bar: At 300 ft, it's one of the world's longest. All of Mildura turns out to drink at its 27 taps.

On the banks of the Murray, the **Golden River Zoo** has an extensive collection of native and exotic birds in walk-through aviaries, as well as daily shows featuring pumas, dingoes, and monkeys. Camel and train rides along the river are available during school holidays. ✉ *Flora Ave.,* ☎ *03/5023–5540.* 🎫 *$8.50.* ⊙ *Daily 9–5:30.*

Among Mildura's paddle steamers, the **PS Avoca** is one of the oldest still operating on the river. Built in 1877, this steamer has been immaculately restored and now carries more than 200 passengers on a variety of daytime sightseeing cruises that include lunch and live entertainment—and bands or shows on evening dinner cruises. The Thursday dinner cruise is designed for families. ⊠ *Mildura Wharf,* ☎ *03/5021– 1166.* ☛ *Lunch cruise $25, dinner cruise $34–$37.* ☉ *Lunch cruise Tues.–Sun. at noon; dinner cruise Wed. and Sat. at 7:30, Thurs. at 7.*

Lindemans Karadoc Winery is one of the largest and most sophisticated facilities in Victoria. This winery produces much of Lindemans' bulk wines, which end up being drained from "Château Cardboard" dispensers in Ozzie households, but the entire range of Lindemans' respected wines can be sampled here, among them chardonnay, semillon-chardonnay, riesling, and a couple of cabernet blends. ⊠ *Karadoc Rd., Karadoc, 10 km (6 mi) from Mildura* ☎ *03/5024–0357.* ☉ *Weekdays 9–5, weekends 10–4:30.*

Mildara Blass Winery produces about a third of the Lindemans output, with a range including excellent Church Hill Chardonnay, Fumé Blanc, and Cabernet-Merlot. Mildara Blass also makes fine sherry and superb brandy. You can take a guided tour of the facilities where the liquor ages in oak casks. ⊠ *Wentworth Rd., Merbein, 13 km (8 mi) from Mildura,* ☎ *03/5025–2303.* ☛ *Tour $2.* ☉ *Weekdays 9–5 (tours at 11, 2, and 3:30), Sat. 11–4, Sun. noon–4.*

☾ A popular option for kids, the **Aquacoaster** is a big complex of pools that includes an enormous water slide. ⊠ *18 Orange Ave., Mildura,* ☎ *03/5023–3663.* ☛ *$8.* ☉ *Weekdays 2:30–6, weekends 1:30–6:30, school holidays 10–12:30 and 1:30–6:30.*

Dining and Lodging

$$ ✕ **Rendezvous.** A Mildura institution for more than 40 years, the formal restaurant and adjoining pub-style bistro also include a partner, the modern bar and café called Liaison. The restaurant's menu features traditional dishes as well as more adventurous offerings, many of them Thai or Indian in provenance, others with an intriguing mixed birth, such as chili calamari marinated in balsamic vinegar and served on a bed of feta cheese. ⊠ *34 Langtree Ave.,* ☎ *03/5023–1571. AE, DC, MC, V. Closed Sun. No lunch Sat.*

$ 🖭 **Chaffey International Motor Inn.** Rooms and facilities at this modern, centrally located motel are well above average for country Victoria—and certainly better than those at any other motel in town. From Friday through Sunday room rates drop by more than $20. ⊠ *244 Deakin Ave.,* ☎ *03/5023–5833,* 🆉 *03/5021–1972. 32 rooms with bath. Restaurant, bar, pool, spa. AE, DC, MC, V.*

$ 🖭 **Mildura Country Club Resort.** This modern motel has spacious grounds, a large swimming pool, pleasantly decorated rooms, and a resortlike atmosphere, but what really sets it apart is the surrounding golf course. All rooms open to the 18-hole course. ⊠ *12th St. Extension,* ☎ *03/5023–3966,* 🆉 *03/5021–1751. 40 rooms with bath. Restaurant, bar, pool, exercise room. AE, DC, MC, V.*

Murray River Region A to Z

Arriving and Departing
BY CAR
Beechworth and Rutherglen are on opposite sides of the Hume Freeway, the main Sydney–Melbourne artery. Allow four hours for the journey from Melbourne, twice that from Sydney. Echuca is a three-hour drive from Melbourne, reached most directly by the Northern Highway (Hwy. 75).

BY TRAIN

Trains run to most of the major towns in the region, including Echuca, Rutherglen, Swan Hill, and Mildura, but not Beechworth. This reasonable access is most useful if you do not have a car or want to avoid the long-distance drives.

Getting Around

BY CAR

The wide open spaces of the northeast wineries and Murray River districts make driving the most sensible and feasible means of exploration. There is enough scenic interest along the way to make the long drives bearable, especially if you trace the river route. The direct run from Melbourne to Mildura is quite daunting (557 km–348 mi), however, but those towns accessed by the Hume Highway are easily reached from the capital city.

BY TRAIN

As with most country Victorian areas, direct train access from Melbourne to the main centers is reasonable, but getting between towns isn't as easy. The train to Swan Hill or Mildura may be an appealing option for those utterly discouraged by the long drive and the prospect of traveling through remote desert country.

Contacts and Resources

EMERGENCIES

Ambulance, fire brigade, and **police.** ☎ *000.*

GUIDED TOURS

The **Gray Line** (☎ 03/9663–4455) operates one-day tours of Echuca, departing Melbourne on Wednesday and Sunday at 8:45 AM. The cost is $79.

VISITOR INFORMATION

Beechworth Tourist Information Centre. ✉ *Ford and Camp Sts.,* ☎ *03/ 5728–1374.* ⊙ *Daily 9:30–5:30.*
Echuca Tourist Information Centre. ✉ *Leslie St. and Murray Esplanade,* ☎ *03/5480–7555.* ⊙ *Weekdays 9–5, weekends 10–4.*
Mildura Tourist Information Centre. ✉ *Langtree Mall,* ☎ *03/5023–3619.* ⊙ *Weekdays 9–12:30 and 1–4, weekends 10–4.*
Rutherglen Tourist Information Centre. ✉ *Walkabout Cellars, 84 Main St.,* ☎ *03/6032–9784.* ⊙ *Daily 9–6.*
Swan Hill Regional Information Office. ✉ *306 Campbell St., Swan Hill,* ☎ *03/5032–3033.*

ALPINE NATIONAL PARK

The name Alpine National Park actually applies to three loosely connected areas in eastern Victoria that follow the peaks of the Great Dividing Range. This section covers the area, formerly called Bogong National Park, that contains the highest of the Victorian Alps. Its many outdoor activities include excellent walking trails among the peaks, fishing (license required), horseback riding, mountaineering, and skiing.

The land around here is rich in history. *Bogong* is an Aboriginal word for "big moth," and it was to Mt. Bogong that Aborigines came each year after the winter thaw in search of bogong moths, considered a delicacy. Aborigines were eventually displaced by cattlemen who brought their cattle here to graze. Since the creation of the park, grazing has become more limited.

Stately snow gums grace the hills throughout the year, complemented by a budding array of alpine wildflowers in bloom from October

through March. There are half- and full-day trails scattered throughout the scenic area for bushwalkers, many of them in the Falls Creek
area south of Mount Beauty. The popular Bogong High Plains Circuit
is a tough trail ascending Mount Bogong. You could easily spend a week
or more hiking the trails that crisscross this park.

In winter the area is completely covered in snow, and bushwalkers put
on cross-country skis, especially at Falls Creek and Mount Hotham.
If you've skied the Rockies or the European alps, the Victorian alternative will be a bit disappointing, and it doesn't seem to justify the prices
charged at local resorts. Cross-country skiing is the best way to take
in the Down-Under snowscape, enhanced by the exotic shapes of the
gum trees.

Dining and Lodging
The town of Bright is reasonably well supplied with dining possibilities. **Simone's** (✉ Ovens Valley Motel Inn, Ovens Highway, Bright, ☎
03/5755–2022) is a remarkable find with its classic osso buco, gnocchi, panna cotta, and tempting daily specials. **Rebekka's** (✉ 98 Gavan
St, Bright, ☎ 03/5750–1251) has fixed-price menus with a regional
emphasis. Try the twice-baked Milawa goat cheese soufflé.

For places to stay, old cattlemen's huts are scattered throughout the
park and may be used by hikers free of charge. These, however, are
often occupied, and shelter is never guaranteed. Bush camping is permitted throughout the park, and there is a basic campground at Raspberry Hill.

Hotels, motels, commercial camping, and caravan parks are in the major
towns around the park, including Bright, Mount Beauty, Harrietville,
Anglers Rest, Glen Valley, and Tawonga, as well as in the ski resorts
of Falls Creek, Mount Buller, and Mount Hotham year-round.

Skiing
Ski resorts are open at Falls Creek, Mt. Buller, Mt. Buffalo, and Mt.
Hotham in winter.

Arriving and Departing
BY BUS
Bus services operate from Albury on the New South Wales border in
the north. During ski season, buses depart from Mount Beauty for Falls
Creek and Mt. Hotham and depart from Melbourne for Falls Creek.

BY CAR
Alpine National Park is 323 km (200 mi) northeast of Melbourne, and
you can reach it two ways. If you want to go to the park taking a very
small detour through the historic town of Beechworth (☞ The Murray River Region, *above*), take the Hume Freeway (Rte. 31) north out
of Melbourne and turn southeast onto the Ovens Highway at Wangaratta. Beechworth is about a 30-km (18-mi) detour off the Hume.
You can also follow the Princes Highway east from Melbourne through
Sale and Bairnsdale. Pick up the Omeo Highway north from here to
Omeo, and then head west to Cobungra and Mt. Hotham. The turnoff
for Falls Creek is another 39 km (24 mi) north of Omeo.

Visitor Information
Alpine National Park. The ranger station for the park is on Mount Beauty,
and there are information centers in Bright, Omeo, and Falls Creek.
Check the station at Mount Beauty for ranger-led programs that might
be scheduled. ✉ *Box 180, Mount Beauty, VIC, 3699,* ☎ *03/5757–
2693.*
Department of Conservation and Natural Resources. ✉ *240 Victoria
Parade, East Melbourne,* ☎ *03/9412–4011.*

WILSON'S PROMONTORY NATIONAL PARK

★ This southernmost granite peninsula once connected Tasmania with mainland Australia, and you'll find botanical and geological odds and ends common both to the mainland and the wayward island. **Wilson's Promontory** is well endowed with wildlife. More than 180 species of bird have been sighted here, and Corner Inlet, along Five Mile Beach, is a seabird sanctuary. Near the visitor center at Tidal River, you'll probably sight tame marsupials, including kangaroos, wombats, and koalas. Wilson's "Prom" is Victoria's most popular national park because it has most of everything, from remarkable granite outcroppings and upcroppings (tors) to wonderfully secluded beaches.

There are more than 20 well-marked trails here, some meandering past pristine beaches and secluded coves excellent for swimming, others more strenuous. One tough but popular trail is the 9½-km (6-mi) Sealer's Cove Walk, which traverses the slopes of Mt. Wilson Range before descending through Sealer's Swamp to the tranquil Sealer's Cove. The Lilly Pilly Gully nature walk, a 5-km (3-mi) trip among tree ferns and giant mountain ash, gives a good introduction to the park's plant and animal life with the aid of informative signs posted along the way. And from the top of Mt. Oberon on a good day, you'll be able to see across the Bass Straight all the way to Tasmania

Dining and Lodging

There's not much to be said about food in the area, unless you catch and cook it yourself. In Foster, north of the national park, try **Black Cherry** (☎ 03/5682–2110), which is open for lunch daily and dinner on Saturday only. The **Foster Motel** (☎ 03/5682–2022) and the **Wilson's Promontory Motel** (☎ 03/5682–2055) also have reasonable dining rooms.

With 500 campsites, the well-known Tidal River campground is among Australia's largest. Reservations at this popular spot during peak summer and holiday periods are hard to come by and should be made well in advance. During peak season (December through February and holiday weekends) sites cost $12.50 per night for up to three persons, $2.50 for each additional person. Off-season rates are $6.50 per night per person, $2.50 per night for each additional person. Stiff cancellation fees apply. Reserve with the **Tidal River park office** (☎ 03/5680–9555).

Heated apartments and lodges accommodating from two to six people are available at Tidal River. Between September and April, these can be reserved only on a weekly basis. Otherwise, the minimum booking period is from Friday night through Sunday night. Rates are $205 per week in a two-person lodge, $565 per week in a six-person lodge. Lodges and apartments may be reserved up to 12 months in advance through the **Victoria Tourist Information Centre** (✉ Town Hall, Swanston St. Walk and Little Collins St., ☎ 03/9658–9968 or 03/9658–9940), which is open weekdays 8:30–5:30, Saturday 8:30–5, and Sunday 9–5.

Single-room motor huts at Tidal River contain two double bunk beds, a hot plate, heaters, and running cold water. Blankets and linen are not provided. Toilets and showers are available at the campground. The trailers cost $34 for four-berth and $51 for six-berth huts and can be booked through the **Tidal River park office** (☎ 03/5680–9555).

Early in 1997 the Victorian Government scrapped a plan for a four-star lodge at the Prom after widespread protests by conservationists.

The government, however, intends to proceed with a 45-bed lodge for hikers, a new walking trail, and other developments. Environmental groups plan to continue their opposition to construction work at the park.

Arriving and Departing

BY CAR

To get to Wilson's Prom, 231 km (143 mi) south of Melbourne, take the Princes Highway to Dandenong, and then the South Gippsland Highway south to Meeniyan or Foster. Tidal River is another 70 km (44 mi) from there. There is no public transportation to the park.

Visitor Information

Wilson's Promontory National Park. The park headquarters has a variety of guidebooks for the park and interesting displays. ✉ *Tidal River, VIC, 3960,* ☎ *03/5680–9555.*

Department of Conservation and Natural Resources. ✉ *240 Victoria Parade, East Melbourne,* ☎ *03/9412–4011.*

In case you want to see the world.

At American Express, we're here to make your journey a smooth one. So we have over 1,700 travel service locations in over 120 countries ready to help. What else would you expect from the world's largest travel agency?

do more

AMERICAN EXPRESS

Travel

In case you want to be welcomed there.

We're here to see that you're always welcomed at establishments everywhere. That's why millions of people carry the American Express® Card – for peace of mind, confidence, and security, around the world or just around the corner.

do more

Cards

In case you're running low.

We're here to help with more than 118,000 Express Cash locations around the world. In order to enroll, just call American Express before you start your vacation.

do more

Express Cash

And just in case.

We're here with American Express® Travelers Cheques
and Cheques *for Two*.® They're the safest way to carry
money on your vacation and the surest way to get a
refund, practically anywhere, anytime.
Another way we help you...

do more

Travelers
Cheques

6 Tasmania

From the Freycinet Peninsula to the
Nut to the wilds of Southwest
National Park, Tasmania is a place of
unsurpassable natural beauty. The
island is a hiker's dream. For time-
travelers, convict lore from the state's
early days as a penal colony is a
stinging contrast to the well-preserved
old towns where the rest of us would
have lived. But the greatest call comes
from the great outdoors—Tasmania is
rich with coastal and inland parks
both known and loved, and wilderness
still unexplored.

Updated by
Gary Walsh

ABOUT THE SIZE of Scotland, and with a population of less than a half million, the island of Tasmania is an unspoiled reminder of a simpler, slower lifestyle. It has been called the England of the south, as it, too, is richly cloaked in mists and rain, and an evening chill is not uncommon even in summer. Where the English tradition of a Christmas roast may strike one as strange during a steamy Sydney summer, such rites appear natural amid Tasmania's lush quilt of lowland farms and villages. Even towns look English, with their profusion of Georgian cottages and buildings, the preservation of which testifies to Tasmanians' attachment to their past.

There are other parts of that past that many may wish to forget. Tasmania was first settled by Aborigines who crossed a land bridge from Australia some 23,000 years ago, before it washed out. Europeans discovered it in 1642, when Abel Tasman arrived at its southwest coast, but not until 1798 was Tasmania (then called Van Diemen's Land) thought to be an island. Much of the island's subsequent history is violent. The entire population of full-blooded Aborigines was wiped out, and the establishment in 1830 of a penal settlement at Port Arthur for the colony's worst offenders ushered in a new age of cruelty. Tragically, on one horrific day in April 1996, a lone gunman brought that brutality back when he randomly shot and killed 35 people, most of them in the penal settlement's café. That murderer is now serving life imprisonment without parole.

The last convict was shipped to Port Arthur more than 140 years ago, and today, walking through the lovely park at Port Arthur or the personable streets of Hobart, it is difficult to picture Tasmania as a land of desperation and death. That is the great dichotomy of this island, however, for in many ways Tasmania is still wild and untamed. It is one of the most mountainous islands in the world. Parts of the southwest wilderness have never been explored, with access barred by impenetrable rain forests. Of all the states, Tasmania has set aside the greatest percentage of land as national parks. If you're planning a trip to these parks in the mountains of Tasmania, be prepared for sudden climatic changes—a snowstorm in summer is not unusual. More than that of any other Australian state, the Tasmanian climate is greatly influenced by Antarctica.

Pleasures and Pastimes

Dining
The superb and bounteous produce of the sea is the platform on which Tasmania's culinary fame is based. Far-sighted entrepreneurs saw the value of farming seafood—Atlantic salmon in particular—and created a rich industry. Tasmanian dairy produce is also a delight. The cheeses and thick double cream of King Island are specially worth seeking out. In wines, too, Tasmania is at the Australian forefront, with small producers making quality reds and whites for Australian and international consumption.

CATEGORY	COST*
$$$$	over $40
$$$	$25–$40
$$	$10–$25
$	under $10

per person, excluding drinks and service

Lodging

Tasmania has held onto many of the architectural gems of its past. Something of an industrial backwater, and with only a small population to support, the state has rarely found it necessary to demolish the old to make way for the new. Many cottages built during the first days of the colony are now bed and breakfasts, guest houses, and self-catering apartments. They are found in the best preserved towns and villages, as well as in such major cities as Hobart and Launceston. Nowhere else in Australia will the colonial past seem as alive and as close.

CATEGORY	COST*
$$$$	over $200
$$$	$130–$200
$$	$75–$130
$	under $75

All prices are for a standard double room.

Outdoor Activities and Sports

Tasmania is a hiker's state, with some of Australia's best and most challenging walking terrain. The wilderness of the state's southwest is still virtually untracked, and it is the domain of some serious trekkers. You'll find less strenuous but still relatively pristine walking around Cradle Mountain and on the lovely Freycinet Peninsula on the island's east coast. The island is also great for cycling, diving, rafting, and trout fishing. For information on bicycling, bushwalking, diving, and rafting in Tasmania's great outdoors beyond what appears in this chapter, *see* Chapter 13.

Exploring Tasmania

Tasmania is compact in size—the drive from southern Hobart to northern Launceston takes little more than two hours—but the hilly terrain and winding roads make exploration of some areas of the state more time-consuming, and breathtaking. In the great, untrammelled southwest, there are no roads and few bush-walking trails, so even the wild, fast-running rivers of the region become key elements in transportation. Elsewhere, the landscape ranges from perfectly tame to entirely wild—from classic rural farmland tableaux to the most impenetrable mountain ranges in Australia.

Great Itineraries

If it's the genteel Tasmania of colonial times that you're after, concentrate on Hobart, nearby Richmond, the historic towns of the central region of the state, and the not-to-be-missed Port Arthur. To fully explore the more remote areas, especially the southwest wilderness, you need to allocate more time than a superficial glance at the map might make you think.

IF YOU HAVE 3 DAYS

Spend your first day in and around ⚏ **Hobart.** On foot, explore the docks, Salamanca Place, and the colonial architecture of Battery Point, taking time out for a cruise on the Derwent in an historic vessel. In the afternoon, drive to Richmond and stroll its excellently preserved 19th-century streetscape. On the second day head for ⚏ **Port Arthur,** with a stop at the Bush Mill Steam Railway and Settlement. Spend the day exploring the ruins, including a cruise to the Isle of the Dead convict burial ground. On your final day, return slowly to Hobart, taking in some of the other sights of the Tasman Peninsula en route, and drive to the summit of Mount Wellington, where, if the clouds cooperate, there is a wonderful panorama of the city in its lovely seaside setting.

Tasmania

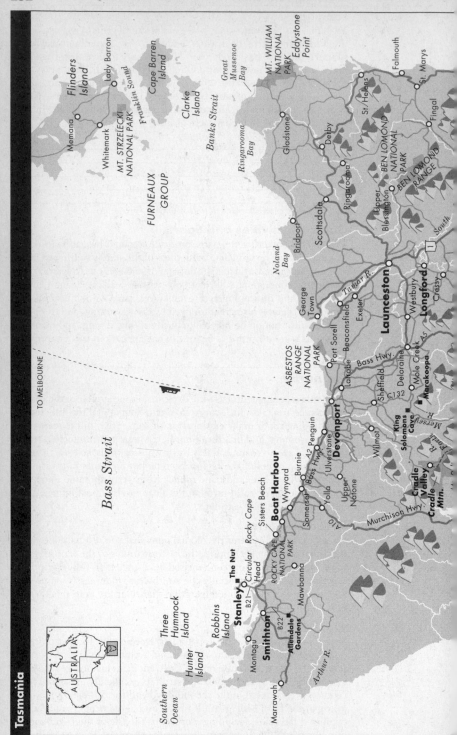

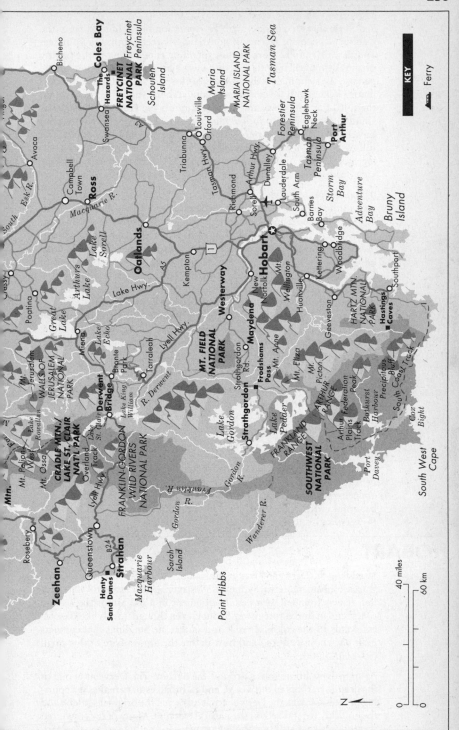

IF YOU HAVE 5 DAYS

See ▣ **Hobart** on day one, with an excursion to Richmond or, to the Cadbury chocolate factory if you have a sweet tooth. On your second day, drive to ▣ **Port Arthur,** spending time taking in the beauty of the Tasman Peninsula on the way. The gorgeous setting of the penal settlement makes the horrors of the past seem all the more dramatic. Hikers and lovers of exquisite scenery should leave early on the third day and drive to ▣ **Coles Bay** on the **Freycinet Peninsula.** Climb the steep path to the outlook over impossibly perfect Wineglass Bay, and descend to the pure white sands for a swim in the ocean. The following day, drive slowly back to Hobart through the historic villages of ▣ **Ross** and **Oatlands,** topping off the day by taking in the view from Mount Wellington.

IF YOU HAVE 10 DAYS

Extra time gives you the chance to see the wonders of the west coast. Explore ▣ **Hobart** and Richmond before heading south to the Tasman Peninsula and ▣ **Port Arthur.** Return to Hobart on day three, with an ascent of Mount Wellington. Depart early the next morning for ▣ **Strahan,** on the west coast, via the peculiarly appealing moonscape of Queenstown, where mining has scarified the once green mountainsides. Spend two nights at Strahan, with time for a leisurely cruise on the Gordon River, before driving north to ▣ **Stanley,** a lovely village set beneath the rocky majesty of The Nut. Continue east to ▣ **Launceston** before turning inland to ▣ **Cradle Mountain** and its fantastic bushwalking and superb scenery. After two nights, circle back to Hobart along the historic central route.

When to Tour Tasmania

Winter can draw freezing blasts from the Antarctic—this is not the time of year for the highlands or wilderness areas. It's better in the colder months to enjoy the warm interiors of colonial cottages and open fireplaces of welcoming pubs. The east coast is generally mild, more protected from the weather than the west, which is struck by the roaring 40s—weather-bearing winds that for thousands of miles blow across the southern 40s latitudes, unobstructed by land masses. Summer can be surprisingly hot—bushfires are not uncommon—but temperatures are generally lower than on the Australian mainland. Early autumn is beautiful, with deciduous trees in full color. Spring, with its wildflowers, is also lovely.

HOBART

Straddling the Derwent River at the foot of Mount Wellington's forested slopes, Hobart may rival Sydney as Australia's most beautiful state capital. It was founded as a penal settlement in 1803 and is the second oldest city in the country after Sydney, even though it feels like the oldest. Many of the colonial brick and sandstone buildings that convicts built have been restored and now define the atmosphere of this small city of 185,000.

As in Sydney, life revolves around the harbor. The Derwent is one of the deepest harbors in the world, and its broad estuary makes it a sporting paradise. It was the Derwent that attracted the original settlers, and they quickly capitalized on the natural treasure. Many of the converted warehouses that still line the wharf were formerly used to store Hobart's major exports—fruit, wool, and corn—as well as the products of the whaling fleet that used the city as a base.

Hobart comes alive between Christmas and the New Year (when it's summer Down Under) during the annual Sydney-to-Hobart yacht race.

The race dominates conversations among Hobart's citizens, who descend on Constitution Dock for a three-day fête (what they call a "quiet little drink"). Otherwise, Hobart *is* a quiet city whose nightlife is largely confined to the action at the Wrest Point Casino in Sandy Bay.

Exploring Hobart

Numbers in the text correspond to numbers in the margin and on the Downtown Hobart map.

A Good Walk

Begin by the city's focal point at the docks, the old warehouses of **Macquarie Wharf**. Spend a couple of hours at the **Tasmanian Museum and Art Gallery** ③, opposite **Constitution Dock** ④, before following the line of the wharves to **Salamanca Place** ⑦, Hobart's most vibrant shopping district and gathering place. At the end of Salamanca Place, follow Castray Esplanade to the south, turn left into Clarke Avenue and then right into Secheron Road, where you'll find the **Maritime Museum of Tasmania** ⑧. After your visit, stroll farther along Secheron Road to Mona Street and turn right. Follow Mona Street onto Hampden Road, which leads to the **Narryna Van Diemen's Land Memorial Folk Museum** ⑨ and a fascinating array of antiques shops, charming cottages, and other historic buildings. Head back toward Castray Esplanade, but this time turn left into Runnymede Street and the delightful **Arthur's Circus** ⑩ around the green, before returning to Salamanca Place.

TIMING

The dock and wharf area is always busy—on weekdays with fishing vessels and commuter boats, on weekends with pleasure craft and sightseeing ferries. Saturday is the optimum time for Salamanca Place, when the area's morning market is set up, although the craft and art galleries are more pleasant when crowds are smaller. You can easily spend an hour or two in each of the museums, more if you want to see their collections in depth.

Sights to See

⑩ **Arthur's Circus** is an enchanting collection of tiny houses and cottages set in a circle around a village green in Runnymede Street, in the heart of historic Battery Point, Hobart's best-preserved suburb. Built in the 1840s and 1850s, most of these houses have been nicely restored.

⑤ The busy waterfront at **Brooke Street Pier** is the departure point for harbor cruises. ⊠ *Franklin Wharf.*

☾ **Cadbury-Schweppes chocolate factory.** Very few children (or adults!) will be able to resist a tour of the best chocolate and cocoa factory in Australia. Book well in advance through the Visitors' Information Centre (☎ 03/6249–0111). ⊠ *Claremont, 12 km (7½ mi) north of Hobart.* ☞ *$10.* ☉ *Tour weekdays 9, 9:30, 10:30, and 1.*

② With its giant clock reenacting the nursery rhyme every hour, **Cat and Fiddle Arcade** is kitsch but entertaining—worth a stop if you're in the area at the right time. ⊠ *Elizabeth St. between Liverpool and Bathurst Sts.*

④ Yachts competing in the annual Sydney-to-Hobart race moor at the colorful **Constitution Dock** marina during the first week of January. Buildings fronting the dock are century-old reminders of Hobart's trading history. ⊠ *Hunter and Davey Sts.*

⑧ **Maritime Museum of Tasmania** is located in the 1831 Secheron House, a fine example of Georgian architecture. The museum houses one of the best maritime collections in Australia, including figureheads, whal-

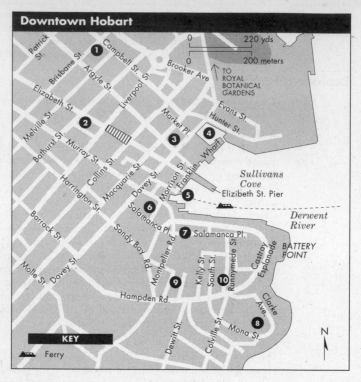

Downtown Hobart

KEY

🚢 Ferry

N

ing implements, models, and photographs dating to 1804. ⊠ *21 Secheron Rd.,* ☎ *03/6223–5082.* 🖾 *$4.* ☉ *Daily 10–4:30.*

⑨ Narryna Van Diemen's Land Memorial Folk Museum. Museum exhibits depict the life of Tasmania's pioneers. ⊠ *103 Hampden Rd.,* ☎ *03/ 6234–2791.* 🖾 *$5.* ☉ *Weekdays 10:30–5, weekends 2–5.*

⑥ Parliament House, built by convicts in 1840 as a customs house, did not acquire its present function until 1856. Contact the Clerk of the House (☎ 03/6233–2374) if you want to watch a session of parliament from the viewing gallery. The grounds of Parliament House are maintained by the Royal Botanic Gardens. ⊠ *Morrison St. between Murray St. and Salamanca Pl.*

❶ Penitentiary Chapel and **Criminal Courts.** Built and used during the early convict days, these buildings vividly portray Tasmania's penal, judicial, and religious heritage in their courtrooms, old cells, and underground tunnels. If you want to get spooked, come for the nighttime ghost tour. ⊠ *Brisbane and Campbell Sts.,* ☎ *03/6231–0911 or 03/ 6273–3361.* 🖾 *$6. Ghost tour $7.* ☉ *Tour weekdays 10–3.*

★ **❼** Old whaling ships used to dock at **Salamanca Place.** Today many of the warehouses along the street that were once used by whalers have been converted into excellent crafts shops, art galleries, and restaurants. On Saturday it is the site of a boisterous morning market, where dealers of a wide assortment of Tasmanian arts and crafts, as well as old records, books, and antiques, display their wares. Keep an eye open for items made from Tasmanian timber.

NEED A
BREAK?

Retro Cafe is among the most stylish and coolly casual of Salamanca Place's busy cafés with sidewalk tables. ⊠ *Salamanca Pl. and Montpelier Retreat,* ☎ *03/6223-3073.*

❸ Overlooking Constitution Dock, **Tasmanian Museum and Art Gallery** has a collection of exhibits on Tasmania's history. It is the best place in Hobart to learn about Tasmania's Aborigines and the island's unique wildlife. ⊠ *40 Macquarie St.*, ☎ *03/6223–1422.* ☞ *Free.* ☉ *Daily 10–5.*

Ⓒ **Tudor Court** is a cutesy, rather twee replica of an English Tudor village. It's very well put together, but kids are more likely to find it memorable than adults. ⊠ *827 Sandy Bay Rd.*, ☎ *03/6225–1194.* ☞ *$3.* ☉ *Daily 9–5:30.*

OFF THE
BEATEN PATH

Royal Tasmanian Botanical Gardens spread across the largest area of open land in Hobart: Part of the Queens Domain, the well-tended gardens are rarely crowded and are a welcome relief from the city. Exotic plants represent the English horticultural tradition, and there are interesting native Tasmanian species as well. One section has been specially designed for wheelchairs. The Japanese Garden is dominated by a miniature Mt. Fuji. Children love the flowered clock. A museum and education center is open daily noon–4. ⊠ *Adjacent to Government House at Tasman Bridge*, ☎ *03/6234-6299.* ☉ *Daily 8–4:45.*

AROUND HOBART
26 km (16 mi) northeast of Hobart via Eastern Outlet Rd.

Richmond. This village just 25 minutes' drive from Hobart has become a major tourist magnet. On weekends you might alternately struggle to find a place to park the car and jostle with crowds on the town's long main street, which has been populated with craft, antiques, and souvenir shops, cafés and restaurants. To get the best sense of Richmond's character and historic importance, wander in a little from the main drag. **Richmond Bridge**, a picturesque counterpoint to the town's church-spired skyline, is Australia's oldest bridge, a convict-built stone structure dating from 1823. **Richmond Jail** (⊠ 37 Bathurst St., ☎ 03/6260–2127) is well preserved and full of evocative historical interpretive materials. Note also **St. John's Roman Catholic Church**, another Richmond entry in the oldest in Australia category.

Dining

$$$$
★
✕ **Alexander's Restaurant.** Located at the historic Lenna of Hobart hotel, Alexander's draws locals and guests to taste some of Tasmania's finest cuisine. Start your meal with, say, pigeon consommé; quail filled with duck liver and grapes and served with port and orange sauce; or beef and vegetable terrine in aspic atop finely diced tomato. For a main course there are such beautifully presented dishes as baked salmon served with garlic-flavored mash and a sweet capsicum (pepper) coulis or venison with baked peaches, spaetzle (Hungarian pasta), and pepper sauce. A sweet finale might be toffee-coated strawberries with Grand Marnier ice cream or cherries poached in spiced wine with sabayon and cardamom ice cream. ⊠ *Lenna of Hobart, 20 Runnymede St., Battery Point*, ☎ *03/6223–2911. Reservations essential. Jacket required. AE, DC, MC, V.*

$$$$
★
✕ **Dear Friends.** One of the most elegant restaurants in Tasmania, this converted flour mill by the wharf is famous for nouvelle cuisine, and each meal is a carefully and artistically arranged. Tables are widely spaced among Old World furniture and antique bric-a-brac. Game dishes, such as roasted venison, are a specialty, as are Atlantic salmon and lamb cutlets. The wine list features Tasmania's best. ⊠ *18 Brook St.*, ☎ *03/6223–2646. Reservations essential. Jacket required. AE, DC, MC, V. Closed Sun.*

$$$$ ✕ **Wrest Point Revolving Restaurant.** Breathtaking views of the city easily justify a visit to this revolving restaurant atop one of Hobart's tallest buildings. Luckily, the food is equally rewarding. Tables are widely spaced around a mirrored central column, and all have views. Specialties include the City Lights dinner—a three-course meal based on seasonal produce—and prawns flambéed at the table with a great deal of pomp. As an appetizer, try the smoked Tasmanian salmon. ⊠ *Wrest Point Hotel, 410 Sandy Bay Rd.,* ☎ *03/6225–0112. Reservations essential. Jacket required. AE, DC, MC, V.*

$$$ ✕ **Drunken Admiral.** The atmosphere here is noisy and raucous. The walls and every other available space are hung with seafaring paraphernalia. With all this naval kitsch, you would expect the food to be of secondary importance, but it's not. Each nautically named dish is well prepared. Try the Sydney-to-Hobart seafood platter, a combination of hot and cold delicacies, or Castaway Tom Sawyer's seafood cauldron, filled with a delicious combination of seasonal fish and shellfish. ⊠ *17–19 Hunter St., Old Hobart Town,* ☎ *03/6234–1903. Reservations essential. AE, MC, V.*

$$$ ✕ **Mures Upper Deck Restaurant.** Situated on the upper floor of the
★ Mures Fish House complex on the wharf, the Upper Deck has superb views of the waterfront. Because the interior, made of Tasmanian wood, tended to amplify diners' chatter, huge stuffed fishes were suspended from the ceiling to combat the noise, and the restaurant is now famous for these flying undersea creatures. Try the superb flathead, the house version of a local fish, trevalla—panfried with smoked trout pâté and Brie—or seafood tagliatelle, a mixture of fish, shellfish, bacon, mushrooms, onions, and cream served over pasta. Downstairs, **Mures Lower Deck** (☎ 03/6231–2121) is a less expensive alternative: You'll get a number with your order and take your food out by the dock or to tables outside. ⊠ *Victoria Dock,* ☎ *03/6231–1999. AE, DC, MC, V. No credit cards downstairs.*

$$$ ✕ **Sisco's Restaurant.** This is one of the best Spanish and Mediterranean
★ restaurants in Australia, as the crowds that flock here on Friday and Saturday nights attest. The decor is distinctly Iberian, with soft lighting, stucco walls, Spanish tiles, and heavy wooden tables, and there are strolling guitar players. Sisco's is renowned for air-dried ham, homemade pork sausages, stuffed squid, and river trout. ⊠ *121 Macquarie St.,* ☎ *03/6223–2059. AE, DC, MC, V. Closed Sun.*

$$ ✕ **Aegean Restaurant.** Don't go to this lively Greek restaurant looking for romance. This is the place to bring a large group—the larger the better—for a meal interspersed with belly dancing, plate throwing, and traditional Greek dancing. During lulls, enjoy moussaka, vegetarian platters, marinated chicken livers, or grilled chicken. ⊠ *121 Collins St.,* ☎ *03/6231–1000. AE, DC, MC, V. BYOB (wine only). Closed Sun. and Mon.*

$$ ✕ **Ali Akbar.** A roaring fire and Lebanese music welcome you to this
★ traditional restaurant in northern Hobart. White tablecloths and fresh flowers add to the appealing atmosphere. Here you'll find some great modern interpretations of traditional dishes—and superb use of local produce. Typical Lebanese dishes include *maqlubat-al-qarnabeet* (a mixture of cauliflower, pine kernels, and spiced rice) and *sambousek* (yeast pastry filled with feta cheese, egg, and parsley). After 9 PM you can order the banquet plate, a combination of various hot and cold dishes. ⊠ *321 Elizabeth St.,* ☎ *03/6231–1770. Reservations essential. AE, DC, MC, V. BYOB. Closed Mon.*

$$ ✕ **Riviera Ristorante.** On the wharf across the street from the Sheraton Hobart, this simply decorated restaurant is always busy and noisy. And you can expect to stand in line for tables packed together on the restaurant's bare floor. The wait is worthwhile. All the food, includ-

ing the pasta, is very tasty. There are 15 choices of pizza and 16 different sauces to accompany four types of pasta. Try pasta *tricolore*—three types of pasta served with three sauces. ✉ *15 Hunter St., Sullivans Cove,* ☎ *03/6234–3230. Reservations not accepted. AE, MC, V.*

Lodging

$$$$ ⊞ **Grand Chancellor Hotel.** Across the street from the old wharf and
★ some of the best restaurants in Hobart, this monolith seems a bit out of place amid Hobart's quaint colonialism. What it lacks in period charm, however, it more than makes up for in luxury. All rooms have a large wooden desk, and thick white bathrobes are provided for guests' use. No detail, it seems, has been forgotten—there is even music in the bathrooms. Some rooms overlook the harbor. ✉ *Box 1601, 1 Davey St., 7001,* ☎ *03/6235–4535 or 1800/22–2229,* FAX *03/6223–8175. 234 rooms with bath. 2 restaurants, beauty salon, massage, sauna, health club. AE, DC, MC, V.*

$$$$ ⊞ **Salamanca Inn.** Close to the Salamanca Place market, these elegant self-contained units are built from Tasmanian timber and incorporate the latest energy-saving devices. The inn was built in 1988, but its architectural design blends in well with this historic district. Queen-size sofa beds, modern kitchens, and free laundry facilities make these apartments perfect for families. Ask for a room on the sunny western side, but don't expect great views from a three-story building. All apartments are serviced by housekeepers. ✉ *10 Gladstone St., 7000,* ☎ *03/6223–3300 or 1800/03–0944,* FAX *03/6223–7167. 60 rooms with bath. Restaurant, pool, spa. AE, DC, MC, V.*

$$$–$$$$ ⊞ **Wrest Point Hotel and Casino.** Built in 1940, this 17-floor luxury hotel earned its renown in 1973, when it opened the first legalized gambling casino in Australia. For lodgings, choose the more expensive tower or the moderately priced motor inn. The higher floors offer enjoyable views of either Mt. Wellington or the Derwent River. Regine's Videoteque and the nightclub are major entertainment spots in Hobart. ✉ *410 Sandy Bay Rd., Sandy Bay 7005,* ☎ *03/6225–0112 or 1800/03–0611,* FAX *03/6225–2424. 278 rooms with bath. Restaurants, room service, indoor pool, beauty salon, tennis court, health club. AE, DC, MC, V.*

$$$ ⊞ **Islington Elegant Private Hotel.** A converted 1845 mansion, this guest
★ house exudes taste from the moment you enter its spacious, high-ceiling, black-and-white tiled entrance hall. Rooms are decorated in a cozy colonial style with Laura Ashley curtains and matching bedspreads. Although it's only minutes from the city center, the hotel seems comfortably isolated, with a lush garden, outdoor pool, and stunning view of Mt. Wellington. Ask for a room with garden access. Personal service is stressed, and guests who are staying for an extended period are picked up from the airport and may even be shuttled into the city. A complimentary Continental breakfast is served in a sunny conservatory. ✉ *321 Davey St., 7000,* ☎ *03/6223–3900,* FAX *03/6234–9053. 8 suites. Pool. DC, MC, V.*

$$$ ⊞ **Lenna of Hobart.** This 19th-century hotel, a short stroll from Bat-
★ tery Point and Salamanca Place, is an eclectic mix of Old World charm and Australian colonial furnishing. Inside this 1874 Italianate mansion, soft lights glow through stained-glass walkways that are lined with urns and Greek statuary. Rooms are furnished with flower-upholstered wicker chairs, canopy beds, and antique-style telephones. Alexander's Restaurant serves some of the best cooking in the state (☞ Dining, *above*). ✉ *20 Runnymede St., 7000,* ☎ *03/6232–3900 or 1800/03–0633,* FAX *03/6224–0112. 50 rooms with bath. Restaurant. AE, DC, MC, V.*

$$ ⌂ **Westside Hotel.** Well-positioned in the center of the city, the modern Westside has functional, rather than stylish, rooms, most of which have good views of the city skyline or harbor. Four executive suites, decorated in various styles from modern to Japanese, have Jacuzzis, and two double rooms are specifically designed for guests with disabilities. ⌧ *156 Bathurst St., 7000,* ☎ *03/6234–6255,* ℻ *03/6234–7884, telex AA58228. 139 rooms with bath. Restaurant, room service. AE, DC, MC, V.*

Cottages and Guest Houses

$$ ⌂ **Barton Cottage.** Built in 1837, this Battery Point lodge maintains
★ its colonial grace while offering modern conveniences. Rooms with such names as Footman, Pantrymaid, and Chambermaid are simply decorated with antiques, and all have private facilities. ⌧ *72 Hampden Rd., 7000,* ☎ *03/6224–1606,* ℻ *03/6224–1724. 6 rooms with bath. No credit cards.*

$$ ⌂ **Colville Cottage.** From the moment you pass through the white picket fence and into the garden surrounding this cottage, you can't help but feel relaxed. The interior isn't fancy, but hardwood floors, fireplaces, fresh flowers, and bay windows create a warm, cozy atmosphere. Afternoon tea is served outside on the veranda. Rates include breakfast. ⌧ *32 Mona St., 7000,* ☎ *03/6223–6968,* ℻ *03/6224–0500. 6 rooms with bath. MC, V.*

$$ ⌂ **Cromwell Cottage.** Built in the 1880s, this simple guest house is remarkable for its colorful rooms. You have the choice of an all-red, an all-yellow (the sunniest), or an all-blue room. Otherwise, ask for the garden room, with its large brass bed and ornate chandeliers. Some of the rooms have a view of the Derwent River. Rates include breakfast. ⌧ *6 Cromwell St., 7000,* ☎ *03/6223–6734. 5 rooms with bath. V.*

$$ ⌂ **Elms of Hobart.** Classified by the National Trust, this immaculately restored heritage mansion in North Hobart offers colonial-style accommodations. There are just four suites on two floors, and all have fireplaces, electric blankets, telephones, and tea makers. ⌧ *452 Elizabeth St., North Hobart,* ☎ *03/6231–3277. 4 suites. Laundry. MC, V.*

$$ ⌂ **Warwick Cottages.** Annie's Room and Pandora's Box are identical cottages built by convicts in 1854. Now they're filled with an assortment of colonial bric-a-brac that lends them their individual charm. Pandora's Box, for example, has an antique meat grinder and old-style carriage lanterns. A winding staircase in each cottage leads to a double bed upstairs, and the ground floor has two single beds. ⌧ *119–121 Warwick St., 7000,* ☎ *018/12–5049,* ℻ *03/6254–1527. 2 units with bath. V.*

Nightlife and the Arts

Hobart's nightlife is very tame. Consult the Friday or Saturday editions of the local newspaper, *The Mercury,* for the latest in evening entertainment. *This Week in Tasmania,* available at most hotels, is a comprehensive guide to current performances and rock and jazz concerts.

Casino

Located in the Wrest Point Hotel, the **Wrest Point Casino** has blackjack, American roulette, minibaccarat, keno, minidice, craps, federal wheel, federal poker and stud poker, and two-up. Maximum stakes are $500 (a special suite on the ground floor caters to high rollers). The Wrest Point also offers late-night comedy and cabaret. **Regines Night Club** is open late for dancing (from 9 PM onward). ⌧ *410 Sandy Bay Rd., Sandy Bay 7005,* ☎ *03/6225–0112 or 008/03–0611.* ☾ *Mon.– Thurs. 1 PM–3 AM, Fri. and Sat. 1 PM–4 AM, Sun. noon–3 AM.*

Music

Out at the **Carlysle Hotel** (⊠ 232 Main Rd., Derwent Park, ☎ 03/6272–0299) every Friday and Saturday night the popular "Sixties in the Suburbs" night is hosted by a local radio station DJ. If you'd prefer something more sedate, try the piano bar at the **Grand Chancellor** (⊠ 1 Davey St., ☎ 03/6235–4535). For the serious bop-till-you-drop set, try **Knopwoods Retreat Hotel** (⊠ Salamanca Pl., ☎ 03/6223–2290), **Round Midnight** (⊠ 39 Salamanca Pl., ☎ 03/6223–2491), and **Stoppy's Waterfront Tavern** (⊠ 21 Salamanca Pl., ☎ 03/6223–3799).

The **ABC Odeon** (⊠ 167 Liverpool St., ☎ 03/6235–3634) hosts concerts of the Tasmanian Symphony Orchestra and organizes youth concerts. The ABC and the Conservatorium of Music stage regular lunchtime concerts in the State Library Auditorium on Murray Street.

Theater

Theatre Royal (⊠ 29 Campbell St., ☎ 03/6234–6266), an architectural gem that dates back to 1834—look carefully at the portraits of composers painted on the magnificent dome—puts on plays. Other performances can be seen at the **Playhouse Theatre** (⊠ 106 Bathurst St., ☎ 03/6234–1536).

Wine Bar

Oenophiles should try Tasmanian wine, some of which is exceptional. Look for Pipers Brook, Heemskerk, Freycinet, and Moorilla Estate labels. For sampling in convivial surroundings, try **Nickelby's Wine Bar** (⊠ 217 Sandy Bay Rd., ☎ 03/6223–6030).

Outdoor Activities and Sports

Bicycling

For rentals, try **Peregrine Adventures.** ⊠ *5/13 Beechworth Rd., Sandy Bay,* ☎ *03/6225–0944.*

Bushwalking

A variety of walking tracks are within easy reach of Hobart, including several routes around Mt. Wellington, which you'll need a car to reach. Stop in at the Visitors' Information Centre (☞ Hobart A to Z, *below*) for more information.

Fishing

Tasmania is one of the best places in the world for trout fishing: Lakes and streams are well stocked. The season runs from August through May, and licensed trout-fishing trips can be arranged through the **Tasmanian Travel and Information Centre** (⊠ 20 Davey St., at Elizabeth St., ☎ 03/6230–8233).

Skiing

Tasmanian snowfields are only an hour's drive from Hobart, so if you stay in town, you can get to the slopes early the next day. The main ski area is at Mt. Field, 81 km (50 mi) northwest of Hobart. Contact the Visitors' Information Centre (☞ Hobart A to Z, *below*) for information on conditions, accommodations, and equipment rental.

Spectator Sports

You'll be able to watch cricket, soccer, and Australian-rules football all in Hobart: cricket matches in summer (November–March) at the **Bellerive Oval** (☎ 03/6244–7099) in the Queens Domain, and football matches Saturday afternoons in winter at **North Hobart Sports Ground** (☎ 03/6234–3203). You can buy tickets at the gates.

Swimming

The **Hobart Olympic Pool** (☎ 03/6234–4232) on Domain Road and **Clarence Swimming Centre** (☎ 03/6244–2294) on Riawena Road, Montagu Bay, both welcome visitors. River and ocean beaches are within easy reach of Hobart.

Shopping

Tasmania is noted for its artisans and craftspeople, who use local timber—Huon pine, sassafrass, myrtle—to fashion such items as letter racks and salad bowls. Stores worth a visit include **Aspect Design** (✉ 79 Salamanca Pl., ☎ 03/6223–2642), which stocks blown glass, wooden products, pottery, jewelry, and postcards; **Handmark Gallery** (✉ 77 Salamanca Pl., ☎ 03/6223–7895), which sells Hobart's best wooden jewelry boxes as well as Art Deco–style jewelry, pottery, painting, and sculpture; the **National Trust Gift Shop** (✉ Galleria, 33 Salamanca Pl., ☎ 03/6223–7371), crowded with smaller items, such as lacework and Tasmanian motif tea towels; and **Sullivan's Cove** (✉ 47 Salamanca Pl., ☎ 03/6223–7262), located in a building dating from the 1860s and carrying women's clothing along with crafts and prints.

Hobart A to Z

Arriving and Departing

BY BUS

Tasmanian Redline Coaches (☎ 03/6231–3233 or 1800/03–0033) run daily to towns and cities across the state. Buses also meet the ferry from Victoria that comes into Tasmania's northern port city, Devonport (for ferry information, *see* Northwest Coast A to Z, *below*). Super Tassie Passes, 15-day tickets for unlimited travel around Tasmania, cost $149; 30-day passes cost $199. **Tiger Line** (✉ 4 Liverpool St., ☎ 03/6234–4077 or 1800/03–0620) provides a similar range of intrastate services (including Port Arthur and the east coast). For $140 you can purchase a Wilderness and Highway Pass that gives 14 days' unlimited travel to principal cities and wilderness areas.

BY CAR

If you're arriving in Devonport on the *Spirit of Tasmania* ferry from Melbourne, Hobart is about four hours south by car.

BY PLANE

Hobart International Airport is one hour by air from Melbourne or two hours from Sydney.

On the island, **Airlines of Tasmania** flies between Hobart, Launceston, and the northwest and west coasts. Tickets can also be booked through **Tasmanian Travel and Information Centres** (☞ Visitor Information, *below*) in cities around the island. ☞ Air Travel *in* the Gold Guide for information on airlines.

Between the Airport and Downtown. Hobart International Airport is located 22 km (14 mi) east of Hobart. The trip along the Eastern Outlet Road should take no more than 20 minutes by car. **Tasmanian Redline Coaches** (☞ *above*) has regular shuttle service for $7 per person between the airport and its downtown depot at 199 Collins Street. For small groups, **taxis** are an economical way to travel to the city. Metered taxis are available at the taxi stand in front of the terminal. The fare to downtown Hobart is approximately $25.

Getting Around

BY BUS

The **Metropolitan Transport Trust** (MTT) operates a bus system from downtown Hobart to the surrounding suburbs daily from 6 AM to midnight. Special "Day Rover" tickets for $3.10 permit unlimited use of buses for a day. ⊠ *Inquiries at Metroshop, 18 Elizabeth St.,* ☎ *03/ 6233–4222.*

BY CAR

Unlike mainland Australia, most places in Tasmania are within easy driving distance: rarely more than three or four hours in a stretch, if that. Hobart itself is extremely compact—most sights are easily visited on a walking tour. Looking farther afield, a car allows access to places on the outskirts of the city, as well as to the lookout point atop windy and often snowy Mount Wellington, and the larger opportunity to get out and about on the island. If you drive in the city, watch the one-way street system in the city center, which takes some getting used to.

BY TAXI

You can hail metered taxis in the street, or find them at designated stands and major hotels. Cabs for hire have lighted signs on their roofs. Contact **City Cabs** (☎ 03/6234–3633) or **Taxi Combined** (☎ 03/6234–8444).

Contacts and Resources

B&B RESERVATION AGENCIES

Homehost Tasmania (⊠ Box 780, Sandy Bay 7005, ☎ 03/6224–1612, FAX 03/6224–0472) arranges for visitors to stay in Tasmanian homes, many of which are farms, cottages, and Federation-style houses. Prices are generally inexpensive to moderate, and breakfast is included. Dinners often can be arranged as well.

CAR RENTALS

Cars, campers, caravans, and minibuses are available for hire. The largest companies are **Avis** (☎ 03/6234–4222 or 1800/03–0008), **Budget** (☎ 03/6234–5222 or 03/6213–2727), **Autorent Hertz** (☎ 03/6234–5555 or 13–6039), and **Colonial Thrifty** (☎ 03/6234–1341 or 1800/22–6434). Some lower-priced rental companies include **Lo-Cost Auto Rent** (☎ 03/6231–0550 or 1800/03–0023) and **Range Rent-a-Bug** (☎ 03/6231–0300).

EMERGENCIES

Ambulance, fire brigade, and **police.** ☎ *000.*
St. Helen's Private Hospital. ⊠ *186 Macquarie St.,* ☎ *03/6221–6444.*
Royal Hobart Hospital. ⊠ *48 Liverpool St.,* ☎ *03/6238–8308.*

GUIDED TOURS

Bicycling. Brake Out Cycling Tours (☎ 03/6278–2966) leads tours from Mt. Wellington, Mt. Nelson, and other neighboring scenic areas. The company provides all equipment, and a guide and support vehicle accompany you on the road. Lunch and morning and afternoon teas are included on most tours.

Flightseeing. Par Avion Tours (☎ 03/6248–5390) offers some of the most exciting ways to see Hobart and its surroundings. One flight goes to Melaleuca Inlet on the west coast and includes a boat trip with **Wilderness Tours** around Bathurst Harbour, with stops for bushwalking. The cost is all-inclusive, and lunch and afternoon tea are provided.

Harbor Tours. Transderwent (⊠ Franklin Wharf Ferry Pier, ☎ 03/6223–5893) runs the *MV Emmalisa,* an old-fashioned ferry, daily around Derwent Harbour. Cruises (1¼ hours) include an excellent commentary on Hobart and its environs, and the lunchtime trip includes a hot meal. Fare is $10 ($15 for the lunch cruise). The *MV Cartela* (⊠

Franklin Wharf Ferry Pier, ☎ 03/6223–1914), built in 1912, plies the harbor and D'Entrecasteaux Channel in the morning, at lunch, and in the afternoon. Fares start at $12. The *Rhona H* sailing ship (✉ Franklin Wharf Ferry Pier, ☎ 018/13–3396) takes to the harbor four times daily. The $25 cost includes refreshments.

Orientation Tours. Hobart Sightseeing (✉ 199 Collins St., ☎ 03/6231–3511) runs half-day city sightseeing tours on Tuesday, Thursday, and Saturday mornings, including visits to Battery Point and Salamanca Place. The cost is $23. **TigerLine–Gray Line** (✉ 4 Liverpool St., ☎ 03/6234–4077) buses operate full-day tours every Saturday that take in Salamanca Place, nearby Russell Falls National Park, and Richmond. Fare is $47.

Walking Tours. Walks led by the **National Trust** (☎ 03/6223–7570) provide an excellent overview of Battery Point, including visits to mansions and 19th-century houses. Tours leave the wishing well (near the post office in Franklin Square) at Battery Point every Saturday at 9:30 AM, and the $8 cost includes morning tea. The **National Trust** also conducts daily tours (hourly 10–2) of the old penitentiary, courthouse, and chapel on Campbell Street. ✉ *National Trust, 6 Brisbane St.,* ☎ *03/6223–5200.*

VISITOR INFORMATION
Tasmanian Travel and Information Centre. ✉ *20 Davey St., at Elizabeth St.,* ☎ *03/6230–8233.*

PORT ARTHUR

102 km (63 mi) southeast of Hobart.

When Governor Arthur was looking for a site to dump his worst convict offenders in 1830, the Tasman Peninsula was a natural choice. Joined to the rest of Tasmania only by the narrow Eaglehawk Neck, the spit was easy to isolate and guard. And so Port Arthur was born, a penal colony whose name became a byword for vicious horror and cruelty. Between 1830 and 1877, nearly 13,000 convicts served sentences in Britain's equivalent of Devil's Island, and nearly 2,000 of them died here. Few men escaped—dogs were used to patrol the narrow causeway, and sharks were reputed to infest the waters. Reminders of those dark days remain in some of the names—Dauntless Point, Stinking Point, Isle of the Dead. But today this once foreboding peninsula has become Tasmania's major tourist attraction, filled with beautiful scenery and historic attractions that recapture Australia's difficult beginnings. Although many visitors come here on a day trip from Hobart, consider at least an overnight stay. There is more than enough to do here to occupy a couple of days, and watching afternoon shadows lengthen over the ruins creates a mood much more in keeping with the settlement's doleful past. Walking these grounds at dawn is magical, especially when taking in the view from the knoll behind the church.

Following the bloody rampage of Martin Bryant, Port Arthur's always eerie atmosphere has taken on a more poignant air. In April 1996, he shot 35 people at the historic site and in a nearby village; this was Australia's single worst killing. He was tried, pleaded guilty, and sentenced to life in jail without remission. The café that was the scene of much of the slaughter has been demolished, save for a portion retained as a memorial to the dead.

Exploring Port Arthur

The grounds on which the **Port Arthur Penal Settlement** once stood now compose one of the nicest parks in Tasmania—but be prepared to do a lot of walking among widely scattered sites. When you stand by scenic Carnarvon Bay, it is hard to imagine the bloodshed and misery that existed here. But when you walk into the solitary confinement cells or the main penitentiary, it's hard to fight off the unsettling feeling. Most of the original buildings were damaged by bush fires in 1877, shortly after the settlement was abandoned, but you can still see the beautiful church, round guard house, commandant's residence, model prison, hospital, and government cottages.

The old **lunatic asylum** is now an excellent museum featuring a scale model of the Port Arthur settlement, a video history, and a collection of tools, leg irons, and chains. Along with a walking tour of the grounds and entrance at the museum, admission includes a harbor cruise, of which there are eight daily in summer. There is a separate twice-daily cruise to and tour of the **Isle of the Dead,** which sits in the middle of the bay. It is estimated that 1,769 convicts and 180 free people are buried here, mostly in communal pits. No headstones were used to mark the sites—bodies were simply bundled in sailcloth, thrown in a hole, and sprinkled with quicklime. ✉ *Penal Settlement Tour $13, Isle of the Dead tour $5; admission valid for multiple entries over 24-hr period.* ☉ *Isle of the Dead tour daily at noon and 3.*

☾ **Bush Mill Steam Railway and Settlement** is a great place to learn about a miller's life at the turn of the century. Highlights are a replica steam-powered bush sawmill, with a working steam engine, and a narrow-gauge steam railway that was once used to transport timber. The train runs at least three times daily for rides. ✉ *Arthur Hwy.,* ☎ *03/6250-2221.* ✉ *$12.50.* ☉ *Daily 9–5.*

The **Tasmanian Devil Park** is a wildlife refuge for injured animals of many species. It's probably the best place in the state to see Tasmanian devils (a burrowing carnivorous marsupial about the size of a dog), as well as quolls, boobooks, masked owls, eagles, and other native fauna. The park is unusual in that it conducts "night owl" tours that give you a great chance to observe these mainly nocturnal animals when they are most active. ✉ *Taranna, 11 km (7 mi) north of Port Arthur,* ☎ *03/6250-3203.* ✉ *$8.* ☉ *Peak season, daily 8:30–7:30; off season, daily 9:30–4:30.*

Dining and Lodging

$$ ✗ **Tracks.** This small colonial-style restaurant at the Bush Mill specializes in salads and delicious home-baked scones. Other treats include vegetable stockpot and marinated Scotch fillet, called bushman's steak. Try apple crumble and ice cream for dessert. ✉ *Port Arthur,* ☎ *03/6250-2221. Reservations not accepted. AE, DC, MC, V.*

$$ 🏠 **Cascades Colonial Accommodation.** Part of a onetime convict out-station that dates to 1841, these cottages are comfortable and full of character. Each is equipped with kitchen facilities, and breakfast provisions are included in the room rate. There is also a small museum related to the property on site. ✉ *Nubeena Rd., Koonya (20 km, or 12 mi, north of Port Arthur),* ☎ FAX *03/6250-3121. 4 cottages with bath. No credit cards.*

$$ 🏠 **Port Arthur Motor Inn.** Situated on a ridge behind an old church,
★ this motel overlooks the entire historic Penal Settlement site. The comfortable but somewhat old-fashioned guest rooms sport 1960s decor, with small bathrooms. Although none of the accommodations have good views, the hotel's main restaurant, the Commandant's Table, overlooks the prison ruins, a particularly lovely vista at sunset. The food, sadly, is unworthy of the setting—you would do better to eat in the

much cheaper (but viewless) pub restaurant adjacent. ⊠ *Tasman Hwy., Port Arthur 7182,* ☎ *03/6250–2101 or 1800/03–0747,* FAX *03/6250–2417. 35 rooms with bath. Bar. AE, DC, MC, V.*

$$ ⌂ **Port Arthur Villas.** Two stones' throws from the penal colony site, these apartments are modern, but they have design elements that follow Port Arthur style, such as verandas, old-fashioned brickwork, and pleasant cottage gardens. Studio and two-bedroom apartments are well appointed and have fully equipped kitchens. There are also barbecue facilities and a playground on site. ⊠ *Safety Cove Rd., Port Arthur,* ☎ *03/6250–2239,* FAX *03/6250–2589. 9 apartments. AE, DC, MC, V.*

Port Arthur A to Z

Arriving and Departing
BY CAR

Port Arthur is an easy 90-minute drive from Hobart via the Lyell Highway and the Arthur Highway, but it is worth pausing at such places as Eaglehawk Neck, where tethered guard dogs used to be placed to dissuade escaped convicts from heading farther north. Nearby is the Tessellated Pavement, an interesting geological formation; the Blowhole, spectacular in wild weather; and Tasman Arch, a naturally formed archway.

Getting Around
BY CAR

A private vehicle is essential if you want to explore parts of the Tasman Peninsula beyond the historic settlement.

Contacts and Resources
GUIDED TOURS

The **Port Arthur Penal Settlement** conducts a variety of daily tours around Port Arthur (☞ *above*), as well as popular nightly ghost tours (☎ $10). Guides recount stories of apparitions and supposed hauntings at the site while walking its darkened attractions by torchlight. There is also a self-guided audiocassette tour (☎ $3) that gives visitors a running commentary on the sites at the settlement. ⊠ *Information Office,* ☎ *03/6250–2539.*

Hobart Sightseeing (⊠ 199 Collins St., Hobart, ☎ 03/6231–3511) has full-day tours (☎ $49) of the penal settlement and Bush Mill. **Remarkable Tours** (☎ 03/6250–2359, or book through Port Arthur Information Office, ☎ 03/6250–2539) offers minibus tours from the Port Arthur Penal Settlement to such nearby scenic sites as Remarkable Cave and observation points along the coast. **Tasman Peninsula Detours** (⊠ Port Arthur Settlement, ☎ 03/6250–3355) gives daily four-wheel-drive tours of rain forests, beaches, and the convict ruins. The all-day tour includes morning and afternoon tea, as well as a barbecue lunch with wine. The **Tasmanian Travel and Information Centre** (⊠ 20 Davey St., at Elizabeth St., ☎ 03/6230–8233) organizes day trips from Hobart to Port Arthur by bus.

FREYCINET NATIONAL PARK

It took the early European explorers of Van Diemen's Land four voyages and 161 years to realize that the Freycinet Peninsula, a thickly forested wedge of granite jutting east into the Southern Ocean, was not an island.

In 1642 Abel Tasman saw it through fierce squalls, and thinking it separate from the mainland named it van der Lyn's Island, after a member of the council of governors of the Dutch East India Company. In

1773, Tobias Furneaux in HMS *Adventure*, part of Captain Cook's second world expedition, passed by far enough out to sea to believe Tasman's theory. Twenty-five years later, Matthew Flinders agreed, and it was not until Nicolas Baudin's 1803 hydrographer, Pierre Faure, took a longboat and crew into what is now Great Oyster Bay to prove that van der Lyn's island was in fact a peninsula. It was named the Freycinet Peninsula after the expedition's chief cartographer.

It is ironic that this piece of Tasmania's east coast should have been so misunderstood because of foul weather—the climate here is as benign as anywhere on the island. And that climate, especially in summer, is a reason why the wild Freycinet Peninsula is prime walking terrain.

The road onto the peninsula halts just beyond the township of **Coles Bay,** at a carpark busy with serious hikers strapping on backpacks and lacing boots, and day trippers deciding whether they're up to the steep 30-minute climb to the saddle of a mountain and a lookout platform over the absurdly precise half-moon shape of **Wineglass Bay.** Many stop there, but others plunge down the rocky, precipitous slope to the bay, where talcum-soft white sand meets turquoise water. With the hulking granite bluffs of **Mount Graham** and **Mount Freycinet** looming in the background above a mantle of trees, it couldn't be more spectacular. The walk to the end of Wineglass Bay and back to the carpark takes about 2½ hours.

The many walking trails of the peninsula are well signposted. On a day trip, you can walk across the peninsula at its narrowest point, along the **Isthmus Track** past swamps and myriad waterbirds, to Hazards Beach, which is more protected for swimming than Wineglass Bay. You can then return on the **Hazards Beach Track,** beneath the mighty bulk of the snaggle-toothed Hazards, the daunting granite towers that glower over the national park. This walk takes about 4½ hours.

A longer walk of about six hours takes you along the length of lovely **Hazards Beach,** along which there is evidence of Aboriginal occupation in the numerous shell middens—old refuse heaps—that dot the dunes. A more strenuous walk climbs from the end of Wineglass Bay over the summit of **Mount Graham,** and then to **Cook's Beach,** returning along Hazards Beach. It will take at least seven hours.

Daily entry to the park costs $2.50, $8 for vehicles.

Dining and Lodging

Freelance camping is permitted in the park—walkers should register at the booth in the carpark—and there is a campground inland of Cook's Beach. Water is scarce, particularly in summer, so overnighting is advised only for experienced campers. Walkers can also spend the night inside Cook's Hut, the granite and tin homestead of the 19th-century grazier who attempted to make a living on this marginal land.

$$$ ✕🏨 **Freycinet Lodge.** The lodge's wooden one- and two-bedroom cabins are unobtrusively situated in a densely treed setting overlooking Great Oyster Bay. Simple but comfortable rooms and furnishings are enriched with handsome Tasmanian timber. Secluded balconies are ideal for drinking in the views. Local seafood on the menu is particularly good; meals are not included in room rates. ✉ *Freycinet National Park, Coles Bay 7215,* ☎ *03/6257–0101,* FAX *03/6257–0278. 36 rooms with bath. Restaurant, tennis, recreation room. MC, V.*

Arriving and Departing

BY BUS
Tasmanian Redline Coaches (☎ 03/6234–4577) runs between Hobart and Bicheno, where you can connect with a local bus that runs twice

daily on weekdays, and once on Saturday, to Coles Bay. A shuttle bus
runs from Coles Bay to the carpark within the national park.

BY CAR

Freycinet National Park is 206 km (129 mi) northeast of Hobart and
214 km (134 mi) southwest of Launceston. From either city, it is about
a three-hour drive.

Contacts and Resources

GUIDED TOURS

Freycinet Experience (✉ 22 Brisbane St., Box 1879, Launceston 7250,
☎ 03/6334–4615, FAX 03/6334–5525) runs excellent four-day walks
in the park. Accommodation is in high-quality tent camps and an architectural award–winning timber lodge overlooking the stunning
sands of Friendly Beaches. You have the choice on the second day of
traversing Mount Graham or taking the easier option of following the
beach and bush track. Food is outstanding—you'll taste plenty of Tasmanian seafood, wine, and produce.

VISITOR INFORMATION

Freycinet National Park (☎ 03/6257–0107).

THE MIDLANDS

Tasmania's Midlands is first and foremost pastoral countryside—
green, undulating landscapes set off by views of distant highlands. And
dropping in on the towns that lie off the Midlands Highway is another
way to get a feeling for Tasmania's past—milder than the skull-and-
bones drama of Port Arthur. Oatlands, Ross, and Longford are full of
old buildings, some of which have taken on new lives as bed and
breakfasts.

When the original track of the Hobart-Launceston Highway was finished in 1818, it linked two separately developed (and administered)
colonies. By the middle of the last century it was the best route in Australia, and it was largely bushranger-free. The road now skirts most
of the historic towns, so a journey along the Midlands Highway calls
for short side trips into pieces of history frozen in time and delightfully free of through traffic—you're more likely to encounter mobs of
sheep than lines of cars. The entire strip (Rte. 1) is only 200 km (124
mi) long and can be driven nonstop in less than three hours.

Oatlands

85 km (53 mi) north of Hobart.

Situated alongside Lake Dulverton, this Georgian gem was built during the 1820s to serve the newly arrived local farming community as
a garrison town and to house convicts building the highway. It was
named in June 1821 by Governor Macquarie for what he predicted
would be the best use for the surrounding fertile plains. The whole town
of Oatlands looks rather like an open-air museum, and enough buildings have plaques explaining their significance to reward the most curious wanderer. Since the highway bypassing town was completed, the
main street (inevitably called High Street) has returned to looking
much as it did for the past century.

The most outstanding structure in Oatlands is the **Council Chambers
and Town Hall** (not open to the public), erected in 1880 from local sandstone. In fact, the town of Oatlands has the greatest concentration of
sandstone buildings in Australia—there are more than 150 within a
2-km (1-mi) radius.

Oatlands' oldest building is the **Court House.** The large room at its core was reputedly built in 1829 by two convicts in four months.

Callington Mill (☎ 03/6254–1525; ☉ weekdays 9–5) was completed in 1837 and used wind power to grind grain. With the surrounding mill buildings, it gives a glimpse into early Tasmanian industry.

Of Oatlands' **churches,** Georgian **St. Peter's Anglican** was built in 1838 from a design by John Lee Archer, the colony's civil enginer, who also designed the bridge at Ross. **St. Paul's Catholic** was built in 1848, again of the mellow golden sandstone prevalent in Oatlands. The **Presbyterian Campbell Memorial Church** was erected in 1856 and in 1859 after the original steeple collapsed. Don't miss the row of workers' cottages at the end of High Street.

Dining and Lodging

$$ ✕ **Blossum's of Oatlands.** Unlike most buildings in Oatlands, this one is made of convict-made brick, not sandstone, and it retains the original wooden floors and open fireplaces. The menu changes each week but invariably features rainbow trout and Tasmanian-apple pie topped with rich King Island cream. ✉ *116–118 High St.*, ☎ *03/6254–1516. MC, V.*

$–$$ ✕🏠 **Wilmot Arms Inn.** Built in 1843, Wilmot Arms's term as an inn was interrupted 100 years ago when its proprietor got religion. It is furnished with antiques, a vintage piano, and an open fireplace and is exclusively for nonsmokers. All meals are available, and there's a guest laundry facility. ✉ *Main Rd., Kempton, 32 km (20 mi) south of Oatlands,* ☎ *03/6259–1272. 5 rooms with shared bath. AE, MC, V.*

$$ 🏠 **Amelia Cottage.** Convict-built in 1838, this cottage contains many of its original features including shutters, fuel stove, baker's oven, and flagstone kitchen floor, with modern amenities cleverly concealed. There is a claw-foot bath, even an antique high chair and crib. Toys are provided for children to play with, the nursery being a special feature of the cottage, which can sleep 12 people. ✉ *104 High St, Oatlands.* ☎ *03/6254–1264. 4 cottages. DC, MC, V.*

$ 🏠 **Oatlands Lodge.** The two-story guest house has one of the prettiest interiors in Tasmania, with convict-split sandstone walls complemented by attractive and comfortable country furnishings and quilts. This building is right in the middle of Oatlands, but as the village is no longer on the highway, it's a blessedly tranquil place. Built in 1837, Oatlands Lodge has also served as a shop and a girls' school. All the rooms have en suite bathrooms. A complete English-style breakfast is included. ✉ *92 High St.,* ☎ *03/6254–1444. 4 rooms with bath. MC, V.*

Ross

55 km (34 mi) north of Oatlands, 140 km (87½ mi) north of Hobart.

This pretty village of some 500 residents is Tasmania's most historic town.

Ross Bridge (1836) is John Lee Archer's best-loved work. Graceful arches are highlighted by local sandstone and the decorative carvings of a convicted highwayman, Daniel Herbert, who was given freedom for his efforts. Herbert's work can also be seen throughout the graveyard where he's buried. ✉ *Bridge St.*

The buildings at the intersection of **Church Street** (the main street) and Bridge Street are often said to summarize life neatly. They include the **Man-O-Ross Hotel** (Temptation), the **Town Hall** (Re-creation), the

Catholic Church (Salvation), and the **Old Gaol** (Damnation). Other historic buildings in Ross include the **Macquarie Store,** the **Old Ross General Store,** and the old **Scotch Thistle Inn,** built around 1840. The Man-O-Ross is the town's best option for food of the basic counter meal variety.

The **Tasmanian Wool Centre** was built in 1988 as a bicentennial project to provide information about the wool industry. It's fitting that it should be here: The area produces some of Australia's best superfine wool, which is among the best fine wool in the world (New Zealand, on the other hand, excels at producing coarse wool). The chance to see and feel the difference between various wools and divergent thicknesses of wool (and leave with hands soft with lanoline) is worth the admission fee. In 1989, the record price paid for wool was set for a local bale that fetched more than $300,000—$3,008.50 per kilo. It was made into prestige suit lengths. There is also an excellent crafts shop at the front of the Wool Centre with an extensive range of high-quality goods. ⊠ *Church St.,* ☎ *03/6381–5466.* 🖼 *$4.* ⊙ *Nov.–mid-Apr., daily 9–5:30; mid-Apr.–Oct., daily 10–4.*

Lodging

$$ 🏠 **Colonial Cottages of Ross.** Four self-contained cottages, built between 1830 and 1880 provide charming and historic accommodation. Apple Dumpling Cottage (circa 1880) and Hudson Cottage (circa 1850) can accommodate four adults; Church Mouse Cottage (circa 1840) can take only a couple; and Captain Samuel's Cottage (circa 1830) can accommodate six or more people. ⊠ *Church St.,* ☎ *03/6381–5354,* 🖷 *03/6381–5408. MC, V.*

$ 🏠 **Ross Bakery Inn.** Right next to St. John's Church of England, this colonial sandstone building was erected in 1832 and served as the Sherwood Castle Hotel. It is now a very comfortable four-room guest house with a bakery on the premises. At breakfast you get to taste the daily produce from the wood-fired oven. ⊠ *Church St.,* ☎ *03/6381–5246. 4 rooms with bath. MC, V.*

En Route   North of Ross, **Campbell Town** has two notable firsts. Around 1877, Alfred Barret Biggs, a local schoolteacher who had read of Alexander Graham Bell's invention of the telephone in 1876, built his own telephone, partly out of Huon pine. Using the telegram line at Campbell Town railway station, Biggs called Launceston. That may have been the first telephone call in Australia—or in the Southern Hemisphere. Some of his prototype telephones are in Launceston's Queen Victoria Museum. The facts about Mr. Biggs are nebulous (he also developed telescopes) and, as he died in 1900, unlikely ever to be resolved.

In 1931, Harold Gatty, a local lad, was with American flyer Wiley Post on his record-breaking flight around the world (8 days, 15 hrs, 51 min, and a distance of 27,360 km, or 16,963 mi). In so doing, Gatty became the first navigator to circumnavigate the world. A rather ugly metal globe in the park on the western side of the road, at the northern end of Campbell Town, commemorates his achievement.

Longford

72 km (45 mi) northwest of Ross, 212 km (132½ mi) north of Hobart.

It's worth taking a short detour from the highway to visit another designated Historic Town. Settled in 1813, Longford was one of northern Tasmania's first towns. Between the 1950s and the 1970s, Longford attracted interest with its auto racing road circuit, which has since ceased to exist.

The **Archer family** name is all over Longford, and their legacy is in the town's buildings. Of particular early historic interest is **Christ Church,** built in 1839 and set on spacious grounds. William, who was the first Australian-born architect (of European descent), designed the west window of the church. It is regarded as one of the country's finest. **Panshanger,** a historic villa in neoclassical style, belonged to William Archer's uncle Joseph. **Brickendon** was William's father's.

Thomas Archer originally owned **Woolmers,** now one of the best preserved (and least altered) of the area's homesteads. It is almost surprising to find that there are several historic country estates around Longford not built by Archers. ☎ 03/6391–1251. ⌦ $10. ⊙ 2-hr guided tour of Woolmers and Brickendon Tues., Fri., and Sun.

Longford Wildlife Park is set in natural bushland, with a man-made lake, and is home to free-ranging animals, including deer. ⊠ Pateena Rd., ☎ 03/6391–1630. ⌦ $4. ⊙ Tues.–Sun. 9–5.

Lodging

$$ 🏨 **Racecourse Private Hotel.** Built in 1840, this hotel is classified by the National Trust and has a National Estate listing. It is a very pleasant five-room guest house: Four rooms are upstairs attics, and the fifth is on ground level. There's a log fire in the parlor and an array of photographs depicting the hotel's checkered past. ⊠ 114 Marlborough St., ☎ 03/6391–2352, ⅎ̄Ẋ 03/6391–2430. 5 rooms with bath. AE, DC, MC, V.

Midlands A to Z

Arriving and Departing

BY CAR

The Midland Highway bypasses Oatlands, Ross, and Longford—a good thing—and they all lie just off the highway. Oatlands is only an hour's drive from Hobart. Any of these towns can be part of a day trip from the capital, or stops along the drive between Hobart and Launceston.

Contacts and Resources

GUIDED TOURS

Fielding's Historic Tours, in Oatlands (☎ 03/6254–1135), gives an interesting Convict Tour ($6), and an atmospheric Ghost Tour at 9 PM ($8), which inspects jails and other historic buildings by lamplight. **Specialty Tours of Ross** (☎ 03/6381–5354) on Church Street is operated by Tim Johnson, a local history buff who also operates Colonial Cottages of Ross. His Historic Tour has a minimum rate of $25 for up to five people and $3 for any extra clients. Reservations are essential.

LAUNCESTON

Nestled in a fertile agricultural basin where the South and North Esk rivers join to form the Tamar, the city of Launceston is the commercial center of Tasmania's northern region. Its abundance of unusual markets and shops is concentrated downtown, unlike Hobart's gathering of shops in its historic center, set apart from the commercial district. Launceston is far from bustling, and its remarkable qualities reside in its pleasant parks, turn-of-the-century homes, historic mansions, and private gardens. Perhaps its most compelling asset is the magnificent scenery on which it verges: rolling farmland and the rich loam of English-looking landscapes powerfully set off by the South Esk meandering through towering gorges on its way to that confluence of rivers.

Exploring Launceston

Aside from its parks and gardens, Launceston's main appeal is the sumptuous surrounding countryside.

Almost in the heart of the city, **Cataract Gorge** is one of the most spectacular sights in Australia. The South Esk River flows through the gorge on its way toward the Tamar River. A 1½-km (1-mi) path leads along the face of the cliffs to the Cliff Grounds Reserve, where picnic tables, a pool, and a restaurant are located. The park itself looks like a botanic garden, with ornate gazebos and with peacocks strutting on the open lawns. Take the chairlift in the first basin ($4) for a thrilling aerial view of the gorge. Just over 1,000 ft, it is the longest single chairlift span in the world. Several self-guided nature trails wind through the park as well. ⊠ *Follow Paterson St. across Kings Bridge to gorge,* ☎ *03/ 6331–5915.* ☉ *Daily 9–4:40.*

You can cruise along the Tamar River on the quaint MV **Lady Stelfox.** There's a licensed bar and other refreshments on board. ⊠ *Kings Park at Paterson St.,* ☎ *03/6331–6699.* 🎫 *$6.50.* ☉ *Departures every hr 10:10–3:10.*

Trevallyn Dam, on the western outskirts of Launceston, is located in a stunning wildlife preserve. Boating down the South Esk River is common here, but for a unique adventure, try **cable hang gliding**—a 650-ft flight from the edge of a 60-ft cliff. Strapped into a harness and hooked onto a cable, you'll have the thrill of hang gliding with none of the risks. An 85-year-old woman has taken the ride, as has the owner's dog! ⊠ *Trevallyn Dam Quarry,* ☎ *03/6330–1567.* 🎫 *$9.* ☉ *Dec.–Apr., daily 10–5; May–Nov., weekends and holidays 10–4.*

The **Queen Victoria Museum,** opened in 1891 in honor of Queen Victoria's Golden Jubilee, combines items of Tasmanian historical interest with natural history. The museum has a large collection of stuffed birds and animals (including the now-extinct thylacine, or Tasmanian wolf), as well as a Chinese Joss House and a display of coins. ⊠ *Wellington and Paterson Sts.,* ☎ *03/6331–6777.* 🎫 *Free.* ☉ *Mon.– Sat. 10–5, Sun. 2–5.*

☺ The **Penny Royal World and Gunpowder Mill** is the closest thing to a large amusement park in Tasmania, and families can easily spend an entire day here. Rides in sailboats, barges, and trams are included in the ticket price, as are exhibits in the various buildings. Inspect the foundry, museum, and historic gunpowder mills, where cannon are periodically fired. The admission price also includes a ride on the paddle steamer MV *Lady Stelfox,* which cruises up the Cataract Gorge and into the River Tamar. ⊠ *Paterson St.,* ☎ *03/6331–6699.* 🎫 *$19.50.* ☉ *Daily 9–4:30.*

OFF THE BEATEN PATH	The **Waverly Woollen Mills** are still powered by a waterwheel. Opened in 1874, the mill prides itself on using only the finest Tasmanian wool. A store on the premises sells products made in the mills. ⊠ *Across North Esk River at Tasman Hwy. and Waverly Rd.,* ☎ *03/6339–1106.* 🎫 *$4.* ☉ *Weekdays 9–5.*

Dining

$$$$ ✕ **Fee and Me.** Mark Lunnon's award-winning cuisine, presented in
★   a gracious Georgian-style mansion dating from 1838, is Australian-Mediterranean with Asian overtones. His imaginative dishes include oysters in coconut and chili sauce over vermicelli; crayfish baked with whipped butter of saffron, lime, and crayfish flavors; and roast duck-

ling with green Chartreuse glaze and *rösti* potatoes. For dessert try a citrus concoction of lemon potted cream, orange and mint sorbet, brandied orange segments, lemon-glazed shortbread, or lemon ice-cream wedges. The wine list has a good representation of Tasmanian wine. The restaurant is located on the edge of the Launceston city area. ⊠ *190 Charles St.,* ☎ *03/6331–3195. Jacket and tie. AE, MC, V. Closed Sun.*

$$$$ ✕ **The Terrace.** Launceston Country Club Casino's spacious restaurant was designed for the privacy of its diners. Tables are separated by low walls, and each has its own silver champagne bucket. Specialties include smoked duck breast, local scallops, and Atlantic salmon. Steaks are served panfried or au poivre. Special fixed-price dinners include tickets to the evening's cabaret show. ⊠ *Launceston Country Club Casino, Country Club Ave., Prospect Vale 7250,* ☎ *03/6344–8855. Jacket and tie. AE, DC, MC, V. Closed Sun. and Mon.*

$$$ ✕ **Shrimps.** For the best selection of seafood in Launceston, this is the place to go. Set in a brick building erected by convicts in 1824, the restaurant was preceded by a sweetshop and then a private residence. The tables are small and widely spaced, and the menu is chalked on a large blackboard. Nightly specials include oysters, trevalla, whitebait (a minnow-sized delicacy), mussels, and abalone served fresh from the restaurant's tank. ⊠ *72 George St.,* ☎ *03/6334–0584. AE, DC, MC, V. Closed Sun.*

$$$ ✕ **Victoria's Tassie Fare Restaurant.** Located in historic Albert Hall in the middle of City Park, this is one of the few restaurants in Launceston to include only Tasmanian produce on the menu. The casual garden furniture used at lunch is replaced at night with tables set with white tablecloths and silver table settings. Evening specialties include beef and seafood roasts and Tasmanian scallops. A few pasta and vegetarian dishes appear on the extensive menu. There is a 10% surcharge on Sunday and holidays. ⊠ *Cimetiere and Tamar Sts.,* ☎ *03/6331–7433. AE, DC, MC, V.*

$$ ✕ **Posh Nosh.** This noisy, busy deli puts out some of the best and cheap-
★ est food in Launceston. Everything is served fresh or made on the premises. A delightful place for lunch, it offers specialties that include King Island platter of Brie and smoked beef and a gourmet ploughman's lunch of sea trout. A diverse range of soups is offered, including creole chicken and sweet corn, and potato and leek. The restaurant closes at 5:30. ⊠ *127 St. John St.,* ☎ *03/6331–9180. No credit cards. BYOB. Closed weekends.*

$ ✕ **Ripples.** Part of Ritchie's Mill Arts Centre and directly across from the Penny Royal World, this tiny tearoom is a pleasant lunch or afternoon stopover. It serves the best pancakes and crêpes in town and fine coffee. ⊠ *Paterson St.,* ☎ *03/6331–4153. No credit cards. No dinner.*

Lodging

$$$$ ▣ **Launceston Country Club Casino.** This luxury club and casino located on the outskirts of Launceston has been renovated and modernized. The gold and dark tones have been replaced by softer pastels of gray, blue, and pink. The curved driveway to the club is lined with flowers, and the gardens are beautifully kept. The golf course, one of the best in Australia, attracts visitors from all around. The club offers gambling, dancing, and cabaret shows at night. ⊠ *Country Club Ave., Prospect Vale 7250,* ☎ *03/6344–8855 or 1800/03–0211,* FAX *03/6343–1880, telex 58600. 104 rooms with bath. Room service, indoor pool, sauna, spa, golf course, tennis courts, horseback riding, squash, casino, dance club. AE, DC, MC, V.*

$$$ 🏨 **Launceston Novotel.** This six-story building in the heart of Launceston was designed with elegance in mind. When empty, however, the soaring marble foyer can appear quite daunting. The guest rooms are much more comfortable, decorated in pastels with light-color furniture. Lower floors can be noisy from street activity, so ask for a room on a higher floor—but don't expect a view. One of the hotel entrances leads directly into the Yorktown Mall, a major shopping area in Launceston. ⊠ *29 Cameron St., 7250,* ☎ *03/6334–3434 or 1800/03–0123,* 🖷 *03/6331–7347. 165 rooms with bath. 3 restaurants, room service. AE, DC, MC, V.*

$$ 🏨 **Alice's Place.** Constructed from the remains of three buildings erected during the 1840s, this delightful cottage is best known for its whimsical touches. The drawers of the antique furniture might contain old-fashioned gloves, eyeglasses, or books; an old turtle shell and a deer's head hang on the wall; and Victorian costumes, an old Victrola, and a four-poster canopy bed lend colonial charm. Modern conveniences are cleverly tucked away among the period furnishings—take a bath in a huge old tub and then dry your hair with an electric dryer. ⊠ *17 York St., 7250,* ☎ *03/6334–2231,* 🖷 *03/6334–2696. 1 unit with bath sleeps 4. No credit cards.*

$$ 🏨 **O'Hara's Resort Hotel.** A stone's throw from the Launceston Country Club Casino, this moderately priced complex contains holiday units with fully equipped kitchens. Perfect for families, each wood and brick–lined unit has unobtrusive furnishings with simple bedding, matching curtains, and large picture windows. Guests can play golf on the country club's course and use its other facilities as well. ⊠ *10 Casino Rise, 7250,* ☎ *03/6343–1744,* 🖷 *03/6344–9943. 55 units with bath. Restaurant, pool, tennis court. AE, DC, MC, V.*

$$ 🏨 **Old Bakery Inn.** Guests in this colonial complex can choose from
★ three areas: a converted stable, the former baker's cottage, or the old bakery. A loft above the stables is also available. All rooms are decorated in colonial style, with antique furniture and lace curtains. One room in the old bakery was actually the oven—its walls are 2 ft thick. ⊠ *York and Margaret Sts., 7250,* ☎ *03/6331–7900,* 🖷 *03/6331–7756. 26 rooms with bath. Restaurant. AE, MC, V.*

$$ 🏨 **Prince Albert Inn.** This inn, which first opened in 1855, shines like
★ a gem in the lackluster downtown area that surrounds it. Crossing the threshold of an Italianate facade, you'll enter a Victorian time warp, where wall-to-wall portraits of British royalty hang in the plush dining room. Recent renovations of the seven guest rooms have not broken the spell—lace curtains, velvet drapery, and fluffy comforters maintain the atmosphere—and maximize comfort. Smoking is not allowed in the inn. ⊠ *Tamar and William Sts.,* ☎ *03/6331–1931. 7 rooms with bath. MC, V.*

Nightlife and the Arts

The **Launceston Country Club Casino** has blackjack, American roulette, minibaccarat, keno, minidice, federal and stud poker, federal wheel, and two-up. There is also late-night dancing. ⊠ *Country Club Ave., Prospect Vale 7250,* ☎ *03/6344–8855.* ☉ *Mon.–Thurs. 1 PM–3 AM, Fri. and Sat. 1 PM–4 AM, Sun. noon–3 AM.*

There is no cover charge at **Regine's Discotheque.** ☉ *Wed. and Thurs. 9 PM–4 AM, Fri. and Sat. 10 PM–5 AM, Sun. 9 PM–4 AM.*

The **Silverdome** (⊠ Bass Hwy., ☎ 03/6344–9988) holds regular concerts—everything from classical to heavy metal. The **Princess Theatre** (⊠ Brisbane St., ☎ 03/6337–1270 or 03/6326–3384) features local and imported stage productions.

Shopping

Launceston is a good place to do a little shopping, with most stores centrally located on George Street and in nearby Yorktown Mall. Some of the better arts-and-crafts shops include **National Trust Old Umbrella Shop** (✉ 60 George St., ☎ 03/6331–9248), **Design Centre of Tasmania** (✉ Brisbane and Tamar Sts., ☎ 03/6331–5506), **Emma's Arts** (✉ 78 George St., ☎ 03/6331–5630), and **Gallery Two at Ritchie's Mill Arts Centre** (✉ 2 Bridge Rd., ☎ 03/6331–2339). **The Sheep's Back** (✉ 53 George St., ☎ 03/6331–2539) sells woolen products exclusively.

Sports

Details about upcoming sporting events, including cricket and Australian-rules football, can be found in the Friday *Examiner*.

Launceston A to Z

Arriving and Departing

BY BUS
Hobart Coaches (☎ 03/6334–3600) and **Tasmanian Redline Coaches** (✉ 112 George St., ☎ 03/6331–3233) serve Launceston from Devonport, Burnie, and Hobart.

BY CAR
Highway 1 connects Launceston with Hobart 2½ hours to the south and with Devonport 1½ hours to the northwest.

BY PLANE
The Launceston airport is served by several domestic airlines, including **Airlines of Tasmania, Ansett Australia,** and **Qantas.** ☞ Air Travel *in* the Gold Guide for information on airlines.

Getting Around

BY BICYCLE
Rent bicycles from the **Youth Hostel** (✉ 36 Thistle St., ☎ 03/6344–9779) for $11 per day for a touring bike, or $18 per day for a mountain bike. Costs per week are respectively $65 and $95.

BY TAXI
Central Cabs (☎ 03/6331–3555) and **Taxi Combined** (☎ 03/6331–5555) can be hailed in the street or booked by phone.

Contacts and Resources

CAR RENTAL
Cars, campers, caravans, and minibuses are available for hire at several agencies in Launceston: **Avis** (☎ 03/6391–8314 or 1800/22–5533), **Autorent Hertz** (☎ 03/6335–1111), **Budget** (☎ 03/6334–0099), and **Colonial Thrifty** (☎ 03/6391–8105).

EMERGENCIES
Ambulance, police, and **fire brigade.** ☎ 000.

Launceston General. ✉ *Charles St.,* ☎ *03/6332–7111.*

St. Luke's Hospital. ✉ *24 Lyttleton St.,* ☎ *03/6331–3255.*

St. Vincent's Hospital. ✉ *5 Frederick St.,* ☎ *03/6331–4444.*

GUIDED TOURS
Orientation Tours. A **City Sights** (✉ St. John and Paterson Sts., ☎ 03/6336–3122; ☎ $19; ☉ Nov.–Apr., twice daily) tour of Launceston by replica tram may be booked through the Tasmanian Travel and Information Centre (☞ *below*). **Launceston Historic Walks** (☎ 03/6331–3679; ☎ $10) conducts a leisurely stroll through the historic heart of

the city. Walks leave from the Tasmanian Travel and Information Centre (☞ *below*) weekdays at 9:45.

Outdoor Adventure Tours. Tasmanian Wilderness Travel (☎ 03/6334–4442) leads day tours to Cradle Mountain and the Tamar Valley, from $39.

VISITOR INFORMATION

Tasmanian Travel and Information Centre. ⊠ *St. John and Paterson Sts.,* ☎ *03/6336–3122.*

NORTHWEST COAST

The Northwest Coast of Tasmania is one of the most exciting and least known areas of the state. Most of the local inhabitants are farmers, anglers, or lumberjacks—they're a hardy bunch, but they're also some of the friendliest folk in Tasmania. The rugged coastline here has long been the solitary haunt of abalone hunters, and from the area's lush grazing land comes some of Australia's best beef and cheese. Tasmanian farmers are the only legal growers of opium poppies (for medicinal use) in the Southern Hemisphere, and some of the fields in the northwest are covered with their flowers.

Devonport

89 km (56 mi) northwest of Launceston, 289 km (180 mi) northwest of Hobart.

In the middle of the north coast, Devonport is a sleepy town that's more used to serving local farmers than tourists. You might find, in today's world, that that's just what you're looking for. It is also the Tasmanian port into which the ferry from Melbourne docks (☞ Northwest Coast A to Z, *below*).

Stop at the **Tiagarra Aboriginal Cultural and Art Centre** to see remnants of Tasmania's Aboriginal past, including more than 250 images of rock engravings. ⊠ *Mersey Bluff,* ☎ *03/6424–8250.* ⬚ *$3.* ☉ *Daily 9–6.*

Dining and Lodging

$ ✕ **Rialto Gallery.** Good and simple pasta dishes are the order of the day at this Venetian-style Italian restaurant. Cream-based sauces are favored. Other entrées include such classics as veal scaloppine. ⊠ *159 Rooke St, Devonport,* ☎ *03/6424–6793. DC, MC, V. No lunch weekends.*

$$ ✕▥ **Lighthouse Hotel.** This unexpected delight in the small coastal town
★   of Ulverstone is a very contemporary-looking, salmon-pink building with an enclosed garden atrium. Guest rooms have a predominantly blue color scheme and are furnished with blond-wood pieces. The standard of international cuisine at the resident bistro is very high. ⊠ *33 Victoria St., at Reiby St., Ulverstone 7315, 21 km (13 mi) from Devonport,* ☎ *03/6425–1197,* ℻ *03/6425–5973. 28 rooms with bath. Restaurant, sauna, spa, exercise room. AE, MC, V.*

Shopping

For a large selection of Australian colonial, English, and country cottage furniture and antiques, go to **Thomsons of Devonport** (⊠ *13 Formby Rd.,* ☎ *03/6424–8360*).

En Route   Head west on Bass Highway toward Burnie. If you have time, stop in at **Penguin**—a charming little town that has little penguin statues on its sidewalks acting as litter baskets. It's a quintessential small town—the milk bar is larger than the nearest pub. From Penguin the road leads through the Table Cape region to Wynyard, passing through rich farm country and gentle, rolling hills.

Continue west on the Bass Highway past Wynyard to **Boat Harbour.** This secluded area, popular with summer vacationers, rarely gets cold, even in winter. For a tiny settlement, Boat Harbour has one remarkable find. Jacobs Restaurant at the Boat Harbour Beach Resort (☎ 03/ 6445–1107) serves exceptional, award-winning fare. Local seafood is a specialty.

Beyond Boat Harbour near Sisters Beach is the 10-acre **Birdland Native Gardens,** where you can see native Tasmanian birds flying in open aviaries. The picnic ground here is a fine spot for lunches and afternoon barbecues. ⊠ *Wattle Ave.,* ☎ *03/6445–1270.* 🖾 *$2.* ⊙ *Daily 9–5.*

Stanley

140 km (90 mi) west of Devonport, 430 km (270 mi) northwest of Hobart.

★ The famous "**Nut**"—Tasmania's version of Uluru (Ayers Rock)—is located in Stanley. Perched at the northernmost point of mainland Tasmania, the Nut, a sheer volcanic plug some 12½ million years old, is almost totally surrounded by the sea. Visitors can either walk or take a chairlift ($4 one way, $6 round-trip) to the summit. From the top, walking trails lead in all directions—but hikers should be wary of snakes. Contact Nut Chairlifts (⊠ Box 43, Stanley 7331, ☎ 03/6458–1286) for information.

Stanley, the town at the foot of the Nut, is one of the prettiest villages in Tasmania and a must for anyone traveling in the northwest. It is filled with historic cottages, friendly tearooms, unique shops, and inns.

Dining
$ ✕ **Hursey Seafoods.** Some say the best fish and chips in Tasmania are to be had here, downstairs in the casual café, upstairs in more formal surrounds, or to take out. You can choose your fish and shellfish from tanks at the shop, and all types of seafood are available. Or try out a local specialty, muttonbird (shearwater), but keep in mind that its oily, gamey taste is not for everyone. ⊠ *2 Alexander Terr., Stanley,* ☎ *03/ 6458–1103. MC, V.*

Lodging
$ 🏠 **Touchwood Cottage.** Built in 1836, this is one of Stanley's oldest homes, and it's furnished accordingly with plenty of period pieces. The product of an architect's whimsy (or incompetence), the cottage is known for its doorways of different sizes and oddly shaped living room. It is ideally located near the Nut and the popular Touchwood crafts shop, where guests are entitled to a discount. ⊠ *33 Church St., 7331,* ☎ *03/ 6458–1348. 3 rooms without bath. MC, V.*

Shopping
The **Plough Inn** (⊠ Church St., ☎ 03/6458–1226) has an adequate collection of handicrafts and antiques. **Touchwood Quality Crafts** (⊠ Church St., ☎ 03/6458–1348) has one of the finest selections of Tasmanian crafts in the state.

Smithton

140 km (90 mi) west of Devonport, 510 km (320 mi) northwest of Hobart.

You're climbing out on a limb for natural beauty when you go to **Smithton,** because the town itself has few attractions. You come here to get away, to get outdoors in remote places and explore the rugged North-west Coast. Two nature reserves in the area, **Julius River** and **Milk-shakes Hills,** are worth visiting.

Dining and Lodging

$$–$$$ X📺 **Tall Timbers.** This lodge is one of the finest establishments in the
★ entire northwest region. Built completely of Tasmanian wood, the hotel consists of two buildings: the annex, where rooms are located, and the main house, which has a cozy bar and two restaurants—one for formal dining and the other a huge bistro. Rooms are simply decorated and equipped with the latest energy-saving devices. The staff is young, energetic, and friendly. The restaurant, **Grey's Fine Dining,** has high ceilings, wood walls, and rafters made from Tasmanian timber—even the menu is wooden. Specialties include rock crayfish, chicken breast, rabbit hot pot, and Atlantic salmon. Try crêpes suzette for dessert. ⊠ *Scotchtown Rd., Box 304, 7330,* ☎ *03/6452–2755 or 1800/03–0300,* 🗚 *03/6452–2742. 32 units with bath. AE, DC, MC, V.*

En Route **Allendale Gardens,** south of Smithton, were cultivated as a hobby and
★ have come to rival the Royal Botanic Gardens in Hobart. Around each corner of these private gardens is a surprise—a cluster of native Tasmanian ferns or a thicket of shrubs and flowers. Forest walks of 10–25 minutes' duration take you past trees more than 500 years old. The gardens are filled with more birds than you're likely to see in other areas of Tasmania. ⊠ *Eurebia, Edith Creek 7330, 14 km (9 mi) from Smithton,* ☎ *03/6456–4216.* 🖾 *$5.* ☉ *Sept.–May, daily 9–6.*

Northwest Coast A to Z

Arriving and Departing

BY BUS

Hobart Coaches has offices in Devonport (⊠ King St., ☎ 03/6424–6599) and Burnie (⊠ 54 Cattley St., ☎ 03/6431–1971).

Tasmanian Redline Coaches has offices in Devonport (⊠ 9 Edward St., ☎ 03/6424–5100); Burnie (⊠ 117 Wilson St., ☎ 03/6431–3233); Smithton (⊠ 19 Smith St., ☎ 03/6452–1262); and Queenstown (⊠ Orr St., ☎ 03/6471–1011).

BY FERRY

The *Spirit of Tasmania* makes the 14-hour trip from Melbourne to Devonport three times a week. The ferry carries 1,278 passengers and up to 490 cars. Cabin rates range from $120 to $185 each way; ferrying a car costs between $50 and $70 each way. Facilities include children's playrooms, gift shops, and several restaurants and bars. Advance bookings are essential. ⊠ *Box 323, Port Melbourne, VIC 3207;* ⊠ *Box 168, East Devonport, TAS 7310,* ☎ *03/9645–2766, 03/6427–9751, or 13–2010;* 🗚 *03/646–7450.*

BY PLANE

Devonport and Wynyard are served by several domestic airlines, including **Airlines of Tasmania** and **Kendell Airlines.** ☞ Air Travel *in* the Gold Guide for information on airlines.

Getting Around

BY BICYCLE

Rent bicycles in Devonport at **Hire a Bike** (⊠ 51 Raymond Ave., ☎ 03/6424–3889).

BY CAR

Many of the roads in the northwest are twisty and, in some of the more remote areas, unpaved. A very few may even require four-wheel-drive vehicles. However, two-wheel drive is sufficient for most touring. Be prepared for sudden weather changes—this is one of the colder parts of Tasmania, and snow in the summertime is not uncommon.

Contacts and Resources

CAR RENTALS

Cars, campers, and minibuses are available for rent in Devonport, Burnie, and Wynyard. The numbers of the following companies are for their offices in Devonport: **Autorent Hertz** (☎ 03/6424–1013), **Avis** (☎ 03/6427–9797), **Budget** (☎ 03/6424–7088), **Colonial Thrifty** (☎ 03/6427–9119).

EMERGENCIES

Ambulance, fire brigade, and **police.** ☎ *000*.

GUIDED TOURS

Devonport Aviation conducts scenic flights and departs from both Cradle Valley and Devonport. Flights take visitors over the valley and across to Barn Bluff, Mt. Ossa, the Acropolis, Lake St. Clair, Mt. Olympus, and other sights in the area. Doors on the planes are removable for photography. Thirty- to 90-minute flights are available. ⊠ *Cradle Valley,* ☎ *03/6492–1132;* ⊠ *Devonport,* ☎ *03/6427–9777.*

VISITOR INFORMATION

Tasmanian Travel and Information Centre has offices in Devonport (⊠ 5 Best St., ☎ 03/6424–4466) and Burnie (⊠ 48 Civic Sq., off Little Alexander St., ☎ 03/6434–6111).

WEST COAST

The wildest and least explored countryside in Australia lies on the Tasmanian west coast. Much of the land is national park, and much of that has been protected only after fierce battles between conservationists, loggers, and the state and federal governments. Strahan is the only town of any size on the west coast, and it is the center for cruises onto the pristine and astonishingly beautiful Gordon River and Macquarie Harbor, where the cruel and remote Sarah Island penal settlement had been established in 1821. Convicts worked in hellish conditions to log valuable Huon pine for ships and furniture.

Strahan

305 km (190 mi) northwest of Hobart.

This lovely, lazy fishing port has one of the deepest harbors in the world and a population under 500. It used to be a major port for mining companies, and its waters are still brown from the effect of ore mixing with tannin from surrounding vegetation. The town sits on the edge of Macquarie Harbor, and mixes a still-active fishing industry with tourism. The foreshore walking track gives an excellent picture of Strahan's delightful setting. Cruises along the Gordon River to the ravishingly beautiful World Heritage site in Franklin-Gordon Wild Rivers National Park constitute the main tourist activity here.

Strahan Wharf Centre is both a visitors' center and an interesting museum that concentrates on local subjects and is not afraid to tackle such controversial issues as past conservation battles over the Gordon River and the fate of Tasmania's Aborigines. ☎ *03/6471–7488.* ☜ *Museum $4.50.* ☉ *Daily 10–6.*

Gordon River Cruises has two half-day trips daily (9–2) that travel 24 km (15 mi) up Macquarie Harbour and the Gordon River, and a daily summer-only full-day tour that includes lunch. An informative commentary accompanies the trip past historic Sarah Island and stands of tea, melaleuca, sassafrass, and Huon pine trees. You can get off at Heritage Landing and take a half-hour walk through the vegetation. Reservations are essential. ⊠ *Box 40, Strahan 7468,* ☎ *03/6471–7187.* 🚌 *Full-day $62, half-day $44.*

World Heritage Cruises's MV *Heritage Wanderer* sails daily from mid-August until June, leaving Strahan Wharf at 9 AM and returning at 4:30 PM. Meals and drinks are available on board. The boat goes at a leisurely pace, stopping at Sarah Island, Heritage Landing, and the Saphia Ocean Trout Farm on Macquarie Harbour. ⊠ *Box 93, Strahan 7468,* ☎ *03/6471–7174,* 🖷 *03/6471–7431.* 🚌 *$42.*

West Coast Yacht Charters has daily twilight cruises on Macquarie Harbour, aboard the 60-ft ketch *Stormbreaker,* that include a dinner of the famed local crayfish ($45). The company also operates a two-day sailing excursion ($290) and a morning fishing trip ($35 negotiable cost includes gear, bait, and morning tea). It has newly won permission for overnight cruises on the Gordon River as far as Sir John Falls, a trip designed to pick up whitewater rafters from the Franklin River, but on which passengers from Strahan are welcome. It costs $80; all meals are included. ⊠ *Esplanade, Strahan 7468,* ☎ *03/6471–7422.*

OFF THE BEATEN PATH	North of Strahan are the **Henty Sand Dunes,** accessible by a reasonably good sandy track. The dunes are worth visiting for the desertscape they present.

Dining and Lodging

$$ ✕ **Hamers Hotel.** The crayfish (clawless lobster) salad at this hotel is legendary (and costs $25 for a half cray). However, if you aim your sights lower—to other seafood and steak—food is better than most pub counter meals for about the same price. Dessert includes an array of freshly made cakes. The restaurant is closed daily between 2:30 and 5:30. ⊠ *Esplanade,* ☎ *03/6471–7191. MC, V.*

$$$ ▥ **Franklin Manor.** When it was converted in 1990 from a private home into a guest house, the Manor immediately became *the* place to stay in Strahan. Set in gardens near the harbor, it has open fires and a relaxing lounge. Rooms have TV, telephone, and heated towel rails. The restaurant is known for a refined and comfortable ambience. An à la carte menu includes lobster, oysters, pot-roasted quail, and sea trout. ⊠ *Esplanade, Strahan, 7468,* ☎ *03/6471–7311. 13 rooms with shower. MC, V.*

$$ ▥ **Strahan Motor Inn.** The most popular hotel in Strahan (it's only 1,800 ft from the Gordon River cruise dock), this inn includes a main building and an annex behind. Ask for rooms in the main building overlooking the harbor—rooms in the annex have limited views and are noisier. Colonial furniture and beds with quilt coverings create a welcoming ambience. ⊠ *Jolly St., 7468,* ☎ *03/6471–7160. 50 rooms with shower, 11 with Jacuzzi. Restaurant. AE, DC, MC, V.*

Zeehan

72 km (45 mi) north of Strahan, 375 km (235 mi) northwest of Hobart.

During the past century, silver-lode discoveries transformed Zeehan into one of the state's largest towns—it had 26 hotels—but some 25 years later deposits started to run out, and Zeehan went the way of many failed mining towns.

A drive along Main Street takes you past the transient grandeur of the Grand Hotel and the Gaiety Theatre; both buildings now belong to

Pick up
the phone.

Pick up
the miles.

MCI Calling Card

415 555 1234 2244
J.D. SMITH

WORLDPHONE

Use your MCI Card® to make an international call from virtually anywhere in the world and earn frequent flyer miles on one of seven major airlines.

Enroll in an MCI Airline Partner Program today. In the U.S., call **1-800-FLY-FREE.** Overseas, call MCI collect at **1-916-567-5151.**

1. To use your MCI Card, just dial the WorldPhone access number of the country you're calling from.
   (For a complete listing of codes, visit www.mci.com.)
2. Dial or give the operator your MCI Card number.
3. Dial or give the number you're calling.

# Bahrain	800-002	# Kuwait	800-MCI (800-624)
# Brunei	800-011	Lebanon ∻	600-MCI (600-624)
# China ❖	108-12	# Macao	0800-131
For a Mandarin-speaking		# Malaysia (CC) ♦	800-0012
operator	108-17	# Philippines (CC) ♦	
# Cyprus ♦	080-90000	To call using PLDT ■	105-14
# Egypt ♦	355-5770	To call using PHILCOM ■	1026-14
(Outside of Cairo, dial 02 first)		Philippines IIIC via PLDT	
# Federated States of Micronesia	624	in Tagalog ■	105-15
# Fiji	004-890-1002	Philippines IIIC via PHILCOM	
# Guam (CC)	950-1022	in Tagalog ■	1020-12
# Hong Kong (CC)	800-1121	# Qatar ★	0800-012-77
# India (CC) ❖	000-127	# Saipan (CC) ∻	950-1022
# Indonesia (CC) ♦	001-801-11	# Saudi Arabia (CC)	1-800-11
Iran ∻	(Special Phones Only)	# Singapore	8000-112-112
# Israel (CC)	177-150-2727	# Sri Lanka	440-100
# Japan (CC) ♦		(Outside of Colombo, dial 01 first)	
To call using KDD ■	0039-121▶	# Syria	0800
To call using IDC ■	0066-55-121	# Taiwan (CC) ♦	0080-13-4567
To call using ITJ ■	0044-11-121	# Thailand ★	001-999-1-2001
# Jordan	18-800-001	# United Arab Emirates ♦	800-111
# Korea (CC)		Vietnam ●	1201-1022
To call using KT ■	009-14	Yemen	008-00-102
To call using DACOM ■	00309-12		
Phone Booths ∻	Red Button 03, then press ★		
Military Bases	550-2255		

Is this a great time, or what? :-)

MCI

Urban planning.

CITYPACKS

The ultimate guide to the city—a complete pocket guide plus a full-size color map.

www.fodors.com

Fodor's *The name that means smart travel.*™
At bookstores, or call 1-800-533-6478.

the **West Coast Pioneers' Memorial Museum** and stand empty, awaiting renovation. The museum itself, in the historic old School of Mines Building, has an excellent mineral exhibit among its collections. ⊠ *Main St.,* ☎ *03/6471–6225.* ⊞ *Donations accepted.* ⊙ *Apr.–Oct., daily 8:30– 5; Nov.–Mar., daily 8:30–6.*

For pub food, the **Cecil Hotel** (☎ 03/6471–6221) serves good, hearty fare at reasonable prices.

En Route A brief detour from the highway route between Strahan and Zeehan takes you to **Queenstown,** set amid one of the most astonishing landscapes on earth. Decades of mining have stripped the earth of all vegetation (although some replanting is going on), leaving a stark, unearthly scene.

West Coast A to Z

Arriving and Departing
BY CAR

The West Coast is a long way from everywhere. The road from Hobart winds from the lowlands into the high country, with excellent views of Lake St. Clair and the distant mountains of central Tasmania. From the north, the highway snakes down to Zeehan, with an alternative sandy track (usually passable with a conventional vehicle) between Zeehan and Strahan.

Getting Around
BY BOAT

Cruises are the only way for most people to get a taste of the west coast's stunning wilderness country. Exploration along the Gordon River is deliberately slow, so as not to erode the fragile riverbanks and damage the ecosystem conservationists fought so hard to preserve.

BY CAR

A vehicle is absolutely essential for moving from place to place on the west coast.

Contacts and Resources
EMERGENCIES

Ambulance, fire brigade, and **police.** ☎ *000.*

GUIDED TOURS

Wilderness Air (☎ 03/6471–7280) flies seaplanes from Strahan Wharf over Frenchman's Cap, the Franklin and Gordon rivers, Lake Pedder, and Hells Gates, with a landing at Sir John Falls. It's a great way to see the area's peaks, lakes, coast, and rivers.

CENTRAL TASMANIAN NATIONAL PARKS

Cradle Mountain–Lake St. Clair National Park

★ Cradle Mountain–Lake St. Clair National Park contains the most spectacular alpine scenery in Tasmania and the best mountain trails in Australia. Popular with hikers of all levels of ability, the park has several high peaks, including Mt. Ossa, the highest in Tasmania (more than 5,300 ft). The Cradle Mountain section of the park lies in the north, where the Waldheim Chalet, built by the park's founder, Gustav Weindorfer, stands guard over the valley below.

The southern section of the park, Lake St. Clair, is popular not only for boat trips but also for trails that circumnavigate the lake. Trout fishing is permitted with a license, and boat trips can be arranged from Cynthia Bay.

It is impossible to visit the park without hearing of the **Overland Track.** The most famous trail in Australia, it traverses 85 km (53 mi) from the northern to the southern boundary of the park. Traveled by more than 200 people per week, the trail has several basic accommodation huts that are available on a first-come, first-served basis. Because space in the huts is limited, hikers are advised to bring their own tents. If you prefer to do the walk in comfort—and are prepared to pay for the privilege—there are relatively well-equipped (and heated) private huts managed by Cradle Mountain Huts, a commercial concern (☞ Chapter 13).

The toughest part of the Overland is in the northern section of the park where most hikers begin—a moderately steep climb of Cradle Mountain must be made on the first day. The climbing is not nearly as difficult to bear as the weather, however. Even in summer, frequent storms are guaranteed to douse hikers. The trail, which takes between 5 and 10 days to traverse, passes over and around many of the mountains and lakes in the park as well as through temperate rain forest.

For those who are less adventurous or have less time, the park contains many rewarding shorter trails.

Dining and Lodging

Caravan, car, and bus campgrounds are located 2 km (1 mi) north of the park boundary and provide showers, toilets, laundry facilities, and enclosed cooking shelters with electric barbecues. Usage is free. Tent sites cost $10 per night for two persons. Bunkhouse accommodations are $15 per person per night. Advance booking is essential (☎ 03/6492–1395).

Four-, six-, and eight-bed huts in Cradle Valley must be booked in advance. Rates average about $15 per person per night. Huts can be rented at Cynthia Bay as well.

$$$ ✕▥ **Cradle Mountain Lodge.** This wilderness lodge gave birth to a genre
★ in Australia, and is the most comfortable place to stay at Cradle Mountain. Accommodations are not luxurious, but they are homey. The high-ceiling guest rooms, two per cabin, each have their own kitchenette and are decorated with green and burgundy fabric. The environment is what counts here, and it is magnificent. Many walking trails begin at the lodge door. After a good meal in the dining room, you can walk outside to see a gathering of Tasmania's wildlife come to dine on the lodge's leftovers. Meals are not included in room rates. ✉ *Box 153, Sheffield 7306,* ☎ *03/6492–1303,* ℻ *03/6492–1309. 77 rooms with bath. MC, V.*

Arriving and Departing

BY BUS

Tasmanian Wilderness Transport & Tours (☎ 03/6334–4442) runs to Cradle Mountain from Devonport, Strahan, and Launceston. It also serves Lake St. Clair from Launceston, Devonport, and Hobart. **Tasmanian Redline Coaches** (☎ 03/6234–4577) operates buses daily (except Sunday) from Hobart and Queenstown to Derwent Bridge, near the park entrance.

BY CAR

Getting to the two parks is a two-part activity. **Lake St. Clair** is 173 km (107 mi) from Hobart and can be reached via the Lyell Highway or from Launceston via Deloraine or Poatina. **Cradle Mountain** is located 85 km (53 mi) south of Devonport and can be reached by car via Claude Road from Sheffield or via Wilmot. Both lead 30 km (19 mi) along Route C132 to Cradle Valley. The last 10 km (6 mi) are unpaved.

Mount Field National Park

The first national park created in Tasmania, Mount Field still ranks first in popularity among Tasmanians and visitors alike. The park's easily navigable trails, picnic areas, and well-maintained campsites are ideal for family outings. Many popular animals—including Bennett's and rufous wallabies as well as Tasmanian devils—are often out and about around dusk.

Some 80 km (50 mi) northwest of Hobart, the park contains the most popular ski area in southern Tasmania. Located on Mt. Mawson, it has challenging trails for cross-country skiers and some downhill skiing. For walkers, however, summer is the best time to visit. The most popular trail is the **Russell Falls Nature Walk.** This 1-km (½-mi) path is paved part of the way and is suitable for wheelchairs. Numbered pegs inform walkers about vegetation along the route. The path leads bushwalkers from eucalyptus forest into temperate rain forest and ends at Russell Falls. Along the way, the trail passes the tallest hardwood trees in the world—a variety of eucalyptus known as mountain ash (locally as swamp gum), some of which tower more than 325 ft.

Lodging

A campground and a caravan park, equipped with toilets, hot water, showers, and laundry facilities, are located near the entrance to Mount Field. Firewood is provided free of charge. Fees are $10 for a campsite, $12 for a powered site for two. Minimal grocery supplies may be purchased at the kiosk near the caravan park. Wilderness huts are situated on certain trails throughout the park. They cost $20 for two adults. Check with the ranger about their specific locations.

Arriving and Departing

From Hobart, drive north on the Lyell Highway and then west on Maydena Road. Scheduled buses leave Hobart for the park weekdays, except public holidays.

Visitor Information

Mt. Field National Park. ⊠ *Box 41, Westerway 7140,* ☎ *03/6288–1149.*

SOUTHWEST NATIONAL PARK

The largest park in Tasmania, Southwest encompasses the entire southwestern portion of the state. One of the few areas of Australia with virgin land unaffected by human tampering, the park has trees topping 300 ft in a dense, temperate rain forest. Indeed, its five mountain ranges and more than 50 lakes were unknown to all but the most avid bushwalkers until the park gained notoriety in 1974 with the drowning of Lake Pedder: To boost the power of a nearby hydroelectric dam, the lake was flooded. It is now a much bigger Lake Pedder, about 25 times the size of the original one.

The road into the park passes through rain forest and offers views of rock formations dating back more than 500 million years. In summer, the road is lined with beehives brought here by keepers taking advantage of the blossoms of leatherwood trees.

Southwest is a park for the hardiest of travelers. Only one trail—the Western Arthurs Transverse—is well marked, and it is a seven-day trek.

Parts of it require short ascents, best made with ropes, up steep gullies and cliff faces. The hike should not be attempted by anyone who minds being wet and cold, because the park is often hit with violent storms, snow, and rainfall even in summer. Do not embark on walks in the park without registering (and logging out) with the Tasmanian Police (☎ 03/6230–2111) in Hobart. Admission is $2 per car.

Lodging
Free campsites are available at Lake Pedder, Scott's Peak Dam, and Edgar Dam. Gas, food, and accommodations are available in Strathgordon.

Arriving and Departing
BY BUS
A regularly scheduled minibus is available from **Tasmanian Wilderness Transport and Tours** (☎ 03/6334–4442 or 1800/03–0505) in Hobart on Tuesday, Thursday, and weekends from December through March. The cost is $35 one way or $65 round-trip.

BY CAR
Southwest is located 174 km (108 mi) from Hobart and can be reached by car from the north via Strathgordon Road, passing through Maydena to Frodshams Pass, where a left turn leads to Scott's Peak Road and the park.

BY PLANE
Two companies provide air service into the park at Cox Bight and Melaleuca: **Par Avion** (☎ 03/6248–5390) and **TASAIR** (☎ 03/6248–5088).

Visitor Information
Department of Parks, Wildlife, and Heritage. ⊠ *Box 41, Westerway 7140,* ☎ *03/6233–6191.*

7 Queensland

A fusion of Florida, Las Vegas, and the Caribbean Islands, Queensland is a mecca for crowd lovers and escapists alike, whether you wish to be awash in the Coral Sea, to stroll from cabana to casino with your favorite cocktail, or to cruise rivers and rain forests with crocs and other legendary creatures of the tropics.

Updated by
Jane Carstens

QUEENSLAND is a state of enormous geographic variety—the sheer size of it defies homogeneity. Queensland occupies 1,727,999 square km (667,180 square mi)—more than four times the size of California—and its eastern seaboard stretches 5,200 km (3,234 mi)—about the distance from Rome to Cairo—from the subtropical Gold Coast to the wild and steamy rain forests of the far north. Only in recent years has the northern tip, the Cape York Peninsula, been fully explored, and crocodiles still claim a human victim once in a while. Away from the coastal sugar and banana plantations, west of the Great Dividing Range, Queensland looks as arid and dust-blown as any other part of Australia's interior. Few paved roads cross this semidesert, and, as in the Red Centre, communication with remote farms is mostly by radio and air. Not surprisingly, most of the state's 3.2 million inhabitants reside on the coast.

The Queensland license plate calls this the "Sunshine State," a sort-of Australian Florida—a laid-back stretch of beaches and sun where many Australians head for their vacations. The state has actively promoted tourism, and today such areas as the Gold Coast in the south and Cairns in the north have exploded into mini-Miamis, complete with high-rise buildings, casinos, and beachfront amusements.

At the same time, Queenslanders have been called intensely parochial. This was especially true during the reign of the conservative Sir Joh Bjelke-Petersen, whose 20-year span as premier ended in 1989 when the National Party elected a new leader following an inquiry that revealed corruption in the government and police force. The now famous Fitzgerald Inquiry tarnished Queensland's image, but even Bjelke-Petersen's detractors admired his legacy of a balanced budget and a fiscally sound low-tax economy.

This is the only Australian state that didn't adopt daylight saving time, which means that summertime airline schedules can get confusing. Detractors have smirked that this is because Queenslanders don't like change, but the reality is based on practical concerns: People living in the far reaches of the northwest would have been severely affected. Unless the state were divided in half, its residents would reject the time change because it wasn't advantageous for everyone.

The major attraction for Australians and foreign tourists alike is the Great Barrier Reef. This 1,900-km (1,200-mi) ecological masterpiece supports thousands of animal species. With such an abundance of marine life, it's not surprising that Queensland is a fishing mecca. Cairns and Lizard Island in the far north are renowned for big-game fishing—often enough, black marlin weigh in at more than a half ton. The reef, an integral part of any trip to the state, is discussed separately in Chapter 8.

Queensland was thrust into the spotlight with the Commonwealth Games in 1982 and World Expo 88. These two events exposed Brisbane (pronounced "*briz*-bin") to the wider world and helped bring the city, along with other provincial capitals, to fully fledged social and cultural maturity. Consequently, Queensland is a vibrant place to visit, and Sunshine Staters are far more likely to be city kids who work in modern offices than stereotypical bushies—people with the unsophistication characteristic of lives lived in the bush—who work the land. Whatever their background, Queenslanders are known for their friendliness and hospitality. Typical of lands blessed with hot weather and plenty of sunshine, the pace of life is relaxed and takes on a different perspective.

Pleasures and Pastimes

Dining

After only a few days in Queensland, you'll find that the concept of specialized rural cuisines seems highly unlikely: Steak and seafood predominate once you leave the city limits. There are a few exceptions to that rule, however. Brisbane has its share of new, Mediterranean–Asian–influenced menus, and in Noosa people argue about dishes and spices and the merits of the special local ingredients of "Noosa Cuisine" with a fervor that others reserve for the horse races or football. The state is a great source of produce from land and sea. Cairns and the coast up to Mossman have some fine restaurants. Above that, cooking is decidedly more rustic.

CATEGORY	COST*
$$$$	over $50
$$$	$40–$50
$$	$30–$40
$	under $30

*per person, excluding drinks and service

Diving

Cairns is a great base for divers. The cognoscenti may argue whether the Great Barrier Reef or the Red Sea offers better diving, but the fact remains that the reef is one of the certified wonders of the world.

Fishing

If you're a serious deep-sea angler, Cairns is your mecca. Scores of charter boats leave the city in pursuit of black marlin, tuna, and reef fish.

Lodging

Queensland accommodations run the gamut, from rain-forest lodges, outback pubs, and backpacker hostels to five-star beachside resorts and big-city hotels.

CATEGORY	COST*
$$$$	over $280
$$$	$140–$280
$$	$80–$140
$	under $80

*All prices are for a standard double room.

Queensland's Great Outdoors

From the varied ecosystems of Lamington National Park on the New South Wales Border, to the gorges and Aboriginal rock paintings of Carnarvon northwest of Brisbane, to the rain forests of Daintree National Park north of Cairns, Queensland has one of the most extensive and organized park systems in Australia. Along the east coast, there seems to be a marine park or tiny, island park every few miles.

If you have the time, an explorer's curiosity, or just wish to see one of the world's last wild jungles, take a trip north from Cairns. The remaining pockets of ancient, untouched wilderness that warrant the area's listing as a World Heritage site provide one of the most archetypal Australian adventures that you'll have.

For more information on bicycling, sea kayaking, diving, four-wheel-driving, and sailing in Queensland's great outdoors, *see* Chapter 13.

Reef Visits

Snorkeling, scuba diving, and glass-bottom boat trips on the Great Barrier Reef (☞ Chapter 8) are essential parts of any trip to Queensland.

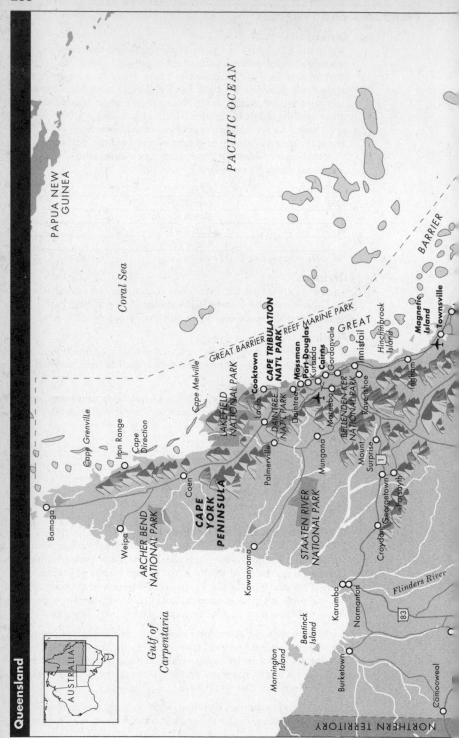

Queensland

PAPUA NEW
GUINEA

PACIFIC OCEAN

Coral Sea

GREAT BARRIER

BARRIER

REEF MARINE PARK

GREAT

Cape Grenville

Iron Range

Cape
Direction

Cape Melville

CAPE TRIBULATION
NAT'L PARK

Mossman

Port Douglas

Cairns

Gordonvale

Innisfail

Hinchinbrook
Island

Magnetic
Island

Townsville

Ingham

Bamaga

Weipa

ARCHER BEND
NATIONAL PARK

CAPE YORK
PENINSULA

Coen

LAKEFIELD
NATIONAL PARK

Laura

Cooktown

Palmerville

DAINTREE
NAT'L PARK

Daintree

Kuranda

Mareeba

Malanda

BELLENDEN KER
NATIONAL PARK

Ravenshoe

Mount
Surprise

STAATEN RIVER
NATIONAL PARK

Mungana

Kowanyama

Croydon

Georgetown

Forsayth

Gulf of
Carpentaria

Mornington
Island

Bentinck
Island

Karumba

Normanton

Flinders River

83

Burketown

Camooweal

AUSTRALIA

NORTHERN TERRITORY

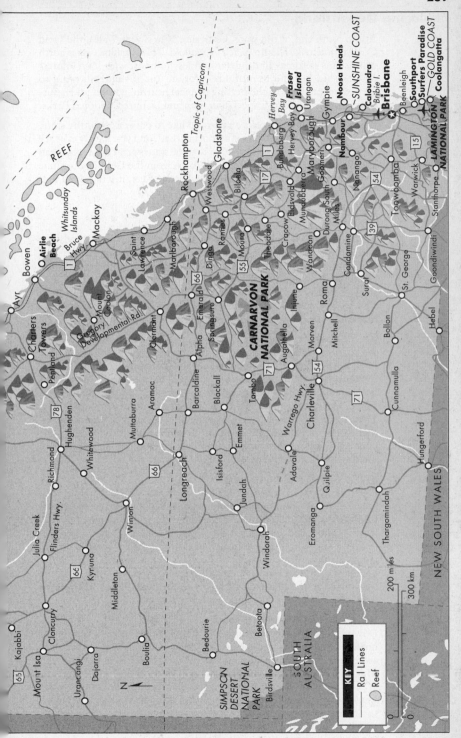

REEF

Tropic of Capricorn

SUNSHINE COAST

Ayr
Bowen
Airlie Beach
Whitsunday Islands
Bruce Hwy.
Mackay
Saint Lawrence
Marlborough
Rockhampton
Westwood
Gladstone
Bilela
Hervey Bay
Bundaberg
Childers
Maryborough
Urangan
Gympie
Noosa Heads
Caloundra
Bribie I.
Nambour
Brisbane
Beenleigh
Southport
Surfers Paradise
GOLD COAST
Coolangatta
LAMINGTON NATIONAL PARK

Charters Towers
Pentland
Hughenden
Gregory Developmental Rd.
Mount Coolon
Clermont
Emerald
Springsure
Rennes
Dingo
Moura
Theodore
Cracow
Biddville
Mundubbera
Durong South
Goomeri
Nanango
Kingaroy
Toogoolawah
Toowoomba
Warwick
Stanthorpe
Goondiwindi

CARNARVON NATIONAL PARK

Julia Creek
Flinders Hwy.
Richmond
Whitewood
Muttaburra
Aramac
Barcaldine
Blackall
Tambo
Augathella
Injune
Roma
Mitchell
Morven
Charleville
Surat
St. George
Hebel
Bollon

Kajabbi
Mount Isa
Cloncurry
Duchess
Kynuna
Middleton
Winton
Longreach
Isisford
Emmet
Jundah
Adavale
Quilpie
Eromanga
Windorah
Cunnamulla
Thargomindah
Hungerford

Urandangi
Dajarra
Boulia
Bedourie
Betoota
Birdsville

SIMPSON DESERT NATIONAL PARK

SOUTH AUSTRALIA

NEW SOUTH WALES

N

200 miles
300 km

KEY
—— Rail Lines
Reef

Exploring Queensland

At the south end of the state, bordering New South Wales, the Gold Coast is much like Miami Beach or Waikiki. The Sunshine Coast north of Brisbane is somewhat quieter and less touristy, with long, almost deserted beaches and beautiful rain forest. And if you really want to get away from it all to the pulsing tropical heart of nature, take yourself north of Cairns to Cape Tribulation and Daintree National Parks.

If you do have a few weeks and would like to cover a lot of the state, avoid driving up the coast—it's a boring road, and you hardly ever see the water. Fly instead. Keep in mind that the state's great distances mean additional transit time. If you want to go from the Gold or Sunshine coasts near Brisbane up to the Great Barrier Reef, it will take a half day or more en route.

Great Itineraries

IF YOU HAVE 3 DAYS

Fly into ⌖ **Cairns** and take a boat out to one of the reef islands (☞ Chapter 8) for a day, then head up to ⌖ **Cape Tribulation** for the next two days to take in the sights and sounds of the rain forest. If you'd rather have a Miami Beach–style trip, fly into ⌖ **Brisbane** and head straight for the glitzy **Gold Coast,** overnighting in ⌖ **Surfers Paradise.** You could end that spree with a final night and day in ⌖ **Lamington National Park** for its subtropical wilderness and bird life.

IF YOU HAVE 5 DAYS

Spend three days on shore and two days on the reef. Take the first night in ⌖ **Brisbane,** then head up the **Sunshine Coast** for a hike up one of the **Glass House Mountains** on the way to ⌖ **Noosa Heads.** Apart from beach- and surf-time, take in some of the Sunshine Coast's monumental kitsch, like the **Big Pineapple** or the House of Bottles or the Big Shell. Then make your way back to Brisbane for a flight to ⌖ **Cairns** and either a boat to the reef or a drive to the **rain forest** north of Cairns for cruising the rivers, listening to the jungle, relaxing on the beach, and looking into the maw of a crocodile.

IF YOU HAVE 7 OR MORE DAYS

Unless you're keen on seeing everything, limit yourself to a couple of areas, such as **Brisbane, the Sunshine Coast,** and the rain forests **North from Cairns,** and take three to four days in each—Queensland's climate is conducive to slowing down. Extended stays will also allow you to take a four-wheel-drive trip all the way to the top of **York Peninsula** from **Cairns,** go for overnight bush walks in national parks, spend a few days on a **dive boat** exploring islands and reefs north of Cairns, trek inland to the Outback's **Carnarvon National Park** and **Undarra lava tubes,** or just lie back and soak in the heat.

When to Tour Queensland

Down Under, the farther north you go, the hotter it gets. Summer is normally sweltering, and the north is plenty warm in winter for ocean swimming. North of Cairns, in fact, the best time for visiting is between May and September, when the daily maximum temperature averages around 80°F (26°C) and the water is comfortably warm. During the wet season up there, from about December through March, expect monsoon conditions. Elsewhere in the state, fall and spring are nicest, in part because October through April, the tropical coast is besieged by deadly box jellyfish that make ocean swimming impossible. The jellies don't drift out to the reef or south of the Tropic of Capricorn, however. Because of school holidays, sea- and reef-side Queensland tend to fill up around Christmas and into January.

BRISBANE

Until the mid-1970s this city, Australia's third largest in population and one of the world's largest in area, still had a country feeling and attitude. During the 1980s, Brisbane underwent an impressive spurt of growth and modernization that culminated in today's pleasantly contemporary cityscape of pedestrian plazas, riverside vistas, and café culture. Much of this occurred as a response to Brisbane's hosting Expo '88, an event that put the city on the world map and made its residents more aware of the wider world.

Brisbane was founded as a penal colony for prisoners who had committed crimes after their arrival in Australia. The waterway across which the city sprawls was discovered by two escaped convicts in 1823, and the penal settlement was established on its banks the following year, 32 km (20 mi) from Moreton Bay.

Few historic buildings have survived the wrecker's ball, and today's city is very much a product of recent development. Far surpassing the architecture are the open spaces: Brisbane is beautifully landscaped, brimming with jacarandas, tulip trees, flame trees, oleanders, frangipani, and the ever-stunning bougainvillea. In summer the city broils, and although the climate is pleasant at other times of the year, there is never any doubt that this is a subtropical region.

Exploring Brisbane

Numbers in the text correspond to numbers in the margin and on the Brisbane map.

City Center

Brisbane's inner-city landmarks—a combination of Victorian, Edwardian, and slick high-tech architecture—are best explored on foot. Most of them lie within the triangle formed by Ann Street and the bends of the Brisbane River.

A GOOD WALK

Start at **St. John's Anglican Cathedral** ①, near the corner of Wharf and Ann streets. Like so many other grand edifices in Australia, this building was never completed—although work has resumed on the unfinished western end. Inside the cathedral grounds, the **Deanery** has been finished, in fact long before the first stone for the cathedral was laid. This house, originally built as a doctor's residence, became a temporary government house when Queensland was proclaimed a separate colony from New South Wales in 1859. The proclamation of separation was read from its veranda.

Walk southeast along Wharf Street, across Queen Street, down Eagle Street, and southwest on Elizabeth Street to **Old St. Stephen's Church** ②, which stands in the shadow of St. Stephen's Catholic Cathedral. Both buildings are in Gothic Revival style. The church is believed to have been designed by Augustus Pugin, a noted English architect who designed much of London's Houses of Parliament.

One block northwest of the church, and worlds away in terms of style, is the **National Bank Building** ③. Don't miss a look at the doors and interior of this Classical palazzo if you're at all interested in architecture. Continue southwest along Queen Street for one block to **MacArthur Chambers** ④, General Douglas MacArthur's main Pacific office during World War II and one of Brisbane's earliest office blocks.

Head northwest along Edward Street and turn right into Adelaide Street. On the left look for **Anzac Square and the Shrine of Remem-**

Brisbane

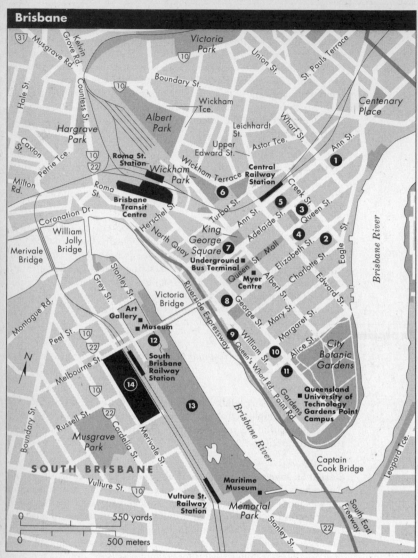

Anzac Square and the
Shrine of
Remembrance, **5**

Brisbane City Hall, **7**

Brisbane Convention
and Exhibition
Centre, **14**

MacArthur
Chambers, **4**

Mansions in George
Street, **10**

National Bank
Building, **3**

Old Commissariat
Store, **9**

Old Windmill, **6**

Parliament House, **11**

Queensland Cultural
Centre, **12**

St. John's Anglican
Cathedral, **1**

St. Stephen's
Church, **2**

South Bank
Parklands, **13**

Treasury Building, **8**

brance ⑤), built in memory of Australian casualties in World War I. The circular Doric Greek Revival Cenotaph is particularly handsome, and there are lawns around the memorial if you'd like to take a break. On April 25, Anzac Day, a moving dawn service is held here in remembrance of Australia's fallen soldiers.

Return to Edward Street and head northwest to Wickham Terrace. Turn left and follow the street as it curves to the **Old Windmill** ⑥, also known as the Observatory. This is one of only two remaining convict-built buildings from the days when Brisbane was a penal settlement, called Moreton Bay, which was set up to take Sydney's particularly recalcitrant convicts.

Back on Edward Street, walk two blocks southeast and turn right into Adelaide Street. Past David Jones department store and abutting King George Square is the classical, temple-fronted, bell-towered **Brisbane City Hall** ⑦, one of Australia's largest city halls. Consider taking the lift to the bell tower for great views of the city—when the bells aren't ringing.

From City Hall, walk over to the Queen Street Mall between George and Edward streets for a choice of places to wet your whistle or have a bite of lunch. There is often free entertainment at lunch hour (noon–1).

Head south to George Street, then turn left and continue to the **Treasury Building** ⑧, alias the Conrad Treasury Casino. Continue southeast on William Street, which runs behind the Treasury Building, to the **Old Commissariat Store** ⑨, which is the city's other surviving convict-built structure. Today it houses the Royal Historical Society of Queensland along with its museum and library. Farther along William Street, turn left into Margaret Street and then right into George Street. **The Mansions in George Street** ⑩, built of brick and sandstone just before the turn of this century, are former town houses now occupied by offices, a restaurant, a book shop, and the National Trust gift shop.

For a break from the city streets, cross Alice Street and step into the **City Botanic Gardens** that stretch over to the river. There are some venerable trees in the garden that are well worth extending your walk to see, as well as a charming restaurant-cum-café tucked away at the back of the gardens. Back out on Alice Street, at the end of William Street amid tropical palms, is the splendid French Renaissance **Parliament House** ⑪, which earned its colonial designer a meager 200-guinea salary. If Queensland's Parliament is in session, you can look in on the proceedings from a visitor's gallery.

Return to Queen Street along George Street and walk over Victoria Bridge. Across the Brisbane River, the sleek **Queensland Cultural Centre** ⑫ extends for a block on either side of Melbourne Street. Plan to spend time here exploring the expansive rooms of the Queensland Art Gallery (open daily 10–5) or the Queensland Museum natural history exhibits (open daily 9–5), perhaps picking up a reminder of your visit at the complex's shops.

Just south of the Cultural Centre along the river is **South Bank Parklands** ⑬. An enormously popular destination for Brisbane folk and visitors alike, it contains a sprawling beach lagoon, popular for swimming (and complete with lifeguard), a wildlife sanctuary, a replicated rain forest, an insect and butterfly house, cafés and restaurants, along with plenty of places to sit and relax.

TIMING

Without pausing at any of the attractions, this walk would take almost two hours and includes a hike up a small hill to get to the Old Windmill. The place that will take the most exploring is South Bank Parklands, especially if you are there when the markets are operating (Friday night, Saturday, and Sunday). During Brisbane's blistering summer it's a good idea to carry water, as the humidity can be quite draining. Winter on the other hand is quite pleasant, and the boardwalk along the river at South Bank is a great place to enjoy the sun and city views.

SIGHTS TO SEE

⑤ Anzac Square and the Shrine of Remembrance. Walking paths through Anzac Square stretch across green lawns, directing all eyes toward the shrine, which is constructed of Queensland sandstone; an eternal flame burns within for Australian soldiers who died in World War I. Equally spine-tingling is the **Shrine of Memories,** a crypt below the flame, which stores soil samples labeled "forever Australian" that were collected from battlefields on which Australian soldiers perished. ⊠ *Adelaide St. between Edward and Creek Sts.* ⊙ *Shrine weekdays 11–3.*

⑦ Brisbane City Hall. Once referred to as the "million pound town hall" because of the massive funds poured into its construction, this community center built in 1930 has been a major symbol of Brisbane's civic pride. The substantial Italianate city hall is in fact one of Australia's largest. Visitors and locals "ooh" and "aah" at the grand pipe organ and circular concert hall. Other features include an observation platform affording superb city views and a ground-floor museum and art gallery. You can tour both the building and its huge clock tower, home to one of Australia's largest civic clocks. ⊠ *King George Sq., Adelaide St.,* ☎ *07/3404–4048.* ⊙ *Weekdays 8–5; tours at 10, noon, and 2.* ⌨ *City Hall free; tour $4.*

NEED A BREAK?

The **Queen Street Mall** is a two-block pedestrian boulevard stretching from George Street to Edward Street. It features a wide selection of places to eat, ranging from take-out food to elegant restaurants. Also remember that the **David Jones** department store (on the mall) has a well-stocked food hall, where you can assemble your own picnic to eat in nearby King George Square with locals on their lunch break.

⑭ Brisbane Convention and Exhibition Centre. For a slice of Australiana in the form of the Bridal and Honeymoon Spectacular or the Motor Show, this imposing building covers 4½ acres and is equipped with 4 exhibition halls, a 4,000-seat Great Hall, and a Grand Ballroom. ⊠ *Glenelg and Merivale Sts.,* ☎ *1800/03–6308.*

④ MacArthur Chambers. As commander-in-chief of the Allied Forces fighting in the Pacific, General Douglas MacArthur came to Australia from the Philippines, leaving the Japanese in control there with his notorious vow, "I shall return." This present-day office building was MacArthur's World War II headquarters. ⊠ *Queen St., entrance at 201 Edward St.*

⑩ Mansions in George Street. Constructed in 1890, these were originally six fashionable town houses—worth a detour even if they're out of your way. These splendid Victorian terrace houses with elegant wrought-iron lace trim house the National Trust gift shop, restaurants, bookshops, and professional offices. ⊠ *40 George St.*

③ National Bank Building. Brisbane's National Bank went up in 1885 and is one of the country's finest Italian Renaissance–style structures. Aside from the majestic entrance hall with its ornate ceilings and eye-catching dome, the most interesting features are the front doors, which were crafted from a single cedar trunk. ⊠ *308 Queen St.* ⊙ *Weekdays 9–4.*

⑨ Old Commissariat Store. Convict-built in 1829, this was the first stone building in Brisbane. It has served variously as a customs house, storehouse, and immigrants' shelter. Currently the headquarters of the Royal Historical Society of Queensland, it is built on the spot where Brisbane's original timber wharf was located. ⊠ *115 William St.,* ☎ *07/3221–4198.* ▣ *Donations accepted.* ⏱ *Tues.–Fri. 11–2.*

6 **Old Windmill.** From the streets below, the view of the windmill at the top of Edward Street is now almost obscured by trees. It is the oldest of the few remaining convict buildings in Brisbane. The poorly designed 1928 windmill never worked very well; whenever the wind died down, convicts were forced to power a treadmill to crush grain for the colony's bread, thus tagging this landmark the "Tower of Torture." When fire erupted across the city in 1864, scorching almost everything in its path, the windmill survived with only minimal damage. Stripped of its blades, the tower now looks a lot like a lighthouse. The large copper ball on top of the building used to drop at 1 PM every day so people could set their watches accurately. As early as 1930, experimental television broadcasts were beamed from here to Ipswich, 33 km (20 mi) away. Entering the building isn't allowed. ⊠ *Wickham Park, Wickham Terr.*

⑪ **Parliament House.** Opened in 1868, this stone-clad building, with a Mt. Isa copper roof, has had a relatively new legislative annex added. The interior is fitted with polished timber, brass, and frosted and engraved glass. If State Parliament is sitting, you can observe the action from the visitors' gallery. Afterward, wander through the adjacent City Botanic Gardens. ⊠ *George and Alice Sts.,* ☎ *07/3226–7111.* ⏱ *Tour weekdays at 10:30, 11:15, 2:30, 3:15, and 4:15.*

⑫ **Queensland Cultural Centre.** The Queensland Art Gallery, the Queensland Museum, the State Library, the Performing Arts Complex, and a host of restaurants, cafés, and shops—you'll find all of these inside the Queensland Cultural Center. On weekdays at noon there are free tours of the Performing Arts Complex, on which backstage peeks are often included at the 2,000-seat Concert Hall and Cremorne Theatre. The cultural center is on the west side of the Brisbane River near Victoria Bridge. ⊠ *Melbourne St.,* ☎ *07/3840–7303 art gallery, 07/3840–7601 museum, 07/3840–7785 library, 07/3840–7444 or 1800/77–7699 performing arts complex.* ▣ *Free.* ⏱ *Gallery daily 10–5; museum daily 9–5; library Mon.–Thurs. 10–8 and Fri.–Sun. 10–5.*

❶ **St. John's Anglican Cathedral.** Built in 1901 with porphyry rock, this is a fine example of Gothic Revival architecture. Free guided tours are available by request at the cathedral weekdays from 10 to 4. Services are held Sunday morning at 7:30 and 9:30.

Inside the cathedral grounds is the **Deanery,** which predates the construction of the cathedral by almost 50 years. The proclamation declaring Queensland separate from New South Wales was read from the building's east balcony on June 6, 1859. The building served as Government House for Queensland for three years after the declaration. Unfortunately, the interior isn't open to the public. ⊠ *373 Ann St.*

❷ **St. Stephen's Church.** The tiny old church that adjoins St. Stephen's Catholic Cathedral opened in May 1850. This is Brisbane's oldest house of worship, a particularly fine example of Gothic Revival architecture. The church is no longer open to the public. ⊠ *Elizabeth St. near Creek St.*

⑬ **South Bank Parklands.** One of the most appealing urban parks in Australia, Brisbane's World Expo '88 site reopened with its current identity in 1992. In it you can experience various ecosystems. The Gondwana Wildlife Sanctuary is home to more than 700 Australian animal species, from Tasmanian Devils, crocodiles, possums, and feather gliders to pythons and parrots, all living in a replica Daintree forest. The Butterfly and Insect House fosters almost 850 varieties of butterflies as well as the weird and wonderful insects that inhabit Australia. Aside from many shops and restaurants, the 40-acre complex includes an artificial beach beside a swimming lagoon, a Nepalese-style carved-wood pagoda, and cycling paths, and provides excellent views of the city center. The parklands, which feature Friday night Lantern Markets, and a weekend Crafts Village, lie alongside the river just south of the Cultural Centre. ☎ 07/3867–2000, 07/3867–2051 entertainment information. ✉ Sanctuary $10, butterfly house $6.50. ✆ Parklands daily 5 AM–midnight, sanctuary daily 8–5:30, butterfly house daily 8–5, Lantern Markets Fri. 5 PM–10 PM, Crafts Village Sat. 10–5, Sun. 9–5.

❽ Treasury Building. Prominently placed overlooking the river and surrounded by bronze figurative statuary, this massive Italian Renaissance edifice stands on the site of the officers' quarters and military barracks from the original penal settlement. In April 1995, after a $330 million conversion, the building reopened as **Conrad Treasury Casino.** It aims for the more dignified European style of gambling rather than the Las Vegas glitz of Jupiters on the Gold Coast (☞ Lodging and Nightlife and the Arts, below). ✉ William and Elizabeth Sts.

Around Brisbane

Ⓒ Australian Woolshed. The woolshed presents a slice of Australiana that is fascinating for both children and adults. In a one-hour stage show, eight rams from the major sheep breeds found in Australia perform. This is not a circus, however, but an opportunity to gain insight into the dramatically different appearances—and personalities—of sheep. There is also a koala sanctuary, where, for a fee of $7.50, you can be photographed holding a koala. Barbecue lunches are available, and there is an extensive crafts shop. Australian Woolshed can be reached by train to Ferny Grove Station or by taxi (about a $15 ride). ✉ 148 Samford Rd., Ferny Hills, ☎ 07/3351–5366. ✉ $12. ✆ 9:30–5, shows daily at 10, 11, 2.

★ Lone Pine Koala Sanctuary. Queensland's most famous fauna park, founded in 1927, claims to be the oldest animal sanctuary in the world. The real attraction for most visitors is the koalas, although there are also emus, wombats, and kangaroos. Some of the animals can be petted, and for $8 visitors can have a quick cuddle and their photo snapped with a koala. One way to get to the park is by ☞ **cruise boat.** ✉ Jesmond Rd., Fig Tree Pocket, ☎ 07/3222–7278. ✉ $12. ✆ Daily 7:30–4:45.

Cruise boats travel daily to the Lone Pine Koala Sanctuary from North Quay next to the Victoria Bridge in Brisbane proper. Mirimar Cruises, ☎ 07/3221–0300. ✉ $15 round-trip.

Popcorn Factory. Come watch kernels pop and puff at Australia's largest popcorn manufacturer. Overhead walkways allow you to view the entire process; then you can select your favorite at the on-site confectionery shop. ✉ 358 Nudgee Rd., Hendra, ☎ 07/3268–4877. ✉ Free. ✆ Daily 8–6.

Dining

Asian

By Jacki
Passmore

Updated by
Jane Carstens

$$

✗ **Oriental Bangkok Restaurant.** Only a pleasant 20-minute walk from the central business district, this Thai restaurant serves meals as good as any in Bangkok. Begin with hot-and-sour soup or creamy chicken soup with Thai ginger, then sample one of the curries or salads. The seafood salad, with fresh prawns, is a sensation of complementary citrus flavors, and roast duck curry and whole coral trout Thai style are unforgettable entrées. The staff recommends a slightly sweet and fruity

Brisbane Dining and Lodging

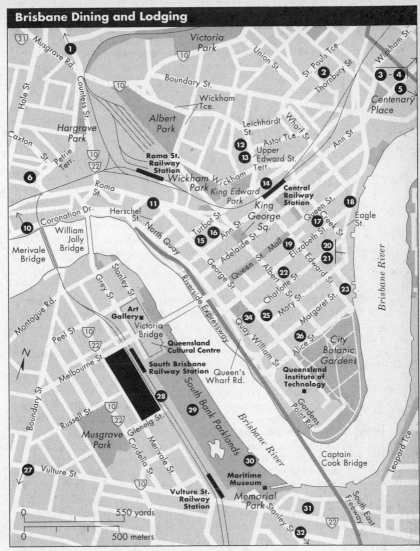

wine, such as gewürztraminer, to complement hot and spicy curries. ⊠ *454 Upper Edward St.,* ☎ *07/3832–6010. AE, DC, MC, V. Closed Sun. No lunch.*

$ ✕ **Kim Thanh Chinese & Vietnamese Restaurant.** Great food at bar-
★   gain prices has made this restaurant an institution among Brisbane diners. Re-decorated after a fire in 1992, the owners re-instated its famous
kitsch decorations—like the large bamboo shrimps perched on the wall.
There is a huge variety of Vietnamese and Chinese dishes, and after
tasting the Mongolian lamb on a hot plate, *goi cuon* (transparent
spring rolls), and barbecued prawns wrapped in sugarcane, you may
want to change the rest of your itinerary to stay here and trawl the
rest of the menu. Take-away is also available. ⊠ *99 Hardgrave Rd.,
West End,* ☎ *07/3844–4954. AE, DC, MC, V.*

$ ✕ **Malaysian Experience.** Unfortunately situated beside the Legal and
General building carpark, this authentic restaurant has an award-winning chef who once cooked for Malaysian royalty. Here you can tuck
into noodles, *laksa* (Malaysian curry soup), claypot chicken, and curries that come straight from the Malay peninsula. ⊠ *80 Jephson St.,
Toowong,* ☎ *07/3870–2624. Reservations essential. AE, DC, MC, V.
No lunch Sun.*

Australian

$$$ ✕ **About Face.** In the skilled hands of chef Peter Davison, this innova-
★   tive restaurant—a one-time tavern dating from 1878—serves an intrigu-
ing Pacific Rim menu, melding Asian, French, and even Australian flavors
and techniques. Favorites are fresh grilled West Australian sardines in
herbed macadamia crust on gaufrette crisps with lemon hollandaise, and
Rannoch Farm Quail with Vietnamese spices. Leave room for one of
the sensational desserts. The restaurant, a previous finalist as Aus-
tralia's Restaurant of the Year, is a 10-minute drive from the city cen-
ter. ⊠ *252 Kelvin Grove Rd., Kelvin Grove,* ☎ *07/3356–8605.
Reservations essential. AE, DC, MC, V. BYOB. No lunch Sat.–Thurs.*

$$$ ✕ **Summit Restaurant.** Perched beside the lookout on the side of Mt.
Coot-tha, this restaurant offers unbeatable views of the city, especially
at night with Brisbane's shimmering lights all around. The original building dates from 1925 and has been patronized by such lights and dig-
nitaries as Katharine Hepburn, Princess Alexandra, and King Peter of
Yugoslavia. At this lofty height, start with cream of macadamia nut
soup followed by char-grilled lamb medallions, then end with a tropical fruit ice cream served in a coconut shell. Taxi fare to the Summit
from the city is about $15. ⊠ *Sir Samuel Griffith Dr., Mt. Coot-tha
Lookout,* ☎ *07/3369–9922,* FAX *07/3369–8937. AE, DC, MC, V.*

$$$ ✕ **Tables of Toowong.** Chef Russell Armstrong's irrepressible culinary
★   imagination, coupled with bold use of Asian spices, French technique,
and fine local produce, places him on the cutting edge of modern Aus-
tralian cuisine. His list of "Just Dishes"—a sort-of tasting menu of ap-
petizer-size portions—includes confit of Atlantic salmon with grilled
fennel, artichokes and potato mash, or milk-fed veal carved over gor-
gonzola-creamed polenta, or fried eggplant and grilled asparagus with
Chianti roasting jus. Even his desserts are like an edible fireworks dis-
play, a spectacular explosion of color and flavor. This culinary bounty
resides in a tastefully converted, Queenslander-style wooden house about
15 minutes from the city center. Bring along a top Australian wine to
round out the meal. ⊠ *85 Miskin St., Toowong,* ☎ *07/3371–4558.
Reservations essential. AE, DC, MC, V. BYOB. Closed Sun. and Mon.
No lunch Sat. in Dec., or Tues.–Thurs. and Sat. Jan.–Nov.*

$$$ ✕ **Victoria's.** This elegant hotel restaurant continues to offer fine din-
ing: there's talent aplenty in the kitchen, a wine list to compete with
the best in the country, comfortable furnishings at large, well-spaced

tables, and impeccable yet friendly service. Look for smoked and sugar-cured Tasmanian salmon and outstanding rare roasted pigeon stuffed with tasso ham and served with kumquats and glazed pears. ⊠ *Brisbane Hilton, Queen St. Mall, Brisbane,* ☎ *07/3231–3131. Reservations essential. AE, DC, MC, V. Closed Sun. No lunch Sat.*

Australian Rustic

$$ ✕ **Ned Kelly's Bushtucker Restaurant.** This slice of Australiana is Brisbane's only authentic bushtucker restaurant and steak house. The outback-theme, wood and corrugated-iron building sets the stage for a menu of Australian game meats—kangaroo, crocodile, buffalo, and emu—char-grilled as steaks or kebabs. Such bushmen's meals as steak-and-kidney pie, barbecued Moreton Bay bugs (a type of lobster), and dumplings in golden syrup supplement the huge, sizzling slabs. If you're feeling gutsy, try the witchety-grub (a kind of moth larvae) soup that tastes surprisingly like another Australian icon—Vegemite. ⊠ *Boardwalk, South Bank Parklands, South Brisbane,* ☎ *07/3846–1880. AE, DC, MC, V.*

Brasseries

$–$$ ✕ **Indigo.** This stylish bistro has flourished under chef Gillian Hurst's talents. It produces sophisticated meals, with frequent menu changes accompanied by a solid wine list. An open kitchen and bar, as well as a small pantry shop outside selling bottled goods and cakes, complement the establishment's intimate atmosphere. If they're on the menu when you visit, try butterfly wings of pickled beetroot under a warm potato cake, or, after dinner, arborio-rice ice cream in layered sheets of almond wafers. ⊠ *695 Brunswick St., New Farm,* ☎ *07/3254–0275. AE, DC, MC, V. No lunch Sun.*

$ ✕ **Brasserie Indochine.** This upmarket inner-city brasserie with minimalist decor is equipped with an open stainless steel kitchen and lots of glass everywhere. Thai-born executive chef Timmy Kemps develops her dishes by preparing an Asian dish and presenting it in a French fashion, or vice versa. Thai tofu pancake of coconut and pickled radish over salad and hot-sour sauce, as well as an oyster salad with chili and coconut dressing and kaffir lime leaf are superb. ⊠ *307 Queen St.,* ☎ *07/3229–4033. Reservations essential. AE, DC, MC, V.*

$ ✕ **Fiasco's.** The dining and bar area of the decrepit Morrison Hotel was imaginatively refurbished by a Queensland restaurateur and is now one of the hippest spots in town. The menu owes its focus to a wood-fired pizza oven, which turns out thin-crusted pies topped with Cajun chicken, smoked salmon, or Thai marinated meats, as well as rolled focaccia with fillings as cross-cultural as the clientele. This original Fiasco's is still on the south side of town; a second, larger branch is at North Quay and Turbot Street just a few minutes from downtown. ⊠ *640 Stanley St., South Brisbane,* ☎ *07/3391–1413. Reservations essential. Closed Sun. and early Jan.*

International

$$$$ ✕ **Michael's Riverside Restaurant.** Michael Platsis owns four very different restaurants, all in the Riverside Centre, and the jewel of the bunch is this silver-service establishment. You'll find a sweeping view of the Brisbane River and an unusual touch in the trolley of fresh, beautifully arranged seafood that's wheeled to your table along with the menu to aid in choosing your meal. Try a collage of Queensland seafood or the mud-crab claws steamed with black beans, ginger, and shallots. No worries about BYOB here: Michael's has what might be the best wine cellar in town. ⊠ *Riverside Centre, 123 Eagle St., Brisbane,* ☎ *07/3832–5522. Reservations essential. AE, DC, MC, V. No lunch Sat., no dinner Sun.*

$$$$ ✕ **Siggi's at the Heritage.** Socialites rub shoulders with visiting celebrities and high-powered businesspeople at this supremely comfortable no-smoking restaurant in the luxurious **Heritage Hotel** (☞ Lodging, *below*). As befits the restaurant's setting, the service is impeccable, and the decor of the adjacent dining and bar areas makes full use of the architecture of the 19th-century Port of Brisbane Office in which they are placed. The compact, classically based menu changes frequently and is supplemented on Wednesday and Thursday evenings with a tasting menu that sets numerous small courses before you. Look for asparagus and crab salad with caviar crème fraîche, and spring lamb on roasted marinated eggplant with a pinot jus. Desserts are just as worthy. ✉ *Edward and Margaret Sts.,* ☎ *07/3221–4555. Reservations essential. AE, DC, MC, V. Closed Sun. and Mon.*

$$ ✕ **Oxley's on the River.** A five-minute taxi ride from the city center takes you to the only restaurant in Brisbane that's built right on the river. By day the dining room is sun filled and has a bird's-eye view of river traffic; by night, light from the city and the moon dimple the water and lend an intimate, romantic ambience. Oxley's traditional char-grilled New York–cut sirloin, Queensland barramundi, mud crab, and fillets of coral trout stuffed with a ragout of seafood are all rightly famed. ✉ *330 Coronation Dr., Milton,* ☎ *07/3368–1866. AE, DC, MC, V.*

Italian

$$ ✕ **Il Centro.** No expense has been spared in fitting this handsome Eagle
★ Street Pier eatery with gleaming wood floors, terra-cotta and dark blue tiles, enormous windows that take advantage of the river view, and undercover outdoor seating. Wondrous aromas spill out of an open kitchen into the stylish, buzzy dining room. The seasonal menu presents excellent fare—try the sand-crab lasagna and pan-fried chicken saltimbocca on a warm salad of pumpkin, asparagus, and rocket. Then throw your diet out the window and try gelato or semifreddo with vanilla, butterscotch, and honeycomb. There is also an excellent wine list. ✉ *1 Eagle St., Eagle Street Pier,* ☎ *07/3221–6090. AE, DC, MC, V. No lunch weekends.*

Mediterranean

$$$$ ✕ **Baguette Bar Café.** Formerly a restaurant that was an institution for
★ 20 years on the Brisbane culinary scene, Baguette has undergone a transformation to a trendy bar and café complete with a vivid citrus decor and modern menu that has retained its original Asian and French influences. Chef Hans Kern's sambal prawns on lime-scented coconut rice with spinach and mushroom risotto alone is worth the 15-minute drive from town. Baguette still has its enterprising wine list and professional service, and the bar doubles as a gallery for local art. ✉ *150 Racecourse Rd., Ascot,* ☎ *07/3268–6168. AE, DC, MC, V.*

$$ ✕ **Peperinas Restaurant and Tapas Bar.** Jose and Ali Fernandes run
★ the only genuine tapas bar in town. This charming, Spanish-style restaurant is a short taxi ride from the heart of the city. The glass-enclosed courtyard is a favorite among lunching businesspeople, and nonsmokers appreciate the three casually elegant, smoke-free dining rooms. On balmy nights the best tables are outdoors under the peperina trees. Order a bottle of Rioja and savor rosemary-seared baby lamb cutlets, grilled Spanish sausage, or barbecued sardines with lemon and garlic while seated under the stars. ✉ *140 Sylvan Rd., at Milton Rd., Toowong,* ☎ *07/3870–9981. AE, DC, MC, V. Closed Sun. and early Jan. No lunch Sat.*

$$ ✕ **Sirocco Mediterranean Café.** No article of Mediterranean kitsch has been left out of this South Bank Parklands eatery. Nonetheless, the place to be seen is in the more nautical outdoor area noshing on slivers of pita dipped into *melitzanosaláta* (eggplant dip). Heartier options include

souvlaki, marinated baby octopus, and large seafood platters. ⊠ *South Bank Parklands,* ☎ *07/3846–1803. AE, DC, MC, V.*

$ ✗ **Grape Wine & Food Bar.** Located in the historic Wickham Hotel, this smallish bistro shares its space with a wine bar, art gallery, wobbly staircase, and alarmingly slanted verandas, but its creative fare has people coming back again and again. Try goat cheese ravioli with pear compote, tomato extract, and black pepper alongside something from the superb wine list, which has plenty of varieties by the glass. ⊠ *308 Wickham St., Fortitude Valley,* ☎ *07/3852–1301. AE, DC, MC, V. Closed Sun. and Mon. No lunch Sat. or Tues.*

Seafood

$$–$$$ ✗ **Pier 9 Oyster Bar and Seafood Grill.** The city's best-looking seafood
★ place prepares a host of fish dishes, from fish-and-chips to lobsters, in considerable style. The dining room's glass walls admit plenty of sunshine and have fine river views. Only the best of the catch from the Northern Territory to Tasmania is served here, and several types of fresh oysters are delivered daily and shucked to order. Marinated seviche and tartare of gravlax are made on the premises. Blackened barramundi is a favorite among Brisbane diners. There is a sizable Australian wine list, with four or five always available by the glass. ⊠ *1 Eagle St., Eagle Street Pier,* ☎ *07/3229–2194. AE, DC, MC, V.*

Lodging

$$$$ 🏨 **Conrad Treasury Brisbane.** Like the Treasury Casino, Brisbane's
★ newest top hotel finds itself within a beautiful, sandstone example of Edwardian Baroque architecture. The rooms are exceptionally modern in facilities provided—luxurious bathrooms, personal bars, coffeemakers, electronic keys, individually controlled air-conditioning, and a wide range of movies to watch. All rooms have antique furnishings and the hotel has five very different restaurants (Marco Polo's east-west fusion cuisine is notable), to suit all budgets and tastes. ⊠ *William St., 4000,* ☎ *07/3306–8888,* FAX *07/3306–8880. 81 rooms with bath, 16 suites. 5 restaurants, 4 bars. AE, DC, MC, V.*

$$$$ 🏨 **The Heritage.** Located on the riverfront next to the City Botanic Gar-
★ dens, this is arguably Brisbane's finest hotel. Its soaring lobby, full of artwork, flower arrangements, and an expanse of natural woods, is warm and inviting, and it is a popular gathering spot. Guest rooms are decorated in neoclassical style in muted yellow and beige and come with the services of a butler (one for each of the 21 floors). Every room has clear views over the river. There are two no-smoking floors. The staff's attention to detail is already legendary; if you require a fax machine in your room, your fax number will be the same on subsequent visits. The hotel's signature restaurant, Siggi's (☞ Dining, *above*), has one of Queensland's best wine cellars. ⊠ *Edward and Margaret Sts.,* ☎ *07/3221–1999 or 1800/77–3700,* FAX *07/3221–6895 or 1800/77–3900. 232 rooms with bath, 20 suites. 3 restaurants, 3 bars, pool, sauna, spa, exercise room. AE, DC, MC, V.*

$$$$ 🏨 **Sheraton Brisbane Hotel & Towers.** Despite its position directly
★ above the city's main commuter rail station, this high-rise hotel is a quiet and extremely pleasant place to stay. The travertine marble floor of the mezzanine lobby is complemented by plenty of brass and natural timber, and there is a spectacular skylit atrium. Floors 27 through 29 constitute the pricier Sheraton Towers, where service and comfort are extended to include personalized registration and use of the exclusive Towers Club lounge on the 27th floor as well as facilities on the lower floors. Decorated in soft pastels, the rooms in both sections of the hotel are spacious and elegant, with marble bathrooms and small sitting areas. ⊠ *249 Turbot St., 4000,* ☎ *07/3835–3535,* FAX *07/3835–4960. 392*

rooms with bath, 26 suites. 3 restaurants, pool, beauty salon, exercise room. AE, DC, MC, V.

$$$–$$$$ ⛉ **Brisbane Hilton.** Designed by award-winning and controversial Australian architect Harry Seidler, this eye-catching, curved 25-story building has an imposing atrium that ranks among the largest in the Southern Hemisphere. All rooms open onto the atrium, are spacious and well appointed, and feature small sitting areas. The Queen Street Mall is at the hotel's back door, and the recently revamped Wintergarden shopping center is housed on the first three floors of the hotel. ✉ *190 Elizabeth St., 4000,* ☎ *07/3231–3131,* 𝔽𝔸𝕏 *07/3231–3199. 322 rooms with bath. 2 restaurants, 5 bars, pool, tennis court, health club, dance club. AE, DC, MC, V.*

$$$ ⛉ **Carlton Crest Hotel.** Refurbished in 1995, the Carlton Crest is op-
★   posite City Hall, close to the center of town. The hotel consists of two towers and a central lobby that is elegantly furnished with French-style sofas and carpets. The Crest Tower rooms are on the small side, but the bathrooms are spacious, where the Carlton Tower executive rooms are furnished in earthy tones and are (understandably) quite spacious. Oliver's Restaurant, which has a large glass-enclosed balcony adjacent to the sidewalk, is worth patronizing both for its international fare and for the people-watching potential of its balcony. ✉ *Ann and Roma Sts., 4000,* ☎ *07/3229–9111 or 1800/77–7123,* 𝔽𝔸𝕏 *07/3229–9618. 432 rooms with bath, 6 suites. 3 restaurants, 3 bars, pool, gymnasium, sauna. AE, DC, MC, V.*

$$$ ⛉ **Quay West.** Opposite Brisbane's Botanic Gardens, this 1995-built hotel exudes a sense of taste with pressed metal ceilings, sandstone floors and columns, hammered iron decorations, and white louvered shutters. The warm, earthy tones and soft pastels of the decor complement the sandstone, and the suites are fitted with plantation teak furniture and raw silk drapes. They include fully equipped kitchens and laundries. Level one of the hotel has a tropically landscaped area surrounding the heated pool, which has five sandstone carvings of merino rams that form an interesting waterfall. A poolside pergola is supported by intricately carved early–19th-century teak columns from South Africa. ✉ *132 Alice St., 4000,* ☎ *07/3853–6000,* 𝔽𝔸𝕏 *07/3853–6060. 134 suites. Restaurant, bar, pool, spa, gymnasium, sauna. AE, DC, MC, V.*

$$$ ⛉ **Royal Albert Boutique Hotel.** This heritage-listed building is situated right in the heart of Brisbane city and offers more than you would expect from a standard hotel room. The larger-than-average rooms all have a self-contained kitchen and laundry, and the reproduction antique furniture and cream-and-plum plush carpets add elegant finishing touches. Being a small hotel, the staff are very friendly and take pride in greeting guests by name. There is a licensed brasserie on the ground floor. ✉ *Elizabeth and Albert Sts., 4000,* ☎ *07/3291–8888,* 𝔽𝔸𝕏 *07/3229–7705. 27 rooms with bath, 28 suites, 4 apartments. Restaurant. AE, DC, MC, V.*

$$$ ⛉ **Rydges South Bank.** Sandwiched between the Brisbane Convention and Exhibition Centre and South Bank Parklands, this 1996-vintage Brisbane Rydges is an excellent choice for business or holiday travelers. The rooms are predominantly olive green and pale yellow, and have modern furnishings and computer work stations in case you bring your laptop with you. The in-house Chinese restaurant, Peking House, has earned a reputation for fine food. Although there is no pool in the complex, Kodak Beach at South Bank is very close, and it's a fine place to swim. ✉ *9 Glenelg St., 4101,* ☎ *07/3255–0822,* 𝔽𝔸𝕏 *07/3255–0899. 238 rooms with bath and shower, 65 suites. 2 restaurants, 2 bars, gymnasium, sauna, spa. AE, DC, MC, V.*

$$–$$$ ⛉ **Brisbane City Travelodge.** Located in the Brisbane Transit Centre just a short walk from the business district, this 18-story hotel caters

to businesspeople. The dark glass exterior is lackluster, but the use of wicker in the lounge area gives the lobby a distinctive Queensland flavor. Furnished in shades of beige and blue, rooms are unusually large and comfortable. Standard double rooms have queen-size beds; king studios have king-size beds. The hotel's Verandah Café is open and airy; the Drawing Room Restaurant is formal and elegant; and the Jazz 'n' Blues Club is a casual, locally popular spot for drinks and live music. ⊠ *Roma and Hershel Sts., 4000,* ☎ *07/3238–2222,* FAX *07/3238–2288. 191 rooms with bath, 2 suites. 2 restaurants, 3 bars, sauna, laundry service. AE, DC, MC, V.*

$$ ⊞ **Bellevue Hotel.** The rooms in this modern, multistory hotel are rather plain, but the heart of Brisbane location is hard to beat. Despite their lack of character, rooms have a large number of modern amenities. ⊠ *103 George St., 4000,* ☎ *07/3221–6044,* FAX *07/3221–7474. 100 rooms with bath. Restaurant, coffee shop, pool, laundry. AE, DC, MC, V.*

$$ ⊞ **Hillcrest Central Apartments.** With the construction of new apartments in front of this nine-story complex, some of its river and city views have been interrupted—but not all. Hillcrest is located close to the South Bank Parklands, and its apartments have modern Italian decor in pale shades of yellow and blue-gray, with sliding glass doors leading onto private balconies. Each apartment has a fully equipped kitchen and color TV. Large family units with two bedrooms are available, as are studios and one-bedrooms that can sleep as many as six people. ⊠ *311 Vulture St., South Brisbane, 4000,* ☎ *07/3846–3000 or 1800/ 07–7777,* FAX *07/3846–3578. 16 rooms with bath, 64 apartments. Restaurant, pool, sauna, tennis court, laundry. AE, DC, MC, V.*

$$ ⊞ **Thornbury House.** At first glance this historic B&B looks tiny, but its looks are deceiving—the 19th-century merchant's house has three levels. Inside, buttermilk-color walls, polished floors, thick carpets, and wooden furniture give it old-world charm. And where that charm translates into sharing bathrooms (one room has its own bath), the waffle-weave bathrobes supplied for guests are a thoughtful comfort. The tariff includes a full breakfast, which you can enjoy in the garden courtyard. A more formal sitting room, where you'll find complimentary port on a sideboard, is provided for quiet evenings. ⊠ *1 Thornbury St., 4000,* ☎ *07/3832–5985,* FAX *07/3832–7255. 9 rooms, 1 with private bath. AE, MC, V.*

$ ⊞ **Annie's Shandon Inn.** A five-minute walk from the railway station,
★ this small, modern, B&B-style lodge has pleasant rooms decorated with Laura Ashley–style wallpaper. Continental breakfast is included in room rates, and local tour buses conveniently stop outside. ⊠ *405 Upper Edward St., 4000,* ☎ *07/3831–8684,* FAX *07/3831–3073. 19 rooms, 4 with bath. AE, MC, V.*

Nightlife and the Arts

The Arts
Concerts, ballet, opera, theater, jazz, and other events are listed in the Saturday edition of the *Courier–Mail* newspaper. Thursday's paper includes a free What's On magazine, which is a comprehensive entertainment guide for Brisbane.

The **Performing Arts Complex** (⊠ Melbourne St., ☎ 07/3840–7444 or 1800/77–7699) at the city's cultural heart, hosts both international and Australian entertainers and performing troupes. The **Art Gallery** (⊠ Melbourne St., ☎ 07/3840–7303) hangs an interesting range of permanent and visiting exhibitions. A listing of events is available at the **Queensland Cultural Centre** (⊠ Stanley St., ☎ 07/3840–7200) and most of the better hotels.

Nightlife

Conrad Treasury Casino. With a dress code that prohibits collarless shirts, shorts, and sporting footwear, this *is* a European-style casino. The Conrad Treasury has three levels of gaming, with a total of 104 tables and more than 1,000 machines. Games include roulette, blackjack, baccarat, mini-baccarat, craps, big six, keno, and two-up. For high rollers there is the exclusive Club Conrad (reserved for members), and there are three restaurants and four bars in the complex. ⊠ *William and Elizabeth Sts.,* ☎ *07/3306–8888.* ⊘ *Daily.*

Friday's caters to a sophisticated clientele in the 30-something age group. Overlooking the Brisbane River, the club has special nights during the week, such as cocktail nights and wine nights (for the 40-somethings). There is a cover charge of $7 on Friday and Saturday nights, and the rest of the week there are charges for the various activities. ⊠ *123 Eagle St.,* ☎ *07/3832–2122.* ⊡ *$7.* ⊘ *Daily 11 AM–late.*

Hogie's Pool Bar & Nightclub, Brisbane's newest nightspot, has an American-style pool room upstairs, open seven nights; there's no cover charge. The nightclub downstairs is decorated in stark warehouse style—the building was originally an electricity substation. ⊠ *127 Charlotte St.,* ☎ *07/3221–5555.* ⊡ *$4–$6.* ⊘ *Wed.–Sat. 8 PM–4 AM.*

Breakfast Creek Hotel is a classic old Australian pub that has hardly changed during the last century. Popular with blue-collar workers, the bar serves pub food and steaks. There is a restaurant in the garden outside. ⊠ *2 Kingsford-Smith Dr., Breakfast Creek,* ☎ *07/3262–5988.* ⊘ *Daily 10–10.*

Outdoor Activities and Sports

Cricket

Queensland Cricketer's Club provides playing schedules and ticket information for the nation's favorite sport. ⊠ *Vulture St., East Brisbane,* ☎ *07/3391–6533.*

Fishing

Anne's Sportfishing Charters can arrange any local on-water activity. Anne Donaldson, the proprietor, is also quite helpful in dispensing advice to visitors about fishing trips and local regulations. ⊠ *24 Grattan Terr., Wynnum,* ☎ *07/3396–2149,* 𝕱𝕬𝕏 *07/3393–0558.*

Golf

To play a round of golf at one of the city's premier courses contact **Indooroopilly Golf Club** (⊠ Meiers Rd., Indooroopilly, ☎ 07/3870–3728) or **Royal Queensland Golf Club** (⊠ Curtin Ave., Eagle Farm, ☎ 07/3268–1127).

Rugby

Rugby League, a professional variation of rugby, is played in winter in Australia. For match programs and information call **Queensland Rugby Football League Limited** ☎ 0055/34–212. Rugby Union, a game more familiar to Americans, is also popular. Call **Queensland Rugby Union Limited** (☎ 07/3250–6100).

Tennis

For information about playing at Brisbane's municipal or private courts or for details of upcoming tournaments, contact **Queensland Lawn Tennis Club.** ⊠ *316 Milton Rd., Milton,* ☎ *07/3369–5325.*

Walking

The National Trust publishes an informative *Historic Walks* brochure that is available from the Queensland Government Travel Centre and some hotels. ⊠ *Edward and Adelaide Sts.,* ☎ *13–1801.*

Shopping

Department Stores

The famous **David Jones** and **Myer** department stores are downtown on Queen Street.

Discount Stores

Stones Corner, a business and residential area about 10 km (6 mi) south of the city center, is a popular shopping area where a variety of shops have opened discount outlets selling goods that are either seconds or end-of-season ranges: Country Road, Sportsgirl, Esprit, and Table Eight are a few of the brands available. Housewear stores are also represented. ✉ *Logan and Old Cleveland Rds., Stones Corner.*

Malls and Arcades

The **Queen Street Mall** is considered the best downtown shopping area, with numerous buskers, flower stalls, and a generally festive atmosphere. **Myer Centre** (✉ Queen, Elizabeth, and Albert Sts.) houses the national department store of the same name, as well as boutiques, specialty shops, delis, restaurants, cinemas, and an upstairs amusement park. The historic and aesthetically pleasing **Brisbane Arcade** joins Queen Street Mall and Adelaide Street and features elegant designer boutiques and jewelry shops. **Rowes Arcade** (✉ 235 Edward St.) is a renovated 1920s ballroom and banquet hall. **Wintergarden Complex** (Queen Street Mall) was renovated in 1996 and has a range of boutiques and specialty shops, as well as a food court. **Broadway on the Mall** connects via a walkway to David Jones, and it has a very good food center on the lower ground floor. **The Pavilion** (✉ Queen and Albert Sts.) has two levels of exclusive shops. **T&G Arcade** (✉ 141 Queen St.) is a less-hurried area of specialty shops and restaurants. **Savoir Faire** (✉ 20 Park Rd., Milton) is an upscale shopping area 10 minutes from the business district. **Chopstix** (✉ 249 Brunswick St., Fortitude Valley) is a collection of 20 Asian shops and restaurants in the heart of Chinatown.

Markets

The Riverside Centre (✉ 123 Eagle St.) is home to the **Cat's Tango Riverside Markets,** an upscale arts-and-crafts market, which is open Sunday 8–4. **South Bank Parklands** has a Friday night Lantern Market that is open 5–10, and a Crafts Village that sells good quality home-made clothing and arts and crafts on Saturday 10–5, Sunday 9–5.

Specialty Stores

ABORIGINAL CRAFTS

Queensland Aboriginal Creations sells genuine Aboriginal hunting paraphernalia and boomerangs, woomeras, didgeridoos, bark paintings, pottery, and carvings. ✉ *135 George St.,* ☎ *07/3224–5730.*

ANTIQUES

Brisbane Antique Market, near the airport, collects more than 40 dealers' antiques, collectibles, and jewelry under one roof. ✉ *791 Sandgate Rd., Clayfield,* ☎ *07/3262–1444.*

Cordelia Street Antique and Art Centre, housed inside an old church, purveys an interesting range of antiques and jewelry ✉ *Cordelia and Glenelg Sts.,* ☎ *07/3844–8514.*

AUSTRALIAN PRODUCTS

Cotton Wool sells high-quality pure Australian wool sweaters and other knitwear. Overseas shipping is available. ✉ *Brisbane Arcade, Queen Street Mall,* ☎ *07/3221–0484.*

Greg Grant Country Clothing specializes in the legendary Drizabone oilskin coats, Akubra and leather hats, whips, R.M. Williams boots, and moleskins. ✉ *Myer Centre, Queen St.,* ☎ *07/3221–4233.*

OPALS

Quilpie Opals has a large selection of Queensland boulder opals as well as high-grade opals, available as individual stones or already set. ⊠ *Lennons Hotel, 68 Queen Street Mall,* ☎ *07/3221–7369.*

SOUVENIRS

The National Trust Gift Shop sells quality Australian-made handicrafts, plus postcards, books, and novelty items. ⊠ *The Mansions, 40 George St.,* ☎ *07/3221–1887.*

Brisbane A to Z

Arriving and Departing

BY BUS

Long-distance bus companies serving Brisbane include **Greyhound Pioneer Australia** (⊠ Brisbane Transit Centre, Roma St., ☎ 07/3258–1670 or 13–2030), and **McCafferty's** Express Coaches (⊠ Brisbane Transit Centre, Roma St., ☎ 07/3236–3035 or 13–1499).

BY CAR

Brisbane is 1,002 km (622 mi) from Sydney along Highway 1. An inland route from Sydney follows Highway 1 to Newcastle and then heads inland on Highway 15.

BY PLANE

Brisbane International Airport is served by a multitude of international airlines. ☞ Air Travel *in* the Gold Guide for information on international as well as domestic carriers.

Between the airport and center city. Brisbane International Airport is 9 km (6 mi) from the city center. **Coachtrans** (☎ 07/3236–1000) provides a daily bus service, called Sky Trans, to and from city hotels every 30 minutes between 5 AM and 8:30 PM. The fare is $6 per person one way, $11 round-trip.

Taxis to downtown Brisbane cost approximately $25.

BY TRAIN

Railways of Australia run nightly service between Sydney and Brisbane (14 hours). The *Sunlander* and the luxurious *Queenslander* trains make a total of four runs a week between Brisbane and Cairns in the north. Other long-distance passenger trains are the *Spirit of Capricorn* between Brisbane and Rockhampton (daily departures), the *Inlander* between Townsville and Mt. Isa (four times per week), and the *Spirit of the Outback* between Brisbane and Longreach (twice per week). Packages, such as Reef and Rail or Outback Aussies Adventures are also available. Trains depart from the Roma Street Station. For details contact Queensland Rail (⊠ 305 Edward St., ☎ 07/3235–2222) or the **City Booking Office** (☎ 13–2232).

Getting Around

BY BUS

Whether or not Brisbane's buses properly serve regular commuters is one question. For vacationers, stops are well signposted and the buses mostly run to schedule, so buses can be a good way to get around. For routes, schedules, and fares, call **Trans Info** (13–1230).

BY CAR

All major car-rental agencies have offices in Brisbane, including **Avis** (☎ 1800/22–5533), **Thrifty** (☎ 1800/65–2008), **Hertz** (☎ 07/3221–6166 or 13–3039), and **Budget** (☎ 13–2727). Four-wheel-drive vehicles are available.

Taxis are metered and relatively inexpensive. They are available at designated taxi stands outside hotels, downtown, and at the railway station, although it is usually best to phone for one. The best taxi companies in Brisbane are **Yellow Cabs** (☎ 07/3391–0191) and **Black and White Cabs** (☎ 13–1008).

Contacts and Resources

EMERGENCIES
Ambulance, fire brigade, and **police.** ☎ *000.*
Royal Brisbane Hospital. ☎ *07/3253–8111.*

GUIDED TOURS
Australian Pacific Day Tours (✉ Brisbane Transit Centre, Roma St., Level 3, ☎ 07/3236–4165 or 1800/36–1788) offers a range of half- or full-day tours of Brisbane, as well as trips to the Gold Coast, Noosa Heads, and the Sunshine Coast.

City Sights open tram-style buses, run by the Brisbane City Council, make half-hourly circuits of city landmarks and other points of interest. They leave from Post Office Square every 40 minutes, starting at 9 AM, with a break from 12:20 to 1:40. You can buy tickets on the bus, and you can get on or off at any of the 19 stops. ✉ *Brisbane City Council, 69 Ann St.,* ☎ *13–1230.* 🖭 *$15.*

Kookaburra Queen, a paddle wheeler, runs daily morning tea and buffet-, seafood lunch-, and dinner-cruises along the Brisbane River. They also have afternoon tea on Sunday. The cruises often feature live entertainment. ✉ *Eagle Street Pier, Creek and Eagle Sts.,* ☎ *07/3221–1300.* 🖭 *$20–$50 per person.*

VISITOR INFORMATION
Out and About in Brisbane, a free pocket guide available at most hotels, lists events, services, and attractions in the city.
Brisbane Visitors and Convention Bureau. ✉ *Box 12260, Elizabeth St.; Brisbane City Hall, Adelaide St.,* ☎ *07/3221–8411; Queen Street Mall,* ☎ *07/3229–5918; at airport,* ☎ *07/3860–4688.*
Queensland Government Travel Centre provides information about all of Queensland. ✉ *Edward and Adelaide Sts., GPO Box 9958, 4001,* ☎ *13–1801.*

CARNARVON NATIONAL PARK

Despite its remote location 700 km (437 mi) northwest of Brisbane—*way* off the beaten path—**Carnarvon National Park** is one of the most popular parks in central Queensland. Its 21 km (13 mi) of walking tracks are suitable for the whole family, with only a few side tracks that involve difficult ascents. Even on hot days, the park's shady gorges are cool and refreshing.
Carnarvon is famous for its ancient Aboriginal paintings, particularly those in the Art Gallery and Cathedral Cave. Both galleries span more than 165 ft of sheer sandstone walls covered with red ochre stencils of ancient Aboriginal life—among them weapons and hands. An extensive boardwalk system with informational plaques allows easy access to the fragile paintings.

Several popular walking trails wend through the park, most of them branching off the main trail, which begins near the campground. The 18½-km (11½-mi) round-trip trail to Cathedral Cave leapfrogs back and forth across the Carnarvon Creek at well-placed, round boulders. Except at stream crossings, the trail is flat and well marked. Side trips off the main trail lead to the popular Moss Garden, a collection of sandstone walls blanketed in green moss, and the Amphitheater, an enclosed gorge accessible by a 30-ft steel ladder. Take water with you when hiking, because creek water is not potable. Carnarvon is best visited during the dry season, April through October, when most roads to the park are passable.

Lodging

One main campground (☎ 079/84–4505) at Carnarvon is at the end of the only road into the park. Fees are $3 per person per night for up to six people, and facilities include cold-water showers and toilets. Bookings are essential; if you plan to visit during school holiday periods, call up to nine months in advance. Safari cabin accommodation is available at the **Carnarvon Gorge Oasis Lodge** (☎ 079/84–4503), where rates are $150 per person, including full board and activities. There are 23 cabins, and the lodge also has a general store that sells food staples as well as fuel, gas, and ice.

Arriving and Departing

A four-wheel-drive vehicle is recommended for travel to Carnarvon, especially right after the wet season (January–late April), when many roads may still be flooded. Two-wheel-drive vehicles are adequate during the height of dry season. From Brisbane, take the Warego Highway 486 km (302 mi) west to Roma, then 271 km (168 mi) north toward Injune and Carnarvon. The final 70 km (44 mi) are rather rough. Be sure to bring food for at least two extra days in case of road flooding.

Visitor Information

Carnarvon National Park, Department of Environment, Western Region. *Gorge section,* ☎ *079/84–4505. Mt. Moffatt section,* ☎ *076/26–3581.*

GOLD COAST AND
LAMINGTON NATIONAL PARK

For many years this was the fastest growing playground in Australia. As a result, skyscraper condominiums jostle for waterfront positions, casting giant afternoon shadows onto the beaches, and the streets are lined with souvenir shops, fast-food stalls, and restaurants. The area can be garish, glitzy, and even crass—but it is never, *never* dull. Don't come here if you want to get away from it all, because life on the Gold Coast is a nonstop party.

An hour south of Brisbane, the Gold Coast officially comprises the 32 km (20 mi) from Southport to Coolangatta, but it has sprawled almost as far inland as Nerang. It is without doubt the most developed tourist destination in Australia, its popularity ensured by 300 days of sunshine a year and an average temperature of 75°F (24°C). Christmas and June through August are peak seasons.

Away from the Gold Coast scene, Lamington National Park is an interesting tropical–subtropical–temperate ecological border zone. That makes for a complex abundance of plant and animal life that's astounding. The park is on the Queensland–New South Wales border, about a three-hour trip from Brisbane, or about an hour from Surfers Paradise.

For the sake of putting some form on the twisting ribbon of development that is the Gold Coast, this section is arranged as if you were approaching the area by road from Brisbane and following the coast from north to south, down as far as the New South Wales border.

Coomera

48 km (36 mi) south of Brisbane.

🐨 **Dreamworld.** In just one day at this family theme park, you can thrill on the fastest, tallest ride in the world, The Tower of Terror, then take on action rides like the Wipeout and Thunderbolt. You can also watch Bengal tigers play and swim with their handlers on Tiger Island, cuddle a koala in Koala Country, or journey into a fragile world on the Creature Cruise. There are entertaining shows, costumed characters roaming the park, and an amazing six-story IMAX screen theater. The park is 40 minutes outside Brisbane and 20 minutes from Surfers Paradise along the Pacific Highway. ⊠ *Dreamworld Pkwy.,* ☎ *07/5588–1111 or 1800/07–3300.* 🎟 *$39.* ☉ *Daily 10–5; Main St., Plaza Restaurant, and Koala Country daily 9–5.*

Oxenford

2 km (1¼ mi) south of Coomera.

🐨 **Warner Bros. Movie World** is one of the most popular tourist attractions in Australia and is one of the few movie theme parks outside the United States. The park incorporates Warner Roadshow Movie World Studios, where you can see the actual Riddler's Lair set from *Batman Forever,* and learn how the special effects for the movie were produced. The park is also home to the Lethal Weapon ride, which is the only suspended looping coaster in Australia. Other highlights include the *Police Academy* stunt show and the Batman Adventure ride. There is a good children's section and plenty of shops selling Warner Brothers' souvenirs. ⊠ *Pacific Hwy.,* ☎ *07/5573–3999 or 07/5573–8485.* 🎟 *$37.* ☉ *Daily 9:30–5:30. Closed Dec. 25–Apr. 25.*

🐨 When you're looking for **Wet 'n' Wild Water Park,** keep your eyes out for Matilda, the giant kangaroo mascot of the 1982 Brisbane Commonwealth Games. The park has magnificent water slides, as well as a wave pool with 3-ft-high surf. One favorite attraction is the Dive-in-Movies, where a giant screen at the back of the wave pool shows recent releases Saturday night from September to April and every night in January. And of course there's Calypso Beach, a tropical island fringed with white sandy beaches, surrounded by a slow-moving river where guests can laze about in brightly colored tubes. ⊠ *Pacific Hwy.,* ☎ *07/5573–2277.* 🎟 *$21.* ☉ *Sun.–Fri. 10–5, Sat. 10–9.*

Hope Island

6 km (4 mi) east of Oxenford.

Home to a five-star Hyatt Regency hotel, **Sanctuary Cove** (☎ 07/5530–8400) is a huge resort area with two golf courses, an outstanding marina, and a shopping center filled with boutiques, restaurants, a cinema, health club, and a small brewery. It is the result of a 1980s experiment in forming a very exlusive community within a secure enclave. Most residents travel around the village in golf carts, saving their cars for the times when they have to venture out into the wider world. It's reached by turning north off the highway at Oxenford.

Lodging

$$$$ 🏨 **Hyatt Regency Sanctuary Cove.** Set in landscaped tropical gardens,
★ this opulent low-rise hotel resembles a monumental Australian colonial mansion. Five three-story guest courts are luxuriously appointed, each with its own large, private balcony. The main lobby building, known as the Great House, leads past a cascading waterfall to the courtyard and swimming pool–spa area. There's also a sandy beach lagoon fed

with filtered saltwater next to the resort's main harbor. A walkway from the hotel leads directly into the village. ⊠ *Manor Circle, Casey Rd.,* ☎ *07/5530–1234,* FAX *07/5530–8056. 247 rooms with bath. 3 restaurants, 2 bars, sauna, spa, 18-hole golf course, tennis, bowling, squash, deep-sea fishing. AE, DC, MC, V.*

Southport

16 km (10 mi) southeast of Oxenford.

In Southport, look for the turnoff to **the Spit,** a natural peninsula pointing north where you'll find some of the town's best attractions.

Seaworld is Australia's largest marine park. Six daily shows feature whales, dolphins, sea lions, and water-skiing. There is a large number of rides, including a monorail, a corkscrew roller-coaster, and some exceptional water slides, and Dolphin Cove, the largest natural dolphin lagoon in the world, opened in 1996. Limited numbers of visitors, aged 14 years or more, can swim with the dophins. All rides except helicopter and parasailing flights are included in the ticket price. ⊠ *The Spit, Main Beach,* ☎ *07/5588–2222.* ➽ *$37.* ☉ *Daily 9:30–5.*

Fisherman's Wharf (☎ *07/5532–7944*), a complex of shops and restaurants next to Seaworld, has marvelous views across the water and is a great place to stop for a snack. A public saltwater swimming pool is on site.

Dining and Lodging

$–$$ ✕ **Grumpy's Wharf Restaurant.** The seafood here is inspired and widely regarded as the best on the coast, and it comes with a view of boats moored at the wharf. You may have a hard time choosing between mixed seafood platters and seafood risotto. Don't expect pretty decor (it could use sprucing up) or a quick dine and dash, as service tends to be slow. ⊠ *66–70 Seaworld Dr., The Spit,* ☎ *07/5532–2900. AE, DC, MC, V.*

$$$$ 🖼 **Sheraton Mirage.** A low-rise building nestled amid lush gardens and
★ fronting a secluded beach, this top-flight resort has a distinctly Australian look. Rooms are tastefully furnished in soft colors and overlook gardens, the Pacific Ocean, or vast saltwater lagoons. A suspension bridge over the road links the resort with the elegant Marina Mirage shopping and restaurant center, although you would be wise to sample the excellent fare at the resort's own restaurants first. Don't miss the weekly poolside barbecue in summer. ⊠ *Seaworld Dr., the Spit, Broadwater, 4217,* ☎ *07/5591–1488,* FAX *07/5591–2299. 323 rooms with bath, 40 suites. Restaurants, coffee shop, pool. AE, DC, MC, V.*

Boating

You can rent yachts and cabin cruisers from **Popeye's Boat Hire.** ⊠ *Mariner's Cove, 212 Seaworld Dr., Main Beach,* ☎ *07/5591–2553 or 07/5532–5822.*

Fishing

Doug and Paul's Gold Coast Fishing Tackle can provide tackle and advice about local fishing hot spots. ⊠ *20 Nind St.,* ☎ *07/5531–0755.*

Nightlife and the Arts

For the most elegant disco on the Gold Coast, head for **Rolls** nightclub. The decor is built around a glorious vintage Rolls-Royce that is fitted with a small table so that you can enjoy your snacks and drinks in its ultimate luxury. This is the place to come for champagne, cocktails, light supper, and live music. ⊠ *Sheraton Mirage, Seaworld Dr., Broadwater Spit,* ☎ *07/5591–1488.*

Shopping

The most elegant shopping center on the Gold Coast is the **Marina Mirage,** where you'll find such designer boutiques as Yves Saint Laurent, Aigner, Louis Vuitton, and Hermès, along with fine antiques, beach and leisure wear, perfume, and duty-free goods. There are fine restaurants and marina facilities as well. ⊠ *74 Seaworld Dr., Broadwater Spit,* ☎ *07/5577-0088.*

Paradise Waters

5 km (3 mi) south of Southport.

One of those suburbs that exists in its own right but is small enough to be left off most maps, Paradise Waters is the site for the Gold Coast's Sunbelt Indy Carnival races in late March.

Dining

$$$–$$$$ ✕ **Grissini.** You can see the experienced touch of Sydney's Percuoco
   ★ family (of the Buon Ricordo) in this new Italian-style waterfront restaurant. One standard here is spaghetti *in cartoccio* (with cracked pepper, tomatoes, seafood, and olive oil, wrapped and baked in paper), or try the menu *di degustazione* (tasting menu) to sample a variety of dishes. ⊠ *Nelson Bldg., Admiralty Dr., Paradise Waters,* ☎ *07/5532-5788. AE, DC, MC, V.*

Main Beach

6 km (4 mi) south of Southport.

Along with being a residential area full of high-rise apartments and houses, Main Beach is a popular swimming spot for Brisbane residents who are looking for good surf without the crowds of Surfers Paradise. Tedder Avenue at Main Beach is one of the local haunts. It has a strip of elegant coffee shops and cafés separate from the tourist areas, which makes it the spot to get the measure of real-time Gold Coast life.

Surfers Paradise

8 km (5 mi) south of Southport; 72 km (45 mi) south of Brisbane.

In Surfers Paradise park as close to Cavill Avenue as possible—this is the heart of town, a tawdry collection of high-rises overlooking the beach, where bodies bake in the sand under signs warning of the risks of skin cancer.

If your thirst for the bizarre isn't satisfied by the crowds in Surfers Paradise, the displays at **Ripley's Believe It or Not Museum** will take you that extra mile. ⊠ *Raptis Plaza, Cavill Mall,* ☎ *07/5592-0040.* ⊡ *$9.95.* ⊙ *Daily 9 AM–11 PM.*

Dining and Lodging

$$$ ✕ **Danny's.** In a spacious and elegant room overlooking the river,
  ★ guests are seated in comfortable booths while a trio plays Continental and Latin American music. The menu includes memorable international and Italian dishes, such as *capeletti* (small hats of pasta filled with ricotta cheese, cream, and mushrooms) and sautéed baby veal in white wine, lemon, and rosemary. Danny's continues to serve the pasta that well-fed tenor Luciano Pavarotti says is his favorite: spinach spaghetti with Moreton Bay bugs (a type of lobster). For dessert, have Mamma's homemade gelato. ⊠ *Tiki Village, Cavill Ave., Riverfront,* ☎ *07/5538-2818. AE, DC, MC, V.*

$$$ ✕ **Mango's.** The Santa Fe decor is one striking feature of this Nerang River–front restaurant, which comes as well with palm trees, thatched

roof, exposed beams, and waterfall. Even though the restaurant seats 400, the candle-lit tables and clever layout make dinners as intimate as you want them to be. The menu is swimming with seafood dishes, so try grilled spring water barramundi, or poached prawn, scallop, oysters, Moreton Bay bugs and fish in a champagne citrus sauce. ⊠ *Tiki Village, Cavill Ave. (river end)*, ☎ *07/5531–6177. AE, DC, MC, V.*

$$ ✕ **Shogun.** Incongruously set in the middle of a light industrial area,
★ this little Japanese restaurant may serve the best Japanese fare on the Gold Coast. Walk through a classic garden to the Oriental dining room, where you are served such traditional delicacies as *shishamon* (grilled marinated fish filled with roe), tempura, yakitori, and *chawan mushi* (steamed egg soup with small pieces of fish and prawns). ⊠ *90 Bundall Rd.*, ☎ *07/5538–2872. AE, DC, MC, V. Closed Mon. No lunch.*

$–$$ ✕ **Hard Rock Cafe Surfers.** Packed with the usual rock memorabilia, this has been one of the hottest spots on the coast since it opened in 1996. You'll walk into the Pray for Surf bar and Hard Rock Shop on the ground floor; the café, with its stone sculpted Cadillac canopies and a Hall of Fame dedicated to surfing memorabilia, resides on the second floor. The menu is very American, with a few locally named dishes thown in—try the Shark Repellent cocktail and the Aussie burger. A children's menu is also available. ⊠ *Cavill Ave. and Gold Coast Hwy.*, ☎ *07/5539–9377. AE, MC, V.*

$$$ 🏨 **Marriott Surfers Paradise Resort.** Unlike many of its Gold Coast peers,
★ this hotel has a grand style, from the use of sandstone and polished natural wood to the lobby's giant columns and grand circular staircase, which is cooled by a colorful Indian punkah. The guest rooms, all large and decorated in gentle hues of beige, light plum, and moss green, have walk-in closets, marble bathrooms, and safes. The hotel is close to both the Nerang River and the beach, and all rooms have balconies and ocean views. It's a five-minute walk to the ocean, but the hotel has its own beach on a saltwater lagoon that is deep enough for scuba lessons and is well stocked with brilliantly colored marine fish. The freshwater outdoor pool is surrounded by gardens. There are dive and water sports shops on the premises, and you can hire board-sailing equipment, water skis, and catamarans on the river. ⊠ *158 Ferny Ave., 4217*, ☎ *07/5592–9800, * FAX *07/5592–9888. 330 rooms with bath, 13 suites. 2 restaurants, 3 bars, in-room VCRs, pool, sauna, spa, steam room, 2 tennis courts, exercise room, baby-sitting. AE, DC, MC, V.*

$$–$$$ 🏨 **Moroccan Beach Resort.** Located opposite a patrolled section of the beach, these white Mediterranean-style apartments offer a stark contrast to the blue skies and water. Of the development's three towers, the pick of them is the Esplanade, which has absolute beach frontage. The hotel-style rooms are quite small—but comfortable—and the one- and two-bedroom apartments are spacious and luxuriously appointed with a tangerine, white, and blue color scheme. Apartments come with a well-equipped kitchen and laundry facilities. Outside, there is a common barbecue area. ⊠ *9 Elkhorn Ave., Surfers Paradise*, ☎ *07/ 5526–9400, * FAX *07/5526–9700. 180 rooms and apartments with bath. 3 heated pools, 3 whirlpools, wading pool. AE, DC, MC, V.*

$$ 🏨 **ANA Hotel Gold Coast.** This 22-story hotel is one of the best managed establishments in Surfers Paradise. A minute's walk from the beach and Cavill Avenue, the hotel is perfect if you like being in the center of the action, especially when it comes to the Sunbelt Indy Carnival. This ANA has a winning position overlooking the Gold Coast's annual late-March racing event, and bookings for that time are advised well in advance. Rooms have soft pastel decor with blond-wood furniture and balconies with views over central Surfers Paradise. Service is impeccable. ⊠ *22 View Ave., 4217*, ☎ *07/5579–1000, * FAX *07/5570–*

1260. 403 rooms with bath, 17 suites. 3 restaurants, 3 bars, pool, 2 tennis courts, sauna, exercise room. AE, DC, MC, V.

Nightlife and the Arts

New nightspots spring up in Surfers Paradise all the time. Some of the long-running favorites are **Melba's On The Park** (⊠ 46 Cavill Ave., ☎ 07/5538–7411), **The Penthouse Nightclub** (⊠ Orchid Ave., ☎ 07/5538–1388), and **Bensons Nightclub** (⊠ 22 Orchid Ave., ☎ 07/5538–7600).

Shopping

Raptis Plaza (⊠ Between Cavill Mall and the Esplanade, ☎ 07/5592–2133) is filled with enticing boutiques and coffee shops. **The Paradise Centre** (⊠ Cavill Ave., ☎ 07/5592–0155) has 120 shops and restaurants, as well as an extensive amusement arcade. **Surfers Paradise Beach Front Markets** sell locally made arts and crafts every Friday night (5:30–10) on the boardwalk at the beach end of Cavill Mall (☎ 07/5581–7510).

Ashmore

7 km (4.5 mi) west of Surfers Paradise.

Lodging

$$$–$$$$ ⌹ **Royal Pines Resort.** Nestled beside the Nerang River, this resort offers the best of everything: 495 acres of manicured gardens, two golf courses, small lakes, and a marina that has access to the Nerang River and the ocean. The rooms are nicely decorated with pastel colors and natural wood furnishings—the Junior suites, which have spas overlooking the golf courses, are the ones to reserve. Other highlights include two undercover tennis courts and a floating restaurant and café. The resort hosts major golf events, and it even has its own white church, which is popular for weddings. ⊠ *Ross St., ☎ 07/5597–1111 or 1800/07–4999,* FAX *07/5597–2277. 329 suites. 9 restaurants, 2 bars, 3 pools, 2 18-hole golf courses, 5 tennis courts, health club, marina. AE, DC, MC, V.*

Broadbeach

8 km (5 mi) south of Southport.

Dining and Lodging

$$$ ✕⌹ **Hotel Conrad and Jupiters Casino.** This award-winning hotel-casino always seems to be bustling, especially in the sprawling lobby, where people always seem congregated, waiting to head to a restaurant, bar, or into the main gambling rooms. Gamblers can try their hand at the casino's 100 gaming tables or feed coins into more than 100 gaming machines; high-rollers should steer straight for the lavishly appointed Club Conrad. Located within the complex are six restaurants, including the buffet-style Food Fantasy, which is a Gold Coast favorite for families, and Andiamo, a local Italian star. ⊠ *Broadbeach Island, Gold Coast Hwy., 4218, ☎ 07/5592–1133 or 008/07–4344,* FAX *07/5592–8219. 609 rooms, 29 suites, 2 penthouses. 6 restaurants, 9 bars, coffee shop, sauna, whirlpool, tennis, squash. AE, DC, MC, V.*

Nightlife

Jupiter's Casino in Broadbeach provides flamboyant around-the-clock entertainment. The Casino features 100 gaming tables on two levels, and includes blackjack, baccarat, craps, sic-bo, pai gow, keno, plus more than 100 gaming machines, which are open 24 hours a day, 7 days a week. Fortunes Nightclub is on the top level of the complex and is open nightly, and the 950-seat showroom often features glitzy Las Vegas–style productions. ⊠ *Gold Coast Hwy., ☎ 07/5592–1133.*

Shopping

Oasis Shopping Centre. This development is the retail heart of beach-side Broadbeach, with over 100 retailers as well as an attractive mall where coffee shops stand umbrella-to-umbrella along the edge. A monorail runs from the center to Conrad Jupiters and the Pan Pacific Hotel. ⊠ *Victoria Ave.,* ☎ *07/5592–3900.*

Pacific Fair. This sprawling outdoor shopping center is Queensland's largest, and its major retailers and 260 specialty shops should be enough to satisfy even die-hard shoppers. There are also undercover malls, landscaped grounds with three small lakes, a children's park, and village green. ⊠ *Hooker Blvd., adjacent to Jupiter's Casino,* ☎ *07/5539–8766.*

Elanora

15 km (9 mi) south of Surfers Paradise.

Directly behind Palm Beach, and midway between Burleigh Heads and Currumbin, Elanora is one of several Gold Coast areas set back from the beach that have been extensively developed over the years by the addition of landfill, canals, and marinas.

Lodging

$$ ⊡ **Isle of Palms.** Ideal if you want to get away from the madding
★ crowd, this complex of luxury town houses is a short distance outside Elanora on a man-made island. It's 2 km (1 mi) from the surf beach, and the resort has its own private beaches, a heated rock lagoon, and a swimming pool with an outdoor whirlpool. You can fish from the jetties or windsurf on the quiet waters of the lake. Most of the town houses have views of the waterfront, some look onto courtyard gardens instead. Spacious, airy, and gracefully furnished in pastel motifs, all town houses are equipped with full kitchens and laundry facilities. ⊠ *Coolgardie St., 4221,* ☎ *07/5598–1733,* 𝔽𝔸𝕏 *07/5598–1653. 174 suites. Restaurant, 2 pools, 2 tennis courts. AE, DC, MC, V.*

Burleigh Heads

9 km (6 mi) south of Surfers Paradise.

Presented to the National Parks and Wildlife Association by wildlife
ℭ naturalist David Fleay, **Fleay's Wildlife Park** consists of wetlands, eucalypts, and rain forests in their natural states and 4 km (2½ mi) of magnificent bushwalks. You'll see koalas, swamp wallabies, brolgas, ibises, platypuses, swans, and crocodiles. The park is just west of town. ⊠ *W. Burleigh Rd.,* ☎ *07/5576–2411 or 07/5576–2767.* 🎫 *$9.50.* ☉ *Daily 9–5.*

Currumbin

6 km (4 mi) south of Burleigh Heads.

Across the creek from Palm Beach on the Gold Coast Highway is the
ℭ community of Currumbin and the **Currumbin Sanctuary.** What started off as a bird park in 1947 is now a 70-acre National Trust Reserve that is home to huge flocks of Australian lorikeets, as well as other exotic birds, bilbies, kangaroos, and koalas. Aboriginal dancers also perform daily. Try to be on hand between 8 AM and 9 AM or 4 PM and 5 PM when the lorikeets arrive to be fed. The park's lovely grounds are ideal for picnics, and there is a café/restaurant on site. ⊠ *28 Tomewin St., off Gold Coast Hwy.,* ☎ *07/5534–1266.* 🎫 *$16.* ☉ *Daily 8–5.*

Coolangatta

25 km (16 mi) south of Surfers Paradise; 97 km (61 mi) south of Brisbane.

This southernmost Gold Coast border town blends into its New South Wales neighbor, Tweed Heads. It's a pleasant town, with a state-line lookout at the Captain Cook memorial at Point Danger.

Dining

$$–$$$ ✕ **Oskar's on the Beach.** One of the few restaurants overlooking
★   Coolangatta Beach, Oskar's serves food worthy of the many awards it has won. Try the warm seafood salad with pink peppercorn dressing, or splendid green prawns dipped in coconut and macadamia nuts and fried in beer batter. The wine selection is excellent, too. ⊠ *Marine Parade,* ☎ *07/5536–4621. AE, DC, MC, V.*

Gold Coast Hinterland–Lamington National Park

A visit to the Gold Coast wouldn't be complete without a short journey to nearby **Lamington National Park.** Be forewarned, however, that this can induce culture shock: The natural grandeur of the rain forest contrasts dramatically with the man-made excesses of the coastal strip. The valleys and peaks of Lamington are home to two types of dense rain forest: the warm tropical variety common in Queensland, and remnants of the cooler subtropical rain forest that blanketed Australia when it was still part of the ancient, Southern Hemisphere supercontinent of Gondwanaland between 50 and 100 million years ago. There is a third forest culture in the park as well, as this is the northernmost point in Australia where the Antarctic beech grows. You'll find it only at higher elevations.

Bushwalkers are well served here, with 160 km (100 mi) of walking tracks that lead to streams, cascades, and waterfalls, through eroded caves, along cliffs, and into fern-filled gullies. The park is a bird-watcher's delight, with more than 200 species identified, including 14 parrot, 16 honeyeater, and 5 owl species. Flashy crimson rosellas are particularly noticeable—the park is home to thousands of these birds, which are not shy about eating out of people's hands. Campers shouldn't be surprised to see brushtail and ringtail possums lurking around the campground at night.

Only two roads lead into the park, one ending at Binna Burra in the northeast, and the other at Green Mountains Lodge (O'Reilly's Mountain Resort) in the south. Several trails wind through the park from these two privately run facilities. The Border Track is a 43-km (26½-mi) round-trip walk that connects the two lodges and takes two days to complete. Other trails branch off this one and lead to some of the more than 500 waterfalls in the park. The Senses Track at Binna Burra is a short loop of either 1,300 or 2,300 ft. Designed for the blind, ropes guide walkers to Braille informational signs that dot the trail (parts of the trail have been in disrepair, so check in advance if the ropes are intact). If you don't read Braille, a tape-recorded commentary is also available. Both resorts include introductory walks through the rain forest in their rates.

Rain is likely to fall at any time of the year, but April through October is usually the driest period. The park is 2,805 ft above sea level, so evenings are generally cool. Also, bring appropriate hiking boots for solid footing on park trails.

Dining and Lodging

There are two lodges to choose from in the Lamington area. Both have budget and higher-price accommodations. Binna Burra also has a campground that charges $12 per night for two people. You can pick up gasoline and supplies in Canungra.

$$$$ ✕▣ **O'Reilly's Rainforest Guesthouse** has three styles of cabins, ranging from a 1930s-style house with shared bathroom for $110 per person up to a mountain-style unit with private bathroom for $160 per person. These rates include all meals and activities, such as guided forest walks. The resort is 109 km (68 mi) from Brisbane via Route 1 through Oxenford and Canungra. The road is twisting and steep, and too narrow for RVs. ✉ *Green Mountains, via Canungra 4275,* ☎ *07/ 5544–0644. 45 rooms with bath. AE, DC, MC, V.*

$$$ ✕▣ **Binna Burra Mountain Lodge** has three levels of cabins, and tariffs range from $105 for shared accommodations with a shared bathroom to $185 for the sole use of a cabin with a private bathroom. These prices include all meals and guided activities, such as guided bushwalks and mountain biking. To reach Binna Burra, 98 km (61 mi) south of Brisbane, take Route 1 to Nerang, then follow back roads through Beechmont to the lodge; or turn off of Route 1 at Oxenford and drive past Canungra. The lodge also operates a Binna Burra bus that makes a daily return trip to the Surfers Paradise Transit Centre. ✉ *Binna Burra, Beechmont,* ☎ *07/5533–3622. 41 cabins with bath. Library, gift shop, laundry service. AE, DC, MC, V.*

Arriving and Departing

Access to O'Reilly's Mountain Resort from Brisbane is via Route 13 through Tamborine and Canungra. The road is twisting and steep, and too narrow for RVs—four-wheel-drive vehicles are recommended. To reach Binna Burra, drive south on Route 13 and turn off at Beaudesert to Nerang and the park.

Buses leave Brisbane for O'Reilly's ($35 round-trip) Sunday through Friday at 9:30 AM (✉ Allstate Scenic Tours, Transit Centre, Roma St., Brisbane 4000, ☎ 07/3285–1777).

Visitor Information

Department of Environment and Heritage. ✉ *160 Ann St., Brisbane,* ☎ *07/3227–8185.*

Gold Coast A to Z

Arriving and Departing

BY BUS

Long-distance buses traveling between Sydney and Brisbane stop at Coolangatta and Surfers Paradise. **McCafferty's** (☎ 07/5538–2700 or 13–1499) and **Murrays Coaches** (07/5526–3822) operate between Brisbane's Roma Street transit center and the Gold Coast. **Greyhound Pioneer Australia** (✉ 6 Beach Rd., Surfers Paradise, ☎ 13–2030) runs an express coach from the Gold Coast to Brisbane International Airport and Coolangatta Airport, as well as day trips that cover southeast Queensland with daily connections to Sydney and Melbourne.

BY CAR

The Gold Coast begins 65 km (40 mi) south of Brisbane. Take the Pacific Highway (Hwy. 1) south to the Gold Coast Highway, which runs through the towns of Southport, Surfers Paradise, and Coolangatta. From Brisbane International Airport take the Toll Road over the Gateway Bridge to avoid having to drive through Brisbane, then follow the signs to the Gold Coast.

BY PLANE

☞ Air Travel *in* the Gold Guide for information on airlines serving **Coolangatta Airport.**

Getting Around

The **Surfside Buslines** (☎ 07/5536–7666) runs an excellent bus service every 15 minutes between Gold Coast attractions, along the strip between Tweeds Head and Southport.

BY CAR

All major car-rental agencies have offices in Brisbane and at the airport. On the Gold Coast itself, hire cars from **Avis** (✉ Ferny and Cypress Aves., Surfers Paradise, ☎ 07/5536–3511), **Budget** (✉ Ferny and Norfolk Aves., ☎ 07/5538–1330; airport, ☎ 07/5536–5377), **Hertz** (✉ Gold Coast Hwy., 13–3039), and **Thrifty** (✉ 3006 Gold Coast Hwy., ☎ 07/5538–6511; airport, ☎ 07/5536–6955). Four-wheel-drive vehicles are available.

Contacts and Resources

EMERGENCIES

Ambulance, fire brigade, and **police.** ☎ *000.*
Gold Coast Hospital. ☎ *07/5571–8211.*
Tweeds Head Hospital. ☎ *07/5536–1133.*

GUIDED TOURS

Terranora Coach Tours (✉ 85 Anne St., Southport, ☎ 07/5538–7113) and **Coachtrans** (552 Reserve Rd., Coomera ☎ 1300/36–1788) have a variety of day tours of the Gold Coast.

VISITOR INFORMATION

Gold Coast Information Centres. ✉ *Beach House Plaza, Marine Parade, Coolangatta,* ☎ *07/5536–7765;* ✉ *Cavill Mall Kiosk, Surfers Paradise,* ☎ *07/5538–4419.*
Gold Coast Tourism Bureau. ✉ *64 Ferny Ave., Level 2, Surfers Paradise 4217,* ☎ *07/5592–2699.*

SUNSHINE COAST

One hour from Brisbane by car to its southernmost point, the Sunshine Coast is a 60-km (36-mi) stretch of white sand beaches, inlets, lakes, and mountains. It begins at the Glass House Mountains in the south and extends to Rainbow Beach in the north. Kenilworth is its inland extent, 40 km (25 mi) west of the ocean. Except for a few touristy eyesores, it has avoided the high-rise glitz of its southern cousin, the Gold Coast. You'll find a quieter, more relaxing pace here, with abundant national parks, secluded coves, and magnificent rain forests spilling down to the ocean.

The Sunshine Coast is generally for the physically active—swimming and surfing are superb, and sports facilities are every bit as good as those on the Gold Coast. It's also the place to find some monumental Ozzie kitsch, like the Ettamogah Pub, Big Pineapple, the House of Bottles, and the Big Shell.

Our coverage follows the inland Bruce Highway north, then turns seaward to Noosa Heads, returning south along the ocean shore.

Numbers in the margin correspond to points of interest on the Sunshine Coast map.

En Route The Bruce Highway runs north from Brisbane through flat eucalyptus country and past large stands of pine. Shortly after the Caboolture turnoff, 44 km (27 mi) north of Brisbane, you will come to a region that was once home to a large Aboriginal population but is now a prosperous dairy center. Here also is the turnoff to **Bribie Island,** 25 km

(15 mi) to the east, which has magnificent beaches, some with glass-calm waters and others with rolling Pacific surf.

Glass House Mountains

⑭ *65 km (44 mi) north of Brisbane.*

More than twenty million years old, the Glass House Mountains consist of nine dramatic, conical outcrops. Pick a peak and go for a climb. Some are gently sloped, while others are serious enough to attract intrepid rock climbers. The mountains are also a favorite destination for experienced hang-glider pilots. About half an hour outside Brisbane to the west of the Bruce Highway, the cones lie along the old main road.

The **Queensland Reptile and Fauna Park** has a collection of Australian animals, including pythons, taipans, adders, kangaroos, crocodiles, emus, and wallabies. Guided tours are offered twice daily, and there are plenty of walking trails for you to explore by yourself. ✉ *Beerwah, north of Glass House Mountains from Caboolture,* ☎ *07/5494–1134.* ☞ *$12.* ⊙ *Daily 9–5.*

Palmview

21 km (13 mi) north of Glass House Mountains, 82 km (51 mi) north of Brisbane.

There's a large, red-roof parody of a classic Australian pub on the left side of the Bruce Highway a few kilometers north of Palmview. A veteran car is perched precariously on the roof, and the whole building ⑮ appears on the verge of collapse. This is the **Ettamogah Pub,** whose name and design are based on the famous pub featured for decades in the work of Australian cartoonist Ken Maynard. It has an upstairs bistro, a beer garden, and a bar.

The **Aussie World** amusement area behind Ettamogah Pub has a large shed with pool tables as well as long wooden tables that form the pub's beer garden. There are also camel and pony rides, an extensive souvenir outlet, opal shop, and **Aboriginal Cultural Centre** (☎ 07/5494–5444) that displays Aboriginal art. An Aboriginal artist is usually on hand demonstrating indigenous art-making, and the Baribunma Dance Troupe gives twice daily performances. Tours through the center highlighting Aboriginal and Torres Straight Islander lifestyles are also available. ✉ *Bruce Hwy.,* ☎ *07/5494–5444.* ⊙ *Mon.–Sat. 9 ᴀᴍ–10 ᴘᴍ, Sun. 9–9.*

Forest Glen

10 km (6 mi) northwest of Palmview.

⑯ The expansive **Forest Glen Sanctuary** is a drive-through park that covers 52 acres of forest and pastureland where rusa, fallow, chital, and red deer will come right up to your car, especially if you have purchased a 50¢ feed bag. The park is also home to emus, peacocks, and other bird life. A nocturnal house has a wide variety of Australian night animals, such as possums, gliders, and owls. Koala shows are given daily at 11 and 4; a wombat show is featured at 12:30. ✉ *Bruce Hwy.,* ☎ *07/5445–1274.* ☞ *$10.* ⊙ *Daily 9–5.*

⑰ The **Moonshine Valley Winery** produces surprisingly good wines made from locally grown fruit. Tastings are offered of fortified ginger wine, Mulberry Rose, and Tom Cobb, a genuine Australian spirit that tastes like strong bourbon. The winery also adjoins Georges, an Italian trattoria, which serves tasty pasta. Georges is only open for lunch on

The Sunshine Coast

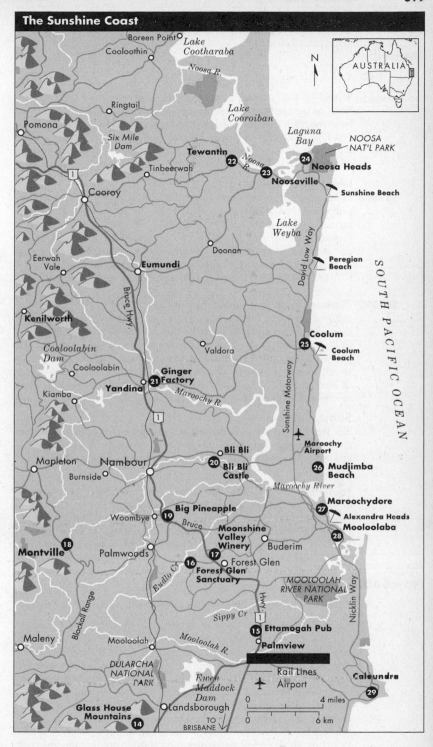

Boreen Point
Cooloothin
Lake Cootharaba
Noosa R.
N
AUSTRALIA

Ringtail
Lake Cooroiban

Pomona
Six Mile Dam
Tinbeerwah
Tewantin **22**
Noosa R.
23 Noosaville
Laguna Bay
24 Noosa Heads
NOOSA NAT'L PARK

Cooroy
Sunshine Beach

Eerwah Vale
Eumundi
Doonan
Lake Weyba

Kenilworth
Bruce Hwy.
Peregian Beach

Cooloolabin Dam
Valdora
Coolum **25**
Coolum Beach

Cooloolabin
Ginger Factory **21**
Yandina
Maroochy R.

Kiamba

SOUTH PACIFIC OCEAN

Sunshine Motorway

Mapleton
Nambour
Bli Bli
Maroochy Airport

Burnside
20 Bli Bli Castle
26 Mudjimba Beach

Maroochy River

Big Pineapple **19**
Maroochydore **27**
Alexandra Heads
Mooloolaba
28

Woombye
Bruce
Moonshine Valley Winery
Buderim

Montville **18**
Palmwoods
17
Forest Glen
MOOLOOLAH RIVER NATIONAL PARK

Eudlo Cr
16 Forest Glen Sanctuary

Blackall Range
Nicklin Way

Maleny
Mooloolah
Sippy Cr
Hwy.
15 Ettamogah Pub
Palmview

Mooloolah R.

DULARCHA NATIONAL PARK
Ewen Maddock Dam
Rail Lines
Airport
Caloundra
29

Glass House Mountains
14
Landsborough
TO BRISBANE

0   4 miles
0   6 km

weekends and for dinner from Wednesday to Saturday. ⊠ *Bruce Hwy.,* ☎ *07/5445–1198.* ☉ *Daily 10–5.*

Montville

⑱ *16 km (10 mi) northwest of Forest Glen.*

Settled in 1887, this quaint mountain village is called the creative heart of the Sunshine Coast. There are panoramic views of the coast from the main street, which has been built with a blend of Tudor, Irish, and English cottages of log or stone; Bavarian and Swiss houses; and old Queenslanders. Shops in town are filled with a browser's delight of curiosities and locally made crafts.

Dining and Lodging

$$–$$$ ✗ **Mirrabelle.** The much-loved Mirabelle always appeals with its wooden floors, exposed beams, and a wall of glass windows that afford spectacular coastal views. The food is no less a pleasure, with favorites that include moussaka of local scallops with salmon taramasalata and tomata salsa, as well as steamed rhubarb and amaretto pudding with butterscotch sauce. Take-aways are also available. ⊠ *96 Main St.,* ☎ *07/5442–9489. MC, V. No lunch Mon. or Tues., no dinner Sun.–Tues.*

$$–$$$ 🏠 **Montville Country Cabins.** Built from local timber, all seven of these cabins are perched on a gentle hill that has a pond at its base, and their cottage furniture and quaint touches, such as cane baskets and log fires, or hot tubs with bush views, make for a perfect, private romantic getaway. The property, which is just 5 km (3 mi) from Montville's main street, adjoins the Obi Obi National Park and attracts a prolific range of birdlife. Cabins come with a fully equipped kitchen. ⊠ *396 Western Ave.,* ☎ *074/5442–9484,* ℻ *07/5442–9213. 7 cabins. MC, V.*

Shopping

The small, ivy-covered **Herb Garden** cottage shop is packed with such goods as natural skin care products, books, aromatherapy supplies, candles, decorator pieces, and handcrafted jewelry. ⊠ *Main St.,* ☎ *07/5442–9190.*

The Dome. About 1 km (½ mi) north of the town, this gallery consists of three separate businesses: Ardleigh gallery and design studio has a range of hand printed silks, wooden items, and other Australian crafts; Gallery D, which features glass, sculpture, paintings, and ceramics; and Pantano Glass Blowing Studio, where you can watch artisans handblow glass pieces. ⊠ *Montville North,* ☎ *07/5442–9244.*

Nambour

9 km (6 mi) north of Forest Glen, 101 km (63 mi) north of Brisbane.

🌀 ⑲ Sunshine Plantation is home of the impossible-to-miss **Big Pineapple.** The 50-ft superkitsch fiberglass monster towers over the highway, and you can climb inside to learn how pineapples are grown. The plantation is a tourist-oriented operation, incorporating a large souvenir shop, jewelry store, arts and crafts shop, large selection of foods, restaurants, flume rides, and train rides. It is also a good place to see how macadamia nuts and other tropical fruits are cultivated. If that's not enough, take a ride on the Nutmobile for a trip to the Magic Macadamia Nut. Other rides include Tomorrow's Harvest, a boat ride through an undercover hydroponic garden, and a cane train ride. ⊠ *Bruce Hwy., 6 km (4 mi) south of Nambour,* ☎ *07/5442–1333.* 🏠 *Entry free, rides $5–$6 each.* ☉ *Daily 9–5.*

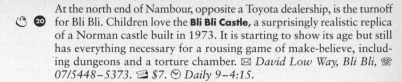

At the north end of Nambour, opposite a Toyota dealership, is the turnoff for Bli Bli. Children love the **Bli Bli Castle,** a surprisingly realistic replica of a Norman castle built in 1973. It is starting to show its age but still has everything necessary for a rousing game of make-believe, including dungeons and a torture chamber. ⊠ *David Low Way, Bli Bli,* ☎ *07/5448–5373.* ☞ *$7.* ⊘ *Daily 9–4:15.*

Yandina

9 km (6 mi) north of Nambour.

㉑ The **Ginger Factory** is one of the legendary establishments of Queensland tourism, and it now goes far beyond its original factory door sale of ginger. Of course, there's a restaurant and a large shop area selling ginger in all forms—from crystallized to various jams and marmalades. There's also a miniature train ride ($4) and the Bunya Park Wildlife Sanctuary ($5). You'll also find a viewing deck overlooking the ginger factory itself and a ginger theaterette. ⊠ *50 Pioneer Rd. (Coolum Rd.), 1 km (½ mi) east of Bruce Hwy.,* ☎ *07/5446–7100.* ☞ *Free.* ⊘ *Daily 9–5.*

Dining

$$$ ✕ **Spirit House.** The owners here, who spent five years in Thailand, have done a remarkable job of transplanting Thai cuisine on Queensland soil. Set in a beautiful rain forest garden, with a nursery and art gallery on site, the restaurant is perched over a duck pond. Try peanut-crusted chicken breast with a salad of glass noodles and a fragrant coconut cream sauce, then move on to sticky rice with fresh mangoes and coconut cream for dessert. ⊠ *4 Ninderry Rd.,* ☎ *07/5446–8994. MC, V. No dinner Sun.–Tues.*

Eumundi

18 km (11 mi) north of Nambour, 21 km (13 mi) southwest of Noosa Heads.

One of the best open **street markets** on the Sunshine Coast is held on Saturday from 6:30 AM to 12:30 PM on Memorial Drive in Eumundi, where you'll find wares by local craftspeople and lots of local color. ☎ *07/5442–8581.*

Lodging

$$ 🏠 **Taylor's Damn Fine Bed & Breakfast.** Damn fine indeed. The main house is a gracious old Queenslander filled with an eclectic blend of retro and country furnishings that do manage to work together. All spacious bedrooms have their own bathrooms—four have double beds, one has twin beds—and two of the rooms are adjacent to the main house in a restored railway carriage. The house overlooks 4 acres of lush paddock that borders the North Maroochy River, where you can take a short rain forest walk. Saturday morning, you can take a free horse and carriage ride to the Eumundi market. There is also a pool and par-3 practice range. Taylor's is a short stroll from Eumundi's main street, and 15 minutes to Noosa. Dinner is available by prior arrangement. ⊠ *15 Eumundi–Noosa Rd.,* ☎ *07/5442–8685,* ℻ *07/5442–8168. 5 rooms with bath. No credit cards.*

Tewantin

㉒ *18 km (11 mi) northeast of Eumundi, 7 km (4 mi) west of Noosa Heads.*

Tewantin is the proud home of the **House of Bottles and Bottle Museum,** one big "bottle building" constructed from 35,000 bottles of different sizes and shapes. More than 5,000 other bottle-art exhibits are featured, but it's all looking a bit dusty these days. ⊠ *19 Myles St.,* ☎ *07/5447–1277.* ⊠ *$3.* ⊙ *Daily 9–5.*

The Sunshine Coast has an obsession with monstrously proportioned kitsch, and Tewantin is right on the cutting edge. Not content with its big bottle, the town also claims the **Big Shell Museum and Hattery.** This attraction (which you enter through a giant cement shell) has displays of local crafts, as well as seashells, an extensive range of them being Australian, coral, and other marine items. It also has surprisingly reasonably priced hats. ⊠ *Gympie and Hay Sts.,* ☎ *07/5447–1268.* ⊠ *Free.* ⊙ *Sun.–Fri. 9–5.*

Boating
You can rent sailboats at **Boreen Point,** north of Tewantin on the western side of Lake Cootharaba. ☎ *07/5485–3213.*

Dining
$$ ✕ **Jetty Licensed Restaurant.** For a romantic lunch, take a boat from
★ Tewantin to the Jetty, upriver from town on the edge of Lake Cootharaba. Simple fare, based on seafood and local produce, is served on a glassed-in veranda overlooking the lake. The menu changes continually, but always uses only local produce. Typical dishes include grilled barramundi, Moreton Bay bugs, and grilled prawns. This spot is a favorite with locals and is licensed, with a range of reasonably priced wines. ⊠ *Boreen Parade, Boreen Point (21 km, or 13 mi, from Tewantin by road),* ☎ *07/ 5485–3167. MC, V. No lunch Mon. or Tues., no dinner Sun.–Thurs.*

River Cruises
Everglades Water Bus Co. conducts combined boat–four-wheel-drive tours from Harbour Town Jetty in Tewantin to the Everglades, Cooloola National Park, Cherry Venture, Bubbling Springs, and Coloured Sands. Another boat takes you to the Jetty Restaurant ($22 return) in Boreen Point. ⊠ *Harbour Town Marina,* ☎ *07/5447–1838.*

Noosaville

㉓ *4 km (2½ mi) east of Tewantin, 3 km (2 mi) west of Noosa Heads.*

A small town dotted with small hotels and apartment complexes, Noosaville is the access point for trips to the **Teewah Coloured Sands,** an area built up with multicolored sands that were created by natural chemicals in the soil. Dating from the Ice Age, some of the 72 different hues of sand form cliffs rising to 600 ft.

Dining
$$ ✕ **Chilli Jam Thai.** With its strong foodie cult, it's not surprising to find
★ that the Sunshine Coast has an exceptionally good Thai restaurant. Indeed, it was voted the best restaurant in the region in 1995. Located above a corner store, the simplicity of painted-wooden-table–with–cotton-throw decor impresses you the way the food will. But the chef here was originally at Sydney's renowned Darley St. Thai, and the pedigree shows. There are about 12 appetizers and as many main dishes—and most are quite tempting. Sour orange curry of salmon with fish broth, tamarind, tofu, and Asian greens is one standout. ⊠ *195 Weyba Rd., at Swan St.,* ☎ *07/5449–9755. MC, V. Closed Mon. No lunch.*

Golf
The **Noosa Valley Country Club** accepts visiting players. ⊠ *92 Valley Dr., Doonan,* ☎ *07/5449–1411.*

River Cruises
Cooloola Cruises drives through the Everglades and the Noosa River and Lakes. The Cooloola Safari is the most comprehensive and ad-

venturous tour, combining a cruise with a four-wheel-drive trip to
Coloured Sands, Cherry Venture, and the rain forest, and including barbecue lunch and morning and afternoon teas. ⊠ *Gympie Terr.,* ☎ *07/
5449–9177.* 🖃 *Safari $80.*

Noosa Heads

㉔ *39 km (24 mi) northeast of Nambour, 17 km (11 mi) north of Coolum,
140 km (88 mi) north of Brisbane.*

Noosa Heads is one of the most stylish resort areas in Australia. Although the country's new money tends to head for the glitter of the Gold
Coast's Surfers Paradise, the old money retreats to Noosa. Set beside
the calm waters of Laguna Bay at the northern tip of the Sunshine Coast,
the town consisted of nothing more than a few shacks just a dozen or
so years ago. Surfers discovered it first, lured by the spectacular waves
that curl around the sheltering headland of Noosa National Park.
Today, Noosa Heads is a charming mix of surf, sand, and sophistication. Elegant boutiques and restaurants lure you in from the streets. Lovely
trails wind through nearby Noosa National Park's rain forest, leading
to beautiful coves with white sand beaches and crashing surf. Views along
the trail from Laguna Lookout to the top of the headland take in miles
of magnificent beaches, ocean, and dense vegetation.

Dining and Lodging

$$–$$$ ✕ **Saltwater.** Upstairs and down, at café–style tables inside or on a plant-
fringed open balcony overlooking Hastings Street, the seafood here is
consistently delectable. Try Tasmanian roe on scallops that are flame
grilled and served with a sun-dried-tomato bread crust, or fillets of Noosa
River mullet marinated in mild, pink tandoori spices and yogurt and
served over fragrant jasmine rice. Proprietor Steve Cross also owns a
winery in Victoria, which accounts for Saltwater's own brand wine. Take-
away raw and cooked seafood is also available if you want a picnic on
the beach. ⊠ *8 Hastings St.,* ☎ *07/5447–2234. AE, DC, MC, V.*

$$–$$$ ✕ **Eduardo's Café.** If you were any closer to the beach, you'd need a
★ towel at this relaxed café. The decor is simple, bordering on spartan,
but the food is very good. For breakfast you might like to try banana
pancakes with a warm honey and lemon-mint fruit salad. Lunch tends
toward spinach and ricotta gnocchi or whitebait fritters. Dinner becomes more formal and somewhat more expensive with the house specialty being a seafood curry served with rice and *papadam* (peppered
flatbread). ⊠ *Tingirana Arcade, 25 Hastings St.,* ☎ *07/5447–5875.
AE, DC, MC, V.*

$–$$ ✕ **Artis Café and Bar.** This A-frame café serves art and jazz alongside
innovative modern Australian cuisine. It's a light and airy setting—more
so, of course, on the outdoor terrace. Dishes to seek out include freshwater redclaw lobster lasagna served with a saffron–sweet corn–
chili–and–coriander compote and salmon caviar. ⊠ *8 Noosa Dr.,* ☎
07/5447–2300. AE, DC, MC, V. Reservations essential for lunch.

$–$$ ✕ **Cafe Vespa.** There's a relaxed and comfortable ambience to this up-
stairs Bay Village Mediterranean restaurant, decorated with flower-filled
planters. The menu offers pasta, wood-fired pizza, and, among other
dishes, mushroom, pea, and spinach risotto. ⊠ *Bay Village, Hastings
St.,* ☎ *07/5447–2473. AE, DC, MC, V.*

$ ✕ **Aromas.** Another of the successful Aromas cafés that were started
in Brisbane in the early 80s, this one has a loyal clientele who come
for the film-noir ambience and great people-watching. Come for breakfast, a good selection of cakes, biscuits, and light meals, and an excellent selection of coffees and alcoholic beverages. ⊠ *32 Hastings St.,*
☎ *07/5474–9788. AE, DC, MC, V. Open daily 7* AM*–late.*

$$$$ ⊞ **Sheraton Noosa Resort.** This six-story, horseshoe-shape complex faces
★   fashionable Hastings Street on one side and the river on the other. There
are various themes at play here, from the hard-to-miss pink and blue
exterior to the room decor appelations, such as Napoléon and Josephine,
Miss Scarlet, Rudolph Valentino—you get the picture (sorry about the
pun). In fact it is hard to find fault with the rooms, each of which has
a balcony and a Jacuzzi. Eight two-story celebrity suites are also available. ⊠ *Hastings St., 4567,* ☎ *07/5449–4888,* ℻ *07/5449–2230. 169
rooms with bath. Pool, sauna, health club. AE, DC, MC, V.*

$$$ ⊞ **Netyana Noosa.** This low-rise beachfront complex of suites is pop-
ular among Australian managerial types. There is one staff member for
every two visitors, and guests are pampered with soft bathrobes, English
toiletries, and in-room hair dryers. All suites have verandas large enough
for room-service dining. The Presidential suite has a private terrace with
an outdoor Jacuzzi, and a magnificent dining room in which the resort
chef will serve specially prepared dinners on request. ⊠ *75 Hastings St.,
4567,* ☎ *07/5447–4722,* ℻ *07/5447–3914. 48 suites. Restaurant, bar,
2 pools, sauna, exercise room, laundry. AE, DC, MC, V.*

$ ⊞ **Halse Lodge.** If you are looking for cheap accommodation in a per-
fect location in the heart of Noosa, aim for Halse Lodge. This 1880
heritage-listed building is the last timber structure in Noosa, and it is
southeast Queensland's longest serving guest house. The rooms are clean
and the shared bathrooms modern, and the large utility rooms are dot-
ted with pictures of Noosa from yesteryear. Accommodation is in two
double rooms, two others with two bunks, and the remainder are dor-
mitory-style. Next to the main building is Bishop's Cottage, a converted
church with two large fully self-contained rooms. The whole complex
is a long stone's throw from Hastings Street, set in 2 acres of garden
and rain forest overlooking town. The per-person flat rate includes Con-
tinental breakfast, and the lodge has a licensed bar. ⊠ *Halse Lane, 4567,*
☎ *07/5447–3377. 16 bunk rooms share bath. Bar. MC, V.*

Shopping

Hastings Street has the best shopping in the area, with chic boutiques,
basic beach shops, bookshops, and houseware stores. ⊠ *Hastings St.,
Noosa Heads.*

Water Sports

Sea Wind Charters and Holiday Tours rents a variety of yachts and Jet
Skis. The company also has a half-day cruise ($65) during which you
can snorkel, and the captain teaches sailing fundamentals. The com-
pany also organizes scuba-diving lessons, daily boat dives, and equip-
ment rental. ⊠ *10 Cooloosa St., Sunshine Beach,* ☎ *07/5447–3042.*

Peregian Beach

10 km (6 mi) south of Noosa Heads.

Peregian Beach is a cluster of holiday units along the beach, a small
row of shops, and scattering of homes spreading inland. The old
Homestead restaurant a few kilometers west is its outstanding feature.

Dining

$$ ✕ **Peregian Park Homestead.** Located 5 km (3 mi) from Peregian Beach
★   along an unpaved road, this restaurant is not one you are likely to stum-
ble upon. The trip is worth getting lost, however, for this is a real find—
a traditional old Queenslander-style home with a wide veranda
overlooking a lake for summertime dining and log fires in winter. The
fixed menu consists of soup, an appetizer, main course, dessert, and coffee, with two choices each for starters and mains. For the price ($38
per person), the cuisine is surprisingly sophisticated, with fresh At-

lantic salmon with tomato dressing on a bed of wong bok, or beef tenderloin over braised greens and creamy mashed potato with mustard-scented jus. Be sure to bring your own wine. ⊠ *Monak Rd., accessible from Woodland Dr. or Murdering Creek Rd.,* ☎ *07/5448–1628. MC, V. BYOB. No lunch Mon.–Sat., no dinner Sun.–Thurs.*

Coolum

㉕ *17 km (11 mi) south of Noosa, 25 km (16 mi) northeast of Nambour.*

At the center of the Sunshine Coast, Coolum makes an ideal base from which to explore the surrounding countryside. Coolum also has what is probably the finest beach along the Sunshine Coast—and a placid, easygoing pace.

Dining and Lodging

$$$ ✕☷ **Hyatt Regency Resort.** Spread out at the foot of Mount Coolum,
★ this is one of the best health spa–resorts in Australia. The spa has everything a fitness fanatic could want—several pools, aerobics rooms, a supervised exercise room, squash, Jacuzzis, cold plunge baths, and massage facilities. The resort also has a championship 18-hole golf course designed by Robert Trent Jones, Jr., lighted tennis courts, a beach club, and a mile of ocean surf. Accommodations consist of a series of villas, each containing two to six apartments. Set amid gardens overlooking the tennis courts or the golf course, the villas are grouped in clusters around their own swimming pools and clubhouses, where complimentary Continental breakfast and pre-dinner champagne are served. One- and two-bedroom apartments, decorated in soft pastel colors with comfortable, modern furniture and marble bathrooms, are available. Boutiques, a deli, a wine shop, and sidewalk restaurants with umbrella-shaded tables are arranged around a village square within the complex. The only drawback to the resort is the amount of walking involved between facilities in the 370-acre complex. ⊠ *Warran Rd., Coolum Beach, 4573,* ☎ *07/5446–1234,* ℻ *07/5446–2957. 330 apartments. 8 restaurants, 8 pools, 9 tennis courts, golf course, dance club. AE, DC, MC, V.*

Mudjimba Beach

㉖ *9 km (5.6 mi) north of Maroochydore.*

Lodging

$$$ ☷ **Novotel Twin Waters Resort.** Nestled amid 660 private acres, this Novotel was built around a 15-acre saltwater lagoon bordering both the Maroochy River and Mudjimba Beach (a boardwalk joins the resort and the beach). The resort, more of a family place than the glitzier Hyatt in Coolum Beach, is well spread out over this area, and features a separate golf club that offers an 18-hole championship course—one of the top 10 in the country—that is home to kangaroos and ducks. The saltwater lagoon is the site of much water-based activity, such as catamaran sailing, windsurfing, and canoeing, all of which are free of charge to guests. It also has an excellent restaurant, Lily's-on-the-Lagoon, which is perched over one section of the lake. ⊠ *Ocean Drive, Mudjimba Beach.,* ☎ *07/5448–8000,* ℻ *07/5448–8001. 244 rooms with bath, 130 suites. 3 restaurants, 4 bars, pool, whirlpool, driving range, 6 tennis courts, water sports. AE, DC, MC, V.*

Maroochydore

㉗ *18 km (11 mi) south of Coolum, 21 km (13 mi) north of Caloundra, 18 km (11 mi) east of Nambour.*

Maroochydore has been a popular beach resort for several years and suffers its fair share of high-rise towers. Nevertheless, with its location at the mouth of the Maroochy River, the town has excellent surfing and swimming beaches.

Dining and Lodging

$$$ ✕ **Signatures.** It may be a little difficult to find Signatures: You have to go through a car park just off First Avenue. However, the food is well worth the effort, as is the setting—the deck overlooks the Maroochy River and the surf beyond. There's a rather New Orleans feel to the decor, with dark wood posts, painted wooden walls, crystal glasses, and black plates on lace tablecloths. The theme to the restaurant is that each dish is named after a Hollywood or television star, or a supermodel. The W.C. Fields is honey mango duck while the James Dean is prawns, scallops, Moreton Bay lobster, and crabmeat in a light mornay sauce topped with macadamia nuts. Signatures is fully licensed. ⊠ *6 Duporth Ave., ☎ 07/ 5443–6401. AE, MC, V. No lunch weekends, no dinner Sun.*

$$–$$$$ 🏨 **Catalina Resort.** This high-rise complex is one block from the beach, and because the thick seaside vegetation shields views from other lodgings, this is one of the few places that actually has sea views. Each apartment is furnished differently, and beach views start on the sixth floor. All apartments are self-contained with kitchen and laundry and are serviced weekly. ⊠ *6th Ave., ☎ 07/5443–8666, 📠 07/5443–7942. 51 apartments. Pool, sauna, whirlpool, tennis court, recreation room. AE, DC, MC, V.*

Outdoor Activities and Sports

FISHING

Rods and reels are available at **Fishing World.** ⊠ *22 1st Ave., ☎ 07/ 5447–2714.*

GOLF

The **Headland Golf Club** is only a few kilometers inland from Maroochydore, and it accepts visiting players. ⊠ *Golf Links Rd., Buderim, ☎ 07/5443–2714.*

TENNIS

Courts and coaching are available at **Alinga Tennis Centre.** ⊠ *121 Sugar Rd., ☎ 07/5443–4584.*

Shopping

The best shopping centers on the Sunshine Coast include **Sunshine Plaza** (Aerodrome Rd.), in Maroochydore, with several major department stores.

En Route For the best surfing in the southern part of the Sunshine Coast, head for the beach at **Alexandra Headland,** 5 km (3 mi) south of Maroochydore.

Mooloolaba

㉘ *5 km (3 mi) south of Maroochydore.*

Mooloolaba—the port for the local prawning and fishing fleets, as well as deep-sea charter boats—has one particularly notable attraction: **Underwater World,** with its walk-through aquarium. In a clear acrylic underwater tunnel you'll stare face-to-face with giant sharks, stingrays, and other local marine species. The marine complex, one of the best in Australia, has a shark feeding, a crocodile lagoon, a seal show, an Oceanarium, Ocean Discover Centre, and Theatre of the Sea. If marine life interests you, plan to spend time here. ⊠ *Parkyn Parade, ☎ 07/5444–8488. 🎫 $16.50, free after 5. ☉ Daily 9–6.*

Boating

You can hire motorboats with a canopy from **Sunlover Boat Hire.** ⊠ *The Wharf, Parkyn Parade,* ☎ *07/5444–4744.*

Fishing

Deep-sea fishing charters can be arranged through **Mooloolaba Reef and Game Charters.** ⊠ *33 Jessica Blvd.,* ☎ *07/5444–3735.*

Nightlife

Friday's On the Wharf is a popular nightspot. ⊠ *Parkyn Parade,* ☎ *07/5444–8383.*

Rock On Nightclub is a scene for younger revelers. ⊠ *Esplanade,* ☎ *07/5478–3422.*

Shopping

The **Wharf Shopping Centre** is a re-creation of a 19th-century fishing village with boutiques, souvenir shops, food outlets, a games arcade, and a tourist information center. ⊠ *Parkyn Parade.*

Caloundra

㉙ *21 km (13 mi) south of Maroochydore, 56 km (35 mi) south of Noosa, 91 km (57 mi) north of Brisbane.*

It's not just excellent beaches that makes Caloundra so popular. The town is also an ideal family destination, free of the glitz of the more touristy Queensland resorts. Retirees have been moving here for some time now, and it is also with Brisbanites, many of whom have Caloundra weekend houses or apartments.

Sunshine Coast A to Z

Arriving and Departing

BY BUS

Coachtrans offers daily bus service from Brisbane Airport and the Roma Street Transit Centre in Brisbane to Caloundra, Mooloolaba, Maroochydore, Noosa, and Tewantin. ☎ *07/3236–1000.*

BY PLANE

☞ Air Travel *in* the Gold Guide for information on airlines serving Maroochydore Airport. Note that it is almost as convenient to fly into Brisbane, which is only an hour's drive away.

BY TRAIN

Trains leave regularly from **Roma Street Station** (⊠ Roma St., ☎ 07/3235–2222) in Brisbane en route to Nambour in the heart of the Sunshine Coast. However, once in Nambour you will need a car, so it makes more sense to drive from Brisbane or take a bus right to your destination.

Getting Around

BY CAR

A car is a necessity on the Sunshine Coast. The traditional route to the coast has been along the Bruce Highway (Hwy. 1) to the Glass House Mountains, and turn off at Cooroy that makes about a two-hour drive from Brisbane to Noosa, the heart of the area. However, the motorway, which was a tollway until 1996, may be marginally faster—turn off the Bruce Highway at Tanawah (toward Mooloolaba) and follow the signs to the motorway. The most scenic route is to turn off the Bruce Highway to Caloundra and follow the coast to Noosa Heads.

Contacts and Resources

CAR RENTAL

All major companies have offices in Brisbane (☞ Brisbane A to Z, *above*). The following international companies have local offices: **Avis** (✉ Maroochydore and airport, ☎ 07/5443–5055), **Budget** (✉ Maroochydore, ☎ 07/5443–6555), **Hertz** (✉ Noosa Heads, ☎ 07/5449–2033; airport, ☎ 07/5443–8799), and **Thrifty** (✉ Maroochydore and airport, ☎ 07/5443–1733 or 1800/65–2008).

EMERGENCIES

Ambulance, fire brigade, and **police.** ☎ *000*.
Caloundra Hospital. ☎ *07/5491–1888*.
Nambour Public Hospital. ☎ *07/5470–9600*.

GUIDED TOURS

Adventures Sunshine Coast has one-day trips from **Noosa Heads** and **Caloundra** that take you to rain forests, the mountains, Barrier Reef islands, and other points of interest. ✉ *69 Alfriston Dr., Buderim,* ☎ *07/5444–8824.*

Black Thunder Ballooning (☎ 07/5494–9699 or 1800/81–6623) floats over the Sunshine Coast from **Caboolture** for $150 for three quarters of an hour, including the traditional champagne celebration.

Great Gourmet Adventure Tours (☎ 07/5449–9087; Thurs. only; ⊠ $170), hosted by local journalist and personality Helen Flanagan, chart the path of local food from paddock to plate for about eight serious foodies at a time. Gourmands are taken to a crayfish farm, a tropical orchard where morning tea is served, a spice farm, and after lunch an authentic gold rush pub. The highlight is the four-course lunch, presented on tables overlooking a lake, which serves up everything you've seen growing in the paddocks in the morning. Variations, such as lunching at The Jetty restaurant or flying to Fraser Island for lunch, can be arranged.

Tropical Coast Tours runs regular tours to attractions around the Sunshine Coast, Brisbane, and the Gold Coast. ✉ *Harbour Town, Weyba Rd., Noosa Heads,* ☎ *07/5449–0822.*

VISITOR INFORMATION

Caloundra City Tourist Information Centre. ✉ *7 Caloundra Rd., Caloundra,* ☎ *07/5491–0202.*
Maroochy Information Centre. ✉ *6th Ave., Maroochydore,* ☎ *07/5479–1566.*
Noosa Heads Tourist Information Centre. ✉ *Hastings St., Noosa Heads,* ☎ *07/5447–4988.*

FRASER ISLAND

Some 200 km (125 mi) north of Brisbane, Fraser Island is both the largest of Queensland's islands and the most unusual. Instead of coral reefs and coconut palms, it has wildflower-dotted meadows, freshwater lakes, a teeming and exotic bird population, dense stands of rain forest, towering sand dunes, and sculpted, multicolor sand cliffs along its east coast—a lineup that has won the island a place on UNESCO's World Heritage list. The surf fishing is legendary, and humpback whales and their calves can be seen wintering in Hervey Bay between May and September. The island also has interesting Aboriginal sites that have been here for millennia.

Once you've seen Fraser's 140-km (90-mi) east coast—nearly one continuous beach—it will come as no surprise that this is the world's largest sand island. But these are beaches like few others anywhere else. Colors stray from the typical beige to deep rust and sugar white, and shapes range from sensuous drifts to huge dunes.

Fraser's east coast marks the intersection of two serious Australian passions: an addiction to the beach and a love affair with the motor vehicle. Unrestricted vehicle access means that this coast has become a giant sandbox for four-wheelers. If you prefer your wilderness *sans* dune-buggying, head for the unspoiled interior of the island.

Exploring Fraser Island

Highlights of a drive north along the east coast include the rusting hulk of the **Maheno,** lying half-buried in the sand, a roost for seagulls and a prime hunting ground for anglers when the tailor are running. North of the *Maheno* wreck are the **Pinnacles**—also known as the Cathedrals— a stretch of dramatic, deep red cliffs.

Great Sandy National Park covers the top third of the island. The park's beaches around Indian Head are known for their shell middens—basically attractive garbage heaps that were left behind after Aboriginal feasting. The head's name is another kind of relic: Captain James Cook saw Aborigines standing on the headland as he sailed past, and he therefore named the area after inhabitants he believed to be "Indians." Farther north, past Waddy Point, is one of Fraser Island's most magnificent variations on sand: Wind and time have created enormous dunes, which are constantly swept clean of footprints by a breeze that blows off Hervey Bay. The southern border of the park is just past the Cathedral Beach Resort. ☎ *07/4127–9177.*

The center of the island is a quiet, natural garden of paperbark swamps, giant satinay and brush box forests, wildflower heaths, and 40 freshwater lakes—including the spectacularly clear **Lake McKenzie,** which is ringed by a beach of incandescent whiteness.

The island's excellent network of walking trails converges at **Central Station,** a former logging camp at the center of the island. Services here are limited to a map board, parking lot, and campground. It's a promising place for spotting dingo, however. Comparative isolation has meant that Fraser Island's dingoes are the most purebred on the east coast of Australia; to ensure the future of the breed, domestic dogs are not permitted on the island. The dingoes here are unfazed by human contact, but they are still wild animals: Don't feed them, and keep a close eye on children.

Two noteworthy walking tracks lead from **Central Station:** A boardwalk heads south to **Wanggoolba Creek,** a favorite spot of photographers; this little stream snakes through a green palm forest, trickling over a bed of white sand between clumps of the rare angiopteris fern. A slightly longer trail leads north to **Pile Valley,** where you'll find a stand of giant satinay trees. This timber is so dense and durable that it was shipped to Egypt to be used as pilings for the Suez Canal.

Dining and Lodging

Apart from the Kingfisher Bay Resort, accommodations on Fraser Island are limited to campsites and the bungalows along the island's eastern beaches. Camping is permitted only in designated areas.

$$ ✕🏨 **Fraser Island Retreat.** This is the pick of the east coast accommodations. Formally known as Happy Valley Resort, it is in fact more of a retreat than a resort, with its breezy one- and two-bedroom bungalows with polished timber floors and bamboo furnishings. The on-site restaurant has a pleasant atmosphere and food that is nothing to write home about. A small store sells groceries and fishing supplies, as well as gas and diesel. ☎ *07/4127–9144,* FAX *07/4127–9131. 9 rooms with shower. Restaurant, bar. AE, MC, V.*

$$$ 🏨 **Kingfisher Bay Resort & Village.** Since this resort opened in mid-1992, the island has had man-made accommodations to match those bequeathed by Mother Nature. Wrapped around a bay on the island's west coast, this is a stylish, high-tech marriage of glass, stainless steel, dark timber, and corrugated iron; although the two-story structures are by no means inconspicuous, developers have succeeded in attractively integrating the resort with its environment. The resort has 152 hotel rooms, over 100 self-contained villas, a 100-bed wilderness lodge for groups, and a team of highly skilled rangers who conduct a variety of four-wheel-drive guided tours. They also offer a daily range of free nature walks and activities, and children can join in a free junior ranger progam on weekends and during Australian school holiday periods. Three-day wilderness adventures are also offered ($225), during which you stay in the wilderness lodge and embark on three days of exploring the island with a ranger. Four-wheel-drive vehicles are also available for individual hire. Meals are not included in room rates, but they are reasonably priced. ⊠ *GPO Box 913, Brisbane 4001,* ☎ *07/ 4120–3333 or 1800/07–2555,* FAX *07/3221–3270. 152 rooms with bath, 100 villas, 100-bed lodge. 3 restaurants, bar, 4 pools, spa, tennis courts. AE, DC, MC, V.*

$ 🏕 **Camping.** The Department of Environment runs 11 campsites on the island. Those at Dundabara and Waddy Point have showers and toilets, and some wood is supplied. Permits for the Cathedral Beach Camping Park, a privately managed site that's one of the best on the island, are also available from the park's service offices in Torquay and in Rainbow Beach on the mainland. ⊠ *Department of Environment, Hervey Bay City Council, 10 Bideford St., Torquay,* ☎ *07/4125– 0222.* ⊙ *Weekdays 9–5.* ⊠ *Rainbow Beach Rd., Rainbow Beach,* ☎ *07/5486–3160.* ⊙ *Daily 7–4.*

Fraser Island A to Z

Arriving and Departing
Hervey Bay is both the expanse of water between Fraser Island and the Queensland coast and the generic name given to a conglomeration of four nearby coastal towns—Urangan, Pialba, Scarness, and Torquay—that have grown into a single settlement. This township is the jumping-off point for most excursions to Fraser Island. Travelers should be aware, however, that maps and road signs usually refer to individual town names, not Hervey Bay.

BY BUS
McCafferty's Express Coaches (☎ 13–1499) and **Greyhound Pioneer** (☎ 07/3058–1670) run between Brisbane and Hervey Bay, where the bus terminal is near the Fraser Island ferry dock.

BY CAR
Although the southernmost tip of Fraser Island is 200 km (125 mi) north of Brisbane, the best access to the island is from the Hervey Bay area, another 90 km (56 mi) away. Take the Bruce Highway to Maryborough, then follow signs to Urangan.

BY FERRY
Vehicle ferries run to Fraser Island from Mary River Heads (12 km, or 7 mi, south of Urangan) and Inskip Point (opposite the island's south-

ern tip). Round-trip fare is $30 one way or $60 return including the driver, and $4 for each additional passenger. ☎ 07/25–5155.

The *Kingfisher* passenger ferry runs between Urangan and North White Cliffs, near Kingfisher Bay Resort. ✉ *Urangan harbor,* ☎ *07/4125–5155.* 🖃 *$28.* ⊙ *Departs daily at 6:45, 8:30, noon, 4, 6:30, and 10.*

BY PLANE

Sunstate Airlines (☎ 13–1313) has several flights daily between Brisbane and Hervey Bay Airport on the mainland.

Getting Around

BY CAR

Despite the island's free-range feeling, the rules of the road still apply: Wear seat belts, drive on the left, obey the speed limit—and remember that the island has a serious accident rate of about one per week. Watch out for creek crossings and keep an eye on the tide. Tide tables are available from ranger stations or from any shop on the island. It is generally advised to keep your vehicle off the beach for three hours before high tide and four hours after.

Contacts and Resources

CAR RENTAL

Four-wheel-drive rentals may be cheaper on the mainland, but factoring in the ferry ticket makes it less expensive to get your rental on-island. **Kingfisher Bay Resort & Village** (☎ 07/4120–3333) leases four-wheel-drive vehicles for $150 per day. **Fraser Island Retreat** (☎ 07/4127–9144) rents four-wheelers for the same price, but it's difficult to get there unless you're already four-wheel equipped.

GUIDED TOURS

Fraser Island Discovery Tours has three-day safaris to Fraser Island from Brisbane. A maximum of 16 passengers tour the island by four-wheel-drive vehicle and spend two nights at the Cathedral Beach campground. ☎ 07/3821–1694. 🖃 $320.

Whale-Watching Tours. Air Fraser Island operates whale-watching flights of 45 minutes or more across Hervey Bay between July and October. Aircraft seat six people. ☎ 07/4124–3549. 🖃 *Prices start at $40 per person, minimum 4 people.*

Mimi MacPherson's Whale-Watching Expeditions. Elle's sister has been running this successful operation from Hervey Bay since 1989. Tours depart daily from Urangan Boat Harbour at Hervey Bay between July to October. ☎ 07/4124–7247. 🖃 $62–$65.

VISITOR INFORMATION

Fraser Coast Tour Booking Office and Whale Watch Centre is a good source of information, maps, and brochures. The center will also help you with tour and accommodations bookings. ✉ *Buccaneer Ave., Urangan,* ☎ 07/4125–3287.

Hervey Bay Tourist Office. ✉ *46 Main St., Shop 4, Pialba,* ☎ 07/4124–2448.

TOWNSVILLE AND MAGNETIC ISLAND

By Jane Carstens and David McGonigal

Townsville is Australia's largest tropical city, with a population of 130,000. Unlike tourist-heavy Cairns to the north, it relies on its deepwater port from which sugar, beef, wool, and the mineral wealth of Mount Isa are exported. In fact, the city is the commercial capital of the north and a major center for education, scientific research, and defense. Townsville is built around the pink granite outcrop of Castle Hill, the first feature one notices about the place, which rises from otherwise featureless coastal plains to just under 300 meters (1,000 ft). On the banks of the boat-filled Ross Creek, Townsville is a pleasant city, an urban sprawl of palm-fringed malls, white lattice verandas on historic colonial buildings, and lots of parkland and gardens. If you want to get into the *real* Australian tropical life, this is the place to visit. It isn't fancy, but there is a fair amount to see, including the Great Barrier Reef Wonderland aquarium. Townsville is also the stepping off point for Magnetic Island, one of the largest Queensland islands.

Magnetic Island is essentially an island suburb, where the sounds of birds and other wildlife replace the sounds of the city. Captain James Cook bestowed the title Magnetic on the island in the erroneous belief that the ironstone deposits caused his compass to err. He was wrong, but the name stuck, and today 2,500 people call the island home.

The terrain of Magnetic Island is well suited for bushwalking—it's hilly rather than mountainous—and 75% of it is national park. There are some great jungle walks and a serrated coastline of rocky headlands sheltering palm-shaded beaches. Wallabies, koalas, possums, and a great variety of birds make up the wild population of the island. Reefs protect the shoreline, but, unlike islands farther offshore, marine stingers can infest the beaches between October and April.

Townsville

Townsville's focal point is **Flinders Mall,** a tropically landscaped shopping mall in the heart of the city center. On Sunday morning it is the venue for the **Cotters Market,** an arts and crafts offering of locally made items, as well as food and entertainment.

Most visitors head for the top of **Castle Hill,** 1 km (½ mi) from the city center on foot, or about 4 km (2½ mi) by car, on a steep walking track that doubles as one of the most scenic jogging routes in Queensland. If you're game, branch off onto one of several goat tracks that lead up the pink granite hill. However you get to the top, the summit provides great views of the city as well as the islands of the Great Barrier Reef. While you're perched on top, think about the proud local resident who, along with various scout troops, spent years in the 1970s piling rubble onto the peak to try to add the 23 ft that would officially make it Castle Mountain. Technically speaking, a rise has to exceed 1,000 ft to be called a mountain—and this one tops out at just 977 ft.

Great Barrier Reef Wonderland is Townsville's most spectacular attraction. Right on the waterfront, only a few minutes' walk from the city center, it has a perspex walkway in which you seemingly walk under the sea. It also has the largest natural coral aquarium in the world: a living slice of the Great Barrier Reef. There are over 100 species of hard coral, 30 soft corals, and hundreds of fish species. Also included in the general admission fee are an Omnimax Theatre and the Museum of Tropical Queensland, a division of the Queensland Museum. A ferry terminal and shopping mall are also parts of the complex. ⊠ *Finders St.,* ☎ *07/4721–2411.* ☎ *$28.* ☉ *Daily 9–5.*D/ rd

Take a walk along **Flinders Street** to look at some of Townsville's turn-of-the-century colonial architecture. **Magnetic House** still has a hitching rail. **Queens Building** is in Classical Revival style. The apparently immovable **masonry clock tower** (⊠ Flinders and Denham Sts.) of the post office was erected in 1889 but taken down during World War II so it wouldn't be a target for air raids. It was put up again in 1964.

The National Trust has placed three very different dwellings alongside each other at the **Castling Street Heritage Centre** (☎ 07/4772–5195, ☉ Wed. 10–2 and weekends 1–4). The 1884 worker's dwelling is a simple cottage that has been refurnished. The 1921 farmhouse is a typical example of the house occupied by early Queensland farmers. Currajong is a grand residence that was built in 1888. It has been completely restored and furnished. ⊠ *5 Castling St., West End,* ☎ *077/72–5195.* ⊙ *Wed. 10–2, weekends 1–4.*

Townsville Common, also known as the Townsville Environment Park, is an important bird sanctuary. One may doubt the wisdom of encouraging birds to live at the seaward end of the airport runway, but they don't seem to mind. It's hard not to be impressed by the profusion of spoonbills, jabiru storks, pied geese, herons, and ibis, plus the occasional wallabies, goannas, and even an echidna, and children will be fascinated by the sight of large brolgas performing their elegant dances. The best time to visit is either at dawn or dusk. Most of the birds leave these swamplands from May through August, the dry months, but they're all back by October. To get to the Common, take a taxi past the airport. Access is free.

OFF THE
BEATEN PATH

Billabong Sanctuary is an extensive nature park inhabited by crocodiles, koalas, wombats, dingoes, and wallabies. There is also quite a range of bird life: the large local cassowaries, kookaburras with their distinctive laugh, and beautiful red-tailed black cockatoos. The setting of the 22-acre property is close to the creatures' natural habitat. Twice daily educational shows give you the chance to learn more about native animals and their habits and include koala feeding, crocodile feeding, and handling snakes. ⊠ *Bruce Hwy., Nome, 17 km (10 mi) south of Townsville,* ☎ *07/4778-8344.* ⊠ *$16.* ⊙ *Daily 8–5.*

Dining

$$$ ✕ **Flutes.** The decor here may not be striking, but service is excellent. Try such starters as prawns tempura in chili plum sauce, and such main courses as Spanish mackerel fillets slowly cooked in a tomato and olive sauce with herbs, or a combination of king prawns and local sea bugs (lobster) sautéed in rich garlic and cheese sauce served with a wild pilaf rice. ⊠ *Townsville Reef International, 63 The Strand,* ☎ *07/4721–1777. AE, DC, MC, V. No lunch.*

$$$ ✕ **Meltons.** Colorful decor and a consistently high standard of award-
★ winning fare make this Townsville's finest restaurant. The menu is true to the supply of local beef and seafood from the nearby Great Barrier Reef. Try char-grilled whole calamari with baked plum tomatoes, or seared fillet of grass-fed beef on mashed sweet potato with a dijon-seeded mustard jus, and finish with baked passion-fruit soufflé with yogurt and mint. ⊠ *Sheraton Breakwater Casino-Hotel, Sir Leslie Thiess Dr.,* ☎ *07/4722–2333. AE, DC, MC, V. Closed Sun. and Mon. No lunch.*

$$ ✕ **Pinocchio's on Flinders.** Warm terra-cotta and moss green colors cre-
★ ate an inviting ambience in this intimate restaurant. In the upstairs section, original local art provides a charming touch. Among a good selection of seafood, steak, and pasta dishes, pan-fried calamari with a light salad is a favorite, as is the Reef and Beef: top grade eye fillet served with Australian lobster, prawns, scallops, and béarnaise sauce. ⊠ *223 Flinders St. E,* ☎ *07/4771 2209. Reservations essential. No lunch Sat.–Wed.*

Lodging

$$$$ 🏨 **Sheraton Breakwater Casino-Hotel.** When it opened in the 1980s, this Sheraton seemed to change the tourism profile of Townsville by providing international level facilities in what was at the time a rather sleepy town. It has also dominated Townsville's waterfront vista and, although it has a rather bland, block-shaped architectural design, it manages to look sophisticated against the adjacent marina. This waterfront

location translates into great views across to Magnetic Island from all
11 floors. Inside, rooms are decorated in bright tropical reds, blues,
and greens and are larger than standard hotel rooms. This is a busy
hotel—with North Queensland's first casino attracting many patrons—
but rooms are pleasantly quiet. ⊠ *Box 1223, Sir Leslie Thiess Dr., 4810,*
☎ *07/4722–2333. 192 rooms with shower and bath, 16 suites. 3 restaurants, 5 bars, casino, in-room VCR, pool, spa, sauna, tennis courts,
exercise room. AE, DC, MC, V.*

$$ ☒ **Townsville Reef International.** This four-story beachfront hotel over-
★ looking Cleveland Bay is a pleasant modern property with a high stan-
dard of service. It has typical Queensland decor, with lots of lattice, tropical
prints, and muted grays and greens. From Flutes restaurant (☞ Din-
ing, *above*) and the palm trees shading the pool, to private balconies
overlooking the bay and Magnetic Island, this Best Western is a fine
place to stay. ⊠ *63 The Strand,* ☎ *07/4721–1777. 45 rooms with shower
and bath. VCRs, pool, whirlpool, laundry. AE, DC, MC, V.*

$$ ☒ **Townsville Travelodge.** This circular 20-story building is a Townsville
landmark, its sugar shaker resemblance a tribute to one of the city's
industries. Its prime advantage is its location in the heart of the city
center. Refurbished in 1996 with vibrant reef colors and cane furniture, the hotel's rooms have good views of the city and waterfront. Popular among business travelers, it is a favorite for functions and
conferences. ⊠ *Flinders Mall,* ☎ *07/4772–2477. 159 rooms with
bath, 39 suites. 2 restaurants, 3 bars, pool, laundry. AE, DC, MC, V.*

$ ☒ **Seagull's Resort on the Seafront.** This very pleasant, two-story
★ brick complex and its large, unusually shaped pools sit in three acres
of rock and palm tree–studded tropical gardens. The hotel rooms are
spacious and have cane furniture and a pastel color scheme. Self-contained apartments are also available. On site, Seagull's à la carte restaurant serves generous portions alfresco. House specialties include a
chilled seafood platter, as well as prawn and scallop brochettes. The
resort is 2½ km (1½ mi) from the city center and about a two-minute
walk to the beach. ⊠ *74 The Esplanade,* ☎ *07/4721–3111. 70 rooms
with shower. Restaurant, bar, in-room VCRs, 2 pools, tennis court, playground, laundry. AE, DC, MC, V.*

Nightlife and the Arts

The **Civic Theatre** (⊠ Boundary St., ☎ 07/4772–2677) hosts some of
the state's finest performing artists, and the **Breakwater Entertainment
Centre** (Sir Leslie Thiess Dr., ☎ 07/4771–4000), which can seat 4,000,
has hosted such international acts as Tom Jones and Tina Turner. The
center is also the home of the Sun's National Basketball League team.

For gamblers, the main attraction in Townsville is the **Sheraton Breakwater Hotel & Casino** (☞ Lodging, *above*), which has a full range of
gaming opportunities including mini baccarat, sic bo, blackjack,
roulette, keno, and slot machines, as well as the uniquely Australian
game of two up.

Outdoor Activities and Sports

BEACHES

Townsville is blessed with a long golden strand of swimming beach along
the northern edge of the city. There is no surf, as the beach is sheltered
by the reef and Magnetic Island.

DIVING

Because it's surrounded by tropical islands and warm waters, it's no
surprise that Townsville is an important diving center. A bonus is that
diving courses and excursions here are not as crowded or frenetic as
in the hot spots of Cairns or the Whitsunday Islands.

The wreck of the Yongala steamship that sank just south of Townsville in 1911 lies in 99 ft of water about 16 km (11 mi) off shore, 60 km (40 mi) from Townsville. Now the abode of a vast variety of marine life, it is one of Australia's best dive sites and can be approached as either a one- or two-day trip. All local dive operators offer trips out to the site.

The world-renowned **Mike Ball Dive Expeditions** (⊠ 252 Walker St., ☎ 07/4772–3022) has three-day trips ($390) to the Yongala every Tuesday, and on one Friday per month, which include on-board meals, linen, tanks, and weight belts. Extra gear can also be hired.

Other major dive operators are **Pro-Dive Townsville** (⊠ Great Barrier Reef Wonderland, Flinders St., East, ☎ 07/4721–1760) and **Sun City Watersports** (⊠ Tobruk Pool, the Strand, ☎ 07/4771–6527).

FISHING

Fringe Benefits Charters (⊠ 36 Yarrawonga Dr., ☎ 07/4771–5579) and **Coral Sea Fishing Charters** (⊠ 7 Fletcher St., ☎ 018/778–534) offer game fishing and reef fishing trips. **True Blue Charters** (⊠ 65 Gilbert Crescent, Yarrawonga, ☎ 07/4771–5474) will arrange whatever sort of fishing you like, whether it's out to the reef or along coastal estuaries.

GOLF

Rowes Bay Golf Course offers 18 holes with a new par 3, 9-hole course. ⊠ *Pallarenda,* ☎ *07/4774–1188.*

Willows Golf Club is an 18-hole championship course. ⊠ *19th Ave., Kirwan,* ☎ *07/4773–4777.*

Shopping

Flinders Street Mall is the main shopping area of Townsville, a bright and sunny street closed to vehicular traffic. Look for **Cat and Fiddle Centre** (⊠ 401 Flinders St.) and **Northtown on the Mall** (⊠ 280 Flinders St.).

Magnetic Island

The bulk of Magnetic Island's 52 square km (20 square mi) is national parkland, laced with miles of walking trails and rising to a height of 1,640 ft on Mount Cook. The terrain is punctuated with huge granite boulders and softened by tall hoop pines, euclaypt forest, and small patches of rain forest. The park is a haven for wildlife, including rock wallabies, koalas, and an abundance of bird life.

The 2,500-odd year-round residents live on the eastern shore, where you'll also stay while on holiday. The main settlements are Picnic Bay, Arcadia, Nelly Bay, and Horseshoe Bay. But don't look for the high-rises of the Gold Coast or the luxurious resorts of the Whitsundays—Magnetic Islanders live here for the relaxed lifestyle and natural surroundings.

One way to get an overview of Magnetic Island is to ride an **Explorer Leisure Tours** bus with driver commentary—your ticket then allows unlimited travel on the bus to return to the places you like most. ⊠ *44 Mandalay Ave., Nelly Bay,* ☎ *07/4778–5130.* $9.

The beaches all around the island are another reason to visit. Alma Bay's beach near Arcadia is good for swimming and snorkeling. Near the northeastern corner of the island, Radical Bay has a small, some would say ideal, beach surrounded by tree-covered rock outcrops. Horseshoe Bay has the largest beach, with boat rentals as well. There is good snorkeling at Nelly Bay, and Geoffrey Bay has a well-marked snorkel trail. Free self-guiding trail cards that identify various corals and sea life are available from the information center adjacent to the Picnic Bay Jetty.

Hiking trails on the island are relatively easy. A track to West Point from Picnic Bay leads through interesting terrain to good birding spots (3 hrs round trip). The most popular walk is to World War II gun emplacements overlooking Horseshoe and Florence Bays. This trip takes 45 minutes each way at a leisurely pace. The best views are on the Nelly Bay to Arcadia walk and are rewarding if you take the higher ground. There are altogether 24 km (16 mi) of tracks on island.

The walking trails of the island run under gum trees that are home to many koalas. The **Koala Park Oasis** in Horseshoe Bay is North Queensland's largest koala sanctuary, where you can see and touch koalas. ☎ 07/4778–5260. ⌨ $7. ⏱ Daily 9–5.

Dining and Lodging

Magnetic Island's lodgings are specifically for vacationers, but they are geared largely to the needs of Australians on holidays rather than international visitors. As a result they tend to be less expensive.

$ ✗▦ **Arcadia Hotel Resort.** This pleasant resort is opposite both Geoffrey and Alma bays. The original single-story wooden building stands adjacent to one of two pools, and the 1980s saw the addition of the motel-style terrace rooms. Unfortunately, their decor is uninspiring, with mission brown, red, and green colors at odds with each other. The bar-restaurant area is next to a pool and is open to the public. Dining here is a casual affair and the food—predominately steak, seafood, and salads—is good value for the money. The resort also has a shopping arcade with a dive center, and other shops and restaurants are close by. ⌑ Marine Parade, Arcadia 4819, ☎ 07/4778–5177, ℻ 07/4778–5897. 27 rooms with shower. Restaurant, bistro, in-room VCRs, 2 pools, laundry service. AE, DC, MC, V.

$$ ▦ **Magnetic International Resort.** The first four-star facility to open on Magnetic Island, this resort is nestled amid 11 acres of lush gardens 2 km (1.2 mi) from the beach. Rooms follow a pastel yellow color scheme, have kitchenettes, tiled floors, cane furniture, and overlook the gardens. At the resort's terrace restaurant, MacArthur's, beef and seafood are the mainstays of the menu. Try grilled coral trout on a bed of crisp snow peas topped with tiger prawns and finished with a lemon and chive beurre blanc. As for activities, hiking trails into the bush are nearby, and the energetic can take advantage of floodlit tennis courts in the evenings when the temperature is cooler. The resort's bus departs regularly for Arcadia and Picnic bays as well as the beach. ⌑ Mandalay Ave., Nelly Bay, ☎ 07/4778–5200. 96 rooms with shower. Restaurant, bar, pool, 3 tennis courts, recreation room, playground, laundry. AE, DC, MC, V.

Horseback Riding

The pace of life on Magnetic Island is perfectly suited to riding. With **Bluey's Horseshoe Ranch Trail Rides** you can take a one-hour bush ride ($18), a trail in the bush and along the beach ($33), or a more extensive bush and beach ride with a chance to take the horses swimming ($50). ⌑ 38 Gifford St., Horseshoe Bay, ☎ 07/4778–5109. ⏱ Daily.

Water Sports

Horseshoe Bay Watersports offers sailing, paraflying, water-skiing, aquabikes, surfskis, and canoes for hire. ⌑ 97 Horsehoe Bay Rd., ☎ 07/4758–1336.

Townsville and Magnetic Island A to Z

Arriving and Departing

TOWNSVILLE

By Bus. Greyhound Pioneer (☎ 13–2030), **McCafferty's** (☎ 07/4772–5100), and **Bus Australia** (☎ 13–2323) all run regularly from Cairns and Brisbane and to points farther south. *Terminal, ⊠ Palmer and Plume Sts., South Townsville,* ☎ 07/4721–2322.

By Car. Townsville is 1,400 km (870 mi) by road from Brisbane—a colossal, dull drive. The 370 km (230 mi) journey from Townsville to Cairns, with occasional Hinchinbrook Island views, is more appealing.

By Plane. Ansett Australia and **Qantas** fly frequently to Brisbane, Cairns, interstate cities, and overseas destinations. **Flight West** (☎ 13–2392) has a comprehensive flight network throughout Queensland.

Airport Shuttle Service (☎ 07/4775–5544) runs shuttle buses that meet each flight. The cost of the transfer to the city is $7 (one-way). **Standard White Cabs** (⊠ 11 Yeatman St., Hyde Park, ☎ 07/4772–1555) are available from the rank at the airport. If there are none there, there is a free phone to the dispatch radio room. The average cost of the journey to a city hotel is $14.

By Train. The *Queenslander* departs Brisbane each Sunday at 10 AM and arrives in Townsville on Monday at 10:15 AM. For more information call the Railways Information Centre (☎ 07/3235–2222) in Brisbane.

MAGNETIC ISLAND

By Boat. Magnetic Island Ferries (☎ 07/4772–7122) has fast catamaran service every day from Townsville (leaving Great Barrier Reef Wonderland and 168–172 Flinders St. E) to Picnic Bay on the island. There are at least 10 departures daily; the 20-minute trip costs $19. Resorts' minibuses meet each ferry on arrival. **Capricorn Barge Company** (07/4772–5422) runs a car ferry service to Magnetic Island with four departures on weekdays and two on the weekend. Cost is $93 return, which includes up to six passengers. Walk-ons cost $12.

Getting Around

TOWNSVILLE

By Bicycle. Townsville's flat terrain is well suited to cycling. Pick up a rental at **Bicycle Tours** (⊠ 36 Tenth Ave., Railway Estate, ☎ 07/4721–2026).

By Car. Avis (☎ 07/4721–2688 or 07/4775–2888), **Budget** (☎ 07/4713–2727), **Hertz** (☎ 07/4779–2022), **National** (☎ 07/4772–5133), and **Thrifty** (☎ 07/4772–4600) all have rental cars available in Townsville.

By Taxi. You can flag a **Standard White Cab** (⊠ 11 Yeatman St., Hyde Park, ☎ 07/4772–1555) in the street or find one at stands or hotels.

MAGNETIC ISLAND

By Bicycle and Scooter. Magnetic Sports (⊠ 8 The Esplanade, Picnic Bay, ☎ 07/4778–5407) rents bicycles for $5 per half day, $8 per day, or more for mountain bikes and tandems. **Road Runner Scooter Hire** (⊠ The Esplanade, Picnic Bay, ☎ 07/4778–5222) rents scooters by the hour ($12), half-day ($20), day ($25), or longer.

By Bus. Magnetic Island Bus Service (☎ 077/78–5130) runs every half hour between Horseshoe Bay in the north of the island and Picnic Bay in the south. A day pass costs $9.

By Mini Moke. A Mini Moke is a soft-top version of the tiny Minor Mini car. They are ideal if you want to explore the island but don't feel comfortable on two wheels. **Magnetic Island Rent-A-Moke** (⊠ The

Esplanade, Picnic Bay, ☎ (07/4778–5377) has a large fleet for hire ($32 per day). Other vehicles are available at higher rates, but they aren't necessary on this compact island.

By Taxi. Magnetic Island All White Taxi Service (☎ 07/4778–5946) has a stand at the ferry terminal at Picnic Point.

Contacts and Resources

EMERGENCIES
Ambulance, fire brigade, and **police.** ☎ 000.
Townsville Hospital. ✉ *Eyre St.,* ☎ 07/4781–9211.

DOCTORS
Aitkenvale 24 hour Medical Centre (301 Ross River Rd., Aitkenvale, ☎ 07/4775–7444) can provide nonurgent medical assistance.

GUIDED TOURS
Pure Pleasure Cruises (☎ 07/4721–3555) runs from the Great Barrier Reef Wonderland wharf out to its pontoon at Kelso Reef on the outer edge of the Great Barrier Reef. The trip out takes 2½ hours by high speed catamaran. Once there, you have the choice of fishing, snorkeling, diving (if you have a certificate), or viewing the coral through the floor of a glass-bottom boat. Morning and afternoon tea and a tropical buffet lunch are included in the cost ($125). The cat departs daily (except Mon. and Thurs.) at 9 AM, returning at 5:30 PM. Hotel pickups are available.

Coral Princess has a four-day cruise from Townsville to Cairns or one way or return. It is a minicruise ship that carries 54 passengers in great comfort. There are plenty of stops for snorkeling, fishing, and exploring such resort islands as Dunk and Orpheus. The crew includes marine biologists who give lectures and accompany you on excursions. If you are a diver, you can rent equipment on board; if you wish to learn, lessons are available. ✉ *Coral Princess, Breakwater Marina, Townsville 4810,* ☎ 07/4721–1673 or 008/07–9545. 🕮 *From $990 double occupancy (if you also make return journey, cost is 50% of outbound rate).*

VISITOR INFORMATION
Magnetic Island Tourist Bureau is the island's primary oracle. ✉ *26 The Grove, Nelly Bay 4819,* ☎ 07/4778–5596.
National Parks & Wildlife Service's Picnic Bay(☎ 07/4778–5378) has an office in Picnic Bay on Magnetic Island with information on walking trails.
Townsville Enterprise has the widest range of material and information on all local attractions. ✉ *Enterprise House, 3 The Strand, Box 1043, Townsville 4810,* ☎ 07/4771–3061, ☉ *weekdays 8:30–5.*

CAIRNS

Cairns is the capital of the region known as the Far North. The city is closer to Papua New Guinea than it is to most of Australia, and its sense of isolation has only just begun to lessen with its role as an international gateway. Nevertheless, it still feels like a sleepy tropical town. Many older homes are built on stilts to catch ocean breezes, and overhead fans are ubiquitous. The city itself is totally flat, surrounded by rain forest and macadamia, sugarcane, and pineapple plantations. The Coral Sea forms the town's eastern boundary, and to the west are the slopes of the dividing range leading up to the Atherton Tableland.

In many respects, the city is nothing more than a staging post—high-rise hotels, motels, and cheap hostels abound, but most people use the town as a base for exploring the surrounding ocean and rain forest.

So if you want to immerse yourself in Queensland's natural wonders, Cairns is the place to start.

Exploring Cairns

The **Esplanade** and the waterfront are the focal points of life in Cairns. Fronting Trinity Bay, the Esplanade is the site of many of the town's best stores and hotels. It is also where many of the backpackers who throng to Cairns like to gather, giving it a lively, slightly bohemian feel. Trinity Bay is a shallow stretch of hundreds of yards of mangrove flats, uncovered at low tide, that attract interesting bird life. Over the past few years, some of the waterfront has been filled in, and **Pier Market Place,** a shopping-hotel complex, was constructed.

Cairns can trace its beginnings to the point where the Esplanade turns into **Wharf Street.** In 1876 this small area was a port for the gold and tin mined inland. The area later became known as the Barbary Coast because of its criminal element. Today, it's once again a thriving port. Wander onto **Marlin Jetty** where the charter fishing boats are moored. Big-game fishing is a major industry, and fish weighing more than 1,000 pounds have been caught in the waters off the reef. South of Marlin Jetty are the docks for the catamarans that conduct tours of the islands and marine life of the Great Barrier Reef (☞ Cairns A to Z, *below*).

The actual center of Cairns is **City Place,** a quaint pedestrian mall where you can watch the passing parade. Some of the town's few authentic pubs, as well as the major shopping area, are around the square.

The **Cairns Museum** houses a collection of artifacts and photographs of Cairns's history, including a fascinating exhibit on the life of Aborigines in the rain forest. The museum is situated next to City Place on Shields Street. ⊠ *Lake and Shields Sts.,* ☎ *07/4051–5582.* ⊡ *$3.* ☉ *Mon.–Sat. 10–3.*

While you're in Cairns, attend one of the informative and entertaining lectures presented by **Reef Teach** at the City Library. Six nights a week, a marine biologist uses slides and samples of coral—not to mention sterling fish imitations—to inform prospective divers and general sightseers about the Great Barrier Reef's evolution and the unique inhabitants of this delicate marine ecosystem. ⊠ *Cairns City Library, Bolands Centre, 14 Spence St. Reef Teach office,* ⊠ *300 Draper St.,* ☎ *07/4051–6882.* ⊡ *$10.* ☉ *Lecture Mon.–Sat. 6:15 PM–8:30 PM.*

Around Cairns

The 1996 creation of the $9 million **Tjapukai Aboriginal Cultural Park** was overseen by Aboriginal elders, and features three theaters, one of which draws on state-of-the-art holographic technology. A surrounding encampment vignettes aspects of tribal life, including fire-making, didgeridoo playing, preparation of bush foods and medicines, and instruction on how to throw a boomerang and spear. A good range of Aboriginal artworks are on display and for sale. The park moved to its present location at the base of the **Skyrail Rainforest Cableway** (☞ Guided Tours *in* Cairns A to Z, *below*) from a previous home in Kuranda. ⊠ *Kamerunga Rd., Caravonica Lakes, Smithfield (15 km, or 9 mi, north of Cairns),* ☎ *07/4042–9999.* ⊡ *$21.* ☉ *Daily 9–5.*

Bellenden Ker National Park is nestled in the heart of the Atherton Tableland, one of the most densely vegetated areas in Australia. Rain forest dominates Bellenden Ker, from lowland tropical rain forest to the stunted growth on Mt. Bartle Frere, the highest point in Queensland, where you'll find Australia's largest remaining area of upland rain forest. Encompassing both the eastern and western slopes of the Bellenden Ker range, the park is largely undeveloped. It still shows the effects of a major cyclone that hit in 1986 and destroyed much of the vegetation. A profusion of vines has replaced many of the lost trees, temporarily limiting their chances of regenerating.

It has a variety of trails, including a short 2,640-ft paved trail that leads from the parking area to Josephine Falls, which is a fine place to swim. Picnic facilities and toilets are there as well. For the more adventurous, a 30-km (19-mi) return trail leads from the parking area to the summit of Mt. Bartle Frere. The two-day hike has some rough patches along the way, including steep climbs and rock scrambling, but it is well worth the effort for the spectacular view of the surrounding rain forest—unless the mountain is shrouded in fog. Avoid the gympie tree: Its large, round leaves are covered with sharp barbs that inflict a painful sting.

To reach the park, drive 50 km (31 mi) south from Cairns along the Bruce Highway via Babinda. Bush camping is allowed with ranger permission throughout the park, except at Josephine Falls. Permits cost $3 per person per night. Supplies can be bought in Babinda. ⊠ *Bellenden Ker National Park, Box 93, Mirriwinni 4871,* ☎ *07/4067–6304.*

OFF THE BEATEN PATH   A bit far afield, to put it lightly, the **Undara Lava Tubes** are a fascinating geological oddity in the Outback, and they are attracting an ever-increasing number of visitors for day visits and overnight trips. The hollow basalt tubes were created by a volcanic outpouring 190,000 years ago and there are several places where it is possible to walk into the tubes. Leaving the ferns, vines, and wallabies at the entrance behind, one steps onto the smooth and dry tunnel floor. Above, horseshoe bats twitter and flitter in the crannies. Patterns etched in the ceiling by water seepage create an incongruous cathedral effect.

Undara lies on the western side of the ranges, 400 km (248 mi) from Cairns. Day tours to Undara from the city are operated by **Australian Pacific Tours** (⊠ Orchid Plaza, Lake St., ☎ 07/4051-9299) and depart daily between April and November, and on Tuesday, Wednesday, Saturday, and Sunday between December and March. The cost of the tour is $92. There are accommodations at **Lava Lodge** (☎ 07/4097-1411, 🖷 07/4097-1450), which consists of interesting old railway cars converted to comfortable (if compact) motel rooms.

Dining and Lodging

$$$ ✕ **Captain's Table.** On the waterfront in the Radisson Plaza Hotel, this restaurant serves innovative international cuisine. The decor is gracious and elegant, and tables are set with silver cutlery. Many of the dishes have French influences with tropical undertones, and make sure you save room for something sweet—the dessert tray has to be seen to be believed. Try the mouth-watering chocolate mousse cake. ⊠ *Radisson Plaza Hotel at the Pier, Pier Point Rd.,* ☎ *07/4031–1411. AE, DC, MC, V. Closed Sun. No lunch.*

$$ ✕ **Breezes Brasserie.** Ceiling-to-floor windows overlooking Trinity
★   Inlet and the distant mountains set the mood in this attractive restaurant in the **Hilton International Cairns** (☞ Lodging, *below*). The decor is bright, with tropical greenery, white tablecloths, candles, and silver tableware, and you can feast on everything from quick sandwiches to full-course dinners. Its modern Australian fare includes delights such as smoked Tasmanian salmon served with a bug mush (Australian lobster mixed with mashed potato), accompanied by red wine jus. The specialty, however, is seafood, and a spectacular seafood and Asian buf-

fet is available nightly. ⊠ *Cairns Hilton International, Wharf St.,* ☎ *07/4052–6786. AE, DC, MC, V.*

$ ✕ **Gallery Café.** Iron-forged tables and chairs, an outdoor balcony with views of the Coral Sea—this café, right in the middle of the action, can lure you in with either prime people watching or idyllic gazing at ocean-bound yachts. Get out of the travel-food-stomach rut with down-to-earth open sandwiches, noodles, pastas, salads, and excellent cakes. The menu changes frequently. ⊠ *Regional Art Gallery, Abbott and Shield Sts.,* ☎ *07/4031–5889. No credit cards.*

$ ✕ **Red Ochre Grill.** This restaurant uses about 40 different native foods to create modern Australian cuisine. A char-grill fired on mallee roots is used to infuse the dishes with Australian flavors, and you can feast on such dishes as prawn and crocodile gumbo scented with aniseed myrtle (a native myrtle leaf with an anise flavor). As the restaurant's name suggests, the decor is warm-red and terra-cotta, with glass walls providing uninterrupted views of the street. The menu is accompanied by a good wine list. ⊠ *43 Sheilds St.,* ☎ *07/4051–0100. AE, DC, MC, V. No lunch Sun.*

$ ✕ **Roma Roulette.** Popular with locals and visitors alike, this Cairns Italian has an easygoing, informal atmosphere, and smiling chef Antonio often personally advises customers on what to order. Two of the restaurant's favorites are *pasta tricolore* and *scaloppine al vino bianco.* Seafood is also recommended. ⊠ *48A Aplin St.,* ☎ *07/4051–1076. AE, DC, V. BYOB. No dinner Mon. or Tues.*

$$$$ 🏨 **Hilton International Cairns.** An American favorite, the seven-story
★ Hilton curves along the shoreline and offers wonderful sea views, and it is near the business district and a famous game-fishing club. The lobby, which looks out past lush gardens to the ocean, is distinctly tropical, with ceramic floor tiles and an atrium filled with rain-forest palms and ferns. Plants from a rooftop garden hang down long external walkways, and rooms on the lowest level open onto a palm forest on the lobby roof. Decorated in pinks and blue-greens with touches of brown, the rooms are tastefully appointed and furnished. ⊠ *Wharf St., 4870,* ☎ *07/4052–1599,* FAX *07/4052–1370. 264 rooms with bath and shower. Pool, hot tub, sauna, laundry service. AE, DC, MC, V.*

$$$$ 🏨 **Radisson Plaza Hotel at the Pier.** The conservative, low-rise design of this popular hotel is typical of northern Queensland, with an appropriate nautical look, as it overlooks Trinity Bay and Marlin Marina—the main Cairns terminal for cruises to the Barrier Reef. The hotel also adjoins the numerous shops and restaurants of Pier Marketplace. The lobby atrium's tropical theme is so spectacular (or horrific, depending on your view of artificial indoor rain forests) that it's a tourist attraction in its own right. All rooms are spacious, and some designed for guests with disabilities are available. ⊠ *Pier Point Rd., 4870,* ☎ *07/ 4031–1411,* FAX *07/4031–3226. 223 rooms with bath. 2 restaurants, pool, hot tub, laundry, business services. AE, DC, MC, V.*

$$$$ 🏨 **Reef Hotel Casino.** Opened in April 1996, the Reef is part of a $200
★ million entertainment complex in the heart of Cairns. Its features set it apart as the most sophisticated hotel in town: to start, butler service to all rooms, each of which has a Jacuzzi. A rooftop conservatory is a tropical hothouse by day, at night turning into a candlelit dinner theater within a rain forest. Along with a coffee shop, nightclub, and several bars, you'll also find a very good Chinese restaurant, Pacific Flavours Brasserie, and the more dignified Anthias Restaurant. If you arrive before your room is ready or need to check out well before your flight, the Transit Lounge has the facilities of a first-class airport lounge. ⊠ *35-41 Wharf St.,* ☎ *07/4030–8888 or 1800/80–8883,* FAX *07/4030–8788. 128 suites. 4 restaurants, 4 bars, pool, exercise room, casino. AE, DC, MC, V.*

$$$ **⚟ Holiday Inn.** This seven-story hotel is built in a figure eight over-looking Trinity Bay and the Coral Sea. Decorated with a marble floor, luxurious rugs, and cane sofas, the glass-wall lobby overlooks the hotel gardens. Guest rooms are large, decorated in aqua hues with cane chairs and wood tables. The hotel is within walking distance of shops, restaurants, and the business district. ✉ *Esplanade and Florence St., 4870,* ☎ *07/4031–3757,* ☒ *07/4031–4130. 259 rooms with bath. Restaurant, 3 bars, room service, laundry service. AE, DC, MC, V.*

$$$ **⚟ Il Palazzo Boutique Hotel.** Cairns's first boutique hotel is close to the city and offers luxury in a smaller package. A 6½-ft Italian marble replica of Michelangelo's David greets you in the foyer, and other in-triguing *objets* appear throughout the hotel. The suites are spacious, with a soft green color scheme, forged-iron and glass tables, and cane furniture. They all have fully equipped kitchens and laundry machines. ✉ *62 Abbott St., 1800/81–3222. 38 suites. Restaurant, pool, hair and beauty salon. AE, DC, MC, V.*

$$$ **⚟ Pacific International.** Facing the waterfront and the marina, this 11-
★   story hotel has a soaring three-story lobby—with palms, a marble floor, rattan furniture, and two spectacular brass chandeliers—that makes for an impressive entrance. Guest rooms are furnished with cane and rattan chairs, soft pastels, tropical plants, and Gauguin-style prints. All have private balconies, tea and coffee makers, and color TVs. Rooms for guests with disabilities are available. ✉ *Esplanade and Spence St., 4870,* ☎ *07/4051–7888 or 1800/07–9001,* ☒ *07/4051–0210. 176 rooms with bath. Restaurant, 4 bars, coffee shop, beauty salon. AE, DC, MC, V.*

$$ **⚟ Cairns Colonial Club Resort.** Set in 8 acres of lush tropical gardens, this two-story, colonial-style complex won the Beautiful Garden Award for the Cairns area for several years in a row. The resort is built around two saltwater swimming pools, and the public areas and rooms are sim-ply furnished with cane furniture, ceiling fans, and vivid tropical cush-ions. Apartments with cooking facilities are also available. Two rooms offer special facilities for guests with disabilities. A free shuttle makes the 7-km (4-mi) run to the city center hourly, and courtesy airport trans-fers are provided. ✉ *18–26 Cannon St., Manunda, 4870,* ☎ *07/ 4053–5111,* ☒ *07/4053–7072. 264 rooms with bath, 82 apartments. 2 restaurants, 3 bars, room service, 2 pools. AE, DC, MC, V.*

$ **⚟ Hides of Cairns.** Located within a heartbeat of the city center, this three-story circa-1890 structure, with its breezy verandas, is a superb example of colonial outback architecture. An adjoining motel section has modern rooms with tropical decor. Rates include full or Continental breakfast. ✉ *Lake and Shields Sts., 4870,* ☎ *07/4051–1266,* ☒ *07/ 4031–2276. 72 rooms, most with bath and shower. Restaurant, 5 bars, pool, hot tub. AE, DC, MC, V.*

Nightlife

1936. This blend of retro and modern isn't exactly the place to go for a quiet chat, but the live nightly shows and "underworld" feel actu-ally work quite well. ✉ *Reef Casino Hotel, 35-41 Wharf St.,* ☎ *07/ 4030–8717.* ▭ *$5 (free to hotel guests).* ☉ *Nightly 10 PM–3 AM.*

The Pier Tavern overlooking the waterfront, is a more sophisticated, upmarket watering hole—a good place to meet locals. ✉ *The Pier Mar-ketplace, Pierpoint Rd.,* ☎ *07/4031–4677.*

Outdoor Activities and Sports

Adventure Trips

Raging Thunder offers adventure packages that include the Great Bar-rier Reef, whitewater rafting through the rain forest, the Tjapukai

Aboriginal Cultural Park, Kuranda Scenic Railway or Skyrail, and hot air ballooning over the Atherton tablelands—the best of Cairns in one package. ⊠ *87 Hartley St.,* ☎ *07/4051–4911.* ☎ *Double occupancy $646, single $839.*

RNR Rafting runs very exciting one-, two-, and five-day white-water expeditions that are suitable only for the physically fit. ⊠ *81 The Esplanade,* ☎ *07/4051–7777.*

Beaches

Cairns has no beaches of its own, and most visitors head out to the reef to swim and snorkel. Just north of the airport, however, are **Palm Cove, Trinity Beach, Clifton Beach, Kewarra Beach, Yorkey's Knob, Holloway's Beach,** and **Machan's Beach.** Do not swim in these waters from October through May, though, when deadly box jellyfish, called marine stingers, float in the water along the coast. Some beaches have small netted areas, but it is advisable to stick to hotel pools at that time. Stingers stay closer to shore and are not found around the Great Barrier Reef or any nearby islands.

Diving

A large number of diving schools in Cairns offer everything from beginner's lessons to equipment rentals and expeditions for experienced divers. Contact **Deep Sea Divers Den** (⊠ 319 Draper St., ☎ 07/4031–2223), **Don Cowie's Cairns Reef Services** (⊠ Hinds and Shields Sts., ☎ 07/4031–1588), **Pro Dive** (⊠ Marlin Parade, ☎ 07/4031–5255), **Quicksilver Diving Services** (⊠ Marina Mirage, Port Douglas, ☎ 07/4099–5050), and **Sunlover Cruises** (⊠ Trinity Wharf, ☎ 07/4031–1055).

Shopping

Malls

Orchid Plaza (⊠ 79–87 Abbott St., ☎ 07/4051–7788) has 14 clothing stores, several cafés, record stores, a pearl emporium, and post office. **Palm Court** (⊠ 34–42 Lake St.) is a reasonably modern complex offering a variety of specialty shops. Located on the waterfront, **Trinity Wharf** (⊠ Wharf St., ☎ 07/4031–1519) has everything from designer clothes and souvenirs to resort wear, hairdressers, and restaurants. Shoppers can request complimentary transportation from their hotels. On the Esplanade, The **Pier Marketplace** (⊠ Pierpoint Rd., ☎ 07/4051–7244) houses such international chains as Lacoste and Country Road, and the offices of yacht brokers and tour operators. Many of the cafés, bars, and restaurants open onto verandas on the waterside.

Markets

Held Friday afternoons, Saturday all day, and Sunday mornings, **Rusty's Bazaar** is the best street market in Cairns. Everything from homegrown fruit and vegetables to secondhand items and antiques is on sale. ⊠ *Grafton and Sheridan Sts.*

Specialty Stores

The well-respected **Original Dreamtime Gallery of Alice Springs** (⊠ 7/8 Palm Court, Lake St., ☎ 07/4051–3222) has a branch in Cairns selling top-quality artwork created by the Aborigines of the Northern Territory. **Gallery Primitive** (⊠ 26 Abbott St., ☎ 07/4031–1641) has Aboriginal and New Guinean arts and artifacts on display and for sale. **Pier Gallery** (⊠ The Pier Marketplace, ☎ 07/4051–6533) sells paintings by leading local artists. **Australian Craftworks** (⊠ Shop 20, Village La., Lake St., ☎ 07/4051–0725) has one of the finest collections of local crafts. **Gallery Appeal** (⊠ Cairns Regional Gallery, Abbott and Shields Sts., ☎ 07/4041–1044) has a range of quality souvenirs for sale.

Cairns A to Z

Arriving and Departing

BY BUS

Greyhound Pioneer Australia (☎ 13–2030), **Murrays Coaches** ☎ 07/4035–2622), and **McCafferty's** (☎ 07/4051–5899 or 13–1499) operate daily express buses from major southern cities.

BY CAR

The 1,712-km (1,063-mi) route from Brisbane to Cairns runs along the Bruce Highway (Hwy. 1), which later becomes the Captain Cook Highway. Although the entire route is paved, there are many tortuous sections that make driving difficult. Throughout its length, the road rarely touches the coast—so, unless you crave endless fields of sugarcane, it's not even picturesque. Fly to Cairns and rent a car instead.

BY PLANE

☞ Air Travel *in* the Gold Guide for information on airlines.

BY TRAIN

Trains arrive at the Cairns Railway Station on Bunda Street (☎ 07/4052–6249). The *Sunlander* and *Queenslander* trains make the 32-hour journey between Brisbane and Cairns. The *Sunlander* runs three times a week to Cairns. The *Queenslander* has been refurbished to the level of most luxury cruise ships, making the journey equal in comfort to that of the world's great deluxe trains. It runs once a week. ☎ 13–2232.

Getting Around

BY TAXI

Black and White Taxis (☎ 07/4051–5333).

Contacts and Resources

CAR RENTAL

Avis (☎ 07/4051–5911), **Budget** (☎ 07/4051–9222), **Hertz** (☎ 13-3039), and **Thrifty** (☎ 07/4051–8099) have airport locations. Four-wheel-drive vehicles are available.

EMERGENCIES

Ambulance, fire brigade, and **police.** ☎ *000.*
Cairns Base Hospital. ☎ *07/4050–6333.*

GUIDED TOURS

Cableway Tours: In August 1995, a whole new way of seeing the rain forests behind Cairns opened after the expenditure of $35 million to
★ build the remarkable **Skyrail Rainforest Cableway.** The base station is 15 km (9 mi) north of Cairns; from there six-person cable cars lift you on a 7½-km (5-mi) journey across the top of the rain forest canopy to the tiny highland village of Kuranda. There are two stops along the way where you can walk to Barron Falls or into the rain forest. Despite the protests of some conservationists—some of whom glued their hands together around a tree only to discover they had picked a tree that was not to be removed—the Skyrail does provide a unique perspective on this astonishingly rich area. ⊠ *Caravonica Lakes, Kamerunga Rd. and Cook Hwy., Smithfield,* ☎ *07/4038–1555.* ⊠ *One-way $23, round-trip $39.* ☉ *Shows daily at 11 and 1:30.*
Great Barrier Reef Tours: Coral Princess (⊠ Breakwater Marina, Townsville, 4810, ☎ 07/4721–1673 or 1800/079–545) conducts a four-day trip from Cairns to Townsville, vice versa, or round-trip aboard a minicruise ship that carries 54 passengers in great comfort. There are plenty of stops for snorkeling, fishing, and exploring Dunk and Orpheus islands. The crew includes marine biologists who lecture on board and on excursions from the boat. Diving gear can be rented, and lessons are available.

Great Adventures Outer Barrier Reef and Island Cruises (⊠ Wharf St.,
☎ 07/4051–0455 or 1800/07–9080) runs a fast catamaran daily to
Green and Fitzroy islands, Norman Reef, and Moore Reef (where diving and snorkeling, and helicopter overflights are available). Some
trips include barbecue luncheon and coral viewing from an underwater observatory and a semisubmersible.

Ocean Spirit Cruises (⊠ 143 Lake St., ☎ 07/4031–2920) has a full-
day tour aboard the *Ocean Spirit,* the largest sailing vessel of its type
in the world, and the smaller *Ocean Spirit II.* A daily trip to Michaelmas Cay includes four hours at the Great Barrier Reef, coral viewing
in a semisubmersible, swimming and snorkeling, and a fresh seafood
lunch. Introductory diving lessons are available.

Four-Wheel-Drive Tours: Wild Track Adventure Safaris (⊠ Box 2397,
Cairns 4870, ☎ 07/4055–2247, FAX 07/4058–1930) runs trips to the
top of the Cape York Peninsula. For more information, *see* Four-
Wheel-Drive Tours *in* Chapter 13.

Nature Tours: Daintree Wildlife Safari (☎ 07/4098–6125 or 1800/07–
9102) and **Daintree Rainforest River Trains** (☎ 07/4090–7676 or
1800/17–9090) run full-day, half-day, and self-drive tours through mangrove swamps and thick rain forest to see native orchids, birds,
crocodiles, and butterfly farms.

Tropic Wings Coach Tours offers a variety of trips in the Cairns area,
including tours to Atherton Tablelands, waterfalls, Kuranda, Port
Douglas, Daintree Rainforest, the Outback, and the Gulf of Carpentaria west and north of Cairns. ⊠ *278 Hartley St.,* ☎ *07/4035–3555.*

Orientaton Tours: Cairns Explorer Bus Lines runs hourly tours of the
city accompanied by commentary. Passengers can disembark at any point
along the tour and board a later bus. ⊠ *9 Clatcherty St.,* ☎ *07/4055–
1240.* ☞ *$20.* ☉ *Tour hourly Mon.–Sat. 9–4.*

Train Tours: Kuranda Scenic Railway from Cairns to Kuranda is one of
the most scenic rail journeys of the world. Kuranda is the gateway to
the Atherton Tableland, an elevated area of rich volcanic soil that produces some of Australia's finest beef, dairy, and vegetables. Between this
tableland and the narrow coastal strip is a rugged dividing range filled
with waterfalls, lakes, caves, and gorges. The train makes the 1½-hour
ascent through the rain forest via the Barron River Gorge and 15 hand-
carved tunnels. A wide range of tours is available, from full-day rain
forest safaris to simple round-trip train and bus rides. ⊠ *Cairns Railway Station, Bunda St.,* ☎ *07/4052–6250, 07/4055–2222 or 07/
4058–1108 for reservations with Kuranda Connection for Royale
Class.* ☞ *Commentary Class one-way $25, Royale Class one-way $36.*

VISITOR INFORMATION

Far North Queensland Promotion Bureau. ⊠ *Port Authority Bldg., Hartley and Grafton Sts.,* ☎ *07/4051–3588.*

NORTH FROM CAIRNS

The Captain Cook Highway runs from Cairns to Mossman, a relatively
civilized stretch known mostly for the chic resort town of Port Douglas. Past the Daintree River, wildlife parks and sunny coastal villages
fade into one of the most sensationally wild corners of the continent.
If you came to Australia in search of high-octane sun, empty beaches
and coral cays, steamy jungles filled with exotic bird noises and riot-
ing vegetation, and a languid, beachcomber lifestyle, then head straight
for the coast between Daintree and Cooktown.

The southern half of this coastline lies within Cape Tribulation National Park, part of the Greater Daintree Wilderness Area, a region named
to UNESCO's World Heritage list because of its unique ecology. If you

want to get a peek at the natural splendor of the area, then there's no need to go past Cape Tribulation. However, the Bloomfield Track does continue on to Cooktown, a destination that will tack two days onto your itinerary. This wild, rugged country breeds some notoriously maverick personalities and can add a whole other dimension to the Far North Queensland experience.

It is not advisable to tackle the wilderness of the Far North alone. By its very nature, the national park requires an expert interpreter. To untrained eyes, the rain forest can look like nothing more than giant roots underfoot and palm trees overhead. But there is so much within the forest to see, and a guide can help you train your eyes on all that's weird and wonderful. Many tour operators offer day trips across the Daintree River from either Cairns or Port Douglas. After a day with a guide, you'll be prepared to do a little more on your own. Better still, stay a couple of days at Cape Tribulation, leaving your footprints on empty beaches, snorkeling off the coral reefs, and drifting off to sleep while the jungle croaks, drips, and squeaks around you.

Prime time for visiting the area is between May and September, when the daily maximum temperature averages around 80°F (26°C) and the water is comfortably warm. During the wet season, which lasts from about December through March, expect monsoon conditions. Toxic box jellyfish make the coastline unsafe for swimming during the Wet, but the jellies don't drift out as far as the reefs, so you're safe there.

Numbers in the margin correspond to points of interest on the Far North Queensland Coast map.

Palm Cove

㉗ *23 km (14 mi) north of Cairns.*

Palm Cove, a mere 20-minute drive north of Cairns, is one of the jewels of Queensland and an ideal base for exploring the far north. It is an oasis of quietude that those in the know seek out for its magnificent trees, calm waters, and excellent restaurants. The loudest noises you are likely to hear are the singing of birds and the lapping of the Pacific Ocean on the beach.

At the **Outback Opal Mine** you can glimpse huge specimens of this unique Australian gemstone and opalized seashells and fossils. The owners, who were once opal miners at Coober Pedy, show how an opal is formed and then how it is cut and polished. ⊠ *Captain Cook Hwy. next to Wild World Palm Cove,* ☎ *07/4055–3492.* ☞ *Free.* ☉ *Daily 9–5.*

Right on the highway at Palm Cove is **Wild World**, a 10-acre park with a wide variety of Australian wildlife, including kangaroos, crocodiles and other reptiles, pelicans, and cassowaries. Most distinguished among its residents is Sarge, a crocodile that the park claims is more than 100 years old and the largest female in captivity. At 1,540 pounds and more than 17 ft in length, Sarge won't leave many unconvinced. The park also has a snake show, a snake-handling demonstration, trained cockatoos that perform twice daily, and a giant North Queensland canetoad race. ⊠ *Captain Cook Hwy., Palm Cove,* ☎ *07/4055–3669.* ☞ *$16.* ☉ *Daily 8–5.*

Lodging

$$$–$$$$ 🏨 **Novotel Palm Cove Resort.** The villagelike buildings and 100 acres of gardens and golf fairways here are a five-minute walk from the beach. Hotel-style rooms—apartments are also available—are average in size and decorated with pale greens and muted yellows. The furniture is a harmonious mixture of cane and wood. The Palm Cove jetty, where

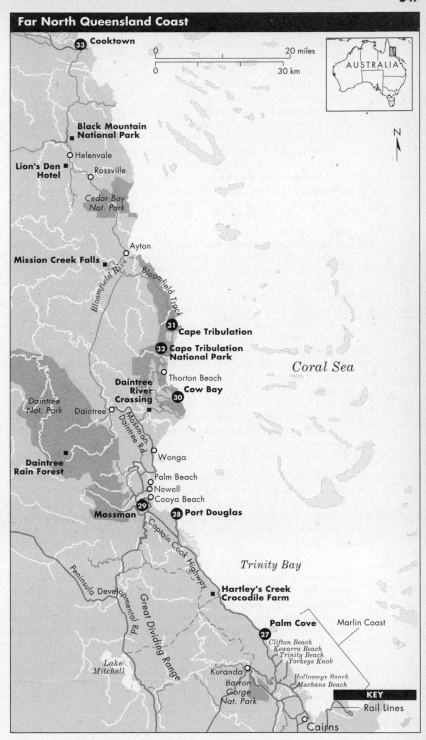

Far North Queensland Coast

33 Cooktown

0 ——— 20 miles
0 ——— 30 km

AUSTRALIA

N

Black Mountain National Park

○ Helenvale

Lion's Den Hotel

○ Rossville

Cedar Bay Nat. Park

○ Ayton

Mission Creek Falls

Bloomfield River

Bloomfield Track

31 **Cape Tribulation**

32 **Cape Tribulation National Park**

○ Thorton Beach

Daintree River Crossing

Cow Bay

30

Daintree Nat. Park

Daintree ○

Mossman–Daintree Rd.

Coral Sea

Daintree Rain Forest

○ Wonga

○ Palm Beach
○ Nowoll
○ Cooya Beach

29

Mossman

28 **Port Douglas**

Captain Cook Highway

Trinity Bay

Hartley's Creek Crocodile Farm

Peninsula Developmental Rd.

Great Dividing Range

Palm Cove

27

Clifton Beach
Kewarra Beach
Trinity Beach
Yorkeys Knob

Marlin Coast

Lake Mitchell

Holloways Beach
Machans Beach

Kuranda ○

Barron Gorge Nat. Park

KEY

—— Rail Lines

○ Cairns

tour operators pick up passengers for trips to the Great Barrier Reef, is just a five-minute walk from the resort. There are also excellent dining facilities, which include a fine poolside Asian restaurant. ⊠ *Coral Coast Dr.,* ☎ *07/4059–1234,* 𝖥𝖠𝖷 *07/4059–1317. 152 rooms, 72 suites, 116 apartments. 2 restaurants, 10 pools, 9-hole golf course, 2 squash courts, 3 tennis courts, dive shop, windsurfing, boating, jetskiing, children's programs. AE, DC, MC, V.*

$$$ 🏨 **Alamanda.** This four-story complex of vacation apartments opens directly onto a large white-sand beach. The white, colonial-style design is enhanced by fine landscaping, with pools, barbecues, and plenty of sunny areas in which to relax. Each suite has a large, private veranda, a comfortable sitting and dining area, two bathrooms, and two or three bedrooms with king-size beds. The furnishings are all custom designed in a cheery, modern style. Kitchens have granite-top counters, and there is a separate laundry room. ⊠ *1 Veivers Rd.,* ☎ *07/4055–3000 or 1800/07–9052,* 𝖥𝖠𝖷 *07/4055–3090. 70 apartments. 3 pools, spa, tennis court. AE, DC, MC, V.*

$$$ 🏨 **Ramada Great Barrier Reef Resort.** Built around a free-form swimming pool that is shaded by giant melaleucas and palm trees, this very pretty low-rise resort is an escapist's delight. You can enjoy all the amenities of a deluxe resort, including private balconies, at a more reasonable rate. ⊠ *Box 122, Vievers Rd. and Williams Esplanade, Palm Cove, 4879,* ☎ *07/4055–3999,* 𝖥𝖠𝖷 *07/4055–3902. 175 rooms with bath, 4 suites. Restaurant, bar, pool, spa, tennis court, baby-sitting, playground, laundry. AE, DC, MC, V.*

$$$ 🏨 **Reef House.** Set amid lovely gardens, this charming hotel seems more ★   like a private club. The main building was constructed in 1885 by a retired politician, and a new wing was added in 1986. The lobby, along with its mural of the Queensland rain forest, is decorated with a superb collection of New Guinea Sepik River handicrafts. The comfortable rooms have a turn-of-the-century atmosphere characterized by mosquito netting, white walls, and pastel furnishings. All rooms have bars and refrigerators. ⊠ *99 Williams Esplanade,* ☎ *07/4055–3633,* 𝖥𝖠𝖷 *07/4055–3305. 70 suites. 3 pools, laundry. AE, DC, MC, V.*

En Route   North of Palm Cove, the Captain Cook Highway swoops toward the ★   sea, a sign announces the beginning of the **Marlin Coast,** and for the next 30 km (19 mi) the road plays hide-and-seek with a glorious stretch of shoreline, ducking inland through tunnels of coconut palm and curving back to the creamy fingers of surf that hiss and froth across the sand.

On Cook Highway, **Hartley's Creek Crocodile Farm** is the home of the renowned Charlie, a saltwater crocodile that is the crocodile held longest in captivity—he's been a "pet" for about 65 years. Apart from Charlie and his hundreds of crocodile mates, visitors can look at many native animals, such as koalas, kangaroos, dingoes, snakes, lizards, and such native birds as the rare cassowary, which is a large and colorful bird found only in New Guinea and parts of northern Australia. All of these animals can be enjoyed in the park's rain forest setting. ⊠ *Cook Hwy., 40 km (24 mi) north of Cairns,* ☎ *07/4055–3576.* 🎫 *$13.* ⏱ *Daily 8–5, crocodile show at 11 and 3, crocodile photos at 4, koalas and dingoes at 1, snake show at 2.*

Port Douglas

㉘ *61 km (38 mi) north of Cairns.*

In the early eighties Port Douglas was a sleepy little fishing village, but today it's one of the "in" places to go in Australia. In fact it's so hot that the Clintons chose to holiday here in November 1996, to recover from the presidential race. The road into town passes through sugar-cane fields then widens and is flanked by palm trees that were planted during World War II for palm oil and then moved here to create this avenue. Known simply as the "Port" to locals, the town has an indefinable mystique. Enough of the old Queensland colonial buildings remain to give it an authentic feel, despite the growing presence of modern resorts and hotels. High-speed cruises leave the Port for the Outer Reef (☞ Guided Tours *in* North from Cairns A to Z, *below*).

Dining and Lodging

$$$$ ✕ **Macrossans.** This modern, glass-walled restaurant in the Sheraton Mirage (☞ *below*) is a study in opulence. High-quality antiques, floor-length white tablecloths, and elegant silver settings complement the cuisine. French dishes prepared with fresh seafood and local produce are appropriately lightened to suit the tropics. The food is beautifully presented, usually with a garnish of exotic fruit. Try Mossman prawns if they are available, and save some room for dessert—chocolate laden black-and-white terrine is the chef's specialty. ⊠ *Port Douglas Rd.,* ☎ *07/4098–5888. AE, DC, MC, V. No lunch.*

$$$ ✕ **Island Point Restaurant.** The Sassi family, the previous owners, have
★ moved on, but the quality of the cuisine at the Island Point remains unchanged. This open-air restaurant is set in a lovely garden and offers views of rain forest, cane fields, and distant mountains. Instead of being a mere sideshow to the view, however, the Italian-based food rises to the challenge, especially with seafood dishes. Barramundi, coral trout, and mudcrabs appear on the menu, and the leader prawns come straight from the Gulf. ⊠ *2 Island Point Rd.,* ☎ *07/4099–5323. AE, DC, MC, V. No lunch Mon.–Thurs.*

$$$ ✕ **Nautilus Restaurant.** Pull up one of the high-back cane chairs out-
★ side under a canopy of magnificent tropical palms in a lush garden setting. The modern Australian cuisine is fresh and original, with plenty of seafood on the menu, and all dishes are beautifully presented. The Nautilus is famous for its mud crabs cooked to order. Try the mille-feuille wonton of marinated barramundi, or leeks and capsicum (sweet peppers) with coconut and lemon dressing, or Thai chicken curry with steamed rice. For dessert, you can't go wrong ordering poached peach with passion fruit sabayon. ⊠ *17 Murphy St.,* ☎ *07/4099–5330. AE, DC, MC, V. No lunch.*

$$$$ 🏨 **Sheraton Mirage.** This is unquestionably the far north's best resort
★ in the most deluxe bracket, and it was the hotel of choice for President and Mrs. Clinton's stay in 1996. If you go for glitz, polished marble, exotic foliage, and lagoon-size pools, then look no further. Elegant guest rooms are decorated with cane furniture upholstered in subtle greens and pinks, and tropical-print bedspreads. Rooms overlook the hotel gardens, golf course, or lagoons that surround the resort. Butlers are available 24 hours a day to assist with everything from replenishing ice buckets to arranging special candlelight dinners in the room. Guests are free to use the gym and tennis courts at the neighboring Mirage Club. ⊠ *Port Douglas Rd., 4871,* ☎ *07/4099–5888,* FAX *07/4099–5398. 298 rooms with bath and shower, 1 suites. Restaurant, 3 bars, coffee shop, pool, exercise room, laundry service. AE, DC, MC, V.*

Shopping

Unquestionably the best and most elegant shopping complex in northern Queensland, the **Marina Mirage** contains 40 fashion and specialty shops for souvenirs, jewelry, accessories, resort wear, designer clothing. ⊠ *Wharf St., Port Douglas,* ☎ *07/4099–5775.*

Mossman

㉙ *14 km (9 mi) northwest of Port Douglas, 75 km (47 mi) north of Cairns.*

A sugar town with a population of less than 2,000—Mossman's appeal lies not in the village itself but 5 km (3 mi) out of town where you find the beautiful waterfalls and river at Mossman Gorge.

Dining and Lodging

$$$$ ╳▣ **Silky Oaks Lodge and Restaurant.** Situated on a hillside surrounded by national parkland, this P&O Resorts hotel is reminiscent of the best African safari lodges. Air-conditioned cabins on stilts overlook either the rain forest and the river below or a natural rock swimming pool. The colonial-style cabins are lined with wood and have exceptionally comfortable beds with tropically inspired decor. Views from the verandas are stunning. Dining in the open-side timber restaurant ($$) is nothing short of idyllic. Dishes range from classical to nouvelle, such as baked barrramundi fillet served on steamed asparagus and with a macadamia nut and lime butter sauce, or rack of lamb marinated in an herb yogurt. The restaurant has an excellent selection of Australian wine. The lodge is the starting point for four-wheel-drive trips into otherwise inaccessible national park rain forest. ⊠ *Finlayvale Rd., Mossman Gorge, 4873,* ☎ *07/4098–1666,* FAX *07/4098–1983. 35 rooms with bath and shower, 25 rooms with spa. Restaurant, bar, pool, tennis court, library. AE, DC, MC, V.*

En Route New species of fauna and flora are still being discovered in **Daintree Rainforest,** and the tropical vegetation is as impressive as anything found in the Amazon Basin. Collect information and maps for exploring from park rangers, since you'll need to detour off the main road to find the best areas for walking. You'll want to explore part of the area in a four-wheel-drive vehicle. Some of the rain forest tracks are unpaved and muddy, and it is often necessary to ford streams. There are also guided four-wheel-drive tours, which include walking within the rain forest. Or at least enjoy a ride on a river boat (☞ North from Cairns A to Z, *below*). The national park is 35 km (22 mi) northwest of Mossman.

The intrepid will follow the Mossman–Daintree Road as it winds through sugarcane plantations and towering green hills to the **Daintree River crossing.** The Daintree is a relatively short river, yet it's fed by heavy monsoonal rains that make it wide, glossy, and brown—and a favorite inland haunt for saltwater crocodiles.

The relationship between the area's reptile and human inhabitants is not always harmonious: During a 1985 New Year's Eve party, a local resident was snatched from the bank of the river, and her enraged companions took their revenge on every crocodile they could find. To dramatize the resulting decline in the crocodile population, local tour operator Brian Strike swam across the river at the ferry crossing—with nary a nibble. Although the waters right at the ferry may have been thinned, during most times of the year you won't have to travel far to spot a croc. ▣ *$5 per vehicle.* ☉ *Ferry crossings every 20 min daily 6 AM–midnight.*

On the north bank of the Daintree River, a sign announces the beginning of **Cape Tribulation National Park** (☞ Cape Tribulation, *below*). The gravel road beyond the ferry crossing has been upgraded and paved—increasing tour traffic had been kicking up dust, which was harmful to the forest's rare flora.

Cow Bay

㉚ *17 km (11 mi) northeast of the Daintree River crossing, 47 km (29 mi) north of Mossman.*

The sweep of sand at Cow Bay is fairly typical of the beaches north of the Daintree, with the advantage that the fig trees at the back of the beach offer welcome shade. Follow Buchanans Creek Road north from the Daintree River crossing, which after about 10 km (6 mi) turns toward the sea and Cow Bay.

Dining and Lodging

$ ✕🏨 **Crocodylus Village.** Set in a rain forest clearing about 3 km (2 mi) from Cow Bay, the Village is highly recommended for adventurous or budget-conscious travelers. Guests are accommodated in large, fixed-site tents, which are raised off the ground and enclosed by a waterproof fabric and insect-proof mesh. Some tents are set up as dormitories with bunk beds, others are private with showers. Both styles are basic, but the entire village is neat and well maintained, and it offers an excellent activities program. Restaurant prices are low, and the atmosphere is friendly and relaxed. The village is enormously popular, so reserve ahead, especially in peak season between June and August. ⊠ *Buchanan Creek Rd., Cow Bay,* ☎ *07/4098–9166,* 🆑 *07/4098–9131. 10 dormitory tents, 2 private tents. Restaurant, bar, pool. MC, V.*

Cape Tribulation

③¹ *27 km (17 mi) north of Cow Bay, 34 km (21 mi) north of the Daintree River crossing, 139 km (87 mi) north of Cairns.*

Cape Tribulation was named by Captain James Cook, who was understandably peeved after a nearby reef inflicted a gaping wound in the side of his ship, HMS *Endeavour,* forcing him to seek refuge at the present-day site of Cooktown. To reach the tiny settlement, set dramatically at the base of Mount Sorrow, proceed north from Cow Bay along a road that plays a game of hide-and-seek with the sea, climbing high over the Noah Range before reaching town.

In many ways, Cape Tribulation is a microcosm of Queensland's diverse climates and terrain. Along this undeveloped coastal strip, rain forest, mangroves, coral, and sea all come together, and the waters have their dangerous appeal, with saltwater crocodiles lurking in larger local streams.

The Cape Tribulation settlement, small enough to shoot past in a blink, is the activities and accommodations base for the surrounding national park. You'll find a shop, a couple of lodges, and that's about it. The cape's natural credentials are impeccable, however. Nowhere else on the Australian coastline do coral reef and rain forest exist in such unspoiled proximity—a happy coincidence that the area's relaxed manners enhance. Until recently, the only tourists who came this way were backpackers who holed up in lodges here for a few dollars a night, and tourism in the area still has a casual, back-to-nature feeling. For example, all of the regional tours—including rain forest walks, reef trips, horseback riding, and fishing—can be booked through the village shop. If you'd rather loaf on the beach, the one nearest to town is about a five-minute stroll along a boardwalk that cuts through a mangrove swamp. The beach to the north of Cape Tribulation is more scenic. Keep in mind that swimming in the ocean from October through April is perilous because of the preponderance of marine stingers.

③² **Cape Tribulation National Park** is an ecological wonderland, a remnant of the forests in which flowering plants first appeared on earth—an evolutionary leap that took advantage of insects for pollination and provided an energy-rich food supply for the early marsupials that were replacing the dinosaurs. Experts can readily identify species of angiosperms, the most primitive flowering plant, many of which are found nowhere else on the planet. If you were searching for the most ancient roots of humankind, sooner or later you would find yourself here, in this very forest.

The park stretches along the coast and west into the jungle from Cow Bay to Aytor. The beach is usually empty, except for the tiny soldier crabs that move about by the hundreds and scatter when approached. Hikers exploring the mangroves are likely to see an incredible assortment of small creatures that depend on the trees for survival. Most evident are mudskippers and mangrove crabs, but keen observers may spot green-backed herons crouched among mangrove roots.

The best time to see the rain forest is in the dry season, May through September. Walking along dry creek beds is the best way to explore the forest—*rain forest,* that is. Bring plenty of insect repellent.

Several tour companies in Cairns offer day trips to the rain forest in four-wheel-drive buses and vans. Contact the **Department of Environment** (⊠ 10-12 McLeod St., ☎ 07/4052–3096).

Dining and Lodging

$$$–$$$$ ✕⚏ **Coconut Beach Rainforest Resort.** The most dignified of accommodations at Cape Tribulation sits swathed in a jungle of fan palms, staghorn ferns, giant melaleucas, and strangler figs, about 2 km (1 mi) south of the cape itself. The centerpiece of the resort is the Long House, a striking, pole-frame building that overlooks the main swimming pool. Stay in individual chalets built in 1994 or in less-expensive, older-style rooms, which are clustered in blocks of three. The resort makes much of its eco-awareness, so the rooms are fan-cooled rather than air-conditioned. The beach is only a two-minute walk away, or you can take advantage of an elevated walkway set into the nearby rain forest canopy, the habitat of most local birds. ⊠ *Box 6903, Cairns 4870,* ☎ *07/4098–0033,* ℻ *07/4098–0047. 67 rooms with shower. Restaurant, bar, pool, mountain bikes. AE, DC, MC, V.*

$$$ ✕⚏ **Ferntree Rainforest Resort.** On the site of an earlier backpackers' lodge, this very comfortable Resort was formerly known as Ferntree Lodge. Its large, split-level villas and bungalows are hunkered in the rain forest, close to the beach. They both make the most of the natural environment. ⊠ *Box 7662, Cairns 4870,* ☎ *07/4098–0000,* ℻ *07/ 4098–0099. 22 bungalows, 20 villas, 8 suites. Restaurant, pool, laundry. AE, DC, MC, V.*

$ ⚐ Camping is permitted at **Noah's Beach** for a nominal fee, about 8 km (5 mi) south of Cape Tribulation. Privately run campgrounds and small resorts can be found along the Daintree Road at Myall Creek and Cape Tribulation.

En Route   The **Bloomfield Track** leads north from Cape Tribulation. Less than 30 km (19 mi) long, it is one of the most controversial strips of roadway in Australia, and it still generates powerful passions. The decision in the early '80s to carve a road through the Daintree wilderness provoked one of the most bitter conservation battles of recent memory. The road went through, but the ruckus was instrumental in securing a World Heritage listing for the Daintree, thereby effectively shutting out logging operations. At Cape Tribulation a sign warns that the track is open only to four-wheel-drive vehicles, and although no one will stop you from driving through in a conventional vehicle, the rough passage over the Cowie Range essentially closes the road to all but the most rugged machines.

Bloomfield River

22 km (14 mi) north of Cape Tribulation.

The **Bloomfield River** is subject to tides at the ford, and you must cross the river only when the water level has dropped sufficiently to allow safe crossing. Extreme care is needed because the submerged causeway can be difficult to follow, and it is fairly common for vehicles to topple off.

Dining and Lodging

$$$$ ✗⊞ **Bloomfield Wilderness Lodge.** This lodge sits in rugged surroundings near the mouth of the Bloomfield River and consists of timber bungalows, each of which has a balcony at the front, lots of open latticework, and a ceiling fan. Activities include guided walks, fishing, beachcombing along small but deserted beaches, and croc-spotting cruises on the Bloomfield River. The most convenient access is by plane from Cairns, with the final trip by boat from the Bloomfield River (arranged by the lodge). Rates include all meals. Children under 14 are not accommodated. ⊠ *Box 966, Cairns 4870,* ☎ *07/4035–9166,* ℻ *07/4035– 9180. 17 rooms with bath. Restaurant, bar, pool. AE, DC, MC, V.*

En Route At the Aboriginal settlement of Wujal Wujal on the north bank of the river, make the short detour inland to **Mission Creek Falls,** where the river is safe for swimming. Some 20 minutes' drive north of the Bloomfield River is a great swimming spot: Pull over to the left where a sign identifies the Cedar Bay National Park and walk down the steep gully to a creek; at the bottom of a small cascade is one of the most perfect swimming holes you're ever likely to find.

About 33 km (20 mi) north of Wujal Wujal at the junction of the rain forest and an area of open woodland is the **Lion's Den Hotel,** a pub whose corrugated-iron walls and tree-stump chairs ooze un-self-conscious character. The walls are covered in graffiti, from the simple KIL-ROY WAS HERE variety to the totally scandalous, and for the price of a donation to the Royal Flying Doctor Service, you can add your own wit to the collection. It's easy to pass a pleasant afternoon here just observing who and what wanders in the door.

At the junction of Northern Road—you'll see it called the Bicentennial National Trail on some maps—and the Cooktown Development Road, jumbled piles of rock beside the road identify **Black Mountain National Park.** The distinctive coloration of these granite boulders is caused by a black algae. Climbing the rocks is difficult and dangerous, and there are stinging trees in the area. For the non-adventurous, the formations are best appreciated from the roadside.

Cooktown

③ *96 km (60 mi) north of Cape Tribulation, 235 km (146 mi) north of Cairns.*

Cooktown is the last major settlement on the east coast of the continent. It is a frontier town on the edge of a difficult wilderness, its wide main street consisting mainly of two-story pubs with four-wheelers parked out front. Despite the temporary air, Cooktown has a long and impressive history. It was here in 1770 that Captain James Cook beached the *Endeavour* to repair her hull. Any tour of Cooktown should begin at the waterfront, where a statue of Captain Cook gazes out to sea, overlooking the spot where he landed.

A town was established a hundred years after Cook's landfall when gold was discovered on the Palmer River. Cooktown mushroomed and quickly became the largest settlement in Queensland after Brisbane, but as in many other mining boomtowns, life was hard and often violent. Chinese miners flooded into the goldfields and anti-Chinese sentiment flared into race riots, echoing events that had occurred at every other goldfield in the country. Further conflict arose between miners and local Aborigines, who resented what they saw as a territorial invasion and the rape of the region's natural resources; such place names as Battle Camp and Hell's Gate testify to the pattern of ambush and revenge.

Cooktown is a sleepy shadow of those dangerous days—when it had 64 pubs on a main street 3 km (2 mi) long—but a significant slice of history has been preserved at the **James Cook Historical Museum,** formerly a convent of the Sisters of Mercy. The museum houses relics of the gold-mining era, Chinese settlement, both world wars, Aboriginal artifacts, canoes, and a notable collection of seashells—not to mention artifacts relating to the intriguing story of Mrs. Watson, who escaped from a party of hostile Aborigines on Lizard Island with her son and a Chinese servant in a huge cooking pot, only to perish of thirst on another island. The museum also contains mementos of Cook's voyage, including the anchor and one of the cannons that were jettisoned when the *Endeavour* ran aground. ⊠ *Helen St.,* ☎ *07/4069–5386.* 🖃 *$5.* ⊙ *Daily 10–4.*

Lodging

$$ 🏨 **Sovereign Resort.** This attractive, colonial-style hotel in the heart of town is the best bet in Cooktown. Refurbished and extended in 1997, this two-story timber-and-brick affair with verandas across the front, terra-cotta tiles, and soft-color decor gives the air of a plantation house. Appealing guest rooms trimmed with rustic wooden doors, terra-cotta floor tiles, and bright blues and reds overlook tropical gardens at the rear of the building. ⊠ *Charlotte St.,* ☎ *07/4069–5400. 29 rooms with bath and shower. Restaurant, bar, pool. AE, MC, V.*

En Route   From Cooktown, the northern tip of the Australian mainland is still some 800 km (500 mi) distant via the road that runs along the middle of Cape York. Access to the **Cape York Peninsula** used to be granted to only a lucky (or crazy) few, but new roads now make it relatively easy to travel in a four-wheel-drive vehicle from Cairns right to the tip of the Cape.

North from Cairns A to Z

Arriving and Departing

BY BUS

Coral Coaches (☎ 07/4031–7577) runs buses between Cairns, Port Douglas, and Cape Tribulation.

KCT Connections (☎ 07/4031–2990) operates package tours that include bus transport from Cairns and overnight dormitory accommodations at either the Jungle Lodge or Crocodylus Village in Cow Bay (☞ *above*). Cost of a one-night stay is $74; two nights is $86.

Strikies Safaris (☎ 07/4099–5599) operates an air-conditioned bus service between Cairns and Cooktown along the inland route.

BY CAR

To head north by car from Cairns, take Florence Street from the Esplanade for four blocks and then turn right into Sheridan Street, which is the beginning of northbound Highway 1. Highway 1 leads past the airport and forks 12 km (7 mi) north of Cairns; take the right fork for Cook Highway, which goes as far as Mossman. From Mossman, the turnoff for the Daintree River crossing is 29 km (17 mi) north on the Daintree–Mossman Road. Except for four-wheel-drive vehicles, rental cars are not permitted on the narrow, twisting road north of the Daintree River.

Hinterland Aviation (☎ 07/4035–9323) links Cairns with Cow Bay—the airport for Cape Tribulation—and the Bloomfield River. The flight to Cow Bay costs $60 per person each way. To Bloomfield, the cost is $75. Both airfields are isolated dirt strips, and passengers must arrange onward transport to their destination in advance. In-flight coastal views are spectacular.

Getting Around

The **Coral Coaches** bus (☎ 07/4031–7577) travels between the Daintree Ferry crossing and Cape Tribulation twice daily in each direction.

Contacts and Resources

CAR RENTAL

Avis (☎ 07/4051–5911) has four-wheel-drive Toyota Landcruisers for rent from Cairns; the cost varies daily depending on availability of vehicles. For other car rental information, *see* Cairns A to Z, *above.*

EMERGENCIES

Be advised that doctors, ambulances, firefighters, and police are scarce to nonexistent between the Daintree River and Cooktown.

Ambulance, fire brigade, and **police.** ☎ *000.*
Mossman Police. ☎ *07/4098–1200.*
Port Douglas Police. ☎ *07/4099–5220.*
Mossman District Hospital. ☎ *07/4098–2444.*
Cooktown Hospital. ✉ *07/4069–5433.*

GUIDED TOURS

Australian Wilderness Safari has a one-day wildlife and wilderness trip into Cape Tribulation National Park—as well as tours of the Daintree Rainforest—aboard air-conditioned four-wheel-drive vehicles. All tours are led by naturalists and include use of binoculars and reference books. Morning tea or lunch is included. This is one of the longest-established rain forest tours and one of the best. ☎ *07/4098–1766.* ▧ *From Cairns $120, from Port Douglas $110.*

The **Crocodile Express** is a flat-bottom boat, which cruises the Daintree River on crocodile-spotting excursions. The boat departs from the Daintree River crossing at 9:30, 10:30, and 2:30 for a one-hour cruise. Trips also depart from the Daintree Eco Centre, 3 km (2 mi) upstream from the village of Daintree, hourly from 9:30 to 3:30 for a two-hour cruise. ☎ *07/4098–6120.* ▧ *1-hr cruise $12, 1½-hr cruise $15.*

Kuku-Yalanji Dreamtime Tours. Kuku-Yalanji Aborigines are the indigenous inhabitants of the land between Cooktown in the north, Chillagoe in the west, and Port Douglas in the south. Guides from this tribe will take you on a one-hour walk through stunning rain forest and point out such significant features as cave paintings and special Aboriginal sites. They also tell you about traditional bush tucker and medicine. Afterward, tea and damper are served under a bark warun (shelter), where you can chat with your guide and ask questions. ✉ *Gorge Rd., 24 km (15 mi) northwest of Port Douglas,* ☎ *07/4098–1305.* ▧ *$15.* ⊙ *Weekdays 8:30–5; walks at 10, 11:30, 1, and 2:30.*

Native Guide Safari Tours is operated by Hazel Douglas, an Aboriginal woman whose knowledge and passion for her ancestral homeland—which extends from Mossman to Cooktown—set this one-day tour apart. After departing from Port Douglas, you'll sample some of the edible flora of the Daintree region, learn how Aboriginal people maintained the balance of the rain forest ecosystem, and hear legends that have been passed down over thousands of years. Be sure to pack swimwear, insect repellent, and good walking shoes. A maximum of 11 passengers is allowed on each tour. ☎ FAX 07/4098–2206 or ☎ 07/4099–4144. ✉ *$105 ($115 from Cairns) includes picnic lunch.*

Strikies Safaris operates a two-day, four-wheel-drive safari along the coast from Cairns to Cooktown. ☎ 07/4099–5599. ✉ *$199, excluding accommodations.*

VISITOR INFORMATION
Cooktown Travel. ✉ *Charlotte St., Cooktown,* ☎ 07/4069–5377.

8 The Great Barrier Reef

Lady Elliot Island

Lady Musgrave Island

Heron and Wilson Islands

Great Keppel Island

Brampton Island

Lindeman Island

Long Island

Hamilton Island

South Molle Island

Daydream Island

Hayman Island

Orpheus Island

Dunk Island

Bedarra Island

Fitzroy Island

Lizard Island

MORE THAN 2,000 km (1,200 mi) long and as much as 80 km (50 mi) wide, the Great Barrier Reef parallels the Queensland seaboard from the Sunshine Coast near Brisbane as far north as Papua New Guinea. It is the world's largest living organism, composed of billions of coral polyps whose structures shelter countless plants and animals. The Great Barrier Reef is the richest marine resource in the world—and you won't find more remarkable diving and snorkeling anywhere on earth. Much of the reef has been incorporated into the Great Barrier Reef Marine Park, and strict laws govern its preservation. At the same time, the reef is attracting more and more vacationers, to whom a host of island resorts now cater. Although the islands that these resorts occupy are billed as Great Barrier islands, most are not on the reef at all but close to shore. Hamilton Island, for instance, is more than 70 km (43 mi) from the reef. Still, they do have fringing coral, the variety that grows in the islands' sheltered coves and can be every bit as fascinating as the main reef.

Updated by
Jane Carstens

This chapter is arranged in three geographical sections covering islands off the mid-Queensland coast from south to north. The sections group together islands that share a common port or jumping-off point. Addresses for resorts often include the word "via" to indicate which port town to use to reach the island.

Pleasures and Pastimes

Dining

Food is an important part of any vacation. On the Barrier Reef it's likely to be a highlight. Australia's wide open spaces and benign climate produce a remarkable range of fresh produce. The seas and shoals that surround these islands deliver an equally munificent bounty of seafoods: crayfish, scallops, and countless fish feature on most menus.

At many resorts, rates include all meals, which are served in the dining room, although outdoor barbecues and seafood buffets are also commonplace. Some resorts offer more than one choice of restaurant, as well as a premium restaurant for which you pay extra. Keep in mind that special package rates are generally available.

CATEGORY	COST*
$$$$	over $50
$$$	$40–$50
$$	$30–$40
$	under $30

*per person, excluding drinks and service

Island Time

Life in and around the reefs may be the reason that most people visit Queensland's island chain, but flora and fauna on the islands themselves can be fascinating. Some islands have rain forests, or hills and rocky areas, or those postcard perfect beaches. In other words there is more to do on land than just relax—the choice is yours.

Lodging

You can't exactly pick and choose among different hotels on a Great Barrier Reef island—a resort and its island are basically one entity. So choose an island based on your taste and budget. Many islands cater to those wanting peace and tranquillity, whereas others attract a crowd wanting just the opposite. An island generally has only one resort, although the resort may offer a variety of accommodations.

The Great Barrier Reef

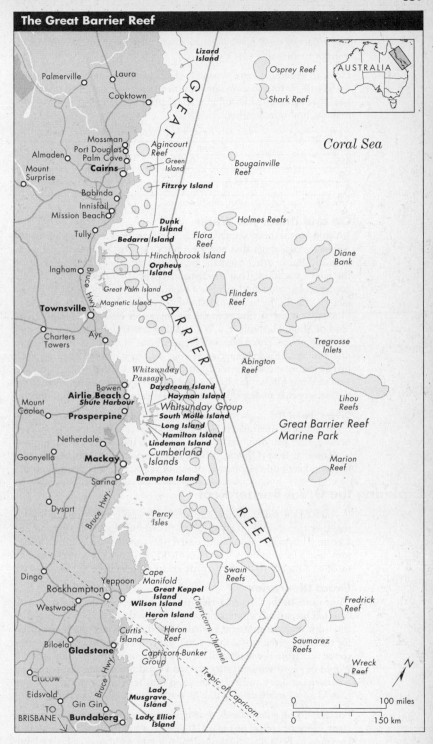

Lizard Island

Osprey Reef

Shark Reef

AUSTRALIA

Coral Sea

Palmerville
Laura
Cooktown

Mossman
Port Douglas
Almaden
Palm Cove
Cairns
Mount Surprise

Agincourt Reef
Green Island
Bougainville Reef

Fitzroy Island

Babinda
Innisfail
Mission Beach
Tully

Dunk Island
Bedarra Island
Flora Reef
Holmes Reefs

Hinchinbrook Island
Orpheus Island

Ingham
Great Palm Island
Magnetic Island

Diane Bank

Flinders Reef

Townsville

Charters Towers
Ayr

Tregrosse Inlets

Whitsunday Passage
Daydream Island
Hayman Island
Whitsunday Group
South Molle Island
Long Island
Hamilton Island
Lindeman Island
Cumberland Islands

Abington Reef

Lihou Reefs

Bowen
Airlie Beach
Shute Harbour
Prosperpine

Great Barrier Reef Marine Park

Mount Coolon

Netherdale

Goonyella
Mackay
Sarina

Brampton Island

Marion Reef

Dysart

Percy Isles

R E E F

Dingo
Cape Manifold
Yeppoon
Rockhampton
Westwood

Swain Reefs

Great Keppel Island
Wilson Island
Heron Island

Fredrick Reef

Curtis Island
Heron Reef
Capricorn Channel

Biloela
Gladstone

Capricorn-Bunker Group

Saumarez Reefs

Clucow
Eidsvold
Tropic of Capricorn

Wreck Reef

Gin Gin
Lady Musgrave Island

TO BRISBANE
Bundaberg
Lady Elliot Island

Bruce Hwy.

G R E A T   B A R R I E R

0   100 miles
0   150 km

With some exceptions, such sporting activities as sailing, snorkeling, and tennis are normally included in basic rates. However, trips to the Great Barrier Reef, fishing charters, scuba diving, and other sports requiring fuel usually cost extra.

Dress in general is resort casual, which for everyone is the next step up from T-shirts and jeans. As for amenities, rooms in most resorts are equipped with air-conditioning, telephones, televisions, tea and coffee makers, and refrigerators.

CATEGORY	COST*
$$$$	over $400
$$$	$300–$400
$$	$150–$300
$	under $150

All prices are for a standard double room.

On and Under the Water

Visiting any of these islands by definition requires a journey across the water. In some cases that may be a ferry ride (or a flight) of just a few minutes. But in other cases the trip to the island can be a highlight of the whole vacation. That's particularly true if you elect to fly by helicopter to Heron Island or pick a window seat for the flight to Lizard Island: you'll take in a wonderland of reefs and coral cays layered in blue and turquoise. But even taking the water taxi from Hamilton Island or Shute Harbour to a Whitsunday resort will demonstrate why so many people come here and charter a yacht to cruise the Whitsunday Passage. Once you arrive at your resort, it's very tempting to let inertia set in and stay settled until it's time to leave—but try not to. You've come all the way to Queensland, so get out on the water to see the variety that makes this string of islands and islets so special.

Divers' note: If you are certified or plan to get certification for scuba diving while in Australia, bring a physician's statement from home confirming that you don't have any conditions that would endanger you underwater. Resort diving, where you are paired off with an instructor who keeps an eye on you, does not require medical certification.

Exploring the Great Barrier Reef

If you had the time, money, and patience, you could string a holiday together that would take you to all the island resorts of this chapter. The map linking these various coastal ports and offshore resorts would look like a lace-up boot 1,600 km (1,000 mi) long. It would also take most of a month to do if you only spent a night in each place.

Great Itineraries

Most visits to the Great Barrier Reef combine time on an island with time in Queensland's mainland towns and parks. But keep in mind that staying a night or more on any island will give you a much better feel for this part of the world than you'll get from any number of day trips to the reef from the mainland. With a week or more on your hands, it would be worthwhile to stay on two very different islands: perhaps a southern coral cay and a mountainous northern one, in which case you should allow as much as a day to get from one island to the next.

For divers, consider islands that have fringing reef around them, like Lady Elliot or Heron or Lizard. If you're after the good life, look into Hayman or Bedarra or Lizard islands. If you want to do a little island-hopping, pick the closely arranged Whitsunday Group islands.

IF YOU HAVE 1 DAY
Take an early boat from **Cairns** to **Fitzroy Island,** or from **Shute Harbour** to **Daydream Island.** Spend a couple of hours snorkeling, take a walk around the island to get a look at island wilds, then find a quiet beach for a daydream afternoon. Or take a boat to a pontoon on the outer reef for a day on and in the water. A helicopter flight back will provide an astounding view of the reef and islands from above.

IF YOU HAVE 3 DAYS
Pick one island that has the water sports and on-land activities you appreciate—flora and fauna, beaches and pools, or resort nightlife—and give yourself a taste of everything. Carefully choosing an island will allow you to enjoy every moment while you're there.

IF YOU HAVE 7 OR MORE DAYS
Planning a full week on an island means that you're probably a serious diver, a serious lounger, or both. So pick an island that has fringing coral, such as **Lady Elliot, Heron,** or **Lizard,** plan to spend a day or two out on the reef itself, and you'll have the diving experience of a lifetime. If you take more time on an island, choose one that has terrain to explore and great beaches.

When to Tour the Great Barrier Reef

The great majority of Barrier Reef islands lie north of the Tropic of Capricorn and have a distinctly monsoonal climate. In summer, expect some tropical downpours during your trip, but they are unlikely to last more than a few hours. And count on it being hot everywhere—hotter the farther north you go. If you're aiming for a northern island, you'll find that the warm days, clear skies, and balmy nights of winter are ideal. If you choose an island on the southern end of the chain, keep in mind that some winter days are too cool for swimming, and summertime is deliciously hot, with no lack of the attendant thunderstorms of a subtropical climate.

Remember that Australian seasons are the reverse of the northern hemisphere: summer runs from December to February, winter from June through August. North of the Tropic of Capricorn, daytime temperatures in winter rarely fall below 81°F (27°C).

MACKAY–CAPRICORN ISLANDS

Lady Elliot Island

★ Lady Elliot is a 100-acre coral cay on the southern tip of the Great Barrier Reef, lying within easy reach of Bundaberg on the Queensland coast. Fringed on all sides by the reef and graced with a white coral beach, this oval isle is diving heaven. Its clear, calm waters afford superb views of schools of mantas, turtles, morays, wobbegong sharks, and millions of tropical fish. If you want to get away from it all, wildlife easily outnumbers the 140 guests on this vacation spot. Even the top-level lodgings pale in comparison to those on other islands. And Lady Elliot is one of the few islands in the area where camping (modified) is part of the resort's offering. There are no televisions, there's only one guest telephone, and social activities revolve around diving, reef walking, and the island's lively bar and restaurant. Between October and April, Lady Elliot becomes a busy breeding ground for birds and sea turtles.

Dining and Lodging

$$ ✕🏨 **Lady Elliot Island Resort.** Don't go to Lady Elliot if you're looking for luxury. You'll stay in simple waterfront cabins with polished wood floors. The cabins are sparsely furnished with plastic chairs and

pine furniture and are serviced at least twice weekly. Campers stay in permanent oceanfront safari tents and share facilities. Dinner and breakfast are included in the basic price and served in the dining room; they tend to be simple (with an emphasis on grilled dishes, salads, and seafood) and served buffet style. ⌗ *Box 206, Torquay, Queensland 4655,* ☏ *071/25–5344 or 1800/07–2200. 24 rooms with shower, 14 tent-cabins, 6 lodge rooms. Pool, 2 bars, laundry. AE, DC, MC, V.*

Outdoor Activities and Sports

Certified divers can rent equipment at the resort's dive shop. Scuba-diving lessons can be arranged through Lady Elliot's excellent dive school for $440 per person. Visitors coming for this five-day program must plan to stay from Sunday to Saturday and bring a medical report and two passport photos. In addition, the resort offers reef walks, glass-bottom boat rides ($10), and island walks.

Arriving and Departing

BY PLANE
Lady Elliot is the only coral cay with its own airstrip. Small aircraft make the 80-km (50-mi) flight from Hervey Bay, Bundaberg, and Gladstone, coastal towns about 320 km (200 mi) north of Brisbane. Daily flights run from Bundaberg, Hervey Bay, and Brisbane. A round-trip fare for the 30-minute flight from Bundaberg or the 35-minute flight from Hervey Bay to Lady Elliot on **Whitaker Air** (☏ 071/25–5344 or 800/07–2200) costs $130. There are strict limitations on luggage—only 22 pounds per person are allowed. Be sure to confirm your transfer flight to the island with Whitaker Air as you cannot arrive on the island by boat.

Day Trips

You can arrange a day trip to Lady Elliot through the resort. It will include the flight, lunch, a glass-bottom boat ride, a reef walk (if tides are appropriate), and snorkeling gear. The cost is $120 per person from Bundaberg or Hervey Bay for the flight, lunch, and use of snorkeling gear (☏ 071/25–5344 or 1800/07–2200).

Lady Musgrave Island

Lady Musgrave Island sits at the southern end of the Great Barrier Reef Marine Park about 40 km (25 mi) north of Lady Elliot Island. The island is a true coral cay of 35 acres—just 500 yards wide—and it is surrounded by 5 km (3 mi) of coral reef and a massive, 3,000-acre safe lagoon. When day-trippers, yachties, divers, and campers converge, traffic on Lady Musgrave gets heavy. But the island offers some of the best diving and snorkeling in Queensland. In quiet times campers have a chance to come to terms with the great variety of life surrounding a tiny speck of land in the Pacific.

In summer (November through March), the island is a bird and turtle rookery. You can expect to find such species as white-capped noddies, wedge-tailed shearwaters, and green and loggerhead turtles. There is also an abundance of flora, including cassurina and pisonia trees.

Camping

The island is uninhabited and has only basic facilities (one toilet block and emergency radio equipment) for campers. Camping permits are available from the Queensland Marine Park Authority (☏ 079/76–0766) at a cost of $2 per person per night. Because numbers are restricted to 50 people, early bookings are advisable. Commercial tour operators will transport all camping equipment (including a small dinghy) and deliver fresh water, milk, bread, and other supplies on their regular trips.

Arriving and Departing

You can reach the island on the catamaran **MV *Lady Musgrave,*** or the trimaran **MV *Spirit of Musgrave,*** which depart from **Port Bundaberg** 20 minutes northeast of Bundaberg, each Monday, Tuesday, Wednesday, Thursday, and Saturday at 8:30 AM, returning at 5:45 PM. The trip takes 2½ hours in each direction and costs $105 for day-trippers, $205 for campers to secure return passage. Scuba diving (including equipment) is an extra $50. Coach pickup from accommodations in Bundaberg is available for $7 per person. ⊠ *1 Quay St., Bundaberg,* ☎ *07/ 4152–9011 or 1800/07–2110.*

Bundaberg Seaplane Tours. The flight ($165 per person round-trip) from Bundaberg to Lady Musgrave takes about 30 minutes and seats up to four passengers. Pickup from your accommodation is included, and a picnic lunch is served on the island. ☎ *07/4155–2068.*

Heron Island

★   Whereas most resort islands lie well inside the shelter of the distant reef, Heron, the most famous of the Queensland islands, is actually part of the reef. Seventy km (43 mi) northeast of Gladstone, Heron is ideal if you want to learn about indigenous life on a coral island.

Thousands of green turtles and a large number of loggerhead turtles make their home there, and the island becomes a vast breeding ground in October and November. Staff from the resort will escort you out to watch the turtles come ashore, nest, and lay their eggs. In February and March you can watch the last eggs being laid and the first hatchlings emerge. Between July and October (September is best), humpback whales pass here on their journey from the Antarctic.

The waters are spectacular, teeming with fish and coral, and ideal for snorkeling. The area around the channel leading to the resort is particularly good. Farther out toward the reef the ocean becomes more agitated, with a consequent loss of visibility. The water is clearest during June and July and cloudiest during the rainy season from January through March.

Heron Island is also a breeding ground for thousands of birds, including noddy terns, reef herons (hence the island's name), and silver gulls. You'll never be far from the sound or smell of birds.

You won't find a wide range of activities and entertainment on Heron, as on some other islands. And its 40 acres house a maximum of 250 people in Heron Island Resort, the island's only accommodation. But those might be reasons that you decide to come here.

You can visit **Wilson Island,** another Great Barrier Reef Marine Park coral cay, on a day trip from Heron Island. Ten km (6 mi) to the south, it's an attractive adjunct of the Heron Island Resort, which controls access to it. In January and February, Wilson Island becomes the breeding ground for roseate terns.

Dining and Lodging

$$$–$$$$ ✕⊡ **Heron Island Resort.** Set among palm trees and connected by sand paths, the accommodations here range from simple cabins with shared bathrooms to large, comfortable suites. With private balconies, cane furniture, and pastel or vibrant reef-inspired decor, the modern suites are worth the extra expense. There are no telephones or TVs in guest rooms. An airy bar and a coffee shop whose seaward side is made primarily of glass were added in 1992. These are the best spots to wind down after a day outdoors—organized entertainment here is sparse,

although the resort does screen excellent movies about the reef and diving. Meals are included in the resort's basic rate, but food isn't going to lure you away from the reef. The restaurant serves typical island cuisine, with an emphasis on salads, barbecued seafood, and steaks. Breakfast and lunch are served buffet style. ⊠ *P&O Resorts, Level 10, 160 Sussex St., Sydney, NSW 2000,* ☎ *13–2469; 408/335–4954 or 800/225–9849 in the U.S. 1 beach house, 86 suites, 30 cabins. Restaurant, bar, pool, tennis courts, laundry. AE, DC, MC, V.*

Outdoor Activities and Sports
Snorkeling and diving lessons are offered by the dive shop. Open-water diving courses are available for about $395. The resort also offers excursions for experienced divers: One-tank boat dives cost about $35; three-day packages are available for $192.

Nondivers who want to explore the reef's underwater world can board a semisubmersible sub that offers tours from Heron Island twice daily, or go on one of the guided reef walks. Heron also has a large pool, table tennis, tennis courts, and a game room.

Beach fishing and spear fishing are prohibited.

Arriving and Departing
BY BOAT

The *Reef Adventurer* (☎ 079/72–5166), a high-speed catamaran, has a two-hour run to Heron Island from **Gladstone** for $72 one way or $144 round-trip. The trip can be rough, and some visitors have problems with gas fumes and seasickness.

BY HELICOPTER

Lloyd's Helicopter Service (☎ 079/78–1177) has a 20-minute helicopter flight to Heron Island from Gladstone, a town on the Queensland coast, for $228 one way or $377 round-trip. The baggage restriction is 15 kg (33 lb) per person and one piece of hand luggage. Lockup facilities for excess baggage are available free of charge.

Great Keppel Island

Over the years the Great Keppel Island Resort has garnered a reputation similar to Fort Lauderdale's at spring break. Crowds are smaller, but it is a party place. Guests tend to be young singles, although the resort does draw its share of young families. Like its sister resort at Dunk Island (☞ *below*), Great Keppel has a following that returns year after year. Only 13 km (8 mi) off the coast and 48 km (30 mi) northeast of Rockhampton, the island was originally a sheep station, and the old homestead remains on the hill that overlooks the island. Great Keppel is large—8 km (5 mi) wide and 11 km (7 mi) long—and there are several private residences in addition to the resort. Unfortunately, it's 40 km (25 mi) from the Great Barrier Reef, which makes any trip out there lengthy. It does have a fair amount to offer, though, both on shore and off: 17 stunning beaches, a wide array of walks and trails, and excellent coral growth in many sheltered coves. An underwater observatory at nearby Middle Island allows you to watch marine life without getting wet. A confiscated Taiwanese fishing boat has been sunk alongside the observatory to provide shelter to myriad tropical fish.

Dining and Lodging
$–$$ ✕⊡ **Great Keppel Island Resort.** The bungalows and two-story accommodations of Great Keppel stand among gardens (adjacent to the airstrip) and extend up the island's hills. Rooms are comfortable and decorated in cheery pinks and greens, with natural timber and spacious balconies. The Hillside Villas are air-conditioned and have wonderful

views but are some distance from the beach. The Admiral Keppel restaurant, set in a large, open room overlooking the beach and the bay, has both smorgasbord and à la carte dining. The menu is a mélange of Continental and island cooking and changes daily according to the availability of fresh ingredients. Barbecues and buffets predominate, and there are occasional theme dinners. ⊠ *CMB, Great Keppel Island, Rockhampton, Queensland 4702,* ☎ *079/39–5044, 800/227–4411 in the U.S. 192 rooms with shower. 4 bars, 3 pools, 3 tennis courts, 6-hole golf course, squash. AE, DC, MC, V.*

Outdoor Activities and Sports

Great Keppel Island offers almost every conceivable sport. Included in the basic rate are snorkeling, fishing, sailing, windsurfing, tennis, squash, golf, archery, basketball, baseball, volleyball, and badminton. You'll pay an extra fee for any activity that requires fuel, including island cruises, Barrier Reef cruises, motor boating, and parasailing. Camel rides along the beach, tandem skydiving, and scuba-diving lessons are also available.

Arriving and Departing

BY BOAT

Keppel Tourist Services (☎ 079/33–6744) has two vessels that serve the island from **Rosslyn Harbour** near Rockhampton and Yeppoon. It also operates a round-trip coach pickup ($13) between Rockhampton hotels and Rosslyn Harbour. The *Spirit of Keppel* departs at 11:30 and 3:30 and costs $20 each way or $25 return. The larger *Reefcat* departs at 9:15, and it stops at a purpose-built pontoon near the island for snorkeling and swimming. A tour of the underwater observatory costs $10 for guests and nonguests alike.

BY PLANE

Qantas (☎ 13–1313) offers connecting flights from **Rockhampton** to the island for $82.50 each way.

Brampton Island

Actually part of the Cumberland Islands near the southern entrance to the Whitsunday Passage, 195-acre Brampton Island is one of the prettiest in the area. Seven coral-and-white sandy beaches ring the island, and the hilly interior's rain forests are populated by kangaroos, colorful rainbow lorikeets, and butterflies. Most of the island is designated national park. The resort has a loyal clientele that returns annually, attracted by a vacation style far less structured than on other resort isles. There is live entertainment every evening and a variety of theme nights, dancing, and floor shows. The biggest attraction, of course, is the water—especially snorkeling over the reef between Brampton and adjoining Carlisle islands.

Dining and Lodging

$–$$ ✕🏨 **Brampton Island Resort.** Popular with overseas visitors in the 30 to 50 age group, this resort offers comfort and quiet. Rooms are in large, Polynesian-style buildings, many of which directly face the beach. High ceilings and verandas give rooms an airy atmosphere, which is enhanced by rattan furniture, ceiling fans, and soft gray-and-pink decor. Some rooms are as high as 10 ft off the ground, allowing ocean breezes to waft underneath. The restaurant at Brampton Island serves a buffet breakfast, smorgasbord lunch, and an à la carte dinner featuring local seafoods. Meal packages can be purchased for $75 for breakfast, lunch, and dinner, or $55 for breakfast and dinner only. An "Island Night" is held Saturday, during which the chefs prepare a huge seafood dinner. They will also cook any fish you catch. The dining room is part of the entertainment complex that overlooks the main beach, with magnificent views of the Whitsunday Passage. Keep in mind that you can also arrange beach picnics. ⊠ *Brampton Island, via Mackay, Queensland 4740,* ☎ *079/51–4499, 800/227–4411 in the U.S.,* 𝔽𝔸𝕏 *079/51–4097. 108 rooms with shower. 2 bars, 2 pools, golf, laundry. AE, DC, MC, V.*

Outdoor Activities and Sports
Brampton Island's huge array of facilities and activities includes free tennis courts, a six-hole golf course, archery, table tennis, beach volleyball, snorkeling, sailing, and windsurfing. For an extra charge, the resort also has fishing trips, waterskiing, and tube rides.

Arriving and Departing
BY BOAT
Roylen Cruises (☎ 079/55–3066) has daily service from **Mackay** to Brampton Island on the *Spirit of Roylen* for $50 per adult and $25 per child round-trip. Boats leave daily at 9 AM.

BY PLANE
Qantas (☎ 13–1313) flies to Brampton via the coastal town of **Mackay** for $79.50 one way. From Mackay, passengers make the 35-km (22-mi) flight to Brampton aboard a Twin Otter light aircraft.

Guided Tours
Brampton Island is 50 km (31 mi) from the Great Barrier Reef. Fast-cat outer reef day trips aboard the *Spirit of Roylen* depart Monday, Wednesday, and Friday at 10:15; return at 4:30; and cost $75. The Waiben Day Cruise takes people to nearby islands for $85. You can also take the Bushy Atoll trip ($190), which involves catching a seaplane to the outer Reef, landing on the water, then snorkeling over the coral (wet suit hire $10). A two- to three-hour fishing trip ($20) aboard a glass-bottom boat departs twice weekly; the cost includes bait, tackle, and, in the evening, a chef's preparation of your own catch of the day in the Salt Water Rocks Cafe.

CENTRAL ISLANDS

Lindeman Island

Lindeman Island is one of the largest islands (2,000 acres) of the Whitsunday Group. More than half of the island is national park, with 20 km (12 mi) of walking trails that wind through tropical growth and up hills that reward a climb with fantastic views. Bird-watching is excellent here, and yet the blue tiger butterflies that you can see in Butterfly Valley may be even more impressive than the birds. Seven sandy beaches and superb snorkeling around the fringing reefs are added attractions. The island is located 40 km (25 mi) northeast of Mackay at the southern entrance to the Whitsunday Passage.

The **Club Med Village** runs a Petit Club for children ages 1 to 3, a Mini-Club for children ages 4 to 7, and a Kids' Club for those 8 to 12 (but there are no care facilities for children under 1 year). Swimming, tennis, and archery are among the planned events, and there are also hikes into the national park and boat trips around the island.

Dining and Lodging
$$$ ✕🏨 **Club Med Lindeman Island.** This resort sits on the southern end of the island and has rain-forest plantings of palm trees in its grounds. All rooms in the building's three floors overlook the sea (each has a balcony or patio), and all border the beach and pool. Away from the main village are the golf clubhouse, sports center, disco, and restau-

rant. Entertainment includes cabaret shows in the theater. ⊠ *Club Med, Lindeman Island via Mackay, Queensland 4741,* ☎ *079/46–9333,* FAX *070/46–9598. 224 rooms with shower or shower and bath. Restaurant, 4 bars, 2 pools, laundry. AE, DC, MC, V.*

Outdoor Activities and Sports

Club Med includes in the basic price use of its six lighted tennis courts, paddle skis, snorkeling equipment, catamarans, and Windsurfers, as well as archery, cricket, volleyball, basketball, football, badminton, hiking, aquagym, and aerobics.

Lindeman has one of the most picturesque nine-hole golf courses anywhere. For an additional fee, resort and refresher scuba diving courses are provided, and there are diving excursions to the outer reef by air (30 minutes each way) and boat (two hours each way).

Arriving and Departing

BY BOAT

Boats regularly serve the island from the small port at **Shute Harbour** (36 km/22 mi east of Proserpine), which is the major coastal access point for all the resorts in the Whitsunday region. The trip takes about an hour and costs $24 one-way or $44 round-trip. There are also direct half-hour water-taxi transfers from Hamilton Island airport (☎ 079/46–9333).

BY PLANE

Island Air Taxis (☎ 079/46–9933) planes fly to the Lindeman airstrip upon demand. The one-way cost is $75 from Proserpine, $55 from Shute Harbour, $40 from Hamilton Island, and $95 from Mackay.

Long Island

This aptly named, narrow mainland island lies just off the coast south of Shute Harbour. Although it's 40 km (26 mi) long, it's a mere 655 ft wide at the Palm Bay resort. It has large areas of thick, undisturbed rain forest, which is protected as national parkland, through which there are walking trails. Over the years the island has seen several styles of resort; the most dramatic conclusion to any of them came when the original Palm Bay, which opened in 1933, was leveled by a cyclone in 1970. Today there are two very different resorts here.

Dining and Lodging

$$ ✕🔟 **Club Crocodile Long Island Resort.** A constant stream of guests flies into the Hamilton Island airport, then takes the transfer boat to this resort. Previously known as Whitsunday Long Island Resort, it is geared to families, and has child care facilities available. It's not the place to go for a quiet time communing with nature, because all interest is directed outdoors, particularly in water sports. ⊠ *PMB 26, via Mackay, Queensland 4740,* ☎ *079/46–9400,* FAX *079/46–9555. 160 units with shower. Restaurant, café, grill, pool, sauna, spa, tennis, exercise room, laundry. AE, DC, MC, V.*

$$ ✕🔟 **Palm Bay.** Much smaller than the Club Crocodile resort, Palm Bay is also much quieter. The six Polynesian-style bungalows and eight cabins stand scattered along a sandy beach near a large bay. You have the choice of taking an accommodations package that includes meals in the restaurant (more home-style than haute), or paying a room-only rate and purchasing individual meals, or buying supplies at the resort's Island Trader store. The store has reasonable prices and a fair selection—but if you crave something particular, you'd better bring it along. All nonmotorized activities are included in the rate, such as canoeing, paddle skiing, and windsurfing. ⊠ *Palm Bay Hideaway, PMB 28, via Mackay, Queensland 4740,* ☎ FAX *079/46–9233 or 1800/33–4009. 14 units with shower. Pool, spa, cooking facilities, laundry. AE, DC, MC, V.*

Arriving and Departing

BY BOAT

Reach Long Island by **Whitsunday All Over and Water Taxi** (☎ 079/
46–9499) from either **Shute Harbour** or **Hamilton Island.** Boats leave
Shute Harbour at 7:15, 9:15, 1:30, 4, and 5:15, and the 15-minute trip
costs $24 round-trip. A water taxi meets each flight into Hamilton Is-
land, and the 30- to 45-minute transfer to either resort costs $41 one
way for adults.

Hamilton Island

Originally, the construction of this resort island was surrounded with
controversy: The original developer paid scant attention to conservationists, dynamiting the top off one of the hills to make a helipad, building a seawall to prevent the tides from draining the swimming area,
dredging a boat marina, erecting a high-rise apartment tower, and
then removing the side of another hill to accommodate a runway for
what would be the Whitsundays' major airport. Despite its shaky
start, over 80 percent of this Whitsunday group island has been carefully preserved in its natural state, which translates into beautiful
beaches, native bush trails, and spectacular lookouts.

The island has the greatest range of activities and amenities of any
Queensland resort. In addition to an extensive sports complex and Barrier Reef excursions, there are six different types of accommodation,
10 restaurants, a full range of shops and boutiques, and a 200-acre
fauna park. The nightlife ranges from Bohemes Dance Club, which
swings into the wee hours three nights a week, to the Mantaray Café.

Hamilton Island is divided into two distinct areas: the resort—a combination of high-rise and cottage accommodations that overlook Catseye Beach—and the boat harbor—flanked by restaurants, shops, an
ice cream parlor, a fish-and-chips carryout, and the best bakery in the
Whitsundays. The whole complex is in the midst of a $40 million re-
development program, started in late 1996, so some accommodations
and restaurants may be closed while they are being refurbished.

☾ The **Hamilton Island Day Care** (☎ 079/46–9999, ext. 8546) caters to
children 4 years old and younger with a range of organized activities
supervised by a qualified staff. **Kid's Club** is for 5- to 14-year-olds, and
activities include indoor-outdoor basketball, arts and crafts, snorkeling, fishing, tennis, and Sega Mega Drive. Programs are included in
the rates, but are subject to availability.

Dining

$$$ ✕ **Outrigger Restaurant.** Large glass panels with louvered windows give
this elegant restaurant an unobstructed view of Catseye Beach. High
timber ceilings and plenty of tile and wood set the scene for predom-
inantly French cuisine, which is largely set to work on seafood. Try
such innovative dishes as Naga à la Nage, poached salmon served with
its own cooking bouillon, pink peppercorns, cucumber, and basil;
Coupe Mont Blanc, fresh fruit sorbets doused with champagne and al-
mond tile biscuits; *coquillage en feuillette,* a puff-pastry boat filled with
oysters, scallops, and lobster on julienne of leeks all set on champagne
and green peppercorn sauce; or *langouste grillée aux petites légumes
et sauce Robert,* grilled lobster with vegetables and Dijon mustard sauce.
✉ *Main resort complex,* ☎ *079/46–9999. AE, DC, MC, V. Closed
Mon. No lunch.*

$$$ ✕ **Romano's Italiano Restaurant.** With polished wood floors and a bal-
cony overlooking the harbor, Romano's is the place to come for a qui-
eter meal. The kitchen produces such dishes as pollo Zeeland (chicken

breasts sautéed with mushrooms) and fettuccine *boscaiola*. ⊠ *Front St., Harbourside,* ☎ *079/46–9999. AE, DC, MC, V.*

$ ✕ **Toucan Tango Restaurant and Bar.** Overlooking the waters of both Catseye Beach and the main resort, this restaurant, formally called Tradewinds Restaurant, features vibrant summer colors, high ceilings, timber furniture, and floor rugs that combine to create a cool, tropical theme. It is the relaxed dining option, with plenty of barbecue dishes, Mediterranean fare and pasta, and a salad and dessert bar. ⊠ *Main resort complex,* ☎ *079/46–9999. AE, DC, MC, V.*

Lodging

Make reservations for all accommodations on Hamilton Island with the Hamilton Island Resort (☎ 1800/07–5110).

$$$$ 🏨 **Hamilton Island Resort.** Overlooking Catseye Beach, this complex has the widest selection of any Queensland island resort: seven types of lodging ranging from high-rise towers to privately owned homes. Guests in all the resort's lodges and towers have access to a host of services and amenities, including a beauty salon, professional masseuse, nightclub, piano bar with live entertainment, art gallery, and doctor. Unlike the rates at many other resorts in the region, those here cover only accommodations, not meals or activities. ⊠ *Hamilton Island Resort, PMB, Post Office, Hamilton Island, Queensland 4803,* ☎ *079/46–9999 or 1800/07–5110,* FAX *079/46–8888. AE, DC, MC, V.*

$$$$ 🏨 **Illalangi.** A privately owned home in the super luxury class, Illalangi is rented by the resort on the owner's behalf. It is a four-bedroom, three-bathroom house with a formal dining area, a breakfast room, and an ultramodern kitchen and laundry room. A landscaped pool and a sauna are located within the grounds. Guests are attended by a butler and have use of a six-seat minibus. A chef and a maid can be hired.

$$$$ 🏨 **Yacht Harbour Towers.** In this unmistakable white high rise overlooking the marina, five owners rent out their four-bedroom apartments during their absence. Although all are furnished differently, each is 3,500 square ft and comes complete with marble floors, a balcony, four bathrooms, a fully equipped kitchen, and a laundry room. The $1,980-per-day rate includes the use of a personal golf cart. *6 apartments with 4 baths each.*

$$–$$$$ 🏨 **Hamilton Towers.** This high rise, completed in August 1990, is the newest complex on the island. Papered in off-white and beige with fawn tiles and blond wood furniture, rooms are enlivened by bedspreads with cool, tropical patterns and dark green curtains. All rooms have two queen-size beds and balconies with ocean views. The towers house a bar, restaurant, and lobby shop. *368 rooms, 18 suites.*

$$$ 🏨 **Bougainvillaea Lodge.** Rooms in the two-story complex overlooking Hamilton's Catseye Beach have tile floors, wicker furniture, and sliding doors onto private balconies. Decorated in earth tones, each room contains two queen-size beds. The complex also has a number of rooms specially designed for guests with disabilities. *60 rooms with shower.*

$$$ 🏨 **Whitsunday Apartments.** Looking out over the Coral Sea toward Whitsunday Island, these twin 13-story towers consist of self-contained apartments. The one-bedroom apartments come complete with fully equipped kitchens, balconies, and dining and sitting areas. Although there is only one bedroom, they can accommodate up to five people with the aid of two sofa beds. *168 apartments with shower.*

$$ 🏨 **Bures.** The steeply sloping roofs and small balconies of this complex resemble Polynesian huts. Each of these small, individual units contains a king-size bed, a small bar, and a furnished patio. *31 units with bath, 20 with shower.*

Outdoor Activities and Sports

Hamilton Island charges a fee for almost all activities. Nevertheless, the resort's sports complex is one of its greatest strengths, with a fully equipped gym, aerobics classes, and squash and tennis courts. The island has one of the largest freshwater swimming pools in the Pacific area, and five smaller pools—one with a spa—are scattered throughout the resort. There is also an 18-hole miniature golf course, a driving range, tandem skydiving, clay pigeon and rifle range shooting, and archery. Reserve ahead through the Tour Booking Desk.

FISHING

The island's deep-sea game fishing boat, *Renegade,* will take you in search of the marlin, sailfish, Spanish mackerel, and tuna that thrive in the waters of the Whitsundays in November. Charters for six people can be arranged through Hamilton Island's Tour Booking Desk. $1,090 full day, $690 half day.

SCUBA DIVING

If you've never dived before, Hamilton has an introductory scuba course, which includes pool instruction, equipment rental, and a dive with a qualified diver. If you are already qualified, all equipment can be rented and a variety of diving trips arranged.

TENNIS

The resort has six floodlit tennis courts. Twice-weekly social nights feature a tennis tournament involving guests and resort pros, followed by cold drinks and steak sandwiches from the barbecue.

WATER SPORTS

You can rent Jet Skis, catamarans, paddle skis, and Windsurfers. Waterskiing, parasailing, and snorkeling are also easily arranged, and instruction is available. Book the above activities through the resort's Tour Booking Desk (☎ 079/46–8535).

Shopping

The island has a waterfront shopping area with restaurants, a bakery, butcher, general store, bank, art gallery, pharmacy, and post office. Several stores selling men's and women's clothing and a fast photo service are located off the lobby in the main complex.

Arriving and Departing

BY BOAT

Fantasea Cruises' catamaran **2000** makes the 35-minute journey from **Shute Harbour** twice daily. ☎ *079/46–5111.* *Round-trip $35.*

BY PLANE

Hamilton is the only Queensland island with an airport large enough to accommodate commercial jets. **Ansett Australia** (☎ 13–1344) operates direct flights to the island from **Sydney** (two hours), **Cairns,** and **Brisbane** (1½ hours). Flights from **Melbourne** connect through Sydney or Brisbane. Boat transfers to all other Whitsunday resort islands can be made from the wharf adjoining the airport.

Guided Tours

Helijet Whitsunday flies guests from Hamilton Island, Shute Harbour, or any of the Whitsunday Islands on a Reef Discovery Flight to the Hardy Reef Lagoon on the outer barrier reef. The tour lasts approximately three hours. ☎ *079/46–8249.* *$360.*

Fantasea Cruises runs reef trips daily, leaving Hamilton Harbour at 8:30 AM for the 75-km (46-mi) trip to the company's own pontoon on magnificent Hardy Reef Lagoon, and returning at 5. For 2½ hours, you can swim or snorkel around the reef, or ride in a glass-bottom boat or submarine. A buffet lunch is included. *Tour Booking Desk,* ☎ *079/ 46–8535.* ✉ *$112 plus reef tax and administration fee ($3).*

The catamaran *1000* sails daily to **Whitehaven Beach,** a 6½-km (4-mi) stretch of glistening white silica that has to be seen to be believed. The cruise leaves the harbor at 12:15 PM for the 30-minute trip to the beach, returning to Hamilton about 4:15 PM. ✉ *$35.*

A large number of vessels at Hamilton Island are available for **charter and group trips.** Call Sun Sail (☎ 079/46–8699) or Moorings (☎ 079/ 46–8044) for information.

South Molle Island

Times past in Australia saw Aborigines come to South Molle to collect basalt to use for their axes. Much later it became the first of the Whitsundays to be used for grazing—hence its extensive grassy tracts. Now the island is a national park with a single resort that is popular with families. And the resort is on an exceptional part of South Molle: Bauer Bay at the northern end. Sheltered between two headlands, the bay often remains calm when wind is ripping the rest of the Whitsundays. South Molle is a relatively large island (1,040 acres) not far from Shute Harbour.

Dining and Lodging

$$ ✕🏠 **South Molle Island Resort.** From the water it doesn't look very large; only when you explore the complex do you realize that there are more than 200 guest rooms. The resort nestles in a bay at the northern end of the island with a long jetty reaching out into deep water beyond the fringing reef. Standards for facilities are high, and they appeal to young couples, families (there is full child-care service), and retirees alike. Every room has a balcony. Several standards of accommodation are available. All meals in the dining room and most activities are included in the rate; as at most other resorts, only sports requiring fuel cost extra. Apart from the Island Restaurant and Bar, the A La Carte is the signature restaurant. South Molle is understated in promoting itself, but it's one of the most pleasant resorts in the Whitsundays. ✉ *South Molle Island, via Shute Harbour, Queensland 4711,* ☎ *079/46–9433. 202 units with shower. Pool, sauna, spa, 9-hole golf course, 2 tennis courts, squash, exercise room, water sports, laundry. AE, DC, MC, V.*

Arriving and Departing
BY BOAT
The island's own boats will bring you from **Shute Harbour,** or take **Whitsunday All Over and Water Taxi** (☎ 079/46–9499) from **Hamilton Island** (☞ *above*). The former leave Shute Harbour at 9, 12:30, and 5. The 30-minute trip costs $30 for adults round-trip, $15 for children. A water taxi meets each flight into Hamilton Island; the 30-minute transfer costs $41 each way for adults.

Daydream Island

Every part of this little island in the heart of the Whitsundays is incorporated into the resort, yet somehow it manages to keep the original feel of a tropical paradise—much of the rain forest is intact and there are lush gardens everywhere. The island is divided, with 301 guest accommodations at the northern end and a day-visitor center in the south. The nightly entertainment, reasonable cost, and wide range of activities keep guests returning year after year.

☺ There is free **child care** every day providing a range of activities; each evening there is a Rascal Kids' Dinner Restaurant, free for children between six months and three years, and $6 all you can eat for children between 4–14 years.

Dining and Lodging

$$ ✕⌑ **Daydream Island Resort.** In spite of the difference in price and size, the three types of accommodations offered are all well appointed by Barrier Reef island standards. The Garden rooms do not offer views of the ocean, but they make up for this with their pool and tropical garden views. The Ocean View and larger Sunlover suites view the Whitsunday Passage, and the superluxurious, multilevel Royal suite sits right on the beach. All rooms have modern, light-color furnishings. Food is not included in the basic price of the resort; guests can choose between the Waterfall Café Restaurant, bistro meals in the Tavern nightclub, the coffee shop, and the more elegant Sunlover Restaurant, where seafood is the specialty. ✉ *Daydream Island, PMB 22, via Mackay, Queensland 4740,* ☎ *079/48–8488 or 800/07–5040. 301 rooms. 2 pools, sauna, 2 whirlpools, 2 tennis courts, exercise room, dive shop. AE, DC, MC, V.*

Outdoor Activities and Sports

Most sports are included in room rates. The most popular are tennis, badminton, volleyball, windsurfing, parasailing, fishing, snorkeling, and waterskiing. Much of the daily resort activity takes place at the centrally located swimming pool and bar.

A day trip to the reef for scuba diving costs $80, or $100 if you make two dives. If you have no diving experience, a $60 two-hour introductory diving course qualifies you to dive on the reef with supervision from an instructor the next day.

Arriving and Departing

BY BOAT

Whitsunday All Over and Water Taxi (☎ 079/46–9499) runs regularly to Daydream from **Shute Harbour** ($24 round-trip). The company also offers transit from **Hamilton Island** (☞ Hamilton Island, *above*) for $40 each way.

BY PLANE

Although most people come by boat from **Hamilton Airport,** an alternative is to fly **Ansett Australia** (☎ 13–1344) or **Qantas** (☎ 13–1313) to **Proserpine** on the mainland. Then catch a bus to **Shute Harbour** with **Whitsunday Shuttle Service,** and a boat from Shute Harbour to the island.

Day Trips

Only 20 minutes by boat from Shute Harbour, Daydream is one of the few islands where day visits are not merely allowed but actively encouraged. As a day visitor you won't be permitted to use resort facilities, but there is a separate visitor center: a miniresort that has a pool, cash bar, and late-night disco. Water sports are available for a fee. In addition, there are many boutiques and shops.

From Daydream Island you can take most of the excursions to the outer reef available from Shute Harbour—the resort picks up from the island.

Hayman Island

★   Quite simply, Hayman Island is one of the finest resorts in the world. Situated in the northern approaches to the Whitsunday Passage, it caters to people for whom luxury is a priority. The architecture of the hotel is superb—with reflecting pools, sandstone walkways, manicured tropical gardens, and sparkling waterfalls. The atmosphere is closer to an exclusive club than a resort.

Swimming pools at Hayman are delights. One wing of the hotel has a huge seawater lagoon with walkways leading across it to a central island that, in turn, encircles a large, pentagon-shape freshwater pool. Deck chairs are arranged under the shelter of palms and umbrellas. The hotel's other wing features another freshwater pool partly surrounded by tropical gardens, and a vast fishpond across which white swans glide.

Hayman Island is a 900-acre crescent with a series of hills along its spine. The area around the resort is rather arid, but there are beautiful walking trails through the rain forest on the other side of the island. The view of the Whitsunday Passage from the hills is unbeatable. The main beach is right in front of the hotel, but more secluded beaches, as well as fringing coral, can be reached on foot or by boat.

Hayman has its own marina with a sheltered anchorage for the island's diving and cruise boats, charter vessels, and yachts. The resort also has a nightclub. Several boutiques selling clothing, perfume, cosmetics, and jewelry are located in the hotel's shopping arcade, and there is an organized children's activity center.

Dining
The base rate at the Hayman Island Resort includes only a buffet breakfast. Otherwise, you sign for meals, charges being added to your hotel bill. Reservations are recommended for all restaurants and can be booked through the resort's operator.

$$$$ ✕ **La Fontaine.** With Waterford chandeliers and Louis XVI decor, this elegant French restaurant is the resort's culinary showpiece. The cuisine rivals the finest restaurants on the mainland and features such innovative dishes as *suprême de volaille et langouste en crème d'Algues* (chicken breast and wing stuffed with lobster in cream sauce) and *noisettes d'agneau rôties à la compote d'échalote* (roast medallions of lamb with compote of shallots and red capsicum coulis). Dinner is usually accompanied by live music. Private rooms are available. No lunch. Jacket required.

$$$$ ✕ **Oriental Seafood Restaurant.** This Asian restaurant overlooks one of the most authentic Japanese gardens in Australia. Black lacquer chairs, shoji screens, and such superb Japanese artifacts as Buddhist statues give this outstanding restaurant a comfortably exotic ambience. Try *hoi man poo* (Thai-style mussels in black bean sauce), shark-fin soup, or jellyfish vinaigrette. No lunch. Long pants are required.

$$ ✕ **Beach Pavilion.** Popular with guests coming directly from the beach or the pool for lunch or for sunset cocktails, this restaurant serves snacks, hamburgers, steaks, and a variety of other dishes in a pleasantly informal atmosphere.

$$ ✕ **Coffee House.** Serving dishes that range from simple sandwiches and cakes baked in the hotel's kitchens to full meals, this coffee shop offers a choice between indoor seating and breezy, sunlit outdoor tables.

$$ ✕ **La Trattoria.** With its red-and-white-check tablecloths and furnishings, this classic provincial Italian restaurant could easily be in Sorrento or Portofino. Seated either inside or outdoors, diners can choose from an extensive list of pastas and traditional Italian dishes. Prices are very reasonable. No lunch.

$$ ✕ **Planters.** This Australian restaurant uses rattan furniture, ceiling fans, and hibiscus artwork to create a relaxed local mood. You can feast on seafood or such specialties as kangaroo, emu, and buffalo. No lunch.

Lodging
$$$$ ⊞ **Hayman Island Resort.** It seems that money can buy almost everything. Asian artifacts, European tapestries, Persian rugs, and exquisite objets d'art enliven the lobby, restaurants, and rooms, which virtually

echo from the amount of marble adorning the walls and floor. Set in tropical gardens next to the pool and lagoon areas, Palm Garden rooms have garden views and their own terraces, and Beachfront Rooms allow you to walk from your terraces straight onto the coral-sand beach. For utter luxury, nothing could top the 11 Penthouse Suites, each of which is decorated in a different style, ranging from Californian to Moroccan, French to Australian. ✉ *Hayman Island, Great Barrier Reef, Queensland 4801,* ☎ *079/40–1234,* FAX *079/40–1567. Airline-accommodations packages,* ✉ *Hayman Island Reservations* ☎ *1800/ 07–5175, 800/366–1300 in the U.S. 203 rooms, 11 penthouses. AE, DC, MC, V.*

Outdoor Activities and Sports

All nonmotorized water sports on Hayman Island—such as catamarans, Windsurfers, and paddle skis—as well as use of the putting green, table tennis, dart board, basketball, and badminton facilities are included in guests' rates. Fees apply for squash, tennis, golf, and parasailing. A coral-viewing trip aboard the *Reef Dancer* ($50 per person) departs daily at 9, 10:45, and 1:30. A Whitehaven Beach Cruise ($120) departs Tuesday and Thursday at 9:45.

Adjacent to the marina, the resort's water-sports center has a training tank for diving lessons. A dive shop sells everything from snorkels to complete wet suits and sports clothing. The marina organizes parasailing, waterskiing, sailing, boating, windsurfing, and snorkeling. Fishing trips, as well as trips to the reef for scuba diving and coral viewing, can be arranged through the hotel's Recreation Information Centre (☎ 079/40–1723).

Arriving and Departing

Hayman does not have an airstrip of its own. Instead, take **Ansett Australia** (☎ 13–1344) to **Hamilton Island,** where you'll board one of Hayman's three luxury motor yachts, *Sun Eagle, Sun Goddess,* or *Sun Paradise.* Australian Sparkling Wine is served during the 35- to 60-minute trip to the island. On arrival at the wharf, guests are driven to the resort about 1 km (½ mi) away. Make sure you are ticketed all the way to Hayman Island including the motor yacht leg, or the luxury motor yacht will cost $320 for the round-trip journey to Hayman from Hamilton Island.

Guided Tours

Reef Goddess, Hayman Island's own boat, makes Great Barrier Reef excursions every day (except Tuesday and Thursday, when it goes to Whitehaven Beach for $130 including lunch) from 10 to 4. The $165-per-person charge includes snorkeling, some drinks, and a light lunch. There is a dive master on board, and the day-trip cost for divers is $185 (plus $40 for gear hire).

The $345 **Heli Reef** helicopter tour (☎ 079/46–9102) includes an aerial sweep of the Great Barrier Reef, snorkeling (equipment supplied), lunch, and coral viewing from the submarine at the Fantasy pontoon in Hardy Reef. Certified divers can dive for an additional $55. Flights take off daily.

The Hayman Island **Coral Air Whitsunday** seaplanes also fly over the reef. After a two-hour aerial tour, the plane lands in the sheltered waters of Hardy Reef Lagoon, where you board a semisubmersible boat for a tour of the reef. More adventurous passengers can snorkel or reef walk (gear is available). The cost of the tour is $240 for adults; reserve at the concierge desk.

CAIRNS ISLANDS

Orpheus Island

Volcanic in origin, this narrow island—11 km (6 mi) long and 1 km (½ mi) wide—uncoils like a snake in the waters between Halifax Bay and the Barrier Reef. Although patches of rain forest exist in the island's deeper gullies and around the sheltered bays, Orpheus is a true Barrier Reef island, ringed by seven unspoiled sandy beaches and superb coral. Incredibly, 340 of the known 350 species of coral grace Orpheus's waters. James Cook University has a Marine Research Station on the island.

Dining and Lodging

$$$$ ✕⊡ **Orpheus Island Resort.** If you are looking for glitzy accommodation surrounded by restaurants, bars, and boutiques, then this is *not* the place to go. Orpheus is for people who want to get away from it all. It offers privacy, sophistication, and total relaxation in an unspoiled environment.

Situated on the west coast of the island right on the beach, the resort itself is a cross between a South Seas island and an elegant Italian hotel, with terra-cotta floors, Persian rugs, and comfortable rattan furniture. Choose between beachfront terrace rooms, grouped four to a building; studio units in five groups of three; or two freestanding bungalows, which have queen-size beds, sitting areas, and whirlpool baths. All are beachfront rooms. Six luxury Mediterranean-style villas, on the hill behind the resort, are available from $550 per person per night and are absolutely stunning. There are no nightclubs, and rooms are TV- and telephone-free. Instead, a recreation room with TV, video games, gym equipment, and a billiard table is provided. Guests can also go bushwalking.

Although a full array of activities and water sports is offered, you might find yourself content to laze about, waiting for the next culinary offering. All à la carte meals and snacks are included in the price, and the cuisine at Orpheus is superior. The resort's chefs create dishes that emphasize seafood from the nearby reef. Given enough time, the kitchen will also accommodate special orders. Much of the cuisine reflects both European and tropical Queensland influences, and you can choose from such dishes as deviled king prawns, sautéed scallops with ginger and broccoli, and broiled barramundi with capers, beets, and ginger. The restaurant also has an extensive list of Australian wine, and because the resort houses a maximum of 74 guests, dinners tend to be friendly and intimate. Even buffet breakfasts are sumptuous and, on request, the kitchen will prepare gourmet picnic hampers. Potted plants, large palms, and blond wicker and wood give the open-sided dining room a distinctly tropical feel.

The resort has various value-for-money packages that are worth looking into. Day-trippers are not permitted, and the resort does not cater to children under 15. ⊠ *Orpheus Island, PMB 15, Townsville Mail Centre, Queensland 4810,* ☎ *077/77−7377 or 1800/07−7167,* ҒAX *077/ 77−7533. 23 rooms with bath, 8 with shower. AE, DC, MC, V.*

Outdoor Activities and Sports

The resort has two freshwater swimming pools, a Jacuzzi, a tennis court, and a host of walking trails that wind through the large national park. Snorkeling and diving from the island's beaches are spectacular, and at low tide the coral is exposed outside the resort so you can actually go reef walking. Most activities, such as waterskiing, windsurfing, sailing, canoeing, boating, and rides in a glass-bottom boat, are included in the room rate.

Outer reef fishing charters (for additional fee; minimum numbers required; trips subject to weather conditions) can also be arranged.

Arriving and Departing

BY PLANE

Orpheus Island is situated 24 km (15 mi) offshore opposite the town of Ingham, and about 80 km (50 mi) northeast of **Townsville. Nautilus Aviation's** (☎ 077/25–6056) 25-minute flights from Townsville to Orpheus aboard its seaplanes cost $270 per person round-trip; from **Cairns** an hour-long round trip costs $420 per person. Book flights when you make your reservation with Orpheus Island Resort.

Guided Tours

The coral around Orpheus is some of the best in the area, and cruises to the outer reef can be arranged through the resort. Whereas most of the islands are more than 50 km (31 mi) from the reef, Orpheus is just 15 km (9 mi) away.

Dunk Island

Dunk Island—which provided the setting for E.J. Banfield's 1908 escapist classic *Confessions of a Beachcomber*—is divided by a hilly spine that runs its entire length. The eastern side is mostly national park, with dense rain forest and secluded beaches accessible only by boat. Beautiful paths have been tunneled through the rain forest, along which you might see the large blue Ulysses butterfly, whose wingspan can reach 6 inches. Dunk Island Resort's prize-winning gardens are some of the best maintained in Australia, and the cascading series of swimming pools is a delight. The atmosphere is informal—guests are not required to change for dinner—and light entertainment is offered every night in the main lounge. The resort is on the western side of the island overlooking the mainland. Managed by Qantas, it's particularly popular with middle-income Australians and families. Situated 5 km (3 mi) off the coast of Queensland's tropical north, Dunk is, at 3,000 acres, the largest of the Family Group islands.

Dining and Lodging

$$ ✕🖬 **Dunk Island Resort.** Set among coconut palms, flowering hibiscus, and frangipani, the resort overlooks the waters of Brammo Bay. Guests have a choice of four types of accommodation. The Bayview Villas are the island's newest and best. At the end of each block, they have grand beach views. Each has a single and a queen bed. Only slightly less expensive than the villas, the Beachfront Units offer the best value and the most privacy. These spacious rooms have latticed balconies, cool tile floors, modern wicker furniture, and pink-and-cream decor. The Garden Cabanas do not have beach views but are located instead among tropical gardens. High ceilings and large sliding-glass doors create a sense of airiness, augmented by a simple decor that relies on light colors, woven mats, and basic tiling. Housed in two-story buildings, the less-expensive Banfield Units also have balconies overlooking the resort's gardens, and double family rooms are available for couples with children. Keep in mind that in this very wet climate, some of the garden accommodations can feel very damp. Rooms are serviced daily.

If you choose a full-board package (an extra $82 per day), meals—but not cold drinks—are included in the price. EJ's Australiana Restaurant is the resort's main dining spot. Overlooking lovely gardens and a shoreline lit by gas flares at night, this open-air restaurant has a South Seas atmosphere enhanced by wood beams, cane furniture, and plentiful potted plants. Meals at the resort's signature à la carte restaurant, the Rainforest Brasserie, are extra, however. Cascade's Restaurant is the romantic alternative on Dunk Island. Amid a riot of tropical plants, you sit in comfortable cream-color chairs at tables set with pink napery and elegant silverware. Terra-cotta tiles and a stunning view of the resort's swimming pools add to the restaurant's elegance. ✉ *Dunk Island, Queensland, PMB 28, via Townsville 4810,* ☎ *070/68–8199,* ℻ *070/ 68–8528, 800/227–4411 in the U.S. 148 rooms with shower. 2 pools, spa, tennis, squash, golf, laundry. AE, DC, MC, V.*

Outdoor Activities and Sports

In addition to reef cruises and fishing charters, the resort has a full range of water sports, including snorkeling, sailing, windsurfing, water skiing, and parasailing. The resort rates include all sports except horseback riding, scuba diving, clay target shooting, and activities that require fuel.

The inner reef trip ($110 per person) to Beaver Cay aboard the MV *Quickcat* departs at 10:30, returns at 4:30, and includes snorkeling, a glass-bottom boat ride, morning and afternoon tea, and a buffet lunch.

Dunk Island also has a six-hole golf course, skeet shooting, horseback riding, archery, two squash courts, and four tennis courts. And there is freshwater swimming in huge cascading pools.

You also can wander throughout the island along prepared trails with the help of a map provided by the resort. All walks are graded according to difficulty. Some of the harder ones—particularly to the top of Mount Koo-ta-loo—have beautiful views.

Arriving and Departing

BY BOAT

The catamaran **MV** *Quick Cat* (☎ 070/68–7289) departs Clump Point Jetty in **Mission Beach** daily at 10 for the 15-minute ride to Dunk Island, returning at 4:30. Round-trip fare is $24.

BY PLANE

Dunk Island has its own grass landing strip. **Sunstate Airlines** (☎ 070/ 860–4577) serves the island daily from **Cairns** and **Townsville.** One-way fare is $130 from Cairns and $129.50 from Townsville.

Guided Tours

MV *Quick Cat* (☎ 070/68–7289; 🚢 $105 adults), a large passenger catamaran, runs daily to the reef some 35 km (22 mi) away, leaving Dunk Island at 11:30 and returning at 4:30.

Bedarra Island

Within the confines of this tiny, 247-acre island you'll come across natural springs, a dense rain forest, and eight separate beaches. At 5 km (3 mi) off the northern Queensland coast, this is also the site of one of the Barrier Reef's smallest and finest resorts: Bedarra Bay is situated on the eastern side of the island, connected to the now-closed Bedarra Hideaway resort by a trail that winds through the interior rain forest. Another Qantas resort, this tranquil getaway is popular with affluent executives who want complete escape. It's the only Great Barrier Reef resort with an open bar, and the liquor (especially champagne) flows freely. Bedarra accommodates only 32 people, and you'll stay in your own freestanding villa hidden amid thick vegetation, a stone's throw away from golden sandy beaches with fringing coral less than 65 ft from shore. This is not a place to look for organized activity. Privacy and quiet are what Bedarra is all about: There are no discos or nightclubs, and you are discouraged from bringing children.

Dining and Lodging

$$$$ ✕⊡ **Bedarra Bay.** This resort vies with Lizard, Hayman, and Orpheus
★   islands to take the title as the most expensive in Queensland. It attracts
wealthy travelers seeking a discreet retreat, a quiet, luxurious holiday.
Elevated on stilts, duplex villas blend into the island's dense vegetation. Polished wood floors, ceiling fans, and exposed beams set the tone
for bright, airy suites that bear little resemblance to standard hotel rooms.
Each villa has its own balcony with a view of the ocean, and a queen-
size bed.

All meals and drinks are included in the price. The resort is limited to
32 guests, which means that food preparation is free of the institutional
blandness sometimes found at larger resorts. Despite the full à la carte
menu, you are urged to request whatever dishes you want. The emphasis is on fresh seafood and tropical fruit, including such dishes as
freshly made pasta with skewered lobster, prawns, and chicken. Breakfast includes splendid thick muesli and such morning treats as eggs Bene-
dict. The restaurant at Bedarra Bay is modern and airy, set in a round
timber building with tile floors and plenty of natural wood. The restaurant flows onto a deck that overlooks the pool. The bar is wide open
and well stocked. ⊠ *Bedarra Island, PMB 40, via Townsville 8810,*
☎ *070/68–8233,* ℻ *070/68–8215, 800/227–4411 in the U.S. 16 villas with bath. AE, DC, MC, V.*

Outdoor Activities and Sports
Snorkeling around the island is good, although the water can get
cloudy. In addition, you can windsurf, sail, fish, or boat. There are also
swimming pools and floodlit tennis courts. Fishing charters can be organized.

Arriving and Departing
Bedarra Island is just a few minutes by boat from **Dunk Island** (☞ *above*),
at which you arrive before transferring to a small boat for the 20-minute
ride to Bedarra. The cost is $70 round trip.

Guided Tours
To get to the Barrier Reef from Bedarra you have to return to Dunk
Island, from which all reef excursions depart.

Fitzroy Island

This rugged, heavily forested national park has a good fringing reef,
which is excellent for snorkeling and diving. On-island, the principal
walking trail, a two-hour loop, takes you past a lighthouse and onto
a lookout almost 900 ft above the surrounding waters. There's also
an interpretive center that explains the major features of life on the island, as well as its history. In spite of the fact that it's a mere 45-minute
cruise from the tourist center of Cairns, Fitzroy has remained distinctly low-key.

Overall, Fitzroy is a good option if you're looking for a more affordable island. The resort opened in 1981, and the island is still best known
as a popular day trip from Cairns (☞ Great Barrier Reef A to Z, *below*).

Dining and Lodging
$$$ ✕⊡ **Fitzroy Island Resort.** This is a casual affair of eight beach cab-
ins, each with two bedrooms furnished in natural woods and bright
prints. The Rainforest Restaurant within the resort serves well-presented
meals. The island also has camping facilities and bunkhouse accom-
modations for backpackers. ⊠ *Fitzroy Island, Box 2120, Cairns,
Queensland 4870,* ☎ *070/51–9588,* ℻ *070/52–1335. 8 units with
shower. Pool, dive shop, laundry. AE, DC, MC, V.*

Arriving and Departing

The boat for Fitzroy departs daily at 8:30 and 10:30 from Great Adventures in **Cairns.** ✉ *Wharf St., Cairns,* ☎ *070/51–0455.* 🚢 *Round-trip $30.*

Lizard Island

The farthest north of any of the Barrier Reef resorts, Lizard Island Lodge is small, secluded, and very upmarket. Only 64 guests can be accommodated at any one time. This is a place to relax and unwind, safely protected from business pressures and prying eyes. As on Qantas' other luxury hideaway, Bedarra Island, standards are exceptionally high.

The island itself is large and quite different from the other Barrier Reef islands: Composed mostly of granite, it has a remarkable diversity of vegetation and terrain, and grassy hills give way to rocky slabs interspersed with valleys of rain forest. The whole island is a national park ringed by miles of white-sand beaches, and it may have the best examples of fringing coral of any of the resort islands. Excellent walking tracks lead to key lookouts with spectacular views of the coast. The highest point, Cooks Look (1,180 ft), is the historic spot from which, in August 1770, Captain James Cook of the *Endeavour* finally spied a passage through the reef that had held him captive for a thousand miles. Lizards, for which he named the island, often bask on the lodge's front lawn.

Diving and snorkeling in the crystal-clear waters off Lizard Island are a dream. Twenty km (12 mi) from Lizard is the Cod Hole, rated by divers among the best sites in the world. Here you will find giant potato cod that swim up to be fed and petted—an awesome experience, considering these fish weigh more than 250 pounds and are more than 6 ft long! In the latter part of the year, when black marlin are running, Lizard Island becomes the focal point for big-game anglers from around the world.

Dining and Lodging

$$$$ ✗🏨 **Lizard Island Lodge.** In 1995 eight new villas were built on Lizard Island's Sunset Point. With views over the turquoise bay from the sail-shaded deck of each villa, this may well be Queensland's most idyllic location. The 40 rooms are self-contained, large and comfortable, decorated in pastel blue, green, and white. Each has its own verandah, polished wood floors and blinds, and soft furnishings with Balarinji Aboriginal motifs. The two Anchor Bay suites, separate from the other units, have living rooms and are closer to the beach. All rooms have king- or queen-size beds. To keep the sense of isolation, there are no televisions in the rooms.

The cost of meals (but not drinks) is included in the base rate. In recent years the quality of the cooking, always high, has been elevated further. The resort has a spacious dining room with a modern tropical decor accented by cane-back chairs and ceiling fans. The restaurant has also been opened up to admit the ocean breeze, and to better offer diners splendid views across the gardens and palms to the water. There is also dining on the verandah. Seafood is the foundation for the restaurant's cuisine. Although the menu changes daily, diners can expect such dishes as New Zealand green-lipped mussels poached in white wine and served with a light cream and garlic sauce, fresh coral trout panfried and served with a passion-fruit sauce, or tournedos of Northern Territory buffalo on a bed of mushrooms accompanied by a tomato sauce. Vegetarian dishes are also available. The menu is complemented by an excellent wine list. Upon request, the chef will prepare picnic baskets with a bottle of chilled wine. ✉ *Lizard Island Lodge, PMB 40, Cairns, Queensland 4870,* ☎ *070/60–3999, 800/227–4411 in the U.S. 40 rooms with shower. Bar, pool, tennis, laundry. AE, DC, MC, V.*

Outdoor Activities and Sports

The lodge has an outdoor pool, a tennis court, catamarans, outboard dinghies, windsurfers, and fishing and archery supplies. There is superb snorkeling around the island's fringing coral.

DEEP-SEA GAME FISHING

Lizard Island is one of the big-game fishing centers in Australia: Several world records were set in 1991, 1992, 1993, and 1995. Fishing is best between August and December, and marlin weighing more than 1,200 pounds is no rarity here. A day's fishing on the outer reef, including use of tackle, costs $1,495. In marlin season, between September and December, an entire heavy-tackle boat can be rented for $1,100 per day. Inner reef and night fishing are also available. One day's inner reef fishing with light tackle costs $975.

SCUBA DIVING

The resort will arrange supervised scuba diving trips to both the inner and outer reef, as well as local dives and night dives. Introductory and refresher courses are available. A full-certification scuba course lasting four or five days costs $650 and includes all equipment and local dives.

Arriving and Departing

Lizard Island has its own small airstrip served by **Sunstate Airlines** (☎ 070/860–4577). Daily flights from **Cairns** cost $383 round-trip.

Guided Tours

The reefs around the island have some of the best marine life and coral anywhere. The 16-km (10-mi) trip to the outer Reef ($150) will take you to snorkeling and diving locations, including world famous Cod Hole, where crew feed the giant potato cod and the Maori wrasse. Inner Reef trips are available for $110. Glass-bottom boat and snorkeling trips and the use of motorized dinghies are included in guests' rates.

GREAT BARRIER REEF A TO Z

Arriving and Departing

Regular boat and air service are available to most of the Great Barrier Reef resorts. But because all of the destinations are islands, they require extra travel time, sometimes as much as a day. Plan on scheduling the last leg of your trip for the early morning, when most charters and launches depart. In some cases travel is limited to certain days of the week, so coordinate international and domestic flights, as well as helicopters and launches, accordingly. In many cases it is necessary to stay overnight at a nearby mainland city before taking the last leg to the island. For information about reaching the various islands, *see* Arriving and Departing *in* individual island headings.

The Queensland towns that serve as jumping off points for the reef islands covered in this chapter include Townsville, Bundaberg, Gladstone, Rockhampton, Yeppoon, Mackay, Proserpine, Shute Harbour, and Cairns. Information on some of these towns themselves appears in Chapter 7, *above.*

Getting Around

By Chartered Boat

In recent years sailing around the Great Barrier Reef islands in your own boat has become very popular, and there are a number of charter companies that rent out yachts and cabin cruisers.

For uncrewed charters, contact **Australian Bareboat Charters** (✉ Box 357, Airlie Beach, Queensland 4802, ☎ 079/46–9381 or 1800/07–5000), **Club Seafarer** (✉ 2/809 Botany Rd., Rosebery, NSW 2018, ☎ 02/9693–5899 or 1800/22–1484), **Cumberland Charter Yachts** (✉ Box 49, Abel Point Marina, Airlie Beach, Queensland 4802, ☎ 079/46–7500 or 1800/07–5101), **Queensland Yacht Charters** (✉ Box 293, Airlie Beach, Queensland 4802, ☎ 079/46–7400 or 1800/07–5013), and **Whitsunday Rent a Yacht** (✉ PMB 25, via Mackay, Queensland 4741, ☎ 079/46–9232 or 1800/07–5111).

Crewed charters are available from **Club Seafarer** (☞ *above*) or **Sunsail Australia** (✉ Box 65, Hamilton Island, Queensland 4803, ☎ 079/46–9900 or 1800/80–3988).

Camping

Brochures and guides to the Queensland coast often leave the impression that you have the choice of staying either on the mainland or at an island resort, but for the adventurous there is a third option. On many uninhabited islands lying within national parks, you are allowed to camp, as long as you have permission from the **National Parks and Wildlife Service.** For details or to find out which regional office looks after a particular island, contact the service's head office in Brisbane. ✉ *Dept. of Environment, Box 155, Brisbane Albert St., Queensland 4002,* ☎ *07/3227–8185.*

The myriad islands of the Whitsunday Group are especially popular with young campers. For more information, contact the **Whitsunday Information Centre of the Department of Environment,** 3 km (2 mi) from Airlie Beach toward Shute Harbour. ✉ *Box 332, Airlie Beach, Queensland 4802,* ☎ *079/46–7022,* ℻ *079/46–7023.*

Contacts and Resources

Emergencies

Emergencies are handled by the front desk of the resort on each island. Each resort can summon aerial ambulances or doctors. Hamilton Island has its own doctor.

Guided Tours

FROM CAIRNS

Coral Princess (✉ Breakwater Marina, Townsville, Queensland 4810, ☎ 077/21–1673 or 1800/07–9545) conducts a four-day trip from Cairns to Townsville, vice versa or round-trip aboard a mini cruise ship that carries 54 passengers in great comfort. There are plenty of stops for snorkeling, fishing, and exploring Dunk and Orpheus islands. The crew includes marine biologists who lecture on board and on excursions from the boat. Diving gear and lessons are available. Townsville departures are Tuesday and Sunday, Cairns departures are Thursday and Saturday. Deluxe accommodation is $1,276, State $1,116 and Cabin $960.

Great Adventures (✉ Wharf St., ☎ 070/51–5644 or 1800/07–9080) operates fast catamaran service daily to Green and Fitzroy islands, Norman Reef, and Moore Reef (where diving and snorkeling, and helicopter overflights are available). Some trips include barbecue luncheon and coral viewing from an underwater observatory and a semisubmersible.

Ocean Spirit Cruises (⊠ 143 Lake St., ☏ 070/31–2920 or 1800/64–4227) offers a variety of tours aboard the *Ocean Spirit*, the largest sailing catamaran of its type in the world, and the smaller *Ocean Spirit II*. A daily trip to Michaelmas Cay or Upolu Cay includes four hours at the Great Barrier Reef, coral viewing in a semisubmersible, swimming and snorkeling, and a fresh seafood lunch. Introductory diving lessons are available.

Quicksilver Connections (☏ 070/99–5500) operates tours to the reef from Cairns, Palm Cove, and Port Douglas (☞ From Port Douglas, *below*).

FROM MACKAY

Roylen Cruises (⊠ Box 169, via Mackay 4740, ☏ 079/55–3066 or 1800/07–5032) operates daily cruises to Brampton Island from Mackay, proceeding on to Credlin Reef on Monday, Wednesday, and Friday. Trips include coral viewing at the underwater observatory; snorkeling and scuba-diving gear are available for hire.

FROM MISSION BEACH

The **Quick Cat** (☏ 070/68–7289) catamaran drives to Dunk Island and continues on to the Great Barrier Reef for snorkeling and coral viewing.

FROM PORT DOUGLAS

Quicksilver Connections (⊠ Marina Mirage, Port Douglas, ☏ 070/99–5500) runs day trips aboard their high-speed catamaran MV *Quicksilver* to their large floating dual level pontoon on Agincourt Reef. Once there, guests can swim, snorkel or scuba dive around the reef or board the *Quicksilver Sub*, which is a semisubmersible that provides superb underwater views through its keel windows. 10-minute Helicoptor Reef flights are also available from a landing platform on the pontoon, and costs $79 per person.

FROM TOWNSVILLE

Coral Princess (⊠ Breakwater Marina, Queensland 4810, ☏ 077/21–1673 or 1800/07–9545) operates cruises to Cairns (☞ From Cairns, *above*).

Pure Pleasure Cruises (☏ 077/21–3555) has day cruises from the Great Barrier Reef Wonderland wharf to the company's pontoon at Kelso Reef, on the outer edge of the Reef. The trip takes 2½ hours by high-speed catamaran. Once there, you have 3½ hours to enjoy fishing, snorkeling, diving, or viewing the reef through the floor of a glass-bottom boat. Morning and afternoon tea and a buffet lunch are included in the cost ($120).

Visitor Information

Queensland Tourist and Travel Corporation (⊠ Government Travel Centre, Adelaide and Edward Sts., Brisbane, ☏ 13–1801).

9 Adelaide and South Australia

Come to park-enveloped Adelaide for its biennial Festival of Arts or simply for a calmer urban experience. Elsewhere in the state, step back in time on the quiet, entirely relaxing Kangaroo Island; explore some of Australia's most celebrated wineries in the Clare and Barossa valleys; unwind on a Murray River cruise, as your own pilot if you choose; gaze at the great variety of Australian wildlife; live underground with opal miners; or tramp around one of the best Outback national parks.

By Michael
Gebicki

Updated by
Gary Walsh

OFTEN CALLED the city of churches or the Festival City—a reference to the biennial Festival of Arts—Adelaide is easy to explore. We have William Light, the first surveyor-general of the colony, to thank for that. In 1836, on a flat saucer of land between the Mount Lofty Ranges and the sea, Light laid out the city center—one square mile divided into a grid of broad streets running north to south and east to west—and surrounded it with parks. He put a large square at the center and other squares in each quarter of the city.

Today Light's plan is recognized as a work that was far ahead of its time. Largely due to his foresight, this city of a million people moves at a leisurely pace, free of the typical urban menace of traffic jams and glass canyons. The rest of South Australia gives even more reason to cherish this poise and gentility, for Adelaide stands on the very doorstep of the harshest, driest land in the most arid of the earth's populated continents.

Nearly 99% of South Australia's residents lives in the fertile south around Adelaide. Hugging the shoreline—wary of moving too close to the barren, jagged hills and stony deserts of the parched interior—they've left the northern half of the state virtually unchanged since the first settlers arrived here. Heat and desolate desert terrain have thwarted all but the most determined efforts to conquer the land. Indeed, "conquer" is too strong a word for what is often little better than subsistence. In Coober Pedy, an opal mining town in the far north, residents live underground to avoid temperatures that top 48°C (118°F).

The scorched hills of the Flinders Ranges, north of Adelaide, hold Aboriginal cave paintings and fossil remains from the ages when the area was an ancient seabed. Beyond that is Lake Eyre, a great salt lake that in 1989 filled with water for only the third time in its recorded history. The Nullarbor ("treeless") Plain stretches west, plodding across state lines in its tirelessly flat, ruthlessly arid march into Western Australia.

By comparison, Adelaide is a veritable Eden, but reminders of the harsh desiccated land on which the city verges abound. Notice that poles supporting electric wires are made from steel and cement rather than wood. Timber is precious. Toward the end of summer it is quite common to find trees in the city parks crowded with brilliantly colored parrots, which have fled to these oases from the desert. For many residents, the most urgent concern is not rising crime or property taxes but bush fire. The city is still haunted by the memory of the Ash Wednesday bush fires that devastated the Adelaide Hills at the end of the long, hot summer of 1983 and cast a pall of smoke over the city that blotted out the sun.

Yet South Australia is, perhaps ironically, well equipped for the good life. It produces most of the country's wine, and the sea ensures a plentiful supply of lobster and tuna. Cottages and guest houses tucked away in the countryside around Adelaide are among the most charming and relaxing in the country. Although the state doesn't have attractions on the scale of Sydney Harbour or the Great Barrier Reef, and it draws far fewer visitors than the eastern states, you're likely to come away from here with the feeling that you've discovered one of Australia's best-kept secrets.

Pleasures and Pastimes

The Arts

Adelaide's Festival Centre is the focus of the city's cultural life, and its name hints at the highlight of South Australia's arts calendar, the bi-

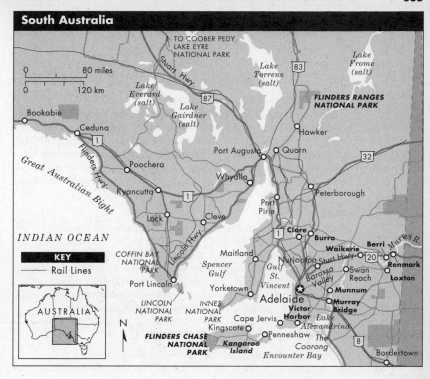

South Australia

ennial Adelaide Festival, a tremendously successful festival that was the forerunner to other artistic celebrations throughout Australia. On off-festival years, Adelaide hosts the Womad celebration of world music. Country towns and regions all have their own smaller festivals, the most notable of which is the Barossa Music Festival.

Dining

South Australia, along with the Northern Territory, led the way in educating the Australian palate in the pleasures of bush tucker—the wild foods found in the Australian countryside that have been used for millennia by the Aboriginal people. Kangaroo, crocodile, emu, and other exotic fare was introduced to a skeptical public that now embraces it wholeheartedly (although some question the ethics of using native animals for food) and seeks ever more inventive preparations of native ingredients. Local seafood is featured on many menus, especially tuna caught in the waters of Spencer Gulf and the Great Australian Bight.

CATEGORY	COST*
$$$$	over $40
$$$	$30–$40
$$	$20–$30
$	under $20

*per person, excluding drinks and service

Lodging

Adelaide's accommodations are bargains compared with those in any other Australian capital city. Even so, you might consider staying outside the city in the Adelaide Hills, which offer the best of both worlds: easy access to the pleasures of the city as well as to the vineyards, orchards, and rustic villages that are tucked away in this idyllic, rolling landscape. Wonderfully restored historic homes and guest houses are plentiful in Adelaide and throughout the state.

CATEGORY	COST*
$$$$	over $175
$$$	$100–$175
$$	$60–$100
$	under $60

*All prices are for a standard double room.

Outdoor Activities and Sports

Kangaroo Island's Flinders Chase and the Outback's Flinders Ranges national parks are great places to take in the geographical variety of South Australia—from coastal land and seascapes to rugged Outback mountain terrain. Cleland Conservation Park is one of the best ways to see the full spectrum of native wildlife. Especially when active, always carry water in this dry state and drink often. Australian Rules football and cricket are the main spectator sports.

Wine

South Australia is considered Australia's premium wine producer. The great vintages of the Barossa Valley, Clare Valley, McLaren Vale, and Coonawarra are treasured by wine enthusiasts worldwide, and many South Australian producers and wines have been awarded international honors. In general, reds are marginally more highly regarded than whites. Whether or not you make it to any vineyard tasting rooms, you'll have plenty of opportunities in restaurants to sample both.

Exploring Adelaide and South Australia

South Australia might neatly be partitioned into two—the dry, hot north, and the greener, more temperate south. The green belt includes Adelaide and its surrounding hills and orchards, the Barossa and Clare valleys' vineyards, the beautiful Fleurieu Peninsula, and the Murray River's towering cliffs and lakes. Offshore, the seals and seascapes of Kangaroo Island live in their delightfully cocooned way as a memory of the pace of times past. Heading up to the almost extraterrestrial Coober Pedy is one way to get a glimpse of life in the Outback.

Great Itineraries

The majority of the state's attractions are close to Adelaide, within an easy half-day's journey. To capture the essence of South Australia's character, you need at least to explore the nearby Adelaide Hills. An Outback journey provides an intense contrast—wide horizons, trackless deserts, and barren, starkly beautiful mountain regions.

IF YOU HAVE 3 DAYS

Spend a day around ⛿ **Adelaide**—a leisurely pace befits the almost countrylike atmosphere of the city—with a tram car excursion to the beach suburb of Glenelg. Spend the next day in the ⛿ **Adelaide Hills,** strolling the historic streets of Hahndorf, and taking in the panorama from the summit of Mount Lofty, before tasting the great wines of the Barossa Valley.

IF YOU HAVE 5 DAYS

The pleasures of ⛿ **Adelaide** and its suburbs (take some time to walk around the 19th-century streetscapes of North Adelaide) will fill a day. On day two, make for the ⛿ **Adelaide Hills** and on the following day visit the ⛿ **Barossa Valley** wineries and historic villages, perhaps overnighting on a vineyard estate. Then drive, take the fast ferry, or fly to ⛿ **Kangaroo Island** and savor its wildlife and fierce beauty.

IF YOU HAVE 7 DAYS

Spend a day in ⛿ **Adelaide,** nosing through museums and perhaps picnicking on the banks of the Torrens River. Next morning, head into the leafy ⛰ **Adelaide Hills,** where car buffs will love the National Motor Museum. On day three, descend to the ⛰ **Barossa Valley,** where the German influence is all-pervading and the free tastings at dozens of wineries are a temptation you needn't resist. Then take the ferry south of Adelaide to ⛰ **Kangaroo Island,** where two days and nights will give you time to nudge into its remote corners and provide a verdant respite before plunging into the Outback at extraordinary ⛰ **Coober Pedy** (consider flying to maximize your time). There you can live, eat, and shop underground, as the locals do, and fossick (rummage) for opal gemstones. If you're a hiker, consider spending a couple of days at **Flinders Ranges National Park,** one of the country's finest Outback parks.

When to Tour South Australia

The major festivals, the Adelaide Festival and Womad, are held in March, when the fiercest of the summer heat has abated. Adelaide has the least rainfall of all Australian capital cities, so at any time of the year you are likely to encounter dry weather. In high summer the midday heat should be avoided throughout the state, when the Outback especially is too hot for comfortable touring. If exploring the interior, wait for winter, which is pleasantly warm. For photographs, the brilliant late afternoon Outback light is magical. Summers are exceedingly hot and dry in South Australia, and winters can be very cold. The best times to visit national parks here are spring and autumn.

ADELAIDE

Adelaide's eminently sensible, thoroughly regimented grid pattern of streets at its center makes for easy exploration. And the lovely streetscapes have an appeal that transcends the attractions arrayed along them. The entire city center is an island surrounded by parks, with the meandering Torrens River flowing through the heart of the green belt—at its finest passing the Festival Centre and the picturesque Adelaide Oval.

Exploring Adelaide

City Center

Numbers in the text correspond to numbers in the margin and on the Adelaide map.

A GOOD WALK

Victoria Square ① is Adelaide's geographical heart, and a perfectly appropriate place to begin a walking tour. Head north along King William Street, with the **General Post Office** ② on your left. Directly opposite is the **Old Treasury Building Museum** ③, parts of which date from 1839. The **Town Hall** ④, built from designs by Edmund Wright, mayor of Adelaide in 1859, is next door.

Turn right into Grenfell Street. Two blocks beyond Hindmarsh Square on the right is the **Tandanya Aboriginal Cultural Institute** ⑤, which showcases the work of Australia's indigenous people. Turn left down East Terrace and left again into Rundle Street, which becomes Rundle Mall, Adelaide's main shopping strip. At King William Street, turn right and walk a block to North Terrace.

Dominating this busy corner is the formidable Greco-Roman facade of **Parliament House** ⑥. To its left is Old Parliament House, the historic rooms of which used to house a museum (it is no longer open to the public). The **South African War Memorial** ⑦, a bronze statue of a mounted trooper commemorating the Boer War, stands opposite. Walk up Kintore Avenue, past the white marble facade of the **City of Ade-**

Adelaide

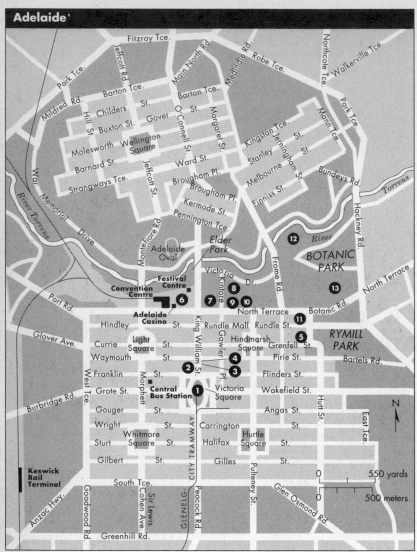

Art Gallery of South Australia, **10**

Ayers House, **11**

Botanic Gardens, **13**

General Post Office, **2**

Migration Museum, **8**

Old Treasury Building Museum, **3**

Parliament House, **6**

South African War Memorial, **7**

South Australian Museum, **9**

Tandanya Aboriginal Cultural Institute, **5**

Town Hall, **4**

Victoria Square, **1**

Zoological Gardens, **12**

laide Lending Library to the **Migration Museum** ⑧, one of Australia's most evocative and affecting museums.

Return to North Terrace, walk past the **Royal Society of the Arts** and the library, and turn left at the grassy courtyard to the **South Australian Museum** ⑨, which holds a particularly rich collection of Aboriginal artifacts. Next along North Terrace is the **Art Gallery of South Australia** ⑩, with its neoclassical facade, recently enhanced by a long overdue expansion. Continue on North Terrace and cross to **Ayers House** ⑪, once the scene for the highlights of Adelaide's social calendar and the home of seven-time state premier Sir Henry Ayers.

Cross North Terrace and walk along Frome Road, the shady avenue that leads to the **Zoological Gardens** ⑫. As well as an extensive collection of native animals, the zoo conducts breeding programs for threatened species such as the red panda and the Persian leopard. From the zoo you can return to the city either by the footpath that follows the River Torrens through a pretty park or aboard one of the Pop-Eye launches that run to the Festival Centre.

TIMING
A walk past, rather than through, Adelaide's attractions will take only a couple of hours. The South Australian Museum deserves at least 90 minutes, as does the Art Gallery. The more eclectic contents of the Migration Museum repay detailed viewing. In summer, time your visits to indoor attractions such as museums and the art gallery so you are under cover at the hottest time of day. It may be unpleasantly hot in the Botanic Gardens and the zoo, where the animals will be seeking the shade even if you are not.

SIGHTS TO SEE

⑩ **Art Gallery of South Australia.** Many famous Australian painters are represented in this collection, including Tom Roberts, Margaret Preston, Clifford Possum Tjapaltjarri, Russell Drysdale, and Sidney Nolan. The newest wing, opened in 1996, houses Aboriginal artifacts and Australiana. ⊠ *North Terr.*, ☎ *08/8223–7200.* ☉ *Daily 10–5, tour free.* ☉ *Tour weekdays 11 and 1, weekends 1 and 3.*

⑪ **Ayers House.** Between 1855 and 1897, this sprawling colonial structure was the home of Sir Henry Ayers, the premier of the state and the man for whom Uluru was renamed Ayers Rock. Ayers made his fortune from the copper mines at Burra, which enabled him to build this 41-room mansion. Most of the rooms have been restored with period furnishings, although few of the pieces actually belonged to the Ayers family. The admission price includes a one-hour tour. Since 1970, the house has been the headquarters of the National Trust of South Australia, caretaker of the state's historic buildings. Two restaurants are located inside Ayers House: the elegant, café-style Conservatory and the opulent Henry Ayers Restaurant. Both are operated independently. ⊠ *288 North Terr.*, ☎ *08/8223–1234.* ⊠ *$5.* ☉ *Tues.–Fri. 10–4, weekends 1–4.*

⑬ **Botanic Gardens.** These magnificent formal gardens include roses, giant water lilies, an avenue of Moreton Bay figs, an Italianate garden, acres of green lawns, and duck ponds. The latest additions to the gardens are a palm house and the Bicentennial Conservatory, an enormous glass dome that provides a high-humidity, high-temperature environment for rain-forest species. Guided tours leave from the Simpson Kiosk in the center of the gardens Tuesday and Friday at 10:30. The **Botanic Gardens Restaurant** (☞ *Dining, below*) at the center of the grounds has one of the prettiest views of any city restaurant, and good food to go with it. ⊠ *North Terr.*, ☎ *08/8228–2311.* ☉ *Gardens weekdays 7–sunset, weekends 9–sunset.*

② **General Post Office.** Constructed in 1867, this is one of a series of historic Victorian-era buildings on King William Street. ⊠ *Franklin and King William Sts.*

PIE FLOATER CARTS – A meat pie submerged in pea soup, the floater is South Australia's distinguished contribution to the culinary arts. Many locals insist that you have not really been to Adelaide unless you've tasted this dish, and the traditional place to try one is from the pie cart found at Adelaide Casino between 6 PM and 1 AM. Other nocturnal stands can be found on Grote Street just off Victoria Square and outside the General Post Office in Franklin Street.

⑧ **Migration Museum.** This fine facility chronicles the origins, hopes, and fates of some of the millions of immigrants who have settled in Australia over the past two centuries. The museum is starkly realistic, and the bleak welcome that awaited many migrants as recently as the 1970s is graphically illustrated in the reconstructed quarters of a migrant hostel. The museum is housed in the historic buildings of the Destitute Asylum, which is where many found themselves when the realities of Australian life failed to match their expectations. For anyone interested in the evolution of Australian society, this is a fascinating and rewarding museum. ⊠ *82 Kintore Ave.,* ☎ *08/8223–8748.* ▧ *Free.* ☉ *Weekdays 10–5, weekends 1–5.*

③ **Old Treasury Building Museum.** The exploration and survey of South Australia is a story of quiet heroism, and the museum is dedicated largely to the memory of explorers who feature prominently in the state's history, such as Charles Sturt, whose explorations of the Murray and Darling rivers contributed to the understanding of Australia's greatest river system, and Edward Eyre, who in 1840–1841 walked the desert from Adelaide to Perth. Included in the display of gleaming brass surveying equipment is Light's theodolite, which was used in the planning of Adelaide. ⊠ *Flinders and King William Sts.,* ☎ *08/8226–4130.* ▧ *Free.* ☉ *Weekdays 10–4.*

⑥ **Parliament House.** This parliament building was constructed in two stages, 50 years apart. The west wing was completed in 1889 and the east wing opened in 1939. The 10 Corinthian columns are the most striking aspect of its classical design. Alongside it is **Old Parliament House,** which dates from 1843. ⊠ *North Terr. between King William and Montefiore Sts.*

⑦ **South African War Memorial.** This statue was unveiled in 1904 to commemorate the volunteers of the South Australian Bushmen's Corps who fought with the British in the Boer War. Through the gates behind the statue you can catch a glimpse of **Government House,** the official residence of the state governor, which was completed in 1878. ⊠ *King William St. and North Terr.*

⑨ **South Australian Museum.** Don't be put off by the dusty, rather jumbled and old-fashioned displays of this extensive collection of Melanesian artifacts—the objects deserve careful inspection. Unfortunately the museum lacks the space to display more than a fraction of its outstanding Aboriginal anthropological collection. ⊠ *North Terr.,* ☎ *08/8223–8911.* ▧ *Free.* ☉ *Daily 10–5.*

⑤ **Tandanya Aboriginal Cultural Institute.** The first major Aboriginal cultural facility of its kind in Australia, Tandanya houses a high-quality changing exhibition of works by Aboriginal artists, a theater for dance and music performances, and an excellent gift shop. ⊠ *253 Grenfell St.,* ☎ *08/8223–2467.* ▧ *$4.* ☉ *Daily 10–5.*

4 Town Hall. This imposing building was constructed in 1863 in Renaissance style, modeled on buildings in Genoa and Florence. ✉ *King William St.,* ☎ *08/8203–7777.*

NEED A
BREAK?

The Bull and Bear Ale House is the perfect spot for a respite. The house specialty is Two Dogs alcoholic lemonade, made on the premises and cold and refreshing straight from the tap. It's best not to inquire about the source of the distinctive name unless you are prepared for a ribald joke about Native Americans. ✉ *91 King William St.,* ☎ *08/8231-5795.*

1 Victoria Square. Here is the very heart of Adelaide. The fountain in the square uses the Torrens, Onkaparinga, and Murray rivers as its theme. The square itself is surrounded by some excellent examples of Adelaide's colonial buildings constructed from local stone, although over the years many have been replaced by office blocks. One of the few grand survivors is the three-story stone **Torrens Building** on the east side of the square.

12 Zoological Gardens. Adelaide's zoo is small, but the landscaping and lack of crowds make this a pleasant place to see Australian fauna. You might particularly enjoy the aviary of Australian birds. ✉ *Frome Rd.,* ☎ *08/ 8267–3255.* 🎟 *$9.* ⊙ *Daily 9:30–5 (until 8 Wed. and Sun. in Jan.).*

From the zoo you can return to the city either by the footpath that follows the river Torrens through a pretty park or aboard one of the **Pop-Eye** launches. The boats travel between the front gate of the zoo and Elder Park, in front of the Festival Centre (☞ The Arts, *below*), the setting for most of the mainstream events of the Adelaide Festival. 🎟 $2. ⊙ Boats depart weekdays hourly 11:25–3:25, weekends every 20 min 11–5.

Around Adelaide

Cleland Conservation Park. Just a half hour drive from Adelaide, Cleland is one of the most unusual parks in Australia. It has only a few bushwalking trails, and its main attraction is its Native Wildlife Park. Developed in the 1960s, the zone is divided into five separate environments through which animals roam freely. This is one of the few places where you are guaranteed to see wombats, emus, and many species of kangaroo. Swampy billabongs harbor waterfowl difficult to spot elsewhere, and enclosures protect endangered species, such as yellow-footed rock wallabies and Cape Barren geese. Two major walking tracks in the park are open if you're interested in exploring the terrain outside the Wildlife Zone. Both are steep climbs offering panoramic views of neighboring Adelaide. Night walks led by rangers are also rewarding. Contact Adelaide Sightseeing (☎ 08/8231–4144) for information on tours to the park. ✉ *From Adelaide follow Greenhill Rd. and turn right at Summit Rd., or take Southeastern Fwy. and turn left through Crafers to Summit Rd.,* ☎ *08/8339–2444.* 🎟 *Park admission $7.50.* ⊙ *Daily 9–5 (Fri. and Sat. 9–7 during daylight savings time); closed fire-ban days.*

Camping is not permitted in the Cleland Conservation Park, but there is a self-catering youth hostel nearby. Reserve through the **Youth Hostel Association of South Australia.** ✉ *38 Sturt St., Adelaide 5000,* ☎ *08/231–5583.*

Magic Mountain. This beachside amusement park in Glenelg has video games, a huge water slide, and assorted amusement park rides. A tram runs from Victoria Square to Glenelg. The fare is $2.70. ✉ *Colley Reserve, Glenelg,* ☎ *08/8294–8199.* 🎟 *Most rides $2–$4 each.* ⊙ *Late Sept.–Easter, weekdays 10–10 or later, weekends 10–midnight.*

Port Dock Station. Steam buffs will delight in the historic collection of locomotive engines and rolling stock located in the former Port Adelaide railway yard. The finest of its kind in Australia, the collection includes enormous "Mountain"-class engines, the small engines that were used to pull suburban trains, and the historic "Tea and Sugar"— once the lifeline for the railway camps scattered across the deserts of South and Western Australia. ✉ *Lipson St., Port Adelaide,* ☎ *08/8341–1690.* 🎟 *$6.* ⊘ *Daily 10–5.*

🏛 **South Australian Maritime Museum.** Located inside a restored stone warehouse, the museum brings maritime history vividly to life with ships' figureheads, relics from shipwrecks, intricate scale models, slot machines from a beachside amusement park, and a full-size sailing coaster. In addition to the main display in the warehouse, the museum also includes a lighthouse, a collection of historic sailing vessels, and a steam tug tied up at the wharf nearby. ✉ *117 Lipson St., Port Adelaide,* ☎ *08/8240–0200.* 🎟 *$7.* ⊘ *Daily 10–5.*

Dining

By Jacquie van Santen

Updated by Gary Walsh

$$$$
★

✕ **Blake's.** This sophisticated spot, the Hyatt Regency Adelaide's (☞ Lodging, *below*) finest, is perfect for a big night out. Rough timber and small, cozy spaces create a relaxed, intimate atmosphere. Highlights of the main-course menu are blackened fish with vegetable couscous and lemongrass butter sauce, and braised duck on lentils with ginger sauce, and a tandoor oven permits such novelties as clay-roasted fillet of lamb with tomato and bean salsa, and roasted quail breasts on snow-pea sprouts with oyster mushrooms. The impressive wine list includes some of the finest wine makers in the country. ✉ *Hyatt Regency Adelaide, North Terr.,* ☎ *08/8238–2381. Reservations essential. AE, DC, MC, V. Closed Sun. No lunch.*

$$$$
★

✕ **Grange Restaurant.** The best in-house restaurant of any hotel in town, the Hilton's (☞ Lodging, *below*) upbeat brasserie has a casual, contemporary flair that's right for any time of day. Mediterranean and Asian cooking styles fuse on a menu that lists ragout of possum with root vegetables and basil noodles, and red roasted snapper with green chili, coriander snow-pea shoots, and calamari shavings. Executive chef Cheong Liew also cooks such exotica as braised shark lips, mughlai-style pigeon, and saltwater duck. ✉ *Hilton International Adelaide, 233 Victoria Sq.,* ☎ *08/8217–0711. AE, DC, MC, V. No dinner Sun.*

$$$
★

✕ **Chloe's.** Grand dining, a modern French menu, and the all-seeing eyes of owner and maître d' Nick Papazahariakis are the ingredients that define this glamorous and polished yet unpretentious restaurant. The dining-room appointments—Georgian chairs, crystal decanters, Lalique chandeliers, and gleaming silver—give any meal a sense of occasion, and prices are surprisingly modest. Panfried duck breast with game wonton, and fresh date tart with lemon glaze are signature dishes on a menu that draws its inspiration from European and Eastern cuisine. The 20,000-bottle cellar—a must-see for patrons—showcases Australia's best labels, plus some top-notch French favorites. ✉ *36 College Rd., Kent Town,* ☎ *08/8363–1001. AE, DC, MC, V. Closed Sun. No lunch Sat.*

$$$

✕ **Magic Flute.** This elegantly appointed, long-established restaurant houses a less expensive café. The menu includes roasted milk-fed lamb with mushroom ragout, in addition to peppered venison fillet with *rösti* potatoes and a black-currant sauce. The restaurant, which has an enclosed courtyard, is closed Sunday and serves dinner only. In the café, look to the specials board rather than the à la carte menu for inspiration. Desserts, particularly crème brûlée, are always worthy. ✉ *109 Melbourne St., North Adelaide,* ☎ *08/8267–3172. Reservations essential. AE, DC, MC, V.*

Adelaide Dining and Lodging

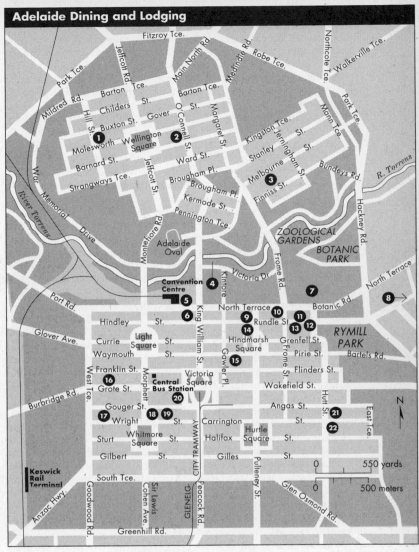

Dining

Amalfi Pizzeria
Ristorante, **10**
Blake's, **5**
Boltz Café, **11**
Botanic Gardens
Restaurant, **7**
Chloe's, **8**
Grange Restaurant, **20**
Jasmin, **14**

Jolley's Boathouse, **4**
La Guillotine, **19**
Magic Flute, **3**
Mona Lisa's
Bistro, **21**
Nediz tu, **22**
The Oxford, **2**
Red Ochre Grill, **18**
Ruby's Café, **13**
Universal Wine
Bar, **12**

Lodging

Adelaide's Bed and
Breakfast, **16**
Directors Studios and
Suites, **17**
Earl of
Zetland, **15**
Hilton
International
Adelaide, **20**
Hyatt Regency
Adelaide, **3**

The Mansions, **9**
North Adelaide
Heritage
Apartments, **1**
Stamford Plaza, **6**

$$$ ✕ **Mona Lisa's Bistro.** One of Adelaide's more adventurous restaurants, the Mona Lisa offers a refreshing change of pace for jaded palates. You can choose from a number of imaginative combinations, such as lamb shanks with Algerian spices; chicken with semolina gnocchi and braised leeks, and twice-cooked duck with glazed kumquats and onion tart. The decor is smart and modern with a touch of rusticity—stone walls, brick floor, bare wooden tables set with starched white napery and sparkling wineglasses. ✉ *160 Hutt St.,* ☎ *08/8223–3733. AE, DC, MC, V.*

$$$ ✕ **Nediz tu.** The starchy white interior punctuated by dramatic floral
★   arrangements conveys a note of sanctity, and all who come must be prepared to worship at one of Australia's altars of gastronomy. The kitchen operates under the direction of award-winning chefs Le Tu Thai and Kate Sparrow, who combine the rigor of Sino-Vietnamese cooking with the classical flavors of France. Appetizers might include chili squid with whitebait (a delicious, minnow-size fish), and goat cheese croquettes with avocado mousse and eggplant. Among the entrées are such dishes as lobster mille-feuille with champagne butter, and roast squab with parsley ravioli in truffle-scented sauce. Desserts like the celebrated passion-fruit tart, as well as hot kumquat soufflé and vanilla-bean ice cream, round out this exotic menu. Smoking is not permitted until after 10:30 PM. ✉ *170 Hutt St.,* ☎ *08/8223–2618. Reservations essential. MC, V. Closed Sun. and Mon. No lunch.*

$$ ✕ **Amalfi Pizzeria Ristorante.** Along with the low prices, bustle, no-frills atmosphere, and menu of Italian favorites, this mid-city bistro serves up a few surprises. The flavors here speak of sunlight: The specials board might list linguine with fresh blue swimmer crab, chicken breast stuffed with cheese and wrapped in prosciutto, or barbecued, chili-infused squid with char-grilled vegetables. Pasta dishes are large and the pizza is some of the best in town. ✉ *29 Frome St.,* ☎ *08/8223–1948. Reservations not accepted. AE, DC, MC. Closed Sun. No lunch Sat. or Mon.*

$$ ✕ **Boltz Café.** With semi-industrial decor—dull blue-green paint, exposed ducts, metal and vinyl chairs—medium-volume rock music, and a midnight closing time, this café targets the young and vibrant. The menu lists a choice of salad, pizza, focaccia, and such crowd pleasers as fish-and-chips, chicken curry, and ribs. You'll also find dishes like warm chicken salad with pickled pears, roasted walnuts, mixed greens, and blue cheese dressing. There is live entertainment some nights, when a cover charge of $12–$15 per person may apply. The coffee is great. ✉ *286 Rundle St.,* ☎ *08/8232–5234. Reservations not accepted. AE, MC, V. No dinner Sun.*

$$ ✕ **Botanic Gardens Restaurant.** This delightful place sits in the heart of the idyllic Adelaide Botanic Gardens and serves modern Australian cuisine with Asian and southern European influences, along with some of the finest vintages from South Australia's smaller wineries. Main dishes include soy and lime braised oxtail with crispy spiced polenta, and pork fillet with a steamed ginger bun and chilli black bean sauce. In addition to daily lunch, a traditional afternoon tea of scones, jam, and cream is served. ✉ *North Terr.,* ☎ *08/8223–3526. Reservations essential. AE, DC, MC, V. No dinner.*

$$ ✕ **Jasmin.** Traditional Indian prints and artifacts give an authentic ambience to this celebrated restaurant. Jasmin specializes in Punjabi cooking and offers more than 200 wines from some of Australia's smaller vineyards. Tandoor-style fish and chicken are recommended, as is vegetable curry. ✉ *31 Hindmarsh Sq.,* ☎ *08/8223–7837. AE, DC, MC, V. Closed Sun. and Mon. No lunch Sat.*

$$ ✕ **Jolley's Boathouse.** Blue canvas deck chairs and white-painted timber create a relaxed, nautical air, befitting the restaurant's position overlooking the river Torrens. The menu emphasizes such grilled delicacies as yearling sirloin with sage and parsnip cake, and braised veni-

son shank tart with caramelized onions and seeded mustard. The restaurant is very popular for Sunday lunch, and it's quite romantic on a warm evening. ⊠ *Jolley's La.,* ☎ *08/8223–2891. AE, DC, MC, V. No dinner Sun.–Tues.*

$$ ✕ **La Guillotine.** This pleasantly rustic restaurant is a long-standing traditional French favorite. Tables on a balcony overlook Gouger Street, Adelaide's bustling market center, others are in a courtyard garden. Highlights include frogs legs in brioche crumbs with a tomato, ginger, and coriander coulis, and kangaroo fillet char-grilled with a cherry and port glaze. Profiterole is a signature dessert. ⊠ *125 Gouger St.,* ☎ *08/8212–2536. Reservations essential. AE, DC, MC, V. Closed Sun. No lunch Sat.–Tues.*

$$ ✕ **Red Ochre Grill.** Restaurateur and chef Andrew Fielke is on a cru-
★ sade to transpose bush tucker (or creative native, as it's now known) from campfires to starched white tablecloths. Examples of his success include yabby tails with tomato and lemon myrtle jelly, and yam gnocchi flavored with sun-dried tomatoes, Warrigal olives, and Parmesan. Items from the barbie include grilled emu steak, tomato and eggplant galette with a bush-tomato glaze, and lamb medallions with artichokes, sage, and Illawarra plums. Kangaroo Island chicken breast with wattle-seed coriander crust, wild-mint harissa glaze, and preserved wild lime is beatific. An adjoining café offers a less extensive version of the menu. ⊠ *129 Gouger St.,* ☎ *08/8212–7266. AE, DC, MC, V. No lunch Sat. Closed Sun.*

$$ ✕ **Ruby's Café.** Sunday brunch is an institution at this chrome and vinyl 1950s-style café. Lemon-scented chicken, kangaroo fillet with fresh egg noodles, and ham, potato, and pea soup, as well as traditional puddings (banana, vanilla, toffee), are among the items on the menu. ⊠ *255B Rundle St.,* ☎ *08/8224–0365. MC, V. BYOB. No lunch Mon.–Sat.*

$$ ✕ **Universal Wine Bar.** This high-gloss, split-level bar-café with giant
★ mirrors and exposed wine racks along one wall remains a favorite of Adelaide's café society. Main meals include char-grilled quail and radicchio, grilled goat cheese salad, and duck dishes—but grazing is the name of the game here. The bar plate—an antipasto platter that usually features such exotic treats as witloof with balsamic dressing and kangaroo pastrami—is a meal for two. Don't miss the grape cake. You can choose from a wide and interesting selection of wines by the glass. This is a place to see and be seen. ⊠ *285 Rundle St.,* ☎ *08/8232–5000. AE, DC, MC, V. Closed Sun.*

$ ✕ **The Oxford.** One of Adelaide's best-value restaurants is in the midst of a burgeoning café scene in North Adelaide. The Oxford specializes in such inventive dishes as spatchcock (young chicken) with chili lemon butter, red Thai-style braised duck-leg curry, and oxtail Lyonnaise with salsa verde. At the same time, the traditional Caesar salad is as good as any you will find. ⊠ *101 O'Connell St., North Adelaide,* ☎ *08/8267–2652. AE, DC, MC, V. No lunch Sat. or dinner Sun.*

Lodging

$$$$ 🏨 **Hilton International Adelaide.** Overlooking Victoria Square in the heart of the city, this Hilton has extensive facilities and a highly professional staff. Guest rooms are large, comfortable, well maintained, and warm. Corner rooms are slightly larger than standard rooms. The best views, of the Adelaide Hills, are from rooms on the east side of the hotel above the 10th floor. The superb Grange Restaurant (☞ Dining, *above*), is on site. ⊠ *Box 1871, 233 Victoria Sq., 5001,* ☎ *08/8217–0711,* 𝖥𝖠𝖷 *08/8231–0158. 387 rooms with bath. 3 restaurants, 2 bars, pool, spa, tennis court, exercise room, nightclub. AE, DC, MC, V.*

$$$$ ⚑ **Hyatt Regency Adelaide.** Adelaide's premier hotel, this statuesque
★ atrium-style building has a luxurious and convenient blend of service,
comfort, facilities, and location. The hotel's octagonal towers create
unusual room shapes—a welcome change from the uniformity of most
other accommodations. The best view is from the riverside rooms
above the eighth floor. Four Regency Club floors have extra facilities,
including separate concierge service as well as complimentary Continental breakfast and evening aperitifs and hors d'oeuvres. The hotel
also includes a first-rate international restaurant, Blake's (☞ Dining,
above), as well as one of the finest Japanese restaurants in Adelaide.
⊠ *North Terr., 5000,* ☎ *08/8231–1234,* FAX *08/8231–1120. 369
rooms with bath. 3 restaurants, room service, sauna, spa, exercise
room, nightclub. AE, DC, MC, V.*

$$$$ ⚑ **Stamford Plaza.** Set in a prime location on North Terrace, the Stamford has excellent facilities. The rooms and decor have a cool, contemporary style. Those on the northern side of the hotel above the 10th
floor overlook Government House and the parks that border the Torrens River. ⊠ *150 North Terr., 5000,* ☎ *08/8217–7552,* FAX *08/8231–
7572. 334 rooms with bath. 4 restaurants, bar, pool, sauna, spa,
exercise room, nightclub. AE, DC, MC, V.*

$$ ⚑ **Adelaide's Bed and Breakfast.** An intimate alternative to the big
hotels, this stone guest house evokes its Victorian ancestry with bold
colors and big brass beds. Of the four upstairs bedrooms, those at the
front are larger but more affected by traffic noise during the daytime.
For a small surcharge, you can have the ground-floor bedroom with
its own bathroom. The house is a 10-minute walk from the city cen-
ter and about ¾ km (½ mi) from the main attractions in North Ter-
race. ⊠ *239 Franklin St., 5000,* ☎ *08/8231–3124,* FAX *08/8212–7974.
5 rooms, 1 with bath. Restaurant. AE, DC, MC, V.*

$$ ⚑ **Directors Studios and Suites.** The rooms in this smart, modern hotel
★ rival those in many of the city's luxury hotels. The absence of expan-
sive public areas, however, means the room rate is about half that of
the others. The functional but stylish layout features corridors enclosed by a glass roof and miniature tropical gardens. Apart from
standard hotel-style rooms, studio apartments include kitchenettes
and baths as well as showers, which easily justify their marginally higher
price. Of these, numbers 301 and 302 are more spacious and have city
views. Traveling executives form a large part of the clientele. A pub
with a dining room, open for all meals, adjoins the hotel. ⊠ *259
Gouger St., 5000,* ☎ *08/8231–3572,* FAX *08/8231–5989. 16 rooms and
36 studios with bath. AE, DC, MC, V.*

$$ ⚑ **The Mansions.** If you are looking for self-catering accommodations
that combine a central location with good value, these studio and one-
bedroom serviced apartments are spacious, comfortable, and equipped
with complete kitchen facilities, although furnishings and decor are to-
tally lacking in personality. If you intend to do your own cooking, pay
the slightly higher cost for a one-bedroom apartment. The hotel has
no dining facilities, but the Hindley Street restaurant district is within
easy walking distance, and Rundle Mall, the main shopping area, is
less than 50 yards from the front door. ⊠ *21 Pulteney St., 5000,* ☎
08/8232–0033, FAX *08/8223–4559. 50 apartments. Sauna, spa. AE,
MC, V.*

$$ ⚑ **North Adelaide Heritage Apartments.** Tucked away in a leafy cor-
★ ner of the city, these apartments and cottages have character, a dash
of luxury, and a reasonable price tag. The creation of antiques dealers
Rodney and Regina Twiss, the Heritage Apartments vary in size, but
each has a bath, sitting room, kitchen, and from one to three bedrooms.
Furnishings are in opulent late-Victorian style. The most intriguing of
the cottages is the Friendly Meeting Chapel, a former Forresters Lodge

meeting hall turned into an open-plan apartment. The city is about 2 km (1.2 mi) away, and none of the apartments is more than a 10-minute walk from a bus stop. Breakfast is available at a minimal charge. ⊠ *109 Glen Osmond Rd., Eastwood, 5061,* ☎ *08/8272–1355,* FAX *08/ 8272–6261. 6 cottages, 5 apartments. MC, V.*

$ ⊞ **Earl of Zetland.** Located above a pub in the busy mid-city, the rooms and furnishings in the Earl are comfortable and slightly old-fashioned, but so is the price. Perhaps its greatest attraction is its four bars, one of which offers a range of 275 malt whiskeys—a choice unrivaled in the Southern Hemisphere. ⊠ *Gawler Pl. and Flinders St., 5000,* ☎ *08/8223–5500,* FAX *08/8223–5243. 30 rooms with bath. 4 bars. AE, DC, MC, V.*

Nightlife and the Arts

The Arts

For a listing of performances and exhibitions, look to the entertainment pages of ***The Advertiser.*** Tickets for concerts and plays can be purchased from Bass ticket agencies, which are located at the Festival Centre, Myer Center Point, Hindley Street, Rundle Street, and Her Majesty's Theatre. For credit card bookings, call **Bass Dial 'n' Charge.** ☎ *08/8413–1246.* ☉ *Mon.–Sat. 9–6. AE, DC, MC, V.*

The biggest arts festival in the country, the three-week **Adelaide Festival,** which takes place in March in even-numbered years only, is a cultural smorgasbord of outdoor opera, classical music, jazz, art exhibitions, comedy, and cabaret presented by some of the world's top artists. In past years musicians and writers have included Dublin's Abbey Theatre, Kiri Te Kanawa, Placido Domingo, Billy Connolly, Muddy Waters, and Salman Rushdie. The festival features events as diverse as Writers' Week and a food fair, when a city street is taken over by food stalls devoted to gourmet grazing. For information on festival events, contact the South Australian Government Travel Centre (☞ Adelaide A to Z, *below*).

The Adelaide Festival Centre is the city's major venue for the performing arts. The **State Opera,** the **South Australian Theatre Company,** and the **Adelaide Symphony Orchestra** perform here regularly. On the lighter side, the center also hosts champagne brunches on Sunday morning in the bistro (☎ 08/8216–8744), and outdoor rock-and-roll, jazz, and country music concerts in the amphitheater. The complex includes **Lyrics** restaurant (☎ 08/8216–8720). ⊠ *King William Rd.,* ☎ *08/8216–8600.* ☉ *Box office Mon.–Sat. 9:30–8:30.*

In odd-numbered years the three-day **Womadelaide Festival** of world music takes place in late February or early March, with stages erected in the Botanic Gardens and crowds of 60,000 plus. Performers have included Peter Gabriel and Nusrat Fateh Ali Khan.

Nightlife

CASINO

Compared to Las Vegas the action inside the **Adelaide Casino** is sedate, but this stately sandstone building is undoubtedly one of Adelaide's main draws. All the major casino games are played here, as well as a highly animated Australian two-up, in which you bet against the house on the fall of two coins. The casino complex includes five bars and a restaurant. ⊠ *North Terr.,* ☎ *08/8212–2811.* ☉ *Mon.–Thurs. 10– 4, continuously Fri. 10 AM–Mon. 4 AM.*

CLUBS

In nightclubs, cover charges vary according to the night and the time of evening. A listing of nightlife for the coming week can be found in

The Guide, a pullout section of the Thursday edition of *The Advertiser.* The daily edition lists attractions for that day.

Adelaide's bright young things can generally be found nightclubbing along **Hindley Street** or relaxing in the trendy cafés of **Rundle Street.**

Margaux's on the Square is a plush, elegant nightclub and a regular haunt for the city's sophisticates. ✉ *Hilton Hotel, Queens Sq.,* ☏ 08/ 8217–0711. ▱ *$5–$15.* ⊙ *Thurs.–Sat. 9 PM–3 AM.*

Cargo Club attracts a stylish clientele with live funk, jazz, and soul music. ✉ *213 Hindley St.,* ☏ 08/8231–2327. ⊙ *Tues.–Sat. 10 PM–dawn.*

Mystics, dark, stylish, and intimate, attracts a sleek, over-25 crowd with disco and live music. ✉ *Stamford Plaza Hotel, North Terr.,* ☏ 08/8217– 7552. ⊙ *Fri. and Sat. 8 PM–3 AM.*

The Old Lion Hotel in North Adelaide showcases live Australian bands for a young crowd. ✉ *163 Melbourne St., North Adelaide,* ☏ 08/8267– 3766. ⊙ *Wed.–Sun. 8 PM–late.*

Outdoor Activities and Sports

Beaches

Adelaide's coastline from North Haven to Brighton is practically one long beach—a distance of about 25 km (15 mi). There is no surf, but the sand is clean. The most popular spots are those to the west of the city, including **Henley Beach** and **West Beach.** Farther south, **Glenelg** has a carnival atmosphere that makes it a favorite with families.

Cricket

The main venue for interstate and international competition is the **Adelaide Oval.** ✉ *War Memorial Dr. and King William St.,* ☏ 08/8231– 3759.

Football

Australian Rules football is the most popular winter sport in South Australia. Games are generally played on Saturday either at **Football Park** (✉ Turner Dr., West Lakes, ☏ 08/8268–2088) or the **Adelaide Oval** (☞ *above*). The Adelaide Crows team plays in the national AFL competition, generally every second Sunday at Football Park. The Port Adelaide Power joined the league in 1997, which ensures a national league game virtually every week in Adelaide. Games are popular: Tickets for AFL matches are very hard to come by. The season runs from the beginning of April to the end of August. Finals are held in September, and local teams will play a match or two then if they qualify.

Golf

Situated close to town, the **City of Adelaide Golf Links** has two short 18-hole courses and a full championship course. You can hire clubs and carts from the pro shop. ✉ *War Memorial Dr., North Adelaide,* ☏ 08/8231–2359. ▱ *Greens fee weekdays $14, weekends $17, par-3 course $8.*

Running

The parks north of the city have excellent running routes, especially the track beside the river Torrens.

Tennis

Located just across the Torrens from the city, the **Memorial Drive Tennis Courts** has hard and grass courts. ✉ *War Memorial Dr., North Adelaide,* ☏ 08/8231–4371. ▱ *$12 per hr until 5 PM, $18 until 10 PM.* ⊙ *Weekdays 9 AM–10 PM, Sun. 9–5.*

Shopping

Jewelry and Gems
South Australia is the world's largest source of **opals.** Excellent selections of opals and other gems can be found at Opal Field Gems (✉ 29 King William St., 3rd floor, ☎ 08/8212–5300) and the Opal Mine (✉ 30 Gawler Pl., ☎ 08/8223–4023). For high-quality **antique jewelry** try the Adelaide Exchange (✉ 10 Stephens Pl., behind David Jones department store, ☎ 08/8212–2496) and Megaw & Hogg Antiques (✉ 26 Leigh St., off Hindley St., ☎ 08/8231–0101).

Malls
Adelaide's main shopping area is **Rundle Mall** (✉ Rundle St. between King Williams and Pulteney Sts.), a pedestrian plaza lined with boutiques and department stores. Shops in this area are open Monday–Thursday 9–5:30, Friday 9–9, Saturday 9–5. Sunday hours are irregular. For information on specific shops in this area, visit the Rundle Mall Information Centre in the booth near the corner of King William Street. The center is open weekdays 9–5 and weekends 10–1.

Markets
Central Market is the largest produce market in the Southern Hemisphere. The stalls in this sprawling complex also sell T-shirts, records, and electrical goods. ✉ *Victoria Sq.* ⊙ *Tues. 7–5:30, Thurs. 11–5:30, Fri. 7 AM–9 PM, Sat. 7–1.*

Market Adventures is a behind-the-scenes guided tour of the market led by respected food authority Graeme Andrews. You can meet stall holders, share their knowledge, and taste the wares. ☎ *018/842–242.* ✉ *$20.* ⊙ *Tues. and Thurs. at 10:30 and 1:30, Fri. at 10 and 2.*

Adelaide A to Z

Arriving and Departing
BY BUS
The **Central Bus Station** (☎ 08/8415–5533; ⊙ 6 AM to 10 PM) is near the city center at 101 Franklin Street. It is the terminal for all intercity bus companies: **Greyhound/Pioneer** (☎ 13–2030), **Premier** (☎ 08/8233–2744), and **Stateliner** (☎ 08/8415–5555).

BY CAR
Adelaide has excellent road connections with other states. Highway 1 links the city with Melbourne, 728 km (455 mi) southeast, and with Perth, 2,724 km (1,700 mi) to the west via the vast and bleak Nullarbor Plain. The Stuart Highway provides sealed road access to the Red Centre. Alice Springs is 1,542 km (963 mi) north of Adelaide.

BY PLANE
Adelaide Airport is 6 km (3¾ mi) west of the city center. The international and domestic terminals are about ¼ mi apart. International airlines serving Adelaide are **British Airways, Singapore Airlines, Japan Air Lines,** and **Qantas.** Domestic airlines flying into Adelaide include **Ansett Australia, Air Kangaroo Island, Augusta Airways, Kendell,** and **Qantas.** ☞ Air Travel *in the* Gold Guide *for airline telephone numbers.*

The **Transit Bus** (☎ 08/8381–5311) costs $6 and links the airport terminals with the city hotels and the rail and bus stations. On weekdays the bus leaves the terminals at 30-minute intervals between 7:30 AM and 1:30 PM and 4:30 PM and 9 PM. Between 1:30 and 4:30, the bus departs at one-hour intervals. On weekends the bus departs every hour between 7:30 AM and 8:30 PM. **Taxis** are available from the stands outside the air terminal buildings. The fare to the city is about $13.

BY TRAIN

The station for interstate and country trains is the **Keswick Rail Terminal,** just west of the city center. The terminal has a small café and snack bar, and taxis are available from the rank outside (☎ 08/8217–4111). The ***Overlander*** makes daily 12-hour runs between Melbourne and Adelaide. The ***Ghan*** (Rail Australia, ☎ 13–2232 or 1800/88–8480) makes the 20-hour journey to Alice Springs weekly from November through April, and at least twice weekly from May through October. The ***Indian Pacific*** links Adelaide with Perth (37½ hours) and Sydney (28 hours) twice a week.

Getting Around

BY BICYCLE

Adelaide's parks, flat terrain, and wide, uncluttered streets make it a perfect city for two-wheel exploring. **Pulteney Street Cycles** rents 21-speed mountain bikes for $15 per day, $70 per week, including a helmet. ⊠ *309 Pulteney St.,* ☎ *08/8223–6380.* ⊙ *Daily 9–5:30.*

BY BUS AND TRAIN

The public transportation network is divided into three zones, and fares are calculated according to the number of zones traveled. The area within a 5-km (3-mi) radius of the city center is Zone 1. Between 9 AM and 3 PM on weekdays, the fare for any bus journey within Zone 1 is $1.60; at other times the fare is $2.70. Tickets are available from most railway stations and from the TransAdelaide Information Centre. A surcharge of approximately 10% is added to tickets purchased on board a bus, train, or tram. Anyone who expects to travel frequently can economize with a **Multitrip Ticket** ($16.80), which allows 10 rides throughout the three bus zones. Off-peak Multitrip tickets are $10.40. Another economical way to travel is with the **Daytrip Ticket,** which allows unlimited bus, train, and tram travel throughout Adelaide and most of its surroundings after 9 AM. It costs $5 for adults.

The free **City Loop Bus** makes almost 30 stops in downtown Adelaide, including Hindley Street, Victoria Square, and Rundle Mall. The bus runs on the half hour in both directions Monday–Thursday 8:30–6, Friday 8:30 AM–9 PM, and Saturday 9–5. Buses have ramp access for wheelchairs and baby carriages.

If you think you'll make extensive use of Adelaide's public buses, purchase a copy of the Public Transport map for 30¢, also available from the **TransAdelaide Information Centre.** ⊠ *Currie and King William Sts.,* ☎ *08/8210–1000.* ⊙ *Weekdays 9–5, Sat. 9–noon.*

BY TAXI

Taxis can be hailed on the street, booked by phone, or collected from a rank. It is often difficult to find a cruising taxi beyond the central business district. Some taxis will accept credit cards. **Suburban Taxi Service** (☎ 08/8211–8888)offers a reliable booking service.

BY TRAM

One of the city's last surviving trams runs between Victoria Square and the lively beachside suburb of Glenelg. The fare is $2.70.

Contacts and Resources

CAR RENTALS

The following have offices both at the airport and downtown: **Avis** (⊠ 136 North Terr., ☎ 08/8410–5727 or 1800/22–5533), **Budget** (⊠ 274 North Terr., ☎ 13–2727, **Thrifty** (⊠ 100 Franklin St., ☎ 08/8211–8788 or 800/65–2008).

Police, fire, or **ambulance.** ☎ *000.*
Royal Adelaide Hospital. ⊠ *North Terr. and Frome Rd.,* ☎ *08/8223–0230.*

GUIDED TOURS

Orientation Tours. The **Adelaide Explorer** is a replica tram that takes passengers on a two-hour tour of the highlights of the city and Glenelg, Adelaide's seaside suburb. Passengers may leave the vehicle at any of the attractions along the way and join a following tour. ⊠ *14 King William St.,* ☎ *08/8364–1933.* 🚋 *$22.*
Adelaide Sightseeing operates a morning city sights tour. The company also has trips to ☞ **Cleland Conservation Park** outside of Adelaide. ⊠ *101 Franklin St.,* ☎ *08/8231–4144.* 🚋 *$27.*
Festival Tours operates a morning city tour that takes in all the highlights, including the view from Light's Vision lookout and a visit to St. Peter's Cathedral. ⊠ *18 King William St.,* ☎ *08/8374–1270.* 🚋 *$26.*

TRAVEL AGENCIES

American Express Travel. ⊠ *13 Grenfell St.,* ☎ *08/8212–7099.*
Thomas Cook. ⊠ *45 Grenfell St.,* ☎ *08/8212–3354.*

VISITOR INFORMATION

South Australian Government Travel Centre. ⊠ *1 King William St.,* ☎ *08/8212–1505.*
State Information Centre has travel books and brochures on South Australia and an especially good range of hiking and cycling maps. ⊠ *77 Grenfell St.,* ☎ *08/8204–2900.*
What's on in Adelaide (☎ *08/8411–699*) is a recorded information service that covers current events and attractions in both the city and the Adelaide Hills.

THE ADELAIDE HILLS

The green slopes, wooded valleys, and gardens brimming with flowers of the Adelaide Hills are a pastoral oasis in this desert state. The combination of orchards, vineyards, avenues of tall conifers, and town buildings of rough-hewn stone gives this region a distinctly European feel and makes the hills one of the best reasons to visit Adelaide. During the steamy summer months these hills, barely 15 km (10 mi) from the heart of Adelaide, are consistently cooler than the city.

To reach the Hills, follow Payneham Road northeast from Adelaide to Gorge Road, which leads to Torrens Gorge. This delightful drive leads through a succession of orchards, vineyards, and historic towns, with the Torrens river flashing through the trees.

Birdwood

44 km (27 mi) east of Adelaide.

Birdwood was originally named Blumberg (Hill of Flowers), but it was renamed during the First World War in honor of the commander of the Australian military forces. The town's historic flour mill, built in 1852, now has a new role as the home of Australia's best motoring museum.

The **National Motor Museum** is a must for automobile enthusiasts and has enough general interest to captivate those usually unmoved by motor vehicles. This outstanding collection includes the first vehicle to cross Australia (1908); the first Holden, Australia's indigenous automobile, off the production line (1948); and hundreds of other historic autos and motorcycles. ⊠ *Main St., Birdwood,* ☎ *08/8568–5006,* FAX *08/8568–5195.* 🖛 *$8.* ⊙ *Daily 9–5.*

Mount Lofty

30 km (19 mi) southwest of Birdwood, via Mount Torrens and Lobethal, 16 km (10 mi) southeast of Adelaide.

There are splendid views of Adelaide from the lookout at the 2,300-ft peak of **Mount Lofty.** Much of the surrounding area was devastated during the Ash Wednesday bush fires of 1983; you can see the skeletal remains of some historic mansions behind the television antennas just below the summit.

Dining and Lodging

$$$$ ✕ **Hardy's.** The formal dining room inside Mount Lofty Country House is one of the highlights of this elegant country-house hotel. Although it reflects the opulence of the restaurant, the international menu is also stylishly modern. Try locally farmed venison fillet served on a beetroot, Spanish onion, and chili risotto with butternut squash mousseline and sweet pepper sauce. The wine list includes South Australia's finest. ⊠ *74 Summit Rd., Crafers,* ☎ *08/8339–6777. Reservations essential. Jacket required. AE, DC, MC, V.*

$$$ ✕ **Uraidla Aristologist.** Food is taken very seriously indeed at this
★   small, rustic country restaurant that evokes the flavors and scents of rural Tuscany. Typical selections from the changing, fixed-price menu are anchovy dip with fresh vegetables, osso bucco with tomatoes, pumpkin pasta, fried zucchini flowers, and oxtail with peeled grapes. Many vegetables and herbs come from gardens that surround the pretty two-story restaurant. Allow several hours for the experience of dining here. ⊠ *Greenhill and Basket Range Rds., Uraidla, 5 km (3 mi) from Mount Lofty,* ☎ *08/8390–1995. Reservations essential. MC, V. Closed Mon.–Thurs. No lunch Fri.*

$$$$ 🏠 **Mercure Grand Hotel Mount Lofty House.** This is country living at its finest. Enjoy the sophisticated pleasures of gourmet dining and thoughtful service at this refined country house against a backdrop of rolling hills and crisp mountain air. The house sits in a commanding position just below the summit of Mt. Lofty, overlooking the patchwork of vineyards, farms, and bushland in the Piccadilly Valley. The house itself is surrounded by informal gardens and shaded by giant sequoias. Guest rooms are large and well furnished. ⊠ *74 Summit Rd., Crafers 5152,* ☎ *08/8339–6777,* FAX *08/8339–5656. 30 rooms with bath. Restaurant, bar, pool. AE, DC, MC, V.*

Mylor

10 km (6 mi) south of Mount Lofty via the town of Crafers, the South Eastern Freeway, and Stirling; 25 km (15 mi) southeast of Adelaide.

Mylor is a picturesque little village, merely a speck on the map. It's worth visiting for the role that a wildlife sanctuary in its midst is playing in the preservation of native animals.

At **Warrawong Sanctuary** there are no koalas to cuddle, but this is one of the few chances you will have to see kangaroos, wallabies, bandicoots, and platypuses in their native habitat. Without human feeding, and European-introduced cat, fox, and rabbit predation and food-source competition, native species have flourished on this 35-acre property of rain forest, gurgling streams, and black-water ponds. There are guided walks around the property morning and evening, and because most of the animals are nocturnal, the evening walk is the most rewarding for wildlife watching. There is also a walk-and-dinner package available. Reservations for walks are essential. ⊠ *Stock Rd., Mylor,* ☎ *08/ 8370–9422.* 🖾 *Dawn and evening walks $15, walk-and-dinner $28.50 including drinks.*

Bridgewater

6 km (4 mi) north of Mylor, 22 km (14 mi) southeast of Adelaide.

Bridgewater came into existence in 1841 as a place of refreshment for bullock teams fording Cock's Creek. It was officially planned in 1859 by the builder of the first Bridgewater mill.

It would be difficult to miss the handsome 130-year-old **stone flour mill** with its churning waterwheel that stands at the entrance to the town. These days the mill houses the first-class Granary Restaurant (☞ Dining and Lodging, *below*) and serves as the shopfront for Petaluma Wines, one of the finest labels in the state. The prestigious Croser champagne is matured on the lower level of the building, and you can tour the cellars by appointment. ⊠ *Mt. Barker Rd., Bridgewater,* ☎ *08/8339– 3422.* ⊙ *Wine tasting daily 10–5.*

Dining and Lodging

$$ ✕ **Granary Restaurant.** More commonly known as Bridgewater Mill,
★ this stylish restaurant inside a converted flour mill is one of the best in the state. The contemporary Australian menu is small and limited to lunch, but the food is as fresh, original, and as well presented as the surroundings. Imaginative use is made of local produce in such dishes as goat cheese baked with eggplant and roasted capsicum, and miniature oyster pie served with mushrooms and chervil cream. In summer, book ahead to get a table on the deck beside the waterwheel. If you're feeling flush, ask to see the special wine list. ⊠ *Mt. Barker Rd., Bridgewater,* ☎ *08/8339–3422. AE, DC, MC, V. Closed Tues. No dinner.*

$ ✕ **Aldgate Pump.** This friendly country pub has a huge menu that ranges from a hearty moussaka to Thai curries and salad dishes. The bistro overlooks a shady beer garden, but the restaurant is slightly more formal—and more expensive. ⊠ *1 Strathalbyn Rd., Aldgate, 2 km (1.25 mi) from Bridgewater,* ☎ *08/8339–2015. Reservations not accepted. AE, DC, MC, V.*

$$ 🏠 **Aldgate Village Inn.** Formerly the Aldgate general store, this rustic, century-old stone building provides atmospheric lodgings in the pretty village of Aldgate. Guest rooms are simply but neatly furnished, and breakfast is included in the tariff. An apartment offers more spacious accommodation at a higher price. Its greatest asset is its tranquil location, surrounded by wooded hills, just a 20-minute drive from the city of Adelaide. ⊠ *2 Strathalbyn Rd., Aldgate 5154,* ☎ *08/8370–8144. 5 rooms with bath. MC, V.*

Hahndorf

7 km (4 mi) east of Bridgewater, 29 km (18 mi) southeast of Adelaide.

Hahndorf is a picture-perfect village that might have sprung to life from the cover of a chocolate box. Founded 150 years ago by German settlers, Hahndorf consists of a single shady main street lined with stone-and-timber shops and cottages. Most old shops have become arts-and-crafts galleries and antiques stores, although German traditions survive in cake shops and a butcher's shop. The village is extremely crowded Sundays.

The **Hahndorf Academy** contains several works by Sir Hans Heysen, a famous Australian landscape painter who lived in this area at the turn of the century. ⊠ *68 Main St.,* ☎ *08/8388–7250.* ⊡ *$2.* ☼ *Daily 10:15–5.*

Lodging

$$$ ⊡ **Apple Tree Cottage and Gum Tree Cottage.** This is your chance to
★   escape to your own country cottage in idyllic surroundings. Set in rolling countryside on a cattle stud farm near the historic village of Hahndorf, both cottages come with antique furnishings, open log fires, well-equipped kitchens, and air-conditioning. Apple Tree Cottage is a two-story Georgian farmhouse surrounded by a lake and gardens close to an orchard. Gum Tree Cottage was built only a few years ago, but the stonework, red-gum beams, and post-and-rail fence suggest a pioneer's house of the last century. During your stay, you can row to the large dam next to the house or stretch out in a hammock slung underneath a walnut tree. Adelaide is about 40 minutes away by car. Rates include supplies for a full breakfast. ⊠ *Box 100, Oakbank 5243, 10 km (6 mi) northeast of Hahndorf,* ☎ *08/8388–4193. 2 cottages. No credit cards.*

Adelaide Hills A to Z

Getting Around

BY BUS

The Adelaide Hills are served by the Adelaide suburban network, but buses, particularly to some of the more remote attractions, are limited. ☞ Arriving and Departing *in* Adelaide A to Z, *above.*

BY CAR

The best way to explore the area is by car, which gives you the freedom to explore the country lanes and villages that are an essential part of the hills experience. ☞ Car Rentals *in* Adelaide A to Z, *above.*

Contacts and Resources

GUIDED TOURS

Adelaide Sightseeing (☎ 08/8231–4144) runs a daily afternoon coach tour of the Adelaide Hills and historic Hahndorf village ($28 adults). The tour departs from the Central Bus Station at 101 Franklin Street.

VISITOR INFORMATION

Adelaide Hills Tourist Information Centre. ⊠ *64 Main St., Hahndorf,* ☎ *08/8388–1185.*

THE BAROSSA VALLEY

Some of Australia's most famous vineyards are found in the Barossa Valley, less than an hour's drive northeast of Adelaide. The wide, shallow valley's 50 wineries produce a huge array of wine, from aromatic Rhine Riesling that sells for $6 a bottle to Seppelts Para Port for up to $3,000 to Penfold's Grange Hermitage—Australia's most celebrated wine.

What sets the Barossa apart is not so much the quality of its wine as its cultural roots. The area was settled by Silesian immigrants who left the German-Polish border region to escape religious persecution. These conservative, hardworking farmers brought traditions that you can't miss in the solid bluestone architecture, the tall, slender spires of the Lutheran churches, and the Black Forest cake that has taken the place of Devonshire tea. All of this gives the Barossa a character and identity that no other wine-growing area of Australia possesses. Although it would be a shame to go to the Barossa and not taste the wine, its scenery, history, architecture, and distinctive cuisine can appeal to anyone.

The Barossa lives, thinks, and breathes wine, and any tour of the area will usher you into the mysterious world of wine tasting. The haze of jargon enshrouding this rite might seem obscure and intimidating at first, but keep in mind that the heady passion uniting wine lovers could take you by surprise. If you are new to the process, relax and let your sense of taste guide you.

Every winery in the Barossa operates sale rooms, which will usually have between 6 and 12 varieties of wine available for tasting. Generally, you will begin with a light, aromatic white, such as Riesling, move on through heavier white, and then repeat the process with red wine. Sweet and fortified wine should be left until last. You are not expected to sample the entire range; to do so would overpower your taste buds. It's far better to give the tasting-room staff some idea of your personal preferences and let them suggest wine for you to taste.

Numbers in the margin correspond to points of interest on the Barossa Valley map.

Lyndoch

① *58 km (44 mi) northeast of Adelaide.*

This pleasant little town, surrounded by vineyards, as most are in the Barossa Valley, owes the spelling of its name to a draftsman's error. It was meant to be named Lynedoch, after the British soldier Lord Lynedoch.

Dining and Lodging

$$ ✕🏠 **Miners Cottage.** It would be hard to imagine a more romantic hide-
★ away than this peaceful country charmer. Set among giant gum trees above a billabong, the small, century-old stone cottage consists of a slate-floor kitchen sitting room, a bedroom, and a bath. The decor is delightful—lace, antiques, tiny windows, thick stone walls, and a veranda at the back that overlooks a swimming pool in the garden below. The cottage is situated on a 66-acre farm in rolling country with a number of fine walks close by. Dinner is available by prior arrangement. ✉ *Box 28, 10 km (6 mi) from Lyndoch, Cockatoo Valley 5351,* ☎ *08/8524–6213,* FAX *08/8524–6650. Pool. MC, V.*

$$ 🏠 **Warrenda Cottage and the Dairy.** Warrenda is a perfect choice if you are looking for family-size space in rustic, pastoral surroundings. The three-bedroom, century-old house is furnished with red-gum tables and pine dressers complemented by white, sponged walls and country scenes out the windows. There are mosquito nets and linen sheets on the beds and a huge, old-fashioned bathroom with its own fireplace. Breakfasts include home-cured bacon and preserves made from fruit grown on the property. The Dairy is a romantic one-bedroom cottage decorated in Mediterranean style and furnished with 18th-century antiques. ✉ *Box 391, Lyndoch 5351,* ☎ FAX *08/8524–4507. MC, V.*

Tanunda

13 km (8 mi) north of Lyndoch, 70 km (44 mi) north of Adelaide.

The cultural heart of the Barossa, Tanunda is its most German settlement. The four Lutheran churches in the town testify to its German heritage, reinforced by the proliferation of German pastries, breads, and wursts—not to mention the wine—in Tanunda's main street. Many of the valley's best wineries are close by.

② The **Grant Burge** winery is the label of one of the most successful of the young, independent winegrowers of the Barossa. Grant Burge pro-

The Barossa Valley

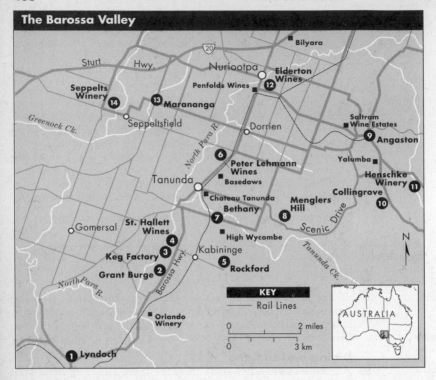

duces mainly white wine, and his Semillon and Rhine Riesling in particular are highly regarded by wine judges. The style of this wine maker is reflected in the tasting room, which uses the traditional bluestone architecture of the Barossa to striking effect. ⊠ *Jacobs Creek, 5 km (3 mi) from Tanunda,* ☎ *08/8563–3700.* ⊙ *Daily 10–5.*

❸ The **Keg Factory** uses traditional methods to make oak casks for Barossa wineries. You can watch coopers working the American and French oak staves inside the iron hoops. The small port kegs make a wonderful souvenir of the Barossa. ⊠ *St. Halletts Rd.,* ☎ *08/8563–3012.* ⊙ *Mon.–Sat. 8–5.*

❹ **St. Hallett Wines** uses 100-year-old vines for its signature Old Block Shiraz, a classic and fantastic Australian red. This is one of the area's best wineries. Taste the wine in the comfortable Old Block Cellar, where a log fire encourages wintertime lingering. Poacher's Blend Semillon and Barossa Valley Shiraz are also good choices. The homemade Farm Follies range of produce makes a tasty souvenir. ⊠ *St. Halletts Rd.,* ☎ *08/8563–2319.* ⊙ *Oct.–June, daily 10–5; July–Sept., Sun. 11–5.*

❺ **Rockford** is another small wine maker, with tasting room to match in a small, dark stone barn. Rockford's specialty is heavy, rich wine made from some of the oldest vines in the Barossa. These vines bear small quantities of fruit with intense flavor and often survive only in areas as small as a single acre, which makes them uneconomical for anyone but a small scale, dedicated winery to handle. So you won't find this wine distributed far and wide. A range of notable wine has appeared under the Rockford label, and nobody should miss the opportunity to taste the cabernet sauvignon and Basket Press Shiraz, an outstanding example of this most traditional of Australian varieties. Call in advance to arrange a tasting. ⊠ *Krondorf Rd.,* ☎ *08/8563–2720.*

❻ Peter Lehmann Wines. Peter Lehmann is a larger-than-life Barossa character whose wine consistently wins awards and medals. The tasting room is among the most pleasant in the valley, and staff are friendly and informative. Look for semillons, shiraz, cabernet malbec, and Cellar Collection wines. ✉ *Para Rd.,* ☎ *08/8563–2500.* ☉ *Weekdays 9:30–5, weekends 10:30–4:30.*

Dining and Lodging

$$$ ✕ **Lanzerac.** The earthy flavors of French and Italian provincial cooking are rekindled in this former barn, which is a local favorite. Typical dishes are carpaccio of Atlantic salmon, eye fillets of venison with pasta, and wok-fried pigeon. ✉ *Menge Rd.,* ☎ *08/8563–0499. MC, V. No dinner Mon. or Tues.*

$$ ✕ **1918 Bistro and Grill.** Housed in a restored villa, this pretty, rusticated restaurant makes exemplary use of the distinctive regional produce of the Barossa Valley, which ranges from olive oil to almonds to sausages. Dishes might include leek risotto with lemon parsley and Parmesan or char-grilled snapper with leek, mint, and pea vinaigrette. The restaurant is partly owned by Robert O'Callaghan of Rockford Winery, so, as you might expect, the wine list is outstanding. ✉ *94 Murray St.,* ☎ *08/8563–0405. AE, DC, MC, V.*

$$$ 🏠 **Lawley Farm.** Built around a courtyard shaded by peppercorn trees,
★ these charming stone cottages have been assembled from barns that date from the pioneering days of the Barossa. Surrounded by vineyards and orchards in the shadow of the Barossa Range, their rustic character is enhanced by antique furnishings and a family of peacocks that rules the grounds. The Lyndoch Suite, with massive ceiling beams from local wineries, and the sunny Bethany suite are particularly appealing. The Krondorf Suite is the original 1852 cottage, with a wood-burning stove and low-beam doors. ✉ *Box 103, Krondorf Rd., 5352,* ☎ 🖷 *08/8563–2141. 7 suites. Spa. MC, V.*

$ 🏠 **Blickinstal.** These motel-style units are set on a farm on the lower slopes of the Barossa Ranges. The name means "look into the valley," which perfectly describes the view of almond trees and vineyards. Guest rooms have a contemporary, functional design, and each has kitchen facilities. ✉ *Box 17, Rifle Range Rd., 5352,* ☎ *08/8563–2716. 4 rooms with bath. MC, V.*

Bethany

❼ *4 km (2½ mi) southeast of Tanunda, 70 km (44 mi) northeast of Adelaide.*

The village of Bethany was the original German settlement in the Barossa. Those who established the town in 1842 divided the land exactly as they did in their Silesian homeland—with the farmhouses side by side at the front of long, narrow strips of land that run down to Bethany Creek. Today Bethany is a sleepy hollow, eclipsed in size and importance by the nearby towns. Its one shop, the Bethany Art and Craft Gallery, is set in a garden brimming with flowers.

❽ Menglers Hill is the best spot from which to view a panorama of the Barossa. The parking lot near the summit overlooks the patchwork of vineyards in the valley below. Like so much of South Australia, the Barossa suffers from a shortage of rain; in summer the landscape is scorched brown. Only the vineyards—most of which are irrigated—stand out as bright green rectangles.

Angaston

9 *17 km (11 mi) north of Bethany, 86 km (54 mi) northeast of Adelaide.*

This part of the Barossa was settled largely by immigrants from the British Isles, and the architecture of Angaston differs noticeably from the low stone buildings of the German towns.

10 **Collingrove.** Until 1975, this patrician country house was the ancestral home of the Angas family, the descendants of George Fife Angas, one of the founders of South Australia. The family carved a pastoral empire from the colony and at the height of their fortunes controlled 14.5 million acres from this house. Today the house is administered by the National Trust, and you can inspect the Angas family portraits and memorabilia, including Dresden china, a hand-painted Louis XV cabinet, and Chippendale chairs. The veranda at the front of the house overlooks formal gardens. You can also overnight at Collingrove (☞ *below*). ⊠ *Eden Valley Rd.,* ☎ *08/8564–2061.* ⌑ *$3.* ⊙ *Oct.–June, weekdays 1–4:30, weekends 11–4:30; July–Sept., Mon.–Thurs. 1– 4:30, weekends 11–4:30.*

11 Stephen and Prue Henschke, the wine makers of **Henschke Winery,** were named International Red Wine Makers of the Year 1994–1995 at London's International Wine Challenge. Taste the magnificent Hill of Grace, a superb wine by any standards, and you will understand why Henschke is the Barossa's premium winery. Other great reds include Cyril Henschke Cabernet Sauvignon and Mount Edelstone Shiraz. And don't miss out on their Semillon. The winery is 4 km (2½ mi) from Keyneton on a passable dirt road. ⊠ *Keyneton, 11 km (7 mi) from Angaston,* ☎ *08/8564–8223.* ⊙ *Weekdays 9–4:30, Sat. 9–noon.*

OFF THE
BEATEN PATH
From Henschke Winery, turn right into the dirt road and left at the second road, Gnadenberg Road, along which you will see the **Hill of Grace** vineyard opposite pretty **Gnadenberg Zion Church** (1860). Turn left into Lindsay Park Road, passing the famous Lindsay Park horse stud farm, and return to Angaston.

Dining and Lodging

$$$$ ✕ **The Vintners.** This relaxed, sophisticated restaurant combines the
★ techniques of French and Asian cooking using the finest local produce. Local trout, lamb, kangaroo, and homemade sausages—with seasonings that hail from Paris to Penang—appear on a menu that appeals to conservative as well as creative tastes. Try Tuscan scalded cream with caramel sauce for dessert. The fabulous wine list comes with enthusiastic and eloquent advice from front-of-house manager Doug Coats. ⊠ *Nuriootpa Rd.,* ☎ *08/8564–2488. AE, DC, MC, V. Closed Mon. No dinner Tues.–Thurs.*

$$ ✕⌑ **Collingrove.** This stately country house, situated on undulant
★ grazing land, was built more than a century ago by the Angas family, one of South Australia's pioneering dynasties. Guests stay in the former servants' quarters at the back of the house, where large, comfortable rooms are furnished in a rustic style with antique iron bedsteads, cane chairs, and pine wardrobes. The house operates under the auspices of the National Trust and is open to the public during the day; when it is closed to the public, you as a guest can look through it and use the former library as a lounge. Dinner is available by prior arrangement. ⊠ *Eden Valley Rd., 5353,* ☎ ℻ *08/8564–2061. 4 rooms share 3 baths. Spa. AE, DC, MC, V.*

Shopping

Bethany Art and Craft Gallery is housed in Angaston's Old Police Station and Courthouse, an 1855 building with stone walls 20 ft thick. What was once the prisoners' exercise yard—now covered with translucent roofing—is used to exhibit the work of some of the finest artisans in Australia. ⌧ *12 Washington St., Angaston,* ☎ *08/8564–3344.* ⊙ *Daily 10–5.*

Nuriootpa

6 km (4 mi) northwest of Angaston, 74 km (46 mi) northeast of Adelaide.

Long before it was the Barossa's commercial center, Nuriootpa was used as a place of bartering by local Aboriginal tribes, hence its name: Nuriootpa means "meeting place."

⑫ **Elderton Wines.** This is another of the small "boutique" wineries of the area, and its elegant wine has rapidly garnered an enviable reputation. Elderton's award-winning range of red, white, and sparkling wine is excellent. The winery's full-bodied reds are of particular note. Elderton conducts a 20-minute tour of its vineyard, starting from its tasting rooms, but only by appointment. ⌧ *Murray St. and New Rd.,* ☎ *08/8562–1058.* ⊙ *Weekdays 8:30–5, weekends 11–4.*

Marananga

⑬ *6 km (4 mi) west of Nuriootpa, 68 km (43 mi) northeast of Adelaide.*

The tiny hamlet of Marananga inhabits one of the prettiest corners of the Barossa. The original name for this area was Gnadenfrei, which means "Freed by the Grace of God"—a reference to the religious persecution the German settlers suffered under the Prussian kings before they emigrated to Australia. Marananga, the Aboriginal name, was adopted in 1918, when a wave of anti-German sentiment spurred many name changes in the closing days of World War I. The barn at the lower end of the parking lot is one of the most photogenic in the Barossa.

Marananga marks the beginning of a 3-km (2-mi) avenue of date palms planted during the depression as a work-creation scheme devised by the Seppelts, a wine-making family. Look for the Doric temple on the hillside to the right—it's the Seppelt family mausoleum.

⑭ The avenue of date palm trees ends at **Seppelts Winery,** one of the most magnificent in the Barossa. Joseph Seppelt was a Silesian farmer who arrived in Australia in 1849 and purchased land in the Barossa. Under the control of his son, Benno, the wine-making business flourished, and today the winery and its splendid grounds are a tribute to the family's industry and enthusiasm. Fortified wine is a Seppelts specialty: This is the only winery in the world that has vintage ports for every year as far back as 1878. Along with port, the winery's sauvignon blanc, chardonnay, and cabernet are well worth tasting. Seppelts runs an excellent tour of the winery, which takes you from the crushing area to the fermentation tanks and the maturation cellars, where the fortified wine is stored and the air is filled with rich, spicy aromas. The 45-minute tour also includes an inspection of the Seppelts carriage museum, which houses some of the finest horse-drawn vehicles in the country. ⌧ *Seppeltsfield, 3 km (2 mi) from Marananga,* ☎ *08/8562–8028.* ⌧ *Tour $3.* ⊙ *Weekdays 8:30–5, Sat. 10:30–4:30, Sun. 11–4; tour weekdays at 11, 1, 2, and 3 and weekends at 11:30, 1:30, and 2:30.*

Dining and Lodging

$ ✕ **Barossa Picnic Baskets.** These baskets come stuffed with all the meat, pâté, cheese, salad, and fruit needed for a perfect lunch outdoors. Three feasts are available, including a vegetarian basket, and each comes with a bottle of wine and a map directing you to picnic spots. Go and get yourself a basket! ⊠ *Gnadenfrei Estate,* ☎ *08/8562–2522. AE, DC, MC, V.*

$$$$ ✕⊞ **The Lodge.** This rambling, aristocratic bluestone homestead was
★   built in 1903 for one of the 13 children of Joseph Seppelt, the founder of the showpiece winery across the road. Its lawns, rose garden, native woodland, and its orchards of plum, peach, pear, almond, and apple trees are all quite lovely. Inside, the house has a library, wine cellar, formal dining room, and a sitting room furnished with big, comfortable sofas. Located off a lounge room at the rear of the house, four guest bedrooms are large, luxuriously equipped, and furnished in period style. Meals make good use of local produce—smoked salmon from the Adelaide Hills, meats from the German butcher down the road, and local olives. Communal dinners vary from formal banquets to barbecues. Unfortunately, children are not welcome. ⊠ *RSD 120, Seppeltsfield via Nuriootpa, 5355,* ☎ *08/8562–8277,* ℻ *08/8562–8344. 4 rooms with bath. Pool, tennis court. MC, V. Closed Tues. and Wed. except by appointment.*

$$$ ⊞ **Hermitage of Marananga.** Located on a quiet back road, this hilltop inn has large, modern guest rooms furnished with a sense of style that sets them apart from standard motel rooms. ⊠ *Box 330, Seppeltsfield and Stonewell Rds., Tanunda 5352, Marananga,* ☎ *08/ 8562–2722,* ℻ *08/8562–3133. 10 rooms with bath. Restaurant, pool, spa. AE, DC, MC, V.*

Shopping

Pooters Old Wares, situated in a charming corrugated-iron building, houses a fascinating treasury of handmade furniture and farm implements—much of it unearthed from the cellars of the local German community. ⊠ *Seppeltsfield Rd.,* ☎ *08/8562–2538.* ☉ *Tues.–Thurs. and weekends 11–5.*

Barossa Valley A to Z

Arriving and Departing

BY CAR

The most direct route from Adelaide to the Barossa Valley is via the town of Gawler. From the center of Adelaide, drive north on King William Road. About 1 km (½ mi) past the Torrens River Bridge, take the right fork onto the Main North Road. After 6 km (3 mi) this road forks to the right—follow signs to the Sturt Highway and the town of Gawler. At Gawler, leave the highway and follow the signs to Lyndoch on the southern border of the Barossa. The 50-km (31-mi) journey should take just less than an hour. A more attractive, if circuitous, route winds through the northern portion of the Adelaide Hills, traveling through Chain of Ponds and Williamstown to Lyndoch.

Getting Around

BY CAR

The widespread nature of the Barossa wineries means a car is by far the best way of getting around. But remember, if you intend to taste wines at a number of vineyards, there are stiff penalties for driving under the influence of alcohol, and random breath testing has been known to occur. ☞ Car Rentals *in* Adelaide A to Z, *above.*

Contacts and Resources

EMERGENCIES
Police, fire or **ambulance.** ☎ *000.*

GUIDED TOURS
Festival Tours (☎ 08/8374–1270) operates a full-day tour of the Barossa from Adelaide for $54, including lunch. Tours depart from 18 King William Street. **Barossa Valley Tours** (☎ 08/8562–1524) operates a six-hour coach tour of the wineries and churches of the Barossa for $30, lunch included, with pickup in Lyndoch, Tanunda, Angaston, and Nuriootpa.

VISITOR INFORMATION
Barossa Wine and Tourism Association. ⊠ *66–68 Murray St., Tanunda 5352,* ☎ *08/8563–0600.*

THE CLARE VALLEY

The Clare is the "other" South Australia grape-growing valley. Smaller and less well known than the Barossa, the Clare Valley nonetheless holds its own. Its robust reds and delicate whites are among the country's finest, and the Clare is generally regarded as the best area in Australia for fragrant, flavorsome rieslings. Almost on the fringe of the vast inland deserts, the Clare is a narrow sliver of fertile soil about 30 km (19 mi) long and 5 km (3 mi) wide, with a micro-climate that makes it ideal for premium wine making.

The first vines were planted here as early as 1842, but it is only in the last decade that the Clare Valley's viticultural reputation has taken its place on the national stage. The mix of small family wineries and large-scale producers, historic settlements and grand country houses, snug valleys and dense native forest has rare charm. And beyond the northern edge of the valley, where the desert takes hold, there is the fascinating copper mining town of Burra, which makes for a natural adjunct to any Clare Valley sojourn.

Auburn

110 km (66 mi) north of Adelaide.

Auburn, the southern gateway to the Clare Valley, initially developed as an overnight halt for wagon trains carting the copper ore of Burra down to Port Wakefield. The historic buildings of the St. Vincent Street and Main North Road precinct are worth a look for their superb stonework. Auburn was the birthplace of Australian poet C. J. Dennis—the town's heritage walk includes the home in which he was born.

The **Kollektakan Memorabilia Museum** is the first in Australia dedicated to Coca-Cola products. There are three rooms filled with Coca-Cola bottles and cans, advertisements, packaging and history, and an outlet where you can buy, surprise, Coke products. ⊠ *36 Main North Rd., Auburn,* ☎ *08/8849–2373.* 🎫 *$2.* ⏱ *Daily 9:30–5:30.*

Jeffrey Grosset established his small, highly regarded **Grosset Wines** in 1981 in an old butter factory. His wines include Polish Hill and Watervale Rieslings, a late-harvest riesling, and Gaia, a blend of cabernet sauvignon, cabernet franc, and merlot grapes. The vineyard, at 570 meters (1,870 feet) elevation, is the highest in the Clare Valley. Tours are available by appointment. ⊠ *King St., Auburn, 08/8849–2175.* ⏱ *Sept.– until vintage is sold out, Wed.–Sun. 10–5.*

Watervale

8 km (5 mi) north of Auburn, 118 km (71 mi) north of Adelaide.

This tiny hamlet amid acres of vines is fitted with a number of heritage-listed buildings in a very pretty setting.

Crabtree of Watervale winery, perhaps uniquely among Australian wineries, welcomes children, who are encouraged to explore the property and make friends with its many animals while adults enjoy tasting the vineyard's produce. Tastings and sales are in the original cellars (1870s), which offer a superb view of the surrounding valleys. The riesling is especially good, as are the shiraz and cabernet sauvignon. ⊠ *North Terr.,* ☎ *08/8843–0069.* ⊙ *Daily 9–5, vineyard tour by appointment.*

The cellar buildings of historic **Quelltaler Estate** date in part from 1863. There is a lovely picnic area in front of the cellar door sales area, but of greatest interest is the small wine museum, which includes early wine-making equipment. Try the fruity riesling and full-flavored reds. ⊠ *Quelltaler Rd.,* ☎ *08/8843–0003.* ⊙ *Weekdays 9–5, Sat. 11–4, Sun. noon–4.*

Sevenhill

8 km (5 mi) north of Watervale, 126 km (76 mi) north of Adelaide.

Sevenhill is the geographic center of the Clare Valley, and the location of the first winery in the region, established by Jesuit priests in 1851 to produce altar wine. The area had been settled by Austrian Jesuits three years earlier, who named their seminary after the seven hills of Rome. They also, rather optimistically, named a local creek the Tiber.

If you have the inclination or opportunity to visit only one Clare winery, make it **Sevenhill Cellars.** This was the creation of the Jesuits, and they still run the show. In the 1940s the winery branched into commercial production, which today accounts for 75% of its business. By appointment, you can receive a guided tour from the charming wine maker Brother John May (it may be the only winery tour in the world where the farewell is "God bless you"). Otherwise you are free to roam the cellars and winery. The original cellars, musty and cool even in midsummer, are reached by a stepladder. Don't miss St. Aloysius Church, built of stone quarried on the property, and its crypt, in which Jesuits have been interred since 1865. ⊠ *College Rd., Sevenhill,* ☎ *08/8843–4222.* ⊙ *Weekdays 8:30–4:30, Sat. 9–4.*

Skillogalee Winery is not only known for its excellent wines—its restaurant is the Clare Valley's number one dining experience (☞ Dining and Lodging, *below*). Wine tasting takes place in a small room of a 140-year-old cottage (the restaurant occupies the others). Try the excellent shiraz, cabernet, and riesling. ⊠ *Hughes Park Rd.,* ☎ *08/8843–4311.* ⊙ *Daily 10–5.*

Jeanneret Wines is one of the youngest producers in the valley—its first sales were in 1994. Nestled in a heavily treed area on the edge of the Spring Gully Conservation Park, it is worth visiting for the setting alone. There is a charming picnic spot beneath gum trees, which is a perfect place to enjoy a newly purchased bottle of riesling or shiraz. ⊠ *Jeanneret Rd.,* ☎ *08/8843–4308.* ⊙ *Daily 11–5.*

Dining and Lodging

$–$$$ ✕ **Skillogalee Winery.** This Clare Valley darling fills the rooms of a
★   140-year-old cottage and spills onto a beautiful veranda overlooking
           the vineyard. For a light meal, try the vine pruner's lunch—chef Diana

Palmer's spin on the British ploughman's lunch. More substantial fare includes braised oxtail and a fragrant chicken curry. Sticky toffee pudding is a dessert favorite. The restaurant serves lunch, morning and afternoon teas. ⊠ *Hughes Park Rd.,* ☎ *08/8843–4311.* ⊘ *Daily 10–5.*

$$$$ 🏠 **Thorn Park Country House.** Saved from ruin by owners David Hay
★ and Michael Speers, Thorn Park is one of Australia's finest bed-and-breakfasts. The lovely 135-year-old house is furnished with exquisite taste and the finest antiques. The sitting room and small library are particularly charming, and the grounds, filled with hawthorns, elms, and heritage roses, are equally impressive. Houseguests can enjoy a superb dinner and an incredibly indulgent cooked breakfast—David also runs occasional cooking schools. ⊠ *College Rd.,* ☎ *08/8843–4304. 5 rooms with bath. MC, V.*

Mintaro

10 km (6 mi) southeast of Sevenhill, 126 km (76 mi) north of Adelaide.

Originally a stop on the Burra–Port Wakefield copper ore route, Mintaro later became known for its enormous slate deposit, which was used internationally for pool tables and locally for building. The tiny town is beautifully preserved; its one street, lined with shops and houses, is heritage listed. Go for a stroll to enjoy its discreet charm.

Rather grander than the cottages of Mintaro hamlet is **Martindale Hall.** This gracious manor house, which dates from 1879, was built by Edmund Bowman in an attempt to lure his fiancée to move from England to the colonies. He failed. Bowman subsequently spent his time buying property and enjoying sport and society, but his fortune dwindled because of debt and drought, and he was forced to sell the hall in 1891. Decades later, in 1965, Martindale Hall was willed to the University of Adelaide. Today it is furnished in period style, and doubles as an upscale bed-and-breakfast. The building featured in director Peter Weir's first film, *Picnic at Hanging Rock.* ⊠ *Via Mintaro,* ☎ *08/ 8843–9088.* 💶 *$5.* ⊘ *Weekdays 11–4, weekends noon–4.*

Clare

20 km (12 mi) northeast of Mintaro, 136 km (82 mi) north of Adelaide.

The bustling town of Clare is the commercial center for the Clare Valley. Unusual for ultra-English South Australia, many of its early settlers were Irish. Thus we have the valley's name, after the Irish county Clare, as well as place names such as Armagh and Donnybrook.

The **Old Police Station Museum** has an interesting collection of memorabilia from Clare's early days, as well as Victorian furniture and clothing, horse-drawn vehicles, and agricultural machinery. The 1850 stone building was Clare's first courthouse and police station. ⊠ *West Terr.,* ☎ *08/8842–2376.* 💶 *$2.* ⊘ *Weekends 10–noon and 2–4.*

Wendouree Cellars is one of the smallest wineries in the Clare, but, as it dates from 1895, it is also one of its most historic, and as a result treasured. Renowned for producing big wines from very old vines— its shiraz is particularly worthy—Wendouree also makes a fine cabernet sauvignon and an exceptional Cabernet Malbec blend. ⊠ *Wendouree Rd., Clare, 08/8842–2896.* ⊘ *Mon.–Sat. 10–4:30.*

On the fringe of Clare is **Leasingham Wines,** among the biggest producers in the valley. The winery began operation in 1893, which makes it one of the oldest vineyards. The tasting room is in an attractive old still house. Leasingham's reputation of late has been forged by its red wines, particularly the peppery shiraz. ⊠ *7 Dominic St., Clare,* ☎ *08/8842–2555.* ⊙ *Weekdays 8.30–5, weekends 10–4.*

Bungaree Station was established in 1841 when this site was chosen by grazier George Hawker and his two brothers for an enormous sheep farm. Today the property, though vastly smaller, remains in the family. In its heyday it had a shearing complex, manager's house and farm cottages, the local council chamber, and a church, all of which have been preserved as a living museum. There is a self-guided cassette tour of the historic buildings, and rustic accommodation is available. ⊠ *Off Main Rd., 12 km (7½ mi) north of Clare,* ☎ *08/8842–2677.* 🎫 *$8, including cassette tour.* ⊙ *By appointment.*

Burra

44 km (32 mi) northeast of Clare, 156 km (99½ mi) north of Adelaide.

Burra isn't strictly part of the Clare Valley, but it's an important adjunct to any visit to the Clare. Burra, like many Australian towns, developed because of mineral wealth. In this case it was copper, which for a time in the early 1850s made Burra Australia's largest inland town, and its seventh largest settlement overall. The ore ran out quickly, however—the biggest mine closed just 32 years after it opened—and Burra settled into a comfortable existence as a service town.

The innovative **"Burra Passport,"** a guidebook and key that provides information about and entry to the town's main attractions, makes touring the place simple and enjoyable. The passport costs $20, and you can purchase it at the tourist office in Market Square (⊙ Daily 9–4).

The key that comes with the Burra Passport allows access to the **Burra Mine Site,** the open cut, so-called Monster Mine that contains many relics of the early days, including a powder magazine, machinery, chimneys, and the Enginehouse Museum. ⊠ *West and Linkson Sts., Burra,* ☎ *08/8892–2056.* 🎫 *$3.* ⊙ *Weekdays 12:30–2:30, weekends 12:30–3:30.*

The **Bon Accord Mine** (⊠ Linkston St.), unlike the phenomenally successful Monster Mine, was a failure, but the canny Scottish owners made the best of a bad lot by selling the mine shaft, which hit the water table, to the town as a water supply, and subdividing the land for housing. The old mine is now an interesting museum. Entry is additional to the passport.

Redruth Gaol (⊠ Tregony St.), a colonial prison that later served as a girls' reformatory, houses an informative display on its checkered history. The jail appeared in the Australian film *Breaker Morant.* The **Unicorn Brewery Cellars** (⊠ Bridge Terr.) are cool and inviting in the desert heat of a Burra summer, even though there's no longer any beer in the house. The brewery lasted for 30 years from 1873 and was regarded as one of Australia's best producers.

During the mining period, as many as 2,000 miners lived in dugout homes on the banks of Burra Creek. Two of these tiny dwellings remain, accessed by the Burra Passport. One of them, **Hampton,** is a sad, windswept, and evocative place. It was built as a village for English miners (there were separate Cornish, Scottish, Welsh, and colonial settlements) but was eventually abandoned. The ruins of the village, mainly the foundations of homes, are a stark reminder of the transitory nature of colonial industry, and in a way, of life. To get there, drive north on Tregony Street from Redruth Gaol and take the first right turn. At the T-junction, turn left into the Hampton carpark.

Malowen Lowarth is one of several dozen cottages at Paxton Square built between 1849 and 1852 as housing for miners who had moved from the creek dugouts. It is now owned by the National Trust, and operates as a museum featuring period furniture and fittings. Entry is additional to the Burra passport. ⊠ *Paxton Sq.,* ☎ *08/8892–2154.* 🖾 *$2.* ⊙ *Sat. 1–3, Sun. 10:30–2:30, or by appointment.*

Clare Valley A to Z

Arriving and Departing

BY CAR

The Clare Valley is about 90 minutes' drive from Adelaide via the Main North Road. From the center of Adelaide, head north on King William Street through the heart of North Adelaide. King William becomes O'Connell Street. After crossing Barton Terrace, look for the Main North Road signs on the right. The road passes through the satellite town of Elizabeth, bypasses the center of Gawler, and then runs due north to Auburn, the first town of the Clare Valley when approaching from the capital. Main North Road continues down the middle of the valley to Clare. From Clare town, follow signs to Burra, on the Barrier Highway.

Getting Around

BY CAR

As with the Barossa, a car is essential for exploring the Clare Valley in any depth. Note again that penalties are severe for drunk driving. Taste wine in moderation. ☞ Car Rentals *in* Adelaide A to Z, *above.*

Contacts and Resources

EMERGENCIES

Police, fire or **ambulance.** ☎ *000.*

VISITOR INFORMATION

Clare Valley Tourist Information Center. ⊠ *Town Hall, 229 Main North Rd., Clare,* ☎ *08/8842–2131.*

FLEURIEU PENINSULA

The Fleurieu has traditionally been seen as Adelaide's backyard. Generations of Adelaide families have vacationed in the string of beachside resorts between Goolwa, near the mouth of the Murray River, and Victor Harbor. It is so close to Adelaide and so easy to get to that its appeal has been somewhat overlooked in the recent past. No longer. The wineries of the McLaren Vale attract connoisseurs, the beaches and bays bring in surfers, swimmers, and sun bakers, and towns like Victor Harbor are being rediscovered by new generations of visitors.

You can easily combine a day trip to the Fleurieu with one or more nights on Kangaroo Island. The ferry from Cape Jervis, at the end of the peninsula, takes one hour to reach Penneshaw on the island. If you are traveling during Australian holiday periods, reserve space on the ferry in advance.

McLaren Vale

39 km (24 mi) south of Adelaide.

There are more than 50 wineries in this town. The first vines were planted just to the north at Reynella in 1838 by Englishman John Reynell, who had collected them en route from the Cape of Good Hope. The McLaren Vale has always been known for its big reds, shiraz notably, but in recent years more white varietals have been planted and softer reds developed.

Chapel Hill Winery is a small, somewhat exclusive vineyard, with the tasting room set in an old, hilltop chapel. Wine maker Pam Dunsford was the queen of the district's first bushing festival in 1991, a celebration of the new vintage. Wines include rich shiraz and cabernet sauvignon, as well as a fine late harvest white. The grapes for the sweet white are (deliberately) affected by a fungus known as the noble rot, which produces a rich, luscious dessert wine. ⊠ *Chapel Hill Rd., McLaren Vale,* ☎ *08/8323–8429.* ⊙ *Weekdays 9–5, weekends 11–5.*

At **d'Arenberg Wines,** family run since 1912, excellent wine is complemented by a fine restaurant. The splendidly named Chester d'Arenberg Osborn is the wine maker, known for quality whites, including a Noble Riesling (botrytis affected) and a wide range of reds and fortified wines. d'Arry's Verandah Restaurant overlooks the vineyards and the valley to the sea. Recent dishes on the menu, which changes daily, have included roasted pigeon or venison, loin of goat, deep-fried fish, or saltbush hogget. A two-course meal is $30, $40 for three courses. ⊠ *Osborn Rd.,* ☎ *08/8323–8206.* ⊙ *Winery daily 10–5. No lunch Mon. or Tues. No dinner weekdays.*

The most historic of McLaren Vale's wineries is **Seaview,** which was established in 1850. The large tasting room is particularly impressive, lined with old carved wine vats. You can look around the winery and its historic buildings, but there are no organized tours. The winery produces a delicious array of whites, including fantastic sparkling wines, and a couple of reds. ⊠ *Chaffey's Road,* ☎ *08/8323–8250.* ⊙ *Weekdays 9–4:30, Sat. 10–5, Sun. 11–4.*

The restored cellars of **Wirra Wirra Vineyards** were built in 1894, and they couldn't be more appealing than in winter, when a roaring fire is burning. Try riesling, cabernet sauvignon, shiraz, the good value Church Block Dry Red, and a méthode champenoise white. ⊠ *McMurtrie Rd.,* ☎ *08/8323–8414.* ⊙ *Mon.–Sat. 10–5, Sun. 11–5.*

Goolwa

44 km (26 mi) southeast of McLaren Vale, 83 km (49 mi) south of Adelaide.

Beautifully situated near the mouth of the mighty Murray River, Goolwa grew fat on the river paddle steamer trade last century. At one point it boasted 88 pubs. Today its envious position, close to the sea, Lake Alexandrina, and the lovely Coorong National Park, has seen tourist business replace river trade as the main source of income. South Australia's first railway line was built in 1854 to Port Elliot, Goolwa's sea port.

Signal Point is an excellent interpretive center on Goolwa Wharf that uses audiovisual techniques to tell stories of the indigenous Ngarrindjeri people and of the river trade. The River Museum highlights artifacts, charts, paintings, and models. ⊠ *Goolwa Wharf,* ☎ *08/8555–3488.* ⊠ *$5.* ⊙ *Daily 10–5.*

Goolwa Wharf is the launch for daily cruises on the **PS Mundoo,** a replica paddle steamer that makes half- and full-day trips to Currency Creek, Narnu Bay, the Mundoo Channel, and the Goose and Goat Islands. The **MV Aroona** cruises past the Murray mouth to the wild Coorong Peninsula, where you can step ashore and cross to the ocean. ⊠ *Goolwa Wharf,* ☎ *08/8555–2203.* ⊠ *Coffee cruise $12, lunch cruise $18, pelican-feeding cruise on MV Aroona $10.*

Coorong National Park is a sliver of land—stretching southeast of the Fleurieu Peninsula and completely separate from it—that hugs the

South Australian coast for more than 150 km (94 mi). Most Australians became aware of the Coorong's beauty from the 1970s film *Storm Boy,* which told the story of a boy's friendship with a pelican. These mighty birds are one reason why the Doorong is a wetland area of world standing. Birdwatching is excellent, but the beaches and dunes have plenty of appeal even if you aren't interested in birdlife. The area was also a major habitation for Aborigines, and shell middens give abundant evidence of their life here. The mainland side of the park, which you would reach driving straight from Adelaide, is off of Princes Highway south of the fishing town of Meningie.

Victor Harbor

16 km (10 mi) west of Goolwa, 83 km (49 mi) south of Adelaide.

In some ways, Victor Harbor has come full circle. In the 1830s the town was a major whaling center, from which whalers set out to hunt the southern right whale. The species was so named because it was considered the "right" whale to kill—it was slow, easy to target, and its flesh had a high oil content that caused the whale to float after being harpooned. The leviathans came to Encounter Bay (named for the meeting here in 1802 of English and French explorers Matthew Flinders and Nicholas Baudin) to breed in the winter and early spring. Their great numbers made whaling a profitable trade, but the last whale was killed in the bay in 1878. Within that 50-year period the southern right was nearly hunted to extinction. Now the blessed creatures are back— as many as 40 at a time—and Victor Harbor is again capitalizing on their presence.

The **South Australian Whale Center** tells the often graphic story of the whaling industry along the SA coast, particularly in Encounter Bay. The interpretive displays are excellent, spread over three floors, and deal with dolphins, seals, and penguins—all of which can be seen in these waters—as well as whales. In whale-watching season (generally June through September), the center has information on sightings. ✉ *Railway Terr.,* ☎ *08/8552–5644.* ☞ *$5.* ⊙ *Daily 9–5.*

Visit **The Bluff,** a few kilometers west of Victor Harbor, to see where whalers once stood lookout for their prey. Today the granite outcrop, also known as Rosetta Head, serves the same purpose in very difference circumstances.

Granite Island is linked to the mainland by a causeway, along which a double-decker tram trundles, pulled by Clydesdale horses. A large colony of fairy penguins lives on the island. They are best seen at dusk. You can walk to the summit of the island, or take a chairlift if you're flagging. ☎ *08/8552–1777.* ☞ *Return tram trip $3, including chairlift.*

The steam powered **Cockle Train** travels the original route of South Australia's first railway line on its journey to Goolwa. Extended from Port Elliot to Victor Harbor in 1864, the line traces the lovely Southern Ocean beaches on its 16 km (10 mi) route. The train runs over Easter and during school holidays, and on selected Sundays. ☞ *Return fare $12.* ☎ *08/8231–1707.*

Head to **Urimbirra Wildlife Park** if you feel like gawking at a menagerie of native Ozzie animals and birds, more than 70 species in all. Among the collection at this open range zoo are kangaroos, saltwater and freshwater crocodiles, pelicans (which you can see in the wild in Coorong National Park to the south), and Cape Barren Geese. ✉ *Adelaide Rd.,* ☎ *08/8554–6554.* ☞ *$5.* ⊙ *Daily 10–5.*

Fleurieu Peninsula A to Z

Arriving and Departing
BY CAR

The Fleurieu is an easy drive south from Adelaide—McLaren Vale it-self is little more than half an hour away. Leave central Adelaide along South Terrace or West Terrace, linking with the Anzac Highway, which heads toward beachside Glenelg. At the intersection with the Main South Road, turn left. This road will take you almost to the town of McLaren Vale. After a detour to visit the wineries, watch for signs for Victor Harbor Road. About 20 km (12 mi) south, the highway splits—one road heads for Victor Harbor, the other for Goolwa. Those two places are connected by a major road that follows the coastline. Drivers making for Cape Jervis and the Kangaroo Island ferry should stay on the Main South Road.

Getting Around
BY CAR

A car is the best means to visit the Fleurieu Peninsula, especially if you wish to visit any wineries, which are not served by public transport. ☞ Car Rentals *in* Adelaide A to Z, *above.*

Contacts and Resources
EMERGENCIES

Police, fire or **ambulance.** ☎ *000.*

VISITOR INFORMATION

Goolwa Tourist Information Center. ✉ *Old Library Bldg., Cadell St. and Goolwa Terr.,* ☎ *08/8555–1144.*
Victor Harbor Tourist Information Center. ✉ *10 Railway Terr.,* ☎ *08/ 8552–4255.*

KANGAROO ISLAND

Kangaroo Island, Australia's third largest island, is barely 16 km (10 mi) from the Australian mainland, yet the distance between the two places far exceeds that in years. Kangaroo Island belongs to another age—a folksy, friendly, less sophisticated time when you'd leave your car unlocked and wave to other drivers as they passed.

The island's interior is stark and barren for the most part, but the coast-line is sculpted into a series of bays and inlets teeming with bird and marine life. In fact the wildlife is probably the greatest attraction. In a single day you can stroll along a beach crowded with sea lions and watch koalas, kangaroos, pelicans, sea eagles, and fairy penguins in their native environment.

Kangaroo Island has a turbulent history. At the beginning of the 19th century it was a haven for escaped convicts and sailors who had de-serted their whaling ships—some of them from North American ports. These castaways preyed on the coastal Aborigines and made a living from trading sealskin. Eventually their raids became too bold, and the colonial government sent an armed expedition to the island in 1827. Most of the renegades were dragged away to Sydney in chains, and the island was left with a population of less than a dozen.

Many people treasure Kangaroo Island for what it lacks. Although it's just a two- to three-hour trip from Adelaide, there are no resorts and virtually no nightlife, and its only luxuries are salty sea breezes, sparkling clear water, and solitude.

Exploring Kangaroo Island

The towns and most of the accommodations are located in the eastern third of the island. The most interesting sights are on the southern coast, so it's advisable to tour the island in a clockwise direction—leaving the beaches of the north coast for later in the day. You can take in a fair amount in a single day, but allow three days at least to explore more of the island. Except in the main towns, gas stations and shops are scarce. Before heading out for the day, you should have a full tank of gas and a picnic lunch. Many of the roads are loose gravel, so take care when driving.

National parks on the island have the most to offer. At the start of your journey, it is advisable to purchase an **Island Pass** ($15), available from any national park ranger station or from the Environment and Natural Resources office (✉ 27 Dauncey St., Kingscote, ☎ 08/8552–2381). The pass covers all national park entry fees, vehicle fees, ranger-guided tours, and camping fees for 14 nights, and it is valid from July 1 to June 30 of the following year.

Kingscote

121 km (75 mi) southwest of Adelaide.

Ferries from Port Adelaide and Glenelg arrive in Kingscote, the largest town on Kangaroo Island. It has a more substantial character than its sister towns Penneshaw and American River. Reeves Point, at the northern end of town, marks the beginning of South Australia's colonial history. It was here that settlers landed in 1836 and established the first official town in the new colony, but you'll have to use your imagination to appreciate this. Little remains of the original settlement, which was abandoned barely three years after it began, due to poor soil and a lack of fresh water. The town comes alive in mid-February for a weekend of horse races.

☾ Throughout January, rangers from the **Environment and Natural Resources Service** run an extensive program of events designed to introduce children to the nature and history of the island. Events include lighthouse tours, tidal-pool walks, and evenings on the beach to watch fairy penguins waddle ashore. ✉ *Government Office Bldg., 27 Dauncey St., ☎ 08/8552–2381.*

Dining and Lodging

$$ ✕ **Cygnet Cafe.** Kangaroo Island's first quality dining experience is a classy café transformed from a former gas station. The cuisine, which draws its influences from such places as Asia and North Africa, is as innovative as the interior design with its dazzling use of color. The menu changes fortnightly, but you will always find spicy Malay chicken curry and wonderful, rich, brandy chocolate prune cake on the list. Local products are used extensively: Kangaroo Island cream, sheep's milk yogurt, mutton, turkey, and corn-fed chicken. ✉ *Playford Hwy., Cygnet River, 13 km (8 mi) west of Kingscote, ☎ 08/8552–9187. AE, DC, MC, V. No dinner Mon. or Tues.*

$$$$ ▦ **The Settlement.** Set in hilly grazing country above one of the finest beaches on the island, these two adjacent cottages are perfect for a total getaway. Of the two, the stone Settlers Cottage is the more modern and better equipped. Each cottage sleeps up to six. Dinner is available on request. ✉ *Middle River, N. Coast Rd. via Kingscote 5223, ☎ 08/8553–6237. No credit cards.*

$$$ ⊞ **Sorrento Resort.** Overlooking a beach that is home to a colony of fairy penguins, Sorrento offers motel rooms and one-, two-, or three-bedroom units with their own cooking facilities. Village rooms are less expensive and are not serviced daily, but they have a garden setting that is preferable to the neat, clean, but rather charmless motel rooms. ⊠ *Box 352, North Terr., Penneshaw 5222, 59 km (37 mi) east of Kingscote,* ☎ *08/8553–1028,* FAX *08/8553–1024. 18 rooms with bath, 9 apartments. Restaurant, bar, pool, sauna, spa, tennis court. AE, DC, MC, V.*

$$ ⊞ **Wanderers Rest.** The size, furnishings, and stylish decor of these motel rooms make this one of the best bargains on the island. ⊠ *Box 34, Bayview Rd., American River 5221, 39 km (24 mi) west of Kingscote,* ☎ *08/8553–3140,* FAX *08/8553–3282. 8 rooms with bath. Restaurant, bar, pool, spa. AE, DC, MC, V.*

$ ⊞ **Barbaree Cottage.** Despite its unimposing exterior, this cottage is cozy and comfortable and provides self-catering accommodations for up to six people. Located about 5 km (3 mi) from American River, it is pleasantly close to the main farmhouse on an exposed promontory above a lagoon where black swans and pelicans come to fish. The lagoon is a declared aquatic reserve. ⊠ *Box 30, Pelican Lagoon, American River 5221, 39 km (24 mi) west of Kingscote,* ☎ *08/8553–3190. No credit cards.*

Seal Bay Conservation Park

60 km (37 mi) southwest of Kingscote via the Playford Hwy.

This is one of the most accessible sea lion colonies anywhere—and the sight of these animals lazing on the beach, suckling their young, and bodysurfing in the waves is the highlight of any trip to Kangaroo Island. Australian sea lions, which recover here from their long and strenuous fishing trips, allow humans to approach within about 15 ft. The colony numbers approximately 500, and about a hundred sea lions can usually be found on the beach, except on stormy days, when they take shelter in the sand dunes. You can visit the beach only in a tour party led by a park ranger, but apart from the busy summer holiday period, you are usually allowed to wander the beach freely (albeit under the watchful eye of the ranger). The slope from the ranger station to the beach is moderately steep, and there are steps at the bottom. ⊠ *Seal Bay,* ☎ *08/8552–8233.* 🎫 *Tour $7.50.* ☉ *Tour Dec. and Jan., daily every 15–30 min 9–4:30; Feb.–Nov., daily every 45 min 9–4:30.*

Little Sahara

7 km west of Seal Bay, 67 km (42 mi) southwest of Kingscote.

Towering white sand dunes cover several square miles here, and a short walk is hard to resist—but even a glimpse of the sea is a long way off. To get here from Seal Bay Road, turn left onto the South Coast Highway and continue until just before a one-lane bridge. Turn left onto the rough track that leads to Little Sahara.

Vivonne Bay

60 km (37 mi) southwest of Kingscote, 181 km (113 mi) southwest of Adelaide.

There isn't much here besides a jetty, a few crayfish boats, and a beach that disappears into the distance, but if you continue to **Point Ellen,** views of the bay and of Vivonne Bay Conservation Park are superb.

Hanson Bay

20 km (12 mi) west of Vivonne Bay, 80 km (125 mi) southwest of Kingscote.

A narrow, winding road ends at Hanson Bay, a perfect little sandy cove. The gentle slope of the beach and the rocky headlands on either side provide safe swimming. On the far side of the headland to the east are several secluded beaches, although these are more exposed, and riptides make swimming dangerous. You can catch salmon from these beaches. Limestone caves, the Kelly Hill Caves, are also nearby.

Lodging

$$ ☒ **Hanson Bay Cabins.** These neat, self-contained log cabins are set in coastal heath land near Flinders Chase National Park, one of the most isolated spots on the island. A pristine white-sand beach, where swimming is safe for children, is 50 yards away. ☒ *10 McKenna St., Hanson Bay, Kensington Park 5068,* ☎ *08/8333–0646. 6 cabins. No credit cards.*

Fishing

Fishing is excellent on the island's beaches, bays, and rivers. Crayfish can be caught from the rocks, sea salmon and mullet from beaches, and bream in rivers. The island's deep-sea fishing fleet holds several world records for tuna. No permit is required, although restrictions do apply on the size and quantity of fish you can keep. Rent boats and fishing tackle from the **Tacklebox Boat Hire** (☒ American River Wharf, ☎ 08/8553–3150).

Flinders Chase National Park

80 km (48 mi) west of Kingscote, 200 km (120 mi) southwest of Adelaide.

Some of the most beautiful coastal scenery in Australia is on the western end of Kangaroo Island at Flinders Chase National Park. The rest of the island is widely cultivated and grazed, but the park has maintained much of its original vegetation since it was declared a national treasure in 1919.

The seas crashing onto the southern coast of Australia are merciless, and their effects are visible in the oddly shaped rocks off the coast of Kangaroo Island. At Cape du Couedic, on the island's southwestern shore, for instance, a limestone promontory has been carved from underneath, producing what is now known as **Admiral's Arch.** About 4 km (2½ mi) east along the coast are **Remarkable Rocks**—huge boulders balanced precariously on the promontory of Kirkpatrick Point.

Starting in the 1920s, animals from the mainland were introduced to the island. Today a large population of koalas and Cape Barren geese live in the park. Much of the wildlife is so tame that a barricade had to be constructed at the Rocky River Campground to keep humans in and kangaroos and geese out.

Flinders Chase has several **walking trails,** ranging from 3 to 7 km (2 to 4 mi) in length, which take anywhere from one to three hours to complete. The trails meander along the rivers to the coast, passing mallee scrub and sugar gum forests. The 3-km (2-mi) Rocky River Walking Trail leads to a powerful waterfall before ending on a quiet sandy beach. Self-guided walks can be taken along the river valleys and beach.

The park is on the western end of the island, bounded by the Playford and West End highways. ☒ *$6.50 per vehicle.*

Lodging

All accommodations within the national park are controlled by the Department of Environment & Natural Resources. Camping is allowed only at designated sites for $2 per tent site at Rocky River and at bush campground, plus $2 for each adult and $1 for each child. Cottages listed below are simply but comfortably furnished, with rustic sofas, chairs, and tables: appealing for their rural charm and setting. Except for Hartley Hut, all have cooking facilities. Prices listed below apply per adult, per night.

⊡ **Old Homestead and Mays Cottage.** Built by the Mays family for their family and their mailman, these can be rented on a nightly basis. The Homestead (which sleeps six) rents for $25 a night. Mays Cottage (which sleeps four) rents for $10.

⊡ **Karatta, Parndana and Troubridge Cottages.** Located at Cape du Couedic, 20 km (12½ mi) from the Rocky River Headquarters, each sleeps six and costs $27.40.

⊡ **Flinders Light Cottage.** The lodge at Cape Borda sleeps six and rents for $25.

⊡ **Hartley Hut.** This hut at Cape Borda sleeps four and rents for $15.

⊡ **Seymour and Thomas Cottages.** These lighthouse cottages at Cape Willoughby rent for $25.

Visitor Information

Environment & Natural Resources Service. ⊠ *27 Dauncey St., Kingscote,* ☎ *08/8552–2381.*

Snellings Beach

50 km (31 mi) west of Kingscote.

Surrounded by high, rolling pastures, Snellings is broad and sandy, one of the best beaches on the island. Swimming is safe, but there are no facilities. ⊠ *N. Coast Rd.*

Kangaroo Island A to Z

Arriving and Departing

BY CAR FERRY

Vehicular ferries allow access for cars through either Kingscote or Penneshaw. The most popular option is the ferry from Cape Jervis at the tip of the Fleurieu Peninsula, about a 90-minute drive from Adelaide.

The **MV *Philanderer III*** and **MV *Island Navigator*** (☎ 13–1301) make the one-hour crossing between Cape Jervis and Penneshaw. There are three sailings per day between March and December, and up to 10 per day in summer months. These ferries are by far the most popular means of transport between the island and the mainland, and reservations are advisable during the summer vacation period. The one-way crossing costs $60 per vehicle, $30 per person. The **MV *Island Seaway*** (☎ 08/8447–5577), another ferry, makes the seven-hour journey between Port Adelaide and Kingscote. The fare is $62 per vehicle, and $25.50 for each adult.

BY PASSENGER FERRY

Fast Ferries (☎ 08/295–2688) operates daily cruiser trips from Glenelg (accessible from Adelaide by tram) to Kingscote, taking just over two hours. The one-way fare is $40, return is $69.

BY PLANE

Kendell Airlines flies daily between Adelaide and Kingscote, the island's main airport. The one-way fare is $79. Ask about the availability of 14-day advance purchase fares, which cost $53. Flights to the island take about 40 minutes. ☞ Air Travel *in* the Gold Guide for airline telephone numbers.

Getting Around

BY BUS

Apart from a bus service that connects Kingscote, American River, and Penneshaw, there is no public transport on the island.

BY CAR

The main attractions are widely scattered and the most practical way to see them is either on a guided tour or by car.

Contacts and Resources

CAR RENTALS

Budget Rent-a-Car. ⊠ *76 Dauncey St., Kingscote 5223,* ☎ *08/8552–3133.*

GUIDED TOURS

Adventure Charters of Kangaroo Island (⊠ Kingscote 5223, ☎ 08/8552–9119, FAX 08/8552–9122) offers island tours ranging from one to three days, as well as a three-day trip that combines walking and four-wheel-driving. Sea fishing, cliff climbing, kayaking, and diving tours can also be arranged. **Australian Odysseys** (⊠ Box 494, Penneshaw 5222, ☎ 08/8553–1294) operates four-wheel-drive tours. **The Island Travel Centre** (⊠ 27 Gresham St., Adelaide, ☎ 08/8212–4550) is an Adelaide travel agent specializing in tours and transport to Kangaroo Island as well as accommodations there. **Kangaroo Island Sealink** (⊠ Box 570, Penneshaw 5222, ☎ 13–1301 or 08/8552–2274) operates a one-day coach tour of the island in conjunction with the ferry service from Cape Jervis. It costs $135.

Kendell Airlines (☞ Arriving and Departing, *above*) also packages its air services in conjunction with the tours offered by various travel operators on the island. Choices include a standard one-day island bus tour or a four-wheel-drive tour with the emphasis on adventure. The coach tour costs $69, the four-wheel-drive tour $160. Airfare is additional. You can also construct individual itineraries.

VISITOR INFORMATION

Dudley Council Office. ⊠ *Middle Terr., Penneshaw 5222,* ☎ *08/8553–1011.*

THE MURRAY RIVER

The "Mighty Murray" is the longest river in Australia and among the longest rivers on the planet. From its source in the Snowy Mountains of New South Wales, it travels some 2,415 km (1,500 mi) through 11 locks before it enters the ocean southeast of Adelaide. As pioneers settled the interior, the river became a major artery for their cargoes of wool and livestock. During the second half of the 19th century, the river reverberated with the churning wheels of paddle steamers and the shrieks of their whistles. This colorful period ended when railways shrank the continent at the turn of the century, easing the difficulty of overland transport and reducing dependence on the river. Today the Murray is a sporting paradise for water-skiers, boaters, and anglers.

The Murray's role as an industrial waterway may be over, but it remains a vital part of the economy and life of South Australia. It provides water for the vast irrigation schemes that have turned the desert into a fruit bowl—as well as supplying Adelaide with its domestic water. The Riverland region is one of the country's largest producers of citrus fruits and supplies more than 40% of the nation's wine—although the quality of Riverland wine doesn't compare with the wine of the Barossa.

In spite of what the railroads did to river traffic, or perhaps because of it, the only way to see the river properly is to spend a few days on a boat. At this stretch of the Murray, a car is a less efficient and less appealing way to travel through the countryside. A trip down the broad brown river is still an adventure; the history of the little towns on its banks, along with river culture and its importance to South Australia, merits some study. Most rewarding, however, is the area's natural beauty. Couched within high ochre cliffs, the Murray is home to river red gums, still lagoons, and abundant bird life.

There are two ways to take a trip up or down river. You can either ride on a riverboat and let someone else do the driving and the cooking, or choose to pilot a houseboat yourself. *See* Murray River A to Z, *below,* for information on both options.

Renmark

256 km (160 mi) east of Adelaide.

Heading upstream from Renmark toward Wentworth in Victoria, the Murray River is at its tranquil best, gliding between tall cliffs and spilling out across broad lakes filled with bird life. No towns lie along this section of the river, so this is the route to take for peace and quiet. Downstream from Renmark the river is more populated, although only during peak summer periods does the Murray become even remotely crowded.

Sitting on a bend in the river lined with willow trees, Renmark is a busy town, one of the most important on the Murray—a center for the fruit industry, the mainstay of the Riverland region. Fruit growing began here in 1887, when the Canadian Chaffey brothers were granted 250,000 acres to test their irrigation plan. One of the original wood-burning water pumps they devised can still be seen on Renmark Avenue.

Olivewood, the original homestead of Charles Chaffey, is run by the National Trust and is open to visitors. ⊠ *21st St.,* ☎ *08/8586–6175.* ☜ *$3.50.* ⊙ *Thurs.–Mon. 10–4.*

Dining is less than spectacular in Renmark. Consider trying the Greek food at **Sophia's Restaurant,** or the buffet dinners at the **Renmark Club.**

Berri

52 km (28 mi) downstream from Renmark, 236 km (148 mi) northeast of Adelaide.

Berri was once a refueling station for the river steamers and today is the economic heart of the Riverland. Wine production is the major industry—the town's Berri Estates is the largest single winery in the southern hemisphere.

For anyone who wants to see what the Riverland is all about, the **Berrivale Orchards** showroom has a 15-minute video on various stages of the fruit-growing process. ⊠ *Sturt Hwy.,* ☎ *08/8582–1455.* ⊙ *Weekdays 8:30–4:30, Sat. 9–noon.*

The **Riverland Display Centre** has an exhibition of classic cars and motorcycles. ⊠ *Sturt Hwy.,* ☎ *08/8582–2325.* ☜ *$2.* ⊙ *Daily 10–4.*

Loxton

43 km (23 mi) downstream from Berri, 255 km (159 mi) east of Adelaide.

Loxton is a hard-working town, one of the most attractive on the river, surrounded by orchards and the vineyards of the Penfold winery, one of Australia's mass producers.

In Loxton's **Historical Village,** many of the town's 19th-century buildings have been reconstructed beside the river. ⊠ *East Terr.,* ☎ *08/8584-7194.* ✆ *$5.* ☉ *Weekdays 10–4, weekends 10–5.*

In East Terrace, the **Loxton Hotel-Motel** ☎ 08/8584–7266) serves reasonable counter meals, and the **Loxton Palace** (☎ 08/8584–6825) is a standard Chinese restaurant.

Waikerie

120 km (65 mi) downstream of Loxton, 177 km (111 mi) northeast of Adelaide.

The teeming bird life in this part of the river gave the town of Waikerie its name—the Aboriginal word means "many wings." Surrounded by irrigated citrus orchards and vineyards overlooking the river red gums and cliffs of the far bank, the town is also a center for gliding.

Waikerie Gliding Club's joy flights are a great way to see the river and the rich farmland along its banks. ⊠ *Sturt Hwy., Box 320, 5330,* ☎ *08/8541–2644.* ✆ *20-min flight $45.*

En Route   Cruising downstream between Waikerie and Swan Reach you approach the tiny settlement of **Morgan.** When you round the bend in the river and catch a glimpse of this sleepy little backwater, it's hard to believe that it was once the state's second busiest port. In Morgan's heyday at the end of the last century, freight from the upper reaches of the Murray was unloaded here and sent by train to Port Adelaide. The demise of river traffic put an end to its prosperity. Fortunately the towering wharves, railway station, and the shops and hotels along Railway Terrace have been preserved largely in their original state.

Swan Reach, not surprisingly named for its bird population, lies 51 km (29 mi) downstream from Morgan. This quiet town overlooks some of the prettiest scenery on the Murray. Below town, the river makes a huge curve—known as the Big Bend—before flowing onward.

Mannum

195 km (122 mi) downstream from Waikerie, 84 km (53 mi) east of Adelaide.

Murray River paddle steamers had their origins in Mannum when the first riverboat, the *Mary Ann,* was launched in 1853. The town has a number of reminders of its past, including the paddle steamer *Marion,* now a floating museum. ⊠ *William Randell's Wharf.* ✆ *$2.* ☉ *Daily 10–4.*

SJ's Brasserie, on Randell Street, is regarded as Mannum's finest restaurant; **Captain Randell's Restaurant** has a fine position on the wharf overlooking the river and the ferry traffic.

Murray Bridge

35 km (22 mi) downstream from Mannum, 78 km (49 mi) east of Adelaide.

Murray Bridge is the largest town on the South Australian section of the river, and its proximity to Adelaide makes it a popular spot for fishing, waterskiing, and picnicking—crowds get heavy on weekends.

Dining alternatives are reasonably extensive in Murray Bridge. The **Amorosa** in Bridge Street serves good Italian food. The **Oriental Garden**, in Adelaide Road, and the **Happy Gathering**, in First Street, are the town's Chinese offerings.

Murray River A to Z

Arriving and Departing

BY BUS

Stateliner Coaches (⊠ 111 Franklin St., Adelaide, ☎ 08/8415–5555) operates a daily service between Adelaide and the towns of Berri and Renmark. The one-way fare from Adelaide to Renmark–Berri is $26.50. The trip takes 3½ hours to Berri, 4 to Renmark.

BY CAR

Leave Adelaide by Main North Road and follow signs to the Sturt Highway and the town of Gawler. This highway continues east to Renmark. Allow 3½ hours for the 295-km (185-mi) trip to Renmark.

Getting Around

BY BOAT

Cruise vacations on the river are available aboard large riverboats or in rented houseboats. The latter sleep 4 to 10 people and range in quality from basic to luxurious.

BY CAR

Although the Sturt Highway crosses the river several times between Waikerie and Renmark, and smaller roads link more isolated towns along the river, the most impressive sections of the Murray can be seen only from the water. If you've rented a car, drive to Mannum, Berri, or Renmark and hook up with a river cruise or rent a houseboat to drive yourself along the river.

Contacts and Resources

BOAT RENTALS

During peak summer holiday season, a deluxe eight-berth houseboat costs about $1,200 per week, and a four-berth boat goes for $650. Off-peak prices drop by as much as 20%. Water and power for lights and cooking are carried on board. No previous boating experience is necessary—the only requirement is a driver's license.

Houseboats are supplied with basic safety equipment, such as life preservers, with which you should familiarize yourself before departure. Treat your houseboat as your home, and safeguard personal effects by locking all doors and windows before venturing away from the vessel.

Liba-Liba has a fleet of 30 houseboats for rent and is based in both Renmark and Wentworth, at the junction of the Murray and Darling rivers in southwestern New South Wales, which is useful if you want to sail one-way only. ⊠ *Box 1, Jane Eliza Landing, Renmark 5341,* ☎ *08/8586–6734.*

Swan Houseboats are among the most comfortable, well-equipped, and luxurious accommodations on the river. ⊠ *Box 345, Murray River, near Sturt Hwy., Berri 5343,* ☎ *1800/08–3183.*

PS *Murray Princess* is a copy of a Mississippi River paddle wheeler that makes five-day and weekend cruises from Mannum. All cabins are air-conditioned and include en suite bathrooms. Passengers have access to a spa and sauna. For reservations, contact Captain Cook Cruises. ⊠ *96 Randell St., Mannum 5238,* ☎ *1800/80–4843 or 08/8569–2511.*

Proud Mary offers two- to five-night cruises upstream from Murray Bridge, which is only a 45-minute drive from Adelaide. You travel in comfortable, air-conditioned cabins. The cost is from $490 per person on a twin-share basis. For reservations, contact Proud Australia Holidays. ⊠ *23 Leigh St., Level 2, Adelaide 5000,* ☎ *08/8231–9472.*

Berri Tourist and Travel Centre. ⊠ *24 Vaughan Terr.,* ☎ *08/8582–1655.* **Renmark Information Centre.** ⊠ *Murray Ave.,* ☎ *08/8586–6703.*

THE OUTBACK

South Australia is the country's driest state, and its Outback is a largely featureless expanse of desert, the only vegetation being scrubby salt-bush and hardy eucalypt trees holding on in the normally dried-up water courses. The landscape is marked by geological uplifts, abrupt transitions between plateaus broken at the edges of ancient, long-inactive fault lines. These uplifts are all the more dramatic for their unexpectedness when you come across them. Few roads track through this desert wilderness—the main highway is the Stuart, which runs all the way to Alice Springs in the Northern Territory.

The people of the Outback are as hardy as the terrain. They are also often eccentric, colorful characters, who will happily bend a visitor's ear over a drink in the local pub. These remote, isolated communities attract loners, adventurers, fortune-seekers, and people simply on the run. In this unyielding country of big sky and vast distances, you've got to be tough to survive.

Coober Pedy

850 km (530 mi) northwest of Adelaide.

Known as much for the troglodytic lifestyle of its inhabitants—all 2,500 of them, most of whom live underground in dugouts gouged from the line of hills running through town—as for its opal riches, Coober Pedy is arguably Australia's most singular place. The town's flat landscape is given perspective by a ring of mullock heaps, pyramidal piles of rock and sand left over after mining shafts are dug. Opals are Coober Pedy's reason for existence—here is the world's richest opal field.

Opal was discovered here in 1915, and miners returning from the Great War introduced the first dugout homes, forced underground by the searing heat. In midsummer outside temperatures can reach 48°C (118°F); inside the dugouts, the air remains a constant 22°–24°C (72°–75°F). Australia has 95% of the world's opal deposits, and Coober Pedy has the bulk of that wealth. Mining is controlled so that small operators, not large conglomerates, do the digging and discover the riches.

Big finds are big news, but it is not only licensed miners who strike it rich—dugout home extension has been particularly popular since one local found a $40,000 seam of opal while hacking out a new room. Working mines are off limits to visitors, although if you befriend a miner in the pub chances are you'll be invited for an off-the-record hard hat tour.

Coober Pedy is a brick and corrugated-iron settlement propped unceremoniously on a scarred desert landscape. It is not pretty in any conventional sense—it's a town built for efficiency, not beauty. It works, and that's what matters for local residents. But its ugliness has a kind of bizarre appeal.

Keep in mind that this is a macho kinda town, and single women are generally advised to use common sense in dealings with men in the Outback.

Exploring

Noodling—fossicking (rummaging) for opal gemstones—is encouraged and requires no permit, provided you are not on a pegged claim and use no digging devices, but care needs to be taken as disused shafts are unmarked and not filled in. The Jeweler's Shop mining area on the edge of town is the most popular area for noodling. Don't expect to make your fortune there, however.

Although most of Coober Pedy's underground devotions are decidedly secular in nature, the town does have five underground churches. **St. Peter and St. Paul's** Catholic Church is a listed Heritage building, and the **Catacomb** Anglican Church is notable for its altar fashioned from a windlass (a winch) and lectern made from a log of mulga wood. The newest church, the **Serbian Orthodox,** is perhaps the most striking, with its scalloped ceiling, rock-carved icons, and brilliant stained-glass windows.

Aboriginal-owned **Umoona Opal Mine and Museum** is an enormous underground complex with a mine and display home as well as opal sales and souvenirs. ⊠ *Hutchinson St.,* ☎ *08/8672–5288.* ▨ *Free, mine tour $5.* ⊙ *Daily 8–7; mine tour daily at 10, noon, 2, and 4.*

The **Old Timers Mine** is an original opal mine turned into a museum. Two underground houses, furnished in 1920s and 1980s styles, are part of the complex, which exhibits mining equipment and memorabilia in a network of hand-dug tunnels and shafts. ⊠ *Crowders Gully,* ☎ *08/8672–5555.* ▨ *$5.* ⊙ *Fall–spring, daily 9–5; summer, daily 9–2.*

Outside of Town

Breakaways. This striking series of rock formations, known locally as the Moon Plain, is reminiscent of the American West, with buttes and jagged hills erupting from the desert. There are fossils and patches of petrified forest in this strange landscape, which has appealed to filmmakers of apocalyptic films. *Mad Max 3—Beyond Thunderdome* was filmed around here, as was the Australian film about the dawn of the nuclear age, *Ground Zero.* The scenery is especially evocative early in the morning. The Breakaways area is 30 km (19 mi) northeast of Coober Pedy.

Dog Fence. An extraordinary measure designed to protect the valuable sheep-grazing land to the south from marauding dingoes, this fence runs 5,600 km (3,500 mi)—9,600 km (6,000 mi) by some people's reckoning—from far away Queensland. It is a simple wire fence, and its arrow-straight run across this barren country gives it a sad, lonely grandeur. You'll find it in the Breakaways area, 30 km (19 mi) northeast of Coober Pedy.

Dining and Lodging

$$ ✕ **Umberto's.** Perched atop the monolithic Desert Cave Hotel, this restaurant oddly fails to take advantage of its prime position—there are no views from the tables—but the food compensates for the lack of outlook. Try kangaroo fillet with a port wine and red currant glaze, or crocodile fried in tempura batter with a light honey, soy, and ginger dip-

ping sauce. Uncommonly good food for an Outback town. ⊠ *Desert Cave Hotel, Hutchinson St.,* ☎ *08/8672–5688. AE, DC, MC, V.*

$ ✗ **Last Resort Café.** The place for wonderful breakfasts—the patented "hangover" breakfast is highly recommended by locals in the know—great cakes and ice creams. Very friendly, casual ambience. ⊠ *Post Office Hill Rd.,* ☎ *08/8672–5072. No dinner.*

$ ✗ **Old Miner's Dugout Café.** Run by an expat American, the café is renowned for its kangaroo with potato and salad, and Anne's Ambrosia chocolate cake. Most dishes are home-style productions. ⊠ *Hutchinson St.,* ☎ *08/8672–5541. Closed Sun. No lunch.*

$$$ ▦ **Desert Cave Hotel.** Most visitors to Coober Pedy want the chance to live underground, so here's your opportunity. Underground rooms (there are 19 in all) are spacious and well appointed, with red striated rock walls. There is no natural light, so the rooms may be a little dark for some people's taste, and some may find the atmosphere claustrophobic. Aboveground rooms are also available. ⊠ *Hutchinson St.,* ☎ *08/8672–5688,* FAX *08/8672–5198. 50 rooms with bath. Restaurant, pool, shops. AE, DC, MC, V.*

$$ ▦ **Coober Pedy Opal Fields Motel.** No underground rooms here, but another form of construction uses nature for insulation. Rammed earth is the building method, and the decor of the guest rooms carries through the earthy feel using desert colors. Two-bedroom apartments are available, complete with cooking facilities. ⊠ *St. Nicholas St.,* ☎ *086/72–3003,* FAX *08/8672–3004. 20 rooms with bath. Restaurant. AE, DC, MC, V.*

$$ ▦ **Underground Motel.** A little way out of the center, this motel has excellent views of the Breakaways rock formations from its underground rooms, each of which is uniquely shaped. Guest rooms are simply but comfortably furnished. A kitchen is provided, as are breakfast makings. ⊠ *Catacomb Rd.,* ☎ *08/8672–5324,* FAX *08/8672–5911. 8 rooms with bath. AE, DC, MC, V.*

Shopping

You will find more than 30 shops selling opals in Coober Pedy. One of the best is the **Opal Cutter** (⊠ Post Office Hill Rd., ☎ 08/8672–3086), where stones valued from $7 to $25,000 are offered for sale, and owners Piet and Barbara Lamont are very helpful and informative. Stop by for a daily display of opal cutting at 5 PM. Another good option is the **Opal Factory** (⊠ Hutchison St., ☎ 08/8672–5300), where you can see the world's largest opal matrix.

Underground Books (⊠ Post Office Hill Rd., ☎ 08/8672–5558) has an excellent selection of books, but the best buy is one of proprietor Peter Caust's superb postcards, which capture the essence of the desert landscape.

Flinders Ranges National Park

Extending from the northern end of Gulf St.Vincent, the Flinders Ranges consist of a chain of desert mountains—and one of the most impressive outback parks in the country. These dry, craggy mountain peaks, once the bed of an ancient sea, have been cracked, folded, and sculpted by millions of years of rain and sun. This furrowed landscape of deep valleys is covered with cypress pine and casuarina, which slope into creeks lined with river red gums. The area is utterly fascinating—both for geologists and for anyone else who revels in wild, raw scenery and exotic plant and animal life.

The scenic center of the Flinders Ranges is **Wilpena Pound,** an 80-sq-km (207-sq-mi) bowl ringed by red hills that curve gently upward, only to fall off in the rims of sheer cliffs. The only entrance to the Pound is a narrow cleft through which the Wilpena Creek sometimes trickles.

The numerous steep trails of Flinders Ranges make them a **bushwalking** mecca, even though the park has few amenities. Water in this region is scarce and should be carried at all times. The best time for walking in the area is during the relatively cool months between April and October. This is also the wettest time of year, so you should be prepared for rain. Between September and late October, wildflowers bring a flush of color to the hillsides.

The most spectacular of the park's walking trails leads to the summit of **St. Mary's Peak** (3,840 ft)—the highest point in the Pound's rim and the second tallest peak in South Australia. The more scenic of the two routes to the summit is the outside trail; give yourself a full day to get up and back. The final ascent is difficult, but views from the top—including the distant white glitter of the salt flats on Lake Frome—make the climb worthwhile.

Arriving and Departing

Flinders Ranges National Park is 460 km (285 mi) north of Adelaide via the Princes Highway to Port Augusta, and then east toward Quorn and Hawker. A four-wheel-drive vehicle is highly recommended for traveling on the many gravel roads in the area.

Dining and Lodging

Between April and the end of November, nightly motel rates (including Continental breakfast) at the ⊡ **Wilpena Pound Holiday Resort** (☎ 08/8648–0004) are $88 for a double room and $80 for a single. Stays of three nights or more are rewarded with a 20% discount. In the heat of summer, the room rate falls to $75 for doubles and $69 for singles. A licensed restaurant serves breakfast, lunch, and dinner, with fair quality meals. The campground at Wilpena is operated by the motel. Powered campsites are $16 per night for two people, and $2 for each additional person. The resort operates a general store and gas pumps.

⚠ **Cooinda Campsite** is the only bush campsite within the Pound, although camping with a permit is allowed throughout the rest of the park. A small rock hole about 2,790 ft from Cooinda is usually filled with fresh water. Otherwise, you must carry water into the campsite.

Visitor Information

Flinders Ranges National Park. ☎ *08/8648–0048*.
National Parks and Wildlife Service. ✉ *55 Grenfell St., Adelaide 5000,* ☎ *08/8207–2000*.

The Outback A to Z

Arriving and Departing

BY BUS
Buses leave the Central Bus Terminal in Adelaide for **Flinders Ranges National Park** on Thursday and Friday, returning to Adelaide on Thursday and Sunday. ☞ Arriving and Departing *in* Adelaide A to Z, *above*.

BY CAR
The main road to **Coober Pedy** is the Stuart Highway from Adelaide, 850 km (530 mi) to the south. Alice Springs is 700 km (437 mi) north of Coober Pedy. The drive from Adelaide to Coober Pedy takes about nine hours on a very good quality road. To the Alice, it is about seven hours.

BY PLANE
Kendell Airlines flies daily between Coober Pedy and Adelaide, via the township of Olympic Dam, which serves the uranium mine at Roxby Downs. ☞ Air Travel *in* the Gold Guide for airline telephone numbers.

Getting Around

BY CAR

A rental car is the best way to see Coober Pedy and its outlying attractions. Rental vehicles are in extremely short supply in town, so hire elsewhere. Although some of the roads are unsealed—those to the Breakaways and the Dog Fence, for example—surfaces are generally suitable for conventional vehicles. Check on road conditions with the police if there has been substantial rain.

Contacts and Resources

EMERGENCIES

Police, fire, or **ambulance.** ☎ *000.*

GUIDED TOURS

★ The **Coober Pedy–Oodnadatta Mail Run** tour is a bona fide Australian classic. You'll join the Outback postman in town in his four-wheel-drive vehicle for a 600-km (375-mi) odyssey to tiny Outback settlements and cattle stations. The route passes historic ruins and monuments, part of the Overland Telegraph Line and the original line of the Ghan railway. You visit South Australia's smallest town (William Creek, pop. 7) and its biggest cattle station, Anna Creek. This is a trip not to be missed. ☎ *800/06–9911 or 086/72–5558.* ✉ *$60, $89 with lunch (less expensive lunch options are available en route).*

Perentie Outback Tours operates three-day camping tours to the Painted Desert, Oodnadatta, and the Ghan railway ruins. ☎ *08/8672–5558.* ✉ *$395.*

VISITOR INFORMATION

Tourist Information Office. ✉ *Hutchinson St., Coober Pedy,* ☎ *08/8672–5298.*

10 The Red Centre

The light in the Red Centre—named for the deep color of its desert soils—has a purity and vitality that photographs only begin to approach. Like the ancient desert landscapes, the quality of light is humanized in the heritage of the Aboriginal people who have occupied this vast territory for tens of thousands of years. Uluṟu, also known as Ayers Rock, is a great symbol in Aboriginal traditions, as are so many sacred sites among the Centre's mountain ranges, gorges, dry riverbeds, and spinifex plains. At the center of all this lies Alice Springs, Australia's only desert city.

By Chips
Mackinolty

AUSTRALIA'S RED CENTRE APPEARS at first sight to be harsh and unforgiving—it is, after all, at the heart of some of the world's largest deserts in the middle of the driest continent in the world. The apparent desolation of the spinifex plains conceals a richness and beauty of plant and animal life that has adapted over millennia to survive and thrive in an environment of extremes. Nights in winter can reach the freezing point, and summer days can soar above 110°F. And with such little rain, the pockets of water to be found in isolated gorges and saltpans are precious indicators of surprisingly varied life-forms. Like so many deserts, when you stop to look at the Red Centre closely, you'll find that it is full of beauty and tremendous vitality.

The essence of this land of contrasts is epitomized in the paintings of the reknowned Aboriginal landscape artist Albert Namatjirra and his followers. Viewed away from the desert, their images of the MacDonnell Ranges appear at first to be garish and unreal in their depiction of mountain ranges of purples and reds and stark white ghost gum trees. To see the real thing makes it difficult to imagine them painted in any other way. This is a place where expectations can easily be turned upside down.

Uluru—pronounced *oo*-loo-*roo*—what Anglos have dubbed Ayers Rock, that great stone monolith that rises above the surrounding plains, is but one focus in the Red Centre. The rounded forms of Kata Tjuta (*ka*-ta *tchoo*-ta) are another. The cliffs, gorges, and mountain chains of the MacDonnell Ranges that straddle the desert and Watarrka National Park, or Kings Canyon, are other worlds to explore as well.

Pleasures and Pastimes

Camping

Under a full moon and the Milky Way, camping out in the desert is an experience that you will carry with you for the rest of your life: There are far more stars visible in the southern hemisphere than there are in the north, like the fascinating Magellanic clouds. Nights can be very cold in winter, but happily the native mulga wood supplies the best fire in the world, burning hot and long for cooking and for curling up next to in your sleeping bag—a tent is an unnecessary accoutrement. Pick dry, sandy riverbeds to avoid ants and tall ghost gums for shade in the daytime.

Dining

Although restaurants in Alice Springs and at Ayers Rock Resort are unlikely to surprise visitors with innovative cuisine, they do serve food rarely seen on menus outside Australia, including crocodile, kangaroo, and camel.

CATEGORY	COST*
$$$$	over $45
$$$	$35–$45
$$	$25–$35
$	under $25

per person, excluding drinks

Lodging

The tourism boom of the 1980s resulted in the rapid growth of accommodations in Alice Springs and at Ayers Resort. Several of the newer and better hotels are located out of walking distance from the downtown area.

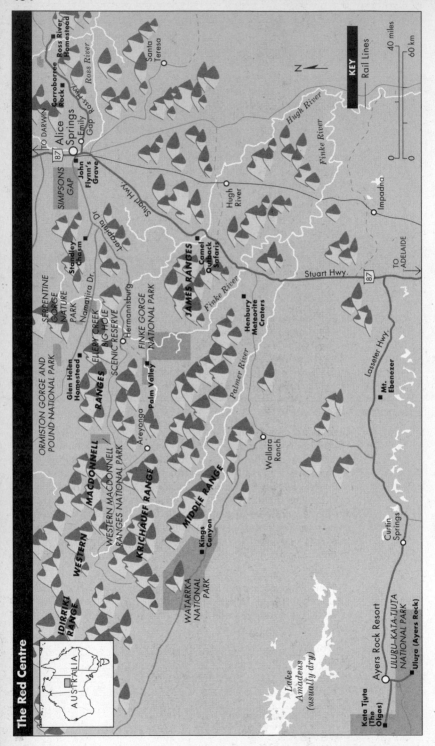

The Red Centre

KEY

Rail Lines

40 miles

60 km

Ross River Homestead

Corroboree Rock

Santa Teresa

TO DARWIN

Alice Springs

Emily Gap

Ross River

87

Ross River

John Flynn's Grave

SIMPSONS GAP

Stuart Hwy.

Hugh River

Finke River

Impadna

Standley Chasm

Namatjira Dr.

Hugh River

TO ADELAIDE

SERPENTINE GORGE NATURE PARK

Jaronga Dr.

JAMES RANGES

Camel Outback Safaris

Stuart Hwy.

87

ORMISTON GORGE AND POUND NATIONAL PARK

ELLERY CREEK BIG HOLE

Hermannsburg

Finke River

Henbury Meteorite Craters

Glen Helen Homestead

RANGES

SCENIC RESERVE

FINKE GORGE NATIONAL PARK

Palmer River

Mt. Ebenezer

Lasseter Hwy.

WESTERN

MACDONNELL

WESTERN MACDONNELL RANGES NATIONAL PARK

Palm Valley

Areyonga

MIDDLE RANGE

Wallara Ranch

KRICHAUFF RANGE

Curtin Springs

IDIRRIKI RANGE

Kings Canyon

WATARRKA NATIONAL PARK

AUSTRALIA

Lake Amadeus (usually dry)

Ayers Rock Resort

ULURU-KATA-TJUTA NATIONAL PARK

Uluru (Ayers Rock)

Kata Tjuta (The Olgas)

CATEGORY	COST*
$$$$	over $200
$$$	$140–$200
$$	$80–$140
$	under $80

All prices are for a standard double room, excluding the NT Tourism Marketing Levy of 5%.

Photography, Video, and Filming

Landscape photography in the Red Centre is challenging and rewarding: Amazing light and intense colors change through the day, and your efforts will yield far more meaningful memories of your travels than store-bought souvenirs. Sunset at Uluṟu is but one of hundreds of panoramic sights that will inspire you to pick up your camera and shoot. Heat and dust can be a problem, so be sure to take insulated, dust-proof bags for your cameras and film stock.

Exploring the Red Centre

The primary areas of interest in the ponderous middle of Oz are Alice Springs, which is flanked by the intriguing eastern and western Mac-Donnell Ranges, and Ayers Rock Resort and Uluṟu–Kata Tjuṯa National Park. Unless you have more than three days, focus on only one of these areas.

Great Itineraries

It doesn't take long for the beauty of the desert to enthrall your senses. Still, allow yourself enough time in the Red Centre to really let it soak in. If you don't fly right into the Ayers Rock Resort, you'll start in Alice Springs, around which you'll find some spectacular scenery. Poke around town for a day, then head out to the nearby hills.

To get a grip on Australia's notorious "tyranny of distance" and allow yourself the unique cultural experience of roadhouse Outback pubs, consider driving from the Alice to Uluṟu. Take in all of the open space and the interesting sights along the way. And when you get to the great Rock, don't forget that the other otherworldly landscape of Kata Tjuṯa (the Olgas) is just down the road.

IF YOU HAVE 3 DAYS

You can hardly ignore one of Australia's great icons: Uluṟu. Drive straight down from Alice Springs to 🎥 **Ayers Rock Resort** for lunch, followed by a circuit of the Rock, and a look at the **Aboriginal Cultural Centre** near its base. On the next day it's worth an early start to catch dawn at **Kata Tjuṯa** and an exploration of its extraordinary domes. End the day with **sunset at the Rock.** Return to Alice Springs via **Wallara Ranch** and the **Henbury Meteor Craters.** If you fly in and out of Ayers Resort and have more time, take a **Mala or Uluṟu Experience walk** and a **flight-seeing** tour of the area.

If you opt to spend your days around 🎥 **Alice Springs,** take the first day in town, walking around the city center and shopping, in the afternoon heading out to the **Alice Springs Telegraph Station Historical Reserve** or **MacDonnell Siding** to look at the Old Ghan train. The next day drive out into either the eastern or western MacDonnell Ranges to explore the gorges and gaps and dip into a water hole. Overnight at the 🎥 **Glen Helen Homestead.** Make your way back to town through the mountain scenery on the third day.

IF YOU HAVE 5 DAYS

Combine the two itineraries above, taking in the best of Alice Springs and the MacDonnell Ranges before heading down to the Rock. If you

want to take in more of the desert, start out in Uluṟu as above but head
west at **Wallara Ranch** for the ⛰ **Watarrka National Park** for a day
and two nights exploring **Kings Canyon** by yourself or with one of the
Aboriginal guided tours available. Surprisingly little-visited, Kings
Canyon is one of the hidden wonders of central Australia.

IF YOU HAVE 7 DAYS

Start with two days in and around ⛰ **Alice Springs,** then turn south
and west to spend two days and a night in ⛰ **Watarrka National Park.**
For the remaining three days, knock around ⛰ **Uluṟu–Kata Tjuṯa Na-
tioal Park,** leaving yourself at least a few hours for absorbing the
sounds and silence of the desert. Fly out from the resort to your next
location.

When to Tour the Red Centre

Winter, May through August, is the best time to visit—nights are crisp
and cold, and days are pleasantly warm. High summer temperatures
may be too much to cope with for most people, despite extensive air-
conditioning at resorts.

Hiking or climbing in the desert carries certain dangers, among them
dehydration. Carry plenty of water, even for short trips, and let park
rangers, police, or cattle-station owners know where you're going
when you undertake long walks.

ALICE SPRINGS

Once a ramshackle collection of dusty streets and buildings, Alice
Springs—known colloquially as the Alice—has been transformed in recent decades into an incongruously suburban tourist center in the middle of the desert. A focus of ceremonial activities for the Arrernte
Aboriginal tribe, its ancient sites lie cheek by jowl with air-conditioned
shops and hotels. Dominated by the MacDonnell Ranges—which
change color according to time of day from brick red to purple—the
other striking feature of the town is the Todd River. Water rarely runs
in the desert, and the deep sandy beds of the Todd, fringed by majestic ghost gum trees, suggest a timelessness far different from the bus-
tle of the nearby town. The Todd's dry riverbed is the scene for one of
the Alice's more bizarre celebrations—September's Henley-on-Todd Regatta. A lighthearted send-up of England's staid boating classic, entrants
must grab their bottomless homemade boats and run to the finishing
line. The only time in the last quarter century this event has not been
run is 1994—unexpected and embarrassing rains filled the river and
caused its cancellation!

Until the 1970s the Alice was a frontier town servicing the region's pastoral industry, and life was tough. During World War II it was one of
the few (barely) inhabited stops on the 3,024-km (1,875-mi) supply
lines between Adelaide and the front line of Darwin. First established
at the Old Telegraph Station as the town of Stuart, it was moved and
renamed Alice Springs in 1933 after the wife of the telegraph boss,
Charles Todd. The town's position in the center of the continent as a
communications link has always been important. Today the town
hosts both the U.S. secret-communications base of Pine Gap just out
of town, as well as the only Aboriginal-owned satellite television network, which broadcasts across nearly half of Australia.

*Numbers in the margin correspond to points of interest on the Alice
Springs map.*

Exploring Alice Springs

City Center

❸ **Adelaide House** was the first Alice Springs hospital. Designed by the Reverend John Flynn and run by the Australian Inland Mission (which Flynn established) from 1926 to 1939, the hospital used an ingenious system of air tunnels and wet burlap bags to cool the rooms. It's now a museum devoted to the mission and pioneering days in Alice Springs. Getting back to John Flynn, it would be difficult to overstate his contribution to the settlement of inland Australia. The stone hut at the rear of Adelaide House was the site of the first field radio transmission in 1926, which made viable his concept of a flying doctor. The Royal Flying Doctor Service continues to maintain its "mantle of safety" over Australia's remote settlements. ⌧ *Todd Mall,* ☎ *08/8952–1856.* ▧ *$3.* ⊙ *Mar.–Nov., weekdays 10–4, weekends 10–noon.*

❶ **Anzac Hill,** just north of downtown, has an excellent view of Alice Springs and the surrounding area, including the MacDonnell Range south of town. From atop the hill, note that **Todd Mall** is one block west of the Todd River, which at best flows only a few days a year. The hill is a good place from which to begin a walking tour. To reach the top, head up Lions Walk, which starts opposite the Catholic church on Wills Terrace downtown.

❷ The Alice Plaza Building contains the **Museum of Central Australia**'s art and natural history collections. The museum's animal and mineral specimens are very interesting. ⌧ *Todd Mall between Wills Terr. and Parsons St.,* ☎ *08/8951–5335.* ▧ *$2.* ⊙ *Weekdays 9–5, weekends 10–5.*

❹ The wide, simple roof lines of the **Old Court House** are typical of the Pioneering style of architecture. The building is still the Crown Law Department, so it can be viewed only from the outside. ⌧ *Parsons and Hartley Sts.*

❼ There is, alas, little at the **Old Hartley Street School** that recalls the blackboards and lift-top integrated desks and benches in use in the year 1929, when Miss Pearl Burton was installed in the building as the first teacher. But it's worth a peek anyway. The school is also the headquarters of the Alice Springs National Trust branch, and brochures on local sights are available. ⌧ *Hartley St.,* ☎ *08/8952–4516.* ▧ *Free.* ⊙ *Weekdays 10:30–2:30.*

Artist Henk Guth found canvases too restrictive for his vision of central Australia, so he painted his panoramic, unstintingly realistic work **❽** in the round. **Panorama Guth,** inside an unusual crenellated building, has a circumference of 200 ft and stands 20 ft high. There is also an odd collection of Aboriginal artifacts downstairs. ⌧ *65 Hartley St.,* ☎ *08/8952–2013.* ▧ *$3.* ⊙ *Mon.–Sat. 9–5, Sun. noon–5.*

The high white picket fence on the corner of Parsons and Hartley marks **❺** the **Residency.** Built in 1927 for John Cawood, the first government resident to be appointed to central Australia, it is now a museum with displays depicting the social and economic history of the area. ⌧ *Parsons and Hartley Sts.* ▧ *Donations accepted.* ⊙ *Weekdays 9–4, weekends 10–4.*

❾ Directed from the **Royal Flying Doctor Service (RFDS)** radio base, doctors use aircraft to make house calls on settlements and homes hundreds of miles apart. There is a display of historical material, an audiovisual show, and tours every half hour during the midyear season. Like the School of the Air (☞ *below*), the RFDS is still a vital part of life in the Outback. ⌧ *Stuart Terr.,* ☎ *08/8952–1129.* ▧ *$3.* ⊙ *Mon.–Sat. 9–4, Sun. 1–4.*

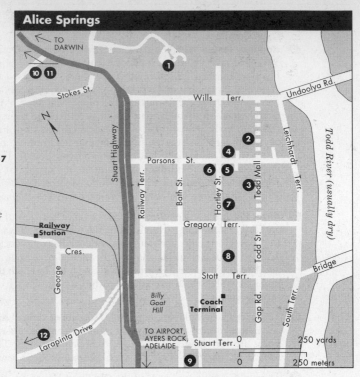

6 The 1908 **Stuart Town Gaol** is the oldest surviving building in Alice Springs—and it looks it. With almost no air coming through its tiny barred windows, imprisonment here on a long, hot summer day was punishment indeed. ⊠ *Parsons St.* ☎ *$2.* ☉ *Weekdays 10–12:30, Sat. 9:30–noon.*

The **Todd Mall** pedestrian area is the heart of Alice Springs, lined with cafés, galleries, banks, and tourist shops. ⊠ *Todd St. between Wills and Gregory Terrs.*

Around Alice

10 Just north of town, **Alice Springs Telegraph Station Historical Reserve** is the site of the first white settlement in the area—the original Alice Springs and the spring itself. The telegraph station buildings have been restored and are now evocative reminders of the Red Centre as it existed at the turn of the century. Within the buildings, exhibits of life at the station and a display of early photographs chronicle its history from 1872. There are pleasant picnic areas on the grassy banks of the river. ⊠ *Follow Stuart Hwy. 3 km (2 mi) north to track on right, or follow riverside walk 3 km (2 mi) from Wills Terr.,* ☎ *08/8952–1013.* ☎ *$4.* ☉ *Apr.–Sept., daily 8–7; Oct.–Mar., daily 8 AM–9 PM.*

11 Operating in many remote areas of Australia, the **School of the Air** has an ingenious way of teaching students separated by hundreds of miles. Children take their classes by correspondence course, supplemented by lessons over the Royal Flying Doctor radio network. Observing the teacher-student relationship by way of radio is fascinating. ⊠ *Head St.,* ☎ *08/8951–6800.* ☎ *Donations accepted.* ☉ *During school term, weekdays 8:30–4:30, Sat. 8:30–4:30, Sun. 1:30–4:30.*

12 The **Strehlow Research Centre,** a distinctive, multiroof building with a huge, curved, rammed-earth wall, commemorates the work of

Theodor Strehlow (b. 1908). The anthropologist grew up with and later spent many years studying the Aranda people, central Australia Aborigines who have traditionally lived on the land extending north to central Mount Stuart and south beyond the border with South Australia. The center's collection, which consists chiefly of "men's-only" ceremonial artifacts, cannot be displayed because of its contemporary religious significance. Still, the exhibits that are open to the public give rare insight into the beliefs of the Aranda people, their homelands, and their special association with Dr. Strehlow, who actually became their *ingkata*, their ceremonial chief. ✉ *Larapinta Dr., southwest of town,* ☎ *08/8951–8000.* 🎫 *$4.* ⊙ *Daily 10–5, last admission 4:30.*

At central Australia's only winery, aptly called **The Winery,** bush balladeer Ted Egan entertains Monday–Thursday during the busy season (April–October). You might catch him off-season, too—call ahead. ✉ *Petrick Rd., off Stuart Hwy.,* ☎ *08/8955–5133.* ⊙ *Daily 9–5.*

OFF THE BEATEN PATH

MACDONNELL SIDING – is the resting place of the now-restored *Old Ghan* train. Named after the Afghans who led camel trains on the route from Adelaide, the train began passenger service on August 6, 1929. Over the next 51 years the *Ghan* provided a vital, if erratic, link with the south. In times of flood it could take up to three months to complete the journey. Service on the new *Ghan* began in 1980 (☞ Arriving and Departing *in* Alice Springs A to Z, *below*).

Between April and November you can take a trip on the *Old Ghan,* 6 km (10 mi) along the original track to Mt. Ertiva. There are morning rides Wednesdays at 10 ($12 per person) and evening dinner rides. One of the dinner rides takes you to a bush setting for a camp-oven roasted meal with entertainment ($49); another is a round-trip back to MacDonnell Siding for a more formal dinner ($90). Reservations are advised (☎ 08/8955–5047, ℻ 08/8955–5220).

The **Road Transport Hall of Fame** is another feature of the MacDonnell Siding. It is a monument to the unsung heroes and pioneers of Australia's Trucking Industry, which has been vital in opening up the country. ✉ *MacDonnell Siding, Stuart Hwy., 10 km (6 mi) south of town,* ☎ *08/ 8952–7161.* 🎫 *Old Ghan $3, Hall of Fame $3.* ⊙ *Old Ghan daily 9– 5, Hall of Fame daily 8:30–5.*

Dining

$$$ ✕ **Overlander Steakhouse.** When local residents take out-of-town guests to a restaurant, this is often the one they choose. The atmosphere is clearly Outback, with an abundance of old saddles, lamps, artifacts, and equipment from local cattle stations, plus live entertainment every night in the form of Australian folk singing. Overall, the Overlander *is* a folkloric experience that maintains a satisfactory standard of cooking and presentation. It has a full range of Northern Territory specialties, including an appetizer of vol-au-vent filled with crocodile that lets the unusual chicken-fish flavor of this white meat come through. For non-residents, one inevitable main course is the mixed grill of buffalo, kangaroo, camel, and barramundi. Drover's Blowout is a set menu with a taste of everything for $35. ✉ *72 Hartley St.,* ☎ *08/8952–2159. AE, DC, MC, V.*

$$ ✕ **Balloons.** This relaxing bistro, located in the Plaza Hotel, is enhanced by a serene view of the hotel lawns, bounded by the impressive MacDonnell Range. The menu has a strong French flair but utilizes some distinctly local ingredients. There is also a buffet lunch and, on Sunday, a champagne brunch. ⊠ *Plaza Hotel, Barrett Dr.,* ☎ *08/8952–8000. AE, DC, MC, V.*

$$ ✕ **Ristorante Puccini.** Dark wood paneling, subdued lighting, and
★   friendly service are complemented by first-rate Italian cuisine that, in
the middle of the Outback, is nothing short of a revelation. For starters
at this bistro-brasserie, try carpaccio with pine nuts, or fettuccine Cal-
abrese, tossed in hot chili, spices, tomatoes, and black pepper. Barra-
mundi baked in lemon, garlic, and vermouth is very good; so, too, are
tournedos *funghi*—medallions of grain-fed beef with brandy and mush-
rooms. ⊠ *Todd Mall and Parsons St.,* ☎ *08/8953–0935. AE, DC, MC,
V. Closed Sun.*

$ ✕ **Oriental Gourmet.** The best Chinese food in the Red Centre is found
in this restaurant. There are no surprises on the menu—honey prawns,
beef with black bean sauce, duck with lemon sauce, and the like—but
all the dishes are fresh, simple, and soundly prepared. ⊠ *80 Hartley
St.,* ☎ *08/8953–0888. AE, MC, V. No lunch.*

Lodging

Hotels and Motels

$$$$ ▦ **Plaza Hotel Alice Springs.** With pastel hues and landscaped lawns,
★   this hotel is by far the best in Alice Springs, even if it is a mile from
town—a longish walk or a $6 cab ride. The rooms are softly ap-
pointed with bleached wood and enhanced by views overlooking the
pool and the low, barren mountains behind the hotel. The Plaza also
offers an eclectic menu at Balloons (☞ Dining, *above*). ⊠ *Barrett Dr.,
0870,* ☎ *08/8952–8000,* ℻ *08/8952–3822. 235 rooms with bath, 7
suites. 2 restaurants, 2 bars, pool, sauna, tennis courts, health club.
AE, DC, MC, V.*

$$$ ▦ **Alice Springs Pacific Resort.** On the east bank of the Todd River across
from the main downtown area, this hotel has spacious and airy reception
and restaurant areas that are graced with high ceilings and filled with
potted palms. Many of the rooms open directly onto a large lawn; all
are plainly furnished in cane with green carpeting. ⊠ *34 Stott Terr.,
0870,* ☎ *08/8952–6699 or 1800/80–5055,* ℻ *08/8953–0995. 108
rooms with bath. 2 bars, pool, laundry. AE, DC, MC, V.*

$$ ▦ **Desert Rose Inn.** This motel provides the best value for families stay-
★   ing in Alice Springs. Budget rooms are cramped, and standard rooms
are unexceptional, but the deluxe family rooms are spacious and well
furnished. Exposed brick walls set the tone for deluxe rooms, which
contain a double bed, two single beds, balcony, and kitchenette with
sink, microwave, and breakfast table. ⊠ *15–17 Railway Terr., 0870,*
☎ *08/8952–1411 or 1800/89–6116,* ℻ *08/8952–3232. 73 rooms,
most with bath or shower. Restaurant, pool, laundry. DC, MC, V.*

$$ ▦ **Diplomat Hotel Alice Springs.** The location of the Diplomat is ideal,
★   especially if you don't have a car. It's only 300 ft from the town cen-
ter, just far enough away to be quiet in the evening. All 90 rooms are
comfortable: carpeted, decorated with dark bedspreads and drapes, and
air-conditioned. Avoid ground-floor rooms if you want privacy—their
full glass doors open onto the central pool–car park area. The staff is
friendly. ⊠ *Gregory Terr. and Hartley St.,* ☎ *08/8952–8977 or 1800/
80–4885,* ℻ *08/8953–0225. Bar, pool, laundry. AE, DC, MC, V.*

$$ ▦ **Outback Motor Lodge.** This motel offers simple, clean accommoda-
tions. The only public areas are the lawn around a small pool and the
office. There is no dining room, but all rooms have kitchen facilities. A
Continental breakfast is available. ⊠ *South Terr., 0870,* ☎ *08/8952–
3888 or 1800/89–6133,* ℻ *08/8953–2166. 42 rooms with shower. Pool,
laundry. AE, DC, MC, V.*

$$ ⊡ **Vista Alice Springs.** Built in 1987, the Vista is shadowed by the mountain range that forms the southern periphery of the town. Apart from the pool-barbecue area at the back of the hotel, there are few public areas. Rooms have bare brick walls, comfortable modern furnishings, and molded fiberglass bathrooms. The downtown area is 2½ km (1½ mi) away, but the hotel provides courtesy transport. ⊠ *Stephens Rd., 0870,* ☎ *08/8952–6100 or 1800/81–0664,* FAX *08/8952–1988. 140 rooms with bath. Restaurant, bar, pool, spa, tennis court, laundry. AE, DC, MC, V.*

$ ⊡ **Melanka Lodge.** Just south of the main shopping area, Melanka offers a range of accommodations, including dormitories and double rooms for backpackers, standard rooms, and 60 deluxe rooms with private bathrooms. ⊠ *94 Todd St., 0870,* ☎ *08/8952–2233 or 1800/89–6110,* FAX *08/8952–3819. 112 rooms, 49 with shower. Restaurant, bar, 2 pools, laundry. AE, DC, MC, V.*

$ ⊡ **YHA Hostel.** This facility is in the center of town. ⊠ *Leichhardt Terr. and Parsons St., 0870,* ☎ *08/8952–8855,* FAX *08/8952–4144. 1 room, 15 4-bed dormitories. Pool, recreation room, air-conditioning, laundry.*

Caravan Park

$ △ **MacDonnell Range Holiday Park.** Tucked behind the ranges 5 km
★   (3 mi) south of town, this is an extensive, well-planned park. There is little shade, however. Most of the sites have electrical hookup, and about one-third have a private shower and toilet. ⊠ *Palm Pl. off Ross Hwy.,* ☎ *08/8952–6111 or 1800/80–8373,* FAX *08/8952–5236. 230 sites, 68 with bath. 2 pools, laundry. MC, V.*

Nightlife

Lasseters Hotel Casino operates from midday into the wee hours with the full range of games: blackjack, roulette, slot machines, keno, and the Australian game of two-up. ⊠ *Barrett Dr.,* ☎ *08/8950–7777.*

Outdoor Activities and Sports

Ballooning

At dawn on most mornings, hot-air balloons can be seen in the sky around Alice Springs. **Outback Ballooning** will pick you up from your hotel about one hour before dawn and return you between 9 AM and 10 AM. The $130 fee covers 30 minutes of flying time and a champagne and chicken breakfast. ⊠ *18 The Links, Desert Springs, Alice Springs,* ☎ *08/8952–8723.*

Golf

Alice Springs Golf Club welcomes visitors. Clubs and motorized buggies are available for hire. Greens fees are $15 for 9 holes, $25 for 18. ⊠ *Cromwell Dr.,* ☎ *08/8952–5440.*

Tennis

The public tennis courts in **Traeger Park** (⊠ entrance on Traeger Ave.) can be rented from the caretaker at the courts. The **Vista** and **Plaza** hotels have tennis courts for guests' use (☞ Lodging, *above*).

Shopping

Apart from the ubiquitous souvenir shops, whose T-shirt designs have reached the level of an art form, the main focus of shopping in Alice Springs is Aboriginal art and artifacts. Central Australian Aboriginal art is characterized by intricate patterns of dots, commonly called sand paintings because they were originally drawn on sand as ceremonial devices. Prices for paintings on canvas range from less than a hundred dollars to several thousand, but these prices are considerably lower than they are elsewhere in Australia. Two of the better galleries are the **Aboriginal Desert Art Gallery** (✉ 87 Todd St., ☎ 08/8953–1005) and the **Original Dreamtime Art Gallery** (✉ 63 Todd Mall, opposite Flynn Church, ☎ 08/8952–8861). The latter is particularly impressive for the number of important Aboriginal artists it represents.

Alice Springs A to Z

Arriving and Departing

BY BUS

Interstate buses operated by **Greyhound** (☎ 08/8952–7888) arrive and depart from outside **Melanka Lodge** (✉ 94 Todd St.). The **AAT Kings** terminal is just up the road at (✉ 74 Todd St., ☎ 08/8952–1700). The **McCafferty's Buses** (☎ 08/8952–3952) office and terminal are located at 91 Gregory Terrace.

BY CAR

There is only one road into Alice Springs, and it runs north to south— the Stuart Highway, commonly called the Track. The town center lies east of the highway. The 1,610-km (1,000-mi) drive from Adelaide takes about 24 hours; from Darwin the 1,515 km (940 mi) is about 100 km (62 mi) shorter than from the south.

BY PLANE

Alice Springs Airport is 15 km (9 mi) southeast of the center of town. The bright and cool passenger terminal is a welcome relief for anyone who sweated through the shedlike structure it replaced. The local airport is currently served by **Ansett Australia** and **Qantas** The flight from either Sydney or Melbourne takes 2¾ hours; from Brisbane, three hours; from Adelaide, two hours. ☞ Air Travel *in* the Gold Guide for airline telephone numbers.

Alice Springs Airport Shuttle Service has a shuttle bus that meets every flight. The ride to your hotel costs $9 each way. On request, the bus will also pick you up at your hotel and take you to the airport. ✉ *113 Todd St., ☎ 08/8953–0310.*

Alice Springs Taxis (☎ 08/8952–1877) maintains a taxi stand at the airport. The fare to most parts of town is $18–$20.

BY TRAIN

It's impossible to miss your stop at Alice Springs—it's the end of the line. The *Ghan* (Rail Australia, ☎ 13–2232 or 1800/88–8480), named after the Afghan camel-train drivers who traveled the route before the railway, provides one of the world's classic rail journeys. It's comfortable and well run, although the food does tend toward standard fare. The train leaves Adelaide at 2 PM each Thursday, arriving in Alice Springs at 10 AM Friday. The return train leaves Alice Springs at 2 PM Friday, arriving in Adelaide at 11:45 AM Saturday. Between April and December there is an additional departure from both Adelaide (each Monday) and from Alice Springs (each Tuesday), and departure and arrival times are the same as those of the regular service. Alice Springs's railway station is 2½ km (1½ mi) west of Todd Mall.

Getting Around

BY CAR

If you want to get out and around town into the desert, renting a car is a smart idea. And looking farther down the road, it's 440 km (273 mi) from Alice Springs to Ayers Rock Resort. There are also interesting natural wonders to take in on the way down: another reason to rent a car. The trip takes about five hours (☞ On the Way to Uluru, *below*). The road is paved and in very good condition.

When traveling off the few paved roads, be sure to carry survival rations, water, and spares. Rental cars cannot be driven out of the Northern Territory except by special arrangement.

Contacts and Resources

CAR RENTAL

Several rental-car companies have offices in Alice Springs: **Avis** (☎ 08/8953–5533), **Budget** (☎ 08/8952–8899), **Hertz** (☎ 08/8952–2644), **Territory Rent-a-Car** (☎ 08/8952–9999), and **Thrifty** (☎ 08/8952–2400).

DENTISTS

Department of Health Dental Clinic. ☎ 08/8951–6713.

DOCTORS

Central Clinic. ✉ 76 Todd St., ☎ 08/8952–1088.

EMERGENCIES

Ambulance, fire brigade, and **police.** ☎ 000.
Hospital. ☎ 08/8951–7777.

GUIDED TOURS

The **Alice Wanderer** (☎ 08/8952–2111) completes an hourly circuit (with commentary) of most tourist attractions in and around Alice Springs between 9 and 5 daily. You can leave and rejoin the bus whenever you like for a flat daily rate.

Several companies offer half-day tours of Alice Springs. All tours include visits to the Royal Flying Doctor Service Base, the School of the Air, the Old Telegraph Station, and the Anzac Hill scenic lookout. **AAT Kings** (✉ 74 Todd St., ☎ 08/8952–1700, or 1800/33–4009) runs three-hour tours to the School of the Air, Telegraph Station, Royal Flying Doctor's Base, Strehlow Centre, and Anzac Hill. There is also a half-day Aboriginal Dreamtime tour to a bush site outside town, where local Aborigines explain their way of life, show how to find bush foods, and demonstrate how their weapons (including boomerangs) are made and used. Courtesy hotel pickup is provided (💳 $43 for town tours, $67 for Dreamtime tour; the two can be combined for $99). **Tailormade Tours & Airport Limousines** (✉ 23 Gosse St., ☎ 08/8952–1731 or 1800/80–6641) offers a three-hour coach tour that covers the same sights as AAT Kings's tour (💳 $40). The company will also provide a chauffeur-driven, air-conditioned car for city sightseeing at $62 per hour.

PHARMACIES

Alice Springs Pharmacy. ✉ Shop 19, Hartley St., ☎ 08/8952–1554.
Plaza Amcal Chemist. ✉ Alice Plaza, Todd Mall, ☎ 08/8953–0089.

ROAD ASSISTANCE

Road Conditions Information (☎ 22–32–32) provides the latest information about conditions on the many unpaved roads in the area. In the event of a breakdown, contact the **Automobile Association of N.T.** (✉ Shop 4, 105 Gregory Terr., ☎ 08/8953–1322). Its agent for vehicle recovery is located at 58 Sargent Street.

VISITOR INFORMATION

The **Central Australian Tourism Industry Association** dispenses information, advice, and maps. ✉ Gregory Terr. and Hartley St., ☎ 08/8952–5199.

For additional information on buildings of heritage significance in and around Alice Springs, contact the **National Trust.** ✉ Old Hartley Street School, Hartley St., ☎ 08/8952–4516. ☺ Weekdays 10:30–2:30.

SIDE TRIPS FROM ALICE SPRINGS

Eastern MacDonnell Ranges—Ross Highway

★ East of the Alice, spectacular scenery and Aboriginal rock art found in the MacDonnell Ranges are well worth a day or more's exploring, and many sights are closer to town than those in the western ranges. Emily Gap (a sacred site), Jessie Gap, Undoolya Gap, and Corroboree Rock (a particularly interesting formation) are all located within the first 44 km (27 mi) east of Alice Springs. Beyond that, Trephina Gorge and John Hayes Rockhole (both with very good walks), N'Dhala Gorge Nature Park (with numerous hide-and-seek Aboriginal rock carvings), and Ross River Homestead (with overnight lodging; ☞ *below*), are 76 km (47 mi) and farther out.

Dining and Lodging

$$ ✕⊞ **All Seasons Ross River Homestead Resort.** Situated among rugged ranges next to the river after which it is named, this resort is a place to experience the remote Outback in relative comfort, and with plenty to keep you occupied. Accommodations are basic redwood cabins, each with its own bathroom. A bar and restaurant are on the premises, and horse and camel riding are also offered. Camping facilities are also available. ⊠ *Ross River Rd., NT 0870, 85 km (53 mi) east of Alice Springs,* ☎ *08/8956–9711,* ☒ *08/8956–9823. 30 5-person cabins with bath. Pool, spa. MC, V.*

Western MacDonnell Ranges

★ The MacDonnell Ranges west of Alice Springs are, like the eastern ranges, broken by a series of chasms and gorges, many of which can be visited in a single day, depending on your stamina. To reach them, drive out of town on Larapinta Drive, the western continuation of Stott Terrace.

On the way out to the ranges, **Alice Springs Desert Park** provides an informative way to understand the ecology of 70% of the Australian landmass—that is, the desert. The park opened in 1997, and its core exhibit area of 75 acres presents 120 animal and 320 plant species in the range of Australian ecosystems and includes the largest nocturnal house in the southern hemisphere. The park is also one of the leading research centers on desert ecologies. ⊠ *Larapinta Dr. (6½ km, or 4 mi, from Alice Springs's center), Box 1046, Alice Springs, NT 0871,* ☎ *08/8951–8788,* ☒ *08/8951–8720.* ☞ *$12.* ☉ *Daily 9–9.*

John Flynn's Grave is situated on a rise with the stark ranges behind, and the setting is memorable. The grave is unmistakable, too: a rock cairn with a large round stone, one of the Devil's Marbles from near Tennant Creek, on top. ⊠ *6 km (4 mi) from Alice Springs on left.*

Simpsons Gap National Park isn't dramatic, but it is the closest gorge to town. Stark white ghost gums, red rocks, and the purple-hazed mountains give visitors a taste of the scenery to be seen farther into the ranges. The gap itself can be crowded, but it's only 200 yards from the car park. ⊠ *24 km (15 mi) west of Alice Springs, then 5⅓ km (3½ mi) on side road.* ☞ *Free.* ☉ *8–8.*

Standley Chasm is one of the most impressive canyons. At midday, when the sun is directly overhead, the 10-yard-wide canyon glows red from the reflected light. The walk from the car park takes about 20 minutes and is rocky toward the end. There is a kiosk at the park entrance. ⊠ *48 km (30 mi) west of Alice Springs, then 9 km (5½ mi) on side road.* ☎ *08/8956–7440.* ☞ *$3 per person.* ☉ *Daily 7:30–6.*

Namatjira Drive

Beyond **Standley Chasm** (☞ *above*) the mileage starts adding up, and be prepared for rough road conditions.

Ellery Creek Big Hole Scenic Reserve is believed to have the coolest swimming hole in the Red Centre. ⊠ *48 km (30 mi) west of Alice Springs 6½ km (4 mi) past Standley Chasm Rd., take Namatjira Dr.*

Serpentine Gorge requires a swim—which can be quite refreshing—through the gorge to get the best perspective on the place. ⊠ *106 km (66 mi) west of Alice Springs on Namtjira Dr., then 4 km (2½ mi) on rough track.*

Ormiston Gorge and Pound National Park is one of the few really breathtaking sights of the western ranges. Unfortunately, it can be crowded at times. There are several walks, including the Pound Walk, in the park. ⊠ *135 km (84 mi) west of Alice Springs on Namatjira Dr.*

Glen Helen Gorge National Park has the most substantial gorge of all, a good water hole, and the rather sporadic coursing of the Finke River. ⊠ *140 km (87 mi) west of Alice Springs on Namatjira Dr.*

DINING AND LODGING

$–$$ ✕🗊 **Glen Helen Homestead.** A variety of accommodations are available at the homestead, from motel and lodge rooms to hostel and camping facilities. Considering its remove from civilization, **Cloudy's** restaurant on site comes pretty well recommended. ⊠ *Namatjira Dr., 135 km (84 mi) west of Alice Springs,* ☎ *08/8956–7489.*

Hermannsburg and Beyond

Another alternative after passing **Standley Chasm** (☞ *above*) is to continue on Larapinta Drive in the direction of **Hermannsburg,** which has tearooms, a supermarket, and a service station. The buildings of the early Lutheran Mission have been restored (the mission is open Tuesday–Sunday, and admission is free). ⊠ *132 km (82 mi) from Alice Springs.*

You need a four-wheel-drive vehicle to continue past Hermannsburg to **Palm Valley** in **Finke Gorge National Park.** The valley is a remnant of a time when Australia had a moister climate and supported palm trees over large areas. The trees here are the unique *Livistonia mariae*, a type of cabbage palm, which have survived as a species for more than 10,000 years. Palm Valley is like a slice of the tropical north dropped into the middle of the Red Centre.

ULURU AND KATA TJUTA

It isn't too difficult to see why the Aborigines attach spiritual significance to Uluru (Ayers Rock). Rising more than 1,100 ft from the flat surrounding plain, it is one of the world's largest monoliths. More impressive than its size, however, is its color—a glowing red that changes constantly throughout the day. Kata Tjuta (the Olgas), 53 km (33 mi) west, is a series of 36 gigantic rock domes that hide a maze of fascinating gorges and crevasses. The names Ayers Rock and The Olgas are used to describe these two wonders out of familiarity alone—at the sites themselves, you'll find that the Aboriginal Uluru and Kata Tjuta are the respective names of preference.

Uluru and Kata Tjuta have very different compositions: The great monolith is a type of sandstone called arkose, and the rock domes are composed of conglomerate. For a long time it was thought that they sit upon the sandy terrain like pebbles. That isn't the case. Both formations are the tips of tilted rock strata that extend into the earth for thousands of meters; perhaps two-thirds of each formation extends below the surface. During a period of intense geological activity more than 300 million years ago, the strata were tilted—the arkose by nearly 90 degrees and the conglomerate only about 15 degrees. The rock surrounding the formations had been fractured, and thus it quickly eroded away, leaving the present structures standing as separate entities about 40 million years ago.

Both of these intriguing sights lie within Uluru–Kata Tjuta National Park, which is protected as a World Heritage Site. As such it is one of only two parks in the world recognized in this way for both its landscape and cultural values. All tourist facilities lie just outside of the national park at the Ayers Rock Resort. The whole experience is a bit like seeing the Grand Canyon turned inside out, and you'll remember a visit here for a lifetime.

On the Way to Uluru

The 440-km (273-mi) drive to Uluru from Alice Springs along the Stuart and Lasseter highways takes about five hours, but there are interesting sights along the way if you're prepared to make a few detours.

Camel Outback Safaris is owned by a local legend, Noel Fullerton, who raises and trains his own camels for tourist expeditions. Day rides are available from 7:30 AM to 5 PM. The duration of the rides varies from one hour to 14 days. For rides of half a day (which include a light lunch) or longer, be sure to book in advance. ⊠ *93 km (58 mi) south of Alice Springs,* ☎ *08/8956–0925.*

The **Henbury Meteorite Craters,** a group of 12 depressions between 6 and 600 ft across, were probably formed by a meteorite shower about 5,000 years ago. One of them is 60 ft deep. ⊠ *134 km (83 mi) south of Alice Springs take exit to Kings Canyon and continue 13 km (8 mi).*

★ **Kings Canyon,** in Watarrka (formerly Kings Canyon) National Park, is one of the finest sights in Central Australia. Sheltered within the sheer cliff walls of the canyon is a world of ferns and rock pools, permanent springs, and woodlands. Several walking tracks wind through the gorge and along the ridge tops. The main path is the 6-km (4-mi) Canyon Walk, which starts with a fairly steep climb to the top of the escarpment and leads to a delightful water hole in the so-called Garden of Eden at the approximate middle of the four-hour walk.

Watarrka National Park is now accessible by car on the **Mereenie Track** from Glen Helen. To make this loop around the Western MacDonnell Ranges, you'll need an Aboriginal Land Entry Permit, which can be obtained free of charge from the **Central Australian Tourism Industry Association** (☎ 08/8952–5199) in Alice Springs. ⊠ *134 km (83 mi) south of Alice Springs take exit to Kings Canyon and continue 200 km (124 mi) west.*

Dining and Lodging

$$$$ ╳⊞ **Kings Canyon Resort.** Only 6 km (4 mi) from the canyon, this recently built accommodation is the only place to stay within Watarrka National Park. All rooms are air-conditioned, with satellite TV, refrigerators, and direct-dial phones. There are souvenir and provision shops. **Carmichael's** ($$) is the premier restaurant, with seating for 250 and a feature wall of Aboriginal art that provides a counterpoint to the sweeping desert views through the large windows. If you are on a budget, there are two- and four-bed backpacker rooms as well as a large, well-equipped campground adjoining. ⊠ *Ernest Giles Rd., Wattarka National Park. Mailing address: PMB 136, Alice Springs, NT 0871,*

☎ 08/8956–7442 or 1800/81–7622, FAX 08/8956–7410. 96 rooms with
shower, 4 suites, 36 4-bed rooms. Restaurant, 2 bars, café, pool, laundry. AE, DC, MC, V.

Uluru and Kata Tjuta

Allow about 20 minutes to drive to Uluru from the Ayers Rock Resort
area; Kata Tjuta will take another 30 minutes. The park entrance fee
of $15 is valid for a week. The sunset-viewing area is 13 km (8 mi)
from the resort on the way to Uluru.

Uluru

★ There is an inevitable sensation of excitement as you approach the great
rock—Uluru just keeps looming larger and larger. After entering the
park through a toll gate, you'll come upon the serpentine shape of the
Uluru–Kata Tjuta Cultural Centre, two buildings that reflect the Kuniya
and Liru stories of two ancestral snakes whose activities come together on the southern side of Uluru. Located on the right hand side
of the road just before you reach the rock, the cultural center houses
displays depicting Aboriginal history and knowledge of the park's
flora and fauna, along with information on the return of the park to
Aboriginal ownership in 1985. Comprehensive explanatory material
is available at the station, as are descriptions of local plant and animal life. The center opened in October 1995, and it incorporates the
park's ranger station.

As you work your way around Uluru, you'll notice that your perspective
of the great rock changes significantly. Four hours will allow you to
walk the 10 km (6 mi) around the rock with time to explore the several deep crevices along the way; or you can drive around it on the paved
road. Be aware that some places are Aboriginal sacred sites and cannot be entered. These are clearly signposted. There is some Aboriginal art to be found in caves at the base of the rock. If you're comparing
notes on native rock art, the work here is neither as extensive nor as
impressive as those in Kakadu National Park at the top of the Northern Territory (☞ Chapter 11). It is nonetheless interesting to look at.

Only one trail leads to the top of the rock. The Aboriginal owners of
Uluru don't encourage people to climb it. They don't prohibit it either,
but the ranger station displays a well-reasoned argument why you should
reconsider your intentions to ascend.

If you do decide to mount, the climb from the base is about 1½ km
(1 mi), and the round-trip walk takes about two hours. Be careful:
The ascent is very steep. Climbers have fallen to their deaths or had
heart attacks; even experienced hikers should use the safety chain on
the steep initial incline. Don't attempt the climb if you aren't in good
condition. You'll also need to be well prepared with solid hiking
boots, a hat, sunscreen, and drinking water. Once you are on top of
the rock, the trail is much easier. You can sign a guest book at the summit. In summer the climb is prohibited during the middle of the day.

The other popular way of experiencing Uluru is far less taxing but no
less intense: watching the sun set against it from one of the two sun-
set-viewing areas. As the last rays of the sun strike, the rock seems lit
from within: It positively glows. Just as quickly, the light is extinguished,
and the color changes to a somber mauve and finally to black.

SHOPPING
The Cultural Centre (☎ 08/8956–3138) houses the **Ininti Store** (☎ 08/
8956–2214), which sells a range of souvenirs, and the adjoining
Maruku Arts and Crafts Centre (☎ 08/8956–2558), which is owned

by Aborigines and sells Aboriginal painting and handicrafts. There is also a display of traditional huts and shelters.

Kata Tjuṯa

★ In many ways, Kata Tjuṯa is more satisfying to explore than Uluṟu. The rock is one immense block, so you feel as if you're always on the outside looking in. But you can really come to grips with Kata Tjuṯa. As the Aboriginal name, *Kata Tjuṯa* (many heads), suggests, this is a jumble of huge rocks containing numerous hidden gorges and chasms. There are three main walks. The first is from the car park into **Olga Gorge,** the deepest valley between the rocks. This is a mile walk, and the round-trip journey takes about one hour. From the parking lot farther along, the walk to **Kata Tjuṯa Lookout** is about a mile round-trip and takes about an hour. More rewarding but also more difficult is a walk that continues through the major cleft between the Olgas known (for reasons not obscure) as the **Valley of the Winds.** Experienced walkers can complete this 6-km (4-mi) walk in about four hours. Remember to carry at least a quart of water for each hour of walking and avoid activity during the hottest part of the day.

Ayers Rock Resort

Dining and Lodging

This is a planned resort. You can choose from five types of accommodation, priced on a descending scale from the luxurious rooms of the Sails in the Desert to the campsites of the Ayers Rock Campground. All reservations can be made through a central reservation service, Southern Pacific Hotels' Travelex (☎ 1300/363–300 in Australia), or through the resort's central reservations service in Sydney (☎ 02/9360–9099).

The choice of dining is limited to hotel restaurants and the less expensive **Gecko's Cafe** (☎ 08/8956–2562), which serves lunch and dinner in Continental style with gourmet, wood-fired pizza and pasta, coffee, and cakes. It's open from 8 AM to 10 AM for coffee and pastries, then from 10 AM to midnight for full service. If you eat outside of your hotel, you can have the meals billed to your room. Not to be missed is the "**Sounds of Silence**" Dinner in the Desert for $90, where you dine under the open sky, surrounded by the vastness of central Australia.

CATEGORY	COST*
$$$$	over $240
$$$	$180–$240
$$	$110–$180
$	under $110

All prices are for a standard double room, excluding the NT Tourism Marketing Levy of 5%.

HOTELS AND MOTELS

Because of the transient nature of the staff at this resort-only area, you might find the quality of service at the following establishments to be uneven.

$$$$ 🕾 **Sails in the Desert.** With architectural shade sails (for protection from
★   the sun), manicured lawns, Aboriginal artwork, and a wide range of facilities, this three-story hotel clearly aspires to be the best address at the resort. Open-air stairways and passages contribute to the overall sense of space and light. Rooms are decorated in ochre shades and have balconies overlooking the central lawns and gardens. A viewing tower looks out toward Uluṟu in the distance. Sails in the Desert also has the best restaurant, the Kuniy ($$$), which serves such specialties as barramundi, buffalo, and kangaroo. Two other restaurants, the Desert Rose

and the Rock Pool (both $$), are also on the property. ⊠ *Yulara Dr.,
0872;* ☎ *08/8956–2200, 08/8956–2494, or 1800/08–9622;* FAX *08/
8956–2018. 228 rooms with bath, 2 suites, 6 deluxe rooms with
whirlpool on balcony. 3 restaurants, 3 bars, piano bar, pool, tennis courts,
putting green, travel services. AE, DC, MC, V.*

$$$ ⊞ **Desert Gardens.** If you prefer a smaller hotel, the two-story Desert
Garden has very good overall quality and service. Like Sails in the Desert,
it is built around a lawn, pool, and extensive gardens with native
flora. The modern rooms are small but comfortable and well kept. The
hotel is located near the visitor center and the Shopping Square. The
Whitegums ($$$) is open for breakfast and dinner, serving light sal-
ads of local fruits, nuts, and berries. The Bunya Bar ($) serves lunch
and dinner, with an emphasis on fresh, healthy, affordable meals and
a relaxed atmosphere. The Palya Bar serves snacks and drinks at pool-
side. ⊠ *Yulara Dr., 0872,* ☎ *08/8956–2100,* FAX *08/8956–2156. 160
rooms with bath. Restaurant, bar, pool, 2 tennis courts, laundry. AE,
DC, MC, V.*

$$ ⊞ **Outback Pioneer Hotel and Lodge.** Although the theme is the Out-
★ back of the 1860s, complete with rustic decor and bush games in the
evening, you won't be roughing it here. Situated on the other side of
the resort from hotels and the Shopping Square, the lodge is served by
a shuttle bus that runs to the other properties every 15 minutes. Guests
at the adjoining Outback Pioneer Lodge, a fully air-conditioned budget accommodation, have access to all of the hotel's facilities. The Bough
House, open daily for breakfast, lunch, and dinner, offers hearty central Australian dishes as well as lighter food. The Pioneer Self-Cook
Barbecue's fully equipped kitchen ($) is open from noon into the night.
As the name suggests, you buy a cut of meat and cook it yourself, and
alcoholic drinks are available with the barbecue facility. There is also
a kiosk open daily from morning till night where you can buy light
meals, snacks, and soft drinks. ⊠ *Yulara Dr., 0872,* ☎ *08/8956–
2170,* FAX *08/8956–2320. 125 rooms, 224 dormitory beds, 20 cabins.
Pool, laundry. AE, DC, MC, V.*

$ ⊞ **Emu Walk Apartments.** These one- and two-bedroom apartments
have fully equipped kitchens (down to champagne glasses), living
rooms, and daily maid service. Each unit has a sofa bed, so one bedrooms can sleep four, and the balconied two-bedrooms can accommodate
six or eight. There's no restaurant on site, but you are welcome to dine
in any of the resort's eateries. ⊠ *Yulara Dr., 0872,* ☎ *08/8956–2000,*
FAX *08/8956–2328. 56 apartments. AE, DC, MC, V.*

$ ⊞ **Spinifex Lodge.** Originally used to house resort-area staff, most of
the rooms in this lodge have two single beds or two bunk beds and
most of the amenities you would expect in a good hotel, plus kitchenettes and daily maid service. Bathrooms are shared. ⊠ *Yulara Dr.,
0872,* ☎ *08/8956–2131,* FAX *08/8956–2163. 68 rooms without bath.
Laundry. AE, DC, MC, V.*

CARAVAN PARK

$ ⚠ **Ayers Rock Campground.** This large campground has 240 sites for
campers, 500 tent sites, and 10 air-conditioned cabins. The area has
rolling green lawns, refrigerators, tables and chairs, and an Outback-
style barbecue shelter. It is the only site for private camping in the area.
⊠ *Yulara Dr., 0872,* ☎ *08/8956–2055,* FAX *08/8956–2260. Pool,
laundry. MC, V.*

Child Care

☼ The resort area's hotels have joined to form a free **Kids Only Club** for
5- to 12-year-olds that operates daily from 8 to noon and from 6 to
10 PM during peak holiday seasons. Activities include sports, excursions to the rock, and forays for bush tucker. Reservations should be

made the evening before through reception at your hotel. The **Child Care Centre** will look after children between the ages of three months and eight years on weekdays between 8 AM and 5:30 PM. Child minding is available outside these times by arrangement with the center. ⊠ *Next to Community Hall,* ☎ *08/8956–2097.*

Shopping

Until recently, Ayers Rock Resort had a news agency, a very reasonably priced supermarket (open 8 AM–9 PM), and a couple of souvenir shops. Then the **Mulgara Gallery and Craft Works Gallery** (☎ 08/8956–2460) opened in the foyer of the Sails in the Desert Hotel. It specializes in high-quality Australian arts and crafts, including Aboriginal works and opal jewelry. A lack of competition ensures that the art is likely to cost more here than in Alice Springs. Several new stores have opened, however, including food shops and a tourist information center, and each of the hotels has an Ayers Rock Logo Shop, selling Australian-made garments and leather goods.

Uluru and Kata Tjuta A to Z

Arriving and Departing

BY BUS
Bus companies traveling to Ayers Rock Resort from Alice Springs include **AAT Kings** (☎ 08/8952–1700) and **Greyhound Pioneer** (☎ 08/8952–7888).

BY CAR
It is 440 km (273 mi) from Alice Springs to Ayers Rock Resort; the trip takes about five hours. The road is paved and in fine condition.

BY PLANE
Connellan Airport is 5 km (3 mi) north of the resort complex. It is served by **Ansett Australia** and **Qantas. Kendall Airlines** has a Saturday service to the Rock from Adelaide via Coober Pedy. ☞ Air Travel *in* the Gold Guide for airline telephone numbers.

Between the Airport and Yulara. AAT Kings (☎ 08/8952–1700) has a complimentary shuttle bus that meets every flight.

Getting Around

BY BUS
AAT Kings (☎ 08/8952–1700) offers a range of daily local tours.

BY CAR
From the resort it's about 19 km (12 mi) to Uluru or 53 km (33 mi) to Kata Tjuta. The road to Kata Tjuta is sealed. Routes between the hotels and the sights are clearly marked, and because prices are competitive with those for the bus tours—especially for larger parties—renting a car may be your most thrifty and convenient option. There are several car-rental companies at the resort: **Avis** (☎ 08/8956–2266), **Territory Rent-a-Car** (☎ 08/8956–2030), and **Hertz** (☎ 08/8956–2244). For a chauffeur-driven limousine, contact **V.I.P. Chauffeur Cars** (☎ 08/8956–2283).

BY TAXI
Sunworth Transport Service (☎ 08/8956–2152) can whisk you from the resorts to the sights for much less than the cost of a guided bus tour. Plus, you can go at your own convenience.

Guided Tours and Programs
Flightseeing Tours. An ideal view of Uluru and Kata Tjuta is from the air. A variety of light-plane tours are offered (with courtesy pickup from your hotel included), from half-hour flights over Ayers Rock and the

Olgas to 110-minute flights that also fly over Kings Canyon. Prices range from $65 to $175 per person. Contact **Airnorth** (☎ 08/8956–2093) or **RockAyer** (☎ 08/8956–2345). Helicopter flights are more expensive: $75 per person for 15 minutes over Ayers Rock or $100 for 20 minutes over the Olgas. A flight over both sights costs $145 per seat. The local operators are **Jayrow** (☎ 08/8956–2077 or 1800/65–0057, FAX 08/8956–2060) and **RockAyer** (☎ 08/8956–2345).

General Tours. Anangu Tours (☎ 08/8956–2123, FAX 08/8956–3136) has a number of excellent offerings: the Uluru Breakfast Tour ($78) which includes a restaurant breakfast and Aboriginal guided tour, the Kuniya Sunset Tour ($65), the Anangu Culture Pass ($120), the self-drive Liru Tour ($39), and the self-drive Kuniya Tour ($39). Guides are Aboriginal people who work with interpreters.

Motorcycle Tour. The normally fine climate of the desert makes **Uluru Motorcycle Tours** (☎ 08/8956–2019, FAX 08/8956 2196) enjoyable (and popular) and provides the chance for some very different vacation photographs. Guides communicate with their passengers by helmet intercoms. Prices range from $70 for the Uluru Cruise to $85 to view sunrise over the Rock to $145 for a three-hour tour to the Olgas.

Slide Shows. Several free slide shows about local wildlife and flora are given at the auditorium near the resort's visitor center opposite the Desert Gardens Hotel on Yulara Drive.

Stargazing. Central Australia has some of the clearest and cleanest air in the world—just look up into the night sky. A small observatory with a good telescope has been set up within the grounds of the resort for just that purpose. Viewing times vary with the seasons; sessions last for about an hour, and can be booked through **Uluru Experience** (☎ 1800/80–3174; ☞ $20).

Walking Tours. The **Mala Walk** (☎ 08/8956–2299; ☞ free) is led by Aboriginal rangers who show you the land from their perspective. The walk starts from the base of the climbing trail. **Uluru Experience** (☎ 1800/80–3174) specializes in small group tours at Uluru with guides who have extensive local knowledge. Tours, which should be booked at least a day ahead, include a 10-km (6-mi) walk around the base of Uluru. The Uluru Walk gives fascinating insight into the significance of the area to the Aboriginal people. It departs daily, includes breakfast, and costs $64. A tour of the remarkable, flat-top Mt. Conner, which continues on to the Curtin Springs cattle station for dinner, costs around $120.

Contacts and Resources

EMERGENCIES

Ambulance, fire brigade, and **police.** ☎ *000.*

Ambulance. ☎ *08/8956–2286.*

Police. ☎ *08/8956–2166.*

Medical Clinic. ✉ *Flying Doctor Base, near police station, 08/8956–2286 emergencies.* ☉ *Weekdays 9–noon and 2–5, weekends 10–11.*

VISITOR INFORMATION

The **Uluru–Kata Tjuta Cultural Centre** (☎ 08/8956–2299) is on the park road just before you reach the rock. It also contains the park's ranger station.

A **Visitors Centre** (☎ 08/8957–7377) is opposite the Desert Gardens Hotel on Yulara Drive.

11 Darwin, the Top End, and the Kimberley

From sunset over Darwin Harbour to sunrise over the rocky domes and towers of Purnululu National Park, the Top End and the Kimberley's stunning and diverse landforms are virtual timelines of life on the planet, tracing the ancient and living heritage of Aboriginal rock art alongside contemporary pursuits. Darwin and Broome—both far closer to the cities of Asia than to any Australian counterparts—host the most racially diverse populations of the nation: Aborigines, Anglos, and Asians sharing a relaxed tropical lifestyle.

THE TOP END is a geographic description—but it is also a state of mind. Isolated from the rest of Australia by thousands of miles of desert and lonely scrubland, "Top Enders" are different and proud of it. From the remote wetlands and stone country of Arnhem Land—home to thousands of Aboriginal people—to the lush tropical city of Darwin, the Top End is a gateway to a region where people from 70 different national and cultural backgrounds live in what they regard as the "real" Australia. It's an isolation that contributes to strong feelings of independence from the rest of the country—"Southerners" are regarded with a mixture of pity and ridicule.

By David McGonigal and Chips Mackinolty

It is also a region of extremes—of geography and climate. The people of the Top End spend more time than other Australians enjoying the outdoors, through sport, a wide variety of community celebrations and, simply, "going bush" for weekends of fishing, hiking, and exploring the many national parks.

Although Aboriginal people recognize up to six different seasons, for most people the year is divided into the "Wet" and the "Dry." The Dry is a period of idyllic weather with warm days and cool nights. So to make up for those eight months of the year where there is barely a cloud in the sky, the Wet season brings monsoonal storms that dump an average 65 inches of rain in a few short months—and even the rain is warm! Heralded by the notorious heat and humidity of the "build up," the Wet is a time of year when roads can be washed out and rivers become impassable for months at a time, and the region faces the ever present threat of cyclones.

It was during the Wet of 1974–75 that Cyclone Tracy ripped through Darwin with winds of 136 mph, killing 66 people and destroying or damaging over 80% of its buildings. In this time of year spectacular electrical storms light up the skies and the region between Darwin and Kakadu National Park, which has the world's highest recorded rate of lightning strikes—up to 1,000 during a single storm.

The starkness of the isolation of the Top End and Western Australia's Kimberley is reflected in its tiny population. Where the Northern Territory occupies one sixth of Australia's landmass, its population of 170,000 makes up less than one hundredth of the continent's citizenry—an average density of 1 person per 8 square km (3 square mi). In many areas kangaroos and cattle outnumber the locals: the Kimberley, an area of land larger than the state of Kansas, is home to only 30,000 people. Traveling by road from Darwin to Broome is the best way to see the Kimberley, but you'll pass through only nine communities in 2,016 km (1,250 mi), from such tiny settlements as Timber Creek to the "big" towns, such as Katherine.

The Kimberley possesses some of the most spectacular landscapes in Australia. A land of rugged ranges, tropical wetlands, and desert, of vast cattle stations and wonderful national parks, including the bizarre red-and-black-striped sandstone domes and towers of Purnululu National Park that are among Australia's most beautiful sights, the Kimberley still has the feel of the frontier about it. Like Top Enders, the people of the Kimberley region see themselves as living in a land apart from the rest of the nation, and it's easy to see why—landscape and distance combine to make the Kimberley one of the world's few uniquely open spaces.

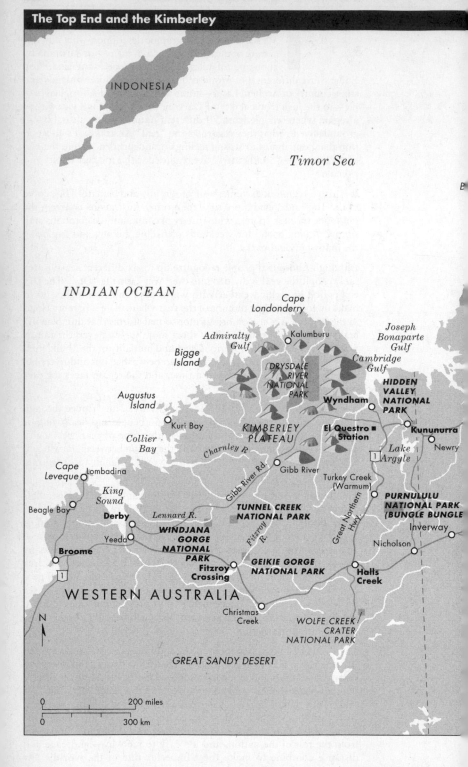

INDONESIA

Timor Sea

INDIAN OCEAN

Cape Londonderry

Kalumburu

Admiralty Gulf

Joseph Bonaparte Gulf

Bigge Island

DRYSDALE RIVER NATIONAL PARK

Cambridge Gulf

HIDDEN VALLEY NATIONAL PARK

Augustus Island

Wyndham

Kuri Bay

KIMBERLEY PLATEAU

El Questro ■ Station

Kununurra

Collier Bay

Charnley R.

Newry

Lake Argyle

Gibb River

Turkey Creek (Warmum)

Cape Leveque Lombadina

Gibb River Rd.

PURNULULU NATIONAL PARK (BUNGLE BUNGLE

Beagle Bay

King Sound

Lennard R.

TUNNEL CREEK NATIONAL PARK

Inverway

Derby

Fitzroy R.

Nicholson

Yeeda

WINDJANA GORGE NATIONAL PARK

Broome

Fitzroy Crossing

GEIKIE GORGE NATIONAL PARK

Halls Creek

N

WESTERN AUSTRALIA

Christmas Creek

WOLFE CREEK CRATER NATIONAL PARK

GREAT SANDY DESERT

0   200 miles
0   300 km

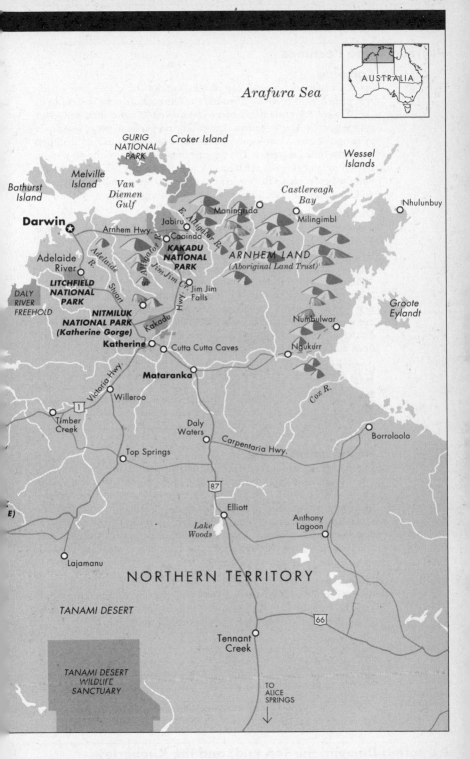

Arafura Sea

AUSTRALIA

GURIG NATIONAL PARK

Croker Island

Melville Island

Van Diemen Gulf

Bathurst Island

Wessel Islands

Nhulunbuy

Castlereagh Bay

Maningrida

Milingimbi

Darwin

Jabiru

Cooinda

E. Alligator R.

Arnhem Hwy.

Adelaide R.

KAKADU NATIONAL PARK

ARNHEM LAND
(Aboriginal Land Trust)

Adelaide River

Stuart Hwy.

S. Alligator R.

Jim Jim Cr.

Groote Eylandt

LITCHFIELD NATIONAL PARK

DALY RIVER FREEHOLD

Jim Jim Falls

NITMILUK NATIONAL PARK
(Katherine Gorge)

Kakadu Hwy.

Numbulwar

Katherine

Cutta Cutta Caves

Ngukurr

Mataranka

Cox R.

Victoria Hwy.

Willeroo

Daly Waters

Carpentaria Hwy.

Borroloola

Timber Creek

1

Top Springs

87

Elliott

Anthony Lagoon

Lake Woods

Lajamanu

E)

NORTHERN TERRITORY

TANAMI DESERT

66

Tennant Creek

TANAMI DESERT WILDLIFE SANCTUARY

TO ALICE SPRINGS

Note: ☞ Chapter 13 for more information on four-wheel-driving in the Top End and the Kimberley's great outdoors.

Pleasures and Pastimes

Camping

From Darwin to Broome, camping out under the stars is one of the real pleasures of traveling through the Outback. It's not much fun in the Wet—if the rains don't carry you away the mosquitos will—but camping in the Dry is perfect. Depending on personal taste, you don't even need a tent. Most locals just take a swag—heavy canvas wrapped around a rolled mattress. The region abounds in out-of-the-way spots to pull up and sleep in the open. Wherever you go, ask a local to tell you the best place to throw down your swag, brew a billy (pot) of tea, and contemplate the glories of the southern night skies.

Dining

The menus in Darwin seem to indicate that there is little the average Territorian won't eat—buffalo, crocodile, camel, and kangaroo are all frequently featured. Barramundi is one of the tastiest fish in the world. Buffalo can be tough, but a tender piece is like a gamey piece of beef. Opinion is divided about crocodile—it, too, can be tough, but (like every other reptile, it seems) a good piece tastes like chicken. Since 1996 a new "eating precinct" has developed in Darwin's Cullen Bay. Only five minutes from the city, near where Darwin Harbour cruises embark, a cluster of restaurants overlooking the marina provide a range of indoor and outdoor eating venues.

CATEGORY	COST*
$$$$	over $45
$$$	$30–$45
$$	$20—$30
$	under $20

*per person, excluding drinks and service

Hiking and Walking

The national parks of the Top End and Kimberley are ideal for hiking—Australians call it bushwalking—and the parks will suit a variety of fitness levels. Major rock-art sites in Kakadu, for example, incorporate bushwalks from an hour or so to a half day in length. Park rangers supply maps and route information for walks that last overnight and longer. The rugged adventures require care and planning, but you'll be rewarded with unforgettable memories of trekking through some of the most remote places on earth.

Lodging

Apart from Darwin hotels and Top End resorts, accommodations fall into the more basic category. With the local scenery as spectacular as it is, however, those shouldn't be discouraging words.

CATEGORY	COST*
$$$$	over $160
$$$	$100–$160
$$	$60–$100
$	under $60

*All prices are for a standard double room, excluding the NT Tourism Marketing Levy of 2.5%.

Exploring Darwin, the Top End, and the Kimberley

The telltale recurring phrase "tyranny of distance" was first used to describe Australia's relationship to the rest of the world. In many ways it still describes the Top End and Kimberley, with vast distances setting this region apart from the rest of the nation. This is not a region that you can justly contemplate—nor travel, for that matter—in a few days. And especially if you plan to get out to the Kimberley, you should consider seeing it over a couple of weeks and combining it with a visit to the Red Centre for full effect. There are a number of organized tours of varying lengths that may suit the time you have available, but for independent travelers the following are suggested.

Great Itineraries

IF YOU HAVE 3 DAYS

Limit your time to the Top End and **Kakadu** and **Litchfield Parks.** Start from Darwin just after dawn and head east on the Arnhem Highway to **Fogg Dam** to view the birdlife. Continue into the park and picnic at the rock art site at **Ubirr.** Take a **scenic flight** in the afternoon, then a trip to the **Bowali Vistor's Centre,** and overnight at **Jabiru.** On the second day, head to **Nourlangie Rock** and **Anbangbang Billabong,** then continue to the **Yellow Water** cruise at **Cooinda** and stay there for the night. A visit to the **Aboriginal Cultural Centre** is a must on the third day, followed by a drive to **Litchfield National Park** via Batchelor. Depending on your time, a visit to any one of **Florence, Tjaynera,** or **Wangi Falls** for a picnic lunch followed by a stop at **Tolmer Falls** before returning to Darwin will conclude a somewhat hectic but rewarding survey of the Top End.

IF YOU HAVE 5 DAYS

Darwin should still be your starting point. To get straight into the Outback, start with a leisurely visit to **Litchfield National Park,** entering through the town of Batchelor. Don't miss a swim at the **Florence Falls** plunge pool and a picnic at **Petherick's Rain Forest.** Leave Litchfield on the back road to visit the **Territory Wildlife Park** at Berry Springs and on to stay at the **South Alligator Holiday Village.** An early start on day two will allow you to reach the Kakadu rock art site at **Ubirr** not too long after dawn, if you're ambitious. After Ubirr, stop at **Bowali Visitors Centre** before continuing to **Nourlangie Rock** and **Anbangbang Billabong** for lunch. In the early afternoon visit the **Aboriginal Cultural Centre,** then take the evening **Yellow Water** cruise at **Cooinda,** where you can overnight. On the third day head down the Kakadu Highway to the less-visited southern half of Kakadu National Park, swim at Gumlom Falls and lunch across the South Alligator at Bukbukluk. After lunch drop into the old gold mining town of **Pine Creek** before continuing to **Edith Falls.** Camp there in **Nitmiluk (Katherine Gorge) National Park** or head into **Katherine** for the night. Next morning hire a canoe or take a cruise up Katherine Gorge in Nitmiluk National Park; after lunch head south to **Cutta Cutta Caves** and the thermal pools at **Mataranka** and stay the night at the **Mataranka Homestead.** The return trip to Darwin will give you a chance to explore some of the small roads down "the Track," as the Stuart Highway is called. A diversion from **Hayes Creek** along the path of the old highway to Adelaide River is a beautiful alternative way back to the city.

IF YOU HAVE 10 DAYS

With 10 days, you have a chance to break off from the shorter itineraries and head west to the Kimberley. From Mataranka or Litchfield National Park, go to **Katherine** and take the Victoria Highway for lunch at the Highway Inn in the spectacular gorge country at the Victoria River Crossing, passing then through mesa formations and **Timber Creek** to **Kununurra** for the night. On the sixth day, take in the spectacular landscapes of **Purnululu National Park** by four-wheel-drive or with a guided tour, and spend the night in **Halls Creek.** It'll be a long haul west the seventh day on the Great Northern Highway, but you can make it to **Geikie Gorge National Park** for an afternoon boat tour, a welcome and interesting respite before heading off to camp the night at **Windjana Gorge.** Another early start will get you to **Broome** to poke around in the old pearling town. Slow down and take a fishing charter the next day. The return trip through **Derby** and back along the Gibb River Road with an overnight camp at the **El Questro Cattle Station** reveals the Kimberley at its most remote and spectacular. Continue back to Darwin from El Questro. A couple of alternatives: Spend more time at Purnululu National Park and stop your westward trip through the Kimberley at El Questro. Or go ahead and trek all the way to Broome, and fly back to Darwin from there.

When to Tour the Top End

Unless you are used to extreme heat and humidity, the best time to tour is in the Dry, roughly May to August, with inland nights in July becoming quite chilly. On the road, early starts beat the heat and get you to swimming holes in the middle of the day—the crucial time for cooling off. Most boat tours in the region run throughout the day, but early mornings and evening cruises are best for several reasons: to avoid the heat, to see animals when they are out feeding, to catch sunrises and sunsets, and to take advantage of the ideal light for photography (by noon the light is often harsh and flat).

DARWIN

There is no other city in Australia that dates its history by a single cataclysmic event. For the people of Darwin—including the vast majority who weren't here at the time—everything is dated as "before Tracy" or "after Tracy." It wasn't just the death toll. Officially 66 people died on that terrible Christmas Eve, compared to the 243 who died on 1942's first day of Japanese bombing raids. It was the immensity of the destruction wrought by Cyclone Tracy that has marked Australia's northern capital. Casualties of war are one terrible thing; but the helplessness of an entire population faced with natural disaster is something else again. Within a week of Tracy, Australia's biggest peacetime airlift reduced the population from 47,000 people to 12,000, with many refusing to return to a city that, for them, had died.

It's a tribute to those who stayed and those who have come to live here after Tracy that the rebuilt city now thrives as an administrative and commercial center for northern Australia. Old Darwin has been replaced by something of an edifice complex—such buildings as Parliament House and the Supreme Court seem all a bit too grand for such a small city, especially one that prides itself on its relaxed and informal atmosphere. It is a melting pot of Aborigines, Asians, and Anglos living together in an alluring combination of Outback openness and cosmopolitan multiculturalism.

The seductiveness of contemporary Darwin lifestyles belies a Top End history of failed attempts by Europeans dating back to 1824 to establish an enclave in a climate that was harsh and unyielding to new arrivals. Established in 1869, the original settlement of Palmerston was built on land that had changed little in 15 million years—a parcel of mangrove wetlands and rain forest. It was not until 1911, after it had already weathered the disastrous cylones of 1878, 1882, and 1897, that the town was named after the scientist who had visited these shores aboard the *Beagle* in 1839.

Today Darwin is the best place from which to explore the beauty and diversity of Australia's Top End, as well as the wonders of Kakadu, Nitmiluk (Katherine Gorge), and the mighty Kimberley region.

Exploring Darwin

The orientation point for visitors is the Mall at Smith Street. Normally crowded with locals in shorts and T-shirts, groups of Aborigines, and well-dressed office workers, this is a place where cowboy meets croissant. The downtown grid of streets around the Mall is at the very tip of a peninsula; most of the suburbs and outlying attractions are out beyond the airport.

Numbers in the text correspond to numbers in the margin and on the Darwin map.

A Good Walk

From the Smith Street Mall head southwest down Knuckey Street across Mitchell Street. On the right, at the intersection with the Esplanade, is the 1925 **Lyons Cottage** ① museum, which focuses on local history, including early settlement, pearling, and relations with Indonesian and Chinese groups. On the other side of Knuckey Street is an old house elevated on columns—the style used to be a regular feature of Darwin. This is the **Old Admiralty House** ②. Farther southeast on the Esplanade, the 1936 **Hotel Darwin** ③ also has an old-timey look that will take you back to Darwin's early days.

The Esplanade winds around the hotel to a cairn known as the **Overland Telegraph Memorial** ④, site of Australia's first telegraph connection with the rest of the world in 1871. Remember that prior to the telegraph, all communication to and from the island continent had to be made by ship. Facing the memorial is **Government House** ⑤, which has remarkably withstood the ravages of cyclones and Japanese bombing in World War II.

On the opposite side of the Esplanade between Mitchell and Smith streets are the **Old Police Station and Court House** ⑥, which date to 1884, with their long veranda and old stone facades. They currently function as governmental offices. **Survivor's Lookout** ⑦, a memorial to the victims of Japan's first bombing of Australia in 1942, is across the road.

To get to the wharf area, take the stairs down the cliff face. Directly at the bottom of the stairs is the entrance to Darwin's **World War II Storage Tunnels** ⑧, which secured fuel stores in World War II. Inside there are photographs of Darwin during wartime.

A walk of 435 ft to the east leads to **Stokes Hill Wharf** ⑨. The wharf now has a dual function: serving ships and serving locals with restaurants, weekend markets, and a good fishing spot. For a different perspective on fish, stop in at the wharf's **Indo Pacific Marine** ⑩. Inside you'll find a vast tank in which a coral-reef ecosystem and its astonishing collection of fish reside. In the same building, the **Australian Pearling Exhibition** ⑪ has a lively presentation of northern Australia's history of hunting and cultivating pearls.

Returning up the cliff to Smith Street, look on the right-hand side of the street for **Christ Church Cathedral** ⑫. **Browns Mart** ⑬, which in its current incarnation is a theater, is on the same side of Smith Street farther down.

Stop in at the **Victoria Hotel,** across Bennett Street on the left-hand side of Smith Street, and proceed to the balcony for a drink—a fine way to conclude a walking tour of Darwin.

460

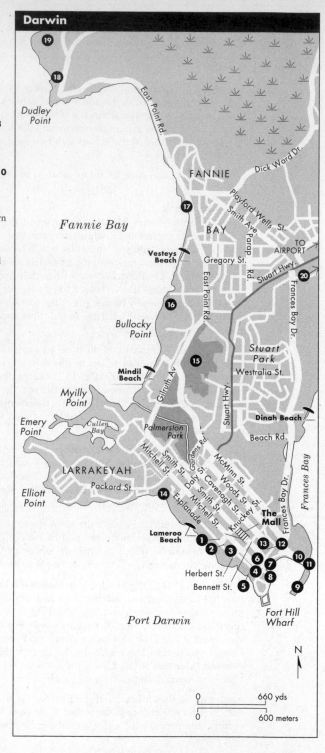

City Center

⑪ The **Australian Pearling Exhibition** displays 100 years of history of the hunt for pearls in Australia's northern waters. Exhibits cover everything from pearl farming to pearl jewelry settings. ⊠ *Stokes Hill Wharf,* ☎ *08/8941–2177.* ⊠ *$6.* ⊙ *Daily 10–5.*

⑬ **Browns Mart,** erected in 1885, has seen duty as an emporium, a mining exchange, and currently as a theater. ⊠ *Smith St. and Harry Chan Ave.*

NEED A BREAK? The balcony of the **Victoria Hotel** is a good place for a little refreshment. A Darwin institution since its construction in 1894, the Vic has been hit by every cyclone and rebuilt afterward—most recently in 1978. ⊠ *Bennett and Smith Sts.*

⑫ The Anglican **Christ Church Cathedral** was largely destroyed by Cyclone Tracy, and the remains of the original 1902 structure have been incorporated into the new building. ⊠ *Smith St. and Esplanade south.*

⑤ **Government House,** Darwin's oldest building, has been the home of the administrator for the area since 1870. The grounds are not open to the public, but most of the building can be seen over the picket fence. Despite being bombed by Japanese aircraft in 1942 and damaged by the cyclones of 1897, 1937, and 1974, it looks much as it did in 1879 when it was first completed. The house faces the ☞ **Overland Telegraph Memorial.**

③ When the **Hotel Darwin** first opened in 1883, it set new standards for lodging in Darwin, including "accommodation suitable for ladies." The present building, erected in 1936, takes up the better part of a block. It still has period charm, with plenty of wicker, cane, and potted palms (☞ Lodging, *below*). ⊠ *10 Herbert St. and Esplanade,* ☎ *08/8981–9211.*

⑩ If you'd rather ogle fish than eat them, visit the ☞ **Stokes Hill Wharf's Indo Pacific Marine.** Housed in a huge, glass-sided tank is the only self-contained coral-reef ecosystem in the southern hemisphere. Among the exotic corals are reef fish and other marine life. ⊠ *Stokes Hill Wharf,* ☎ *08/8981–1294.* ⊠ *$11.* ⊙ *Daily 10–5.*

① There are several buildings dating back to the early settlement of northern Australia in downtown Darwin. **Lyons Cottage** was built in 1925 for executives of the British-Australian Telegraph Company (B.A.T.). The stone building is now a historical museum with exhibits on life in Darwin, the Macassans, the Chinese, pearl diving, the early explorers, and the operation of the telegraph. ⊠ *74 Esplanade,* ☎ *08/8981–1750.* ⊠ *Free.* ⊙ *Daily 10–5.*

② The **Old Admiralty House** is elevated on columns, a design well suited to Darwin's steamy climate. This style of building was once common in Darwin, but the home is one of only a few of its kind to survive Cyclone Tracy in 1974. The Old Admiralty House was built in 1937 to provide lodging for the naval officer commanding northern Australia ⊠ *Knuckey St. and Esplanade.*

⑥ The 1884 **Old Police Station and Court House,** with their long verandas and old stone facades, were both reconstructed after Cyclone Tracy to serve as offices for the Northern Territory administrator. ⊠ *Esplanade south between Mitchell and Smith Sts.*

④ The Esplanade zigzags around the Hotel Darwin to a cairn known as the **Overland Telegraph Memorial** on the harbor side of the street. This is where the first international telegraph cable came ashore from Java in 1871—a monumental event in Australia's history, providing the first direct link with the mother country, England. Before that, information and orders from "home" took months to arrive by ship.

⑨ Stokes Hill Wharf has a number of restaurants and outdoor performance areas where concerts and arts-and-crafts markets are held most weekends during the Dry. It's also a favorite spot for Darwinites to fish: When the mackerel are running, you can join scores of locals over a few beers in late-night fishing parties. The wharf is a working pier as well with berths for cargo ships, trawlers, and defense vessels.

⑦ The **Survivor's Lookout** overlooks the site of World War II's first Japanese bombing raid on Australia and commemorates those who died, including sailors of the USS *Peary*. The shaded viewing platform holds a panoramic illustrated map describing the events of that fateful day. The lookout is also the gateway, via stairs down the cliff face, to the wharf precinct. ⊠ *Esplanade south.*

⑧ Darwin's **World War II Storage Tunnels** were built to store and protect fuel from the many Japanese bombing raids on the city. Carved into solid rock, the main tunnel is 22 ft high and extends 210 ft under the city. There is a self-guided tour of the dimly lit tunnels, which now house extensive photographic records of the war period. ⊠ *Entrance at bottom of stairs below Survivor's Lookout, Esplanade south,* ☎ *018/89– 5982.* 🎟 *$4.*

Around Darwin
Darwin's other interesting sights are scattered along a line from downtown to the end of East Point, about 8 km (5 mi) away.

⑭ At **Aquascene,** on the northwestern end of the Esplanade, visitors have the chance to hand-feed thousands of fish. Starting with a few mullet over 30 years ago, fish have been coming here to be hand-fed. At high tide, people wade into the water with buckets of bread to feed the schools of batfish, bream, catfish, milkfish, and mullet that now come inshore in a feeding frenzy. ⊠ *Doctors Gully, Esplanade,* ☎ *08/8981–7837,* FAX *08/8941–8844.* 🎟 *$4.* ☯ *Hrs depend on tides.*

⑳ At the impressive **Australian Aviation Heritage Centre,** displays trace the history of flight in the Northern Territory, which, because of its isolation and sparse population, played an important role in the expansion of aviation in Australia. Planes on exhibition here include a massive B-52 bomber on permanent loan from the United States—one of very few not on U.S. soil—as well as a Japanese Zero shot down on the first day of bombing raids in 1942. ⊠ *557 Stuart Hwy., Winnellie, 8 km (5 mi) down Stuart Hwy. from town,* ☎ *08/8947–2145.* 🎟 *$8.* ☯ *Daily 8:30–5.*

☾ The Crocodile Farm. More than just a tourist park, this farm supplies much of the crocodile meat you'll find on menus around the Territory. It is also a research station studying both fresh- and saltwater crocodiles. The best time to visit is during the daily feeding and tour at 2 PM when the generally immobile reptiles become active in the presence of food. There is an extra feeding session at noon on weekends. ⊠ *40 km (25 mi) south on Stuart Hwy.,* ☎ *08/8988–1450.* 🎟 *$9.50.* ☯ *Daily 10– 4, tour daily on the hr.*

⑮ Darwin's Botanic Gardens is an ideal spot in which to escape the tropical heat. Originally started in 1879, the gardens were like so much else largely destroyed by Cyclone Tracy. They have been replanted with large collections of figs and palms (400 species), as well as a wetland flora area, a rain forest, and a waterfall. The greenhouse displays ferns and orchids. ⊠ *Gardens Rd.,* ☎ *08/8981–1958.*

⑱ East Point Road leads past the beaches of Fannie Bay onto the headland occupied by the **East Point Reserve.** This is a pleasant expanse of small beaches, cliffs, lawns, and forest, where wallabies can be seen grazing at dawn and dusk.

⑰ If the sordid stuff of prison life stirs your blood, take a trip out to **Fannie Bay Gaol** (pronounced like jail), which served as a prison from 1883 to 1979. It is now a museum where you can look into the former gaol's living conditions as well as the gallows where the last execution in the Northern Territory was performed in 1952. ⊠ *E. Point Rd., Fannie Bay,* ☎ *08/8999–8290.* ▣ *Free.* ⊙ *Daily 10–5.*

⑲ The **Military Museum** at East Point has an interesting collection of artillery and vehicles. ⊠ *E. Point Rd.,* ☎ *08/8981–9702.* ▣ *$5.* ⊙ *Daily 9:30–5.*

⑯ The **Museum and Art Gallery of the Northern Territory** is most notable for its Gallery of Aboriginal Man, including an exceptional collection of bark paintings. The displays of Aboriginal art and culture provide solid insight into the lives of the most ancient inhabitants of the Top End. Most fascinating, perhaps, are the exhibits about the devastating, Christmas 1974 Cyclone Tracy. Other exhibits deal with natural history, Pacific Island cultures, maritime displays, and visual arts. The stuffed remains of Sweetheart, a 17-ft crocodile taken from a Top End water hole, are also on display. ⊠ *Conacher St., Bullocky Point, Fannie Bay,* ☎ *08/8999–8201.* ▣ *Free except for some traveling exhibits.* ⊙ *Weekdays 9–5, weekends 10–5.*

Ⓒ **Territory Wildlife Park.** In addition to its water buffalo, dingoes, and water birds, this large park has an underwater viewing area from which to observe freshwater fish and a nocturnal house kept dark for viewing animals that are active only at night. Visitors ride around the 960-acre park on a train. Allow at least two hours to tour the park. ⊠ *Berry Springs, turnoff 47 km (29 mi) south of Darwin on Stuart Hwy.,* ☎ *08/8988–6000.* ▣ *$12.* ⊙ *Daily 8:30–4.*

OFF THE BEATEN PATH — Built as a water supply for the ill-fated rice-growing project of Humpty Doo in the late 1950s, **Fogg Dam** has remained untouched by commercialism in its remote location 68 km (42 mi) east of Darwin. The project failed largely because the birds of the region regarded the rice crop as a rather tasty smorgasbord. The birds have remained, and they provide an unforgettable sight at sunrise and sunset during the Dry. Exercise care driving through this swampland, however, and wear clothes that you don't mind getting dirty.

To get to the Dam from Darwin, take the Stuart Highway to the Arnhem Highway. After 24 km (15 mi) turn left and continue for another 4 mi; then turn right and drive the last half mile to the dam.

Dining

City Center

$$$$ ✕ **Siggi's.** With a classic French menu that changes every few weeks,
★ Siggi's may be the finest restaurant in Darwin. In a faintly Asian setting, diners enjoy privacy in large, softly lit cubicles separated by glass panels. The seasonal menu features such dishes as barramundi with prawns, panfried buffalo fillet with blackberry sauce, and ragout of chicken with leek and mango in a martini sauce. ⊠ *Beaufort Hotel, Esplanade,* ☎ *08/8980–0800 or 1800/89–1119. AE, DC, MC, V. Closed Sun. and Mon. No lunch.*

$$-$$$ ✕ **Christo's on the Wharf.** Part of the Wharf Precinct, Christo's has
Darwin's most unusual setting. Situated at the end of a commercial wharf
in a renovated corrugated-iron storage shed, this large restaurant is dominated by a traditional Macassarese fishing prau seized by Australian
customs in 1990. Open to sea breezes, it is an ideal place to escape from
Darwin's summer heat without being confined by air-conditioning.
Seafood takes the foreground, and such Greek dips as *taramousalata*
can be followed by chili bugs (small lobsters), lightly cooked calamari,
or garlic prawns, a specialty of the house. ✉ *Stokes Hill Wharf,*
☎ *08/8981–8658. AE, DC, MC, V.*

$$-$$$ ✕ **Hanuman Thai and Nonya Restaurant.** Hanuman sets a standard
★   for dining in Darwin. Dark furniture and deep peacock-blue walls with
touches of gold provide atmosphere for fine food and a wine list that
includes the best from every grape-growing region in Australia. By drawing on Thai and Nonya (Malaysian) culinary traditions, Hanuman's
chefs turn locally produced herbs, vegetables, and seafood into a wide
range of innovative dishes. Of special note are Hanuman oysters,
lightly cooked in a spicy coriander-and-lemongrass sauce; barramundi
baked with ginger flower; *tom yum* soups; and any of the many curries. ✉ *28 Mitchell St.,* ☎ *08/8941–3500. AE, DC, MC, V.*

$$ ✕ **Lindsay Street Cafe.** Lush tropical gardens surround this old-style,
★   elevated Darwin house. The bottom-level café serves some of Darwin's
more exotic cuisine, adaptations of Asian and European food to trop-
ical climes. The menu is regularly updated, but some perennial customer
favorites include rice pancakes with paw-paw salad, shallots, and oys-
ter mushrooms, and grilled escallope of kangaroo with lemongrass-and-
red-wine sauce, cracked coriander, and sweet pickled mango slices. ✉
2 Lindsay St., ☎ *08/8981–8631. MC, V. Closed Sun. and Mon. No
lunch Sat.*

$$ ✕ **Tonkris Restaurant.** Established in 1994, the Tonkris is a welcome
addition, with its traditional northern Italian country cooking and an
excellent selection of wine. Dine outdoors or in air-conditioned comfort. Along with a range of pasta dishes—the marinara makes best use
of local produce—meat dishes are superbly cooked and presented. ✉
MLC Bldg., 79 Smith St., ☎ *08/8981–0778. AE, MC, V.*

$ ✕ **Roma Bar.** The decorative theme of the Roma Bar seems only acci-
dentally Italian, and the clientele is similarly eclectic: Office workers,
lawyers, and magistrates from the surrounding business district mingle with artists, entertainers, and students. Visitors enjoy the good coffee and somewhat rowdy hubbub of business-suited and barefoot
Darwinites in their natural habitat. The food is the kind of straightforward fare that you might be craving—like fresh tossed green salads, pasta, and focaccia. ✉ *30 Cavenagh St.,* ☎ *08/8981–6729. No
credit cards.*

Cullen Bay

$$-$$$ ✕ **Scales on Cullen.** For a lazy Sunday lunch or nighttime dining,
★   Scales serves a unique blend of Italian-style cooking with the best of
fresh Australian produce, seafood in particular. One local favorite is
spaghetti topped with giant sea scallops, prawns, green-lip mussels, and
a fresh basil and tomato sauce. Also look for marinated char-grilled
lamb fillet served with oven-dried tomatoes, taramasalata, and yogurt
and cucumber dressing. Dine under cover or on the boardwalk overlooking the marina. The wine list is limited but well chosen. ✉ *The
Rocks, 54 Marina Blvd., Cullen Bay,* ☎ *08/8981–6522. AE, MC, V.*

$$ ✕ **Yots Café.** Darwin's first wood-fired pizza oven comes with some
★   of the city's most exotic decor—plenty of stainless steel, marble, and
luxuriant, polished wood. The pizzas are well above the average: Try
a tiger prawn, pesto, and pine-nut pie with marinated artichoke and

shaved Parmesan cheese. Main courses are equally satisfying, such as one of the best versions of the Top-End favorite, oven-baked barramundi served with char-grilled foccacia wedges. ✉ *The Rocks, 54 Marina Blvd., Cullen Bay,* ☎ *08/8981–4433. MC, V.*

Lodging

City Center

$$$$ 🏨 **Beaufort Hotel.** With its colorful, round exterior, this is the most
★ striking and unusual hotel in Darwin, as well as the most expensive. Built in 1986 and completely refurbished in 1994, the Beaufort has five floors of guest rooms around a central foyer. The rooms are decorated in subtle greens and pinks with plenty of natural wood and have panoramic views over the city or harbor. ✉ *Esplanade 0800,* ☎ *08/8980–0800 or 1800/89–1119,* 𝖥𝖠𝖷 *08/8980–0888. 164 rooms with bath, 32 suites. 3 restaurants, 3 bars, pool, 2 saunas, exercise room, shops, nightclub, laundry. AE, DC, MC, V.*

$$$$ 🏨 **MGM Grand Darwin Casino.** Shaped like pyramids with square tops, this casino and the smaller adjoining hotel are two of the most distinctive structures in the city. Set amid lush lawns and gardens, the three-story hotel is *the* luxury resort in Darwin, and it has the city's only beachfront accommodations. Well-appointed rooms combine a tropical feeling with dark marble, cherry-wood furniture, and Italian designer lighting fixtures. ✉ *Gilruth Ave., Mindil Beach 0800,* ☎ *08/8943–8888,* 𝖥𝖠𝖷 *08/8943–8999. 79 rooms with bath, 18 suites. Restaurant, 7 bars, pool, sauna, tennis courts, exercise room. AE, DC, MC, V.*

$$$$ 🏨 **Plaza Hotel.** Central to the business district, this 12-story hotel built in 1986 is the highest in Darwin. Rooms offer a pleasant mixture of art deco–style lamps and cool pastel furnishings. With its raised piano bar and elegant armchairs, the high-ceiling lobby can seem a bit formal if you're coming straight from a fishing trip or the mud pools of Kakadu. Equally posh, if improbably named, is the hotel's gourmet restaurant, Igunana. ✉ *32 Mitchell St., 0800,* ☎ *08/8982–0000 or 1800/89–1107,* 𝖥𝖠𝖷 *08/8981–1765. 221 rooms with bath, 12 suites. 2 restaurants, bars, pool, exercise room. AE, DC, MC, V.*

$$$ 🏨 **Darwin Travelodge.** Built in 1974, this 10-story hotel offered the best accommodations in Darwin until a rash of new hotels and resorts went up during the mid-'80s. Nevertheless, the views of the city or Fannie Bay from rooms on floors 6–10 are still the best in town. The lobby is decorated in warm tropical colors with cane chairs. The color scheme is continued in the rooms, each of which has its own small bar. ✉ *122 Esplanade, 0800,* ☎ *08/8981–5388,* 𝖥𝖠𝖷 *08/8981–5701. 170 rooms with bath, 2 suites. Restaurant, bar, pool, laundry. AE, DC, MC, V.*

$$$ 🏨 **Novotel Atrium.** Vying for the title of Darwin's prettiest hotel, the
★ Atrium is served by glass elevators, its seven floors opening onto a central, vine-hung atrium. In the foyer, set around a tiny artificial stream amid palm trees and ferns, are the hotel's bars and restaurants. Guest rooms are attractive and airy, decorated in pastel blues, and each has its own kitchenette. ✉ *Peel St. and Esplanade, 0800,* ☎ *08/8941–0755,* 𝖥𝖠𝖷 *08/8981–9025. 140 rooms with bath, 4 suites. 2 restaurants, bar, pool, laundry. AE, DC, MC, V.*

$$ 🏨 **Hotel Darwin.** Once the grande dame of Darwin, this two-story colonial hotel has faded with time. The Green Room—the bar where much of the city's business has been discussed over the years—is still a pleasant indoor-outdoor area next to the pool. The rooms belong to an earlier era and their carpets are worn, but they have a pleasant view over the garden or pool. Despite its slightly run-down look, the hotel maintains some of its colonial character, including ample use of wicker and cane. ✉ *10 Herbert St., 0800,* ☎ *08/8981–9211,* 𝖥𝖠𝖷 *08/8981–9575.*

66 rooms with shower, 7 with bath. Restaurant, bar, nightclub, pool, laundry. AE, DC, MC, V.

$$ ⚏ **Top End Hotel and Best Western.** Overlooking a central garden and
★ pool, this two-story hotel has a country ambience that belies its position only a few minutes' walk from the Mall at Smith Street. The rooms have cane furnishings and a warm color scheme. All ground-floor rooms open onto the central lawn and pool, and those upstairs have private balconies. ⊠ *Mitchell and Daly Sts., 0800,* ☎ *08/8981–6511 or 1800/62–6151,* FAX *08/8941–1253. 40 rooms without bath. Restaurant, 4 bars, pool, laundry. AE, DC, MC, V.*

$ ⚏ **YHA Hostel.** This hostel provides the cheapest accommodations in town for members of the Youth Hostel Association only. Totally rebuilt and expanded in 1996, the YHA supplies basic but clean, bright, and airy accommodation. You need to supply or rent sheets, but you'll have all of the other basics, including cooking facilities. ⊠ *69A Mitchell St., 0800,* ☎ *08/8981–3995,* FAX *08/8981–6674. 292 beds in 96 rooms share bathrooms. Laundry. AE, MC, V.*

Gurig National Park

$$$$ ✕⚏ **Seven Spirit Bay.** A couple of hundred miles northeast of Darwin
★ on the Cobourg Peninsula is an international resort accessible only by a one-hour light-plane flight. Seven Spirit Bay may well be the most remote resort on earth. The Cobourg Peninsula has miles of pristine bays and beaches, colonial ruins, and exotic wildlife. The resort spreads over several acres in Gurig National Park and consists of groups of individual hexagonal huts linked to the main complex by winding paths. Each hut contains a single spacious room and each has its own fenced outdoor bathroom. The main building is drab outside, but the polished timbers, high ceilings, and bright coverings inside draw your eyes to the glass doors leading out to the deck and pool and the ocean beyond. There is a resident naturalist, and excursions include photographic tours and bushwalks to see wildlife such as dingo dogs, wallabies, goannas (large lizards), crocodiles, as well as introduced animals now wild such as water buffalo and Timorese ponies. Other tours are available on inquiry. The dining room serves some of the Territory's best meals. Seafood comes from the surrounding waters, herbs are from the gardens, and the light, modern Australian dishes put traditional bush foods as well as Indonesian and Malaysian techniques to work. All meals are included in the rate. ⊠ *Reservations, Seven Spirit Wilderness Pty. Ltd., Box 4721, Darwin 0801,* ☎ *08/8979–0277 or 1800/89–1189,* FAX *08/8979–0284. 24 rooms with bath. Bar, pool.*

Nightlife and the Arts

Bars and Lounges

For a quiet beer visit the **Top End Best Western** (⊠ Daly and Mitchell Sts., ☎ 08/8981–6511). If you feel like having a Guinness, **Shenanigans Hotel** (⊠ 69 Mitchell St., ☎ 08/8981–2100) has it on tap. It's also the only place in town you can get those other two famous Irish beers, Kilkenny and Harp. Continuing the international flavor is a bar alternately called **The World Travellers Bar** or **Herbie's** (⊠ Mitchell and Herbert Sts., ☎ 08/8981–9211), attached to the Hotel Darwin. It is a well-known haunt for world-weary travelers on a tight budget. If you're after a late night and a friendly (albeit very smoky) game of pool, try **Squire's Tavern** (⊠ 3E Edmund St., ☎ 08/8981–9761). If you're feeling young and hip, step next door to **The Time** (⊠ 3E Edmund St., ☎ 08/8981–9761) nightclub where you can dance the night away to techno and funk. For a more sedate evening, visit **Petty Sessions** (⊠ Shop 2, NT House, Mitchell St., ☎ 08/8941–2000).

Casino

MGM Grand Hotel Casino is Darwin's most popular source of evening entertainment. ⊠ *Gilruth Ave.,* ☎ *08/8946–2666.*

Theaters and Concerts

The **Darwin Entertainment Centre** (⊠ 93 Mitchell St., ☎ 08/8981–1222), next door to the Beaufort Hotel, has a large theater that regularly stages concerts, dance, and drama. It also doubles as booking office for other touring concerts in town—especially those at the **Amphitheatre,** Australia's best outdoor concert venue (entrance next to Botanical Gardens, Gardens Road). Check the *Northern Territory News* or the *Sunday Territorian* for current shows, or call the center.

Outdoor Activities and Sports

Bicycling

Darwin is fairly flat, so cycling is a good way to get around—except during the Wet, when you are pretty likely to get soaked. Rent bicycles from **Darwin Bike Hire,** next door to Shenannigans Hotel on Mitchell Street.

Fishing

The best-known fish of the Top End, barramundi, which grows to up to 110 pounds, is an excellent fighting fish and tastes great on the barbie afterward. Fishing safaris can be arranged through **Big Barra** (☎ 08/8932–1473, ℻ 08/8932–1473) and **NT Barra Fishing Trips** (☎ 08/ 8945–1841). For ocean game-fishing contact **Predator Charters** (mobile ☎ 0419/41–8800).

Golf

You can rent clubs at all three of the following courses. The only 18-hole course in Darwin is **Darwin Golf Club** (⊠ Links Rd., Marrara, ☎ 08/8927–1322); greens fees are $13 for 9 holes and $20 for 18, and the club has motorized carts for hire at $15 and $20. The **Gardens Park Golf Links** (⊠ Botanic Gardens, ☎ 08/8981–6365) is a 9-hole course; fees are $10 for adults. **Palmerston Golf and Country Club** (⊠ Dwyer Crescent, Palmerston, ☎ 08/8932–1324) also has only 9 holes, however with different tees you can play 18. Greens fees are $10 for 9 holes and $15 for 18.

Health and Fitness Clubs

Several hotels have their own gyms. The most central commercial gym is **Time Out Fitness Centre.** ⊠ *5-2798 Dashwood Pl.,* ☎ *08/8941–8711.* ⊙ *Weekdays 6:30 AM–8 PM, Sat. 9–6, Sun. 10–2.*

Motorscooting

If you don't want to hire a car, a small motorbike is the next best thing. It's a cheap way to get around—although not advisable during the Wet for obvious reasons. **Freedom Cycles** hire small motor scooters for reasonable rates. ⊠ *90 Mitchell St.,* ☎ *08/8981–9995.*

Running

The waterfront park parallel to the Esplanade is a good area for running within the city. For a longer run, the beachfront parks along the shores of Fannie Bay to East Point provide generally flat terrain and a great view.

Tennis

Several hotels have tennis courts (☞ Lodging, *above*), and there are four courts at the **Darwin Tennis Centre.** ⊠ *Gilruth Ave., the Gardens,* ☎ *08/8985–2844.*

Water Sports

Marine stingers (jellyfish) and other hazards restrict water activities around Darwin. The **beaches** of Fannie Bay, such as Mindil and Vesteys, and those of Nightcliff are no less popular, however, especially on weekends.

For **diving,** contact **Cullen Bay Dive** (⊠ 66 Marine Blvd., Cullen Bay, ☎ 08/8981–3049) or **Sand Pebbles Dive Shop** (⊠ De Latour St., Coconut Grove, ☎ 08/8948–0444).

To rent **sailboats,** contact **Darwin Sailing Club** (☎ 08/8981–1700 or 015/61–0753).

Shopping

Aboriginal Art

As in Alice Springs, the best buys in Darwin are Aboriginal paintings and artifacts. A visit to the **Museum and Art Gallery of the Northern Territory** (☞ Around Darwin, *above*) will give you a good idea of the highest standards attainable. The extensive Aboriginal art collection on public display at the **Supreme Court** (⊠ State Sq., Mitchell St.) is complemented by a spectacular floor mosaic of an Aboriginal desert "dot" painting. The best commercial galleries in Darwin are the **Raintree Aboriginal Art Gallery** (⊠ Shop 1, 18 Knuckey St., ☎ 08/8981–2732), and **Framed Gallery** (⊠ 55 Stuart Hwy., ☎ 08/8981–2994).

Markets

For Darwin locals, markets have become as much a form of popular entertainment as they are a shopping venue. Up to a fifth of the city's population may show up for the movable feast that is the **Mindil Beach Sunset Markets** (⊠ Mindil Beach, ☎ 08/8981–3454), an extravaganza that takes place every Thursday evening during the Dry (Apr.–Oct.). After the hard work of snacking at hundreds of food stalls, shopping at artisans' booths, and watching singers, dancers, and musicians, Darwinites unpack tables, chairs, and bottles of wine and then watch the sun plunge into the harbor.

Other markets for food, secondhand items, and crafts stands include the **Big Flea Market** (⊠ Rapid Creek Shopping Centre, Trower Rd., Rapid Creek, ☎ 08/8985–5806), which specializes in Asian-influenced produce and cuisine. Hours are Sunday 8–1. The **Parap Market** (⊠ Parap Sq., Parap) is open Saturday 8–2. The **Palmerston Night Market** (⊠ Frances Mall, ☎ 08/8932–2623) is open Friday 5:30–9:30.

Darwin A to Z

Arriving and Departing

BY BUS

Greyhound Pioneer (☎ 08/8981–8700) terminates at the new Mitchell Street Shopping Precinct, which is the old **Darwin Transit Centre** (⊠ 69 Mitchell St.), and **McCafferty's** (☎ 08/8941–0911) terminates at 71 Smith Street in the middle of town.

BY CAR

The Stuart Highway is Darwin's land connection with the rest of Australia, and anyone arriving by car will enter the city on this road. Darwin is 1,706 km (1,058 mi) by road from Alice Springs and 4,095 km (2,539 mi) from Sydney.

BY PLANE

Darwin's International Airport is serviced from overseas by **Ansett Australia, Qantas,** and **Singapore Airlines.** Domestic carriers flying into

Darwin are **Qantas Australian** and **Ansett Australia.** ☞ Air Travel *in* the Gold Guide for airline telephone numbers.

Between the Airport and Downtown. Airport Transfers (☎ 08/8945– 1000) has regular bus service between the airport and the downtown area. The cost is $8 per person or $12 for two people traveling together.

The airport is 13 km (8 mi) northeast of the city **by car.** After leaving the terminal, turn left into McMillans Road and left again into Bagot Road. Continue until you cross the overpass that merges into the Stuart Highway, which later becomes Daly Street. Turn left into Smith Street to reach the Smith Street Mall in the heart of the city.

Taxis are available from the taxi rank at the airport. The journey downtown costs about $15.

Getting Around

BY BUS

The bus network in Darwin links the city with its far-flung suburbs. The main bus terminal (Buslink, ☎ 08/8947–0577) for city buses is on Harry Chan Avenue, near the Bennett Street end of Smith Street Mall.

BY CAR

The best way to get around Darwin is by car. Rental car companies include **Avis** (✉ Airport, and 145 Stuart Hwy., Stuart Park, ☎ 08/8981– 9922); **Brits-Rentals** (✉ 44–46 Stuart Hwy., Stuart Park, ☎ 08/8981– 2081); **Budget** (✉ Airport, and 108 Mitchell St., ☎ 08/8981–9800); **Hertz** (✉ Airport, and Smith and Daly Sts., Darwin, ☎ 08/8941–0944); **Territory Rent-a-Car** (✉ Airport, and 64 Stuart Hwy., Stuart Park, ☎ 08/8981–8400); and **Thrifty** (✉ Airport, and 89 Smith St., Darwin, ☎ 08/8981–8555). Four-wheel-drive vehicles are available.

BY TAXI

Contact **Darwin Radio Taxis** (☎ 08/8981–8777), **Darwin Combined Taxis** (☎ 08/8941–1777), or **Taxinet North** (☎ 08/8943–8008).

Contacts and Resources

EMERGENCIES

Ambulance, fire brigade, and **police.** ☎ *000.*
Royal Darwin Hospital (☎ 08/8922–8888) has a 24-hour emergency room.
Night & Day Medical & Dental Surgery. ✉ *Casuarina Shopping Centre,* ☎ *08/8927–1899.*
Trower Road A/H Medical Service. ✉ *Trower Rd.,* ☎ *08/8927–6905.*

GUIDED TOURS

Every day but Sunday, **Darwin Day Tours** (☎ 08/8981–8696) conducts half-day tours ($29) morning and afternoon. For $5 more you can extend the afternoon tour to take in the sunset with a glass of champagne. Tours include: historic buildings, the main harbor, the Botanic Gardens, the Museum and Art Gallery of the Northern Territory, the East Point Military Reserve, and the Fannie Bay Gaol Museum. Fish-feeding at Aquascene is sometimes included, depending on the tides.

Daytime and sunset cruises around one of the most beautiful and unspoiled harbors in the world are available on **Darwin Harbor Tours'** *Darwin Duchess.* There's a licensed bar on board. ✉ *Stokes Hill Wharf,* ☎ *08/8978–5094.* 🎫 *$25.*

VISITOR INFORMATION

Darwin Region Tourism Association. ✉ *Beagle House, Mitchell and Knuckey Sts.,* ☎ *08/8981–4300.*

KAKADU NATIONAL PARK

Kakadu National Park is a jewel in the array of Top End parks, and many visitors come to the Top End just to experience this tropical wilderness. Located 256 km (159 mi) east of Darwin, the park covers 20,082 square km (7,720 square mi) and protects a large system of unspoiled rivers and creeks, as well as a rich Aboriginal heritage that extends back to the earliest days of humankind. The superb gathering of Aboriginal rock art may be Kakadu's highlight.

Two major types of **Aboriginal artwork** are found here. The Mimi style is the oldest—it is believed to be up to 20,000 years old—and uses red-ochre stick figures to depict hunting scenes and other pictures of Aboriginal life. Aborigines believe that Mimi spirits created these images. The more recent artwork, known as X-ray painting, dates back less than 9,000 years and depicts freshwater animals—especially fish, turtles, and geese—living in floodplains created after the last ice age. The animals are drawn complete with heart, spinal cord, lungs, and intestines.

Most of the region is virtually inaccessible during the Wet, so it is strongly advisable to visit the park between May and September. As the dry season progresses, water holes (called billabongs) become increasingly important to the more than 280 species of birds that inhabit the park: Huge flocks can be found at Yellow Water, South Alligator River, and Magela Creek. If you do visit during the Wet, scenic flights over the wetlands and Arnhem Land escarpment provide unforgettable moments.

Most of the park is owned by Aboriginal traditional owners and managed by a board with an Aboriginal majority membership, and visitor access is restricted to certain areas.

Orientation

The Bowali Kakadu National Park Visitors Information Centre and the Warradjan Aboriginal Cultural Centre are two good places to get your bearings before heading into the park.

The **Bowali Kakadu National Park Visitors Information Centre** opened mid-1994. State-of-the-art audiovisual displays, as well as more traditional exhibits, offer an introduction to the park's several ecosystems and to its bird population, the world's most diverse. The park's Aboriginal owners contribute to the flora and fauna information and provide some insight into their culture's traditional hunting practices, land management techniques, and use of raw materials. ☎ 08/8938–1100. ۞ Daily 8–5.

Warradjan Aboriginal Cultural Centre. Opened in 1995 at Yellow Water near Cooinda, the Cultural Centre—named after the pig-nose turtle unique to the Top End—is an excellent experience of local native culture. Displays take you through the Aboriginal Creation period, following the path of the creation ancestor Rainbow Serpent through the ancient landscape of Kakadu. It also shows many of the important stories associated with the Park and the activities of the Nayuhyunggi (first people) who created the land, plants, and animals, and who gave people laws to live by. ☎ 08/8979–0051. ۞ Daily 9–5.

Exploring

★ Like the main Kakadu escarpment, **Nourlangie Rock** is a remnant of an ancient plateau that is slowly eroding away, leaving sheer cliffs rising high above the floodplains. The main attraction here is the **Anbangbang Gallery,** an excellent frieze of Aboriginal rock paintings near the main parking lot. To reach the area, drive 19 km (12 mi) from the Park Headquarters down the Kakadu Highway to the left-hand turnoff to Nourlangie Rock. A parking area 11 km (7 mi) down this paved road is accessible year-round.

Ubirr has an even more impressive array of Aboriginal paintings scattered through six shelters in the rock. The main gallery contains a 49-ft frieze of X-ray paintings depicting animals, birds, and fish. A half-mile path around the rock leads to all the galleries. Ubirr is 43 km (27 mi) north of the Park Headquarters along a paved road.

The best way to gain a true appreciation of the natural beauty of Kakadu is to visit the **waterfalls** running off the escarpment. Some 39 km (24 mi) south of the Park Headquarters along the Kakadu Highway, a track leads off to the left toward Jim Jim and Twin falls. This unpaved road is suitable only for four-wheel-drive vehicles and is closed in the Wet. Even in good conditions, the 60-km (37-mi) ride to Jim Jim takes about two hours. The Twin Falls car park is 10 km (6 mi) farther on.

★ From the parking area at **Jim Jim Falls,** you have to walk a half mile over boulders to reach the falls and the plunge pool it has created at the base of the escarpment. On the right-hand side before the main pool is a beautiful sandy beach shelving to a pleasant, shallow swimming area. After May, the water flow over the falls may cease but the pools remain well worth visiting.

★ **Twin Falls** is more difficult to reach, but the trip is rewarding. After a short walk from the parking lot, you must swim along a small creek for a few hundred yards to reach the falls—many people use inflatable air beds as rafts to float their lunch and towels in. As you approach, the ravine opens up dramatically to reveal a beautiful sandy beach scattered with palm trees, as well as the crystal waters of the falls spilling onto the end of the beach. If you are feeling energetic, swim across the large pool to a track leading up to the top of the falls. On top, the river has worn the rocks smooth, creating fantastic stone sculpture.

In the Dry you can continue down the road to Pine Creek, a worthwhile shortcut if you are heading from Kakadu to Katherine (or vice versa).

Dining and Lodging

$$$–$$$$ ×⛺ **Frontier Kakadu Village** is a 138-room hotel with a pool, spa, barbecue, and laundry. Two room sizes are available: double rooms with one queen-size and one single bed, and family rooms with a queen and two single beds. Room rates are significantly higher during the Dry. ⊠ *2½ km (1½ mi) before Arnhem Hwy. crosses South Alligator River,* ☎ *08/8979–0166 or 1800/81–8845. Restaurant, café. AE, DC, MC, V.*

$$$$ ⛺ **Gagudju Crocodile Hotel.** The best of the area's three hotels is this unusual 100-room place, shaped like a crocodile. The reception is through the mouth, the swimming pool is in the open courtyard in the belly, and the gardener's shed is at the end of the tail. ⊠ *Flinders St., Jabiru,* ☎ *08/8979–2800. 100 rooms. Restaurant, tavern, pool. AE, DC, MC, V.*

$$$ ⛺ **Gagudju Lodge Cooinda.** Conveniently located near Yellow Water is a 48-room facility with its own pool, bars, restaurant, and barbecue. ⊠ ☎ *08/8979–0145 or 800/50–0401* FAX *08/8979–0148. AE, MC, V.*

$ ⛺ **Campgrounds** at Merl, Muirella Park, Mardugal, and Gunlom have toilets, showers, and water. A fee of $7 per tent per night is charged. There are privately operated camping grounds available at Frontier Kakadu Village and the Gagudju Lodge Cooinda.

Kakadu A to Z

Arriving and Departing

From Darwin take the Arnhem Highway east to Jabiru. Although four-wheel-drive vehicles are not necessary to travel to the park, they are a necessity for many of the unsealed roads within, including the track to Jim Jim Falls. The entrance fee is $15 per person.

Guided Tours

AERIAL TOURS

Kakadu Air Services (☎ 08/8979–2731, 08/8979–2411, or 1800/ 08–9113) flies out of Jabiru and Darwin.

BOAT TOURS

★ The **Gagudju Lodge Cooinda** arranges boat tours of **Yellow Water,** the major water hole during the Dry, where innumerable birds and crocodiles gather. There are six tours throughout the day; the first (6:45 AM) is the coolest. ☎ *08/8979–0111.* ☒ *$26.50.*

GENERAL TOURS

Park rangers conduct free walks and tours at popular locations throughout the Dry. You can pick up a program at the entry station or at either of the visitor centers. **Billy Can Tours** (☒ Box 4407, Darwin 0801, ☎ 08/8981–9813 or 1800/81–3484, FAX 08/8941–0803) provides a range of two- and three-day camping and accommodation tours in Kakadu, including special wet-season tours and tours that combine excursions to Kakadu with ☞ Litchfield and ☞ Nitmiluk (Katherine Gorge) national parks. **Odyssey Safaris** (☒ Box 3012, Darwin 0801, ☎ 08/8948–0091 or 1800/89–1190, FAX 08/8948–0646) offers quality deluxe four-wheel-drive tours into Kakadu as well as other areas of northern Australia including the ☞ Kimberley, and Litchfield and Nitmiluk national parks.

Visitor Information

Darwin Region Tourism Association. ☒ *Beagle House, Mitchell and Knuckey Sts., Darwin 5744,* ☎ *08/8981–4300.*
Bowali Kakadu National Park. ☒ *Box 71, Jabiru 0886,* ☎ *08/8938– 1100.*

LITCHFIELD NATIONAL PARK

Litchfield, one of the Northern Territory's newest parks, is also one of the most accessible from Darwin. Convenience hasn't spoiled the park's beauty, however: Almost all of the park's 1,340 square km (515 square mi) are covered by an untouched wilderness of monsoonal rain forests, rivers, and escarpment—cliffs formed by erosion. The highlights of this dramatic landscape are four separate spectacular waterfalls supplied by natural springs year-round from aquifers deep under the plateau. And the park is crocodile-free.

Exploring

Lovely trails lead to **Florence, Tjaynera,** and **Wangi Falls,** all of which have secluded plunge pools at their base. **Tolmer Falls** looks out over a natural rock arch and is within a short walk of the parking lot. Near Tolmer Falls—although accessible only by four-wheel-drive vehicles— is a series of large, freestanding sandstone pillars known as the **Lost City.** The living landscape is no less unusual: Look for groves of extremely slow-growing **cycad palms,** an ancient plant species that is unique to the area; some of the larger specimens here are thought to be hundreds of years old.

Magnetic Termite Mounds, which have an eerie resemblance to eroding grave markers, dot the black-soil plains of the northern part of the park. To avoid being crisped by the hot tropical sun, termites have learned to orient their mounds so that they face north–south, leaving only a thin edge exposed to direct light.

Dining and Lodging

If you want to stay in Litchfield National Park, you'll have to camp. Sites are available at Florence Falls, Wangi Falls, Buley Rockhole, and Sandy Creek. These **campgrounds** are basic—Buley has no shower facilities and Sandy Creek is accessible only by four-wheel-drive vehicles—but the price can't be beat. You'll never pay more than $5 per person per night. Contact the Parks and Wildlife Commission (☎ 08/8976–0282) for more information.

In Batchelor, you'll find a couple of restaurants and a number of caravan parks, as well as the moderately priced **Rum Jungle Motor Inn.** ⊠ *220 Rum Jungle Rd., Batchelor 0845,* ☎ *08/8976–0123,* FAX *08/ 8976–0230. 22 rooms. Restaurant, pool. MC, V.*

Arriving and Departing

Litchfield is an easy 122 km (76 mi) from Darwin. Take the Stuart Highway 85 km (53 mi) south to the turnoff for the town of **Batchelor,** and continue on the Batchelor Road to the park's northern border. As you enter the park you will see a sign telling you to tune your radio to 88 on the FM dial. This station provides up-to-date information on the park, such as current road and campsite conditions, and how to get to the park's main areas of interest. Most parts of the park are accessible by conventional vehicles; four-wheel-drive vehicles are advised after the rains and are necessary to enter the park from **Berry Springs** or Adelaide River. You can make a loop through the park by connecting the Batchelor and Berry Springs entrances.

Guided Tours

Billy Can Tours provides a number of tours to Litchfield, along with those that combine Litchfield with Kakadu and Nitmiluk (Katherine Gorge) national parks. ⊠ *Box 4407, Darwin 0801,* ☎ *08/8981–9813 or 1800/81–3484,* FAX *08/8941–0803.*

Visitor Information

Parks and Wildlife Commission of the Northern Territory. ⊠ *Box 45, Batchelor 0845,* ☎ *08/8976–0282.*

KATHERINE

327 km (203 mi) southeast of Darwin.

If you're heading west to the Kimberley or south to the Red Centre, Katherine River is the last permanently flowing water till you get to Adelaide—2,741 km (1,700 mi) to the south! A veritable oasis, Katherine is the crossroads of the region, making it the second largest town in the Top End with a booming population of 10,500. Named in 1862 by the European explorer John McDouall Stuart after the daughter of his patron, the town was first established to service the Overland Telegraph that linked the south with Asia and Europe. It was the site of the first cattle and sheep runs in the Top End, and the Springvale Homestead 8 km (5 mi) west of town is the oldest still standing in the Northern Territory.

Katherine is now a regional administrative and supply center for the cattle industry, as well as being the site for the largest military air base in northern Australia. As befits its status as an oasis, the focus of the town is on the Katherine River, which is popular for its fishing, swimming, and canoeing. In a region best known for the spectacular 13 gorges of Nitmiluk National Park, Katherine provides a base for such regional phenomena as Cutta Cutta Caves, the small town Mataranka, and interesting local Aboriginal culture.

Among other things, Katherine is home to the world's largest school classroom, the **Katherine School of the Air,** which broadcasts to about 100 students over 301,000 square km (115,700 square mi) of isolated cattle country. Tours are available on weekdays from April through to October. ⊠ *Giles St.,* ☎ *08/8972–1833.*

<table>
<tr><td>OFF THE
BEATEN PATH</td><td>The region is a focus for Aboriginal cultures quite different from that of the rest of the Top End and the Red Centre—and an increasing number of tours are available that are owned and operated by Aboriginal people themselves. Manyallaluk Tours (☎ 08/8975–4727 or 1800/64–4727, FAX 08/8975–4724) is 110 km (68 mi) by road east of Katherine. The community of Manyallaluk is on Aboriginal-owned land and hosts a series of half- to four-day tours focusing on bush tucker (food), art and artifact manufacture, and extensive rock-art sites with Aboriginal guides. You can drive yourself in a conventional vehicle or take advantage of community four-wheel-drive buses.</td></tr>
</table>

Dining and Lodging

$$–$$$ ✕🖼 **Knotts Crossing Resort.** Consistently the best accommodation in Katherine, with prices ranging from budget to executive, Knotts Crossing has well-designed rooms in low-slung cabins, and a pool and outside bar that are a welcome oasis after a hot day. Katie's bistro serves by far the best local fish around. ⊠ *Cameron and Giles Sts., Katherine 0850,* ☎ *08/8972–2511,* FAX *08/8972–2628. 95 rooms. Restaurant, bar, pool. AE, DC, MC, V.*

Nitmiluk (Katherine Gorge) National Park

31 km (19 mi) north of Katherine.

One of the Territory's most famous parks, Nitmiluk—named after a *cicada* dreaming site at the mouth of the first gorge—is now owned by the local Jawoyn Aboriginal tribe and leased back to the Parks and Wildlife Commission. Katherine Gorge, the park's European name, is derived from the area's most striking feature: The power of the Katherine River in flood during the Wet has created an enormous system of gorges—13 in all—connected by the river. Rapids separate the gorges, much to the delight of experienced canoeists, and there really is no better way to see the gorges than by boat. Regularly scheduled flat-bottom tour boats take visitors on all-day safaris to the fifth gorge, a trip that requires hiking to circumnavigate each rapid. During the Wet, jet boats provide access into the flooded gorges. In general the best time to visit is during the Dry, from May through early November.

For the more adventurous traveler, Katherine Gorge National Park offers some of the best **bushwalking** trails in the Top End. Ten well-marked walking tracks, ranging from one hour to five days, lead hikers on trails parallel to the Katherine River and north toward Edith Falls at the edge of the park. Some of the longer, overnight walks lead past Aboriginal paintings and through swamps, heathlands, and small patches of rain forest. Hikers out for the day may want to carry inflatable rafts with them so they can float downstream back to the campground.

Canoes can be rented from the **Nitmiluk Centre** (☎ 08/8972–3604) or at the gorge boat ramp from $23 per half day for a single canoe to $48 per day for a two-person canoe. A $20 deposit is required for all same-day hire; that becomes $60 if you are going on a longer overnight trip up the gorge. Fishing is permitted at Katherine, but be sure to check with the ranger about license and size requirements.

Camping
The campground and most other facilities at Katherine Gorge are privately owned. Campsites located near the Katherine River cost $8 per person per night. Bush camping along the river past the second set of rapids is allowed with the ranger's permission.

Cutta Cutta Caves

29 km (18 mi) south of Katherine via the Stuart Highway.

This series of limestone caverns is home to the rare Ghost and Orange Horseshoe bats, which inhabit the stalactites. There are ranger-led tours during the Dry, and the caves are closed in the wettest of the Wet. ☎ 08/8972–1940.

Mataranka

105 km (65 mi) southeast of Katherine.

The tiny township of Mataranka is the original center of Australia's literary expression for the Outback of the "never never"—as in Jeannie Gunn's novel, *We of the Never Never,* about turn-of-the-century life in the area. West of the upper reaches of the Roper River, Mataranka was a major army base during World War II and its most famous attraction, the **Mataranka Thermal Pool,** was first developed as a recreation site by American troops during that period.

Katherine A to Z

Arriving and Departing
BY BUS
Greyhound Pioneer (☎ 08/8981–8700) runs between Darwin and Alice Springs with a stop at Katherine.

BY CAR
Katherine is 327 km (203 mi) southeast of Darwin via the Stuart Highway. Driving to Katherine will allow you to stop along the way at ☞ **Litchfield National Park** and get around easily to Nitmiluk and other sights nearby. And you may want to continue on to Kununurra, 564 km (350 mi) west, or to Alice Springs, 1,145 km (710 mi) to the south.

BY PLANE
Air North Regional (☎ 08/8945–2866) serves Katherine, and **Ansett** takes bookings for weekday morning and evening flights to Katherine on local commuter airlines. The airport is about 10 minutes south of town.

Contacts and Resources
CAR RENTAL
Avis, Budget, Hertz, and **Territory Rent-a-Car** all have offices at the airport. ☞ Darwin A to Z, *above,* for telephone numbers.

EMERGENCIES
Katherine Hospital. ☎ 08/8973–9211.
Police. ☎ 08/8972–0111.

GUIDED TOURS
Nitmiluk Tours (☎ 08/8972–1044) offers tours ranging from two hours ($27), four hours ($41), and eight hours ($69) up the Kather-

ine River aboard a flat-bottom boat. The fit and adventurous may wish to consider the dry-season-only **Manyallaluk Four-Day Trekking Adventure** (☎ 08/8975–4727 or 1800/64–4727, FAX 08/8975–4724). Led by Aboriginal guides, this 31-km (19-mi) trek starts from Eva Valley Station, east of the park across the top of the Katherine River escarpment, and travels by boat down the gorge system to the entrance of Nitmiluk National Park. **Billy Can Tours** (✉ Box 4407, Darwin 0801, ☎ 08/8981–9813 or 1800/81–3484, FAX 08/8941–0803) has tours that combine excursions to Nitmiluk with Litchfield and Kakadu national parks.

VISITOR INFORMATION

Katherine Visitors Information Centre. ✉ *Lindsay St. and Stuart Hwy.,* ☎ *08/8972–2650.*

Parks and Wildlife Commission of the Northern Territory can provide information on Nitmiluk National Park. ✉ *Box 344, 0851,* ☎ *08/8973–8888 or 08/8973–8899.*

THE KIMBERLEY

Perched on the northwestern hump of the loneliest Australian state, half the distance to Indonesia that it is to Sydney, the Kimberley remains a frontier of sorts. The first European explorers, dubbed by one of their descendants as "cattle kings in grass castles," ventured into the heart of the region in 1879 to establish cattle runs. They subsequently became embroiled in one of the country's longest-lasting guerilla wars between white settlers and Aboriginal people, who were led by Jandamarra of the Bunuba people.

The Kimberley remains sparsely populated, with only 30,000 people living in an area of 351,200 square km (135,000 square mi)—that's 12 square km (4½ square mi) per person. The region is dotted with cattle stations and raked with desert ranges, rivers, tropical forests, and towering cliffs. Several of the country's most spectacular national parks are here, including Purnululu (the Bungle Bungles)—a vast area of bizarrely shaped and colored rock formations that became widely known to white Australians only as late as 1983. Facilities in this remote region are few, but if you're looking for a genuine bush experience, the Kimberley represents the opportunity of a lifetime.

This section begins in Kununurra, just over the northwestern border of the Northern Territory, in Western Australia.

Kununurra

376 km (233 mi) west of Katherine, 710 km (440 mi) southwest of Darwin.

Population 2,000, Kununurra is the eastern gateway to the Kimberley. It is a modern planned township with little of inherent or historical interest, developed in the 1960s for the nearby Lake Argyle and Ord River irrigation scheme. The town is the base for adventure activities (☞ Four-Wheel-Drive Tours *in* Chapter 13). Nearby **Hidden Valley National Park** contains good examples of the strange banded sandstone towers and cliffs typical of the Kimberley, along with pleasant walks.

Dining and Lodging

$$$ ✕ **George Room in Gulliver's Tavern.** Lots of dark jarrah timber gives the George Room an old English atmosphere in keeping with its name. Although the tavern alongside offers simple counter meals, the George aims for greater things. And though the Continental-style food is good,

service can be erratic. The menu features northern Australian specialties, such as beef à la Ord, locally fattened grilled beef served with fresh mushrooms and onions, and the favorite fish dish, barramundi brushed with butter and wine, coated in bread crumbs, then topped with cheese and grilled. ⊠ *196 Cottontree Ave.,* ☎ *08/9168–1666. AE, DC, MC, V. Closed Sun. No lunch.*

$$ ✕ **Chopsticks Chinese Restaurant.** This restaurant is the most pleas-
★ ant dining surprise in the Kimberley. Ozzie country-town Chinese cooking is generally mediocre or worse, but the food here is uniformly excellent. All tables are outdoors, either along the covered veranda or in the courtyard, with pleasant views over gardens illuminated by colored lights. China's spicier dishes and various Szechuan specialties are well worth trying, like honey chili king prawns or excellent chili mussels served on a sizzling platter with vegetables. The lightly battered barramundi served with lemon or any of a variety of sauces is memorable. ⊠ *Country Club Private Hotel, 76 Coolibah Dr.,* ☎ *08/9168–1024. AE, DC, MC, V.*

$$ 🏨 **Kimberley Court.** Separated from Kununurra's shopping center by
★ a wide park, this small hotel has a relaxed atmosphere that makes it almost impossible not to meet fellow guests. Every room opens onto a cool veranda, and the central courtyard is filled with tropical plants, a pond, and a small aviary. Deluxe rooms are twice as large as standard rooms and come with a kitchenette and whirlpool bath. The swimming pool is a nice place to relax at the end of a hot day. The Kimberley Court may not be the place for a high-powered holiday, but this hotel succeeds where the vast majority fail—it feels like a home away from home. ⊠ *Box 384, Erythrina St., 6743,* ☎ *08/9168–1411,* FAX *08/9168–1055. 31 rooms with shower or bath. Coin laundry. MC, V.*

$ 🏨 **Kununurra Backpackers.** This outfit provides quality, low-cost accommodations in shared, twin, or single rooms from $14 per night. Budget safaris also operate out of here—including trips to the Bungle Bungle Range. ⊠ *Nutwood Crescent, 6743,* ☎ *08/9169–1998 or 1800/64–1998,* FAX *08/9168–3998. 50 beds share baths. Pool. MC, V.*

Shopping
Waringarri (⊠ Speargrass Rd., Kununurra, ☎ 08/9168–1528) has a large selection of Aboriginal art in a spacious gallery.

Gibb River Road and El Questro

Gibb River Road, the cattle-carrying route through the heart of the Kimberley, provides an alternative to the Great Northern Highway between Kununurra–Wyndham and Derby. The unpaved 700-km (434-mi) road runs through a remote area, and the trip should be done only with a great deal of caution. The road is passable by conventional vehicles only after it's been recently graded. At other times you need a four-wheeler, and in the Wet it's impassable. At any time in any vehicle, a breakdown would be a real problem.

Should you decide to take the Gibb River Road, consider stopping for some R&R at **El Questro Cattle Station and Wilderness Park,** a working ranch in some of the most rugged country in Australia. Besides providing an opportunity to see Outback station life, El Questro has a full complement of such recreational activities as fishing and swimming, and horse, camel, and helicopter rides. On individually tailored walking and four-wheel-drive tours through the bush, you can bird-watch or look at ancient spirit figures depicted in the unique *wandjina* style of Kimberley Aboriginal rock painting—one of the world's most striking forms of spiritual art. The turnoff for El Questro is 27 km (17 mi) down the Gibb River Road as you head west from Kununurra.

Dining and Lodging

$–$$$$ ⊡ **El Questro Cattle Station.** Accommodations on the huge station run
★ the gamut from luxury to bare bones: Staying at the Homestead can
be very expensive—$640 per person per night for double accommo-
dation or $200 for single accommodation, with a two-night mini-
mum—but its location at the top of a cliff face above the Chamberlain
River rates as one of the most spectacular in Australia, and the price
includes all drinks and food, room service, laundry, most activities, and
transportation to and from Kununurra, about 50 km (31 mi) away.
Nearby are the considerably less expensive bungalows ($65 per per-
son twin share) and the campground ($7.50 per person), which is a
great deal—30 secluded sites are right on the river, and barbecue and
bathroom facilities are available. At the Emma Gorge Resort, which
is in a different section of the station and has a licensed restaurant, fam-
ily cabins sleeping four are available for $146. ⊠ *Box 909, Banksia
St., Kununurra 6743;* ☎ *08/9169–1777,* ℻ *08/9169–1383 reserva-
tions; 08/9161–4318,* ℻ *08/9161–4355 bungalows and campground;*
☎ ℻ *08/9161–4388 Emma Gorge Resort.*

Wyndham

103 km (64 mi) northwest of Kununurra.

The small, historic port on the Cambridge Gulf was established in 1886
to service the Halls Creek goldfields, and it looks as if nothing much
has happened in Wyndham in the century since. The wharf is the best
location in the Kimberley for spotting saltwater crocodiles as they
bask on the mud flats below.

Purnululu (Bungle Bungle) National Park

202 km (125 mi) south and southwest of Wyndham and Kununurra.

★ **Purnululu National Park** covers nearly 3,120 square km (1,200 square
mi) in the southeast corner of the Kimberley. Australians of European
descent first "discovered" its great beehivelike domes—their English
name is the Bungle Bungles—in 1983, proving how much about this
vast continent remains outside of "white" experience. The local Kidja
Aboriginal tribe knew about these scenic wonders long ago, of course,
and called the area Purnululu.

The park's orange silica- and black lichen-striped mounds bubble up
on the landscape. Climbing is not permitted because the sandstone en-
crusted beneath the thin layer of lichen and silica is fragile and would
quickly erode without protection. Walking tracks follow rocky, dry creek
beds. One popular walk leads hikers along the **Piccaninny Creek** to **Pic-
caninny Gorge,** passing through gorges with towering 328-ft cliffs to
which slender fan palms cling.

The Bungle Bungles are best seen from April through October and are
closed from January through March. The park charges an entrance fee
of $11 for adults and $1 for children. Anyone who has the time and
a sense of adventure should spend a few days at Purnululu National
Park. Facilities are primitive (☞ Lodging, *below*), but the setting and
experience are incomparable.

Lodging

Camping is permitted only at two designated campgrounds at Purnu-
lulu National Park. None of the campsites has facilities—both the
Bellbyrn Creek and Walardi campgrounds have simple pit toilets—and
fresh drinking water is available only at the Belburn Creek. The near-

est accommodations are in Kununurra (☞ The Kimberley, *above*), and most visitors fly in from there.

Arriving and Departing

BY CAR

The Bungle Bungles are 252 km (156 mi) south of Kununurra along the Great Northern Highway. A rough, 55-km (34-mi) unpaved road, negotiable only in a four-wheel-drive vehicle, is the last stretch of road leading to the park from the turnoff at Turkey Creek–Warmum Community. That part of the ride takes about 2½ hours.

BY PLANE

The ideal way to see the park is to arrive by air. There is an airstrip at Purnululu National Park suitable for light aircraft, but access is restricted by the authorities. Recently several operators have been given permission to fly clients from Kununurra, Broome, and Halls Creek to the airstrip, where they are collected by guides with four-wheel-drive vehicles. The most popular of these fly-drive tours between April and December includes one night of camping in the park. The two companies operating these trips are **East Kimberly Tours** (⊠ Box 537, Kununurra, WA 6743, ☎ 08/9168–2213) and **Halls Creek and Bungle Bungle Tours** (⊠ Box 58, Halls Creek, WA 6770, ☎ 08/9168–6217, or mobile 015/ 99–3509).

Guided Tours

AERIAL TOURS

Alligator Airways (⊠ Box 10, Kununurra, WA 6743, ☎ 08/9168–1575) operates both fixed-wing float planes from Lake Kununurra and land-based flights from Kununurra airport. **Slingair Tours** (☎ 08/9169–1300) conducts two-hour economy flights over the Bungle Bungles for $150 for adults. A more expensive alternative is to take a helicopter flight with **Slingsby Helicopters** (☎ 08/9168–1811).

FOUR-WHEEL-DRIVE TOURS

East Kimberley Tours (☞ *above*) runs from Kununurra into the Bungle Bungle massif. Based to the south in ☞ Halls Creek, **Halls Creek and Bungle Bungle Tours** also has a range of tours to the park.

Visitor Information

Department of Conservation and Land Management, State Government Offices. ⊠ *Box 942, Kununurra, WA 6743,* ☎ *08/9168–0200.*

Halls Creek

363 km (225 mi) southwest of Kununurra.

Old Halls Creek is the site of the short-lived Kimberley gold rush of 1885. Set on the edge of the Great Sandy Desert, the town has been a crumbling shell since its citizens decided in 1948 to move 15 km (9 mi) away to the site of the present Halls Creek, which has a better water supply. The old town is a fascinating place to explore, however, and small gold nuggets are still found in the surrounding gullies.

Halls Creek is the closest town to the **Wolfe Creek Meteorite Crater,** the world's second largest. The crater is a half mile wide, and, like its counterpart in Arizona, its shape has been well preserved in the dry desert air.

Dining and Lodging

$$ 🏨 **Kimberley Hotel.** If you arrive by aircraft, you'll practically bump
★ into the Kimberley Hotel—it's located right at the end of the runway! Fortunately for the hotel's guests, the airstrip is used irregularly and only by light planes, so noise isn't a problem. With its lawns, airy rooms,

and swimming pool, the hotel is something of an oasis in this dusty town on the edge of the desert. Originally a simple Outback pub with a few rooms, it was completely renovated in 1987 and is now a surprisingly pleasant place to rest. Staying in one of the old, cheaper rooms would be a false economy—the newer ones, with their pine furnishings, tile floors, and peach decor, are among the best in the region. The high-ceiling restaurant, which overlooks the lawns and pool, has an excellent wine list and serves some of the best meals in town. ⊠ *Box 244, Roberta Ave., 6770,* ☎ *08/9168–6101,* FAX *08/9168–6071. 40 rooms with shower. Restaurant, pool, hot tub. MC, V.*

Fitzroy Crossing

290 km (180 mi) west of Halls Creek, 381 km (236 mi) east of Broome.

The main attraction of Fitzroy Crossing is **Geikie Gorge National Park,** which cuts through one of the best preserved fossilized coral reefs in the world. The town has a couple of basic motels and restaurants.

Geikie Gorge National Park

16 km (10 mi) north of Fitzroy Crossing.

Geikie Gorge is part of a 350-million-year-old reef system formed from fossilized layers of algae—evolutionary precursors of coral reefs—when this area was still part of the Indian Ocean. The limestone walls you see now were cut and shaped by the mighty Fitzroy River. During the Wet, the normally placid river roars through the region, threatening to uproot the river red gums that line its banks. The walls of the gorge are stained red from iron oxide, except where they have been leached to their original white by the floods, which have washed as high as 52 ft from the bottom of the gorge.

When the Indian Ocean receded, it left a number of stranded sea creatures, which managed to adapt to their new conditions. Geikie is one of the few places in the world where freshwater barramundi, mussels, stingrays, and prawns are found. The park is also home to the freshwater archerfish, which can spit water as far as a yard to knock insects out of the air. Aborigines call this place Kangu, meaning "big fishing hole."

Both sides of the gorge are wildlife sanctuaries that are off-limits to visitors, except for a small area on the western bank at the end of a mile-long trail. The only way to see the gorge is aboard one of the daily boat tours led by park rangers, at 8, 11, and 3. The 1½-hour flat-bottom boat trip costs $15. The rangers are extremely knowledgeable and helpful in pointing out the vegetation, strange limestone formations, and the many freshwater crocodiles along the way. Tourists get to see only a part of the noisy fruit bat colony—estimated at 600,000—that inhabits the region.

Arriving and Departing

BY CAR

From Broome, follow the Great Northern Highway east 381 km (236 mi) to Fitzroy Crossing, then 16 km (10 mi) north on a paved side road to the park. Since 1989 camping has not been permitted at the gorge, so you must stay in Fitzroy Crossing.

Visitor Information

National Park Ranger. ⊠ *Box 37, Fitzroy Crossing, WA 6765,* ☎ *08/ 9191–5121.*

Tunnel Creek and Windjana Gorge National Parks

Tunnel Creek is 111 km (69 mi) north of Fitzroy Crossing; Windjana Gorge is 145 km (90 mi) northwest of Fitzroy Crossing.

On the back road between Fitzroy Crossing and the coastal town of Derby are two other geological oddities. **Tunnel Creek** was created when a stream cut an underground course through a fault line in a formation of limestone. You can follow the tunnel's path on foot along the stream for a half mile, with the only natural light coming from those areas where the tunnel roof has collapsed. Flying foxes and other types of bats inhabit the tunnel. About a hundred years ago a band of outlaws and their Aborigine leader Jundumurra, nicknamed "Pigeon," used the caves as a hideout.

Windjana Gorge has cliffs nearly 325 ft high, which were carved out by the flooding of the Lennard River. During the Wet, the Lennard is a roaring torrent, but it dwindles to just a few still pools in the Dry.

Derby

242 km (150 mi) west of Fitzroy Crossing, 226 km (140 mi) northeast of Broome, 921 km (571 mi) west of Kununurra via Halls Creek, 758 km (470 mi) west of Kununurra via the Gibb River Road.

With its port, Derby has long been the main administrative and economic center of the western Kimberley, as well as a convenient base from which to explore the nearby gorge national parks—**Geikie Gorge, Windjana Gorge,** and **Tunnel Creek.** Without much else to recommend it, the town is known for its giant boab trees—kin to Africa's baobab trees—which have enormously fat trunks. The hollow trunk of one of these trees was reputedly used as a prison at one time. Known as the Prison Tree, this boab has a circumference of 45 ft and is 6 km (4 mi) south of town.

Dining and Lodging

$$ ✗⬚ **Spinifex Hotel.** You'll find basic accommodation here, with friendliness that typifies the Outback pub. The bar serves solid if uninspired food known as a counter meal, and it's a great place to be on Thursday night for the Smorgasbord or on Friday night, when many in the town gather for live music. Standard motel-style rooms and hostel-style dormitory accommodations are available. ✉ *Clarendon St., 6728,* ☎ *08/9191–1233,* FAX *08/9191–1576. 19 rooms with bath, 12 dormitory beds. Bar. MC, V.*

Broome

216 km (134 mi) southwest of Derby, 1,048 km (650 mi) southwest of Kununurra via Halls Creek, 1,610 km (1,000 mi) southwest of Katherine, 1,935 km (1,200 mi) southwest of Darwin.

Broome is the holiday capital of the Kimberley. It's the only town in the region with sandy beaches, so it has seen the growth of several resorts, a crocodile farm, and a large, if sparsely populated, zoo. Until the recent tourist boom, Broome had depended on pearling for its livelihood. Early in the century, 300 to 400 sailing boats employing 3,000 men provided most of the world's mother-of-pearl shell. Many of the pearlers were Japanese, Malay, and Filipino, and the town is still multiracial today. Each August during the famous Shinju Matsuri (Pearl Festival), Broome looks back to the good old days. All but a few of the traditional old wooden luggers have disappeared, and Broome cultivates most of its pearls at nearby Kuri Bay. The town itself has retained a faint air of its boisterous shantytown days, with wooden side-walks and a charming Chinatown.

Although there are no scheduled boat cruises, there are several boat charter operations in Broome and Derby for single-day or extended **fishing expeditions.** The myriad empty islands and deserted beaches off the coast and the 35-ft tides that surge through here creating waterfalls and whirlpools in the narrows make the Kimberley coast an adventurer's delight. Broome marks the end of the Kimberley.

From here it's another 2,212 km (1,372 mi) south to Perth, or 2,000 km (1,240 mi) back to Darwin.

Dining and Lodging

$$$–$$$$ ✕ **Club Restaurant.** In keeping with the standards of the Cable Beach Club (☞ *below*), where it is located, this restaurant is Broome's premier dining establishment. Dark wood beams and plenty of antiques figure into the sophisticated decor. The menu changes every few days, and the chef prides himself on using only fresh ingredients. If it's available, try zucchini stuffed with chicken mousse or fried prawns with coconut. Other innovative dishes include pigeon with garlic and marsala, and a crayfish salad with a champagne vinaigrette. ⊠ *Cable Beach Club, Cable Beach Rd.,* ☎ *08/9192–2505 or 1800/09–5508,* FAX *08/9192–2249. Reservations essential. AE, DC, MC, V.*

$$ ✕ **Conti Bar and Bistro.** This sparkling bistro at the Mercure Inn Continental Hotel gets its brightness from terra-cotta tiles and tables and
★   its view of palms and the hotel pool through the plate-glass windows. The blackboard menu changes regularly, but the cuisine is Continental with an emphasis on seafood. ⊠ *Mercure Inn Continental Hotel, Weld St.,* ☎ *08/9192–1002. AE, DC, MC, V.*

$$$$ ⊞ **Cable Beach Club.** Just a few minutes out of town opposite the broad,
★   beautiful Cable Beach—the only sandy beach near any Kimberley town—this resort is the area's most luxurious accommodation. Built in 1988, the club has 77 single and 7 double bungalows spread through tropical gardens, as well as 176 studio rooms and three suites. The decor is colonial with a hint of Asia, and the extensive resort facilities include two pools and 12 tennis courts. The fine Club Restaurant is also on the premises (☞ *above*). ⊠ *Box 1544, Cable Beach Rd., 6725,* ☎ *08/9192–2505 or 1800/09–5508,* FAX *08/9192–2249. 258 rooms with bath, 3 suites. Restaurant, pool, 12 tennis courts, children's programs, laundry. AE, DC, MC, V.*

$$$ ⊞ **Mangrove Hotel.** Situated on a rise overlooking Roebuck Bay, this highly regarded hotel has the best location of any accommodations in Broome. All the spacious rooms have private balconies, many of which overlook the bay. The pool is set in a large, palm-shaded area of lawn. ⊠ *Box 84, Carnarvon St., 6725,* ☎ *08/9192–1303 or 1800/09–4818,* FAX *08/9193–5169. 68 rooms with shower. Restaurant, bar, pool. AE, DC, MC, V.*

Shopping

Aboriginal Art

Prices for Aboriginal art in the Kimberley are generally well below those in Darwin or Alice Springs. **Kimberley Kreations** (⊠ Carnarvon St., ☎ 08/9192–2260) specializes in Kimberley arts and crafts. **Kreations Gallery** (⊠ 60 Hammersley St., ☎ 08/9193–5811, FAX 08/9192–1995) regularly holds exhibitions by local artists, including Aborigines.

Jewelry

The number of jewelry stores in Broome is completely out of proportion to the size of the town. **Paspaley Pearling** (⊠ 2 Short St., Chinatown, ☎ 08/9192–2203) specializes in high-quality, very expensive pearls and jewelry. The same is true of **Linneys** (✉ Dampier Terr., ☎ 08/9192–2430), the **Pearl Emporium** (✉ Dampier Terr., ☎ 08/9192–1531), and **Broome Pearls** (✉ Dampier Terr., ☎ 08/9192–1295).

The Kimberley A to Z

Arriving and Departing

BY BUS

Greyhound Pioneer (☎ 08/8981–8700) runs the 2,000 km (1,240 mi) between Darwin and Broome.

BY CAR

The distances in this part of the continent are indeed tyrannical, in other words colossal. If you're planning to drive, be prepared for this. From Darwin to Kununurra and the eastern extent of the Kimberley is 903 km (560 mi). From Darwin to Broome on the far side of the Kimberley is 2,000 km (1,240 mi). The route runs from Darwin to Katherine along the Stuart Highway, and then along the Victoria Highway to Kununurra. The road is paved all the way but quite narrow in parts—especially so, it may seem, when a road train (an extremely long truck) is coming the other way—so drive with care. Fuel and supplies can be bought at the small settlements along the way, and you should always keep your supplies in abundance.

BY PLANE

Ansett flies from Darwin to Kununurra, Derby, and Broome.

Contacts and Resources

EMERGENCIES

For emergency assistance, go to the casualty section of a local hospital or call the **Royal Flying Doctor Service.** ✉ *Derby,* ☎ *08/9191–1211.*

Broome District Hospital. ✉ *Anne St.,* ☎ *08/9192–1401.*
Derby Regional Hospital. ✉ *Loch St.,* ☎ *08/9193–3333.*
Kununurra District Hospital. ✉ *Coolibah Dr.,* ☎ *08/9168–1522.*

GUIDED TOURS

AAT King's (✉ City Office, 14 Knuckey St., Darwin, NT 0800, ☎ 08/8947–1207, FAX 08/8941–3386) conducts tours throughout the Kimberley. For more information or to book a tour, the contact is the Darwin office. **Amesz Tours** (✉ Box 1060, Midlands, WA 6056, ☎ 09/9250–2577 or 1800/99–9204, FAX 09/9250–2634) runs a 13- or 18-day safari from Broome to Darwin that travels right across the Kimberley and the Top End to Kakadu. Amesz also offers a 13-day tour in a four-wheel-drive vehicle that covers the region in more detail with a smaller group. **Belray Diamond Tours** (✉ Box 10, Kununurra 6743, ☎ 08/9168–1014) offers an interesting daily air tour (subject to numbers) from Kununurra to the Argyle Diamond Mine—the world's largest diamond mine, producing about 6½ tons of diamonds a year.

VISITOR INFORMATION

Broome Tourist Bureau. ✉ *Box 352, Great Northern Hwy., Broome 6725,* ☎ *091/92–2222,* FAX *08/9192–2063.*
Derby Tourist Bureau. ✉ *2 Clarendon St., Derby 6728,* ☎ *091/91–1426,* FAX *08/9191–1609.*
Kununurra Tourist Bureau. ✉ *Coolibah Dr., Kununurra 6743,* ☎ *08/9168–1177,* FAX *091/68–2598.*
Western Australian Tourism Commission. ✉ *16 St. Georges Terr., Perth 6000,* ☎ *09/9220–1700 or 1800/99–3333,* FAX *09/9220–1702.*

12 Perth and Western Australia

Despite the tyranny of distance, those who make it to the "undiscovered country" are stunned by the diversity of places to go and things to do. Relax on far-flung beaches; go snorkeling around the numerous islands; overnight for an idle wander around Fremantle; hop a train to Kalgoorlie for a weekend on the goldfields; explore the historic towns, wineries, and seaside national parks of the Southwest; wonder at coastal limestone formations in Naumbung National Park; or swim with dolphins, manta rays, and whale sharks at Monkey Mia or Ningaloo Reef Marine Park.

By Helen Ayers
and Lorraine
Ironside

ALTHOUGH the existence of the south land—*terra australis*—was known long before Dutch seafarer Dirk Hartog first landed on the coast of "New Holland" in 1616 in today's Shark Bay, the panorama was so bleak he didn't even bother to plant his flag and claim it for the Dutch crown. It took an intrepid English seaman, William Dampier, to see past the daunting prospect of endless beaches, rugged cliffs, heat, flies, and sparse scrubby plains to lay claim to the land on behalf of a nation 12,000 mi away. Although his faith has been rewarded, still nothing can quite prepare you for what lies beyond the city of Perth. The scenery is magnificent, from the awesome, rugged north to the green sweep of the southern plains. But the sheer emptiness—the utter silence broken only by the mournful cry of the crow circling high overhead wherever you wander throughout this vast state—beggars description.

Western Australia is a state blessed by wealth and cursed by distance—in every direction Perth is 2,000 mi from any other major city in the world. And the place itself is *huge*. Its million square miles make up 33% of the Australian continent, yet it is home to just 1.2 million people. Sheep stations here can be the size of Kentucky. And although the 21st century is just around the corner, denizens of the state often feel theirs is an undiscovered country.

Perched as it is on the edge of the continent, Perth is much closer to Indonesia than to its overland Australian cousins. Such social isolation would ordinarily doom a community to life as a backwater, and for most of its existence Perth has been just that. The gold rush of the 1890s brought a boom to the city, but it did little to change Perth's insularity. The discovery of vast mineral deposits in the 1970s, however, jump-started the state into catching up with the rest of the country. It is a young city, the destination of a new breed of hopefuls from the east coast and abroad, lured by the city's energy and uninhibited lifestyle. About half the population is under 24 years of age, and a third are teenage.

The city has fantastic beaches, a beautiful river, and a Mediterraneanlike climate that averages eight hours of sunshine a day—although in January and February, the heat becomes oppressive when temperatures climb above the century mark. It is then that the Southwest region, with its lush farmland, vineyards, hillsides profuse with wildflowers, and a spectacular coastline, provide a cool escape from the city.

It is to the hot, dry north and to the east, though, that the city looks for its wealth, out in the fly-blown desert that constitutes the majority of Western Australia. In the 1890s it was the goldfields verging on the treeless wastes of the Nullarbor Plain; today it is the Pilbara, the richest source of iron ore in the world. Here, huge machines capable of lifting 5 tons at a time gouge 24,000 tons of rock out of the earth each day. The air conditioner is the most precious possession in the Pilbara, where the mercury frequently hits 120°F. Wages are high, but there is little for employees to buy in the small, company-operated towns. No one thinks twice about driving 1,000 mi round-trip for a long weekend.

For many, work on Western Australia's strip mines or natural gas wells is a necessary hardship that they endure before scuttling back to easy living in Perth. The basic tenet of Western Australian life remains the same: To make money, you have to dig!

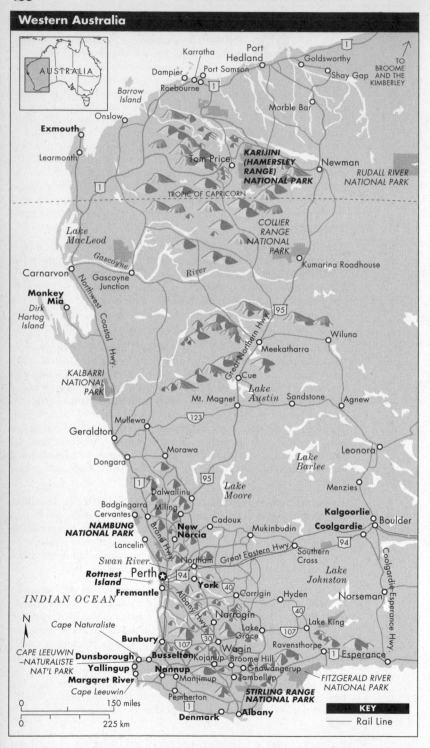

Western Australia

AUSTRALIA

TO BROOME AND THE KIMBERLEY

Karratha
Port Hedland
Goldsworthy
Shay Gap
Dampier
Port Samson
Roebourne
Barrow Island
Marble Bar
Onslow

Exmouth

Learmonth

Tom Price
KARIJINI (HAMERSLEY RANGE) NATIONAL PARK
Newman
RUDALL RIVER NATIONAL PARK

TROPIC OF CAPRICORN

Lake MacLeod
COLLIER RANGE NATIONAL PARK
Gascoyne

Carnarvon
Gascoyne Junction
River
Kumarina Roadhouse

Monkey Mia
Dirk Hartog Island

Northwest Coastal Hwy.

95

Wiluna

Meekatharra

KALBARRI NATIONAL PARK

Great Northern Hwy.

Cue
Lake Austin
Sandstone
Agnew

Mt. Magnet

Mullewa
123

Geraldton
Morawa
Lake Barlee
Leonora

Dongara

95
Lake Moore
Menzies

Dalwallinu
Badgingarra
Cervantes
Miling
Cadoux
Kalgoorlie
Coolgardie
Boulder

NAMBUNG NATIONAL PARK
Lancelin
New Norcia
Mukinbudin
94

Brand Hwy.
Northam
Great Eastern Hwy.
Southern Cross
Lake Johnston
Coolgardie-Esperance Hwy.

Swan River
Rottnest Island
Perth
94
York
40
Corrigin
Hyden
Norseman

Fremantle

INDIAN OCEAN
N

Cape Naturaliste
Albany Hwy.
Narrogin
40
Lake King

CAPE LEEUWIN –NATURALISTE NAT'L PARK
30
Lake Grace
107
Ravensthorpe
1
Esperance

Bunbury
107
Wagin
Dunsborough
Busselton
Kojanup
Broome Hill
Gnowangerup
FITZGERALD RIVER NATIONAL PARK
Yallingup
Nannup
Manjimup
Tambellup
Margaret River
Cape Leeuwin
Pemberton
STIRLING RANGE NATIONAL PARK

0   150 miles
0   225 km
Denmark
Albany

KEY
—— Rail Line

The Kimberley region in Western Australia's tropical north is closer geographically and in character to the Northern Territory city of Darwin than it is to Perth. For this reason, information about Broome and the Kimberley is included in Chapter 11.

Pleasures and Pastimes

Beaches
You'll find some of Australia's finest beaches in Western Australia, stretching from the snow-white salt beaches of Frenchman's Bay in the south to beyond Port Hedland in the north. In just a day's drive from Perth, you can enjoy a sojourn just about anywhere along the coast in the Southwest, or escape to the life-size chessboard feeling of the beach where the Pinnacles stand watch.

Dining
Although Perth's cuisine has been shaped by such external influences as the postwar European immigration and the recent influx of Asian migrants, an indigenous West Coast cuisine is emerging. Like much of the innovative cooking in Australia, this style fuses Asian, European, and native Australian herbs and spices with French technique to bring out the best in what is grown locally. In Western Australia's case, that means some of the country's finest seafood, as well as beef, lamb, kangaroo, venison, and emu.

CATEGORY	COST*
$$$$	over $60
$$$	$45–$60
$$	$25–$45
$	under $25

*per person, excluding drinks and service

Lodging
Perth has experienced a hotel trade boom at all levels, from the luxurious to the frill-free. In the countryside, B&Bs are a great alternative. In farther-flung parts of the state—and there are plenty of those—much of the lodging is motel style.

CATEGORY	COST*
$$$$	over $125
$$$	$90–$125
$$	$50–$90
$	under $50

*All prices are for a standard double room.

Outdoor Activities and Sports
Western Australia's national parks are full of natural wonders—among them fascinating rock formations, exotic birdlife, and incredible wildflowers in spring. The parks are some of the best in Australia, in some cases because they are remote and uncrowded. Some of these aren't within easy reach of Perth, so you should plan in advance for long drives.

Lovers of water sports will be very much at home in Western Australia. For wind-in-your-hair types, you can get your fill of jet skiing and parasailing in Perth. Underwater types should seriously consider going all the way north to Exmouth to take the dive of a lifetime with whale sharks at Ningaloo Reef Marine Park. And in certain towns in the Southwest, surfing is a way of life.

Note: ☞ Chapter 13, for more information on diving and four-wheel-driving in Western Australia's great outdoors.

Exploring Perth and Western Australia

Most trips to Western Australia begin in Perth. Apart from its own points of interest, there are a few great day trips to take from the city: to Rottnest Island, the historic towns of New Norcia or York, and a day or overnight excursion north to the coastal Nambung National Park. The port city of Fremantle is a good place to unwind, and you can extend a jaunt there with a tour of the Southwest, with its history, seashore, parks, wildflowers, and first-rate wine. The old goldfields towns east of Perth are a slice of the dust-blown Australia of yore. There are also a few long-distance forays worth your while: to the meetings of land- and sea-creatures at Monkey Mia and at Ningaloo Reef Marine Park, and to the ancient rock formations inland at Karijini National Park.

Great Itineraries

Planning your time out west is a matter of choosing a couple of areas to concentrate on—it's unlikely you'll cover the whole state, even if you decide to permanently relocate. There are a few questions that will help narrow down your choices. Do you have but a few days to spend in and around Perth and Fremantle? Does the thought of cooler air and the coastal scenery of the Southwest appeal to you, or would you rather get in a car and drive to far reaches east or north? Or do you want to trek north along the coast to Monkey Mia or Exmouth to frolic in and under the waves with amazing sea creatures? Those are your basic options; here are a few possible combinations.

IF YOU HAVE 3 DAYS

Spend most of the first day knocking around **Perth**'s city center, or take the train to pleasantly restored **Fremantle** to stroll through the streets and stop for breaks at sidewalk cafés. In the evening in either city, have dinner overlooking the water. Over the next two days, take a ferry to **Rottnest Island** and cycle around, walk on the beach, fish, or try to spot the small local marsupials that are called quokkas, and either stay the night or come back to town. If you're feeling ambitious you could drive the couple of hours north to **Nambung National Park** to see the Pinnacles, interesting coastal rock formations that look like anything from tombstones to trance-state druids moving en masse to the sea, depending on your mood. The historic towns of **York** and **New Norcia** also make for good day trips from Perth.

IF YOU HAVE 5 DAYS

This in-between-length trip allows you to take on some of the larger distances in Western Australia, provided that you have the right mode of transportation. Fly north to **Monkey Mia** to learn about and interact with dolphins or to **Exmouth** to dive with whale sharks and watch the annual coral spawning. Or fly to the **Southwest** coastal area and pick up a car, then drive to see spring wildflowers, wineries, and national parks—and generally enjoy the good life. You'll have enough time for a day or two around Perth before getting in a car and heading east to the old goldfield towns of **Kalgoorlie** and **Coolgardie.** It may remind you of America's Wild West—except that camel teams used to pull into town—but this is pure Oz all the way.

IF YOU HAVE 7 OR MORE DAYS

Now you can consider all options, mixing a few of the three- and five-day activities. Of course, you could opt to spend the entire week leisurely making your way along the coast of the **Southwest,** tasting the wine at the vineyards of **Margaret River** and around **Albany,** checking out the caves and seashore of **Cape Leewin–Naturaliste National Park,** heading inland to tramp around the fascinating landscape and outstanding spring wildflowers of **Stirling Range National Park.** If you plan to go as far north as **Karijini (Hamersley Range) National Park** for its stunning gorges and rock-scapes—taking a plane will save days on the road getting there—you may want to continue to the Western Australian city of Broome and the Kimberley region, even beyond them to Darwin (☞ Chapter 11).

When to Tour Perth and Western Australia

Generally speaking, it's best to avoid summer travel in Western Australia. Only the Southwest is even slightly bearable. This is no news when you know that the mercury can hang around over 100°F—for weeks at a time. It's always cooler at the coast, but spring and fall are the ideal months for touring in the south. Spring wildflowers in the Southwest are well worth seeing if you're in the state September to November. If you're going north, the best times to visit are May to August, during the dry season. Nights inland in July can be chilly.

PERTH

Orbiting Earth in 1962, John Glenn was surprised to see a beacon of light shining up from the black void of a Western Australian night. That beacon was Perth, whose residents had turned on every light in the city as a greeting, prompting Glenn to dub it the City of Lights. In many ways Perth remains Australia's city of lights, for just as its citizens reached out to the future then, so do they now. In its early days Perth was a poor country cousin. The gold rush at the turn of the century changed that for a time, and the more recent minerals boom of the '70s has utterly transformed the city. Buoyed by its mineral wealth and foreign investment, Perth continues to grow steadily. High-rise buildings dot the skyline, and an influx of immigrants has given the city a healthy diversity. And despite the expansion, the city has maintained its relaxed pace of living. Residents live for the water: Half of Perth is always heading for its boats, the old joke goes, while the other half is already on them. And who can blame them? Some of the finest beaches, sailing, and fishing in the world are on the city's doorstep. It's no accident that the 1983 America's Cup was won by a contender from Perth.

For all its modernity, Perth is not a driver's town. Traveling around downtown is easiest on foot. The main thoroughfare is St. George's Terrace, an elegant street along which many of the most intriguing sights are located. Perth's literal highlight is King's Park, a 1,000-acre garden atop Mount Eliza affording a panoramic view of the city.

Exploring Perth

Because of its relative colonial youth, Perth has an advantage over most other capital cities. Where others grew into being along with civilization, Perth was laid out with elegance and foresight. Streets were planned so that pedestrian traffic could flow smoothly from one avenue to the next. Most of the points of interest are in the downtown area not far from the banks of the Swan River.

City Center

Perth's major business thoroughfare is St. George's Terrace. A pleasant blend of old and new, the city center is located along this street as well as on parallel Hay and Murray streets.

Numbers in the text correspond to numbers in the margin and on the Perth map.

A GOOD WALK
Home to almost a million people, Perth is a compact city best explored on foot. Though the city was carefully planned and its streets follow

a grid system, Perth has managed to avoid the sterile orderliness of Canberra. Its public buildings, however, are not nearly as grand as those in Melbourne, which is not surprising considering that Perth was a poor country cousin until the gold rush at the turn of the century and the more recent minerals boom of the 1970s. Today it's a pleasant, easily negotiated blend of old and new. Begin your tour in the major downtown area, on the north bank of the Swan River.

Our walking tour begins on Forrest Place at the **General Post Office** ①, a solid sandstone edifice facing **Citiplace** ②, one of the city's bustling pedestrian malls. Head east along Murray Street, passing the new **Forrest Chase Shopping Plaza** ③. Beyond that, near the corner at Irwin Street, three blocks away, is the great **Old Fire Station** ④, which is now full of historic fire-fighting artifacts that you can look in on.

Continue east on Murray Street to Victoria Square, one of Perth's finest plazas, which is dominated by **St. Mary's Cathedral** ⑤. Turn right into Victoria Avenue for a block, then right again on Hay Street, passing two of Perth's newer buildings—the **Central Fire Station** ⑥ (480 Hay St.) on your right and the **Law Courts** ⑦ (30 St. George's Terr.) on your left. Turn left into Pier Street and head toward St. George's Terrace. On the corner, adjacent to **St. George's Cathedral** ⑧, is the **Deanery,** one of Perth's oldest houses.

Look across St. George's Terrace for the Gothic Revival turrets of **Government House** ⑨, then stroll through **Sterling Gardens** on your way to **Supreme Court Gardens** ⑩, where you should look for the stately presence of Moreton Bay fig trees. At the western end of the gardens is the charming Georgian **Francis Burt Law Centre** ⑪. Across Barrack Street, the glass pyramid of **Alan Green Conservatory** ⑫ has been plunked down on the Esplanade's lawns.

Return to Howard Street and turn left into St. George's Terrace for a walk past many of Perth's newest and most impressive office buildings, including the notable **R&I Tower** ⑬ (108 St. George's Terr.) on the corner of William Street. Continuing on St. George's Terrace, the 1854 **Old Perth Boys School** ⑭ is another of Perth's Gothic Revival buildings. As you continue along the terrace, you will pass the **Cloisters** ⑮ (200 St. George's Terr.) on your right, built by high school boys four years after the Old Perth Boys School went up. At the top of the terrace is the lone remnant of the former Pensioner Forces headquarters, the **Barracks Arch** ⑯, which stands in front of **Parliament House** ⑰.

For a detour into the greener reaches of Perth, head down Harvest Terrace to Malcolm Street, then circle the roundabout to get to **King's Park.** The Botanic Garden within its bounds is a great place for an introduction to Western Australia's flora and natural bushland, and the native wildflowers in spring are well worth the trip. You can return to the city on the No. 33 bus.

From Barrack's Arch, turn around and walk back along St. George's Terrace to Milligan Street and turn left. When you reach Hay Street, turn right and walk toward the opulent Edwardian exterior of **His Majesty's Theatre** ⑱ at the King Street corner. Continue to the Hay Street Mall, one of many city streets closed to traffic, where you'll find **London Court** ⑲, a shopping arcade running north to south between Hay Street and St. George's Terrace. Stop by on the quarter hour for some mechanical-horological entertainment. Finally, at the intersection of Hay and Barrack streets, **Town Hall** ⑳ is another of Perth's handsome convict-built structures.

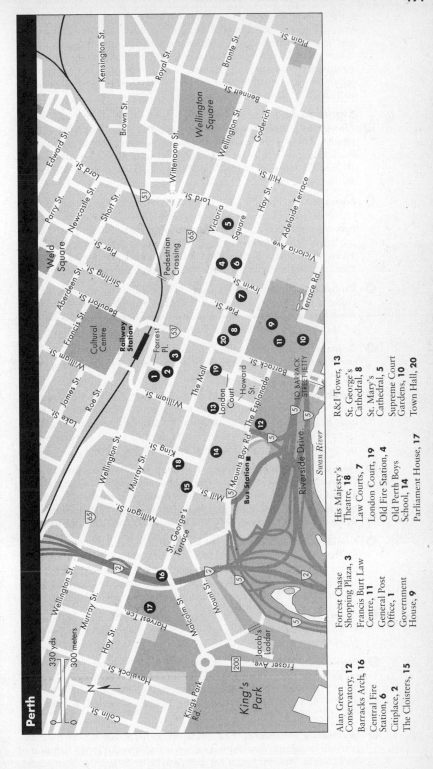

Perth

0 330 yds
0 300 meters

Alan Green
Conservatory, **12**
Barracks Arch, **16**
Central Fire
Station, **6**
Citiplace, **2**
The Cloisters, **15**

Forrest Chase
Shopping Plaza, **3**
Francis Burt Law
Centre, **11**
General Post
Office, **1**
Government
House, **9**

His Majesty's
Theatre, **18**
Law Courts, **7**
London Court, **19**
Old Fire Station, **4**
Old Perth Boys
School, **14**
Parliament House, **17**

R&I Tower, **13**
St. George's
Cathedral, **8**
St. Mary's
Cathedral, **5**
Supreme Court
Gardens, **10**
Town Hall, **20**

TIMING

It would take 90-some minutes to merely pace off the above route. You can lengthen that to any degree by stopping in shops and gardens and musuems, or by taking a detour down Barracks Street to the river. Temperatures from December through February make all but early morning strolls very uncomfortable, which follows from the general principle to visit Western Australia in its spring or fall.

Sights to See

⑫ **Alan Green Conservatory.** A glass pyramid that dominates the neat Esplanade lawns, the conservatory houses a wide variety of rare and remarkable exotic plants in a carefully controlled environment. ⊠ *William St. and Esplanade,* ☎ *08/9265–3145.* ☎ *Free.* ☼ *Mon.–Sat. 10–5, Sun. 2–6.*

⑯ **Barracks Arch.** This, the city's oddest architectural curiosity, stands more or less in front of the seat of government—the highway actually comes between them. This brick monument is all that remains of the headquarters of the Pensioner Forces, which was demolished in 1966. The Tudor-style edifice, built in the 1860s in Flemish bond brickwork, is a memorial to the earliest settlers. ⊠ *St. George's Terr. and Malcolm St.*

❻ **Central Fire Station.** This relatively new building, of no particular architectural or historical merit, nevertheless provides a distinctive landmark for the odd visitor who gets disoriented or doesn't speak English. ⊠ *Hay St. between Twin and Victoria Sts.*

❷ **Citiplace.** This pedestrian mall has become the stage for a wide variety of street theater and free outdoor concerts. ⊠ *Forrest Pl. opposite post office.*

⑮ **The Cloisters.** Erected in 1858 to serve as the city's first boys' high school, the Cloisters remnant now stands in memory of its former life. The facade has been preserved as the front for a multistory shop and office complex distanced far enough by elevators so as not to compromise its remaining heritage value. ⊠ *200 St. George's Terr.*

❸ **Forrest Chase Shopping Plaza.** This shop-plex, with its myriad merchants and Myer department store (☞ Shopping, *below*), was considered important enough to warrant a royal opening at the hands of Elizabeth II, by the Grace of God, Queen of Australia, during a state visit to Australia. ⊠ *Murray St. between Forrest Pl. and Barrack St.*

⑪ **Francis Burt Law Centre.** A former courthouse and the oldest public city building, this charming 1836 Georgian building sits in the **Supreme Court Gardens.** The building now contains the **W.A. Law Museum** memorabilia and an audiovisual presentation. ⊠ *Supreme Court Gardens,* ☎ *08/9325–4787.* ☎ *Free.* ☼ *Feb.–Dec., Tues. and Thurs. 10–2.*

❶ **General Post Office.** The handsome, colonnaded sandstone building forms an impressive backdrop to the city's major public square, ☞ **Citiplace.** ⊠ *Forrest Pl.*

❾ **Government House.** Built between 1859 and 1864, this is the official residence of the governor and home to members of the royal family during visits to Perth. It was constructed in a Gothic Revival style, with arches and turrets reminiscent of the Tower of London. ⊠ *Supreme Court Gardens.*

⑱ **His Majesty's Theatre** at the King Street corner is among Perth's most gracious buildings, and restoration has transformed it into a handsome home for the Western Australian opera and ballet companies. Tour guides are usually available; call ahead. ⊠ *825 Hay St.,* ☎ *08/9322–2929.* ☎ *Free.* ☼ *Weekdays 10–4.*

☼ **It's a Small World.** A wonderland for children and their parents, this museum of toys and miniatures from around the world displays doll-houses, train stations, and a Formula 1 racing car just 6½ ft long. ⊠ *12 Parliament Pl.,* ☎ *08/9322–2020.* 🎟 *$5.* ☼ *Sun.–Fri. 10–5, Sat. 2–5.*

7 **Law Courts.** Here, over the last four years, some of the nation's no longer wealthy entrepreneurs, along with two of the state's premiers (one a former ambassador to Ireland) and a deputy-premier have been sentenced to terms of imprisonment for mismanaging their own and the publics' financial affairs. The debacle was so widespread it became known under the collective title of W.A. Inc., and it took a Royal Commission (the equivalent of a Senate Inquiry) to winkle out why the public purse had gone from prosperity to poverty in less than 10 years. Repercussions still echo in the corridors of power at both state and federal levels. ⊠ *30 St. George's Terr.*

19 **London Court.** A magnet for buskers and anyone with a camera, this outdoor shopping arcade was built in 1937 by gold-mining entrepreneur Claude de Bernales. Along its length you'll find statues of Sir Walter Raleigh and Dick Whittington, the legendary lord mayor of London. Costumed mechanical knights joust with one another when the clock strikes the quarter hour. Its mock-Tudor facade is considered less than attractive by many, but most Western Australians stoutly defend it. The row of shops runs north to south between Hay Street Mall and St. George's Terrace.

4 **Old Fire Station.** The old limestone fire station is a fine colonial structure. No longer operational, it is now a museum housing a photographic exhibit of the history of the fire brigade—from its beginnings, when it used horses and carts, to the present day—as well as a splendid display of old vehicles and equipment. ⊠ *Murray and Irwin Sts.,* ☎ *08/9323–9300.* 🎟 *Free.* ☼ *Weekdays 10–3.*

14 **Old Perth Boys School.** Erected in 1854 in the Gothic Revival style so popular with colonial architects, the old school is yet another example of the acquired masonry skills of those early convicts, many of whom were Irish political prisoners. It is now used as the gift shop for the National Trust in Western Australia. ⊠ *139 St. George's Terr.,* ☎ *08/9321–2754.* ☼ *Weekdays 9–5.*

17 **Parliament House.** From its position at the top of St. George's Terrace, Parliament House dominates Perth's skyline and serves as a respectable backdrop for the ☞ **Barracks Arch** remnant. Shady old Moreton Bay Fig Trees and landscaped gardens make the lodge of Western Australian government one of the most pleasant aspects in the city. Yet because of its location atop the main thoroughfare, and because the freeway comes between it and the city proper, Parliament House doesn't get much pedestrian traffic. Call the Parliamentary Information Officer to arrange a weekday tour. ⊠ *St. George's and Harvest Terrs.,* ☎ *08/9222–7222.*

Perth Concert Hall. At the time it was built in the '60s, this small concert hall by world standards was considered both elegant and architecturally impressive. Although its architectural merit may seem questionable to some, its acoustics are clear, and it still serves as the city's focus for the arts. ⊠ *5 St. George's Terr.,* ☎ *08/9325–9944.*

13 **R&I Tower.** The 1988 tower wraps around the historic old **Palace Hotel**, now used for bank offices. The hotel is a fine example of the ornate architecture that once dominated the city. ⊠ *St. George's Terr. and William St.*

8 St. George's Cathedral. The church and its **Deanery** form one of the city's most distinctive old world complexes. Built during the late 1850s as a home for the first dean of Perth, the Deanery is one of the few remaining houses in Western Australia from this period. It is now used as offices for the Anglican Church. ⊠ *Pier St. and St. George's Terr.*

5 St. Mary's Cathedral. Victoria Square, one of Perth's most appealing plazas, is the happy home of St. Mary's. Its environs house the headquarters for the Catholic Church.

Scitech Discovery Centre is an interactive display of science and technology that entertains children of all ages while they learn. ⊠ *City West, West Perth,* ☎ *08/9481–6295.* ⊡ *$10.* ☉ *Daily 10–5.*

10 Supreme Court Gardens. This favorite lunch spot for hundreds of office workers is home to some of the finest Moreton Bay fig trees in the state. In the rear of the gardens is a band shell used for summer concerts. ⊠ *Barrack St. and Adelaide Terr.*

20 Town Hall. During the 1860s, convict labor built this hall in the style of a Jacobean English market. ⊠ *Hay and Barrack Sts.*

Around Perth

Cohunu Wildlife Park. Don't come to Cohunu just for a cuddle session with a live koala (daily between 11 and 4); take time to view other native animals in natural surroundings, ride a miniature railway, and wander through the largest aviary in the Southern Hemisphere, too. ⊠ *Mills Rd., Gosnells,* ☎ *08/9390–6090.* ⊡ *$9.* ☉ *Daily 10–5.*

Museum of Childhood. Recognized internationally as a pioneer in the conservation of childhood heritage in Australia, the museum is an enchanting hands-on journey for both children and parents. Among its most prized exhibits is an original alphabet manuscript written, illustrated, and bound by William Makepeace Thackeray in 1833. And there are displays of dolls from around the world. ⊠ *Edith Cowan University Campus, Bay Rd., Claremont,* ☎ *08/9442–1373.* ⊡ *$2.* ☉ *Weekdays 10–4.*

Underwater World. Ride a moving walkway through a submerged acrylic tunnel to view some 2,500 examples of 200 marine species, including sharks and stingrays. A dolphin pool allows you to see these marine mammals up close. ⊠ *Hillary's Boat Harbour, West Coast Hwy.,* ☎ *08/9447–7500.* ⊡ *$13.90.* ☉ *Daily 9–5.*

Whiteman Park. This enormous recreation area has barbecue facilities and picnic spots, cycle trails, vintage trains and electric trams, and historic wagons and tractors. In an arts-and-crafts section of the park, you can watch potters, blacksmiths, leather workers, toy makers, printers, and stained-glass artists at work. Naturally, wildlife includes kangaroos. ⊠ *Lord St., Whiteman Park,* ☎ *08/9249–2446.* ⊡ *$3 per car.* ☉ *Daily 9–6.*

Dining

By Peter Forrestal and Helen Ayers

Dining out in Perth is the only consistent form of entertainment in the state, and it can be expensive. At the same time, new restaurants, snack bars, and food halls spring up incessantly, providing a fair amount of culinary variety to choose from. Northbridge, northwest of the railway station, is the new dining and nightclubbing center of Perth, where reasonably priced restaurants proliferate.

Asian

$$ ✕ Emperor's Court. One of the most awarded Asian restaurants in Perth, Emperor's Court serves a variety of provincial Chinese dishes, from

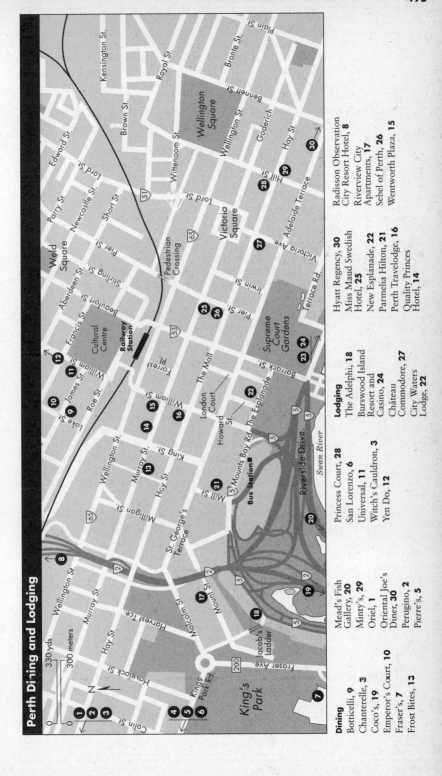

Perth Dining and Lodging

Dining

Botticelli, 9
Chanterelle, 3
Coco's, 19
Emperor's Court, 10
Fraser's, 7
Frost Bites, 13

Mead's Fish
Gallery, 20
Minty's, 29
Oriel, 1
Oriental Joe's
Diner, 30
Perugino, 2
Pierre's, 5

Princess Court, 28
San Lorenzo, 6
Universal, 11
Witch's Cauldron, 3
Yen Do, 12

Lodging

The Adelphi, 18
Burswood Island
Resort and
Casino, 24
Château
Commodore, 27
City Waters
Lodge, 22

Hyatt Regency, 30
Miss Maud Swedish
Hotel, 25
New Esplanade, 22
Parmelia Hilton, 21
Perth Travelodge, 16
Quality Princes
Hotel, 14

Radisson Observation
City Resort Hotel, 8
Riverview City
Apartments, 17
Sebel of Perth, 26
Wentworth Plaza, 15

ever popular hot and spicy Szechuan fare to the sweet and savory southern food of Canton to the imperial tastes of old Peking. The Hong Kong Dim Sum and Yum Cha is the most highly prized in Perth, and you can find it on the luncheon menu. Western Australian seafood appears frequently in an array of dishes, from fish to seasonal mud crabs, crayfish, and yabbies—the combinations seem endless. ⊠ *66 Lake St., Northbridge,* ☎ *08/9328–1628. AE, DC, MC, V.*

$$ ✕ **Princess Court.** At Perth's choice for karaoke, tuck into tasty Chinese food before you get into some sing-a-long and dancing, which can make for a fun night on the town. Hong Kong–trained chefs prepare an excellent barbecued Peking duck, and locally caught Western Australian seafood is the perfect ingredient for whole baked fish, or garlic prawns—possibly the best in the city. Crayfish and mud crabs are available seasonally. ⊠ *326 Hay St., at Hill St., Perth,* ☎ *08/9325–1230 or 08/9325–1529. AE, DC, MC, V.*

$ ✕ **Oriental Joe's Diner.** This theme restaurant in the Hyatt Regency serves tasty Asian food at very reasonable prices. Wood, natural brick, terra-cotta, and teak antiques are used to reinforce the theme, and Thai, Indonesian, Malaysian, and Singaporean dishes are whipped up in the display kitchen. Filling soups are complemented by a delicious range of such noodle dishes as *kway teow* (noodles with bean sprouts, prawn, and chicken), or *laksa* (rice noodles in a rich, spicy, coconut-milk soup with chicken, bean curd, and prawns). Also try Thai green chicken curry and *nasi goreng* (Indonesian fried rice) with chicken and beef *satay* (marinated and served with a peanut sauce). ⊠ *99 Adelaide Terr.,* ☎ *08/9225–1268. AE, DC, MC, V. Closed Sun. No lunch Sat.*

$ ✕ **Yen Do.** Although this popular restaurant specializes in Chinese cooking, it also serves Vietnamese, Indian, and Malaysian food. Situated on the outskirts of Northbridge, Yen Do consists of a single large room with an open kitchen area in back. Laminated tables are packed close together, but everything is spotless, and the service is quick and efficient. Most important, the food is consistently good—and cheap. In addition to daily specials there are Chinese noodle dishes; half a dozen soups; such appetizers as spring rolls, satay, curry puffs, and samosa; such specialties as mussels, Mongolian chicken, and, for lunch, curry laksa. ⊠ *416 William St., Northbridge,* ☎ *08/9227–8833. Reservations essential. AE, DC, MC, V. BYOB.*

Australian

$$$ ✕ **San Lorenzo.** This elegant restaurant with its stone paving, limestone walls, wall fountain, and sprawling grapevine, continues to hold pride of place in Perth. Such fare as pork fricassee, with black pudding and mashed potatoes suggests an English culinary style, but anyone who has tried twice-cooked Kervella goat-cheese soufflé—or Moroccan fried chicken with couscous, spicy tomato sauce, eggplant tahini, chick-pea chips, chorizo sausage, and preserved lemon—can attest to the success of contemporary dishes as well. There is a very good wine list, or you can bring your own bottle. San Lorenzo is a 15-minute cab ride from the city. ⊠ *23 Victoria Ave., Claremont,* ☎ *08/9384–0870. Reservations essential. AE, DC, MC, V. Closed Sun. and Mon. No lunch Sat.*

$$$ ✕ **Witch's Cauldron.** All ambience and elegance, this is where the local populace has eaten for 26 years, bewitching it with its bubbling array of fine food. An intimate bar sets the mood for a relaxed lunch or dinner. A house specialty is fresh fish, grilled or fried, and served with lemon sauce. Just dip into the comprehensive à la carte menu, supplemented by daily specials, and find yourself pleasantly satiated. ⊠ *89 Rokeby Rd., Subiaco,* ☎ *08/9381–2508. AE, DC, MC, V. Closed Sun.*

$$ ✕ **Coco's.** A great location on the river in South Perth, trendy patrons, and fine food have made this one of the city's most popular restau-

rants. No one seems to mind that the comfortable furniture is too close together or that the restaurant is often packed and noisy. After all, the floor-to-ceiling windows show off fabulous views of the Perth waterfront and the city skyline, the food is consistently well prepared, and the service is speedy and efficient. There are 15 items on the à la carte menu—many of which are available in either appetizer or main-course portions—as well as daily seafood, beef, and dessert specials. The beef, aged in the restaurant's own cool room, has a formidable reputation: Try char-grilled Waroona rib eye with steamed new potatoes and Madeira and mushroom sauce. Seafood dishes are always fresh, and simply yet imaginatively presented. Dhufish, a local specialty, is particularly good. ⊠ *Southshore Centre, 85 The Esplanade, South Perth,* ☎ *08/9474–3030. Reservations essential. AE, DC, MC, V.*

$$ ✗ **Fraser's.** This elegant, bilevel restaurant has vistas of the city and Swan River. When the weather is good—most of the time in Perth—the large outdoor area fills with happy diners. The menu changes daily and emphasizes local seafood. Recent standouts include lobster chargrilled or panfried with lemon butter sauce, fillet of Atlantic salmon char-grilled and served with fresh asparagus and walnut herb paste, and roast loin of kangaroo with baby beetroot and Spanish onions on a vegetable pancake. ⊠ *Fraser Ave., King's Park,* ☎ *08/9481–7100. Reservations essential. AE, DC, MC, V.*

Brasseries and Cafés

$$ ✗ **Frost Bites.** This is one of the brightest brasseries in town, near the center of the business district. A day-long menu runs the gauntlet from coffee and cakes to char-grilled chicken, from foccacia to spanking-fresh fish, varieties of pizza baked in a wood-fired oven, and salads. At night the emphasis turns to a bar with attitude, where 14 luridly colored portholes deliver dynamite cocktails. Dinner is available on Thursday, and Friday and Saturday nights offer a snack menu only. A bar and billiards area is available for those with more than a meal on their minds. ⊠ *397 Murray St., at Shafto La.,* ☎ *08/9321–3258. AE, DC, MC, V. Closed Sun. No dinner Mon.–Wed.*

$$ ✗ **Oriel.** Ten minutes from the city center lies the quintessential Perth brasserie: Both the dimly lit interior and the outdoor areas are crowded with tables and overflow with people and noise for most of the 24 hours the restaurant is open (breakfast is served 2 AM–11:30 AM). The food is imaginative and tasty. Try carpaccio of ocean trout with crunchy Chinese pastry, virgin olive oil, and roasted peppers, or Provençal lamb burger with eggplant, tomato, greens, bacon, char-grilled onions, and béarnaise sauce. Coffee is always superb, as is the range of cakes, and an impressive wine list offers more than 20 varieties by the glass. ⊠ *483 Hay St., Subiaco,* ☎ *08/9382–1886. Reservations not accepted. AE, MC, V.*

$$ ✗ **Universal.** Renovations to Northbridge's best café have softened the decor, adding warmth and intimacy to the dining room while placing more emphasis on the bar area. You can expect regular changes in the globally influenced menu, too, although char-grilled duck confit, fillet steak with béarnaise sauce, Thai green curry, and Caesar salad are perennial favorites. Risotto, some pasta dishes, fish of the day, and an antipasto bar plate also make frequent appearances. Expect good coffee, tasty cakes, and an extensive wine list, which always includes rare bottles and about 20 varieties available for a reasonable price by the glass. ⊠ *221 William St., Northbridge,* ☎ *08/9227–6771. AE, MC, V.*

French

$$$ ✗ **Pierre's.** A beautifully restored colonial mansion poses as Perth's grandest restaurant. Service is impeccable, the decor opulent, the furniture elegant, the lighting soft—even the tableware is of the highest quality. Chef Gweneal Lesle uses both imported luxuries—snails, foie gras, and Iranian caviar—and such prime local produce as marron (a freshwater crustacean), pigeon, lamb, and venison in his rich, traditional French dishes. Try medallions of marron wrapped in lettuce and served in a shiraz wine–and-crustacean sauce or boned roast pigeon with lentils, chorizo tart, and date purée. Lesle's bread and butter pudding is a subtle rendition of the homey original. The wine list is outstanding. ⊠ *8 Outram St., West Perth,* ☎ *08/9322–7648. Reservations essential. Jacket required. AE, DC, MC, V. No lunch weekends.*

$$ ✕ **Chanterelle.** A Scottish couple, the Peastons, serve high-quality food without pretension at this popular BYOB restaurant in Subiaco, 10 minutes from downtown. Located in a converted house, the elegant dining area offers a happy blend of formality and friendliness. The menu offers rich dishes from the traditional French repertoire, such as a trio of cream soups and some of the best savory and sweet soufflés in town, as well as lighter, more contemporary preparations. Confit of duck and potato terrine with onion marmalade, Atlantic salmon with cucumbers and English spinach, and grilled emu fillet with sautéed beet and deep-fried celery are all noteworthy. ⊠ *210 Rokeby Rd., Subiaco,* ☎ *08/9381–4637. Reservations essential. AE, DC, MC, V. BYOB. Closed Sun. and Mon. No lunch Sat.*

$$ ✕ **Minty's.** Across from the Perth Mint, Minty's is notable for its French windows, intimate dining areas, and large bar, which dominates the entrance hall. The short menu changes every few weeks and is varied enough to satisfy all tastes. Asparagus in a pastry case with mousseline sauce, medallions of lamb with an herb crust, and whole roast pink snapper on a bed of artichokes, mushrooms, and broad beans are typical of Minty's fresh, flavorsome, and well-presented dishes. The wine list is comprehensive, reasonably priced, and includes a dozen kinds of wine by the glass. ⊠ *309 Hay St., East Perth,* ☎ *08/9325–5299. AE, DC, MC, V. Closed Mon. No lunch weekends.*

Italian

$$ ✕ **Botticelli.** This dark, comfortable restaurant in the heart of Northbridge serves traditional Italian food to a faithful clientele. Veal and lamb dishes are a specialty, so consider trying char-grilled lamb chops, veal rib, or veal medallions panfried with hazelnuts and balsamic vinegar. If pasta is more to your taste, order spinach gnocchi with three-cheese sauce, or spaghetti with a chicken and pistachio sauce. The daily antipasto selection is also a good bet. ⊠ *147 James St., Northbridge,* ☎ *08/9328–3422. AE, DC, MC, V. Closed Sun. No lunch Sat.*

$$ ✕ **Perugino.** This Perth institution is an impressive place for business
★   lunches, romantic trysts, or formal dinners, and chef Giuseppe Pagliaricci's use of fresh produce and his imaginative yet simple approach to the cuisine of his native Umbria are the major reasons. Look for *scottadito* (baby goat chops grilled with olive oil and herbs) and *coniglio* (farm-raised rabbit in a tomato sauce with garlic and chilies). The à la carte menu is supplemented with numerous seasonal specials—usually several excellent risotto and pasta dishes in tasty combination with spinach, ricotta, and chicken. The staff is among the most professional, knowledgeable, and good-humored in town. ⊠ *77 Outram St., West Perth,* ☎ *08/9321–5420. Reservations essential. AE, DC, MC, V. Closed Sun. No lunch Sat.*

Seafood

$$$ ✕ **Mead's Fish Gallery.** Visitors to Mead's, a 15-minute cab ride from
★   town, are frequently divided about whether the setting, on the Swan River surrounded by yachts and mansions of W.A.'s elite, or the seafood is more spectacular. Indoor or outdoor dining is available, both around

an enormous tank that harbors fish for viewing, not consuming—though the owners sometimes have difficulty conveying this to a magnificent rufus heron that is a constant visitor. Feast on the likes of sashimi of Tasmanian salmon, Thai parcel of king prawns and snapper served with fresh mango, or char-grilled baby squid in chili, while gazing at a squadron of pelicans gliding lazily over the shallow water of the river. The service, overseen by owners Warren and Linda Mead, is as outstanding as the wine list. ⊠ *15 Johnson Parade, Mosman Park,* ☎ *08/9383–3388. AE, DC, MC, V. Closed Mon. and Tues.*

Lodging

$$$$ ⊞ **Burswood Island Resort and Casino.** In keeping with its architec-
★ tural style, Burswood is genuinely a distinctive luxury resort, from the top of its 10-story glass atrium to the last blade of grass on its 18-hole golf course. The rooms are as lush as the public spaces, each featuring a Japanese-fashioned bathroom with sliding screen doors and a view of either the river or the city. Suites have Jacuzzis. The adjoining casino, basic in comfort and style, is the largest in the southern hemisphere, and it stays open around the clock for roulette, blackjack, baccarat, keno, craps, and two-up, as does its cabaret. ⊠ *Private Bag 456, Great Eastern Hwy., Victoria Park, Bentley 6983,* ☎ *08/9362–7777,* FAX *08/9470–2553. 394 rooms with bath, 16 suites. 6 restaurants, 7 bars, pool, sauna, spa, 18-hole golf course, 4 tennis courts, health club. AE, DC, MC, V.*

$$$$ ⊞ **Hyatt Regency.** With a picture postcard setting on the banks of the
★ Swan River, the Hyatt is within walking distance of Perth's central business district. Rooms are tasteful and spacious. Other facilities include a business center and two floors of Regency Club, the "hotel within a hotel" concept, in which room rates include a complimentary Continental breakfast and drinks and canapés in the evening. Regency Club rooms and suites have a private elevator and stunning views of either Perth or the Swan River. ⊠ *99 Adelaide Terr., Perth 6000,* ☎ *08/9225–1234,* FAX *08/9325–8899 or 08/9325–8785. 367 rooms with bath. 3 restaurants, 2 bars, pool, health club. AE, DC, MC, V.*

$$$$ ⊞ **Parmelia Hilton.** The unique Parmelia is full of antiques, and you'll gaze upon a Chinese silk tapestry or Mussolini's mirror as you await the elevator. Most rooms are furnished in a contemporary style, with blue carpets, cream walls, and rosewood reproduction Queen Anne furniture. Suites are appointed with damask fabrics, original artwork, and antique furniture, and each enjoys river views, and other rooms overlook the hotel pool and cityscape. Now a Hilton, the Parmelia was originally an independent hotel. ⊠ *Mill St., Perth 6000,* ☎ *08/9322–3622,* FAX *08/9481–0857. 222 rooms with bath, 53 suites. Restaurants, bars, pool, sauna, health club. AE, DC, MC, V.*

$$$$ ⊞ **Radisson Observation City Resort Hotel.** Watching the sun sink into
★ the Indian Ocean from this luxury beachside resort is a great experience, as is a meal in the hotel's restaurant, the Ocean Room. The peppermint, salmon, and blue color scheme in public rooms is offset by predominantly pastel guest rooms, each of which has an ocean view. The elegant decor is highlighted by marble bathrooms and mirrored wardrobes. ⊠ *The Esplanade, Scarborough 6019,* ☎ *08/9245–1000,* FAX *08/9245–1345. 336 rooms with bath, 5 suites. 5 restaurants, 4 bars, sauna, spa, 2 tennis courts, exercise room. AE, DC, MC, V.*

$$$ ⊞ **Château Commodore.** One of Perth's older hotels, the Château Commodore enjoys a reputation for quality and has garnered a loyal following. Rooms are spacious and decorated in shades of blue, green, and pink, with white and blue carpets. Request one with a view. ⊠

417 Hay St., Perth 6000, ☎ 08/9325–0461, FAX 08/9221–2448. 133 rooms with bath. Restaurant, pool. AE, DC, MC, V.

$$$ 🏨 **Perth Travelodge.** Within a stone's throw of the central business district, major shopping areas, cinemas, and restaurants, this Travelodge's location is hard to beat. The property proved so popular that 100 rooms were added in 1995. Its spacious rooms are a relaxing pale peppermint with dark blue-green bedspreads. The bar and brasserie, with warm terra-cotta tiles and wrought-iron furniture, have a Mediterranean feel. An added bonus is the only indoor heated hotel pool in Perth. ✉ 778 Hay St., 6000, ☎ 08/9321–9141, FAX 08/9481–2250. 82 rooms with bath, 1 suite. Restaurant, bar, pool, sauna, spa, health club, laundry. AE, DC, MC, V.

$$$ 🏨 **Sebel of Perth.** Quiet and unassuming, this attractive hotel is close to the central business district and entertainment quarter. Ruby's, an award-winning restaurant with a Mediterranean feel, is located adjacent to the hotel. The south side of the building features apricot-color furnishings, and some of the higher floors have fine views of the Swan River; the cooler north side, which most guests find more appealing, is bedecked with green, modern, light wood furniture. The hotel's 32 suites have been fitted with brocade bedspreads and American cherrywood furniture. ✉ 37 Pier St., 6000, ☎ FAX 08/9325–7655. 120 rooms with bath. Restaurant, bar, pool. AE, DC, MC, V.

$–$$$ 🏨 **Wentworth Plaza.** A Federation-era hotel, the Wentworth has been merged with the equally old Royal on Wellington Street to form one large, grand hotel. The Wentworth recaptures period ambience in its rooms, with a variety of accommodations ranging from two-room apartments to single rooms with private bath to traditional rooms on the Royal Hotel side that share facilities. Downstairs, Garage Bar, Horsefeathers, and Moon and Sixpence are popular watering holes where you can rub shoulders with the local populace. Parking is free for hotel guests. ✉ 300 Murray St., Perth, ☎ 08/9481–1000. 96 rooms. 3 bars, coin laundry. AE, DC, MC, V.

$$ 🏨 **Miss Maud Swedish Hotel.** Old World charm and a delicious Nordic
★ breakfast are two things that make this a Perth favorite. In a centrally located 1911 building, the Miss Maud has the Scandinavian feeling you would expect, with pine furniture and a blue-and-gold color scheme. At the Miss Maud Restaurant and Coffee Shop, famous smorgasbord delicacies bring customers back time and again. ✉ 97 Murray St., 6000, ☎ 08/9325–3900, FAX 08/9221–3225. 51 rooms with bath. Restaurant, room service. AE, DC, MC, V.

$$ 🏨 **New Esplanade.** Ideally situated on the Esplanade, this hotel enjoys the same million-dollar view of the Swan River for which flamboyant mining tycoons have forked over fortunes. And it is just a chopstick's toss from the Grand Palace, one of the more popular Chinese restaurants in town. Rooms are comfortable, decorated in shades of green and cream, with contrasting teak woodwork. ✉ 18 The Esplanade, 6000, ☎ 08/9325–2000, FAX 08/9221–2190. 85 rooms with bath. Restaurant, bar. AE, DC, MC, V.

$$ 🏨 **Quality Princes Hotel.** Closer to the shopping and nightclub action than many central city hotels, the Princes is efficient and pleasant, a firm favorite with visiting U.S. military personnel. Rooms are compact but cheerful, decorated with pinks and blues and light, modern furniture. ✉ 334 Murray St., 6000, ☎ 08/9322–2844, FAX 08/9321–6314. 152 rooms, 20 suites. Restaurant, bar. AE, DC, MC, V.

$ 🏨 **The Adelphi.** One of the most delightful aspects of this property is
★ its location. Although the main thoroughfare running alongside it can be noisy, the hotel sits at the bottom of King's Park bluff opposite the duck-filled lakes of the freeway parklands. An enormously popular self-catering facility, its neat and airy rooms, all of which face the city sky-

line, are decorated with chintz sofas, jarrah coffee tables, and gray and pink furnishings. Rooms on the higher floors have views of the river. ⊠ *130A Mounts Bay Rd., 6000,* ☎ *08/9322–4666,* FAX *08/9322–4580. 61 rooms with bath. Laundry. AE, DC, MC, V.*

$ ⊡ **City Waters Lodge.** Though far removed from the excitement of downtown, these self-catering units are nonetheless quite pleasant. Guest rooms are bright and cheerful; some feature rather old, heavy furniture, and others have pine lounges with pretty floral cushions. The lodge is only a short distance from the river, but only three units have views. Request Room 201, which has a separate sitting room. ⊠ *118 Terrace Rd., 6000,* ☎ *08/9325–1566,* FAX *08/9479–1537. 70 rooms with bath. Room service, laundry. AE, MC, V.*

$ ⊡ **Riverview City Apartments.** Situated in one of the city's most prestigious residential areas, these serviced units are just a short stroll from both the city and King's Park. The rooms are clean and adequate, if somewhat dated, and they are equipped with cooking facilities. ⊠ *42 Mount St., 6000,* ☎ *08/9321–8963,* FAX *08/9322–5956. 50 rooms with bath. AE, MC, V.*

Nightlife and the Arts

The arts scene in Perth is dominated by local talent, although the acclaimed **Festival of Perth,** held in February and March in venues throughout the city, attracts world-class names in music, dance, and theater. Further information is available from the Festival of Perth office (⊠ University of Western Australia, Mounts Bay Rd., Crawley 6009, ☎ 08/9386–7977). Full details on all cultural events in Perth are contained in a comprehensive guide in every Saturday edition of *The West Australian.* A free weekly, *X-Press Magazine,* comprehensively lists music, concerts, and movies, runs reviews, and has a gig guide of who's playing at pubs, clubs, and hotels. Both are widely available.

Ballet

The **West Australian Ballet Company,** at His Majesty's Theatre (☞ *above*), runs four annual short seasons, presenting traditional ballets, the best of modern dance (such as Balanchine) and new experimental and contemporary dance, in February, May, June, and October.

Bars

Until the Matilda Bay Brewing Company opened a few years ago, Perth bars were generally lacking in character and charm. The brew pub has set a new standard for drinking establishments in Western Australia, and architect Michael Patroni has transformed a number of Perth's dilapidated bars into stylish, popular spots, like the **Brass Monkey Pub and Brasserie** (⊠ 209 William St., Northbridge, ☎ 08/9227–9596), the **Queen's Tavern** (⊠ 520 Beaufort St., Highgate, ☎ 08/9328–7267), the **Oriel Cafe and Brasserie** (⊠ 483 Hay St., Subiaco, ☎ 08/9382–1886), and the **Vic** (⊠ 226 Hay St., Subiaco, ☎ 08/9380–0868). The **Adelphi** (⊠ 130A Mounts Bay Rd., ☎ 08/9322–3622) in the Hilton is a swank wine bar and coffee shop, where waiters are energetic and beer flows from brass pumps, though the **Astoria** (⊠ 37 Bay View Terr., Claremont, ☎ 08/9384–1372) is *the* place to go, at any hour, among Perth's young socialites. It's the last word in West Coast chic.

Concerts

Regular recitals by the excellent West Australian Symphony Orchestra as well as Australian and international artists are held at the **Perth Concert Hall** (⊠ 5 St. George's Terr., ☎ 08/9325–9944), a modern building overlooking the Swan River.

Nightclubs and Music

Most luxury hotels in Perth have upscale nightclubs that appeal to the over-30 crowd. The **Burswood Island Resort** (✉ Great Eastern Hwy., Victoria Park, ☎ 08/9362–7777) has its Las Vegas–style cabaret, with national and international artists. **Margeaux's** at the Parmelia Hilton (✉ Mill St., ☎ 08/9322–3622), **Chicago's** at the Orchard (✉ 707 Wellington St., ☎ 08/9327–7000), and **Orsini's** at the Sheraton (✉ 207 Adelaide Terr., ☎ 08/9325–0501) have discos for a more sophisticated crowd. Along more sedate lines, the **Piano Bar** at the Sheraton and the **Millstrasse** at the Parmelia Hilton accompany drinks with piano music.

Jazz and blues lovers can slake their thirst at three popular places: **Hyde Park Hotel** (✉ 331 Bulwer St., North Perth, ☎ 08/9328–6166), a no-nonsense Aussie pub with contemporary jazz Monday night and Dixieland Tuesday night; and for blues Tuesday night, the **Charles Hotel** (✉ 509 Charles St., North Perth, ☎ 08/9444–1051) and the **Grosvenor Hotel** (✉ 339 Hay St., ☎ 08/9325–3799). **The Globe** (✉ 393 Murray St., ☎ 08/9481–2521) has a new, stylish mix of '50s, '60s, and '70s decor, plus live bands and DJs, and draws a 20-something crowd. **Exit** (✉ 187 Stirling St., ☎ 08/9227–8200), one of the most popular spots in the Northbridge area, draws the 18–25 age group with Top-40 hits. Midway between Perth and Fremantle is **Club Bay View** (✉ 20 St. Quentin's Ave., Claremont, ☎ 08/9385–1331), an upmarket cocktail bar-cum-nightclub, which caters to the well-heeled stockbroker set.

Opera

The **West Australian Opera Company** presents three seasons annually in April, August, and November—also at His Majesty's Theatre (☞ *below*). The company's repertoire includes classical opera, Gilbert and Sullivan operettas, and occasional musicals.

Theater

His Majesty's Theatre (✉ 825 Hay St., ☎ 08/9322–2929) opened in 1904, was restored in 1980, and is loved by all who have stepped inside. It is the home of most theatrical productions in Perth. **The Playhouse** (✉ Pier St., ☎ 08/9325–3344), the **Regal Theatre** (✉ 47 Hay St., Subiaco, ☎ 08/9381–5522), and the **Hole in the Wall** (✉ 180 Hamersley Rd., Subiaco, ☎ 08/9381–3694) also feature regular productions.

Outdoor Activities and Sports

Australian Rules Football

Legend has it this unique blend of soccer and Gaelic football first came to life in Melbourne as an off-season activity for the Australian cricket team, and until quite recently it was known as Victorian Rules Football. Now a national game with teams competing from every state, the Australian Football League (AFL) plays every second Saturday afternoon throughout the winter (March–September) at Subiaco Oval, and the local league WAFL continues to play every Saturday at various locations around the metropolitan area. For details, contact the **Western Australia Football Commission Inc.** (☎ 08/9381–5599).

Beaches

Perth's beaches and waterways are among its greatest attractions—plan to make an excursion to the seaside during your stay.

Leighton beach is for windsurfers and the astonishing wave jumpers (who ride Windsurfers against the surf to hurl themselves airborne); **Cottesloe** for young matrons and well-heeled stock exchange executives; **North Cottesloe** for dogs and topless bathers, and the popular

Swanbourne for those wearing even less. Traveling north of the city you come to **Scarborough,** the beach favored by teenagers and young adults and **City Beach,** just 11½ km (7 mi) outside Perth, is more sedate. **Trigg** is home to the surfboard crowd.

Bicycling
The vast network of trails in and around the city, particularly in King's Park, makes cycling a pleasure in Perth. Details on trails and free brochures are available from the **Western Australia Tourist Centre** (⊠ Forrest Pl. and Wellington St., ☎ 08/9483–1111).

Cricket
The national game is played professionally during the summer at the **Western Australia Cricket Association** (WACA) grounds in Nelson Crescent, East Perth. For further information, contact the WACA (☎ 08/9325–9800).

Golf
Perth is home to numerous public golf courses, and each of them rents out clubs. The 18-hole course at **Burswood Resort** (⊠ Great Eastern Hwy., Victoria Park, ☎ 08/9362–7576) is closest to the city. Call the **Western Australia Golf Association** (☎ 08/9474–1005) for further details. **Golf Escort** (☎ 08/9357–5758) is a unique service for golfers who wish to play on Perth's most exclusive courses, most of which are not normally open to the public. It includes limousine service, quality clubs, a motorized buggy, greens fees, and of course a golfing partner.

Health Clubs
Health clubs with spas, saunas, and exercise equipment are available to guests at most luxury hotels.

Lifesport's fitness center is medically supervised, with aerobics, three Olympic-size heated pools, and an in-house physiotherapist, a dietician, and an exercise physiologist. There is a newer location in Joondalup, the most up-to-the-minute center in the Perth area. It is half an hour by train from the city, if you want to combine a workout with a little sightseeing in Perth's fastest growing suburb. ⊠ *Superdrome, Stephenson Ave., Mt. Claremont,* ☎ *08/9387–2699;* ⊠ *Sanori House, Grand Blvd. and Reid Promenade, Joondalup,* ☎ *09300–3033.* ☜ *$8.* ⊙ *Mon.–Wed. 6 AM–9 PM, Thurs. and Fri. 6 AM–8 PM, Sat. 8–4, Sun. 9–4.*

Lords Sports Club features fitness equipment, aerobics, a heated indoor pool, indoor tennis and squash courts, sauna, and spa. ⊠ *588 Hay St., Subiaco,* ☎ *08/9381–4777.* ☜ *$15.* ⊙ *Weekdays 6 AM–9 PM, weekends 8–6.*

Motorcycling
A perfect way to enjoy Perth's Mediterranean climate comes from **Deluxe Harley Tours** (☎ 08/9221–2525), which offers excursions from one to eight hours on a Harley Davidson bike.

Running
A number of jogging tracks lead along the Swan River and through King's Park.

Swimming
Aside from Perth's glorious beaches, the three Olympic-size pools of **Superdrome** allow for a little inland swimming. ⊠ *Stephenson Ave., Mt. Claremont,* ☎ *08/9441–8222.* ☜ *$3.* ⊙ *Weekdays 5:30 AM–9:30 PM, Sat. 5:30 AM–6 PM, Sun. 8–6.*

Tennis

Tennis West (☎ 08/9472–1195) can provide details on the variety of tennis courts available throughout the metropolitan area.

Water Sports

Parasailing is available on the South Perth foreshore every weekend, weather and winds permitting. Rent through **Flying High Parasailing** (⊠ Narrows Bridge, ☎ 08/9446–1835). Jet Skis allow for a flight across Perth's waters for speed lovers. **Jet Ski** (☎ 018/91–8810) rents the vehicles, vests, and fuel at an hourly rate. If you want to enjoy the Swan River at a more leisurely pace, hire a catamaran or a sailboard from **Funcats** at the **Coode Street jetty.** Advance reservations are essential on weekends. ⊠ *South Perth,* ☎ *018/92–6003.* ⊙ *Daily 9–7:30.*

Shopping

Most centrally located stores are open Monday–Saturday 8–6, though some specialty shops have extended hours. Late-night trading, until 9, is available in the city on Friday, in the suburbs on Thursday. Perth's larger shops generally open 10–5 on Sunday and public holidays (except Christmas, Easter, and Anzac Day). Your hotel will provide more details about Sunday shopping.

Australiana

Australian souvenirs and knickknacks are on sale at small shops throughout the city. **Purely Australian** (☎ 08/9325–4328) carries the most comprehensive range of Oz-abilia in London Court, Hay Street Mall, and City Arcade. **Carillon Arcade** (⊠ Hay St. Mall), in the center of the city, has two distinctively Australian stores: **Australia Presents** (☎ 08/9321–6620) sells a wide range of locally made items among other souvenirs; and **R.M. Williams** (☎ 08/9321–7786) has everything for the Australian sheepman, including moleskin trousers, hand-tooled leather boots, and Akubra hats.

Crafts

You can find authentic Aboriginal artifacts at **Creative Native** (⊠ 32 King St., ☎ 08/9322–3398). Out of town, in Subiaco, a former car dealer's workshop has been transformed into an Outback setting, the backdrop for **Indigenart** (⊠ 115 Hay St., Subiaco, ☎ 08/9388–2899), an art gallery–cum–Aboriginal culture center. Visitors can view artwork and talk with the works' Aboriginal creators. Contemporary and traditional works are complemented by jewelry, fabrics, and clothing. It's a unique journey into the Aboriginal Dreamtime.

Gems

Broome, in the far north of the state, has been regarded as the pearl capital of the world for decades. **Linneys** (⊠ 37 Rokeby Rd., Subiaco, ☎ 08/9382–4077), whose designers and craftsmen have won national awards, has an excellent selection of Broome pearls and will set them in the design of your choice. Opal from South Australia's Coober Pedy is available at the **Opal Centre** (⊠ 47 London Ct., ☎ 08/9325–2486). Prized pink diamonds from the Argyle diamond mines are incorporated in stunning pieces by **Charles Edward Jewellers** (⊠ 45 King St., ☎ 08/ 9321–5111).

Malls

Citiplace, flanked by the Post Office and the new **Forrest Chase** shopping complex, is the largest mall area. **Myer** (☎ 08/9221–3444) and **Aherns** (☎ 08/9323–0101) department stores both open onto the Murray Street pedestrian mall.

Perth A to Z

Arriving and Departing

BY BUS

Greyhound Pioneer Australia (⊠ Upper Level, bus station, Wellington St., ☎ 08/9481–7066) travels to Perth from capital cities around the country.

BY CAR

The **Eyre Highway** crosses the continent from Port Augusta in South Australia to Western Australia's transportation gateway, Norseman. From there, take the Coolgardie–Esperance Highway north to Coolgardie, and the Great Eastern Highway on to Perth. Driving to Perth—2,580 km (1,600 mi) from Adelaide and 4,032 km (2,500 mi) from Sydney—is an arduous journey, which should be undertaken only with a car (and mental faculties) in top condition. Carrying a supply of spares and drinking water is essential. Service stations and motels are situated at regular intervals along the route.

BY PLANE

Perth International Airport is 16 km (10 mi) from the city center, and it is the international gateway to Australia for visitors from Europe, Africa, and Southeast Asia traveling on **Ansett Australia, Qantas, British Airways, Singapore Airlines, Air New Zealand,** and **Japan Airlines,** among others.

Perth's former international airport now serves as the domestic terminal. Situated 11½ km (7 mi) from the city, it is served by **Ansett Australia** and **Qantas. Ansett W.A., Airlink** (the regional subsidiary of **Qantas**), and **Skywest** (☎ 08/9334–2288) connect Perth with other towns within the state. *See* Air Travel *in* The Gold Guide, *above,* for additional airline telephone numbers.

Taxis between the airports and the city cost approximately $25. Shuttle buses offer regular service to the major hotels and city center and cost approximately $7.

BY TRAIN

Crossing the Nullarbor Desert from the eastern states on **Westrail** (⊠ East Perth Terminal, West Parade, ☎ 08/9326–2244 or 13–2232 or 18–/88–8480) is one of the great rail journeys of the world. The *Indian Pacific* makes three-day runs from Sydney on Monday and Thursday and two-day runs from Adelaide on Tuesday and Friday.

Getting Around

BY BICYCLE

Perth's climate and its network of excellent trails make cycling a safe and enjoyable way to discover the city, but be aware, the summer temperature can exceed 100°F in the shade and cycling in the heat of the day is not advisable. Wearing a bicycle helmet is required by law, and carrying water is prudent any time. You can rent a bicycle for about $16 a day from **About Bike Hire** (☎ 08/9221–2665) at the southeastern end of Riverside Drive. Free brochures detailing a wide variety of trails, including stops at historical spots, are available from the **Western Australia Tourist Centre** (⊠ Forrest Pl. and Wellington St., ☎ 08/9483–1111).

BY BUS

The Perth central business district and suburban areas are well connected by the **Metrobus** bus line (☎ 08/913–2213). Tickets are valid for two hours and can be used on Metrobus trains and ferries. The main terminal is at the Perth Central Bus Station on Mounts Bay Road, and buses run daily between 6 AM and 11:30 PM, with reduced service on weekends and holidays.

Rides within the city center are free. **City Clipper** buses circle the city center, running approximately every 10 minutes on weekdays from 7 AM to 6 PM, Saturday 9 AM to 5 PM. Routes and timetables are available from Transperth.

BY CAR
All major car-rental companies, including **Hertz** (☎ 08/9321–7777) and **Avis** (☎ 08/9325–7677), have depots at both the international and domestic airports. A free 72-page booklet, "Self-Drive Tours within WA," suggests itineraries both statewide and around Perth and Fremantle. It is available from the Western Australia Tourist Centre (☞ *below*) and major car-rental companies.

BY FERRY
Perth Water Transport ferries make daily runs from 6:45 AM to 7:15 PM between Barrack Street Jetty in Perth to Mends Street, across the Swan River in South Perth. Reduced service runs on weekends and public holidays.

BY TAXI
Cab fare between 6 AM and 6 PM weekdays is an initial $2.10 plus 83¢ every ⅕ km (½ mi). From 6 PM to 6 AM and on weekends the rate rises to $3.10 plus 83¢ per kilometer. Try **Swan Taxis** (☎ 08/9444–4444) or **Black and White** (☎ 08/9333–3333).

BY TRAIN
Fastrack trains run from Perth to Fremantle, Midland, Armadale, Joondalup, and stations en route weekdays from 5:40 AM to 11:30 PM, with reduced service on weekends and public holidays. Suburban and Bunbury trains depart from the city station on Wellington Street.

Contacts and Resources

DENTISTS
The **Perth Dental Hospital** (✉ 196 Goderich St., ☎ 08/9325–3452) will give details of private practitioners who provide an emergency service.

EMERGENCIES
Police, fire, or **ambulance.** ☎ *000.*

Police. ☎ *08/9222–1111.*

GUIDED TOURS
Boat Tours. Captain Cook Cruises (☎ 08/9325–3341) offers five cruises on the Swan River from Perth to the Indian Ocean at Fremantle. **Classic Boat Charters** (☎ 08/9383–9449) has sunset and dinner cruises on the Swan River aboard a handsome jarrah-and-teak motorboat, built in the '50s and restored and relaunched in 1995. The 39-ft vessel accommodates up to 18 passengers, and Western Australian wine and seafood are emphasized. **Boat Torque** (✉ Barrack Street Ferry Terminal, ☎ 08/9221–5844 and 08/9325–6833, FAX 08/9325–3717) runs to Rottnest Island and has whale-watching and wine cruises as well (☞ *below*).

Wildflower Tours. Springtime in Western Australia (August–November) is synonymous with wildflowers, as 8,000 species blanket an area that stretches 645 km (400 mi) north and 403 km (250 mi) south of Perth. Tours of these areas are popular, and early reservations are essential with **Westrail** (☎ 08/9326–2159), **Feature Tours** (☞ *below*), or **Great Western Tours** (☞ *below*).

Orientation Tours. Australian Pacific (☎ 08/9221–4000), **Great Western Tours** (☎ 08/9421–1411), and **Feature Tours** (☎ 08/9479–4131) run day tours of Perth and its major attractions. Most include visits to major sights outside the city as well, including Atlantis Marine Park and Underwater World in Fremantle, and beaches.

Walking Tours. Guntrip's Walking Tours (☎ 08/9293–1132) offers a two-hour historical walking tour of the city. **King's Park** (☎ 08/9480–3600) is the heart of Perth's bushland, and a walking tour through the area provides an excellent orientation for visitors. Free walking tours are available from April through October daily except Saturday. November through March there is a summer Sunday walk.

Whale-watching. From late October to late November, **Boat Torque** (☞ *above*) heads out to sea for whale-watching off the coast, following the migratory route of humpback whales.

Wine. For a trip up river to one of the wineries, the ferry *Lady Houghton,* another craft in the Boat Torque (☞ *above*) fleet, makes daily trips up-river from the Barrack Street Jetty, serving wine coming and going and lunch at its destination. It also runs to some of the best-known Swan Valley wineries.

HOSPITALS

The emergency rooms are open all night at the **Royal Perth Hospital** (⊠ Wellington St., ☎ 08/9224–2244) and **Sir Charles Gairdner Hospital** (⊠ Verdun St., Nedlands, ☎ 08/9346–3333).

VISITOR INFORMATION

Western Australian Tourist Centre. ⊠ *Forrest Pl. and Wellington St.,* ☎ *08/9483–1111.*

SIDE TRIPS FROM PERTH

Rottnest Island

Sunny Rottnest Island is ideal as a day trip from Perth—it makes for a pleasant cruise down the Swan River or across from Fremantle. It's easy to fall in love with its bleached beaches, rocky coves, and blue-green waters—even its wallabylike quokkas.

The most convenient way to get around Rottnest is by bicycle, as cars are not allowed on the island and bus service is infrequent. A bicycle tour of the island covers 26 km (16 mi) and can be done in as little as three hours, though you really ought to set aside an entire day to enjoy the beautiful surroundings. It's impossible to get lost. The one main road circles the island and will always bring you back to your starting point. Look for rentals at **Rottnest Bike Hire** (☎ 08/9372–9722) in the main settlement at Thomson Bay.

Heading south from Thomson Bay, between Government House and Herschell lakes, you'll encounter a **quokka colony.** Quokkas are marsupials, small wallabies that are easily mistaken for rats. In fact, the island's name means "rat's nest" in Dutch. Well fed by visitors, the quokkas are quite tame.

Past the quokka colony you'll come upon **gun emplacements** from World War II, and as you continue south to **Bickley Bay,** you'll be able to spot the wreckage of ships that came to rest on Rottnest's rocky coastline.

Follow the main road past Porpoise, Salmon, Strickland, and Wilson bays to **West End,** the westernmost point on the island and another graveyard for unfortunate vessels. If you've brought a fishing rod, now is the time to unpack it. As you head back to the Thomson Bay settlement, you'll pass a dozen rocky inlets and bays, the prettiest of which, **Parakeet Bay,** is situated at the northernmost tip of the island.

Back at the main settlement, visit the **Rottnest Museum** (☎ 08/9372–9753), which provides an intriguing account of the island's convict history. You might also like to stop in at the **Rottnest Island Bakery** (☎ 08/9292–5023), famous throughout the state for its mouthwatering breads and buns.

Dining and Lodging

$$ ✕🍽 **Brolly's.** The Rottnest Hotel (affectionately known as the Quokka Arms after the island's small marsupials) has one fine restaurant and one that is more casual. At the latter, patrons barbecue their own steaks or seafood before helping themselves to the salad bar, whereas the former has a more typical à la carte menu. ⊠ *Rottnest Hotel, Thomson Bay, Rottnest,* ☎ *08/9292–5011. Reservations essential. AE, MC, V.*

$$ ✕🍽 **Rottnest Island Lodge.** The kitchen at this hotel dining room specializes in seafood. ⊠ *Rottnest Island Lodge, Thomson Bay, Rottnest,* ☎ *08/9292–5161. Reservations essential. AE, DC, MC, V.*

Rottnest A to Z

ARRIVING AND DEPARTING
Boat Torque Cruises (☎ 08/9221–5844) runs ferries to Rottnest Island from both Perth's Barrack Street Jetty and from Fremantle. Speedy air service to the island is available on the **Rottnest Airbus** (☎ 08/9478–1322).

EMERGENCIES
Rottnest Nursing Post (☎ 08/9292–5030). Dial **000** to request emergency assistance from an operator.

GUIDED TOURS
The **Rottnest Island Board** (⊠ Thomson Bay, ☎ 08/9372–9727) runs a daily two-hour coach tour of the island's highlights, including convict-built cottages, World War II gun emplacements, and salt lakes. The **Oliver Hill Railway** made its debut in late 1994, utilizing 6 km (3¾ mi) of reconstructed railway line to the island's gun batteries. Frequent two-hour tours visit the World War II gun emplacements and tunnels.

VISITOR INFORMATION
Rottnest Island Centre (⊠ Thomson Bay, ☎ 08/9372–9752).

York

90 km (56 mi) east of Perth.

Founded in the 1830s, this town stands as an excellent example of historic restoration. It sits in the lovely Avon Valley east of Perth, and its restored main street, Avon Terrace, still evokes the days of the 1890s gold rush. The tiny town is easy to explore on foot and contains lovely local sandstone edifices. The **York Motor Museum** (⊠ Avon Terr., ☎ 08/9641–1288) is open daily and houses more than 150 classic and vintage cars, motorcycles, and even some horse-drawn vehicles. Motorcoach rides are available. If you plan to spend the night, you might consider the lovely colonial **Settler's House** (⊠ Avon Terr., ☎ 08/9641–1096), a romantic hostelry with four-poster beds.

If you don't have a car, **Westrail** (☎ 08/9326–2159) provides bus service to York from Perth.

New Norcia

129 km (80 mi) north of Perth.

In 1846 a small band of Benedictine monks arrived in Australia to establish a mission for Aborigines. They settled in New Norcia and eventually built boarding schools and orphanages. Today the brothers in the monastic community continue to live a simple life of prayer and work—their devotion and labor produce the best olive oil in the state, pressed from the fruit of century-old trees. The original schools have developed into a Catholic college attended by more than 200 students. Follow the New Norcia Heritage Trail to explore the monastery, church, old mill, hotel, and jail, in addition to the museum and art gallery, which house unique collections of European and Australian paintings. Overnight visitors may stay in a small guest house (☎ 08/9654–8056) adjacent to the monastery. Though spartan, it gives an idea of the monastic life led by the Benedictines. ⊠ *From Perth, follow Great Northern Hwy. (Rte. 95) north to New Norcia.*

Nambung National Park

245 km (152 mi) north of Perth.

Located on the Swan coastal plain, Nambung National Park is best known for the Pinnacles Desert situated in the center of the park. Over the years, wind and drifting sand have sculpted forms that loom as high as 15 ft, or merely poke out of the sand three or four inches. These eerie limestone forms, which look like African anthills, are the fossilized roots of ancient coastal plants fused with sand.

You can walk among the pinnacles on a 1,650-ft-long trail from the parking area or drive the Pinnacles Desert Loop (not suitable for large RVs or buses). If you have more time, look for some of the more than 100 species of birds that live around the park's coastal dunes and splendid beaches. Fishing is permitted at Hangover Bay and Kangaroo Point. The best time to visit the park is August through October, when the heath is ablaze with wildflowers. Entrance fees are $3 per car or $2 per bus passenger.

Lodging

Accommodations are available in Cervantes at the **Cervantes Motel** (☎ 08/9652–7145) or the **Cervantes Caravan Park** (☎ 08/9652–7060). There are toilets near the Pinnacles, but camping is not permitted in the park.

Arriving and Departing

From Perth, travel north about 193 km (120 mi) on the Brand Highway toward Badgingarra, then turn west toward Cervantes and south into the park.

Tours of the park can be arranged in Perth through the **Western Australian Tourist Centre** (⊠ Forrest Pl., Perth 6000, ☎ 08/9483–1111) or in Cervantes through the **Caravan Park** or the **service station** (☎ 08/9652–7041).

Visitor Information

Contact the **Department of Conservation and Land Management** (⊠ Box 62, Cervantes, 6511, ☎ 08/9652–7043).

FREMANTLE

Fremantle is the jewel in Western Australia's crown. Located about 19 km (12 mi) southwest of Perth, it is a city busy reinventing itself, at the same time retaining its identity as a place where locals know each other and smile and say hello as they pass in the street.

It's a far cry from the barren sandy plain that greeted the first wave of English settlers back in 1829, at the newly constituted Swan River Colony. Most of them were city dwellers, and after five months at sea in sailing ships, the salt-marsh flats where they landed sorely tested their fortitude. With tents to live in and packing cases for chairs, they found no edible crops, and the nearest fresh water was 32 mi—and a tortuous trip up the salty waters of the Swan—away. As a result they soon moved the settlement upriver to the vicinity of present-day Perth. Fremantle remained the location of the seaport, however, and it is to this day Western Australia's premier port.

World War II saw the first major stirring in Fremantle, when the slumbering colonial port city provided a welcome landfall for American servicemen assigned to the Antipodes. Postwar immigration then added a new impetus. The last major change was wrought in 1983 when the city's *Australia II* snatched America's Cup from Newport.

Though Western Australia's hold on the "Auld Mug" was short lived, there was no stopping Fremantle's comeback once it began. Today "Freo" is a city of gurus and greens, truckies and dockers, yuppies and workers, academics and dropouts. It has a multicultural mix of people living amicably side by side. And local architects have brought about a stunning transformation of the town without defacing the colonial streetscape. In the leafy suburbs, every other house is a restored 19th-century gem.

Exploring Fremantle

An ideal place to start a leisurely stroll around town is **South Terrace,** known as cappuccino strip. Alongside locals, soak up the ambience as you weave through sidewalk cafés or browse in bookstores, art galleries, and souvenir shops. No matter how aimlessly you meander, you'll invariably end up where you began, along the broad sidewalk of cappuccino strip.

Between Phillimore Street and Marine Terrace in the **West End,** you'll find a collection of some of the best preserved heritage buildings in the state. The Fremantle Railway Station on Elder Place is a good place to start a walk.

Fremantle also has plenty to entertain children, from pools to a puppet theater to a clutch of museums that are informative and fun. South Beach and Port Beach provide sun, sand, and surf, and numerous parks around the city are well equipped with playground equipment. The Esplanade Park is the venue for the numerous outdoor activities, including the January Sardine Festival, as well as a weekend funfair.

Sights to See

Outside the port gates on the western end of town is **Arthur's Head,** with its row of cottages built to house employees of the Customs Department. Nearby **J-Shed** houses the workshop of perhaps the nation's foremost exponent of public art, the sculptor Greg James. His extraordinarily lifelike figures grace a number of Perth and metropolitan sites, including King's Square.

At **Bather's Beach,** you can view the work of potter Joan Campbell in her seafront studio, or pause for fresh fish-and-chips or the ubiquitous hamburger as you watch the tide roll in from the old sea wall. Try dangling your feet from the wooden jetty rebuilt on the spot where it stood in the days of tall ships. ⊠ *Waterfront at end of Marine Terr.*

If your interest turns to reptilian carnivores, **Fremantle Crocodile Park** is home to 200 salt- and freshwater crocodiles. Feedings take place between Tuesday and Sunday at 11:30 and 2. ✉ *Mews Rd.,* ☎ *08/ 9430–5388.* 🎟 *$8.* ⊙ *Weekdays 10–4, weekends 10–5.*

Like most of Fremantle, the fine, Gothic Revival **Fremantle Museum** was built by convicts last century. First used as a lunatic asylum (the ghosts of one or two demented souls are said to haunt the halls), by 1900 it was overcrowded and was nearly shut down. It eventually became a home for elderly women until 1942, when the U.S. Navy made it into their local headquarters. Artifacts trace the early days of Fremantle's settlement in one wing and another houses the **Fremantle Art Centre.** The complex contains a restaurant and gift shop, and Sunday afternoon courtyard concerts are a regular feature. ✉ *Ord and Finnerty Sts.,* ☎ *08/9430–7966.* ⊙ *Mon.–Wed. 10:30–5, Thurs.–Sun. 1–5.*

The 1855 **Fremantle Prison** was decommissioned in 1991 and opened to unbound visitors the following year. Guided tours provide a fascinating glimpse of the state's oldest prison, including its famous classic-art cell, a superb collection of drawings made by some unknown convict to decorate his cell. His work has been the inspiration for a new generation of artists, and the iron doors that once slammed shut on convicts at nightfall now slam shut on the work of artists and craftspeople who use the cells as studios by day. Reservations for candlelight tours on Wednesday and Friday are essential. ✉ *Fairbain St.,* ☎ *08/9430–7177.* 🎟 *$10.* ⊙ *Daily 10–6.*

In **Fremantle Market** you can browse in the Victorian building for everything from potatoes to paintings, incense to antiques, sausages to Chinese take-away. A small café and bar make it a lively place to take time out to refresh yourself while musicians entertain. ✉ *South Terr. and Henderson St.,* ☎ *08/9335–2515.* ⊙ *Fri. 9–9, Sat. 9–5, Sun. 10–5.*

In the center of the business district, **High Street Mall** lately has become the haunt of retired Italian fishermen whiling away their days in conversation. They're a part of the local color in the mall. ✉ *High, Market, William, and Adelaide Sts.*

One of the oldest commercial heritage-listed structures in Western Australia is **Moores' Building.** It is currently an exhibition and performance space. ✉ *46 Henry St., Fremantle,* ☎ *08/9335–8366.* ⊙ *Daily 10–5.*

A landmark of early Fremantle atop the limestone cliff known as Arthur's Head, the curious, 12-sided **Round House** was built in 1831 *by* convicts to house convicts. It is the state's oldest surviving structure. From its ramparts, you'll get a vista of High Street until it disappears over the horizon—not to mention the Indian Ocean. Underneath, a tunnel was carved through the cliff to allow easy access to ships lying at anchor off the coast from town. No longer needed for commercial traffic, the tunnel is still open to users of Bather Beach. ✉ *West end of High St.*

St. John's Anglican Church and the ☞ town hall are the focal points of the central business district in the midst of **King's Square.** The square, bounded by High, Queen, and William streets, makes a perfect place for a rest, shaded as it is by the spreading branches of 100-year-old Moreton Bay fig trees and spaced with specially designed, medieval-style benches to complete the picture of Old World elegance.

Ċ **Spare Parts Puppet Theatre.** This imaginative children's theater stages productions several times a year. Spare Parts has built up an international reputation and regularly tours abroad. The foyer is a showplace for its puppetry. ⊠ *1 Short St., opposite railway station, Fremantle,* ☎ *08/9430–4771.* ⊙ *Daily 10–5.*

Perhaps no city sight is more enchanting than the row of perfectly preserved **Warders Quarters** cottages on Henderson Street—and yet they are a grim reminder of the colonial past. Here, convicts hued blocks from the limestone cliffs so that they could build houses for the warders standing guard over them. Hard alongside the rows of terraced-limestone cottages stand the "new" courthouse and the police station and the grim walls of the now decommissioned prison, much of which the convicts also built.

The **W.A. Maritime Museum** offers a fascinating glimpse into the state's nautical past, with a reconstruction of the Dutch vessel *Batavia* and relics from the Dutch and colonial ships that came to grief on Western Australia's rocky coastline. A changing gallery of prints and photographs complements the exhibition. ⊠ *1 Cliff St.,* ☎ *08/9431–8444.* ▢ *Donation accepted.* ⊙ *Mon.–Thurs. 10:30–5, Fri.–Sun. 1–5.*

NEED A
BREAK?

Culley's Tea Rooms is the only remaining old-fashioned cake and pie shop serving its daily-baked fare over the counter or at table accompanied by a pot of freshly brewed tea or coffee. Lunch prices are as low as $4.50 and the quality high—just as one would expect from a family business over 60 years old. ⊠ *116 High Street Mall, Fremantle,* ☎ *08/ 9335-1286.* ⊙ *Weekdays 9–5:30, Sat. 9–noon.*

Dining

$$$ ✕ **Chunagon.** This large Japanese restaurant has superb views of the Fremantle boat harbor on one side and the ocean on the other. Choose from a range of *teppanyaki* (Japanese barbecue) menus—including the house special, grilled crayfish—or from the à la carte menu, which features tempura, teriyaki, and sashimi and sushi dishes. Rice-paper–screen tatami rooms host à la carte diners, and a special teppanyaki area allows you to watch as your meal is barbecued with great theatricality. ⊠ *46 Mews Rd.,* ☎ *08/9336–1000. AE, DC, MC, V.*

$$$ ✕ **Granita's.** Take an old biscuit factory and a lot of creativity and what was considered the wrong end of South Terrace becomes the in place. Granita's specializes in Italian snacks and pasta for lunch, with a full à la carte menu at night. Seafood and pasta are house specialties—try Italian dishes with an Australian signature, such as *sardine di Fremantle,* grilled sardines served with garlic butter and balsamic vinegar; *farfalle dockers,* butterfly shape pasta with caviar, chilli, garlic, parsley, and olive oil; or *schiacciata di manzo,* thinly sliced fillet steak with brandy, balsamic vinegar, cream, onions, and parsley. Granita's has an excellent cellar of mostly Australian wine and beer. ⊠ *330 South Terr., at Jenkins St.,* ☎ *08/9336–4660. AE, MC, V.*

$$ ✕ **Surf Club.** With a kiosk, an à la carte restaurant, and a café designed for families—there's a playground and plenty of shade under a large, tensile, fabric canopy—the Surf Club has something for everyone. Though situated just feet from the shoreline, the café and restaurant are protected by walls of glass, which let in ocean views while shutting out the wind. The regular menu, supplemented by about 10 daily specials, emphasizes excellent local seafood: Dhufish, red emperor, and mulloway are presented grilled, panfried, or cooked in batter. The Waroona sirloin, and char-grilled chicken in soy and honey, are also worth trying. ⊠ *Port Beach Rd., North Fremantle,* ☎ *08/9430–6866. Reservations essential. AE, DC, MC, V. Closed Mon.*

$$ ✕ **Williams.** An unpretentious exterior masks one of the best seafood restaurants in town. Inside, one large room houses a comfortable bar area and elegantly decorated tables. The à la carte menu is quite small and includes non-seafood dishes; a long list of specials changes regularly. These might include fresh fillet of pink snapper panfried in Cajun spices, or local cobbler fillet deep-fried in light beer batter with chili-plum dipping sauce, or a trio of king prawns, Moreton Bay bugs (a small lobster), and yabbies (small, sweet, freshwater crayfish) char-grilled and served with a soy and honey glaze. ⊠ *82 Stirling Hwy., North Fremantle,* ☎ *08/9430–5233. Reservations essential. AE, DC, MC, V. Closed Sun. No lunch Sat.*

Lodging

$$$$ ⊞ **Esplanade Hotel.** This hotel and convention center, which incorporates part of an original colonial hotel, has offered seafront accommodation and spectacular ocean views to West Australians for over a century. Rooms are pleasantly furnished, and if the prospect of a smallish standard room is unappealing, studios are also available. ⊠ *Marine Terr. and Essex St. (Box 1102), 6160* ☎ *08/9432–4000,* FAX *08/ 9430–4539. 2 restaurants, café, 2 pools. AE, DC, MC, V.*

$$$$ ⊞ **Fremantle Biscuit Factory Apartments.** These modern, two-story, serviced apartments, most with sea view, contain everything needed for a short- or long-term stay. All apartments are nicely furnished and offer a choice of one, two, or three bedrooms. Fully equipped living areas include remote control television, video, and CD/stereo, and kitchens come with ovens, dishwashers, and microwaves. Laundry facilities are available, and there is intercom security to each room. ⊠ *330 South Terr., South Fremantle 6162,* ☎ *08/9430–5255,* FAX *08/9430–5266. AE, MC, V.*

$$$ ⊞ **Fothergills.** This historic, 100-year-old classic limestone house stands opposite the old Fremantle prison just a few-minutes' walk from the heart of town. Service and food are wonderful at this B&B, and the house's balconies afford stunning views of the harbor. Breakfast is included in the room rate. ⊠ *20–22 Ord St., Fremantle 6160,* ☎ FAX *08/ 9335–6784. AE, DC, MC, V.*

$$$ ⊞ **Moonrakers.** Proprietor Sally Gordon and her awesome Afghan hound Alf (an acronym for "alien life form") both welcome you into their elegant, single-story Victorian abode. Tuck yourself into one of the four-poster beds and wake to the fragrance of a cottage garden. There is also a poolside cottage with its own bath. This B&B is within easy walking distance of cappuccino strip. The room rate includes breakfast. ⊠ *79 South St., South Fremantle,* ☎ FAX *08/9336–2266. Pool. MC, V.*

Nightlife

Fremantle never closes down—that is the perception of whoever drops in on the city. Cappuccino strip opens at 7 AM and closes around 3 AM. There is nothing more pleasant after a day when the temperature has hit 100 or more degrees than to sit at the sidewalk tables of Old Papas, Ginos, The Dome, Rossini's, or Miss Maud's, where everything from breakfast to late night vino is served seven days a week.

Bars
In its heyday Fremantle had as many as 17 nineteenth-century hosteleries to service weary commercial travelers and workers with a burning thirst after a day on the docks, in the tanneries, or any of the myriad factories with which the town hummed. Many pubs remain, as much a part of the fabric of Fremantle life as they ever were.

National Hotel. Describing itself as "Friends of the Guinness," the National has live Irish music as an entertainment feature Saturday and Sunday. ⊠ *98 High St.,* ☎ *08/9335–1786.*

Rosie O'Grady's. It used to be the Federal, a fine old Australian Hotel, but times have changed the old Australian ambience into a newer Irish pub. ⊠ *William St. opposite town hall, Fremantle,* ☎ *08/9335–1645.*

Sail and Anchor. Thanks to its range of home-brewed beers, this remains a popular watering hole. ⊠ *64 South Terr.,* ☎ *08/9335–8433.*

Music

Fly By Night Musicians Club. Many local bands and soloists owe their big breaks to the smoke-free Fly By Night. ⊠ *Parry St., Fremantle,* ☎ *08/9430–5976.*

Shopping

Most shops are open daily 9–5:30, with late night shopping on Thursday. Additionally, Fremantle's South Terrace Piazza has a host of out-of-the-ordinary gift stores. Some shops can send your purchases overseas.

Bannister Street Craftworks. In a restored 19th-century warehouse a group of craftspeople have gathered in their own workshops to turn out everything from screen printing to woodworks, hand-blown glass, leather goods, and souvenirs. The artists, working as a cooperative, invite you to come in and watch as they demonstrate their skills, or just to browse among the delightful exhibits. ⊠ *8–12 Bannister St.,* ☎ *08/9336–2035.*

Heartworks sells crystals, music, books, local works of art, and Aboriginal crafts. ⊠ *Shop 8, South Terrace Piazza,* ☎ *08/9430–4949.*

Into Camelot. This medieval-style dress shop sells romantic wedding gowns and cloaks, street and evening wear, and peasant smocks for all occasions. Period boots, classic Saxon and Celtic jewelry, masks feathered and plain, are all available at affordable prices. ⊠ *9 South Terr.,* ☎ FAX *08/9335–4698.*

☾ **The Pickled Fairy & Other Myths.** The first shop of its kind in the world, and still only one of two, the "faery" shop is a children's paradise. The fairy theme is everywhere, and Celtic jewelry is sold along with books on magic and mythology. ⊠ *Shop 7B, South Terrace Piazza,* ☎ *08/9430–5821.*

☾ **Timothy's Toys** carries a wide range of wooden toys hand-made on the premises, along with a selection of imported toys. ⊠ *Croke La.,* ☎ *08/9335–5044.* ☽ *Mon.–Sat. 9–5, Sun. 1:30–5.*

Fremantle A to Z

Arriving and Departing

Fremantle is well served by both train and bus. Trains depart approximately every 20 minutes from the **Perth Central Station** on Wellington Street, and bus information is available from **Transperth** (☎ 13–2213).

Contacts and Resources

EMERGENCIES

Police, fire, ambulance. ☎ *000.*

Fremantle Hospital. ⊠ *Alma St., Fremantle,* ☎ *08/9431–3400.*

GUIDED TOURS

Fremantle Trams (⊠ William St., ☎ 08/9339–8719) provides a number of tours, including sightseeing trips along the harbor, a fish-and-chip tour, and a history trail. Trams leave from the Town Hall on the hour. **Pride of the West Stagecoach** (✉ Marine Terr., ☎ 08/9417–5523) offers tours around town in replica Cobb & Co. horse-drawn carriages.

VISITOR INFORMATION

Fremantle Town Hall Information Centre. ✉ *William St.,* ☎ *08/9430– 2222.*

THE SOUTHWEST

Western Australia is famous for its farm, station, and country retreats in a variety of rural settings, from the lush farmlands of the Southwest's Denmark to the 2,500-acre cattle stations in the forbidding Northwest. Considering that contrast, it's not surprising that the southwest continues to be the state's most popular rural getaway. The combination of fine vineyards, rugged coastal cliffs, rolling green fields, majestic forests, and a Mediterranean climate is truly delightful. Cape Leeuwin–Naturaliste and Stirling Range national parks, located on the coast near Margaret River and inland north of Albany, respectively, are also worth visiting.

Bunbury

184 km (114 mi) south of Perth, 53 km (33 mi) north of Busselton.

Bunbury is the major seaport of the Southwest. While here, visit the **King Cottage Museum,** a pretty family home built in 1880 using a Flemish bond-brick design. Today it is furnished with a valuable collection of pioneer artifacts from the area. ✉ *77 Forrest Ave.,* ☎ *08/9721– 3929.* 🎟 *$2.* ☉ *Weekends 2–4 or by appointment.*

Dining

$$ ✕ **Memories of the Bond Store.** The century-old Customs Bond Store
★ provides a handsome home for one of the state's finest country brasseries. The menu, which chef Mark Viskovich changes regularly, centers on local venison, emu, crocodile, and kangaroo; Viskovich also serves substantial soups, at least one Asian and one Cajun dish, and the standout Bond burgers, made with buffalo meat and accompanied by wild mushrooms. The wine list is eclectic without being extensive, and a lovely outdoor area seats 40. ✉ *22 Victoria St.,* ☎ *08/ 9791–2922. AE, DC, MC, V.*

En Route From Bunbury, follow Route 10 through the only natural **tuart forest** in the world. These magnificent trees have been standing on this land for 400 years.

Busselton

53 km (33 mi) south of Bunbury.

Busselton was settled by the Bussell family in 1834, and it is among the state's oldest towns. Its history and that of the southwest dairy industry's early years are recorded in the **Old Butter Factory.** ✉ *Peel Terr.,* ☎ *08/9754–2166.* 🎟 *$2.* ☉ *Wed.–Mon. 2–5,*

Dining and Lodging

$$ ✕ **Newton House.** The finest restaurant in the region is housed in a charm-
★ ing, whitewashed 1851 colonial cottage with polished wooden floors and open fireplaces. Master chef Stephen Reagan, who has a string of culinary awards to back up his reputation, makes magic from regional produce whether he's putting together a simple Devonshire tea or stylish entrées of marron and asparagus or excellent local beef. The menu changes

regularly and is never less than exciting. ⊠ *Bussell Hwy., Vasse,* ☎ *08/ 9755–4485. MC, V. BYOB. No dinner Sun.–Wed.*

$$–$$$ 🏠 **Prospect Villa.** This two-story 1850s house is close to town and within walking distance of the Geographe Bay beaches. Laura Ashley fabrics decorate the rooms and Victorian bric-a-brac provides an atmospheric backdrop for a comfortable B & B. Rates include Continental breakfast. ⊠ *1 Pries Ave., Busselton,* ☎ *08/9752–1509, 08/9752–2273 after 7 PM. 4 rooms with bath. AE, MC, V.*

$$ 🏠 **Jacaranda Guesthouse.** Three-course country dinners make this guest house an ideal holiday retreat. A guest's lounge and the old-world bedrooms are quite pleasant, and the house is just 15 minutes away from numerous Margaret River wineries. Full breakfast is included in the rate, and lunch baskets are available on request. Coach tours leave from the guest house daily. ⊠ *30 West St., Busselton,* ☎ *08/9752– 1246,* 🖷 *08/9754–2910. 8 rooms, 4 with private bath. AE, MC, V.*

Dunsborough

21 km (13 mi) west of Busselton, 8 km (5 mi) east of Yallingup.

Dunsborough is another captivating seaside town. One of the local curiosities is the **Hutchings Antique Shop and Museum**, which contains, among other odd items, the largest private collection of mounted wildlife in the state. ⊠ *58 Gifford Rd.,* ☎ *08/9755–3098.* ⊙ *Aug.– May, Sat.–Mon. 9:30–4:30.*

Dining and Lodging

$$ ✕ **Ibis Café.** This simple café's philosophy is reflected in its surroundings—don't mind the decor, concentrate on the food. Contained within a small shop in the village center, the Ibis has garnered a reputation for excellent fare at reasonable prices. Its menu changes with the seasons, using local produce woven into pasta, salad, popular Asian dishes, and grilled seafood, meat, and vegetables. Dessert cakes and tarts are delicious, and the cheese board presents the region's finest. ⊠ *Dunsborough Shopping Village,* ☎ *08/9755–3381. MC, V. BYOB. No dinner Sun. during winter.*

$$ 🏠 **Windmill Cottages.** Rammed-earth construction, verandas, and the colonial styling of these cottages makes them an appealing option. Tucked into the bushland not far from Geographe Bay, these one- and two-story self-contained cottages sleep from four to eight people and allow you to prepare your own meals in fully equipped kitchens. Linens are serviced daily, and shops are just a five-minute walk away. There is a minimum two-night stay, and special weekly rates are available. ⊠ *Yungarra Dr., Dunsborough,* ☎ *08/9755–3258,* 🖷 *08/9756–8173. 4 cottages. MC, V.*

Cape Leeuwin—Naturaliste National Park

The northernmost part of the park is 266 km (165 mi) south of Perth.

Located on the southwest tip of the continent, this 150-km (93-mi) stretch of coastline is one of Australia's most fascinating areas. The limestone Leeuwin-Naturaliste Ridge directly below the park contains more than 360 known caves. Evidence dates both human and animal habitation here beyond 40,000 years ago.

The coastal scenery changes drastically from north to south: rocks at some points, calm sandy beaches at others, all interspersed with heathlands, eucalyptus forests, and swamps. It would take days to explore all the intricacies of this park.

Four major caves between Margaret River and Augusta are easily accessible: **Yallingup** (with its massive stalagmites, stalactites, delicate straws, and shawl formations), **Mammoth Lake** (where stalagmites and stalactites are reflected in the cave's pools of water), and **Jewel** (near Augusta). Bats live in the caves, as do primitive crustaceans and insects that have evolved in the dark to be sightless and colorless. Three caves—Bride's, Giant's, and Calgardup—which require flashlights, sturdy shoes, and protective clothing, are for the adventurous only. Spelunkers in Bride's Cave should have roping experience. *Yallingup,* ⊠ *Caves Rd.,* ☎ *08/9755–2152.* ▣ *$6.* ☉ *Daily 9:30–3:30. Mammoth,* ▣ *$7.* ☉ *Daily 9:30–3:30. Lake,* ☎ *08/9757–7543.* ▣ *$7.* ☉ *Daily 10:00–3:30. Jewel,* ☎ *08/9758–4541.* ▣ *$8.* ☉ *Daily 9:30–3:30.*

The view from the top of the lighthouse at Cape Leeuwin allows you to witness the meeting of two oceans, the Southern and the Indian. At some places, this alliance results in giant ocean swells that smash among the rocks. At others, small coves are blessed with calm waters ideal for swimming and fishing. Back at the north end of the park, Smith's Beach in Yallingup is a popular surfing hangout.

Caves Road leads to several lookout points, including Boranup Lookout (a 1,980-ft trail overlooking Hamelin Bay) and Boranup Forest, where karri, one of the largest trees in the world, grows. North in Yallingup, a mile-long trail leads from Cape Naturaliste to Canal Rocks, passing rugged cliffs, quiet bays, and curving beaches.

Lodging

If you don't plan to camp, there is plenty of lodging available in the Margaret River area (☞ Dining and Lodging, *above and below*).

⚠ **Campgrounds** with toilets, showers, and an information center are located north in Injidup. Campsites cost $5 for two adults, $3 for each additional adult.

Visitor Information

District manager (⊠ Queen St., Busselton 6280, ☎ 08/9752–1255).

Margaret River

181 km (112 mi) south of Perth, 39 km (24 mi) south of Busselton, 39 km (24 mi) north of Augusta, 377 km (234 mi) west of Albany.

Some of Australia's finest wines are grown by numerous wineries here, most of which are open for tastings and sales. **Cape Mentelle** (⊠ Wallcliffe Rd., ☎ 08/9757–2070) is one of the most notable in the area. The rammed-earth winery and tasting rooms, so typical of the buildings in the Margaret River district, are as handsome and memorable as the wine. The Cullen name is one of the most respected in Australia. Wine maker Di Cullen and her daughter Vanya at **Cullens Willyabrup Wines** (⊠ Caves Rd., Willyabrup, ☎ 08/9755–5277) produce medal-winning vintages on a former sheep and cattle farm. **Leeuwin Estate** (⊠ Gnarawary Rd., ☎ 08/9757–6253) is a fine winery, where the grounds provide a magical setting for annual concerts of such international artists as George Benson, Dionne Warwick, and Diana Ross. **Vasse Felix** (⊠ Harmans Rd. S, Cowaramup, ☎ 08/9755–5242) has an excellent restaurant within picturesque grounds. A brochure with details on individual cellars is available from the **Augusta/Margaret River Tourist Bureau.** ⊠ *Bussell Hwy., Margaret River,* ☎ *08/9757–2911.* ☉ *Daily 9–5.*

A few minutes' walk from the center of Margaret River is the **Old Settlement Craft Village,** which consists of a house, farm buildings, and machinery from the 1920s. This and other "group settlement" farms were built by English veterans of World War I recruited by the Australian government to establish a dairy industry in the then-virgin bush of the southwest. Parcels of 160–180 acres were allocated to each family, but groups of families generally worked collectively to clear the land. The Craft Village traces this history, as well as the less utopian fallout that resulted from various plots, lies, and cover-ups engineered by the government to dupe innocent newcomers—none of whom knew anything about farming. This conspiracy-laden past has given way to a benign present: Now a blacksmith gives demonstrations five days a week, and high-quality crafts items are available from the crafts and souvenir shop. ⊠ *Bussell Hwy., Margaret River,* ☏ *08/9757–2775.* ⊞ *$4.* ☉ *Daily 10–5 (closed Fri. during school year).*

Also in Margaret River, **Eagle's Heritage** is a rehabilitation center for sick and injured birds of prey that provides a unique opportunity to see and handle birds from the largest collection of raptors in Australia. ⊠ *Boodijup Rd.,* ☏ *08/9757–2960.* ⊞ *$4.* ☉ *Daily 10–5.*

Dining and Lodging

$$$$ ✕ **1885.** This restaurant, in a 100-year-old home filled with antiques and candlelight, has a well-deserved reputation. If 200 labels in the wine cellar aren't reason enough to make the three-hour drive from Perth, then the excellent food is. The menu focuses on fresh market produce, such as crayfish, and there's sublime goat cheese. ⊠ *Farrelly St.,* ☏ *08/9757–3177. Reservations essential. AE, DC, MC, V.*

$$$ ✕ **Flutes Cafe.** The pastoral setting here—over the dammed waters of ★ the Willyabrup Brook, surrounded by the Brookland Valley Vineyard—is almost as compelling as the food. Dee and Malcolm Jones prepare local *yabbies* (freshwater crayfish), hearty steak and red wine pies, and spicy curries with aplomb. Their scones, cakes, and muffins are thoroughly delectable. ⊠ *Caves Rd., Willyabrup,* ☏ *08/9755–6250. Reservations essential. AE, DC, MC, V.*

$$ ✕ **Flame Tree Restaurant.** When the chef has a name as Scottish as Hamish McLeay, diners could be forgiven for thinking that they were about to enjoy anything but modern Australian food. Yet he and his wife, Jane, consistently serve some of the best food in the region, especially fresh produce, with all dishes available in appetizer or entrée portions. A pretty outdoor seating area has room for 60. ⊠ *Bussell Hwy., Cowaramup,* ☏ *08/9755–5422. MC, V. BYOB. No dinner Thurs.*

$$$$ ⛬ **Gilgara Homestead.** This 1987 replica of an 1870 station homestead on 23 gently rolling acres provides a bucolic atmosphere for a maximum of 14 guests. The award-winning property has pretty, romantic rooms furnished with antiques and lace and scented with lavender, so it's no surprise that honeymooners choose to stay here. A rose-covered veranda, open fireplaces, and a cozy lounge add to the charm. Because owner Pamela Kimmel fosters local fauna, you might breakfast surrounded by spectacular blue wrens—the outstanding avians of the area. Local kangaroos make regular forays to the front door. You can also play bocce or aqua golf on the lake, although the owners have yet to teach the ducks to retrieve stray balls. Rates include a full breakfast. Bringing children is discouraged. ⊠ *Caves and Carter Rds., 6285,* ☏ *08/9757–2705,* ⅿ *08/9757–3259. 6 rooms with bath. Dining room. AE, MC, V. BYOB.*

$$$ ⛬ **Cape Lodge.** Early morning calls come from a chorus of kook- ★ aburras, and evening is heralded by caroling magpies at this lovely, award-winning property in the heart of Margaret River. The decor has a Dutch-Indonesian theme with colonial furniture, captain's chairs, and rattan settees; each of the airy rooms is also festooned with plump pro-

teas cultivated on the property. Guests can be found canoeing on the lake, napping in front of the gargantuan, marble open fire, or snacking on a sumptuous full breakfast, which is included in the room rate. Dinner is not offered because Cape Lodge is surrounded by a clutch of fine restaurants, but owner Jo Johnson will provide picnic baskets and supper platters or a room-service dinner from the Wildwood Brasserie next door. Within easy walking distance is Driftwood Estate Vineyard, with a restaurant seating 160. Bringing children to the lodge is discouraged. ⊠ *Caves Rd., Yallingup 6282,* ☎ *08/9755–6311,* FAX *08/9755–6322. 15 rooms with bath. Pool. AE, DC, MC, V.*

$$ 🔁 **1885 Inn.** In the modern extension of a huge 100-year-old Victorian home, canopy beds, bay windows, and hand-carved marble-top washstands blend well with the feeling of the original house. Each suite opens onto a lovely garden filled with rhododendrons, waterfalls, and dovecotes. ⊠ *Farrelly St., 6285,* ☎ *08/9757–3177,* FAX *08/9757–3076. 24 rooms. Restaurant. AE, DC, MC, V.*

$ 🔁 **Waterfall Cottages.** Built in 1995, this small, rustic clutch of eight self-contained cottages enjoys a bucolic setting in the heart of the district. Four semidetached dwellings accommodate two each, and four larger cottages include mezzanine floors and sleep six. Rendered walls and traditional iron roofs give a colonial feel, and floor-to-ceiling windows afford lake, waterfall, or bushland views. If you choose not to cook in the well-equipped kitchens, the township and a raft of local restaurants are just a stroll away. ⊠ *Kevill Rd., 6285* ☎ *08/9757–3228,* FAX *08/9757–2658. 8 cottages with bath. Pool, tennis court. AE, V.*

Nannup

100 km (62 mi) east of Margaret River, 71 km (44 mi) southeast of Busselton, 219 km (136 mi) northwest of Denmark.

Nannup is a small, beautiful town amid paddock and pine. There are a number of scenic drives in the area.

Dining and Lodging

$$ 🔁 **The Lodge.** Built in 1987 from century-old materials, the Lodge at Nannup has garnered its share of awards. The charming colonial building, with its exposed beams and stone fireplaces, is set amid 10 timbered acres overlooking the Blackwood Valley, 282 km (175 mi) south of Perth. Nearby you'll find tennis, golf, and horseback riding. Rates include a full hot breakfast, and owners Bill and Tania Jones will indulge you with the dinner of your choice. They emphasize fresh local produce, with organically grown vegetables from the garden. The Lodge doesn't permit smoking indoors, and bringing children is discouraged. ⊠ *Grange Rd., 6275,* ☎ *08/9756–1276,* FAX *08/9756–1394. 7 rooms, 5 with private bath, 2 with non-adjoining private bath. Restaurant, pool. MC, V.*

En Route South and east of Nannup on Route 10, **Pemberton** makes a great place for a stop on the way to Denmark and Albany. It is known for the karri forests in which stand some of the tallest trees in the world. A few miles outside this timber town, rejoin Highway 1 and drive along through the "Rainbow Coast's" rolling green countryside.

Denmark

197 km (122 mi) east of Pemberton, 55 km (34 mi) west of Albany.

Denmark is a quaint old town nestling on a river—"where forest meets the sea" as the town motto goes. It's an ideal place to pause a day or two to enjoy such places as the historic butter factory or the studios tucked away on hillside farms along with the cattle.

Have a picnic alongside the river, or follow its course to the sparkling white beaches and clear waters of Wilson's Inlet, where the swimming is superb. Popular ecological tours include one by the government-run **Landcare** to local farms and the river catchment area. Tours and farm stay, motel, or chalet accommodation can be arranged through the **Denmark Tourist Bureau.** ⊠ *Strickland Str.,* ☎ *08/9848–2055.*

The **Denmark Winery, Craft, and Gallery** now occupies Denmark's old butter factory. Among other items, the gallery sells the superb wine of Michael and Alison Goundrey, whose winery is north of Denmark in Mount Barker. Sample their '94 Unwooded chardonnay, the '93 Langton chardonnay, or the '89 Windy Hill cabernet, if bottles are available, while you inspect the work of local craftspeople and watercolorist Alexander E. Hills. ⊠ *11 North St.,* ☎ *08/9848–2525.* ⊙ *Mon.–Sat. 10–4:30, Sun. 11–4:30.*

Lodging

$–$$ ⊞ **Rannoch West Holiday Farm.** A classic farm stay, family-operated Rannock West tends livestock close to the famed Valley of the Giants forest. Natural attractions abound in the area, as do wineries. Choose to lodge in the homestead on a bed-and-breakfast basis, or take one of two self-catering pioneer cottages within the picturesque grounds. Rooms have their own baths. Full breakfast is included in the rates, and dinner is available separately upon request. ✕ *South Coast Hwy., Denmark,* ☎ *08/9840–8032. 3 rooms (2 with private bath), 2 cottages. No credit cards.*

$$ ⊞ **Riverview Cottage.** This aptly named stone cottage, which is well suited for a romantic getaway, offers uninterrupted river views as well as the delightful possibility of paddling to the nearby town by canoe. Homemade bread and butter is provided on the first night to make you feel welcome. The cycle and walkway to town passes through verdant bushland. There is a fully equipped kitchen in the cottage, and you are also welcome to barbecue in the cottage grounds. ⊠ *96 Scotsdale Rd., Denmark,* ☎ *08/9848–1873. No credit cards.*

Albany

410 km (254 mi) south of Perth via Rte. 30, 55 km (34 mi) east of Denmark, 377 km (234 mi) east of Margaret River.

Albany lies on the southernmost tip of Western Australia's rugged coastline. It was the earliest settlement in Western Australia, founded in 1826 as a penal outpost. Originally named Frederickstown after Frederick, Duke of York and Albany, in 1831 it was proclaimed a part of the Swan River Colony and renamed Albany by Governor James Stirling. With the establishment of the whaling fleet in the 1840s it soon became a boomtown.

Centred in Albany's fine harbor, whalers brought in up to 850 sperm whales every season until the practice was stopped in 1978. In 1994 whales were seen in King George Sound for the first time since that cessation. The old whaling station has been converted to a museum, **Whaleworld.** ⊠ *Cheynes Beach,* ☎ *08/9844–4021.* ☞ *$5.* ⊙ *Daily 9–5, ½-hr tours every hr on the hr 10–4.*

The Old Gaol on Stirling Terrace was built in 1851 and served as the district jail from 1872 until it was closed in the '30s. Restored by the Albany Historical Society in 1968, it now contains a collection of social and historical artifacts. The price of admission also entitles ticket holders to visit **Patrick Taylor Cottage,** a wattle-and-daub dwelling (a very interesting twig-and-mud structure) built on Duke Street in 1832 and believed to be the oldest in the district. It contains more than 2,000 items, including period costumes, old clocks, silverware, and kitchenware. ⊠ *Stirling Terr., Albany,* ☎ *08/9841–1401.* ▣ *$3.50.* ☉ *Daily 10–4:15.*

The **Residency Museum,** one of the finest small museums in Australia, is a focal point for both the social and natural history of the Albany region. It's housed in the former offices of the Government Resident; the lovely sandstone building has sweeping views of the harbor. The saddlery adjoining the museum is also interesting. ⊠ *Residency Rd., Albany,* ☎ *08/9841–4844.* ▣ *Free.* ☉ *Daily 10–5.*

The wattle-and-daub cottage built for the original government resident, Captain Sir Richard Spencer, can be seen at the **Old Farm, Strawberry Hill.** Enjoy Devonshire teas in the adjoining historic miner's cottage. ⊠ *Middleton Rd., Albany,* ☎ *08/9841–3735.* ▣ *$3.* ☉ *July–May, daily 10–5.*

☾ Adjacent to the Residency Museum is a faithful replica of the brig **Amity,** on which Albany's original settlers arrived. The replica was built in 1975 by local artisans using timber from the surrounding forest. If you board the ship, climb below deck and try to imagine how 45 men, plus livestock, fit into such a small craft. ⊠ *Port Rd., Albany,* ☎ *08/9841–6885.* ▣ *$1.50.* ☉ *Daily 9–5.*

The **American Naval Lookout** offers unparalleled views of the harbor and the nearby **Military Institute and Guard House** are two of the superbly restored buildings forming the Princess Royal Fortress, which was built in 1833 to house a permanent garrison and to protect the strategically valuable port. Two gun batteries were concealed in the hillside, and during World War II a signal lookout and a new command post were added.

The coastline around Albany is spectacular. Be sure to spend some time in the peninsular **Torndirrup National Park.** North of Albany, about 39 km (24 mi), **Porongurup National Park**'s ancient granite formations are also well worth a visit. Farther up the road, ☞ **Stirling Range National Park** is a mountainous haven for wildflowers and orchids.

Dining and Lodging

$$ ✕ **Genevieves.** The restaurant takes its name from a veteran English motorcar made famous by a movie in the 1950s. Come for delicious bistro-style breakfasts and à la carte dining. All produce is local, and seafood served is caught daily in the pristine waters of King George Sound. Among other entrées, local venison with nutmeg is superb. The cellar master principally stores vintage Australian wines. ⊠ *Esplanade Hotel, Middleton Beach, Albany,* ☎ *08/9842–1711,* FAX *08/9841–7527. AE, D, MC, V.*

$$ ✕ **Kooka's.** This engaging colonial cottage is dominated by kookaburras (Australian kingfishers) of every description—on lampshades and trays, as salt cellars, teapots, and ornaments. There's even a live one in the garden at the rear. The food is wholesome country fare, prepared with flair and expertise by the English and Scottish chefs. Local produce is the order of the day, especially rabbit, venison, kangaroo, and spanking fresh oysters and mussels. Patrons have been known to travel from miles around for the chilli crab or fillet of beef in black currant and whiskey sauce. ⊠ *204 Stirling Terr.,* ☎ *08/9841–5889. AE, DC, MC, V. BYOB. Closed Sun. and Mon. No lunch Sat.*

$$ ✕ **Penny Post.** Located in the historic old Post Office building, this upscale but casual restaurant has enormous character and serves the sort of food that wins awards again and again. An extensive menu of traditional and nouvelle cuisine includes char-grilled steaks and locally caught oysters, prawns, and crayfish. Pretty, colonial dining-room

decor completes the experience. ⊠ *33 Stirling Terr.,* ☎ *08/9841–1045. Reservations essential. AE, DC, MC, V.*

$ ✕ **Earl of Spencer.** Sitting high on a hill overlooking a harbor of spectacular proportions, this pub was constructed in the 1870s and became one of Albany's most popular meeting places. Renowned for its fine ale, it continues to exude character. Its restoration has earned it a fistful of awards, and you won't find a better vantage point from which to appreciate this handsome seaside town. Pasta and steaks are its specialties. ⊠ *Earl and Spencer Sts.,* ☎ *08/9841–1322. AE, DC, MC, V.*

$$$ ☐ **Esplanade Hotel.** Perhaps the last surviving example of a tradi-
★   tional Australian family hotel, this colonial-style, boutique hotel is reminiscent of Albany's first Esplanade, a grand turn-of-the-century building. Guest rooms and suites are immaculate and well appointed. Request a Middleton Beach view and in winter be sure to spend some time before a roaring log fire in the lounge reading room. ⊠ *Middleton Beach, Albany 6330,* ☎ *08/9842–1711,* ℻ *08/9841–7527. 40 rooms with bath, 8 suites. Restaurant, bars, pool, sauna, tennis courts, health club, coin laundry. AE, DC, MC, V.*

$$ ☐ **Albany Mountside.** This classic colonial house has sweeping views of Princess Royal Harbour and Mount Clarence, and it's a short walk from the historic precinct. Rooms are neatly appointed, including the library–guest lounge. Breakfast is served in a spacious room overlooking the harbor. Children, but not pets, are welcome. Breakfast is included in the room rate. ⊠ *189 Grey St. W, Albany 6330,* ☎ *08/9841–8824. 4 rooms, one with private bath. No credit cards.*

Nightlife and the Arts

The **Town Hall** served as the center for local government for several decades until it was no longer needed whereupon, in 1983, it became a performing arts theater, and the performance venue for the Albany Light Opera Company. Programs change regularly. ⊠ *York St.,* ☎ *08/ 9841–1661.* ☉ *Weekdays noon–5, Sat. 9–11.*

The Albany Cottage Hospital, circa 1887, is now the home of the **Vancouver Arts Centre,** just one of the many arts and crafts galleries with which the town abounds.

Outdoor Activities and Sports

Grove Park Golf Course. The 18-hole course is about 10 km (6 mi) from Albany. Clubs, bags, and caddies can be hired. ☎ *08/9844–4277.*

Middleton Beach Park has a playground at either end, one for 8–12-year-olds, and one for toddlers–7-year-olds, strategically placed just across the road from a fast-food outlet with café service in its own garden-dining area.

Stirling Range National Park

403 km (250 mi) south of Perth, 71 km (44 mi) north of Albany.

During the height of the wildflower season (September and October), the Stirling Ranges, north of Albany, rival any botanical park in the world. Rising from the flat countryside, the ranges fill the horizon with a kaleidoscope of color. The Stirlings are considered the only true mountain range in southwest Australia. They were formed by the uplifting and buckling of sediments laid down by a now dry ancient sea. More than 1,000 wildflower species have been identified, including 69 species of orchid. This profusion of flowers attracts equal numbers of insects, reptiles, and birds, as well as a host of nocturnal honey possums. Emus and kangaroos are frequent visitors as well.

An extensive road system makes travel from peak to peak easy. Treks begin at designated parking areas. Don't be fooled by apparently short distances—a 3-km (2-mi) walk up 3,541-ft Bluff Knoll takes about three hours round-trip. Take plenty of water and wet-weather gear—the park's location near the south coast makes Stirling subject to sudden storms. Before attempting longer hikes, register your intended routes in the ranger's log book, and log out upon return.

Lodging

Albany is close enough to serve as a base for day hikes (☞ Dining and Lodging *in* Albany, *above*).

⚠ The only camping within the park is at **Moingup Springs,** which provides toilets, water, and barbecues. Burning wood is prohibited. Fees are $5 per night for two adults, $3 for additional adults. The privately owned **Stirling Range Caravan Park** (✉ Borden 6333, ☎ 08/9827–9229) is just north of the park's boundary opposite Bluff Knoll on Chester Pass Road, where hot and cold showers, laundry facilities, swimming pool, powered and unpowered sites, chalets, and cabins are available. Campfires are permitted. Camping fees are $8 for two adults; other accommodation starts at $22 per night.

Arriving and Departing

From Perth, the park can be reached by traveling along the Albany Highway to Kojonup, proceeding east via Broome Hill and Gnowangerup, and then veering south through Borden onto the Albany Road.

Visitor Information

Stirling Range National Park. ✉ *Amelup via Borden, 6338,* ☎ *08/9827–9230.*

Southwest A to Z

Getting Around

BY CAR

A comprehensive network of highways makes exploring the southwest practical and easy. Take Highway 1 down the coast from Perth to Bunbury, switch to Route 10 through Busselton and Margaret River, and on to Bridgetown, where you rejoin Highway 1 south to Albany.

BY PLANE

Skywest (☎ 08/9334–2288) provides regular service to the southern coastal town of Albany. **South-West Airlines** (☎ 08/9777–1747) runs a twice-daily service from Perth to Bunbury.

Contacts and Resources

EMERGENCIES

Police, fire, ambulance. ☎ *000.*

Regional hospitals can be found in Bunbury (☎ 08/9721–4911), Margaret River (☎ 08/9757–2000), and Albany (☎ 08/9841–2955).

GUIDED TOURS

Gourmet Tours of Australia (☎ 057/77–3503, ℻ 057/77–3896) offers a unique six-day cycling tour of the Southwest during wildflower season (Sept.–Oct.) through Margaret River's vineyards and restaurants. **Skywest** (☎ 08/9334–2288) provides a variety of three- to five-day packages throughout the southwest region, utilizing coaches and hotels or four-wheel-driving and camping. **Westrail** (☎ 08/9326–2159) runs regular tours of the southwest, with departures from the East Perth rail terminal.

VISITOR INFORMATION

The W.A. Tourism Commission operates a comprehensive network of travel centers throughout the region. Its central office (⊠ Forrest Pl. and Wellington St., Perth, ☎ 08/9483–1111) has an excellent library of free information for visitors, including much about bed-and-breakfast and farm-stay accommodations throughout the region.

Farm and Country Holidays (⊠ Tony Jenour, c/o Post Office, Burekup, WA 6227, ☎ 08/9726–3012, FAX 08/9726–3397) has extensive details of farm-stay accommodations throughout the state, from small holdings with rustic cottages to sheep stations of more than 654,000 acres where you stay in sheep shearers' quarters and enjoy the chance to participate in station activities.

THE GOLDFIELDS

Since the day Paddy Hannan stumbled over a gold nugget on the site of what is now Kalgoorlie, Western Australia's goldfields have ranked among the richest in the world. In their heyday, more than 100,000 men and women were scattered throughout the area, all hoping to make their fortunes. It's still an astonishingly productive area, though today the population of Kalgoorlie and Boulder has fallen to 30,000, and many other communities are now nothing more than ghost towns.

The goldfields still appeal to Australians, however. Kalgoorlie—locals call it Kal—retains the rough-and-ready atmosphere of a frontier town, with streets wide enough to accommodate the camel teams that were once a common sight here. Open-cut mines gouge the earth everywhere, and a nugget or two might still be found if you have time, patience, and a reliable metal detector.

Kalgoorlie

602 km (373 mi) east of Perth, 39 km (24 mi) east of Coolgardie.

Built from local pink stone, Kalgoorlie's **Post Office** has dominated Hannan Street since it was constructed in 1899. Opposite the post office is the **York Hotel,** one of the few hotels in Kalgoorlie to remain untouched by time. Take a look at its fine staircase and intricate cupola.

A block south, the stamped-tin ceiling of **Kalgoorlie Town Hall,** built in 1908, is an excellent example of a common style used around the goldfields. The cast-iron Victorian seats in the balcony were imported from England at the turn of the century.

Outside sits **Paddy Hannan,** arguably the most photographed statue in the nation. This life-size bronze of the town's founder, holding a water bag that contains a drinking fountain, is a replica; the original, which had suffered the vagaries of wind, weather, and the occasional vandal, has been moved inside the Town Hall.

The **Museum of the Goldfields** is housed partly within the historic British Arms—once the narrowest pub in the southern hemisphere. This outstanding small museum paints a colorful portrait of life in this boisterous town. Climb to the top of the massive steeple rising over the main mine shaft for a panoramic view of both the city and the Mt. Charlotte Mine. The hands-on exhibits are a hit with children. ⊠ *17 Hannan St.,* ☎ *08/9021–8533.* 🎟 *Donation accepted.* ☉ *Daily 10–4:30.*

Hannan's North Tourist Mine is an absorbing complex, built over the oldest workings in the town. It provides a comprehensive look at the century-old goldfields, with audiovisual displays, a reconstructed prospector's camp, heritage buildings, and the opportunity to go underground. ⊠ *Eastern Bypass Rd.,* ☎ *08/9091–4074.* ⊡ *$14.* ⊙ *Daily 9:30–4:30.*

Dining and Lodging

$$$$ ✕ **Amalfi.** The flocked wallpaper may not suit everyone's taste, but appreciation for Amalfi's food must be universal. This Italian restaurant has been serving the best scaloppine in town for years. ⊠ *409 Hannan St.,* ☎ *08/9021–3088. Reservations essential. AE, DC, MC, V.*

$$ ✕ **Basil's on Hannan.** This pretty café in the heart of town owes its
★ Mediterranean feel to terra-cotta, wrought-iron, indoor-garden decor, and its goldfields authenticity to the corrugated-metal ceiling. The food is equally casual, with veal dishes and a wide range of pasta dishes as the specialties. The popular Sunday brunch offers something different for Kalgoorlie—namely foccacia, seafood fettuccine, and a renowned Caesar salad. ⊠ *168 Hannan St.,* ☎ *08/9021–7832. AE, MC, V. BYOB. No dinner Sun.*

$ ✕ **Exchange Hotel.** The miners in Kalgoorlie favored slaking their thirst before filling their bellies, but here you can do both at once. A superb example of a goldfields pub, the redecorated Exchange is replete with exquisite stained glass and pressed-tin ceilings. The best counter meals (grills and salads) in the area are served here. The public bar gives an idea of the rough-and-ready goldfields of old, though the scantily clad bar girls may not suit some tastes. ⊠ *Hannan and Maritana Sts.,* ☎ *08/9021–2833. No credit cards.*

$$$ ▦ **Plaza Motel.** This modern hotel complex has a quiet location on a tree-lined street, just a stone's throw from busy Hannan Street. Air-conditioned rooms, furnished in blues, grays, and dusty mauves, are neat but uninspired, with beige furniture and brown-tile bathrooms. All rooms in the four-story building have balconies, and the higher floors enjoy views over the low-rise town. ⊠ *45 Egan St.,* ☎ *08/9021–4544,* FAX *08/9091–2195. 100 rooms with bath. Restaurant, room service, pool. AE, DC, MC, V.*

$$ ▦ **York Hotel.** The historic York, dating from 1901, once contained a 47- by 20-ft billiards room. That is long gone, but the hotel has retained its lovely stained-glass windows and pressed-tin ceilings. Its staircase and dining room are a historian's dream. Rooms are small but functional, and rates include breakfast. ⊠ *259 Hannan St.,* ☎ *08/9021–2337. 16 rooms share 6 baths. Restaurant. AE, DC, MC, V.*

Coolgardie

561 km (348 mi) east of Perth, 39 km (24 mi) west of Kalgoorlie.

Located 40 km (25 mi) west of Kalgoorlie on the Great Eastern Highway, tiny **Coolgardie** is probably the best-maintained ghost town in Australia. A great deal of effort has gone into preserving this historic community—there are some 150 historical markers placed around the town.

The Coolgardie Railway Station operated until 1971 and is now home to the **Railway Station Museum**'s display on the history of rail transport. The museum also includes a display of photographs, books, and artifacts that together offer a gripping portrayal of a famous mining rescue that was once carried out in these goldfields. ⊠ *Woodward St.,* ☎ *08/9026–6388.* ⊡ *Donations accepted.* ⊙ *Sat.–Thurs. 8:30–4:30.*

One of the most unusual museums in Australia, **Ben Prior's Open Air Museum** features the machinery, boilers, and other equipment used to mine the region at the turn of the century, as well as a variety of other relics from Coolgardie's boom years. Items include large covered wagons, old cars, and statues of explorers. ⊠ *Bayley St., no phone.* 🎫 *Free.* ☉ *Daily until dusk.*

The stark, weathered headstones in the **Coolgardie Cemetery,** off the Great Eastern Highway about a half mile east of town, recall stories of tragedy and the grim struggle for survival in a harsh, unrelenting environment. Many of the graves remain unmarked because the identities of their occupants were lost during the wild rush to the eastern goldfields. Look for the graves of several Afghan camel drivers at the rear of the cemetery.

Also on the Great Eastern Highway, 3 km (2 mi) west of Coolgardie, is the **Coolgardie Camel Farm,** which offers a look at the animals that played a vital role in life here. If the roads in town seem overly wide, you'll realize that such dimensions were necessary to accommodate these great beasts. A variety of camel rides are offered, including rides around the yard and one-hour, day-long, or overnight treks. Longer treks allow the chance to hunt for gems and gold. ⊠ *Great Eastern Hwy.,* ☎ *08/9026–6159.* 🎫 *$2.* ☉ *Daily 9–5.*

Goldfields A to Z

Arriving and Departing

BY BUS

Greyhound Pioneer Australia (☎ 08/9481–7066) runs out to the 330-mi-distant goldfields.

BY PLANE

Ansett W.A. and **Airlink,** the Qantas regional subsidiary, operate a daily service to Kalgoorlie. The flight takes an hour. ☞ Air Travel *in* the Gold Guide for airline telephone numbers.

BY TRAIN

The Prospector is an appropriate name for the train that runs a daily seven-hour service between Perth and Kalgoorlie. Clean and efficient, it departs from the East Perth Railway Terminal (☎ 08/9326–2244).

Getting Around

The center of Kalgoorlie is compact enough to explore on foot. Hannan Street, named after the man who discovered gold here, is the main thoroughfare and contains the bulk of the hotels and places of interest. Taxis (☎ 08/9021–2177) are available around the clock.

Contacts and Resources

EMERGENCIES

Police, fire, ambulance. ☎ *000.*
Kalgoorlie Regional Hospital. ☎ *08/9080–5888.*

GUIDED TOURS

All-inclusive package tours from Perth are available by plane, rail, and bus with the companies mentioned under Arriving and Departing, *above.*

Goldfields Air Services (☎ 08/9093–2116) offers an air tour that gives you a bird's-eye view of the open-cut mining technique now used instead of more traditional shaft mining. By the turn of the century a pit measuring 8 km by 5 km (5 mi by 3 mi) is expected to run adjacent to the town. **Goldrush Tours** (⊠ Palace Chambers, Maritana St., Kalgoorlie, ☎ 08/9021–2954) runs an excellent series of tours on the goldfields' history and ghost towns, the profusion of wildflowers in the area, and the nearby ghost town of Coolgardie. Boulder, located just south of Kalgoorlie, is home to the **Loop Line Railroad,** whose train the *Rat-*

tler offers tours of the Golden Mile by rail. The train leaves from the
Boulder Railway Station (✉ Burt St., ☎ 08/9093–1157).

The **Kalgoorlie/Boulder Tourist Bureau** (✉ 250 Hannan St., ☎ 08/9021–
1966) has a staff as enthusiastic and welcoming as they are knowledgeable.

KARIJINI NATIONAL PARK

*1,411 km (875 mi) northwest of Perth, 285 km (177 mi) south of Port
Hedland.*

The huge rocks, crags, and gorges that make up the Hamersley Range
in the northwestern corner of the state are among the most ancient land
surfaces in the world. Sediments deposited by an inland sea more than
2½ billion years ago were forced up by movements in the earth's crust
and slowly weathered by natural elements through succeeding centuries.
Much of the 320-km (200-mi) range is being mined for its rich iron
deposits, but a small section is incorporated into the national park. Towering cliffs, lush fern-filled gullies, and richly colored stone make this
one of the most beautiful parks in Australia.

Karijini's trails are rated easy, moderate, and difficult; all require
sturdy shoes, and you should carry plenty of drinking water to avoid
the dangers of dehydration. Gorges can be reached only on foot from
parking areas. Dales Gorge is the most popular and easily accessible.
The walk is a one-hour return trip from the parking area and ends at
the only permanent waterfall in the park, Fortescue Falls. Ferns and
mosses line the gorge walls, providing a stunning contrast with the arid
landscape outside the park. This walk can be lengthened by hiking downstream to Circular Pool. Other gorges in the park are far more challenging and should be undertaken only by experienced hikers, who must
brave freezing water, cling to rock ledges, and scramble over boulders
through the Joffre, Knox, and Hancock gorges. Notify the ranger before hiking into any of these gorges.

Because summer temperatures often top 110°F, it's best to visit during the cooler months, from April through early November.

Lodging
🏕 Camping is permitted only in designated sites at Yampire Gorge,
Circular Pool, Joffre Turnoff, and Weano. Campsites have no facilities except toilets, but gas barbecues are available for free. The burning of wood is prohibited. Nightly fees are $5, plus $3 for each
additional adult.

Food and supplies can be purchased in Wittenoom, where hotel and
motel accommodations can be arranged as well. Drinking water is available at Yampire and Joffre roads.

Arriving and Departing
This ever so remote park is best reached by flying from Perth to Port
Hedland and renting a car from there, or by flying to Broome (☞ Chapter 11) and driving 551 km (342 mi) on the Great Northern Highway
to Port Hedland. Turn south from Port Hedland to the park.

There are organized tours from Perth; contact the **Western Australian
Tourist Centre** (✉ Forrest Pl., Perth 6000, ☎ 08/9483–1111) for details.

Visitor Information

Contact the **Department of Conservation and Land Management** (⊠ Box 835, Karratha, 6714, ☎ 08/9186–8288).

MONKEY MIA AND NINGALOO REEF

Monkey Mia

985 km (611 mi) north of Perth.

Monkey Mia is the setting for one of the world's most extraordinary natural wonders, for nowhere else do wild dolphins interact so freely with human beings. In 1964 a woman from one of the makeshift fishing camps in the area hand-fed one of the dolphins that regularly followed the fishing boats home. Other dolphins followed that lead, and an extensive family of wild dolphins now come of their own accord to be fed. For many, standing in the shallow waters of Shark Bay to hand-feed a dolphin is the experience of a lifetime. There are no set feeding times—dolphins show up at any hour of the day at the public beach, where park rangers feed them. Rangers will share their food with visitors who want to get close to the sea creatures. There is also a Dolphin Information Centre, which has videos and information. ⊠ *Follow Hwy. 1 north from Perth for 806 km (500 mi) to Denham/Hamelin Rd., then follow signs,* ☎ *08/9948–1366.* ☉ *Information center daily 7–6.*

Arriving and Departing

Skywest (☎ 08/9334–2288) offers a thrice-weekly flight to Shark Bay airport, which serves the Monkey Mia world heritage area and provides easy access to the dolphins and the rare stromatolites at **Hamelin Pool.**

Ningaloo Reef Marine Park

1,512 km (938 mi) north of Perth.

Some of Australia's most pristine coral reef runs 251 km (156 mi) along the coast of the Exmouth Peninsula, very far north of Perth. A happy conjunction of migratory routes and accessibility make it one of the best places on earth to see huge manta rays, giant whale sharks, humpback whales, nesting turtles, and the annual coral spawning. **Exmouth Diving Centre** (⊠ Box 573, Exmouth, 6707, ☎ 08/9949–1201, FAX 08/9949–1680) offers complete diving packages. (☞ Diving *in* Chapter 13 for a full description of diving with whale sharks.) A unique tour, inaugurated in early 1993, allows a handful of travelers to assist in the tagging of the giant loggerhead and hawksbill turtles that come ashore to nest in December and January. This hands-on opportunity, organized by officers of the Department of Conservation and Land Management, is available nowhere else in the country. For more information, contact **Coate's Wildlife Tours** (☎ 08/9324–2552, FAX 08/9324–2238). ⊠ *Follow North West Coastal Hwy. north 1,170 km (726 mi) to Minilya turnoff; Exmouth is 374 km (232 mi) farther north.*

13 Adventure Vacations

Antarctica

Bicycling

Bushwalking (Hiking)

Camel Trekking

Cross-Country Skiing

Diving

Four-Wheel-Drive Tours

Gliding

Horseback Riding

Rafting

Sailing

Sea Kayaking

By David
McGonigal

Updated by
Anne
Matthews

YOU'LL MISS AN IMPORTANT ELEMENT of Australia if you don't get away from the cities to explore "the bush" that is so deeply ingrained in the Down Under character. Australians pride themselves on their ability to cope in the great outdoors even if, in many cases, this has never been tested beyond lighting the backyard barbecue. Nevertheless, the heroes of modern Australia are those men and women who opened this vast, unforgiving land to European settlement—like Ludwig Leichhardt, who pioneered the 4,800-km (3,000-mi) route between Brisbane and Port Essington (Darwin) in 1844, only to vanish without a trace during a transcontinental trek in 1848, or Robert O'Hara Burke, who died in 1861 after completing a south–north transcontinental trip with camels.

Many of the adventure vacations today were journeys of exploration only a generation ago. Even now, the four-wheel-drive vehicle is a necessity, not a plaything, in the great heart of Australia. Indeed, the country retains a raw element that makes it ideally suited to adventure vacationing. You can still travel for hours or days in many places without seeing another person or any sign of human habitation. From the tropical jungles of the north to the deserts of the Red Centre to the snowfields of New South Wales and Victoria, one is constantly reminded of how ancient this country is. The mountains you walk or ride through are rounded with age, and the animals and flora you encounter are themselves reason enough to travel to Australia.

You can always choose to travel without a guide, and you can get into some of the activities listed below on your own. The advantage of using a guide in such cases is often educational. You'll learn more about where you are by having a knowledgeable local by your side than you could traveling on your own. If you go out with a guide early in your trip, you can get an introduction to a part of Australia that you might apply to later parts of your trip when you are on your own in the bush.

Adventure vacations are commonly split into soft and hard adventures. A hard adventure requires a substantial degree of physical participation. You may not have to be perfectly fit, but in a few cases, prior experience is a prerequisite. In soft adventures the destination rather than the means of travel is often what makes it an adventure. With most companies, the adventure guides' knowledge of flora and fauna—and love of the bush—is matched by a level of competence that ensures your safety even in dangerous situations. The safety record of Australian adventure operators is very good. Visitors should be aware, however, that most adventure-tour operators require you to sign waiver forms absolving the company of responsibility in the event of an accident or a problem. Australian courts normally uphold such waivers except in cases of significant negligence.

Tour Operators

There are far more adventure-tour operators in Australia than we can include in this chapter. Most are small and receive little publicity outside their local areas, so contact the relevant state tourist office if you have a specific adventure interest. Here are the addresses of the major adventure-tour operators mentioned in the following pages. U.S. addresses are given when available.

Adventure Associates. ⊠ Box 612, Bondi Junction, NSW 2022, ☎ 02/9389–7466, FAX 02/9369–1853.
Adventure Center. ⊠ 1311 63rd St., Number 200, Emeryville, CA 94608, ☎ 510/654–1879, FAX 510/654–4200.

Adventure Charters of Kangaroo Island. ⊠ *Box 169, Kingscote, Kangaroo Island, SA 5223,* ☎ *08/8553–9119,* FAX *08/8553–9122.*

Alice Springs Camel Outback Safaris. ⊠ *PMB 74, via Alice Springs, NT 0872,* ☎ *08/8956–0925,* FAX *08/8956–0909.*

Bicheno Dive Centre. ⊠ *2 Scuba Ct., Bicheno, TAS 7215,* ☎ *03/6375–1138,* FAX *03/6375–1504.*

Blue Mountains Adventure Company. ⊠ *Box 242, Katoomba, NSW 2780,* ☎ *02/4782–1271.*

Bogong Horseback Adventures. ⊠ *Box 230, Mt. Beauty, VIC 3699,* ☎ *03/5754–4849,* FAX *03/5754–4181.*

Brake Out Cycling Tours. ⊠ *Box 427, Kingston, TAS 7050,* ☎ *03/6229–1999,* FAX *03/6229–8019.*

Cradle Mountain Huts. ⊠ *Box 1879, Launceston, TAS 7250,* ☎ *03/6331–2006,* FAX *03/6331–5525.*

Croydon Travel. ⊠ *34 Main St., Croydon, VIC 3136,* ☎ *03/9725–8555,* FAX *03/9723–9560.*

Dive Adventures. ⊠ *9th level, 32 York St., Sydney, NSW 2000,* ☎ *02/9299–4633,* FAX *02/9299–4644.*

Dive Travel Australia. ⊠ *Shop 3, 50 Kalang Rd., Elanora Heights, NSW 2101,* ☎ *02/9970–6311,* FAX *02/9970–6197.*

East Kimberley Tours. ⊠ *Box 537, Kununurra, WA 6743,* ☎ *08/9168–2213,* FAX *08/9168–2544.*

Ecotrek: Bogong Jack Adventures. ⊠ *Box 4, Kangarilla, SA 5157,* ☎ *08/8383–7198,* FAX *08/8383–7377.*

Equitrek Australia. ⊠ *5 King Rd., Ingleside, NSW 2101,* ☎ *02/9913–9408,* FAX *02/9970–6303.*

Exmouth Diving Centre. ⊠ *Box 573, Exmouth, WA 6707,* ☎ *08/9949–1201,* FAX *08/9949–1680.*

Freycinet Experience. ⊠ *Box 43, Battery Point, TAS 7004,* ☎ *1800/50–6003 or 03/6223–7565,* FAX *03/6224–1315.*

Frontier Camel Tours. ⊠ *Box 2836, Alice Springs, NT 0871,* ☎ *08/8953–0444,* FAX *08/8955–5015.*

Great Aussie Pub Crawls on Horseback. ⊠ *Box 379, Glen Innes, NSW 2370,* ☎ *02/6732–1599,* FAX *02/6732–3538.*

Halls Creek and Bungle Bungle Tours. ⊠ *Box 2615, Broome, WA 6725,* ☎ *08/9168–6217,* FAX *08/9168–6222.*

Himalayan Travel. ⊠ *110 Prospect St., Stamford, CT 06901,* ☎ *203/359–3711.*

Intrepid Tours. ⊠ *Box 31, Quorn, SA 5433,* ☎ *08/8648–6277,* FAX *08/8648–6357.*

King Island Dive Charters. ⊠ *Box 1, Currie, King Island, TAS 7256,* ☎ *03/6461–1133,* FAX *03/6461–1293.*

Lake Keepit Soaring Club. ⊠ *Box 111, Manilla, NSW 2346,* ☎ *02/6769–7640 or 02/6769–7514,* FAX *02/6785–1880.*

Morrell Adventure Travel. ⊠ *1/8 Newcastle St., Rose Bay, NSW 2029,* ☎ *02/9388–1200,* FAX *02/9388–1318.*

Osprey Wildlife Expeditions. ⊠ *Box 738, Stirling, SA 5152,* ☎ *and* FAX *08/8388–2552.*

Outback Camel Company. ⊠ *PMB 53, Waikerie, SA 5330,* ☎ *08/8543–2280.*

Packsaddlers. ⊠ *Megalong Rd., Megalong Valley, NSW 2785,* ☎ *02/4787–9150,* FAX *02/4787–9158.*

Paddy Pallin Jindabyne. ⊠ *PMB 5, Jindabyne, NSW 2627,* ☎ *02/6456–2922,* FAX *02/6456–2836*

Peregrine Adventures. ⊠ *258 Lonsdale St., Melbourne, VIC 3000,* ☎ *03/9663–8611,* FAX *03/9663–8618, or book through Himalayan Travel (☞ above).*

Port Macquarie Camel Safaris. ⊠ *11 Chalmers St., Port Macquarie, NSW 2444,* ☎ *02/6583–7650,* FAX *02/6583–7650.*

Pro Dive Travel. ⊠ *Suite 1–5, Level 7, Dymocks Building, 428 George St., Sydney, NSW 2000,* ☎ *02/9232–5733,* FAX *02/9232–5788.*

Reynella Rides/Kosciusko Trails. ⊠ *Bolaro Rd., Adaminaby, NSW 2630,* ☎ *02/6454–2386,* FAX *02/6454–2530.*

Southern Cross Gliding Club. ⊠ *Box 132, Camden, NSW 2570,* ☎ *02/ 4655–8882 or 02/9949–2057.*

Stoneys' Bluff & Beyond Trailrides. ⊠ *Box 287, Mansfield, VIC 3722,* ☎ *03/5775–2954,* FAX *03/5775–2598.*

Tasmanian Expeditions. ⊠ *110 George St., Launceston, TAS 7250,* ☎ *1800/03–0230 or 03/6334–3477,* FAX *03/6334–3463.*

Tourism Commission of New South Wales. ⊠ *13737 Fiji Way, Suite C10, Marina del Rey, CA 90292,* ☎ *310/301–1903,* FAX *310/301–0913.*

Waikerie International Soaring Centre. ⊠ *Box 320, Waikerie, SA 5330,* ☎ *08/8541–2644,* FAX *08/8541–2761.*

Walkabout Gourmet Adventures. ⊠ *Box 52, Dinner Plain, VIC 3898,* ☎ *03/5159–6556,* FAX *03/5159–6508.*

White Water Rafting Professionals. ⊠ *Box 133, Coffs Harbour, NSW 2450,* ☎ *02/6651–4066,* FAX *02/6651–5699.*

Whitsunday Adventure Sailing. ⊠ *Box 519, Airlie Beach, QLD 4802,* ☎ *07/4946–1777,* FAX *07/4946–1668.*

Wild Escapes. ⊠ *Box 116, Asquith, NSW 2077,* ☎ *02/9482–2881,* FAX *02/9477–3114.*

Wild Track Adventure Safaris. ⊠ *Box 2397, Cairns, QLD 4870,* ☎ *07/4055–2247,* FAX *07/4058–1930.*

World Expeditions. ⊠ *441 Kent St., 3rd floor, Sydney, NSW 2000,* ☎ *02/9264–3366,* FAX *02/9261–1974.*

Antarctica

Australia is perfectly located as a stepping off point for trips to Antarctica, the pristine frozen adventureland to its south. Indeed, Australia claims the largest share of Antarctica for administrative purposes, with the Australian Antarctic Territory comprising 42% of the continent. Ice breakers regularly depart from the Tasmanian port of Hobart carrying ice-fanciers down to the Ross Sea where, besides the regular Antarctic wonders of penguins and icebergs, they visit the historic huts of Scott and Shackleton, looking just as they did the day the explorers left. They also call into the wildlife-rich sub-Antarctic Macquarie, Campbell, and Aucklands islands.

Contact Adventure Associates or World Expeditions for more information—and do so early as every voyage fills up quickly.

A faster and cheaper, if less satisfying, option is to take a one-day Qantas over-flight of Antarctica organized by Croydon Travel. Taking off from Sydney, Melbourne, or Perth, you fly directly to the ice continent. There are a variety of flight plans, but all fly low so you have good views of the mountains and ice. You're still too high to see animals, however. It's worthwhile paying extra for a window seat not over the wing. Although it's better to set foot on the last wild continent, the great majority of those who take the flights return very enthusiastic.

Season: November–March.
Locations: Cruises from Hobart; flights from Sydney, Melbourne, and Perth, with connections from other Australian cities.
Cost: From $800 for one day to $15,000 for three weeks.
Tour Operators: Adventure Associates, Croydon Travel, World Expeditions.

Bicycling

Cycling is an excellent way to explore a small region, allowing you to cover more ground than on foot and observe far more than you could from the window of a car or bus. Riding down quiet country lanes is a great way to relax and get fit at the same time. Cycling rates as a hard adventure because of the amount of exercise.

New South Wales

Morrell Adventure Travel has several tours that include all meals, a support vehicle, guides, mountain bikes, group camping gear, and national park entry fees (where applicable). Its main cycling region is the Snowy Mountains, but it also operates a day ride on the state's South Coast, a weekend ride exploring the Southern Highlands (an area of large manor houses, spectacular formal gardens, and rolling farmland), and a seven-day trip from Canberra to Kosciusko National Park. Blue Mountains Adventure Company offers several one-day rides on mountain bikes through these plunging walled valleys that border Sydney, actually ridges left from a collapsed plateau rather than mountains. The trips include a spectacular ride along Narrow Neck and a ride through a glowworm tunnel.

Season: Year-round.
Locations: Blue Mountains, Snowy Mountains, Southern Highlands.
Cost: From $45 for half a day to $80 for one day and $650 for seven days.
Tour Operators: Blue Mountains Adventure Company, Morrell Adventure Travel.

Tasmania

Tasmania is small enough to make cycling a pleasant option. The classic tour is Tasmanian Expeditions' Cycle Tasmania, an eight-day trip from Launceston that leads through pastoral lands down to the fishing villages of the east coast. Terrain includes undulating hills, full-scale mountains, coastal plains, and dense temperate rain forests. Tasmanian Expeditions also has a very similar 14-day tour, Tasmanian Panorama, which includes cycling, bushwalking, and rafting. Intended for beginners, the trip covers some of the best adventures Tasmania has to offer: walking in the Cradle Mountain area and the Walls of Jerusalem National Park, cycling down the east coast, and rafting on the relatively peaceful Picton River. All of these tours are sold also by World Expeditions. For a shorter ride, join Brake Out for its half-day ride down Mt. Wellington, which looms behind Hobart.

Season: November–March.
Locations: Central Tasmania and the north and east coasts.
Cost: From $25 for a half-day tour to $1,000 for eight days or $1,650 for two weeks, including camping equipment, support vehicle, bicycles, and all meals.
Tour Operators: Adventure Center, Brake Out Cycling Tours, Tasmanian Expeditions, World Expeditions.

Queensland

Rising up behind the coastal town of Cairns, the Atherton Tableland is a mixture of tropical rain forests and sleepy towns—an area to be savored rather than rushed through—reached on board a steam train that labors up the steep gradient from Cairns onto the escarpment. The tablelands themselves are relatively level and ideal for cycling. Staying overnight in quaint old wooden pubs, swimming in cool highland ponds, exploring a huge curtain fig tree, and then heading off for the next pub are all great ways to attain a Queensland frame of mind. Peregrine Adventures also includes this mountain biking excursion as a part of a more extensive seven-day adventure trip, with walking, canoeing, and reef excursions.

Season: Year-round.
Location: Atherton Tableland.
Cost: $275 for two days, $1,050 for the seven-day combination trip.
Tour Operator: Peregrine Adventures.

South Australia

South Australia offers gentle cycling on quiet country roads, particularly on Kangaroo Island and around the famous wine regions of the Barossa and Clare valleys, as well as more challenging mountain bike expeditions into the rugged Flinders Ranges, far to the north of Adelaide. Ecotrek: Bogong Jack Adventures has a range of such cycling trips—varying from weekends in the wine areas to longer rides on Kangaroo Island and in the Flinders Ranges.

Season: April–October.
Locations: Barossa Valley, Clare Valley, Flinders Ranges, Kangaroo Island.
Cost: From $250 for a weekend to around $960 for a seven-day Kangaroo Island cycle safari.
Tour Operator: Ecotrek: Bogong Jack Adventures.

Bushwalking (Hiking)

The Australian bush is unique. The olive-green foliage of the eucalypts seems drab at first, but when you walk into a clearing carpeted with thick grass and surrounded by stately blue gums, its special appeal jumps out at you. The bush is a bright and noisy place, too—crimson- and harlequin-hue parrots screech from the canopy overhead, and kookaburras laugh hysterically from the treetops. Chances are good that you will cross paths with kangaroos, wallabies, goannas, and even echidnas (spiny anteaters). This is a land of a million oddities that is best appreciated on foot. An easy ramble with a picnic lunch through the Blue Mountains of New South Wales can be every bit as rewarding as a challenging 21-km (13-mi) hike to a muddy camp in the Tasmanian wilderness. Depending on the type of walk, therefore, bushwalking can be a soft or hard adventure. Associated high-adrenaline hard adventures are *abseiling* (rappelling) and canyoning—forms of vertical bushwalking well suited to some parts of Australia, notably the Blue Mountains of New South Wales.

New South Wales

The scope for casual bushwalking in New South Wales is extensive. The best one-day walks in the Blue Mountains originate in Blackheath and wind through Grand Canyon or Blue Gum Forest. The Snowy Mountains beyond Perisher are also excellent for walking, as are the national parks to the north—especially Barrington Tops, a mysterious place of narrow paths running through huge rain forests, past streams shaded by giant tree ferns and tall hardwoods. The same areas are ideal for longer treks, too. The advantage of joining an adventure tour is the experience and knowledge of the guides, who identify the animals and plants that you encounter along the way and who show you places of interest off the main trails. The camping equipment provided by tour operators is a welcome alternative to buying it in Australia (where prices for outdoor gear are high) or bringing it from home.

Sydney's Morrell Adventure Travel operates four-day to one-week camping and lodge-based walking tours in the Snowy Mountains between November and April, as does Paddy Pallin, an excellent locally based adventure company. The deeply eroded sandstone canyons of the Blue Mountains are perfect for abseiling down sheer vertical crags and through deep, clean canyons. There is intense competition between tour operators in this area, so a full day of canyoning in the spectacular Grand Canyon or the sublime Claustral Canyon costs less than $100, including lunch. Blue Mountains Adventure Company has more than a dozen different canyoning, climbing, and abseiling programs around this area.

Season: Year-round.
Locations: Blue Mountains, Snowy Mountains, Barrington Tops.
Cost: From $39 for a half day or, on average, about $100 per day, including packs, camping equipment, guide, and food.
Tour Operators: Blue Mountains Adventure Company, Morrell Adventure Travel, Paddy Pallin Jindabyne.

Victoria

Victoria's alpine region offers a range of bushwalking vacations to suit every taste. Ecotrek: Bogong Jack Adventures leads challenging treks to the summit of the state's three highest peaks and several other, less demanding but equally beautiful walks through forests of mountain ash and snow gums. Some of these walks involve camping, though other trips include accommodation in country lodges. Walkabout Gourmet Adventures has an epicurean five-day bushwalking experience, during which you'll stay in a country resort and eat good food and drink nice wine while seeing wildlife and relaxing. These gourmet adventures are designed for healthy, active people, and the number of walkers in any group is kept under 16.

Season: October–May.
Locations: Alpine National Park and the Victorian Alps.
Cost: From $50 for a day walk to $940 for eight days.
Tour Operators: Adventure Center, Ecotrek: Bogong Jack Adventures, Walkabout Gourmet Adventures.

Tasmania

Until recently, some of the best overnight walks in Tasmania were major expeditions suitable only for the highly experienced and very fit. Plenty of these treks are still available, including the nine-day South Coast Track trip operated by Tasmanian Expeditions. The trail includes some easy stretches along pristine, secluded beaches, as well as difficult legs through rugged coastal mountains. You must fly into this remote area—it's the combination of difficult trails and extreme isolation that gives this walk spice.

A much easier walk is conducted on the Freycinet Peninsula, about 97 km (60 mi) north of Port Arthur on the east coast. Much of it can be explored only on foot: The road ends at the pink granite domes of the Hazards, which form a rampart across the top of the peninsula. If you take the time to venture beyond them, you will discover a world of pristine bush where wallabies loll, and white sand beaches fringe crystal clear water. One organized walk, led by Freycinet Experience, lasts four days, the average walk per day covering only 10 km (6 mi). Participants carry very light packs and spend the first two nights in comfortable standing camps, complete with wooden platforms, beds, and pillows. The final night is in a Tasmanian hardwood lodge that is furnished with scatter rugs and wood furniture and situated to take advantage of the best views. The cost is $995.

The best-known walk in Tasmania is the trail from Cradle Mountain to Lake St. Clair. It's so popular that boardwalks have been placed along some sections to prevent the path from turning into a quagmire. The walk starts and finishes in dense forest, but much of it runs along exposed highland ridges. The construction of the Cradle Mountain Huts several years ago made this trail far more accessible. However, these huts are available only to hikers on one of Cradle Mountain Huts' escorted walks. The huts are basic, but they provide a level of comfort unimaginable to anyone forced to camp in the mud of the area's mountain ranges. Huts are well heated and extensively supplied; there are even warm showers. Other operators continue to conduct camping tours along the trail as well as elsewhere in Tasmania. The rapid weather changes typical of this area present an extra challenge, but the spectacular mountain scenery makes any discomfort that the cold or wet causes worthwhile.

Season: November–May.
Locations: Central highlands; south, east, and west coasts.
Cost: From about $130 per day, including camping equipment and meals, to $1,350 for the six-day Cradle Mountain Huts walk or $1,600 for a comprehensive 14-day tour of the island.
Tour Operators: Cradle Mountain Huts, Freycinet Experience, Peregrine Adventures, Tasmanian Expeditions, World Expeditions.

South Australia

There is a wide range of walking opportunities in South Australia, including spectacular coastal walks and the remarkable Heysen Trail, which traverses nearly 2,000 km (1,240 mi) of the semiarid Flinders Ranges and the more gentle Mount Lofty Ranges. In addition to their Heysen Trail itineraries, Ecotrek: Bogong Jack Adventures operates walks on Kangaroo Island and in the rugged Gammon Ranges.

Season: April–October.
Locations: Flinders Ranges, Gammon Ranges, Kangaroo Island.
Cost: From $410 for four days to $720 for seven days.
Tour Operator: Ecotrek: Bogong Jack Adventures.

Camel Trekking

Riding a camel is rather like riding two horses strapped together at right angles. Surprisingly, though, sitting astride a wide, padded, camel saddle is more comfortable than riding horseback, and the animals aren't nearly as aggressive as many people believe. In fact, they can be quite endearing, although they do have revolting personal habits. The night silence of your desert campsite will regularly be broken by the sound of camels regurgitating, followed by their dawn screams as they object to waking from their dreams of desert oases. Strange as it may seem, a camel trek is an extremely pleasant way to spend a week or two, and it beautifully recaptures the experience of desert travel as it was in the past. Australian camels come from Afghan stock (hence the name of the *Ghan* train, which follows the old desert route of the Afghan camel trains from Adelaide to Alice Springs), and many now roam wild in the Outback. Camel treks rate as soft adventure.

New South Wales

Located on the north coast of New South Wales, 419 km (260 mi) north of Sydney, Port Macquarie is a long way from any desert. But it does have an impressive array of expansive, long sandy beaches. Ron Keating set up his camel operation in 1990 and it has now won several tourism awards. The first day of the Overnight Camel Safari weekend takes you to a camp by a freshwater lagoon behind the dunes. All meals (which include local prawns and oysters), drinks, and camping equipment are provided. On day two, you can relax around the beach and campside until morning tea, then ride back to Port Macquarie in time for lunch.

Season: Year-round for individuals, for groups only during school holidays.
Location: Port Macquarie.
Cost: $175 for a 24-hour overnight trip.
Tour Operator: Port Macquarie Camel Safaris.

South Australia

The major camel-tour operator in South Australia, Rex Ellis has a fascination with the Outback that led him to make the only north–south boat crossing of normally dry Lake Eyre. Between April and October, his camel farm in the Flinders Ranges operates rides from a few hours to eight days. For the more adventurous traveler, he operates a series of camel expeditions over the winter months that strike deep into the desert. These include three weeks in the remote Simpson Desert, 16 days in Sturts Stony Desert and Coongie Lakes, and three weeks along the banks of Coopers Creek. The success of these trips relies on the spirit of adventure of the expedition members, to say nothing of the camels' unique ability to cope with arid conditions.

Season: Year-round.
Location: Flinders Ranges.
Cost: From $25 for 1½ hours to about $2,500 for up to three weeks.
Tour Operator: Outback Camel Company.

Northern Territory–The Red Centre

With his long white beard and collection of outback yarns, Noel Fullerton of Alice Springs Camel Outback Safaris is one of the Northern Territory's most colorful characters. He obtained his first camel in 1969, and his company now conducts camel rides of an hour or a day along with a series of camel safaris through the Red Centre from his farm outside Alice Springs (☞ Chapter 10). After a riding accident a few years ago, Noel now leads only occasional trips himself—others are led by his family and staff. Among the places these treks visit is Rainbow Valley, remote gorge country that includes the oldest watercourse in the world and an ancient stand of palms.

Located conveniently close to Alice Springs, Frontier Camel Tours offers a very popular "Take A Camel Out To Dinner" tour, as well as short camel rides that operate every morning and afternoon. Longer safaris include a trek into the Western MacDonnell Ranges, and a six-day Simpson Desert expedition that passes the spectacular 190-ft-high sandstone monolith of Chambers Pillar.

Season: April–September (weekly departures), October–March (every two weeks).
Location: Alice Springs.
Cost: From $45 for a half-day ride to about $330 for three days or $750–$900 for a week.
Tour Operators: Adventure Center, Alice Springs Camel Outback Safaris, Frontier Camel Tours, World Expeditions.

Cross-Country Skiing

Unlike the jagged peaks of alpine regions elsewhere in the world, the ancient Australian Alps have rounded summits, making them ideal for cross-country skiing. Although cross-country doesn't offer the same adrenaline rush as downhill skiing, there are no expensive lift tickets to buy—your legs do the work. Although crowds build up on the slopes, cross-country skiers have a chance to get away from the hordes and experience the unforgettable sensation of skiing through forests of eucalyptus trees, with their spreading branches, pale leaves, and impressionistic bark patterns. Cross-country skiing is hard adventure, even though many tours are arranged so that skiers stay in lodges every night. The joy of leaving the first tracks across new snow and the pleasure afforded by the unique scenery of the Australian snowfields is tempered by the remarkable fatigue that your arms and legs feel at the end of the day—an exhilarating combination.

New South Wales

Some 450 km (279 mi) south of Sydney, Jindabyne is the major gateway to the Snowy Mountains. Morrell Adventure Travel has a large range of camping and lodge-based cross-country ski programs throughout the Snowys. It also has a one-day backcountry tour from Thredbo for downhill skiers. Paddy Pallin Jindabyne is an offshoot of Australia's most respected outdoor-equipment retail store. It has a complete range of ski tours and cross-country instructional programs. Most of the courses are based out of a lodge, but there are also two- and five-day camping tours across the snow trails of the Main Range.

Season: July–September.
Location: Snowy Mountains.
Cost: From $32 for a half day of instruction to $700 for a seven-day tour.
Tour Operators: Morrell Adventure Travel, Paddy Pallin Jindabyne.

Victoria

Ecotrek: Bogong Jack Adventures offers a comprehensive program of lodge-based trips, camping expeditions, skiing instruction, and snow-craft courses. Groups are kept small (fewer than 15 people), and there are enough instructors to ensure that you learn quickly. Building snow caves and mastering the art of survival in the snow are excellent skills—even if Australia seems like a strange place to learn them. In reality, however, the open, gentle slopes here are ideal for learning how to ski cross-country. The scenery of the Victorian Alps is dramatic, with the valley sides rising steeply to high-country plains. A major advantage of skiing in Victoria is that the lodges where skiers stay are close to the snowfields. These comfortable lodges are located below the snow line, and evenings by the fire and the inevitable camaraderie of the group make these stays most enjoyable.

Season: July–September.
Locations: Mansfield, Mt. Beauty, Falls Creek, Mt. Hotham.
Cost: From about $270 for a weekend course to $700 for a five-day and $1,000 for an eight-day course or tour.
Tour Operator: Ecotrek: Bogong Jack Adventures.

Diving

Australia is one of the world's premier diving destinations. Much of the attention centers on Queensland's Great Barrier Reef, but there is very good diving elsewhere as well—including Tasmania and Western Australia (☞ *below*) and Lord Howe Island (☞ Chapter 3). Australian diving operations are generally well run and regulated, and equipment is modern and well maintained. Because it's a competitive industry, most instructors are good at their jobs. Of course, although this competition (especially in Queensland) creates lower prices, it also reduces service. Anyone planning on learning to dive in Australia should closely examine what operators provide (especially the number of open-water dives) rather than basing a decision solely on cost.

Tasmania

Australia's most southern state is not the obvious place to go diving. However, Tasmania's east coast has a remarkably sunny climate and some exceptional kelp forests, magnificent sponge gardens, anemone, basket stars, squid octopus, and butterfly perch. In winter there's a chance that you will dive with the dolphins and whales that call in here on their migration from Antarctica. And King Island in Bass Strait, off the north coast, has some very good wreck diving. Overall, Tasmania possesses Australia's most wreck-strewn coastline—there are more than 20 sites to choose from, including the wreck of the *Cataraqui,* the country's worst maritime disaster.

Season: Mainly summer, but the best east coast conditions are during winter.
Locations: Bicheno, King Island.
Cost: From $105 per day, including two boat dives and all equipment.
Tour Operators: Bicheno Dive Centre, King Island Dive Charters.

Queensland

The main diving centers in Queensland are the island resorts: Cairns (☞ Chapter 7) and the Whitsunday islands and Port Douglas (☞ Chapter 8). For further details on dive operators there, refer to those chapters.

Season: Year-round.
Locations: All along the coast and Great Barrier Reef islands.

Cost: From $50 for a single dive and from $120 for a day trip that includes a boat cruise and two dives. Five-day certification courses start at around $400.

Tour Operators: Dive Adventures, Dive Travel Australia, Pro Dive Travel.

Western Australia

Whale sharks are the world's largest fish. A large one weighs 40 tons and is 50 ft long. It *is* in the shark family, but it is also completely harmless. Like many whales, whale sharks live on tiny krill—not fish, seals, or people. From about March through May each year, more than 100 whale sharks can be found along the Western Australian coast near Exmouth. The exact season varies—depending on the time of the spawning of the coral of Ningaloo Reef. Exmouth is the only place in the world where you can be sure of encountering whale sharks.

If you decide to swim with them, it's as if you have adopted a puppy the size of a truck—or have your own pet submarine. Government regulations prohibit touching them or swimming closer to them than a meter (about a yard). It's an expensive day of diving because you need a large boat to take you out to the sharks, a spotter plane to find them, and a runabout to drop you back in front of their path. Although most of the day is spent with whale sharks, it begins with a dive on Ningaloo Reef. The diversity of coral and marine life here isn't as remarkable as at the Great Barrier Reef, but there is a spectacular juxtaposition of large open-water fish and huge schools of bait fish. Outside of whale-shark season you can encounter a passing parade of humpback whales (from July through September) and nesting turtles (from November through February).

Season: March–June.
Location: Exmouth.
Cost: $299 (including transfer to the boat, an optional dive on Ningaloo Reef, a salad lunch, and soft drinks. It also includes the cost of the spotter aircraft, the runabout to keep you in contact with the whale shark, and the whale shark interaction license fee.)
Tour Operator: Exmouth Diving Centre.

Four-Wheel-Drive Tours

Australia is a vast land with a small population, so many Outback roads are merely clearings through the bush. Black soil that turns into skid pans after rain, the ubiquitous red dust of the center, and the continent's great sandy deserts make a four-wheel-drive vehicle a necessity for exploring the more remote countryside. Outback motoring possesses a real element of adventure—on some roads it's standard practice to call in at the few homesteads along the way so they can initiate search procedures if you fail to turn up at the next farm down the track. At the same time, the laconic Aussies you meet in such places are a different breed from urban Australians, and time spent with them is often memorable. Despite the rugged nature of many of the bush tracks that pass for roads in Australia, four-wheel-drive tours are definitely soft adventure.

Queensland

The most northerly point of the Australian mainland, Cape York is the destination sought by every four-wheel-drive enthusiast in Australia. After passing through the rain forest north of Port Douglas, the track travels through relatively dry vegetation the rest of the way. Several galleries of spectacular Aboriginal rock paintings are here, as are a historic telegraph station and the notorious Jardine River, whose shifting bottom made fording very tricky in the past. Until a few years ago, reaching the Cape was a major achievement; now a ferry service across the Jardine makes it easier, but Cape York is still frontier territory—a land of mining camps, Aboriginal settlements, and enormous cattle stations. For all intents and purposes, civilization stops at Cooktown. Wild Track offers you the option of flying to Cape York and driving back to Cairns on a one-week trip, or driving both ways over two weeks. Shorter trips of one, two, or three days' duration are also available.

Season: Mainly May–November.
Location: North of Cairns.
Cost: From $179 for a one-day trip and from $1,399 for seven days to $1,999 for a two-week return trip.
Tour Operator: Wild Track Adventure Safaris.

South Australia

Unless you have the time to walk, the rugged areas of South Australia are best explored by four-wheel-drive vehicle. Kangaroo Island supports a huge variety of animals, including kangaroos, koalas, fur seals, penguins, and sea lions, as well as such bizarre natural features as huge limestone arches and weather-worn rocks that resemble Henry Moore sculptures. Adventure Charters of Kangaroo Island operates a series of tours, the most comprehensive being a three-day, two-night package.

Alternatively, if you head north, the desert starts relatively near Adelaide. The Flinders Ranges are a low finger of mountains stretching into the desert. Their most notable feature is Wilpena Pound, a huge natural amphitheater filled with small trees and grasses overlooking the barren plains below. Intrepid Tours offers a series of one-day and overnight tours throughout this region.

Season: Year-round.
Locations: Kangaroo Island, Flinders Ranges.
Cost: From $383 for one day and $784 for the three-day trip on Kangaroo Island (prices include airfares to the island), or $566 for a four-day tour through the Outback.
Tour Operators: Adventure Charters of Kangaroo Island, Intrepid Tours.

Northern Territory

Although the number of tourists at Kakadu National Park has risen dramatically each year, some sites can still be reached only by four-wheel-drive vehicle, including Jim Jim Falls and Twin Falls—two of Australia's most scenic attractions. At both of these falls, the water plunges over the escarpment to the flood plains beneath. Below the picturesque falls are deep, cool pools and beautiful palm-shaded beaches. The Adventure Center has comprehensive tours of this remarkable area. World Expeditions has a one-week adventure safari into the wilderness of Kakadu and the remote Cobourg Peninsula.

The **Darwin Region Tourism Association** (✉ 38 Mitchell St., Darwin, NT 0800, ☎ 08/8981–4300, FAX 08/8981–0653) can provide more information about the numerous tour operators based in Darwin.

Season: April–October.
Locations: Throughout the Northern Territory, but mainly in Kakadu.
Cost: From about $625 for six days to $1,390 for 14 days.
Tour Operators: Adventure Center, World Expeditions.

Western Australia–The Kimberley

Most of the four-wheel-drive adventures in Western Australia take place in the Kimberley region in the far north (☞ Chapter 11). The only practical time to visit the Kimberley is during the Dry, May through November, because roads are very often flooded during the Wet.

The Kimberley boasts Australia's richest Aboriginal cultural heritage, and the extraordinary rock art here can be explored in World Expeditions' four-wheel-drive trip to the Bungle Bungles and to the remote, little-explored Keep River National Park on the Northern Territory–Western Australian border. This company also offers an exciting trip from Broome into the Kimberley and Mitchell Plateau area.

East Kimberley Tours and Halls Creek and Bungle Bungle Tours have a range of expeditions into the Bungle Bungles, most of which involve flying, being met at the airstrip, and continuing on a one- or two-day exploration of the massif. If you stay overnight, accommodations are at the operators' permanent camp. At least three days are required if you wish to drive the rough road into Bungle Bungle.

Season: May–November.
Location: The Kimberley.
Cost: From $400 for three days to $700 for six days, and from $1,400 for eight days to $2,745 for a 13-day tour.
Tour Operators: East Kimberley Tours, Halls Creek and Bungle Bungle Tours, World Expeditions.

Horseback Riding

Trail bikes and four-wheel-drive vehicles have slowly been replacing horses on Australian farms and stations over the past 20 years. On the plains and coastal lowlands the transformation is complete, but horses are still part of rural life in the highlands, and it is here that the best horseback adventures are to be found. On a horse trek you come closer to the life of the pioneer Australian bushmen than in any other adventure pursuit. Indeed, the majority of treks are led by Australians with close links to the traditions of bush life.

Riding through alpine meadows and along mountain trails, and sleeping under the stars is an excellent way to see the Australian bush. A typical horseback vacation lasts several days, and the food and equipment for each night's camp is brought in by packhorse or four-wheel-drive vehicle. Although a cook, a guide, and all specialist equipment are provided, participants are expected to help look after the horses. An Australian saddle is a cross between the high Western saddle and the almost flat English one. The horses are normally real workhorses, not riding hacks, and they are used to rough bush work. These trips are essentially soft adventures, for most of the work is done by the horses—it's just hard to convince your cramping leg muscles of this after a long day in the saddle.

New South Wales
The Great Dividing Range, which extends right through New South Wales, has some excellent trails for horseback riding. Almost every country town has a riding school with horses for hire, but a few long rides are particularly outstanding. In the Snowy Mountains high country, a six-day summer ride from Reynella homestead through Kosciusko National Park covers terrain ranging from open plains to alpine forests. Riders camp out in some of the most beautiful valleys in the park—valleys not easily accessible except by horse. A hundred years ago this was the stuff of pioneer legend.

One of the best stables in the Blue Mountains is Packsaddlers in the Megalong Valley, which conduct regular one-, two-, and three-day rides through the rugged countryside to Cox's River. Leaving the farmlands behind and descending through the forest into the river valley, you enter a part of the country that has changed little since European settlers first arrived in Australia. Although you're only a few hours due west of Sydney, eating a lunch from a saddlebag by the river while the horses graze nearby is a memorable bush experience.

One of the most unusual rides in Australia is the "Pub Crawl on Horseback," a 150-km (93-mi) ride through the New England Ranges to Sydney's north, with nights spent at old bush pubs along the early stagecoach routes. The tour emphasizes the bush experience, not drinking, because riding into a tiny village and booking into a historic pub is thrill enough. All the communities en route could fairly be described as one-horse towns—at least until your posse hits town.

In addition to its variety of New South Wales riding trips, Equitrek Australia offers riding in South Australia, Queensland, Western Australia, and the Northern Territory.

Season: All year, but mainly November–April.
Locations: Blue Mountains, Snowy Mountains, New England Highlands.
Cost: From $60 to $100 for a day ride to $200 for a weekend and $1,000 for a week.
Tour Operators: Equitrek Australia, Great Aussie Pub Crawls on Horseback, Packsaddlers, Paddy Pallin Jindabyne, Reynella Rides.

Victoria
An important part of the Australian rural mythology is an A.B. (Banjo) Paterson 1895 poem entitled "The Man from Snowy River," based on the equestrian feats of riders in the Victorian high plains who rounded up stock and horses from seemingly inaccessible valleys. For those who wish to emulate the hero of that work, several operators have rides of 2 to 10 days in the area. Part of the journey is spent above the tree line, where, as Banjo Paterson said, "the horses' hooves strike firelight from the flintstones every stride." Accommodations are either in tents or in the original bushmen's huts that dot the high country.

Season: October–May.
Location: Victorian high plains.
Cost: $65–$150 per day.
Tour Operators: Bogong Horseback Adventures, Stoneys' Bluff & Beyond Trailrides.

Rafting

The exhilaration of sweeping down into the foam-filled jaws of a rapid is always tinged with fear—white-water rafting is, after all, much like being tossed into a washing machine. Although this sort of excitement appeals to many people, the attraction of rafting in Australia involves much more. As you drift downriver during the lulls between the white water, it's wonderful to sit back and watch the wilderness unfold, whether it's stately river gums overhanging the stream, towering cliffs, or forests of eucalyptus on the surrounding slopes. Rafting means camping by the river at night, drinking billy tea brewed over the camp-fire, going to sleep with the sound of the stream in the background, or sighting an elusive platypus at dawn. The juxtaposition of action and serenity gives rafting an enduring appeal that leads most who try it to seek out more rivers with more challenges. Rivers here are smaller and trickier than the ones used for commercial rafting in North America, and rafts usually hold only four to six people. Rafting companies provide all rafting and camping equipment—you only need clothing that won't be damaged by water (cameras are carried in waterproof bar-rels), a sleeping bag (in some cases), and sunscreen. Rafting qualifies as hard adventure.

New South Wales

The upper reaches of Australia's longest waterway, the Murray River, are open for rafting between September and November, when the stream is fed by melting snow. The river is cold, but the rapids are chal-lenging, and the Australian Alps appear in all their spring glory.

The Gwydir River is fed by a large dam, and the scenery downriver is mainly pastoral, but the river has a series of challenging rapids. The Shoalhaven south of Sydney passes through some of the most impres-sive scenery in the coastal ranges.

The Nymboida River flows through beautiful subtropical rain forest near Coffs Harbour and is the warmest river with white water in the state. World Expeditions runs all of these rivers, Whitewater Rafting Professionals only operate on the Nymboida.

Season: Generally September–May.
Locations: The Murray River in the southern part of New South Wales, the Shoalhaven and Gwydir rivers in the center, and the Nymboida River in the north.
Cost: From $115 to $165 for a one-day Nymboida or Shoalhaven trip to about $260–$300 for a weekend. All camping and rafting equip-ment is supplied.
Tour Operators: White Water Rafting Professionals, World Expeditions.

Victoria

The driving time from Melbourne to Victoria's rafting rivers is gener-ally less than from Sydney to the main New South Wales rafting loca-tions. Nevertheless, you need to budget at least a weekend for the trip and be prepared to camp out. The scenery ranges from the rugged Alps of the north to the pastoral areas of eastern Victoria. The Mitta Mitta River is invariably rafted as a two-day trip.

Season: Mainly July–December.
Locations: Mitta Mitta, Thomson, Murray, and Snowy rivers.
Cost: From $270 for a weekend.
Tour Operators: Peregrine Adventures, World Expeditions.

Tasmania

The most exciting white-water rafting gives an instant adrenaline rush. Fortunately, most rivers provide plenty of quiet reaches where you can regain your breath and appreciate the scenery. Nowhere is this more true than on the Franklin River, which has the most spectacular and rewarding rafting in Australia. Deep rocky chasms, grand forested valleys, beautiful sandy beaches, and miles of untouched wilderness make the Franklin something special. The river leads through a truly remote area of Tasmania—there are few places where you can join or leave the river. You have the choice of exploring either the lower or upper parts of the Franklin, or the entire navigable length. By far the most rewarding option is covering the entire river. The combination of isolation, beauty, difficult rapids, and strenuous portages ensures that rafters finish the trip with a real feeling of achievement. It's a difficult and challenging journey that should be tackled only by people who are reasonably fit and comfortable in the bush.

Season: November–March.
Location: Franklin River, west coast.
Cost: From about $1,000 for five days to $1,560–$1,750 for 11–13 days.
Tour Operators: Peregrine Adventures, Tasmanian Expeditions, World Expeditions.

South Australia

The Nullarbor Plain is a flat, treeless desert that stretches for nearly 1,000 miles through Western Australia and South Australia. Below its arid surface, however, lies the largest underground lake in the Southern Hemisphere. On one of the most unusual adventure trips in Australia, participants descend belowground to explore several huge caves, both on foot and by raft. Although only a few of the eight days are spent underground (none of the campsites are underground), they are the most memorable. Swimming in Weebubblie Cave is an unbelievably strange sensation; the water in another cave is so clear that you feel as if you are space-walking through liquid crystal; and an 8-km (5-mi) trail winds through another cavern. No previous caving experience is required, and you won't have to squeeze through any tight spaces if you don't want to. The tour also includes a trip to vantage points along the coast overlooking the breeding grounds of the southern right whale, as well as a visit to an underground rock gallery of Aboriginal paintings in the Great Victoria Desert. Unlike most rafting trips, this is soft adventure.

Season: July–October.
Location: Nullarbor Plain.
Cost: $1,300 for nine days.
Tour Operator: Osprey Wildlife Expeditions.

14 Portraits of Australia

The Shocking Truth About Australian Wine

Five Thousand Miles from Anywhere

Pillars of Fire Across the Plains

The First Australians

THE SHOCKING TRUTH ABOUT AUSTRALIAN WINE

IF THE STORY of Australian wine were poured into a single glass, it would not be pale, structured, and elegant, but jumping with life, enchantingly precocious—and slightly shocking.

Taste it. Roll it around your tongue. Sit down at a table and team it with a Tasmanian lobster salad, or a dozen freshly opened Nambucca Heads oysters, or Australia's newest national dish: seared kangaroo with beetroot. The marriage of Australian food and wine is not a fleeting, passionate affair, it is the real thing, a solid, meaningful, and long-lasting partnership.

But don't expect this wine-and-food matchmaking to fall into safe, comfortable little pinot noir–and–pigeon holes.

Prepare to be thoroughly taken aback, or at least a touch startled, as the new breeds from Australia's wine makers rise up to meet the challenge of an exciting new generation of chefs who need wines to work magic with the feisty, spice- and herb-laden flavors of Asia and the Mediterranean in their cooking. Today's lighter, more refreshing wine styles have left traditional wine-and-food pairing theories dragging their heels in the dust.

Like the one that states only semidry white wine can be drunk with Asian food, or the one about not teaming red wine with fish.

James Halliday, whose bright-tasting Coldstream Hills Pinot Noir from Victoria's Yarra Valley regularly turns up on the country's hottest wine lists, suggests his pinot not only works well with Chinese food (especially Cantonese roast duck), but that it is also a perfect partner for the rich flesh of farmed Atlantic salmon. Likewise, Bannockburn Pinot Noir from Geelong, Dromana Estate Pinot Noir from the Mornington Peninsula, and Piper's Brook Pellion from Northern Tasmania show similar compatibility.

Neil Perry, the swashbuckling, pony-tailed chef of Sydney's groundbreaking Rockpool and Wockpool restaurants, also throws rules out the window, favoring a big, bold Oakridge Yarra Valley Cabernet with his grilled swordfish steak and mushroom potsticker dumplings—or a nicely complex Evans and Tate Margaret River Chardonnay with his Chinese roast duck and sea scallops.

Japanese-born chef Tetsuya Wakuda of the much-loved Tetsuya's restaurant regularly teams his delicate, Japanese-influenced food with one of Australia's brave new sauvignon blancs. A far cry from the "asparagus and cat's piss" wines that have earned sauvignon blanc the scorn of critics around the world, these are beautifully balanced, food-friendly wines. Wakuda suggests a Willespie Sauvignon Blanc from the Margaret River in Western Australia with his warmed salad of tiger prawns and asparagus, and a delicately perfumed Gembrook Hill Sauvignon Blanc from the Yarra Valley with his signature confit of Tasmanian Ocean Trout with konbu, capers, and parsley oil.

He is also a keen advocate of cool-climate gerwurtztraminers. And the coupling of his Spring Bay scallops with coriander, lemongrass, and ginger with the character-laden Henschke Joseph Hill Gerwurtztraminer from South Australia's Eden Valley is nothing short of inspired.

"These wines work better than sake," Wakuda claims, with a glass in his hand and a grin on his face.

Searching out a truly Australian wine style is loaded with even more surprises. From the wineries of Northeast Victoria, an area known for its full-bodied reds, come some truly remarkable fortified tokays and muscats, all with a delicious, wild, untamed quality that is so rich and sticky you don't know whether to drink them—or spread them. Among the more notable varieties are the All Saints Classic Release Tokay, Campbell's Liquid Gold, and Tokay Bailey's Old Muscat. Believe it or not, these are perfect with Australia's distinctive farmhouse cheeses, such as Milawa Gold (North East Victoria), Yarra Valley Persian Fetta, and Meredith Blue (from Victoria's Western District).

Practically unknown beyond these shores is what was once affectionately but euphemistically known as sparkling burgundy, an effervescent red made mainly from shiraz grapes using the traditional méthode champenoise. A dense yet lively wine with fresh, fruity tones, it is particularly suited to game and turkey and is now an integral part of a festive Australian Christmas dinner. Look for labels such as Seppelts Harpers Range, Yalumba Cuvée Two, and Hugh Hamilton Sparkling Shiraz.

Then there are the classic rieslings of the Barossa and Clare valleys of South Australia, first introduced by German and Silesian settlers last century. Today, wines such as Heggies Riesling, Petaluma Riesling, and Wirra Wirra Hand Picked Riesling are just as much at home with Middle Eastern merguez sausage and cous cous as they are with knackwurst and sauerkraut.

Also very Australian in style are the big, oaky Semillons of the Hunter Valley (try Tyrrell's Vat 1 Semillon and Lindeman's Hunter River Semillon) and the powerful steak-and-braised-meat–loving cabernets from the rich, red "terra rossa" soil of the Coonawarra district in South Australia. These wines, including Petaluma Coonawarra, Lindeman's Pyrus, and Hollick Coonawarra, have a habit of knocking first-timers' socks off.

THAT SAID, Australian wines have been stopping people in their tracks ever since the first grapes were grown in the first governor's garden back in 1788.

Certainly, the French wine judges at the prestigious Vienna Exhibition of 1873 got the shock of their lives when faced with a group of "Hermitage" wines from Bendigo in Victoria. In fact, they refused even to judge them at first, claiming that wines so French could not possibly have come from Australia.

To this day, French judges remain bewildered by the quality of many Australian varietals. French wine companies, on the other hand, have been expanding their territories to Australia in a series of ambitious joint ventures. The results are some impressive sparkling wines, including Domaine Chandon from the Yarra Valley

and Jansz from the Pipers River area of Tasmania.

In 1951, more surprises were in store for French and Australian critics alike when an enterprising South Australian wine maker named Max Schubert produced a red wine so strikingly original and powerful that it singlehandedly changed the face of Australian wine making. Made from Syrah, or Shiraz grapes, Grange Hermitage (or Grange as it is now known) is by far Australia's most famous wine, yet nobody quite knew what to make of it at first.

"Schubert, I congratulate you," said one skeptic. "A very good, dry port, which no one in their right mind will buy, let alone drink."

Another respected wine man labeled the astonishingly robust and powerful wine as "a concoction of wild fruits and berries with crushed ants predominating."

Fortunately, Schubert persisted with his wine, creating what is now generally regarded as the quintessentially Australian red, and one of the finest wines in the world.

As a breed, the Australian shiraz style is well worth getting to know. It has delicious pepper-berry characteristics and food-friendly companionability. Fortunately, not all Australian shiraz carries the now astronomic Grangelike price tags. In fact, other Schubert-inspired wines, such as Penfold's bins 128 and 389, are far more accessible, as are a clutch of worthy labels that includes Elderton Shiraz from the Barossa Valley, Brokenwood Graveyard Vineyard from the Hunter Valley, and Seppelt Great Western Shiraz from the Grampians in Victoria.

For an old-world variety, shiraz is very much at home with modern Australian cooking, working beautifully with a Moroccan-inspired lamb tagine, Mediterranean-style roasted goat, pasta, and yes, even kangaroo with beetroot.

So there you have it. If you are about to embark on your own personal discovery of Australian wines, you have been warned. Now get ready to be amazed, astonished, and shocked—into having another glass.

— Terry Durack

FIVE THOUSAND MILES FROM ANYWHERE

START WITH THE LIGHT. Everything starts with the light here.

In the hour before nightfall, what Hollywood calls the "magic hour," the buildings in Australia start to glow with an unearthly light, and the gold-touched clouds look like something Blake might have imagined in his highest moments. The sky becomes a canvas on which absent gods are doodling: over here, patches of tropical blue; over there, shafts of silver slanting through the slate-gray clouds; everywhere, double rainbows arcing over gray Victorian monuments and avenues of palms. Yet this is hardly a warming scene. Rather, the Australian twilight has the same chilly strangeness, the same otherworldly calm—the same off-the-edge-of-the-earthliness—as Iceland in midsummer: a cold and science-fictive beauty. And as the night begins to descend, it seems as if the land is reclaiming itself, and Australia is more than ever a place emptied out of people, some dark, elemental presences awakened behind the placid surfaces of its newborn world.

The light in Australia is like nothing else on earth—as befits, perhaps, a country that feels as if it has fallen off the planet. "Australia's like an open door with the blue beyond," wrote D. H. Lawrence. "You just walk out of the world and into Australia." And the startled intensity of the heavens hints at all the weird paradoxes of this young old land of sunny ironists, a British California caught between a world it has abandoned and one it has yet to colonize. In the vast open blueness of Australia, the only presiding authority, it often seems, is the light.

Australia is, of course, the definitive—perhaps the ultimate—*terra incognita*, its very name derived from the Latin phrase *terra australis incognita*, or unknown land of the south. Captain Cook first bumped into the land of anomalies while trying to observe a transit of the planet Venus. And even today the world's largest island seems to occupy a huge open space in the mind, beyond the reach of our sights. Australia, for one thing, borders nothing and is on the way to nowhere. It feels, in every sense, like the last place on earth. Colonized originally by the British as a place for posthumous lives—a kind of Alcatraz on an epic scale—Australia has always seemed the natural setting for post-apocalyptic imaginings, from Lawrence's utopian visions to Nevil Shute's nuclear wasteland to the haunted deathscape of Mad Max.

What little we know of this tabula rasa, moreover, has generally sounded like fiction. "In Australia alone," as Marcus Clarke wrote, "is to be found the Grotesque, the Weird, the strange scribblings of Nature learning to write." The flattest and driest of the continents defies all the laws of probability with its natural—or unnatural—wonders: not just the world's only egg-laying mammals (the echidna and the duckbill platypus) but the wombat and the wallaby, the koala, the kangaroo, the kookaburra, and the quokka. A land of extremes, it is also one of inversions, an antipodean place where Christmas is celebrated in midsummer and the water goes the wrong way down the drain, a looking-glass world in which trees lose their bark but not their leaves, and crows, it is said, fly backwards (to keep the dust from their eyes). Even the country's social origins are the stuff of Restoration comedy, a down-underworld in which convicts were known as "government men" and thieves were appointed as magistrates—less the Promised than the Threatened Land.

Yet it is in the nature of Lonely Places to attract people, in large part because of their loneliness, and the greatest reason of all for Australia's appeal is, in the end, the very thing that has outlawed it for so long: the tyranny of distance. People are realizing that Australia is so far from the world that it is the ideal place for people who wish to get away from the world, do nothing, and watch others do the same.

This article was written for the Australian bicentennial in 1988. In the time that's elapsed since then, some of the names have changed, but the spirit of terra australis *as Iyer described it lives on.*

The quietness, and unhurried spaciousness, of the Empty Continent can make one feel as if one has all the time in the world—indeed, as if time and the world have both been annulled: "rush hour" is not a term in common currency here. And though irreverence is an Australian article of faith, the most urbanized society on earth (70% of Aussies live in eight major cities) is increasingly endowed with all the gentrified accoutrements of a brunch culture: hotels so untouched they feel like resorts, towns that are drawing-board models of clean lines and open spaces, people who are devoted to life, liberty, and the pursuit of happiness. Not the least of the ironies governing a nation whose founding fathers were convicts is, in fact, that it is now most noted for its air of freedom, safety, and civic order.

IN AUSTRALIA'S laid-back sense of come-as-you-are palliness, many foreign observers have found a model of democracy in action, a natural kind of Whitmanesque fraternalism free of ideological baggage. Calling a spade a spade is a national habit, after all, and nothing seems to anger the Australian but pretension. Though Lawrence may have been merely being Lawrence when he claimed that Australians were such natural democrats that they did not even like to go upstairs, it is certainly true that a visitor is more likely to be called "mate" than "sir."

Yet if Australians' customs are often as unbuttoned as those of the American West, their manners are generally a little more reserved; touched with le vice anglais of self-containment, theirs is still a place of semidetached men in semidetached houses. And even though its feeling of space and ease, like its gold rush past and its sense of limitless future, gives Australia a somewhat Californian air, it feels more provisional, more pressureless than the frontier states of America, less troubled by introspection or ambition. Here, in fact, is a world that makes California seem positively frantic by comparison. In his novel Bliss, a typically Australian compound of irony, fancy, and profanity, Peter Carey shrewdly depicts his homeland as a mythic Eden "on the outposts of the American Empire . . . [with] business more or less done in the

American style, although without quite the degree of seriousness the Americans liked."

Australia, moreover, still holds to its fondness for the piratical, a sense that distinction lies not in the flaunting but in the flouting of refinement. The country delights in the marginal, glories in its freedom from convention, is determined to be different. There is a store in Sydney (as in London) exclusively for left-handers, and the sign in a Melbourne bookshop canvasses members for a Lost in Space club. And Australia's traditional images of rowdy nonconformity are still in constant evidence. The larrikin lives on in the 11-year-old busker in earrings and rattail haircut who plays drinking songs in front of Sydney harbor while his Fagin looks on from the shadows; the convict and prospector are remembered in the dark humor of the names that overbrood the landscape—Lake Disappointment, Cape Grim, Double Crossing Creek; and the ocker asserts his skeptical down-to-earthiness with the bumper sticker EVERYBODY NEEDS TO BELIEVE IN SOMETHING. I BELIEVE I'LL HAVE ANOTHER BEER. In this seriously macho culture, you see more men in earrings than anywhere else—less a statement of fashion, one senses, than a badge of defiant rebelliousness.

To some extent, too, the myths of frontier still animate the culture. Many young Australians continue to take off around the world, treating jobs as way stations and anywhere as home, while many retirement couples take to their mobile homes and circumnavigate the land. And though the country feels less restless than America, it is surely just as mobile. Everywhere there are dreams of long horizons: a concierge is studying Chinese to expand his prospects; a cabbie is working 60 hours a week in the hope of visiting South America; a waiter at an exclusive French restaurant simply picks up his camera and guitar and heads off for a new life in the Outback.

Mike, a rugged, long breeched man who runs a riding stable outside Melbourne, recalls how he came here alone on a boat at the age of 14, propelled by grand dreams awakened by Zane Grey. "There was a feeling that I could do nothing in England; and no matter how well I did at school, I could never go to university. That was just something that people like me didn't do. But over here, anything is possible. No way I could start up a place like this in England."

Besides, with its reverence for unorthodoxy and its sense of being away from it all, Australia remains an ideal retreat for odd men out. At times, in fact, one has the impression that it is less a culture than an aggregation of subcultures, a society of fringes—of surfers, cowboys, boozers, and hippies. Alternative lifestyles are the norm in many places, and the prospect of starting a new life has natural appeal for those committed to Rebirthing. The lush rolling hills known as the Rainbow Region, an hour west of the Gold Coast, have become a perfect haven for back-to-the-land purists and hypnotherapists, and the local bulletin board offers all the Oriental arts, from tai chi to tae kwon do. (The Breath of Life Relaxation and Healing Centre promises "Reiki healing" and "Lazaris videos"—all of this next to Woolworth's!) Still, mellowness here takes on a decidedly Aussie twang: "Shoplifting gives you bad karma!" advises a trendy Asian boutique in Sydney. "And if I catch you, I'll make sure you get it in this life—you Rat Fink! Sincerely, Sandi."

At the same time, Australia, like many a colony, has never entirely left behind the country that abandoned it here. As the relentlessly clever Tasmanian-born critic Peter Conrad points out in his half-autobiography, *Down Home,* Australians wistfully tried to assuage their homesickness by reinventing the motherland here—Tasmania alone has "a cliffless Dover, a beachless Brighton, an unindustrial Sheffield." A local newspaper may have no qualms about describing the visiting Duchess of York as "astonishingly frumpish," yet still her befreckled visage adorns at least three magazine covers in a single week. And even as the tattoo-and-bare-skin crowd is crowding in to see Mick Jagger (who once acted as the country's favorite outlaw, Ned Kelly) perform at the National Tennis Center, hundreds of well-behaved families are lining up to visit Prince Andrew's boat, docked down the coast in Tasmania.

TODAY, in many ways, Australia seems to reflect the eccentric ways of a Western European society set down in the middle of a Lonely Place: hotels as imaginatively designed as pavilions in some world's fair; cities that offer Balkan, Burmese, Mauritian, Uruguayan, and Seychellian cuisine; casinos that are typically down-home affairs where neither solemnity nor discretion is held in high regard ("Not a Poker Face in Sight," promises the Adelaide casino). Nearly all the heads in Australian bars are frothy, and tattooed bikers down 3.3-pint "stubbies" of Foster's in dusty outposts like the Humpty Doo Bar, where a bulletin board advertises pigs and a sign warns customers tersely, "Don't Ask for Credit as Refusal Often Offends." Australian entertainment, in fact, is nothing if not straightforward: a slim tourist brochure in Melbourne includes 22 full ads for escort agencies.

For the historically minded traveler, the main lure of the place may well be Tasmania, the oldest convict settlement after Sydney, and one of those out-of-the-way places that many people want to visit because of their vague sense that no one has visited them before. With its blustery skies and lowering, snowcapped Mount Wellington, Tasmania is in some respects an inversion of the mainland, itself an inversion of England, and so ends up a little like the mother country. But its green and pleasant land is scarred with the remnants of its gloomy penal past: the gutted gray buildings at Port Arthur, the graves on the Isle of the Dead, and all the other grisly mementos of a place once known as "Hell on Earth."

By contrast, the social history of modern Australia—and of many places like it—is summarized most tidily in the main shopping street in Adelaide, the wondrously compact little town laid out in a square by a man named Light. The thoroughfare begins life as Hindley Street, a rough-and-tumble desolation row of sailors' haunts—video arcades, take-away joints, and tawdry souvenir shops. The names say it all: the Box Adult Book Shop, Joynt Venture smoking paraphernalia, For Roses Tattoo Studio, the Sweetheart cocktail lounge, the Pop-in Coffee Lounge, and Crazy Horse Striptease Revue. Then, downtown, it turns into Rundle Mall, a gleaming, pedestrian-only monument to civic order, the sort of middling Middle Australian area you expect to find in any suburban center: Florsheim Shoes, Thomas Cook Travel, Standard Books, Woolworth's, and—on both sides of the central intersection—the Golden Arches.

Finally, on its eastern edge, Rundle Mall opens up into Rundle Street, a SoHoian anthology of today: the Appar-allel boutique, Known Space books, the Campari bistro, Al Fresco gelateria, the Australian School of Meditation, Bryan's Hairdressers, the Bangkok restaurant, Kelley's Grains and Seeds—one long neon-and-mannequin line of vintage clothes stores and veggie restaurants, culminating (as it must culminate) in the New Age Emporium. This street alone, it seems, tells the story of how the twenties became the fifties became the eighties, or how raffishness turned into Standard Shopping Center and then was reborn as Authentic Renovated and Redecorated Raffishdom.

As for the booming present tense, it is best inspected in the one area that contradicts the quiet and unpeopled air of the continent—and also, not coincidentally, the one area expressly designed for foreigners: the 21-mile Floridian motel-and-minigolf seaside strip known as the Gold Coast, an hour south of Brisbane. Centered on the town of Surfers Paradise, a place as self-effacing as its name, the Coast has become a furious riot of development, disco music pulsing through its glassy new arcades, Porsches cruising along its jungle of high-rises, a seemingly unending stretch of traffic-choked boulevards littered with ice cream parlors, Spanish-style motels, and Pizza Huts. There is a wax museum here, and Kenny Koala's Dreamworld. Ripley's Believe It or Not! is scheduled to open any day. And in truth, Surfers Paradise—or should it be called Surface Paradise?—has all the wound-up frenzy of an amusement park writ huge, a neo–Atlantic City tricked up in Miami Vice colors and high-tech accessories. Nothing is missing here, it seems, except surfers, perhaps, and paradise.

IN THE END, the greatest marvels of Australia reside simply in its land—the silence and the sky. For more than a day, you can travel through the Outback, a parched white land of ghosts, of blanched trees twisted at odd angles across a plain as vast and mysterious as Africa. Nothing breaks the vacancy but a dead cow, an upturned car, a stray eagle.

Everywhere there is only emptiness and flatness. And then, rising up unanswerably against a diorama-bright landscape of shocked blue and thick red, Ayers Rock, old and mute and implacable, in powerful counterpoint to the young, pretty, somewhat uninflected society all around. The sacred rock is one of those rare places with a genuine sense of mystery: it casts a larger shadow than any postcard could suggest.

Or awaken one Edenic morning in Kakadu to see the sun gilding the swampy billabong, jabirus hovering above the water in the golden, gauzy early light. Two hours later, on the South Alligator River, listen to a guide reciting names as if riffling through the multicolored pages of some children's picture book: pelicans and egrets and snakebirds are here; pied herons, masked plovers, and migrant warders from Siberia; lotus birds are among the mango trees, and white-breasted sea eagles (with a wingspan of 6 feet), glossy ibises (with sickle-shaped beaks), and whistling ducks ("not capable of quacking"). There are blue-winged kookaburras in the sky, and sulphur-crested cockatoos; frill-necked lizards along the riverbank, and even lazy crocodiles sunbathing just 10 feet from the boat. At dusk, the birds honk and squawk above a huge, pink-flowering lily pond, and flocks of black magpie geese and silver-winged corellas fly across the face of a huge full moon that sits in the middle of the darkening sky, catching the silver of their wings. In the daily enchantment of dusk, a visitor begins, at last, to catch the presence of an Australia within, a *terra incognita* deep inside, and a loneliness that will stay with him even when he leaves. In the twilight of Australia, the foreigner can catch an intimation of what Melville calls "the great America on the other side of the sphere," and so a sense of how everything brings him back to the natural state where he began: a lonely person in a Lonely, Lonely Place.

— Pico Iyer

Pico Iyer is a longtime essayist for *Time* and a contributing editor to *Condé Nast Traveler*, *Civilization*, and *Tricycle: The Buddhist Review*. His books include *Cuba and the Night*, *Falling off the Map*, from which this excerpt was taken, *The Lady and the Monk*, and *Video Night in Kathmandu*.

PILLARS OF FIRE ACROSS THE PLAINS

THE WESTERN PLAINS of New South Wales are grasslands. Their vast expanse flows for many hundreds of miles beyond the Lachlan and Murrumbidgee rivers until the desert takes over and sweeps inland to the dead heart of the continent. In a good season, if the eyes are turned to the earth on those plains, they see a tapestry of delicate life—not the luxuriant design of a book of hours by any means, but a tapestry nonetheless, designed by a spare modern artist. What grows there hugs the earth firmly with its extended system of roots above which the plant life is delicate but determined. After rain there is an explosion of growth. Nut-flavored green grass puts up the thinnest of green spears. Wild grains appear, grains which develop bleached gold ears as they ripen. Purple desert peas weave through the green and gold, and bright yellow bachelor's buttons cover acres at a time, like fields planted with mustard. Closest to the earth is trefoil clover, whose tiny, vivid green leaves and bright flowers creep along the ground in spring, to be replaced by a harvest of seed-filled burrs in autumn—burrs that store within them the energy of the sun as concentrated protein. At the edges of pans of clay, where the topsoil has eroded, live waxy succulents bearing bright pink and purple blooms, spreading like splashes of paint dropped in widening circles on the earth.

Above the plants that creep across the ground are the bushes, which grow wherever an indentation in the earth, scarcely visible to the eye, allows for the concentration of more moisture from the dew and the reluctant rain. There is the ever-present round mound of prickly weed, which begins its life a strong acid green with hints of yellow, and then is burnt by the sun or the frost to a pale whitish yellow. As it ages, its root system weakens so that on windy days the wind will pick it out of the earth and roll it slowly and majestically about like whirling suns in a Van Gogh painting.

The creatures that inhabit this earth carry its colors in their feathers, fur, or scales. Among its largest denizens are emus, 6-foot-high flightless birds with dun-gray feathers and tiny wings, and kangaroos. Kangaroos, like emus, are silent creatures, 2 to 8 feet tall, and ranging in color from the gentlest dove-gray to a rich red-brown. Both species blend with their native earth so well that one can be almost upon them before recognizing the familiar shape. The fur of the wild dogs has the familiar yellow of the sun-baked clay, and the reptiles, snakes, and goannas look like the earth in shadow. All tread on the fragile habitat with padded paws and claws that leave the roots of grass intact.

On the plains, the earth meets the sky in a sharp black line so regular that it seems as though drawn by a creator interested more in geometry than the hills and valleys of the Old Testament. Human purposes are dwarfed by such a blank horizon. When we see it from an island in a vast ocean we know we are resting in shelter. On the plains, the horizon is always with us and there is no retreating from it. Its blankness travels with our every step and waits for us at every point of the compass. Because we have very few reference points on the spare earth, we seem to creep over it, one tiny point of consciousness between the empty earth and the overarching sky. Because of the flatness, contrasts are in a strange scale. A scarlet sunset will highlight gray-yellow tussocks of grass as though they were trees. Thunderclouds will mount thousands of feet above one stunted tree in the foreground. A horseback rider on the horizon will seem to rise up and emerge from the clouds. While the patterns of the earth are in small scale, akin to complex needlepoint on a vast tapestry, the sky is all drama. Cumulus clouds pile up over the center of vast continental spaces, and the wind moves them at dramatic pace along the horizon or over our heads. The ever-present red dust of a dry earth hangs in the air and turns all the colors from yellow through orange and red to purple on and off as the clouds bend and refract the light. Sunrise and sunset make up in drama for the fact that there are so few songbirds in that part of the bush. At sunrise, great shafts of gold precede the baroque sunburst. At sunset, the cumulus ranges through the shades of a Turner seascape before the sun dives below the earth leaving no afterglow, but at the horizon, tongues of fire.

The primal force of the sun shapes the environment. With the wind and the sand it bakes and cleanses all signs of decay. There is no cleansing by water. The rivers flow beneath the earth, and rain falls too rarely. In the recurring cycles of drought the sand and dust flow like water, and like the floods of other climates they engulf all that lies in their path. Painters find it hard to capture the shimmer of that warm red earth dancing in the brilliant light, and to record at the same time the subtle greens and grays of the plants and trees. Europeans were puzzled by the climate and vegetation, because the native eucalyptus trees were not deciduous. The physical blast of the sun in hot dry summers brought plants to dormancy. Slow growth followed in autumn, and a burst of vigorous growth after the brief winter rainy season. Summer was a time of endurance for all forms of life as moisture ebbed away and the earth was scorched. Winter days were like summer in a northern climate, and spring meant the onset of unbroken sunshine. On the plains, several winters might go by without a rainy season, and every 20 years or so the rain might vanish for a decade at a time. When that happened, the sun was needed to cleanse the bones of dead creatures, for the death toll was immense.

The oldest known humans on the continent left their bones on the western plains. Nomadic peoples hunted over the land as long as 40 thousand years ago. They and their progeny left behind the blackened stones of ovens, and the hollowed flat pieces of granite they carried from great distances to grind the native nardoo grain. Their way of life persisted until white settlers came by bullock wagon, 130 years ago, to take possession of the land. They came to graze their flocks of sharp-hooved sheep and cattle, hoping to make the land yield wealth. Other great inland grasslands in Argentina, South Africa, or North America were settled by pastoralists and ranchers who used forced labor: Indian peons, Bantus, or West African slaves. On Australia's great plains there were no settled native people to enslave. The settlers moved onto the plains long after the abandonment of transportation from Great

Britain, the last form of forced labor available in the Antipodes. As a result, the way of life that grew up for white settlers was unique.

A man could buy the government leasehold for hundreds of thousands of acres of grassland at a modest price if he settled the land and undertook to develop it. Others, beyond the reach of government scrutiny, simply squatted with their flocks on likely looking land. The scale of each holding was beyond European dreams of avarice. Each settler could look out to the vacant horizon knowing that all he saw was his. To graze the unfenced land required a population of sheepherders, or, as they came to be called, boundary riders. A settler would need 12 to 15 hands for his several hundred thousand acres, but most would live out on the "run" (sheep run) at least a day's ride from the main settlement. The hands were solitary males, a freewheeling rural proletariat, antisocial, and unconcerned with comfort or the domestic pleasures. Their leisure went in drink and gambling, and their days in a routine of lonely and backbreaking work. The main house would be spare and simple also, its roof of iron and its walls of timber laboriously transported from the coast. The garden would be primitive and the boss's recreations would be little different from his hands'. If he shared his life with a wife and children, they lived marginally on the edge of his world of male activity. There was no rain for orchards, no water for vegetable gardens, and no society for entertaining. Women worked over wood stoves in 100° heat and heated water for laundry over an open fire. There was little room for the culinary arts, because everyone's diet was mutton and unleavened bread, strong black tea, and spirits. The ratio of women to men was as distorted in this wave of settlement as anywhere in the settlement of the New World.

THE PATTERN of the year followed the seasons. If the rains came, they fell in the winter. Lambing was planned for the spring, when the grass was at its best, and the last winter showers might have left some tender growth for young lambs to nibble before their teeth developed. If seasons cooperated, the lambs were well grown, able to walk great distances for their food and water by the time the summer set in. In February, before the summer reached its peak, the lambs were shorn, and the faces and withers of the grown sheep were trimmed so that flies could not infest the places where sweat and urine soiled their fleeces. In June, in midwinter, when it was less harmful to move the animals over distances and hold them penned in yards, the grown sheep were brought to a shearing shed and shorn. If there had been an uninterrupted supply of nourishment through the year, their fleece would be 7 inches thick, unstained by dust, and carrying an unbroken staple that meant it could be easily combed to spin the finest yarn. If the land they grazed did not carry enough herbage throughout the year, the staple of their fleeces would show a break to mark the point where the food supply had faltered. When the staple was broken it could not be so easily combed, and the yarn it produced, being of less high quality, sold for less. If there were too many breaks it might not repay the cost of producing it.

A pastoralist could follow several economic strategies. Fewer sheep could be grazed over a set area of land, moved to fresh pasture whenever their nourishment required, and thus produce smaller amounts of more valuable wool. More sheep could be grazed over land they would crop bare in a year, for a larger volume of less valuable wool. The land that was grazed out each year succumbed quickly to drought. The land that was grazed in careful rotation might not succumb for as long as four or five years, for the unbroken root systems of the plants would hold the ground. One thing was certain. If the drought was long enough, sheep and cattle would, in their hunger, drag up the roots of the herbage, their sharp hooves would loosen the topsoil, and it would begin to blow away in the wind. The grasslands the earliest settlers saw had never been cropped by ruminant animals. No sharp hooves had ever disturbed the soil. It looked rich and indestructible, but in reality it was one of the most delicately balanced environments on the planet.

THE CHANCE to acquire title to a western land lease was the chance of a lifetime. In the expansive environment of the 1900s, men who felt lucky to be alive looked at the plains and dreamed about finally achieving economic independence. Perhaps, if things went well, their children could live the life of Australia's pastoral elites. For the returned soldiers [from the 1914–1918 War], class consciousness was more or less set aside, but most knew they wanted private schools for their children, fashionable clothes for their wives to wear to the races, a fancy horse or two in the stables, and freedom from worry about money.

The voices that exclaimed over the follies of brass hats or swore poetically about the stubborn ways of sheep and cattle did so in a melange of accents. Some carried a Scots burr, some a trace of a Yorkshire flat a; some spoke grammatically and displayed the manners produced by attendance at one of Australia's private schools. Most spoke broad Australian: picturesque in image, laced with the rhyming slang of Cockney London and the poetic black humor of the Irish. Their manners and their clothes were deliberately working-class. At night when they sat with their wives beside their crackling static-blurred radios, they waited for Big Ben to chime and then heard the impeccable British accents of the BBC announcer reading the news. With that voice they absorbed a map of the world that placed their near neighbor, Japan, in the Far East, and located distant Turkey in the Near East. So far as Australia was concerned its map was also clear and idiosyncratic. There were Sydney, Melbourne, and Adelaide on the southeast coast, and the bush. Other places existed–small country towns, the new federal capital planned at Canberra, the Snowy Mountains with their huge areas of snow and ice, industrial seaports like Newcastle, near the coalfields. They did not register because there were really only two places in the westerner's consciousness: the bush, and the metropolis at the end of the railway line where the wool was sold.

The city was a place of unaccustomed leisure for people who labored hard seven days a week. For the men there were cheerful drinking occasions before the wool sales or the agricultural shows. For the women there were the shops, the doctors and dentists for the children, and the luxury of restaurants, fresh fruit and vegetables, seafood, flower stands. For the children there were the marvels of electric lights, neon signs, moving pictures, and unlimited candy stores. These were balanced but not outweighed by the ministrations of the dental and medical professions and the ominous crowds. For everyone there were the sore feet and aching legs that came from wearing one's best shoes on hard pavements, and the unaccustomed feel of city clothes.

Everyone much preferred the rare occasions of leisure and festivity at home. There were picnic races, a bush festivity that involved horse racing by day, cheerful and alcoholic gambling and dances by night. A district might band together to stage a gymkhana, where the jockeys were not professionals and the horses were local products. Every half dozen stations would have somewhere a vestigial race track, barely a trace in the soil, with some rickety shelters from the sun and some kind of access to water. Bookmakers thrived as people cheerfully gambled away the year's profits in big bets, unconsciously recognizing that there were few other really satisfying diversions. Old lumber and battered corrugated iron would be pieced together to make a community hall in the middle of nowhere, and dances would be arranged by the Country Women's Association, or the Returned Soldiers' League. Musicians would materialize, and the men would appear in unaccustomed suits accompanied by wives in long dresses. People starved for company danced happily till dawn, reluctant to go home. Supper would be a feast at which every woman's prowess in the kitchen was assessed, and none of the hardworking revelers needed to worry about dieting.

Before they set out in the lightening sky, they stood to attention for "God Save the King," and if the evening had become an occasion for remembering 1914–1918, they sang "Land of Hope and Glory," evoking the memory, not so much of England, but of her mighty Empire, of which Australia was the proudest part. Anyone who mocked these loyalties learned quickly that he or she did not belong.

The cars would sweep home over the dusty roads, their lights visible like pillars of fire across the plains. If one arrived home first, one could stand on one's veranda and watch the other departures, visible for 20 miles or so. On regular nights there were only the stars, the cry of a fox, and the sound of the wind. Then if a car traveled very late at night it meant an emergency. Distant watchers would crane their heads to see where it went, and wonder what had gone wrong.

— Jill Ker Conway

Born in Hillston, New South Wales, Jill Ker Conway graduated from the University of Sydney in 1958 and received her Ph.D. from Harvard University in 1969. From 1964 to 1975 she taught at the University of Toronto and was vice president there before serving for 10 years as President of Smith College. Since 1985 she has been a visiting scholar and professor in MIT's Program in Science, Technology and Society. She now lives in Boston.

THE FIRST AUSTRALIANS

DURING THE COURSE of the 20th century, a sea change has occurred in the way in which much of the world views the colonization of indigenous peoples. Attention has turned to how colonization so dramatically—often tragically—changed the lives of original inhabitants. The Aboriginal and Torres Strait Islander peoples of Australia, the most recently colonized continent, have shared a tragic history since the first Europeans arrived at what was to be the penal colony of New South Wales in 1788. Only in recent decades has a majority of Australians acknowledged the brutal results of that arrival, and only in recent years has there been a popular appreciation of the wealth and diversity of the cultures of the first Australians.

There is still debate in archeological and anthropological circles about where Aboriginal peoples came from, but it is widely assumed that they migrated from somewhere in Southeast Asia. Evidence of habitation in the Kakadu area of the Northern Territory stretches beyond 60,000 years, and recent research in southern New South Wales suggests human activity from 120,000 years before the present.

The actual size of the pre-European population will never be known. Common estimates have suggested 300,000 people, but recent research has argued for as many as 1,000,000. Population densities varied widely, from 3 to 10 people per 2 square miles in coastal and riverine areas to 0.15 people per 2 square miles in deserts.

What is certain is that Australian Aboriginal people represent the oldest continuous cultural traditions on earth: Kangaroo-tooth headbands similar to those worn by men and women in the Central Desert in the 19th century have been found at Kow Swamp in Victoria and have been dated at 12,000 to 15,000 years old. Australian archaeologists have found evidence of the world's first ritual burial ceremonies and recorded the oldest rock art sites in the world.

Torres Strait Islanders, from the islands north of the Cape York Peninsula, where Australia comes within 100 miles of Papua New Guinea, have occupied their traditional lands and seas for at least 10,000 years. Quite distinct from mainlander Aborigines, Torres Strait Islanders are ethnically, linguistically, and culturally related to the Melanesian peoples of Papua New Guinea and the South Pacific.

Contrary to popular belief, Aboriginal groups often met travelers and explorers long before the British landed. Dutch documents from 1451 record voyages of Macassans seeking trepang in their prahus—southwest Indonesians trading for sea slugs in their light sailing vessels—to "Marege," as the Macassans called Australia. The relationship was friendly and profitable for both groups: For at least 350 years thousands of trepangers (sea slug traders) visited and made exchanges with northern Aboriginal groups during the annual harvests. There was even some intermarriage. Numerous Macassan words remain in use in local languages and have continued to influence cultural activities to this day. It was not until the newly federated Australia banned this trade at the beginning of this century that Macassans stopped visiting Australia. Recently, there have been family reunions between Indonesians and Arnhem Landers (Arnhem Land is an Aboriginal land reserve encompassing the northeastern spur of the Northern Territory), as this history of interaction has finally been officially acknowledged.

Europeans long characterized Aboriginals as nomadic peoples who wandered around aimlessly, but it is now clear that semi-nomadic indigenous groups were practicing highly sophisticated systems of ecological and economic management. It has been suggested that in the traditional economy people had to work little more than 20 hours a week to support themselves—that is how effective their methods were—using their close knowledge of the environment to harvest the natural resources of traditional clan estates. In recent years there has been something of a revolution in the understanding of Australian ecologies as Western scientists have begun to examine and utilize Aboriginal knowledge about the continent.

Perhaps as a consequence of the time freed by their efficient economic systems, Aboriginal groups developed some of the world's most elaborate religious, legal, and social philosophies. Inextricably linked with knowledge of the environment, complex kinship systems evolved to describe and regulate human societies and their relationship with the land, flora and flora, and annual cycles. Across the continent, groups' religious and legal structures intertwined with land tenure systems, ceremonies, and ritual exchange.

ABORIGINAL AUSTRALIA possessed as many as 250 different languages and 700 dialects—complex languages that reflect the cultural diversity of far-flung indigenous groups and their deep knowledge of the continent's varied ecosystems. (And although it is believed that there is a common ancestor for these languages, no link has yet been found with any outside linguistic groups.) Within pre-European Australia, trading networks—many of which are still intact—spanned the entire continent, from as far as Broome in westernmost Kimberley to southern Queensland. Goods, ideas, religious knowledge, and news were all mediums of exchange. As a result of these networks, many groups around the continent received word of the arrival of "the white man"—including information about introduced animals and the threat of firearms—decades before actual contact.

That contact was devastating for native Australians. Traditional lands were appropriated across Australia from 1788 until this century. Consequent disruptions of traditional economies led to widespread starvation. The spread of introduced disease decimated populations even before the arrival of the frontier violence that came as colonizers pushed their way across the continent. Whatever the original Aboriginal population of Australia might have been, by the 1950s the number dropped to 50,000 or less.

Frontier violence has remained part of a hidden history in Australia. Although European settlement was largely seen as having been peaceful, it is now clear that thousands died in encounters with "hostile" Aborigines, who resisted encroachment on their lands. It is suggested that in Queensland alone over 10,000 Aborigines and 1,000 Europeans died as a result of these conflicts. Massacres of Aboriginal people occurred in central Australia and the Kimberley as late as the 1920s.

In the belief that Aboriginal people would eventually die out, European settlers established a system of government reserves and church missions from the late 19th century in order to "protect" this "dying race." In the 1890s and again after World War I some of these reserves were closed down and the land given over to European farmers, forcing many Aboriginal people into fringe camps at the edge of country towns. By the 1930s government policy had shifted toward what was called assimilation—forcing Aboriginal people into becoming "like white Australians." This involved separating tens of thousands of Aboriginal children from their parents to be institutionalized in homes and missions.

By the 1960s it was clear that the Aboriginal race would not "die off," nor would they abandon their remaining lands and culture—hence the beginnings of the modern Aboriginal land rights movement. In 1963, Aboriginal people of northeast Arnhem Land (the northernmost part of the Northern Territory) presented the Federal Government with a petition painted on bark, protesting against the resumption of some of their reserve for a bauxite mine. Their pleas and a subsequent court case failed. But their action ultimately led to the establishment in 1976 of Australia's first Aboriginal land rights legislation for the Northern Territory. The 1970s also saw a nine-year strike by Aboriginal stockmen in the Northern Territory in a campaign for the return of their traditional lands, a "Freedom Ride" in western New South Wales protesting Aboriginal living conditions, and the establishment of the first national lobby group of Aboriginal people and Torres Strait Islanders. Since then, Aboriginal and Torres Strait Islander peoples have been active on a broad range of social and political fronts for recognition of their rights.

In a 1967 national referendum, Australians voted overwhelmingly to amend the Australian constitution in order to include Aboriginal people in the national census and allow the Federal Government to legislate in favor of Aboriginal people—a power previously held by the states. Four years later, Aboriginal people established the "Tent Embassy" outside the national parliament as a symbol of cultural revival and the struggle for land rights. In that year an Aboriginal flag was designed, and it eventually became a national symbol for indigenous Australians. A flag for the Torres Strait Islander people was designed in 1992 as an emblem of Australia's other indigenous group.

To this day, Australia remains the only English-speaking colonized country that has failed to reach a treaty with its indigenous peoples. In 1992, the need for some official recognition of Aboriginal rights received a dramatic boost with what is known as the Mabo decision. After a 10-year case in the High Court—the Australian equivalent of the U.S. Supreme Court—Torres Strait Islander Eddie Koiki Mabo and others established that under traditional law indigenous Australians still hold "native title" to traditional lands they have maintained continuous contact with since 1788. This overturned the concept that Australia was *terra nullius,* an empty land, on the arrival of Europeans.

In late 1996, a further High Court ruling, known as the Wik decision, established that native titles could coexist with titles on pastoral leasehold land (an Australian form of title that covers huge tracts of cattle country across the continent). This practical, "mixed use" resolution cedes some rights to Aboriginals, at a time when any cession is a step forward, but as a compromise measure it fails to fully recognize their traditional claim to the land.

The Mabo and Wik decisions have changed the relationship between indigenous Australians and those who have arrived in the country in the last 200 years, and have provoked long and at times bitter debate. The issue of reconciliation between indigenous and nonindigenous Australians is likely to dominate Australian politics for years to come.

THE FACTS of Aboriginal life in much of Australia are hard. Indigenous people still suffer appalling conditions of poverty. Life expectancy is some 20 years lower than that for the rest of the population, and disease and malnutrition levels rival those of Third World countries. Education standards are low, community infrastructure is often nearly nonexistent, and Aboriginal people have far higher levels of unemployment than other Australians. Discrimination is not uncommon, and Aboriginals are over-represented in the prison system.

Nonetheless, since the early 1970s government has recognized that Aboriginal self-determination is a key to turning around the legacy of indigenous dispossession. Throughout the nation, Aboriginal-controlled organizations are at the forefront of developing health and education programs, establishing economic enterprises, and promoting cultural maintenance and revival programs. Aboriginal people have also become prominent in international indigenous forums, such as the United Nations, and have built strong links with native groups overseas, such as the Inuit of Canada and the Lakota Sioux and Cree nations in the United States.

It is in the arts that Aboriginal and Torres Strait Islander people have achieved national prominence, and the peoples' enormous regional differences reflect the diversity of ancient and contemporary indigenous cultures. Aboriginal art, dance, and music now occupy center stage in Australian culture: It is estimated that there are 7,000 practicing visual artists and craftspeople out of a total indigenous population of 250,000. And sales of Aboriginal art now reach as high as $100 million a year. Major exhibitions of Aboriginal art have been held in the United States and Europe in recent years, bringing the work of the world's oldest cultures to international attention.

This cultural acceptance of Aborigines and Torres Strait Islanders has given them and their heritage a significant boost in recent years. This, as well as other political and social gains, point to a future in which indigenous people can occupy their rightful place as the First Australians.

— Chips Mackinolty

INDEX

WHEREVER YOU TRAVEL, *H*ELP IS NEVER FAR AWAY.

From planning your trip to

providing travel assistance along

the way, American Express®

Travel Service Offices are

always there to help

you do more.

American Express Travel Service
Offices are found in central locations
throughout Australia.

do more AMERICAN EXPRESS

Travel

http://www.americanexpress.com/travel